THE
BIBLE COMMENTARY

F. C. COOK, *Editor*

ABRIDGED AND EDITED

BY J. M. FULLER

I SAMUEL—ESTHER

BAKER BOOK HOUSE
Grand Rapids, Michigan

Library of Congress Catalog Card Number: 55-11630

ISBN: 0-8010-0555-8

First Printing, February 1953
Second Printing, March 1957
Third Printing, April 1959
Fourth Printing, March 1961
Fifth Printing, February 1963
Sixth Printing, March 1965
Seventh Printing, June 1967
Eighth Printing, April 1969
Ninth Printing, June 1970
Tenth Printing, October 1971
Eleventh Printing, July 1973
Twelfth Printing, July 1974

PHOTOLITHOPRINTED BY CUSHING - MALLOY, INC.
ANN ARBOR, MICHIGAN, UNITED STATES OF AMERICA
1974

SAMUEL.

INTRODUCTION.

The double name of these Books, the First and Second Book of Samuel,[1] as they are called in the printed Hebrew Bible, and the First and Second Book of Kings, as they are called in the Vulgate, well marks the two principal features which characterize them. They contain the record of the life and ministry of Samuel, the great Prophet and Judge of Israel, and they also contain the record of the rise of the Kingdom of Israel. If again the Books of Samuel are taken as forming one history with the Books of Kings (the present line of division between 2 Sam. and 1 K. being an arbitrary one), then the division into four Books of Kings is a natural one. But if these Books are looked upon rather as an isolated history, then the name of Samuel is properly affixed to them, not only because he stands out as the great figure of that age, but because his administration of the affairs of Israel was the connecting link, the transitional passage, from the rule of the Judges to the reign of the Kings, distinct from each, but binding the two together.

The important place to be filled by Samuel in the ensuing history is seen at once in the opening chapters of the Book which bears his name. Further, the fact that Samuel's birth of her that had been barren is represented in Hannah's song as typical of the triumphs of the Church and of the Kingdom of Christ, is another indication of the very distinguished place assigned to Samuel in the economy of the Old Testament, borne out by the mention of him in such passages as Ps. xcix. 6; Jer. xv. 1; Acts iii. 24. Though, however, Samuel's personal greatness is thus apparent, it is no less clearly marked that his place is one not of *absolute* but of *relative* importance. When we view the history as a whole, the eye does not rest upon Samuel, and stop there, but is led on to the throne and person of David as typical of the Kingdom and Person of Christ. An incidental mark of this subordination may be seen in the fact that the Books of Samuel are really a continuation of the Book of Ruth; a Book which derived its significance from its containing a history of David's ancestors and genealogy. Clearly, therefore, in the mind of the sacred historian, the personal history of Samuel was only a link to connect David with the Patriarchs, just as the subsequent history connects David himself with our Lord Jesus Christ.

But a still more remarkable and conclusive proof of the same subordination may be found in the circumstance, that it is only the closing years of Saul's reign of which any account whatever is given in

---

[1] In the Heb. MSS. the two make only one Book of Samuel.

this Book. For after having related a few facts connected with the beginning of Saul's reign, the historian passes over some 20 or 30 years (Acts xiii. 21) to relate an occurrence in the last quarter of Saul's reign, God's rejection of Saul from the kingdom, and His choice of " a man after His own heart " to be king in Saul's room (xiii. 13, 14).

The contents of the Books of Samuel consist mainly of three portions, (i.) the history of Samuel's life and judgeship from 1 Sam. i. to xii. inclusive ; (ii.) the history of Saul's reign from xiii. 1 to xv. 35; (iii.) the history of David from xvi. 1 to the end of the second Book ; this latter portion not being completed till 1 K. ii. 11.

The sources from which the narrative is derived, were probably (1), the Book of Jasher (2 Sam. i. 18); (2), David's Psalms (2 Sam. xxii., xxiii.); (3), the Chronicles of king David (1 Chr. xxvii. 24); (4), the Book of Samuel the Seer; (5), the Book of Nathan the Prophet ; (6), the Book of Gad the Seer (1 Chr. xxix. 29, 2 Chr. ix. 29); (7), the national collection of genealogies.

Those sections which give full details of the sayings and doings of Samuel, are conjectured to be extracted from " the Book of Samuel the seer" (e.g. i.–xii.). Those sections which contain narratives in which Nathan bears a part (2 Sam. vii., xi., xii., 1 K. i. ii.) may be referred to the " Book of Nathan the seer." Such passages as 2 Sam. xxi., xxii. 5, xxiv., &c., are pretty certainly from the Book of Gad the Seer. We seem to see extracts from the Chronicles of the kingdom in such passages as 1 Sam. xiii. 1, and xi. 1–11, 15, xiv. 47–52, 2 Sam. ii. 8-11, iii. 1-5, v. 4–16, viii., xx.

23–26, xxi. 15–22, xxiii. 8–39 ; while the song of Hannah (1 Sam. ii. 1–10), the elegy on the death of Abner (2 Sam. iii. 33, 34), and the two Psalms (2 Sam. xxii., xxiii. 1–7), may, as well as the elegy on Saul and Jonathan, be taken from the Book of Jasher.

It is difficult to decide when the final arrangement of the Books of Samuel, in their present shape, was made. The series of historical books from Judges to the end of 2 Kings is formed on one plan, so that each book is a part of a connected whole. This would point to the time of Jeremiah the Prophet, as that when the whole historical series from Judges to Kings inclusive was woven into one work. In his use of the work of contemporary writers, the final compiler left out large portions of the materials before him.[2]

The chief quotations and resemblances from the Books of Samuel in the New Testament are[3] found in the writings of St. Luke and St.

---

[2] e.g. The whole of the beginning and middle of Saul's reign ; the omission of the destruction of the Gibeonites (only incidentally referred to in chap. xxi.) ; the early history of Eli (who is mentioned quite suddenly in 1 Sam. i. 3); the transactions of Samuel's judgeship (of which only a few incidents are recorded) ; the details of David's wars with Moab and Edom; and many circumstances in the reign of David of which we have a full account in the Books of Chronicles.

[3] Matt. i. 6, xii. 3, 4 ; Mark ii. 25, 26 ; Luke i. 32, 33, 46, 47, 48, 68, vi. 3, 4 ; Acts ii. 30, iii. 24, vii. 46, xiii. 20–22; Rom. xi. 1, 2 ; 2 Cor. vi. 18; Heb. i. 5; Rev. xix. 9, xxi. 5, 7, xxii. 6. There is also a remarkable similarity in the phraseology of such passages as 1 Sam. i. 17, xx. 42, and Luke vii. 50, viii. 48; 1 Sam. ii. 1, and Luke i. 46, 47; 1 Sam. ii. 26, and Luke ii. 52 ; 1 Sam. xiv. 45 ; 2 Sam. xiv. 11, and Luke xxi. 18 ; Acts xxvii. 34; 1 Sam. xxv. 32, and Luke i. 68 ; 2 Sam. i. 16, and Acts xviii. 6 ; 2 Sam. xiv, 17, and Gal. iv. 14 ; 2 Sam. xvi. 10, and Matt. viii. 29 ; Luke viii. 28.

Paul. The title THE CHRIST ("the anointed"), given to the Lord Jesus (Matt. i. 16, ii. 4, xvi. 16; Luke ii. 26; John i. 20, 41, xx. 31; Acts ii. 30), is first found in 1 Sam. ii. 10; and the other designation of the Saviour as the SON OF DAVID (Matt. ix. 27, xv. 22, xxi. 9, 15, xxii. 42), is derived from 2 Sam. vii. 12--16.

In these books are passages which occur in duplicate elsewhere, chiefly in the Books of Chronicles and Psalms ; and a careful comparison of these duplicate passages throws great light upon the manner in which the sacred historians used existing materials, incorporating them word for word, or slightly altering them for the sake of explanation, as seemed most expedient to them. It illustrates also the errors and fluctuations of scribes in transcribing MSS., especially in regard to proper names.

For these duplicate passages, and also on the chief quotations from other books in the Old Testament, consult the marginal references.

The style of the Books of Samuel is clear, simple, and forcible, and the Hebrew remarkably pure and free from Chaldaisms. The chief difficulties are the geographical statements of 1 Sam. ix., x., the very difficult poem in 2 Sam. xxiii. 1–7, and the account of the mighty men which follows it, 8--39. There are also some manifest corruptions of the text;[4] but contradictions or disagreements of any kind in the statements of the Books of Samuel, as compared with each other, or with the Books of Chronicles, do not exist.

The time included in the history of these Books cannot be exactly defined, from the lack of any systematic chronology in them. But it may be estimated roughly at about 130 years, made up of the following subdivisions, the precise length of the first of which is a matter of conjecture :—

	Years.
The life of Samuel up to Saul's election to be king (1 Sam. viii. 1, 5), say	50
Saul's reign (Acts xiii. 21) .	40
David's reign (2 Sam. v. 4) .	40
	130

[4] e.g. 1 Sam. xiii. 1; 1 Sam. vi. 19; 2 Sam. xv. 7; 2 Sam. xxi. 8; 2 Sam. xxiii. 8; of the other mighty men in the same list; the names *Ishbi-benob* and *Jaare-oregim*, 2 Sam. xxi. 16, 19.

THE FIRST BOOK

OF

SAMUEL,

OTHERWISE CALLED, THE FIRST BOOK OF THE KINGS.

CHAP. 1. NOW there was a certain man of Ramathaim-zophim, of mount Ephraim, and his name *was* ^aElkanah, the son of Jeroham, the son of Elihu, the son of Tohu, the son of Zuph, ^ban 2 Ephrathite : and he had two wives; the name of the one *was* Hannah, and the name of the other Peninnah : and Peninnah 3 had children, but Hannah had no children. ¶ And this man went up out of his city ^c¹yearly ^dto worship and to sacrifice unto the LORD of hosts in ^eShiloh. And the two sons of Eli, Hophni and 4 Phinehas, the priests of the LORD, *were* there. And when the time was that Elkanah ^foffered, he gave to Peninnah his wife, 5 and to all her sons and her daughters, portions : but unto Hannah he gave ²a worthy portion; for he loved Hannah :

a 1 Chr. 6. 27, 34.
b Ruth 1. 2.

c Ex. 23. 14. Deut. 16. 16. Luke 2. 41.
d Deut. 12. 5, 6, 7.
e Josh. 18. 1. Judg. 21. 19.
f Deut. 12. 17, 18. & 16. 11.

¹ Heb. *from year to year.*   ² Or, *a double portion.*

I. 1. Ramathaim-zophim may signify "the two hills (ix. 11-13) of the watchmen," so called from its being a post from which the watchmen looked out. But since *Zuph* is the name of the head of the family, it is more probable that *Zophim* means the *Zuphites, the sons of Zuph* (see *Zophai,* 1 Chr. vi. 26), from whom the land about Ramah was called "the land of Zuph," ix. 5.

There is reason to believe that Elkanah —*an Ephrathite,* or inhabitant of Bethlehem (xvii. 12, Ruth i. 2) and of the territory of the tribe of Ephraim (1 K. xi. 26)—the father of Samuel, represents the fifth generation of settlers in Canaan, and therefore that Samuel was born about 130 years after the entrance into Canaan,—four complete generations, or 132 years,—and about forty years before David.

2. *he had two wives*] Cp. Gen. iv. 19. This was permitted by the law (Deut. xxi. 15), and sanctioned by the practice of Jacob (Gen. xxix.), Ashur (1 Chr. iv. 5), Shaharaim (1 Chr. viii. 8), David (1 Sam. xxv. 43), Joash (2 Chr. xxiv. 3), and others.

Hannah, i.e. Beauty or *charm,* is the same as *Anna* (Luke ii. 36). *Peninnah, i.e.* a *Pearl,* is the same name in signification as *Margaret.*

The frequent recurrence of the mention of barrenness in those women who were afterwards famous through their progeny (as Sarah, Rebekah, Rachel) coupled with the prophetic language of Hannah's song in the 2nd chapter, justifies us in seeking a mystical sense. Besides the apparent purpose of marking the children so born as raised up for special purposes by Divine Providence, the weakness and comparative barrenness of the Church of God, to be fol-

lowed at the set time by her glorious triumph and immense increase, is probably intended to be foreshadowed.

3. It is likely that during the unsettled times of the Judges (Judg. xxi. 25) the attendance of Israelites at the three Festivals (Ex. xxxiv. 23, Deut. xvi. 16) fell into desuetude or great irregularity, and this one feast (see marg. ref.), which may have coincided with the Feast of Pentecost or Tabernacles, may have been substituted for them.

the LORD *of Hosts*] This title of Jehovah which, with some variations, is found upwards of 260 times in the O. T., occurs here for the first time. The meaning of the word *hosts* is doubtless the same as that of *army* (Dan. iv. 35) and includes all the myriads of holy Angels who people the celestial spheres (1 K. xxii. 19). It is probably with reference to the idolatrous worship of the Host of Heaven that the title *the Lord of Hosts* was given to the true God, as asserting His universal supremacy (see Neh. ix. 6). In the N. T. the phrase only occurs once (Jam. v. 4).

and the two sons, &c.] It should be, "**and there the two sons of Eli, Hophni and Phinehas, were priests to the Lord,**" *i.e.* performed the functions of priests, in the old age of Eli (iv. 18), who is represented (*v.* 9) as sitting on a seat in the temple. The reading of the Greek Version "Eli was there, and his two sons, H. and Ph., priests of the LORD," is quite unnecessary, and indeed destroys the sense. The information here given concerning the sons of Eli is followed up in ii. 12, seq.

5. *a worthy portion*] Probably as in the margin. Naturally she would have had a single

6 *g*but the LORD had shut up her womb. And her adversary also
  [1h]provoked her sore, for to make her fret, because the LORD had
7 shut up her womb. And *as* he did so year by year, [23]when she
  went up to the house of the LORD, so she provoked her; there-
8 fore she wept, and did not eat. Then said Elkanah her husband
  to her, Hannah, why weepest thou? and why eatest thou not? and
  why is thy heart grieved? *am* not I [i]better to thee than ten sons?
9 ¶ So Hannah rose up after they had eaten in Shiloh, and after
  they had drunk. Now Eli the priest sat upon a seat by a post
10 of [k]the temple of the LORD. [l]And she *was* [4]in bitterness of
11 soul, and prayed unto the LORD, and wept sore. And she
  [m]vowed a vow, and said, O LORD of hosts, if thou wilt indeed
  [n]look on the affliction of thine handmaid, and [o]remember me,
  and not forget thine handmaid, but wilt give unto thine handmaid [5]a man child, then I will give him unto the LORD all the
  days of his life, and [p]there shall no razor come upon his head.
12 ¶ And it came to pass, as she [6]continued praying before the
13 LORD, that Eli marked her mouth. Now Hannah, she spake in
  her heart; only her lips moved, but her voice was not heard:
14 therefore Eli thought she had been drunken. And Eli said unto
  her, How long wilt thou be drunken? put away thy wine from
15 thee. And Hannah answered and said, No, my lord, I *am* a
  woman [7]of a sorrowful spirit: I have drunk neither wine nor
  strong drink, but have [q]poured out my soul before the LORD.
16 Count not thine handmaid for a daughter of [r]Belial: for out
  of the abundance of my [8]complaint and grief have I spoken
17 hitherto. Then Eli answered and said, [s]Go in peace: and [t]the
  God of Israel grant *thee* thy petition that thou hast asked of
18 him. And she said, [u]Let thine handmaid find grace in thy
  sight. So the woman [x]went her way, and did eat, and her
19 countenance was no more *sad*. ¶ And they rose up in the
  morning early, and worshipped before the LORD, and returned,

g Gen. 30. 2.
h Job 24. 21.

i Ruth 4. 15.

k ch. 3. 3.
l Job 7. 11.
  & 10. 1.
m Gen.28.20.
n Gen. 29.32.
  Ex. 4. 31.
  2 Sam.16.12.
  Ps. 25. 18.
o Gen. 8. 1.
  & 30. 22.
p Num. 6. 5.
  Judg. 13. 5.

q Ps. 62. 8.
  & 142. 2.
r Deut. 13.
  13.
s Judg. 18. 6.
  Mark 5. 34.
  Luke 7. 50.
  & 8. 48.
t Ps. 20. 4, 5.
u Gen.33.15.
  Ruth 2. 13.
x Eccles.9.7.

---

[1] Heb. *angered her.*
[2] Or, *from the time that she, &c.*
[3] Heb. *from her going up.*
[4] Heb. *bitter of soul,* 2 Sam. 17. 8.
[5] Heb. *seed of men.*
[6] Heb. *multiplied to pray.*
[7] Heb. *hard of spirit.*
[8] Or, *meditation.*

---

portion of the sacrifice (cp. ix. 23), but because
of his love to her he gave her a double portion,
enough for two people (cp. Gen. xliii. 34).

7. *And as he did so,* &c.] It should rather
be " **And so she did year by year, as often
as she went up to the House of the Lord,
so she provoked her.**" Though the verb is
masculine, Peninnah must be the subject,
because *as often as* SHE *went up* follows. The
Vulgate has "*they* went up."

9. *after they had eaten,* &c.] Rather,
"**after she had eaten and after she had
drunk,**" which is obviously right. Hannah,
in the bitterness of her spirit, could not
enjoy her feast, and so, after eating and
drinking a little, she arose and went to the
temple, leaving her husband and Peninnah
and her children at table, where she still
found them on her return (*v.* 18).

upon a seat, &c.] Rather, "**upon the
throne,**" the pontifical chair of state (iv.
13), which was probably set at the gate
leading into the inner court of the Tabernacle.

the temple of the LORD] The application of
the word *temple* to the Tabernacle is found
only here, iii. 3, and Ps. v. 7 : and the use
of this word here is thought by some an indication of the late date of the composition
of this passage.

11. Vows are characteristic of this particular age of the Judges. (Cp. Judg. xi.
30, xxi. 5 ; 1 Sam. xiv. 24.) For the law of
vows in the case of married women, see
Num. xxx. 6-16 ; and for the nature of the
vow, see marg. reff.

15. See *v.* 2 and note. She means that
wine was not the cause of her present dis-
composure, but grief of heart.

18. A beautiful example of the composing influence of prayer. Hannah had
cast her burden upon the Lord, and so her
own spirit was relieved of its load. She
now returned to the family feast, and ate
her portion with a cheerful heart. (Acts ii.
46, 47.)

The word *sad* is not in the Hebrew text,
but it fairly supplies the meaning intended.

ʸ Gen. 4. 1.
ᶻ Gen. 30.
22.

ᵃ ver. 3.

ᵇ Luke 2. 22.
ᶜ ver. 11. 28.
ch. 2. 11, 18.
& 3. 1.
ᵈ Ex. 21. 6.
ᵉ Num. 30. 7.
ᶠ 2 Sam. 7.
25.
ᵍ Deut. 12.
5, 6, 11.
ʰ Josh. 18. 1.

ⁱ Luke 2. 22.
ᵏ Gen. 42.
15.
2 Kin. 2. 2.
ˡ Matt. 7. 7.
ᵐ ver. 11. 22.
ⁿ Gen. 24.
26, 52.

ᵃ Phil. 4. 6.
ᵇ See Luke
1. 46. &c.
ᶜ Ps. 92. 10.
& 112. 9.
ᵈ Ps. 9. 14.
See Rev. 7.
10.
ᵉ Ex. 15. 11.
Deut. 3. 24.
Ps. 86. 8.
ᶠ Deut. 4. 35.
2 Sam. 22.
32.
ᵍ Ps. 94. 4.
Mal. 3. 13.
Jude 15.

and came to their house to Ramah: and Elkanah ʸknew
20 Hannah his wife; · and ᶻthe LORD remembered her. Wherefore
it came to pass, ¹when the time was come about after Hannah
had conceived, that she bare a son, and called his name
²Samuel, *saying*, Because I have asked him of the LORD.
21 ¶ And the man Elkanah, and all his house, ᵃwent up to offer
22 unto the LORD the yearly sacrifice, and his vow. But Hannah
went not up; for she said unto her husband, *I will not go up*
until the child be weaned, and *then* I will ᵇbring him, that he
23 may appear before the LORD, and there ᶜabide ᵈfor ever. And
ᵉElkanah her husband said unto her, Do what seemeth thee
good; tarry until thou have weaned him; ᶠonly the LORD
establish his word. So the woman abode, and gave her son
24 suck until she weaned him. ¶ And when she had weaned him,
she ᵍtook him up with her, with three bullocks, and one ephah
of flour, and a bottle of wine, and brought him unto ʰthe house
25 of the LORD in Shiloh: and the child *was* young. And they
26 slew a bullock, and ⁱbrought the child to Eli. And she said, O
my lord, ᵏ*as* thy soul liveth, my lord, I *am* the woman that
27 stood by thee here, praying unto the LORD. ˡFor this child I
prayed; and the LORD hath given me my petition which I asked
28 of him: ᵐtherefore also I have ³lent him to the LORD; as long
as he liveth ⁴he shall be lent to the LORD. And he ⁿworshipped
the LORD there.

CHAP. 2. AND Hannah ᵃprayed, and said,
        ᵇMy heart rejoiceth in the LORD,
        ᶜMine horn is exalted in the LORD:
        My mouth is enlarged over mine enemies;
        Because I ᵈrejoice in thy salvation.
2   ᵉ*There is* none holy as the LORD ·
        For *there is* ᶠnone beside thee:
        Neither *is there* any rock like our God.
3   ᵍLet *not* ⁵arrogancy come out of your mouth:
        For the LORD *is* a God of knowledge,
        And by him actions are weighed.

¹ Heb. *in revolution of days.*   *have obtained by petition,*   *tained by petition shall*
² That is, *Asked of God.*   *to the LORD.*   *be returned.*
³ Or, *returned him, whom I*   ⁴ Or, *he whom I have ob-*   ⁵ Heb. *hard.*

---

20. *Samuel*] *i.e. heard of God*, because
given in answer to prayer. The names
Ishmael and *Elishama* have the same etymology.
22. *until the child be weaned*] Hebrew
mothers, as elsewhere in the East, usually
suckled their children till the age of two
complete years, sometimes till the age of
three.
26. *as thy soul liveth*] This oath is peculiar
to the Books of Samuel, in which it occurs
six times, and to the Books of Kings, in
which however it is found only once. See
note to *v.* 11.
II. **1.** The song of Hannah is a prophetic
Psalm. It is poetry, and it is prophecy.
It takes its place by the side of the songs of
Miriam, Deborah, and the Virgin Mary, as
well as those of Moses, David, Hezekiah, and
other Psalmists and Prophets whose inspired

odes have been preserved in the Bible. The
peculiar feature which these songs have in
common is, that springing from, and in
their first conception relating to, incidents
in the lives of the individuals who composed
them, they branch out into magnificent descriptions of the Kingdom and glory of
Christ, and the triumphs of the Church, of
which those incidents were providentially
designed to be the types. The perception
of this is essential to the understanding of
Hannah's song. Cp. the marg. reff. throughout.
2. *any rock, &c.*] The term *rock* as applied to God is first found in the song of
Moses (see Deut. xxxii. 4 note), where the
juxtaposition of *rock* and *salvation* in *v.* 15,
he lightly esteemed the rock of his salvation,
seems to indicate that Hannah was acquainted with the song of Moses.

4	^hThe bows of the mighty men *are* broken,

4   ^hThe bows of the mighty men *are* broken,
     And they that stumbled are girded with strength.   *h* Ps. 37. 15.

5   ⁱ *They that were* full have hired out themselves for bread ;   *i* Ps. 34. 10.
     And *they that were* hungry ceased :   See ver. 36.
     So that ^kthe barren hath born seven ;   *k* Ps. 113. 9.
     And ^lshe that hath many children is waxed feeble   Gal. 4. 27. / *l* Isai. 54. 1.

6   ^mThe LORD killeth, and maketh alive :   Jer. 15. 9.
     He bringeth down to the grave, and bringeth up.   *m* Deut. 32. 39.

7   The LORD ⁿmaketh poor, and maketh rich :   Job 5. 18.
     ^oHe bringeth low, and lifteth up.   Hos. 6. 1. / *n* Deut. 8.18.

8   ^pHe raiseth up the poor out of the dust,   *o* Ps. 75. 7.
     And lifteth up the beggar from the dunghill,   *p* Ps. 113. 7, 8.
     ^qTo set *them* among princes,   Dan. 4. 17.
     And to make them inherit the throne of glory :   Luke 1. 52.
     For ^rthe pillars of the earth *are* the LORD'S,   *q* Job 36. 7.
     And he hath set the world upon them.   *r* Job 38. 4. / Ps. 24. 2.

9   ^sHe will keep the feet of his saints,   Heb. 1. 3.
     And the wicked shall be silent in darkness ;   *s* Ps. 91. 11. & 121. 3.
     For by ^tstrength shall no man prevail.   *t* Zech. 4. 6. / 2 Cor. 12. 9.

10   The adversaries of the LORD shall be broken to pieces ;   *u* ch. 7. 10.
     ^uOut of heaven shall he thunder upon them :   Ps. 18. 13.
     ^xThe LORD shall judge the ends of the earth ;   *x* Ps. 96. 13.
     And he shall give strength unto his king,
     And ^yexalt the horn of his anointed.   *y* Ps. 89. 24.

11 ¶ And Elkanah went to Ramah to his house. ^zAnd the child   *z* ver. 18.
12 did minister unto the LORD before Eli the priest. ¶ Now the   ch. 3. 1.
     sons of Eli *were* ^asons of Belial ; ^bthey knew not the LORD.   *a* Deut.13.13.
13 And the priest's custom with the people *was, that,* when any   *b* Judg. 2.10.
     man offered sacrifice, the priest's servant came, while the flesh   Jer. 22. 16.
14 was in seething, with a fleshhook of three teeth in his hand ; and   Rom. 1. 28.
     he struck *it* into the pan, or kettle, or caldron, or pot ; all that
     the fleshhook brought up the priest took for himself. So they
15 did in Shiloh unto all the Israelites that came thither. Also   *c* Lev. 3. 3,
     before they ^cburnt the fat, the priest's servant came, and said to   4, 5, 16.
     the man that sacrificed, Give flesh to roast for the priest ; for he
16 will not have sodden flesh of thee, but raw. And *if* any man

---

5. See an instance in *v.* 36. See, too, in Ezek. xiii. 19, another example of hire paid in bread.

ceased] *i.e.* were at rest, did no work. The general sense is expressed by the translation of the Latin Version, " they were filled."

10. *he shall give strength,* &c.] This is a most remarkable passage, containing a clear and distinct prophecy of the Kingdom and glory of the Christ of God. (Cp. Luke i. 69, 70).

11. The word *minister* is used in three senses in Scripture : (1) of the service or ministration of both priests and Levites rendered unto the Lord (Ex. xxviii. 35, 43): (2) of the ministrations of the Levites as rendered to the priests, to aid them in Divine Service (Num. iii. 6) : (3) of any service or ministration, especially one rendered to a man of God, as that of Joshua to Moses (Num. xi. 28). The application of it to Samuel as ministering to the Lord

before Eli the priest accords *most exactly* with Samuel's condition as a Levite.

12. *sons of Belial*] See marg. reff. note. The phrase is very frequent in the books of Samuel. In the N. T., St. Paul contrasts Christ and Belial, as if Belial were the name of an idol or the personification of evil (2 Cor. vi. 15). This probably led to the use of the term Belial in the A. V., instead of expressing its meaning, which is *mischief, wickedness.*

13. The Law of Moses defined exactly what was to be the priest's portion of every peace offering (Lev. vii. 31-35), as it also gave express directions about the burning of the fat (ib. 23-25, 31). It was therefore a gross act of disobedience and lawlessness on the part of Hophni and Phinehas to take more than the Law gave them. In-cidental evidence is afforded by this passage to the existence of the Levitical Law at this time.

said unto him, Let them not fail to burn the fat [1]presently, and
then take *as much* as thy soul desireth; then he would answer
him, *Nay;* but thou shalt give *it me* now: and if not, I will
17 take *it* by force. Wherefore the sin of the young men was very
great [d]before the LORD: for men [e]abhorred the offering of the
18 LORD. ¶ [f]But Samuel ministered before the LORD, *being* a
19 child, [g]girded with a linen ephod. Moreover his mother made
him a little coat, and brought *it* to him from year to year,
when she [h]came up with her husband to offer the yearly
20 sacrifice. And Eli [i]blessed Elkanah and his wife, and said,
The LORD give thee seed of this woman for the [2]loan which is
[k]lent to the LORD. And they went unto their own home.
21 And the LORD [l]visited Hannah, so that she conceived, and
bare three sons and two daughters. And the child Samuel
22 [m]grew before the LORD. ¶ Now Eli was very old, and heard all
that his sons did unto all Israel; and how they lay with [n]the
women that [3]assembled *at* the door of the tabernacle of the
23 congregation. And he said unto them, Why do ye such
things? for [4]I hear of your evil dealings by all this people.
24 Nay, my sons; for *it is* no good report that I hear: ye make the
25 LORD's people [5]to transgress. If one man sin against another,
the judge shall judge him: but if a man [o]sin against the LORD,
who shall intreat for him? Notwithstanding they hearkened
not unto the voice of their father, [p]because the LORD would

[d] Gen. 6. 11.
[e] Mal. 2. 8.
[f] ver. 11.
[g] Ex. 28. 6. 2 Sam. 6. 14.
[h] ch. 1. 3.
[i] Gen. 14. 19.
[k] ch. 1. 28.
[l] Gen. 21. 1.
[m] Gen. 21. 8. ver. 26. Luke 1. 80. & 2. 40.
[n] See Ex. 38. 8.
[o] Num. 15. 30.
[p] Josh. 11. 20. Prov. 15. 10.

[1] Heb. *as on the day.*
[2] Or, *petition which she asked, &c.*
[3] Heb. *assembled by troops.*
[4] Or, *I hear evil words of you.*
[5] Or, *to cry out.*

---

17. *the offering of the* LORD] *Minchah*, here in the general sense of *gift* or *offering* to God (cp. Mal. i. 10, 11, iii. 3). In its restricted sense, it is used of the meat offerings, the unbloody sacrifices, and is then coupled with bloody sacrifices, sacrifices of *slain* beasts. (See *v.* 29.)

18. *girded with a linen ephod*] This was the usual dress of the priests. It does not appear whether Levites wore an ephod properly. Possibly it was a mark of Samuel's special dedication to the Lord's service that he wore one. (See marg. ref.). The ephod was sometimes used as an idolatrous implement (Judg. viii. 27).

19. *a little coat*] The robe of the ephod was also one of the garments worn by the High Priest (see Ex. xxviii. 31 note). This pointed mention of the ephod and the robe as worn by the youthful Samuel, seems to point to an extraordinary and irregular priesthood to which he was called by God in an age when the provisions of the Levitical law were not yet in full operation, and in which there was no impropriety in the eyes of his contemporaries, seeing that nonconformity to the whole Law was the rule rather than the exception throughout the days of the Judges.

21. See marg. reff. The words *before the* Lord have special reference to his residence at the Tabernacle.

22. *women that assembled*] Or, "**served.**" See marg. ref. and note. Probably such service as consisted in doing certain work for the fabric of the Tabernacle as women are wont to do, spinning, knitting, embroidering, mending, washing, and such like.

25. The sense seems to be, If one man sin against another, the judge shall amerce him in the due penalty, and then he shall be free; but if he sin against the Lord, who shall act the part of judge and arbiter for him? His guilt must remain to the great day of judgment.

because the LORD *would slay them*] There is a sense in which whatever comes to pass is the accomplishment of God's sovereign will and pleasure, and all the previous steps, even when they involve moral causes, by which this will and pleasure are brought about, are in this sense also brought about by God. How this truth, which reason and revelation alike acknowledge, consists with man's free will on the one hand; or, when the evil deeds and punishment of a sinner are some of the previous steps, with God's infinite mercy and love on the other, is what cannot possibly be explained. We can only firmly believe both statements, (1) that God hath no pleasure in the death of him that dieth, and that He willeth not the death of a sinner, but rather that he should be converted and live; (2) that the sins and the punishments of sin are accomplishments of God's eternal purpose (cp. marg. reff,, and Isai. vi. 9, 10; Mark iv.

26 slay them.   ¶And the child Samuel *q*grew on, and was *r*in
27 favour both with the LORD, and also with men.   ¶*s*And there
came a man of God unto Eli, and said unto him, Thus saith the
LORD, *t*Did I plainly appear unto the house of thy father, when
28 they were in Egypt in Pharaoh's house? And did I *u*choose
him out of all the tribes of Israel *to be* my priest, to offer upon
mine altar, to burn incense, to wear an ephod before me? and
*x*did I give unto the house of thy father all the offerings made
29 by fire of the children of Israel? Wherefore *y*kick ye at my
sacrifice and at mine offering, which I have commanded in *my*
*z*habitation; and honourest thy sons above me, to make yourselves fat with the chiefest of all the offerings of Israel my
30 people? Wherefore the LORD God of Israel saith, *a*I said indeed
that thy house, and the house of thy father, should walk before
me for ever: but now the LORD saith, *b*Be it far from me; for
them that honour me *c*I will honour, and *d*they that despise me
31 shall be lightly esteemed. Behold, *e*the days come, that I will
cut off thine arm, and the arm of thy father's house, that there
.32 shall not be an old man in thine house. And thou shalt see *¹*an
enemy *in my* habitation, in all *the wealth* which *God* shall give
Israel: and there shall not be *f*an old man in thine house for
33 ever. And the man of thine, *whom* I shall not cut off from

q ver. 21.
r Prov. 3. 4.
Luke 2. 52.
Acts 2. 47.
Rom. 14. 18.
s 1 Kin. 13.1.
t Ex. 4. 14.
u Ex. 28. 1.
Num. 16. 5.
& 18. 1.
x Lev. 7. 34,
35.
Num. 18.
8—19.
y Deut. 32.
15.
z Deut. 12.
5, 6.
a Ex. 29. 9.
b Jer. 18. 9.
c Ps. 18. 20.
& 91. 14.
d Mal. 2. 9.
e 1 Kin. 2. 27.
Ezek. 44. 10.
See ch. 4.
11, 18, 20.

f See Zech.
8. 4.
1 Sam. 22.18.

¹ Or, *the affliction of the*   *wealth which God would*
  tabernacle, for all the   *have given Israel.*

12; Rom. ix. 15). It may be explained
by saying that in the case of Hophni
and Phinehas God's *will* to slay them was
founded upon His foreknowledge of their
impenitence; while from another point of
view, in which God's *will* is the fixed point,
that impenitence may be viewed in its relation to that fixed point, and so dependent
upon it, and a necessary step to it.

26. *And the child Samuel*, &c.] The account of our Lord's growth (Luke ii. 52)
is very similar; "And Jesus increased in
wisdom and stature, and in favour with
God and man." The literal version of the
passage before us is, "The child Samuel
advanced and grew and was good (or accept-
able), both with the Lord, and also with men."

27. *a man of God*] See Judg. xiii. 6 note.
The sudden appearance of the only prophet
of whom mention is made since Deborah,
without name, or any notice of his country,
is remarkable.

28. *an ephod*] The High Priest's ephod,
in which was Urim and Thummim.

did I give, &c.] The bountiful provision
made by God for His priests is mentioned
as the great aggravation of the covetousness
of Eli's sons (cp. 2 Sam. xii. 7-9).

29. *Wherefore kick ye*] See marg. ref.
The well-fed beast becomes unmanageable
and refractory, and refuses the yoke, and
bursts the bonds (Jer. v. 5). So the priests,
instead of being grateful for the provision
made for them, in their pampered pride
became dissatisfied, wantonly broke the
laws of God which regulated their share of
the offerings, and gave themselves up to an
unbridled indulgence of their passions and
their covetousness.

honourest thy sons above me] What restrained Eli from taking vigorous action
to vindicate God's honour, was his unwillingness to lose for his sons the lucrative
office of the priesthood. He was willing to
rebuke them, he was grieved at their mis-
deeds, but he was not willing to give up the
wealth and plenty which flowed into his
house from the offerings of Israel.

30. *be it far from me*] The phrase so ren-
dered is a favourite one in the Books of
Samuel, where it occurs ten or eleven times.
It is variously rendered in the A. V., *God
forbid*, and *Be it far from me, thee*, &c. Lit.,
Be it an abomination to me.

31. *I will cut off thine arm*, &c.] A strong
phrase for breaking down the strength and
power, of which the arm is the instrument
in man (cp. Zech. xi. 17). See *v.* 33.

32. The original text is rather obscure
and difficult of construction, but the A. V.
probably gives the sense of it. The marg.
gives another meaning.

in all the wealth, &c.] The allusion is particularly to Solomon's reign, when Zadok
was made priest instead of Abiathar, 1 K.
ii. 26, 27. (See 1 K. iv. 20, seq.) The
enormous number of sacrifices then offered
must have been a great source of wealth to
the priests (1 K. viii. 63-66).

33. The meaning is explained by *v.* 36.
Those who are not cut off in the flower of
their youth shall be worse off than those
who are, for they shall have to beg their
bread. (Cp. Jer. xxii. 10.)

mine altar, *shall be* to consume thine eyes, and to grieve thine heart: and all the increase of thine house shall die [1]in the
34 flower of their age. And this *shall be* [g]a sign unto thee, that shall come upon thy two sons, Hophni and Phinehas; [h]in one
35 day they shall die both of them. And [i]I will raise me up a faithful priest, *that* shall do according to *that* which *is* in mine heart and in my mind: and [k]I will build him a sure house; and
36 he shall walk before [l]mine anointed for ever. [m]And it shall come to pass, *that* every one that is left in thine house shall come *and* crouch to him for a piece of silver and a morsel of bread, and shall say, [2]Put me, I pray thee, into [3]one of the priests' offices, that I may eat a piece of bread.

CHAP. 3. AND [a]the child Samuel ministered unto the LORD before Eli. And [b]the word of the LORD was precious in those days;
2 *there was* no open vision. And it came to pass at that time, when Eli *was* laid down in his place, [c]and his eyes began to wax
3 dim, *that* he could not see; and ere [d]the lamp of God went out [e]in the temple of the LORD, where the ark of God *was*, and
4 Samuel was laid down *to sleep;* that the LORD called Samuel:
5 and he answered, Here *am* I. And he ran unto Eli, and said, Here *am* I; for thou calledst me. And he said, I called not;
6 lie down again. And he went and lay down. And the LORD called yet again, Samuel. And Samuel arose and went to Eli, and said, Here *am* I; for thou didst call me. And he answered,
7 I called not, my son; lie down iagan. [4]Now Samuel [f]did not yet know the LORD, neither was the word of the LORD yet
8 revealed unto him. And the LORD called Samuel again the third time. And he arose and went to Eli, and said, Here *am* I; for thou didst call me. And Eli perceived that the LORD

Marginal references (left):

g 1 Kin. 13.
3.
h ch. 4. 11.
i 1 Kin. 2. 35.
1 Chr. 29. 22.
Ezek. 44. 15.
k 2 Sam. 7.
11, 27.
1 Kin. 11. 38.
l Ps. 2. 2.
& 18. 50.
m 1 Kin. 2. 27.

a ch. 2. 11.
b Ps. 74. 9.
Amos 8. 11.
c Gen. 27. 1.
ch. 2. 22.
d Ex. 27. 21.
e ch. 1. 9.

f See Acts
19. 2.

---

[1] Heb. *men.*
[2] Heb. *Join.*
[3] Or, *somewhat about the*

priesthood.
[4] Or, *Thus did Samuel before he knew the* LORD,

and before the word of the LORD *was revealed unto him.*

---

thine eyes...thine heart] For a similar personification of the tribe or family, see Judg. i. 2–4.

35. Zadok is meant rather than Samuel. The High Priesthood continued in the direct descendants of Zadok as long as the monarchy lasted (see 1 Chr. vi. 8–15).

Mine anointed, in its first sense obviously means the kings of Israel and Judah (Ps. lxxxix. 20; Zech. iv. 14). But doubtless the use of the term MESSIAH (Χριστὸς) here and in *v.* 10, is significant, and points to the Lord's Christ, in Whom the royal and priestly offices are united (Zech. vi. 11–15: see marg. reff.). In this connexion the substitution of the priesthood after the order of Melchisedec for the Levitical may be foreshadowed under *v.* 35 (see Heb. vii.).

36. *a piece*] The word is only found here; but is thought to be connected in etymology and in meaning with the *Gerah*, the smallest Hebrew coin, being the twentieth part of the shekel. The smallness of the sum asked for shows the poverty of the asker.

III. 1. See marg ref. note. Josephus says that Samuel's call to the prophetic office happened when he had just comp'eted his twelfth year (cp. Luke ii. 42).

was precious] (or *rare*) The song of Hannah, and the prophecy of the "man of God" (ii. 27 note), are the only instances of prophecy since Deborah. Samuel is mentioned as the first of the series of Prophets (Acts iii. 24).

no open vision] Better rendered, "**There was no vision promulgated** or **published.**" (Cp. 2 Chr. xxxi. 5.)

2. The passage should be rendered thus: —"And it came to pass at that time that Eli was sleeping in his place; and his eyes had begun to grow dim; he could not see. And the lamp of God was not yet gone out, and Samuel was sleeping in the temple of the Lord where the ark of God was; and the Lord called Samuel, &c." Eli's old age and dimness of sight is probably mentioned as the reason why Samuel thought Eli had called him. Being a blind and feeble old man, he was likely to do so if he wanted anything, either for himself, or for the service of the temple.

7. *did not yet know the* LORD] *i.e.* in His supernatural communication, as follows at the end of the verse. The text rendering of this verse is better than that of the margin.

9 had called the child. Therefore Eli said unto Samuel, Go, lie down: and it shall be, if he call thee, that thou shalt say, Speak, LORD; for thy servant heareth. So Samuel went and lay down
10 in his place. And the LORD came, and stood, and called as at other times, Samuel, Samuel. Then Samuel answered, Speak:
11 for thy servant heareth. ¶And the LORD said to Samuel, Behold I will do a thing in Israel, *g*at which both the ears of
12 every one that heareth it shall tingle. In that day I will perform against Eli *h*all *things* which I have spoken concerning
13 his house: ¹when I begin, I will also make an end. ²*i*For I have told him that I will *k*judge his house for ever for the iniquity which he knoweth; because *l*his sons made themselves
14 ³vile, and he ⁴ᵐrestrained them not. And therefore I have sworn unto the house of Eli, that the iniquity of Eli's house
15 ⁿshall not be purged with sacrifice nor offering for ever. ¶And Samuel lay until the morning, and opened the doors of the house of the LORD. And Samuel feared to show Eli the vision.
16 Then Eli called Samuel and said, Samuel, my son. And he
17 answered, Here *am* I. And he said, what *is* the thing that *the* LORD hath said unto thee? I pray thee hide *it* not from me °God do so to thee, and ⁵more also, if thou hide *any* ⁶thing from
18 me of all the things that he said unto thee. And Samuel told him ⁷every whit, and hid nothing from him. And he said, ᴾIt
19 *is* the LORD: let him do what seemeth him good. ¶And Samuel ᑫgrew, and ʳthe LORD was with him, ˢand did let none
20 of his words fall to the ground. And all Israel from Dan even to Beer-sheba knew that Samuel *was* ⁵established *to be* a
21 prophet of the LORD. And the LORD appeared again in Shiloh: for the LORD revealed himself to Samuel in Shiloh by ᵘthe word

g 2 Kin. 21. 12.
Jer. 19. 3.
h ch. 2. 30— 36.
i ch. 2. 29.
k Ezek. 7. 3. & 18. 30.
l ch. 2. 12.
m ch. 2. 23.

n Num. 15. 30, 31.
Isai. 22. 14.

o Ruth 1. 17.

p Job 1. 21. & 2. 10.
Ps. 39. 9.
Isai. 39. 8.
q ch. 2. 21.
r Gen. 39. 2, 21, 23.
s ch. 9. 6.
t Judg. 20. 1.
u ver. 1, 4.

Heb. *beginning and ending.*	³ Or, *accursed.*	⁶ Or, *word.*	
¹²Or, *and I will tell him, &c.*	⁴ Heb. *frowned not upon them.*	⁷ Heb. *all the things,* or, *words.*	
	⁵ Heb. *so add.*	⁸ Or, *faithful.*	

---

10. A Personal Presence, not a mere voice, or impression upon Samuel's mind, is here distinctly indicated. (Cp. Gen. xii. 7 note; Rev. i. 1, xxii. 16.)

11. More accurately, "**the which whosoever heareth both his ears shall tingle.**" This expressive phrase occurs again twice (marg. reff.) with reference to the destruction of Jerusalem by Nebuchadnezzar. It is remarkable that Jeremiah repeatedly compares the destruction of Jerusalem with the destruction of Shiloh (Jer. vii. 12, 14, xxvi. 6, 9. Cp. Ps. lxxviii. 60–64).

12. *when I begin, &c.*] Literally, as in the margin: meaning, I will go through with the performance from first to last.

13. *made themselves vile*] Rather, *have cursed themselves, i.e.* brought curses upon themselves.

he restrained them not] In the sense of punishing. He did not remove them from their office, which he ought to have done.

14. See marg. reff. The sin of the sons of Eli could not be purged by the appointed sacrifices of the Law. In blessed contrast with this declaration is the assurance of the N. T. (1 John i. 7; Acts xiii. 39).

15. *opened the doors*] We learn thus incidentally the nature of some of Samuel's duties. This duty was quite Levitical in its character. In the interval between Josh a and David, when the Tabernacle was stationary for the most part, it may have lost something of its *tent* character, and among other changes have had doors instead of the hanging

Samuel feared to show Eli the vision] Here was Samuel's first experience of the Prophet's cross: the having unwelcome truth to divulge to those he loved, honoured, and feared. Cp. the case of Jeremiah (Jer. xv. 10, xvii. 15-18, xx. 7–18).

18. *It is the* LORD, &c.] Compare the devout submission of Aaron (Lev. x. 3), and of Hezekiah (2 K. xx. 19). And, for the highest conceivable submission to the will of God, cp. Luke xxii. 42.

20. *from Dan, &c.*] See Judg. xx. 1 note.

21. The state described in *v.* 7 was henceforth reversed. Samuel now knew the Lord, and the Word of the Lord was revealed unto him.

_a_ ch. 5. 1.
& 7. 12.

4 of the LORD. AND the word of Samuel ¹²came to all Israel.
¶ Now Israel went out against the Philistines to battle, and
pitched beside ᵃEben-ezer : and the Philistines pitched in Aphek.

2 And the Philistines put themselves in array against Israel :˙and
when ³they joined battle, Israel was smitten before the Philistines:
and they slew of ⁴the army in the field about four thousand men.

3 ¶ And when the people were come into the camp, the elders of
Israel said, Wherefore hath the LORD smitten us to day before
the Philistines? Let us ⁵fetch the ark of the covenant of the
LORD out of Shiloh unto us, that, when it cometh among us, it

4 may save us out of the hand of our enemies. So the people sent
to Shiloh, that they might bring from thence the ark of the

_b_ 2 Sam. 6. 2.
Ps. 80. 1.
& 99. 1.
_c_ Ex. 25. 18.
Num. 7. 89.

covenant of the LORD of hosts, ᵇwhich dwelleth _between_ ᶜthe
cherubims: and the two sons of Eli, Hophni and Phinehas, _were_

5 there with the ark of the covenant of God. ¶ And when the ark
of the covenant of the LORD came into the camp, all Israel

6 shouted with a great shout, so that the earth rang again. And
when the Philistines heard the noise of the shout, they said,
What _meaneth_ the noise of this great shout in the camp of the
Hebrews? And they understood that the ark of the LORD was

7 come into the camp. And the Philistines were afraid, for they
said, God is come into the camp. And they said, Woe unto us!

8 for there hath not been such a thing ⁶heretofore. Woe unto
us! who shall deliver us out of the hands of these mighty Gods?
these _are_ the Gods that smote the Egyptians with all the

_d_ 1 Cor. 16.
13.

9 plagues in the wilderness. ᵈBe strong, and quit yourselves like
men, O ye Philistines, that ye be not servants unto the Hebrews,

_e_ Judg. 13. 1.

ᵉas they have been to you : ⁷quit yourselves like men, and fight.

---

¹ Or, _came to pass._   _spread._   ⁶ Heb. _yesterday,_ or, _the_
² Heb. _was._   ⁴ Heb. _the array._   _third day._
³ Heb. _the battle was_   ⁵ Heb. _take unto us._   ⁷ Heb. _be men._

IV. 1. Some attach the opening words to
the close of ch. iii., as the complement of
what is there said, "The Lord revealed
himself to Samuel...in Shiloh, and the word
of Samuel went forth to all Israel." If
placed at the commencement of ch. iv.,
and in connexion with what follows, they
are to be understood in the sense that
Samuel called all Israel to battle against
the Philistines. (Cp. vii. 5.) But this is
not the natural interpretation of the words,
which seem clearly to belong to what went
before.

The mention of the Philistines connects
the narrative with Judg. xiii.-xvi. Since
the Philistine servitude lasted forty years
(Judg. xiii. 1), and seems to have terminated in the days of Samuel (vii. 13, 14)
in about the 20th year of his judgeship
(vii. 2); and since it had already begun
before the birth of Samson (Judg. xiii. 5),
and Samson judged Israel twenty years "in
the days of the Philistines" (Judg. xv. 20),
it seems to follow that the latter part of the
judgeship of Eli and the early part of that
of Samuel must have been coincident with
the life-time of Samson.

Eben-ezer] (or, _the stone of help_) The place
was afterwards so named by Samuel. See

marg. reff. _Aphek_, or _the fortress_, was
probably the same as the _Aphek_ of Josh.
xii. 18. It would be towards the western
frontier of Judah, not very far from Mizpeh
of Benjamin, and near Shiloh (_v._ 4).

3. In the evening of the defeat of the
Israelites the elders held a council, and
resolved to send for the Ark, which is described in full, as implying that in virtue
of the Covenant God could not but give
them the victory (cp. Num. x. 35; Josh.
iii. 10).

4. _the people sent_] The expression is very
indicative of the political state so frequently
noted by the writer of the Book of Judges,
"In those days there was no king in
Israel."

6. _of the Hebrews_] This was the name by
which the Israelites were known to foreign
nations (cp. Ex. i. 15, ii. 6).

8. This is a remarkable testimony on the
part of the Philistines to the truth of the
events which are recorded in the Pentateuch. The Philistines would of course
hear of them, just as Balak and the people
of Jericho did (Num. xxii. 5; Josh. ii. 10).

with all the plagues, &c.] Rather, "with
every kind of plague," equivalent to _with
utter destruction._

10 And the Philistines fought, and *f*Israel was smitten, and they
   fled every man into his tent: and there was a very great
   slaughter; for there fell of Israel thirty thousand footmen.
11 And *g*the ark of God was taken; and *h*the two sons of Eli,
12 Hophni and Phinehas, [1]were slain. ¶And there ran a man of
   Benjamin out of the army, and *i*came to Shiloh the same day
13 with his clothes rent, and *k*with earth upon his head. And
   when he came, lo, Eli sat upon *l*a seat by the wayside watching:
   for his heart trembled for the ark of God. And when the man
14 came into the city, and told *it*, all the city cried out. And
   when Eli heard the noise of the crying, he said, What *meaneth*
   the noise of this tumult? And the man came in hastily, and
15 told Eli. Now Eli was ninety and eight years old; and *m*his
16 eyes [2]were dim, that he could not see. And the man said unto
   Eli, I *am* he that came out of the army, and I fled to day out of
17 the army. And he said, *n*What [3]is there done, my son? And
   the messenger answered and said, Israel is fled before the Philistines, and there hath been also a great slaughter among the
   people, and thy two sons also, Hophni and Phinehas, are dead,
18 and the ark of God is taken. And it came to pass, when he
   made mention of the ark of God, that he fell from off the seat
   backward by the side of the gate, and his neck brake, and he
   died: for he was an old man, and heavy. [4]And he had judged
19 Israel forty years. ¶And his daughter in law, Phinehas' wife,
   was with child, *near* [5]to be delivered: and when she heard the
   tidings that the ark of God was taken, and that her father in
   law and her husband were dead, she bowed herself and tra-
20 vailed; for her pains [6]came upon her. And about the time of
   her death *o*the women that stood by her said unto her, Fear
   not; for thou hast born a son. But she answered not, [7]neither
21 did she regard *it*. And she named the child, [8]*p*I-chabod, saying,
   *q*The glory is departed from Israel: because the ark of God was
22 taken, and because of her father in law and her husband. And
   she said, The glory is departed from Israel: for the ark of God
   is taken.

f ver. 2.
Lev. 26. 17.
Deut. 28. 25.
Ps. 78. 9, 62.
g ch. 2. 32.
Ps. 78. 61.
h ch. 2. 34.
Ps. 78. 64.
i 2 Sam. 1. 2.
k Josh. 7. 6.
2 Sam.13.19.
Neh. 9. 1.
Job 2. 12.
i ch. 1. 9.

m 1 Kin. 14.
4.

n 2 Sam.1.4.

o Gen. 35.
17.

p ch. 14. 3.
q 2 Kin. 17.
23.
Ps. 26. 8.

---

[1] Heb. *died*.
[2] Heb. *stood*.
[3] Heb. *is the thing*.
[4] He seems to have been

a Judge to do justice
 only, and that in South
 west *Israel*.
[5] Or, *to cry out*.
[6] Heb. *were turned*.

[7] Heb. *set not her heart*.
[8] That is, *Where is the
 glory?* or, There is *no
 glory*.

---

12. Runners who were swift of foot, and
could go long distances were important and
well-known persons (cp. 2 Sam. xviii. 19–
31). There seem to have been always professional runners to act as messengers with
armies in the field (2 K. xi. 4, 6, 19, A. V.
guards).

earth upon his head] In token of bitter
grief. Cp. marg. reff.

15. *dim*] Rather, "set." The word is
quite different from that so rendered in
iii. 2. The phrase seems to express the
fixed state of the blind eye, which is not
affected by the light. Eli's blindness, while
it made him alive to sounds, prevented his
seeing the rent garments and dust-be-
sprinkled head of the messenger of bad
tidings.

18. A comparison of 2 Sam. xviii. 4, explains exactly the meaning of the *side of*

the gate, and Eli's position. His seat or
throne, without a back, stood with the side
against the jamb of the gate, leaving the
passage through the gate quite clear, but
placed so that every one passing through
the gate must pass in front of him.

forty years] This chronological note connects this Book with that of Judges. (Cp.
Judg. iii. 11, &c.) It is an interesting question, but one very difficult to answer, how
near to the death of Phinehas, the son of
Eleazar the High Priest, Eli's forty years of
judgeship bring him. It is probable that at
least one high priesthood intervened.

21. *is departed*] Properly, "**Is gone into
captivity**."

22. The lesson of the ruin brought upon
Churches by the covetousness and pro-
fligacy of their priests, which is here taught
us so forcibly, and which has been again and

a ch. 4. 1.
b Judg. 16.
23.

c Isai. 19. 1.
& 46. 1, 2.
d Isai. 46. 7.

e Jer. 50. 2.
Ezek. 6. 4.
Micah 1. 7.

f See Zeph.
1. 9.
g ver. 7. 11.
Ex. 9. 3.
Acts 13. 11.
h ch. 6. 5.
i Ps. 78. 66.

k Deut. 2. 15.
ch. 7. 13.
& 12. 15.
i ver. 11.
m ver. 6.
Ps. 78. 66.

n ver. 6, 9.

a Gen. 41. 8.
Matt. 2. 4.

CHAP. 5. AND the Philistines took the ark of God, and brought it
2 *a*from Eben-ezer unto Ashdod. When the Philistines took the
ark of God, they brought it into the house of *b*Dagon, and set
3 it by Dagon. And when they of Ashdod arose early on the
morrow, behold, Dagon *was* *c*fallen upon his face to the earth
before the ark of the LORD. And they took Dagon, and *d*set
4 him in his place again. And when they arose early on the
morrow morning, behold, Dagon *was* fallen upon his face to the
ground before the ark of the LORD; and *e*the head of Dagon
and both the palms of his hands *were* cut off upon the threshold;
5 only ¹*the stump of* Dagon was left to him. Therefore neither
the priests of Dagon, nor any that come into Dagon's house,
6 *f*tread on the threshold of Dagon in Ashdod unto this day. ¶ But
*g*the hand of the LORD was heavy upon them of Ashdod, and he
*h*destroyed them, and smote them with *i*emerods, *even* Ashdod
7 and the coasts thereof. And when the men of Ashdod saw that
it was so, they said, The ark of the God of Israel shall not abide
with us : for his hand is sore upon us, and upon Dagon our god.
8 They sent therefore and gathered all the lords of the Philistines
unto them, and said, What shall we do with the ark of the God
of Israel ? And they answered, Let the ark of the God of Israel
be carried about unto Gath. And they carried the ark of the
9 God of Israel about *thither*. And it was *so*, that, after they had
carried it about, *k*the hand of the LORD was against the city
*l*with a very great destruction : and *m*he smote the men of the
city, both small and great, and they had emerods in their secret
10 parts. ¶ Therefore they sent the ark of God to Ekron. And it
came to pass, as the ark of God came to Ekron, that the Ekronites cried out, saying, They have brought about the ark of the
11 God of Israel to ²us, to slay us and our people. So they sent
and gathered together all the lords of the Philistines, and said,
Send away the ark of the God of Israel, and let it go again to his
own place, that it slay ³us not, and our people : for there was a
deadly destruction throughout all the city ; *n*the hand of God
12 was very heavy there. And the men that died not were smitten
with the emerods : and the cry of the city went up to heaven.

CHAP. 6. AND the ark of the LORD was in the country of the
2 Philistines seven months. And the Philistines *a*called for the
priests and the diviners, saying, What shall we do to the ark of

---

¹ Or, *the fishy part.*   ³ Heb. *me not, and my.*
² Heb. *me, to slay me and my.*

---

again illustrated in Jews and Christians, is
too solemn and important to be overlooked.
When the glory of holiness departs from
what should be a holy community, the glory
of God's Presence has already departed,
and the outward tokens of His protection
may be expected to depart soon likewise.
(Cp. Ezek. x 18, xi. 23 ; Rev. ii. 5.) But
though particular churches may fall, our
Lord's promise will never fail the Catholic
Church (Matt. xxviii. 20).

V. **2.** They brought it into the house of
Dagon (see marg. ref.) in order to enhance
the triumph of the gods of the Philistines
over the God of Israel. (Cp. xxxi. 9 Judg.
xvi. 23 ; Isai. xxxvii. 12.)

5. This custom still existed among the
worshippers of Dagon so late as the reign
of Josiah (see marg. ref.).

6. *emerods*] A corruption of *hemorrhoids.*
It is mentioned (Deut. xxviii. 27) among
the diseases with which God threatened to
punish the Israelites for disobedience.

8. The "lords" (see Judg. iii. 3) were very
unwilling to give up their triumph, and,
with the common heathen superstition,
imagined that some local bad luck was
against them at Ashdod. The result was to
bring the whole Philistine community under
the same calamity.

VI. **2.** The word for *priest* here is the
same as that used for the priests of the true
God ; that for *diviners* is everywhere used of
idolatrous or superstitious divining. Three

3 the LORD? tell us wherewith we shall send it to his place. And
they said, If ye send away the ark of the God of Israel, send it
not *empty; but in any wise return him *a trespass offering:
then ye shall be healed, and it shall *be known to you why his
4 hand is not removed from you. Then said they, What *shall be*
the trespass offering which we shall return to him? They
answered, Five golden emerods, and five golden mice, *according*
to the number of the lords of the Philistines: for one plague *was*
5 on ¹you all, and on your lords. Wherefore ye shall make images
of your emerods, and images of your mice that ¹mar the land; and
ye shall *give glory unto the God of Israel: peradventure he will
*lighten his hand from off you, and from off *your gods, and from
6 off your land. Wherefore then do ye harden your hearts, *as
the Egyptians and Pharaoh hardened their hearts? when he had
wrought ²wonderfully among them, ¹did they not let ³the people
7 go, and they departed? Now therefore make *a new cart, and
take two milch kine, *on which there hath come no yoke, and tie
8 the kine to the cart, and bring their calves home from them: and
take the ark of the LORD, and lay it upon the cart; and put
*the jewels of gold, which ye return him *for* a trespass offering,
in a coffer by the side thereof; and send it away, that it may
9 go. And see, if it goeth up by the way of his own coast to
*Beth-shemesh, *then* ⁴he hath done us this great evil: but if
not, then *we shall know that *it is* not his hand *that* smote us;
10 it *was* a chance *that* happened to us. ¶And the men did so;
and took two milch kine, and tied them to the cart, and shut up
11 their calves at home: and they laid the ark of the LORD upon
the cart, and the coffer with the mice of gold and the images of
12 their emerods. And the kine took the straight way to the way
of Beth-shemesh, *and* went along the highway, lowing as they
went, and turned not aside *to* the right hand or *to* the left;
and the lords of the Philistines went after them unto the

b Ex. 23. 15.
Deut. 16. 16.
c Lev. 5. 15,
16.
d ver. 9.

e See ver.
17, 18.
Josh. 13. 3.
Judg. 3. 3.
f ch. 5. 6.

g Josh. 7. 19.
Isai. 42. 12.
Mal. 2. 2.
John 9. 24.
h See ch. 5.
6, 11.
Ps. 39. 10.
i ch. 5. 3, 4,
7.
k Ex. 7. 13.
l Ex. 12. 31.
m 2 Sam.6.3.
n Num. 19. 2.
o ver. 4, 5.

p Josh.15.10.
q ver. 3.

¹ Heb. *them.*
² Or, *reproachfully.*

³ Heb. *them.*
⁴ Or, *it.*

---

modes of divination are described (Ezek.
xxi. 21, 22), by arrows, by teraphim, and
by the entrails of beasts. (Cp. Ex. vii. 11;
Dan. ii. 2).

3. *send it not empty*] See marg. reff. The
heathen idea of appeasing the gods with
gifts, and the scriptural idea of expressing
penitence, allegiance, or love to God, by
gifts and offerings to His glory and to the
comfort of our fellow worshippers, coincide
in the practical result.

4. It was a prevalent custom in heathen
antiquity to make offerings to the gods expressive of the particular mercy received.
Thus those saved from shipwreck offered
pictures of the shipwreck, &c., and the
custom still exists among Christians in certain countries.

The plague of the mice is analogous to
that of the frogs in Egypt. The destructive
power of field-mice was very great.

7. *a new cart ... kine on which there hath
come no yoke*] This was so ordered in reverence to the Ark, and was a right and true
feeling. See Mark xi. 2; Matt. xxvii. 60.

For the supposed peculiar virtue of *new*
things, see Judg. xvi. 7, 11.

9. Bethshemesh was the first Israelitish
town they would come to, being on the border of Judah. (See marg. ref.)

12. *lowing as they went*] Milch kine had
been chosen on purpose to make the sign
more significant. Nature would obviously
dispose the kine to go towards their calves;
their going in an opposite direction was
therefore plainly a Divine impulse overruling their natural inclination. And this is
brought out more distinctly by the mention
of their lowing, which was caused by their
remembering their calves.

and the lords, &c.] This circumstance of
the five satraps of the Philistines accompanying the Ark in person both made
it impossible for the Israelites to practise
any deceit (cp. Matt. xxvii. 63-66), and is
also a striking testimony to the agitation
caused among the Philistines by the plagues
inflicted on them since the Ark had been in
their country.

13 border of Beth-shemesh. And *they of* Beth-shemesh *were* reaping their wheat harvest in the valley: and they lifted up their
14 eyes, and saw the ark, and rejoiced to see *it*. And the cart came into the field of Joshua, a Beth-shemite, and stood there, where *there was* a great stone: and they clave the wood of the cart, and offered the kine a burnt offering unto the LORD.
15 And the Levites took down the ark of the LORD, and the coffer that *was* with it, wherein the jewels of gold *were*, and put *them* on the great stone: and the men of Beth-shemesh offered burnt offerings and sacrificed sacrifices the same day

r Josh. 13. 3.
16 unto the LORD. And when *r*the five lords of the Philistines

s ver. 4.
17 had seen *it*, they returned to Ekron the same day. ¶ *s*And these *are* the golden emerods which the Philistines returned *for* a trespass offering unto the LORD; for Ashdod one, for Gaza one, for Askelon one, for Gath one, for Ekron one;
18 and the golden mice, *according to* the number of all the cities of the Philistines *belonging* to the five lords, *both* of fenced cities, and of country villages, even unto the ¹great *stone* of Abel, whereon they set down the ark of the LORD: *which stone remaineth* unto this day in the field of Joshua, the Beth-shemite.

t See Ex. 19. 21.
Num. 4. 5.
2 Sam. 6. 7.
19 ¶ And *t*he smote the men of Beth-shemesh, because they had looked into the ark of the LORD, even he smote of the people fifty thousand and threescore and ten men: and the people lamented, because the LORD had smitten *many* of the people
20 with a great slaughter. And the men of Beth-shemesh said,

u 2 Sam. 6. 9.
Mal. 3. 2.
x Josh. 18. 14.
u"Who is able to stand before this holy LORD God? and to
21 whom shall he go up from us? And they sent messengers to the inhabitants of *x*Kirjath-jearim, saying, The Philistines have

¹ Or, *great stone*.

---

13. The whole population was in the field. The harvest work was suspended in an instant, and all the workmen ran to where the Ark was.

14. *a great stone*] (Cp. Gen. xxviii. 18; Judg. xiii. 19). This great stone was probably used as an altar on this occasion, and the kine stopping at it of their own accord was understood by the Bethshemites as an intimation that they were to offer sacrifices on it to the Lord God of Israel, Who had so wonderfully brought back the Ark from its captivity.

and they clave the wood of the cart, &c.] A similar expedient was resorted to by Araunah (2 Sam. xxiv. 22), and by Elisha (1 K. xix. 21).

15. The word *Levites* here probably means priests (Ex. iv. 14), sons of Levi, since Bethshemesh was one of the cities of the priests (Josh. xxi. 13-16). The burnt offering of the kine was not in any sense the offering of the men of Bethshemesh, but rather of the Philistine lords to whom the cart and the kine belonged. But the Bethshemites themselves, in token of their gratitude for such a signal mercy, now offered both burnt offerings and sacrifices, probably peace offerings, and doubtless feasted together with great joy and gladness (see 1 K. viii. 62-66; Ezr. vi. 16, 17). There is no-

thing whatever in the text to indicate that these sacrifices were offered otherwise than in the appointed way by the priests.

18. *the great stone of Abel*, &c.] Probably so called from the *lamentation* described in *v*. 19.

19. *fifty thousand and three score and ten*] Read *three score and ten*, omitting *fifty thousand*, which appears to have crept into the text from the margin. It is not improbable that in their festive rejoicing priests, Levites, and people may have fallen into intemperance, and hence into presumptuous irreverence (cp. Lev. x. 1, 9). God had just vindicated His own honour against the Philistines; it must now be seen that He would be sanctified in them that come nigh Him (Lev. x. 3). It is obvious to observe how the doctrine of Atonement, and its necessity in the case of sinners, is taught in this and similar lessons as to the awful HOLINESS of God.

21. *Kirjath-jearim*] See Josh. ix. 17 note. It has been thought that there was a high place at Kirjath-jearim (the *hill*, ch. vii. 1), the remnant of its old heathen sanctity when it was called Kirjath-Baal, *the city of Baal* (see Josh. xviii. 14; 2 Sam. vi. 2); and that for this reason it was selected as a proper place to send the Ark to.

brought again the ark of the LORD : come ye down, *and* fetch
7 it up to you. AND the men of *ᵃ*Kirjath-jearim came, and
fetched up the ark of the LORD, and brought it into the house
of *ᵇ*Abinadab in the hill, and sanctified Eleazar his son to keep
2 the ark of the LORD. ¶ And it came to pass, while the ark
abode in Kirjath-jearim, that the time was long ; for it was
twenty years : and all the house of Israel lamented after the
3 LORD. And Samuel spake unto all the house of Israel, saying,
If ye do *ᶜ*return unto the LORD with all your hearts, *then* *ᵈ*put
away the strange gods and *ᵉ*Ashtaroth from among you, and
*ᶠ*prepare your hearts unto the LORD, and *ᵍ*serve him only :
and he will deliver you out of the hand of the Philistines.
4 Then the children of Israel did put away *ʰ*Baalim and Ash-
5 taroth, and served the LORD only. ¶ And Samuel said, *ᶦ*Gather
all Israel to Mizpeh, and I will pray for you unto the LORD.
6 And they gathered together to Mizpeh, *ᵏ*and drew water, and
poured *it* out before the LORD, and *ˡ*fasted on that day, and said
there, *ᵐ*we have sinned against the LORD. And Samuel judged
7 the children of Israel in Mizpeh. ¶ And when the Philistines
heard that the children of Israel were gathered together to
Mizpeh, the lords of the Philistines went up against Israel.
And when the children of Israel heard *it*, they were afraid of
8 the Philistines. And the children of Israel said to Samuel,
¹*ⁿ*Cease not to cry unto the LORD our God for us, that he will

ᵃ ch. 6. 21.
Ps. 132. 6.
ᵇ 2 Sam. 6. ∴.
ᶜ Deut. 30.
2—10.
1 Kin. 8. 48.
Isai. 55. 7.
Hos. 6. 1.
Joel 2. 12.
ᵈ Gen. 35. 2.
Josh. 24. 14,
23.
ᵉ Judg. 2. 13.
ᶠ 2 Chr. 30.
19.
Job 11. 13.
ᵍ Deut. 6. 13.
Matt. 4. 10.
ʰ Judg. 2. 11.
ᶦ Judg. 20. 1.
2 Kin. 25. 23.
ᵏ 2 Sam. 14.
14.
ˡ Neh. 9. 1.
Dan. 9. 3.
ᵐ Judg. 10.
10.
1 Kin. 8. 47.
Ps. 106. 6.

ⁿ Isai. 37. 4.

¹ Heb. *Be not silent from us from crying.* See Ps. 28. 1.

VII. 1. This verse belongs more properly
to ch. vi. Abinadab and his sons were
probably of the house of Levi. The catastrophe at Beth-shemesh must inevitably
have made the Israelites very careful to pay
due honour to the Ark in accordance with
the Law : but to give the care of the Ark to
those who were not of the house of Levi
would be a gross violation of the Law.

2. *and all the house of Israel lamented, &c.*]
The occupation of the country about Shiloh
by the Philistines (*v.* 3) was partly the
reason for the Ark being kept so long at
Kirjath-jearim. But another reason seems
to have been the fall of the Israelites into
idolatry, which made them neglect the Ark,
and brought upon them this Philistine servitude ; probably the last twenty years of
the Philistine oppression described in Judg.
xiii. 1, which is there expressly connected
with Israelite idolatry. Now, probably,
through the exhortations of Samuel, coupled
with the chastening of the Philistine yoke,
the Israelites repented and turned again to
the God of their fathers.

3-5. Cp. marg. reff. Twenty years of
Samuel's life had passed away since the last
mention of him (iv. 1). Now he appears in
the threefold character of Prophet, Judge,
and the acknowledged leader of the whole
people. His words were an answer to a
profession of repentance on the part of Israel, the practical proof of which would be
the putting away all their false gods. (Cp.
Judg. vi. 10 note.)

I will pray for you, &c.] So Moses prayed

for the people at Rephidim (Ex. xvii. 11,
12), and for Miriam (Num. xii. 13) ; so Elijah prayed at Carmel (1 K. xviii. 36, 42) ;
so Ezra prayed at the evening sacrifice
(Ezr. ix. 5) ; so the High Priest prayed for
the house of Israel on the Day of Atonement ;
and so does our Lord Jesus Christ ever live
at God's right hand to make intercession
for us.

6. Two rites are brought together here
which belong especially to the Feast of Tabernacles and the Day of Atonement, respectively, viz. drawing and pouring out water,
and fasting. Hence some think that Samuel
chose the Feast of Tabernacles, and the fast
which preceded it, as the occasion for assem-
bling the people. Others explain the pouring out water as the pouring out the heart
in penitence as it were water ; or, as a symbolical act expressing their ruin and help-
lessness (2 Sam. xiv. 14) ; or as typifying their
desire that their sins might be forgotten "as
waters that pass away" (Job xi. 16).

and Samuel judged] This seems to denote
the *commencement* of Samuel's Judgeship
civil and military, as having taken place at
Mizpeh on this occasion. As civil Judge he
did exactly what Moses did (Ex. xviii. 13-
16) ; as military Judge he did what Othniel,
Ehud, Barak, and Gideon had done before
him, organized and marshalled the people
for effectual resistance to their oppressors,
and led them out to victory.

7. This implies a united invasion by the
whole Philistine force. Hence the *terror*
of the Israelites. (Cp. Judg. xv. 11.)

9 save us out of the hand of the Philistines. And Samuel took
a sucking lamb, and offered *it for* a burnt offering wholly unto
the LORD: and °Samuel cried unto the LORD for Israel; and
10 the LORD ¹heard him. And as Samuel was offering up the
burnt offering, the Philistines drew near to battle against Israel:
ᵖbut the LORD thundered with a great thunder on that day
upon the Philistines, and discomfited them; and they were
11 smitten before Israel. And the men of Israel went out of
Mizpeh, and pursued the Philistines, and smote them, until
12 *they came* under Beth-car. Then Samuel ᵠtook a stone, and set
it between Mizpeh and Shen, and called the name of it ²Eben-
13 ezer, saying, Hitherto hath the LORD helped us. ʳ¶ So the
Philistines were subdued, and they ˢcame no more into the
coast of Israel: and the hand of the LORD was against the
14 Philistines all the days of Samuel. And the cities which the
Philistines had taken from Israel were restored to Israel, from
Ekron even unto Gath; and the coasts thereof did Israel deliver
out of the hands of the Philistines. And there was peace be-
15 tween Israel and the Amorites. ¶ And Samuel ᵗjudged Israel
16 all the days of his life. And he went from year to year ³in
circuit to Beth-el, and Gilgal, and Mizpeh, and judged Israel in
17 all those places. And ᵘhis return *was* to Ramah; for there *was*
his house; and there he judged Israel; and there he ˣbuilt an
altar unto the LORD.

Marginal references:

° Ps. 99. 6.
Jer. 15. 1.

ᵖ See Josh.
10. 10.
Judg. 4. 15.
2 Sam. 22.
14, 15.

ᵠ Gen. 28.
18.
& 31. 45.
Josh. 4. 9.
ʳ Judg. 13. 1.
ˢ ch. 13. 5.

ᵗ ch. 12. 11.
Judg. 2. 16.

ᵘ ch. 8. 4.
ˣ Judg. 21. 4.

¹ Or, *answered.*   ² That is, *The stone of help:*   ³ Heb. *and he circuited.*
ch. 4. 1.

---

9. Samuel's preparation for intercessory prayer, viz. the offering up an atoning sacrifice, is most significant (cp. Luke i. 9, 10). The term here used for a *lamb* does not occur in the Pentateuch; indeed it is only found besides this place in Isai. lxv. 25. The offering is in accordance with Levit. xxii. 27.

the LORD *heard him*] Better as in marg. The *answer* was not simply the granting the asked-for deliverance, but the great thunder (*v.* 10), which was "the voice of the Lord," the same voice with which the Lord answered Moses (Ex. xix. 19; Ps. xcix. 6).

11. *Beth-car*] This place is nowhere else mentioned. It seems to have stood on a hill overhanging the road from the Philistine territory to Mizpeh, and close to Ebenezer, iv. 1.

12. *Shen* was a *tooth-* or sharp-pointed rock (see xiv. 4), nowhere else mentioned and not identified.

13. *all the days of Samuel*] Not (as in *v.* 15), all the days of his *life*, but all the days of his *government*, when as Judge he ruled over Israel, before they asked for a king.

14. This shows the vigour and success of Samuel's government. He seems not only to have expelled the Philistines from the interior of the Israelitish country, but to have attacked them in their own land, and taken from them the cities, with the adjacent territory, which properly belonged to Israel, but which the Philistines had taken possession of. In this war the Amorites, finding

the Philistines worse masters than the Israelites, made common cause with Samuel, and assisted the Israelites in their wars against the Philistines.

15. *Samuel judged Israel*, &c.] The repetition of the phrase in *vv.* 16, 17, in connexion with Samuel's circuit, is a proof that it is his civil judgeship which is meant. The military leadership of course belonged to Saul, when he became king.

16. *Gilgal*] It is uncertain whether Gilgal in the valley of the Jordan, or the modern Jiljûlieh, the Gilgal of 2 K. ii. 1, iv. 38, be meant; but far more probably the former (see xi. 14 and note).

17. *and there he built an altar*] Whether this altar was in connexion with the Tabernacle or not we have no means of deciding, since we are in complete ignorance as to where the Tabernacle was at this time, or who was High Priest, or where he resided. It is quite possible that Samuel may have removed the Tabernacle from Shiloh to some place near to Ramah; and indeed it is in itself improbable that, brought up as he was from infancy in the service of the Tabernacle, he should have left it. At the beginning of Solomon's reign we know it was at Gibeon, close to Ramah (1 K. iii. 4; 2 Chr. i. 3–6). If the Tabernacle had been at Shiloh at this time, it is likely that Shiloh would have been one of the places at which Samuel judged Israel. But Shiloh was probably waste, and perhaps unsafe on account of the Philistines.

Снар. 8. AND it came to pass, when Samuel was old, that he *a*made
2 his *b*sons judges over Israel. Now the name of his firstborn was
Joel; and the name of his second, Abiah : *they were* judges in
3 Beer-sheba. And his sons *c*walked not in his ways, but turned
aside *d*after lucre, and *e*took bribes, and perverted judgment.
4 Then all the elders of Israel gathered themselves together, and
5 came to Samuel unto Ramah, and said unto him, Behold, thou
art old, and thy sons walk not in thy ways : now *f*make us a
6 king to judge us like all the nations. ¶ But the thing ¹dis-
pleased Samuel, when they said, Give us a king to judge us.
7 And Samuel prayed unto the LORD. And the LORD said unto
Samuel, Hearken unto the voice of the people in all that they
say unto thee : for *g*they have not rejected thee, but *h*they have
8 rejected me, that I should not reign over them. According to
all the works which they have done since the day that I brought
them up out of Egypt even unto this day, wherewith they have
forsaken me, and served other gods, so do they also unto thee.
9 Now therefore ²hearken unto their voice : ³howbeit yet protest
solemnly unto them, and *i*shew them the manner of the king
10 that shall reign over them. ¶ And Samuel told all the words of
11 the LORD unto the people that asked of him a king. And he
said, *k*This will be the manner of the king that shall reign over
you : *l*He will take your sons, and appoint *them* for himself, for
his chariots, and *to be* his horsemen ; and *some* shall run before
12 his chariots. And he will appoint him captains over thousands,
and captains over fifties ; and *will set them* to ear his ground,
13 and to reap his harvest, and to make his instruments of war,
14 *to be* confectionaries, and *to be* cooks, and *to be* bakers. And *m*he
will take your fields, and your vineyards, and your oliveyards,
15 *even* the best *of them*, and give *them* to his servants. And he
will take the tenth of your seed, and of your vineyards, and
16 give to his ⁴officers, and to his servants. And he will take your
menservants, and your maidservants, and your goodliest young
17 men, and your asses, and put *them* to his work. He will take
18 the tenth of your sheep : and ye shall be his servants. And ye

a	Deut.16.18.
	2 Chr. 19. 5.
b	See Judg. 10. 4.
c	Jer. 22. 15.
d	Ex. 18. 21. 1 Tim. 3. 3.
e	Deut.16.19. Ps. 15. 5.
f	ver. 19, 20. Deut. 17. 14.
g	See Ex. 16. 8.
h	ch. 10. 19. & 12. 17, 19.
	ver. 11.
k	See Deut. 17. 16, &c. ch. 10. 25.
l	ch. 14. 52.
m	1 Kin. 21. 7. See Ezek. 46. 18.

¹ Heb. *was evil in the eyes of Samuel.*
² Or, *obey.*
³ Or, *notwithstanding when thou hast solemnly pro-tested against them, then*
thou shalt shew, &c.
⁴ Heb. *eunuchs*, Gen. 37. 36.

VIII. **1.** This verse implies a long period,
probably not less than twenty years, of
which we have no account except what is
contained in the brief notice in vii. 13–
17. The general idea conveyed is of a time
of peace and prosperity, analogous to that
under other Judges.

2. The mention of Beer-sheba, on the
extreme southern frontier of Judah, as the
place where Samuel's sons judged Israel is
remarkable. It was probably due to the recovery of territory from the usurpation of
the Philistines (vii. 14).

6. See marg. which implies that the thing
spoken of caused anger, indignation, or some
revulsion of feeling (see Gen. xxi. 11,
12). The answer of the Lord (*v.* 7) shows
that Samuel's personal feelings had been
hurt. They were soothed by being reminded of the continued ingratitude of the

people to God Himself, upon Whom, in
fact, a greater slight was put by this very
request for a king " like all the nations,"
than upon Samuel (cp. Matt. x. 24 ; John
xv. 18, 20). For a comment on this transaction, see Hos. xiii. 9–11 ; Acts xiii.
21, 22.

12. This organization was as old as the
time of Moses (Num. xxxi. 14 ; Deut. i.
15), and prevailed among the Philistines
also (xxix. 2). The civil and military divisions were identical, and the civil officers
were the same as the captains of thousands, hundreds, fifties, and tens, in time
of war.

to ear his ground] Literally, " **to plough
his ploughing**." *To ear* is an old English
word, now obsolete, for *to plough*.

14–18. See illustrations in marg. reff. ;
1 K. v. 13-18, xii. 4.

shall cry out in that day because of your king which ye shall
have chosen you; and the LORD [n]will not hear you in that day.
19 ¶ Nevertheless the people [o]refused to obey the voice of Samuel;
20 and they said, Nay; but we will have a king over us; that we
also may be [p]like all the nations; and that our king may judge
21 us, and go out before us, and fight our battles. And Samuel
heard all the words of the people, and he rehearsed them in the
22 ears of the LORD. And the LORD said to Samuel, [q]Hearken
unto their voice, and make them a king. And Samuel said unto
the men of Israel, Go ye every man unto his city.

CHAP. 9. NOW there was a man of Benjamin, whose name *was*
[a]Kish, the son of Abiel, the son of Zeror, the son of Bechorath,
2 the son of Aphiah, [1]a Benjamite, a mighty man of [2]power. And
he had a son, whose name *was* Saul, a choice young man, and a
goodly: and *there was* not among the children of Israel a good-
lier person than he: [b]from his shoulders and upward *he was*
3 higher than any of the people. And the asses of Kish Saul's
father were lost. And Kish said to Saul his son, Take now one
4 of the servants with thee, and arise, go seek the asses. And he
passed through mount Ephraim, and passed through the land
of [c]Shalisha, but they found *them* not: then they passed through
the land of Shalim, and *there they were* not: and he passed through
5 the land of the Benjamites, but they found *them* not. *And* when
they were come to the land of Zuph, Saul said to his servant
that *was* with him, Come, and let us return; lest my father leave
6 *caring* for the asses, and take thought for us. And he said unto
him, Behold now, *there is* in this city [d]a man of God, and *he is* an
honourable man; [e]all that he saith cometh surely to pass: now
let us go thither; peradventure he can shew us our way that we
7 should go. Then said Saul to his servant, But, behold, *if* we go,
[f]what shall we bring the man? for the bread [3]is spent in our
vessels, and *there is* not a present to bring to the man of God:
8 what [4]have we? And the servant answered Saul again, and said,
Behold, [5]I have here at hand the fourth part of a shekel of

[n] Prov. 1. 25, 26, 27. Isai. 1. 15. Mic. 3. 4.
[o] Jer. 44. 16.
[p] ver. 5.
[q] ver. 7. Hos. 13. 11.
[a] ch. 14. 51. 1 Chr. 8. 33.
[b] ch. 10. 23.
[c] 2 Kin. 4. 42.
[d] Deut. 33. 1. ch. 2.
[e] ch. 3. 19.
[f] See Judg. 6. 18. & 13. 17. 1 Kin. 14. 3. 2 Kin. 4. 42. & 8. 8.

[1] Or, *the son of a man of Jemini.*
[2] Or, *substance.*
[3] Heb. *is gone out of, &c.*
[4] Heb. is *with us.*
[5] Heb. *there is found in my hand.*

20. *fight our battles*] It appears from xii. 12, that the warlike movements of Nahash had already begun to excite alarm.

22. A repetition for the third time (*vv.* 7, 9) of the expression of God's will in the matter, marks Samuel's great unwillingness to comply with the people's request. Besides the natural aversion which he felt to being thrust aside after so many years of faithful and laborious service, and the natural prejudice which he would feel at his age against a new form of government, he doubtless saw how much of the evil heart of unbelief there was in the desire to have a visible king for their leader, instead of trusting to the invisible Lord Who had hitherto led them. But God had His own purpose in setting up the kingdom which was to be typical of the kingdom of His only begotten Son.

IX. **1.** The genealogy of Saul is here given as far as Aphiah (*Abiah*, 1 Chr. vii. 8), who was of the house of Becher the son of Benjamin (Gen. xlvi. 21). *Kish* (1 Chr. ix. 35-39) was the son of *Ner* the son of *Jehiel*, (or, *Abiel* here and xiv. 51), the first settler (*father*, 1 Chr. ix. 35) at Gibeon, or Gibeah of Saul, and who married *Maachah*, a daughter or granddaughter of Caleb. If so, it is obvious that the names of several generations are omitted between Kish and Abiel, and among them that from which the family of Matri (x. 21) was called.

4. The land of Shalisha was somewhere near Gilgal, *i.e.* Jiljûlieh. It is thought to derive its name from *three* (Shalosh) wadys which unite in the wady of Karawa. The situation of Shalim is not known: its etymology connects it more probably with the land of Shual (xiii. 17), apparently round Taiyibeh, which was about nine miles from Gibeah.

Zuph (*v.* 5), see i. 1 note.

7. Presents of bread or meat were as common as presents of money. (Cp. Ezek. xiii. 19; Hos. iii. 2.)

8. *the fourth part of a shekel*] In value about sixpence. Probably the shekel, like

silver: *that* will I give to the man of God, to tell us our way.
9 (Beforetime in Israel, when a man *º*went to enquire of God, thus he spake, Come, and let us go to the seer: for *he that is* now
10 *called* a Prophet was beforetime called *ʰ*a Seer.) Then said Saul to his servant, ¹Well said; come, let us go. So they went unto
11 the city where the man of God *was*. ¶*And* as they went up ²the hill to the city, *ⁱ*they found young maidens going out to draw
12 water, and said unto them, Is the seer here? And they answered them, and said, He is; behold, *he is* before you: make haste now, for he came to day to the city; for *ᵏthere is* a ³sacri-
13 fice of the people to day *ˡ*in the high place: as soon as ye be come into the city, ye shall straightway find him, before he go up to the high place to eat: for the people will not eat until he come, because he doth bless the sacrifice; *and* afterward they eat that be bidden. Now therefore get you up; for about ⁴this
14 time ye shall find him. And they went up into the city: *and* when they were come into the city, behold, Samuel came out
15 against them, for to go up to the high place. ¶*ᵐ*Now the LORD had ⁵told Samuel in his ear a day before Saul came, saying,
16 To morrow about this time I will send thee a man out of the land of Benjamin, *ⁿ*and thou shalt anoint him *to be* captain over my people Israel, that he may save my people out of the hand of the Philistines: for I have *º*looked upon my people, because
17 their cry is come unto me. And when Samuel saw Saul, the LORD said unto him, *ᵖ*Behold the man whom I spake to thee of! this same
18 shall ⁶reign over my people. Then Saul drew near to Samuel in the gate, and said, Tell me, I pray thee, where the seer's house
19 *is*. And Samuel answered Saul, and said, I *am* the seer: go up before me unto the high place; for ye shall eat with me to day, and to morrow I will let thee go, and will tell thee all that *is* in thine
20 heart. And as for *q*thine asses that were lost ⁷three days ago, set not thy mind on them; for they are found. And on whom *ʳis* all the desire of Israel? *Is it* not on thee, and on all thy
21 father's house? And Saul answered and said, *ˢAm* not I a Benjamite, of the *ᵗ*smallest of the tribes of Israel? and *ᵘ*my family the least of all the families of the tribe of Benjamin? wherefore

º Gen. 25.22.

ʰ 1 Chr. 9. 2.
& 26. 28.
& 29. 29.
2 Chr. 16. 7, 10.
Isai. 30. 10.
ⁱ Gen. 24. 11.

ᵏ Gen. 31. 51.
ch. 16. 2.
ˡ 1 Kin. 3. 2.

ᵐ ch. 15. 1.
Acts 13. 21.

ⁿ ch. 10. 1.

º Ex. 2. 25.
& 3. 7, 9.

ᵖ ch. 16. 12.
Hos. 13. 11.

q ver. 3.

ʳ ch. 8. 5, 10.
& 12. 13.
ˢ ch. 15. 17.
ᵗ Judg. 20.
46, 47, 48.
Ps. 68. 27.
ᵘ See Judg.
6. 15.

¹ Heb. *Thy word is good.*
² Heb. *in the ascent of the city.*
³ Or, *feast.*
⁴ Heb. *to day.*
⁵ Heb. *revealed the ear of Samuel.* See Ruth 4. 4 note.
⁶ Heb. *restrain in.*
⁷ Heb. *to day three days.*

---

our early English silver coins, was divided into four quarters by a cross, and actually subdivided, when required, into half and quarter shekels.

9. This is manifestly a gloss inserted in the older narrative by the later editor of the sacred text, to explain the use of the term in *vv.* 11, 18, 19. It is one among many instances which prove how the very letter of the contemporary narratives was preserved by those who in later times compiled the histories. We cannot say exactly when the term *seer* became obsolete. See marg. reff.

13. *before he go up*] By this phrase we see that the high place was in the highest part of the city. Like the "house of the god Berith" (Judg. ix. 46), it was probably the citadel of Ramah. There was connected with the altar a room large enough for

thirty people to dine in (*v.* 22).

16. *that he may save my people out of the hand of the Philistines,* &c.] These words are not very easily reconcileable with vii. 13. It is possible that the aggressive movements of the Philistines, after the long cessation indicated by vii. 13, coupled with Samuel's old age and consequent inability to lead them to victory as before, were among the chief causes which led to the cry for a king. If this were so, the Philistine oppression glanced at in this verse might in a general survey be rather connected with Saul's times than with Samuel's.

21. The tribe of Benjamin, originally the smallest of all the tribes (Num. i. 36), if Ephraim and Manasseh are reckoned as one tribe, had been nearly annihilated by the civil war recorded in Judg. xx. It had of

22 then speakest thou [1]so to me ? ¶ And Samuel took Saul and his servant, and brought them into the parlour, and made them sit in the chiefest place among them that were bidden, which *were* 23 about thirty persons. And Samuel said unto the cook, Bring the portion which I gave thee, of which I said unto thee, Set it by thee. 24 And the cook took up *x*the shoulder, and *that* which *was* upon it, and set *it* before Saul. And *Samuel* said, Behold that which is [2]left ! set *it* before thee, *and* eat: for unto this time hath it been kept for thee since I said, I have invited the people. So Saul 25 did eat with Samuel that day. ¶ And when they were come down from the high place into the city, *Samuel* communed 26 with Saul upon *v*the top of the house. And they arose early: and it came to pass about the spring of the day, that Samuel called Saul to the top of the house, saying, Up, that I may send thee away. And Saul arose, and they went out both of them, he 27 and Samuel, abroad. *And* as they were going down to the end of the city, Samuel said to Saul, Bid the servant pass on before us, (and he passed on,) but stand thou still [3]a while, that I may shew thee the word of God.

CHAP. 10. THEN *a*Samuel took a vial of oil, and poured *it* upon his head, *b*and kissed him, and said, *Is it* not because *c*the LORD 2 hath anointed thee *to be* captain over *d*his inheritance ? When thou art departed from me to day, then thou shalt find two men by *e*Rachel's sepulchre in the border of Benjamin *f*at Zelzah ; and they will say unto thee, The asses which thou wentest to seek are found : and, lo, thy father hath left [4]the care of the asses, and sorroweth for you, saying, What shall I do for my 3 son ? Then shalt thou go on forward from thence, and thou shalt come to the plain of Tabor, and there shall meet thee three men going up *g*to God to Beth-el, one carrying three kids, and another carrying three loaves of bread, and another 4 carrying a bottle of wine : and they will [5]salute thee, and give thee two *loaves* of bread ; which thou shalt receive of their

Marginal references

x Lev. 7. 32, 33.
Ezek. 24. 4.

y Deut. 22. 8.
2 Sam. 11. 2.
Acts 10. 9.

a ch. 9. 16.
& 16. 13.
2 Kin. 9. 3, 6.
b Ps. 2. 12.
c Acts 13. 21.
d Deut. 32. 9.
Ps. 78. 71.
e Gen. 35.
19, 20.
f Josh. 18.
28.

g Gen. 28. 22.
& 35. 1, 3, 7.

---

[1] Heb. *according to this word?*   [3] Heb. *to day.*   [5] Heb. *ask thee of peace*
[2] Or, *reserved.*   [4] Heb. *the business.*   as Judg. 18. 15.

---

course not recovered from that terrible calamity in the time of Saul, and was doubtless literally much the smallest tribe at that time. Nothing could be more improbable, humanly speaking, than that this weak tribe should give a ruler to the mighty tribes of Joseph and Judah.

22. *the parlour*] The **hall** or *cell* attached to the chapel on the high place, in which the sacrificial feast was wont to be held. (Cp. 1 Chr. ix. 26.)

24. *the shoulder and its appurtenances,* would give the sense accurately. The right shoulder was the priest's portion in the Levitical sacrifices. Probably it was Samuel's own portion in this case, and he gave it to Saul as a mark of the highest honour.

26. *to the top of the house*] "**On the top.**" The bed on which Saul slept was on the top of the house. It is very common in the East to provide extra sleeping accommodation by placing a tent or awning on the house-top.

X. 1. *Is it not because,* &c.] Samuel

answers Saul's tacit or expressed wonder, by telling him why he did as he did. (Cp. ix. 21.)

2. How should Saul know that what Samuel said was the word of the Lord ? Samuel gives him a sign, "Thou shalt find two men," &c. (Cp. Judg. vi. 36–40 ; Isai. vii. 11–14 ; John vi. 30 ; Mark xi. 2, xiv. 13, &c.)

Zelzah] A place absolutely unknown.

3. *The plain of Tabor*] It should be "**the oak or terebinth**" *of Tabor* (Judg. iv. 11 note). It has been ingeniously conjectured that *Tabor* is either a different form of *Deborah*, or a corruption of it, and that the *oak*, or *terebinth of Tabor*, is the same as *Allon-bachuth*, the oak under which Deborah was buried, and which lay *beneath Bethel* (Gen. xxxv. 8). The terebinth, where the three men came upon Saul, must have been at some point previous to that where the road leading northwards from Jerusalem branches ; when they reached that point they would go on with their offerings to Bethel, he would pursue his journey to Gibeah.

5 hands. After that thou shalt come to [h]the hill of God, [i]where *is* the garrison of the Philistines : and it shall come to pass, when thou art come thither to the city, that thou shalt meet a company of prophets coming down [k]from the high place with a psaltery, and a tabret, and a pipe, and a harp, before them ;

6 [l]and they shall prophesy : and [m]the Spirit of the LORD will come upon thee, and [n]thou shalt prophesy with them, and shalt be

7 turned into another man. And [l]let it be, when these [o]signs are come unto thee, [2]*that* thou do as occasion serve thee ; for [p]God

8 *is* with thee. And thou shalt go down before me [q]to Gilgal ; and, behold, I will come down unto thee, to offer burnt offerings, *and* to sacrifice sacrifices of peace offerings : [r]seven days shalt thou tarry, till I come to thee, and shew thee what thou shalt

9 do. ¶ And it was *so*, that when he had turned his [3]back to go from Samuel, God [4]gave him another heart : and all those signs

10 came to pass that day. And [s]when they came thither to the hill, behold, [t]a company of prophets met him ; and [u]the Spirit of

11 God came upon him, and he prophesied among them. And it came to pass, when all that knew him beforetime saw that, behold, he prophesied among the prophets, then the people said, [5]one to another, What *is* this *that* is come unto the son of Kish ? [x]Is

12 Saul also among the prophets ? And one [6]of the same place answered and said, But [y]who *is* their father ? Therefore it

Side references:
[h] ver. 10.
[t] ch. 13. 3.
[k] ch. 9. 12.
[l] Ex. 15. 20, 21.
2 Kin. 3. 15.
1 Cor. 14. 1.
[m] Num. 11. 25.
ch. 16. 13.
[n] ver. 10.
ch. 19. 23, 24.
[o] Ex. 4. 8.
Luke 2. 12.
[p] Judg. 6. 12.
[q] ch. 11. 14, 15.
& 13. 4.
[r] ch. 13. 8.
[s] ver. 5.
[t] ch. 19. 20.
[u] ver. 6.
[x] ch. 19. 24.
Matt. 13. 54, 55.
John 7. 15.
Acts 4. 13.
[y] Isai. 54. 13.
John 6. 45.
& 7. 16.

[1] Heb. *it shall come to pass, that when these signs, &c.*
[2] Heb. *do for thee as thine*
[3] Heb. *shoulder.*
[4] Heb. *turned.*
hand shall find, Judg. 9. 33.
[5] Heb. *a man to his neighbour.*
[6] Heb. *from thence.*

---

5. *hill of God*] Rather, "**Gibeah** " *of God*, and so in *v.* 10. Two things are clear ; *one* that Saul had got home when he got to Gibeah of God, for there he found his uncle, and no further journeying is so much as hinted at, and the same word *Gibeah* describes his home at *v.* 26. The *other* that there was a high place at Gibeah just above the city, from which he met the company of prophets *coming down*. Hence it is obvious to conclude that the name *Gibeah of God* (which occurs nowhere else) was sometimes given to *Gibeah of Saul* on account of the worship on its high place, or, possibly, that the name *Gibeah of God* described the whole hill on a part of which the city Gibeah stood.

where is the garrison of the Philistines] It seems strange that Samuel should give this description of Gibeah to Saul, who must have been so well acquainted with it. Possibly they may be explanatory words inserted by the narrator with reference to xiii. 2.

Musical instruments were the accompaniments of the prophetic song (1 Chr. xiii. 8, xxv. 3). The *Psaltery* is a kind of lyre with ten strings, in the shape of an earthen wine bottle (*nebel*, whence νάβλα), which was something like a sugar-loaf or a delta. The *tabret* is a kind of drum or tambourine, or timbrel, usually played by dancing women (Ex. xv. 20 : Judg. xi. 34. Cp. Jer. xxxi. 4). The *pipe* (*chalil*, literally the *bored* or *pierced* instrument) is a kind of flute used on

occasions of joy and mirth (Isai. v. 12 ; 1 K. i. 40 ; Ps. lxviii. 25). The *harp* (*cinnor*, whence the Greek κινύρα) was a stringed instrument, and that played upon by David (xvi. 16, xix. 9 ; Ps. xliii. 4, lvii. 8).

6. *will come upon thee*] The word rendered *come*, means to *come* or *pass upon*, as fire does when it breaks out and spreads (Amos v. 6) ; hence it is frequently used of the Spirit of God passing upon any one. (See Judg. xiv. 19, xv. 14 ; below *v.* 10, xi. 6, xvi. 13.)

shalt be turned into another man] This is a remarkable expression, and occurs nowhere else. It describes the change in point of mental power and energy which would result from the influx of the Spirit of the Lord (*v.* 9). In the case of Samson it was a supernatural bodily strength ; in the case of Saul a capacity for ruling and leading the people of which before he was destitute, and which the Spirit wrought in him. (Cp Acts i. 8 ; Isai. xi. 2-4.)

8. *seven days shalt thou tarry*, &c.] The appointment here made is not to be confounded with that mentioned in marg. ref.

12. *But who is their father ?*] This is a very obscure phrase. If by *father* be intended the head or leader (cp. 1 Chr. xxv. 6 ; 2 K. ii. 12) of the prophets, the question means : " What kind of leader can they have to admit such a person as Saul into the company ?" Some Versions read *Who is his father ?* in the sense : " Who would have

13 became a proverb, *Is* Saul also among the prophets ? And when he had made an end of prophesying, he came to the high place.
14 ¶ And Saul's uncle said unto him and to his servant, Whither went ye ? And he said, To seek the asses : and when we saw
15 that *they were* no where, we came to Samuel. And Saul's uncle
16 said, Tell me, I pray thee, what Samuel said unto you. And Saul said unto his uncle, He told us plainly that the asses were found. But of the matter of the kingdom, whereof Samuel spake,
17 he told him not.   ¶ And Samuel called the people together *z* unto
18 the Lord *a* to Mizpeh ; and said unto the children of Israel, *b* Thus saith the Lord God of Israel, I brought up Israel out of Egypt, and delivered you out of the hand of the Egyptians, and out of the hand of all kingdoms, *and* of them that oppressed
19 you : *c* and ye have this day rejected your God, who himself saved you out of all your adversities and your tribulations ; and ye have said unto him, *Nay,* but set a king over us. Now therefore present yourselves before the Lord by your tribes, and by
20 your thousands.   And when Samuel had *d* caused all the tribes
21 of Israel to come near, the tribe of Benjamin was taken. When he had caused the tribe of Benjamin to come near by their families, the family of Matri was taken, and Saul the son of Kish was taken : and when they sought him, he could not be
22 found. Therefore they *e* enquired of the Lord further, if the man should yet come thither. And the Lord answered, Behold,
23 he hath hid himself among the stuff. And they ran and fetched him thence : and when he stood among the people, *f* he was higher than any of the people from his shoulders and upwards.
24 And Samuel said to all the people, See ye him *g* whom the Lord hath chosen, that *there is* none like him among all the people ?
25 And all the people shouted, and said, *h* 1 God save the king. Then Samuel told the people *i* the manner of the kingdom, and wrote *it* in a book, and laid *it* up before the Lord. And Samuel sent
26 all the people away, every man to his house.   ¶ And Saul also went home *k* to Gibeah ; and there went with him a band of
27 men, whose hearts God had touched. *l* But the *m* children of Belial said, How shall this man save us ? And they despised him, *n* and brought him no presents. But *2* he held his peace.

z Judg. 11.
11.
& 20. 1.
ch. 11. 15.
a ch. 7. 5, 6.
b Judg. 6. 8,
9.
c ch. 8. 7, 19.
& 12. 12.

d Acts 1. 24,
26.

e ch. 23. 2,
4, 10, 11.

f ch. 9. 2.
g 2 Sam. 21.
6.
h 1 Kin. 1.
25, 39.
2 Kin. 11.
12.
i See Deut.
17. 14, &c.
ch. 8. 11.
k Judg. 20.
14.
ch. 11. 4.
l ch. 11. 12.
m Deut. 13.
13.
n 2 Chr.17.5.
Matt. 2. 11.

1 Heb. *Let the king live.*   *2* Or, *he was as though he had been deaf.*

expected Kish to have a son among the prophets ? " (Cp. Matt. xiii. 54, 55.)

14. From the order of the narrative, and the mention of Saul's servant, it looks as if Saul found his uncle at the high place. Perhaps some solemnity similar to that mentioned in ix. 19 was going on at this time, in which the prophets had been taking part.

19. For the use of "thousand " as equivalent to "family," see xxiii. 23 ; Judg. vi. 15 marg. In Num. i. 16 it may mean whole tribes.

20. *caused...to come near...was taken*] The Heb. phrases are exactly the same as in Josh. vii. 16, 17, where the A.V. renders the first has *brought*.

21. *the family of Matri*] This name occurs nowhere else among the families of Benjamin, or in the genealogy of Saul. (See ix. 1 note.)

22. *among the stuff*] Rather, "**the baggage.**" The assembly was like a camp, and

the baggage (impedimenta) of the whole congregation was probably collected in one place, where the waggons were arranged for protection.

25. *the manner of the kingdom*] *i.e.* the just prerogative of the kingdom, the law, or bill of rights, by which the king's power was limited as well as secured. It is not improbable that what Samuel wrote was simply a transcript of Deut. xvii. 14-20, which he *laid up before the Lord, i.e.* placed by the side of the Ark of the Covenant with the copy of the Law (see Deut. xxxi. 26). It would be ready for reference if either king or people violated the "law of the kingdom."

26. *a band of men*] Rather, "**the host,**" "men of valour." There seems to be an opposition intended between the *valiant men* and the *children of Belial* (*v.* 27 ; see marg. ref. note).

27. *presents*] The *minchah* was the token of homage and acknowledgment from the

Chap. 11. THEN ^aNahash the Ammonite came up, and encamped against ^bJabesh-gilead : and all the men of Jabesh said unto
2 Nahash, ^cMake a covenant with us, and we will serve thee. And Nahash the Ammonite answered them, On this *condition* will I make *a covenant* with you, that I may thrust out all your right
3 eyes, and lay it *for* ^da reproach upon all Israel. And the elders of Jabesh said unto him, ¹Give us seven days' respite, that we may send messengers unto all the coasts of Israel : and then, if *there be* no man to save us, we will come out to thee.
4 ¶ Then came the messengers ^eto Gibeah of Saul, and told the tidings in the ears of the people: and ^fall the people lifted up
5 their voices, and wept. And, behold, Saul came after the herd out of the field ; and Saul said, What *aileth* the people that they weep? And they told him the tidings of the men of Jabesh.
6 ^gAnd the Spirit of God came upon Saul when he heard those
7 tidings, and his anger was kindled greatly. And he took a yoke of oxen, and ^hhewed them in pieces, and sent *them* throughout all the coasts of Israel by the hands of messengers, saying, ⁱWhosoever cometh not forth after Saul and after Samuel, so shall it be done unto his oxen. And the fear of the LORD fell on the
8 people, and they came out ²with one consent. And when he numbered them in ^kBezek, the children ^lof Israel were three hundred thousand, and the men of Judah thirty thousand.
9 ¶ And they said unto the messengers that came, Thus shall ye say unto the men of Jabesh-gilead, To morrow, by *that time* the sun be hot, ye shall have ³help. And the messengers came and
10 shewed *it* to the men of Jabesh ; and they were glad. Therefore the men of Jabesh said, To morrow ^mwe will come out unto

Marginal references:
^a 2 Sam. 10.1.
^b Judg. 21. 8.
^c Gen. 26. 28.
Ex. 23. 32.
1 Kin. 20.34.
Job 41. 4.
Ezek. 17. 13.
^d Gen. 34.14.
ch. 17. 26.

^e ch. 10. 26.
& 15. 34.
2 Sam. 21. 6.
^f Judg. 2. 4.
& 21. 2.

^g Judg. 3.10.
ch. 10. 10.
& 16. 13.
^h Judg. 19.
29.
ⁱ Judg. 21.
5, 8, 10.

^k Judg. 1. 5.
^l 2 Sam. 24.
9.

^m ver. 3.

---

¹ Heb. *Forbear us.*   ² Heb. *as one man,* Judg. 20. 1.   ³ Or, *deliverance.*

---

subject to the sovereign, and from the tributary nation to their suzerain. (See 2 Sam. viii. 2, 6 ; Judg. iii. 17, 18 ; 1 K. iv. 21 ; 2 K. xvii. 4, &c. ; Ps. lxxii. 10 ; Isai. xvi. 1.) Saul dissembled his resentment, and waited for the favourable tide which soon came with the invasion of Nahash.

XI. **1.** Nahash was king of the children of Ammon, as appears from xii. 12. He seems to have been connected with the family of David, since Abigail, David's sister, was "the daughter (perhaps *granddaughter*) of Nahash" (2 Sam. xvii. 25 ; 1 Chr. ii. 16, 17) ; and, perhaps, in consequence of this connexion, he and his family were very friendly to David (2 Sam. xvii. 27).

Jabesh-Gilead must have been re-peopled after its destruction (see marg. ref.). The Ammonites and Moabites resented the possession of Gilead by the Israelites (Judg. x. 6-18, xi.).

3. *the elders*] Observe the universal form of civil government among the Israelites, by elders (Judg. viii. 14, 16, &c.).

4. They came to Gibeah on account of the connexion between the Benjamites and the people of Jabesh (Judg. xxi.).

in the ears of the people] They did not even inquire for Saul, so little was he looked upon as king. Verse 5 shows how com-

pletely he was still in a private and humble station.

6. This time the Spirit of God came upon him, as upon the Judges before him, as a Spirit of supernatural energy and power.

7. Though not expressly stated, it is doubtless implied that he sent the portions by the messengers to the twelve tribes, after the analogy, and probably in imitation, of Judg. xix. 29. He made use of the revered name of Samuel to strengthen his own weak authority. Samuel accompanied Saul in the expedition (*v.* 12).

8. *he numbered them*] This was done to see who was absent (cp. Judg. xxi. 9).

Bezek has been conjectured to be the name of a district rather than of a town. Two villages retained the name in the time of Eusebius seventeen miles from Nablous, on the way to Beth-shean.

the children of Israel and the men of Judah] This looks like the language of later times, times perhaps subsequent to the establishment of the two kingdoms of Israel and Judah. Israel here (including Benjamin) is as ten to one compared with Judah. This is about the true proportion.

9. The distance from Bezek to Jabesh-Gilead would perhaps be about twenty miles.

10. *To-morrow*] Probably the last of the

ⁿ See ch. 31. 11.
ᵒ Judg.7. 16.

ᵖ ch. 10. 27.
ᵍ See Luke 19. 27.
ʳ 2 Sam. 19. 22.
ˢ Ex. 14. 13. ch. 19. 5.
ᵗ ch. 10. 8.
ᵘ ch. 10. 17.
ˣ ch. 10. 8.

ᵃ ch. 8. 5, 19. 20.
ᵇ ch. 10. 24.
ᶜ Num. 27. 17.
ch. 8. 20.
ᵈ ch. 8. 1.
ᵉ ver. 5.
ch. 10. 1.
ᶠ Num. 16. 15.
Acts 20. 33.
ᵍ Deut. 16. 19.

ʰ John 18. 38.
Acts 23. 9.

you, and ye shall do with us all that seemeth good unto you.
11 And it was *so* on the morrow, that *ⁿ*Saul put the people *ᵒ*in three companies; and they came into the midst of the host in the morning watch, and slew the Ammonites until the heat of the day: and it came to pass, that they which remained were
12 scattered, so that two of them were not left together. ¶ And the people said unto Samuel, *ᵖ*Who *is* he that said, Shall Saul reign
13 over us? *ᵍ*bring the men, that we may put them to death. And Saul said, *ʳ*There shall not a man be put to death this day:
14 for to day *ˢ*the LORD hath wrought salvation in Israel. Then said Samuel to the people, Come, and let us go *ᵗ*to Gilgal, and
15 renew the kingdom there. And all the people went to Gilgal; and there they made Saul king *ᵘ*before the LORD in Gilgal; and *ˣ*there they sacrificed sacrifices of peace offerings before the LORD; and there Saul and all the men of Israel rejoiced greatly.

CHAP. 12. AND Samuel said unto all Israel, Behold, I have hearkened unto *ᵃ*your voice in all that ye said unto me, and
2 *ᵇ*have made a king over you. And now, behold, the king *ᶜ*walketh before you: *ᵈ*and I am old and grayheaded; and, behold, my sons *are* with you: and I have walked before you
3 from my childhood unto this day. Behold, here I *am*: witness against me before the LORD, and before *ᵉ*his anointed: *ᶠ*whose ox have I taken? or whose ass have I taken? or whom have I defrauded? whom have I oppressed? or of whose hand have I received any ¹bribe ²to *ᵍ*blind mine eyes therewith? and I will
4 restore it you. And they said, Thou hast not defrauded us, nor oppressed us, neither hast thou taken ought of any man's
5 hand. And he said unto them, The LORD *is* witness against you, and his anointed *is* witness this day, *ʰ*that ye have not

---

¹ Heb. *ransom.*   ² Or, *that I should hide mine eyes at him.*

"seven days' respite" (*v.* 3). Their words were spoken in guile, to throw the Ammonites off their guard.

11. The march from Bezek may have begun the night before. This disposition of the forces *in three companies* (imitating Gideon's strategy, cp. marg. ref.) would not have been made till the morning when they were very near the Ammonitish forces. "The morning watch" was the last of the three watches, of four hours each, into which the night was anciently divided by the Hebrews. (See Judg. vii. 19 note.) The time thus indicated would be between two and six in the morning.

13. *There shall not a man,* &c.] An instance of great moderation, as well as good policy, on the part of Saul. Cp. David's conduct (marg. ref.).

14. *let us go to Gilgal*] *i.e.* to Gilgal by Jericho, where was a famous sanctuary, in the tribe of Benjamin.

15. *made Saul king*] The LXX. has another reading, *and Samuel anointed Saul king there.* The example of David, who, besides his original anointing by Samuel (xvi 12, 13), was twice anointed, first as king of Judah (2 Sam. ii. 4), and again as

king over all Israel (do. v. 3), makes it probable that Saul was anointed a second time; but this may be included in the word "made king" (see xii. 3, 5).

XII. **2.** *my sons are with you*] Possibly, however, a tinge of mortified feeling at the rejection of himself and his family, mixed with a desire to recommend his sons to the favour and goodwill of the nation, is at the bottom of this mention of them.

3. *his anointed*] *i.e.* king Saul. The title Messiah, χριστὸς, unctus, or anointed, had been given to the High Priests (Lev. iv. 3: cp. also ii. 10, 35); but this is the earliest instance of an actual king of Israel bearing the title of God's Christ, and thus typifying the true Messiah or Christ of God.

any bribe] Literally, a *ransom*, the fine paid by a criminal in lieu of bonds or death (Ex. xxi. 30), applied to the bribe paid to an unjust judge to induce him to acquit the guilty. (Cp. Am. v. 12.)

to blind, &c.] See marg. The phrase is used of one who averts his eyes, as refusing assistance, or as showing contempt, or, as here, as winking at what is wrong.

found ought ⁱin my hand. And they answered, *He is* witness.

6 ¶And Samuel said unto the people, ᵏ*It is* the LORD that ¹advanced Moses and Aaron, and that brought your fathers up out of the

7 land of Egypt. Now therefore stand still, that I may ˡreason with you before the LORD of all the ²righteous acts of the LORD,

8 which he did ³to you and to your fathers. ᵐWhen Jacob was come into Egypt, and your fathers ⁿcried unto the LORD, then the LORD ᵒsent Moses and Aaron, which brought forth your

9 fathers out of Egypt, and made them dwell in this place. And when they ᵖforgat the LORD their God, ᑫhe sold them into the hand of Sisera, captain of the host of Hazor, and into the hand of ʳthe Philistines, and into the hand of the king ˢof

10 Moab, and they fought against them. And they cried unto the LORD, and said, ᵗWe have sinned, because we have forsaken the LORD, ᵘand have served Baalim and Ashtaroth : but now ˣdeliver us out of the hand of our enemies, and we

11 will serve thee. And the LORD sent ʸJerubbaal, and Bedan, and ᶻJephthah, and ᵃSamuel, and delivered you out of the hand

12 of your enemies on every side, and ye dwelled safe. And when ye saw that ᵇNahash the king of the children of Ammon came against you, ᶜye said unto me, Nay; but a king shall reign

13 over us : when ᵈthe LORD your God *was* your king. Now therefore ᵉbehold the king ᶠwhom ye have chosen, *and* whom ye have desired ! and, behold, ᵍthe LORD hath set a king over

14 you. If ye will ʰfear the LORD, and serve him, and obey his voice, and not rebel against the ⁴commandment of the LORD, then shall both ye and also the king that reigneth over you

15 ⁵continue following the LORD your God : but if ye will ⁱnot obey the voice of the LORD, but rebel against the commandment of the LORD, then shall the hand of the LORD be against you,

16 ᵏas *it was* against your fathers. Now therefore ˡstand and see

17 this great thing, which the LORD will do before your eyes. *Is it* not ᵐwheat harvest to day ? ⁿI will call unto the LORD, and he shall send thunder and rain ; that ye may perceive and see that

i Ex. 22. 4.
k Mic. 6. 4.

l Isai. 1. 18.
Mic. 6. 2.

m Gen. 46.
5, 6.
n Ex. 2. 23.
o Ex. 3. 10

p Judg. 3. 7.
q Judg. 4. 2.
r Judv. 10. 7.
& 13. 1.
s Judg.3.12.
t Judg. 10.
10.
u Judg. 2.13.
x Judg. 10.
15, 16.
y Judg. 6.
14, 32.
z Judg.11.1.
a ch. 7. 13.
b ch. 11. 1.
c ch. 8. 5.
d Judg. 8.23.
ch. 8. 7.
e ch. 10. 24.
f ch. 8. 5.
& 9. 20.
g Hos.13.11.
h Josh.24.14.
Ps. 81. 13.
i Lev. 26.14,
15, &c.
Deut. 28. 15,
&c.
Josh. 24. 20.
k ver. 9.
l Ex. 14. 13.
m Prov.26.1.
n ch. 7. 9, 10.
Jam. 5. 16.

---

¹ Or, *made*.   ² Heb. *righteousnesses*, or,   ⁴ Heb. *mouth*.
³ Heb. *with*.   *benefits*, Judg. 5. 11.   ⁵ Heb. *be after*.

---

6. *advanced*] In the sense of *appointing* them to their office. It is, literally, *made* (see marg.; 1 K. xii. 31; Heb. iii. 2). Samuel's purpose is to impress the people with the conviction that Jehovah was their God, and the God of their fathers ; that to Him they owed their national existence and all their national blessings, and that faithfulness to Him, to the exclusion of all other worship (*v.* 21) was the only safety of the newly-established monarchy. Observe the constant reference to the Exodus as the well-known turning-point of their national life (see iv. 8, vi. 6).

9. According to the present arrangement of the Book of Judges, and the common chronology, the oppression of Sisera must have occurred about 200 years after the entrance into Canaan. But Samuel here places it as the first great servitude, before that under Eglon king of Moab, or that from which Shamgar delivered them. And this is in accordance with the internal evidence of the Book of Judges itself. It is

also the order of Judg. x. 11, except that there the Ammonites (Judg. iii. 13) are placed before the Philistines.

11. *Bedan*] No such name occurs among the Judges who delivered Israel. Some Versions and commentators read Barak, the form of the letters of both words being in Hebrew somewhat similar.

and Samuel] There is nothing improper or out of place in Samuel mentioning his own judgeship. It had supplied a remarkable instance of God's deliverance (vii. 12-15) ; and, as it was the last as well as one of the very greatest deliverances, it was natural he should do so. The passage in Heb. xi. 32 is quite as favourable to the mention of Samuel here as to that of *Samson*, which some propose to read instead of *Samuel*.

17. *wheat harvest*] Between May 15 and June 15. Jerome's testimony (that of an eye-witness) "I have never seen rain in the end of June, or in July, in Judæa" is borne out by modern travellers.

o ch. 8. 7.

p Ex. 14. 31.
See Ezra 10.
9.
q Ex. 9. 28.
Jam. 5. 15.

r Deut. 11
16.
s Jer. 16. 19.
Hab. 2. 18.
1 Cor. 8. 4.
t Ps. 94. 14.
u Josh. 7. 9.
Ps. 106. 8.
Jer. 14. 21.
x Deut. 7. 7.
Mal. 1. 2.
y Acts. 12. 5.
Rom. 1. 9.
Col. 1. 9.
2 Tim. 1. 3.
z Ps. 34. 11.
Prov. 4. 11.

a 1 Kin. 8. 36.
Jer. 6. 16.
b Eccles. 12.
13.
c Isai. 5. 12.
d Deut. 10.
21.
Ps. 126. 2.
e Josh. 24.
20.
f Deut. 28.
36.
a ch. 10. 26.
b ch. 10. 5.

oyour wickedness *is* great, which ye have done in the sight of
18 the LORD, in asking you a king.   ¶ So Samuel called unto the
LORD; and the LORD sent thunder and rain that day: and pall
19 the people greatly feared the LORD and Samuel.   And all the
people said unto Samuel, qPray for thy servants unto the LORD
thy God, that we die not: for we have added unto all our sins
20 *this* evil, to ask us a king.   ¶ And Samuel said unto the people,
Fear not: ye have done all this wickedness: yet turn not aside
from following the LORD, but serve the LORD with all your
21 heart; and rturn ye not aside: sfor *then should ye go* after vain
22 *things*, which cannot profit nor deliver; for they *are* vain.   For tthe
LORD will not forsake his people ufor his great name's sake:
because xit hath pleased the LORD to make you his people.
23 Moreover as for me, God forbid that I should sin against the
LORD 1yin ceasing to pray for you: but zI will teach you the
24 agood and the right way: bonly fear the LORD, and serve him
in truth with all your heart: for cconsider 2how dgreat *things* he
25 hath done for you.   But if ye shall still do wickedly, eye shall
be consumed, fboth ye, and your king.

CHAP. 13.   SAUL 3reigned one year; and when he had reigned two
2 years over Israel, Saul chose him three thousand *men* of Israel;
whereof two thousand were with Saul in Michmash and in mount
Beth-el, and a thousand were with Jonathan in aGibeah of Benjamin: and the rest of the people he sent every man to his tent.
3 ¶ And Jonathan smote bthe garrison of the Philistines that *was*
in 4Geba, and the Philistines heard *of it*.   And Saul blew the
trumpet throughout all the land, saying, Let the Hebrews hear.
4 And all Israel heard say *that* Saul had smitten a garrison of the
Philistines, and *that* Israel also 5was had in abomination with
the Philistines.   And the people were called together after Saul
5 to Gilgal.   And the Philistines gathered themselves together to
fight with Israel, thirty thousand chariots, and six thousand

1 Heb. *from ceasing.*
2 Or, *what a great* thing,
   &c.
3 Heb. *the son of one year
   in his reigning.*
4 Or, *The hill.*
5 Heb. *did stink*, Gen. 34.
   30. Ex. 5. 21.

XIII. 1. The text of this verse, omitted
by the LXX., is held to be corrupt, and
the numerals denoting Saul's age at his
accession as well as the duration of his
reign, are thought to be omitted or faulty.
Saul may have been about 30 at his accession, and have reigned some 32 years,
since we know that his grandson Mephibosheth was five years old at Saul's
death (2 Sam. iv. 4); and 32 added to the
seven and a half years between the death
of Saul and that of Ishbosheth, makes up
the 40 years assigned to Saul's dynasty in
Acts xiii. 21.   Neither is there any clue to
the interval of time between the events recorded in the preceding chapter, and those
which follow in this and succeeding chapters.   But the appearance of Jonathan as a
warrior (*v.* 2) compared with the mention of
Saul as "a young man" (ix. 2); implies an
interval of not less than ten or fifteen years,
perhaps more.   The object of the historian
is to prepare the way for the history of
David's reign.   He therefore passes at once
to that incident in Saul's reign, which led to

his rejection by God, as recorded in *vv.*
13, 14.
2. The state of things which preceded
the events described in this chapter seems
to have been a comparative peace between
Israel and the Philistines, since Saul had
only 3,000 men under arms.   At the same
time Philistine garrisons continued to occupy the country of the Israelites in certain
strong places, whereof one was at Geba
(*Jeba*), in the immediate neighbourhood of
Gibeah (x. 5, xiii. 3), and exactly opposite
Michmash (*Mukhmas*), which was on the
northern edge of the great Wady Suweinit.
3. This was the first act in the war of
independence, and probably the first feat in
arms of the young hero Jonathan.
4. to *Gilgal*]   The Wady Suweinit de-
bouches into the plain of the Jordan in
which Gilgal was situated.   For the sanctity
of Gilgal, see above, xi. 14 note.
5. *thirty thousand chariots*]   Probably a
copyist's mistake for *three hundred*. [Cp., for
a similar numerical variation, 1 Chr. xviii. 4
with 2 Sam. viii. 4.]

horsemen, and people as the sand which *is* on the sea shore in multitude : and they came up, and pitched in Michmash, east-
6 ward from Beth-aven. ¶ When the men of Israel saw that they were in a strait, (for the people were distressed,) then the people *c* did hide themselves in caves, and in thickets, and in rocks, and
7 in high places, and in pits. And *some of* the Hebrews went over Jordan to the land of Gad and Gilead. As for Saul, he *was* yet
8 in Gilgal, and all the people [1]followed him trembling. *d* And he tarried seven days, according to the set time that Samuel *had appointed :* but Samuel came not to Gilgal ; and the people were
9 scattered from him. And Saul said, Bring hither a burnt offering to me, and peace offerings. And he offered the burnt
10 offering. And it came to pass, that as soon as he had made an end of offering the burnt offering, behold, Samuel came ; and Saul went out to meet him, that he might [2]salute him.
11 ¶ And Samuel said, What hast thou done ? And Saul said, Because I saw that the people were scattered from me, and *that* thou camest not within the days appointed, and *that* the Philistines gathered themselves together at Michmash ;
12 therefore said I, The Philistines will come down now upon me to Gilgal, and I have not [3]made supplication unto the LORD : I
13 forced myself therefore, and offered a burnt offering. And Samuel said to Saul, *e* Thou hast done foolishly : *f* thou hast not kept the commandment of the LORD thy God, which he com-
14 manded thee : for now would the LORD have established thy kingdom upon Israel for ever. *g* But now thy kingdom shall not continue : *h* the LORD hath sought him a man after his own heart, and the LORD hath commanded him *to be* captain over his people, because thou hast not kept *that* which the LORD

c Judg. 6. 2.

d ch. 10. 8.

e 2 Chr. 16. 9.
f ch. 15. 11.

g ch. 15. 28.

h Ps. 89. 20.
Acts 13. 22.

[1] Heb. *trembled after him.*   [2] Heb. *bless him.*   [3] Heb. *intreated the face.*

---

eastward from Bethaven] Or more simply "**to the east of Bethaven,**" which (Josh. vii. 2) lay *on the east side of Bethel.* Bethaven [thought to be the same as Deir Diwân] lay between Bethel and Michmash, which had been evacuated by Saul.

6. *in thickets*] Literally, *among thorns.*

high places] Not the *high places* for worship, but holds or towers (Judg. ix. 46, 49) ; that particular kind of tower which was the work of the old Canaanite inhabitants, and which remained as ruins in the time of Saul.

7. The words *some of,* which are the emphatic words in the A.V., as distinguishing those who crossed the Jordan from those who hid themselves, are not in the Hebrew at all. *The Hebrews* seem to be distinguished from *the men of Israel* in v. 6. (Cp. xiv. 21.)

8. *had appointed*] This appointment has of course nothing whatever to do with that made years before (x. 8), the keeping of which is expressly mentioned at the natural time (xi. 15). But Samuel had again, on this later occasion, made an appointment at the end of seven days. It seems to have been as a trial of faith and obedience, under which, this time, Saul unhappily broke down.

9. There is a difference of opinion among commentators whether Saul himself offered

the sacrifices prepared for Samuel, thus entrenching upon the priest's office ; or whether he ordered the priests to sacrifice, as Solomon did. In the latter case his sin consisted in disobeying the word of God, Who had bidden him wait till Samuel came. And this is, on the whole, the more probable ; since Samuel's rebuke says nothing of any assumption of priesthood, such as we read in the case of Uzziah (2 Chr. xxvi. 18).

11. Saul had come from Michmash to Gilgal, expecting to gather the force of the whole nation around him. Instead of that, the people fled, leaving him in the exposed plain with only 600 men (v. 15). The Philistines occupied Michmash, and might at any moment pour down the valley upon Gilgal. Saul's situation was obviously one of extreme peril. A few hours' delay might prove fatal to him and his little army. Hence, he "forced" himself, &c.

13. *Thou hast done foolishly,* &c.] Motives of worldly expediency were not to be weighed against the express commandment of God. All the circumstances and all the dangers were as well known to God as they were to Saul, and God had bidden him wait till Samuel came. Here was exactly the same sin of wilful disobedience which broke out again, and was so severely reproved (xv. 17–23).

15 commanded thee. ¶And Samuel arose, and gat him up from Gilgal unto Gibeah of Benjamin. And Saul numbered the people *that were* ¹present with him, ⁱabout six hundred men.

ch. 14. 2.

16 And Saul, and Jonathan his son, and the people *that were* present with them, abode in ²Gibeah of Benjamin: but the Philis-
17 tines encamped in Michmash. And the spoilers came out of the camp of the Philistines in three companies: one company turned unto the way *that leadeth to* ᵏOphrah, unto the land of
18 Shual: and another company turned the way *to* ˡBeth-horon: and another company turned *to* the way of the border that looketh
19 to the valley of ᵐZeboim toward the wilderness. ¶Now ⁿthere was no smith found throughout all the land of Israel: for the Philistines said, Lest the Hebrews make *them* swords or spears:
20 but all the Israelites went down to the Philistines, to sharpen every man his share, and his coulter, and his axe, and his mat-
21 tock. Yet they had ³a file for the mattocks, and for the coulters, and for the forks, and for the axes, and ⁴to sharpen the goads.
22 So it came to pass in the day of battle, that ᵒthere was neither sword nor spear found in the hand of any of the people that *were* with Saul and Jonathan: but with Saul and with Jonathan
23 his son was there found. ¶ᵖAnd the ⁵garrison of the Philistines went out to the passage of Michmash.

CHAP. 14. NOW ⁶it came to pass upon a day, that Jonathan the son of Saul said unto the young man that bare his armour,

k Josh. 18.
23.
l Josh. 16. 3.
& 18. 13, 14.
ᵐ Neh. 11.
31.
ⁿ See 2 Kin.
24. 14.
Jer. 24. 1.

o 3o Judg.
5. 3.

p ch. 14. 1, 4.

¹ Heb. *found.* ³ Heb. *a file with mouths.* ⁵ Or, *standing camp.*
² Heb. *Geba,* ver. 3. ⁴ Heb. *to set.* ⁶ Or, *there was a day.*

---

15. *Samuel arose*] Saul could not return to his own station at Michmash, seeing it was occupied by the Philistines; so, perhaps by Samuel's advice (since, according to the text, he preceded him thither), he effected a junction with Jonathan at Gibeah. Some would read *Saul* instead of *Samuel.*

17. *the spoilers*] "**The devastator:**" the same word is used of the destroying Angel (Ex. xii. 23). The verse describes the system adopted by the Philistines by which for a time they subjugated the Israelites. From their central camp at Michmash they sent out three bands to kill and lay waste and destroy. One took a northerly direction towards Ophrah,—five miles east of Bethel, identified with *Ephrain* (2 Chr. xiii. 19) and the modern *Taiyibeh,*—and towards the land of Shual, possibly the same as Shalim (ix. 4); the second westward to Beth-horon; and the third eastward, by the unknown valley of Zeboim, toward the wilderness, *i.e.* the Jordan valley, towards Jericho.

19. *there was no smith*] This was the result of the fierce inroads described in the preceding verses, and the method adopted to make the Philistine conquests permanent.

20–21. The best rendering of the passage is perhaps as follows: "But all the Israelites went down to the Philistines to sharpen &c. (*v.* 21), whenever there was bluntness of edge to their shares and coulters and prong-forks and axes, and to point their goads."

Coulters and mattocks were cutting instruments of the type of the share.

22. This seems to be mentioned here, in anticipation of the narrative in the next chapter, to enhance the victory gained, through God's help (xiv. 23), by the comparatively unarmed Israelites over their enemies. What with occasional skirmishes with the Philistines, the necessity of using their arms for domestic purposes, accidental losses, and the ordinary wear and tear, coupled with the impossibility of renewing their arms from the want of smiths and forges, the people that were with Saul and Jonathan came to be very imperfectly armed. It has been observed, moreover, that the Benjamites were more famous for the use of the sling than for any other weapon (Judg. xx. 16), and this would be an additional cause of the paucity of swords and spears.

23. *the passage of Michmash*] The steep and precipitous path from Michmash to Geba, over the valley of Suweinit. The same term is used in Isai. x. 28, 29, where the march of the Assyrian army is described.

XIV. 1. *Now, &c.*] Rather "**and**," since this verse is in immediate dependence upon the preceding. When Jonathan saw the garrison come out again and again, in defiance "of the armies of the living God," at length "upon a day" he determined to attack them.

Come, and let us go over to the Philistines' garrison, that *is* on
2 the other side. But he told not his father. And Saul tarried in
the uttermost part of Gibeah under a pomegranate tree which *is*
in Migron: and the people that *were* with him *were* *ᵃ*about six
3 hundred men; and *ᵇ*Ahiah, the son of Ahitub, *ᶜ*I-chabod's
brother, the son of Phinehas, the son of Eli, the LORD's priest
in Shiloh, *ᵈ*wearing an ephod. And the people knew not that
4 Jonathan was gone. And between the passages, by which
Jonathan sought to go over *ᵉ*unto the Philistines' garrison, *there*
was a sharp rock on the one side, and a sharp rock on the other
side: and the name of the one *was* Bozez, and the name of the
5 other Seneh. The ¹forefront of the one *was* situate northward
over against Michmash, and the other southward over against
6 Gibeah. And Jonathan said to the young man that bare his
armour, Come, and let us go over unto the garrison of these uncircumcised: it may be that the LORD will work for us: for
there is no restraint to the LORD *ᶠ*to save by many or by few.
7 And his armourbearer said unto him, Do all that *is* in thine
heart: turn thee; behold, I *am* with thee according to thy heart.
8 Then said Jonathan, Behold, we will pass over unto *these* men,
9 and we will discover ourselves unto them. If they say thus
unto us, ²Tarry until we come to you; then we will stand still in
10 our place, and will not go up unto them. But if they say thus,
Come up unto us; then we will go up: for the LORD hath delivered them into our hand: and *ᵍ*this *shall be* a sign unto us.
11 ¶ And both of them discovered themselves unto the garrison of
the Philistines: and the Philistines said, Behold, the Hebrews
come forth out of the holes where they had hid themselves.

ᵃ ch. 13. 15.
ᵇ ch. 22. 9,
11, 20.
called *Ahim-*
elech.
ᶜ ch. 4. 21.
ᵈ ch. 2. 28.
ᵉ ch. 13. 23.

ᶠ Judg. 7. 4,
7.
2 Chr. 14. 11.

ᵍ See Gen.
24. 14.
Judg. 7. 11.

¹ Heb. *tooth.*   ² Heb. *Be still.*

---

2. *under a pomegranate*] Cp. xxii. 6; Judg.
iv. 5. Saul was at the northern extremity
of Gibeah, about an hour's march from
Geba, where Jonathan was.

Migron, if the reading is correct, must be
a different place from the Migron of Isai.
x. 28.

3. Whether *Ahiah* or *Ahijah* is the same
person as *Ahimelech the son of Ahitub* (see
marg. ref.), or whether Ahimelech was the
brother or son of Ahijah, and his successor
in the priesthood, it is impossible to say
certainly. Most probably *Ahijah* and
Ahimilech are variations of the same name ;
the latter element in each alone being different, *melech* (king) being substituted for
the divine name *Jah.* Cp. *Eliakim* and
Jehoiakim (2 K. xxiii. 34), *Eliab* and *Eliel*
(1 Chr. vi. 27, 34).

This fragment of a genealogy is a very
valuable help to the chronology. The
grandson of Phinehas, the son of Eli, was
now High Priest ; and Samuel, who was
probably a few years older than Ahitub the
son of Phinehas, was now an old man. All
this indicates a period of about 50 years or
upwards from the taking of the Ark by the
Philistines.

the LORD's *priest in Shiloh*] But as Eli was
so emphatically known and described in
chs. i.—iv., as God's Priest at Shiloh, and

as there is every reason to believe that
Shiloh was no longer the seat of the Ark in
Saul's time (see xxii. ; 1 Chr. xiii. 3-5), it is
better to refer these words to Eli, and not to
Ahiah, to whom the next words, *wearing*
an ephod, apply. (See ii. 28; Judg. i. 1
note.)

4. [The southern cliff was called *Seneh,*
or "the acacia," and the same name still
applies to the modern valley, dotted by
acacias. The northern cliff was named
Bozez or "Shining." The valley runs nearly
due east, and the northern cliff is of ruddy
and tawny tint, crowned with gleaming
white chalk, and in the full glare of the sun
almost all the day. (Conder.)]

6. It is remarkable that the epithet *un-*
circumcised, used as a term of reproach, is
confined almost exclusively to the Philistines. (Cp. xvii. 26, 36; Judg. xiv. 3, xv.
18, &c.) This is probably an indication of
the long oppression of the Israelites by the
Philistines and of their frequent wars.

10. Though it is not expressly said, as in
the case of Gideon (Judg. vi. 34), Othniel
(Judg. iii. 10), and others, that the Spirit
of the Lord came upon him, yet the whole
course of the narrative, especially *vv.* 13-
16, indicates an extraordinary divine interposition.

12 And the men of the garrison answered Jonathan and his armourbearer, and said, Come up to us, and we will shew you a thing.
And Jonathan said unto his armourbearer, Come up after me:
13 for the LORD hath delivered them into the hand of Israel. And
Jonathan climbed up upon his hands and upon his feet, and his
armourbearer after him: and they fell before Jonathan; and
14 his armourbearer slew after him. And that first slaughter,
which Jonathan and his armourbearer made, was about twenty
men, within as it were [1]an half acre of land, *which* a yoke *of*
[h] 2 Kin. 7. 7. Job 18. 11. 15 *oxen might plow*. ¶ And [h]there was trembling in the host, in
[i] ch. 13. 17. the field, and among all the people: the garrison, and [i]the
spoilers, they also trembled, and the earth quaked: so it was
[k] Gen. 35. 5. 16 [2][k]a very great trembling. And the watchmen of Saul in Gibeah
of Benjamin looked; and, behold, the multitude melted away,
[l] ver. 20. 17 and they [l]went on beating down *one another*. Then said Saul
unto the people that *were* with him, Number now, and see who
is gone from us. And when they had numbered, behold,
18 Jonathan and his armourbearer *were* not *there*. And Saul said
unto Ahiah, Bring hither the ark of God. For the ark of God
19 was at that time with the children of Israel. And it came to
[m] Num. 27. 21. pass, while Saul [m]talked unto the priest, that the [3]noise that
was in the host of the Philistines went on and increased: and
20 Saul said unto the priest, Withdraw thine hand. And Saul and
all the people that *were* with him [4]assembled themselves, and
[n] Judg. 7. 22. 2 Chr. 20. 23. they came to the battle: and, behold, [n]every man's sword was
against his fellow, *and there was* a very great discomfiture.
21 Moreover the Hebrews *that* were with the Philistines before that
time, which went up with them into the camp *from the country*
round about, even they also *turned* to be with the Israelites that
22 *were* with Saul and Jonathan. Likewise all the men of Israel
[o] ch. 13. 6. which [o]had hid themselves in mount Ephraim, *when* they heard
that the Philistines fled, even they also followed hard after them
[p] Ex. 14. 30. Ps. 44. 6, 7. Hos. 1. 7. 23 in the battle. [p]So the LORD saved Israel that day: and the
[q] ch. 13. 5. 24 battle passed over [q]unto Beth-aven. ¶ And the men of Israel
[r] Josh. 6. 26. were distressed that day: for Saul had [r]adjured the people,

[1] Or, *half a furrow of an acre of land*, Judg. 7. 21. [2] Heb. *a trembling of God.* [3] Or, *tumult.* [4] Heb. *were cried together.*

---

12. *we will show you a thing*] Said mockingly.

14. *within as it were an half acre*, &c.] The Hebrew s extremely obscure. Hence there is some probability that the true reading is preserved by the LXX. which translates the clause "*with darts and stones and flints of the field*." Others take the words to mean "in about half the time that a yoke of oxen draw a furrow in the field."

15. *the earth quaked*] This naturally increased the panic to the utmost. Cp. vii. 10; Josh. x. 11; Ps. cxiv. 4.

16. *multitude*] The word is in *v.* 19 (margin) rendered *tumult*. It must have the same meaning here. The sentence is obscure and probably corrupt; perhaps it means, *and behold the tumult! and it went on* (increased) *melting away and beating down*.

18. For "the ark," some read "the ephod," owing to the improbability of the Ark being with Saul at this time, and from the verb "Bring hither" being *never* applied to the Ark, but regularly to the ephod (xxiii. 9, xxx. 7). Moreover not the Ark, but the ephod with Urim and Thummim, was the proper instrument for inquiring of the Lord. If, however, the Hebrew text be correct, they must have brought the Ark into Saul's camp from Kirjath-jearim (vii.), possibly to be safe from the Philistines.

19. *Withdraw thine hand*] *i.e.* "Desist from what thou art about." Saul in his impatience to join the battle would not wait for the answer from God, which he had desired Ahijah to enquire for; just as later (*v.* 35) he would not wait to finish the altar which he had begun to build. Had he now waited he would doubtless have avoided the error into which he fell.

20. *assembled themselves*] See marg. Many Versions give the sense "**shouted**," which is far preferable, and only requires a different punctuation.

saying, Cursed *be* the man that eateth *any* food until evening,
that I may be avenged on mine enemies. So none of the people
25 tasted *any* food. *And all *they of* the land came to a wood; and
26 there was *honey upon the ground. And when the people were
come into the wood, behold, the honey dropped; but no man
27 put his hand to his mouth: for the people feared the oath. But
Jonathan heard not when his father charged the people with the
oath: wherefore he put forth the end of the rod that *was* in his
hand, and dipped it in an honeycomb, and put his hand to his
28 mouth; and his eyes were enlightened. Then answered one of
the people, and said, Thy father straitly charged the people
with an oath, saying, Cursed *be* the man that eateth *any* food
29 this day. And the people were ¹faint. Then said Jonathan,
My father hath troubled the land: see, I pray you, how mine
eyes have been enlightened, because I tasted a little of this
30 honey. How much more, if haply the people had eaten freely
to day of the spoil of their enemies which they found? for had
there not been now a much greater slaughter among the Philis-
31 tines? ¶And they smote the Philistines that day from Mich-
32 mash to Aijalon: and the people were very faint. And the
people flew upon the spoil, and took sheep, and oxen, and
calves, and slew *them* on the ground: and the people did eat
33 *them* ᵘwith the blood. Then they told Saul, saying, Behold, the
people sin against the LORD, in that they eat with the blood.
And he said, Ye have ²transgressed: roll a great stone unto me
34 this day. And Saul said, Disperse yourselves among the people,
and say unto them, Bring me hither every man his ox, and
every man his sheep, and slay *them* here, and eat; and sin
not against the LORD in eating with the blood. And all the
people brought every man his ox ³with him that night, and slew
35 *them* there. And Saul ˣbuilt an altar unto the LORD: ⁴the same
36 was the first altar that he built unto the LORD. And Saul said,
Let us go down after the Philistines by night, and spoil them
until the morning light, and let us not leave a man of them.
And they said, Do whatsoever seemeth good unto thee. Then
37 said the priest, Let us draw near hither unto God. And Saul

ˢ Deut. 9. 28.
Matt. 3. 5.
t Ex. 3. 8.
Num. 13. 27.
Matt. 3. 4.

ᵘ Lev. 3. 17.
& 7. 26.
& 17. 10.
& 19. 26.
Deut. 12. 16,
23, 24.

ˣ ch. 7. 17.

---

¹ Or, *weary,* Judg. 4. 21.   ³ Heb. *in his hand.*   ⁴ Heb. *that altar he began*
² Or, *dealt treacherously.*   *to build unto the* LORD.

---

25. *all they of the land*] Lit., *all the land,*
probably meaning all those named in *vv.* 21,
22, who now flocked to the wood as a ren-
dezvous.

26. *the honey dropped*] Rather, "**Behold
a stream of honey.**" The same thing may
be seen in Spain, where in woody and rocky
ground copious streams of honey are often
found.

27. *were enlightened*] *i.e.* he was refreshed,
when he was faint.

28. *And the people were faint*] Read, "**are
faint,**" the words are part of the man's
complaint.

29. *hath troubled*] The same word as was
applied to Achan (Josh. vii. 25), and gave
its name to the valley of Achor. This additional reference to Joshua is remarkable
(cp. *v.* 24).

31. *Aijalon*] The modern Yalo. It lies
upon the side of a hill to the south of a fine

valley which opens from between the two
Bethhorons right down to the western
plain of the Philistines, exactly on the
route which the Philistines, when expelled
from the high country about Michmash and
Bethel, would take to regain their own
country. Aijalon would be 15 or 20 miles
from Michmash.

33. *sin against the* LORD] See marg. ref. *u.*
But the prohibition was older than the
Law of Moses (Gen. ix. 4). Cp. Acts xv.
20, 29.

35. *And Saul built,* &c.] *i.e.* of the great
stone which they had rolled to kill the oxen
and sheep upon, he began to build an altar
to Jehovah (see marg.); but he did not finish
it (cp. 1 Chr. xxvii. 24), in his haste to pursue the Philistines that night.

36. *Then said the priest,* &c.] Ahijah,
with equal courage and faithfulness, worthy
of his office as "the priest," when every

v ch. 28. 6.

z Josh. 7. 14.
ch. 10. 19.

a 2 Sam. 12.
5.

b Prov. 16.
33.
Acts 1. 24.
c Josh. 7. 16.
ch. 10. 20.
d Josh. 7. 19.
e ver. 27.

f Ruth 1. 17.

g ver. 39.

h 2 Sam. 14.
11.
1 Kin. 1. 52.
Luke 21. 18.

i ch. 11. 11.

k 2 Sam. 10.
6.

l ch. 15. 3, 7.
m ch. 31. 2.
1 Chr. 8. 33.

asked counsel of God, Shall I go down after the Philistines?
wilt thou deliver them into the hand of Israel? But *v*he
38 answered him not that day. And Saul said, *z*Draw ye near
hither, all the ¹chief of the people: and know and see wherein
39 this sin hath been this day. For, *a*as the LORD liveth, which
saveth Israel, though it be in Jonathan my son, he shall surely
die. But *there was* not a man among all the people *that*
40 answered him. Then said he unto all Israel, Be ye on one side,
and I and Jonathan my son will be on the other side. And the
41 people said unto Saul, Do what seemeth good unto thee. Therefore Saul said unto the LORD God of Israel, ²*b*Give a perfect *lot*.
*c*And Saul and Jonathan were taken: but the people ³escaped.
42 And Saul said, Cast *lots* between me and Jonathan my son.
43 And Jonathan was taken. Then Saul said to Jonathan, *d*Tell
me what thou hast done. And Jonathan told him, and said, *e*I
did but taste a little honey with the end of the rod that *was* in
44 mine hand, *and*, lo, I must die. And Saul answered, *f*God do
45 so and more also: *g*for thou shalt surely die, Jonathan. And
the people said unto Saul, Shall Jonathan die, who hath wrought
this great salvation in Israel? God forbid: *h*as the LORD
liveth, there shall not one hair of his head fall to the ground;
for he hath wrought with God this day. So the people rescued
46 Jonathan, that he died not. Then Saul went up from following
the Philistines: and the Philistines went to their own place.
47 ¶ So Saul took the kingdom over Israel, and fought against all
his enemies on every side, against Moab, and against the
children of *i*Ammon, and against Edom, and against the kings
of *k*Zobah, and against the Philistines: and whithersoever he
48 turned himself, he vexed *them*. And he ⁴gathered an host, and
*l*smote the Amalekites, and delivered Israel out of the hands of
49 them that spoiled them. ¶ Now *m*the sons of Saul were Jona-

---

¹ Heb. *corners*, Judg. 20. 2.   ³ Heb. *went forth.*
² Or, *Shew the innocent.*   ⁴ Or, *wrought mightily.*

---

one else yielded to Saul's humour, proposed
that they should draw near to God to enquire of Him. (Cp. 1 K. xxii. 7.)

37. *asked counsel*] The technical phrase
for enquiring of God by Urim and Thummim, and applied also to enquiry of other
oracles.

39. Saul's rashness becomes more and
more apparent. He now adds an additional
oath, to bring down yet further guilt in
"taking God's name in vain." The expressions in *vv.* 36, 40, indicate the fear in which
the people stood of Saul. None dared resist
his will.

41. *Give a perfect lot*] The phrase is obscure, but the meaning is probably as in
the margin.

47. Cp. 2 Sam. viii. 15. The preceding
narrative shows that before this time Saul
had been king in name only, since his country was occupied by the Philistines, and he
could only muster 600 men, and those but
half armed and pent up in a narrow stronghold. Now, however, on the expulsion of
the Philistines from his country, and the
return of the Israelites from their vassalage
and from their hiding places (*vv.* 21, 22),

Saul became king in deed as well as in
name, and acted the part of a king through
the rest of his reign in defending his people
against their enemies round about. A comprehensive list of these enemies, including
the Ammonite war which had already been
described (ch. xi.), and the Amalekite war
which follows in ch. xv., is given in *vv.* 47,
48. There is not the slightest indication from
the words whether this "taking the kingdom" occurred soon or many years after
Saul's anointing at Gilgal. Hence some
would place the clause 47–52 immediately
after ch. xi., or ch. xii., as a summary of
Saul's reign. The details of the reign, viz.
of the Philistine war in chs. xiii., xiv., of
the Amalekite war in ch. xv., and the other
events down to the end of ch. xxxi., preceded by the formulary, xiii. 1, would then
follow according to the common method of
Hebrew historical narrative.

Zobah] This was one of the petty Aramæan kingdoms flourishing at this time
(Ps. lx. title). It seems to have been situated between Damascus and the Euphrates.

49. This enumeration of Saul's children
and chief officers is according to the analogy

than, and Ishui, and Melchi-shua: and the names of his two
daughters *were these;* the name of the firstborn Merab, and the
50 name of the younger Michal : and the name of Saul's wife *was*
Ahinoam, the daughter of Ahimaaz : and the name of the
captain of his host *was* [1]Abner, the son of Ner, Saul's uncle.
51 [n]And Kish *was* the father of Saul ; and Ner the father of Abner
52 *was* the son of Abiel. And there was sore war against the
Philistines all the days of Saul : and when Saul saw any strong
man, or any valiant man, [o]he took him unto him.

CHAP. 15. SAMUEL also said unto Saul, [a]"The LORD sent me to
anoint thee *to be* king over his people, over Israel : now therefore hearken thou unto the voice of the words of the LORD.
2 Thus saith the LORD of hosts, I remember *that* which Amalek
did to Israel, [b]how he laid *wait* for him in the way, when he
3 came up from Egypt. Now go and smite Amalek, and [c]utterly
destroy all that they have, and spare them not ; but slay both
man and woman, infant and suckling, ox and sheep, camel and
4 ass. ¶And Saul gathered the people together, and numbered
them in Telaim, two hundred thousand footmen, and ten
5 thousand men of Judah. And Saul came to a city of Amalek,
6 and [2]laid wait in the valley. And Saul said unto [d]the Kenites,
[e]Go, depart, get you down from among the Amalekites, lest I
destroy you with them : for [f]ye shewed kindness to all the
children of Israel, when they came up out of Egypt. So the
7 Kenites departed from among the Amalekites. [g]And Saul
smote the Amalekites from [h]Havilah *until* thou comest to
8 [i]Shur, that *is* over against Egypt. And [k]he took Agag the
king of the Amalekites alive, and [l]utterly destroyed all the

n ch. 9. 1.

o ch. 8. 11.

a ch. 9. 16.

b Ex. 17. 8, 14. Num. 24. 20. Deut. 25. 17, 18, 19.
c Josh. 6. 17.
d Num. 24. 21. Judg. 1. 16. & 4. 11.
e Gen. 18. 25. Rev. 18. 4.
f Ex. 18. 10. Num. 10. 29, 32.
g ch. 14. 48.
h Gen. 2. 11. & 25. 18.
i Gen. 16. 7.
k See 1 Kin. 20. 34, 35.
l See ch. 30. 1.

[1] Heb. *Abiner.*   [2] Or, *fought.*

---

of the subsequent annals of David and
Solomon's reign. But the one here called
Ishui, is elsewhere (marg. reff.) called *Abinadab* ; and a fourth son, *Esh-baal* or *Ish-
bosheth,* is here omitted.

50. The only other *Ahimaaz* mentioned
in Scripture was the son of Zadok the priest.
The word *Ahi* (brother) is frequently found
in composition in names in the High Priest's
family, *e.g.* in Ahijah, Ahimelech. It is
not improbable that Ahimaaz may have
been of this family, as marriages between
the royal and priestly houses were not unusual (2 K. xi. 2 ; 2 Chr. xxii. 11), and perhaps it may have been owing to such a connexion that Ahijah was brought into prominence by Saul. If there be any truth in
the above supposition, it would be an indication that Saul was not married till after
his election to the throne.

51. Read, *And Kish the father of Saul,
and Ner the father of Abner, were the sons of
Abiel.* Ner was Saul's uncle.

XV. 1. The absence of all chronology or
note of time is remarkable.

2. Cp. marg. reff. It appears (xiv. 48)
that this expedition against Amalek was not
made without fresh provocation. Probably
some incursion similar to that described in
ch. xxx. was made by them upon the south
country at a time when they thought the

Israelites were weakened by their contests
with the Philistines.

3. *utterly destroy*] Rather, "**devote to destruction**" (Levit. xxvii. 28 note). When
a city or people were thus made *cherem,*
everything living was to be destroyed, and
no part of the spoil fall to the conquerors
(cp. *v.* 21). The valuables were put into the
sacred treasury.

4. *Telaim*] Probably the same as *Telem*
(Josh. xv. 24), one of the uttermost cities
of Judah, towards the coast of Edom. The
name means *lambs,* and was probably so
called from the numerous flocks.

two hundred thousand, &c.] A wonderful
contrast with the *six hundred men* who composed his whole army before (xiii. 15), and
a proof how completely for a time the Philistines had been driven back. The separate
mention of the men of Judah shows how
little union there was between Judah and
Ephraim even at this time ; a circumstance
which throws light upon the whole after
history.

7. The district here described would
stretch from Havilah on the extreme east to
Shur, either near Suez, or further north on
the coast road from Gaza to Egypt.

8. The saving Agag alive was in direct
violation of the *devotion* to destruction.

9 people with the edge of the sword. But Saul and the people

m ver. 3, 15.

*m*spared Agag, and the best of the sheep, and of the oxen, and
[1]of the fatlings, and the lambs, and all *that was* good, and would
not utterly destroy them : but every thing *that was* vile and
10 refuse, that they destroyed utterly. ¶ Then came the word of

n ver. 35.
2 Sam. 24.
16.
o Josh. 22.
16.
1 Kin. 9. 6.
p ch. 13. 13.
q 2 Sam. 6.8.
r Josh. 15.
55.

11 the LORD unto Samuel, saying, *n*It repenteth me that I have
set up Saul *to be* king : for he is *o*turned back from following
me, *p*and hath not performed my commandments. And it
12 *q*grieved Samuel ; and he cried unto the LORD all night. And
when Samuel rose early to meet Saul in the morning, it was
told Samuel, saying, Saul came to *r*Carmel, and, behold, he set
him up a place, and is gone about, and passed on, and gone
13 down to Gilgal. ¶ And Samuel came to Saul : and Saul said

s Gen. 14.19.
Judg. 17. 2.

unto him, *s*Blessed *be* thou of the LORD : I have performed the
14 commandment of the LORD. And Samuel said, What *meaneth*
then this bleating of the sheep in mine ears, and the lowing of
15 the oxen which I hear ? And Saul said, They have brought

t ver. 9, 21.
Prov. 28. 13.

them from the Amalekites : *t*for the people spared the best of
the sheep and of the oxen, to sacrifice unto the LORD thy God ;
16 and the rest we have utterly destroyed. Then Samuel said unto
Saul, Stay, and I will tell thee what the LORD hath said to me
17 this night. And he said unto him, Say on. ¶ And Samuel said,

u ch. 9. 21.

*u*When thou *wast* little in thine own sight, *wast* thou not *made*
the head of the tribes of Israel, and the LORD anointed thee
18 king over Israel ? And the LORD sent thee on a journey, and
said, Go and utterly destroy the sinners the Amalekites, and
19 fight against them until [2]they be consumed. Wherefore then
didst thou not obey the voice of the LORD, but didst fly upon
20 the spoil, and didst evil in the sight of the LORD ? ¶ And Saul

x ver. 13.

said unto Samuel, Yea, *x*I have obeyed the voice of the LORD,
and have gone the way which the LORD sent me, and have
brought Agag the king of Amalek, and have utterly destroyed

y ver. 15.

21 the Amalekites. *y*But the people took of the spoil, sheep and

---

[1] Or, *of the second sort.*   [2] Heb. *they consume them.*

---

9. *the fatlings*] The present Heb. text
cannot be so rendered. It can only mean
"*the second* best" (cp. marg.), *i.e.* sheep of
the age to cut or shed the two teeth, sheep
in their prime. But it is probable that the
reading is corrupt, and that "fat or dainty
bits" is the true reading.

11. *it grieved Samuel*] "Samuel was
angry, or displeased," as Jonah was (Jon.
iv. 1), and for a similar reason. Samuel
was displeased that the king whom he had
anointed should be set aside. It seemed a
slur on his prophetic office.

he cried unto the LORD] With the wild
scream or shriek of supplication. (See vii.
8, 9, xii. 18.) The phrase and the action
mark Samuel's fervent, earnest character.

12. *a place*] Rather, "a monument." The
Heb. word (*yad*) means *a hand*, but is used
in the sense of *monument*, or *trophy*, in 2
Sam. xviii. 18, where we are told that the
marble pillar which Absalom set up in his
lifetime, was called *Yad Absalom.*

Carmel (see marg. ref.) would be on Saul's
line of march on his return from the country

of the Amalekites, more especially if he
came from the neighbourhood of Akaba.

13. Gilgal being within 15 miles of Ramah, Samuel might easily have come from
Ramah that morning. Self-will and rashness had hitherto been Saul's chief faults.
He now seems to add falsehood and hypo-
crisy.

15. There is something thoroughly mean
in his attempt to shift the responsibility of
what was done from his own kingly shoulders to those of the people. Every word
uttered by Saul seems to indicate the breaking down of his moral character.

16. Samuel now acquiesces in the wisdom
and justice of the sentence which (*v.* 11) he
had so strenuously resisted at first. What
before was known only to the Searcher of
hearts, had now been displayed to Samuel
by Saul himself.

18. *the sinners*] As though God would
justify His commission to destroy them.
(Cp. Gen. xiii. 13.)

21. *the* LORD *thy God*] There is an implied censure of Samuel in this phrase.

oxen, the chief of the things which should have been utterly
22 destroyed, to sacrifice untō the LORD thy God in Gilgal. ¶ And
Samuel said, [z] Hath the LORD *as great* delight in burnt offerings
and sacrifices, as in obeying the voice of the LORD? Behold,
[a] to obey *is* better than sacrifice, *and* to hearken than the fat of
23 rams. For rebellion *is as* the sin of [1] witchcraft, and stubbornness
is as iniquity and idolatry. Because thou hast rejected the
word of the LORD, [b] he hath also rejected thee from *being* king.
24 ¶ [c] And Saul said unto Samuel, I have sinned: for I have transgressed the commandment of the LORD, and thy words: because
25 I [d] feared the people, and obeyed their voice. Now therefore, I
pray thee, pardon my sin, and turn again with me, that I may
26 worship the LORD. And Samuel said unto Saul, I will not
return with thee: [e] for thou hast rejected the word of the LORD,
and the LORD hath rejected thee from being king over Israel.
27 And as Samuel turned about to go away, [f] he laid hold upon the
28 skirt of his mantle, and it rent. And Samuel said unto him,
[g] The LORD hath rent the kingdom of Israel from thee this day,
and hath given it to a neighbour of thine, *that is* better than
29 thou. And also the [2] Strength of Israel [h] will not lie nor repent:
30 for he *is* not a man, that he should repent. Then he said, I
have sinned: *yet* [i] honour me now, I pray thee, before the elders
of my people, and before Israel, and turn again with me, that I
31 may worship the LORD thy God. So Samuel turned again
32 after Saul; and Saul worshipped the LORD. ¶ Then said
Samuel, Bring ye hither to me Agag the king of the Amalekites. And Agag came unto him delicately. And Agag said,
33 Surely the bitterness of death is passed. And Samuel said, [k] As
thy sword hath made women childless, so shall thy mother be
childless among women. And Samuel hewed Agag in pieces

[z] Ps. 50. 8, 9. Prov. 21. 3. Isai. 1. 11. Jer. 7. 22. Mic. 6. 6. Heb. 10. 6. [a] Eccl. 5. 1. Hos. 6. 6. Matt. 5. 24. & 9. 13. [b] ch. 13. 14. [c] See 2 Sam. 12. 13. [d] Ex. 23. 2. Prov. 29. 25. Isai. 51. 12. [e] See ch. 2. 30. [f] See 1 Kin. 11. 30. [g] ch. 28. 17. 1 Kin. 11. 31. [h] Num. 23. 19. Ezek. 24. 14. 2 Tim. 2. 13. Tit. 1. 2. [i] John 5. 44. & 12. 43. [k] Ex. 17. 11. Num. 14. 45. See Judg. 1. 7.

[1] Heb. *divination*, Deut. 18. 10. [2] Or, *Eternity*, or, *Victory*.

Saul says that Samuel blames him for what
was done in honour of Samuel's God; as if
he had more zeal for the glory of God than
was felt by Samuel.

22. *Hath the* LORD, &c.] A grand example
of the moral and spiritual teaching of the
Prophets (see marg. reff.). The tension of
Samuel's spirit, as he is about to pronounce
the sentence of rejection, produces a lyrical
turn of thought and language.

23. The meaning is "Rebellion is as bad
as the sin of divination, and stubbornness is
as bad as worshipping false gods (*iniquity*),
and teraphim (*idolatry*)."

24. *I have sinned*] Cp. *vv.* 25, 30. How
was it that these repeated confessions were
unavailing to obtain forgiveness, when
David's was? (See marg. ref.) Because
Saul only shrank from the *punishment* of
his sin. David shrank in abhorrence from
the sin itself (Ps. li. 4).

29. *the strength of Israel*] A phrase which
occurs only here. The word means, *perpetuity, truth, glory, victory*, and *trust*, or *confidence*.

30. The pertinacity with which Saul
clings to Samuel for support is a striking
testimony to Samuel's integrity. With all

his worldly-mindedness Saul could perceive
and appreciate the purity of Samuel's
character as a man of God.

the LORD *thy God*] As above, *v.* 15.

32. *delicately*] This phrase is very obscure.
The meaning of the word so rendered is
dainties, delights (Gen. xlix. 20; Prov.
xxix. 17; Lam. iv. 5), which hardly gives a
tolerable sense here. Some understand it
"fawningly, flatteringly," with a view of
appeasing Samuel. [Others alter the reading, and translate "in bonds."]

Surely the bitterness, &c.] Agag hopes that
his life will be spared, and so expresses his
confident belief that the bitterness of death
is over.

33. *hewed in pieces*] Only found in this
passage. Samuel thus executed the *cherem*
(*v.* 3) which Saul had violated, and so both
saved the nation from the guilt of a broken
oath, and gave a final example to Saul, but
apparently in vain, of uncompromising
obedience to the commandments of God.
There is something awful in the majesty of
the Prophet rising above and eclipsing that
of the king (cp. 1 K. xxi. 20; Jer. xxxviii.
14 seq.; Dan. ii. 46, iv. 27).

l ch. 11. 4.
m See
ch. 19. 24.
n ver. 11.
ch. 16. 1.
o ver. 11.
a ch. 15. 35.
b ch. 15. 23.
c ch. 9. 16.
2 Kin. 9. 1.
d Ps. 78. 70.
& 89. 19.
Acts 13. 22.

e ch. 9. 12.
& 20. 29.
f Ex. 4. 15.
g ch. 9. 16.

h ch. 21. 1.

i 1 Kin. 2.13.
2 Kin. 9. 22.
k Ex. 19. 10.

l ch. 17. 13.
1 Chr. 27.18.
m 1 Kin. 12.
26.
n Ps. 147. 10.
11.
Luke 16. 15.
o Isai. 55. 8.
p 2 Cor. 10.7.
q 1 Kin. 8.
39.
Ps. 7. 9.
Jer. 11. 20.
Acts 1. 24.
r ch. 17. 13.
s ch. 17. 13.
t ch. 17. 12.

u 2 Sam. 7. 8.
Ps. 78. 70.
x ch. 17. 42.
Cant. 5. 10.

y So ch. 9.
17.
z ch. 10. 1.
Ps. 89. 20.
a See Num.
27. 18.

34 before the LORD in Gilgal. Then Samuel went to Ramah; and 35 Saul went up to his house to *l*Gibeah of Saul. And *m*Samuel came no more to see Saul until the day of his death: nevertheless Samuel *n*mourned for Saul: and the LORD *o*repented that he had made Saul king over Israel.

CHAP. **16**. AND the LORD said unto Samuel, *a*How long wilt thou mourn for Saul, seeing *b*I have rejected him from reigning over Israel? *c*fill thine horn with oil, and go, I will send thee to Jesse the Beth-lehemite: for *d*I have provided me a king among 2 his sons. And Samuel said, How can I go? if Saul hear *it*, he will kill me. And the LORD said, Take an heifer ¹with thee, 3 and say, *e*I am come to sacrifice to the LORD. And call Jesse to the sacrifice, and *f*I will shew thee what thou shalt do: and 4 *g*thou shalt anoint unto me *him* whom I name unto thee. ¶And Samuel did that which the LORD spake, and came to Bethlehem. And the elders of the town *h*trembled at his ²coming, 5 and said, *i*Comest thou peaceably? And he said, Peaceably: I am come to sacrifice unto the LORD: *k*sanctify yourselves, and come with me to the sacrifice. And he sanctified Jesse and his 6 sons, and called them to the sacrifice. ¶And it came to pass, when they were come, that he looked on *l*Eliab, and *m*said, 7 Surely the LORD's anointed *is* before him. But the LORD said unto Samuel, Look not on *n*his countenance, or on the height of his stature; because I have refused him; *o* for *the LORD seeth* not as man seeth; for man *p*looketh on the ³outward appearance, 8 but the LORD looketh on the *q*heart. Then Jesse called *r*Abinadab, and made him pass before Samuel. And he said, Neither hath the 9 LORD chosen this. Then Jesse made *s*⁴Shammah to pass by. And 10 he said, Neither hath the LORD chosen this. Again, Jesse made seven of his sons to pass before Samuel. And Samuel said unto 11 Jesse, The LORD hath not chosen these. ¶And Samuel said unto Jesse, Are here all *thy* children? And he said, *t*There remaineth yet the youngest, and, behold, he keepeth the sheep. And Samuel said unto Jesse, *u*Send and fetch him: for we will 12 not sit ⁵down till he come hither. And he sent, and brought him in. Now he *was* *x*ruddy, *and* withal ⁶of a beautiful countenance, and goodly to look to. *y*And the LORD said, Arise, anoint him: 13 for this *is* he. Then Samuel took the horn of oil, and *z*anointed him in the midst of his brethren: and *a*the Spirit of the LORD

---

¹ Heb. *in thine hand.*
² Heb. *meeting.*
³ Heb. *eyes.*
⁴ *Shimeah*, 2 Sam. 13. 3.
  Shimma, 1 Chr. 2. 13.
⁵ Heb. *round.*
⁶ Heb. *fair of eyes.*

---

35. *Samuel came no more*, &c.] In the sense of visiting or conversing on public affairs.

XVI. **2.** It was the purpose of God that David should be anointed at this time as Saul's successor, and as the ancestor and the type of His Christ. It was not the purpose of God that Samuel should stir up a civil war, by setting up David as Saul's rival. *Secrecy*, therefore, was a necessary part of the transaction. But *secrecy* and *concealment* are not the same as *duplicity* and *falsehood*. Concealment of a good purpose, for a good purpose, is clearly justifiable. There is therefore nothing in the least inconsistent with truth in the occur-

rence here related. Cp. Exod. vii. 16, viii. 1, ix. 13.

4. *trembled*] There was evidently something unusual in Samuel's coming to Bethlehem; and the elders, knowing that Samuel was no longer at friendship with Saul, foreboded some evil.

10. *seven*] *i.e.* including the three who had already passed (cp. Judg. xiv. 17 note). It appears that Jesse had eight sons; but in 1 Chr. ii. 13-15, only seven are ascribed to him.

11. *we will not sit down*, &c.]. Lit., *we will not turn round* to sit at the table.

13. *the Spirit...came upon David*] The exact phrase used of the Judges and Saul.

came upon David from that day forward. So Samuel rose up,
14 and went to Ramah. ¶ *b*But the Spirit of the LORD departed
from Saul, and *c*an evil spirit from the LORD ¹troubled him.
15 And Saul's servants said unto him, Behold now, an evil spirit
16 from God troubleth thee. Let our lord now command thy servants, *which are* *d*before thee, to seek out a man, *who is* a cunning
player on an harp: and it shall come to pass, when the evil
spirit from God is upon thee, that he shall *e*play with his hand,
17 and thou shalt be well. And Saul said unto his servants, Pro-
18 vide me now a man that can play well, and bring *him* to me. Then
answered one of the servants, and said, Behold, I have seen a
son of Jesse the Beth-lehemite, *that is* cunning in playing, and *f*a
mighty valiant man, and a man of war, and prudent in ²matters,
19 and a comely person, and *g*the LORD *is* with him. Wherefore
Saul sent messengers unto Jesse, and said, Send me David thy
20 son, *h*which *is* with the sheep. And Jesse *i*took an ass *laden* with
bread, and a bottle of wine, and a kid, and sent *them* by David
21 his son unto Saul. And David came to Saul, and *k*stood before
him : and he loved him greatly ; and he became his armour-
22 bearer. And Saul sent to Jesse, saying, Let David, I pray thee,
23 stand before me ; for he hath found favour in my sight. And it
came to pass, when *l*the *evil* spirit from God was upon Saul, that
David took an harp, and played with his hand : so Saul was
refreshed, and was well, and the evil spirit departed from him.

CHAP. 17. NOW the Philistines *a*gathered together their armies to
battle, and were gathered together at *b*Shochoh, which *belongeth*
to Judah, and pitched between Shochoh and Azekah, in ³Ephes-
2 dammim. And Saul and the men of Israel were gathered together, and pitched by the valley of Elah, and ⁴set the battle in

b ch. 11. 6.
& 18. 12.
Judg. 16. 20.
Ps. 51. 11.
c Judg. 9. 23.
ch. 19. 9.
d Gen. 41. 16.

e ver. 23.
2 Kin. 3. 15.

f ch. 17. 32,
34, 35, 36.
g ch. 3. 19.
& 18. 12, 14.
h ver. 11.
ch. 17. 15.
i See ch. 10.
27.
k Gen. 43. 11.
& Gen. 41. 46.
1 Kin. 10. 8.
Prov. 22. 29.

l ver. 14, 16.

a ch. 13. 5.
b Josh. 15. 35.
2 Chr. 28. 18.

---

¹ Or, *terrified.*
² Or, *speech.*

³ Or, *The coast of Dam-
mim,* called *Pas-dam-*
mim, 1 Chr. 11. 13.

⁴ Heb. *ranged the battle.*

See x. 6 ; Judg. iii. 10, vi. 34, xi. 29, xiv.
19, xv. 14 ; and notes.

15. The "evil" or *melancholy* spirit here
spoken of was "the Spirit of God," or "of
Jehovah," as being God's messenger and
minister, sent by Him to execute His
righteous purpose upon Saul (see 1 K.
xxii. 19–22 note).

16. The medicinal effects of music on the
mind and body, especially as appeasing
anger, and soothing and pacifying a troubled
spirit, are well known. It is deeply interesting to have the youthful David thus
brought before us, as using music for its
highest purpose, that of turning the soul
to the harmony of peace and love. We may
infer that some of his Psalms, such *e.g.* as
Ps. xxiii., were already composed.

18. *a mighty valiant man,* &c.] David's
reputation for courage, skill, discretion, and
manly beauty, was already great. Since
"the Spirit of the Lord came upon him,"
his natural qualities and powers had been
greatly enhanced. His feat of killing the
lion and the bear (see marg. reff.) had been
performed, like Samson's feats of strength
(Judg. xiv. 6, 19, xv. 14), under the same
supernatural influence, and was probably
more or less known.

21. The difficulty of reconciling this
verse with xvii. 55–58, is met thus : The
words here are the ultimate sequence of
David's first visit to Saul, and of his skill
in music, and are therefore placed here ;
but they did not really come to pass till
after David's victory over Goliath (see xviii.
2). It is quite conceivable that if David
had only played once or twice to Saul,
and then returned to his father's house
for some months, Saul might not recognise
him.

XVII. 1. The narrative reverts to the
Philistine wars (xiv. 52) ; the other introductory details concerning Saul's rejection,
and David's introduction upon the stage of
the history, having been disposed of in the
intermediate chapters.

Shochoh which belongeth to Judah] See
marg. ref. which places Shochoh and Azekah in the *Shephelah* or maritime plain,
and 2 Chr. xxviii. 18, *Shochoh* now *Shu-*
weikeh, "nine miles from Eleutheropolis,"
Jerome.

Ephes-dammim] Called *Happas-dammim*
(Pas-dammim, 1 Chr. xi. 13), *the end of
bloodshed,* now *Damûn,* about 4 miles N.E.
of Shuweikeh.

2. *the valley of Elah*] *i.e.* of the terebinth,

3 array against the Philistines. And the Philistines stood on a
mountain on the one side, and Israel stood on a mountain on
4 the other side : and *there was* a valley between them. ¶And
there went out a champion out of the camp of the Philistines,

c 2 Sam. 21.
19.
d Josh. 13. 3.

named ᶜGoliath, of ᵈGath, whose height *was* six cubits and a
5 span. And *he had* an helmet of brass upon his head, and he
was ¹armed with a coat of mail; and the weight of the coat *was*
6 five thousand shekels of brass. And *he had* greaves of brass
upon his legs, and a ²target of brass between his shoulders.

e 2 Sam. 21.
19.

7 And the ᵉstaff of his spear *was* like a weaver's beam; and his
spear's head *weighed* six hundred shekels of iron : and one bear-
8 ing a shield went before him. And he stood and cried unto the
armies of Israel, and said unto them, Why are ye come out to

set *your* battle in array ? *am* not I a Philistine, and ye ᶠservants
to Saul ? choose you a man for you, and let him come down to
9 me. If he be able to fight with me, and to kill me, then will

g ch. 11. 1.
h ver. 26.
2 Sam. 21.
21.
i ver. 58.
Ruth 4. 22.
ch. 16. 1, 18.
k Gen. 35.19.
l ch. 16. 10,
11.
See
1 Chr. 2. 13.
14, 15.
m ch. 16. 6.
1 Chr. 2. 13.

we be your servants : but if I prevail against him, and kill him,
10 then shall ye be our servants, and ᵍserve us. And the Philistine
said, I ʰdefy the armies of Israel this day; give me a man, that
11 we may fight together. When Saul and all Israel heard those
words of the Philistine, they were dismayed and greatly afraid.
12 ¶ Now David *was* ⁱthe son of that ᵏEphrathite of Beth-lehem-
judah, whose name *was* Jesse ; and he had ˡeight sons : and the
13 man went among men *for* an old man in the days of Saul. And
the three eldest sons of Jesse went *and* followed Saul to the
battle : and the ᵐnames of his three sons that went to the battle
were Eliab the firstborn, and next unto him Abinadab, and the

---

¹ Heb. *clothed.*   ² Or, *gorget.*

---

now called Wady es Sunt, from the acacias
which are scattered in it.

3. [In the middle of the broad open valley
(*v.* 2) is a deep trench (*v.* 3) with vertical
sides, a valley within a valley : the sides
and bed of the trench are strewn with
water-worn pebbles. (Conder.)]

4. *a champion*] Lit., "*a man between
the two camps;*" *i.e.* one who did not
fight in the ranks like an ordinary soldier, but came forth into the space between the hostile camps to challenge the
mightiest man of his enemies to come and
fight him.

Goliath of Gath] One of the places mentioned in Josh. xi. 22 as still retaining a
remnant of the sons of Anak ; Gaza and
Ashdod being the others. The race of
giants (*rephaim*) is mentioned again in the
account of David's Philistine wars (2 Sam.
xxi. 15-22; 1 Chr. xx. 4-8). It appears
from these passages that Goliath had a
brother Lahmi. Four are named as being
"born to the giant in Gath." See Deut. ii.
10, 11, 20, 21, iii. 11-13.

six cubits, &c.] If the *cubit*, the length
from the elbow to the tip of the middle
finger, be about 1½ feet ; and the *span*, the
distance from the thumb to the middle or
little finger, when stretched apart to the
full length, be half a cubit, *six cubits and a
span* would equal about nine feet nine

inches. The bed of Og king of Bashan was
nine cubits long (Deut. iii. 11).

5. *coat of mail*] Or "**breastplate of
scales.**" A kind of metal shirt, protecting
the back as well as the breast, and made of
scales like those of a fish ; as was the corse-
let of Rameses III., now in the British
Museum. The terms, *helmet, coat,* and
clothed (armed A. V.) are the same as those
used in Isai. lix. 17.

five thousand shekels] Probably about 157
pounds avoirdupois (see Ex. xxxviii. 12
note). It is very probable that Goliath's
brazen coat may have been long preserved as
a trophy, as we know his sword was, and so
the weight of it ascertained.

6. *a target,* &c.] Rather, "**a javelin,**" as
in *v.* 45, and placed between the shoulders,
as the quiver was.

7. *spear's-head*] Lit., "**the flame of his
spear,**" the metal part which flashed like a
flame.

six hundred shekels] *i.e.* between seventeen and eighteen pounds avoirdupois.

12. This and the following *vv.* down to
the end of *v.* 31 are omitted in the Vatican
copy of the LXX., as are *vv.* 55-58. The
object of the omission was doubtless to
avoid the apparent inconsistency with regard to Saul's acquaintance with David (see
xvi. 21 note).

14 third Shammah. And David *was* the youngest: and the three
15 eldest followed Saul. But David went and returned from Saul
16 "to feed his father's sheep at Beth-lehem. And the Philistine
drew near morning and evening, and presented himself forty days.
17 ¶ And Jesse said unto David his son, Take now for thy brethren
an ephah of this parched *corn*, and these ten loaves, and run to
18 the camp to thy brethren; and carry these ten ¹cheeses unto the
²captain of *their* thousand, and ᵒlook how thy brethren fare, and
19 take their pledge. ¶ Now Saul, and they, and all the men of
Israel, *were* in the valley of Elah, fighting with the Philistines.
20 And David rose up early in the morning, and left the sheep with
a keeper, and took, and went, as Jesse had commanded him; and
he came to the ³trench, as the host was going forth to the ⁴fight,
21 and shouted for the battle. For Israel and the Philistines had
22 put the battle in array, army against army. And David left
⁵his carriage in the hand of the keeper of the carriage, and ran
23 into the army, and came and ⁶saluted his brethren. And as
he talked with them, behold, there came up the champion, the
Philistine of Gath, Goliath by name, out of the armies of the
Philistines, and spake ᵖaccording to the same words: and David
24 heard *them*. And all the men of Israel, when they saw the man,
25 fled ⁷from him, and were sore afraid. ¶ And the men of Israel
said, Have ye seen this man that is come up? surely to defy
Israel is he come up: and it shall be, *that* the man who killeth
him, the king will enrich him with great riches, and ᵠwill give
him his daughter, and make his father's house free in Israel.
26 And David spake to the men that stood by him, saying, What
shall be done to the man that killeth this Philistine, and taketh
away ʳthe reproach from Israel? for who *is* this ˢuncircumcised
Philistine, that he should ᵗdefy the armies of ᵘthe living God?
27 And the people answered him after this manner, saying, ˣSo
28 shall it be done to the man that killeth him. ¶ And Eliab his
eldest brother heard when he spake unto the men; and Eliab's
ʸanger was kindled against David, and he said, Why camest
thou down hither? and with whom hast thou left those few
sheep in the wilderness? I know thy pride, and the naughtiness

ⁿ ch. 16. 19.

ᵒ Gen. 37. 14.

ᵖ ver. 8.

ᵠ Josh. 15. 16.

ʳ ch. 11. 2.
ˢ ch. 14. 6.
ᵗ ver. 10.
ᵘ Deut. 5. 26.
ˣ ver. 25.

ʸ Gen. 37. 4, 8, 11.
Matt. 10. 36.

---

¹ Heb. *cheeses of milk.*
² Heb. *captain of a thousand.*
³ Or, *place of the carriage,*
⁴ Or, *battle array,* or, *place of fight.*
⁵ Heb. *the vessels from upon*
ch. 26. 5.
⁶ Heb. *asked his brethren of peace,* as Judg. 18. 15.
⁷ Heb. *from his face.*
him.

---

15. *David went,* &c.] "**Was gone**," referring to xvi. 19, 20. Had he been Saul's armour-bearer at this time it is highly improbable that he would have left him to feed sheep.

18. *take their pledge*] *i.e.* bring back what they have to say in return.

20. *the trench*] Rather, "**the waggons**," which were all put together in the camp so as to form a kind of bulwark or fortification (see xxvi. 5, 7). Here David left his "carriage" (*v.* 22), *i.e.* the things which he had carried, "his things" as we should say, or *baggage* (translated *stuff* in x. 22, xxv. 13, xxx. 24). There seems to have been an officer ("the keeper," *v.* 22) in the Hebrew army whose charge it was to guard the baggage.

25. *free in Israel*] In all the other passages (fifteen) where this word occurs, it means *free,* as opposed to being a *slave* (Deut. xv. 12, 13, 18, &c.) Here it may imply a freedom from all such services and burdens as are spoken of in viii. 11-17.

26. *the living God*] This fine expression occurs first in Deuteronomy (marg. ref.), and next in Josh. iii. 10, and 2 K. xix. 4. We find it twice in the Psalms of David (Ps. xlii. 2, lxxxiv. 2), four times in the Prophets, and frequently in the New Testament. It is generally in contrast to false gods (1 Thess. i. 9, &c.).

28. *Why camest thou down?*] From the heights of Bethlehem to the valley of Elah.
thy pride, and the naughtiness of thine heart] See the similar expression, Jer. xlix.

ver. 17.

u ver. 26, 27.

b Deut. 20.
1, 3.
c ch. 16. 18.
d See Num.
13. 31.
Deut. 9. 2.

e Ps. 18. 16,
17. & † 3. 7.
2 Cor. 1. 10.
2 Tim. 4. 17,
18.
f ch. 20. 13.
1 Chr. 22. 11,
16.

g Ps. 123. 3.
1 Cor. 1. 27,
28.
h ch. 16. 12.
i ch. 24. 14.
2 Sam. 3. 8.
2 Kin. 8. 13.
k 1 Kin. 20.
10, 11.

l 2 Sam. 22.
33, 35.
Ps. 124. 8.
2 Cor. 10. 4.
Heb. 11. 33,
34.
m ver. 10.
n Deut. 28.
26.

of thine heart; for thou art come down that thou mightest see the
29 battle. And David said, What have I now done? *z Is there* not a
30 cause? And he turned from him toward another, and *a* spake after
the same [1] manner: and the people answered him again after the
31 former manner. ¶ And when the words were heard which David
32 spake, they rehearsed *them* before Saul: and he [2] sent for him. And
David said to Saul, *b* Let no man's heart fail because of him;
33 *c* thy servant will go and fight with this Philistine. And Saul
said to David, *d* Thou art not able to go against this Philistine to
fight with him: for thou *art but* a youth, and he a man of war
34 from his youth. And David said unto Saul, Thy servant kept
his father's sheep, and there came a lion, and a bear, and took a
35 [3] lamb out of the flock: and I went out after him, and smote him,
and delivered *it* out of his mouth: and when he arose against
me, I caught *him* by his beard, and smote him, and slew him.
36 Thy servant slew both the lion and the bear: and this uncircumcised Philistine shall be as one of them, seeing he hath
37 defied the armies of the living God. David said moreover,
e The LORD that delivered me out of the paw of the lion, and out
of the paw of the bear, he will deliver me out of the hand of
this Philistine. And Saul said unto David, Go, and *f* the LORD
38 be with thee. ¶ And Saul [4] armed David with his armour,
and he put an helmet of brass upon his head; also he armed
39 him with a coat of mail. And David girded his sword upon his
armour, and he assayed to go; for he had not proved *it*. And
David said unto Saul, I cannot go with these; for I have not
40 proved *them*. And David put them off him. And he took his staff
in his hand, and chose him five smooth stones out of the [5] brook,
and put them in a shepherd's [6] bag which he had, even in a scrip;
and his sling *was* in his hand: and he drew near to the Philistine.
41 And the Philistine came on and drew near unto David; and the
42 man that bare the shield *went* before him. ¶ And when the
Philistine looked about, and saw David, he *g* disdained him: for
43 he was *but* a youth, and *h* ruddy, and of a fair countenance. And
the Philistine said unto David, *i Am* I a dog, that thou comest
to me with staves? And the Philistine cursed David by his
44 gods. And the Philistine *k* said to David, Come to me, and I will
give thy flesh unto the fowls of the air, and to the beasts of the
45 field. Then said David to the Philistine, Thou comest to me
with a sword, and with a spear, and with a shield: *l* but I come
to thee in the name of the LORD of hosts, the God of the armies
46 of Israel, whom thou hast *m* defied. This day will the LORD
[7] deliver thee into mine hand; and I will smite thee, and take
thine head from thee; and I will give *n* the carcases of the host

---

[1] Heb. *word.*
[2] Heb. *took him.*
[3] Or, *kid.*

[4] Heb. *clothed David with his clothes.*

[5] Or, *valley.*
[6] Heb. *vessel.*
[7] Heb. *shut thee up.*

---

16. Cp. the envy of Jacob's sons toward Joseph, and of the slanders heaped upon the Son of David in the days of His flesh.

29. *Is there not a cause?*] *i.e.* is not Saul's promise, and the insolence of Goliath, a sufficient cause for what I am about to do?

34. The narrative does not make it certain whether the lion and the bear came on one and the same, or on two different occasions. If it was on one occasion, the pro-

bability would be that the bear, having seized a lamb and carrying it off, a lion appeared to dispute the prize with the bear, or with David after he had taken it from the bear, and that David slew first one and then the other.

35. *his beard*] Put here for *his throat*, or under jaw; neither lion nor bear has a beard properly speaking.

45. *a shield*] "A javelin," see *v.* 6 note.

of the Philistines this day unto the fowls of the air, and to the
wild beasts of the earth ; [v]that all the earth may know that there
47 is a God in Israel. And all this assembly shall know that the LORD
[p]saveth not with sword and spear: for [q]the battle *is* the LORD'S,
48 and he will give you into our hands. ¶ And it came to pass,
when the Philistine arose, and came and drew nigh to meet
David, that David hasted, and ran toward the army to meet
49 the Philistine. And David put his hand in his bag, and took
thence a stone, and slang *it*, and smote the Philistine in his
forehead, that the stone sunk into his forehead ; and he fell
50 upon his face to the earth. So [r]David prevailed over the Philistine with a sling and with a stone, and smote the Philistine, and
51 slew him ; but *there was* no sword in the hand of David. Therefore David ran, and stood upon the Philistine, and took his
sword, and drew it out of the sheath thereof, and slew him, and
cut off his head therewith. ¶ And when the Philistines saw
52 their champion was dead, [s]they fled. And the men of Israel
and of Judah arose, and shouted, and pursued the Philistines,
until thou come to the valley, and to the gates of Ekron. And
the wounded of the Philistines fell down by the way to [t]Shaaraim,
53 even unto Gath, and unto Ekron. And the children of Israel
returned from chasing after the Philistines, and they spoiled
54 their tents. And David took the head of the Philistine, and
brought it to Jerusalem ; but he put his armour in his tent.
55 ¶ And when Saul saw David go forth against the Philistine, he
said unto Abner, the captain of the host, Abner, [u]whose son *is*
this youth ? And Abner said, *As* thy soul liveth, O king, I can-
56 not tell. And the king said, Enquire thou whose son the strip-
57 ling *is*. And as David returned from the slaughter of the
Philistine, Abner took him, and brought him before Saul [x]with
58 the head of the Philistine in his hand. And Saul said to him,
Whose son *art* thou, *thou* young man ? And David answered,
[y]I *am* the son of thy servant Jesse the Beth-lehemite.

CHAP. 18. AND it came to pass, when he had made an end of
speaking unto Saul, that [a]the soul of Jonathan was knit with the
2 soul of David, [b]and Jonathan loved him as his own soul. And
Saul took him that day, [c]and would let him go no more home to
3 his father's house. Then Jonathan and David made a covenant,
4 because he loved him as his own soul. And Jonathan stripped
himself of the robe that *was* upon him, and gave it to David,
and his garments, even to his sword, and to his bow, and to his
5 girdle. ¶ And David went out whithersoever Saul sent him, *and*

Marginal references:

o Josh. 4. 24.
1 Kin. 8. 43.
Isa. 52. 10.
p Hos. 1. 7.
Zech. 4. 6.
q 2 Chr. 20.
15.

r ch. 21. 9.
See Judg. 3.
31.
& 15. 15.
2 Sam. 23.
21.

s Heb. 11.34.

t Josh. 15.
36.

u See ch. 16
21, 22.

x ver. 54.

y ver. 12.

a Gen. 44.30.
b ch. 19. 2.
& 20. 17.
2 Sam. 1. 26.
Deut. 13. 6.
c ch. 17. 15.

---

47. *the* LORD *saveth not with sword*, &c.]
Observe the consistent teaching of such
passages as xiv. 6 ; Ex. xiv. 13–18 ; Judg.
vii. 2, 4, 7 ; Ps. xliv. 6, &c., and their
practical use to the Church as lessons of
trust in God, and distrust of ourselves.
champion] Quite a different word from
that so rendered in *vv.* 4 and 23 ; better
" warrior."
52. *the men of Israel and Judah*] See xv.
4 note.
Shaaraim] A town of Judah in the *Shephelah* (see marg. ref.), at this time probably
in the possession of the Philistines.
54. *Jerusalem*] See Judg. i. 8 note.
his tent] Perhaps the *Tabernacle.* David

had neither tent nor house of his own. It
would be quite in accordance with David's
piety that he should immediately dedicate
to God the arms taken from the Philistine,
in acknowledgment that the victory was not
his own but the Lord's (cp. xxi. 9). *His*
Tabernacle, meaning the Tabernacle which
he had pitched (2 Sam. vi. 17 ; cp. Acts
xv. 16).
55. *whose son*, &c.] See marg. ref. note.
XVIII. 1. *was knit with the soul of David*]
The same forcible phrase occurs of Jacob's
love for Benjamin (marg. ref.). Jonathan's
truly heroic character is shown in this
generous love of David, and admiration of
his great deed.

¹behaved himself wisely: and Saul set him over the men of war, and he was accepted in the sight of all the people, and also in 6 the sight of Saul's servants. ¶ And it came to pass as they came, when David was returned from the slaughter of the ²Philistine, that ᵈthe women came out of all cities of Israel, singing and dancing, to meet king Saul, with tabrets, with joy, and with 7 ³instruments of musick. And the women ᵉanswered one another, as they played, and said,

Saul hath slain his thousands,
And David his ten thousands.

8 And Saul was very wroth, and the saying ⁴ᵍdispleased him: and he said, They have ascribed unto David ten thousands, and to me they have ascribed but thousands: and what can he have 9 more but ʰthe kingdom. And Saul eyed David from that day 10 and forward. ¶And it came to pass on the morrow, that ⁱthe evil spirit from God came upon Saul, ᵏand he prophesied in the midst of the house: and David played with his hand, as at 11 other times: ˡand there was a javelin in Saul's hand. And Saul ᵐcast the javelin; for he said, I will smite David even to the wall with it. And David avoided out of his presence twice. 12 ¶And Saul was ⁿafraid of David, because ᵒthe LORD was with 13 him, and was ᵖdeparted from Saul. Therefore Saul removed him from him, and made him his captain over a thousand; and 14 ᑫhe went out and came in before the people. And David ⁵behaved himself wisely in all his ways; and ʳthe LORD was with 15 him. Wherefore when Saul saw that he behaved himself very 16 wisely, he was afraid of him. But ˢall Israel and Judah loved 17 David, because he went out and came in before them. ¶And Saul said to David, Behold, my elder daughter Merab, ᵗher will I give thee to wife: only be thou ⁶valiant for me, and fight ᵘthe LORD's battles. For Saul said, ˣLet not mine hand be 18 upon him, but let the hand of the Philistines be upon him. And David said unto Saul, ʸWho am I? and what is my life, or my father's family in Israel, that I should be son in law to the 19 king? But it came to pass at the time when Merab Saul's

Margin references

ᵈ Ex. 15. 20.
Judg. 11. 34.

ᵉ Ex. 15. 21.

f ch. 21. 11.
& 29. 5.

ᵍ Eccles. 4. 4.

ʰ ch. 15. 28.

ⁱ ch. 16. 14.

ᵏ ch. 19. 24.
1 Kin. 18. 29.

ˡ ch. 19. 9.
ᵐ ch. 19. 10.
& 20. 33.
Prov. 27. 4.

ⁿ ver. 15. 29.
ᵒ ch. 16. 13.
ᵖ ch. 16. 14.
& 28. 15.

ᑫ Num. 27.
17.
2 Sam. 5. 2.
ʳ Gen. 39. 2.
Josh. 6. 27.
ˢ ver. 5.

ᵗ ch. 17. 25.

ᵘ Num. 32.
20, 27, 29.
ˣ ver. 21.
2 Sam. 12. 9.
ʸ ch. 9. 21.
2 Sam. 7. 18.

---

¹ Or, *prospered*, ver. 14, 15, 30.
² Or, *Philistines.*
³ Heb. *three-stringed instruments.*
⁴ Heb. *was evil in his eyes.*
⁵ Or, *prospered*, ver. 5.
⁶ Heb. *a son of valour.*

---

6. *the Philistine*] Rather as in the margin. The allusion is not to Goliath, but to one of the expeditions referred to in *v.* 5.

singing and dancing] Women used to dance to the sound of the timbrel, and to sing as they danced and played.

instruments of music] The word means, an instrument like the triangle, or with three cords.

7. *as they played*] Or danced with vocal and instrumental music (see Judg. xvi. 25 note).

8. *what can he have*, &c.] Rather, "There is only the kingdom left for him." Cp. for the same sentiment, 1 K. ii 22 "A kingdom (says Camden) brooketh no companion, and majesty more heavily taketh injuries to heart."

10. *he prophesied*] This, as the effect of the evil spirit coming upon him, is singular as regards Saul, but is borne out by what

we read in 1 K. xxii. 22. (Cp. Acts xvi. 16-18, xix. 15; 1 Joh. iv. 1-3). It is impossible to give the sense of *raving* to the word *prophesied*, as though a merely natural state of phrenzy were intended. The *prophesying* here was as directly the effect of the coming of the evil spirit upon Saul, as the *prophesying* in x. 10 was the effect of the Spirit of God coming upon him. At the same time it is quite true that *madness* and *prophesyings* were considered as near akin (see Jer. xxix. 26; 2 K. ix. 11).

17. Saul had not hitherto fulfilled the promise of which David had heard (marg. ref.); nor was it unnatural that Saul should delay to do so, till the shepherd's boy had risen to a higher rank.

18. *what is my life*] i.e. *condition*, or *means of living* (Prov. xxvii. 27 marg.).

19. *Adriel the Meholathite*] The five sons of this marriage perished by the hands of

daughter should have been given to David, that she was given
20 unto *Adriel the *Meholathite to wife. ¶*b*And Michal Saul's
daughter loved David: and they told Saul, and the thing
21 ¹pleased him. And Saul said, I will give him her, that she may
be *c*a snare to him, and that *d*the hand of the Philistines may be
against him. Wherefore Saul said to David, Thou shalt *e*this
22 day be my son in law in *the one of* the twain. ¶And Saul commanded his servants, *saying,* Commune with David secretly, and
say, Behold, the king hath delight in thee, and all his servants
23 love thee: now therefore be the king's son in law. And Saul's
servants spake those words in the ears of David. And David
said, Seemeth it to you *a* light *thing* to be a king's son in law,
24 seeing that I *am* a poor man, and lightly esteemed? And the
servants of Saul told him, saying, ²On this manner spake David.
25 And Saul said, Thus shall ye say to David, The king desireth
not any *f*dowry, but an hundred foreskins of the Philistines, to
be *g*avenged of the king's enemies. But Saul *h*thought to make
26 David fall by the hand of the Philistines. And when his servants told David these words, it pleased David well to be the
27 king's son in law: and *i*the days were not ³expired. Wherefore David arose and went, he and *k*his men, and slew of the
Philistines two hundred men; and *l*David brought their foreskins, and they gave them in full tale to the king, that he might
be the king's son in law. And Saul gave him Michal his
28 daughter to wife. ¶And Saul saw and knew that the LORD
was with David, and *that* Michal Saul's daughter loved him.
29 And Saul was yet the more afraid of David; and Saul became
30 David's enemy continually. Then the princes of the Philistines
*m*went forth: and it came to pass, after they went forth, *that*
David *n*behaved himself more wisely than all the servants of
Saul; so that his name was much ⁴set by.

CHAP. 19. AND Saul spake to Jonathan his son, and to all his
2 servants, that they should kill David. But Jonathan Saul's son
*a*delighted much in David: and Jonathan told David, saying,
Saul my father seeketh to kill thee: now therefore, I pray thee,
take heed to thyself until the morning, and abide in a secret
3 *place,* and hide thyself: and I will go out and stand beside my
father in the field where thou *art,* and I will commune with my
4 father of thee; and what I see, that I will tell thee. ¶And
Jonathan *b*spake good of David unto Saul his father, and said
unto him, Let not the king *c*sin against his servant, against
David; because he hath not sinned against thee, and because

Side notes:
*2 Sam. 21. 8.
a Judg. 7. 22.
b ver. 28.
c Ex. 10. 7.
d ver. 17.
e See ver. 23.

f Gen. 34. 12.
Ex. 22. 17.
g ch. 14. 24.
h ver. 17.

i See ver. 21.
k ver. 13.
l 2 Sam. 3. 14.

m 2 Sam. 11. 1.
n ver. 5.

a ch. 18. 1.

b Prov. 31. 8, 9.
c Gen. 42. 22.
Ps. 35. 12.
Prov. 17. 13.
Jer. 18. 20.

---

¹ Heb. *was right in his eyes.*   ³ Heb. *fulfilled.*   ⁴ Heb. *precious,* ch. 26. 21.
² Heb. *According to these words.*   2 Kin. 1. 13. Ps. 116. 15.

---

the Gibeonites (marg. ref.), where we learn further that the name of Adriel's father, or ancestor, was Barzillai. His birth-place was Meholah, probably the same as Abel-Meholah. (See 1 K. xix. 16 note).

20. *the thing pleased him*] It partly relieved him from the charge of breaking his faith.

21. *in the one of the twain*] Some prefer "the second time" (Job xxxiii. 14). The *first* contract had been broken by giving Merab to Adriel.

23. *a poor man and lightly esteemed*] Cp.

Ps. cxix. 141. Poor, and therefore unable to pay a sufficient dowry. See *v.* 25.

25. *an hundred foreskins*] This is merely another expression of the spirit which led to the constant application of the epithet *uncircumcised* to the Philistines (xiv. 6).

26. *the days were not expired*] David was so rapid in his attack upon the Philistines that he was able to bring the required dowry within the time, and to receive his wife (Michal), before the time had expired within which he was to receive Merab.

d Judg. 9.17.
ch. 28. 21.
e ch. 17. 49.
f ch. 11. 13.
g ch. 20. 32.
h Matt. 27.4.

i ch. 16. 21.
& 18. 2, 13.

k ch. 16. 14.
& 18. 10.

l Ps. 59,
title.

m So Josh.
2. 15.
Acts 9. 24,
25.

n 2 Sam. 2.
22.

o See John
7. 32, 45.
p ch. 10. 5.
1 Cor. 14. 3,
24, 25.
q Num. 11.
25.
Joel 2. 28.

5 his works *have been* to thee-ward very good: for he did put his ᵈlife in his hand, and ᵉslew the Philistine, and ᶠthe LORD wrought a great salvation for all Israel: thou sawest *it*, and didst rejoice: ᵍwherefore then wilt thou ʰsin against innocent 6 blood, to slay David without a cause? And Saul hearkened unto the voice of Jonathan: and Saul sware, *As* the LORD 7 liveth, he shall not be slain. And Jonathan called David, and Jonathan shewed him all those things. And Jonathan brought David to Saul, and he was in his presence, ⁱas ¹in times past. 8 ¶ And there was war again: and David went out, and fought with the Philistines, and slew them with a great slaughter; and they 9 fled from ²him. ¶And ᵏthe evil spirit from the LORD was upon Saul, as he sat in his house with his javelin in his hand: and 10 David played with *his* hand. And Saul sought to smite David even to the wall with the javelin; but he slipped away out of Saul's presence, and he smote the javelin into the wall: and 11 David fled, and escaped that night. ¶ˡSaul also sent messengers unto David's house, to watch him, and to slay him in the morning: and Michal David's wife told him, saying, If thou save not 12 thy life to night, to morrow thou shalt be slain. So Michal ᵐlet David down through a window: and he went, and fled, and 13 escaped. And Michal took an ³image, and laid *it* in the bed, and put a pillow of goats' *hair* for his bolster, and covered *it* 14 with a cloth. And when Saul sent messengers to take David, 15 she said, He *is* sick. And Saul sent the messengers *again* to see David, saying, Bring him up to me in the bed, that I may 16 slay him. And when the messengers were come in, behold, *there was* an image in the bed, with a pillow of goats' *hair* for his 17 bolster. And Saul said unto Michal, Why hast thou deceived me so, and sent away mine enemy, that he is escaped? And Michal answered Saul, He said unto me, Let me go; ⁿwhy 18 should I kill thee? ¶ So David fled, and escaped, and came to Samuel to Ramah, and told him all that Saul had done to him. 19 And he and Samuel went and dwelt in Naioth. And it was told 20 Saul, saying, Behold, David *is* at Naioth in Ramah. And ᵒSaul sent messengers to take David: ᵖand when they saw the company of the prophets prophesying, and Samuel standing *as* appointed over them, the Spirit of God was upon the messengers 21 of Saul, and they also ᑫprophesied. And when it was told

¹ Heb. *yesterday third day.*   ² Heb. *his face.*   ³ Heb. *teraphim*, Gen. 31. 19.
                                                                           Judg. 17. 5.

XIX. **10.** *David fled*] This was the beginning of David's life as a fugitive and outcast, though for no "offence or fault" of his (Ps. lix. 3, Prayer Book Version).

11. Saul's plan was to surround the house at night, and to have David killed as soon as he came abroad unsuspectingly in the morning.

13. *an image*] *Teraphim* (see marg.), an image, or bust in human form, and as large as life, of a kind of household god, to the worship of which the Israelites, and especially women, were much addicted.

a pillow] It was probably a quilt or blanket of goats' hair, and of common use as a bed-covering. Whether Michal drew it over the head of the teraphim, as if for

warmth, and so covered it, or whether she disposed it about the head so as to look like hair, is not clear.

17. *why should I kill thee?*] To avert Saul's anger from herself, she pretended that David had threatened her life unless she facilitated his escape.

18. No such place as Naioth (or Nevaioth) is known, but the word means *dwellings*. Hence it is considered that Naioth was the name of the collegiate residence of the prophets, in, or just outside, Ramah, to which Samuel removed with David from his own house, for greater safety, owing to the sanctity of the place and company.

20. *Samuel standing as appointed*] Rather, "**as overseer, or leader.**"

Saul, he sent other messengers, and they prophesied likewise.
And Saul sent messengers again the third time, and they pro-
22 phesied also. Then went he also to Ramah, and came to a great
well that *is* in Sechu: and he asked and said, Where *are* Samuel
and David ? And *one* said, Behold, *they be* at Naioth in Ramah.
23 And he went thither to Naioth in Ramah: and *r*the Spirit of
God was upon him also, and he went on, and prophesied, until
24 he came to Naioth in Ramah. *s*And he stripped off his clothes
also, and prophesied before Samuel in like manner, and [1]lay
down *t*naked all that day and all that night. Wherefore they
say, *u Is* Saul also among the prophets ?

Chap. 20. AND David fled from Naioth in Ramah, and came
and said before Jonathan, What have I done ? what *is* mine
iniquity ? and what *is* my sin before thy father, that he seeketh
2 my life ? And he said unto him, God forbid; thou shalt not die:
behold, my father will do nothing either great or small, but
that he will [2]shew it me : and why should my father hide this
3 thing from me ? it *is* not *so*. And David sware moreover, and
said, Thy father certainly knoweth that I have found grace in
thine eyes ; and he saith, Let not Jonathan know this, lest he
be grieved: but truly *as* the LORD liveth, and *as* thy soul liveth,
4 *there is* but a step between me and death. Then said Jonathan
unto David, [3]Whatsoever thy soul [4]desireth, I will even do *it* for
5 thee. And David said unto Jonathan, Behold, to morrow *is*
the *a*new moon, and I should not fail to sit with the king at
meat : but let me go, that I may *b*hide myself in the field unto
6 the third *day* at even. If thy father at all miss me, then
say, David earnestly asked *leave* of me that he might run *c*to
Beth-lehem his city : for *there is* a yearly [5]sacrifice there for all
7 the family. *d*If he say thus, *It is* well ; thy servant shall have
peace : but if he be very wroth, *then* be sure that *e*evil is deter-
8 mined by him. Therefore thou shalt *f*deal kindly with thy
servant ; for *g*thou hast brought thy servant into a covenant of
the LORD with thee : notwithstanding, *h*if there be in me
iniquity, slay me thyself ; for why shouldest thou bring me to
9 thy father ? And Jonathan said, Far be it from thee : for if I

r ch. 10. 10.

s Isai. 20. 2.

t Mic. 1. 8.
See 2 Sam.
6. 14, 20.
u ch. 10. 11.

a Num. 10.
10.
& 28. 11.
b ch. 19. 2.
c ch. 16. 4.

d See Deut.
1. 23.
2 Sam. 17. 4.
e ch. 25. 17.
Esth. 7. 7.
f Josh. 2. 14.
g ver. 16.
ch. 18. 3.
& 23. 18.
h 2 Sam. 14.
32.

---

[1] Heb. *fell*, Num. 24. 4.
[2] Heb. *uncover mine ear*, ver. 12. ch. 9. 15.
[3] Or, *Say what is thy mind, and I will do, &c.*
[4] Heb. *speaketh*, or, *thinketh*.
[5] Or, *feast*, ch. 9. 12.

---

22. *to a great well*] Some large well-
known cistern at Sechu, the site of which
is uncertain, which Saul passed on his way
from Gibeah to Ramah.

24. *naked*] *i.e.* without his robe and other
outer garments, but only the shirt. Cp.
marg. reff.

The whole history affords another instance
of the protection of God vouchsafed to
His servants, which forms so frequent a
topic of the Psalms of David.

XX. 1. While Saul was under the con-
straining influence of the spirit of prophecy,
David escaped from Naioth, and, probably
by Samuel's advice, returned to Saul's
court to commune with Jonathan. Nothing
could be a better evidence of his innocence
than thus putting himself in Jonathan's
power. Perhaps something passed between

Samuel and Saul on the subject, since it
appears from *vv.* 5, 25, 27, that Saul expected David at the feast of the new moon.

2. *it is not so*] Jonathan's unwillingness
to believe evil of his father is one of the
many admirable traits in his character.

3. *And David sware moreover*] Rather,
"yet again." He met Jonathan's denial
by repeating his statement and confirming
it with an oath.

5. The new moon, or beginning of each
month, was celebrated with especial sacrifices and blowing of trumpets (marg. reff.).
The feast was kept with great solemnity as
"a day of gladness," and we may presume
that the "peace offerings" offered on the
occasion furnished the tables of those that
offered.

knew certainly that evil were determined by my father to come
10 upon thee, then would not I tell it thee? Then said David to
Jonathan, Who shall tell me? or what *if* thy father answer thee
11 roughly? And Jonathan said unto David, Come, and let us go
out into the field. And they went out both of them into the
12 field. And Jonathan said unto David, O LORD God of Israel,
when I have [1]sounded my father about to morrow any time, *or*
the third *day*, and, behold, *if there be* good toward David, and I

i Ruth 1. 17.   13 then send not unto thee, and [2]shew it thee; *i*the LORD do so
and much more to Jonathan: but if it please my father *to do*
thee evil, then I will shew it thee, and send thee away, that

k Josh. 1. 5.   thou mayest go in peace: and *k*the LORD be with thee, as he
ch. 17. 37.   14 hath been with my father. And thou shalt not only while yet I
1 Chr. 22. 11, 16.   15 live shew me the kindness of the LORD, that I die not: but *also*
l 2 Sam. 9. 1,   *l*thou shalt not cut off thy kindness from my house for ever: no,
3, 7.   not when the LORD hath cut off the enemies of David every one
& 21. 7.   16 from the face of the earth. ¶ So Jonathan [3]made *a covenant*

m ch. 25. 22.   with the house of David, *saying*, *m*Let the LORD even require *it*
See ch. 31. 2.   17 at the hand of David's enemies. And Jonathan caused David
2 Sam. 4. 7.   to swear again, [4]because he loved him: *n*for he loved him as he
& 21. 8.
n ch. 18. 1.   18 loved his own soul. ¶ Then Jonathan said to David, *o*To morrow
o ver. 5.   *is* the new moon: and thou shalt be missed, because thy seat
19 will be [5]empty. And *when* thou hast stayed three days, *then*

p ch. 19. 2.   thou shalt go down [6][7]quickly, and come to *p*the place where
thou didst hide thyself [8]when the business was *in hand*, and
20 shalt remain by the stone [9]Ezel. And I will shoot three arrows
21 on the side *thereof*, as though I shot at a mark. And, behold, I
will send a lad, *saying*, Go, find out the arrows. If I expressly
say unto the lad, Behold, the arrows *are* on this side of thee,
take them; then come thou: for *there is* peace to thee, and [1]no

q Jer. 4. 2.   22 hurt; *q*as the LORD liveth. But if I say thus unto the young
man, Behold, the arrows *are* beyond thee; go thy way: for the

r ver. 14, 15.   23 LORD hath sent thee away. And *as touching* *r*the matter which
See ver. 42.   thou and I have spoken of, behold, the LORD *be* between thee
24 and me for ever. ¶ So David hid himself in the field: and
when the new moon was come, the king sat him down to eat
25 meat. And the king sat upon his seat, as at other times, *even*
upon a seat by the wall: and Jonathan arose, and Abner sat by
26 Saul's side, and David's place was empty. Nevertheless Saul
spake not any thing that day: for he thought, Something hath

s Lev. 7. 21.   27 befallen him, he *is* [8]not clean; surely he *is* not clean. ¶ And it
& 15. 5, &c.   came to pass on the morrow, *which was* the second *day* of the
month, that David's place was empty: and Saul said unto
Jonathan his son, Wherefore cometh not the son of Jesse to

t ver. 6.   28 meat, neither yesterday, nor to day? And Jonathan *t*answered

---

[1] Heb. *searched.*	[4] Or, *by his love toward*	[8] Heb. *in the day of the*
[2] Heb. *uncover thine ear,*	*him.*	*business.*
ver. 2.	[5] Heb. *missed.*	[9] Or, *That sheweth the way.*
[3] Heb. *cut.*	[6] Or, *diligently.*	[1] Heb. *not any thing.*
	[7] Heb. *greatly.*	

14, 15. The general meaning is: Jonathan had a presentiment, doubtless from God, that David would be established upon the throne. By God's mercy he had the comfort, which he well deserved, of knowing that his own posterity would receive kindness at David's hand (see marg. reff.).

19. *the stone Ezel*] It is not mentioned elsewhere, except possibly in *v.* 41, where see note.

26. *he is not clean*] The new moon being a religious feast, and the meat to be eaten being peace-offerings, no one could assist at the feast who had any ceremonial uncleanness upon him (marg. reff.).

Saul, David earnestly asked *leave* of me *to go* to Beth-lehem:
29 and he said, Let me go, I pray thee; for our family hath a
sacrifice in the city; and my brother, he hath commanded me
to be there: and now, if I have found favour in thine eyes, let
me get away, I pray thee, and see my brethren. Therefore he
30 cometh not unto the king's table. ¶ Then Saul's anger was
kindled against Jonathan, and he said unto him, ¹²Thou son of
the perverse rebellious *woman,* do not I know that thou hast
chosen the son of Jesse to thine own confusion, and unto the
31 confusion of thy mother's nakedness? For as long as the son of
Jesse liveth upon the ground, thou shalt not be established, nor
thy kingdom. Wherefore now send and fetch him unto me, for
32 he ³shall surely die. And Jonathan answered Saul his father,
and said unto him, "Wherefore shall he be slain? what hath he
33 done? And Saul ˣcast a javelin at him to smite him: ʸwhere-
by Jonathan knew that it was determined of his father to slay
34 David. So Jonathan arose from the table in fierce anger, and
did eat no meat the second day of the month: for he was grieved
35 for David, because his father had done him shame. ¶ And it
came to pass in the morning, that Jonathan went out into the
field at the time appointed with David, and a little lad with him.
36 And he said unto his lad, Run, find out now the arrows which I
shoot. *And* as the lad ran, he shot an arrow ⁴beyond him.
37 And when the lad was come to the place of the arrow which
Jonathan had shot, Jonathan cried after the lad, and said, *Is*
38 not the arrow beyond thee? And Jonathan cried after the lad,
Make speed, haste, stay not. And Jonathan's lad gathered up
39 the arrows, and came to his master. But the lad knew not any
40 thing: only Jonathan and David knew the matter. And Jonathan gave his ⁵artillery unto ⁶his lad, and said unto him, Go,
41 carry *them* to the city. ¶ *And* as soon as the lad was gone, David
arose out of *a place* toward the south, and fell on his face to the
ground, and bowed himself three times: and they kissed one
another, and wept one with another, until David exceeded.
42 And Jonathan said to David, ᶻGo in peace, ⁷forasmuch as we
have sworn both of us in the name of the LORD, saying, The
LORD be between me and thee, and between my seed and thy
seed for ever And he arose and departed: and Jonathan went
into the city.

ᵘ ch. 19. 5.
Matt. 27. 23.
Luke 23. 22.
ˣ ch. 18. 11.
ʸ ver. 7.

ᶻ ch. 1. 17.

¹ Or, *Thou perverse rebel.*
² Heb. *Son of perverse re-*
 bellion.
³ Heb. is *the son of death.*
⁴ Heb. *to pass over him.*
⁵ Heb. *instruments.*
⁶ Heb. *that* was *his.*
⁷ Or, the LORD be witness
 of that *which, &c.* See
 ver. 23.

---

30. The greatest insult and most stinging
reproach that can be cast upon an Oriental
is to reproach his parents or ancestors (see
Job xxx. 8). Saul means to intimate that
Jonathan was stubborn from his mother's
womb.

41. *a place toward the south*] An unintelligible description; one expects a repetition
of the description of David's hiding-place in
v. 19. The LXX. in both places has *argab,*
a word meaning a *heap of stones.* If this be
the true reading, David's hiding-place was
either a natural cavernous rock which was
called *Argab,* or some ruin of an ancient
building, equally suited for a hiding-place.
bowed himself three times] In token, doubt-

less, of his unshaken loyalty to Jonathan as
the son of his king, as well as his friend;
and in acknowledgment of Jonathan's power
to kill him if he saw fit. (Cp. Gen.
xxxiii. 3).
David exceeded] His affection for Jonathan, coupled with his sense of Saul's injustice and his own injured innocence, fully
accounts for his strong emotion.
42. *Jonathan went into the city*] From
which one may infer, what the after history
also indicates, that Jonathan's filial duty
and patriotism prevented a complete rupture with his father. Jonathan's conduct in
this, as in everything, was most admirable.

a ch. 14. 3, called Ahiah. Called also Abiathar, Mark 2. 26.
b ch. 16. 4.

c Ex. 25. 30.
Lev. 24. 5.
Matt. 12. 4.
d Ex. 19. 15.
Zech. 7. 3.
e ch. 17. 40.

f Lev. 8. 26.
g Mark 2. 25, 26.
Luke 6. 3.
h Lev. 24. 8.

i ch. 22. 9.
Ps. 52, title.

k ch. 17. 2, 50.
l See ch. 31. 10.

m Ps. 56, title.

CHAP. 21. THEN came David to Nob to *a*Ahimelech the priest: and Ahimelech was *b*afraid at the meeting of David, and said unto 2 him, Why *art* thou alone, and no man with thee? And David said unto Ahimelech the priest, The king hath commanded me a business, and hath said unto me, Let no man know any thing of the business whereabout I send thee, and what I have commanded thee: and I have appointed *my* servants to such and 3 such a place. Now therefore what is under thine hand? give *me* five *loaves of* bread in mine hand, or what there is [1]present. 4 And the priest answered David, and said, *There is* no common bread under mine hand, but there is *c*hallowed bread; *d*if the 5 young men have kept themselves at least from women. And David answered the priest, and said unto him, Of a truth women *have been* kept from us about these three days, since I came out, and the *e*vessels of the young men are holy, and *the bread is* in a manner common, [2]yea, though it were sanctified this day 6 *f*in the vessel. So the priest *g*gave him hallowed *bread:* for there was no bread there but the shewbread, *h*that was taken from before the LORD, to put hot bread in the day when it was taken 7 away. Now a certain man of the servants of Saul *was* there that day, detained before the LORD; and his name *was* *i*Doeg, an 8 Edomite, the chiefest of the herdmen that *belonged* to Saul. ¶ And David said unto Ahimelech, And is there not here under thine hand spear or sword? for I have neither brought my sword nor my weapons with me, because the king's business required haste. 9 And the priest said, The sword of Goliath the Philistine, whom thou slewest in *k*the valley of Elah, *l*behold, it *is here* wrapped in a cloth behind the ephod: if thou wilt take that, take *it:* for *there is* no other save that here. And David said, *There is* none 10 like that; give it me. ¶ And David arose, and fled that day for 11 fear of Saul, and went to [3]Achish the king of Gath. And *m*the servants of Achish said unto him, *Is* not this David the king of

[1] Heb. *found.*
[2] Or, *especially when this day there is* other *sanctified in the vessel.*
[3] Or, *Abimelech,* Ps. 34, title.

XXI. 1. Nob was a city of the priests, the High-Priest resided there, and the Tabernacle was pitched there (*vv.* 4, 6, 9, xxii. 10). It was situated on the road from the north to Jerusalem, near Anathoth, and within sight of the holy city (Isai. x. 32; Neh. xi. 32). But the site has not been identified with certainty.

2. A fresh instance of David's unscrupulous readiness of invention (cp. xx. 6).

4. *common*] As opposed to *holy.* (See marg. reff., and cp. the use of the word in Acts x. 14, 15, 28.) It gives an idea of the depressed and poor condition of the priesthood at that time, that Ahimelech should have had no bread at hand except the shew-bread.

5. *the vessels of the young men,* &c.] *i.e.* their clothes (Deut. xxii. 5) or wallets (marg. ref.), or other articles which might be Levitically unclean and need cleansing (Levit. xiii. 58; Exod. xix. 10, &c.; Mark vii. 4), as well as the person.

and the bread, &c.] The meaning is; "Though it is treating it like common

bread to give it to me and my young men, there is fresh Shew-bread baked and put on the table in place of what you give us"; the day being Friday. as is indicated in the verse following.

7. *detained before the* LORD] Either to fulfil a vow (Acts xxi. 23-27), or on account of uncleanness, or under the law of lepers (Levit. xiii. 4, 11, 21), or as a proselyte. It is not impossible that Doeg may have been in custody or in sanctuary for some crime.

9. *wrapped in a cloth behind the ephod*] Rather, "**in the cloak,**" Goliath's military cloak, which was part of the dedicated trophy. The ephod was naturally hung up where the High-Priest alone could get at it.

10. *Achish king of Gath*] It appears from the title that Ps. xxxiv. was composed on this occasion. (See note there.) Nothing can give a more lively impression of the straits to which David was reduced than the fact of his going to the country of the Philistines.

11. *the king of the land*] The Philistines gave him the title which their own lords bore.

the land? did they not sing one to another of him in dances, saying, *n* Saul hath slain his thousands, and David his ten thou-
12 sands? And David *o* laid up these words in his heart, and was
13 sore afraid of Achish the king of Gath. And *p* he changed his behaviour before them, and feigned himself ma d in their hands, and ¹scrabbled on the doors of the gate, and let his spittle fall
14 down upon his beard. Then said Achish unto his servants, Lo, ye see the man ²is mad: wherefore *then* have ye brought him to
15 me? Have I need of mad men, that ye have brought this *fellow* to play the mad man in my presence? shall this *fellow* come into my house?

CHAP. 22. DAVID therefore departed thence, and *a* escaped *b* to the cave Adullam: and when his brethren and all his father's house
2 heard *it*, they went down thither to him. *c* And every one *that was* in distress, and every one that ³*was* in debt, and every one *that was* ⁴discontented, gathered themselves unto him; and he became a captain over them: and there were with him about
3 four hundred men. ¶ And David went thence to Mizpeh of Moab: and he said unto the king of Moab, Let my father and my mother, I pray thee, come forth, *and be* with you, till I know
4 what God will do for me. And he brought them before the king of Moab: and they dwelt with him all the while that David was
5 in the hold. And the prophet *d* Gad said unto David, Abide not in the hold; depart, and get thee into the land of Judah. Then
6 David departed, and came into the forest of Hareth. ¶ When Saul heard that David was discovered, and the men that *were* with him, (now Saul abode in Gibeah under a ⁵tree in Ramah,

n ch. 18. 7.
& 29. 5.
o Luke 2. 19.
p Ps. 34, title.

a Ps. 57, title, & 142, title.
b 2 Sam. 23. 13.
c Judg. 11. 3.

d 2 Sam. 24. 11.
1 Chr. 21. 9.
2 Chr. 29. 25.

---

¹ Or, *made marks.*
² Or, *playeth the mad man.*
³ Heb. *had a creditor.*
⁴ Heb. *bitter of soul.*
⁵ Or, *grove in a high place.*

---

13. *scrabbled*] Literally, made marks (marg.), viz. the mark of the *tau*, which in the ancient Hebrew and Phœnician was in the shape of a cross. (See Ezek. ix. 4.)

on the doors of the gate] The gate of Achish's palace-yard or court, in which the attendants waited. The house itself stood in this court. (Cp. Esth. ii. 19, 21.)

XXII. 1. *to the cave Adullam*] Or rather "**of Adullam.**" Adullam was the name of a town of Judah in the *Shephelah*, not far from Bethlehem, and below it. Innumerable caverns, one nearly 100 feet long, are excavated in the soft limestone hills in the neighbourhood of Beit-Jibrin. [The cave is placed by Ganneau and Conder on the hill (500 feet high) over 'Aid el Ma or Miyeh.] David's brethren and kinsmen joined him partly from sympathy with him, and partly because their own lives were in jeopardy from Saul's furious enmity.

2. *discontented*] See marg. (Cp. xxx. 6; 2 Sam. xvii. 8.) The phrase here denotes those who were exasperated by Saul's tyranny.

3. *Mizpeh of Moab*] A good conjecture connects it with *Zophim* (a word of the same root as Mizpeh) on the top of Pisgah (Num. xxiii. 14). It is probable that David's descent from Ruth the Moabitess may have had something to do with his seeking an asylum for Jesse, Ruth's grandson, in the

land of her birth. It would be very easy to get to the Jordan from the neighbourhood of Bethlehem, and cross over near its embouchure into the Dead Sea.

come forth, and be *with you*] The construction of the Hebrew is very strange. The Vulg., Syriac, and Arabic seem to have read *dwell* instead of *come forth.*

4. *he brought them before,* &c.] The Sept. renders it *he persuaded (the face of) the king.*

4, 5. *in the hold*] Where David was after he left the cave of Adullam, probably in the land of Moab.

The phrase *all the while*, would indicate that David sojourned a considerable time in Moab.

5. *the prophet Gad*] Mentioned here for the first time. One may conjecture that Samuel had sent him privately from Naioth to tell David not to abide in the hold. Whether he stayed with David or returned to the College of the prophets does not appear. For later notices of him see marg. reff.

The forest of Hareth is unknown.

6. *under a tree in Ramah*] Rather, "**under the tamarisk-tree on the high place,**" where he always held such meetings. It was a kind of parliament in the open air, and all his tribesmen gathered round him. (Cp. Judg. iv. 5.)

having his spear in his hand, and all his servants *were* standing
7 about him;) then Saul said unto his servants that stood about
him, Hear now, ye Benjamites; will the son of Jesse *give every
one of you fields and vineyards, *and* make you all captains of
8 thousands, and captains of hundreds; that all of you have conspired against me, and *there is* none that [1]sheweth me that [f]my
son hath made a league with the son of Jesse, and *there is* none
of you that is sorry for me, or sheweth unto me that my son
hath stirred up my servant against me, to lie in wait, as at this
9 day? ¶ Then answered [g]Doeg the Edomite, which was set over
the servants of Saul, and said, I saw the son of Jesse coming to
10 Nob, to [h]Ahimelech the son of [i]Ahitub. [k]And he enquired of
the LORD for him, and [l]gave him victuals, and gave him the
11 sword of Goliath the Philistine. ¶ Then the king sent to call
Ahimelech the priest, the son of Ahitub, and all his father's
house, the priests that *were* in Nob: and they came all of them
12 to the king. And Saul said, Hear now, thou son of Ahitub.
13 And he answered [2]Here I *am*, my lord. And Saul said unto
him, Why have ye conspired against me, thou and the son of
Jesse, in that thou hast given him bread, and a sword, and hast
enquired of God for him, that he should rise against me, to lie
14 in wait, as at this day? Then Ahimelech answered the king,
and said, And who *is so* faithful among all thy servants as
David, which is the king's son in law, and goeth at thy bidding,
15 and is honourable in thine house? Did I then begin to enquire
of God for him? be it far from me: let not the king impute *any*
thing unto his servant, *nor* to all the house of my father: for
16 thy servant knew nothing of all this, [3]less or more. And the
king said, Thou shalt surely die, Ahimelech, thou, and all thy
17 father's house. And the king said unto the [45]footmen that
stood about him, Turn, and slay the priests of the LORD; because their hand also *is* with David, and because they knew
when he fled, and did not shew it to me. But the servants of
the king [m]would not put forth their hand to fall upon the priests
18 of the LORD. And the king said to Doeg, Turn thou, and fall
upon the priests. And Doeg the Edomite turned, and he fell
upon the priests, and [n]slew on that day fourscore and five per-

Marginal references (left):

e ch. 8. 14.

f ch. 18. 3.
& 20. 30.

g ch. 21. 7.
Ps. 52, title,
& ver. 1, 2, 3.
h ch. 21. 1.
i ch. 14. 3.
k Num. 27.
21.
l ch. 21. 6, 9.

m See Exod.
1. 17.

n See ch. 2.
31.

---

[1] Heb. *uncovereth mine ear,*
   ch. 20. 2.

[2] Heb. *Behold me.*
[3] Heb. *little or great.*

[4] Or, *guard.*
[5] Heb. *runners.*

---

7. *ye Benjamites*] Showing how isolated
the tribes still were, and how for the most
part Saul was surrounded by his own tribesmen only.

10. *he enquired of the* LORD, &c.] This
was not true, but Ahimelech's going to
fetch the sword from behind the ephod
might have given occasion to the belief on
Doeg's part that he had put on the ephod to
enquire of the Lord for David.

14. *goeth at thy bidding*] Better, "**has access to thy** (private) **audience,**" or *council*
(cp. 2 Sam. xxiii. 23, marg.).

15. *Did I then begin,* &c.] Some lay the
stress upon the word *begin,* as though Ahimelech's justification was that he had often
before enquired of the Lord for David when
employed on the king's affairs. But it is
much better to understand the words as

Ahimelech's solemn denial of having enquired of the Lord for David, a duty which
he owed to Saul alone as king of Israel.
The force of the word *begin* lies in this, that
it would have been his first act of allegiance
to David and defection from Saul. This he
strenuously repudiates, and adds, *thy servant knew nothing of all this* conspiracy between Jonathan and David of which Saul
speaks : he had acted quite innocently.

18. We are not to suppose that Doeg
killed them all with his own hand. He
had a band of men under his command,
many or all of whom were perhaps foreigners like himself, and very likely of a Be-
douin caste, to whom bloodshed would be
quite natural, and the priests of the Lord
of no more account than so many sheep or
oxen.

19 sons that did wear a linen ephod. *o*And Nob, the city of the   *o* ver. 9, 11.
priests, smote he with the edge of the sword, both men and
women, children and sucklings, and oxen, and asses, and sheep,
20 with the edge of the sword. ¶ *p*And one of the sons of Ahime-   *p* ch. 23. 6.
lech the son of Ahitub, named Abiathar, *q*escaped, and fled after   *q* ch. 2. 33.
21 David. And Abiathar shewed David that Saul had slain the
22 LORD's priests. And David said unto Abiathar, I knew *it* that
day, when Doeg the Edomite *was* there, that he would surely
tell Saul: I have occasioned *the death* of all the persons of thy
23 father's house. Abide thou with me, fear not: *r*for he that   *r* 1 Kin.2.26.
seeketh my life seeketh thy life: but with me thou *shalt be* in
safeguard.

CHAP. 23. THEN they told David, saying, Behold, the Philistines
2 fight against *a*Keilah, and they rob the threshingfloors. There-   *a* Josh.15.44.
fore David *b*enquired of the LORD, saying, Shall I go and smite   *b* ver. 4, 6, 9.
these Philistines? And the LORD said unto David, Go, and   ch. 30. 8.
   2 Sam. 5. 19,
3 smite the Philistines, and save Keilah. And David's men said   23.
unto him, Behold, we be afraid here in Judah: how much more
then if we come to Keilah against the armies of the Philistines?
4 Then David enquired of the LORD yet again. And the LORD
answered him and said, Arise, go down to Keilah; for I will
5 deliver the Philistines into thine hand. So David and his men
went to Keilah, and fought with the Philistines, and brought
away their cattle, and smote them with a great slaughter. So
6 David saved the inhabitants of Keilah. ¶And it came to pass,
when Abiathar the son of Ahimelech *c*fled to David to Keilah,   *c* ch. 22. 20.
7 *that* he came down *with* an ephod in his hand. ¶And it was told
Saul that David was come to Keilah. And Saul said, God hath
delivered him into mine hand; for he is shut in, by entering
8 into a town that hath gates and bars. And Saul called all the
people together to war, to go down to Keilah, to besiege David
9 and his men. ¶And David knew that Saul secretly practised
mischief against him; and *d*he said to Abiathar the priest, Bring   *d* Num. 27.
10 hither the ephod. Then said David, O LORD God of Israel, thy   21.
   ch. 30. 7.

---

19. *both men and women,* &c.] The language employed in the case of the Amalekites (xv. 3) and of Jericho (Josh. vi. 21).
Nothing could be more truculent than Saul's
revenge.

20. *Abiathar*] He may have remained at
Nob to take care of the sanctuary when the
other priests went to Saul, and so escaped.
He continued David's faithful friend
throughout his reign (xxiii. 9, xxx. 7; 2
Sam. xv. 24, 29, 35), but gave offence by
taking Adonijah's part against Solomon (1
K. i. 7, 19, 42), and in consequence was deprived of the high priesthood (1 K. ii. 26, 27).
In Mark ii. 26, he is spoken of as the High-
Priest who gave the Shew-bread to David.
Perhaps he was the instigator of this act of
kindness to David; and for this cause, as
well as his constancy to David, is mentioned
by our Lord instead of Ahimelech. It is also
possible that, as *sagan* to his father, he may
have performed most of the priestly functions, as Hophni and Phinehas did in the lifetime of Eli. Abiathar did not actually join
David till he went to Keilah (marg. ref.).

23. The characteristic generosity of David's disposition breaks out in these words.
He never forgot a friend. (Cp. 2 Sam. i. 26,
ix. 1, &c.) David acknowledges that Saul's
enmity against Abiathar is the consequence
of his enmity against himself, and therefore
David makes common cause with him.

XXIII. 1. David's growing importance,
fugitive as he was, is marked by this appeal
to him for deliverance from the Philistines.
The *threshing floors* were the natural objects
of plunder (Judg. vi. 11). Keilah was in the
Shephelah (marg. ref.), probably close to the
Philistine border, but its site is uncertain.

2, 4, 6. If Gad was with David at the
forest of Hareth (xxii. 5), and there enquired for him of the Lord (*vv.* 2, 4), but did
not accompany him to Keilah, and if Abiathar's flight occurred at the time of David's
being at Keilah, we have an additional
striking instance of God's watchful providential care of David in thus sending Abiathar to supply the place of Gad at so
critical a moment.

servant hath certainly heard that Saul seeketh to come to Keilah,

11 *to destroy the city for my sake. Will the men of Keilah deliver me up into his hand? will Saul come down, as thy servant hath heard? O Lord God of Israel, I beseech thee, tell thy servant.

12 And the Lord said, He will come down. Then said David, Will the men of Keilah ¹deliver me and my men into the hand of

13 Saul? And the Lord said, They will deliver *thee* up. ¶ Then David and his men, *ʃwhich were* about six hundred, arose and departed out of Keilah, and went whithersoever they could go. And it was told Saul that David was escaped from Keilah; and

14 he forbare to go forth. And David abode in the wilderness in strong holds, and remained in *ᵍa* mountain in the wilderness of *ʰ*Ziph. And Saul *ⁱ*sought him every day, but God delivered

15 him not into his hand. ¶ And David saw that Saul was come out to seek his life: and David *was* in the wilderness of Ziph in

16 a wood. And Jonathan Saul's son arose, and went to David into

17 the wood, and strengthened his hand in God. And he said unto him, Fear not: for the hand of Saul my father shall not find thee; and thou shalt be king over Israel, and I shall be next

18 unto thee; and *ᵏ*that also Saul my father knoweth. And they two *ˡ*made a covenant before the Lord: and David abode in the

19 wood, and Jonathan went to his house. ¶ Then *ᵐ*came up the Ziphites to Saul to Gibeah, saying, Doth not David hide himself with us in strong holds in the wood, in the hill of Hachilah,

20 which *is* ²on the south of ³Jeshimon? Now therefore, O king, come down according to all the desire of thy soul to come down;

21 and *ⁿ*our part *shall be* to deliver him into the king's hand. And Saul said, Blessed *be* ye of the Lord; for ye have compassion on

22 me. Go, I pray you, prepare yet, and know and see his place where his ⁴haunt is, *and* who hath seen him there: for it is told

23 me *that* he dealeth very subtilly. See therefore, and take knowledge of all the lurking places where he hideth himself, and come ye again to me with the certainty, and I will go with you: and it shall come to pass, if he be in the land, that I will search

24 him out throughout all the thousands of Judah. ¶ And they arose, and went to Ziph before Saul: but David and his men *were* in the wilderness *º*of Maon, in the plain on the south of

25 Jeshimon. Saul also and his men went to seek *him*. And they told David: wherefore he came down ⁵into a rock, and abode in the wilderness of Maon. And when Saul heard *that*, he pursued

26 after David in the wilderness of Maon. And Saul went on this side of the mountain, and David and his men on that side of the mountain: and David made haste to get away for fear of Saul: for Saul and his men *q*compassed David and his men round

Marginal references

e ch. 22. 19.

ʃ ch. 22. 2. & 25. 13.

ᵍ Ps. 11. 1.
ʰ Josh. 15. 55.
ⁱ Ps. 54. 3, 4.

ᵏ ch. 24. 20.
ˡ ch. 18. 3. & 20. 16.
2 Sam. 21. 7.
ᵐ See ch. 26. 1.
Ps. 54, title.

ⁿ Ps. 54. 3.

º Josh. 15. 55.
ch. 25. 2.

ᵖ Ps. 31. 22.
q Ps. 17. 9.

---

¹ Heb. *shut up.*   ³ Or, *The wilderness?*   ⁴ Heb. *foot shall be.*
² Heb. *on the right hand.*   ⁵ Or, *from the rock, v. 28.*

---

12. The conduct of the men of Keilah would be like that of the men of Judah to Samson their deliverer (Judg. xv. 10–13).

14. Ziph is placed between Hebron and En-gedi (marg. reff.). [The "wood" (*v.* 15) is by Conder taken as a proper name, "Cheresh," and identified with Khoreisa.]

16. A touching example of mutual fidelity between friends. The humility and unselfish love of Jonathan is apparent in *v.* 17.

19. [Hachilah is thought by Conder to be the long ridge called El Kôlah]. For Jeshimon, see marg. and Num. xxi. 20.

24. *the plain*] The Arabah, the desert tract which extends along the valley of the Jordan from the Dead Sea to the Lake of Gennesareth, now called El-Ghor. The word is now given by the Arabs to the valley between the Dead Sea and the Gulf of Akaba.

27 about to take them. ᴿBut there came a messenger unto Saul, saying, Haste thee, and come ; for the Philistines have ¹invaded
28 the land. Wherefore Saul returned from pursuing after David, and went against the Philistines. therefore they called that
29 place ²Sela-hammahlekoth. And David went up from thence, and dwelt in strong holds at ˢEn-gedi.

CHAP. **24.** AND it came to pass, ᵃwhen Saul was returned from ³following the Philistines, that it was told him, saying, Behold,
2 David *is* in the wilderness of En-gedi. Then Saul took three thousand chosen men out of all Israel, and ᵇwent to seek David
3 and his men upon the rocks of the wild goats. And he came to the sheepcotes by the way, where *was* a cave ; and ᶜSaul went in to ᵈcover his feet and ᵉDavid and his men remained in the sides
4 of the cave. ᶠAnd the men of David said unto him, Behold the day of which the LORD said unto thee, Behold, I will deliver thine enemy into thine hand, that thou mayest do to him as it shall seem good unto thee. Then David arose, and cut off the
5 skirt of ⁴Saul's robe privily. And it came to pass afterward, that ᵍDavid's heart smote him, because he had cut off Saul's
6 skirt. And he said unto his men, ʰThe LORD forbid that I should do this thing unto my master, the LORD's anointed, to stretch forth mine hand against him, seeing he *is* the anointed
7 of the LORD. So David ⁵ˈstayed his servants with these words, and suffered them not to rise against Saul. But Saul rose up
8 out of the cave, and went on *his* way. David also arose afterward. and went out of the cave, and cried after Saul, saying, My lord the king. And when Saul looked behind him, David stooped
9 with his face to the earth, and bowed himself. ¶And David said to Saul, ᵏWherefore hearest thou men's words, saying, Behold,
10 David seeketh thy hurt ? Behold, this day thine eyes have seen how that the LORD had delivered thee to day into mine hand in the cave : and *some* bade *me* kill thee : but *mine eye* spared thee ; and I said, I will not put forth mine hand against my lord ;

Marginal references:
ʳ See 2 Kin. 19. 9.
ˢ 2 Chr. 20. 2.
ᵃ ch. 23. 28.
ᵇ Ps. 38. 12.
ᶜ Ps. 141. 6.
ᵈ Judg. 3. 24.
ᵉ Ps. 57. title, & 112, title.
ᶠ ch. 26. 8.
ᵍ 2 Sam. 24. 10.
ʰ ch. 26. 11.
ⁱ Ps. 7. 4. Matt. 5. 44. Rom. 12. 17, 19.
ᵏ Ps. 141. 6. Prov. 16. 28.

---

¹ Heb. *spread themselves upon, &c.*
² That is, *The rock of divisions.*
³ Heb. *after.*
⁴ Heb. *the robe which* was *Saul's.*
⁵ Heb. *cut off.*

---

28. *Sela-hammahlekoth*] See marg. [Identified by Conder with a narrow and impassable gorge between El Kôlah and Maon, called Malâky].
29. En-gedi (*the fountain of the kid*), anciently called Hazezon-Tamar (Gen. xiv. 7) from the palm-trees which used to grow there, still preserves its name in Ain-Djedy. It is about 200 yards from the Dead Sea, about the centre of its western shore. It is marked by great luxuriance of vegetation, though the approach to it is through most dangerous and precipitous passes. The country is full of caverns, which serve as lurking places for outlaws at the present day. One of these, a spacious one called Bir-el-Mauquouchieh, with a well in it suitable for watering sheep, close to the Wady Hasasa, may have been the identical cavern in which David cut off Saul's skirt.
XXIV. **2.** *the rocks of the wild goats*] To signify the craggy precipitous character of the country.

3. *remained in the sides*] Rather, "**were in the sides of the cave dwelling** or abiding there." Some of these caverns are very deep and spacious. Any one near the mouth of the cave would be visible, but those in the recesses would be quite in the dark and invisible, especially if the incident occurred at night. The lviith Psalm, according to the title, was composed on this occasion.
4. *the day of which the LORD said*, &c.] This was the version by David's men of such Divine predictions as xv. 28, xvi. 1, 12. Jonathan's words (xx. 15, xxiii. 17) show clearly that these predictions were known.
5. *David's heart smote him*] He thought the action inconsistent with the respect which he owed to the king.
9. David was quite aware that there were flatterers at Saul's court who were continually inflaming the King's mind by their false accusations against him. This explains the language of many of the Psalms, *e.g.* x. xi. xii. xxxv. and many more.

11 for he *is* the LORD's anointed. Moreover, my father, see, yea,
see the skirt of thy robe in my hand : for in that I cut off the
skirt of thy robe, and killed thee not, know thou and see that
there is [l]neither evil nor transgression in mine hand, and I have
not sinned against thee ; yet thou [m]huntest my soul to take it.
12 [n]The LORD judge between me and thee, and the LORD avenge
13 me of thee : but mine hand shall not be upon thee. As saith
the proverb of the ancients, Wickedness proceedeth from the
14 wicked : but mine hand shall not be upon thee. After whom is
the king of Israel come out? after whom dost thou pursue?
15 [o]after a dead dog, after [p]a flea. [q]The LORD therefore be judge,
and judge between me and thee, and [r]see, and [s]plead my cause,
16 and [l]deliver me out of thine hand. ¶ And it came to pass, when
David had made an end of speaking these words unto Saul, that
Saul said, [t]*Is* this thy voice, my son David? And Saul lifted
17 up his voice, and wept. [u]And he said to David, Thou art [x]more
righteous than I : for [y]thou hast rewarded me good, whereas I
18 have rewarded thee evil. And thou hast shewed this day how
that thou hast dealt well with me : forasmuch as when [z]the
LORD had [2]delivered me into thine hand, thou killedst me not.
19 For if a man find his enemy, will he let him go well away?
wherefore the LORD reward thee good for that thou hast done
20 unto me this day. And now, behold, [a]I know well that thou
shalt surely be king, and that the kingdom of Israel shall be
21 established in thine hand. [b]Swear now therefore unto me by
the LORD, [c]that thou wilt not cut off my seed after me, and that
22 thou wilt not destroy my name out of my father's house. And
David sware unto Saul. And Saul went home ; but David and
his men gat them up unto [d]the hold.

CHAP. 25. AND [a]Samuel died ; and all the Israelites were gathered
together, and [b]lamented him, and buried him in his house at
Ramah. ¶ And David arose, and went down [c]to the wilderness
2 of Paran. And *there was* a man [d]in Maon, whose [3]possessions
were in [e]Carmel ; and the man *was* very great, and he had three
thousand sheep, and a thousand goats : and he was shearing his
3 sheep in Carmel. Now the name of the man *was* Nabal ; and

[l] Ps. 7. 3.
& 35. 7.
[m] ch. 26. 20.
[n] Gen. 16. 5.
Judg. 11. 27.
ch. 26. 10.
Job 5. 8.

[o] ch. 17. 43.
2 Sam. 9. 8.
[p] ch. 26. 20.
[q] ver. 12.
[r] 2 Chr. 24.
22.
[s] Ps. 35. 1.
& 43. 1.
& 119. 154.
Mic. 7. 9.
[t] ch. 26. 17.
[u] ch. 26. 21.
[x] Gen. 38. 26.
[y] Matt. 5. 44.
[z] ch. 26. 23.

[a] ch. 23. 17.

[b] Gen. 21. 23.

[c] 2 Sam. 21.
6, 8.

[d] ch. 23. 29.
[a] ch. 28. 3.
[b] Num. 20.
29.
Deut. 34. 8.
[c] Gen. 21. 21.
Ps. 120. 5.
[d] ch. 23. 24.
[e] Josh. 15.
55.

[1] Heb. *judge*.　　　[2] Heb. *shut up*, ch. 23. 12. & 26. 8.　　　[3] Or, *business*.

---

11. *my father*] The respectful address of a
junior and an inferior (see 2 K. v. 13, and
cp. *v.* 16, xxv. 8).

14. *After whom*, &c.] *i.e.* was it consistent
with the dignity of the king of Israel to
lead armies in pursuit of a weak and helpless individual like David?

21. *Swear now*, &c.] The same request
which Jonathan made (xx. 15). The deep,
genealogical feeling of the Israelites breaks
out here as so often elsewhere.

22. Saul does not appear to have invited
David to return to Gibeah, or to have given
him any security of doing so with safety.
David, with his intuitive sagacity, perceived
that the softening of Saul's feelings was
only momentary, and that the situation remained unchanged.

XXV. 1. *in his house at Ramah*] Probably
in the court or garden attached to his
dwelling-house. (Cp. 2 Chr. xxxiii. 20 ; 2

K. xxi. 18 ; Joh xix. 41.)

the wilderness of Paran] The LXX. has
the far more probable reading *Maon*. The
wilderness of Paran lay far off to the south,
on the borders of the wilderness of Sinai
(Num. x. 12 ; 1 K. xi. 18), whereas the following verse (2) shows that the scene is laid
in the immediate neighbourhood of Maon.
If, however, Paran be the true reading, we
must suppose that in a wide sense the wilderness of Paran extended all the way to
the wilderness of Beersheba, and eastward
to the mountains of Judah (marg. reff.).

2. *Carmel*] Not Mount Carmel on the
west of the plain of Esdraelon, but the
Carmel close to Maon (marg. reff.).

shearing his sheep] Which was always a
time of open-handed hospitality among
flock-masters (Gen. xxxviii. 12, 13 ; 2 Sam.
xiii. 23, 24).

the name of his wife Abigail: and *she was* a woman of good
understanding, and of a beautiful countenance: but the man
was churlish and evil in his doings; and he *was* of the house
4 of Caleb. ¶ And David heard in the wilderness that Nabal did
5 *f* shear his sheep. And David sent out ten young men, and
David said unto the young men, Get you up to Carmel, and go
6 to Nabal, and [1] greet him in my name: and thus shall ye say to
him that liveth *in prosperity*, *g* Peace *be* both to thee, and peace
7 *be* to thine house, and peace *be* unto all that thou hast. And
now I have heard that thou hast shearers: now thy shepherds
which were with us, we [2] hurt them not, *h* neither was there
ought missing unto them, all the while they were in Carmel.
8 Ask thy young men, and they will shew thee. Wherefore let
the young men find favour in thine eyes: for we come in [i] a good
day: give, I pray thee, whatsoever cometh to thine hand unto
9 thy servants, and to thy son David. ¶ And when David's young
men came, they spake to Nabal according to all those words in
10 the name of David, and [3] ceased. And Nabal answered David's
servants, and said, *k* Who *is* David? and who *is* the son of Jesse?
there be many servants now a days that break away every man
11 from his master. *l* Shall I then take my bread, and my water,
and my [4] flesh that I have killed for my shearers, and give *it*
12 unto men, whom I know not whence they *be?* So David's
young men turned their way, and went again, and came and
13 told him all those sayings. And David said unto his men, Gird
ye on every man his sword. And they girded on every man
his sword; and David also girded on his sword: and there went
up after David about four hundred men; and two hundred
14 *m* abode by the stuff. ¶ But one of the young men told Abigail,
Nabal's wife, saying, Behold, David sent messengers out of the
15 wilderness to salute our master; and he [5] railed on them. But
the men *were* very good unto us, and *n* we were not [6] hurt,
neither missed we any thing, as long as we were conversant
16 with them, when we were in the fields: they were *o* a wall unto
us both by night and day, all the while we were with them
17 keeping the sheep. Now therefore know and consider what
thou wilt do; for *p* evil is determined against our master, and
against all his household: for he *is such* a son of *q* Belial, that a
18 *man* cannot speak to him. ¶ Then Abigail made haste, and *r* took
two hundred loaves, and two bottles of wine, and five sheep

f Gen. 38. 13.
2 Sam. 13. 23.

g 1 Chr. 12.
18.
Ps. 122. 7.
Luke 10. 5.
h ver. 15, 21.

i Neh. 8. 10.
Esth. 9. 19.

k Judg. 9. 28.
Ps. 73. 7, 8.
& 123. 3, 4.
l Judg. 8. 6.

m ch. 30. 24.

n ver. 7.

o Ex. 14. 22.
Job 1: 10.

p ch. 20. 7.
q Deut. 13.
13.
Judg. 19. 22.
r Gen. 32. 13.
Prov. 18. 16.

[1] Heb. *ask him in my name
of peace*, ch. 17. 22.
[2] Heb. *shamed.*
[3] Heb. *rested.*
[4] Heb. *slaughter.*
[5] Heb. *flew upon them.*
[6] Heb. *shamed.*

6. *that liveth in prosperity*] The Hebrew
is obscure, and is variously interpreted. The
simplest rendering is, "**And ye shall say
thus about (his) life**," *i.e.* with reference to
his life, health, circumstances, &c.

11. The mention of water indicates a
country where water was scarce (cp. Josh.
xv. 19). Or "bread and water" may be
equivalent to "meat and drink."

14. *railed on them*] The marginal reading, *flew upon them*, is nearer to the original.

16. *a wall*] To protect them from the
attacks of the Bedouins, &c. They had
been as safe with David's men around
them as if they had been dwelling in a
walled town.

18. *two bottles*] Rather, "**two skins**," each
of which would contain many gallons. These
leathern vessels varied in size according to
the skin they were made of, and the use
they were to be put to. The smaller and
more portable kind, which may not improperly be called *bottles*, were made of the
skin of a kid: larger ones of the skin of a
he-goat. The Arabs invariably to this day
carry their milk, water, &c., in such
leathern vessels. One skin of wine was a
handsome present from Ziba, sufficient for
David's household (2 Sam. xvi. 1). The
provisions were all ready to Abigail's hand,
having been provided for the sheep-shearing
feast.

ready dressed, and five measures of parched *corn*, and an hundred
19 ¹clusters of raisins, and two hundred cakes of figs, and laid
them on asses. And she said unto her servants, ˢGo on before
me; behold, I come after you. But she told not her husband
20 Nabal. And it was *so, as* she rode on the ass, that she came
down by the covert of the hill, and, behold, David and his men
21 came down against her; and she met them. ¶ Now David had
said, Surely in vain have I kept all that this *fellow* hath in the
wilderness, so that nothing was missed of all that *pertained*
22 unto him: and he hath ᵗrequited me evil for good. ᵘSo and
more also do God unto the enemies of David, if I ˣleave of all
that *pertain* to him by the morning light ʸany that pisseth
23 against the wall. ¶And when Abigail saw David, she hasted,
and ᶻlighted off the ass, and fell before David on her face, and
24 bowed herself to the ground, and fell at his feet, and said,
Upon me, my lord, *upon* me *let this* iniquity *be:* and let thine
handmaid, I pray thee, speak in thine ²audience, and hear the
25 words of thine handmaid. Let not my lord, I pray thee,
³regard this man of Belial, *even* Nabal: for as his name *is,* so
is he; ⁴Nabal *is* his name, and folly *is* with him: but I thine
handmaid saw not the young men of my lord, whom thou didst
26 send. Now therefore, my lord, ᵃ*as* the LORD liveth, and *as* thy
soul liveth, seeing the LORD hath ᵇwithholden thee from coming
to *shed* blood, and from ⁵ᶜavenging thyself with thine own
hand, now ᵈlet thine enemies, and they that seek evil to my
27 lord, be as Nabal. And now ᵉthis ⁶blessing which thine handmaid hath brought unto my lord, let it even be given unto the
28 young men that ⁷follow my lord. I pray thee, forgive the
trespass of thine handmaid: for ᶠthe LORD will certainly make
my lord a sure house; because my lord ᵍfighteth the battles of
the LORD, and ʰevil hath not been found in thee *all* thy days.
29 Yet a man is risen to pursue thee, and to seek thy soul: but
the soul of my lord shall be bound in the bundle of life with the
LORD thy God; and the souls of thine enemies, them shall he

¹ Or, *lumps.*
² Heb. *ears.*
³ Heb. *lay it to his heart.*
⁴ That is, *Fool.*
⁵ Heb. *saving thyself.*
⁶ Or, *present.*
⁷ Heb. *walk at the feet of &c.* ver. 42. Judg. 4. 10.

---

20. *the covert of the hill*] Probably a defile
or glen, literally *a secret place*, as in xix. 2.
She was riding down into this glen from one
side, while David and his men were descending the opposite hill. It is perhaps mentioned that she came by this *secret place*,
because she chose this path to escape
the observation of her husband or of any one
else.

21. *in vain*] *i.e.* under false expectation.

22. The concluding phrase denotes the
utter destruction of a family, and is rightly
explained to mean "*every male*," perhaps
with the idea, "*down to the very meanest
member of the household*."

26. The passage should be rendered as
follows: *And now my lord, as the Lord
liveth, and as thy soul liveth,* it is the
Lord that *hath withholden thee from coming*
into blood-guiltiness (as in *v.* 33), *and from*
saving *thyself with thine own hand;* and
now all *thine enemies* shall be as Nabal

(whom she considers as utterly impotent
to hurt David, and as already thoroughly
humbled before him), and (so shall be) all
that seek evil to my Lord.

28. *for the* LORD *will make...a sure house*]
Cp. ii. 35, and 2 Sam. vii. 16; 1 K. xi. 38.
Abigail's firm persuasion of David's kingdom stands upon the same footing as
Rahab's conviction of God's gift of Canaan
to the Israelites (Josh. ii. 9–13). Both testified to God's revelation and their own
faith. This is doubtless the reason why
Abigail's speech is recorded.

29. *in the bundle*] Rather, "**the bag**," in
which anything precious, or important to
be preserved, was put, and the bag was then
tied up (cp. Gen. xlii. 35).

the souls...shall he sling out] The comparison is peculiarly appropriate as addressed
to David, whose feat with his sling was so
celebrated (xvii. 49).

30 [i]sling out, [1]*as out* of the middle of a sling. And it shall come
to pass, when the LORD shall have done to my lord according
to all the good that he hath spoken concerning thee, and shall
31 have appointed thee ruler over Israel; that this shall be [2]no
grief unto thee, nor offence of heart unto my lord, either that
thou hast shed blood causeless, or that my lord hath avenged
himself: but when the LORD shall have dealt well with my
32 lord, then remember thine handmaid. ¶ And David said to
Abigail, [k]Blessed *be* the LORD God of Israel, which sent thee
33 this day to meet me: and blessed *be* thy advice, and blessed *be*
thou, which hast [l]kept me this day from coming to *shed* blood,
34 and from avenging myself with mine own hand. For in very
deed, *as* the LORD God of Israel liveth, which hath [m]kept me
back from hurting thee, except thou hadst hasted and come
to meet me, surely there had [n]not been left unto Nabal by the
35 morning light any that pisseth against the wall. So David
received of her hand *that* which she had brought him, and said
unto her, [o]Go up in peace to thine house; see, I have hearkened
36 to thy voice, and have [p]accepted thy person. ¶ And Abigail
came to Nabal; and, behold, [q]he held a feast in his house, like
the feast of a king; and Nabal's heart *was* merry within him,
for he *was* very drunken: wherefore she told him nothing, less
37 or more, until the morning light. But it came to pass in the
morning, when the wine was gone out of Nabal, and his wife
had told him these things, that his heart died within him, and
38 he became *as* a stone. ¶ And it came to pass about ten days
39 *after*, that the LORD smote Nabal, that he died. And when
David heard that Nabal was dead, he said, [r]Blessed *be* the LORD,
that hath [s]pleaded the cause of my reproach from the hand of
Nabal, and hath [t]kept his servant from evil: for the LORD hath
[u]returned the wickedness of Nabal upon his own head. ¶ And
David sent and communed with Abigail, to take her to him to
40 wife. And when the servants of David were come to Abigail
to Carmel, they spake unto her, saying, David sent us unto
41 thee, to take thee to him to wife. And she arose, and bowed
herself on *her* face to the earth, and said, Behold, *let* [x]thine
handmaid *be* a servant to wash the feet of the servants of
42 my lord. And Abigail hasted, and arose, and rode upon an
ass, with five damsels of her's that went [3]after her; and
she went after the messengers of David, and became his wife.
43 ¶ David also took Ahinoam [y]of Jezreel; [z]and they were also

[i] Jer. 10. 18.
[k] Gen. 24. 27. Ex. 18. 10. Ps. 41. 13.
[l] ver. 26.
[m] ver. 26.
[n] ver. 22.
[o] ch. 20. 42. 2 Sam. 15. 9. 2 Kin. 5. 19. Luke 7. 50.
[p] Gen. 19. 21.
[q] 2 Sam. 13. 23.
[r] ver. 32.
[s] Prov. 22. 23.
[t] ver. 26, 34.
[u] 1 Kin. 2. 44. Ps. 7. 16.
[x] Ruth 2. 10, 13. Prov. 15. 33.
[y] Josh. 15. 56.
[z] ch. 27. 3. & 30. 5.

[1] Heb. *in the midst of the bought* (or, hollow) *of a sling*.
[2] Heb. *no staggering*, or, *stumbling*.
[3] Heb. *at her feet*, *v*. 27.

---

37. *he became as a stone*] Probably his violent anger at hearing it brought on a fit of apoplexy to which he was disposed by the drunken revel of the night before. After lying senseless for ten days he died.

40. There is no note of the exact interval that elapsed between Nabal's death and David's hearing of it, or, again, between David's hearing of it and his message to Abigail; nor is there any reason to suppose that the marriage took place with unbecoming haste. The widow of such a husband as Nabal had been could not, however, be expected to revere his memory. After the usual mourning of seven days, she would probably feel herself free to act as custom allowed. (See 2 Sam. xi. 26.)

43. In the list of David's wives Ahinoam is mentioned first (2 Sam. iii. 2; 1 Chr. iii. 1). But this may be only because her son was the first-born. David's now taking two wives was an indication of his growing power and importance as a chieftain. The number was increased to six when he reigned in Hebron (1 Chr. iii. 1), and still further when he became king of all Israel (2 Sam. v. 12, 13). See i. 2 note.

of Jezreel] Not the well-known city of

44 both of them his wives.   But Saul had given *a* Michal his daughter, David's wife, to ¹Phalti the son of Laish, which *was* of *b* Gallim.

CHAP. 26. AND the Ziphites came unto Saul to Gibeah, saying, *a* Doth not David hide himself in the hill of Hachilah, *which is*
2 before Jeshimon? Then Saul arose, and went down to the wilderness of Ziph, having three thousand chosen men of
3 Israel with him, to seek David in the wilderness of Ziph. And Saul pitched in the hill of Hachilah, which *is* before Jeshimon, by the way. But David abode in the wilderness, and he saw
4 that Saul came after him into the wilderness. David therefore sent out spies, and understood that Saul was come in very deed.
5 ¶ And David arose, and came to the place where Saul had pitched: and David beheld the place where Saul lay, and *b* Abner the son of Ner, the captain of his host: and Saul lay in the
6 ²trench, and the people pitched round about him. Then answered David and said to Ahimelech the Hittite, and to Abishai *c* the son of Zeruiah, brother to Joab, saying, Who will *d* go down with me to Saul to the camp? And Abishai said, I will
7 go down with thee. ¶ So David and Abishai came to the people by night: and, behold, Saul lay sleeping within the trench, and his spear stuck in the ground at his bolster: but Abner and the
8 people lay round about him. Then said Abishai to David, God hath ³delivered thine enemy into thine hand this day: now therefore let me smite him, I pray thee, with the spear even to the earth at once, and I will not *smite* him the second time.
9 And David said to Abishai, Destroy him not: *e* for who can stretch forth his hand against the LORD's anointed, and be
10 guiltless? David said furthermore, *As* the LORD liveth, *f* the LORD shall smite him; or *g* his day shall come to die; or he
11 shall *h* descend into battle, and perish. *i* The LORD forbid that I should stretch forth mine hand against the LORD's anointed: but, I pray thee, take thou now the spear that *is* at his bolster,
12 and the cruse of water, and let us go. So David took the spear and the cruse of water from Saul's bolster; and they gat them away, and no man saw *it*, nor knew *it*, neither awaked: for they *were* all asleep; because *k* a deep sleep from the LORD was fallen
13 upon them. ¶ Then David went over to the other side, and

---

¹ *Phaltiel*, 2 Sam. 3. 15.   ² Or, *midst of his carriages*,   ³ Heb. *shut up*, ch. 24. 18.
ch. 17. :0.

Samaria, which gave its name to the plain of Esdraelon, but a town of Judah, near Carmel (marg. ref.).
44. Saul's giving Michal to Phalti was intended to mark the final rupture of his own relations with David (cp. Judg. xiv. 20 ; 2 Sam. iii. 7, xvi. 21). Phalti or Phaltiel was compelled by Abner to restore Michal to David (2 Sam. iii. 15).
Gallim] A city of Benjamin, and in the neighbourhood of another town called *Laish*.
XXVI. The incident related in this chapter of the meeting between Saul and David bears a strong general resemblance to that recorded in ch. xxiv., and is of a nature unlikely to have occurred more than once. Existing discrepancies are explained by the supposition that one narrative relates fully

some incidents on which the other is silent. On the whole the most probable conclusion is that the two narratives relate to one and the same event. (Cp. the two narratives of the Creation, Gen. i. and Gen. ii. 4, seq. ; the two narratives of David's war, 2 Sam. viii. and x. ; and those of the death of Ahaziah, 2 K. ix. 27, seq., and 2 Chr. xxii. 9.)
6. *Ahimelech the Hittite.* Only mentioned here. Uriah was also a Hittite.
Abishai] He was son of Zeruiah, David's sister, but probably about the same age as David. He became very famous as a warrior (2 Sam. xxiii. 18), but was implicated with his brother Joab in the murder of Abner in retaliation for the death of their brother Asahel (2 Sam. iii. 30).

stood on the top of an hill afar off ; a great space *being* between
14 them : and David cried to the people, and to Abner the son of
Ner, saying, Answerest thou not, Abner ?   Then Abner an-
15 swered and said, Who *art* thou *that* criest to the king ?   And
David said to Abner, *Art* not thou a *valiant* man ? and who *is*
like to thee in Israel ? wherefore then hast thou not kept thy
lord the king ? for there came one of the people in to destroy
16 the king thy lord.   This thing *is* not good that thou hast done.
As the LORD liveth, ye *are* [1] worthy to die, because ye have not
kept your master, the LORD's anointed.   And now see where
the king's spear *is*, and the cruse of water that *was* at his
17 bolster.   And Saul knew David's voice, and said, [*l*] *Is* this thy   *l* ch. 24. 16.
voice, my son David ?   And David said, *It is* my voice, my lord,
18 O king.   And he said, [*m*] Wherefore doth my lord thus pursue   *m* ch. 24. 9.
after his servant ? for what have I done ? or what evil *is* in
19 mine hand ?   Now therefore, I pray thee, let my lord the king
hear the words of his servant.   If the LORD have [*n*] stirred thee   *n* 2 Sam. 16.
up against me, let him [2] accept an offering : but if *they be* the   11. & 24. 1.
children of men, cursed *be* they before the LORD ; [*o*] for they   *o* Deut. 4. 28.
have driven me out this day from [3] abiding in the [*p*] inheritance   Ps. 120. 5.
20 of the LORD, saying, Go, serve other gods.   Now therefore, let   *p* 2 Sam. 14.
                                                                        16.
not my blood fall to the earth before the face of the LORD : for   & 20. 19.
the king of Israel is come out to seek [*q*] a flea, as when one doth   *q* ch. 24. 14.
21 hunt a partridge in the mountains.   ¶ Then said Saul, [*r*] I have   *r* ch. 15. 24.
sinned : return, my son David : for I will no more do thee harm,   & 24. 17.
because my soul was [*s*] precious in thine eyes this day : behold, I   *s* ch. 18. 30.
22 have played the fool, and have erred exceedingly.   And David
answered and said, Behold the king's spear ! and let one of the
23 young men come over and fetch it.   [*t*] The LORD render to every   *t* Ps. 7. 8.
man his righteousness and his faithfulness : for the LORD de-   & 18. 20.
livered thee into *my* hand to day, but I would not stretch forth
24 mine hand against the LORD's anointed.   And, behold, as thy
life was much set by this day in mine eyes, so let my life be
much set by in the eyes of the LORD, and let him deliver me
25 out of all tribulation.   Then Saul said to David, Blessed *be*
thou, my son David : thou shalt both do great *things*, and also   *u* Gen. 32.28.
shalt still [*u*] prevail.   So David went on his way, and Saul returned to his place.
CHAP. 27. AND David said in his heart, I shall now [4] perish one
day by the hand of Saul : *there is* nothing better for me than

---

[1] Heb. *the sons of death*,   [2] Heb. *smell*, Gen. 8. 21.   [3] Heb. *cleaving*.
2 Sam. 12. 5.   Lev. 26. 31.   [4] Heb. *be consumed*.

---

15. This incidental testimony to Abner's
great eminence as a warrior is fully borne
out by David's dirge at Abner's death
(2 Sam. iii. 31-34, 38), as well as by his
whole history.   At the same time David's
bantering tone in regard to Abner, coupled
with what he says in *v.* 19, makes it probable that David attributed Saul's persecution of him in some degree to Abner.   Abner
would be likely to dread a rival in the
young conqueror of Judah (cp. 2 Sam.ii. 8).
19. *If the* LORD *have stirred thee up*] The
meaning is clear from the preceding history.
"An evil spirit from God troubling him "
was the beginning of the persecution.   And

this evil spirit was sent in punishment
of Saul's sin (xvi. 1, 14).   If the continued
persecution was merely the consequence of
this evil spirit continuing to vex Saul,
David advises Saul to seek God's pardon,
and, as a consequence, the removal of the
evil spirit, by offering a sacrifice.   But if
the persecution was the consequence of
the false accusations of slanderers, then
" cursed " be his enemies who, by their
actions, drove David out from the only
land where Jehovah was worshipped, and
forced him to take refuge in the country of
heathen and idolaters (cp. Deut. iv. 27,
xxviii. 36).

that I should speedily escape into the land of the Philistines;
and Saul shall despair of me, to seek me any more in any coast
2 of Israel: so shall I escape out of his hand. And David arose,
a *and* he passed over with the six hundred men that *were* with
3 him *b* unto Achish, the son of Maoch, king of Gath. And
David dwelt with Achish at Gath, he and his men, every man
with his household, *even* David *c* with his two wives, Ahinoam
the Jezreelitess, and Abigail the Carmelitess, Nabal's wife.
4 And it was told Saul that David was fled to Gath: and he
5 sought no more again for him. ¶ And David said unto Achish,
If I have now found grace in thine eyes, let them give me a
place in some town in the country, that I may dwell there:
for why should thy servant dwell in the royal city with thee?
6 Then Achish gave him Ziklag that day: wherefore *d* Ziklag per-
7 taineth unto the kings of Judah unto this day. And *1* the time
that David dwelt in the country of the Philistines was *2* a full
8 year and four months. ¶ And David and his men went up, and
invaded *e* the Geshurites, *f* and the *3* Gezrites, and the *g* Amalekites: for those *nations were* of old the inhabitants of the land,
9 *h* as thou goest to Shur, even unto the land of Egypt. And
David smote the land, and left neither man nor woman alive,
and took away the sheep, and the oxen, and the asses, and the
10 camels, and the apparel, and returned, and came to Achish. And
Achish said, *4* Whither have ye made a road to day? And David
said, Against the south of Judah, and against the south of *i* the
11 Jerahmeelites, and against the south of *k* the Kenites. And
David saved neither man nor woman alive, to bring *tidings* to
Gath, saying, Lest they should tell on us, saying, So did David,
and so *will be* his manner all the while he dwelleth in the
12 country of the Philistines. And Achish believed David, saying,
He hath made his people Israel *5* utterly to abhor him; therefore he shall be my servant for ever.
CHAP. 28. AND *a* it came to pass in those days, that the Philistines
gathered their armies together for warfare, to fight with Israel.
And Achish said unto David, Know thou assuredly, that thou

a ch. 25. 13.
b ch. 21. 10.

c ch. 25. 43.

d See Josh.
15. 31.
& 19. 5.

e Josh. 13. 2.
f Josh. 16.10.
Judg. 1. 29.
g Ex. 17. 16.
ch. 15. 7.
h Gen. 25.18.

i See 1 Chr.
2. 9, 25.
k Judg. 1.
16.

a ch. 29. 1.

---

1 Heb. *the number of days.*   *2* Heb. a year *of days:*   *4* Or, *Did you not make a road, &c.*
3 Or, *Gerzites.*   See ch. 29. 3. till 1056.   *5* Heb. *to stink.*

XXVII. 5. David, with characteristic
Oriental subtlety (cp. xxi. 2), suggests as a
reason for leaving Gath that his presence
was burdensome and expensive to the king.
His real motive was to be more out of the
way of observation and control, so as to act
the part of an enemy of Saul, without really
lifting up his hand against him and his own
countrymen of Israel.
6. *Ziklag*] This was properly one of the
cities of Simeon within the tribe of Judah
(marg. reff.), but it had been taken possession
of by the Philistines. The exact situation
of it is uncertain.
unto this day] This phrase, coupled with
the title *the kings of Judah,* implies that
this was written after the revolt of Jeroboam, and before the Babylonish captivity.
8. The Geshurites bordered upon the
Philistines, and lived in the mountainous
district which terminates the desert on the

north-east (marg. ref.). They were a different tribe, or, at least, a different branch
of it, from the Geshurites who lived on the
north-east border of Bashan, and were
Arameans (2 Sam. xv. 8). The Gezrites,
or Gerzites, may be connected with those
who gave their name to Mount Gerizim.
10. *the Jerahmeelites*] *i.e.* the descendants
of Jerahmeel, the son of Hezron, the son of
Perez, the son of Judah (marg. reff.). They
were therefore a portion of the "south of
Judah."
the Kenites] See Num. xxiv. 21, iv. 11
notes; and for their near neighbourhood to
Amalek, see xv. 6.
11. *tidings*] The word is not in the original. The sense rather is "to bring them
to Gath," as captives and slaves. The
prisoners taken would naturally have been
part of the spoil, but David dared not to
bring them to Gath lest his deceit should

2 shalt go out with me to battle, thou and thy men. And David
said to Achish, Surely thou shalt know what thy servant can do.
And Achish said to David, Therefore will I make thee keeper of
3 mine head for ever. ¶ Now *b*Samuel was dead, and all Israel
had lamented him, and buried him in Ramah, even in his own
city. ¶ And Saul had put away *c*those that had familiar spirits,
4 and the wizards, out of the land. And the Philistines gathered
themselves together, and came and pitched in *d*Shunem: and
Saul gathered all Israel together, and they pitched in *e*Gilboa.
5 And when Saul saw the host of the Philistines, he was *f*afraid,
6 and his heart greatly trembled. And when Saul enquired of the
LORD, *g*the LORD answered him not, neither by *h*dreams, nor
7 *i*by Urim, nor by prophets. Then said Saul unto his servants,
Seek me a woman that hath a familiar spirit, that I may go to
her, and enquire of her. And his servants said to him, Behold,
8 *there is* a woman that hath a familiar spirit at En-dor. ¶ And
Saul disguised himself, and put on other raiment, and he went,
and two men with him, and they came to the woman by night:
and *k*he said, I pray thee, divine unto me by the familiar spirit,
9 and bring me *him* up, whom I shall name unto thee. And the
woman said unto him, Behold, thou knowest what Saul hath
done, how he hath *l*cut off those that have familiar spirits, and
the wizards, out of the land: wherefore then layest thou a snare
10 for my life, to cause me to die? And Saul sware to her by the
LORD, saying, *As* the LORD liveth, there shall no punishment
11 happen to thee for this thing. Then said the woman, Whom
shall I bring up unto thee? And he said, Bring me up Samuel.

b ch. 25. 1.

c Ex. 22. 18.
Deut. 18. 10,
11.
d Josh. 19.
18.
2 Kin. 4. 8.
e ch. 31. 1.
f Job 18. 11.
g ch. 14. 37.
Prov. 1. 28.
h Num. 12. 6.
i Ex. 28. 30.
Num. 27. 21.
Deut. 33. 8.

k Deut. 18.
11.
1 Chr. 10. 13.
Isai. 8. 19.
l ver. 3.

---

be discovered. Obviously these tribes were
allies of the Philistines.

XXVIII. 2. *thou shalt know,* &c.] David
dissembled (cp. also xxix. 8), hoping, no
doubt, that something would happen to
prevent his fighting against his king and
country.

keeper of mine head] Captain of his body-
guard.

3. It does not appear when Saul had sup-
pressed witchcraft; it was probably in the
early part of his reign.

familiar spirits ...wizards] *i.e.* ventrilo-
quists...wise or cunning men. See Lev. xix.
31 note.

4. *Gilboa*] Now called *Jebel Fukûah.*
But the ancient name is preserved in the
village of *Jelbon,* situated on the south side
of the mountain. It was separated from
Shunem (see marg. ref.) by the deep valley
of Jezreel. The Philistines either advanced
along the sea-coast, and then entered the
valley of Jezreel from the west, or they
came by the present road right through
Samaria, starting from Aphek (xxix. 1).

6. *when Saul enquired of the* LORD, &c.]
It is said (1 Chr. x. 14) that one reason why
the Lord slew Saul, and gave his kingdom
to David, was because he *enquired not of the
Lord.* The explanation of this apparent
discrepancy is to be found in the fact that
enquiring of the familiar spirit was posi-
tively antagonistic to enquiring of the Lord.
That Saul received no answer—when he "en-

quired of the Lord" *by dreams,* which was
an immediate revelation to himself; *by
Urim,* which was an answer through the
High-Priest clothed in the ephod; or *by
Prophets,* which was an answer conveyed
through some seer speaking by the Word of
the Lord (xxii. 5)—was a reason for self-
abasement and self-examination, to find
out and, if possible, remove the cause, but
was no justification whatever of his sin in
asking counsel of familiar spirits.

7. *enquire*] A different word from that
in *v.* 6, though nearly synonymous with it.
It is more frequently applied to enquiry of
a false god, as *e.g.* 2 K. i. 2; Isai. viii. 19,
xix. 3.

En-dor (see Josh. xi. 2 note) was seven or
eight miles from the slopes of Gilboa, on
the north of little Hermon, where the
Philistines were encamped; so that Saul
must have run great risks in going there.

8. *divine*] Cp. notes to vi. 2; Num. xxiii.
23.

bring me him up] The art of the ventrilo-
quist seems to have been always connected
with necromancy. The Greeks had necromancers who called up departed spirits to
give answers to those who consulted
them.

11. *Bring me up Samuel*] Archbishop
Trench observes, "All human history has
failed to record a despair deeper or more
tragic than his, who, having forsaken God
and being of God forsaken, is now seeking

12 ¶ And when the woman saw Samuel, she cried with a loud voice: and the woman spake to Saul, saying, Why hast thou deceived
13 me? for thou *art* Saul. And the king said unto her, Be not afraid: for what sawest thou? And the woman said unto Saul,

ᵐ Ex. 22. 28.

14 I saw *ᵐ*gods ascending out of the earth. And he said unto her, ¹What form *is* he of? And she said, An old man cometh up;

ⁿ ch. 15. 27.
2 Kin. 2. 8.

and he *is* covered with *ⁿ*a mantle. And Saul perceived that it *was* Samuel, and he stooped with *his* face to the ground, and
15 bowed himself. • ¶ And Samuel said to Saul, Why hast thou dis-

ᵒ Prov. 5. 11,
12, 13.
& 14. 14.
ᵖ ch. 18. 12.
q ver. 6.

quieted me, to bring me up? And Saul answered, *ᵒ*I am sore distressed; for the Philistines make war against me, and *ᵖ*God is departed from me, and *q*answereth me no more, neither ²by prophets, nor by dreams: therefore I have called thee, that thou
16 mayest make known unto me what I shall do. Then said Samuel, Wherefore then dost thou ask of me, seeing the LORD is departed
17 from thee, and is become thine enemy? And the LORD hath done

r ch. 15. 28.

³to him, *r*as he spake by ⁴me: for the LORD hath rent the kingdom out of thine hand, and given it to thy neighbour, *even* to

s ch. 15. 9.
1 Kin. 20. 42.
1. Chr. 10. 13.
Jer. 48. 10.

18 David: *s*because thou obeyedst not the voice of the LORD, nor executedst his fierce wrath upon Amalek, therefore hath the LORD
19 done this thing unto thee this day. Moreover the LORD will also deliver Israel with thee into the hand of the Philistines: and to morrow *shalt* thou and thy sons *be* with me: the LORD also shall deliver the host of Israel into the hand of the Philistines.
20 ¶ Then Saul ⁵fell straightway all along on the earth, and was sore afraid, because of the words of Samuel: and there was no strength in him; for he had eaten no bread all the day, nor all
21 the night. And the woman came unto Saul, and saw that he was sore troubled, and said unto him, Behold, thine handmaid

t Judg. 12. 3.
ch. 19. 5.
Job 13. 14.

hath obeyed thy voice, and I have *t*put my life in my hand, and have hearkened unto thy words which thou spakest unto me.
22 Now therefore, I pray thee, hearken thou also unto the voice of thine handmaid, and let me set a morsel of bread before thee; and eat, that thou mayest have strength, when thou goest on
23 thy way. But he refused, and said, I will not eat. But his servants, together with the woman, compelled him; and he hearkened unto their voice. So he arose from the earth, and sat
24 upon the bed. And the woman had a fat calf in the house; and

---

¹ Heb. *What is his form?*
² Heb. *by the hand of pro-phets.*
³ Or, *for himself,* Prov. 16. 4.
⁴ Heb. *mine hand.*
⁵ Heb. *made haste, and fell with the fulness of his stature.*

---

to move hell; and infinitely guilty as he is, assuredly there is something unutterably pathetic in that yearning of the disanointed king to change words with the friend and counsellor of his youth, and if he must hear his doom, to hear it from no other lips but his" ('Shipwrecks of Faith,' p. 47).

12. It is manifest both that the apparition of Samuel was real, and also that the woman was utterly unprepared for it.

Why hast thou deceived me, &c.] She perhaps inferred that Samuel would have answered the call of none inferior to the king. Or it may be the presence of an inhabitant of the world of spirits brought a sudden illumination to her mind.

13. *gods*] *Elohim* is here used in a general

sense of a *supernatural* appearance, either angel or spirit. Hell, or the place of the departed (cp. *v.* 19; 2 Sam. xii. 23) is represented as under the earth (Isai. xiv. 9, 10; Ezek. xxxii. 18).

17. *to him*] Better, "for Himself," as in the margin.

19. Rather, "will deliver Israel also." Saul had not only brought ruin upon his own house but upon Israel also; and when Saul and Jonathan fell the camp (not "host") would be plundered by the conquerors (xxxi. 8; 2 Sam. i. 10).

23. *the bed*] Rather, "the bench" or divan, such as in the East still runs along the wall, furnished with cushions, for those who sit at meals (Esth. i. 6; Ezek. xxiii. 41).

she hasted, and killed it, and took flour, and kneaded *it*, and
25 did bake unleavened bread thereof: and she brought *it* before
Saul, and before his servants; and they did eat. Then they
rose up, and went away that night.

CHAP. 29. NOW *a*the Philistines gathered together all their armies   *a* ch. 28. 1.
*b*to Aphek: and the Israelites pitched by a fountain which *is* in   *b* ch. 4. 1.
2 Jezreel. And the lords of the Philistines passed on by hundreds,
and by thousands: but David and his men passed on in the rere-
3 ward *c*with Achish. Then said the princes of the Philistines,   *c* ch. 28. 1.
What *do* these Hebrews *here?* And Achish said unto the princes
of the Philistines, *Is* not this David, the servant of Saul the king
of Israel, which hath been with me *d*these days, or these years,   *d* See ch. 27.
and I have *e*found no fault in him since he fell *unto me* unto   7.
4 this day? And the princes of the Philistines were wroth with   *e* Dan. 6. 5.
him; and the princes of the Philistines said unto him, *f*Make   *f* 1 Chr. 12.
this fellow return, that he may go again to his place which thou   19.
hast appointed him, and let him not go down with us to battle,
lest *g*in the battle he be an adversary to us: for wherewith   *g* As ch. 14.
should he reconcile himself unto his master? *should it* not *be*   21.
5 with the heads of these men? *Is* not this David, of whom they
sang one to another in dances, saying, *h*Saul slew his thousands,   *h* ch. 18. 7.
6 and David his ten thousands? ¶Then Achish called David, and   & 21. 11.
said unto him, Surely, *as* the LORD liveth, thou hast been upright, and *1*thy going out and thy coming in with me in the host   *i* 2 Sam. 3.
is good in my sight: for *k*I have not found evil in thee since the   25.
day of thy coming unto me unto this day: nevertheless *l*the   2 Kin. 19. 27.
7 lords favour thee not. Wherefore now return, and go in peace,   *k* ver. 3.
8 that thou *2*displease not the lords of the Philistines. And David
said unto Achish, But what have I done? and what hast thou
found in thy servant so long as I have been *3*with thee unto this
day, that I may not go fight against the enemies of my lord the
9 king? And Achish answered and said to David, I know that
thou *art* good in my sight, *l*as an angel of God: notwithstanding   *l* 2 Sam. 14.
*m*the princes of the Philistines have said, He shall not go up   17, 20.
10 with us to the battle. Wherefore now rise up early in the morn-   & 19. 27.
ing with thy master's servants that are come with thee: and as   *m* ver. 4.
soon as ye be up early in the morning, and have light, depart.

---

[1] Heb. *thou* art *not good in*   [2] Heb. *do not evil in the*   [3] Heb. *before thee.*
the eyes of the lords.   eyes of the lords.

XXIX. 1. *a fountain*] Probably, the fine
spring *Ain-Jalud.* It is impossible to say
what the peculiar circumstances were which
led to the struggle between Israel and the
Philistines taking place so far north as the
plain of Jezreel. Possibly it was connected
with some movements of the Aramaic
tribes to the north of Palestine. See 2
Sam. viii.

2. *the lords*] See Judg. iii. 3 note, as distinguished from ordinary " princes " (*v.* 3).
The military divisions of the Philistine
army were by hundreds and by thousands,
like those of the Israelites (viii. 12). David
and his men formed a body-guard to Achish
(xxviii. 2).

3. *he fell unto me*] The regular word for
deserting and going over to the other side.
See Jer. xxxvii. 13, xxxviii. 19.

6. *as the* LORD *liveth*] The swearing by
JEHOVAH seems strange in the mouth of
a Philistine. But probably not the very
words, but only the sense of this and such
like speeches, is preserved.

8. See *v.* 10 note.

10. *with thy master's servants*] The clue
to this may be found in 1 Chr. xii. 19-21,
where it appears that a considerable number
of Manassites "fell" to David just at this
time, and went back with him to Ziklag. It
is therefore to these new comers that Achish
applies the expression. It is impossible not
to recognize here a merciful interposition of
Providence, by which David was not only
saved from fighting against his king and
country, but sent home just in time to
recover his wives and property from the
Amalekites (xxx.). That David maintained

n 2 Sam. 4. 4.

11 ¶ So David and his men rose up early to depart in the morning, to return into the land of the Philistines. *n*And the Philistines went up to Jezreel.

Chap. 30. AND it came to pass, when David and his men were come

a See ch. 15. 7.
& 27. 8.

to Ziklag on the third day, that the *a*Amalekites had invaded the south, and Ziklag, and smitten Ziklag, and burned it with fire;

2 and had taken the women captives, that *were* therein : they slew not any, either great or small, but carried *them* away, and went

3 on their way. So David and his men came to the city, and, behold, *it was* burned with fire ; and their wives, and their sons,

4 and their daughters, were taken captives. Then David and the people that *were* with him lifted up their voice and wept, until

b ch. 25. 42.
2 Sam. 2. 2.

5 they had no more power to weep. And David's *b*two wives were taken captives, Ahinoam the Jezreelitess, and Abigail the wife

6 of Nabal the Carmelite. And David was greatly distressed ;

c Ex. 17. 4.

*c*for the people spake of stoning him, because the soul of all the people was [1]grieved, every man for his sons and for his daugh-

d Ps. 42. 5.
& 56. 3, 4.
Hab. 3. 17.
e ch. 23. 6.
f ch. 23. 2. 4.

ters : *d*but David encouraged himself in the LORD his God.

7 ¶ *e*And David said to Abiathar the priest, Ahimelech's son, I pray thee, bring me hither the ephod. And Abiathar brought

8 thither the ephod to David. *f*And David enquired at the LORD, saying, Shall I pursue after this troop ? shall I overtake them ? And he answered him, Pursue : for thou shalt surely overtake

9 *them*, and without fail recover *all*. So David went, he and the six hundred men that *were* with him, and came to the brook

10 Besor, where those that were left behind stayed. But David

g ver. 21.

pursued, he and four hundred men : *g*for two hundred abode behind, which were so faint that they could not go over the

11 brook Besor. ¶ And they found an Egyptian in the field, and brought him to David, and gave him bread, and he did eat; and

12 they made him drink water; and they gave him a piece of a cake of figs, and two clusters of raisins : and *h*when he had

h So Judg.
15. 19.
ch. 14. 27.

eaten, his spirit came again to him : for he had eaten no bread,

13 nor drunk *any* water, three days and three nights. And David said unto him, To whom *belongest* thou ? and whence *art* thou ? And he said, I *am* a young man of Egypt, servant to an Amalek-

i 2 Sam. 8. 18.
1 Kin. 1. 38,
44.
Ezek. 25. 16.
Zeph. 2. 5.

ite ; and my master left me, because three days agone I fell

14 sick. We made an invasion *upon* the south of *i*the Cherethites,

[1] Heb. *bitter*, Judg. 18. 25.   ch. 1. 10.   2 Sam. 17. 8.   2 Kin. 4. 7.

---

his position by subtlety and falsehood, which were the invariable characteristics of his age and nation, is not in the least to be wondered at. No sanction is given by this narrative to the use of falsehood.

XXX. 1. *on the third day*] This indicates that Aphek was three days' march from Ziklag, say about fifty miles, which agrees very well with the probable situation of Aphek (iv. 1 note). From Ziklag to Shunem would not be less than eighty or ninety miles.

The Amalekites, in retaliation of David's raids (xxvii. 8, 9), invaded "the south" of Judah (Josh. xv. 21); but owing to the absence of all the men with David there was no resistance, and consequently the women and children were carried off as prey, and uninjured.

7. Abiathar had continued to abide with David, ever since he joined him at Keilah (xxiii. 6). On enquiry of the Lord by the ephod, see Judg. i. 1 note. The answers were evidently given by the Word of the Lord in the mouth of the High-Priest (cp. John xi. 51).

9. *Besor*] Thought to be the stream of the *Wady Sheriah* which enters the sea a little south of Gaza.

12. *three days and three nights*] Indicating that at least so long a time had elapsed since the sack of Ziklag.

14. *the Cherethites*] Here used as synonymous with *Philistines* (*v.* 16). In David's reign the body-guard commanded by Benaiah consisted of Cherethites and Pelethites (= Philistines?) and a picked corps of six hundred men of Gath commanded by **Ittai**

and upon *the coast* which *belongeth* to Judah, and upon the south
15 of *k*Caleb ; and we burned Ziklag with fire. And David said to
him, Canst thou bring me down to this company ? And he said,
Swear unto me by God, that thou wilt neither kill me, nor deliver me into the hands of my master, and I will bring thee
16 down to this company. ¶ And when he had brought him down,
Behold, *they were* spread abroad upon all the earth, *l*eating and
drinking, and dancing, because of all the great spoil that they
had taken out of the land of the Philistines, and out of the land
17 of Judah. And David smote them from the twilight even unto
the evening of [1]the next day : and there escaped not a man of
them, save four hundred young men, which rode upon camels,
18 and fled. And David recovered all that the Amalekites had
19 carried away : and David rescued his two wives. And there
was nothing lacking to them, neither small nor great, neither
sons nor daughters, neither spoil, nor any *thing* that they had
20 taken to them : *m*David recovered all. And David took all the
flocks and the herds, *which* they drave before those *other* cattle,
21 and said, This *is* David's spoil. ¶ And David came to the *n*two
hundred men, which were so faint that they could not follow
David, whom they had made also to abide at the brook Besor :
and they went forth to meet David, and to meet the people that
were with him : and when David came near to the people, he
22 [2]saluted them. Then answered all the wicked men and *men o*of
Belial, of [3]those that went with David, and said, Because they
went not with us, we will not give them *ought* of the spoil that
we have recovered, save to every man his wife and his chil-
23 dren, that they may lead *them* away, and depart. Then said
David, Ye shall not do so, my brethren, with that which the
LORD hath given us, who hath preserved us, and delivered that
24 company that came against us into our hand. For who will
hearken unto you in this matter ? but *p*as his part *is* that goeth
down to the battle, so *shall* his part *be* that tarrieth by the stuff :
25 they shall part alike. And it was *so* from that day [4]forward,
that he made it a statute and an ordinance for Israel unto this
26 day. ¶ And when David came to Ziklag, he sent of the spoil
unto the elders of Judah, *even* to his friends, saying, Behold a
27 [5]present for you of the spoil of the enemies of the LORD ; to
them which *were* in Beth-el, and to *them* which *were* in *q*south

k Josh.14.13,
& 15. 13.

l 1 Thess. 5.
3.

m ver. 8.

n ver. 10.

o Deut. 13.
13.
Judg. 19. 22.

p See Num.
31. 27.
Josh. 22. 8.

q Josh. 19. 8.

---

[1] Heb. *their morrow.*
[2] Or, *asked them how they did*, Judg. 18. 15.
[3] Heb. *men.*
[4] Heb. *and forward.*
[5] Heb. *blessing*, Gen. 33. 11. ch. 25. 27.

---

the Gittite. It would seem from this that
the Cherethites and Philistines were two
kindred and associated tribes, like Angles
and Saxons, who took possession of the
sea-coast of Palestine. The Philistines,
being the more powerful, gave their name
to the country and the nation in general,
though that of the Cherethites was not
wholly extinguished. Many persons connect the name Cherethite with that of the
island of Crete.

20. The meaning is, *and David took all
the sheep and oxen which the Amalekites drove*
(*i.e.* had in their possession) *before that ac-
quisition of cattle* (viz. before what they took
in their raid to the south), *and they* (the

people) *said, This is David's spoil.* This
was his share as captain of the band (cp.
Judg. viii. 24-26). All the other plunder of
the camp—arms, ornaments, jewels, money,
clothes, camels, accoutrements, and so on—
was divided amongst the little army. David's
motive in choosing the sheep and oxen for
himself was to make presents to his friends
in Judah (*vv.* 26–31).

27. *Bethel*] *i.e. Bethuel* (1 Chr. iv. 30),
quite in the south near Beer-sheba, Hormah, and Ziklag ; or *Bethul* (Josh. xix. 4),
one of the cities of the Simeonites.

South Ramoth] Rather, "**Ramoth of the
South** country" (xxvii. 10, xxx. 1, 14), so-
called to distinguish it from Ramoth-Gilead,

r Josh. 15.
48.
s Josh. 13.
16.
t Josh. 15.
50.
u ch. 27. 10.
e Judg. 1.
16.
y Judg. 1.
17.
z Josh. 14.
13.
2 Sam. 2. 1.
a 1 Chron.
10. 1—12.
b ch. 28. 4.
c ch. 14. 49.
1 Chr. 8. 33.
d See
2 Sam. 1. 6,
&c.
e So, Judg.
9. 54.
f ch. 14. 6.
& 17. 26.
g 2 Sam. 1.
14.
h 2 Sam. 1.
10.

28 Ramoth, and to *them* which *were* in ^rJattir, and to *them* which *were* in ^sAroer, and to *them* which *were* in Siphmoth, and to
29 *them* which *were* in ^tEshtemoa, and to *them* which *were* in Rachal, and to *them* which *were* in the cities of ^uthe Jerahmeelites,
30 and to *them* which *were* in the cities of the ^xKenites, and to *them* which *were* in ^yHormah, and to *them* which *were* in Chor-
31 ashan, and to *them* which *were* in Athach, and to *them* which *were* in ^zHebron, and to all the places where David himself and his men were wont to haunt.

CHAP. 31. NOW ^athe Philistines fought against Israel: and the men of Israel fled from before the Philistines, and fell down ¹slain in
2 mount ^bGilboa. And the Philistines followed hard upon Saul and upon his sons; and the Philistines slew ^cJonathan, and
3 Abinadab, and Melchi-shua, Saul's sons. And ^dthe battle went sore against Saul, and the ²archers ³hit him; and he was sore
4 wounded of the archers. ^eThen said Saul unto his armourbearer, Draw thy sword, and thrust me through therewith; lest ^fthese uncircumcised come and thrust me through, and ⁴abuse me. But his armourbearer would not; ^gfor he was sore afraid.
5 Therefore Saul took a sword, and ^hfell upon it. And when his armourbearer saw that Saul was dead, he fell likewise upon his
6 sword, and died with him. So Saul died, and his three sons, and his armourbearer, and all his men, that same day together.
7 ¶ And when the men of Israel that *were* on the other side of the valley, and *they* that *were* on the other side Jordan, saw that the men of Israel fled, and that Saul and his sons were dead, they forsook the cities, and fled; and the Philistines came and dwelt

---

¹ Or, *wounded*.   ² Heb. *shooters, men with bows*.   ⁴ Or, *mock me*.
³ Heb. *found him*.

---

one of the Simeonite cities (Josh. xix. 8). Shimei, the Ramathite (1 Chr. xxvii. 27), who was over David's vineyards, was evidently a native of this Ramath. See below *v.* 28.

Jattir] "In the mountains" of Judah, and one of the priests' cities, is identified with 'Attir, ten miles south of Hebron.

28. *Aroer*] Not Aroer on the Arnon, but (if rightly written) some town in Judah, not elsewhere named.

Siphmoth, Rachal (*v.* 29), and Athach (*v.* 30), are unknown and not elsewhere mentioned; but *Zabdi the Shiphmite* (1 Chr. xxvii. 27), who was over David's wine-cellars, was evidently a native of the first-named place. It is a remarkable proof of the grateful nature of David, and of his fidelity to his early friendships, as well as a curious instance of undesigned coincidence, that we find among those employed by David in offices of trust in the height of his power so many inhabitants of those obscure places where he found friends in the days of his early difficulties. Ezri the son of Chelub, Shimei the Ramathite, and Zabdi the Shiphmite, as well as Ira and Gareb, and Ittai, and Hezrai, and many others, were probably among these friends of his youth.

30. *Chor-ashan*] Perhaps the same as *Ashan* (Josh. xv. 42), in the *Shephelah* of

Judah, inhabited by Simeonites, and one of the priests' cities (1 Chr. iv. 32, vi. 59).

31. *Hebron*] Now El-Khulil (see Gen. xxiii. 2). Hebron was a city of refuge (Josh. xx. 7), and one of the cities of the Kohathites (Josh. xxi. 11). It lies twenty miles south of Jerusalem.

XXXI. 3. *he was sore wounded*] Better, "**he was sore afraid**" (cp. Deut. ii. 25). Saul's *fear* is explained in *r.* 4.

6. *All his men*] This and similar expressions must not be taken too literally (cp. 1 Chr. x. 6). We know that Abner, and Ishbosheth, and many more survived the day of Gilboa.

7. *the men on the other side of the valley*] This must mean to the north of the plain of Jezreel, and would comprise the tribe of Naphtali, and Zabulon, and probably Issachar. But the text of 1 Chr. x. 7 has "that were in the valley," limiting the statement to the inhabitants of the plain of Jezreel.

on the other side Jordan] This phrase most commonly means *on the east of Jordan*, the speaker being supposed to be on the west side. But it is also used of the west of Jordan, as here, if the text be sound.

the Philistines...dwelt in them] One of the principal cities, Beth-shan, fell into their power at once (*v.* 10).

8 in them.   ¶ And it came to pass on the morrow, when the
Philistines came to strip the slain, that they found Saul and his
9 three sons fallen in mount Gilboa.   And they cut off his head,
and stripped off his armour, and sent into the land of the Philistines round about, to *publish* it *in* the house of their idols, and
10 among the people.   *k* And they put his armour in the house of
l Ashtaroth : and *m* they fastened his body to the wall of *n* Beth-
11 shan.   ¶ *o* And when the inhabitants of Jabesh-gilead heard [1] of
12 that which the Philistines had done to Saul; *p* all the valiant
men arose, and went all night, and took the body of Saul and
the bodies of his sons from the wall of Beth-shan, and came to
13 Jabesh, and *q* burnt them there.   And they took their bones, and
r buried *them* under a tree at Jabesh, *s* and fasted seven days.

i 2 Sam.1.20.
k ch. 21. 9.
l Judg. 2. 13.
m 2 Sam. 21.
12.
n Josh.17.11.
Judg. 1. 27.
o ch. 11. 3.
p See ch.
11. 1—11.
2 San.. 2.
4—7.
q 2 Chr. 16.
14.
Jer. 34. 5.
Amos 6. 10.
r 2 Sam. 2.
4, 5.
& 21. 12.
s Gen.50.10.

[1] Or, *concerning him.*

---

10. *in the house of Ashtaroth*] This was
doubtless the famous temple of Venus in
Askelon mentioned by Herodotus as the
most ancient of all her temples.   Hence the
special mention of Askelon (2 Sam. i. 20).
The placing Saul's armour as a trophy in
the temple of Ashtaroth was a counterpart
to the placing Goliath's sword in the Tabernacle (xxi. 9).   In 1 Chr. x. 10 it is added
that they "fastened Saul's head in the
temple of Dagon," probably either in Gaza
(Judg. xvi. 21), or in Ashdod (v. 1–3).   This
was, perhaps, in retaliation for the similar
treatment of Goliath's head (xvii. 54).   The
variations seem to imply that both this narrative and that in 1 Chr. x. are compiled
from a common and a fuller document.

11. *when the inhabitants of Jabesh-Gilead*

heard, &c.]   See ch. xi.   This is a touching
and rare example of national gratitude.

12. *burnt them*]   Burning was not the
usual mode of sepulture among the Hebrews.
But in this case from a pious desire to disguise the mutilation of the headless corpses,
and exempt them from any possible future
insult, the men of Jabesh burnt the bodies,
yet so as to preserve the bones (*v.* 13; 2
Sam. xxi. 12).

13. *under a tree*]   Rather, "**Under the
tamarisk,**" a well-known tree at Jabesh
which was standing when this narrative was
written.

they fasted seven days]   In imitation of the
mourning for Jacob (marg. ref.).   They
would give full honour to Saul though he
was fallen.

THE SECOND BOOK

OF

S A M U E L ,

OTHERWISE CALLED, THE SECOND BOOK OF THE KINGS.

a 1 Sam. 30.
17, 26.

b ch. 4. 10.

c 1 Sam. 4.
12.

CHAP. 1. NOW it came to pass after the death of Saul, when David was returned from *a*the slaughter of the Amalekites, and David 2 had abode two days in Ziklag; it came even to pass on the third day, that, behold, *b*a man came out of the camp from Saul *c*with his clothes rent, and earth upon his head: and *so* it was, when he came to David, that he fell to the earth, and did obeisance.

3 And David said unto him, From whence comest thou? And he 4 said unto him, Out of the camp of Israel am I escaped. And David said unto him, [1]How went the matter? I pray thee, tell me. And he answered, That the people are fled from the battle, and many of the people also are fallen and dead; and Saul and 5 Jonathan his son are dead also. And David said unto the young man that told him, How knowest thou that Saul and 6 Jonathan his son be dead? And the young man that told him

d 1 Sam. 31. 1.

e See
1 Sam. 31.
2, 3, 4.

said, As I happened by chance upon *d*mount Gilboa, behold, *e*Saul leaned upon his spear; and, lo, the chariots and horsemen 7 followed hard after him. And when he looked behind him, he saw me, and called unto me. And I answered, [2]Here *am* I. 8 And he said unto me, Who *art* thou? And I answered him, I 9 *am* an Amalekite. He said unto me again, Stand, I pray thee, upon me, and slay me: for [3]anguish is come upon me, because

f Judg. 9. 54.

10 my life *is* yet whole in me. So I stood upon him, and *f*slew him, because I was sure that he could not live after that he was fallen: and I took the crown that *was* upon his head, and the bracelet that *was* on his arm, and have brought them hither

g ch. 3. 31.

11 unto my lord. ¶Then David took hold on his clothes, and *g*rent 12 them; and likewise all the men that *were* with him: and they mourned, and wept, and fasted until even, for Saul, and for Jonathan his son, and for the people of the LORD, and for the 13 house of Israel; because they were fallen by the sword. ¶And David said unto the young man that told him, Whence *art* thou? And he answered, I *am* the son of a stranger, an Amalekite.

---

[1] Heb. *What was, &c.*
1 Sam. 4. 16.

[2] Heb. *Behold me.*

[3] Or, *my coat of mail, or,*

my embroidered coat hindereth me, that my, &c.

I. 1. *Now it came to pass,* &c.] There is no break whatever between the two books of Samuel, the division being purely artificial.

9. *anguish*] The Hebrew word here used occurs nowhere else, and is of doubtful meaning (cp. marg.). The Rabbins interpret it *cramp,* or *giddiness.*

10. The Amalekite was one of those who came "to strip the slain" on "the morrow" after the battle (1 Sam. xxxi. 8), and had the luck to find Saul and possess himself of his crown and bracelet. He probably started off immediately to seek David, and invented the above story, possibly having

heard from some Israelite prisoner an account of what really did happen.

12. *for Saul,* &c.] David's thoroughly patriotic and unselfish character is strongly marked here. He looked upon the death of Saul, and the defeat of Israel by a heathen foe, with unmixed sorrow, though it opened to him the way to the throne, and removed his mortal enemy out of the way. For Jonathan he mourned with all the tenderness of a loving friend.

13, 14. Whether David believed the Amalekite's story, or not, his anger was equally excited, and the fact that the young man was an Amalekite, was not calculated

14 And David said unto him, [h]How wast thou not [i]afraid to
15 [k]stretch forth thine hand to destroy the LORD's anointed? And
[l]David called one of the young men, and said, Go near, *and* fall
16 upon him. And he smote him that he died. And David said
unto him, [m]Thy blood *be* upon thy head; for [n]thy mouth hath
testified against thee, saying, I have slain the LORD's anointed.
17 ¶ And David lamented with this lamentation over Saul and over
18 Jonathan his son: ([o]also he bade them teach the children of
Judah *the use of* the bow: behold, *it is* written [p]in the book [1]of
Jasher.)

19   The beauty of Israel is slain upon thy high places:
        [q]How are the mighty fallen!
20   [r]Tell *it* not in Gath, publish *it* not in the streets of Askelon;
        Lest [s]the daughters of the Philistines rejoice,
        Lest the daughters of [t]the uncircumcised triumph.
21   Ye [u]mountains of Gilboa, [x]*let there be* no dew,
        Neither *let there be* rain, upon you, nor fields of offerings:
        For there the shield of the mighty is vilely cast away,
        The shield of Saul, *as though he had* not *been* [y]anointed with oil.
22   From the blood of the slain, from the fat of the mighty,
        [z]The bow of Jonathan turned not back,
        And the sword of Saul returned not empty.
23   Saul and Jonathan *were* lovely and [2]pleasant in their lives,
        And in their death they were not divided
        They were swifter than eagles, they were [a]stronger than lions.
24   Ye daughters of Israel, weep over Saul,
        Who clothed you in scarlet, with *other* delights,
        Who put on ornaments of gold upon your apparel.

¹ Or, *of the upright.*   ² Or, *sweet.*

[h] Num. 12. 8.
[i] 1 Sam. 31. 4.
[k] Ps. 105. 15.
[l] ch. 4. 10, 12.

[m] 1 Sam. 26. 9.
1 Kin. 2. 32, 33, 37.

[o] Luke 19. 22.
[o] 1 Sam. 31. 3.
[p] Josh. 10. 13.

[q] ver. 27.

[r] Mic. 1. 10. See Judg. 16. 23.
[s] See Exod. 15. 20. Judg. 11. 34. 1 Sam. 18. 6.
[t] 1 Sam. 31. 4.
[u] 1 Sam. 31. 1.
[x] So Judg. 5. 23.
[y] 1 Sam. 10. 1.
[z] 1 Sam. 18. 4.

[a] Judg. 14. 18.

to calm or check it. That David's temper was hasty, we know from 1 Sam. xxv. 13, 32–34.

16. David might well think his sentence just though severe, for he had more than once expressed the deliberate opinion that none could lift up his hand against the Lord's anointed, and be guiltless (see 1 Sam. xxiv. 6, xxvi. 9, 11, 16).

17. The words *lamented* and *lamentation* must be understood in the technical sense of a *funeral dirge* or *mournful elegy*. (See similar dirges in iii. 33, 34, and 2 Chr. xxxv. 25.) This and the brief stanza on the death of Abner are the only specimens preserved to us of David's secular poetry.

18. *the use of the bow*] Omit "the use of." "The bow" is the name by which this dirge was known, being so called from the mention of Jonathan's bow in *v.* 22. The sense would then be, *And he bade them teach the children of Israel the song called Kasheth* (the bow), *i.e.* he gave directions that the song should be learned by heart (cp. Deut. xxxi. 19). It has been further suggested that in the Book of Jasher there was, among other things, a collection of poems, in which special mention was made of the bow. This was one of them. 1 Sam. ii. 1–10 was another; Num. xxi. 27–30 another; Lament. ii. another; Lament. iii. another; Jacob's blessing (Gen. xlix.); Moses' song

(Deut. xxxii.); perhaps his Blessing (xxxiii. See *v.* 29); and such Psalms as xliv., xlvi., lxxvi., &c.; Habak. iii.; and Zech. ix. 9–17, also belonged to it. The title by which all the poems in this collection were distinguished was *Kasheth* "the bow." When therefore the writer of 2 Sam. transferred this dirge from the Book of Jasher to his own pages, he transferred it, as we might do any of the Psalms, with its title.

the book of Jasher] See marg. ref. note.

19. *The beauty, &c.*] *i.e.* Saul and Jonathan who were the chief ornament and pride of Israel, and slain upon "high places" (*v.* 25), viz. on Mount Gilboa.

20. Gath, the royal city of Achish (1 Sam. xxi. 10, xxvii. 2). Askelon, the chief seat of worship (1 Sam. xxxi. 10 note).

21. *let there be no dew, &c.*] For a similar passionate form of poetical malediction, cp. Job iii. 3–10; Jer. xx. 14–18.

nor fields of offerings] He imprecates such complete barrenness on the soil of Gilboa, that not even enough may grow for an offering of first-fruits. The latter part of the verse is better rendered thus: *For there the shield of the mighty was polluted, the shield of Saul was not anointed with oil, but with blood*). Shields were usually anointed with oil in preparation for the battle (Isai. xxi. 5).

24. The women of Israel are most happily

25 How are the mighty fallen in the midst of the battle!
O Jonathan, *thou wast* slain in thine high places.

26 I am distressed for thee, my brother Jonathan:
Very pleasant hast thou been unto me:
b Thy love to me was wonderful, passing the love of women.

27 *c* How are the mighty fallen,
And the weapons of war perished!

CHAP. 2. AND it came to pass after this, that David *a* enquired of
the LORD, saying, Shall I go up into any of the cities of Judah?
And the LORD said unto him, Go up. And David said, Whither
2 shall I go up? And he said, Unto *b* Hebron. So David went
up thither, and his *c* two wives also, Ahinoam the Jezreelitess,
3 and Abigail Nabal's wife the Carmelite. And *d* his men that
were with him did David bring up, every man with his house-
4 hold: and they dwelt in the cities of Hebron. *e* And the men of
Judah came, and there they anointed David king over the house
of Judah. ¶ And they told David, saying, That *f* the men of
5 Jabesh-gilead *were they* that buried Saul. And David sent
messengers unto the men of Jabesh-gilead, and said unto them,
g Blessed be ye of the LORD, that ye have shewed this kindness
6 unto your lord, *even* unto Saul, and have buried him. And now
h the LORD shew kindness and truth unto you: and I also will
requite you this kindness, because ye have done this thing.
7 Therefore now let your hands be strengthened, and ¹ be ye
valiant: for your master Saul is dead, and also the house of
8 Judah have anointed me king over them. ¶ But *i* Abner the son
of Ner, captain of ² Saul's host, took ³ Ish-bosheth the son of
9 Saul, and brought him over to Mahanaim; and made him king
over Gilead, and over the Ashurites, and over Jezreel, and over

Marginal references (left column):

b 1 Sam. 18.
1, 3.
& 19. 2, 16.
c ver. 19.
a Judg. 1. 1.
1 Sam. 23. 2,
4, 9.

b 1 Sam. 30.
31.
1 Kin. 2. 11.
c 1 Sam. 30.
5.
d 1 Sam. 27.
2, 3.
& 30. 1.
1 Chr. 12. 1.
e ver. 11.
ch. 5. 5.
f 1 Sam. 31.
11, 13.
g Ruth. 2. 20.
& 3. 10.
Ps. 115. 15.
h 2 Tim. 1.
16, 18.

i 1 Sam. 14.
50.

---

¹ Heb. *be ye the sons of valour.*   ² Heb. *the host which was Saul's.*   ³ Or, *Esh-baal,* 1 Chr. 8. 33. & 9. 39.

---

introduced. They who had come out to meet king Saul with tabrets, with joy, and with instruments of music" in the day of victory, are now called to weep over him.

25. *How are the mighty fallen*] The recurrence of the same idea (*vv.* 19, 25, 27) is perfectly congenial to the nature of elegy, since grief is fond of dwelling upon the particular objects of the passion, and frequently repeating them. By unanimous consent this is considered one of the most beautiful odes in the Bible, and the generosity of David in thus mourning for his enemy and persecutor, Saul, enhances the effect upon the mind of the reader.

II. 1. *enquired of the* LORD] Through Abiathar, the High-priest. The death of Saul and Jonathan had entirely changed David's position, and therefore he needed Divine guidance how to act under the new circumstances in which he was placed. Cp. marg. reff.

Hebron was well suited for the temporary capital of David's kingdom, being situated in a strong position in the mountains of Judah, amidst David's friends, and withal having peculiarly sacred associations (see marg. reff. note). It appears to have also been the centre of a district (*v.* 3).

4. David had already been anointed by Samuel (1 Sam. xvi. 13). His first anointing indicated God's secret purpose, his second the accomplishment of that purpose. (Cp. the case of Saul, 1 Sam. x. 1, xi. 14.) David was anointed again king over Israel (*v.* 3). The interval between the anointing of the Lord Jesus as the Christ of God, and His taking to Himself His kingdom and glory, seems to be thus typified.

8. *Mahanaim*] See Gen. xxxii. 2. From *v.* 12 it would seem to have been Ish-bosheth's capital.

9. *the Ashurites*] If the tribe of Asher, the verse indicates the order in which Abner recovered the different districts from the Philistines, and added them to the dominions of Ish-bosheth, beginning with Gilead, and then gradually adding, on the west of Jordan, first the territory of Asher as far as Carmel and the whole plain of Esdraelon, and then the country of Ephraim and Benjamin, being in fact *all Israel*, as distinguished from Judah; and this reconquest may have occupied five years. Ish-bosheth's reign over Israel may not have been reckoned to begin till the conquest was complete.

10 Ephraim, and over Benjamin, and over all Israel. Ish-bosheth
Saul's son *was* forty years old when he began to reign over
Israel, and reigned two years. But the house of Judah followed
11 David. And [k]the [1]time that David was king in Hebron over
12 the house of Judah was seven years and six months. ¶ And
Abner the son of Ner, and the servants of Ish-bosheth the son
13 of Saul, went out from Mahanaim to [l]Gibeon. And Joab the
son of Zeruiah, and the servants of David, went out, and met
[2]together by [m]the pool of Gibeon : and they sat down, the one
on the one side of the pool, and the other on the other side of
14 the pool. And Abner said to Joab, Let the young men now
arise, and play before us. And Joab said, Let them arise.
15 Then there arose and went over by number twelve of Benjamin,
which *pertained* to Ish-bosheth the son of Saul, and twelve of
16 the servants of David. And they caught every one his fellow
by the head, and *thrust* his sword in his fellow's side ; so they
fell down together : wherefore that place was called [3]Helkath-
17 hazzurim, which *is* in Gibeon. And there was a very sore
battle that day ; and Abner was beaten, and the men of Israel,
18 before the servants of David. ¶ And there were [n]three sons of
Zeruiah there, Joab, and Abishai, and Asahel : and Asahel *was*
19 [o]*as* light [4]of foot [5p]as a wild roe. And Asahel pursued after
Abner ; and in going he turned not to the right hand nor to the

k ch. 5. 5.
1 Kin. 2. 11.

l Josh.18.25.

m Jer. 41. 12.

n 1 Chr. 2.16.

o 1 Chr. 12. 8.
p Ps. 18. 33.
Cant. 2. 17.

---

[1] Heb. *number of days.*
[2] Heb. *them together.*
[3] That is, *The field of strong men.*
[4] Heb. *of his feet.*
[5] Heb. *as one of the roes that is in the field.*

---

10. *forty...two*] The numerals are somewhat strange. First, as regards the forty
years. Even assuming that Ish-bosheth's
reign did not commence till five years and a
half after Saul's death, which must have
been the case if the *two years* in the text
gives the true length of his reign, it is
startling to hear of Saul's younger son being
thirty-five years old at his father's death,
born consequently some three years before
his father's accession, and five years older
than David, the bosom friend of his elder
brother Jonathan. The age, too, of Jonathan's child, Mephibosheth, who was five
years old at his father's death, would lead
one to expect rather a less age for his
uncle. Next, as regards the two years.
Since David (cp. *v.* 11; and marg. reff.)
reigned seven years in Hebron over Judah
only, it follows, if the *two years* in the text
are correct, either that an interval of five
years elapsed between Ish-bosheth's death
and David's being anointed "king over all
Israel," or that a like interval elapsed between Saul's death and the commencement
of Ish-bosheth's reign. Of the two the
latter is the more probable, and has the advantage of diminishing Ish-bosheth's age by
between five and six years. But the narrative in chs. iii. iv. of the "long war," of
the birth of David's six sons, and of Abner's
conspiracy and death, seems to imply a
longer time than *two* years, in which case
both the numerals would have to be corrected.

12. This expedition to Gibeon may have

been for the purpose of shifting his metropolis to his own tribe of Benjamin, and to
his family place, "Gibeah of Saul," close to
Gibeon, with the further purpose of attacking the kingdom of David. *To go out* (*vv.*
12, 13) is a technical phrase for going out to
war (1 Sam. xviii. 30).

13. On the east of the hill (El-jib, the
ancient *Gibeon*) is a copious spring, which
issues in a cave excavated in the limestone
rock, so as to form a large reservoir. In the
trees further down are the remains of a pool
or tank of considerable size (120 feet by 110).
This is doubtless "the pool of Gibeon."

sat down] i.e. halted and encamped.

14. *play*] (Cp. Judg. xvi. 25 ; 1 Sam.
xviii. 7). Here, the word is applied to the
serious game of war, to be played by twelve
combatants on each side, with the two
armies for spectators.

16. Cp. Livy's history of the battle between the Horatii and Curiatii. This
combat, like that, may have been proposed
as a means of avoiding the effusion of blood
of two nations united by consanguinity, and
having a common powerful enemy in the
Philistines.

Helkath-hazzurim] i.e. " the part, field, or
plat (Gen. xxiii. 19) of the sharp edges or
blades." This seems, on the whole, the best
explanation of this rather obscure name.

17. Neither side had the advantage in the
combat of twelve a side ; hence the quarrel
was fought out with great fierceness by the
two armies, and the victory was won by
David.

20 left ¹from following Abner. Then Abner looked behind him,
21 and said, *Art* thou Asahel? And he answered, I *am*. And
Abner said to him, Turn thee aside to thy right hand or to thy
left, and lay thee hold on one of the young men, and take thee
his ²armour. But Asahel would not turn aside from following
22 of him. And Abner said again to Asahel, Turn thee aside from
following me: wherefore should I smite thee to the ground?
23 how then should I hold up my face to Joab thy brother? Howbeit he refused to turn aside: wherefore Abner with the hinder
end of the spear smote him ᵖunder the fifth *rib*, that the spear
came out behind him; and he fell down there, and died in the
same place: and it came to pass, *that* as many as came to the
24 place where Asahel fell down and died stood still. Joab also
and Abishai pursued after Abner: and the sun went down when
they were come to the hill of Ammah, that *lieth* before Giah by
25 the way of the wilderness of Gibeon. ¶ And the children of
Benjamin gathered themselves together after Abner, and became
26 one troop, and stood on the top of an hill. Then Abner called
to Joab, and said, Shall the sword devour for ever? knowest
thou not that it will be bitterness in the latter end? how long
shall it be then, ere thou bid the people return from following
27 their brethren? And Joab said, *As* God liveth, unless ʳthou
hadst spoken, surely then ³in the morning the people had ⁴gone
28 up every one from following his brother. So Joab blew a
trumpet, and all the people stood still, and pursued after Israel
29 no more, neither fought they any more. ¶ And Abner and his
men walked all that night through the plain, and passed over
Jordan, and went through all Bithron, and they came to
30 Mahanaim. And Joab returned from following Abner: and
when he had gathered all the people together, there lacked of
31 David's servants nineteen men and Asahel. But the servants of
David had smitten of Benjamin, and of Abner's men, *so that*
32 three hundred and threescore men died. And they took up
Asahel, and buried him in the sepulchre of his father, which
was in Beth-lehem. And Joab and his men went all night, and
they came to Hebron at break of day.

ᵖ ch. 3. 27.
& 4. 6.
& 20. 10.

ʳ ver. 14.
Prov. 17. 14.

¹ Heb. *from after Abner.*   ³ Heb. *from the morning.*   ⁴ Or, *gone away.*
² Or, *spoil*, Judg. 14. 19.

---

21. *his armour*] Rather, as in the marg.; *i.e.*
content thyself with the spoil of some inferior soldier for a trophy.

23. *with the hinder end*, &c.] *i.e.* the
wooden end, which was more or less
pointed to enable the owner to stick it in
the ground (1 Sam. xxvi. 7).

the fifth rib] The word so rendered here
(and in marg. reff.) means the *abdomen*, and
is not etymologically connected with the
Hebrew for *five*, as the translation "*fifth*
rib" supposes, but with a verb meaning *to
be fat*, or *strong*.

24. *Ammah...Giah*] Local, and otherwise
unknown names.

27. Joab's speech means either "*unless
thou hadst spoken* (challenged us to fight, *v.*
14), *the people would have returned from the
pursuit of their brethren* (many hours ago,
even) *this morning;*" or, "*If thou hadst not

spoken* (asked for peace, *v.* 26), *surely the
people would have returned*, &c., *in the morning, i.e.* would not have ceased the pursuit
till the morning." The latter interpretation
is the more accordant with Joab's boastful
character.

29. *through the plain*] See 1 Sam. xxiii.
24. Bithron is unknown. From the expression *all* (the) *Bithron*, it seems likely
that it is a tract of country, intersected by
ravines lying on the east side of Jordan.

32. Joab, having stopped the pursuit,
passed the night with his army on the field
of battle; the next morning he numbered
the missing, and buried the dead; they
carried the body of Asahel to Bethlehem
and buried him there, and then joined
David at Hebron. Hebron would be about
14 miles from Bethlehem, or about five
hours' march.

CHAP. 3. NOW there was long war between the house of Saul and the house of David: but David waxed stronger and stronger, 2 and the house of Saul waxed weaker and weaker. ¶ And *a* unto David were sons born in Hebron: and his firstborn was Ammon, 3 *b* of Ahinoam the Jezreelitess; and his second, [1]Chileab, of Abigail the wife of Nabal the Carmelite; and the third, Absalom the son of Maacah the daughter of Talmai king *c* of Geshur; 4 and the fourth, *d* Adonijah the son of Haggith; and the fifth, 5 Shephatiah the son of Abital; and the sixth, Ithream, by Eglah 6 David's wife. These were born to David in Hebron. ¶ And it came to pass, while there was war between the house of Saul and the house of David, that Abner made himself strong for the 7 house of Saul. And Saul had a concubine, whose name *was* *e* Rizpah, the daughter of Aiah: and Ish-bosheth said to Abner, Wherefore hast thou *f* gone in unto my father's concubine? 8 Then was Abner very wroth for the words of Ish-bosheth, and said, *Am* I *g* a dog's head, which against Judah do shew kindness this day unto the house of Saul thy father, to his brethren, and to his friends, and have not delivered thee into the hand of David, that thou chargest me to day with a fault 9 concerning this woman? *h* So do God to Abner, and more also, except, *i* as the LORD hath sworn to David, even so I 10 do to him; to translate the kingdom from the house of Saul, and to set up the throne of David over Israel and over Judah, 11 *k* from Dan even to Beer-sheba. And he could not answer Abner 12 a word again, because he feared him. ¶ And Abner sent messengers to David on his behalf, saying, Whose *is* the land? saying *also*, Make thy league with me, and, behold, my hand 13 *shall be* with thee, to bring about all Israel unto thee. And he said, Well: I will make a league with thee: but one thing I require of thee, [2]that is, *l* Thou shalt not see my face, except thou first bring *m* Michal Saul's daughter, when thou comest to

a 1 Chr. 3. 1–4.

b 1 Sam. 25. 43.

c 1 Sam. 27. 8.

ch. 13. 37.
d 1 Kin. 1. 5. & 2. 5.

e ch. 21. 8, 10.

f ch. 16. 21.

g Deut. 23. 18.
1 Sam.24.14.
ch. 9. 8.

h Ruth 1. 17.
1 Kin. 19. 2.
i 1 Sam. 15. 28.
1 Chr. 12. 23.

k Judg. 20.1.

l So Gen. 43. 3.
m 1 Sam. 18. 20.

[1] Or, *Daniel*, 1 Chr. 3. 1. [2] Heb. *saying*.

III. 3. *Chileab*] In the duplicate passage (see marg.) David's second son is called *Daniel* (God is my judge), a name given to him in commemoration of the death of Nabal (1 Sam. xxv. 39). *Chileab* seems to be made up of the three first letters of the following Hebrew word, through an error of the transcriber, and intended to be erased.

Talmai king of Geshur] Talmai was the name of one of the sons of Anak at Hebron (Num. xiii. 22); this Talmai was perhaps of the same race.

Geshur] Where he reigned was in Bashan, and we know from Deut. iii. 11, that Og, king of Bashan, was of the "remnant of the giants." See 1 Sam. xxvii. 8 note.

4. *Adonijah*] The same who, when David was dying, aspired to the crown, and was put to death by Solomon.

Shephatiah] "God is judge." This is the same name as *Jehoshaphat*, only with the two elements composing it placed in inverted order. Nothing more is known of him or of his brother Ithream.

6. Render, "**And it came to pass, while the war between the house of Saul and**

the house of David lasted, that Abner assisted the house of Saul."

7. *Rizpah, the daughter of Aiah*] For the sequel of her history, see marg. ref. *Aiah*, was an Edomitish, or rather Horite name (Gen. xxxvi. 24).

8. The words *against Judah* are very obscure. If the text be correct, the words would seem to be Ish-bosheth's, who in his anger had charged Abner with being a vile partisan of Judah: Abner retorts, *Am I* (as you say) *a dog's head which belongeth to Judah*, or *on Judah's side? This day I show you kindness*, &c., *and this day thou chargest me with a fault*, &c.

12. *Whose is the land?*] Meaning, Is not the land thine by God's promise?

13. David's motive in requiring the restitution of Michal was partly his affection for her, and his memory of her love for him; partly the wish to wipe out the affront put upon him in taking away his wife, by obtaining her return; and partly, also, a politic consideration of the effect on Saul's partisans of a daughter of Saul being David's queen.

14 see my face. And David sent messengers to Ish-bosheth
Saul's son, saying, Deliver *me* my wife Michal, which I espoused

n 1 Sam. 18.
25, 27.
o 1 Sam. 25.
44, *Phalti.*

p ch. 19. 16.

q ver. 9.

r 1 Chr. 12.
29.

s ver. 10, 12.

t 1 Kin. 11.
37.

u 1 Sam. 29.
6.
Isai. 37. 28.

15 to me *n*for an hundred foreskins of the Philistines. And Ish-
bosheth sent, and took her from *her* husband, *even* from *o*Phaltiel
16 the son of Laish. And her husband went with her [1]along
weeping behind her to *p*Bahurim. Then said Abner unto him,
17 Go, return. And he returned. ¶ And Abner had communication
with the elders of Israel, saying, Ye sought for David [2]in times
18 past *to be* king over you: now then do *it :* *q*for the LORD hath
spoken of David, saying, By the hand of my servant David I
will save my people Israel out of the hand of the Philistines,
19 and out of the hand of all their enemies. And Abner also
spake in the ears of *r*Benjamin : and Abner went also to speak
in the ears of David in Hebron all that seemed good to Israel,
20 and that seemed good to the whole house of Benjamin. So
Abner came to David to Hebron, and twenty men with him.
And David made Abner and the men that *were* with him a feast.
21 And Abner said unto David, I will arise and go, and *s*will gather
all Israel unto my lord the king, that they may make a league
with thee, and that thou mayest *t*reign over all that thine heart
desireth. And David sent Abner away ; and he went in peace.
22 ¶ And, behold, the servants of David and Joab came from *pursuing* a troop, and brought in a great spoil with them : but
Abner *was* not with David in Hebron ; for he had sent him away,
23 and he was gone in peace. When Joab and all the host that *was*
with him were come, they told Joab, saying, Abner the son of
Ner came to the king, and he hath sent him away, and he is
24 gone in peace. Then Joab came to the king, and said, What
hast thou done ? behold, Abner came unto thee ; why *is* it *that*
25 thou hast sent him away, and he is quite gone ? Thou knowest
Abner the son of Ner, that he came to deceive thee, and to
know *u*thy going out and thy coming in, and to know all that
26 thou doest. ¶ And when Joab was come out from David, he
sent messengers after Abner, which brought him again from the

[1] Heb. *going and weeping.*　　　　[2] Heb. *both yesterday and the third day.*

---

14. *sent messengers to Ish-bosheth*] Not to
Abner, for the league between David and
Abner was a profound secret, but to Ish-
bosheth who, David knew, must act, feeble
as he was, at Abner's dictation. Abner's
first act of overt allegiance to David was
thus done at Ish-bosheth's bidding ; and the
effect of the humiliation laid upon Ish-
bosheth in exposing his weakness to his own
subjects, and so shaking their allegiance to
him, was such that Abner needed to use no
more disguise.

16. *Bahurim*] Best known as the residence of Shimei, and as the place where
Jonathan and Ahimaaz were concealed in a
well on the occasion of David's flight from
Absalom (xvi. 5, xvii. 18). It seems to have
been situated in the southern border of the
tribe of Benjamin, and on the route from
Jerusalem to the Jordan fords, since Phaltiel came *from* Mahanaim (ii. 8).

17. *Ye sought for David,* &c.] Cp. 1 Sam.
xviii. 5. It was only by Abner's great influence that the elders of Israel had been

restrained hitherto from declaring for
David, and this accounts for Ish-bosheth's
helpless submission to his uncle's dictation.

20. *twenty men*] These were doubtless his
official suite as Ish-bosheth's envoy to conduct Michal to David, but privy and consenting to his intrigue with David. It is
remarkable that not a word should be said
about the meeting of David and Michal.

21. Abner repeats the offer (*v.* 12) ; and
the condition of Michal's return (*v.* 13) being
now fulfilled, David accepts it, and the
league between them was solemnly ratified
at David's board, amidst the rites of hospitality.

24. Joab saw that if Abner was reconciled to David, his own post as second in
the state would be forfeited ; and then with
characteristic unscrupulosity he proceeded
to take Abner's life.

26. *the well of Sirah*] Nowhere else mentioned ; according to Josephus, about two
and a half miles from Hebron.

27 well of Sirah: but David knew *it* not. And when Abner was returned to Hebron, Joab *ᶻ*took him aside in the gate to speak with him [1]quietly, and smote him there *ʸ*under the fifth *rib*,
28 that he died, for the blood of *ᶻ*Asahel his brother. ¶And afterward when David heard *it*, he said, I and my kingdom *are* guiltless before the LORD for ever from the [2]blood of Abner the
29 son of Ner: *ᵃ*let it rest on the head of Joab, and on all his father's house; and let there not [3]fail from the house of Joab one *ᵇ*that hath an issue, or that is a leper, or that leaneth on a
30 staff, or that falleth on the sword, or that lacketh bread. So Joab and Abishai his brother slew Abner, because he had slain
31 their brother *ᶜ*Asahel at Gibeon in the battle. ¶And David said to Joab, and to all the people that *were* with him, *ᵈ*Rend your clothes, and *ᵉ*gird you with sackcloth, and mourn before
32 Abner. And king David *himself* followed the [4]bier. And they buried Abner in Hebron: and the king lifted up his voice, and
33 wept at the grave of Abner; and all the people wept. And the king lamented over Abner, and said,
 Died Abner as a *ᶠ*fool dieth?
34 Thy hands *were* not bound, nor thy feet put into fetters:
 As a man falleth before [5]wicked men, *so* fellest thou.
35 ¶And all the people wept again over him. And when all the people came *ᵍ*to cause David to eat meat while it was yet day, David sware, saying, *ʰ*So do God to me, and more also, if I taste
36 bread, or ought else, *ⁱ*till the sun be down. And all the people took notice *of it*, and it [6]pleased them: as whatsoever the king
37 did pleased all the people. For all the people and all Israel understood that day that it was not of the king to slay Abner the
38 son of Ner. ¶And the king said unto his servants, Know ye not that there is a prince and a great man fallen this day in
39 Israel? And I *am* this day [7]weak, though anointed king; and these men the sons of Zeruiah *ᵏbe* too hard for me: *ˡ*the LORD shall reward the doer of evil according to his wickedness.
CHAP. 4. AND when Saul's son heard that Abner was dead in Hebron, *ᵃ*his hands were feeble, and all the Israelites were
2 *ᵇ*troubled. And Saul's son had two men *that were* captains of bands: the name of the one *was* Baanah, and the name of the
 [8]other Rechab, the sons of Rimmon a Beerothite, of the children

ᶻ 1 Kin. 2. 5.
So ch. 20. 9, 10.
ʸ ch. 4. 6.
ᶻ ch. 2. 23.

ᵃ 1 Kin. 2. 32, 33.

ᵇ Lev. 15. 2.

ᶜ ch. 2. 23.
ᵈ Josh. 7. 6.
ch. 1. 2, 11.
ᵉ Gen. 37. 34.

ᶠ ch. 13. 12.

ᵍ ch. 12. 17.
Jer. 16. 7.
ʰ Ruth 1. 17.
ⁱ ch. 1. 12.

ᵏ ch. 19. 7.
ˡ See ch. 19. 13.
1 Kin. 2. 5, 6, 33, 34.
Ps. 28. 4.
& 62. 12.
2 Tim. 4. 14.
ᵃ Ezra 4. 4.
Isai. 13. 7.
ᵇ Matt. 2. 3.

---

[1] Or, *peaceably.*
[2] Heb. *bloods.*
[3] Heb. *be cut off.*
[4] Heb. *bed.*
[5] Heb. *children of iniquity.*
[6] Heb. *was good in their eyes.*
[7] Heb. *tender.*
[8] Heb. *second.*

---

29. The curse of David proves that Joab was not justified as blood-revenger or *Goel* (*v.* 27) in taking away Abner's life.

that leaneth on a staff] Rather, a *crutch.* The phrase denotes one lame or infirm. For similar instances of hereditary disease and poverty as a punishment of great sin, see 1 Sam. ii. 31-33, 36; 2 K. v. 27; John ix. 2.

33. *lamented*] *i.e.* composed and sang the funeral dirge which follows (cp. i. 17).

Died Abner, &c.] *i.e.* The great and noble and valiant Abner had died as ignobly and as helplessly as the meanest churl!

34. *Thy hands were not bound, &c.*] This thought prepares the way for the solution; Abner had been treacherously murdered by wicked men.

35. *to eat meat, &c.*] Fasting was a sign of the deepest mourning (i. 12). The fast lasted till the sun was set.

IV. 2. *Beeroth*] See marg. ref. From Josh. ix. 17, it might have been expected that the population of Beeroth would be Canaanite. But from some unknown cause the Canaanite inhabitants of Beeroth had fled to Gittaim—perhaps the same as Gath —and continued there as sojourners. If this flight of the Beerothites took place at the time of Saul's cruel attack upon the Gibeonites (2 Sam. xxi. 1, 2), Baanah and Rechab may have been native Beerothites, and have been instigated to murder the son of Saul by a desire to avenge the blood of their countrymen. The fact of their being reckoned as Benjamites is quite com-

e Josh. 18. 25.
d Neh. 11. 33.
e ch. 9. 3.

f 1 Sam. 29.
1, 11.

g ch. 2. 23.

h 1 Sam. 19.
2, 10, 11.
& 23. 15.
& 25. 29.

i Gen. 48. 16.
1 Kin. 1. 29.
Ps. 31. 7.
k ch 1. 2, 4,
15.

l Gen. 9. 5,
6.
m ch. 1. 15.

n ch. 3. 32.

a 1 Chr. 11.
1—9.
b Gen. 29. 14.

of Benjamin: (for *e*Beeroth also was reckoned to Benjamin: 3 and the Beerothites fled to *d*Gittaim, and were sojourners there 4 until this day.) ¶ And *e*Jonathan, Saul's son, had a son *that was* lame of *his* feet. He was five years old when the tidings came of Saul and Jonathan *f*out of Jezreel, and his nurse took him up, and fled: and it came to pass, as she made haste to flee, that he fell, and became lame. And his name *was* ¹Mephibo-5 sheth. ¶ And the sons of Rimmon the Beerothite, Rechab and Baanah, went, and came about the heat of the day to the house 6 of Ish-bosheth, who lay on a bed at noon. And they came thither into the midst of the house, *as though* they would have fetched wheat; and they smote him *g*under the fifth *rib*: and 7 Rechab and Baanah his brother escaped. For when they came into the house, he lay on his bed in his bedchamber, and they smote him, and slew him, and beheaded him, and took his head, 8 and gat them away through the plain all night. And they brought the head of Ish-bosheth unto David to Hebron, and said to the king, Behold the head of Ish-bosheth the son of Saul thine enemy, *h*which sought thy life; and the LORD hath avenged my lord the king this day of Saul, and of his seed. 9 ¶ And David answered Rechab and Baanah his brother, the sons of Rimmon the Beerothite, and said unto them, *As* the LORD 10 liveth, *i*who hath redeemed my soul out of all adversity, when *k*one told me, saying, Behold, Saul is dead, ²thinking to have brought good tidings, I took hold of him, and slew him in Ziklag, ³who *thought* that I would have given him a reward for 11 his tidings: how much more, when wicked men have slain a righteous person in his own house upon his bed? shall I not therefore now *l*require his blood of your hand, and take you 12 away from the earth? And David *m*commanded his young men, and they slew them, and cut off their hands and their feet, and hanged *them* up over the pool in Hebron. But they took the head of Ish-bosheth, and buried *it* in the *n*sepulchre of Abner in Hebron.

CHAP. 5. THEN *a*came all the tribes of Israel to David unto Hebron, and spake, saying, Behold, *b*we *are* thy bone and thy

---

¹ Or, *Merib-baal*, 1 Chr. 8. 34. & 9. 40. ² Heb. *he was in his own eyes as a bringer, &c.* ³ Or, *which* was *the reward I gave him for his tidings.*

---

patible with their being Canaanites by blood.

4. This mention of Mephibosheth seems to be inserted here partly to show that with the death of Ish-bosheth the cause of the house of Saul became hopeless, and partly to prepare the way for the subsequent mention of him (ix., xvi. 1-4, xix. 25).

5. *lay on a bed at noon*] Render, "was taking his midday rest," according to the custom of hot countries.

6. *as though they would have fetched wheat*] This is a very obscure passage, and the double repetition in *vv.* 6 and 7 of the murder of the king and of the escape of the assassin, is hard to account for. Rechab and Baanah came into the house under the pretence of getting grain, probably for the band which they commanded, out of the king's storehouse, and so contrived to get access into the king's chamber; or, they found the wheat-carriers (the persons whose business it was to carry in grain for the king's household) just going into the king's house, and by joining them got into the midst of the house unnoticed. If the latter be the sense, the literal translation of the words would be: "*And behold* (or, *and thither*) there came into the midst of the house the carriers of wheat, and they (i.e. Rechab and Baanah) smote him, &c.*"

12. *cut off their hands*, &c.] After they were dead. Their hands and feet were hung up in a place of public resort, both to deter others and also to let all Israel know that David was not privy to the murder of Ish-bosheth.

V. 1. Cp. marg. ref. The chronicler adds some interesting details (xii. 23-40) of the manner in which the various tribes

2 flesh. Also in time past, when Saul was king over us, ^cthou wast he that leddest out and broughtest in Israel: and the LORD said to thee, ^dThou shalt feed my people Israel, and thou shalt
3 be a captain over Israel. ^eSo all the elders of Israel came to the king to Hebron; ^fand king David made a league with them in Hebron ^gbefore the LORD: and they anointed David king
4 over Israel. David *was* thirty years old when he began to
5 reign, ^h*and* he reigned forty years. In Hebron he reigned over Judah ⁱ seven years and six months: and in Jerusalem he reigned
6 thirty and three years over all Israel and Judah. ¶And the king and his men went ^kto Jerusalem unto ^lthe Jebusites, the inhabitants of the land: which spake unto David, saying, Except thou take away the blind and the lame, thou shalt not
7 come in hither: ¹thinking, David cannot come in hither. Nevertheless David took the strong hold of Zion: ^mthe same *is* the
8 city of David. And David said on that day, Whosoever getteth up to the gutter, and smiteth the Jebusites, and the lame and the blind, *that are* hated of David's soul, ⁿ*he shall be chief and captain.* ²Wherefore they said, The blind and the lame shall

Marginal references:
c 1 Sam. 18. 13.
d 1 Sam. 16. 1, 12. Ps. 78. 71. See ch. 7. 7.
e 1 Chr. 11. 3.
f 2 Kin. 11. 17.
g Judg. 11. 11.
h 1 Chr. 26. 31.
& 29. 27.
i ch. 2. 11. 1 Chr. 3. 4.
k Judg. 1. 21.
l Josh. 15. 63. Judg. 1. 8.
& 19. 11.
m 1 Kin. 2. 10.
& 8. 1.
n 1 Chr. 11. 6—9.

¹ Or, *saying, David shall not, &c.*   ² Or, *Because they had said, even the blind and the* lame, *He shall not come into the house.*

---

from both sides of the Jordan came to Hebron to make David king, and of the joyful festivities on the occasion. The consummation to which events in God's Providence had now come. Saul and Jonathan, Abner and Ish-bosheth, were dead; David was already head of a very large portion of Israel; the Philistines, and perhaps the remnant of the Canaanites, were restless and threatening; and it was obviously the interest of the Israelitish nation to unite themselves under the sovereignty of the valiant and virtuous son of Jesse, their former deliverer, and the man designated by the word of God as their Captain and Shepherd. Accordingly he was at once anointed king over all Israel (cp. ii. 4 note).

3. *before the* LORD] Abiathar and Zadok the priests were both with David, and the Tabernacle and Altar may have been at Hebron, though the Ark was at Kirjath-jearim.

4. The age of David is conclusive as to the fact that the earlier years of Saul's reign (during which Jonathan grew up to be a man) are passed over in silence, and that the events narrated from 1 Sam. xiii. to the end of the Book did not occupy above ten years. If David was twenty years old at the time he slew Goliath, four years in Saul's service, four years of wandering from place to place, one year and four months in the country of the Philistines, and a few months after Saul's death, would make up the ten years necessary to bring him to the age of thirty.

6. David immediately after being anointed king of Israel, probably wished to signalise his accession by an exploit which would be popular with all Israel, and especially with

Saul's tribe, Benjamin. He discerned the importance of having Jerusalem for his capital both because it belonged as much to Benjamin as to Judah, and on account of its strong position.

Except thou take away the blind, &c.] Rather, "**and** (the Jebusite) **spake to David, saying, Thou shalt not come hither, but the blind and the lame shall keep thee off,**" *i.e.* so far shalt thou be from taking the stronghold from us, that the lame and blind shall suffice to defend the place.

7. *the stronghold of Zion*] Or *castle* (1 Chr. xi. 5, 7). The ancient Zion was the hill on which the Temple stood, and the castle seems to have been immediately to the north of the Temple. The modern Zion lies to the south-west of the Temple.

the same is the city of David] The name afterwards given to it (*v.* 9), and by which it was known in the writer's time.

8. *i.e.* "Whosoever will smite the Jebusites, let him reach both the lame and the blind, who are the hated of David's soul, by the gutter or water-course, *and he shall be chief.*" The only access to the citadel was where the water had worn a channel (some understand a subterranean channel), and where there was, in consequence, some vegetation in the rock. Joab (see marg. ref.) took the hint, and with all the activity that had distinguished his brother Asahel (ii. 18), climbed up first. *The blind and the lame* are either literally such, placed there in derision by the Jebusites who thought the stronghold impregnable, or they are the Jebusite garrison, so called in derision by David.

Wherefore they said, &c.] *i.e.* it became a proverb (as in 1 Sam. xix. 24). The pro-

9 not come into the house. ¶ So David dwelt in the fort, and
called it [o]the city of David. And David built round about from
10 Millo and inward. And David [1]went on, and grew great, and
11 the LORD God of hosts *was* with him. ¶ And [p]Hiram king of
Tyre sent messengers to David, and cedar trees, and carpenters,
12 and [2]masons: and they built David an house. And David
perceived that the LORD had established him king over Israel,
and that he had exalted his kingdom for his people Israel's
13 sake. ¶ And [q]David took *him* more concubines and wives out of
Jerusalem, after he was come from Hebron: and there were yet
14 sons and daughters born to David. And [r]these *be* the names of
those that were born unto him in Jerusalem; [3]Shammuah, and
15 Shobab, and Nathan, and Solomon, Ibhar also, and [4]Elishua,
16 and Nepheg, and Japhia, and Elishama, and [5]Eliada, and
17 Eliphalet. ¶ [s]But when the Philistines heard that they had
anointed David king over Israel, all the Philistines came up to
seek David; and David heard *of it*, [t]and went down to the hold.
18 The Philistines also came and spread themselves in [u]the valley
19 of Rephaim. And David [x]enquired of the LORD, saying, Shall
I go up to the Philistines? wilt thou deliver them into mine
hand? And the LORD said unto David, Go up: for I will
20 doubtless deliver the Philistines into thine hand. And David
came to [y]Baal-perazim, and David smote them there, and said,
The LORD hath broken forth upon mine enemies before me, as
the breach of waters. Therefore he called the name of that
21 place [6]Baal-perazim. And there they left their images, and
22 David and his men [z][7]burned them. ¶ [a]And the Philistines
came up yet again, and spread themselves in the valley of
23 Rephaim. And when [b]David enquired of the LORD, he said,

[o] ver. 7.
[p] 1 Kin. 5. 2. 1 Chr. 14. 1.
[q] Deut. 17. 17. 1 Chr. 3. 9. & 14. 3.
[r] 1 Chr. 3. 5. & 14. 4.
[s] 1 Chr. 11. 16. & 14. 8.
[t] ch. 23. 14.
[u] Josh. 15. 8. Isai. 17. 5.
[x] ch. 2. 1. 1 Sam. 23. 2, 4. & 30. 8.
[y] Isai. 28. 21.
[z] Deut. 7. 5, 25. 1 Chr. 14. 12.
[a] 1 Chr. 14. 13.
[b] ver. 19.

[1] Heb. *went going and growing.*
[2] Heb. *hewers of the stone of the wall.*
[3] Or, *Shimea*, 1 Chr. 3. 5.
[4] Or, *Elishama*, 1 Chr. 3. 6.
[5] Or, *Beeliada*, 1 Chr. 14. 7.
[6] That is, *The plain of breaches.*
[7] Or, *took them away.*

---

verb seems merely to have arisen from the blind and the lame being the *hated of David's soul*, and hence to have been used proverbially of any that were hated, or unwelcome, or disagreeable.

9. *David dwelt in the fort*] or stronghold, (as in *v.* 7) *i.e.* eventually, when the buildings were completed, which may not have been for two or three years. Millo appears to have been a fortress of some kind, the northern defence of the city of David, and to have been a part of the original Canaanite defences of Zion, as appears probable also from there having been a fortress called the *house of Millo* in the Canaanite city of Shechem. (Judg. ix. 6 note, and 20.) *Millo* may be the native name. Some identify it with the great platform called the Haram es Sherif.

David built round about] Probably meaning built his own house and other houses and streets, all, in short, that caused it to be called *the city of David.* (Cp. 1 Chr. xi. 8.) The buildings were within, on the south of Millo, so as to be protected by it on the north, as they were east, west, and south, by the precipitous ravines.

11. *Hiram king of Tyre*] Now mentioned for the first time. He survived David, and continued his friendship to Solomon (marg. reff.). The news of the capture of the city of the Jebusites had doubtless reached Tyre, and created a great impression of David's power.

17. *the hold*] Not the same place which is so named in *vv.* 7 and 9, but probably the cave (or hold) of Adullam (xxiii. 13). The invasion most probably took place before David had completed his buildings in the city of David; and is probably referred to in xxiii. 8-17.

20. *Baal-perazim*] *Master* or *possessor of breaches*, equivalent to *place of breaches.* It was on a hill near Gibeon (see marg. ref.).

21. *And there they left their images*] An indication of the precipitancy of their flight, and the suddenness with which the Israelites burst upon them like a "breach of waters." The A. V. rendering *burned them*, does not give a translation (cp. marg.), but a gloss, warranted by the explanation given in marg. reff.

23. *the mulberry trees*] Rather, the *Bacah-tree*, and found abundantly near Mecca. It

Thou shalt not go up; *but* fetch a compass behind them, and
24 come upon them over against the mulberry trees. And let it
be, when thou *c*hearest the sound of a going in the tops of the
mulberry trees, that then thou shalt bestir thyself: for then
*d*shall the LORD go out before thee, to smite the host of the
25 Philistines. And David did so, as the LORD had commanded
him; and smote the Philistines from *e*Geba until thou come to
*f*Gazer.

Chap. 6. AGAIN, David gathered together all *the* chosen *men* of
2 Israel, thirty thousand. And *a*David arose, and went with all
the people that *were* with him from ¹Baale of Judah, to bring
up from thence the ark of God, ²whose name is called by the
name of the LORD of hosts *b*that dwelleth *between* the cheru-
3 bims. And they ³set the ark of God *c*upon a new cart, and
brought it out of the house of Abinadab that *was* in ⁴Gibeah:
and Uzzah and Ahio, the sons of Abinadab, drave the new cart.
4 And they brought it out of *d*the house of Abinadab which *was*
at Gibeah, ⁵accompanying the ark of God: and Ahio went
5 before the ark. And David and all the house of Israel played
before the LORD on all manner of *instruments made of* fir wood,
even on harps, and on psalteries, and on timbrels, and on cornets,
6 and on cymbals. ¶And when they came to *e*Nachon's threshingfloor, Uzzah *f*put forth *his hand* to the ark of God, and took
7 hold of it; for the oxen ⁶shook *it*. And the anger of the LORD
was kindled against Uzzah; and *g*God smote him there for *his*
8 ⁷error; and there he died by the ark of God. And David was

c So 2 Kin.
7. 6.
d Judg. 4. 14.
e 1 Chr. 14.
16.
Gibeon.
f Josh. 16. 10.

a 1 Chr. 13.
5, 6.

b 1 Sam. 4. 4.
Ps. 80. 1.
c See Num.
7. 9.
1 Sam. 6. 7.
d 1 Sam. 7. 1.

e 1 Chr. 13.
9, he is
called,
Chidon.
f See Num.
4. 15.
g 1 Sam. 6.
19.

¹ Or, *Baalah*, that is *Kirjath-
jearim*, Josh. 15. 9, 60.
² Or, *at which the name*, even

*the name of the LORD of
hosts, was called upon.*
³ Heb. *made to ride.*
⁴ Or, *The hill.*

⁵ Heb. *with.*
⁶ Or, *stumbled.*
⁷ Or, *rashness.*

is very like the balsam-tree, and probably
derives its name from the exudation of the
sap in drops like tears when a leaf is torn
off. Some think the valley of Baca (Ps.
lxxxiv. 6) was so called from this plant
growing there.

25. *Geba*] Better, as in marg. ref. *Gibeon*.
Gazer should be "**Gezer**" (Josh. x. 33, &c.);
it lay between the nether Bethhoron and the
sea; on the direct route therefore which the
Philistines, fleeing from Gibeon, would take.
The exact site has now been identified (1 K.
ix. 16 note).

VI. 1. *Again*] It should be, "**and David
again gathered**," &c., *i.e.* after the previous gathering, either for his election to
the kingdom (v. 1-3) or for the Philistine
war (v. 17-25), he assembled them again for
the peaceful purpose of bringing up the Ark
to Mount Zion (see marg. ref.). The whole
narrative indicates the progressive consolidation of David's power, and the settlement
of his monarchy on strong foundations.

2. *from Baale of Judah*] See marg. and 1
Sam. vi. 21 note.

whose name, &c.] The literal rendering is,
"**Upon which is called the Name, the
Name of Jehovah of Hosts, Who sits upon
the Cherubim**," i.e. *the Ark which is called
after the Lord of Hosts and bears His Name*
(see Deut. xxviii. 10; 1 K. viii. 43; Isai. iv. 1).

3. *the house of Abinadab in Gibeah*]. Ra-

ther, *on the hill* (as in marg. and 1 Sam. vii.
1). It does not at all follow that Abinadab
was still alive, nor can we conclude from
Uzzah and Ahio being called *sons of Abinadab*, that they were literally his children.
They may well have been sons of Eleazar
and grandsons of Abinadab, or yet more remote descendants; since there is no distinct
evidence that Abinadab was alive even when
the ark was brought to Kirjath-jearim. The
house may have retained the name of "the
house of Abinadab" long after his death.

5. *played*] *i.e.* danced to music vocal and
instrumental (see Judg. xvi. 25 note).

cornets] Rather, from the etymology of
the Heb. word (*to shake*), and their being
coupled with the *cymbals*, and being rendered *sistra* in the Vulg., some kind of instrument with bells or rings, which gave a
sound by being shaken.

6. *shook it*] The use of the Heb. word
here is unusual. Some take the word as in
2 K. ix. 33, and render the passage: *The
oxen were throwing*, or *had thrown* it *down*,
very likely by turning aside to eat what
grain there might be on the threshing-floor.

7. *for his error*] The Heb. is difficult, and
some prefer the reading of the parallel passage, *because...ask* (1 Chr. xiii. 10).

8. *displeased*] Grief allied to *anger* seems
to be intended. Cp. 1 Sam. xv. 11 note.
On the name of the place, cp. v. 20.

h Ps. 119.
120.
See Luke
5. 8, 9.
i 1 Chr. 13.
13.
k 1 Chr. 13.
14.
l Gen. 30. 27.
& 39. 5.

m 1 Chr. 15.
25.

n Num. 4.15.
Josh. 3. 3.
o See 1 Kin.
8. 5.
1 Chr. 15. 26.
p See Exod.
15. 20.
Ps. 30. 11.
q 1 Sam. 2.
18.
1 Chr. 15. 27.
r 1 Chr. 15.
28.
s 1 Chr. 15.
29.
t 1 Chr. 16. 1.
u 1 Chr. 15. 1.
Ps. 132. 8.
x 1 Kin. 8. 5,
62, 63.
y 1 Kin. 8.
55.
1 Chr. 16. 2.
z 1 Chr. 16. 3.

displeased, because the LORD had [1]made a breach upon Uzzah: and he called the name of the place [2]Perez-uzzah to this day.

9 ¶ And [h]David was afraid of the LORD that day, and said, How 10 shall the ark of the LORD come to me? So David would not remove the ark of the LORD unto him into the city of David: but David carried it aside into the house of Obed-edom [i]the 11 Gittite. [k]And the ark of the LORD continued in the house of Obed-edom the Gittite three months: and the LORD [l]blessed 12 Obed-edom, and all his household. ¶ And it was told king David, saying, The LORD hath blessed the house of Obed-edom, and all that *pertaineth* unto him, because of the ark of God. [m]So David went and brought up the ark of God from the house 13 of Obed-edom into the city of David with gladness. And it was *so*, that when [n]they that bare the ark of the LORD had gone six 14 paces, he sacrificed [o]oxen and fatlings. And David [p]danced before the LORD with all *his* might; and David *was* girded 15 [q]with a linen ephod. [r]So David and all the house of Israel brought up the ark of the LORD with shouting, and with the 16 sound of the trumpet. ¶ And [s]as the ark of the LORD came into the city of David, Michal Saul's daughter looked through a window, and saw king David leaping and dancing before the 17 LORD; and she despised him in her heart. ¶ And [t]they brought in the ark of the LORD, and set it in [u]his place, in the midst of the tabernacle that David had [3]pitched for it: and David [x]offered 18 burnt offerings and peace offerings before the LORD. And as soon as David had made an end of offering burnt offerings and peace offerings, [y]he blessed the people in the name of the LORD 19 of hosts. [z]And he dealt among all the people, *even* among the whole multitude of Israel, as well to the women as men, to every one a cake of bread, and a good piece *of flesh*, and a flagon

---

[1] Heb. *broken.*   [2] That is, *The breach of Uzzah.*   [3] Heb. *stretched.*

---

10. Obed-edom was a Levite of the family of Merari, being (1 Chr. xv. 18-24, xvi. 38) a son of Jeduthun, who was a Merarite. He was a porter, a player on the harp, and was one of the Levites specially designated to take part in the musical services on the occasion of bringing up the Ark to Zion, and to minister before it when brought up. He is called a *Gittite* perhaps from *Gath*-Rimmon, in Manasseh, which belonged to the Kohathites (Josh. xxi. 25). Marriage with a Kohathite, or some other cause, would account for his dwelling in a Kohathite city.

12. *with gladness*] Especially with joyful music and song (1 Chr. xv. 16, &c.).

13. The meaning is, not that they sacrificed oxen and fatlings every six steps, which would have been impossible, but that when —after the arrangement made by David for the Levites to carry the Ark (1 Chr. xv. 2, 12, 15) they had borne it successfully and with visible tokens of God's favour, out of the house of Obed-edom and six "steps" on the road to the city of David to the sound of the musical instruments,—then they stopped and offered solemn sacrifices. Possibly "the step" may have had a technical sense, and denoted a certain distance, say a *stadium*. Six such distances would have been nearly

a mile, and if the ground was difficult and steep, the successful progress of " those that bare the ark," so far, would have been a fit cause for a thanksgiving sacrifice.

14. *danced*] The Heb. word is found only here and in *v.* 16. It means "to dance in a circle," hence simply *to dance*. The parallel passage in 1 Chr. xv. 27 gives a widely different sense.

16. *she despised him in her heart*] In the days of Saul the Ark had been neglected (1 Chr. xiii. 3), and Saul had in everything shown himself to be an irreligious king. Michal seems to have been of a like spirit.

The whole section, 2 Sam. vi. 16-36, should be compared with 1 Chr. xv. 29-xvi. 43.

The *peace offerings* were with a special view to feasting the people. (Cp. 1 K. viii. 63-66.)

18. *he blessed the people*] So did Solomon (1 K. viii. 14).

19. *a good piece* of flesh] The word thus paraphrased is only found here and in marg. ref. A piece of meat from the peace offerings is probably meant. From the fact that the chronicler explains the preceding *cake* by the more common word *loaf*, but leaves this obscure word

of wine. So all the people departed every one to his house.
20 ¶ [a]Then David returned to bless his household. And Michal
the daughter of Saul came out to meet David, and said, How
glorious was the king of Israel to day, who [b]uncovered himself
to day in the eyes of the handmaids of his servants, as one of
21 the [c]vain fellows [1]shamelessly uncovereth himself! And David
said unto Michal, *It was* before the LORD, [d]which chose me
before thy father, and before all his house, to appoint me ruler
over the people of the LORD, over Israel: therefore will I play
22 before the LORD. And I will yet be more vile than thus, and
will be base in mine own sight: and [2]of the maidservants which
23 thou hast spoken of, of them shall I be had in honour. Therefore Michal the daughter of Saul had no child [e]unto the day of
her death.

CHAP. 7. AND it came to pass, [a]when the king sat in his house,
and the LORD had given him rest round about from all his
2 enemies; that the king said unto Nathan the prophet, See now,
I dwell in [b]an house of cedar, [c]but the ark of God dwelleth
3 within [d]curtains. And Nathan said to the king, Go, do all that
4 *is* [e]in thine heart; for the LORD *is* with thee. ¶ And it came to
pass that night, that the word of the LORD came unto Nathan,
5 saying, Go and tell [3]my servant David, Thus saith the LORD,
6 [f]Shalt thou build me an house for me to dwell in? Whereas I
have not dwelt in *any* house [g]since the time that I brought up
the children of Israel out of Egypt, even to this day, but have
7 walked in [h]a tent and in a tabernacle. In all *the places* wherein
I have [i]walked with all the children of Israel spake I a word
with [4]any of the tribes of Israel, whom I commanded [k]to feed

[a] Ps. 30, title.
[b] ver. 14, 16.
1 Sam. 19.
24.
[c] Judg. 9. 4.
[d] 1 Sam. 13.
14.
& 15. 28.

[e] See 1 Sam.
15. 35.

[a] 1 Chr. 17.
1, &c.

[b] ch. 5. 11.
[c] See Acts
7. 46.
[d] Ex. 26. 1.
& 40. 21.
[e] 1 Kin. 8.
17, 18.
[f] See 1 Kin.
5. 3.
1 Chr. 22. 8.
[g] 1 Kin. 8.16.
[h] Ex. 40. 18,
19, 34.
[i] Lev. 26.11.
Deut. 23. 14.
[k] ch. 5. 2.
Ps. 78. 71.
Matt. 2. 6.

---

[1] Or, *openly*.
[2] Or, *of the handmaids* of my servants.
[3] Heb. *to my servant to David*.
[4] *any of the judges*, 1 Chr. 17. 6.

---

unexplained, one might infer that it was
already obsolete and unknown in his time.
The LXX. translates it *a cake baked on the
hearth ;* the Vulg. *a piece of roast beef.*

a flagon of wine] Rather, "**a cake**" of
grapes or raisins (Hos. iii. 1; Cant. ii. 5), or
made with oil or mead.

20. *Then David returned,* &c.] He had
passed his house to accompany the Ark to
the tabernacle he had pitched for it, when
Michal saw him dancing. He now returns
to bless his household. He had blessed the
people (*v.* 18), but there were the inmates
of his own house whom the customs of the
age did not allow to be present, and so, with
his usual considerate kindness and affection,
David came to bless them also on this solemn occasion.

21. *play*] See *v.* 5 note. The speech might
be paraphrased, *Before the Lord which chose
me,* &c., *yea, before the Lord have I danced.*
He humbles Michal's pride by the allusion
to her father's rejection, and shows by
Saul's example how little pride contributes
to the stability of greatness. Therefore for
his part he will not think anything done for
the glory of God too mean for him ; and if
he cannot have honour from Saul's daughter, he will be content to be honoured by
the maid-servants.

VII. 1. There is no indication how soon
after the bringing up of the Ark these things
occurred, but it was probably at no long interval.

2. *Nathan the prophet*] Here first mentioned, but playing an important part afterwards (*e.g.* xii. 1; 1 K. i. 10; 1 Chr. xxix.
29; 2 Chr. ix. 29). From the two last passages it appears that he wrote the history
of David's reign, and a part at least of
Solomon's. His distinctive title is *the prophet,* that of Gad *the seer* (cp. 1 Sam. ix. 9).
He was probably much younger than David.
In *v.* 3, he spoke his own private opinion ;
in *v.* 4, this was corrected by the word of
the Lord.

6. *have walked*] Implying the frequent
moving of the tabernacle, in the times of
the Judges, as opposed to a settled resting
in one place. The word *tent,* refers especially to the outward covering of skins, &c.:
the *tabernacle* denotes the framework of
boards and bars. Observe the constant reference to the Exodus and to the details as
given in the Books of Moses.

7. *the tribes of Israel*] The duplicate passage reads *judges* (see marg. and cp. *v.* 11).
But a comparison with such passages as Ps.
lxxviii. 67, 68; 1 K. viii. 16; and 1 Chr.
xxviii. 4, favours the reading "tribes," and

i 1 Sam. 16.
11, 12.
i a 1 Sam. 18.
14.
ch. 5. 10.
n 1Sam.31.6.
Ps. 89. 23.
o Gen. 12. 2.
p Ps. 44. 2.
Jer. 24. 6.
Amos 9. 15.
q Ps. 89. 22.
r Judg. 2.14,
15, 16.
1 Sam. 12. 9,
11.
s ver. 1.
t Ex. 1. 21.
1 Kin. 11. 38.
u 1 Kin. 2. 1.
x Deut.31.16.
1 Kin. 1. 21.
y 1 Kin.8.20.
Ps. 132. 11.
z 1 Kin. 5. 5.
1 Chr. 22. 10.
a ver. 16.
b Ps. 89. 26,
27.
c Ps. 89. 30,
31, 32, 33.

my people Israel, saying, Why build ye not me an house of cedar? 8 Now therefore so shalt thou say unto my servant David, Thus saith the LORD of hosts, *i*I took thee from the sheepcote, [1]from following the sheep, to be ruler over my people, over Israel: 9 and *m*I was with thee whithersoever thou wentest, *n*and have cut off all thine enemies, [2]out of thy sight, and have made thee *o*a great name, like unto the name of the great *men* that *are* in 10 the earth. Moreover I will appoint a place for my people Israel, and will *p*plant them, that they may dwell in a place of their own, and move no more; *q*neither shall the children of wicked- 11 ness afflict them any more, as beforetime, and as *r*since the time that I commanded judges *to be* over my people Israel, and have *s*caused thee to rest from all thine enemies. Also the LORD 12 telleth thee *t*that he will make thee an house. And *u*when thy days be fulfilled, and thou *x*shalt sleep with thy fathers, *y*I will set up thy seed after thee, which shall proceed out of thy bowels, 13 and I will establish his kingdom. *z*He shall build an house for my name, and I will *a*stablish the throne of his kingdom for 14 ever. *b*I will be his father, and he shall be my son. *c*If he commit iniquity, I will chasten him with the rod of men, and 15 with the stripes of the children of men: but my mercy shall not

[1] Heb. *from after.*   [2] Heb. *from thy face.*

---

the phrase is a condensed one, the meaning of which is, that whatever tribe had in times past supplied the ruler of Israel, whether Ephraim in the days of Joshua, or Benjamin in the time of Saul, or Judah in that of David, God had never required any of those tribes to build a house in one of their cities.

an house of cedar] See 1 K. vii. 2, 3, x. 17, 21; Jer. xxii. 14, 23. Beams of cedar marked a costly building. The cedar of Lebanon is a totally different tree from what we improperly call *the red* or *Virginian cedar*, which supplies the sweet-scented cedar wood, and is really a kind of juniper. The cedar of Lebanon is a close-grained, light-coloured, yellowish wood, with darker knots and veins.

10. *Moreover I will appoint*, &c.] It should be: *And I have appointed a place*, &c., *and have planted them*, &c. This was already done by the consolidation of David's kingdom. The contrast between this and *v.* 11 is that of the troublous unsettled times of the Judges and the frequent servitudes of Israel in those times, with the settled prosperity and independence of the kingdom of David and Solomon.

12. The prophet, having detailed God's past mercies to David, now passes on to direct prophecy, and that one of the most important in the Old Testament.

I will set up thy seed] In one sense this manifestly refers to Solomon, David's successor and the builder of the Temple. But we have the direct authority of St. Peter (Acts ii. 30) for applying it to Christ the seed of David, and His eternal kingdom; and the title *the Son of David* given to the

Messiah in the Rabbinical writings, as well as its special application to Jesus in the New Testament, springs mainly from the acknowledged Messianic significance of this prophecy. (See also Isai. lv. 3; Acts xiii. 34.)

13. *He shall build an house*, &c.] For the fulfilment of this in the person of Solomon, see 1 K. viii. 16-20. For its application to Christ, see John i. 12; Eph. i. 20-22; 1 Tim. iii. 15; Heb. iii. 6, &c.; and Zech. vi. 12, 13.

I will stablish the throne of his kingdom for ever] The words *for ever*, emphatically twice repeated in *v.* 16, show very distinctly that this prophecy looks beyond the succession of the kings of Judah of the house of David, and embraces the throne of Christ, according to the Angel's interpretation given in Luke i. 31-33, where the reference to this passage cannot be mistaken. This is also brought out fully in Ps. lxxxix. 29, 36, 37. See also Dan. vii. 13, 14; Isai. ix. 6, 7; Jer. xxiii. 5, 6, xxxiii. 14-21; Ezek. xxxiv. 24; Zech. xii. 7, 8; Hos. iii. 5, &c.

14. *I will be his father*, &c.] In marg. ref. the equivalent expressions are applied to David. In Heb. i. 5, this text is applied to Christ. But in 1 Chr. xvii. 13, xxii. 9, 10, xxviii. 6, it is expressly appropriated to Solomon.

with the rod of men, &c.] *i.e.* such a chastisement as men inflict upon their children, to correct and reclaim them, not to destroy them. The whole clause is omitted in 1 Chr. xvii. 13.

15. *my mercy shall not depart*, &c.] Hence Isaiah's saying, *the sure mercies of David* (lv. 3), *i.e.* unfailing, lasting mercies: mercies

depart away from him, ^das I took *it* from Saul, whom I put away
16 before thee. And ^ethine house and thy kingdom shall be established for ever before thee: thy throne shall be established for
17 ever. According to all these words, and according to all this
18 vision, so did Nathan speak unto David. ¶Then went king
David in, and sat before the Lord, and he said, ^fWho *am* I, O
Lord God? and what *is* my house, that thou hast brought me
19 hitherto? And this was yet a small thing in thy sight, O Lord
God; ^gbut thou hast spoken also of thy servant's house for a
great while to come. ^hAnd *is* this the ¹manner of man, O Lord
20 God? And what can David say more unto thee? for thou,
21 Lord God, ⁱknowest thy servant. For thy word's sake, and
according to thine own heart, hast thou done all these great
22 things, to make thy servant know *them*. Wherefore ^kthou art
great, O Lord God: for ^l*there is* none like thee, neither *is there*
any God beside thee, according to all that we have heard with
23 our ears. And ^mwhat one nation in the earth *is* like thy people,
even like Israel, whom God went to redeem for a people to himself, and to make him a name, and to do for you great things
and terrible, for thy land, before ⁿthy people, which thou re-
deemedst to thee from Egypt, *from* the nations and their gods?
24 For ^othou hast confirmed to thyself thy people Israel *to be* a
people unto thee for ever: ^pand thou, Lord, art become their
25 God. And now, O Lord God, the word that thou hast spoken
concerning thy servant, and concerning his house, establish *it*
26 for ever, and do as thou hast said. And let thy name be magnified for ever, saying, The Lord of hosts *is* the God over
Israel: and let the house of thy servant David be established
27 before thee. For thou, O Lord of hosts, God of Israel, hast
²revealed to thy servant, saying, I will build thee an house:
therefore hath thy servant found in his heart to pray this prayer
28 unto thee. And now, O Lord God, thou *art* that God, and ^qthy
words be true, and thou hast promised this goodness unto thy
29 servant: therefore now ³let it please thee to bless the house of

d 1 Sam. 15.
23, 28.
e Ps. 89. 36,
37.
John 12. 34.

f Gen. 32. 10.

g ver. 12.
h Isai. 55. 8.

i Gen. 18. 19.
Ps. 139. 1.
k 1 Chr. 16.
25.
2 Chr. 2. 5.
Ps. 48. 1.
& 86. 10.
Jer. 10. 6.
l Deut. 3. 24.
1 Sam. 2. 2.
Ps. 89. 6.
Isai. 45. 5.
m Deut. 4. 7,
32, 34.
Ps. 147. 20.
n Deut. 9. 26.
Neh. 1. 10.
o Deut. 26. 18.
p Gen. 17. 7.
Ex. 6. 7.

q John 17. 17.

---

¹ Heb. *law*.   ² Heb. *opened the ear*, Ruth 4. 4.   ³ Heb. *be thou pleased and*
   1 Sam. 9. 15.   *bless*.

---

which are like streams of water that never
dry up (Isai. xxxiii. 16; Jer. xv. 18). This
is explained in *v.* 16, where the word *established* is the same word as is rendered *sure*
in Isaiah.

before thee] *Before Me* is probably the true
reading in *vv.* 15, 16 (if the rest of the text
be sound), according to the analogy of Jer.
xxxv. 19, 1 Sam. ii. 30, 35, and many other
places; whereas the idea contained in the
reading, *before thee*, is unparalleled. But
the reading in 1 Chr. xvii. 13 is quite different: "*As I took it from him that was before thee*," meaning Saul, which gives a very
good sense, and suggests that the text here
may have been corrupted.

18. *sat before the* Lord] In the tent where
the Ark was. Standing or kneeling was the
usual attitude of prayer (1 K. viii. 22, 54,
55; but cp. Ex. xvii. 12). Modern commentators mostly take the word here in
the sense of *waiting, abiding*, not *sitting*:
but *sat* is the natural rendering. David sat
down to meditate, and then rose up to pray.

19. *is this the manner of man*] Cp. 1 Chr.
xvii. 17. Our passage may be thus understood: *But this is the law* (or prerogative) *of
a great man* to found dynasties which are to
last into the far future. David expresses
his astonishment that he, of such humble
birth, and one so little in his own eyes,
should not only be raised to the throne, but
be assured of the perpetuity of the succession in his descendants, as if he were a man
of high degree.

23. *the nations and their gods*] *i.e.* the people and the idols of Canaan.

27. *therefore hath thy servant found in his
heart*, &c.] The promises of God are the
true guide to the prayers of His people. We
may dare to ask anything, how great soever
it may be, which God has promised to give.
In this and the two following verses David
expresses the same wonder at the riches of
God's grace, and the same expectation
founded on that grace, which St. Paul does
in such passages as Eph. i. 5-7, ii. 7, &c.
marg. reff.

thy servant, that it may continue for ever before thee: for thou,
O Lord God, hast spoken *it:* and with thy blessing let the house

r ch. 22. 51.

of thy servant be blessed *r*for ever.

a 1 Chr. 18.
1, &c.

CHAP. **8.** AND *a*after this it came to pass, that David smote the
Philistines, and subdued them: and David took ¹Metheg-ammah

b Num. 24.
17.

2 out of the hand of the Philistines. ¶ And *b*he smote Moab, and
measured them with a line, casting them down to the ground;
even with two lines measured he to put to death, and with one

c ver. 6, &
14.

full line to keep alive. And *so* the Moabites *c*became David's

d Judg. 3.18.
2 Kin. 17. 3.
e 1 Sam. 14.
47.
f See Gen.
15. 18.
g Josh. 11. 6,
9.
h 1 Kin. 11.
23, 24, 25.

3 servants, *and* *d*brought gifts. ¶ David smote also ²Hadadezer,
the son of Rehob, king of *e*Zobah, as he went to recover *f*his
4 border at the river Euphrates. And David took ³from him a
thousand ⁴*chariots*, and seven hundred horsemen, and twenty
thousand footmen: and David *g*houghed all the chariot *horses*,
5 but reserved of them *for* an hundred chariots. *h*And when the
Syrians of Damascus came to succour Hadadezer king of Zobah,
6 David slew of the Syrians two and twenty thousand men. Then
David put garrisons in Syria of Damascus: and the Syrians

i ver. 2.
k ver. 14.
ch. 7. 9.
l See 1 Kin.
10. 16.

*i*became servants to David, *and* brought gifts. *k*And the LORD
7 preserved David whithersoever he went. And David took *l*the
shields of gold that were on the servants of Hadadezer, and
8 brought them to Jerusalem. And from ⁵Betah, and from ⁶Be-
rothai, cities of Hadadezer, king David took exceeding much
9 brass. ¶ When ⁷Toi king of Hamath heard that David had

---

¹ Or, *The bridle of Ammah.*
·² Or, *Hadarezer,* 1 Chr.
18. 3.
³ Or, *of his.*
⁴ As 1 Chron. 18. 4.
⁵ Or, *Tibhath.*
⁶ Or, *Chun,* 1 Chr. 18. 8.
⁷ *Tou,* 1 Chr. 18. 9.

VIII. *Metheg-ammah* must be the name
of some stronghold which commanded Gath,
and the taking of which made David master
of Gath and her towns.

2. David took great numbers of the
Moabites prisoners of war, and made them
lie down on the ground, and then divided
them by a measuring line into three parts,
putting two-thirds to death, and saving
alive one-third. The cause of the war with
the Moabites, who had been very friendly
with David (1 Sam. xxii. 3, 4), and of this
severe treatment, is not known. But it
seems likely, from the tone of Ps. lx. that
David had met with some temporary reverse
in his Syrian wars, and that the Moabites
and Edomites had treacherously taken advantage of it, and perhaps tried to cut off
his retreat.

3. *Hadadezer*] Not (see marg.) *Hadarezer.*
Hadadezer, is the true form, as seen in the
names *Benhadad, Hadad* (1 K. xv. 18, &c.,
xi. 14, &c.). *Hadad* was the chief idol, or
sun-god, of the Syrians.

to recover his border] Literally, *to cause his
hand to return.* The phrase is used sometimes literally, as *e.g.* Ex. iv. 7; 1 K. xiii.
4; Prov. xix. 24; and sometimes figuratively, as Isai. i. 25, xiv. 27; Am. i. 8; Ps.
lxxiv. 11. The exact force of the metaphor
must in each case be decided by the context.
If, as is most probable, this verse relates to
the circumstances more fully detailed in x.
15-19, the meaning of the phrase here will be
when he.(Hadadezer) *went to renew his attack*

(upon Israel), or *to recruit his strength against
Israel, at the river Euphrates.*

4. *seven hundred horsemen*] It should be
seven thousand, as in 1 Chr. xviii. 4.

5. *Syrians of Damascus*] The Syrians
(Aram), whose capital was Damascus, were
the best known and most powerful. Damascus (written Darmesek in marg. reft.,
according to the late Aramean orthography)
is first mentioned in Gen. xv. 2. According
to Nicolaus of Damascus, cited by Josephus,
the Syrian king's name was Hadad.

6. *garrisons*] The word is used for *officers*
in 1 K. iv. 5, 19, and some think that that
is its meaning here. Perhaps, however, it
is best to take it with the A. V. in the same
sense as in 1 Sam. x. 5, xiii. 3.

brought gifts] Rather, " **tribute** " (and in
v. 2); meaning they became subject and tributary.

8. *Betah and Berothai*] These names (see
also marg.) have not been identified with
certainty.

exceeding much brass] " Wherewith Solomon made the brazen sea, and the pillars,
and the vessels of brass " (1 Chr. xviii. 8).
The LXX. and Vulg. both add these words
here, so that perhaps they have fallen out
of the Hebrew text. For the existence
of metals in Lebanon or Antilebanon, see
Deut. viii. 9.

9. *Hamath*] This appears as an independent kingdom so late as the time of Sena-
cherib (Isai. xxxvii. 13). But in the time of
Nebuchadnezzar, both Hamath and Arpad

10 smitten all the host of Hadadezer, then Toi sent [m]Joram his son unto king David, to [1]salute him, and to bless him, because he had fought against Hadadezer, and smitten him : for Hadadezer [2]had wars with Toi.   And *Joram* [3]brought with him vessels of
11 silver, and vessels of gold, and vessels of brass : which also king David [n]did dedicate unto the Lord, with the silver and gold
12 that he had dedicated of all nations which he subdued ; of Syria, and of Moab, and of the children of Ammon, and of the Philistines, and of Amalek, and of the spoil of Hadadezer, son of
13 Rehob, king of Zobah.   ¶ And David gat *him* a name when he returned from [4]smiting of the Syrians in [o]the valley of salt,
14 [p][5]*being* eighteen thousand *men*.   And he put garrisons in Edom ; throughout all Edom put he garrisons, and [q]all they of Edom became David's servants.   [r]And the Lord preserved David
15 whithersoever he went.   ¶ And David reigned over all Israel ; and David executed judgment and justice unto all his people.
16 [s]And Joab the son of Zeruiah *was* over the host ; and [t]Jehosha-
17 phat the son of Ahilud *was* [6]recorder ; and [u]Zadok the son of Ahitub, and Ahimelech the son of Abiathar, *were* the priests ;
18 and Seraiah *was* the [7]scribe ; [x]and·Benaiah the son of Jehoiada *was over* both the [y]Cherethites and the Pelethites ; and David's sons were [8]chief rulers.

Chap. 9. AND David said, Is there yet any that is left of the house of Saul, that I may [a]shew him kindness for Jonathan's sake ?
2 And *there was* of the house of Saul a servant whose name *was* [b]Ziba.   And when they had called him unto David, the king said
3 unto him, *Art* thou Ziba ? And he said, Thy servant *is* he.   And the king said, *Is* there not yet any of the house of Saul, that I may shew [c]the kindness of God unto him ? And Ziba said unto the king, Jonathan hath yet a son, *which is* [d]lame on *his* feet.

Margin references:
[m] 1 Chr. 18. 10, *Hadoram*.
[n] 1 Kin. 7. 51. 1 Chr. 18. 11. & 26. 26.
[o] 2 Kin. 14. 7.
[p] See 1 Chr. 18. 12.
Ps. 60, title.
[q] Gen. 27. 29, 37, 40.
Num. 24. 18.
[r] ver. 6.
[s] ch. 19. 13. & 20. 23.
1 Chr. 11. 6. & 18. 15.
[t] 1 Kin. 4. 3.
[u] 1 Chr. 24. 3.
[x] 1 Chr. 18. 17.
[y] 1 Sam. 30. 14.
[a] 1 Sam. 18. 3.
& 20. 14, 15, 16, 17, 42.
Prov. 27. 10.
[b] ch. 16. 1. & 19. 17, 29.
[c] 1 Sam. 20. 14.
[d] ch. 4. 4.

---

[1] Heb. *ask him of peace.*
[2] Heb. *was a man of wars with.*
[3] Heb. *in his hand were.*
[4] Heb. *his smiting.*
[5] Or, *slaying.*
[6] Or, *remembrancer, or*
writer of chronicles.
[7] Or, *secretary.*
[8] Or, *princes*, ch. 20. 26.

---

appear to have been incorporated in the kingdom of Damascus (Jer. xlix. 23).

10. *Joram*] Or, more probably, *Hadoram.* See marg.

12. *Syria*] Rather, as in 1 Chr. xviii. 11, Edom, which is manifestly the right reading, both because Edom, Moab, and Ammon are so frequently joined together, and because David's Syrian spoil is expressly mentioned at the end of the verse. [The Hebrew letters for Aram (Syria) and Edom are very similar.]

13. *the Syrians*] Read *the Edomites*, as in marg. reff. (cp. Ps. lx. title), and as the context (*v.* 14) requires. For a further account of this war of extermination with Edom, see 1 K. xi. 15, 16. The war with Edom was of some duration, not without serious reverses and dangers to the Israelites (*v.* 2 note). The different accounts probably relate to different parts of the campaign.

16–18. For a similar account of the officers of Solomon's kingdom, see 1 K. iv. 1–6, where Jehoshaphat is still the recorder, and Benaiah is advanced to be captain of the host in the room of Joab. *The recorder* seems to have been a high officer of state, a kind of

chancellor, whose office was to keep a record of the events of the kingdom for the king's information, and hence he would naturally be the king's adviser. See Esth. vi. 1, 2 ; Isai. xxxvi. 22 ; 2 Chr. xxxiv. 8. Such an officer is found among the ancient Egyptians and Persians.

Ahimelech the son of Abiathar] According to 1 Sam. xxii. 9–23, Abiathar, Zadok's colleague, was the son of Ahimelech. Abiathar the son of Ahimelech continued to be priest through the reign of David. (Cp. also 1 K i. 7, 42, ii. 22–27.) It almost necessarily follows that there is some error in the text.

the scribe] Or secretary of state (2 K. xii. 10, xviii. 37), different from the military scribe (Judg. v. 14 note).

18. *the Cherethites and the Pelethites*] See marg. ref. note.

chief rulers] The word *cohen*, here rendered *a chief ruler*, is the regular word for a *priest*. In the early days of the monarchy the word *cohen* had not quite lost its etymological sense, from the root meaning *to minister*, or *manage affairs*, though in later times its technical sense alone survived.

ᵉ ch. 17. 27.

4 And the king said unto him, Where *is* he? And Ziba said unto
the king, Behold, he *is* in the house of ᵉMachir, the son of
5 Ammiel, in Lo-debar. Then king David sent, and fetched him
out of the house of Machir, the son of Ammiel, from Lo-debar.
6 ¶Now when ¹Mephibosheth, the son of Jonathan, the son of
Saul, was come unto David, he fell on his face, and did reverence. And David said, Mephibosheth. And he answered,

ᶠ ver. 1, 3.

7 Behold thy servant! And David said unto him, Fear not: ᶠfor
I will surely shew thee kindness for Jonathan thy father's sake,
and will restore thee all the land of Saul thy father; and thou
8 shalt eat bread at my table continually. And he bowed himself,
and said, What *is* thy servant, that thou shouldest look upon

ᵍ 1 Sam. 24.
14.
ch. 16. 9.
ʰ See ch. 16.
4.
& 19. 29.

9 such ᵍa dead dog as I *am* ? ¶ Then the king called to Ziba, Saul's
servant, and said unto him, ʰI have given unto thy master's son
10 all that pertained to Saul and to all his house. Thou therefore,
and thy sons, and thy servants, shall till the land for him, and
thou shalt bring in *the fruits*, that thy master's son may have

ⁱ ver. 7, 11,
13.
ch. 19. 28.
ᵏ ch. 19. 17.

food to eat: but Mephibosheth thy master's son ⁱshall eat bread
alway at my table. Now Ziba had ᵏfifteen sons and twenty
11 servants. Then said Ziba unto the king, According to all that
my lord the king hath commanded his servant, so shall thy servant do. As for Mephibosheth, *said the king*, he shall eat at
12 my table, as one of the king's sons. And Mephibosheth had a

ˡ 1 Chr. 8. 34.

young son, ˡwhose name *was* Micha. And all that dwelt in the
13 house of Ziba *were* servants unto Mephibosheth. So Mephibo-

ᵐ ver. 7, 10.
ⁿ ver. 3.

sheth dwelt in Jerusalem: ᵐfor he did eat continually at the
king's table: and ⁿwas lame on both his feet.

¹ Called, *Merib-baal*, 1 Chr. 8. 34.

IX. 4. David reaped the fruit of his kindness to Mephibosheth; for, when he fled
from Absalom, Machir, the son of Ammiel,
was one of those who were most liberal in
providing him and his army with neces-
saries (marg. ref.). According to 1 Chr. iii.
5, *Ammiel* (called inversely *Eliam*, xi. 3)
was the father of Bath-sheba. If this be
the same Ammiel, Machir would be Bath-
sheba's brother. However, the name is not
a very uncommon one (Num. xiii. 12 ; 1
Chr. xxvi. 5, &c.).

Lo-debar] Evidently on the east of Jordan,
and in the neighbourhood of Ish-bosheth's
capital, Mahanaim (xvii 27), but not iden-
fied by any modern traveller. Thought by
some, not improbably, to be the same as
Debir (Josh. xiii. 26).

6. *Mephibosheth*] Also called *Merib-baal*
(and *Meri-baal*, probably by a clerical error,
1 Chr. ix. 40). The two names seem to have
the same meaning : *Bosheth*, *shame*, being
the equivalent for *Baal*, and *Mephi* (*scat-
tering* or *destroying*, being equivalent to
Merib (*contending with*). Cp. Ish-bosheth
and Esh-baal, Jerub-baal and Jerub-be-
sheth.

he fell on his face] In fear. Such generosity
to a fallen rival as David showed in restoring him his paternal property seemed to him
scarcely credible.

8. Mephibosheth's humility of expression,

even in the mouth of an Oriental, is painful.
It was perhaps in part the result of his
helpless lameness, and of the other misfor-
tunes of his life.

a dead dog] The wild dogs of the East,
which still abound in every town, are the
natural objects of contempt and dislike.

9. *Saul's servant*] Josephus calls him one
of Saul's freedmen. The difference this
would make in Ziba's position would only
be that instead of paying in the fruits of
the confiscated land to David, he would
have to pay them to Mephibosheth.

1ᴊ. *fifteen sons*, &c.] See xix. 17, marg.
ref.

11. *said the king*] There is nothing in the
Hebrew to warrant the insertion of these
words. The words are, "**So Mephibosheth
ate at my table as one of the king's sons.**"
Only it follows that the narrator is David
himself.

12. Mephibosheth was five years old at
Saul's death. He may have been thirteen
at David's accession to the throne of Israel.
In the eighth year of David's reign over all
Israel he would have been twenty-one. His
having a son at this time indicates that
we are about the tenth year of David's
reign.

Micha] Or *Micah*; who, as far as we know,
was Mephibosheth's only son, and had a
numerous posterity (marg. reff.).

CHAP. 10. AND it came to pass after this, that the [a]king of the
children of Ammon died, and Hanun his son reigned in his
2 stead. Then said David, I will shew kindness unto Hanun the
son of Nahash, as his father shewed kindness unto me. And
David sent to comfort him by the hand of his servants for his
father. And David's servants came into the land of the children
3 of Ammon. And the princes of the children of Ammon said
unto Hanun their lord, [1]Thinkest thou that David doth honour
thy father, that he hath sent comforters unto thee? hath not
David *rather* sent his servants unto thee, to search the city, and
4 to spy it out, and to overthrow it? Wherefore Hanun took
David's servants, and shaved off the one half of their beards,
and cut off their garments in the middle, [b]*even* to their buttocks,
5 and sent them away. When they told *it* unto David, he sent to
meet them, because the men were greatly ashamed: and the
king said, Tarry at Jericho until your beards be grown, and *then*
6 return. ¶And when the children of Ammon saw that they
[c]stank before David, the children of Ammon sent and hired [d]the
Syrians of Beth-rehob, and the Syrians of Zoba, twenty thousand footmen, and of king Maacah a thousand men, and of [2]Ish-
7 tob twelve thousand men. ¶And when David heard of *it*, he
8 sent Joab, and all the host of [e]the mighty men. And the chil-

a 1 Chr. 19.
1, &c.

b Isai. 20. 4.
& 47. 2.

c Gen. 34. 30.
Ex. 5. 21.
1 Sam. 13. 4.
d ch. 8. 3, 5.

e ch. 23. 8.

---

[1] Heb. *In thine eyes doth David.*   [2] Or, *the men of Tob.* See Judg. 11. 3, 5.

X. On comparing this whole chapter with
viii. 3-13, and 1 Chr. xix. with 1 Chr. xviii.,
it seems not improbable that they are two
accounts of one and the same war; the
former account (viii. 3-13) being inserted out
of its chronological order. The numbers
slain on both occasions, 42,000 (viii. 4, 5),
40,000 (x. 18), 700 (viii. 4, x. 18), the seat of
war, the mention of the Euphrates, the
persons engaged—David, Joab, and Abishai on one side, Hadarezer and the vassal
kings on the other—are too similar to make
it probable that they belong to two different wars.

1. *the king*] In marg. ref. *Nahash, king*,
&c. The interval between the two events,
not less than fifty years, and possibly more,
is against his being the same as the Nahash
of 1 Sam. xi.

The Ammonites are almost always
spoken of as *the children of Ammon*, from
the name of their first ancestor Ben-ammi
(Gen. xix. 38).

Hanun] The equivalent of the Cartha-
ginian *Hanno*, from the same root as the
Hebrew, *Hananiah, Johanan, Hannah*, &c.
The same name appears in composition with
Baal in Baal-Hanan, an Aramean king
(Gen. xxxvi. 38, 39).

2. The history does not record any instance of Nahash's kindness to David, but
the enmity of the house of Nahash against
Saul may have disposed him favourably
towards Saul's enemy David, and if there
was any family connexion between David's
house and Nahash (xvii. 25) this may have
increased the friendship.

3. *the princes*, &c.] Cp. Rehoboam's advisers (1 K. xii. 10, 11). It is not improbable

that David's severe treatment of Moab (viii.
2) was in part the cause of the fear of the
Ammonites that a similar treatment was in
store for themselves.

4. In 1 Chr. xix. 4, more concisely
"*shaved.*" Cutting off a person's beard is
regarded by the Arabs as an indignity
equal to flogging and branding among ourselves. The loss of their long garments, so
essential to Oriental dignity, was no less
insulting than that of their beards.

6. *stank*, &c.] A strong figure for to be
odious or *detested.* Cp. marg. reff.

the Syrians of Beth-rehob] If identical with
the Mesopotamians of 1 Chr. xix. 6, Beth-
rehob is the same as *Rehoboth by the river*
(Gen. xxxvi. 37). Others think *Beth-rehob*
(*Rehob v.* 8) the same as the *Rehob* and
Beth-rehob of Num. xiii. 21, near Hamath
(perhaps the modern ruin of Hunin). If
so, Beth-rehob, as well as Tob, must have
been a colony of Aram Naharaim (cp. the
numbers in 1 Chr. xix. 7 and here).

Syrians of Zoba] Cp. 1 Sam. xiv. 47 note.

king Maacah] Read the "**King of Maacah**" (1 Chr. xix. 6, 7). For the position of
Maacah, see Deut. iii. 14; Josh. xii. 5. It
appears to have been a very small state,
since its king only brought a thousand men
into the field.

Ish-tob] See marg. *Tob* was the district
whither Jephthah fled when driven out by
the Gileadites.

7. This sufficiently indicates the greatness
of the danger to Israel from this formidable
league of Ammonites and Syrians.

8. *came out*] From their city, Rabbah
(Deut. iii. 11), 15 or 20 miles from Medeba,
where (1 Chr. xix. 7) the Syrian army was

f ver. 6.
dren of Ammon came out, and put the battle in array at the entering in of the gate: and *f*the Syrians of Zoba, and of Rehob,

9 and Ish-tob, and Maacah, *were* by themselves in the field. When Joab saw that the front of the battle was against him before and behind, he chose of all the choice *men* of Israel, and put *them* in

10 array against the Syrians: and the rest of the people he delivered into the hand of Abishai his brother, that he might put *them* in

11 array against the children of Ammon. And he said, If the Syrians be too strong for me, then thou shalt help me: but if the children of Ammon be too strong for thee, then I will come

g Deut. 31.6.
h 1 Sam. 4. 9.
1 Cor. 16. 13.
i 1 Sam.3.18.
12 and help thee.   *g*Be of good courage, and let us *h*play the men for our people, and for the cities of our God: and *i*the LORD do

13 that which seemeth him good.   ¶And Joab drew nigh, and the people that *were* with him, unto the battle against the Syrians:

14 and they fled before him. And when the children of Ammon saw that the Syrians were fled, then fled they also before Abishai, and entered into the city. So Joab returned from the children

15 of Ammon, and came to Jerusalem.   ¶And when the Syrians saw that they were smitten before Israel, they gathered them-

16 selves together. And Hadarezer sent, and brought out the Syrians that *were* beyond ¹the river: and they came to Helam; and ²Shobach the captain of the host of Hadarezer *went* before

17 them. And when it was told David, he gathered all Israel together, and passed over Jordan, and came to Helam. And the Syrians set themselves in array against David, and fought with

18 him. And the Syrians fled before Israel; and David slew *the men of* seven hundred chariots of the Syrians, and forty thou-

k 1 Chr. 19.
18,
footmen.
sand *k*horsemen, and smote Shobach the captain of their host,

19 who died there. And when all the kings *that were* servants to Hadarezer saw that they were smitten before Israel, they made

l ch. 8. 6.
peace with Israel, and *l*served them. So the Syrians feared to help the children of Ammon any more.

CHAP. 11. AND it came to pass, ³after the year was expired, at the
a 1Chr.20.1.
time when kings go forth *to battle*, that *a*David sent Joab, and

---

¹ That is, *Euphrates.*
² Or, *Shophach*, 1 Chr. 19. 16.
³ Heb. *at the return of the year*, 1 Kin. 20. 22, 26. 2 Chr. 36. 10.

---

encamped. Medeba (modern *Madeba*) was taken from Sihon (Num. xxi. 30), and fell to Reuben (Josh. xiii. 9, 16); in the reign of Ahaz it seems to have returned to Moab (Isai. xv. 2), and in the time of the Maccabees to the Amorites (1 Macc. ix. 36, 37). In Christian times it was a bishop's see.

in the field] *i.e.* in the plain below the round rocky hill on which the city stood.

9. The two armies of the Ammonites and the Syrians were drawn up facing one another; the Ammonites supported by the city Rabbah behind them; the Syrians in great force, with numerous chariots able to manœuvre in the plain in front of Medeba. If Joab advanced against either, he would have the other in his rear.

12. *for the cities of our God*] This rather indicates that the relief of Medeba was one of the immediate objects in view, and consequently that at this time Medeba was still in the possession of the Reubenites. To prevent an Israelite city falling into the hands of a heathen people, and the rites of

Moloch being substituted for the worship of Jehovah, was a very urgent motive to valour.

14. *Joab returned*] The great strength of Rabbah made it hopeless to take it by assault, and the Syrians were not sufficiently broken (*v*. 15) to make it safe to undertake a regular siege.

16. *Helam*] The place is unknown. Some prefer the translation of the Latin Vulgate, *their host came.*

18. *seven hundred chariots*] More probable than the *seven thousand* of 1 Chr. xix. 18. The frequent errors in numbers arise from the practice of expressing numerals by letters, with one or more *dots* or *dashes* to indicate hundreds, thousands, &c.

19. *servants to Hadarezer*] This gives us an idea of the great power of Hadarezer, and consequently of the strength of Israel in David's victorious reign.

XI. 1. *after the year was expired*] The next spring after the escape of the Ammonites into their city (x. 14).

his servants with him, and all Israel; and they destroyed the
children of Ammon, and besieged Rabbah. But David tarried
2 still at Jerusalem. ¶And it came to pass in an eveningtide, that
David arose from off his bed, *b*and walked upon the roof of the
king's house : and from the roof he *c*saw a woman washing her-
3 self; and the woman *was* very beautiful to look upon. And
David sent and enquired after the woman. And *one* said, *Is* not
this ¹Bath-sheba, the daughter of ²Eliam, the wife *d*of Uriah the
4 Hittite? And David sent messengers, and took her; and she
came in unto him, and *e*he lay with her; ³for she was *f*purified
5 from her uncleanness : and she returned unto her house. And
the woman conceived, and sent and told David, and said, I *am*
6 with child. ¶And David sent to Joab, *saying*, Send me Uriah
7 the Hittite. And Joab sent Uriah to David. And when Uriah
was come unto him, David demanded *of him* ⁴how Joab did, and
8 how the people did, and how the war prospered. And David
said to Uriah, Go down to thy house, and *g*wash thy feet. And
Uriah departed out of the king's house, and there ⁵followed him
9 a mess *of meat* from the king. But Uriah slept at the door of
the king's house with all the servants of his lord, and went not
10 down to his house. And when they had told David, saying,
Uriah went not down unto his house, David said unto Uriah,
Camest thou not from *thy* journey? why *then* didst thou not go
11 down unto thine house? And Uriah said unto David, *h*The
ark, and Israel, and Judah, abide in tents; and *i*my lord Joab,
and the servants of my lord, are encamped in the open fields;
shall I then go into mine house, to eat and to drink, and to lie
with my wife? *as* thou livest, and *as* thy soul liveth, I will not
12 do this thing. And David said to Uriah, Tarry here to day also,
and to morrow I will let thee depart. So Uriah abode in Jeru-
13 salem that day, and the morrow. And when David had called
him, he did eat and drink before him; and he made him *k*drunk :
and at even he went out to lie on his bed *l*with the servants of
14 his lord, but went not down to his house. ¶And it came to pass
in the morning, that David *m*wrote a letter to Joab, and sent *it*
15 by the hand of Uriah. And he wrote in the letter, saying, Set
ye Uriah in the forefront of the ⁶hottest battle, and retire ye
16 *i*from him, that he may *n*be smitten and die. ¶And it came to
pass, when Joab observed the city, that he assigned Uriah unto

b Deut. 22. 8.

c Gen. 34. 2.
Job 31. 1.
Matt. 5. 28.

d ch. 23. 39.

e Ps. 51,
title.
Jam. 1. 14.
f Lev. 15. 19,
28.
& 18. 19.

g Gen. 18. 4.
& 19. 2.

h ch. 7. 2, 6.
i ch. 20. 6.

k Gen. 19.
33, 35.
l ver. 9.

m See 1 Kin.
21. 8, 9.

n ch. 12. 9.

---

¹ Or, *Bath-shuah*, 1 Chr. 3. 5.   *purified herself, &c. she*   ⁵ Heb. *went out after him.*
² Or, *Ammiel.*   *returned.*   ⁶ Heb. *strong.*
³ Or, *and when she had*   ⁴ Heb. *of the peace of, &c.*   ⁷ Heb. *from after him.*

---

the children of Ammon] The marg. ref.
supplies the word "*the land of*," which is
obviously the right reading.

David tarried at Jerusalem] The Syrians
being subdued, the war with Ammon was
not of sufficient moment to require David's
personal presence. The whole section relating to David's adultery and Uriah's
death, from this verse to xii. 26, is omitted
in the Book of Chronicles.

2. *an eveningtide*] The evening began at
three o'clock in the afternoon.

3. *Eliam*] Or *Ammiel*, (1 Chr. iii. 5), the
component words being placed in an inverse
order. Bath-sheba was the granddaughter of
Ahithophel (xxiii. 34).

7. David was forced to stoop to falsehood
and dissimulation in the vain hope of hiding
his sin.

8. *a mess of meat*] Cp. Gen. xliii. 34. The
word denotes the honourable portion given
by the host to his chief guest.

11. *the ark*] Perhaps there was a double
purpose in taking the Ark; one, to excite to
the utmost the enthusiam of the people for
its defence and against the Ammonites; the
other, to have the means at hand of *enquiring of the Lord*, which David had found so
serviceable.

16. *observed the city*] In the sense of besieging it closely.

17 a place where he knew that valiant men *were*. And the men of
the city went out, and fought with Joab : and there fell *some* of
the people of the servants of David ; and Uriah the Hittite died
18 also. ¶ Then Joab sent and told David all the things concerning
19 the war ; and charged the messenger saying, When thou hast
20 made an end of telling the matters of the war unto the king, and
if so be that the king's wrath arise, and he say unto thee, Wherefore approached ye so nigh unto the city when ye did fight ?
21 knew ye not that they would shoot from the wall ? Who smote
o Abimelech the son of *p* Jerubbesheth ? did not a woman cast a
piece of a millstone upon him from the wall, that he died in
Thebez ? why went ye nigh the wall ? then say thou, Thy ser-
22 vant Uriah the Hittite is dead also. ¶ So the messenger went,
and came and shewed David all that Joab had sent him for.
23 And the messenger said unto David, Surely the men prevailed
against us, and came out unto us into the field, and we were
24 upon them even unto the entering of the gate. And the shooters
shot from off the wall upon thy servants; and *some* of the king's
servants be dead, and thy servant Uriah the Hittite is dead also.
25 Then David said unto the messenger, Thus shalt thou say unto
Joab, Let not this thing [1] displease thee, for the sword devoureth
[2] one as well as another: make thy battle more strong against
26 the city, and overthrow it : and encourage thou him. ¶ And
when the wife of Uriah heard that Uriah her husband was dead,
27 she mourned for her husband. And when the mourning was
past, David sent and fetched her to his house, and she *q* became
his wife, and bare him a son. ¶ But the thing that David had
done [3] displeased the LORD.

CHAP. 12. AND the LORD sent Nathan unto David. And *a* he
came unto him, and *b* said unto him, There were two men in one
2 city ; the one rich, and the other poor. The rich *man* had
3 exceeding many flocks and herds : but the poor *man* had
nothing, save one little ewe lamb, which he had bought and
nourished up : and it grew up together with him, and with his
children ; it did eat of his own [4] meat, and drank of his own
cup, and lay in his bosom, and was unto him as a daughter.
4 And there came a traveller unto the rich man, and he spared to
take of his own flock and of his own herd, to dress for the way-
faring man that was come unto him ; but took the poor man's
5 lamb, and dressed it for the man that was come to him. ¶ And
David's anger was greatly kindled against the man ; and he said
to Nathan, *As* the LORD liveth, the man that hath done this

o Judg. 9. 53.
p Judg. 6. 32,
Jerubbaal.

q ch. 12. 9.

a Ps. 51,
title.
b See ch. 14.
5, &c.
1 Kin. 20.
35—41.
Isai. 5. 3.

---

[1] Heb. *be evil in thine eyes.*
[2] Heb. *so and such.*
[3] Heb. *was evil in the eyes of.*
[4] Heb. *morsel.*

---

17. *the men of the city went out*] *i.e.* they
made a sally and attacked the troops which
were blockading the city on that side,
chiefly to entice them to pursue them, and
so come within shot of the archers who
lined the wall (*vv.* 20, 24).

there fell some of the people, &c.] They,
too, as well as the brave and faithful Uriah,
were victims of David's cruel artifice.

21. *Who smote Abimelech, &c.*] This
reference indicates the existence in David's
time of the national annals of that period
in an accessible form, and the king's habit

of reading, or having read to him, the history
of his country. (Cp. Esth. vi. 1.)

26. Bath-sheba's mourning, like that of
Abigail (1 Sam. xxv. 39-42), was probably
limited to the customary time of seven days.

XII. 1. Nathan came to David as if to
ask his judicial decision on the case about
to be submitted to him (cp. xiv. 2-11 ; 1 K.
xx. 35-41). The circumstances of the story
are exquisitely contrived to heighten the
pity of David for the oppressed, and his
indignation against the oppressor (1 Sam.
xxv. 13, 22).

6 *thing* ¹shall surely die: and he shall restore the lamb ᶜfourfold, ᶜ Ex. 22. 1.
7 because he did this thing, and because he had no pity. ¶ And Luke 19. 8.
Nathan said to David, Thou *art* the man. Thus saith the LORD
God of Israel, I ᵈanointed thee king over Israel, and I delivered ᵈ 1 Sam. 16.
8 thee out of the hand of Saul; and I gave thee thy master's 13.
house, and thy master's wives into thy bosom, and gave thee
the house of Israel and of Judah; and if *that had been* too little,
I would moreover have given unto thee such and such things.
9 ᵉWherefore hast thou ᶠdespised the commandment of the LORD, ᵉ See 1 Sam.
to do evil in his sight? ᵍthou hast killed Uriah the Hittite with 15. 19.
ᶠ Num. 15.
the sword, and hast taken his wife *to be* thy wife, and hast slain 31.
10 him with the sword of the children of Ammon. Now therefore ᵍ ch. 11. 15,
16, 17, 27.
ʰthe sword shall never depart from thine house; because thou ʰ Amos 7. 9.
hast despised me, and hast taken the wife of Uriah the Hittite
11 to be thy wife. Thus saith the LORD, Behold, I will raise up
evil against thee, out of thine own house, and I will ⁱtake thy ⁱ Deut. 28.
wives before thine eyes, and give *them* unto thy neighbour, and 30.
ch. 16. 22.
12 he shall lie with thy wives in the sight of this sun. For thou
didst *it* secretly: ᵏbut I will do this thing before all Israel, and ᵏ ch. 16. 22.
13 before the sun. ¶ ˡAnd David said unto Nathan, ᵐI have sinned ˡ See 1 Sam.
against the LORD. And Nathan said unto David, The LORD 15. 24.
14 also hath ⁿput away thy sin; thou shalt not die. Howbeit, ᵐ ch. 24. 10.
Job 7. 20.
because by this deed thou hast given great occasion to the Prov. 28. 13.
enemies of the LORD ᵒto blaspheme, the child also *that is* born ⁿ Mic. 7. 18.
15 unto thee shall surely die. And Nathan departed unto his ᵒ Isai. 52. 5.
house. ¶ And the LORD struck the child that Uriah's wife bare Ezek. 36. 20,
23.
16 unto David, and it was very sick. David therefore besought Rom. 2. 24.
God for the child; and David ²fasted, and went in, and ᵖlay all ᵖ ch. 13. 31.
17 night upon the earth. And the elders of his house arose, *and*
went to him, to raise him up from the earth: but he would not,
18 neither did he eat bread with them. And it came to pass on
the seventh day, that the child died. And the servants of
David feared to tell him that the child was dead: for they said,
Behold, while the child was yet alive, we spake unto him, and
he would not hearken unto our voice: how will he then ³vex
19 himself, if we tell him that the child is dead? But when David

---

¹ Or, is *worthy to die*, or, is *a son*
  of death, 1 Sam. 26, 16.

² Heb. *fasted a fast.*
³ Heb. *do hurt.*

---

6. *fourfold*] The exact number prescribed
by the Law (see marg. reff.), and acted upon
by Zaccheus. The LXX. has *sevenfold*, as
in Prov. vi. 31.

8. *and thy master's wives*, &c.] According
to Eastern custom, the royal harem was a
part of the royal inheritance. The prophets
spake in such matters according to the received opinions of their day, and not always
according to the abstract rule of right.
(Cp. Matt. xix. 4–9.)

11. See marg. reff. In both the points of
David's crime the retribution was according
to his sin. His adultery was punished by
Absalom's outrage, his murder by the bloodshed of domestic broils, which cost the lives
of at least three of his favourite sons, Amnon, Absalom, and Adonijah.

13. For a comment on David's words,
read Pss. li. and xxxii.

thou shalt not die] Not spoken of the
punishment of death as affixed to adultery
by the Mosaic Law : the application of that
law (Lev. xx. 10; Deut. xxii. 22; John viii.
5) to an absolute Eastern monarch was out
of the question. The death of the soul is
meant (cp. Ezek. xviii. 4, 13, 18).

16, 17. The death of the infant child of
one of the numerous harem of an Oriental
monarch would in general be a matter of
little moment to the father. The deep
feeling shown by David on this occasion is
both an indication of his affectionate and
tender nature, and also a proof of the
strength of his passion for Bath-sheba. He
went into his most private chamber, his
closet (Matt. vi. 6), and *lay upon the earth*
(xiii. 31), rather **"the ground,"** meaning
the floor of his chamber as opposed to his
couch.

saw that his servants whispered, David perceived that the child
was dead: therefore David said unto his servants, Is the child
20 dead? And they said, He is dead. Then David arose from the
earth, and washed, and [q]anointed *himself*, and changed his
apparel, and came into the house of the LORD, and [r]worshipped:
then he came to his own house; and when he required, they
21 set bread before him, and he did eat. Then said his servants
unto him, What thing *is* this that thou hast done? thou didst
fast and weep for the child, *while it was* alive; but when the
22 child was dead, thou didst rise and eat bread. And he said,
While the child was yet alive, I fasted and wept: [s]for I said,
Who can tell *whether* GOD will be gracious to me, that the child
23 may live? But now he is dead, wherefore should I fast? can I
bring him back again? I shall go to him, but [t]he shall not
24 return to me. ¶ And David comforted Bath-sheba his wife,
and went in unto her, and lay with her: and [u]she bare a son,
and [x]he called his name Solomon: and the LORD loved him.
25 And he sent by the hand of Nathan the prophet; and he called
26 his name [1]Jedidiah, because of the LORD. ¶ And [y]Joab fought
against [z]Rabbah of the children of Ammon, and took the royal
27 city. And Joab sent messengers to David, and said, I have
fought against Rabbah, and have taken the city of waters.
28 Now therefore gather the rest of the people together, and en-
camp against the city, and take it: lest I take the city, and [2]it
29 be called after my name. And David gathered all the people
together, and went to Rabbah, and fought against it, and took
30 it. [a]And he took their king's crown from off his head, the
weight whereof *was* a talent of gold with the precious stones:
and it was *set* on David's head. And he brought forth the spoil
31 of the city [3]in great abundance. And he brought forth the
people that *were* therein, and put *them* under saws, and under
harrows of iron, and under axes of iron, and made them pass
through the brickkiln: and thus did he unto all the cities of the
children of Ammon. So David and all the people returned unto
Jerusalem.

[q] Ruth 3. 3.
[r] Job 1. 20.
[s] See Isai. 38. 1, 5. Jonah 3. 9.
[t] Job 7. 8, 9, 10.
[u] Matt. 1. 6.
[x] 1 Chr. 22. 9.
[y] 1 Chr. 20. 1.
[z] Deut. 3. 11.
[a] 1 Chr. 20. 2.

[1] That is, *Beloved of the* LORD.
[2] Heb. *my name be called upon it.*
[3] Heb. *very great.*

24. *Solomon*] Or "peaceable," a name given to him at his circumcision. Cp. Luke i. 59. The giving of the name *Jedidiah*, by the Lord through Nathan, signified God's favour to the child, as in the cases of Abraham, Sarah, and Israel. The name *Jedidiah* (which contains the same root as the name *David*, viz., "to love") indicated prophetically, what God's Providence brought about actually, viz., the succession and glorious reign of Solomon over Israel.

27. *the city of waters*] The lower town of Rabbah (the modern Ammâm), so called from a stream which rises within it and flows through it. The upper town with the citadel lay on a hill to the north of the stream, and was probably not tenable for any length of time after the supply of water was cut off.

30. *their king's crown*] The word rendered *their king* (*Malcham*) is also the name of the national idol of the Ammonites (Jer. xlix. 1, 3 marg.; Amos i. 15; Zeph. i. 5). Moreover, the weight of the crown, which is calculated to be equal to 100 or 125 pounds weight, is far too great for a man to wear. On the whole, it seems most probable that the idol Malcam is here meant.

31. For the saw as an implement of torture cp. Heb. xi. 37.

harrows of iron] Or rather *thrashing-machines* (Isai. xxviii. 27, xli. 15, &c.).

axes] The word so rendered occurs only here and in 1 Chr. xx. 3. It evidently means some cutting instrument.

made them pass through the brick-kiln] The phrase is that always used of the cruel process of making their children *pass through* the fire to Moloch, and it is likely that David punished this idolatrous practice by inflicting something similar upon the worshippers of Moloch. The cruelty of these executions belongs to the barbarous manners of the age, and was provoked by the conduct

Chap. 13. AND it came to pass after this, [a]that Absalom the son of David had a fair sister, whose name *was* [b]Tamar; and Amnon 2 the son of David loved her. And Amnon was so vexed, that he fell sick for his sister Tamar; for she *was* a virgin; and 3 [1]Amnon thought it hard for him to do any thing to her. But Amnon had a friend, whose name *was* Jonadab, [c]the son of Shimeah David's brother: and Jonadab *was* a very subtil man. 4 And he said unto him, Why *art* thou, *being* the king's son, [2]lean [3]from day to day? wilt thou not tell me? And Amnon 5 said unto him, I love Tamar, my brother Absalom's sister. And Jonadab said unto him, Lay thee down on thy bed, and make thyself sick: and when thy father cometh to see thee, say unto him, I pray thee, let my sister Tamar come, and give me meat, and dress the meat in my sight, that I may see *it*, and eat *it* at 6 her hand. ¶So Amnon lay down, and made himself sick: and when the king was come to see him, Amnon said unto the king, I pray thee, let Tamar my sister come, and [d]make me a couple 7 of cakes in my sight, that I may eat at her hand. Then David sent home to Tamar, saying, Go now to thy brother Amnon's 8 house, and dress him meat. So Tamar went to her brother Amnon's house; and he was laid down. And she took [4]flour, and kneaded *it*, and made cakes in his sight, and did bake the 9 cakes. And she took a pan, and poured *them* out before him; but he refused to eat. And Amnon said, [e]Have out all men 10 from me. And they went out every man from him. ¶And Amnon said unto Tamar, Bring the meat into the chamber, that I may eat of thine hand. And Tamar took the cakes which she had made, and brought *them* into the chamber to Amnon 11 her brother. And when she had brought *them* unto him to eat, he [f]took hold of her, and said unto her, Come lie with me, my 12 sister. And she answered him, Nay, my brother, do not [5]force me; for [g][6]no such thing ought to be done in Israel: do not 13 thou this [h]folly. And I, whither shall I cause my shame to go? and as for thee, thou shalt be as one of the fools in Israel. Now therefore, I pray thee, speak unto the king; [i]for he will

[a] ch. 3. 2, 3.
[b] 1 Chr. 3. 9.

[c] See 1 Sam. 16. 9.

[d] Gen. 18. 6.

[e] Gen. 45. 1.

[f] Gen. 39. 12.

[g] Lev. 18. 9, 11. & 20. 17.
[h] Judg. 19. 23. & 20. 6.
[i] See Lev. 18. 9, 11.

[1] Heb. *it was marvellous,* or, *hidden in the eyes of Amnon.* See Gen. 18. 14.　[2] Heb. *thin.*　[3] Heb. *morning by morning.*　[4] Or, *paste.*　[5] Heb. *humble me,* Gen. 34. 2.　[6] Heb. *it ought not so to be done.*

---

of the Ammonites (x. 1-4; 1 Sam. xi. 1, 2), but is utterly indefensible under the light of the Gospel. If Rabbah was taken before David's penitence, he may have been in an unusually harsh and severe frame of mind. The unpleasant recollection of Uriah's death would be likely to sour and irritate him to the utmost.

XIII. **1.** The history here, down to the end of ch. xxiii. (excepting a few particulars), is omitted in the Book of Chronicles.

3. *Shimeah*] Called *Shamma* (marg. ref.), was Jesse's third son.

subtil] Lit., *Wise.* The word is generally used in a good sense, but here, and in Job v. 13, it means *crafty.*

5, 6. *make thyself sick*] "**Feign thyself to be ill.**" (Cp. xiv. 2.)

that I may see it] He was to feign that he could not fancy anything that came from the kitchen, but that if he saw it cooked he should be able to eat it.

6, 9. *make me cakes…a pan*] The words here used occur nowhere else, and the etymology is doubtful. Some particular kind of cake or pudding is meant (*v.* 8), called a *lebibah ;* according to some, it was, from its etymology, shaped like a heart.

9. The dish into which she poured the *lebibah* was doubtless borne to him by one of the servants into the chamber where he lay, and from which, the doors being open, he could see the outer room where Tamar prepared the meat.

12. Tamar's words are a verbal quotation from Gen. xxxiv. 7. The natural inference is that Tamar knew the passage in Genesis, and wished to profit by the warning it contained. (Cp. also *v.* 13.)

13. *my shame*] Better, "**my reproach.**" Cp. Gen. xxx. 23, xxxiv. 14 ; 1 Sam. xi. 2.

speak unto the king, &c.] It cannot be inferred with certainty from this that marriages were usual among half brothers and

14 not withhold me from thee. Howbeit he would not hearken
unto her voice : but, being stronger than she, ^kforced her, and
15 lay with her. ¶Then Amnon hated her ¹exceedingly; so that
the hatred wherewith he hated her *was* greater than the love
wherewith he had loved her. And Amnon said unto her, Arise,
16 be gone. And she said unto him, *There is* no cause : this evil
in sending me away *is* greater than the other that thou didst
17 unto me. But he would not hearken unto her. Then he called
his servant that ministered unto him, and said, Put now this
18 *woman* out from me, and bolt the door after her. And *she had*

^la garment of divers colours upon her : for with such robes were
the king's daughters *that were* virgins apparelled. Then his
19 servant brought her out, and bolted the door after her. ¶And

Tamar put ^mashes on her head, and rent her garment of divers
colours that *was* on her, and ⁿlaid her hand on her head, and
20 went on crying. And Absalom her brother said unto her,
Hath ²Amnon thy brother been with thee ? but hold now thy
peace, my sister : he *is* thy brother ; ³regard not this thing. So
Tamar remained ⁴desolate in her brother Absalom's house.
21 ¶But when king David heard of all these things, he was very

22 wroth. And Absalom spake unto his brother Amnon ^oneither
good nor bad : for Absalom ^phated Amnon, because he had forced
23 his sister Tamar. ¶And it came to pass after two full years, that
Absalom ^qhad sheepshearers in Baal-hazor, which *is* beside
24 Ephraim : and Absalom invited all the king's sons. And Absalom came to the king, and said, Behold now, thy servant hath
sheepshearers ; let the king, I beseech thee, and his servants go
25 with thy servant. And the king said to Absalom, Nay, my
son, let us not all now go, lest we be chargeable unto thee.
And he pressed him : howbeit he would not go, but blessed him.
26 Then said Absalom, If not, I pray thee, let my brother Amnon
27 go with us. And the king said unto him, Why should he go
with thee ? But Absalom pressed him, that he let Amnon and
28 all the king's sons go with him. ¶Now Absalom had commanded his servants, saying, Mark ye now when Amnon's

¹ Heb. *with great hatred greatly.*　　² Heb. *Aminon.*　　³ Heb. *set not thine heart.*
⁴ Heb. *and desolate.*

sisters in the time of David. The Levitical
law forbade them (marg. ref.), and Tamar
may have merely wished to temporise. On
the other hand, the debasing and unhu-
manizing institution of the harem, itself
contrary to the law of Moses (Deut. xvii.
17), may well have led to other deviations
from its precepts, and the precedent of
Abraham (Gen. xx. 12) may have seemed
to give some sanction to this particular
breach of it.

16. The sense of the passage probably is,
*And she spake with him on account of this
great wrong in sending me away, greater than
the other wrong which thou hast done me* (said
she), *but he hearkened not unto her.* The
Heb. text is probably corrupt, and the
writer blends Tamar's words with his own
narrative.

18. *a garment of divers colours*] See Gen.
xxxvii. 3. Some prefer here (and there) "a
tunic with sleeves," a tunic reaching to the

extremities, *i.e.* the hands and feet, and
worn over the common tunic, in room of a
robe.

19. *laid her hand on her head*] To hold on
the ashes (see marg. reff.).

went on crying] *i.e.* "**went away, crying
out as she went.**"

21. The LXX. adds, what is a good explanation, *but he did not vex the spirit of
Amnon his son, because he loved him, because
he was his first-born.* This want of justice in
David's conduct, and favouritism to Amnon,
probably rankled in Absalom's heart, and
was the first seed of his after rebellion.

23. Sheepshearing was always a time of
feasting (marg. reff.). Baal-hazor is not
known.

26. He mentions Amnon as being the
king's first-born. If he could not have the
king's company, let him at least have that
of the heir apparent, and the king's other
sons.

[r]heart is merry with wine, and when I say unto you, Smite
Amnon; then kill him, fear not: [1]have not I commanded you?
29 be courageous, and be [2]valiant. And the servants of Absalom
did unto Amnon as Absalom had commanded. Then all the
king's sons arose, and every man [3]gat him up upon his mule,
30 and fled. ¶And it came to pass, while they were in the way,
that tidings came to David, saying, Absalom hath slain all the
31 king's sons, and there is not one of them left. Then the king
arose, and [s]tare his garments, and [t]lay on the earth; and all
32 his servants stood by with their clothes rent. And [u]Jonadab,
the son of Shimeah David's brother, answered and said, Let
not my lord suppose *that* they have slain all the young men
the king's sons; for Amnon only is dead: for by the [4]appoint-
ment of Absalom this hath been [5]determined from the day that
33 he forced his sister Tamar. Now therefore [x]let not my lord the
king take the thing to his heart, to think that all the king's
34 sons are dead: for Amnon only is dead. [y]But Absalom fled.
¶And the young man that kept the watch lifted up his eyes,
and looked, and, behold, there came much people by the way
35 of the hill side behind him. And Jonadab said unto the king,
Behold, the king's sons come: [6]as thy servant said, so it is.
36 And it came to pass, as soon as he had made an end of speaking,
that, behold, the king's sons came, and lifted up their voice and
wept: and the king also and all his servants wept [7]very sore.
37 ¶But Absalom fled, and went to [z]Talmai, the son of [8]Ammihud,
38 king of Geshur. And *David* mourned for his son every day. So
Absalom fled, and went to [a]Geshur, and was there three years.
39 And the *soul of* king David [9]longed to go forth unto Absalom:
for he was [b]comforted concerning Amnon, seeing he was
dead.

CHAP. 14. NOW Joab the son of Zeruiah perceived that the king's
2 heart *was* [a]toward Absalom. And Joab sent to [b]Tekoah, and
fetched thence a wise woman, and said unto her, I pray thee,
feign thyself to be a mourner, [c]and put on now mourning
apparel, and anoint not thyself with oil, but be as a woman that

Side notes:
[r] Judg. 19. 6, 9, 22. Ruth 3. 7. 1 Sam. 25. 36. Esth. 1. 10. Ps. 104. 15.
[s] ch. 1. 11. [t] ch. 12. 16. [u] ver. 3.
[x] ch. 19. 19.
[y] ver. 38.
[z] ch. 3. 3.
[a] ch. 14. 23, 32. & 15. 8. [b] Gen. 38. 12.
[a] ch. 13. 39. [b] 2 Chr. 11. 6. [c] See Ruth 3. 3.

[1] Or, *will you not, since I have commanded you?* Josh. 1. 9.
[2] Heb. *sons of valour.*
[3] Heb. *rode.*
[4] Heb. *mouth.*
[5] Or, *settled.*
[6] Heb. *according to the word of thy servant.*
[7] Heb. *with a great weeping greatly.*
[8] Or, *Ammihur.*
[9] Or, *was consumed,* Ps. 84. 2.

---

29. *upon his mule*] So in 1 K. i. 33, 38 the mule is the royal animal on which David himself rides. In 2 Sam. xviii. 9 Absalom rides upon a mule.

32. The history supplies another (cp. *v.* 3) instance of Jonadab's subtlety and sagacity. He at once gave the true explanation of the catastrophe at Baal-hazor, in spite of the false rumour.

by the appointment of Absalom, &c.] Meaning that Absalom's resolution to slay Amnon had been formed at the time, and only waited an opportunity to give expression to it.

34. *Absalom fled*] This is the sequel to *v.* 29. The king's sons rose from table and fled, and Absalom taking advantage of the confusion, also escaped and fled. This information is inserted here to account for the king's sons returning unmolested.

35. The watchman, as his duty was, had sent immediate notice to the king that he saw a crowd approaching (see 2 K. ix. 17-20). Jonadab, who was with the king, was prompt to give the explanation.

37. See marg. ref.

Ammihur (see marg.) is found as a Punic name.

39. *longed to go forth*] Rather, "**longed after Absalom,**" literally, *was consumed in going forth*, with a sense of disappointed hope.

XIV. 2. *Tekoah*] In the south of Judah, six miles from Bethlehem, the modern *Tekua*. The rough, wild district was well suited for the lawless profession of the wise woman; it abounds in caves, as does the country near Endor.

3 had a long time mourned for the dead: and come to the king,
and speak on this manner unto him. So Joab ^dput the words
4 in her mouth. ¶And when the woman of Tekoah spake to the
king, she ^efell on her face to the ground, and did obeisance, and
5 said, ¹Help, O king. And the king said unto her, What aileth
thee? And she answered, ^gI *am* indeed a widow woman, and
6 mine husband is dead. And thy handmaid had two sons, and
they two strove together in the field, and *there was* ²none to part
7 them, but the one smote the other, and slew him. And, behold,
^hthe whole family is risen against thine handmaid, and they
said, Deliver him that smote his brother, that we may kill him,
for the life of his brother whom he slew; and we will destroy
the heir also: and so they shall quench my coal which is left,
and shall not leave to my husband *neither* name nor remainder
8 ³upon the earth. ¶And the king said unto the woman, Go to
9 thine house, and I will give charge concerning thee. And the
woman of Tekoah said unto the king, My lord, O king, ⁱthe
iniquity *be* on me, and on my father's house: ^kand the king and
10 his throne *be* guiltless. And the king said, Whosoever saith
ought unto thee, bring him to me, and he shall not touch thee
11 any more. Then said she, I pray thee, let the king remember
the LORD thy God, ⁴that thou wouldest not suffer ^lthe revengers
of blood to destroy any more, lest they destroy my son. And
he said, ^m*As* the LORD liveth, there shall not one hair of thy
12 son fall to the earth. ¶Then the woman said, Let thine handmaid, I pray thee, speak *one* word unto my lord the king. And
13 he said, Say on. And the woman said, Wherefore then hast
thou thought such a thing against ⁿthe people of God? for the
king doth speak this thing as one which is faulty, in that the
14 king doth not fetch home again ^ohis banished. For we ^pmust
needs die, and *are* as water spilt on the ground, which cannot

Margin references:
d ver. 19.
Ex. 4. 15.

e 1 Sam. 20.
41.
h. 1. 2.
f See 2 Kin.
6. 26, 28.
g See ch. 12.
1.

h Num. 35.
19.
Deut. 19. 12.

i Gen. 27. 13.
1 Sam. 25. 24.
Matt. 27. 25.
k ch. 3. 28,
29.
1 Kin. 2. 33.

l Num. 35.
19.

m 1 Sam. 14.
45.
Acts 27. 34.

n Judg. 20. 2.
o ch. 13. 37,
38.
p Job 34. 15.
Heb. 9. 27.

¹ Heb. *Save.*
² Heb. *no deliverer between them.*
³ Heb. *upon the face of the earth.*
⁴ Heb. *that the revenger of blood do not multiply to destroy.*

**3. *come to the king*] The king as a judge
was accessible to all his subjects (xv. 2; cp.
1 K. iii. 16).

**4. *spake*] Seems to be an accidental error
for *came*, which is found in many MSS. and
Versions.

Help] Lit., *save* (see marg). It is the same
cry as *Hosanna, i.e. save now* (Ps. cxviii. 25).

**7. *the whole family*, &c.] This indicates
that all the king's sons, and the whole
court, were against Absalom, and that the
knowledge of this was what hindered David
from yielding to his affection and recalling
him.

**8. *I will give charge*, &c.] Indirectly grant-
ing her petition, and assenting that her
son's life should be spared.

**9. *the iniquity be on me*, &c.] Cp. the prin-
ciple in Gen. ix. 5, 6; Num. xxxv. 30-34.
The woman therefore says, if there is any
such guilt in sparing my son, may it rest
upon me and my house, not on David and
his throne. Cp. iii. 28. The cunning
speech of the woman extracted a more direct promise of protection from the king
(*v.* 1).

**12. Having at last obtained what she
wanted, the king's oath that her son should
not die, she proceeds to the case of Absalom. The meaning of *v.* 13 may be paraphrased thus:—" If you have done right as
regards my son, how is it that you harbour
such a purpose of vengeance against Absalom as to keep him, one of God's people, an
outcast in a heathen country, far from the
worship of the God of Israel? Upon your
own showing you are guilty of a great fault
in not allowing Absalom to return."

the king doth speak, &c.] Literally, "**And
from the king speaking this word** (this
sentence of absolution to my son) he is **as
one guilty**; *i.e.* the sentence you have pronounced in favour of my son condemns your
own conduct towards Absalom."

his banished] The use of the word as applied to one of the people of God driven
into a heathen land, is well illustrated by
Deut. xxx. 4, 5; Jer. xl. 12; Mic. iv. 6;
Zeph. iii. 19.

**14. *neither doth God respect any person*]
Some prefer the margin: "**And God does
not take away life**, in the case of every sin

be gathered up again; ¹neither doth God respect *any* person: yet doth he *q*devise means, that his banished be not expelled 15 from him. Now therefore that I am come to speak of this thing unto my lord the king, *it is* because the people have made me afraid: and thy handmaid said, I will now speak unto the king; it may be that the king will perform the request of his hand- 16 maid. For the king will hear, to deliver his handmaid out of the hand of the man *that would* destroy me and my son together 17 out of the inheritance of God. Then thine handmaid said, The word of my lord the king shall now be ²comfortable: for *r*as an angel of God, so *is* my lord the king ³to discern good and bad: 18 therefore the LORD thy God will be with thee. ¶Then the king answered and said unto the woman, Hide not from me, I pray thee, the thing that I shall ask thee. And the woman said, Let 19 my lord the king now speak. And the king said, *Is not* the hand of Joab with thee in all this? And the woman answered and said, *As* thy soul liveth, my lord the king, none can turn to the right hand or to the left from ought that my lord the king hath spoken: for thy servant Joab, he bade me, and *s*he put all these 20 words in the mouth of thine handmaid: to fetch about this form of speech hath thy servant Joab done this thing: and my lord *is* wise, *t*according to the wisdom of an angel of God, to know 21 all *things* that *are* in the earth. ¶And the king said unto Joab, Behold now, I have done this thing: go therefore, bring the 22 young man Absalom again. And Joab fell to the ground on his face, and bowed himself, and ⁴thanked the king: and Joab said, To day thy servant knoweth that I have found grace in thy sight, my lord, O king, in that the king hath fulfilled the re- 23 quest of ⁵his servant. So Joab arose *u*and went to Geshur, and 24 brought Absalom to Jerusalem. And the king said, Let him turn to his own house, and let him *x*not see my face. So Ab- salom returned to his own house, and saw not the king's face. 25 ¶⁶But in all Israel there was none to be so much praised as Absalom for his beauty: *y*from the sole of his foot even to the 26 crown of his head there was no blemish in him. And when he polled his head, (for it was at every year's end that he polled *it*: because *the hair* was heavy on him, therefore he polled it:) he weighed the hair of his head at two hundred shekels after the 27 king's weight. And *z*unto Absalom there were born three sons, and one daughter, whose name *was* Tamar: she was a woman

q Num. 35. 15, 25, 28.

r ver. 20. ch. 19. 27.

s ver. 3.

t ver. 17. ch. 19. 27.

u ch. 13. 37.

x Gen. 43. 3. ch. 3. 13.

y Isai. 1. 6.

z See ch. 18. 18.

---

¹ Or, *because God hath not taken away* his *life,* he hath also devised means, *&c.*

² Heb. *for rest.*
³ Heb. *to hear.*
⁴ Heb. *blessed.*
⁵ Or, *thy.*

⁶ Heb. *And as Absalom there was not a beautiful man in all Israel to praise greatly.*

---

that deserves death, *e.g.* David's own case (xii. 13), **but devises devices that the wanderer may not be** for ever **expelled from him,** *i.e.* for the return of penitent sinners."

15. *the people have made me afraid*] She pretends still that her suit was a real one, and that she was in fear of the people ("the whole family," *v.* 7) setting upon her and her son.

17. *as an angel of God*] Rather, as "the" Angel of God; and therefore whatever David decided would be right.

24. *Let him not see my face*] We are not told why David adopted this half-measure.

Possibly Bath-sheba's influence may have been exerted to keep Absalom in disgrace for the sake of Solomon.

26. *two hundred shekels,* &c.] The exact weight cannot be determined. If these *shekels after the king's weight* were the same as *shekels of the sanctuary,* the weight would be about 6 lbs., which is incredible; *twenty* shekels is more probable.

27. *three sons*] These probably died in infancy (see marg. ref.) From Tamar must have been born Maachah, the mother of Abijah, and the favourite wife of Rehoboam (1 K. xv. 2; 2 Chr. xi. 20–22).

a ver. 24.

28 of a fair countenance. ¶ So Absalom dwelt two full years in
29 Jerusalem, *a*and saw not the king's face. Therefore Absalom
sent for Joab, to have sent him to the king; but he would not
come to him: and when he sent again the second time, he would
30 not come. Therefore he said unto his servants, See, Joab's field
is ¹near mine, and he hath barley there; go and set it on fire.
31 And Absalom's servants set the field on fire. Then Joab arose,
and came to Absalom unto *his* house, and said unto him, Where-
32 fore have thy servants set my field on fire? And Absalom
answered Joab, Behold, I sent unto thee, saying, Come hither,
that I may send thee to the king, to say, Wherefore am I come
from Geshur? *it had been* good for me *to have been* there still:
now therefore let me see the king's face; and if there be *any*
33 iniquity in me, let him kill me. So Joab came to the king, and
told him: and when he had called for Absalom, he came to the
king, and bowed himself on his face to the ground before the
king: and the king *b*kissed Absalom.

b Gen. 33. 4.
Luke 15. 20.
a ch. 12. 11.
b 1 Kin. 1. 5.

CHAP. 15. AND *a*it came to pass after this, that Absalom *b*prepared
2 him chariots and horses, and fifty men to run before him. And
Absalom rose up early, and stood beside the way of the gate:
and it was *so*, that when any man that had a controversy ²came
to the king for judgment, then Absalom called unto him, and
said, Of what city *art* thou? And he said, Thy servant *is* of one
3 of the tribes of Israel. And Absalom said unto him, See, thy
matters *are* good and right; but ³*there is* no man *deputed* of the

c Judg. 9. 29.

4 king to hear thee. Absalom said moreover, *c*Oh that I were
made judge in the land, that every man which hath any suit or
5 cause might come unto me, and I would do him justice! And
it was *so*, that when any man came nigh *to him* to do him
obeisance, he put forth his hand, and took him, and kissed him.
6 And on this manner did Absalom to all Israel that came to the

d Rom. 16.
18.
e 1 Sam. 16.
1.

king for judgment: *d*so Absalom stole the hearts of the men of
7 Israel. ¶ And it came to pass, *e*after forty years, that Absalom
said unto the king, I pray thee, let me go and pay my vow,

---

¹ Heb. *near my place.*
² Heb. *to come.*

³ Or, *none will hear thee
from the king* downward.

---

33. *kissed*] This was the pledge of reconciliation. (See marg. reff. and Gen. xlv. 15.)

XV. **1.** *And it came to pass, &c.*] The
working out of Nathan's prophecy (marg.
ref.) is the clue to the course of the narrative. How long after Absalom's return
these events occurred we are not told.

2. *beside the way of the gate*] See Ruth iv.
1 note.

3. To flatter each man by pronouncing a
favourable verdict in his case, to excite a
sense of grievance and discontent by cen-
suring the king for remissness in trying the
causes brought before him by his subjects,
and to suggest a sure and easy remedy for
all such grievances, viz. to make Absalom
king ; all this, coupled with great affability
and courtesy, which his personal beauty and
high rank made all the more effective, were
the arts by which Absalom worked his way
into favour with the people, who were light
and fickle as himself.

6. *stole the hearts*] i.e. *deceived them*, for
so the same phrase means (Gen. xxxi. 20,
26).

7. *forty years*] An obvious clerical error,
though a very ancient one for *four years*,
which may date from Absalom's return
from Geshur, or from his reconciliation with
David, or from the commencement of the
criminal schemes to which *v.* 1 refers.

Hebron] This, as having been the old
capital of David's kingdom and Absalom's
birthplace, was well chosen. It was a natural
centre, had probably many inhabitants discontented at the transfer of the . government to Jerusalem, and contained many of
the friends of Absalom's youth. As the
place of his birth (cp. 1 Sam. xx. 6), it
afforded a plausible pretext for holding
there the great sacrificial feast ("the serving the Lord," *v.* 8), which Absalom pretended to have vowed to hold to the glory
of God.

8 which I have vowed unto the Lord, in Hebron. *f*For thy servant *g*vowed a vow *h*while I abode at Geshur in Syria, saying, If the Lord shall bring me again indeed to Jerusalem, then I

9 will serve the Lord. And the king said unto him, Go in peace.

10 So he arose, and went to Hebron. ¶ But Absalom sent spies throughout all the tribes of Israel, saying, As soon as ye hear the sound of the trumpet, then ye shall say, Absalom reigneth

11 in Hebron. And with Absalom went two hundred men out of Jerusalem, *that were* *i*called; and they went *k*in their simplicity,

12 and they knew not any thing. And Absalom sent for Ahithophel the Gilonite, *l*David's counsellor, from his city, *even* from *m*Giloh, while he offered sacrifices. And the conspiracy was strong; for the people *n*increased continually with Absalom.

13 ¶ And there came a messenger to David, saying, *o*The hearts of

14 the men of Israel are after Absalom. And David said unto all his servants that *were* with him at Jerusalem, Arise, and let us *p*flee; for we shall not *else* escape from Absalom : make speed to depart, lest he overtake us suddenly, and *1*bring evil upon us,

15 and smite the city with the edge of the sword. And the king's servants said unto the king, Behold, thy servants *are ready to do*

16 whatsoever my lord the king shall *2*appoint. And *q*the king went forth, and all his household *3*after him. And the king left *r*ten women, *which were* concubines, to keep the house.

17 ¶ And the king went forth, and all the people after him, and

18 tarried in a place that was far off. And all his servants passed on beside him ; *s*and all the Cherethites, and all the Pelethites, and all the Gittites, six hundred men which came after him

19 from Gath, passed on before the king. Then said the king to *t*Ittai the Gittite, Wherefore goest thou also with us ? return to thy place, and abide with the king : for thou *art* a stranger, and

20 also an exile. Whereas thou camest *but* yesterday, should I this day *4*make thee go up and down with us ? seeing I go

21 *u*whither I may, return thou, and take back thy brethren: mercy and truth *be* with thee. And Ittai answered the king, and said,

f 1 Sam. 16. 2.
g Gen. 28. 20, 21.
h ch. 13. 38.

i 1 Sam. 9. 13. & 16. 3.
Matt. 22. 14.
k Gen. 20. 5.
l Ps. 41. 9. & 55. 12.
m Josh. 17. 51.
n Ps. 3. 1.
o ver. 6.
Judg. 9. 3.
p ch. 19. 9.
Ps. 3, title.

q Ps. 3, title.

r ch. 16. 21, 22.

s ch. 8. 18.

t ch. 13. 2.

u 1 Sam. 23. 13.

---

1 Heb. *thrust.*
2 Heb. *choose.*
3 Heb. *at his feet.*
4 Heb. *make thee wander in going.*

---

12. *Ahithophel*] It has been with great probability supposed that Ahithophel was estranged from David by personal resentment for his conduct in the matter of Bathsheba and Uriah (see xi. 3).

while he offered sacrifices] Rather, that Absalom sent for Ahithophel to be present when he offered the sacrifices ; the intention being that all who partook of the sacrifice should be bound together to prosecute the enterprise. Absalom, too, would take advantage of the excitement of the great feast to inflame the ardour of the guests, and pledge them irrevocably to his cause.

14. *and smite the city*] David's kind nature induced him to spare Jerusalem the horrors of a siege, and the risk of being taken by assault. He had no standing army with which to resist this sudden attack from so unexpected a quarter. Possibly too he remembered Nathan's prophecy (xii. 10–12).

18. *passed on*] Rather, "**crossed**" the brook Kidron, as in *vv.* 22, 23.

Gittites] During David's residence in the country of the Philistines he attached such a band to himself ; and after the settlement of his kingdom, and the subjugation of the Philistines, the band received recruits from Gath, perhaps with the king of Gath's consent. They were now under the command of Ittai the Gittite, a foreigner (*v.* 19), and "his brethren" (*v.* 20). The number 600 probably indicates that this band or regiment of Gittites had its origin in David's band of 600 (1 Sam. xxiii. 13, xxvii. 2). They were at first, it is likely, all Israelites, then Gittites mixed with Israelites, and at last all Gittites.

20. *thou camest but yesterday*] Meaning, "Thou art not a native Israelite, but only a sojourner for a few years, it is not reason therefore that thou shouldst share my calamities. Return to thy place, thy adopted home Jerusalem, and to the king, Absalom" (*vv.* 34, 35).

g Ruth 1. 16,
17.
Prov. 17. 17.
& 18. 24.

*x*As the LORD liveth, and *as* my lord the king liveth, surely in
what place my lord the king shall be, whether in death or life,
22 even there also will thy servant be. And David said to Ittai,
Go and pass over. And Ittai the Gittite passed over, and all
23 his men, and all the little ones that *were* with him. And all
the country wept with a loud voice, and all the people passed
over: the king also himself passed over the brook ¹Kidron, and

y ch. 16. 2.

all the people passed over, toward the way of the *y*wilderness.

z Num. 4. 15.

24 ¶And lo Zadok also, and all the Levites *were* with him, *z*bearing
the ark of the covenant of God: and they set down the ark of
God; and Abiathar went up, until all the people had done
25 passing out of the city. And the king said unto Zadok, Carry
back the ark of God into the city: if I shall find favour in the

a Ps. 43. 3.

eyes of the LORD, he *a*will bring me again, and shew me *both* it,

b Num. 14. 8.
ch. 22. 20.
1 Kin. 10. 9.
2 Chr. 9. 8.
Isai. 62. 4.
c 1 Sam. 3.
18.
d 1 Sam. 9. 9.
e See ch. 17.
17.
f ch. 17. 16.

26 and his habitation: but if he thus say, I have no *b*delight in
thee; behold, *here am* I, *c*let him do to me as seemeth good unto
27 him. The king said also unto Zadok the priest, *Art not* thou a
*d*seer? return into the city in peace, and *e*your two sons with
28 you, Ahimaaz thy son, and Jonathan the son of Abiathar. See,
*f*I will tarry in the plain of the wilderness, until there come
29 word from you to certify me. Zadok therefore and Abiathar
carried the ark of God again to Jerusalem: and they tarried

g ch. 19. 4.
Esth. 6. 12.
h Isai. 20. 2, 4.
i Jer. 14. 3, 4.
k Ps. 126. 6.
l Ps. 3. 1, 2.
& 55. 12, &c.
m ch. 16. 23.
& 17. 14, 23.

30 there. ¶And David went up by the ascent of *mount* Olivet,
²and wept as he went up, and *g*had his head covered, and he
went *h*barefoot: and all the people that *was* with him *i*covered
every man his head, and they went up, *k*weeping as they went
31 up. And *one* told David, saying, *l*Ahithophel *is* among the
conspirators with Absalom. And David said, O LORD, I pray
32 thee, *m*turn the counsel of Ahithophel into foolishness. ¶And
it came to pass, that *when* David was come to the top *of the*

n Josh. 16. 2.
o ch. 1. 2.

mount, where he worshipped God, behold, Hushai the *n*Archite
came to meet him *o*with his coat rent, and earth upon his head:
33 unto whom David said, If thou passest on with me, then thou

p ch. 19. 35.

34 shalt be *p*a burden unto me: but if thou return to the city, and

q ch. 16. 19.

say unto Absalom, *q*I will be thy servant, O king; *as* I *have
been* thy father's servant hitherto, so *will* I now also *be* thy servant: then mayest thou for me defeat the counsel of Ahithophel.
35 And *hast thou* not there with thee Zadok and Abiathar the
priests? therefore it shall be, *that* what thing soever thou shalt

r ch. 17. 15,
16.
s ver. 27.

hear out of the king's house, *r*thou shalt tell *it* to Zadok and
36 Abiathar the priests. Behold, *they have* there *s*with them their
two sons, Ahimaaz Zadok's *son*, and Jonathan Abiathar's *son;*
and by them ye shall send unto me every thing that ye can hear.

t ch. 16. 16.
1 Chr. 27. 33.
u ch. 16. 15.

37 So Hushai *t*David's friend came into the city, *u*and Absalom
came into Jerusalem.

¹ Called, John 18. 1, *Cedron*.   ² Heb. *going up, and weeping*.

---

24. *Abiathar went up*] i.e. continued to
ascend the Mount of Olives. Abiathar was
High Priest (1 K. ii. 35). Perhaps Zadok
is addressed by David (*v.* 25) as the chief
of those who were actually bearing the
Ark.

27. *Art not thou a seer?*] If the text be correct, the sense would be, *Art thou not a
seer? therefore go back to the city, and observe,
and certify me of what thou seest* (*v.* 28).
Others, by a slight alteration of the original

text, read "Art not thou a chief" (priest),
&c.

30. *his head covered*] See marg. reff. and
Jer. xiv. 3, 4; Ezek. xxiv. 17; the sign of
deep mourning.

32. Render ... "**when David was come
to the top** of the mount **where** people **worship God.**" The top here, and in xvi. 1, is
used almost as a proper name. No doubt
there was a high-place upon the top of the
Mount of Olives.

CHAP. 16. AND ^awhen David was a little past the top *of the hill*, behold, ^bZiba the servant of Mephibosheth met him, with a couple of asses saddled, and upon them two hundred *loaves* of bread, and an hundred bunches of raisins, and an hundred of 2 summer fruits, and a bottle of wine. And the king said unto Ziba, What meanest thou by these? And Ziba said, The asses *be* for the king's household to ride on; and the bread and summer fruit for the young men to eat; and the wine, ^cthat 3 such as be faint in the wilderness may drink. And the king said, And where *is* thy master's son? ^dAnd Ziba said unto the king, Behold, he abideth at Jerusalem: for he said, To day shall 4 the house of Israel restore me the kingdom of my father. ^eThen said the king to Ziba, Behold, thine *are* all that *pertained* unto Mephibosheth. And Ziba said, ¹I humbly beseech thee *that I* 5 may find grace in thy sight, my lord, O king. ¶ And when king David came to Bahurim, behold, thence came out a man of the family of the house of Saul, whose name *was* ^fShimei, the son of 6 Gera: ²he came forth, and cursed still as he came. And he cast stones at David, and at all the servants of king David: and all the people and all the mighty men *were* on his right hand and 7 on his left. And thus said Shimei when he cursed, Come out, 8 come out, thou ³bloody man, and thou ^gman of Belial: the LORD hath ^hreturned upon thee all ⁱthe blood of the house of Saul, in whose stead thou hast reigned; and the LORD hath delivered the kingdom into the hand of Absalom thy son: and, ⁴behold, thou *art taken* in thy mischief, because thou *art* a 9 bloody man. ¶ Then said Abishai the son of Zeruiah unto the king, Why should this ^kdead dog ^lcurse my lord the king? let 10 me go over, I pray thee, and take off his head. And the king said, ^mWhat have I to do with you, ye sons of Zeruiah? so let

Margin references (right column):
^a ch. 15. 30, 32.
^b ch. 9. 2.
^c ch. 15. 23. & 17. 29.
^d ch. 19. 27.
^e Prov. 18. 13.
^f ch. 19. 16. 1 Kin. 2. 8, 44.
^g Deut. 13. 13.
^h Judg. 9. 24, 56, 57. 1 Kin. 2. 32, 33.
ⁱ See ch. 1. 16. & 3. 28, 29. & 4. 11. 12.
^k 1 Sam. 24. 14.
^l Ex. 22. 28. 1 Pet. 2. 23.

---

¹ Heb. *I do obeisance.*
² Or, *he still came forth and*
³ Heb. *man of blood.*
⁴ Heb. *behold thee in thy evil.*

XVI. **1.** *a couple of asses saddled*] Those that Mephibosheth and his servant should have ridden. See xix. 26 note.

3. *thy master's son*] Meaning Saul's grandson (ix. 6). David asks the question, evidently hurt at the apparent ingratitude of Mephibosheth. It is impossible to say whether Mephibosheth was quite guiltless or not. If Ps. cxvi. was composed by David, and after the quelling of Absalom's rebellion, *v.* 11 may contain David's confession of his present hasty judgment (*v.* 4) in the matter.

5. *Bahurim*] See iii. 16 note. It seems to have lain off the road, on a ridge (*v.* 13), separated from it by a narrow ravine, so that Shimei was out of easy reach though within hearing, and within a stone's throw (*vv.* 6, 9).

Shimei, the son of Gera] In the title to Ps. vii. he is apparently called "Cush the Benjamite." On Gera, see Judg. iii. 15 note.

7. *Come out*] Rather, "**Go out**," viz. of the land, into banishment. Cp. Jer. xxix. 16.

thou bloody man] See marg. The Lord's word to David (1 Chr. xxii. 8) was probably known to Shimei. and now cast in Da-

vid's teeth by him, with special reference to the innocent blood of Uriah.

8. *all the blood of the house of Saul*] Shimei probably put to David's account the death of Saul, and Jonathan, and Abinadab, and Melchishua, slain in battle by the Philistines with whom David was in league; of Ish-bosheth, slain in consequence of David's league with Abner; that of Abner himself, which he attributed to David's secret orders; and all the 360 slain in the battle between Joab and Abner (ii. 31). Some, too, think that the death of seven men of Saul's immediate family (xxi. 8) had occurred before David's flight, and was referred to by Shimei. Shimei's hatred and virulence is an indication that the Benjamites resented the loss of royalty in their tribe, even in the palmiest days of David's monarchy.

9. *this dead dog*] See marg. ref. and ix. 8 note.

go over] The ravine, possibly with a stream of water (xvii. 20), which lay between them and Shimei.

10. *what have I to do, &c.*] See marg. reff. cp. Matt. viii. 29: John ii. 4, and a similar complaint about the sons of Zeruiah (iii. 39).

n See 2 Kin.
18. 25.
Lam. 3. 38.
o Rom. 9. 20.
p ch. 12. 11.
q Gen. 15. 4.

r Rom. 8. 28.

s ch. 15. 37.

t ch. 15. 37.

u ch. 19. 25.
Prov. 17. 17.

x ch. 15. 34.

v ch. 15. 16.
& 20. 3.
z Gen. 34. 30.
1 Sam. 13. 4.
a ch. 2. 7.
Zech. 8. 13.
b ch. 12. 11,
12.

c ch. 15. 12.

a See Deut.
25. 18.
ch. 16. 14.
b Zech. 13. 7.

him curse, because *n*the Lord hath said unto him, Curse David.
11 *o*Who shall then say, Wherefore hast thou done so? And
David said to Abishai, and to all his servants, Behold, *p*my son,
which *q*came forth of my bowels, seeketh my life: how much
more now *may this* Benjamite *do it?* let him alone, and let him
12 curse; for the Lord hath bidden him. It may be that the
Lord will look on mine [1][2]affliction, and that the Lord will
13 *r*requite me good for his cursing this day. And as David and
his men went by the way, Shimei went along on the hill's side
over against him, and cursed as he went, and threw stones at
14 him, and [3]cast dust. And the king, and all the people that *were*
15 with him, came weary, and refreshed themselves there. ¶And
*s*Absalom, and all the people the men of Israel, came to Jerusa-
16 lem, and Ahithophel with him. And it came to pass, when
Hushai the Archite, *t*David's friend, was come unto Absalom,
that Hushai said unto Absalom, [4]God save the king, God save
17 the king. And Absalom said to Hushai, *Is* this thy kindness
18 to thy friend? *u*why wentest thou not with thy friend? And
Hushai said unto Absalom, Nay; but whom the Lord, and this
people, and all the men of Israel, choose, his will I be, and
19 with him will I abide. And again, *x*whom should I serve?
should I not *serve* in the presence of his son? as I have served in
20 thy father's presence, so will I be in thy presence. ¶Then said
Absalom to Ahithophel, Give counsel among you what we shall
21 do. And Ahithophel said unto Absalom, Go in unto thy father's
*v*concubines, which he hath left to keep the house; and all
Israel shall hear that thou *z*art abhorred of thy father: then
22 shall *a*the hands of all that *are* with thee be strong. So they
spread Absalom a tent upon the top of the house, and Absalom
went in unto his father's concubines *b*in the sight of all Israel.
23 And the counsel of Ahithophel, which he counselled in those
days, *was* as if a man had enquired at the [5]oracle of God: so
was all the counsel of Ahithophel, *c*both with David and with
Absalom.

Chap. 17. MOREOVER Ahithophel said unto Absalom, Let me
now choose out twelve thousand men, and I will arise and
2 pursue after David this night: and I will come upon him while
he is *a*weary and weak handed, and will make him afraid: and
all the people that *are* with him shall flee; and I will *b*smite the
3 king only: and I will bring back all the people unto thee:. the
man whom thou seekest *is* as if all returned: *so* all the people

[1] Or, *tears.*   [2] Heb. *eye,* Gen. 29. 32.   [4] Hcb. *Let the king live.*
[3] Heb. *dusted* him *with dust.*   1 Sam. 1. 11. Ps. 25. 18.   [5] Heb. *word.*

And for a like striking incident in the life
of the Son of David, see Luke ix. 52-56.
  12. *his cursing*] Another reading has *my
curse, i.e.* the curse that has fallen upon me.
David recognises in every word and action
that he was receiving the due reward of
his sin, and that which Nathan had foretold.
  21. Taking possession of the harem was
the most decided act of sovereignty (see 1
K. ii. 22). It was also the greatest offence
and insult that could be offered. Such an
act on Absalom's part made reconciliation
impossible. A further motive has been
found in this advice, viz., the desire on the

part of Ahithophel to make David taste the
bitterness of that cup which he had caused
others (Uriah and all Bath-sheba's family)
to drink, and receive the measure which he
had meted withal.
  XVII. 1. *this night*] The night of the day
on which David fled, and Absalom entered
into Jerusalem. Ahithophel's idea was to
fall upon David by surprise, and in the first
confusion of the surprised army to seize and
kill David only.
  3. *the man whom thou seekest*] viz., David.
Ahithophel means to say: "If I can only
smite David, there will be no civil war, all
the people will peaceably submit."

4 shall be in peace. And the saying [1]pleased Absalom well, and
5 all the elders of Israel. ¶ Then said Absalom, Call now Hushai
6 the Archite also, and let us hear likewise [2]what he saith. And
  when Hushai was come to Absalom, Absalom spake unto him,
  saying, Ahithophel hath spoken after this manner: shall we do
7 *after* his [3]saying? if not; speak thou. And Hushai said unto
  Absalom, The counsel that Ahithophel hath [4]given *is* not good
8 at this time. For, said Hushai, thou knowest thy father and
  his men, that they *be* mighty men, and they *be* [5]chafed in their
  minds, as *c* a bear robbed of her whelps in the field: and thy   *c* Hos. 13. 8.
  father *is* a man of war, and will not lodge with the people.
9 Behold, he is hid now in some pit, or in some *other* place: and it
  will come to pass, when some of them be [6]overthrown at the
  first, that whosoever heareth it will say, There is a slaughter
10 among the people that follow Absalom. And he also *that is*
  valiant, whose heart *is* as the heart of a lion, shall utterly *d* melt: *d* Josh. 2. 11.
  for all Israel knoweth that thy father *is* a mighty man, and *they*
11 which *be* with him *are* valiant men. Therefore I counsel that
  all Israel be generally gathered unto thee, *e* from Dan even to   *e* Judg. 20. 1.
  Beer-sheba, *f* as the sand that *is* by the sea for multitude; and   *f* Gen. 22. 17.
12 [7]that thou go to battle in thine own person. So shall we come
  upon him in some place where he shall be found, and we will
  light upon him as the dew falleth on the ground: and of him
  and of all the men that *are* with him there shall not be left so
13 much as one. Moreover, if he be gotten into a city, then shall
  all Israel bring ropes to that city, and we will draw it into the
14 river, until there be not one small stone found there. ¶ And
  Absalom and all the men of Israel said, The counsel of Hushai
  the Archite *is* better than the counsel of Ahithophel. For *g* the   *g* ch. 15. 31,
  LORD had [8]appointed to defeat the good counsel of Ahithophel,   34.
  to the intent that the LORD might bring evil upon Absalom.
15 ¶ *h* Then said Hushai unto Zadok and to Abiathar the priests,   *h* ch. 15. 35.
  Thus and thus did Ahithophel counsel Absalom and the elders
16 of Israel; and thus and thus have I counselled. Now therefore
  send quickly, and tell David, saying, Lodge not this night *i* in   *i* ch. 15. 28.
  the plains of the wilderness, but speedily pass over; lest the

---

[1] Heb. *was right in the eyes*   [3] Heb. *word?*   [6] Heb. *fallen.*
    of, &c. 1 Sam. 18. 20.   [4] Heb. *counselled.*   [7] Heb. *that thy face,* or,
[2] Heb. *what* is *in his*   [5] Heb. *bitter of soul.* Judg.   *presence go, &c.*
    mouth.   18. 25.   [8] Heb. *commanded.*

---

7. *at this time*] Rather, "**The counsel which Ahithophel has given this time is not good.**" He contrasts it with that given before (xvi. 21), which was good. This gave an appearance of candour to his conduct, and so gave weight to his dissent. Observe the working of David's prayer (xv. 31).

9. *some pit, or in some other place*] The Hebrew has *in one of the pits,* or *in one of the places.* Hence *place* must have some defined meaning. It probably is used here, as elsewhere, for a *dwelling-house* or *village,* which might in that district be fortified houses (*v.* 12; 1 Sam. xxvi. 25). Hushai's argument is that there was no chance of seizing David by surprise as Ahithophel suggested. There was sure to be sharp fighting, and the terror of the

names of David, Joab, Abishai, Ittai, and their companions, would magnify the first few blows received into a victory, and Absalom's men would flee in panic. It is likely that Absalom was not a man of courage, and Hushai, knowing this, adroitly magnified the terror of the warlike prowess of David and his mighty men.

12. *as the dew*] Like the drops of dew, in the vast number of our host, and in our irresistible and unavoidable descent upon our enemies.

16. Hushai, like a wise and prudent man, knowing, too, Absalom's weak and fickle character, would not depend upon the resolution, taken at his instigation, not to pursue the king, but took instant measures to advertise David of his danger.

king be swallowed up, and all the people that *are* with him.
17 ¶ *k*Now Jonathan and Ahimaaz *l*stayed by *m*En-rogel; for they
might not be seen to come into the city: and a wench went and
18 told them; and they went and told king David.   Nevertheless a
lad saw them, and told Absalom: but they went both of them
away quickly, and came to a man's house *n*in Bahurim, which
19 had a well in his court; whither they went down. And *o*the
woman took and spread a covering over the well's mouth, and
spread ground corn thereon; and the thing was not known.
20 And when Absalom's servants came to the woman to the house,
they said, Where *is* Ahimaaz and Jonathan? And *p*the woman
said unto them, They be gone over the brook of water. And
when they had sought and could not find *them*, they returned to
21 Jerusalem.   And it came to pass, after they were departed, that
they came up out of the well, and went and told king David,
and said unto David, *q*Arise, and pass quickly over the water:
22 for thus hath Ahithophel counselled against you.   Then David
arose, and all the people that *were* with him, and they passed
over Jordan: by the morning light there lacked not one of them
23 that was not gone over Jordan.   ¶ And when Ahithophel saw
that his counsel was not [1]followed, he saddled his *ass*, and arose,
and gat him home to his house, to *r*his city, and [2]put his household in order, and *s*hanged himself, and died, and was buried in
24 the sepulchre of his father.   ¶ Then David came to *t*Mahanaim.
And Absalom passed over Jordan, he and all the men of Israel
25 with him.   And Absalom made Amasa captain of the host
instead of Joab: which Amasa *was* a man's son, whose name
was Ithra an Israelite, that went in to *u*[3]Abigail the daughter of
26 [4]Nahash, sister to Zeruiah Joab's mother.   So Israel and Ab-

k ch. 15. 27, 36.
l Josh. 2. 4, &c.
m Josh. 15. 7. & 18. 16.
n ch. 16. 5.
o See Josh. 2. 6.

p See Exod. 1. 19.
Josh. 2. 4, 5.

q ver. 15, 16.

r ch. 15. 12.
s Matt. 27. 5.
t Gen. 32. 2.
Josh. 13. 26.

u 1 Chr. 2. 16, 17.

---

[1] Heb. *done.*   [2] Heb. *gave charge concerning his house*, 2 Kin. 20. 1.   [3] Heb. *Abigal.*   [4] Or, *Jesse.* See 1 Chr. 2. 13, 16.

---

17. *En-rogel*] See marg. ref.
a wench] Heb. "**the maid servant**," viz.,
of the High-Priest, either Zadok or Abiathar, or possibly one employed in some service in the Temple courts. (1 Sam. ii. 22
note.)
and they went and told king David] As
related afterwards (*v.* 21). Here mentioned
by anticipation.
18. *Bahurim*] See marg. ref.   They were
not all Shimeis in Bahurim.
19. *a covering*] Heb. "**the covering**,"
perhaps *the hanging* or *awning* at the door of
the house, as the word seems to mean when
spoken of the Tabernacle.
ground corn] Or *peeled barley*, which she
spread out as if for the purpose of drying it
in the sun.
20. As soon as ever she had hid the men
she went into the house, as if busy about her
usual occupations. Had Absalom's servants,
who had had information from some of the
people of Bahurim that the men had come
to this house, found her in the court it
might have directed their attention to the
peeled barley.
over the brook of water] Cp. xvi. 9 note. The
word for *brook* (*Michal*) occurs only here.
One has been found in this very district,

still so called. The woman showed great
presence of mind and adroitness in not
denying that they had been there.
23. *to his city*] To Giloh (marg. ref.).
Ahithophel was probably influenced by deep
mortification at the slight put upon him by
rejecting his counsel. He is a memorable
example of the impotence of worldly wisdom.
Cp. marg. ref.
24. *Mahanaim*] See ii. 8. The same reasons which induced Abner to choose it for
Ishbosheth probably made it a good rally-
ing point for David. It was a strong city,
in a well-provisioned country, with a mountainous district for retreat in case of need,
and with a warlike and friendly population.
25. *Ithra an Israelite*] Or *Jether the Ishmeelite* (1 Chr. ii. 17). *Ithra* and *Jether* are
practically the same names. *Israelite* in the
text is wrong. It should be either *Ishmaelite*
or *Jezreelite* (iii. 2).
Abigail the daughter of Nahash] If Zeruiah
and Abigail were Jesse's daughters, the
only probable way of reconciling our text
with 1 Chr. ii. 16, 17, is to suppose that
Nahash was Jesse's wife. If Zeruiah and
Abigail were only sisters of David by the
mother, then Nahash might be the name of
her first husband.

27 salom pitched in the land of Gilead. ¶ And it came to pass, when David was come to Mahanaim, that *Shobi the son of Nahash of Rabbah of the children of Ammon, and *Machir the son of Ammiel of Lo-debar, and *Barzillai the Gileadite of

28 Rogelim, brought beds, and ¹basons, and earthen vessels, and wheat, and barley, and flour, and parched *corn*, and beans, and

29 lentiles, and parched *pulse*, and honey, and butter, and sheep, and cheese of kine, for David, and for the people that *were* with him, to eat: for they said, The people *is* hungry, and weary, and thirsty, *a*in the wilderness.

CHAP. 18. AND David numbered the people that *were* with him, and set captains of thousands and captains of hundreds over

2 them. And David sent forth a third part of the people under the hand of Joab, and a third part under the hand of Abishai the son of Zeruiah, Joab's brother, *a*and a third part under the hand of Ittai the Gittite. And the king said unto the people, I

3 will surely go forth with you myself also. *b*But the people answered, Thou shalt not go forth : for if we flee away, they will not ²care for us ; neither if half of us die, will they care for us : but now *thou art* ³worth ten thousand of us : therefore now *it is*

4 better that thou *succour us out of the city. And the king said unto them, What seemeth you best I will do. And the king stood by the gate side, and all the people came out by hundreds

5 and by thousands. And the king commanded Joab and Abishai and Ittai, saying, *Deal* gently for my sake with the young man, *even* with Absalom. *c*And all the people heard when the king gave all the captains charge concerning Absalom.

6 ¶ So the people went out into the field against Israel : and the

7 battle was in the *d*wood of Ephraim ; where the people of Israel

x See ch. 10. 1. & 12. 29.
y ch. 9. 4.
z ch. 19. 31, 32.
1 Kin. 2. 7.

a ch. 16. 2.

a ch. 15. 19.

b ch. 21. 17.

c ver. 12.

d Josh. 17. 15, 18.

¹ Or, *cups.*
² Heb. *set their heart on us.*
³ Heb. *as ten thousand of us.*
⁴ Heb. *be to succour.*

---

27. Shobi's father may have been the king of the Ammonites, and Shobi appointed by David as tributary king or governor of Ammon after he took Rabbah (xii. 29). On the other hand, Nahash may have been a common name among the Ammonites, and the Nahash of *v.* 25 may have been of that nation.

On Machir, see marg. ref.

Barzillai was ancestor, through a daughter, to a family of priests, who were called after him *sons of Barzillai*, and who returned from captivity with Zerubbabel, but were not allowed to officiate as priests, or eat of the holy things, through defect of a proper register (Ezr. ii. 61–63). It is likely that being wealthy they had neglected their priestly privileges, as a means of maintenance, before the Captivity.

Rogelim was situated in the highlands of Gilead, but the exact situation is not known. It means *the fullers*, being the plural of the word *Rogel*, in *En-Rogel, v.* 17.

29. *cheese of kine*] Or, as others, *milch cows*, which is more in accordance with the context, being coupled with *sheep*, and is more or less borne out etymologically by the Arabic. God's care for David was evident in the kindness of these people.

XVIII. 2. *a third part*] This seems to have been a favourite division with the Hebrew commanders (see Judg. vii. 16, ix. 43 ; 1 Sam. xi. 11 ; 2 K. xi. 5, 6) and with the Philistines also (1 Sam. xiii. 17).

3. *succour us out of the city*] David, with a reserve, would hold the city, and either support the bands in case of need, or receive them within the walls should they be compelled to flee.

6. *against Israel*] Implying that the revolt was in a great measure that of the ten tribes, Saul's party, against the kingdom.

the wood of Ephraim] This would naturally be sought in the west of Jordan (marg. ref.). But on the other hand it seems certain that the scene of this battle was on the east of Jordan. It seems therefore inevitable to conclude that some portion of the thick wood of oaks and terebinths which still runs down to the Jordan on the east side was for some reason called *the wood of Ephraim*, either because it was a continuation on the east side of the great Ephraimitic forests on the west, or because of some transaction there in which Ephraim had taken part, such as the slaughter of the Midianites (Judg. vii. 24, 25), or their own slaughter (Judg. xii. 6).

were slain before the servants of David, and there was there a
8 great slaughter that day of twenty thousand *men*. For the battle
was there scattered over the face of all the country: and the
wood [1]devoured more people that day than the sword devoured.
9 ¶ And Absalom met the servants of David. And Absalom rode
upon a mule, and the mule went under the thick boughs of a
great oak, and his head caught hold of the oak, and he was
taken up between the heaven and the earth; and the mule that
10 *was* under him went away. And a certain man saw *it*, and told
11 Joab, and said, Behold, I saw Absalom hanged in an oak. And
Joab said unto the man that told him, And, behold, thou sawest
him, and why didst thou not smite him there to the ground?
and I would have given thee ten *shekels* of silver, and a girdle.
12 And the man said unto Joab, Though I should [2]receive a thousand *shekels* of silver in mine hand, *yet* would I not put forth

ver. 5.

mine hand against the king's son: *e*for in our hearing the king
charged thee and Abishai and Ittai, saying, [3]Beware that none
13 *touch* the young man Absalom. Otherwise I should have
wrought falsehood against mine own life: for there is no matter
hid from the king, and thou thyself wouldest have set thyself
14 against *me*. Then said Joab, I may not tarry thus [4]with thee.
And he took three darts in his hand, and thrust them through
the heart of Absalom, while he *was* yet alive in the [5]midst of
15 the oak. And ten young men that bare Joab's armour com-
16 passed about and smote Absalom, and slew him. ¶ And Joab
blew the trumpet, and the people returned from pursuing after
17 Israel: for Joab held back the people. And they took Absalom,

f Josh. 7. 26.

and cast him into a great pit in the wood, and *f*laid a very great
heap of stones upon him: and all Israel fled every one to his
18 tent. ¶ Now Absalom in his lifetime had taken and reared up

g Gen. 14. 17.
h See ch. 14.
27.

for himself a pillar, which *is* in *g*the king's dale: for he said, *h*I
have no son to keep my name in remembrance: and he called
the pillar after his own name: and it is called unto this day,

---

[1] Heb. *multiplied to devour.*   [3] Heb. *Beware whosoever*   [4] Heb. *before thee.*
[2] Heb. *weigh upon mine hand.*   ye be of, &c.   [5] Heb. *heart.*

---

8. *the battle was scattered*] Probably Absalom's forces were far more numerous than
David's; but, most likely by Joab's skilful
generalship, the field of battle was such
that numbers did not tell, and David's
veteran troops were able to destroy Absalom's rabble in detail. The wood entangled
them, and was perhaps full of pits, pre-
cipices, and morasses (*v.* 17).

9. It would seem that the two things
which his vain-glory boasted in, the royal
mule, and the magnificent head of hair, by
which he was caught in the "oak" (rather,
terebinth or turpentine tree), both contributed to his untimely death.

11. *ten shekels*] [About 25 shillings.] The
word *shekel* is understood, as in Gen. xx. 16,
xxxvii. 28. See Ex. xxxviii. 24 note.

a girdle] Girdles were costly articles of
Hebrew dress used to put money in (Matt.
x. 9), and given as presents (1 Sam.
xviii 4).

13. The man gives a remarkable incidental

testimony to David's sagacity and penetra-
tion (cp. xiv. 19), and to Joab's known un-
scrupulousness.

14. *I may not tarry*, &c.] *i.e.* lose time in
such discourse.

16. *blew the trumpet*] To stop the pursuit
and slaughter (ii. 28, xx. 22).

17. *a great heap of stones*] See marg. ref.
This kind of monument is common to
almost all early nations.

18. *the king's dale*] Anciently the *valley*
of *Shaveh* (marg. ref.), and apparently in
the near neighbourhood of Sodom; but the
exact site is not known. It quite agrees
with Absalom's preference for Hebron (xv.
7), that his monument should be reared by
him in the south. If Absalom's monument
be placed in the ravine of the Kedron, the
king's dale here is a different place from the
dale of Shaveh.

Absalom's place] Literally, *Absalom's hand.*
(1 Sam. xv. 12 note.)

19 Absalom's place. ¶ Then said Ahimaaz the son of Zadok, Let
me now run, and bear the king tidings, how that the LORD
20 hath [1]avenged him of his enemies. And Joab said unto him,
Thou shalt not [2]bear tidings this day, but thou shalt bear tidings
another day: but this day thou shalt bear no tidings, because
21 the king's son is dead. Then said Joab to Cushi, Go tell the king
what thou hast seen. And Cushi bowed himself unto Joab, and
22 ran. Then said Ahimaaz the son of Zadok yet again to Joab,
But [3]howsoever, let me, I pray thee, also run after Cushi. And
Joab said, Wherefore wilt thou run, my son, seeing that thou
23 hast no tidings [4]ready? But howsoever, said he, let me run.
And he said unto him, Run. Then Ahimaaz ran by the way of
24 the plain, and overran Cushi. ¶ And David sat between the
two gates: and [i]the watchman went up to the roof over the gate
unto the wall, and lifted up his eyes, and looked, and behold a
25 man running alone. And the watchman cried, and told the
king. And the king said, If he be alone, there is tidings in his
26 mouth. And he came apace, and drew near. And the watchman saw another man running: and the watchman called unto
the porter, and said, Behold another man running alone. And
27 the king said, He also bringeth tidings. And the watchman
said, [5]Me thinketh the running of the foremost is like the
running of Ahimaaz the son of Zadok. And the king said, He
28 is a good man, and cometh with good tidings. ¶ And Ahimaaz
called, and said unto the king, [6][7]All is well. And he fell down
to the earth upon his face before the king, and said, Blessed be
the LORD thy God, which hath [8]delivered up the men that lifted
29 up their hand against my lord the king. And the king said,
[9]Is the young man Absalom safe? And Ahimaaz answered,
When Joab sent the king's servant, and me thy servant, I saw
30 a great tumult, but I knew not what it was. And the king said
unto him, Turn aside, and stand here. And he turned aside, and

i ch. 13. 34.
2 Kin. 9. 17.

---

[1] Heb. judged him from the hand, &c.
[2] Heb. be a man of tidings.
[3] Heb. be what may.
[4] Or, convenient.
[5] Heb. I see the running.
[6] Or, Peace be to thee.
[7] Heb. Peace.
[8] Heb. shut up.
[9] Heb. Is there peace.

---

19. Ahimaaz was a well-known runner (v. 27). Speed was a heroic virtue in those simple times (cp. ii. 18). In Hezekiah's reign (2 Chr. xxx. 6, 10) we find an establishment of running post-men; and the same name (runners) is given (Esth. iii. 13) to the Persian posts, though at that time they rode on mules and camels.

bear tidings] The original word is used almost exclusively of bearing good tidings, and hence is rendered in the LXX. (though not always) εὐαγγελίζεσθαι (iv. 10; 1 Sam. xxxi. 9). In v. 21, it is not carry the good tidings, but tell, simply announce.

21. *Cushi*] "The Cushite," a foreign slave, perhaps of Joab's, whom he did not scruple to expose to David's anger. If, however, it is a name, it must be rendered Haccushi. In the title to Ps. vii., "Cush, the Benjamite," cannot mean this Cushi, since the contents of the Psalm are not suitable to this occasion.

23. *the plain*] The floor of the valley through which the Jordan runs. The Cushite did not run by that road, but took the road over the hills, which may well have been the shorter but also the more difficult road. The two roads would probably meet a short distance from Mahanaim. These words, which have been thought to prove that the battle took place on the west of Jordan, are a clear proof that it took place on the east, because if the runners had had to cross the Jordan, they must both have come by the same road, which it is clear they did not.

28. *Ahimaaz called*] This marks the eager haste with which, before he had quite reached the king, he shouted out the pithy decisive word of good tidings, Shalom! Peace!

hath delivered] See marg. The figure seems to be that of confining a person within the power of his enemy, in opposition to giving him his liberty "in a large room," to work what mischief he pleases.

31 stood still. And, behold, Cushi came; and Cushi said, ¹Tidings, my lord the king: for the Lord hath avenged thee this day of 32 all them that rose up against thee. And the king said unto Cushi, *Is* the young man Absalom safe? And Cushi answered, The enemies of my lord the king, and all that rise against thee 33 to do *thee* hurt, be as *that* young man *is*. And the king was much moved, and went up to the chamber over the gate, and

k ch. 19. 4.

wept: and as he went, thus he said, *k*O my son Absalom, my son, my son Absalom! would God I had died for thee, O Absalom, my son, my son!

CHAP. 19. AND it was told Joab, Behold, the king weepeth and 2 mourneth for Absalom. And the ²victory that day was *turned* into mourning unto all the people: for the people heard say that 3 day how the king was grieved for his son. And the people gat

a ver. 32.
b ch. 15. 30.
c ch. 18. 33.

them by stealth that day *a*into the city, as people being ashamed 4 steal away when they flee in battle. But the king *b*covered his face, and the king cried with a loud voice, *c*O my son Absalom, 5 O Absalom, my son, my son! ¶ And Joab came into the house to the king, and said, Thou hast shamed this day the faces of all thy servants, which this day have saved thy life, and the lives of thy sons and of thy daughters, and the lives of thy wives, 6 and the lives of thy concubines; ³in that thou lovest thine enemies, and hatest thy friends. For thou hast declared this day, ⁴that thou regardest neither princes nor servants: for this day I perceive, that if Absalom had lived, and all we had died 7 this day, then it had pleased thee well. Now therefore arise, go forth, and speak ⁵comfortably unto thy servants: for I swear by the Lord, if thou go not forth, there will not tarry one with thee this night: and that will be worse unto thee than all the 8 evil that befell thee from thy youth until now. Then the king arose, and sat in the gate. And they told unto all the people, saying, Behold, the king doth sit in the gate. And all the people came before the king: for Israel had fled every man to his tent. 9 ¶ And all the people were at strife throughout all the tribes of Israel, saying, The king saved us out of the hand of our enemies, and he delivered us out of the hand of the Philistines; and now

d ch. 15. 14.

10 he is *d*fled out of the land for Absalom. And Absalom, whom we anointed over us, is dead in battle. Now therefore why 11 ⁶speak ye not a word of bringing the king back? ¶ And king David sent to Zadok and to Abiathar the priests, saying, Speak unto the elders of Judah, saying, Why are ye the last to bring the king back to his house? seeing the speech of all Israel is 12 come to the king, *even* to his house. Ye *are* my brethren, ye

e ch. 5. 1.

are ⁿmy bones and my flesh: wherefore then are ye the last to

---

¹ Heb. *Tidings is brought.*
² Heb. *salvation,* or, *deliverance.*
³ Heb. *By loving, &c.*
⁴ Heb. *that princes or servants* are *not to thee.*
⁵ Heb. *to the heart of thy servants,* Gen. 34. 3.
⁶ Heb. are *ye silent?*

---

31. *tidings,* &c.] Rather, " Let my lord the king receive the good tidings."
33. There is not in the whole of the O. T. a passage of deeper pathos than this. Cp. Luke xix. 41. In the Hebrew Bible this verse commences the nineteenth chapter. The A. V. follows the Greek and Latin Versions.
5. Had Absalom gained the victory, it is likely that, according to the manner of

Oriental despots, he would have sought to secure his throne by killing all possible competitors (Judg. ix. 5; 1 K. xv. 29).
8. David saw the justice of what Joab said, and the new danger which threatened him if he did not rouse himself from his grief.
for Israel, &c.] Not David's followers, but as before (xvii. 26, xviii. 6, 17), Absalom's army.

13 bring back the king? *f*And say ye to Amasa, *Art* thou not of   *f* ch. 17. 25.
   my bone, and of my flesh? *g*God do so to me, and more also,   *g* Ruth 1. 17.
   if thou be not captain of the host before me continually in the
14 room of Joab. And he bowed the heart of all the men of Judah,
   *h*even as *the heart of* one man; so that they sent *this word* unto   *h* Judg. 20.1
15 the king, Return thou, and all thy servants. So the king
   returned, and came to Jordan. And Judah came to *i*Gilgal, to   *i* Josh. 5. 9.
16 go to meet the king, to conduct the king over Jordan. ¶And
   *k*Shimei the son of Gera, a Benjamite, which *was* of Bahurim,   *k* ch. 16. 5.
   hasted and came down with the men of Judah to meet king   1 1 in. 2. 8.
17 David. And *there were* a thousand men of Benjamin with him,
   and *l*Ziba the servant of the house of Saul, and his fifteen sons   *l* ch. 9. 2, 10.
   and his twenty servants with him; and they went over Jordan   & 16. 1, 2.
18 before the king. And there went over a ferry boat to carry
   over the king's household, and to do *1*what he thought good.
   And Shimei the son of Gera fell down before the king, as he was
19 come over Jordan; and said unto the king, *m*Let not my lord   *m* 1 Sam. 22.
   impute iniquity unto me, neither do thou remember *n*that which   15.
   thy servant did perversely the day that my lord the king went   *n* ch. 16. 5,
   out of Jerusalem, that the king should *o*take it to his heart.   6, &c.
20 For thy servant doth know that I have sinned: therefore,   *o* ch. 13. 33.
   behold, I am come the first this day of all *p*the house of Joseph   *p* See ch. 16.
21 to go down to meet my lord the king. But Abishai the son of   5.
   Zeruiah answered and said, Shall not Shimei be put to death
22 for this, because he *q*cursed the LORD's anointed? And David   *q* Ex. 22. 28.
   said, *r*What have I to do with you, ye sons of Zeruiah, that ye   *r* ch. 16. 10.
   should this day be adversaries unto me? *s*shall there any man   *s* 1 Sam. 11.
   be put to death this day in Israel? for do not I know that I   13.
23 *am* this day king over Israel? Therefore *t*the king said unto   *t* 1 Kin. 2. 8,
   Shimei, Thou shalt not die. And the king sware unto him.   9, 37, 46.
24 ¶And *u*Mephibosheth the son of Saul came down to meet the   *u* ch. 9. 6.
   king, and had neither dressed his feet, nor trimmed his beard,

1 Heb. *the good in his eyes.*

---

13. *of my bone,* &c.] Render as in preceding verse, "**art thou not my bone and my flesh?**" It is curious to note how the phrase is used in v. 1 of common descent from Israel, in *v.* 12 of the closer kindred of the tribe of Judah, and in this verse of the yet nearer kindred between David and Amasa his sister's son.

captain...in the room of Joab] It is very plain that David felt the weight of Joab's overbearing influence to be very oppressive (cp. *v.* 22, iii. 39, xvi. 10). He was, at this time, very angry with Joab for killing Absalom; and so, thinking it of vital importance to win over Amasa and the army of Judah, he did not scruple to offer him Joab's high post.

16. Shimei being aware that Judah was unanimous in recalling the king, lost no time in trying to make his peace with David, by bringing a large Benjamite force with him.

17. *before the king*] *i.e.* "**to meet the king.**" Cp. xx. 8. The king was on the east bank, and they crossed over (by the ford) from the west bank to go to him.

18. *as he was come over Jordan*] Render, "**when he was crossing**," *i.e.* just embarking for the purpose of crossing. The scene still lies on the east bank. Shimei left nothing undone to soften, if possible, David's resentment.

20. This is the first time that the *house of Joseph*, or *Joseph*, stands for all the ten tribes of which Ephraim was the head and leader. While Saul of Benjamin was king, or while Mahanaim was the capital of his son's kingdom, it was not natural so to name them, nor does it seem so at first sight in the mouth of Shimei the Benjamite. But it is very possible that he used the phrase for the purpose of exculpating himself and his own tribe from having taken the initiative in the rebellion, and of insinuating that they were drawn away by the preponderating influence of the great house of Joseph. On the other hand, the phrase may be an indication that the passage was written after the separation of the kingdom of Israel, when the phrase was a common one.

24. *beard*] The *moustache*, the beard of the upper lip. The fact related in this

nor washed his clothes, from the day the king departed until the
25 day he came *again* in peace. And it came to pass, when he
was come to Jerusalem to meet the king, that the king said unto
26 him, *x* Wherefore wentest not thou with me, Mephibosheth? And
he answered, My lord, O king, my servant deceived me: for thy
servant said, I will saddle me an ass, that I may ride thereon,
27 and go to the king; because thy servant *is* lame. And *v* he hath
slandered thy servant unto my lord the king; *z* but my lord the
king *is* as an angel of God: do therefore *what is* good in thine
28 eyes. For all *of* my father's house were but ¹dead men before
my lord the king: *a* yet didst thou set thy servant among them
that did eat at thine own table. What right therefore have I
29 yet to cry any more unto the king? And the king said unto
him, Why speakest thou any more of thy matters? I have said,
30 Thou and Ziba divide the land. And Mephibosheth said unto
the king, Yea, let him take all, forasmuch as my lord the king
31 is come again in peace unto his own house. ¶ And *b* Barzillai
the Gileadite came down from Rogelim, and went over Jordan
32 with the king, to conduct him over Jordan. Now Barzillai was
a very aged man, *even* fourscore years old: and *c* he had provided the king of sustenance while he lay at Mahanaim; for he
33 *was* a very great man. And the king said unto Barzillai, Come
thou over with me, and I will feed thee with me in Jerusalem.
34 And Barzillai said unto the king, ²How long have I to live,
35 that I should go up with the king unto Jerusalem? I *am* this
day *d* fourscore years old: *and* can I discern between good and
evil? can thy servant taste what I eat or what I drink? can I
hear any more the voice of singing men and singing women?
wherefore then should thy servant be yet a burden unto my lord
36 the king? Thy servant will go a little way over Jordan with
the king: and why should the king recompense it me with such
37 a reward? Let thy servant, I pray thee, turn back again, that I
may die in mine own city, *and be buried* by the grave of my father
and of my mother. But behold thy servant *e* Chimham; let him
go over with my lord the king; and do to him what shall seem
38 good unto thee. And the king answered, Chimham shall go
over with me, and I will do to him that which shall seem good
unto thee: and whatsoever thou shalt ³require of me, *that* will
39 I do for thee. And all the people went over Jordan. And
when the king was come over, the king *f* kissed Barzillai, and
40 blessed him; and he returned unto his own place. Then the
king went on to Gilgal, and ⁴Chimham went on with him: and

x ch. 16. 17.
y ch. 16. 3.
z ch. 14. 17, 20.
a ch. 9. 7, 10, 13.
b ch. 17. 27. 1 Kin. 2. 7.
c ch. 17. 27.
d Ps. 90. 10.
e 1 Kin. 2. 7. Jer. 41. 17.
f Gen. 31. 55.

¹ Heb. *men of death,* 1 Sam. 26. 16.
² Heb. *How many days are the years of my life.*
³ Heb. *choose.*
⁴ Heb. *Chimhan.*

verse tends to clear Mephibosheth from the suspicion of unfaithfulness to David.

26. What appears to have happened is, that when Mephibosheth ordered Ziba to saddle the asses and ride with him to join David, Ziba left him under pretence of obeying, but instead laded the asses with provisions, and went off alone with them, thus making it impossible for Mephibosheth to follow.

29. Unable to get to the bottom of the story, and perhaps unwilling to make an enemy of Ziba, David compromised the matter by dividing the land, thus partially

revoking his hasty sentence (xvi. 4). We still see the impatient temper of David.

37. *Chimham*] From marg. reff. it appears that Chimham, having accepted David's offer, came and settled near Bethlehem. His house was still called after him at the time of the Captivity.

39. The *people* is the term especially applied in this narrative to David's followers (xv. 17, xvi. 14, xvii. 2, xviii. 1, 2, xix. 2, 3). They crossed by the ford, while David and his household, accompanied by Barzillai and Chimham, came over in the ferry.

all the people of Judah conducted the king, and also half the
41 people of Israel. ¶ And, behold, all the men of Israel came to
the king, and said unto the king, Why have our brethren the
men of Judah stolen thee away, and *g*have brought the king, *g* ver. 15.
and his household, and all David's men with him, over Jordan?
42 And all the men of Judah answered the men of Israel, Because
the king *is* *h*near of kin to us : wherefore then be ye angry for *h* ver. 12.
this matter? have we eaten at all of the king's *cost?* or hath he
43 given us any gift? And the men of Israel answered the men
of Judah, and said, We have ten parts in the king, and we have
also more *right* in David than ye : why then did ye ¹despise us,
that our advice should not be first had in bringing back our
king? And *i*the words of the men of Judah were fiercer than *i* See Judg.
the words of the men of Israel. 8. 1.
 & 12. 1.
Chap. 20. AND there happened to be there a man of Belial, whose
name *was* Sheba, the son of Bichri, a Benjamite : and he blew a
trumpet, and said, *a*We have no part in David, neither have we *a* ch. 19. 43.
inheritance in the son of Jesse : *b*every man to his tents, O *b* 1 Kin. 12.
2 Israel. So every man of Israel went up from after David, *and* 16.
followed Sheba the son of Bichri : but the men of Judah clave 2 Chr. 10. 16.
3 unto their king, from Jordan even to Jerusalem. ¶ And David
came to his house at Jerusalem ; and the king took the ten
women *his* *c*concubines, whom he had left to keep the house, *c* ch. 15. 16.
and put them in ²ward, and fed them, but went not in unto & 16. 21, 22.
them. So they were ³shut up unto the day of their death,
4 ⁴living in widowhood. ¶ Then said the king to Amasa, *d*⁵As- *d* ch. 19. 13.
semble me the men of Judah within three days, and be thou
5 here present. So Amasa went to assemble *the men of* Judah :
but he tarried longer than the set time which he had appointed
6 him. And David said to Abishai, Now shall Sheba the son of
Bichri do us more harm than *did* Absalom : take thou *e*thy lord's *e* ch. 11. 11.
servants, and pursue after him, lest he get him fenced cities, 1 Kin. 1. 33.
7 and ⁶escape us. And there went out after him Joab's men, and
the *f*Cherethites, and the Pelethites, and all the mighty men : *f* ch. 8. 18.
 1 Kin. 1. 38.

¹ Heb. *set us at light.*　　³ Heb. *bound.*　　⁶ Heb. *deliver himself from*
² Heb. *an house of ward.*　　⁴ Heb. *in widowhood of life.*　　*our eyes.*
　　　　　　　　　　⁵ Heb. *Call.*

---

41. It seems that David and his whole
party made a halt at Gilgal (*v.* 15 ; 1 Sam.
xi. 14), and possibly made some solemn
agreement there about the kingdom. But
while they were there, *all the men of Israel,*
representatives from the tribes not included
in *half the people of Israel* (*v.* 40), came
up in great wrath at finding that the
restoration had been accomplished without
consulting them, and accused the men of
Judah of unfair dealing.

XX. 1. *the son of Bichri,* &c.] Rather, *a*
Bichrite, formed like the names *Ahohite,*
Hachmonite, &c. (xxiii. 8, 9), and so called
from Becher, the son of Benjamin (Gen.
xlvi. 21 ; 1 Chr. vii. 6-8) Saul was also of
this family. It is evident that the transfer
of the royalty from their tribe to that of
Judah still rankled in the hearts of many
Benjamites (xvi. 8 note).

2. *from Jordan,* &c.] The men of Israel
only escorted David from Jordan to Gilgal,

and there left him ; but the men of Judah
in a body went with him all the way to
Jerusalem.

4. *to Amasa,* &c.] Evidently feeling his
way towards fulfilling the promise to Amasa
(marg. ref.).

5. *he tarried*] The cause of Amasa's
delay is not stated. It may have been the
unwillingness of the men of Judah to place
themselves under his orders, or it may have
been caused by a wavering or hesitation in
loyalty. This last is evidently insinuated
in *v.* 11, and no doubt this was the pretext,
whether grounded in fact or not, by which
Joab justified the murder of Amasa before
David.

6. *to Abishai*] Probably, as the king was
on bad terms with Joab, and wished to
deprive him of his post as captain of the
host, he gave his orders to Abishai, and
weakly connived at the execution of them
by Joab, which was inevitable.

and they went out of Jerusalem, to pursue after Sheba the son
8 of Bichri. ¶When they *were* at the great stone which *is* in
Gibeon, Amasa went before them. And Joab's garment that
he had put on was girded unto him, and upon it a girdle *with* a
sword fastened upon his loins in the sheath thereof; and as he
9 went forth it fell out. And Joab said to Amasa, *Art* thou in
health, my brother? *g*And Joab took Amasa by the beard with
10 the right hand to kiss him. But Amasa took no heed to the
sword that *was* in Joab's hand: so *h*he smote him therewith *i*in
the fifth *rib*, and shed out his bowels to the ground, and ¹struck
him not again; and he died. So Joab and Abishai his brother
11 pursued after Sheba the son of Bichri. And one of Joab's men
stood by him, and said, He that favoureth Joab, and he that *is*
12 for David, *let him go* after Joab. And Amasa wallowed in
blood in the midst of the highway. And when the man saw
that all the people stood still, he removed Amasa out of the
highway into the field, and cast a cloth upon him, when he saw
13 that every one that came by him stood still. When he was
removed out of the highway, all the people went on after Joab,
14 to pursue after Sheba the son of Bichri. And he went through
all the tribes of Israel unto *k*Abel, and to Beth-maachah, and
all the Berites: and they were gathered together, and went also
15 after him. And they came and besieged him in Abel of Beth-
maachah, and they *l*cast up a bank against the city, and ²it
stood in the trench: and all the people that *were* with Joab
16 ³battered the wall, to throw it down. ¶Then cried a wise woman
out of the city, Hear, hear; say, I pray you, unto Joab, Come

g Matt. 26.
49.
Luke 22. 47.
h 1 Kin. 2. 5.
i ch. 2. 23.

k 2 Kin. 15.
29.

l 2 Kin. 19.
32.
Isai. 37. 33.

---

¹ Heb. *doubled not his stroke.*　² Or, *it stood against the outmost wall.*　³ Heb. *marred to throw down.*

---

8. *Amasa went before them*] Rather, "**advanced to meet them.**" Amasa was no doubt returning to Jerusalem, according to his orders (*v.* 4), and was probably much surprised to meet the army in march. Joab's resolution was quickly taken.

and Joab's garment, &c.] Render, *And Joab was girded with his military garment, as his clothing, and upon it*—*i.e.* the military garment—(or *him*), *the girdle of a sword fastened on his loins in its sheath, and as he went forth* (to meet Amasa) *it fell* out of the sheath. What appears to have happened is that, by accident or design, Joab's sword fell out of the scabbard on the ground as he was going to meet Amasa, and that he picked it up with his left hand so as to leave his right hand free for the customary salutation (*v.* 9). This awakened no suspicion in Amasa's mind. Cp. the case of Ehud, Judg. iii. 21.

11. *He that favoureth Joab,* &c.] This speech, addressed to Amasa's followers as well as Joab's, shows very distinctly that the rivalry between Joab and Amasa, and David's purpose to make Amasa captain in Joab's room, were well known; and shows also the real reason why Joab slew Amasa. What is added, *and he that is for David,* was intended to identify Joab's cause with David's, and also to insinuate that

Amasa had not been loyal to David (*v.* 5 note).

12. *all the people,* &c.] *i.e.* the levies which Amasa had been leading to Jerusalem; they were irresolute as to what they should do, and the stoppage at Amasa's body very nearly led to their refusing to follow Joab. But upon the prompt removal and hiding of the body they passed on and followed Joab, their old captain.

14. *Abel*] More commonly called (*v.* 15) *Abel-Beth-maachah* to distinguish it from other places of the name of *Abel* (a grassy plain). It is represented by the modern Abil-el-Kamh, a Christian village on the N.W. of lake Huleh, the ancient Merom. Cp. 2 Chr. xvi. 4, *Abel-maim,* Abel by the water.

and all the Berites] What this means is utterly unknown. Many approve of the reading of the Latin Version, connecting it with what follows: "*And all the choice young men mustered and followed him.*"

15. *cast up a bank*] See marg. reff. The throwing up of mounds against the walls of besieged places by the besiegers is well illustrated in the Assyrian sculptures.

the trench] The *pomœrium,* or fortified space outside the wall. When the mound was planted in the pomœrium the battering engines were able to approach close to the wall to make a breach.

17 near hither, that I may speak with thee. And when he was
come near unto her, the woman said, *Art* thou Joab? And he
answered, I *am he.* Then she said unto him, Hear the words
18 of thine handmaid. And he answered, I do hear. Then she
spake, saying, [1]They were wont to speak in old time, saying,
They shall surely ask *counsel* at Abel: and so they ended *the*
19 *matter.* I *am one of them that are* peaceable *and* faithful in
Israel: thou seekest to destroy a city and a mother in Israel:
20 why wilt thou swallow up *m* the inheritance of the LORD? And
Joab answered and said, Far be it, far be it from me, that I
21 should swallow up or destroy. The matter *is* not so: but a
man of mount Ephraim, Sheba the son of Bichri [2]by name, hath
lifted up his hand against the king, *even* against David: deliver
him only, and I will depart from the city. And the woman said
unto Joab, Behold, his head shall be thrown to thee over the
22 wall. Then the woman went unto all the people *n* in her wisdom.
And they cut off the head of Sheba the son of Bichri, and cast *it*
out to Joab. And he blew a trumpet, and they [3]retired from
the city, every man to his tent. And Joab returned to Jeru-
23 salem unto the king. ¶ Now *o* Joab *was* over all the host of
Israel: and Benaiah the son of Jehoiada *was* over the Cherethites
24 and over the Pelethites: and Adoram *was* *p* over the tribute:
25 and *q* Jehoshaphat the son of Ahilud *was* [4]recorder: and Sheva
26 *was* scribe: and *r* Zadok and Abiathar *were* the priests: *s* and Ira
also the Jairite was [5]a chief ruler about David.

CHAP. 21. THEN there was a famine in the days of David three
years, year after year; and David [6]enquired of the LORD. And

m 1 Sam. 26.
19.
ch. 21. 3.

n Eccles. 9.
14, 15.

o ch. 8. 16,
18.
p 1 Kin. 4. 6.
q ch. 8. 16.
1 Kin. 4. 3.
r ch. 8. 17.
1 Kin. 4. 4.
s ch. 23. 38.

[1] Or, *They plainly spake in*
the beginning, saying,
Surely they will ask of
Abel, and so make an end:
[2] Heb. *by his name.*
[3] Heb. *were scattered.*
[4] Or, *remembrancer.*
[5] Or, *a prince,* Gen. 41.
45. Ex. 2. 16.
[6] Heb. *sought the face, &c.*
See Num. 27. 21.
See Deut. 20. 11.

---

18. This was an old proverb. Abel, like
Teman, and some other places, was once
famous for the wisdom of its inhabitants
(1 K. iv. 30, 31). The wise woman was
herself a remnant of this traditional wisdom.

19. *I am one,* &c.] The woman speaks in
the name of the whole city, which she
means to say was peaceable and loyal.

20. Joab's character is strongly brought
out in the transaction. Politic, decided,
bold, and unscrupulous, but never needlessly
cruel or impulsive, or even revengeful. No
life is safe that stands in his way, but from
policy he never sacrifices the most insig-
nificant life without a purpose. (Cp. ii.
27-30.)

23. *now Joab,* &c.] This is by no means
an unmeaning repetition. Joab had been
dismissed to make room for Amasa, and
was now, as the result of his successful expedition against Sheba, and the death of
Amasa, reinstated in his command. Moreover, this was a fresh beginning of David's
reign, and therefore a statement of his chief
officers is as proper as in viii. 16, when he
had just established himself on the throne
of Israel. Cp. 1 K. iv. 2-6.

24. *Adoram*] Not mentioned before by

name or office. Apparently, therefore, the
office was not instituted till the latter part
of David's reign, and its duties probably
were the collection of the tribute imposed
upon vanquished nations, or the command
of the forced levies employed in public
works. Adoram was stoned to death in the
beginning of the reign of Rehoboam (1 K.
xii. 18).

26. *Ira the Jairite*] Not mentioned before:
perhaps the same as *Ira an Ithrite* (marg.
ref.), *i.e.* an inhabitant of Jattir in the hill
country of Judah (Josh. xv. 48; 1 Sam.
xxx. 27). Perhaps we ought to read *Ithrite*,
for *Jairite*.

a chief ruler...about David] More simply
and clearly, "**was David's cohen**" (viii. 18
note). In the early part of David's reign
his own ons were *cohanim* (chief rulers).
The deaths of Amnon and Absalom, and
the dissensions in the family, had probably caused the change of policy in this
respect.

XXI. 1. There is no note of time whatever, nor any clue as to what part of David's
reign the events of this chapter ought to be
assigned.

enquired of the LORD] Heb. "**sought the**
face of the Lord," quite a different phrase

the LORD answered, *It is* for Saul, and for *his* bloody house,
2 because he slew the Gibeonites. And the king called the
Gibeonites, and said unto them; (now the Gibeonites *were* not

a Josh. 9. 3,
15, 16, 17.

of the children of Israel, but *a*of the remnant of the Amorites;
and the children of Israel had sworn unto them: and Saul
sought to slay them in his zeal to the children of Israel and
3 Judah.) Wherefore David said unto the Gibeonites, What
shall I do for you? and wherewith shall I make the atonement,

b ch. 20. 19.

4 that ye may bless *b*the inheritance of the LORD? And the
Gibeonites said unto him, ¹We will have no silver nor gold of
Saul, nor of his house; neither for us shalt thou kill any man
in Israel. And he said, What ye shall say, *that* will I do for
5 you. And they answered the king, The man that consumed us,
and that ²devised against us *that* we should be destroyed from
6 remaining in any of the coasts of Israel, let seven men of his
sons be delivered unto us, and we will hang them up unto the

c 1 Sam. 10.
26.
& 11. 4.
d 1 Sam. 10.
24.
e 1 Sam.18.3.
& 20. 8,15,42.
& 23. 18.
f ch. 3. 7.

LORD *c*in Gibeah of Saul, *d*³*whom* the LORD did choose. And
7 the king said, I will give *them*. ¶ But the king spared Mephibosheth, the son of Jonathan the son of Saul, because of *e*the
LORD's oath that *was* between them, between David and Jona-
8 than the son of Saul. But the king took the two sons of *f*Rizpah the daughter of Aiah, whom she bare unto Saul, Armoni
and Mephibosheth; and the five sons of ⁴Michal the daughter of

---

¹ Or, It is *not silver nor gold that we have to do with Saul or his house,*   *neither* pertains it *to us to kill, &c.*   ² Or, *cut us off.*
³ Or, *chosen of the LORD.*
⁴ Or, *Michal's sister.*

---

from that so often used in Judges (*e.g.* i. 1)
and the Books of Samuel, and probably
indicating that this chapter is from a different source; an inference agreeing with
the indefinite "*in the days of David,*" and
with the allusion to the slaughter of the
Gibeonites, which has not anywhere been
narrated.

and for his bloody house] Lit., *the house
of blood, i.e.* the house or family upon
which rests the guilt of shedding innocent
blood.

2. The way in which the writer here
refers to the history of the league with the
Gibeonites (Josh. ix.) shows that the Book
of Joshua was not a part of the same work
as the Books of Samuel.

of the Amorites] The Gibeonites were
Hivites (Josh. ix. 7, xi. 19); and in many
enumerations of the Canaanitish nations
the Hivites are distinguished from the
Amorites. But *Amorite* is often used in a
more comprehensive sense, equivalent to
Canaanite (as Gen. xv. 16; Deut. i. 27), and
denoting especially that part of the Canaanite nation which dwelt in the hill country
(Num. xiii. 29; Deut. i. 7, 20, 24), and so
includes the Hivites.

4. *no silver, nor gold,* &c.] Money payments as a compensation for blood-guilt
were very common among many nations.
The law, too, in Num. xxxv. 31, 32, pre-
supposes the existence of the custom which
it prohibits. In like manner the speech of

the Gibeonites implies that such a payment
as they refuse would be a not unusual proceeding.

*neither ... shalt thou kill any man in Is-
rael*] They mean that it is not against the
nation of Israel, but against the individual
Saul, that they cry for vengeance. The
demand for Saul's sons is exactly similar to
that which dictated David's own expression
in xxiv. 17, "*against me, and against my
father's house.*"

6. *seven men*] Seven was a sacred number
not only with the Hebrews but with other
Oriental nations (Num. xxiii. 1, 29), and is
therefore brought in on this occasion when
the judicial death of the sons of Saul was a
religious act intended to appease the wrath
of God for the violation of an oath (Num.
xxv. 4).

whom the LORD did choose] Rather, "**the
Lord's chosen,**" or elect. The same phrase
is applied to Moses (Ps. cvi. 23), to the Israelites (Isai. xliii. 20), and to Christ (Isai.
xlii. 1).

7. *the LORD's oath*] The calamity brought
upon Israel by Saul's breach of the oath to
the Gibeonites would make David doubly
careful in the matter of his own oath to
Jonathan.

8. *Rizpah*] See marg. ref. A foreign origin
was possibly the cause of the selection of
Rizpah's sons as victims.

sons of Michal] An obvious error for
Merab (1 Sam. xviii. 19 note).

Saul, whom she ¹brought up for Adriel the son of Barzillai the
9 Meholathite : and he delivered them into the hands of the
Gibeonites, and they hanged them in the hill ᵍbefore the LORD :
and they fell *all* seven together, and were put to death in the
days of harvest, in the first *days*, in the beginning of barley
10 harvest.   ¶ And ʰRizpah the daughter of Aiah took sackcloth,
and spread it for her upon the rock, ⁱfrom the beginning of
harvest until water dropped upon them out of heaven, and
suffered neither the birds of the air to rest on them by day, nor
11 the beasts of the field by night. And it was told David what
Rizpah the daughter of Aiah, the concubine of Saul, had done.
12 ¶ And David went and took the bones of Saul and the bones of
Jonathan his son from the men of ᵏJabesh-gilead, which had
stolen them from the street of Beth-shan, where the ˡPhilistines
had hanged them, when the Philistines had slain Saul in Gilboa :
13 and he brought up from thence the bones of Saul and the bones
of Jonathan his son ; and they gathered the bones of them that
14 were hanged.   And the bones of Saul and Jonathan his son
buried they in the country of Benjamin in ᵐZelah, in the
sepulchre of Kish his father : and they performed all that the
king commanded.   And after that ⁿGod was intreated for the
15 land.   ¶ Moreover the Philistines had yet war again with Israel ;
and David went down, and his servants with him, and fought
16 against the Philistines : and David waxed faint. And Ishbi-
benob, which *was* of the sons of ²the giant, the weight of whose
³spear *weighed* three hundred *shekels* of brass in weight, he being
17 girded with a new *sword*, thought to have slain David. But
Abishai the son of Zeruiah succoured him, and smote the

ᵍ ch. 6. 17.

ʰ ver. 8.
ch. 3. 7.
ⁱ See Deut.
21. 23.

ᵏ 1 Sam. 31.
11, 12, 13.
ˡ 1 Sam. 31.
10.

ᵐ Josh. 18.
28.

ⁿ So Josh. 7.
26.
ch. 24. 25.

---

¹ Heb. *bare to Adriel*, 1   ² Or, *Rapha*.   ³ Heb. *the staff*, or, *the
Sam. 18. 19.   head.*

---

9. *in the first days*] The barley harvest
(about the middle or towards the end of
April) was earlier than the wheat harvest
(Ex. ix. 31; Ruth i. 22).
  10. *dropped*] Rather, "**poured**," the proper word for heavy rain (Ex. ix. 33). The
"early rain," or heavy rain of autumn,
usually began in October, so that Rizpah's
devoted watch continued about six months.
How rare rain was in harvest we learn from
1 Sam. xii. 17, 18; Prov. xxvi. 1. The
reason of the bodies being left unburied,
contrary to Deut. xxi. 23, probably was that
the death of these men being an expiation
of the guilt of a violated oath, they were to
remain till the fall of rain should give the
assurance that God's anger was appeased,
and the national sin forgiven.
  birds of the air...beasts of the field] It is
well known how in the East, on the death
e.g. of a camel in a caravan, the vultures
instantly flock to the carcase. (Cp. Matt.
xxiv. 28.)
  12. *from the street of Beth-shan*] This was
the wide. place just inside the gate of an
Oriental city, bounded therefore by the
city wall (cp. marg. ref.). Here, as the
place of concourse, the Philistines had fastened the bodies.
  15. This, like the preceding paragraph

(1-14), is manifestly a detached and uncon-
nected extract. It is probably taken from
some history of David's wars, apparently
the same as furnished the materials for chs.
v., viii., and xxiii. 8-39. There is no direct
clue to the time when the events here related
took place, but it was probably quite in the
early part of David's reign, while he was
still young and active, after the war described in ch. v. The Book of Chronicles
places these Philistine battles immediately
after the taking of Rabbah of the Ammonites (1 Chr. xx. 4-8), but omits David's ad-
venture (15-17).
  16. *Ishbi-benob*] A corrupt reading. The
whole passage should perhaps run thus :
"*And David waxed faint. So they halted in
Gob* (as in *rr.* 18, 19). *And there was a man
(in Gob) which was of the sons of the giant,*
&c."
  sons of the giant] The *giant* here (*rr.* 18,
20, 22) is *ha-Raphah,* whence the *Rephaim*
(Gen. xiv. 5; Deut. ii. 11). The sons of Ha-
raphah, or Rephaim, are different from the
Nephilim, or Giants (Gen. vi. 4; Num. xiii.
33). The sons of Anak were not strictly
Rephaim, but Nephilim.
  three hundred shekels of brass] About eight
pounds. Goliath's spear's head weighed *six
hundred shekels of iron.*

Philistine, and killed him. Then the men of David sware unto
him, saying, °Thou shalt go no more out with us to battle, that
18 thou quench not the *p*1light of Israel. ¶*q*And it came to pass
after this, that there was again a battle with the Philistines at
Gob: then *r*Sibbechai the Hushathite slew 2Saph, which *was* of
19 the sons of 3the giant. And there was again a battle in Gob
with the Philistines, where Elhanan the son of 4Jaare-oregim, a
Beth-lehemite, slew *s the brother of* Goliath the Gittite, the staff
20 of whose spear *was* like a weaver's beam. ¶And *t*there was yet
a battle in Gath, where was a man of *great* stature, that had on
every hand six fingers, and on every foot six toes, four and
21 twenty in number; and he also was born to 5the giant. And
when he 6defied Israel, Jonathan the son of *u*Shimeah the
22 brother of David slew him. ¶*x*These four were born to the
giant in Gath, and fell by the hand of David, and by the hand
of his servants.

CHAP. 22. AND David *a*spake unto the LORD the words of this
song in the day *that* the LORD had *b*delivered him out of the
2 hand of all his enemies, and out of the hand of Saul: and he
said,

¶*c*The LORD *is* my rock, and my fortress, and my deliverer;
3   The God of my rock; *d*in him will I trust:
He is my *e*shield, and the *f*horn of my salvation, my high
   *g*tower, and my *h*refuge,
My saviour; thou savest me from violence.
4   I will call on the LORD, *who is* worthy to be praised:
So shall I be saved from mine enemies.
5   ¶ When the 7waves of death compassed me,
The floods of 8ungodly men made me afraid;
6   The 9*i*sorrows of hell compassed me about;
The snares of death prevented me;
7   In my distress *k*I called upon the LORD,
And cried to my God:

Marginal references (left column):

o ch. 18. 3.
p 1 Kin. 11. 36.
& 15. 4.
Ps. 132. 17.
q 1 Chr. 20. 4.
r 1 Chr. 11. 29.
s See 1 Chr. 20. 5.
t 1 Chr. 20. 6.

u 1 Sam. 16. 9, *Shammah*.
x 1 Chr. 20. 8.

a Ex. 15. 1.
Judg. 5. 1.
b Ps. 34. 19.

c Deut. 32. 4.
Ps. 18. 2, &c.
d Heb. 2. 13.
e Gen. 15. 1.
f Luke 1. 69.
g Prov. 18. 10.
h Ps. 9. 9.
Jer. 16. 19.

i Ps. 116. 3.

k Ps. 120. 1.
Jonah 2. 2.

Footnotes:

1 Heb. *candle*, or, *lamp*.
2 Or, *Sippai*.
3 Or, *Rapha*.
4 Or, *Jair*.
5 Or, *Rapha*.
6 Or, *reproached*, 1 Sam. 17. 10, 25, 26.
7 Or, *pangs*.
8 Heb. *Belial*.
9 Or, *cords*.

---

18. *a battle in Gob*] In the parallel passage (marg. ref.), *Gezer* is named as the field of this battle. Gath is however named (*vv.* 20, 22) in a way to make it probable that Gath was the scene of all the battles. The LXX. in this verse has *Gath*.

19. The Hebrew text is manifestly very corrupt. First, for *Jaare-oregim*, 1 Chr. xx. 5 gives us the reading *Jair*. *Oregim* has evidently got in by a transcriber's error from the line below, where *oregim* is the Hebrew for *weavers*. Again, the word *the Bethlehemite* is very doubtful. It is supported by xxiii. 24, but it is not found in the far purer text of 1 Chr. xx. 5, but instead of it we find the name of the Philistine slain by Elhanan, *Lahmi the brother of Goliath the Gittite*. It is probable, therefore, that either the words *the Bethlehemite*, are a corruption of *Lahmi*, or that the recurrence of *Lahmi*, and the termination of *Beth-lehemite* has confused

the transcriber, and led to the omission of one of the words in each text.

22. *four*] Not necessarily meaning that they were brothers, but that they were all of the race of the Giant, all Rephaim. The word *four* is omitted in the parallel passage, only the three last being mentioned in that chapter.

XXII. 1. This song, which is found with scarcely any material variation as the XVIIIth Psalm, and with the words of this first verse for its title, belongs to the early part of David's reign when he was recently established upon the throne of all Israel, and when his final triumph over the house of Saul, and over the heathen nations (*vv.* 44-46), Philistines, Moabites, Syrians, Ammonites, and Edomites, was still fresh (ch. xxi.). For a commentary on the separate verses the reader is referred to the commentary on Ps. xviii.

And he did [l]hear my voice out of his temple,
And my cry *did enter* into his ears.
8 Then [m]the earth shook and trembled;
[n]The foundations of heaven moved
And shook, because he was wroth.
9 There went up a smoke [1]out of his nostrils,
And [o]fire out of his mouth devoured:
Coals were kindled by it.
10 He [p]bowed the heavens also, and came down;
And [q]darkness *was* under his feet.
11 And he rode upon a cherub, and did fly:
And he was seen [r]upon the wings of the wind.
12 And he made [s]darkness pavilions round about him,
[2]Dark waters, *and* thick clouds of the skies.
13 Through the brightness before him were [t]coals of fire kindled.
14 The LORD [u]thundered from heaven,
And the most High uttered his voice.
15 And he sent out [x]arrows, and scattered them;
Lightning, and discomfited them.
16 And the channels of the sea appeared,
The foundations of the world were discovered,
At the [y]rebuking of the LORD,
At the blast of the breath of his [3]nostrils.
17 ¶ [z]He sent from above, he took me;
He drew me out of [4]many waters;
18 [a]He delivered me from my strong enemy,
And from them that hated me: for they were too strong for me.
19 They prevented me in the day of my calamity:
But the LORD was my stay.
20 [b]He brought me forth also into a large place:
He delivered me, because he [c]delighted in me.
21 [d]The LORD rewarded me according to my righteousness:
According to the [e]cleanness of my hands hath he recompensed me.
22 For I have [f]kept the ways of the LORD,
And have not wickedly departed from my God.
23 For all his [g]judgments *were* before me:
And *as for* his statutes, I did not depart from them.
24 I was also [h]upright [5]before him,
And have kept myself from mine iniquity.
25 Therefore [i]the LORD hath recompensed me according to my righteousness;
According to my cleanness [6]in his eye sight.
26 ¶ With [k]the merciful thou wilt shew thyself merciful,
And with the upright man thou wilt shew thyself upright.
27 With the pure thou wilt shew thyself pure;
And [l]with the froward thou wilt [7]shew thyself unsavoury.
28 And the [m]afflicted people thou wilt save:
But thine eyes *are* upon [n]the haughty, *that* thou mayest bring *them* down.
29 For thou *art* my [8]lamp, O LORD:
And the LORD will lighten my darkness.

[l] Ex. 3. 7. Ps. 34. 6.
[m] Judg. 5. 4. Ps. 77. 18.
[n] Job 26. 11.
[o] Ps. 97. 3. Hab. 3. 5.
[p] Ps. 144. 5. Isai. 64. 1.
[q] Ex. 20. 21. 1 Kin. 8. 12.
[r] Ps. 104. 3.
[s] Ps. 97. 2.
[t] ver. 9.
[u] Judg. 5. 20. 1 Sam. 2. 10. Ps. 29. 3. Isai. 30. 30.
[x] Deut. 32. 23. Ps. 7. 13.
[y] Ex. 15. 8. Ps. 106. 9. Nah. 8. 4. Matt. 8. 26.
[z] Ps. 144. 7.
[a] ver. 1.
[b] Ps. 31. 8.
[c] ch. 15. 26. Ps. 22. 8.
[d] 1 Sam. 26. 23. 1 Kin. 8. 32. Ps. 7. 8.
[e] Ps. 24. 4.
[f] Gen. 18. 19. Ps. 119. 3.
[g] Deut. 7. 12. Ps. 119. 30.
[h] Gen. 6. 9. Job 1. 1.
[i] ver. 21.
[k] Matt. 5. 7.
[l] Lev. 26. 23.
[m] Ex. 3. 7. Ps. 72. 12.
[n] Job 40. 11. Isai. 2. 11. Dan. 4. 37.

[1] Heb. *by*.
[2] Heb. *binding of waters*.
[3] Or, *anger*, Ps. 74. 1.
[4] Or, *great*.
[5] Heb. *to him*.
[6] Heb. *before his eyes*.
[7] Or, *wrestle*, Ps. 18. 26.
[8] Or, *candle*, Job 29. 3. Ps. 27. 1.

30 For by thee I have ¹run through a troop :
   By my God have I leaped over a wall.

^o Deut. 32. 4.   31 ¶ *As for* God, ^ohis way *is* perfect ;
Rev. 15. 3.   ^pThe word of the LORD *is* ²tried :
^p Ps. 12. 6.   He *is* a buckler to all them that trust in him.
Prov. 30. 5.

^q 1 Sam. 2. 2.   32 For ^qwho *is* God, save the LORD ?
Isai. 45. 5.   And who *is* a rock, save our God ?

^r Ex. 15. 2.   33 God *is* my ^rstrength *and* power :
Ps. 27. 1.   And he ^{3 s}maketh my way ^tperfect.
Isai. 12. 2.
^s Heb. 13. 21.   ·34 He ⁴maketh my feet ^ulike hinds' *feet :*
^t Deut.18.13.   And ^xsetteth me upon my high places.
Ps. 101. 2.
^u ch. 2. 18.   35 ^yHe teacheth my hands ⁵to war ;
Hab. 3. 19.   So that a bow of steel is broken by mine arms.
^x Deut. 32.
13.   36 Thou hast also given me the shield of thy salvation :
Isai. 33. 16.   And thy gentleness hath ⁶made me great.
^y Ps. 144. 1.   37 Thou hast ^zenlarged my steps under me ;
^z Prov. 4. 12.   So that my ⁷feet did not slip.

38 ¶I have pursued mine enemies, and destroyed them ;
   And turned not again until I had consumed them.

39 And I have consumed them, and wounded them, that they
      could not arise :
^a Mal. 4. 3.   Yea, they are fallen ^aunder my feet.
^b Ps. 18. 32.   40 For thou hast ^bgirded me with strength to battle :
^c Ps. 44. 5.   ^cThem that rose up against me hast thou ⁸subdued under me.
^d Gen. 49. 8.   41 Thou hast also given me the ^dnecks of mine enemies,
Josh. 10. 24.   That I might destroy them that hate me.

42 They looked, but *there was* none to save :
   Even ^eunto the LORD, but he answered them not.
^e Job 27. 9.
Prov. 1. 28.   43 Then did I beat them as small ^fas the dust of the earth,
Isai. 1. 15.   I did stamp them ^gas the mire of the street, *and* did spread
^f 2 Kin. 13.7.   them abroad.
Dan. 2. 35.
^g Isai. 10. 6.   44 ^hThou also hast delivered me from the strivings of my people,
Mic. 7. 10.   Thou hast kept me *to be* ⁱhead of the heathen :
^h ch. 3. 1.   ^kA people *which* I knew not shall serve me.
ⁱ ch. 8. 1—
14.   45 ⁹Strangers shall ¹²submit themselves unto me :
Ps. 2. 8.   As soon as they hear, they shall be obedient unto me.
^k Isai. 55. 5.
46 Strangers shall fade away,
   And they shall be afraid ^lout of their close places.
^l Mic. 7. 17.
47 ¶The LORD liveth ; and blessed *be* my rock ;
   And exalted be the God of the ^mrock of my salvation.
^m Ps. 89. 26.
48 It *is* God that ³avengeth me,
   And that ⁿbringeth down the people under me,
ⁿ Ps. 144. 2.   49 And that bringeth me forth from mine enemies :
   Thou also hast lifted me up on high above them that rose up
      against me :
^o Ps. 140. 1.   Thou hast delivered me from the ^oviolent man.

^p Rom.15. 9.   50 Therefore I will give thanks unto thee, O LORD, among ^pthe
      heathen,
   And I will sing praises unto thy name.

^q Ps. 144. 10. 51 ^q*He is* the tower of salvation for his king :
^r Ps. 89. 20.   And sheweth mercy to his ^ranointed,
^s ch. 7. 12.   Unto David, and ^sto his seed for evermore.
Ps. 89. 29.

---

¹ Or, *broken a troop.*   ⁶ Heb. *multiplied me.*   ² Heb. *lie :* See Deut. 33.
² Or, *refined.*   ⁷ Heb. *ankles.*   29. Ps. 66. 3. & 81. 15.
³ Heb. *riddeth,* or, *looseth.*   ⁸ Heb. *caused to bow.*   ³ Heb. *giveth avengement*
⁴ Heb. *equalleth.*   ⁹ Heb. *Sons of the stranger.*   *for me,* 1 Sam. 25. 39.
⁵ Heb. *for the war.*   ¹ Or, *yield feigned obedience.*   ch. 18. 19, 31.

CHAP. 23. NOW these *be* the last words of David.
David the son of Jesse said,
   a And the man *who was* raised up on high,
   b The anointed of the God of Jacob,
   And the sweet psalmist of Israel, said,

2   *c* The Spirit of the LORD spake by me,
   And his word *was* in my tongue.

3   The God of Israel said,
   d The Rock of Israel spake to me,
   ¹ He that ruleth over men *must be* just,
   Ruling *e* in the fear of God.

4   And *f* he shall be as the light of the morning, *when* the sun
   riseth,
   Even a morning without clouds ;
   As the tender grass *springing* out of the earth by clear
   shining after rain.

5   Although my house *be* not so with God ;
   g Yet he hath made with me an everlasting covenant,
   Ordered in all *things*, and sure :
   For *this is* all my salvation, and all *my* desire,
   Although he make *it* not to grow.

6   But *the sons* of Belial *shall be* all of them as thorns thrust
   away ;
   Because they cannot be taken with hands :

7   But the man *that* shall touch them must be ² fenced with
   iron and the staff of a spear ;
   And they shall be utterly burned with fire in the *same* place.

8 ¶ These *be* the names of the mighty men whom David had :
   ³ The Tachmonite that sat in the seat, chief among the captains ;

a ch. 7. 8, 9.
Ps. 78. 70.
& 89. 27.
b 1 Sam. 16.
12, 13.
Ps. 89. 20.
c 2 Pet. 1. 21.

d Deut. 32.
4, 31.
ch. 22. 2, 32.
e Ex. 18. 21.

f Prov. 4. 18.
Hos. 6. 5.
Ps. 72. 6.
Isai. 44. 3.

g Ps. 89. 29.
Isai. 55. 3.

---

¹ Or, *Be thou ruler, &c.*,
  Ps. 110. 2.
² Heb. *filled.*
³ Or, *Joshebbassebet the*
   Tachmonite, head of the
   three.

XXIII. 1. *the last words of David*] i.e.
his last Psalm, his last "words of song"
(xxii. 1). The insertion of this Psalm, which
is not in the Book of Psalms, was probably
suggested by the insertion of the long Psalm
in ch. xxii.
  David the son of Jesse said, &c.] The
original word for *said* is used between 200
and 300 times in the phrase, "saith the
Lord," designating the word of God in the
mouth of the prophet. It is only applied
to the words of a man here, and in the strikingly similar passage Num. xxiv. 3, 4, 15, 16,
and in Prov. xxx. 1 ; and in all these places
the words spoken are inspired words. The
description of David is divided into four
clauses, which correspond to and balance
each other.
  4. Comparisons illustrating the prosperity
of the righteous king.
  5. *although my house, &c.*] The sense of
this clause (according to the A.V.) will be
that David comparing the actual state of
his family and kingdom during the latter
years of trouble and disaster with the prophetic description of the prosperity of the
righteous king, and seeing how far it falls
short, comforts himself by the terms of

God's covenant (vii. 12–16) and looks forward to Messiah's kingdom. The latter
clause, *although he make it not to grow*, must
then mean that, although at the present
time the glory of his house was not made to
grow, yet all his salvation and all his desire
was made sure in the covenant which would
be fulfilled in due time. But most modern
commentators understand both clauses as
follows : *Is not my house so with God that He
has made with me an everlasting covenant,
&c. ? For all my salvation and all my desire,
will He not cause it to spring up ?* viz., in the
kingdom of Solomon, and still more fully
in the kingdom of Christ.
  8. The duplicate of this passage is in 1
Chr. xi., where it is in immediate connexion
with David's accession to the throne of
Israel, and where the mighty men are
named as those by whose aid David was
made king. The document belongs to the
early part of David's reign. The text of
vv. 8, 9 is perhaps to be corrected by comparison with 1 Chr. xi. 11, 12.
  chief among the captains] There is great
doubt about the exact meaning of this
phrase. (1) The title is given to two other
persons, viz., to Abishai in *v.* 18 ; 1 Chr. xi.

the same *was* Adino the Eznite: [1]*he lift up his spear* against
9 eight hundred, [2]whom he slew at one time. ¶ And after him

ʰ 1 Chr. 11.
12.
& 27. 4.

was ʰEleazar the son of Dodo the Ahohite, *one* of the three
mighty men with David, when they defied the Philistines *that*
were there gathered together to battle, and the men of Israel
10 were gone away: he arose, and smote the Philistines until his
hand was weary, and his hand clave unto the sword: and the
LORD wrought a great victory that day; and the people returned

i 1 Chr. 11.
27.
k See 1 Chr.
11. 13, 14.

11 after him only to spoil. ¶ And after him *was* iShammah the
son of Agee the Hararite. kAnd the Philistines were gathered
together [3]into a troop, where was a piece of ground full of
12 lentiles: and the people fled from the Philistines. But he stood
in the midst of the ground, and defended it, and slew the Philis-

l 1 Chr. 11.
15.

13 tines: and the LORD wrought a great victory. ¶ And [4]three of
the thirty chief went down, and came to David in the harvest

m 1 Sam. 22. 1.
n ch. 5. 18.
& 21. 16.
o 1 Sam. 22.
4, 5.

time unto ᵐthe cave of Adullam: and the troop of the Philis-
14 tines pitched in ⁿthe valley of Rephaim. And David *was* then
in ᵒan hold, and the garrison of the Philistines *was* then *in*
15 Beth-lehem. And David longed, and said, Oh that one would
give me drink of the water of the well of Beth-lehem, which *is*
16 by the gate! And the three mighty men brake through the
host of the Philistines, and drew water out of the well of Beth-
lehem, that *was* by the gate, and took *it*, and brought *it* to
David: nevertheless he would not drink thereof, but poured it

---

[1] See 1 Chron. 11. 11.   [2] Heb. *slain*.   [4] Or, *the three captains*
27. 2.   [3] Or, *for foraging*.   *over the thirty*.

20, and to Amasa in 1 Chr. xii. 18. (2)
The word translated *captain*, is of uncertain
meaning, and the orthography repeatedly
fluctuates throughout this and the duplicate
passage in 1 Chr. xi., between *Shalish* a
captain, and *Sheloshah* three. (3) If, however, the text of Chronicles be taken as the
guide, then the sense of *captain* will not
come into play, but the word will be a
numeral throughout, either *three* or *thirty*,
and will describe David's band of thirty
mighty men, with a certain triad or triads
of heroes who were yet more illustrious
than the thirty. In the verse before us,
therefore, for *chief among the captains*, we
should render, *chief of the thirty*.

eight hundred] The parallel passage in
1 Chr. has *three hundred*, as in *v*. 18. Such
variations in numerals are very frequent.
Compare the numbers in Ezr. ii. and
Neh. vii.

9. *gone away*] Rather, "**went up**" to
battle (v. 19; 2 K. iii. 21, &c.) against them.
These words and what follows as far as *troop*
(*v*. 11) have fallen out of the text in Chronicles. The effect of this is to omit Eleazar's
feat, as here described, to attribute to him
Shammah's victory, to misplace the flight
of the Israelites, and to omit Shammah altogether from the list of David's mighty men.

11. *Hararite*] Interpreted to mean *moun-
taineer*, one from the hill country of Judah
or Ephraim.

13. The feat at Bethlehem by three of the
thirty was the occasion of their being formed

into a distinct triad; Abishai (*v*. 18), Benaiah (*v*. 20), and a third not named, were
probably the three.

in the harvest time] An error for *to the
rock* (cp. marg. ref.).

the troop of the Philistines] The word
rendered *troop* occurs in this sense only
here (and, according to some, in *v*. 11), and
perhaps in Ps. lxviii. 11. In 1 Chr. xi:, as in
v. 16 of this chapter the reading is *host*
or *camp*, which may be the true reading
here.

pitched] The same Hebrew word as *encamped* in 1 Chr. xi. 15.

valley of Rephaim] Or Giants. See xxi.
16 note.

14. *in an hold*] In "**the hold**" (1 Chr. xi.
16) close to the cave of Adullam (marg. ref.
note). It shows the power and daring of
the Philistines that they should hold a post
so far in the country as Bethlehem.

15. A cistern of deep, clear, cool water,
is called by the monks, David's Well, about
three-quarters of a mile to the north of
Bethlehem. Possibly the old well has been
filled up since the town was supplied with
water by the aqueduct.

16. *brake through the host*] Their camp
was pitched in the valley of Rephaim (*v*.
13; 1 Chr. xi. 15). It follows from this
that the way from Adullam to Bethlehem
lay through or across the valley of Rephaim.

poured it out unto the LORD] It was too
costly for his own use, none but the Lord

17 out unto the LORD. And he said, Be it far from me, O LORD,
that I should do this: *is not this* [p]the blood of the men that [p] Lev. 17. 10.
went in jeopardy of their lives? therefore he would not drink it.
18 These things did these three mighty men. And [q]Abishai, the [q] 1 Chr. 11. 20.
brother of Joab, the son of Zeruiah, was chief among three.
And he lifted up his spear against three hundred, [1]*and* slew
19 *them*, and had the name among three. Was he not most
honourable of three? therefore he was their captain: howbeit
20 he attained not unto the *first* three. ¶ And Benaiah the son of
Jehoiada, the son of a valiant man, of [r]Kabzeel, [2]who had done [r] Josh. 15. 21.
many acts, [s]he slew two [3]lionlike men of Moab: he went down [s] Ex. 15. 15.
21 also and slew a lion in the midst of a pit in time of snow: and 1 Chr. 11. 22.
he slew an Egyptian, [4]a goodly man: and the Egyptian had a
spear in his hand; but he went down to him with a staff, and
plucked the spear out of the Egyptian's hand, and slew him
22 with his own spear. These *things* did Benaiah the son of
23 Jehoiada, and had the name among three mighty men. He was
[5]more honourable than the thirty, but he attained not to the
24 *first* three. And David set him [t]over his [6 7]guard. ¶ Asahel the [t] ch. 8. 18. & 20. 23.
brother of Joab *was* one of the thirty; [u]Elhanan the son of [u] ch. 21. 19.
25 Dodo of Beth-lehem, [x]Shammah the Harodite, Elika the Haro- [x] See 1 Chr.
26 dite, Helez the Paltite, Ira the son of Ikkesh the Tekoite, 11. 27.
27, 28 Abiezer the Anethothite, Mebunnai the Hushathite, Zalmon
29 the Ahohite, Maharai the Netophathite, Heleb the son of
Baanah, a Netophathite, Ittai the son of Ribai out of Gibeah of
30 the children of Benjamin, Benaiah the Pirathonite, Hiddai of
31 the [8]brooks of [y]Gaash, Abi-albon the Arbathite, Azmaveth the [y] Judg. 2. 9.
32 Barhumite, Eliahba the Shaalbonite, of the sons of Jashen,

[1] Heb. *slain.*
[2] Heb. *great of acts.*
[3] Heb. *lions of God.*
[4] Heb. *a man of countenance,* or *sight:* called, 1 Chr. 11. 23. *a man of* great *stature.*
[5] Or, *honourable among the thirty.*
[6] Or, *council.*
[7] Heb. *at his command,* 1 Sam. 22. 14.
[8] Or, *valleys,* Deut. 1. 24.

---

was worthy of it. For libations, see Judg. vi. 20 note.

17. Better as in 1 Chr. xi. 19.

18. *three*] "**The three**" (*v.* 22). It was Abishai's prowess on this occasion that raised him to be chief of this triad.

19. *i.e. Was he not the most honourable of the three of the second order, howbeit he attained not to the three,* the triad, viz. which consisted of Jashobeam, Eleazar, and Shammah. That two triads are mentioned is a simple fact, although only five names are given.

20. *Benaiah the son of Jehoiada*] He commanded the Cherethites and Pelethites all through David's reign (viii. 18, xx. 23), and took a prominent part in supporting Solomon against Adonijah when David was dying, and was rewarded by being made captain of the host in the room of Joab (1 K. i. 8, 26, 32-40, ii. 25-35, iv. 4). It is possible that Jehoiada his father is the same as Jehoiada (1 Chr. xii. 27), leader of the Aaronites, since "Benaiah the son of Jehoiada" is called *a chief priest* (1 Chr. xxvii. 5).

two lion-like men] The Hebrew word Ariel, means literally *lion of God,* and is interpreted to mean *an eminent hero.* Instances occur among Arabs and Persians of the surname "lion of God" being given to great warriors. Hence it is supposed that the same custom prevailed among the Moabites. But the Vulgate has "two lions of Moab," which seems to be borne out by the next sentence.

slew a lion, &c.] Rather, "**the**" lion, one of those described above as *a lion of God,* if the Vulgate Version is right. Apparently in a severe winter a lion had come up from its usual haunts to some village in search of food, and taken possession of the tank or cistern to the terror of the inhabitants, and Benaiah attacked it boldly and slew it.

23. *David set him over his guard*] *Made him of his privy council,* would be a better rendering. See 1 Sam. xxii. 14 note. This position, distinct from his office as captain of the Cherethites and Pelethites, is clearly indicated (1 Chr. xxvii. 34).

24, &c. The early death of Asahel (ii. 32) would make it very likely that his place in the 30 would be filled up, and so easily account for the number 31 in the list. Cp. throughout the list in 1 Chr. xi.

33 Jonathan, Shammah the Hararite, Ahiam the son of Sharar
34 the Hararite, Eliphelet the son of Ahasbai, the son of the
35 Maachathite, Eliam the son of Ahithophel the Gilonite, Hezrai
36 the Carmelite, Paarai the Arbite, Igal the son of Nathan of
37 Zobah, Bani the Gadite, Zelek the Ammonite, Nahari the

ch. 20. 26. 38 Beerothite, armourbearer to Joab the son of Zeruiah, *z*Ira an
a ch. 11. 3, 6. 39 Ithrite, Gareb an Ithrite, *a*Uriah the Hittite: thirty and seven
in all.

a ch. 21. 1.   **CHAP. 24.** AND *a*again the anger of the LORD was kindled against
b 1 Chr. 27.   Israel, and [1]he moved David against them to say, *b*Go, number
23, 24.   2 Israel and Judah. For the king said to Joab the captain of the
host, which *was* with him, [2]Go now through all the tribes of
c Judg. 20. 1. Israel, *c*from Dan even to Beer-sheba, and number ye the people,
d Jer. 17. 5.   3 that *d*I may know the number of the people. And Joab said
unto the king, Now the LORD thy God add unto the people, how
many soever they be, an hundredfold, and that the eyes of my
lord the king may see *it:* but why doth my lord the king delight
4 in this thing? Notwithstanding the king's word prevailed
against Joab, and against the captains of the host. ¶ And Joab
and the captains of the host went out from the presence of the
5 king, to number the people of Israel. And they passed over
e Josh. 13. 9, Jordan, and pitched in *e*Aroer, on the right side of the city that
16.   6 *lieth* in the midst of the [3]river of Gad, and toward *f*Jazer: then
f Num. 21.   they came to Gilead, and to the [4]land of Tahtim-hodshi; and they
32, 32. 1.

---

[1] *Satan.* See 1 Chr. 21. 1.   [3] Or, *valley.*   [4] Or, *nether land newly*
[2] Or, *Compass.*   *inhabited.*

---

36. It is remarkable that we have several foreigners at this part of the list: Igal of Zobah, Zelek the Ammonite, Uriah the Hittite, and perhaps Nahari the Berothite. The addition of Zelek to the mighty men was probably the fruit of David's war with Ammon (viii. 12, x., xii. 26-31).

39. *thirty and seven in all*] This reckoning is correct, though only 36 *names* are given, the names of only two of the second triad being recorded, but 31 names are given from *v.* 24 to the end, which, added to the two triads, or six, makes 37. Joab as captain of the whole host stands quite alone. In 1 Chr. xi. 41-47, after Uriah the Hittite, there follow sixteen other names, probably the names of those who took the places of those in the former list, who died from time to time, or who were added when the number was less rigidly restricted to thirty.

XXIV. **1.** *And again the anger of the LORD was kindled against Israel*] This sentence is the heading of the whole chapter, which goes on to describe the sin which kindled this anger, viz. the numbering of the people (1 Chr. xxi. 7, 8, xxvii. 24). There is no note of time, except that the word *again* shows that these events happened *after* those of ch. xxi. (Cp. also *v.* 25 and xxi. 14.)

and he moved David] In 1 Chr. xxi. 1 the statement is, *and an adversary* (not *Satan*, as A. V., since there is no article prefixed, as in Job i. 6, ii. 1, &c.) *stood up against Israel and moved David*, just as (1 K. xi.

14, 23, 25) first Hadad, and then Rezon, is said to have been *an adversary* (Satan) to Solomon and to Israel. Hence our text should be rendered, *For one moved David against them.* We are not told whose advice it was, but some one, who proved himself an enemy to the best interests of David and Israel, urged the king to number the people.

2. 1 Chr. xxi. 2, supplies some missing words. This passage should run, as at *v.* 4, *And the king said to Joab and to the princes of the host who were with him*, &c. (cp. 1 Chr. xxvii. 22). They were employed *with Joab* as his assistants in the numbering, exactly as in the previous numbering (Num. i. 4) when a prince was appointed from each tribe to be *with* Moses and Aaron.

5. *Aroer*] Aroer on the Arnon (Deut. ii. 36 note). Aroer itself stood on the very edge of the precipitous cliff of the valley; and in the valley beneath, possibly in an island in the stream, stood another city which is here alluded to.

river] Rather, " the **valley** " (marg.). They passed from Aroer, northward to Gad, and so pitched at Jazer (see marg. reff.), which is on the frontier of Gad and Reuben.

6. *to Gilead*] Jazer was in the plain. They passed from thence to the mountain district of Gilead.

the land of Tahtim-hodshi] The text here is corrupt, as no such land is known. Possibly the right reading is *the land of the*

7 came to ^gDan-jaan, and about to ^hZidon, and came to the strong hold of Tyre, and to all the cities of the Hivites, and of the Canaanites: and they went out to the south of Judah, *even* to
8 Beer-sheba. So when they had gone through all the land, they came to Jerusalem at the end of nine months and twenty days.
9 And Joab gave up the sum of the number of the people unto the king: ⁱand there were in Israel eight hundred thousand valiant men that drew the sword; and the men of Judah *were* five
10 hundred thousand men.   ¶ And ^kDavid's heart smote him after that he had numbered the people. And David said unto the LORD, ^lI have sinned greatly in that I have done: and now, I beseech thee, O LORD, take away the iniquity of thy servant;
11 for I have ^mdone very foolishly. For when David was up in the morning, the word of the LORD came unto the prophet ⁿGad,
12 David's ^oseer, saying, Go and say unto David, Thus saith the LORD, I offer thee three *things;* choose thee one of them, that I
13 may *do it* unto thee. So Gad came to David, and told him, and said unto him, Shall ^pseven years of famine come unto thee in thy land? or wilt thou flee three months before thine enemies, while they pursue thee? or that there be three days' pestilence in thy land? now advise, and see what answer I shall return to him
14 that sent me. And David said unto Gad, I am in a great strait: let us fall now into the hand of the LORD; ^qfor his mercies *are*
15 ¹great: and ^rlet me not fall into the hand of man. ¶ So ^sthe LORD sent a pestilence upon Israel from the morning even to the time appointed: and there died of the people from Dan even to
16 Beer-sheba seventy thousand men. ^tAnd when the angel stretched out his hand upon Jerusalem to destroy it, ^uthe LORD repented him of the evil, and said to the angel that destroyed the people, It is enough: stay now thine hand. And the angel

¹ Or, *many.*

Marginal references:
g Josh. 19. 47.
Judg. 18. 29.
h Josh.19.28.
Judg. 18. 28.

i See 1 Chr. 21. 5.

k 1 Sam.24.5.

l ch. 12. 13.
Ps. 32. 5.

m 1 Sam. 13. 13.
n 1 Sam.22.5.
o 1 Sam. 9. 9.
1 Chr. 29. 29.

p See 1 Chr. 21. 12.

q Ps. 103. 8, 13, 14.
& 119. 156.
r See Isai. 47. 6.
Zech. 1. 15.
s 1Chr.21.14.
& 27. 24.
t Ex. 12. 23.
1 Chr. 21. 15.
u Gen. 6. 6.
1 Sam.15.11.
Joel 2. 13, 14.

Hittites (Judg. i. 26); *hodshi* may be a fragment of a sentence which mentioned in what month (*hodesh*) they arrived there, just as v. 8 relates that they returned to Jerusalem at the end of nine *months.*

Dan-jaan] The Versions read *Dan-jaar, i.e.* Dan in the wood. Whatever is the meaning of *Jaan,* there can be little doubt that Dan (the ancient Laish) is meant (marg. reff.), both from its position and importance as the northern boundary of Israel, and from its connexion with Zidon.

7. *the strong hold of Tyre*] "**The fenced city,**" as it is generally rendered throughout the Historical Books.

the cities of the Hivites] Gibeon, Chephirah, Beeroth, and Kirjath-jearim, and perhaps Shechem, besides those at the foot of Hermon and Lebanon, of which we do not know the names. This continuance of distinct communities of Hivites so late as the end of David's reign is remarkable.

9. 1 Chr. xxvii. 23 indicates sufficiently why the numbering was sinful. It is also stated in 1 Chr. xxi. 6, that Joab purposely omitted Levi and Benjamin from the reckoning.

eight hundred thousand ...five hundred thousand] In Chronicles the numbers are differently given. It is probable therefore that the Chronicler has included in his statement of the sum total some numbers which are not included here.

11. *David's seer*] Marg. reff. From the latter passage it is probable that we have here Gad's narrative.

13. Cp. Ezek. xiv. 13-21. The *seven* years of famine correspond with the *seven* years of famine in Gen. xli. 27, 30, and with the same number of years in 2 K. viii. 1. But in Chronicles, it is *three years,* which agrees better with the *three* months and *three* days. The whole passage is amplified in Chronicles, which has less the aspect of an original text than this.

15. *the time appointed*] Perhaps "*the time of the assembly,*" meaning the time of the evening sacrifice, at three o'clock, when the people assembled for prayer, more commonly described as *the time of the evening oblation* (Dan. ix. 21; 1 K. xviii. 29, 36; Acts iii. 1; Luke i. 10).

seventy thousand] It is the most destructive plague recorded as having fallen upon the Israelites. In the plague that followed the rebellion of Korah there died 14,700 (Num. xvi. 49); in the plague, on account of Baal-Peor, 24,000 (Num. xxv. 9; 1 Cor. x. 8).

*1 Chr. 21.
15,
Ornan:
See ver. 18.
2 Chr. 3. 1.
y 1 Chr. 21.
17.
z 1 Chr. 21.
18, &c.

a See Gen.
23. 8—16.
b Num. 16.
48, 50.

c 1 Kin. 19.
21.

d Ezek. 20.
40, 41.

e See 1 Chr.
21. 24, 25.

f ch. 21. 14.
v ver. 21.

of the LORD was by the threshingplace of *x*Araunah the Jebusite.
17 And David spake unto the LORD when he saw the angel that
smote the people, and said, Lo, *v*I have sinned, and I have done
wickedly: but these sheep, what have they done? let thine
hand, I pray thee, be against me, and against my father's house.
18 ¶ And Gad came that day to David, and said unto him, *z*Go up,
rear an altar unto the LORD in the threshingfloor of ¹Araunah
19 the Jebusite. And David, according to the saying of Gad, went
20 up as the LORD commanded. And Araunah looked, and saw the
king and his servants coming on toward him: and Araunah went
out, and bowed himself before the king on his face upon the
21 ground. And Araunah said, Wherefore is my lord the king
come to his servant? *a*And David said, To buy the threshing-
floor of thee, to build an altar unto the LORD, that *b*the plague
22 may be stayed from the people. And Araunah said unto David,
Let my lord the king take and offer up what *seemeth* good unto
him: *c*behold, *here be* oxen for burnt sacrifice, and threshing
23 instruments and *other* instruments of the oxen for wood. All
these *things* did Araunah, *as* a king, give unto the king. And
Araunah said unto the king, The LORD thy God *d*accept thee.
24 And the king said unto Araunah, Nay; but I will surely buy *it*
of thee at a price: neither will I offer burnt offerings unto the
LORD my God of that which doth cost me nothing. ¶ So *e*David
bought the threshingfloor and the oxen for fifty shekels of silver.
25 And David built there an altar unto the LORD, and offered
burnt offerings and peace offerings. *f*So the LORD was intreated
for the land, and *v*the plague was stayed from Israel.

¹ Heb. *Araniah.*

---

17. Cp. the passage in Chronicles. The
account here is abridged; and *v.* 18 has
the appearance of being the original statement.

20. *and his servants*] In Chronicles *his
four sons,* viz. David's. It is very possible
that David may have taken his sons with
him, as well as his elders, and Gad's original
narrative may have mentioned the circumstance, which the compiler of this chapter
did not care to specify, and so used the
general term *his servants.*

22. *here be oxen*] Those, viz., which were
at that very time threshing out the grain in
Araunah's threshing-floor (1 Chr. xxi. 20;
Deut. xxv. 4).

threshing-instruments] This was a kind of
sledge with iron teeth (Isai. xli. 15). It
was drawn by two or four oxen over the
grain on the floor.

other instruments of the oxen] *i.e. the
harness of the oxen,* of which the yoke, and

perhaps some other parts, would be made
of wood (marg. reff.; 1 Sam. vi. 14).

23. Either, "*the whole O king does Araunah give unto the king;*" or (2) *the whole did
king Araunah give to the king.* The former
is preferable.

24. *fifty shekels of silver*] In Chronicles,
six hundred shekels of gold by weight. In
explanation, it is supposed—that the fifty
shekels here mentioned were gold shekels,
each worth twelve silver shekels, so that
the fifty gold shekels are equal to the
600 silver; that our text should be rendered, *David bought the threshing-floor and
the oxen for money,* viz., *fifty shekels;* and
that the passage in Chron. should be rendered, *David gave to Ornan gold shekels of
the value* (or weight) *of 600 shekels.* What
is certain is that our text represents the
fifty shekels as the price of the threshing-
floor and the oxen.

KINGS.

INTRODUCTION TO BOOKS I. AND II.

THE Greek translators, known as the LXX., who separated the "Book of the Law of Moses" into five parts, and the "Book of Samuel" into two, made the division, which is now almost universally adopted, of the original "Book of Kings" into a "First" and a "Second Book." The separation thus made was followed naturally in the early Latin Versions, which were formed from the Greek ; and when Jerome set forth the edition now called "The Vulgate," he followed the custom which he found established. The general adoption of the Vulgate by the Western Church caused the arrangement introduced by the LXX. to obtain almost universal acceptance.

The work is named from its contents, since the entire subject of the whole is the history of the "Kings" of Israel and Judah from the accession of Solomon to the Babylonish captivity.

1. The unity of the work is proved by the marked and striking simplicity and regularity of the plan. The work is, from first to last a history of the kings in strict chronological order, on the same system, and on a uniform scale. Exceptions to this uniformity in the larger space bestowed on the reigns of a few monarchs[1] are due to the principle of treating with the greatest fulness the parts of the history theocratically of most importance.

A second evidence of unity is the general uniformity of style and language—a uniformity admitted by all writers, and one which is only slightly infringed in two or three instances, where the irregularity may be accounted for by a diversity in the sources used by the author and a close following of the language which he found in those sources.[2]

To these general heads of evidence may be added certain peculiarities of thought or expression which pervade the two Books, all of them indicating with greater or less certainty a single author.[3]

---

[1] As Solomon (1 K. i.-xi.), Jeroboam (1 K. xii. 25-xiv. 20), Ahab (1 K. xvi. 29-xxii. 40), Jehoram (2 K. iii.-ix. 26), Hezekiah (2 K. xviii.-xx.), and Josiah (2 K. xxii. and xxiii.).

[2] e. g. In the first chapter of the First Book peculiarities of diction occur which connect it with the Books of Samuel, and are sufficiently explained by the supposition that in this part of his work the author of Kings drew from a source which had been used also by the author of Samuel. The narratives in 2 Kings iv. 1-37, and viii. 1-6, contain some remarkable Aramaic forms, which have been regarded as evidences of late composition, but which are, it is probable, provincialisms—peculiarities of an Israelite author contemporary (or nearly so) with Elisha, whose words the compiler of Kings preserved unaltered.

[3] e. g. The formulæ which introduce and close the reign of almost every king, or which describe the ordinary sinfulness of the Israelite monarchs ; others are less palpable and evident, and therefore the more thoroughly to be relied

2. Some have thought from the continuity of the narrative, from the general resemblance of the style, and from the common employment of a certain number of words and phrases, that the six "Books," commencing with Judges and terminating with the Second Book of Kings, are the production of a single writer, and constitute in reality a single unbroken composition. Others consider these arguments far from conclusive. The continuity of the narrative is formal, and may be due to the after arrangements of a reviser, such as Ezra is commonly believed to have been.

So far as the mere idiom of the language goes, it is perhaps true that we cannot draw a marked line between Kings and Samuel. But many of the traits most characteristic of the writer of Kings are wholly wanting in the other (and probably earlier) composition. For these and other reasons the "Books of Kings" may claim distinctness and separateness.[4]

3. There are two grounds upon which, apart from all traditional notices, the date of a historical work may be determined, viz., the peculiarities of the diction, and the contents.

The language of Kings belongs unmistakably to the period of the Captivity. It is later than that of Isaiah, Amos, Hosea, Micah, Joel, and Nahum, earlier than that of Chronicles, Ezra, Nehemiah, Haggai, and Zechariah.[5] In general character it bears a close resemblance to the language of Jeremiah and Ezekiel; and may be assigned to the sixth century before our era.

The result obtainable from the contents is similar, only somewhat more definite. Assuming the last detached section of the work (2 K. xxv. 27–30) to be an integral portion of it, we obtain the year B.C. 561—the first year of Evil-Merodach—as the earliest possible date of the completion of the composition.[6] Again, from the fact that the work contains no allusion at all to the return of the Jews from their Captivity, we obtain for the latest possible date the year B.C. 538, the year of the return under

---

upon : such as the habit of express allusion to the Law of Moses (1 K. ii. 3, vi. 12, &c. ; 2 K. x. 31, xi. 12, &c.); the perpetual reference to God's choice of David and of Jerusalem (1 K. viii. 16, 29, ix. 3, &c ; 2 K. xx., xxi. 4); the constant use of the phrase "man of God," (which occurs in Kings at least fifty-three times, and in twelve distinct chapters. In Samuel it is used about five times in two chapters. In Chronicles it is used six times—in four chapters) ; the habit of frequently prefixing the word "king" to the names of monarchs ; and the like.

[4] *e. g.* References to the Book of the Law, so constant in Kings, nowhere occur in Samuel. Samuel is incomplete and vague in respect of dates, which in Kings are given with extraordinary precision. The author of Samuel nowhere makes any mention of his sources, while the author of Kings is constantly alluding to his.

The favourite usages of the writer of Kings, such as his employment of the phrase "man of God," and his habit of prefixing the word "king" to the names of monarchs, although not absolutely unknown to the writer of Samuel, are with him comparatively rare and unfamiliar. Each character who is brought upon the scene, however familiar to one acquainted with Samuel, is given a descriptive epithet, such as, "the prophet," "the priest," "the son of," &c., as if previously unknown, when first introduced.

[5] The words and phrases which have been thought to indicate a later date than the time of the Captivity can be shown, in almost every instance, to have been in use during that time, or even previously.

[6] The rest of the work may have been written as early as B.C. 580, and the section in question may have been added afterwards.

Zerubbabel : or in other words between the death of Nebuchadnezzar and the accession of Cyrus in Babylon. Linguistic and other considerations favour the belief that the actual completion was early in this period—about B.C. 560; and it is not improbable that the greater part of the work was written as early as B.C. 580—*i.e.* some twenty years previously.

4. Jewish tradition assigns the authorship of Kings to Jeremiah ; and there are very weighty arguments in favour of this view. There is a very remarkable affinity between the language of Kings and that of the admitted writings of the Prophet.[7] The matter moreover, of the two works, so far as the same events are treated, is in the closest harmony,[8] those points being especially singled out for insertion, of which Jeremiah had personal knowledge and in which he took peculiar interest. Another argument of very considerable force is drawn from the entire omission of any notice at all of Jeremiah in Kings, which would have been very strange and unnatural in any other historian, considering the important part which Jeremiah played in the transactions of so many reigns, but which is completely intelligible on the hypothesis of his authorship of Kings : it is then the natural fruit and sign of a becoming modesty and unselfishness.

Still, though Jeremiah's author-

ship appears, all things considered, to be highly probable, we must admit that it has not been proved, and is therefore to some extent uncertain.

5. The author of Kings cites as authorities on the subject-matter of his history three works : (1) the "Book of the Acts of Solomon" (xi. 41) ; (2) the "Book of the Chronicles of the Kings of Israel" (xiv. 19, &c.) ; and (3) the "Book of the Chronicles of the Kings of Judah" (xiv. 29, &c.). His own history was, at least in part, derived from these works. Lesser works were also open to him.[9] Further, the writer had probably access to a work of a different character from any of those quoted by the author of Chronicles, namely, a collection of the miracles of Elisha, made probably in one of the schools of the Prophets.

Hence the sources of Kings may be considered threefold, consisting, first, of certain general historical documents called the "Books of the Chronicles of the Kings;" secondly, of some special treatises on the history of particular short periods; and, thirdly, of a single work of a very peculiar character, the private biography of a remarkable man.

The "Books of the Chronicles of the Kings" were probably of the nature of public Archives,[1]—State-annals, that is, containing an ac-

---

[7] *e. g.* Cp. 2 K. xvii. 14 and Jer. vii. 26 ; 2 K. xvii. 15 and Jer. ii. 5 ; 1 K. viii. 25 and Jer. xxxiii. 17 ; 2 K. xxi. 12 and Jer. xix. 3 ; 2 K. xxii. 17 and Jer. vii. 20, &c.

[8] Compare 2 K. xxiii. 34 with Jer. xxii. 12 ; 2 K. xxiv. 1 with Jer. xxv. 1-9 ; 2 K. xxiv. 7 with Jer. xlvi. 2-12 ; 2 K. xxv. 1-12 with Jer. xxxix. 1-10, &c.

[9] Such as the following :—"The Chronicles of King David" (1 Chr. xxvii. 24), "The Acts of Samuel the Seer," "The Acts of Nathan the Prophet," "The Acts of Gad the Seer" (1 Chr. xxix. 29), "The Prophecy of Ahijah the Shilonite," "The Visions of Iddo the Seer against Jeroboam the Son of Nebat" (2 Chr. ix. 29), "The Acts of Shemaiah the Prophet," "Iddo the Seer on Genealogies" (2 Chr. xii. 15), "The Commentary of the Prophet Iddo" (2 Chr. xiii. 22), and the like.

[1] See Esther ii. 23, vi. 1, x. 2.

count of the chief public events in the reign of each king, drawn up by an authorised person. With the Israelites the authorised person was probably in almost every case a Prophet. The Prophets regarded this as one of their principal duties, as we see by the examples of Isaiah (2 Chr. xxvi. 22 ; Is. xxxvi.--xxxviii.), Jeremiah (xxxix.--xliii. 7 ; lii.), and Daniel (i.--vi.). At the close of every reign, if not even in its course, an addition was probably made to the " Book of the Chronicles of the Kings " by the Prophet who held the highest position at the period.[2]

But the Prophets, in addition to these formal official writings, composed also historical works which were on a somewhat larger scale, and were especially more full in the account which they gave of religious matters. Cp. for example, the difference between the prophetical monograph and the drier abstract of the " Book of the Chronicles," contained in the historical chapters of Isaiah (xxxvi.--xxxix.), and the parallel chapters of the Second Book of Kings (xviii.--xx.). Cp. also Jer. xxxix.--xliv. with 2 K. xxv. 1--26. Further, comparing generally the

history as given in Chronicles with the corresponding history in Kings, the author of Chronicles seems to have followed generally the separate works of the various prophetical writers :[3] the author of Kings, mainly the official documents. In Chronicles nothing is more noticeable than the greater fulness of the *religious* history of Judah.[4] This came chiefly from the several prophetical works, and marks a contrast between their character and the ordinary character of the State-annals.

The writer of Kings was *mainly* a compiler. He selected, arranged, and wove into a whole, the various narratives of earlier writers whereof he made use. This is evident, both from the retention of obsolete or provincial forms in particular narratives, and from the occurrence of a number of statements which were inappropriate at the time when the compiler wrote.[5] The close verbal agreement between 2 Kings xviii. 15--xx. 19, and Isaiah xxxvi.--xxxix., can only have arisen from the writer's extracting without alteration Isaiah's

---

[2] Thus the "Book of the Acts of Solomon" was perhaps begun by Nathan, and was concluded either by Ahijah the Shilonite or by Iddo the Seer (2 Chr. ix. 29). The "Book of the Chronicles of the Kings of Judah" was probably the work of Shemaiah (2 Chr. xii. 15), Iddo (do. xiii. 22), Jehu the son of Hanani (do. xx. 34), Isaiah (do. xxvi. 22), Jeremiah, and others of the prophetical order, each of whom wrote the history of the king or kings with whom he was himself contemporary. Similarly with the "Book of the Chronicles of the Kings of Israel," Israelitish prophets such as Ahijah, Micaiah the son of Imlah (1 K. xxii. 8), Elisha, and Jonah (2 K. xiv. 25), composed portions.

[3] See the " Introd. to Chronicles," and compare 1 Chr. xxix. 29 ; 2 Chr. ix. 29, xii. 15, xiii. 22, &c.
[4] See particularly 1 Chr. xxii. 1--19, xxviii. 1--21, xxix. 1--22 ; 2 Chr. ii. 3--16, xiii. 4--18, &c.
[5] Of this kind are the following :--1. The statement in 1 K. viii. 8, that the staves of the Ark continued where they were placed by Solomon. 2. The statement that the bondage of the Amorites, Hivites, &c., continued (1 K. ix. 21). 3. The assertion that Israel was still in rebellion against the house of David (do. xii. 19). 4. The declaration that Selah (Petra) kept the name of Joktheel, which Amaziah gave it (2 K. xiv. 7). 5. The assignment of a preference over all other kings of Judah, previous and subsequent, both to Hezekiah (2 K. xviii. 5) and to Josiah (ib. xxiii. 25).

account of the reign of Hezekiah as it occurred in the State-annals: and the verbal agreement between great part of Chronicles and Kings, is often best accounted for by supposing that the two writers made *verbatim* extracts from the same authority.

On the other hand the writer of Kings sometimes departed from the wording of his authors, and substituted expressions purely his own.[6]

And there are passages evidently original.[7] It is on these parts of the work that the argument in favour of Jeremiah's authorship especially rests.

6. Philologically speaking the general condition of the text is good.[8] But the historian has to lament an unsoundness, which, though affecting in no degree the religious character of the books, detracts from their value as documents wherein is contained an important portion of the world's civil history. The numbers, as they have come down to us in Kings, are untrustworthy, being in part self-contradictory, in part

opposed to other scriptural notices,[9] in part improbable, if not even impossible.[1] The defect would seem to have arisen from two causes, one common to the Hebrew Scriptures, the other peculiar to these Books. The common cause is corruption, partly from the fact that error in them is rarely checked by the context, partly from the circumstance that some system of abbreviated numerical notation[2] has been adopted by professional scribes, and that the symbols employed by them have been mistaken one for another. The peculiar cause of error seems to have been insertions into the text of chronological notes originally made in the margin by a commentator. The first date which occurs (1 K. vi. 1) seems to be a gloss of this cha-

---

[6] *e. g.* The phrase " across the river " (1 K. iv. 24) would not have been used to designate the tract west of the Euphrates by a Jew writing in Palestine in the reign of Solomon or Rehoboam. A contemporary of Jeroboam would not have spoken of " the cities of *Samaria* " (do. xiii. 32). The annals of Joash, son of Jehoahaz, did not, we may be sure, contain a statement that " God cast not Israel from his presence *as yet* " (2 K. xiii. 23).

[7] Besides the *formulæ* at the beginning and end of reigns, the same hand may be traced in 2 K. xvii. 7-41, xxi. 7-16, xxiii. 26, 27, xxiv. 3, 4, 6-20, xxv. 1-30.

[8] Almost the only passages where the question of the true reading is of much importance are 1 K. xi. 25, and 2 K. xvi. 6, in both which cases it is suspected that " Edom," should be read for " Syria."

[9] The date in 1 K. vi. 1, contradicts the Chronology of Judges and Samuel, as well as Acts xiii. 20 ; 1 K. xiv. 21, is at variance with ch. xii. The accession of Jehoram is variously placed in 2 K. i. 17 and 2 K. iii. 1 ; 2 K. xv. 1 is irreconcilable with 2 K. xiv. 23 ; xvii. 1 with xv. 30, &c.

[1] Thus Josiah (according to the present numbers) must have been born to Amon when the latter was sixteen, Jehoiakim to Josiah when Josiah was fourteen, and Hezekiah to Ahaz when Ahaz was only *eleven!* See 2 K. xviii. 2 note.

[2] Abbreviated forms of numerical notation are exceedingly ancient, and appear to have prevailed in all the great Oriental monarchies, notably in Egypt and Babylonia. The Hebrews certainly employed letters for numbers, in the same way as they do at present, as early as the time of the Maccabees; and it is probable that they employed either this or some other method of abbreviation from a much earlier date, perhaps even from the time of the Exodus. The full expression of the numbers in the sacred text belongs probably to the Talmudical period of superstitious regard for the mere letter of Scripture—the time when the characters were counted, when central letters were determined, and the practice commenced of writing them large.

racter, and it may be suspected that to a similar origin is due the whole series of synchronisms between the dynasties of Israel and Judah. It is probable that the original work gave simply the years assigned to each king in the " Books of the Chronicles," without entering upon the further question, in what regnal year of the contemporary monarch in the sister kingdom each prince ascended the throne. The chief difficulties of the chronology, and almost all the actual contradictions, disappear if we subtract from the work these portions.[3]

Excepting in this respect, the Books of Kings have come down to us, as to all essentials, in a thoroughly sound condition. The only place where the LXX. Version differs importantly from the Hebrew text is in 1 Kings xii., where a long passage concerning Jeroboam, the son of Nebat, not now found in the Hebrew, occurs between *vv.* 24 and 25. But this passage is clearly no part of the original narrative. It is a story after the fashion of the apocryphal Esdras, worked up out of the Scripture facts, with additions, which the Alexandrian writer may have taken from some Jewish authority whereto he had access, but which certainly did not come from the writer of Kings. None of its facts except possibly a single one—the age, namely, of Rehoboam at his accession[4]—belongs

to the real narrative of our historian.

7. The primary character of the work is undoubtedly historical. It is the main object of the writer to give an account of the kings of Israel and Judah from Solomon's accession to the captivity of Zedekiah.

The history is, however, written —not, like most history, from a civil, but from a religious point of view. The Jews are regarded, not as an ordinary nation, but as God's people. The historian does not aim at exhibiting the mere political progress of the kingdoms about which he writes, but intends to describe to us God's treatment of the race with which He had entered into covenant. Where he records the events of the civil history, his plan is to trace out the fulfilment of the combined warning and promise which had been given to David (2 S. vii. 12–16).

Hence events, which an ordinary historian would have considered of great importance, may be (and are) omitted by our author from the narrative ; or touched slightly and hastily.[5] As a general rule, the military history of the two kingdoms, which was no doubt carefully recorded in the " Books of the Chronicles," is omitted by

---

[3] As for instance in 1 K. xvi. 22, 23 :—" So Tibni died, and Omri reigned. [In the thirty and first year of Asa king of Judah] Omri reigned over Israel twelve years." Here the removal of the words in brackets would evidently improve the sense.

[4] See note on 1 K. xii. 8, 10.

[5] Thus he takes no notice at all of the expedition of Zerah the Ethiopian (2 Chr. xiv. 9–15, xvi. 8) ; of Jehoshaphat's war with Moab, Ammon, and Edom (2 Chr. xx. 1–25) ; of Uzziah's successes against the Philistines (do. xxvi. 6–8) ; r of Manasseh's capture by the Assyrians do. xxxiii. 11–13). He treats with the utmost brevity the conquest of Jerusalem by Shishak (1 K. xiv. 25, 26), the war between Abijam and Jeroboam (do. xv. 7), that of Amaziah with Edom (2 K. xiv. 7), and that of Josiah with Pharaoh-Nechoh (do. xxiii. 29) ; events treated at length in the parallel passages of the Book of Chronicles.

the writer of Kings, who is content for the most part to refer his readers to the State-annals for the events which would have made the greatest figure in an ordinary secular history.

On the other hand, the special aim of the writer induces him to assign a prominent place and to give a full treatment to events which a secular historian would have touched lightly or passed over in silence. The teaching of the prophets, and their miracles, were leading points in the religious history of the time ; it was owing to them especially that the apostacy of the people was without excuse ; therefore the historian who has to show that, despite the promises made to David, Jerusalem was destroyed, and the whole twelve tribes carried into captivity, must exhibit fully the grounds for this severity, and must consequently dwell on circumstances which so intensely aggravated the guilt of the people.

The character of the history that he has to relate, its general tendency and ultimate issue, naturally throw over his whole narrative an air of gloom. The tone of the work thus harmonises with that of Jeremiah's undoubted writings, and furnishes an additional argument in favour of that Prophet's authorship.

The style of Kings is, for the most part, level and uniform—a simple narrative style. Occasionally a more lofty tone is breathed, the style rising with the subject-matter, and becoming in places almost poetical (1 K. xix. 11, 12 ; 2 K. xix. 21–31). The most striking chapters are the eighth, eighteenth, and nineteenth of the First Book ; the fifth, ninth, eight-

eenth, nineteenth, and twentieth of the Second.

8. The general authenticity of the narrative contained in our Books is admitted. Little is denied or questioned but the miraculous portions of the story, which cluster chiefly about the persons of Elijah and Elisha. Some critics admitting that the narrative generally is derived from authentic contemporary documents—either State-annals cr the writings of contemporary Prophets—maintain that the histories of Elijah and Elisha come from an entirely different source, being (they hold) collections of traditions respecting those persons made many years after their deaths, either by the writer of Kings or by some other person, from the mouths of the common people. Hence, according to them, their "legendary" or "mythical" character.

But there are no critical grounds for separating off the account of Elijah, or more than a small portion of the account of Elisha,[6] from the rest of the composition. The history of Elijah especially is so intertwined with that of the kingdom of Israel, and is altogether of so public a nature, that the "Chronicles of the Kings of Israel" would almost necessarily have contained an account of it ; and an important part of the history of Elisha is of a similar character. Further, it is quite gratuitous to imagine that the account was not a contemporary one, or that it was left for a writer living long subsequently to collect into a volume the doings of these remarkable personages. The proba-

---

[6] 2 K. iv. 1–37, and viii. 1–6, form the exceptions to the general rule.

bility is quite the other way. As the Prophets themselves were the historians of the time, it would be only natural that Elisha should collect the miracles and other remarkable deeds of Elijah ; and that his own should be collected after his decease by some one of the "sons of the Prophets." Add to this that the miracles, as related, have all the air of descriptions derived from eye-witnesses, being full of such minute circumstantial detail as tradition cannot possibly preserve. The whole result would seem to be that (unless we reject miracles altogether as unworthy of belief on account of an *à priori* impossibility) the account of the two great Israelite Prophets in Kings must be regarded as entitled to acceptance equally with the rest of the narrative.

Both internal consistency and probability, and also external testimony, strongly support the general authenticity of the secular history contained in Kings. The empire of Solomon is of a kind with which early Oriental history makes us familiar ; it occurs exactly at a period when there was room for its creation owing to the simultaneous weakness of Egypt and Assyria ; its rapid spread, and still more rapid contraction, are in harmony with our other records of Eastern dominion ; its art and civilization resemble those known to have prevailed about the same time in neighbouring countries. The contact of Judæa with Egypt, Assyria, and Babylonia, during the period covered by our Books agrees with the Egyptian annals, and in some respects is most strikingly illustrated by the cuneiform inscriptions. Berosus, Manetho, Me-

nander, Dius—the heathen historians of Babylon, Egypt, and Tyre—join with the monuments in the support which they furnish to our author's truthfulness and accuracy, as the comment appended to the text will prove abundantly.

Even the broader features of the chronology are both internally probable, and externally confirmed by the chronologies of other countries. The interval between the accession of Solomon and the captivity of Zedekiah is given as $433\frac{1}{2}$ years,[7] which is divided among twenty-one monarchs, who belong to eighteen (or, excluding Jehoiachin, to seventeen) generations. This allows for each generation the very probable term of $25\frac{1}{2}$ years. During the portion of the history where the chronology is double, and where the chief internal difficulties occur, the divergence of the two schemes is but slight, amounting to no more than about twenty years in 240 or 250. Egyptian annals confirm approximately the Biblical dates for Shishak's invasion, and So's alliance. The Assyrian annals agree with the Hebrew in the date of the fall of Samaria, and in exhibiting Hazael and Jehu, Tiglath-Pileser and Ahaz, Sennacherib and Hezekiah, Esarhaddon and Manasseh, as contemporaries. The chronological difficulties, where such exist, do not at all exceed those with which every reader of profane historians is familiar, and which, in fact, pervade the whole of ancient chron-

---

[7] This number is obtained by adding together the years of the kings of Judah. If parts of years are throughout counted as full years, this number is somewhat in excess. Clinton makes the actual time 429 years.

ology. They are partly to be accounted for by diversities in the mode of reckoning;[8] while occasionally no doubt they result from a corrupt reading, or from an unauthorised interpolation.

[8] In some systems, fractions of years are reckoned as years; in others, they are omitted altogether. In some, years are longer; in others, shorter than the true astronomical year. The differences which result from these causes mount up to something considerable in the course of centuries.

THE FIRST BOOK

OF THE

KINGS,

COMMONLY CALLED, THE THIRD BOOK OF THE KINGS.

CHAP. 1. NOW king David was old *and* [1]stricken in years; and they covered him with clothes, but he gat no heat. Wherefore his
2 servants said unto him, [2]Let there be sought for my lord the king [3]a young virgin: and let her stand before the king, and let her [4]cherish him, and let her lie in thy bosom, that my lord the
3 king may get heat. So they sought for a fair damsel through-
out all the coasts of Israel, and found Abishag a *a*Shunammite,
4 and brought her to the king. And the damsel *was* very fair, and cherished the king, and ministered to him: but the king
5 knew her not. ¶Then *b*Adonijah the son of Haggith exalted himself, saying, I will [5]be king: and *c*he prepared him chariots
6 and horsemen, and fifty men to run before him. And his father had not displeased him [6]at any time in saying, Why hast thou done so? and he also *was* a very goodly *man;* *d*and *his mother*

a Josh. 19. 18.

b 2 Sam. 3. 4.
c 2 Sam.15. 1.

d 2 Sam. 3. 3, 4.
1 Chr. 3. 2.

[1] Heb. *entered into days.*
[2] Heb. *Let them seek.*
[3] Heb. *a damsel, a virgin.*
[4] Heb. *be a cherisher unto him.*
[5] Heb. *reign.*
[6] Heb. *from his days.*

I. 1. *Now*] Rather, "and." The conjunction has here, probably, the same sort of connecting force which it has at the opening of Joshua, Judges, 1 Samuel, &c., and implies that the historian regards his work as a *continuation* of a preceding history.

king David] The expression "king David," instead of the simpler "David," is characteristic of the writer of Kings. (See Introd., p. 264, notes 3, 4.) The phrase is comparatively rare in Chronicles and Samuel.

stricken in years] David was perhaps now in his 71st year. He was thirty years old when he was made king in Hebron (2 Sam. v. 4); he reigned in Hebron seven years and six months (2 Sam. ii. 11; 1 Chr. iii. 4); and he reigned thirty-three years at Jerusalem (2 Sam. v. 5). The expression had hitherto been used only of persons above eighty (Gen xviii. 11, xxiv. 1; Josh. xiii. 1, xxiii. 1): but the Jews at this time were not long-lived. No Jewish monarch after David, excepting Solomon and Manasseh, exceeded sixty years.

clothes] Probably "bed-clothes." The king was evidently bed-ridden (*v.* 47).

2. As the Jewish Law allowed polygamy, David's conduct in following—what has been said to have been—physician's advice, was blameless.

5. The narrative concerning Abishag, the Shunammite (see marg. ref. *a*), is introduced as necessary for a proper understanding of Adonijah's later history (see ii. 13–

25.) But even as it stands, it heightens considerably the picture drawn of the poor king's weak and helpless condition, of which Adonijah was not ashamed to take advantage for his own aggrandisement. Adonijah was born while David reigned at Hebron, and was therefore now between thirty-three and forty years of age. He was David's fourth son, but had probably become the eldest by the death of his three older brothers. He claimed the crown by right of primogeniture (ii. 15), and secretly to his partisans (cp. *v.* 10) announced his intention of assuming the sovereignty. It was well known to him, and perhaps to the Jews generally, that David intended to make Solomon his successor (*v.* 13).

to run before him] That is, he assumed the same *quasi*-royal state as Absalom had done, when he contemplated rebellion (2 Sam. xv. 1).

6. *had not displeased him*] i.e. "His father had never checked or thwarted him all his life."

a very goodly man] Here, too, Adonijah resembled Absalom (2 Sam. xiv. 25). The Jews, like the other nations of antiquity, regarded the physical qualities of rulers as of great importance, and wished their kings to be remarkable for strength, stature, and beauty (1 Sam. ix. 2). Adonijah's personal advantages no doubt helped to draw the people to him.

his mother, &c.] i.e. Haggith bare Adonijah after Maacah bare Absalom (2 Sam. iii. 3, 4). The words in italics are not in the

7 bare him after Absalom. And [1]he conferred with Joab the son
of Zeruiah, and with *Abiathar the priest: and [f]they [2]following
8 Adonijah helped *him*. But Zadok the priest, and Benaiah the
son of Jehoiada, and Nathan the prophet, and [g]Shimei, and
Rei, and [h]the mighty men which *belonged* to David, were not
9 with Adonijah. And Adonijah slew sheep and oxen and fat
cattle by the stone of Zoheleth, which *is* by [3]En-rogel, and
called all his brethren the king's sons, and all the men of Judah
10 the king's servants: but Nathan the prophet, and Benaiah, and
the mighty men, and Solomon his brother, he called not.
11 ¶ Wherefore Nathan spake unto Bath-sheba the mother of
Solomon, saying, Hast thou not heard that Adonijah the son of
12 [i]Haggith doth reign, and David our lord knoweth *it* not? Now
therefore come, let me, I pray thee, give thee counsel, that thou
mayest save thine own life, and the life of thy son Solomon.
13 Go and get thee in unto king David, and say unto him, Didst
not thou, my lord, O king, swear unto thine handmaid, saying,
[k]Assuredly Solomon thy son shall reign after me, and he shall
14 sit upon my throne? why then doth Adonijah reign? Behold,
while thou yet talkest there with the king, I also will come in
15 after thee, and [4]confirm thy words. ¶ And Bath-sheba went in

e 2 Sam. 20.
25.
f ch. 2. 22,
28.
g ch. 4. 18.
h 2 Sam. 23.
8.

i 2 Sam. 3. 4.

k 1 Chr. 22. 9.

---

[1] Heb. *his words were
with Joab.*
[2] Heb. *helped after Adonijah.*
[3] Or, *The well Rogel*, 2 Sam.
17. 17.
[4] Heb. *fill up.*

---

original; hence some, by a slight alteration,
read "David begat him."

7. Joab's defection on this occasion, after
his faithful adherence to David during the
troubles caused by Absalom (2 Sam. xviii.
2–17), may be accounted for by his fear that
Solomon would be a "man of rest" (1 Chr.
xxii. 9) and by his preference for the character of Adonijah. He may also have
thought that Adonijah, as the eldest son
(*v.* 5), had almost a right to succeed.

Abiathar's defection is still more surprising than Joab's. For his history, see
1 Sam. xxii. 20 note. Hitherto David and
he had been the firmest of friends. It has
been conjectured that he had grown
jealous of Zadok, and feared being sup-
planted by him.

8. There is some difficulty in understanding how Zadok and Abiathar came to be
both "priests" at this time, and in what
relation they stood to one another. The
best explanation seems to be that Abiathar
was the real High-Priest, and officiated at
the Sanctuary containing the Ark of the
Covenant in Zion, while Zadok performed
the offices of chief priest at the Tabernacle
of Witness at Gibeon (1 Chr. xvi. 39).

For Benaiah, see 2 Sam. viii. 18, xx. 23,
xxiii. 20, 21. For Nathan, see 2 Sam. vii.
2, 3, 17, xii. 1–15, 25. As privy to all
David's plans (*v.* 24), he had no doubt fully
approved the order of succession which the
king was known to intend.

Shimei and Rei] Shimei and Rei are
perhaps David's two brothers, Shimma and
Raddai (1 Chr. ii. 13, 14).

mighty men] Probably the company of 600,
originally formed during David's early wan-

derings (1 Sam. xxv. 13, xxvii. 2), and
afterwards maintained as the most essential element of his standing army.

9. Adonijah's feast was probably of a
sacrificial character, and intended to inaugurate him as king. Cp. the "sacrifices"
of Absalom (2 Sam. xv. 12).

Zoheleth] No satisfactory explanation has
been given of this name. Large blocks of
stone always attract attention in the East,
and receive names which are often drawn
from some trivial circumstance. Sinai and
Palestine are full of such *Hajars*, which
correspond to the *Ebens* or "stones" of
Holy Scripture. (Cp. Gen. xxviii. 22; Josh.
iv. 9; 1 Sam. vi. 14.) For En-Rogel, see
marg. ref.

11. *the son of Haggith*] Cp. marg. ref.
This expression was well chosen to touch
the pride of Bath-sheba. "Adonijah; not
thy son, but the son of thy rival, Haggith."

12. It would have been in accordance
with general Eastern custom for Solomon
to suffer death, if Adonijah had succeeded
in his attempt. But to have executed his
mother also would have been an unusual
severity. Still, such cases sometimes occurred: Cassander put to death Roxana,
the widow of Alexander the Great, at the
same time with her son, the young Alexander.

14. *confirm thy words*] "Establish" them,
by giving a second testimony. Nathan
thinks it best to move David's affections
first through Bath-sheba, before he comes
in to discuss the matter as one of state
policy, and to take the king's orders upon it.

15. *into the chamber*] The "**bed-chamber**"

unto the king into the chamber: and the king was very old;
16 and Abishag the Shunammite ministered unto the king. And
Bath-sheba bowed, and did obeisance unto the king. And the
17 king said, [1]What wouldest thou? And she said unto him, My
[l] ver. 13, 30. lord, [l]thou swearest by the LORD thy God unto thine handmaid,
saying, Assuredly Solomon thy son shall reign after me, and he
18 shall sit upon my throne. And now, behold, Adonijah reigneth;
[m] ver. 7, 8, 9, 25. 19 and now, my lord the king, thou knowest *it* not: [m]and he hath
slain oxen and fat cattle and sheep in abundance, and hath
called all the sons of the king, and Abiathar the priest, and
Joab the captain of the host: but Solomon thy servant hath he
20 not called. And thou, my lord, O king, the eyes of all Israel
are upon thee, that thou shouldest tell them who shall sit on
21 the throne of my lord the king after him. Otherwise it shall
[n] Deut. 31. 16. ch. 2. 10. come to pass, when my lord the king shall [n]sleep with his
fathers, that I and my son Solomon shall be counted [2]offenders.
22 ¶ And, lo, while she yet talked with the king, Nathan the
23 prophet also came in. And they told the king, saying, Behold
Nathan the prophet. And when he was come in before the
king, he bowed himself before the king with his face to the
24 ground. And Nathan said, My lord, O king, hast thou said,
Adonijah shall reign after me, and he shall sit upon my throne?
[o] ver. 19. 25 [o]For he is gone down this day, and hath slain oxen and fat
cattle and sheep in abundance, and hath called all the king's
sons, and the captains of the host, and Abiathar the priest;
[p] 1 Sam. 10. 24. and, behold, they eat and drink before him, and say, [p][3]God
26 save king Adonijah. But me, *even* me thy servant, and Zadok
the priest, and Benaiah the son of Jehoiada, and thy servant
27 Solomon, hath he not called. Is this thing done by my lord the
king, and thou hast not shewed *it* unto thy servant, who should
28 sit on the throne of my lord the king after him? ¶ Then king
David answered and said, Call me Bath-sheba. And she came
29 [4]into the king's presence, and stood before the king. And the
[q] 2 Sam. 4. 9. king sware, and said, [q]*As* the LORD liveth, that hath redeemed

[1] Heb. *What to thee?*
[2] Heb. *sinners.*
[3] Heb. *Let king Adonijah live.*
[4] Heb. *before the king.*

---

or "**inner chamber.**" Abishag was a disinterested witness present, who heard all that Bath-sheba said to David.

16. Bath-sheba bowed, like the woman of Tekoah (2 Sam. xiv. 4), with the humble prostration of a suppliant. Hence the king's question, "What wouldest thou?"

20. *tell them who shall sit on the throne*] Side by side with what may be called the natural right of hereditary succession, there existed in the old world, and especially in the East, a right, if not of absolutely designating a successor, yet at any rate of choosing one among several sons. Thus Cyrus designated Cambyses; and Darius designated Xerxes; and a still more absolute right of nomination was exercised by some of the Roman emperors.

21. *shall sleep*] This euphemism for death, rare in the early Scriptures,—being found only once in the Pentateuch (marg. ref.), and once also in the historical books before Kings (2 Sam. vii. 12),—becomes in Kings and Chronicles the ordinary mode of speech (see ii. 10, xi. 43, &c.; 2 Chr. ix. 31, xii. 16, &c.). David uses the metaphor in one psalm (Ps. xiii. 3). In the later Scriptures it is, of course, common. (Jer. li. 39; Dan. xii. 2; Matt. ix. 24; John xi. 11; 1 Cor. xi. 30, xv. 51; 1 Thess. iv. 14, &c.)

22. Nathan came into the palace, not into the chamber, whither he might not enter unannounced. Bath-sheba retired before Nathan entered, in accordance with Oriental ideas of propriety. So, when Bath-sheba was again sent for (*v.* 28), Nathan retired (cp. *v.* 32).

24. *hast thou said*] **Thou hast said.** In the original no question is asked. Nathan assumes, as far as words go, that the king has made this declaration. He wishes to draw forth a disclaimer.

29. "As the Lord liveth" was the commonest form of oath among the Israelites (*e.g.* Judg. viii. 19; 1 Sam. xiv. 39, xix. 6).

30 my soul out of all distress, ʳeven as I sware unto thee by the   ʳ ver. 17.
LORD God of Israel, saying, Assuredly Solomon thy son shall
reign after me, and he shall sit upon my throne in my stead;
31 even so will I certainly do this day. Then Bath-sheba bowed
with *her* face to the earth, and did reverence to the king, and
32 said, ˢLet my lord king David live for ever. ¶And king David   ˢ Neh. 2. 3.
said, Call me Zadok the priest, and Nathan the prophet, and   Dan. 2. 4.
Benaiah the son of Jehoiada. And they came before the king.
33 The king also said unto them, ᵗTake with you the servants of   ᵗ 2 Sam. 20,
your lord, and cause Solomon my son to ride upon ¹mine own   6.
34 mule, and bring him down to ᵘGihon: and let Zadok the priest   ᵘ 2 Chr. 32.
and Nathan the prophet ˣanoint him there king over Israel: 30.
and ʸblow ye with the trumpet, and say, God save king Solo-   ˣ 1 Sam.10.1.
                                                                     ch. 19. 16.
35 mon. Then ye shall come up after him, that he may come and   2 Kin. 9. 3.
sit upon my throne; for he shall be king in my stead: and I   ʸ 2 Sam. 15.
have appointed him to be ruler over Israel and over Judah.   10.
36 And Benaiah the son of Jehoiada answered the king, and said,   2 Kin. 9. 13.
                                                                     & 11. 14.
37 Amen: the LORD God of my lord the king say so *too*. ᶻAs the   ᶻ Josh. 1. 5,
LORD hath been with my lord the king, even so be he with   17.
Solomon, and ᵃmake his throne greater than the throne of my   1 Sam. 20.13.
                                                                     ᵃ ver. 47.
38 lord king David. ¶So Zadok the priest, and Nathan the prophet, ᵇand Benaiah the son of Jehoiada, and the Cherethites,   ᵇ 2 Sam. 8.
and the Pelethites, went down, and caused Solomon to ride   18.
                                                                     & 23, 20—23.
39 upon king David's mule, and brought him to Gihon. And
Zadok the priest took an horn of ᶜoil out of the tabernacle, and   ᶜ Ex. 30. 23.
                                                                     Ps. 89. 20.

¹ Heb. *which* belongeth *to me:* See Esth. 6. 8.

It was peculiar to David to attach a further
clause to this oath—a clause of thankfulness
for some special mercy (1 Sam. xxv. 34), or
for God's constant protection of him (here
and in 2 Sam. iv. 9).

31. A lower and humbler obeisance than
before (*v.* 16). In the Assyrian sculptures
ambassadors are represented with their
faces actually touching the earth before the
feet of the monarch.

32. The combination of the High-Priest,
the Prophet, and the captain of the body-
guard (the Cherethites and Pelethites, *v.*
38), would show the people that the proceedings had the king's sanction. The
order of the names marks the position of
the persons with respect to the matter in
hand.

33. Mules and horses seem to have been
first employed by the Israelites in the
reign of David, and the use of the former
was at first confined to great personages
(2 Sam. xiii. 29, xviii. 9). The Rabbins tell
us that it was death to ride on the king's
mule without his permission; and thus it
would be the more evident to all that the
proceedings with respect to Solomon had
David's sanction.

Gihon] Probably the ancient name of the
valley called afterwards the Tyropœum,
which ran from the present Damascus Gate,
by Siloam, into the Kedron vale, having
the Temple hill, or true Zion, on the left,
and on the right the modern Zion or an-

cient city of the Jebusites. The upper
"source" of the "waters of Gihon," which
Hezekiah stopped (see marg. ref.), was probably in the neighbourhood of the Damascus Gate.

34. *anoint him*] Inauguration into each
of the three offices [those of prophet, priest,
and king] typical of the Messiah, or
Anointed One, was by anointing with oil.
Divine appointment had already instituted
the rite in connexion with the kingly office
(2 Sam. ii. 4); but after Solomon we have
no express mention of the anointing of kings,
except in the three cases of Jehu, Joash, and
Jehoahaz (2 K. ix. 6, xi. 12, xxiii. 30), who
were all appointed irregularly. At the time
of the Captivity, kings, whose anointing has
not been related in the historical books, still
bear the title of "the anointed of the Lord."
(Lam. iv. 20; Ps. lxxxix. 38, 51.)

35. *over Israel and over Judah*] There is
no anticipation here of the subsequent division of the kingdom; the antithesis between
Judah and Israel already existed in the
reign of David (2 Sam. ii. 9, xix. 11).

37. *As the* LORD *hath been with my lord*]
This phrase expresses a very high degree
of Divine favour. It occurs first in the
promises of God to Isaac (Gen. xxvi. 3, 24)
and Jacob (Gen. xxviii. 13). See further
marg. reff.

39. *the tabernacle*] Probably that which
David had made for the Ark of the Covenant on Mount Zion (2 Sam. vi. 17). For

d 1 Chr. 29.
22.
e 1 Sam. 10.
24.

^danointed Solomon. And they blew the trumpet; ^eand all the
40 people said, God save king Solomon. And all the people came
up after him, and the people piped with ¹pipes, and rejoiced
with great joy, so that the earth rent with the sound of them.
41 ¶And Adonijah and all the guests that *were* with him heard *it*
as they had made an end of eating. And when Joab heard the
sound of the trumpet, he said, Wherefore *is this* noise of the
42 city being in an uproar? And while he yet spake, behold,
Jonathan the son of Abiathar the priest came: and Adonijah

f 2 Sam. 18.
27.

said unto him, Come in; for ^fthou *art* a valiant man, and
43 bringest good tidings. And Jonathan answered and said to
Adonijah, Verily our lord king David hath made Solomon king.
44 And the king hath sent with him Zadok the priest, and Nathan
the prophet, and Benaiah the son of Jehoiada, and the Cherethites, and the Pelethites, and they have caused him to ride upon
45 the king's mule: and Zadok the priest and Nathan the prophet
have anointed him king in Gihon: and they are come up from
thence rejoicing, so that the city rang again. This *is* the noise

g 1 Chr. 29.
23.
h ver. 37.

46 that ye have heard. And also Solomon ^gsitteth on the throne
47 of the kingdom. And moreover the king's servants came to
bless our lord king David, saying, ^hGod make the name of
Solomon better than thy name, and make his throne greater

i Gen. 47. 31.

than thy throne. ⁱAnd the king bowed himself upon the bed.
48 And also thus said the king, Blessed *be* the LORD God of Israel,

k ch. 3. 6.
Ps. 132. 11.

which hath ^kgiven *one* to sit on my throne this day, mine eyes
49 even seeing *it*. ¶And all the guests that *were* with Adonijah
50 were afraid, and rose up, and went every man his way. And
Adonijah feared because fo Solomon, and arose, and went, and

l ch. 2. 28.

51 ^lcaught hold on the horns of the altar. And it was told Solomon, saying, Behold, Adonijah feareth king Solomon: for, lo,
he hath caught hold on the horns of the altar, saying, Let king
Solomon swear unto me to day that he will not slay his servant
52 with the sword. And Solomon said, If he will shew himself a

m 1 Sam. 14.
45.
2 Sam.14.11.
Acts 27. 34.

worthy man, ^mthere shall not an hair of him fall to the earth:
53 but if wickedness shall be found in him, he shall die. So king
Solomon sent, and they brought him down from the altar.

¹ Or, *flutes*.

---

the holy oil, see marg. reff. That it was
part of the regular furniture of the Tabernacle appears from Ex. xxxi. 11, xxxix.
38.

40. *piped with pipes*] Some prefer "danced
with dances"—a meaning which the Hebrew would give by a change in the pointing, and the alteration of one letter. But
the change is unnecessary. (Flute-) pipes
were known to the Israelites (1 Sam. x. 5);
they were very ancient in Egypt, and were
known also to the Assyrians.

the earth rent] If the present Hebrew
text is correct we have here a strong instance of Oriental hyperbole. But it is
suspected that there is a slight corruption,
and that the verb really used meant "re-
sounded."

42. Jonathan had acted in a similar
capacity, as a carrier of intelligence, in the
time of Absalom's attempt (2 Sam. xv. 36,
xvii. 17); but at that time, like his father,

he was faithful to David, and "a valiant
man," "a virtuous man," or "a man of
worth." (See *v.* 52; Prov. xii. 4.)

43. *Verily*] "Nay, but" [or, "Not so"].

47. *the king bowed himself*] The king worshipped God and prayed that it might be
so. Cp. Gen. xlvii. 31, with marg. ref.,
Heb. xi. 21.

50. On the "horns" of the Altar, see
Ex. xxvii. 2 note. The Altar to which
Adonijah fled was probably in the "Taber-
nacle" already referred to (*v.* 39).

52. *there shall not an hair, &c.*] This was a
proverbial expression, meaning "he shall
suffer no hurt at all." Solomon's clemency
in pardoning Adonijah is very remarkable. In the East not only are pretenders
almost always punished with death, but it
has often been the custom for each king
upon his accession to put to death all his
brothers as mere possible pretenders.

And he came and bowed himself to king Solomon: and Solomon said unto him, Go to thine house.

CHAP. 2. NOW [a]the days of David drew nigh that he should die; 2 and he charged Solomon his son, saying, [b]I go the way of all the earth : [c]be thou strong therefore, and shew thyself a man; 3 and keep the charge of the LORD thy God, to walk in his ways, to keep his statutes, and his commandments, and his judgments, and his testimonies, as it is written in the law of Moses, that thou mayest [d][1]prosper in all that thou doest, and whither-4 soever thou turnest thyself: that the LORD may [e]continue his word which he spake concerning me, saying, [f]If thy children take heed to their way, to [g]walk before me in truth with all their heart and with all their soul, [h]there shall not [2]fail thee 5 (said he) a man on the throne of Israel. Moreover thou knowest also what Joab the son of Zeruiah [i]did to me, and what he did to the two captains of the hosts of Israel, unto [k]Abner the son of Ner, and unto [l]Amasa the son of Jether, whom he slew, and [3]shed the blood of war in peace, and put the blood of war upon his girdle that was about his loins, and in his shoes that were on 6 his feet. Do therefore [m]according to thy wisdom, and let not

a Gen. 47. 29.
Deut. 31. 14.
b Josh. 23.
14.
c Deut. 17.
19, 20.
d Deut. 29. 9.
Josh. 1. 7.
1 Chr. 22. 12,
13.
e 2 Sam. 7.
25.
f Ps. 132. 12.
g 2 Kin.20.3.
h 2 Sam. 7.
12, 13.
ch. 8. 25.
i 2 Sam. 3.
39.
& 19. 5, 6.
k 2 Sam. 3.
27.
l 2 Sam. 20.
10.
m ver. 9.
Prov. 20. 26.

[1] Or, *do wisely*, 1 Sam. 18. 5, 14, 30. [2] Heb. *be cut off from thee from the throne.* [3] Heb. *put.*

II. The events related in 1 Chr. xxviii. and xxix. had occurred in the interval which separates the last and this present chapter.

2. David appears to have in his thoughts the Divine address to Joshua. Without following it servilely, he reproduces several of its leading expressions and sentiments (cp. marg. reff.). Solomon's youth clearly constituted one of the chief difficulties of his position. If he was about nineteen or twenty, and known to be of a pacific disposition (1 Chr. xxii. 9), then to have to rule over the warlike and turbulent Hebrew nation, with a strong party opposed to him, and brothers of full age ready to lead it, was evidently a most difficult task. Hence he is exhorted, though in years a boy, to show himself in spirit "a man."

3. The "statutes" have been explained to be the positive ordinances of the Law; the "commandments" the moral precepts, not to steal, &c.; the "judgments" the laws belonging to civil government; and the "testimonies" the laws directing the commemoration of certain events. Cp. Ps. xix. 7, 8.

4. *that the* LORD *may continue his word*] The original promise given to David indirectly, through Nathan (2 Sam. vii. 11-17), and apparently unconditional, afterwards was made conditional upon continued obedience. (See marg. ref. *f.*) David reminds Solomon of this, in order to impress upon him a powerful motive to continue faithful and obedient.

5. In his directions with respect to certain important persons, David, anxious for the security of his young successor's king-

dom, allows old animosities to revive, and is willing to avenge himself indirectly and by deputy, though he had been withheld by certain scruples from taking vengeance in his own person. We must not expect Gospel morality from the saints of the Old Testament. They were only the best men of their several ages and nations. The maxim of "them of old time," whether Jews or Gentiles, was "Love your friends and hate your enemies" (see Matt. v. 43) ; and David perhaps was not in this respect in advance of his age. Joab's chief offence against David, besides his two murders, was no doubt his killing Absalom (2 Sam. xviii. 14). Another serious crime was his support of the treasonable attempt of Adonijah (i. 7). But besides these flagrant misdemeanours, he seems to have offended David by a number of little acts. He was a constant thorn in his side. He treated him with scant respect, taking important steps without his orders (2 Sam. iii. 26), remonstrating with him roughly and rudely (do. *vv.* 24 and 25), almost betraying his secrets (do. xi. 19-21), and, where he disliked the orders given him, disobeying them (1 Chr. xxi. 6). David allowed his ascendancy, but he chafed against it, finding *this* "son of Zeruiah," in particular "too hard" for him (marg. ref.).

put the blood of war upon his girdle, &c.] Meaning "The blood of Amasa spirted all over the girdle to which the sword of Joab was attached; and the sandals on his feet were reddened with the stains left by the falling corpse."

6. *his hoar head*] Joab, though the nephew of David, was probably not very

7 his hoar head go down to the grave in peace. But shew kindness unto the sons of ⁿBarzillai the Gileadite, and let them be of those that ᵒeat at thy table: for so ᵖthey came to me when I
8 fled because of Absalom thy brother. And, behold, *thou hast* with thee ᵠShimei the son of Gera, a Benjamite of Bahurim, which cursed me with a ¹grievous curse in the day when I went to Mahanaim: but ʳhe came down to meet me at Jordan, and ˢI sware to him by the LORD, saying, I will not put thee to
9 death with the sword. Now therefore ᵗhold him not guiltless: for thou *art* a wise man, and knowest what thou oughtest to do unto him; but his hoar head ᵘbring thou down to the grave with
10 blood. ¶So ˣDavid slept with his fathers, and was buried in
11 ʸthe city of David. And the days that David ᶻreigned over Israel *were* forty years· seven years reigned he in Hebron, and
12 thirty and three years reigned he in Jerusalem. ¶ᵃThen was Solomon upon the throne of David his father; and his kingdom
13 was established greatly. ¶And Adonijah the son of Haggith came to Bath-sheba the mother of Solomon. And she said, ᵇComest
14 thou peaceably? And he said, Peaceably. He said moreover,
15 I have somewhat to say unto thee. And she said, Say on. And he said, Thou knowest that the kingdom was ᶜmine, and *that* all Israel set their faces on me, that I should reign: howbeit the kingdom is turned about, and is become my brother's: for ᵈit
16 was his from the LORD. And now I ask one petition of thee,
17 ²deny me not. And she said unto him, Say on. And he said, Speak, I pray thee, unto Solomon the king, (for he will not say thee nay,) that he give me ᵉAbishag the Shunammite to wife.
18 And Bath-sheba said, Well; I will speak for thee unto the king.
19 ¶Bath-sheba therefore went unto king Solomon, to speak unto him for Adonijah. And the king rose up to meet her, and ᶠbowed himself unto her, and sat down on his throne, and caused a seat to be set for the king's mother; ᵍand she sat on his right
20 hand. Then she said, I desire one small petition of thee; *I pray thee,* say me not nay. And the king said unto her, Ask on, my
21 mother: for I will not say thee nay. And she said, Let Abishag the Shunammite be given to Adonijah thy brother to wife.
22 And king Solomon answered and said unto his mother, And why dost thou ask Abishag the Shunammite for Adonijah? ask

ⁿ 2 Sam. 19.
31, 38.
ᵒ 2 Sam. 9.
7, 10.
& 19. 28.
ᵖ 2 Sam. 17.
27.
ᵠ 2Sam.16.5.
ʳ 2 Sam. 19.
18.
ˢ 2 Sam. 19.
23.
ᵗ Ex. 20. 7.
Job 9. 28.
ᵘ Gen. 42.
38.
& 44. 31.
ˣ ch. 1. 21.
Acts 2. 29.
& 13. 36.
ʸ 2 Sam. 5. 7.
ᶻ 2 Sam. 5. 4.
1 Chr. 29. 26,
27.
ᵃ 1Chr.29.23.
2 Chr. 1. 1.
ᵇ 1 Sam. 16.
4, 5.
ᶜ ch. 1. 5.

ᵈ 1 Chr.22.9,
10.
& 28. 5—7.
Prov. 21. 30.
Dan. 2. 21.
ᵉ ch. 1. 3, 4.

ᶠ Ex. 20. 12.
ᵍ See Ps. 45.
9.

¹ Heb. *strong.*   ² Heb. *turn not away my face,* Ps. 132. 10.

greatly his junior, David being the youngest of the family, and Zeruiah, as is most likely, one of the eldest.

7. One of the sons of Barzillai here intended was probably Chimham (see marg. ref.). Who the others were is not known. The family continued down to the return from the Captivity, and still held property in Israel (cp. Ezra ii. 61 and Nehemiah vii. 63).

9. *hold him not guiltless*] i.e. "Do not treat him as an innocent man. Punish him as in thy wisdom thou deemest best. Not capitally at once; but so that he may be likely to give thee in course of time a just occasion to slay him." So, at least, Solomon seems to have understood the charge. (See *vv.* 36-46.)

11. *forty years*] In all forty years and

six months. See 2 Sam. v. 5, and 1 Chr. iii. 4. The Jewish writers almost universally omit the fractions of a year.

12. The "establishment" of the kingdom here intended is probably its universal acceptance both by the tribe of Judah and the other Israelites.

16. *deny me not*] Lit., as in the margin, *i.e.* "make me not to hide my face through shame at being refused."

19. *a seat*] Or, "a throne." We have here a proof of the high dignity of the Queen-mother. Cp. also xv. 13; 2 K. xi. 1-3. In the Persian Court the Queen-mother had often the chief power.

22. *ask for him the kingdom also*] Bath-sheba had not seen anything dangerous or suspicious in Adonijah's request. Solomon, on the contrary, takes alarm at once. To

for him the kingdom also ; for he *is* mine elder brother; even
for him, and for *ʰ*Abiathar the priest, and for Joab the son of

23 Zeruiah. ¶ Then king Solomon sware by the LORD, saying, *ⁱ*God
do so to me, and more also, if Adonijah have not spoken this

24 word against his own life. Now therefore, *as* the LORD liveth,
which hath established me, and set me on the throne of David
my father, and who hath made me an house, as he *ᵏ*promised,

25 Adonijah shall be put to death this day. And king Solomon
sent by the hand of Benaiah the son of Jehoiada ; and he fell

26 upon him that he died. ¶ And unto Abiathar the priest said the
king, Get thee to *ˡ*Anathoth, unto thine own fields ; for thou *art*
¹worthy of death : but I will not at this time put thee to death,
*ᵐ*because thou barest the ark of the Lord GOD before David my
father, and because *ⁿ*thou hast been afflicted in all wherein my

27 father was afflicted. So Solomon thrust out Abiathar from
being priest unto the LORD ; that he might *ᵒ*fulfil the word of
the LORD, which he spake concerning the house of Eli in Shiloh.

28 ¶ Then tidings came to Joab : for Joab *ᵖ*had turned after Adonijah, though he turned not after Absalom. And Joab fled unto
the tabernacle of the LORD, and *ᑫ*caught hold on the horns of

29 the altar. And it was told king Solomon that Joab was fled
unto the tabernacle of the LORD ; and, behold, *he is* by the altar.
Then Solomon sent Benaiah the son of Jehoiada, saying, Go,

30 fall upon him. And Benaiah came to the tabernacle of the
LORD, and said unto him, Thus saith the king, Come forth. And
he said, Nay ; but I will die here. And Benaiah brought the
king word again, saying, Thus said Joab, and thus he answered

31 me. And the king said unto him, *ʳ*Do as he hath said, and fall
upon him, and bury him ; *ˢ*that thou mayest take away the
innocent blood, which Joab shed, from me, and from the house

ʰ ch. 1. 7.
ⁱ Ruth 1. 17.

ᵏ 2 Sam. 7.
11, 13.
1 Chr. 22.10.

ˡ Josh. 21.18.

ᵐ 1 Sam.
23. 6.
2 Sam. 15.
24, 29.
ⁿ 1 Sam. 22.
20, 23.
ᵒ 1 Sam. 2.
31—35.
ᵖ ch. 1. 7.
ᑫ ch. 1. 50.

ʳ Ex. 21. 14.
ˢ Num.35.33.
Deut. 19. 13.

¹ Heb. *a man of death.*

---

ask for Abishag was to ask for the kingdom.
To the Oriental mind a monarch was so
sacred, that whatever was brought near to
him was thenceforth separate from common
use. This sacred and separate character
attached especially to the Royal harem.
The inmates either remained widows for the
rest of their lives, *or became the wives of the
deceased king's successor.* When a monarch
was murdered, or 'dethroned, or succeeded
by one whose title was doubtful, the latter
alternative was almost always adopted (cp. 2
Sam. xii. 8, xvi. 22). Public opinion so closely
connected the title to the crown and the
possession of the deceased monarch's wives,
that to have granted Adonijah's request
would have been the strongest encourage-
ment to his pretensions. Solomon, seeing
this, assumes that Adonijah cherishes a
guilty purpose, that there has been a fresh
plot, that Abiathar and Joab—Adonijah's
counsellors in the former conspiracy (i.
7)—are privy to it, and that the severest
measures are necessary to crush the new
treason.

23. *against his own life*] Adonijah had forfeited his life by his former conduct, and his
pardon had been merely conditional (i. 52).

24. The phrase "making a house" means
"continuing the posterity" of a person,
and, in the case of a royal person,
"maintaining his descendants upon the
throne."

26. For Anathoth and the allusions in
this verse, see marg. reff.

27. *that he might fulfil the word of the
LORD*] We need not understand this as
stating that the fulfilment of the old prophecy was Solomon's motive, or even one
of his motives. The reference is to the
overruling providence of God, which thus
brought about the fulfilment of the prophecy. (Cp. Matt. i. 22, ii. 15, xxvii. 35,
&c.) The deposition of Abiathar involved
the rejection of the house of Ithamar (1 Chr.
xxiv. 3), to which Eli belonged, and the re-
establishment of the High-Priesthood in the
line of Eleazar.

28. Joab followed the example of Adonijah (marg. ref.). The Tabernacle was now
at Gibeon (iii. 4 ; 1 Chr. xvi. 39).

31. It was only a murderer to whom the
Tabernacle was to be no protection (marg.
ref.). Hence the reference to the "innocent blood."

t Judg. 9.
24, 57.
Ps. 7. 16.
u 2Chr.21.13.
x 2Sam.3.27.
y 2 Sam. 20.
10.

z 2Sam.3.29.
a Prov. 25.5.

32 of my father. And the LORD *t*shall return his blood upon his own head, who fell upon two men more righteous *u*and better than he, and slew them with the sword, my father David not knowing *thereof, to wit,* *x*Abner the son of Ner, captain of the host of Israel, and *y*Amasa the son of Jether, captain of the 33 host of Judah. Their blood shall therefore return upon the head of Joab, and *z*upon the head of his seed for ever: *a*but upon David, and upon his seed, and upon his house, and upon 34 his throne, shall there be peace for ever from the LORD. So Benaiah the son of Jehoiada went up, and fell upon him, and slew him: and he was buried in his own house in the wilderness.

b Num. 25.
11, 12, 13.
1 Sam. 2. 35.
See 1 Chr. 6.
53.
& 24. 3.
c ver. 27.
d 2Sam.16.5.
ver. 8.
e 3 Sam. 15.
23.
f Lev. 20. 9.
Josh. 2. 19,
2 Sam.1. 16.
g 1 Sam.
27. 2.

35 And the king put Benaiah the son of Jehoiada in his room over the host: and *b*Zadok the priest did the king put in the room 36 of *c*Abiathar. ¶And the king sent and called for *d*Shimei, and said unto him, Build thee an house in Jerusalem, and dwell 37 there, and go not forth thence any whither. For it shall be, *that* on the day thou goest out, and passest over *e*the brook Kidron, thou shalt know for certain that thou shalt surely die: 38 *f*thy blood shall be upon thine own head. And Shimei said unto the king, The saying *is* good: as my lord the king hath said, so will thy servant do. And Shimei dwelt in Jerusalem many days. 39 And it came to pass at the end of three years, that two of the servants of Shimei ran away unto *g*Achish son of Maachah king of Gath. And they told Shimei, saying, Behold, thy servants *be* 40 in Gath. And Shimei arose, and saddled his ass, and went to Gath to Achish to seek his servants: and Shimei went, and 41 brought his servants from Gath. And it was told Solomon that Shimei had gone from Jerusalem to Gath, and was come again. 42 And the king sent and called for Shimei, and said unto him, Did I not make thee to swear by the LORD, and protested unto thee, saying, Know for a certain, on the day thou goest out, and walkest abroad any whither, that thou shalt surely die? and thou 43 saidst unto me, The word *that* I have heard *is* good. Why then hast thou not kept the oath of the LORD, and the commandment 44 that I have charged thee with? The king said moreover to

h 2 Sam.
16. 5.

Shimei, Thou knowest *h*all the wickedness which thine heart is privy to, that thou didst to David my father: therefore the LORD

i Ps. 7. 16.
Ezek. 17.19.
k 2 Sam. 7.
13. Ps. 89. 4.

45 shall *i*return thy wickedness upon thine own head; and king Solomon *shall be* blessed, and *k*the throne of David shall be es- 46 tablished before the LORD for ever. So the king commanded Benaiah the son of Jehoiada; which went out, and fell upon

l ver. 12.
2 Chr. 1. 1.

him, that he died. And the *l*kingdom was established in the hand of Solomon.

---

32. *shall return his blood*] i.e. "his shedding of blood."

33. *upon the head of his seed*] Cp. marg. ref. Nothing further is heard of Joab's descendants in the history.

34. Retribution overtook Joab on the very scene (Gibeon) of the most treacherous of his murders. It was at the "great stone which is in Gibeon" that Joab slew Amasa (2 Sam. xx. 8–10).

35. The High-Priesthood had been for some time in a certain sense divided between Zadok and Abiathar. (See i. 8 note). Henceforth Zadok became sole High-Priest.

36. The object, apparently, was to keep Shimei under the immediate eye of the government. Shimei's old home, Bahurim, lay east of Jerusalem, on the road to Jericho (2 Sam. xvii. 18), and could only be reached by crossing the Kedron valley. Solomon assumes, that, if he quits the city, it will probably be in this direction (*v.* 37).

39. *Achish*] Possibly the Achish of marg. ref., but more probably the grandson of the former Achish.

42. *Did I not make thee to swear*] The LXX. add to *v.* 37 a clause stating that Solomon "made Shimei swear" on the day when he commanded him to reside at Jerusalem.

CHAP. 3. AND ^aSolomon made affinity with Pharaoh king of Egypt, and took Pharaoh's daughter, and brought her into the ^bcity of David, until he had made an end of building his ^cown house, and ^dthe house of the LORD, and ^ethe wall of Jerusalem round 2 about. ^fOnly the people sacrificed in high places, because there was no house built unto the name of the LORD, until those days. 3 And Solomon ^gloved the LORD, ^hwalking in the statutes of David his father : only he sacrificed and burnt incense in high places. 4 ¶ And ⁱthe king went to Gibeon to sacrifice there ; ^kfor that *was* the great high place: a thousand burnt offerings did Solomon 5 offer upon that altar. ^lIn Gibeon the LORD appeared to Solomon ^min a dream by night: and God said, Ask what I shall 6 give thee. ⁿAnd Solomon said, Thou hast shewed unto thy ser-.vant David my father great ¹mercy, according as he ^owalked before thee in truth, and in righteousness, and in uprightness of heart with thee; and thou hast kept for him this great kindness,

¹ Or, *bounty*.

a ch. 7. 8.
& 9. 24.
b 2 Sam. 5.7.
c ch. 7. 1.
d ch. 6.
e ch. 9. 15.
f Lev. 17. 3.
ch 22. 43.
g Deut. 6. 5.
& 30. 16.
Ps. 31. 23.
Rom. 8. 28.
1 Cor. 8. 3.
h ver. 6. 14.
i 2 Chr. 1. 3.
k 1Chr.16.39.
l ch. 9. 2.
2 Chr. 1. 7.
m Num.12.6.
Matt. 1. 20.
n 2 Chr. 1.
8, &c.
o ch. 2. 4.
Ps. 15. 2.

III. 1. What Pharaoh is meant is uncertain. It must have been a predecessor of Shishak (or Sheshonk), who invaded Judæa more than forty years later (xiv. 25) ; and probabilities are in favour, not of Psusennes II., the last king of Manetho's 21st dynasty, but of Psinaces, the predecessor of Psusennes. This, the Tanite dynasty, had become very weak, especially towards its close, whence we may conceive how gladly it would ally itself with the powerful house of David. The Jews were not forbidden to marry foreign wives, if they became proselytes. As Solomon is not blamed for this marriage either here or in ch. xi., and as the idol temples which he allowed to be built (xi. 5–7) were in no case dedicated to Egyptian deities, it is to be presumed *t*hat his Egyptian wife adopted her husband's religion.

the city of David] The city, situated on the eastern hill, or true Zion, where the Temple was afterwards built, over against the city of the Jebusites (ix. 24 ; cp. 2 Chr. viii. 11).

2. The word "only" introduces a contrast. The writer means to say that there was one exception to the flourishing condition of things which he has been describing, viz., that "the people sacrificed in high-places." (Compare the next verse.) The Law did not forbid "high-places" directly, but only by implication. It required the utter destruction of all the high-places which had been polluted by idolatrous rites (Deut. xii. 2) ; and the injunction to offer sacrifices nowhere except at the door of the Tabernacle (Lev. xvii. 3–5) was an indirect prohibition of them, or, at least, of the use which the Israelites made of them ; but there was some real reason to question whether this was a command intended to come into force until the "place" was chosen "where the Lord would cause His name to dwell." (See Deut. xii. 11, 14.) The result was that high-places were used for the wor-

ship of Jehovah, from the time of the Judges downwards (Judg. vi. 25, xiii. 16 ; 1 Sam. vii. 10, xiii. 9, xiv. 35, xvi. 5 ; 1 Chr. xxi. 26), with an entire unconsciousness of guilt on the part of those who used them. And God so far overlooked this ignorance that He accepted the worship thus offered Him, as appears from the vision vouchsafed to Solomon on this occasion. There were two reasons for the prohibition of high-places ; first, the danger of the old idolatry creeping back if the old localities were retained for worship ; and, secondly, the danger to the unity of the nation if there should be more than one legitimate religious centre. The existence of the worship at high-places did, in fact, facilitate the division of the kingdom.

4. *Gibeon*] The transfer to Gibeon of the "Tabernacle of the congregation," and the brazen "Altar of burnt offerings" made by Moses, which were removed thither from Nob (cp. 1 Sam. xxi. 6, with marg. reff. *i*, *k*), had made it "the *great* high-place," more sacred, *i.e.*, than any other in the Holy Land, unless it were Mount Zion whither the Ark had been conveyed by David. For the position of Gibeon, see Josh. ix. 3 note.

a thousand burnt offerings did Solomon offer] Solomon presented the victims. The priests were the actual sacrificers (viii. 5). A sacrifice of a thousand victims was an act of royal magnificence suited to the greatness of Solomon. So Xerxes offered 1000 oxen at Troy. If the offerings in this case were "whole burnt offerings," and were all offered upon the Altar of Moses, the sacrifice must have lasted several days.

5. *the* LORD *appeared unto Solomon in a dream*] Cp. marg. reff. and Gen. xv. 1, xxviii. 12, xxxvii. 5.

6. *this great kindness*] David himself had regarded this as God's crowning mercy to him (i. 48).

p ch. 1. 48.

q 1 Chr. 29.1.
r Num.27.17.

s Deut. 7. 6.

t Gen. 13. 16.
& 15. 5.
u 2 Chr.1.10.
Pro. 2. 3—9.
Jam. 1. 5.
x Ps. 72. 1.
y Heb. 5. 14.
z Jam. 4. 3.

a 1 John 5.
14, 15.
b ch. 5. 12.
& 10. 24.
Eccles. 1. 16.

c Matt. 6. 33.
Eph. 3. 20.
d ch.4. 21,24.
Prov. 3. 16.

e ch. 15. 5.
f Ps. 91. 16.
Prov. 3. 2.
g So Gen.
41. 7.

that thou *p*hast given him a son to sit on his throne, as *it is* this
7 day. And now, O LORD my God, thou hast made thy servant
king instead of David my father: *q*and I *am but* a little child:
8 I know not *how* *r*to go out or come in. And thy servant *is* in
the midst of thy people which thou *s*hast chosen, a great people,
9 *t*that cannot be numbered nor counted for multitude. *u*Give
therefore thy servant an ¹understanding heart *x*to judge thy
people, that I may *y*discern between good and bad: for who is
10 able to judge this thy so great a people? ¶And the speech
11 pleased the LORD, that Solomon had asked this thing. And God
said unto him, Because thou hast asked this thing, and hast *z*not
asked for thyself ²long life; neither hast asked riches for thyself,
nor hast asked the life of thine enemies; but hast asked for thy-
12 self understanding ³to discern judgment; *a*behold, I have done
according to thy words: *b*lo, I have given thee a wise and an understanding heart; so that there was none like thee before thee,
13 neither after thee shall any arise like unto thee. And I have
also *c*given thee that which thou hast not asked, both *d*riches,
and honour: so that there ⁴shall not be any among the kings
14 like unto thee all thy days. And if thou wilt walk in my ways,
to keep my statutes and my commandments, *e*as thy father
15 David did walk, then I will *f*lengthen thy days. And Solomon
*g*awoke; and, behold, *it was* a dream. And he came to Jerusalem, and stood before the ark of the covenant of the LORD,
and offered up burnt offerings, and offered peace offerings, and

¹ Heb. *hearing.*   ² Heb. *many days.*   ³ Heb. *to hear.*
⁴ Or, *hath not been.*

---

7. See ii. 2 note, and on the hyperbole
contained in the phrase "little child," cp.
Gen. xliii. 8; Ex. xxxiii. 11.

how to go out or come in] This expression
is proverbial for the active conduct of
affairs. (See marg. ref.)

8. Cp. marg. reff. Solomon regards the
promises as fulfilled in the existing greatness and glory of the Jewish nation.

9. One of the chief functions of the
Oriental monarch is always to hear and
decide causes. Hence supreme magistrates
were naturally called "judges." (See Introd. to Book of Judges.) In the minds
of the Jews the "judge" and the "prince"
were always closely associated, the direct
cognisance of causes being constantly taken
by their chief civil governors. (See Ex.
ii. 14, xviii. 16, 22; 1 Sam. viii. 20; 2 Sam.
xv. 2-6.)

good and bad] i.e. "right and wrong,"
"justice and injustice."

10. Although Solomon's choice was made
"in a dream" (*v*. 5), we must regard it as
springing from his will in some degree, and
therefore as indicative of his moral character.

11. *thine enemies*] e.g. Hadad the Edomite (xi. 14-22) and Rezon the son of Eliadah
(do. *vv*. 23-25), whom Solomon might well
have wished to remove.

12. *a wise and an understanding heart*]
Solomon's wisdom seems to have been both
moral and intellectual (see iv. 29-34). But

it was moral wisdom alone which he requested, and which was promised him.
The terms translated "wise" and "understanding," both denote *practical* wisdom.
(See Gen. xli. 33, 39; Deut. iv. 6; Prov.
i. 2, &c.)

*neither after thee shall any arise like unto
thee*] i.e. in the knowledge of what was in
man, and in the wisdom to direct men's
goings, he was to be the wisest of *all* mere
men. In such wisdom the world would
know one only "greater than Solomon"
(Matt. xii. 42; Luke xi. 31).

13. A striking illustration of that law
of the Divine government to which Christ
referred (marg. ref.).

14. *I will lengthen thy days*] The promise
here was only conditional. As the condition was not observed (xi. 1-8), the right to
the promise was forfeited, and it was not
fulfilled. Solomon can scarcely have been
more than fifty-nine or sixty at his death.

15. Solomon determined to inaugurate
his reign by a grand religious ceremonial at
each of the two holy places which at this
time divided between them the reverence
of the Jews. Having completed the religious service at Gibeon, where was the
Tabernacle of the Congregation, he proceeded to Jerusalem, and sacrificed before
the Ark of the Covenant, which was in
Mount Zion (2 Sam. vi. 12). A great feast
naturally followed on a large sacrifice of
peace-offerings. In these the sacrificer

16 [h]made a feast to all his servants. ¶ Then came there two women, *that were* harlots, unto the king, and [i]stood before him.

17 And the one woman said, O my lord, I and this woman dwell in one house; and I was delivered of a child with her in the house.

18 And it came to pass the third day after that I was delivered, that this woman was delivered also: and we *were* together; *there was* no stranger with us in the house, save we two in the house.

19 And this woman's child died in the night; because she overlaid

20 it. And she arose at midnight, and took my son from beside me, while thine handmaid slept, and laid it in her bosom, and laid

21 her dead child in my bosom. And when I rose in the morning to give my child suck, behold, it was dead: but when I had considered it in the morning, behold, it was not my son, which I did

22 bear. And the other woman said, Nay; but the living *is* my son, and the dead *is* thy son. And this said, No; but the dead *is* thy son, and the living *is* my son. Thus they spake before the king.

23 ¶ Then said the king, The one saith, This *is* my son that liveth, and thy son *is* the dead: and the other saith, Nay; but thy son

24 *is* the dead, and my son *is* the living. And the king said, Bring

25 me a sword. And they brought a sword before the king. And the king said, Divide the living child in two, and give half to the

26 one, and half to the other. Then spake the woman whose the living child *was* unto the king, for [k]her bowels [1]yearned upon her son, and she said, O my lord, give her the living child, and in no wise slay it. But the other said, Let it be neither mine

27 nor thine, *but* divide *it*. Then the king answered and said, Give her the living child, and in no wise slay it: she *is* the mother

28 thereof. And all Israel heard of the judgment which the king had judged; and they feared the king: for they saw that the

4 [l]wisdom of God *was* [2]in him, to do judgment. SO king Solo-

2 mon was king over all Israel. ¶ And these *were* the princes

3 which he had, Azariah the son of Zadok [3]the priest, Elihoreph and Ahiah, the sons of Shisha, [4]scribes; [a]Jehoshaphat the son

Margin references:

[h] So Gen 40. 20. ch. 8. 65. Esth. 1. 3. Dan. 5. 1. Mark 6. 21.

[i] Num. 27. 2.

[k] Gen. 43. 30. Isai. 49. 15. Luke 1. 7, 8. 2 Cor. 7. 15

[l] ver. 9, 11, 12.

[a] 2 Sam. 8. 16. & 20. 24.

---

[1] Heb. *were hot.*   [2] Heb. *in the midst of him.*   [3] Or, *the chief officer.*
[4] Or, *secretaries.*

---

always partook of the flesh of the victim, and he was commanded to call in to the feast the Levite, the stranger, the fatherless, and the widow (Deut. xiv. 29). Cp. 2 Sam. vi. 19; 1 Chr. xvi. 3.

28. *the wisdom of God*] i.e. "Divine wisdom," "a wisdom given by God" (*v.* 12). The ready tact and knowledge of human nature exhibited in this pattern judgment, and its peculiar fitness to impress Orientals, have generally been admitted.

IV. 1. Solomon, that is, was king over "*all* Israel" from the first; not like David, who for seven and a half years reigned over Judah only. This feature well introduces the glory of Solomon and the organisation of the Court, of which the historian in this chapter intends to give us a general sketch. Solomon constitutes certain "princes" or officers of the first rank, deriving their station from him, and probably holding it during pleasure.

Azariah, the son of Zadok, the priest] "The priest" here belongs to Azariah, not

to Zadok. The term used (*cohen*) means sometimes a priest, sometimes a civil officer, with perhaps a semi-priestly character. (See 2 Sam. viii. 18 note.) In this place it has the definite article prefixed, and can only mean "the High-Priest." Azariah, called here the *son*, but really the *grandson*, of Zadok, seems to have succeeded him in the priesthood (1 Chr. vi. 10). His position as High-Priest at the time when this list was made out gives Azariah the foremost place in it.

3. Shisha, or Shavsha (1 Chr. xviii. 16), seems also to have been called Sheva (2 Sam. xx. 25), and Seraiah (2 Sam. viii. 17).

The "scribes" were probably royal "secretaries" (marg.), who drew up the king's edicts, wrote his letters, and perhaps managed his finances (xii. 10). They were among his most influential councillors.

By "recorder" or "remembrancer" (marg.), we must understand "Court annalist" (marg. ref. *a*).

b ch. 2, 35.
c See ch. 2.27.
d ver. 7.
e 2 Sam. 8. 18.
& 20. 26.
f 2 Sam. 15.
37.
& 16. 16.
1 Chr. 27. 33.
g ch. 5. 14.

4 of Ahilud, the ¹recorder. And ᵇBenaiah the son of Jehoiada
was over the host: and Zadok and ᶜAbiathar *were* the priests:
5 and Azariah the son of Nathan *was* over ᵈthe officers: and Za-
bud the son of Nathan *was* ᵉprincipal officer, *and* ᶠthe king's
6 friend: and Ahishar *was* over the household: and ᵍAdoniram
7 the son of Abda *was* over the ²tribute. ¶And Solomon had
twelve officers over all Israel, which provided victuals for the
king and his household: each man his month in a year made
8 provision. And these *are* their names: ³The son of Hur, in
9 mount Ephraim · ⁴the son of Dekar, in Makaz, and in Shaalbim,
10 and Beth-shemesh, and Elon-beth-hanan: ⁵the son of Hesed, in
Aruboth; to him *pertained* Sochoh, and all the land of Hepher:
11 ⁶the son of Abinadab, in all the region of Dor; which had
12 Taphath the daughter of Solomon to wife: Baana the son of
Ahilud; *to him pertained* Taanach and Megiddo, and all Beth-
shean, which *is* by Zartanah beneath Jezreel, from Beth-shean
to Abel-meholah, *even* unto *the place that is* beyond Jokneam:

h Num. 32.
41.

13 ⁷the son of Geber, in Ramoth-gilead; to him *pertained* ʰthe
towns of Jair the son of Manasseh, which *are* in Gilead; to him

---

¹ Or, *remembrancer.*
² Or, *levy.*
³ Or, *Ben-hur.*
⁴ Or, *Ben-dekar.*
⁵ Or, *Ben-hesed.*
⁶ Or, *Ben-abinadab.*
⁷ Or, *Ben-geber.*

---

4. It is curious to find Abiathar in this list of princes, after what has been said of his disgrace (ii. 27, 35). Some have supposed that after a while Solomon pardoned him. Perhaps the true explanation is that the historian here enumerates all those who were accounted "princes" in any part of Solomon's reign.

5. *the son of Nathan*] It is uncertain whether the Nathan of this verse is the Prophet or the son of David (2 Sam. v. 14). While on the one hand the position of "king's friend" is more likely to have been held by a contemporary, which the Prophet's son would have been, than by one so much younger as the son of a younger brother; on the other hand the title *cohen* seems to point to a member of the royal family. (See the next note.) Azariah who was "over the officers" was chief, that is, of the "officers" mentioned in *vv.* 8–19, as appears from the identity of the term here used with the title by which they are designated in *v.* 7.

principal officer] Or, *cohen.* The fact that the title *cohen* was borne by sons of David (2 Sam. viii. 18), who could not be priests in the ordinary sense of the word, seems to identify the Nathan of this verse with David's son (2 Sam. v. 14) rather than with the Prophet.

6. *over the household*] Comptroller of the household, like the "Steward" of the Persian Court. On the importance of this office, see 2 K. xviii. 18, and cp. Is. xxii. 15–25.

the tribute] The marginal reading, "levy," is preferable. The reference is to the forced labourers whom Solomon employed in his great works (marg. ref.).

7. The requirement of a portion of their produce from subjects, in addition to money payments, is a common practice of Oriental monarchs. It obtained in ancient, and it still obtains in modern, Persia.

8. In this arrangement of the territory into twelve portions, the divisions of the tribes seem to have been adopted as far as could be managed without unfairness. The prefecture of Ben-Hur corresponded nearly to the territory of Ephraim; that of Ben-Dekar to Dan; that of Ben-Hesed to Judah; those of Ben-Abinadab and Baana to Cis-Jordanic Manasseh; that of Ben-Geber to Manasseh beyond Jordan; of Abinadab to Gad; of Ahimaaz to Naphtali; of Baanah to Asher; of Jehoshaphat to Issachar; of Shimei to Benjamin; and of Geber to Reuben. The order in which the prefectures are mentioned is clearly not the geographical. Perhaps it is the order in which they had to supply the king's table.

9. For some of the names, see Josh. xix. 41–43.

10. *Sochoh*] See Josh. xv. 35.

11. *Dor*] See Josh. xi. 2 note. It has always been a practice among Oriental potentates to attach to themselves the more important of their officers by giving them for wives princesses of the royal house. Hence the union here between Ben-Abinadab (probably Solomon's first cousin, cp. 1 Sam. xvi. 8) and Taphath. Cp. *v.* 15.

12. On these cities see Josh. xii. 21, iii. 16; Judg. vii. 22; Josh. xxi. 22.

13. It will be observed that five out of the twelve prefects are designated solely by their father's names, Ben-Hur, &c., while one (Ahimaaz, *v.* 15) has no such designa-

also *pertained* [i]the region of Argob, which *is* in Bashan, three-
14 score great cities with walls and brasen bars : Ahinadab the son
15 of Iddo *had* [1]Mahanaim : Ahimaaz *was* in Naphtali ; he also
16 took Basmath the daughter of Solomon to wife : Baanah the son
17 of Hushai *was* in Asher and in Aloth : Jehoshaphat the son of
18 Paruah, in Issachar : Shimei the son of Elah, in Benjamin :
19 Geber the son of Uri *was* in the country of Gilead, *in* [k]the
country of Sihon king of the Amorites, and of Og king of
Bashan ; and *he* *was* the only officer which *was* in the land.
20 ¶ Judah and Israel *were* many, [l]as the sand which *is* by the sea
21 in multitude, [m]eating and drinking, and making merry. And
[n]Solomon reigned over all kingdoms from [o]the river unto the
land of the Philistines, and unto the border of Egypt : [p]they
brought presents, and served Solomon all the days of his life.
22 ¶ And Solomon's [2]provision for one day was thirty [3]measures
23 of fine flour, and threescore measures of meal, ten fat oxen, and
twenty oxen out of the pastures, and an hundred sheep, beside
24 harts, and roebucks, and fallowdeer, and fatted fowl. For he
had dominion over all *the region* on this side the river : from

[i] Deut. 3. 4.

[k] Deut. 3. 8.

[l] Gen. 22. 17.
Prov. 14. 28.
[m] Ps. 72. 3.
[n] 2 Chr. 9.26.
Ps. 72. 8.
[o] Gen. 15. 18.
Josh. 1. 4.
[p] Ps. 68. 20.

[1] Or, *to Mahanaim.* [2] Heb. *bread.* [3] Heb. *cors.*

---

tion. Probably the document, which the
author of the Book of Kings consulted, had
contained originally the proper name and
father's name of each prefect; but it was
mutilated or illegible in places at the time
when he consulted it. If *it* was in the
shape of a *list*, a single mutilation at one
corner might have removed four of the six
wanting names.

14. See margin. Ahinadab had the territory from the places last mentioned as far
as Mahanaim (Gen. xxxii. 2).

19. The meaning of the last clause is
somewhat doubtful. On the whole, our
Version may well stand as nearly correct.
The writer has assigned to Geber a wide
stretch of territory ; and, anticipating surprise, assures his readers " (there was but)
one officer who (purveyed) in this land."

20. There is some doubt about the proper
arrangement of the remainder of this chapter. The best alteration, if we alter the
Hebrew order at all, would be to place *vv.*
20 and 21 after *v.* 25.

many, &c.] See iii. 8 note ; and cp. Ps.
cxxvii., which is traditionally ascribed to
Solomon, and which celebrates the popu-
lousness and security of Israel in his day.

21. Solomon's empire, like all the great
empires of Asia down to the time of the
Persians, consisted of a congeries of small
kingdoms, all ruled by their own kings (*v.*
24), who admitted the suzerainty of the
Jewish monarch, and paid him " presents,"
i.e. an annual tribute (see x. 25).

unto the land of the Philistines] There is
no word corresponding to "unto" in the
Hebrew. The construction should be,
"Solomon reigned over all the kingdoms
from the river (*i.e.* the Euphrates : see
marg. reff.), *over* the land of the Philistines,"

&c. The writer draws attention to the fact
that the extent of Solomon's kingdom was
in accordance with the promises made to
Abraham, Moses, and Joshua.

22. *thirty measures*] (marg. *cors*) The *cor*,
which was the same measure as the homer,
is computed, on the authority of Josephus,
at 86 English gallons, on the authority of
the Rabbinical writers at 44. Thirty *cors*,
even at the lower estimate, would equal
1,320 gallons, or 33 of our "sacks ; " and the
90 *cors* of fine and coarse flour would altogether equal 99 sacks. From the quantity
of flour consumed, it has been conjectured
that the number of those who fed at the
royal board was 14,000.

23. *harts*, &c.] The exact sorts of wild
land animals here intended are very uncertain. Perhaps it would be best to translate "wild-goats, gazelles, and wild oxen,"
which abounded in the wilder parts of
Syria, whence Solomon would be supplied.
(See *v.* 24.) [Yahmûr, or the "roebuck,"
gives its name to a valley in a wooded
district, south of Carmel (Conder).] The
use of game at the royal banquets of Assyria
appears in the sculptures.

24. *on this side the river*] *i.e.* the region
west of the Euphrates.

Tiphsah, or Tiphsach, the place on the
Euphrates called Thapsacus. The word
means "ford," or "passage," being formed
from *pasach*, "to pass over" (cp. "paschal").
It is the modern *Suriyeh*, forty-five miles
below Balis, at the point where the Euphrates changes its course from S. to S.E.
by E. The stream is fordable here, and
nowhere else in this part of its course.
Solomon's possession of Thapsacus would
have been very favourable to his schemes
of land commerce (ix. 19).

q Ps. 72. 11.
r 1Chr. 22. 9.
s See Jer.23.6
t Mic. 4. 4.
Zech. 3. 10.
u Judg. 20. 1.
x ch. 10. 26.
2 Chr. 1. 14.
y See Deut.
17. 16.
z ver. 7.
a ch. 3. 12.
b Gen. 25. 6.
c See Acts 7.
22.
d ch. 3. 12.
e 1Chr.15.19.
Ps. 89, title.
f See 1 Chr.
2. 6.
& 6. 33.
& 15. 19.
Ps. 88,
title.
g Prov. 1. 1.
Eccles.12.9.
h Cant. 1. 1.

Tiphsah even to Azzah, over *q* all the kings on this side the river:
25 and *r* he had peace on all sides round about him. And Judah
and Israel *s* dwelt [1] safely, *t* every man under his vine and under
his fig tree, *u* from Dan even to Beer-sheba, all the days of Solo-
26 mon. ¶ And *x* Solomon had forty thousand stalls of *y* horses for
27 his chariots, and twelve thousand horsemen. And *z* those officers
provided victual for king Solomon, and for all that came unto
king Solomon's table, every man in his month: they lacked no-
28 thing. Barley also and straw for the horses and [2] dromedaries
brought they unto the place where *the officers* were, every man
29 according to his charge. ¶ And *a* God gave Solomon wisdom and
understanding exceeding much, and largeness of heart, even as
30 the sand that *is* on the sea shore. And Solomon's wisdom ex-
celled the wisdom of all the children *b* of the east country, and
31 all *c* the wisdom of Egypt. For he was *d* wiser than all men;
e than Ethan the Ezrahite, *f* and Heman, and Chalcol, and Darda,
the sons of Mahol: and his fame was in all nations round about.
32 And *g* he spake three thousand proverbs: and his *h* songs were a

---

[1] Heb. *confidently.*　　　　[2] Or, *mules,* or, *swift beasts,* Esth. 8. 14. Mic. 1. 13.

---

to Azzah] *i.e.* Gaza.

all the kings] Cp. Josh. xii. 9-24. In
Philistia, small as it was, there were five
kings (1 Sam. vi. 18). Syria was divided
into numerous small states, as many as
thirty-two kings being mentioned on one
occasion (xx. 1). The Hittites were ruled
by a great number of chieftains or princes
(x. 29; 2 K. vii. 6). Twelve are mentioned
in the Assyrian inscriptions.

25. *under his vine,* &c.] This phrase seems
to have been common among the Jews, and
even among neighbouring nations (2 K.
xviii. 31), to express a time of quiet and
security. It is used by the prophets in
descriptions of the Messianic kingdom
(marg. reff.).

26. In 2 Chr. ix. 25, the number of stalls
for Solomon's chariot horses is stated at
4,000, instead of 40,000. The number in
the present passage is probably a corruption. Solomon's chariots were but 1,400
(x. 26; 2 Chr. i. 14), for which 40,000 horses
could not possibly be required. The Assyrian
chariots had at most three horses apiece,
while some had only two. 4,000 horses
would supply the full team of three to 1,200,
and the smaller team of two to 200 chariots.
The number 4,000 is in due proportion to
the 12,000 horses for cavalry, and is in
accordance with all that we know of the
military establishments of the time and
country. Cp. 2 Chr. xii. 3; 2 Sam. viii. 4.

28. Barley is to this day in the East the
common food of horses.

dromedaries] **Coursers.** The animal intended is neither a camel nor a mule, but a
swift horse.

the place where the officers were] Rather,
"places where the horses and coursers
were," *i.e.* to the different cities where they
were lodged.

29. *largeness of heart*] What we call

"great capacity." The expression which
follows is common in reference to numerical multitude (*v.* 20), but its use here
to express mere amplitude or greatness is
peculiar.

30. *children of the east country*] Rather,
"of the East"—the *Beni Kedem*—a distinct tribe, who occupied both sides of the
Euphrates along its middle course (marg.
ref.). They were mostly nomads, who
dwelt in tents (Jer. xlix. 28, 29). Job belonged to them (Job i. 3), as did probably
his three friends; and, perhaps, Balaam
(Num. xxiii. 7). They must have been
either Arabs or Aramæans. We may see
in the Book of Job the character of their
"wisdom." Like Solomon's, it was chiefly
gnomic but included some knowledge of
natural history. The "wisdom of Egypt"
was of a different kind. It included magic
(Gen. xli. 8; Ex. vii. 11), geometry, medi-
cine, astronomy, architecture, and a dreamy
mystic philosophy, of which metempsy-
chosis was the main principle. It is not
probable that Solomon was, like Moses
(marg. ref.), deeply versed in Egyptian
science. The writer only means to say that
his wisdom was truer and more real than
all the much-praised wisdom of Egypt.

31. It is most probable that the persons
with whom Solomon is compared were contemporaries, men noted for "wisdom,"
though there is no other mention of them.

his fame was in all nations] See below,
ch. x.

32. *proverbs*] In the collection which
forms the "Book of Proverbs," only a
small portion has been preserved, less certainly than one thousand out of the three.
Ecclesiastes, if it be Solomon's, would add
between one and two hundred. But the
great bulk of Solomon's proverbs has
perished.

33 thousand and five. And he spake of trees, from the cedar tree that *is* in Lebanon even unto the hyssop that springeth out of the wall : he spake also of beasts, and of fowl, and of creeping
34 things, and of fishes. And *i*there came of all people to hear the wisdom of Solomon, from all kings of the earth, which had heard of his wisdom.

CHAP. 5. AND *a*Hiram king of Tyre sent his servants unto Solomon ; for he had heard that they had anointed him king in the
2 room of his father : *b*for Hiram was ever a lover of David. And
3 *c*Solomon sent to Hiram, saying, Thou knowest how that David my father could not build an house unto the name of the LORD his God *d*for the wars which were about him on every side, until
4 the LORD put them under the soles of his feet. But now the LORD my God hath given me *e*rest on every side, *so that there is*
5 neither adversary nor evil occurrent. *f*And, behold, I [1]purpose to build an house unto the name of the LORD my God, *g*as the LORD spake unto David my father, saying, Thy son, whom I will set upon thy throne in thy room, he shall build an house
6 unto my name. Now therefore command thou that they hew me *h*cedar trees out of Lebanon ; and my servants shall be with thy servants : and unto thee will I give hire for thy servants according to all that thou shalt [2]appoint : for thou knowest that *there is* not among us any that can skill to hew timber like unto

i ch. 10. 1.
2 Chr. 9.
1, 23.

a 2 Chr. 2, 3,
Huram.

b 2 Sam. 5 11.
1 Chr. 14. 1
c 2 Chr. 2. 3.

d 1 Chr. 22.8.
& 28. 3.

e ch. 4. 24.
1 Chr. 22. 9.
f 2 Chr. 2. 4.
g 2 Sam. 7.13.
1 Chr. 17. 12.
& 22. 10.

h 2 Chr.2.
8, 10.

---

[1] Heb. *say.*   [2] Heb. *say.*

---

songs] Of these, Canticles is probably one (marg. ref.) : Pss. lxxii. and cxxvii. *may* also be of the number. Probably the bulk of Solomon's songs were of a secular character, and consequently were not introduced into the Canon of Scripture.

33. *trees,* &c.] A keen appreciation of the beauties of nature, and a habit of minute observation, are apparent in the writings of Solomon that remain to us. The writer here means to say that Solomon composed special works on these subjects. The Lebanon cedars were the most magnificent of all the trees known to the Hebrews, and hence represent in the Old Testament the grandest of vegetable productions. (Ps. civ. 16 ; Cant. v. 15 ; Ezek. xxxi. 3, &c.) For the hyssop, see Ex. xii. 22 note.

of beasts, and of fowls, and of creeping things, and of fishes] This is the usual Biblical division of the animal kingdom (Gen. i. 26, ix. 2 ; Ps. cxlviii. 10).

V. 1. *Hiram, king of Tyre*] Menander of Ephesus, who wrote a history of Tyre in Greek, founded upon native Tyrian documents, about B.C. 300, mentioned this Hiram as the son of Abibaal king of Tyre, and said that he ascended the throne when he was nineteen ; that he reigned thirty-four years, and, dying at the age of fifty-three, was succeeded by his son Baleazar. Menander spoke at some length of the dealings of Hiram with Solomon.

sent his servants] This appears to have been an embassy of congratulation.

3. Solomon's presumption that Hiram knew David's design has not appeared in

the previous history, but it is in accordance with 1 Chr. xxii. 4.

4. The contrast is not between different periods of Solomon's reign, but between his reign and that of his father.

evil occurrent] Rather, **evil occurrence.**

5. *as the LORD spake*] See marg. reff. vii. 13, and cp. 1 Chr. xxii. 10.

6. Solomon's message to Hiram and Hiram's answer (*vv.* 8, 9) are given much more fully in 2 Chr. ii. 3–16.

cedar-trees] The Hebrew word here and elsewhere translated "cedar," appears to be used, not only of the cedar proper, but of other timber-trees also, as the fir, and, perhaps, the juniper. Still there is no doubt that the real Lebanon cedar is most commonly intended by it. This tree, which still grows on parts of the mountain, but which threatens to die out, was probably much more widely spread anciently. The Tyrians made the masts of their ships from the wood (Ezek. xxvii. 5), and would naturally be as careful to cultivate it as we have ourselves been to grow oak. The Assyrian kings, when they made their expeditions into Palestine, appear frequently to have cut it in Lebanon and Hermon, and to have transported it to their own capitals.

skill to hew timber like unto the Sidonians] The mechanical genius and nautical skill of the Phœnicians generally, and of the Sidonians in particular, is noticed by Homer and Herodotus. In the reign of Hiram, Sidon, though perhaps she might have a king of her own, acknowledged the supremacy of Tyre.

7 the Sidonians.   ¶ And it came to pass, when Hiram heard the
words of Solomon, that he rejoiced greatly, and said, Blessed *be*
the LORD this day, which hath given unto David a wise son over
8 this great people.   And Hiram sent to Solomon, saying, I have
¹considered the things which thou sentest to me for : *and* I will
do all thy desire concerning timber of cedar, and concerning
9 timber of fir.   My servants shall bring *them* down from Lebanon

ⁱ 2 Chr. 2.16.   unto the sea : ⁱand I will convey them by sea in floats unto the
place that thou shalt ²appoint me, and will cause them to be discharged there, and thou shalt receive *them :* and thou shalt accom-

ᵏ See Ezra,   10 plish my desire, ᵏin giving food for my household.   So Hiram
3. 7.
Ezek. 27. 17.   gave Solomon cedar trees and fir trees *according to* all his desire.
Acts 12. 20.   11 ⁱAnd Solomon gave Hiram twenty thousand ³measures of wheat
ⁱ See 2 Chr.   *for* food to his household, and twenty measures of pure oil : thus
2. 10.
12 gave Solomon to Hiram year by year.   And the LORD gave

ᵐ ch. 3, 12.   Solomon wisdom, ᵐas he promised him: and there was peace
between Hiram and Solomon; and they two made a league
13 together.   ¶ And king Solomon raised a ⁴levy out of all Israel ;
14 and the levy was thirty thousand men.   And he sent them to
Lebanon, ten thousand a month by courses : a month they were

ⁿ ch. 4. 6.   in Lebanon, *and* two months at home : and ⁿAdoniram *was* over

ᵒ ch. 9. 21.   15 the levy.   ᵒAnd Solomon had threescore and ten thousand that
2 Chr. 2.
17, 18.   bare burdens, and fourscore thousand hewers in the mountains,

---

¹ Heb. *heard.*   ² Heb. *send.*   ³ Heb. *cors.*   ⁴ Heb. *tribute* of men.

---

9. See marg. ref.   The timber was first
carried westward from the flanks of Lebanon to the nearest part of the coast, where
it was collected into floats, or rafts, which
were then conveyed southwards along the
coast to Joppa, now *Jaffa*, whence the land
journey to Jerusalem was not more than
about forty miles.   A similar course was
taken on the building of the second Temple
(Ezr. iii. 7).

food for my household]   The Phœnician
cities had very little arable territory of
their own, the mountain range of Lebanon
rising rapidly behind them ; and they must
always have imported the chief part of
their sustenance from abroad.   They seem
commonly to have derived it from Judæa
(marg. reff.).   Hiram agreed now to accept
for his timber and for the services of his
workmen (*v.* 6) a certain annual payment of
grain and oil, both of them the best of their
kind, for the sustentation of his Court.
This payment was entirely distinct from
the supplies furnished to the workmen
(marg. ref. *l*).

11. The number of measures of wheat
was considerably less than Solomon's own
annual consumption, which exceeded 32,000
cors (iv. 22) ; but the small amount of
twenty *cors* of oil, which seems at first
sight scarcely to match with the 20,000
cors of wheat, will not appear improbable,
if we consider that the oil was to be " pure "
—literally " beaten "—*i.e.* oil extracted from
the olives by pounding, and not by means
of the press.

year by year]   *i.e.* during all the years that
Solomon was engaged in building and was
helped by Hiram.

12. *the* LORD *gave Solomon wisdom*]   It
seems to be implied that Solomon's Divine
gift of wisdom enabled him to make such
favourable arrangements with Hiram.

13. *a levy out of all Israel*]   This was,
apparently, the first time that the Israelites
had been called upon to perform forced
labour, though it had been prophesied (1
Sam. viii. 16).   David had bound to forced
service " the *strangers* " (1 Chr. xxii. 2) ;
but hitherto the Israelites had escaped.
Solomon now, in connexion with his proposed work of building the Temple, with the
honour of God as an excuse, laid this burthen upon them.   Out of the 1,300,000 able-
bodied Israelites (2 Sam. xxiv. 9), a band of
30,000—one in forty-four—was raised, of
whom one-third was constantly at work in
Lebanon, while two-thirds remained at
home, and pursued their usual occupations.
This, though a very light form of task-
work, was felt as a great oppression, and
was the chief cause of the revolt of the ten
tribes at Solomon's death (xii. 4).

15. *that bare burdens*, &c.]   Cp. marg.
reff.   These labourers, whose services were
continuous, consisted of " strangers "—" the
people that were left of the Amorites,
Hittites, Perizzites, Hivites, and Jebusites "—whom Solomon, following the example of his father (1 Chr. xxii. 2), condemned to slavery, and employed in this
way.

16 beside the chief of Solomon's officers which *were* over the work, three thousand and three hundred, which ruled over the people 17 that wrought in the work. And the king commanded, and they brought great stones, costly stones, *and* ᵖhewed stones, to 18 lay the foundation of the house. And Solomon's builders and Hiram's builders did hew *them*, and the ¹stone-squarers; so they prepared timber and stones to build the house.

CHAP. 6. AND ᵃit came to pass in the four hundred and eightieth year after the children of Israel were come out of the land of Egypt, in the fourth year of Solomon's reign over Israel, in the month Zif, which *is* the second month, that ᵇhe ²began to build 2 the house of the LORD. ¶And ᶜthe house which king Solomon built for the LORD, the length thereof *was* threescore cubits, and the breadth thereof twenty *cubits*, and the height thereof 3 thirty cubits. And the porch before the temple of the house,

p 1 Chr. 22.2.

a 2 Chr. 3. 1, 2.

b Acts 7. 47.

c See Ezek. 41. 1, &c.

---

¹ Or, *Giblites*: as Ezek. 27. 9.　　　　² Heb. *built.*

---

16. Comparing this verse and ix. 23 with 2 Chr. ii. 18, viii. 10, the entire number of the overseers will be seen to be stated by both writers at 3,850; but in the one case nationality, in the other degree of authority, is made the principle of the division.

17. Some of these "great, hewed (no *and*) stones," are probably still to be seen in the place where they were set by Solomon's builders, at the south-western angle of the wall of the Haram area in the modern Jerusalem. The largest yet found is 38 ft. 9 in. long, and weighs about 100 tons.

18. *the stone-squarers*] The Gebalites (see marg.), the inhabitants of Gebal, a Phœnician city between Beyrout and Tripolis, which the Greeks called Byblus, and which is now known as *Jebeil.*

VI. 1. *in the four hundred and eightieth year*] It is upon this statement that all the earlier portion of what is called the "received chronology" depends. Amid minor differences there is a general agreement, which justifies us in placing the accession of Solomon *about* B.C. 1000 [B.C. 1018. Oppert.] But great difficulties meet us in determining the sacred chronology anterior to this. Apart from the present statement, the chronological data of the Old Testament are insufficient to fix the interval between Solomon's accession and the Exodus, since several of the periods which make it up are unestimated. Hence chronologists who based entirely on the "received chronology" upon this verse. But the text itself is not free from suspicion. (1) It is the sole passage in the Old Testament which contains the idea of dating events from an era. (2) It is quoted by Origen *without the date*, and seems to have been known only in this shape to Josephus, to Theophilus of Antioch, and to Clement of Alexandria. (3) It is hard to reconcile with other chronological statements in the Old and New Testament. Though the Books of Joshua, Judges, and Samuel furnish us with no exact chronology, they still supply important chronological data—data which seem to indicate for the interval between the Exodus and Solomon, a period considerably exceeding 480 years. For the years actually set down amount to at least 580, or, according to another computation, to 600; and though a certain deduction might be made from this sum on account of the round numbers, this deduction would scarcely do more than balance the addition required on account of the four unestimated periods. Again, in the New Testament, St. Paul (according to the received text) reckons the period from the division of Canaan among the tribes in the sixth year of Joshua (Josh. xiv.), to Samuel the Prophet, at 450 years, which would make the interval between the Exodus and the commencement of the Temple to be 579 years. On the whole, it seems, therefore, probable that the words "in the four hundred and eightieth year, &c.," are an interpolation into the sacred text, which did not prevail generally before the third century of our era.

2. The size of Solomon's Temple depends upon the true length of the ancient cubit, which is doubtful. It has been estimated as somewhat less than a foot, and again as between 19 and 20 inches, a difference of nearly 8 inches, which would produce a variation of nearly 40 feet in the length of the Temple-chamber, and of 46 in that of the entire building. It is worthy of remark that, even according to the highest estimate, Solomon's Temple was really a *small* building, less than 120 feet long, and less than 35 broad. Remark that the measures of the Temple, both "house" and porch (*v.* 3), were exactly *double* those of the older Tabernacle (Ex. xxvi. 18 note). This identity of proportion amounts to an undesigned coincidence, indicating the thoroughly historical character of both Kings and Exodus.

d See Ezek.
40. 16.
k 41. 16.
e See Ezek.
41. 6.
f ver. 16, 19,
20, 21, 31.

g See Deut.
27. 5, 6.
ch. 5. 18.

k ver. 14, 38

twenty cubits *was* the length thereof, according to the breadth of the house ; *and* ten cubits *was* the breadth thereof before the house.

4, 5 And for the house he made *d*1 windows of narrow lights. And ²against the wall of the house he built *e*³chambers round about, *against* the walls of the house round about, *both* of the temple

6 *f* and of the oracle : and he made ⁴chambers round about : the nethermost chamber *was* five cubits broad, and the middle *was* six cubits broad, and the third *was* seven cubits broad : for without *in the wall* of the house he made ⁵narrowed rests round about, that *the beams* should not be fastened in the walls of the house.

7 And *g*the house, when it was in building, was built of stone made ready before it was brought thither : so that there was neither hammer nor axe *nor* any tool of iron heard in the house,

8 while it was in building. The door for the middle chamber *was* in the right ⁶side of the house : and they went up with winding stairs into the middle *chamber*, and out of the middle into the

9 third. *h*So he built the house, and finished it ; and covered the

---

¹ Or, *windows broad* within, and *narrow* without: or, *skewed* and *closed*.
² Or, *upon*, or, *joining to*.
³ Heb. *floors*.
⁴ Heb. *ribs*.
⁵ Heb. *narrowings*, or, *re batements*.
⁶ Heb. *shoulder*.

---

4. *windows of narrow lights*] Either (as in marg.) windows, externally mere slits in the wall. but opening wide within, like the windows of old castles : or, more probably, "windows with fixed lattices." The windows seem to have been placed high in the walls, above the chambers spoken of in *vv.* 5–8.

5. *chambers*] (Marg. floors). Rather, **a lean-to**, which completely surrounded three sides of the building, the north, the west, and the south.

6. In order to preserve the sanctity of the Temple, and at the same time allow the attachment to it of secular buildings—  sleeping apartments, probably, for the priests and other attendants — Solomon made "rebatements" in the wall of the Temple, or in other words built it externally in steps, thus :— The beams, which formed the roof of the chambers and the floors of the upper stories, were then laid on these steps or "rests" in the wall, not piercing the wall, or causing any real union of the secular with the sacred building. It resulted from this arrangement that the lowest chambers were the narrowest, and the uppermost considerably the widest of all, the wall receding each time by the space of a cubit.

7. The spirit of the command (marg. reff.), was followed. Thus the fabric rose without noise.

8. *The door for the middle chamber*] i.e. the door which gave access to the mid-most "set of chambers." The chambers on the

ground-floor were possibly reached each by their own door in the outer wall of the lean-to. The middle and upper floors were reached by a single door in the right or south wall, from which a winding staircase ascended to the second tier, while another ascended from the second to the third. The door to the stairs was in the outer wall of the building, not in the wall between the chambers and the Temple. That would have desecrated the Temple far more than the insertion of beams.

9. *he built the house, and finished it*] i.e. the external shell of the house. The internal fittings were added afterwards. See *vv.* 15–22.

covered the house] Roofed it with a wooden roof, sloped like our roofs.

The annexed diagram of a section of the Temple will illustrate *vv.* 2–10. The numbers give the dimensions in cubits.

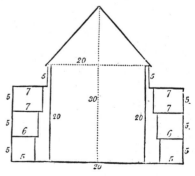

10 house ¹with beams and boards of cedar. And *then* he built
   chambers against all the house, five cubits high: and they rested
11 on the house with timber of cedar. ¶ And the word of the LORD
12 came to Solomon, saying, *concerning* this house which thou art
   in building, ⁱif thou wilt walk in my statutes, and execute my
   judgments, and keep all my commandments to walk in them;
   then will I perform my word with thee, ᵏwhich I spake unto
13 David thy father: and ˡI will dwell among the children of
14 Israel, and will not ᵐforsake my people Israel. ¶ ⁿSo Solomon
15 built the house, and finished it. And he built the walls of the
   house within with boards of cedar, ²both the floor of the house,
   and the walls of the cieling: *and* he covered *them* on the inside
   with wood, and covered the floor of the house with planks
16 of fir. And he built twenty cubits on the sides of the house,
   both the floor and the walls with boards of cedar: he even built
   them for it within, *even* for the oracle, *even* for the ᵒmost holy
17 *place*. And the house, that *is*, the temple before it, was forty

ⁱ ch. 2. 4.
& 9. 4.
ᵏ 1 Chr. 22. 10.
ˡ Lev. 26. 11.
2 Cor. 6. 16.
Rev. 21. 3.
ᵐ Deut. 31. 6.
ⁿ ver. 38.
ᵒ Ex. 26. 33.
Lev. 16. 2.
ch. 8. 6.
2 Chr. 3. 8.
Ezek. 45. 3.
Heb. 9. 3.

---

¹ Or, *the vaultbeams and the*   ² Or, *from the floor of the*   and so ver. 16.
  cielings with cedar.   *house unto the walls, &c.,*

---

12. The meaning is, "So far as this house goes, thou art obedient (2 Sam. vii. 13; 1 Chr. xvii. 12, &c.); if thou wilt be obedient in other things also, then will I perform My word," &c., God's promises being always conditional. The promises made to David were—(1) that he should be succeeded by one of his sons (2 Sam. vii. 12; Ps. cxxxii. 11); (2) that the kingdom should be established in the line of his descendants for ever, if they were faithful (Ps. cxxxii. 12); and (3) that the Israelites should be no more afflicted as beforetime (2 Sam. vii. 10). These promises are now confirmed to Solomon, but on the express condition of obedience, and two further promises are added.

13. The first promise to "dwell among" the Israelites had been made to Moses (Ex. xxv. 8, xxix. 45), but had not been repeated to David. The next promise, "I will not forsake, &c.," if not absolutely new, seems to have been more positive and general than previous similar promises (Deut. xxxi. 6, 8; Josh. i. 5). God will not *at any time or under any circumstances* wholly forsake Israel.

15. The description of this verse applies to the main chamber of the Temple, the Holy Place, only. The writer in *v.* 16 describes the Holy of Holies.

The marginal rendering of this verse is right, and not the rendering in the text.

fir] Rather, "**juniper.**" See v. 8 note.

16. The meaning is, that at the distance of 20 cubits, measured along the side walls of the house from the end wall, Solomon constructed a partition, which reached from the floor to the ceiling and had a doorway in it. He thus made within the house, a sanctuary for a Holy of Holies.

17. Cp. the diagram.

GROUND PLAN OF TEMPLE.
1. Holy of Holies, Oracle or Sanctuary.
2. Holy Place, or Main-chamber.
3. Porch.   4. Priests' Chambers.
5. Position of Altar of incense.

18 cubits *long*. And the cedar of the house within *was* carved with
¹knops and ²open flowers: all *was* cedar; there was no stone
19 seen. And the oracle he prepared in the house within, to set
20 there the ark of the covenant of the LORD. And the oracle in
the forepart *was* twenty cubits in length, and twenty cubits in
breadth, and twenty cubits in the height thereof: and he overlaid it with ³pure gold; and *so* covered the altar *which was of*
21 cedar. So Solomon overlaid the house within with,pure gold:
and he made a partition by the chains of gold before the oracle;
22 and he overlaid it with gold. And the whole house he overlaid
with gold, until he had finished all the house: also ᵖthe whole
23 altar that *was* by the oracle he overlaid with gold. ¶ And
within the oracle ᵠhe made two cherubims *of* ⁴⁵olive tree, *each*
24 ten cubits high. And five cubits *was* the one wing of the
cherub, and five cubits the other wing of the cherub: from the
uttermost part of the one wing unto the uttermost part of the
25 other *were* ten cubits. And the other cherub *was* ten cubits:
26 both the cherubims *were* of one measure and one size. The
height of the one cherub *was* ten cubits, and so *was it* of the
27 other cherub. And he set the cherubims within the inner
house: and ʳ⁶they stretched forth the wings of the cherubims,
so that the wing of the one touched the *one* wall, and the wing
of the other cherub touched the other wall; and their wings
28 touched one another in the midst of the house. And he overlaid
29 the cherubims with gold. ¶ And he carved all the walls of the
house round about with carved figures of cherubims and palm
30 trees and ⁷open flowers, within and without. And the floor of

p Ex. 30. 1,
3, 6.

q Ex. 37. 7,
8, 9.
2 Chr. 3. 10,
11, 12.

r Ex. 25. 20.
& 37. 9.
2 Chr. 5. 8.

---

¹ Or, *gourds*.   ⁴ Or, *oily*.   ⁶ Or, *the cherubims stretched*
² Heb. *openings of flowers*.   ⁵ Heb. *trees of oil*.   *forth their wings*.
³ Heb. *shut up*.   ⁷ Heb. *openings of flowers*.

---

18. *knops and open flowers*] Rather,
"**gourds and opening flower-buds.**" Imitations of the vegetable world are among
the earliest of architectural ornaments.
They abound in the architecture of Egypt
and Persia. In that of Assyria they occur
more sparingly.

20. *the fore part*] Perhaps "the interior."

and so covered, &c.] Rather, "and **he
covered the altar** (of incense) **with cedar.**"
The altar was doubtless of stone, and was
covered with cedar in preparation for the
overlaying with gold. This overlaying was
not gilding, but the attachment of thin
plates of gold, which had to be fastened on
with small nails. Such a mode of ornamentation was common in Babylonia, in Assyria, and in Media.

21. *the house*] *i.e.* the main chamber.

the chains of gold] Omit "the." Their
object was to form a barrier between the
Holy Place and the Holy of Holies.

22. The lavish use of the precious metals
in ornamentation was a peculiar feature of
early Oriental architecture. Recent re-
searches have given reason to believe that
two stages of the great temple at Borsippa
—now known as the Birs Nimrud—had respectively a gold and a silver coating.

23. *two cherubims*] The pattern of the
Tabernacle was followed (marg. ref.), but
without servile imitation. The original
cherubs were entirely of gold. These, being
so much larger, were of wood, merely overlaid with a golden plating. The arrangement of the wings, and the direction of the
faces, seem also to have been different.
Moses' cherubim "covered with their wings
over the mercy seat;" Solomon's stretched
out theirs to the full (*v.* 27), so that the four
wings, each five cubits long (*v.* 24), extended across the whole Sanctuary, the
width of which was twenty cubits (*v.* 20).
The former looked toward one another, and
were bent downward towards the mercy
seat; the latter looked outward, towards
the great chamber. (See 2 Chr. iii. 13, and
note.)

of olive-tree] The oleaster or wild olive,
not the cultivated species.

29. Palms, cherubs, and flowers — the
main decorations of Solomon's Temple—
bear considerable resemblance to the ornamentation of the Assyrians, a circumstance
which can scarcely be accidental.

within and without] *i.e.* both in the inner
chamber, or Holy of Holies, and in the outer
one.

31 the house he overlaid with gold, within and without. ¶And for
the entering of the oracle he made doors of olive tree: the lintel
32 *and* side posts were ¹a fifth part *of the wall.* The ²two doors also
were of olive tree; and he carved upon them carvings of cherubims and palm trees and ³open flowers, and overlaid *them* with
gold, and spread gold upon the cherubims, and upon the palm
33 trees. So also made he for the door of the temple posts *of* olive
34 tree, ⁴a fourth part *of the wall.* And the two doors *were of* fir
tree: the *two leaves of the one door *were* folding, and the two
35 leaves of the other door *were* folding. And he carved *thereon*
cherubims and palm trees and open flowers: and covered *them*
36 with gold fitted upon the carved work. And he built the inner
court with three rows of hewed stone, and a row of cedar beams.
37 ¶ᵗIn the fourth year was the foundation of the house of the
38 Lord laid, in the month Zif: and in the eleventh year in the
month Bul, which *is* the eighth month, was the house finished
⁵throughout all the parts thereof, and according to all the fashion
7 of it. So was he ᵘseven years in building it. BUT Solomon
was building his own house ᵃthirteen years, and he finished all
2 his house. ¶ He built also the house of the forest of Lebanon;

*ˢ Ezek. 41.
23, 24, 25.*

ᵗ ver. 1.

*ᵘ Compare
ver. 1.
ᵃ ch. 9.10.
2 Chr. 8. 1.*

¹ Or, *fivesquare.*
² Or, *leaves of the doors.*
³ Heb. *openings of flowers.*
⁴ Or, *foursquare.*
⁵ Or, *with all the appurtenances thereof, and with
all the ordinances thereof.*

31. *a fifth part*] Better than the margin. The meaning seems to be that the
lintel was one-fifth of the width of the wall,
and each door-post one-fifth of its height.
Thus the opening was a square of four
cubits, or of six feet.

32. *The two doors*] *i.e.* two leaves which
met in the middle, as in the Assyrian gateways generally.

spread gold] The doors were not simply
sheeted with gold, like the floors (*v.* 30),
but had the gold hammered to fit the forms
of the palms, cherubs, and flowers carved
upon them. (*v.* 35.) Such hammered metal-
work, generally in bronze, has been found
in tolerable abundance among the Assyrian
remains.

33. *the door of the temple*] The door, that
is, which led from the porch into the great
chamber of the Temple. Its posts were "a
fourth part of the wall," or, "five cubits
high," which was, therefore, the height of
the doorway.

34. *fir-tree*] Rather, **juniper** (v. 8 note).
Each door was made in two parts, which
folded back one on the other like shutters,
by means of hinges. The weight of the
doors no doubt made it inconvenient to
open the whole door on every occasion.

36. *the inner court*] An *outer* court is mentioned in 2 Chr. iv. 9. The inner court is
probably identical with the "higher court"
of Jeremiah (xxxvi. 10), being raised above
the outer, as were sometimes the inner
courts of Assyrian palaces. The court
seems to have surrounded the Temple. Its
dimensions may be reasonably presumed to
have been double those of the court of the
Tabernacle, *i.e.* 100 cubits on each side of

the Temple, and 200 cubits at the ends; or,
about 720 feet long by 360 broad.

with three rows of hewed stone] Either a
fence enclosing the court, or the area of the
court, which was possibly formed by three
layers of hewn stone placed one above the
other, and was then boarded on the top
with cedar planks. Such a construction
would no doubt be elaborate; but if it was
desired to elevate the inner court above the
outer, this is the way in which it would be
likely to have been done. The Temple
would be placed, like the Assyrian palaces,
on an artificial platform; and the platform,
being regarded as a part of the sacred building, would be constructed of the best material.

28. *seven years*] More exactly, "seven
years and six months," since Zif was the
second, and Bul the eighth month. (*v.* 1.)

VII. **1.** *thirteen years*] The thirteen
years, *i.e.* counting from the end of the
seven (vi. 38). Solomon's buildings thus
occupied him twenty years (ix. 10; 2
Chr. viii. 1), from the fourth year of his
reign to the twenty-fourth. The difference
in the time taken by the Temple and the
palace is to be accounted for, (1) by the long
period of preparation which preceded the
actual building of the former (1 Chr. xxii.
2-4; 1 K. v. 13-18); and (2) by the greater
size of the palace, which consisted of several
large ranges of buildings. (See the next
note.)

2. Many have supposed that the buildings
mentioned in *vv.* 1, 2, 8, were three entirely
distinct and separate buildings. But it is
perhaps best to consider the "house" of
v. 1 as the palace proper—Solomon's own

the length thereof *was* an hundred cubits, and the breadth thereof fifty cubits, and the height thereof thirty cubits, upon four rows of cedar pillars, with cedar beams upon the pillars.
3 And *it was* covered with cedar above upon the [1]beams, that *lay*
4 on forty five pillars, fifteen *in* a row. And *there were* windows
5 *in* three rows, and [2]light *was* against light *in* three ranks. And all the [3]doors and posts *were* square, with the windows: and
6 light *was* against light *in* three ranks. And he made a porch of pillars; the length thereof *was* fifty cubits, and the breadth thereof thirty cubits: and the porch *was* [4]before them: and the
7 *other* pillars and the thick beam *were* [5]before them. Then he made a porch for the throne where he might judge, *even* the porch of judgment: and *it was* covered with cedar [6]from one
8 side of the floor to the other. And his house where he dwelt *had* another court within the porch, *which* was of the like work.
b ch. 3. 1.   ¶ Solomon made also an house for Pharaoh's daughter, *b* whom
2 Chr. 8. 11. 9 he had taken *to* wife, like unto this porch. ¶ All these *were of* costly stones, according to the measures of hewed stones, sawed with saws, within and without, even from the foundation unto
10 the coping, and *so* on the outside toward the great court. And

---

[1] Heb. *ribs.*
[2] Heb. *sight against sight.*
[3] Or, *spaces and pillars* were *square in prospect.*
[4] Or, *according to them.*
[5] Or, *according to them.*
[6] Heb. *from floor to floor.*

---

dwelling-house (see *v.* 8); the house of *v.* 2, as the state apartments; and the house for Pharaoh's daughter as the *hareem* or *zenana;* and to regard these three groups of buildings as distinct, though inter-connected, and as together constituting what is elsewhere termed "the king's house" (ix. 10).

the house of the forest of Lebanon] This name was probably given from the supposed resemblance of the mass of cedar pillars, which was its main feature, to the Lebanon cedar forest. Its length of "a hundred cubits," or 150 feet, was nearly twice as long as the entire Temple without the porch. Some of the great halls in Assyrian palaces were occasionally as much as 180 feet. The breadth " of fifty cubits," or 75 feet, is a breadth very much greater than is ever found in Assyria, and one indicative of the employment in the two countries of quite different methods of roofing. By their use of pillars the Jews, like the Persians, were able to cover in a very wide space.

four rows] The LXX. gives "three rows." If the pillars were forty-five (*v.* 3), fifteen in a row, there should have been but three rows, as seems to have been the case in the old palace of Cyrus at Pasargadæ. If there were four rows of fifteen, the number of pillars should have been sixty.

4. Either three ranges of windows, one above the other, on either side of the house; or perhaps the three ranges were one in either side wall, and the third in a wall down the middle of the hall, along the course of the midmost row of pillars. The windows were directly opposite one another, giving what we call a *through* light

5. *all the doors and posts*] The doorways, and the posts which formed them, seem to be intended. These were square at top, not arched or rounded. In Assyrian buildings arched doorways were not uncommon. The doorways also, like the windows, exactly faced one another.

6. Probably the porch of the "House of the Forest." Porches of columns immediately in front of columnar chambers were a favourite feature of Persian architecture. The whole verse should be translated, "**And he made the porch of the pillars in length 50 cubits, and in breadth 30 cubits, and a porch before them** (*i.e.* the pillars), **and pillars, and a base** (or step) **before them.**" Most of the Persepolitan porches had small pillared chambers at some little distance in front of them.

7. The porch or gate of justice still kept alive the likeness of the old patriarchal custom of sitting in judgment at the gate; exactly as the "Gate of Justice" still recalls it at Granada, and the Sublime Porte—"the Lofty Gate"—at Constantinople.

8. *like unto this porch*] *i.e.* of similar materials, hewn stone and cedar. The *zenana* could not have been a mere portico.

9. The stones were uniform—all cut to certain fixed measures of length, breadth, and thickness. They were not squared only on the face which showed, but also on the sides which fell within the wall and were not seen. Saws appear in Assyrian sculptures of the age of Sennacherib; and fragments of an iron saw have been found at Nimrud.

10. See *v.* 17 note.

the foundation *was of* costly stones, even great stones, stones of
11 ten cubits, and stones of eight cubits. And above *were* costly
12 stones, after the measures of hewed stones, and cedars. And
the great*court round about *was* with three rows of hewed
stones, and a row of cedar beams, both for the inner court of the
13 house of the LORD, *c*and for the porch of the house. ¶And king
14 Solomon sent and fetched *d*Hiram out of Tyre. *e*He *was* [1]a
widow's son of the tribe of Naphtali, and *f*his father *was* a man
of Tyre, a worker in brass: and *g*he was filled with wisdom, and
understanding, and cunning to work all works in brass. ¶And
15 he came to king Solomon, and wrought all his work. For he
[2]cast *h*two pillars of brass, of eighteen cubits high apiece: and
16 a line of twelve cubits did compass either of them about. And
he made two chapiters *of* molten brass, to set upon the tops of
the pillars : the height of the one chapiter *was* five cubits, and
17 the height of the other chapiter *was* five cubits: *and* nets of
checker work, and wreaths of chain work, for the chapiters
which *were* upon the top of the pillars ; seven for the one
18 chapiter, and seven for the other chapiter. And he made the
pillars, and two rows round about upon the one network, to

c John 10.23.
Acts 3. 11.
d 2 Chr. 4.11,
Huram:
See ver. 40.
e 2 Chr. 2.14.
f 2 Chr. 4.16.
g Ex. 31. 3.
& 36. 1.
h 2 Kin. 25.
17.
2 Chr. 3. 15.
& 4. 12.
Jer. 52. 21.

[1] Heb. *the son of a widow woman.*   [2] Heb. *fashioned.*

---

12. The palace, like the Temple, had two courts (vi. 36), not, however, one immediately within the other. The lesser court of the palace seems to have been a private inner court among the buildings (*v.* 8). The greater court was outside all the buildings, surrounding the palace on every side. Assyrian palaces had always such an external court, and had generally one or more inner courts or quadrangles.

both for the inner court] By a slight alteration of the text, the meaning would be "as (was done) in the inner court, &c. and in the porch."

13. *Hiram*] A man who bore the same name as the king of Tyre, a master workman, known as Hiram Ab, *i.e.* Master Hiram (2 Chr. ii. 13, iv. 16).

14. Hiram's mother, while by birth of the tribe of Dan, had had for her first husband a man of the tribe of Naphtali. (Cp. this verse and marg. ref.)

all his work] The work that he personally did for Solomon seems to have been limited to metal-work, and indeed to works in brass. (See below, *v.* 45, and cp. 2 Chr. iv. 16.)

15. These famous pillars, which were broken in pieces by the Babylonians when they destroyed Jerusalem (2 K. xxv. 13; Jer. lii. 17), were probably for ornament, standing by themselves under or in front of the porch. It is certain that the Phœnicians used isolated metal columns as sacred ornaments, so that Hiram would be familiar with such a mode of ornamentation. Eighteen cubits appear to have been the height of the shaft only. Adding the capital (*vv.* 16, 19), the entire metal pillar was 27 cubits high ; and if it had a stone base of eight cubits, which would not be greatly out of propor-

tion, the height of 35 cubits (52½ feet, 2 Chr. iii. 15) would have been reached. The height of some of the Persepolitan columns, with which these pillars may be best compared, is 67 feet. The circumference of 12 cubits (18 feet) implies a diameter of about 5 feet 9 inches at the base, which would make the column somewhat heavy in appearance. Egyptian pillars were, however, even thicker in proportion to their height. On the supposition that a portion of the original text has fallen out, this verse has been thus completed : "He cast two pillars of brass ; eighteen cubits was the height of the one pillar, *and eighteen cubits was the height of the other pillar ; and a line of twelve cubits compassed the one pillar*, and a line of twelve cubits compassed the other pillar."

16. The general character of the *chapiters* or capitals, their great size in proportion to the shaft, which is as one to two, and their construction of two quite different members, remind us of the pillars used by the Persians in their palaces, which were certainly more like Jachin and Boaz than any pillars that have reached us from antiquity. The ornamentation, however, seems to have been far more elaborate than that of the Persian capitals.

17. *nets*, &c.] Rather, "Nets chequerwise, and festoons chainwise,"—probably a fine network over the whole, and chainwork hanging in festoons outside.

seven for the one chapiter] The LXX. reading is preferable. "A net for the one chapiter and a net for the other chapiter." Cp. *v.* 41.

18. The pomegranate was one of the commonest ornaments in Assyria. It was used on quivers, on spear-shafts, and mace-heads, in patterns on doorways and pave-

cover the chapiters that *were* upon the top, with pomegranates:
19 and so did he for the other chapiter. And the chapiters that
were upon the top of the pillars *were* of lily work in the porch,
20 four cubits. And the chapiters upon the two pillars *had pomegranates* also above, over against the belly which *was* by the network: and the pomegranates *were* [i]two hundred in rows round
21 about upon the other chapiter. [k]And he set up the pillars in
[l]the porch of the temple: and he set up the right pillar, and
called the name thereof [1]Jachin: and he set up the left pillar,
22 and called the name thereof [2]Boaz. And upon the top of the
pillars *was* lily work: so was the work of the pillars finished.
23 ¶ And he made [m]a molten sea, ten cubits [3]from the one brim
to the other: *it was* round all about, and his height *was* five
cubits: and a line of thirty cubits did compass it round about.
24 And under the brim of it round about *there were* knops compassing it, ten in a cubit, [n]compassing the sea round about: the
25 knops *were* cast in two rows, when it was cast. It stood upon
[o]twelve oxen, three looking toward the north, and three looking
toward the west, and three looking toward the south, and three
looking toward the east: and the sea *was set* above upon them,
26 and all their hinder parts *were* inward. And it *was* an hand
breadth thick, and the brim thereof was wrought like the brim
of a cup, with flowers of lilies: it contained [p]two thousand baths.

Margin notes:
[i] See 2 Chr. 3. 16.
[k] 2 Chr. 3. 17.
[l] ch. 6. 3.
[m] 2 Kin 25. 13. 2 Chr 4. 2. Jer. 52. 17.
[n] 2 Chr. 4. 3.
[o] 2 Chr. 4. 4, 5. Jer. 52. 20.
[p] See 2 Chr. 4. 5.

---

[1] That is, *He shall estab-lish.*   [2] That is, *In it is strength.*   [3] Heb. *from his brim to his brim.*

---

ments, &c. It is doubtful whether a symbolical meaning attached to it, or whether
it was merely selected as a beautiful natural
form.

19. There is a cornice of (so-called) lily-
work at Persepolis, consisting of three
ranges of broadish rounded leaves, one over
the other. Lilies are also represented with
much spirit on a bas-relief from Koyunjik.

20. In this verse also a portion of the
original text is supposed to have fallen out
in consequence of the repetition of words.
The full phrase of the original has been
retained in *vv.* 16 and 17. It may be restored thus:—" And the pomegranates were
two hundred in rows round about *upon the
one chapiter, and two hundred in rows round
about* upon the other chapiter." The "four
hundred" (*v.* 42; 2 Chr. iv. 13), are obtained by counting the pomegranates of both
pillars together. In Jerem. lii. 23, is an
account of the arrangement of a single row
of pomegranates, whereof each pillar had
two.

21. The LXX. in the parallel passage
(marg. ref.), translate Jachin and Boaz by
Κατόρθωσις and Ἰσχύς — " Direction " and
" Strength." The literal meaning of the
names is given in the margin. The meaning was probably " God will establish in
strength " (*i.e.* firmly) the Temple and the
religion connected with it.

23. The "molten sea " of Solomon, so
called from its great size, took the place of
the laver of the Tabernacle (Ex. xxx. 18-21),
which was required for the ablutions of the

priests. It was ten cubits, or fully fifteen
feet, in diameter at top, and therefore forty-
seven feet in circumference, with a depth of
5 cubits, or 7½ feet. As a vessel of these
dimensions, if hemispherical, would certainly not hold 2000 (*v.* 26), much less 3000
(2 Chr. iv. 3) *baths*, the bath equalling 8½ gallons, it is now generally supposed that the
bowl bulged considerably below the brim,
and further, that it had a "foot,"—or basin
which received the water as it was drawn
out by taps from the bowl. The "2000
baths" may give the quantity of water ordinarily supplied to the "sea;" the "3000
baths" the utmost that the laver could any-
how take. Bowls of a considerable size are
represented in the Assyrian bas-reliefs; but
none of such dimensions as Solomon's. The
largest mentioned by the Greeks held only
5400 gallons, less than one-third of the contents of the "molten sea," even according
to the lowest estimate.

24. *knops*] Literally, "gourds," — *i.e.* a
boss or ball ornament encircled the rim of
the bowl in two rows.

25. Josephus charged Solomon with a
breach of the Commandment (Ex. xx. 4, 5),
on account of the oxen here and the lions
for his throne. The charge expresses the
prohibition which some Jews have conceived
the Commandment to urge against the arts
of sculpture and painting.

26. The palm or hand-breadth seems to
have a little exceeded three inches.

with flowers of lilies] Rather, "**in the
shape of a lily flower.**" The rim was

27 ¶ And he made ten bases of brass; four cubits *was* the length of
one base, and four cubits the breadth thereof, and three cubits
28 the height of it. And the work of the bases *was* on this *manner :* they had borders, and the borders *were* between the ledges :
29 and on the borders that *were* between the ledges *were* lions,
oxen, and cherubims : and upon the ledges *there was* a base
above : and beneath the lions and oxen *were* certain additions
30 made of thin work. And every base had four brasen wheels, and
plates of brass : and the four corners thereof had undersetters :
under the laver *were* undersetters molten, at the side of every
31 addition. And the mouth of it within the chapiter and above
was a cubit : but the mouth thereof *was* round *after* the work of
the base, a cubit and an half : and also upon the mouth of it
32 *were* gravings with their borders, foursquare, not round. And
under the borders *were* four wheels ; and the axletrees of the
wheels *were* ¹*joined* to the base : and the height of a wheel *was*
33 a cubit and half a cubit. And the work of the wheels *was* like
the work of a chariot wheel : their axletrees, and their naves,
34 and their felloes, and their spokes, *were* all molten. And *there
were* four undersetters to the four corners of one base : *and* the
35 undersetters *were* of the very base itself. And in the top of the
base *was there* a round compass of half a cubit high : and on the
top of the base the ledges thereof and the borders thereof *were*
36 of the same. For on the plates of the ledges thereof, and on the
borders thereof, he graved cherubims, lions, and palm trees,

¹ Heb. *in the base.*

slightly curved outwards, like the rim of an
ordinary drinking-cup, or the edge of a lily
blossom. See 2 Chr. iv. 5 marg.

27. *ten bases of brass*] These were for the
ten lavers (*v.* 38. See 2 Chr. iv. 6). In
general terms the bases were square stands,
6 feet each way, and 4½ feet high, elabo-
rately ornamented on their four sides, and
resting upon four wheels, 2¼ feet in diameter. Each stand supported a laver 6 feet
high, which contained 40 baths (*v.* 38), or
about 340 gallons.

28. *borders*] Rather, "**panels**" (so *rv.* 32,
35), a set of square compartments between
the "ledges" or borders, or mouldings.
Below the panelling, with its ornamentation of lions, oxen (the two animal forms
which occur most frequently in Assyrian
decoration), and cherubim, was a space de-
corated with "additions of thin work"
(*v.* 29).

Upon the "ledges" (*v.* 29) which surrounded the top of the base there was a
stand for the laver, distinct from the upper
surface of the base.

30. *plates of brass*] Rather, " **brazen
axletrees.**"

The "undersetters" (literally, "shoulders") are conjectured to have been four
brackets, or bars, proceeding from the four
upper corners of the bases, and stretching
upwards to the outer rim of the laver,
which thus rested partly upon them.

at the side of every addition] Rather,
"**each opposite garlands.**" The laver was
ornamented with a garland at the place
where the support reached it.

31. It seems impossible to determine what
is meant by the "mouth" of the laver, or
what by its "chapiter."

32. With the diameter (2¼ ft.) of the
wheel here, may be compared that of the
earliest Assyrian chariot-wheels, which was
under 3 feet ; and that of the front wheels
seen in representations of Assyrian close
carriages, which scarcely exceed ¼th of the
height of the entire vehicle. The wheels of
these moveable lavers appear to have been
a little less than ⅛th of the height of the
whole structure.

34. The undersetters were cast with the
base, not afterwards attached to it, and were
therefore stronger and better able to support the laver.

35. *a round compass*] A circular elevation,
half a cubit high, rather than a circular depression, half a cubit deep. Cp. *v.* 29. The
"ledges" and "borders" of the top of the
base were its "hands" and its "panels."
These "hands," distinct from the "shoulders" (*v.* 30), were probably supports,
adorned with engraved plates (*v.* 36), either
of the elevated circle on which the laver
stood, or of the lower part of the laver itself. Both panels and "hands" were "of
the same," *i.e.* of one piece with the base,
cast at the same time.

36. *according to the proportion of every one*,
i.e. "as large as the room left for them
allowed," implying that the panels were

according to the [1]proportion of every one, and additions round
37 about. After this *manner* he made the ten bases: all of them

38 had one casting, one measure, *and* one size. ¶ Then *q*made he
ten lavers of brass : one laver contained forty baths : *and* every
laver was four cubits : *and* upon every one of the ten bases
39 one laver. And he put five bases on the right [2]side of the
house, and five on the left side of the house: and he set the sea
on the right side of the house eastward over against the south.
40 And [3]Hiram made the lavers, and the shovels, and the basons.
¶ So Hiram made an end of doing all the work that he made king
41 Solomon for the house of the LORD: the two pillars, and the *two*
bowls of the chapiters that *were* on the top of the two pillars ;

and the two *r*networks, to cover the two bowls of the chapiters
42 which *were* upon the top of the pillars ; and four hundred pomegranates for the two networks, *even* two rows of pomegranates
for one network, to cover the two bowls of the chapiters that
43 *were* [4]upon the pillars ; and the ten bases, and ten lavers on the

44, 45 bases ; and one sea, and twelve oxen under the sea ; *s*and
the pots, and the shovels, and the basons : and all these vessels,
which Hiram made to king Solomon for the house of the LORD,

46 *were of* [5]bright brass. *t*In the plain of Jordan did the king cast
them, [6]in the clay ground between *u*Succoth and *x*Zarthan.
47 And Solomon left all the vessels *unweighed*, [7]because they were
exceeding many: neither was the weight of the brass [8]found out.
48 ¶ And Solomon made all the vessels that *pertained* unto the

house of the LORD: *y*the altar of gold, and *z*the table of gold,
49 whereupon *a*the shewbread *was*, and the candlesticks of pure
gold, five on the right *side*, and five on the left, before the oracle,
50 with the flowers, and the lamps, and the tongs *of* gold, and the
bowls, and the snuffers, and the basons, and the spoons, and the
[9]censers *of* pure gold ; and the hinges *of* gold, *both* for the doors
of the inner house, the most holy *place, and* for the doors of the
51 house, *to wit*, of the temple. ¶ So was ended all the work that
king Solomon made for the house of the LORD. And Solomon

brought in the [1]things *b*which David his father had dedicated ;
even the silver, and the gold, and the vessels, did he put among
the treasures of the house of the LORD.

---

[1] Heb. *nakedness.*
[2] Heb. *shoulder.*
[3] Heb. *Hirom:* See ver.13.
[4] Heb. *upon the face of the pillars.*
[5] Heb. *made bright*, or, *scoured.*
[6] Heb. *in the thickness of the ground.*
[7] Heb. *for the exceeding multitude.*
[8] Heb. *searched*, 1 Chr. 22. 14.
[9] Heb. *ash pans.*
[1] Heb. *holy things of David.*

---

smaller than those on the sides of the base, and allowed scant room for the representations.

38. *every laver was four cubits*] Assuming height to be intended, and taking the cubit at 20 inches, the entire height of the lavers as they stood upon their wheeled stands would seem to have been 13 ft. 9 in. It is evident, therefore, that the water must have been drawn from them, as from the "molten sea," through cocks or taps.

40. *lavers*] Rather, according to the true reading, "pots." (Cp. *v.* 45 ; 2 Chr. iv. 16.) The "pots" were the caldrons in which it was usual to boil the peace-offerings. See 1 Sam. ii. 13, 14.

46. *Succoth and Zarthan*] See Judg. vii. 22, viii. 5 note.

47. The brass of which the two pillars, Jachin and Boaz, the brazen sea, and the various vessels were made had been taken by David from two cities belonging to Hadadezer, king of Zobah (1 Chr. xviii. 8).

48. See note to vi. 20 and 2 Chr. iv. 19—22.

49, 50. See notes to Ex. xxv. 31—38. The "bowls" of *v.* 50 were the "bowls" for the tables (Ex. xxxvii. 16), large vases containing oil for the lamps.

51. *the things which David had dedicated*] Not only the things described in 1 Chr. xxviii. 14-18, but also the spoil of the nations which he had subdued (marg. ref.),

CHAP. 8. THEN ^aSolomon assembled the elders of Israel, and all the heads of the tribes, the ¹chief of the fathers of the children of Israel, unto king Solomon in Jerusalem, ^bthat they might bring up the ark of the covenant of the LORD ^cout of the city of
2 David, which *is* Zion.   ¶ And all the men of Israel assembled themselves unto king Solomon at the ^dfeast in the month Ethanim,
3 which *is* the seventh month.   And all the elders of Israel came,
4 ^eand the priests took up the ark.   And they brought up the ark of the LORD, ^fand the tabernacle of the congregation, and all the holy vessels that *were* in the tabernacle, even those did the
5 priests and the Levites bring up.   And king Solomon, and all the congregation of Israel, that *were* assembled unto him, *were* with him before the ark, ^gsacrificing sheep and oxen, that could
6 not be told nor numbered for multitude.   And the priests ^hbrought in the ark of the covenant of the LORD unto ⁱhis place, into the oracle of the house, to the most holy *place, even* ^kunder
7 the wings of the cherubims.   For the cherubims spread forth *their* two wings over the place of the ark, and the cherubims
8 covered the ark and the staves thereof above.   And they ^ldrew out the staves, that the ²ends of the staves were seen out in the ³holy *place* before the oracle, and they were not seen with-
9 out: and there they are unto this day.   ^m*There was* nothing in the ark ⁿsave the two tables of stone, which Moses ^oput there at

a 2 Chr. 5. 2, &c.

b 2 Sam. 6. 17.
c 2 Sam. 5. 7, 9.

d Lev. 23 34. 2 Chr. 7. 8.

e Num. 4. 15. Josh. 3. 3, 6. 1 Chr. 15. 14, 15.
f ch. 3. 4. 2 Chr. 1. 3.

g 2 Sam. 6. 13.

h 2 Sam. 6. 17.
i Ex. 26. 33, 34. ch. 6. 19.
k ch. 6. 27.

l Ex. 25. 14.

m Ex. 25. 21. Deut. 10. 2.
n Deut. 10. 5.
o Ex. 40. 20.

¹ Heb. *princes.*   ² Heb. *heads.*   ³ Or, *ark:* as 2 Chr. 5. 9.

---

and also the vessels of gold, silver, and brass, sent him by Toi king of Hamath, on his victory over Hadadezer. Solomon now brought these into the Temple treasury. A sacred treasury had been established at least as early as the time of Saul, to which Saul himself, Abner, Joab, and others, had contributed (1 Chr. xxvi. 28).

VIII. **1.** There seems to be a contrast here between the more popular proceedings of David (2 Sam. vi. 1), and the statelier system of his son, who merely summons the chief men as representatives of the nation. The rest of the people "assembled themselves" (*v.* 2), and were mere spectators of the solemnity.

2. *the feast in the month Ethanim*] *i.e.* the Feast of Tabernacles, or In-gathering, the commemoration of the dwelling in booths at the time of the Exodus (marg. ref.), and the festival of thanksgiving on account of the completion of harvest (Ex. xxiii. 16; Lev. xxiii. 39; Deut. xvi. 13). It was one of the three on which the people were required to "appear before the Lord."

3. In 2 Chr. v. 4, "*the Levites* took up the ark;" and by the Law the Ark was the special charge of the Kohathites (Num. iii. 31, iv. 15). But all priests were Levites (Josh. iii. 3), though all Levites were not priests. And as Joshua had done (Josh. iii. 6, vi. 6), so Solomon called upon the priests to bear the holy structure, allowing to mere Levites only the inferior honour of helping to transport the Tabernacle and the vessels of the Sanctuary.

4. *and the tabernacle of the congregation*]

Not the tented structure erected for the Ark on Mount Zion (2 Sam. vi. 17) by David, but the original Tabernacle made by Moses, which had hitherto remained at Gibeon (marg. ref.). The Tabernacle and its holy vessels were probably placed in the treasury.

8. It was forbidden to withdraw the staves wholly from the rings (marg. ref.); but they appear to have been now drawn forward in such a way that their ends or heads could be seen from the Holy Place, or great chamber of the Temple, though without their being visible from the porch or vestibule. Either the doorway into the Holy of Holies was not exactly opposite the Ark, but a little on one side; or, though that doorway was in the middle, opposite the Ark, the doorway from the porch into the main chamber was not opposite to it. In Assyrian temples the arrangement of the outer door, the inner door, and the sanctuary, seems to have been designedly such that a mere passer-by on the outside should not obtain even a glimpse of the shrine. It is suggested that the withdrawal of the staves was intended as a sign that the Ark had reached "the place of its rest," and was not to be borne about any more.

there they are unto this day] This is a quotation from an author who lived while the Temple was still standing. See also ix. 21.

9. Comparing this statement with Heb. ix. 4, it would seem that Solomon, now that the sacred chest had reached its final resting-place, and stood in a large chamber surrounded by tables (2 Chr. iv. 8), removed

Horeb, [1]p when the Lord made *a covenant* with the children of
10 Israel, when they came out of the land of Egypt. ¶And it came
to pass, when the priests were come out of the holy *place*, that
11 the cloud q filled the house of the Lord, so that the priests could
not stand to minister because of the cloud : for the glory of the
12 Lord had filled the house of the Lord. r¶ Then spake Solomon,
13 The Lord said that he would dwell s in the thick darkness. t I
have surely built thee an house to dwell in, u a settled place for
14 thee to abide in for ever. ¶ And the king turned his face about,
and x blessed all the congregation of Israel : (and all the congre-
15 gation of Israel stood ;) and he said, y Blessed *be* the Lord God
of Israel, which z spake with his mouth unto David my father,
16 and hath with his hand fulfilled *it*, saying, a Since the day that I
brought forth my people Israel out of Egypt, I chose no city out
of all the tribes of Israel to build an house, that b my name
might be therein ; but I chose c David to be over my people
17 Israel. And d it was in the heart of David my father to build an
18 house for the name of the Lord God of Israel. e And the Lord
said unto David my father, Whereas it was in thine heart to
build an house unto my name, thou didst well that it was in
19 thine heart. Nevertheless f thou shalt not build the house ; but
thy son that shall come forth out of thy loins, he shall build the
20 house unto my name. And the Lord hath performed his word
that he spake, and I am risen up in the room of David my
father, and sit on the throne of Israel, g as the Lord promised,
and have built an house for the name of the Lord God of Israel.
21 And I have set there a place for the ark, wherein *is* h the covenant of the Lord, which he made with our fathers, when he
22 brought them out of the land of Egypt. ¶And Solomon stood
before i the altar of the Lord in the presence of all the congregation of Israel, and k spread forth his hands toward heaven :
23 and he said, Lord God of Israel, l *there is* no God like thee, in

[1] Or, *where.*

the pot of manna and the rod from the interior, and set them elsewhere in the Holy
of Holies.

10. The cloud—the visible symbol of the
Divine Presence—the Shechinah of the Tar-
gums—which had been promised before the
Ark was begun (Ex. xxix. 43), and had filled
the Tabernacle as soon as it was completed
(do. xl. 34), and which had probably been
seen from time to time during the long interval when we have no express mention of
it, now once more appeared in full magnificence, and took, as it were, possession of
the building which Solomon was dedicating.
The Presence of God in the Temple henceforth was thus assured to the Jews, and His
approval of all that Solomon had done was
signified.

11. As in the case of Moses (Ex. xl. 35),
so now the glory of the Lord, the manifestation of the Divine Presence, which the
cloud usually veiled, shone forth from it
with such brilliancy, that mortal man could
not bear the sight.

12. Rather, "**The Lord spake of dwelling in the thick darkness**" (marg. reff.).
Solomon sees in the cloud the visible sym-

bol of God's Presence, and accepts the token
as a proof that He has taken possession of
the house built for Him, and will thenceforth dwell there (*v.* 13).

14. Solomon had spoken the preceding
words, addressed to God, with his face directed to the Holy of Holies. He now
turned round and looked outwards towards
the people. The people "stood" to hear
him—the attitude of respect and attention.
This first blessing seems to have been without speech—an inward prayer accompanied
by the ordinary gesture of blessing.

15. The exact words of 2 Sam. vii. are not
reproduced ; only their general sense is
given. In *v.* 18, what was merely tacitly
implied was regarded as actually "said."

16. The marg. ref. completes the sense of
this verse here. The passage is in accordance with archaic modes of speech, and is
probably the more verbally accurate of the
two.

22. The marg. ref. shows that the king
was so placed as to be seen by all present,
and that, before beginning his prayer, he
knelt down upon his knees (cp. *v.* 54).

23. Cp. Deut. vii. 9.

heaven above, or on earth beneath, *m*who keepest covenant and
mercy with thy servants that *n*walk before thee with all their
24 heart: who hast kept with thy servant David my father that
thou promisedst him: thou spakest also with thy mouth, and
25 hast fulfilled *it* with thine hand, as *it is* this day. Therefore
now, LORD God of Israel, keep with thy servant David my
father that thou promisedst him, saying, *o1*There shall not fail
thee a man in my sight to sit on the throne of Israel; *2*so that
thy children take heed to their way, that they walk before me as
26 thou hast walked before me. *p*And now, O God of Israel, let
thy word, I pray thee, be verified, which thou spakest unto thy
27 servant David my father. ¶ But *q*will God indeed dwell on the
earth? behold, the heaven and *r*heaven of heavens cannot
contain thee; how much less this house that I have builded?
28 Yet have thou respect unto the prayer of thy servant, and to his
supplication, O LORD my God, to hearken unto the cry and to
29 the prayer, which thy servant prayeth before thee to day: that
thine eyes may be open toward this house night and day, *even*
toward the place of which thou hast said, *s*My name shall be
there: that thou mayest hearken unto the prayer which thy
30 servant shall make *t3*toward this place. *u*And hearken thou to
the supplication of thy servant, and of thy people Israel, when
they shall pray *4*toward this place: and hear thou in heaven thy
31 dwelling place: and when thou hearest, forgive. ¶ If any man
trespass against his neighbour, *5*and *x*an oath be laid upon him
to cause him to swear, and the oath come before thine altar in
32 this house: then hear thou in heaven, and do, and judge thy
servants, *y*condemning the wicked, to bring his way upon his
head; and justifying the righteous, to give him according to his
33 righteousness. ¶ *z*When thy people Israel be smitten down
before the enemy, because they have sinned against thee, and
*a*shall turn again to thee, and confess thy name, and pray, and
34 make supplication unto thee *6*in this house: then hear thou in
heaven, and forgive the sin of thy people Israel, and bring them
again unto the land which thou gavest unto their fathers.
35 ¶ *b* When heaven is shut up, and there is no rain, because they
have sinned against thee; if they pray toward this place, and
confess thy name, and turn from their sin, when thou afflictest

m Deut. 7. 9.
Neh. 1. 5.
Dan. 9. 4.
n Gen. 17. 1.
ch. 3. 6.
2 Kin. 20. 3.

o 2 Sam. 7.
12, 16.
ch. 2. 4.

p 2 Sam.7.
25.

q 2 Chr. 2. 6.
Isai. 66. 1.
Jer. 23. 24.
Acts 7. 49.
r 2 Cor.12. 2.

s Deut.12.11.

t Dan. 6. 10.
u 2 Chr.20.9.
Neh. 1. 6.

x Ex. 22. 11.

y Deut. 25. 1.

z Lev. 26. 17.
Deut. 28. 25.
a Lev. 26.
39, 40.
Neh. 1. 9.

b Lev. 26.19.
Deut. 28. 23

---

1 Heb. *There shall not be
cut off unto thee a man
from my sight.*
2 Heb. *only if.*
3 Or, *in this place.*
4 Or, *in this place.*
5 Heb. *and he require an
oath of him,* Lev. 5. 1.
6 Or, *toward.*

---

26. Solomon's prayer is, perhaps, generally for the fulfilment of all the promises made to David in connection
with the building of the Temple. But
there seems to be special allusion in this
verse to the promise recorded in Ps.
cxxxii. 14.
27. *heaven of heavens*] Cp. Deut. x. 14;
Ps. cxlviii. 4. It seems to mean the heaven in its most extended compass. Solomon
combines with his belief in Jehovah's special Presence in the Temple, the strongest
conviction that He is no local or finite deity,
but is ever present everywhere. Cp. Ps.
cxxxix. 7–10.
29. The choice of Jerusalem as the place
seems to have been made by special revela-

tion to David. See Pss. lxxviii. 68, cxxxii.
13; and cp. 1 Chr. xxii. 1.
toward this place] Better (here and in *v.* 30)
than the marginal "in." Wherever they
were, the Jews always worshipped *towards*
the Temple. (See marg. ref.)
and when thou hearest, forgive] Lit.,
"both hear and forgive"—*i.e.*, "hear the
prayer, and forgive the sin" which alone
causes God to chasten men or to withhold
from them His choicest blessings.
31. *the oath come before,* &c.] "The oath"
is equivalent to "the man who swears the
oath." A slight alteration in the present
Hebrew text gives the sense "and he (the
accused) go and swear before thine altar," &c.
The threats and the promises, the punish-

36 them: then hear thou in heaven, and forgive the sin of thy
servants, and of thy people Israel, that thou ^cteach them ^dthe
good way wherein they should walk, and give rain upon thy
land, which thou hast given to thy people for an inheritance.

37 ¶ ^eIf there be in the land famine, if there be pestilence, blasting,
mildew, locust, or if there be caterpiller; if their enemy besiege
them in the land of their ¹cities; whatsoever plague, whatsoever

38 sickness there be; what prayer and supplication soever be made
by any man, or by all thy people Israel, which shall know every
man the plague of his own heart, and spread forth his hands

39 toward this house: then hear thou in heaven thy dwelling place,
and forgive, and do, and give to every man according to his
ways, whose heart thou knowest; (for thou, even thou only,

40 ^fknowest the hearts of all the children of men;) ^gthat they may
fear thee all the days that they live in the land which thou

41 gavest unto our fathers. ¶Moreover concerning a stranger,
that is not of thy people Israel, but cometh out of a far country

42 for thy name's sake; (for they shall hear of thy great name, and
of thy ^hstrong hand, and of thy stretched out arm;) when he

43 shall come and pray toward this house; hear thou in heaven thy
dwelling place, and do according to all that the stranger calleth
to thee for: ⁱthat all people of the earth may know thy name, to
^kfear thee, as do thy people Israel; and that they may know
that ²this house, which I have builded, is called by thy name.

44 ¶ If thy people go out to battle against their enemy, whithersoever thou shalt send them, and shall pray unto the LORD
³toward the city which thou hast chosen, and toward the house

45 that I have built for thy name: then hear thou in heaven their

46 prayer and their supplication, and maintain their ⁴cause.   ¶ If

---

¹ Or, jurisdiction.   ² Heb. thy name is called   ³ Heb. the way of the city.
               upon this house.   ⁴ Or, right.

---

ments and calamities of vv. 31–38 were distinctly named in the Law. See marg. reff.

36. teach them, &c.] Rather, "**when thou
art teaching** them (by thy chastisement)
the good way that they should walk in,"
i.e. when thou art still teaching, not taking
vengeance.

37. in the land of their cities] Literally,
"in the land of their gates." Hence the
marginal translation "jurisdiction," because judgments were pronounced in the
town gates (Deut. xvi. 18). Another reading gives "in one of their cities."

38. know every man the plague of his own
heart] i.e. perceive one's sinfulness, or recognise one's sufferings as Divine chastise-
ments, and sin as their cause.

41. Nothing is more remarkable in the
Mosaic Law than its liberality with regard
to strangers, both in general (Ex. xxii. 21;
Lev. xxv. 35; Deut. x. 19) and in religious
matters (Num. xv. 14–16; Deut. xxxi. 12).
It is quite in the spirit of these enactments
that Solomon, having first prayed to God on
behalf of his fellow-countrymen, should
next go on to intercede for the strangers,
and to ask for their prayers the same acceptance which he had previously begged
for the prayers of faithful Israelites.

for thy name's sake] i.e. "to visit the place
where Thou hast set Thy name" (Cp. Deut.
xii. 5, 11, &c.).

42. great name] A somewhat rare expression. It does not occur at all in the Pentateuch; though "mighty hand" and the
"stretched out arm" are so frequent (Ex.
vi. 6, xiii. 9; Deut. ix. 29); only once in
Joshua (vii. 9); and twice in the Psalms
(lxxvi. 1, xcix. 3). About the time of the
Captivity the use of the phrase became more
common (Ezek. xxxvi. 23; Jer. x. 6, xliv. 26).

43. that all people of the earth may know
thy name, to fear thee] Solomon prays
that the result of Jehovah's hearing the
prayers of heathens addressed towards the
Temple may be the general conversion of
the world to the worship of Him. Cp. Pss.
xcvi., xcviii.

this house, &c.] Lit., as in the margin.
In Scripture, when God's Name is said
to be "called upon" persons or things, it
seems to be meant that God is really present in them, upholding them and sancti-
fying them. This passage therefore means,
that the heathen, when their prayers, directed towards the Temple, are granted, will
have a full assurance that God is present in
the building in some very special way.

they sin against thee, (¹for *there is* no man that sinneth not,) and thou be angry with them, and deliver them to the enemy, so that they carry them away captives ᵐunto the land of the 47 enemy, far or near; ⁿ*yet* if they shall ¹bethink themselves in the land whither they were carried captives, and repent, and make supplication unto thee in the land of them that carried them captives, ᵒsaying, We have sinned, and have done per- 48 versely, we have committed wickedness; and *so* ᵖreturn unto thee with all their heart, and with all their soul, in the land of their enemies, which led them away captive, and �𐞥pray unto thee toward their land, which thou gavest unto their fathers, the city which thou hast chosen, and the house which I have 49 built for thy name: then hear thou their prayer and their sup- plication in heaven thy dwelling place, and maintain their 50 ²cause, and forgive thy people that have sinned against thee, and all their transgressions wherein they have transgressed against thee, and ʳgive them compassion before them who carried them captive, that they may have compassion on them: 51 for ˢthey *be* thy people, and thine inheritance, which thou broughtest forth out of Egypt, ᵗfrom the midst of the furnace 52 of iron: that thine eyes may be open unto the supplication of thy servant, and unto the supplication of thy people Israel, to 53 hearken unto them in all that they call for unto thee. For thou didst separate them from among all the people of the earth, *to be* thine inheritance, ᵘas thou spakest by the hand of Moses thy servant, when thou broughtest our fathers out of Egypt, O Lord 54 God. ¶And it was *so*, that when Solomon had made an end of praying all this prayer and supplication unto the Lord, he arose from before the altar of the Lord, from kneeling on his knees 55 with his hands spread up to heaven. And he stood, ˣand blessed all the congregation of Israel with a loud voice, saying, 56 Blessed *be* the Lord, that hath given rest unto his people Israel, according to all that he promised: ʸthere hath not ³failed one word of all his good promise, which he promised by the hand 57 of Moses his servant. The Lord our God be with us, as he was 58 with our fathers: ᶻlet him not leave us, nor forsake us: that he may ᵃincline our hearts unto him, to walk in all his ways, and to keep his commandments, and his statutes, and his judgments,

l 2 Chr. 6. 36.
Prov. 20. 9.
Eccles. 7. 20.
James 3. 2.
1 John 1. 8, 10.
m Lev. 26. 34, 44.
Deut. 28.
36, 64.
n Lev. 26 40.
o Neh. 1. 6.
Ps. 106. 6.
Dan. 9. 5.
p Deut. 30. 2.
q Dan. 6. 10.

r Ezra 7. 6.
Ps. 106. 46.
s Deut. 9. 29.
Neh. 1. 10.
t Deut. 4. 20.
Jer. 11. 4,

u Ex. 19. 5.
Deut. 4. 20.
& 9. 26, 29.

x 2 Sam. 6. 18.

y Deut. 12. 10.
Josh. 21. 45.

z Deut. 31. 6.
Josh. 1. 5.
Ps. 27. 9.
a Ps. 119. 36.

¹ Heb. *bring back to their heart.*   ² Or, *right.*   ³ Heb. *fallen.*

---

47. *bethink themselves*] Lit., as in margin—*i.e.* "reflect," "consider seriously." Cp. Deut. xxx. 1.

sinned, done perversely, committed wickedness] The words here used seem to have become the standard form of expressing contrition when the time of the Captivity arrived and the Israelites were forcibly removed to Babylon (cp. marg. reff.). The three expressions are thought to form a climax, rising from negative to positive guilt, and from mere wrongful acts to depravation of the moral character.

50. *compassion,* &c.] Not merely such compassion as Evil-Merodach shewed towards Jehoiachin (2 K. xxv. 27-30; Jer. lii. 31-34), but such as Cyrus and Artaxerxes shewed in allowing the captive Jews to return to their own land (Ez. i. 3; Neh. ii. 6).

51. *the furnace of iron*] Egypt is so called as a place of severe trial and affliction.

54. If the prayer of Solomon be, as it has all the appearance of being, a genuine document of the time, preserved in the archives to which the authors of both Kings and Chronicles had access, all theories of the late origin of Deuteronomy must be regarded as baseless. While references are not infrequent to other portions of the Pentateuch, the language of the prayer is mainly modelled upon Deuteronomy, the promises and threats contained in which are continually before the mind of the writer. (See marg. reff.).

58. *incline our hearts*] This is a doctrine which first appears in Scripture in the Davidical Psalms (see marg. ref. and Ps. cxli. 4). Solomon in this prayer seems to be

59 which he commanded our fathers. And let these my words, wherewith I have made supplication before the LORD, be nigh unto the LORD our God day and night, that he maintain the cause of his servant, and the cause of his people Israel [1]at all

b Josh. 4. 24.
1 Sam.17.46.
2 Kin. 19.19.
c Deut. 4.
35, 39.
d ch. 11. 4.
& 15. 3, 14.
2 Kin. 20. 3.
e 2 Chr. 7. 4,
&c.

60 times, as the matter shall require: [b]that all the people of the earth may know that [c]the LORD *is* God, *and that there is* none 61 else. Let your [d]heart therefore be perfect with the LORD our God, to walk in his statutes, and to keep his commandments, as 62 at this day. ¶ And [e]the king, and all Israel with him, offered 63 sacrifice before the LORD. And Solomon offered a sacrifice of peace offerings, which he offered unto the LORD, two and twenty thousand oxen, and an hundred and twenty thousand sheep. So the king and all the children of Israel dedicated the house of the

f 2 Chr. 7. 7.

64 LORD. [f]The same day did the king hallow the middle of the court that *was* before the house of the LORD : for there he offered burnt offerings, and meat offerings, and the fat of the

g 2 Chr. 4. 1.

peace offerings : because [g]the brasen altar that *was* before the LORD *was* too little to receive the burnt offerings, and meat 65 offerings, and the fat of the peace offerings. ¶ And at that time

h ver. 2.
Lev. 23. 34.
i Num. 34. 8.
Josh. 13. 5.
k Gen.15.18.
Num. 34. 5.
l 2 Chr. 7. 8.
m 2 Chr. 7.
9, 10.

Solomon held [h]a feast, and all Israel with him, a great congregation, from [i]the entering in of Hamath unto [k]the river of Egypt, before the LORD our God, [l]seven days and seven days, 66 *even* fourteen days. [m]On the eighth day he sent the people away : and they [2]blessed the king, and went unto their tents joyful and glad of heart for all the goodness that the LORD had done for David his servant, and for Israel his people.

a 2 Chr. 7.
11, &c.
b ch. 7. 1.
c 2 Chr. 8. 6.
d ch. 3. 5.

CHAP. 9. AND [a]it came to pass, when Solomon had finished the building of the house of the LORD, [b]and the king's house, and 2 [c]all Solomon's desire which he was pleased to do, that the LORD appeared to Solomon the second time, [d]as he had appeared unto

---

[1] Heb. *the thing of a day in his day.*   [2] Or, *thanked.*

---

thoroughly penetrated with his father's spirit.   •

61. *as at this day*] *i.e.* "as ye are now doing, in coming with pious intentions to this festival."

63. These numbers have been thought incredible, but they are not impossible. At least 100,000, or 120,000 men (*v.* 65) were assembled ; and as they *all* offered sacrifice with the king (*v.* 62), the number of victims must have been enormous. Part of the flesh of so many victims would be eaten ; but much of the meat may have been privately burnt (Lev. xix. 6), the object of the sacrifice being the glory of God, and not the convenience of the people. Profusion was a usual feature of the sacrifices of antiquity.

64. *the middle of the court*] Or, "the *whole area* of the court "—all the *mid* space within the enclosing walls, which thus became one huge altar, on any part of which victims might be offered at one and the same time.

65. A feast necessarily accompanied such a sacrifice as Solomon was holding. Cp. Lev. xix. 5. On the present occasion there was a double festival—first, the Feast of the Dedication, from the 8th to the 15th of the month Ethanim (or Tisri), and then the

Feast of Tabernacles, from the 15th to the 22nd (*v.* 2). On the day after this, "the eighth day," counting from the commencement of the second seven, and the twenty-third day of the month (marg. ref. *m*), Solomon dismissed the people to their homes.

the entering in of Hamath] Cp. Num. xiii. 21, note and marg. reff. The phrase marks the extreme northern boundary of the Holy Land.

the river of Egypt] The Wady-el-Arish, the only large water-course on this coast (marg. reff.).

66. *their tents*] *i.e.* "their homes." The word "tents" was used for "houses" from an old habit of speech, which had come down from the time when the Israelites were a nomadic nation.

IX. **2.** This appearance is fixed by *v.* 1 to Solomon's twenty-fourth year, the year in which he completed his palace (vi. 37, 38, vii. 1). The fact seems to be that, though the Temple was finished in Solomon's eleventh year, the Dedication did not take place till his twenty-fourth year. The order of the narrative in Kings agrees with this view, since it interposes the account of the building of the palace (vii. 1–12), and of the

3 him at Gibeon. And the LORD said unto him, *e*I have heard thy prayer and thy supplication, that thou hast made before me: I have hallowed this house, which thou hast built, *f*to put my name there for ever; *g*and mine eyes and mine heart shall be

4 there perpetually. And if thou wilt *h*walk before me, *i*as David thy father walked, in integrity of heart, and in uprightness, to do according to all that I have commanded thee, *and* wilt keep

5 my statutes and my judgments: then I will establish the throne of thy kingdom upon Israel for ever, *k*as I promised to David thy father, saying, There shall not fail thee a man upon the throne

6 of Israel. *l*But if ye shall at all turn from following me, ye or your children, and will not keep my commandments *and* my statutes which I have set before you, but go and serve other

7 gods, and worship them: *m*then will I cut off Israel out of the land which I have given them; and this house, which I have hallowed *n*for my name, will I cast out of my sight; *o*and Israel

8 shall be a proverb and a byword among all people : and *p*at this house, *which* is high, every one that passeth by it shall be astonished, and shall hiss; and they shall say, *q*Why hath the LORD

9 done thus unto this land, and to this house? And they shall answer, Because they forsook the LORD their God, who brought forth their fathers out of the land of Egypt, and have taken hold upon other gods, and have worshipped them, and served them : therefore hath the LORD brought upon them all this evil.

10 ¶And *r*it came to pass at the end of twenty years, when Solomon had built the two houses, the house of the LORD, and the

11 king's house, *s*(now Hiram the king of Tyre had furnished Solomon with cedar trees and fir trees, and with gold, according to all his desire,) that then king Solomon gave Hiram twenty cities

12 in the land of Galilee. And Hiram came out from Tyre to see the cities which Solomon had given him; and they ¹pleased him

e 2 Kin. 20.5.
Ps. 10. 17.
f ch. 8. 29.
g Deut. 11.
12.
h Gen. 17. 1.
i ch. 11. 4, 6,
38.
& 14. 8.
& 15. 5.
k 2 Sam. 7.
12, 16.
ch. 2. 4.
& 6. 12
1 Chr. 22. 10.
Ps. 132. 12.
l 2 Sam.7.14.
Ps. 89. 30.
m Deut 4. 26.
2 Kin. 17.23.
& 25. 21.
n Jer. 7. 14.
o Deut. 28.
37.
Ps. 44. 14.
p 2 Chr. 7 21.
q Deut. 29.
24, 25, 26.
Jer. 22. 8,9.

r ch. 36. 37,
38.
& 7. 1.
2 Chr. 8. 1.
s 2 Chr. 8. 2.

¹ Heb. *were not right in his eyes.*

making of the furniture (vii. 13–51), between the completion of the building of the Temple (vi. 38) and the ceremony of the Dedication (viii.).

3. The answer given by God to Solomon's prayer is reported more fully in 2 Chronicles (vii. 12–22).

When God puts His Name in the temple He does it, in intention, *for ever.* He will not arbitrarily withdraw it; there it will remain *for ever*, so far as God is concerned. But the people may by unfaithfulness drive it away (*rv.* 7–9).

and mine eyes and my heart] An answer in excess of the prayer (viii. 29); "Not Mine eyes only, but Mine eyes *and Mine heart.*"

4. See iii. 14. Solomon's subsequent fall lends to these repeated warnings a special interest.

6. *at all turn*] Rather, "If ye shall **wholly** turn from following Me." (See 2 Chr. vii. 19.) The Israelites were not to be cut off, except for an entire defection.

8. The Hebrew text runs—"**And this house shall be high**: every one," &c. The meaning appears to be, "This house shall

be high " (*i.e.* conspicuous) "in its ruin as in its glory."

and shall hiss] In contempt. This expression first appears in the time of Hezekiah (2 Chr. xxix. 8; Mic. vi. 16). It is especially familiar to Jeremiah (xviii. 16, xix. 8, &c.).

10. The "twenty years" are to be counted from the fourth year of Solomon, the year when he commenced the building of the Temple. They are made up of the seven years employed in the work of the Temple (vi. 38), and the thirteen years during which Solomon was building his own house (vii. 1).

11. By the spirit, if not by the letter, of the Law, Solomon had no right to give away these cities, or any part of the inheritance of Israel (Lev. xxv. 13–34). But the exigences of a worldly policy caused the requirements of the Law to be set aside.

12. *they pleased him not*] It is a reasonable conjecture that, when a question arose with respect to a cession of land, Hiram had cast his eyes on the bay or harbour of Acco, or Ptolemais, and was therefore the more disappointed when he received an inland tract of mountain territory.

13 not. And he said, What cities *are* these which thou hast given

t Josh. 19.27.
me, my brother ?   *t*And he called them the land of [1]Cabul unto
14 this day. And Hiram sent to the king sixscore talents of gold.

u ch. 5. 13.
15 ¶ And this *is* the reason of *u*the levy which king Solomon raised;
     for to build the house of the LORD, and his own house, and

x ver. 24.
y Josh. 11. 1.
z Josh.12.21.
a Josh.16.10.
*x*Millo, and the wall of Jerusalem, and *y*Hazor, and *z*Megiddo,
16 and *a*Gezer. *For* Pharaoh king of Egypt had gone up, and
     taken Gezer, and burnt it with fire, *b*and slain the Canaanites

Judg. 1. 29.
b Josh.16.10.
c Josh. 10.10.
     that dwelt in the city, and given it *for* a present unto his daugh-
17 ter, Solomon's wife. And Solomon built Gezer, and *c*Beth-

2 Chr. 8. 5.
d Josh.19.44.
2 Chr. 8. 4.
18 horon the nether, and *d*Baalath, and Tadmor in the wilderness,
19 in the land, and all the cities of store that Solomon had, and

e ch. 4. 26.
     cities for *e*his chariots, and cities for his horsemen, and [2]that

f ver. 1.
     which Solomon *f*desired to build in Jerusalem, and in Lebanon,

---

[1] That is, *Displeasing*, or, *Dirty*.   [2] Heb. *the desire of Solomon which he desired.*

---

13. Cabul is said to be a Phœnician word, and signified " displeasing " (see marg.). There is some reason to believe that the cities thus despised by Hiram were restored to Solomon (2 Chr. viii. 2), and that Solomon rebuilt them and colonized them with Israelites.

14. *Hiram sent sixscore talents of gold*] Apparently, to show that, although disappointed, he was not offended. The sum sent was very large—above a million and a quarter of our money, according to one estimate of the weight of the Hebrew gold talent ; or about 720,000*l.* according to the estimate adopted in Ex. xxxviii. 24-29 note. At any rate, it was more than equal to a sixth part of Solomon's regular revenue (x. 14).

15. *levy*] See marg. ref. note.

Millo] See 2 Sam. v. 9 note. The LXX. commonly render the word ἡ ἄκρα, " the citadel," and it may possibly have been the fortress on Mount Zion connected with the Maccabean struggles (1 Mac. iv. 41, xiii. 49-52). Its exact site has not been determined.

and the wall of Jerusalem] David's fortification (2 Sam. v. 9 ; 1 Chr. xi. 8) had been hasty, and had now—fifty years later—fallen into decay. Solomon therefore had to " repair the breaches of the city of David " (xi. 27).

Hazor, Megiddo, and Gezer were three of the most important sites in the Holy Land. For the two first places, cp. marg. reff. and notes.

Gezer was a main city of the south. It was situated on the great maritime plain, and commanded the ordinary line of approach from Egypt, which was along this low region. The importance of Gezer appears from Josh. x. 33, xii. 12, &c. Its site is near Tell Jezer, and marked now by Abu Shusheh. Though within the lot of Ephraim (Josh. xvi. 3), and specially assigned to the Kohathite Levites (do. xxi. 21), it had never yet been conquered from the old inhabitants (marg. reff.), who con-

tinued to dwell in it till Solomon's time, and apparently were an independent people (*v.* 16).

Pharaoh took it before the marriage of Solomon with his daughter, and gave it " *for a present* "—*i.e.* for a dowry. Though in the East husbands generally pay for their wives, yet dower is given in some cases. Sargon gave Cilicia as a dowry with his daughter when he married her to Ambris king of Tubal : and the Persian kings seem generally to have given satrapial or other high offices as dowries to the husbands of their daughters.

17. *Beth-horon the nether*] See marg. ref. note.

18. *Tadmor*] The Hebrew text here has, as written, Tamor (or Tamar), and as read, Tadmor. That the latter place, or Palmyra, was meant appears, first, from the distinct statement of Chronicles (2 Chr. viii. 4) that Solomon built Tadmor, and the improbability that the fact would be omitted in Kings ; secondly, from the strong likelihood that Solomon, with his wide views of commerce, would seize and fortify the Palmyrene Oasis : and thirdly, from the unanimity of the old Versions in rendering Tamar here by Tadmor. The probability seems to be that Tamar was the original name of the place, being the Hebrew word for " a palm," whence it is generally agreed that the town derived its name. Tadmor was a corrupt or dialectic variety of the word, which was adopted at the city itself, and prevailed over the original appellation. No reference is found to Tadmor in the Assyrian inscriptions, or in any classical writer before Pliny.

19. " The cities of store " contained provisions stored up for the troops (cp. 2 Chr. xxxii. 28). They seem to have been chiefly in the north—in Hamath (2 Chr. viii. 4) and Naphtali (do. xvi. 4). On the " cities for his chariots," see x. 26 note.

By " that which Solomon desired to build " (see marg.) seem to be intended " pleasaunces " in or near the capital, and

20 and in all the land of his dominion. ¶ *And* all the people *that were* left of the Amorites, Hittites, Perizzites, Hivites, and Jebu-
21 sites, which *were* not of the children of Israel, their children *h*that were left after them in the land, *i*whom the children of Israel also were not able utterly to destroy, *k*upon those did
22 Solomon levy a tribute of *l*bondservice unto this day. But of the children of Israel did Solomon *m*make no bondmen: but they *were* men of war, and his servants, and his princes, and his cap-
23 tains, and rulers of his chariots, and his horsemen. These *were* the chief of the officers that *were* over Solomon's work, *n*five hundred and fifty, which bare rule over the people that wrought
24 in the work. ¶ But *o*Pharaoh's daughter came up out of the city of David unto *p*her house which *Solomon* had built for her:
25 *q*then did he build Millo. ¶ *r*And three times in a year did Solomon offer burnt offerings and peace offerings upon the altar which he built unto the LORD, and he burnt incense *¹*upon the altar that *was* before the LORD. So he finished the house.
26 ¶ And *s*king Solomon made a navy of ships in *t*Ezion-geber, which *is* beside Eloth, on the *²*shore of the Red sea, in the land
27 of Edom. *u*And Hiram sent in the navy his servants, shipmen that had knowledge of the sea, with the servants of Solomon.
28 And they came to *x*Ophir, and fetched from thence gold, four hundred and twenty talents, and brought *it* to king Solomon.

CHAP. 10. AND when the *a*queen of Sheba heard of the fame of Solomon, concerning the name of the LORD, she came *b*to prove

g 2 Chr. 8. 7, &c.
h Judg. 1. 21, 27, 29.
& 3. 1.
i Josh. 15.63. & 17. 12.
k Judg. 1. 28.
l See Gen. 9. 25, 26.
Ezra 2.55,58.
Neh. 7. 57.
& 11. 3.
m Lev. 25.39.
n See 2 Chr. 8. 10.
o 2 Chr. 8. 11.
p ch. 7. 8.
q 2 Sam. 5.9.
ch. 11. 27.
2 Chr. 32. 5.
r 2 Chr. 8. 12, 13, 16.
s 2 Chr. 8. 17, 18.
t Num.33.35.
Deut. 2. 8.
u ch. 10. 11.
x Gen.10. 29.
a 2 Chr. 9. 1, &c.
Matt. 12. 42.
Luke 11. 31.
b See Judg. 14. 12.
Prov. 1. 6.

¹ Heb. *upon it.*   ² Heb. *lip.*

---

in the Lebanon range, built specially for the enjoyment of the king.

21. See v. 15 note.

22. Comparing this with v. 13, 14, it would seem that a modified service of forced labour for one-third of each year was not regarded as reducing those who were subject to it to the condition of bondmen.

23. *five hundred and fifty*] See v. 16 note.

24. Cp. marg. ref. Solomon was not satisfied that Pharaoh's daughter should remain in the palace of David, which was on Mount Zion, in the immediate vicinity of the Temple, because he regarded the whole vicinity of the Temple as made holy by the presence of the Ark of God. His own palace was on the other (western) hill, probably directly opposite to the Temple, the valley of the Tyropœum running between them.

25. *three times*] i.e. (see marg. ref.) the three solemn Feasts—the Feast of unleavened bread, the Feast of weeks, and the Feast of tabernacles.

did Solomon offer...and he burnt incense] Not with his own hand, but by his priests (viii. 6; 2 Chr. v. 7-14). In sacred, as in ordinary, history, men are said to do that which they cause to be done.

26. On Ezion-geber and Eloth, see notes to marg. reff. As the entire tract about Elath (Akaba) is destitute of trees, it is conjectured that the wood of which Solomon built his fleet was cut in Lebanon,

floated to Gaza by sea, and thence conveyed across to Ezion-geber, at the head of the Elanitic Gulf, by land carriage. (Cp. 2 Chr. ii. 16.)

27. *shipmen*] See v. 6 note. With respect to the acquaintance of the Phœnicians with this particular sea, it may be observed that they are not unlikely to have had trading settlements there, as they had in the Persian Gulf, even at this early period. The commerce with Ophir was probably an established trade, previously either in their hands or in those of the Egyptians, when Solomon determined to have a share in it. The Egyptians had navigated the other arm of the Red Sea, and perhaps its lower parts, from a much more ancient period.

28. On Ophir, see marg. ref. note. Among the various opinions three predominate; all moderns, except a very few, being in favour of Arabia, India, or Eastern Africa. Arabia's claims are supported by the greatest number.

X. 1. Doubt has arisen whether the "queen of Sheba" was an Ethiopian or an Arabian princess. Both countries profess to have traditions on the subject connecting the queen of Sheba with their history; and in both countries, curiously enough, government by queens was common. But the claims of Arabia decidedly preponderate. The Arabian Sheba was the great spice country of the ancient world; whereas Ethiopia furnished no spices. The Arabian Sheba was an important kingdom. Sheba

2 him with hard questions. And she came to Jerusalem with a
very great train, with camels that bare spices, and very much
gold, and precious stones: and when she was come to Solomon,
3 she communed with him of all that was in her heart. And
Solomon told her all her [1]questions: there was not *any* thing
4 hid from the king, which he told her not. And when the queen
of Sheba had seen all Solomon's wisdom, and the house that he
5 had built, and the meat of his table, and the sitting of his servants, and the [2]attendance of his ministers, and their apparel,
and his [3]cupbearers, *c*and his ascent by which he went up unto
6 the house of the LORD; there was no more spirit in her. And
she said to the king, It was a true [4]report that I heard in mine
7 own land of thy [5]acts and of thy wisdom. Howbeit I believed
not the words, until I came, and mine eyes had seen *it*: and,
behold, the half was not told me: [6]thy wisdom and prosperity
8 exceedeth the fame which I heard. *d*Happy *are* thy men, happy
are these thy servants, which stand continually before thee, *and*
9 that hear thy wisdom. *e*Blessed be the LORD thy God, which
delighted in thee, to set thee on the throne of Israel: because
the LORD loved Israel for ever, therefore made he thee king, *f*to
10 do judgment and justice. And she *g*gave the king an hundred
and twenty talents of gold, and of spices very great store, and
precious stones: there came no more such abundance of spices
as these which the queen of Sheba gave to king Solomon.

c 1Chr.26.16.

d Prov. 8.34.

e ch. 5. 7.

f 2 Sam.8.15.
Prov. 8. 15.
g Ps. 72. 10,
15.

---

[1] Heb. *words.*   [4] Heb. *word.*   [6] Heb. *thou hast added wis-*
[2] Heb. *standing.*   [5] Or, *sayings.*   *dom and goodness to the*
[3] Or, *butlers.*   *fame.*

---

in Ethiopia was a mere town, subject to
Meroë. And it may be doubted whether
the Cushite Sheba of Scripture (Gen. x. 7)
is not rather to be sought on the shores of
the Persian Gulf (do. note), whence no one
supposes "the queen of Sheba" to have
come. If Ophir be placed in Arabia, there
will be an additional reason for regarding Sheba as in the same quarter, because
then Solomon's trade with that place will
account for his fame having reached the
Sabæan princess.

"The fame of Solomon concerning the
name of the Lord," has been variously
explained, and is confessedly very obscure. May it not mean what we should
call "his *religious* fame," as distinct from
his artistic, literary, military, or political
fame—"his fame with respect to God and
the things of God"—or, in other words, "his
moral and religious wisdom?" (cp. *v.* 6).

hard questions] Or "riddles" (Judg. xiv.
12), though not exactly riddles in our sense.
The Orientals have always been fond of
playing with words and testing each other's
wit and intelligence by verbal puzzles of
various kinds. This spirit seems to have
been particularly rife in Solomon's time,
for Josephus records other encounters with
Hiram of Tyre and another Tyrian called
Abdemonus.

2. See *v.* 10 note.

5. *and the meat of his table*] Cp. iv. 22,
23. The scene here described receives very

apt illustration from the Assyrian banquet
scenes, where we have numerous guests
sitting, dressed handsomely in fringed robes,
with armlets upon their arms, and bracelets
round their wrists, attendants standing behind them, and magnificent drinking-cups,
evidently of a costly metal, in the hands of
the guests, which are filled from a great
wine-bowl at one end of the chamber.

and his ascent by which he went up] A rendering preferable to "the *burnt-offering*
which he *offered in.*" The "ascent" was
probably a private way by which the king
passed from his palace on the western
hill, across the ravine (Tyropœum) and up
the eastern hill, to the west side of the
Temple area (cp. marg. ref.).

9. *Blessed be the* LORD *thy God*] This
acknowledgment of Jehovah falls below the
confessions of Hiram (2 Chr. ii. 12) and
Cyrus (Ezr. i. 3). It does not imply more
than an admission of His power as a local
deity; viz. that He is the God of the Jews
and of their country.

10. Strabo relates that the Sabæans were
enormously wealthy, and used gold and
silver in a most lavish manner in their furniture, their utensils, and even on the walls,
doors, and roofs of their houses. That the
gold of Sheba should be given to Solomon
was prophesied by the writer of Ps lxxii.
(see marg. ref.). The immense abundance
of spices in Arabia, and especially in the
Yemen or Sabæan country, is noted by

11 ¶[h]And the navy also of Hiram, that brought gold from Ophir,   [h] ch. 9. 27.
    brought in from Ophir great plenty of [1]almug trees, and pre-
12 cious stones. [i]And the king made of the almug trees [23]pillars   [i] 2 Chr. 9.11.
    for the house of the LORD, and for the king's house, harps also
    and psalteries for singers: there came no such [k]almug trees, nor   [k] 2 Chr. 9.10.
13 were seen unto this day. ¶And king Solomon gave unto the
    queen of Sheba all her desire, whatsoever she asked, beside *that*
    which Solomon gave her [4]of his royal bounty. So she turned
14 and went to her own country, she and her servants. ¶Now the
    weight of gold that came to Solomon in one year was six
15 hundred threescore and six talents of gold, beside *that he had* of
    the merchantmen, and of the traffick of the spice merchants,
    and [l]of all the kings of Arabia, and of the [5]governors of the   [l] 2 Chr. 9. 24.
16 country. ¶And king Solomon made two hundred targets *of*   Ps. 72. 10.
    beaten gold: six hundred *shekels* of gold went to one target.

---

[1] *algum trees,* 2 Chr. 2. 8.   [2] Or, *rails.*   *hand of king Solomon.*
  & 9. 10, 11.   [3] Heb. *a prop.*   [5] Or, *captains.*
                       [4] Heb. *according to the*

---

many writers. According to Strabo, the spice-trade of Arabia was in the hands of two nations, the Sabæans and the Gerrhæans. The spices in which they dealt seem to have been only in part the produce of Arabia itself; some of the most important kinds, as the cinnamon and the cassia, must have been imported from India, since Arabia does not yield them. The chief precious stones which Arabia now yields are the onyx and the emerald. Anciently she is said to have produced other gems. Pearls, too, were readily procurable in Arabia from the Persian Gulf fishery.

11. *the navy of Hiram*] *i.e.* Solomon's navy in the Red Sea, which was chiefly manned by subjects of Hiram. (see marg. ref.)

almug-trees] Probably the sandal-wood tree (*pterocarpus santalinus*). The wood is very heavy, hard, and fine grained, and of a beautiful garnet colour, which, according to the Rabbinical writers, was the colour of the algum. One of the names of the red sandal-wood, in its own native country (India) is *valguka,* a word of which *algum* is a natural corruption.

12. *pillars*] The Hebrew word signifies ordinarily a "prop" (marg.). It is generally supposed to mean in this place a "railing," or "balustrade," a sense which connects and harmonises the present passage with the parallel passage in Chronicles (marg. ref.), where Solomon is said to have made of the almug-wood "stairs" for the Temple and for his own house.

harps] The Jewish harp (*kinnor*) was of a triangular shape, and had ordinarily ten strings. It probably resembled the more ancient harp of the Assyrians, which was played with a plectrum, as was (ordinarily) the *kinnor.*

psalteries] The psaltery, or viol (*nebel,* Gr. νάβλα), was a stringed instrument played with the hand; perhaps a lyre, like those on Hebrew coins, the sounding-board of which is shaped like a jug; or, perhaps, a sort of guitar, with a hollow jug-shaped body at the lower end.

14. *six hundred threescore and six talents of gold*] About 3,646,350*l.* of our money. Solomon's annual revenue exceeded that of Oriental empires very much greater in extent than his, and must have made him one of the richest, if not the very richest, of the monarchs of his time.

15. There is no mention in the original of "*spice* merchants." Two classes of traders are spoken of; but both expressions are general.

kings of Arabia] Rather, "kings of the mingled people" (cp. Jer. xxv. 24). These were probably tribes half Jewish, half Arabian, on the borders of the western desert. They are regarded as Arabs by the author of Chronicles (marg. ref.).

governors] The word used here is thought to be of Aryan origin. It appears to have been a title given by the Persians to petty governors, inferior to the great satraps of provinces. We find it borne by, among others, Tatnai (Ezr. v. 6), Zerubbabel (Hag. i. 1), and Nehemiah (Neh. v. 14). It can scarcely have been in use among the Jews so early as Solomon, and we must therefore suppose it to have been substituted by the writer of Kings for some corresponding Semitic title. The empire of Solomon was not a state governed from a single centre by an organisation of satrapies or provinces (iv. 21 note). But exceptionally, in some parts of the empire, the kings had been superseded by "governors" (cp. xx. 24).

16. The "targets" seem to have been long shields protecting the whole body, while the "shields" of the next verse were bucklers of a smaller size, probably round, and much lighter. They may be compared with the Assyrian long shield, and the ordinary Assyrian round shield. As the amount

m ch. 14. 26.

n ch. 7. 2.

o 2 Chr. 9.
17, &c.

p 2 Chr. 9.
20, &c.

q Gen. 10. 4.
2 Car. 20. 36.

17 And *he made* *m* three hundred shields *of* beaten gold ; three pound
of gold went to one shield : and the king put them in the *n* house
18 of the forest of Lebanon. ¶ *o* Moreover the king made a great
19 throne of ivory, and overlaid it with the best gold. The throne
had six steps, and the top of the throne *was* round ¹behind : and
there were ²stays on either side on the place of the seat, and two
20 lions stood beside the stays. And twelve lions stood there on
the one side and on the other upon the six steps : there was not
21 ³the like made in any kingdom. ¶ *p* And all king Solomon's
drinking vessels *were of* gold, and all the vessels of the house of
the forest of Lebanon *were of* pure gold ; ⁴none *were of* silver :
22 it was nothing accounted of in the days of Solomon. For the
king had at sea a navy of *q* Tharshish with the navy of Hiram :
once in three years came the navy of Tharshish, bringing gold,

---

¹ Heb. *on the hinder part
thereof.*

² Heb. *hands.*

³ Heb. *so.*

⁴ Or, there was *no silver*
in them.

---

of gold used in each of the larger shields was
only 600 shekels—worth from 650*l.* to 700*l.*
of our money—and that used in the smaller
ones was only half as much it is evident
that the metal did not form the substance
of the shields, but was laid as a coating or
plating over them.

17. These shields, together with the 500
taken by David from Hadadezer (2 Sam.
viii. 7) were hung round the outer walls of
a building, reckoned as belonging to the
"house of the Forest of Lebanon," but
separate from it, and called sometimes
"the Tower of David" (Cant. iv. 4), or
from its use "the armoury" (do.; Is. xxii.
8). The practice of hanging shields outside walls for ornamentation seems to have
existed at Tyre (Ezek. xxvii. 10, 11), Rome,
Athens, and elsewhere. Traces of it are
thought to be found in the Assyrian sculptures.

18. It is, on the whole, probable that the
substance of the throne was wood, and that
the ivory, cut into thin slabs, and probably
carved in patterns, was applied externally
as a veneer. This is found to have been the
practice in Assyria. The gold was probably
not placed over the ivory, but covered other
parts of the throne.

19. Representations of thrones are frequent in the Egyptian and Assyrian sculptures. They have no steps up to them, but
frequently stand upon square bases. The
back appears to be flat at the top, not
rounded. Assyrian thrones have "stays"
or arms on either side, and they stand generally upon lion's feet. They are always
accompanied by a footstool.

lions stood beside the stays] The arms of
Assyrian thrones are occasionally supported
by figures of animals. The throne of
Rameses II. at Medinet Abou has a sphinx
at the side and a lion below the sphinx.
The figure of the lion is naturally adopted
by any imaginative race as an emblem of
sovereignty. In the present case its adop-

tion seems to have grown directly out of
the poetic imagery of inspired Prophets,
who, living before the time of Solomon,
had compared Israel (Num. xxiii. 24, xxiv.
9), and more particularly Judah (Gen. xlix.
9), to a lion. The "twelve lions" of *v.* 20
were probably intended to be emblematic
of the twelve tribes. Josephus adds to the
description of Solomon's throne here given,
that the seat was supported by a golden ox
or bull, with its head turned over its
shoulder. As the lion was especially emblematic of Judah, so was the ox or bull of
Ephraim. (Hos. iv. 16, x. 11 ; Jer. xxxi.
18, &c.)

20. Solomon's throne, as described, is
certainly grander than any of which we
have a representation, either in Assyria or
Egypt. Much more, then, would it trans-
cend the thrones in inferior kingdoms.

22. This is given as the reason of the
great plentifulness of silver in the time of
Solomon. The "navy of Tharshish" (not
the same as the navy of Ophir, ix. 26)
must therefore have imported very large
quantities of that metal. Tharshish, or
Tartessus, in Spain, had the richest silver
mines known in the ancient world, and had
a good deal of gold also ; apes and ivory were
produced by the opposite coast of Africa ;
and, if north Africa did not produce "peacocks," which is uncertain, she may have
produced the birds called here *tukkiyim,*
which some translate "parrots," others
"guinea-fowl"—the latter being a purely
African bird. The etymology of the Hebrew
words here rendered "ivory," "apes," and
"peacocks," is uncertain ; but even if of In-
dian origin, the Jews may have derived their
first knowledge of ivory, apes, and peacocks, through nations which traded with
India, and may thus have got the words
into their language long before the time of
Solomon. The names once fixed would be
retained, whatever the quarter whence the
things were procured afterwards.

23 and silver, [1]ivory, and apes, and peacocks. ¶ So [r]king Solomon
exceeded all the kings of the earth for riches and for wisdom.
24 And all the earth [2]sought to Solomon, to hear his wisdom,
25 which God had put in his heart. And they brought every man
his present, vessels of silver, and vessels of gold, and garments,
and armour, and spices, horses, and mules, a rate year by year.
26 ¶ [s]And Solomon [t]gathered together chariots and horsemen : and
he had a thousand and four hundred chariots, and twelve thousand horsemen, whom he bestowed in the cities for chariots, and
27 with the king at Jerusalem. [u]And the king [3]made silver _to be_
in Jerusalem as stones, and cedars made he _to be_ as the syco-
28 more trees that _are_ in the vale, for abundance. ¶ [x][4]And Solomon had horses brought out of Egypt, and [v]linen yarn : the
29 king's merchants received the linen yarn at a price. And a
chariot came up and went out of Egypt for six hundred _shekels_
of silver, and an horse for an hundred and fifty : [z]and so for all

[r] ch.3. 12,13.
& 4. 30.

[s] ch. 4. 26.
2 Chr. 1. 14.
& 9. 25.
[t] Deut. 17.16.
[u] 2 Chr. 1.
15—17.

[x] Deut. 17.
16.
2 Chr. 1. 16.
& 9. 28.
[v] Ezek. 27.7.

[z] Josh. 1. 4.
2 Kin. 7. 6.

---

[1] Or, _elephants' teeth._
[2] Heb. _sought the face of._
[3] Heb. _gave._
[4] Heb. _And the going forth_
of _the horses which was
Solomon's._

23, 24. See marg. reff. By "all the
earth" we are, of course, only to understand
the kings or people of neighbouring nations.

25. _his present_] i.e. his tribute (iv. 21
note). A statement illustrated by Egyptian
and Assyrian sculptures on slabs and obelisks. Tribute-bearers from the subject
kings, bring not only the fixed rate of bul-
lion, but a tribute in kind besides, consisting of the most precious products of their
respective countries.

26. See iv. 26 note. Until the time of
Solomon, war-chariots had not been in use
among the Jews, except to a very small
extent (1 Chr. xviii. 4). Hence, it was
necessary for him to put himself on an
equality in this respect with neighbouring
powers.

cities for chariots] They were probably
fortresses upon the borders of his territory,
in which he maintained the standing army
necessary for the support of his dominion.

27. _made silver as stones_] This strong
hyperbole marks in the most striking way
the great wealth and prosperity of the
capital during Solomon's reign. The lavish
expenditure which impoverished the provinces, and produced, or helped to produce,
the general discontent that led to the out-
break under Jeroboam, enriched the metropolis, which must have profited greatly
by the residence of the court, the constant
influx of opulent strangers, and the peri-
odical visits of all Israelites not hindered
by some urgent reason at the great festivals.

The "sycomore-trees in the vale" (She-
phêlah) are mentioned also in 1 Chr. xxvii.
28. Like the olives and the vines, they
were placed by David under a special overseer, on account of their value. The tree
meant seems to be the sycomore proper, or
"fig-mulberry," which is still common in

Palestine, and is highly esteemed both on
account of its fruit and its timber.

28. The word translated "linen yarn" is
thought now by Hebraists to mean "a
troop" or "**company.**" If the present
reading is retained, they would translate
the passage—"As for the bringing up of
Solomon's horses out of Egypt, _a band_ of
the king's merchants fetched _a band_ (or
troop) of horses at a price." But the reading
is very uncertain. The LXX. had before
them a different one, which they render
"and from Tekoa." Tekoa, the home of
Amos (Am. i. 1), was a small town on the
route from Egypt to Jerusalem, through
which the horses would have naturally
passed. The monuments of the 18th and of
later dynasties make it clear that the horse,
though introduced from abroad, became
very abundant in Egypt. During the
whole period of Egyptian prosperity the
corps of chariots constituted a large and
effective portion of the army. That horses
were abundant in Egypt at the time of the
Exodus is evident from Ex. ix. 3, xiv. 9,
23, 28 ; Deut. xvii. 16. That they continued numerous in later times appears
from frequent allusions, both in the Historical Books of Scripture and in the Prophets, as 2 K. vii. 6, xviii. 24 ; Is. xxxvi. 9 ;
Ezek. xvii. 15, &c. The monuments show
that the horse was employed by the Egyptians in peace no less than in war, private
persons being often represented as paying
visits to their friends in chariots.

29. Taking the shekel at about three
shillings of our money, six hundred silver
shekels would be equal to about 90_l._ ; and
150 shekels to 22_l._ 10_s._ _Average_ price seems
to be in each case intended ; and we may
account for the comparatively high price of
the chariot by supposing that by "chariot"
is intended the entire equipage, including
car, harness, and trained horses, of which

the kings of the Hittites, and for the kings of Syria, did they bring *them* out [1]by their means.

a Neh. 13.26.
b Deut.17.17.

CHAP. 11. BUT [a]king Solomon loved [b]many strange women, [2]together with the daughter of Pharaoh, women of the Moabites, 2 Ammonites, Edomites, Zidonians, *and* Hittites; of the nations

c Ex. 34. 16.
Deut. 7. 3, 4.

concerning which the LORD said unto the children of Israel, [c]Ye shall not go in to them, neither shall they come in unto you : *for* surely they will turn away your heart after their gods : 3 Solomon clave unto these in love. And he had seven hundred wives, princesses, and three hundred concubines : and his wives 4 turned away his heart. For it came to pass, when Solomon was

d Deut.17.17.
Neh. 13. 26.
e ch. 8. 61.
f ch. 9. 4.
g ver. 33.
Judg. 2. 13.
2 Kin. 23.13.

old, [d]*that* his wives turned away his heart after other gods : and his [e]heart was not perfect with the LORD his God, [f]as *was* the 5 heart of David his father. For Solomon went after [g]Ashtoreth the goddess of the Zidonians, and after [3]Milcom the abomination

---

[1] Heb. *by their hand.*   [2] Or, *beside.*   [3] Called *Molech,* ver. 7.

---

there would be two at least, if not three. The "horses" mentioned separately from the chariots are not chariot-horses, but chargers for the cavalry.

the kings of the Hittites] See 2 K. vii. 6 note. The kings intended were probably Solomon's vassals, whose armies were at his disposal if he required their aid.

XI. 1. In noticing successively Solomon's excessive accumulation of silver and gold (x. 14–25), his multiplication of horses (do. 26–29), and his multiplication of wives, the writer has in mind the warning of Moses against these three forms of princely ostentation, all alike forbidden to an Israelite monarch (marg. ref.).

Zidonians] *i.e.* Phœnician women. A tradition states that Solomon married a daughter of Hiram, king of Tyre.

2. *ye shall not go in unto them,* &c.] These words are not a quotation from the Pentateuch. They merely give the general meaning of the two passages prohibiting intermarriage with neighbouring idolators (marg. reff.). Strictly speaking, the prohibition in the Law of intermarriage was confined to the Canaanitish nations. But the principle of the prohibition applied equally to the Moabites, Ammonites, and Edomites, who all bordered on the Holy Land ; and was so applied by Ezra (Ezr. ix. 1) and Nehemiah (Neh. xiii. 23).

3. These numbers seem excessive to many critics, and it must be admitted that history furnishes no parallel to them. In Cant. vi. 8 the number of Solomon's legitimate wives is said to be sixty, and that of his concubines eighty. It is, perhaps probable, that the text has in this place suffered corruption. For "700" we should perhaps read "70."

4. *old*] About fifty or fifty-five. From his age at his accession (ii. 2 note) he could not have been more than about sixty at his death.

The true nature of Solomon's idolatry

was neither complete apostasy—an apostasy from which there could be no recovery ; nor a mere toleration, rather praiseworthy than blameable. Solomon did not ever openly or wholly apostatise. He continued his attendance on the worship of Jehovah, and punctually made his offerings three times a year in the Temple (ix. 25) ; but his heart was not "perfect" with God. The religious earnestness of his younger days was weakened by wealth, luxury, sensualism, an increasing worldliness leading him to worldly policy and latitudinarianism arising from contact with all the manifold forms of human opinion. His lapse into deadly sin was no doubt gradual. Partly from ostentation, partly from that sensualism which is the most common failing of Oriental monarchs, he established a harem on a grand and extraordinary scale. To gratify "strange women," *i.e.* foreigners, admitted either from worldly policy, or for variety's sake, he built magnificent temples to their false gods, right over against Jerusalem, as manifest rivals to "the Temple." He thus became the author of a syncretism, which sought to blend together the worship of Jehovah and the worship of idols—a syncretism which possessed fatal attractions for the Jewish nation. Finally, he appears himself to have frequented the idol temples (*vv.* 5 and 10), and to have taken part in those fearful impurities which constituted the worst horror of the idolatrous systems, thus practically apostatising, though theoretically he never ceased to hold that Jehovah was the true God.

5. *went after*] This expression is common in the Pentateuch, and always signifies actual idolatry (see Deut. xi. 28, xiii. 2, xxviii. 14, &c.).

For Ashtoreth, or Astarte, the goddess of the Zidonians, see Ex. xxxiv. 13 ; Deut. xvi. 21 notes. On the tomb of a Phœnician king, discovered in 1855, on the site of

6 of the Ammonites. And Solomon did evil in the sight of the
LORD, and ¹went not fully after the LORD, as *did* David his
7 father. ʰThen did Solomon build an high place for ʲChemosh,
the abomination of Moab, in ᵏthe hill that *is* before Jerusalem,
and for Molech, the abomination of the children of Ammon.
8 And likewise did he for all his strange wives, which burnt in-
9 cense and sacrificed unto their gods. ¶And the LORD was
angry with Solomon, because ˡhis heart was turned from the
10 LORD God of Israel, ᵐwhich had appeared unto him twice, and
ⁿhad commanded him concerning this thing, that he should not
go after other gods: but he kept not that which the LORD com-
11 manded. Wherefore the LORD said unto Solomon, Forasmuch
as this ²is done of thee, and thou hast not kept my covenant
and my statutes, which I have commanded thee, ᵒI will surely
rend the kingdom from thee, and will give it to thy servant.
12 Notwithstanding in thy days I will not do it for David thy
father's sake: *but* I will rend it out of the hand of thy son.
13 ᵖHowbeit I will not rend away all the kingdom; *but* will give
�q one tribe to thy son for David my servant's sake, and for Jeru-
14 salem's sake ʳwhich I have chosen. ¶And the LORD ˢstirred
up an adversary unto Solomon, Hadad the Edomite: he *was* of
15 the king's seed in Edom. ᵗFor it came to pass, when David
was in Edom, and Joab the captain of the host was gone up to
16 bury the slain, ᵘafter he had smitten every male in Edom; (for
six months did Joab remain there with all Israel, until he had

ʰ Num. 33. 52.
ⁱ Num.21.29. Judg. 11.24.
ᵏ 2 Kin. 23. 13.

ˡ ver. 2, 3.
ᵐ ch. 3. 5. & 9. 2.
ⁿ ch. 6. 12. & 9. 6.

ᵒ ver. 31. ch. 12. 15,16.

ᵖ 2Sam.7.15. Ps. 89. 33.
q ch. 12. 20.
ʳ Deut.12.11.
ˢ 1 Chr. 5.26.
ᵗ 2 Sam.8.14. 1 Chr. 18. 12, 13.
ᵘ Num. 24. 19. Deut. 20. 13.

¹ Heb. *fulfilled not after*, Num. 14. 24.　　² Heb. *is with thee.*

Sidon, mention is made of a temple of Astarte there, which the monarch built or restored; and his mother is said to have been a priestess of the goddess.

Milcom or Molech (*v.* 7) are variants of the term ordinarily used for "king" among the Semitic races of Western Asia, which appears in *Melk*arth (Phœnic.), Abi*melech* (Heb.), Andram*melek* (Assyr.), Abd-ul-*Malik* (Arab.), &c. On the character and worship of Molech, see Lev. xx. 2–5 note.

7. Chemosh (Num. xxi. 29 note), seems to have been widely worshipped in Western Asia. His name occurs frequently on the "Moabite-Stone." Car-Chemish, "the fort of Chemosh," a great city of the northern Hittites, must have been under his protection. In Babylon he seems to have been known as Chomus-belus, or Chemosh-Bel.

the hill] Olivet. At present the southern summit only (the *Mons Offensionis*) is pointed out as having been desecrated by the idol sanctuaries: but the early Eastern travellers tell us that in their time the most northern suburb was believed to have been the site of the high place of Chemosh, the southern one that of Molech only.

13. *one tribe*] i.e. (marg. ref.) the tribe of Judah. Benjamin was looked upon as absorbed in Judah, so as not to be really a tribe in the same sense as the others. Still, in memory of the fact that the existing tribe of Judah was a double one (xii. 21), the prophet Ahijah tore his garment into

twelve parts, and kept back two from Jeroboam (*vv.* 30, 31).

14. The writer has reserved for this place the various troubles of Solomon's reign, not allowing them to interrupt his previous narrative. He has, consequently, not followed chronological order. Hadad's (*v.* 23) and Rezon's opposition belong to the early years of Solomon's reign.

Hadad was a royal title (perhaps, the Syriac name for "the Sun") both in Syria and in Idumæa (cp. Gen. xxxvi. 35; 1 Chr. i. 51).

15. The verse gives certain additional particulars of David's conquest of Edom (marg. reff.). Joab was left, or sent, to complete the subjugation of the country, with orders to exterminate all the grown male inhabitants. It was not very often that David acted with any extreme severity in his wars; but he may have considered himself justified by policy, as he certainly was by the letter of the Law (Deut. xx. 13), in adopting this fierce course against Edom.

was in Edom] Or, according to another reading, "*smote*" Edom.

the slain] Probably the Israelites who had fallen in the struggle. Translate, "when... Joab was gone up to bury the slain, and had smitten every male," &c.

16. *every male in Edom*] i.e. every male whom he could find. As did Hadad and his company (*v.* 17), so others would escape in various directions. The Edomite nation was not destroyed on the occasion.

17 cut off every male in Edom :) that Hadad fled, he and certain
Edomites of his father's servants with him, to go into Egypt;
18 Hadad *being* yet a little child. And they arose out of Midian,
and came to Paran : and they took men with them out of Paran,
and they came to Egypt, unto Pharaoh king of Egypt; which
gave him an house, and appointed him victuals, and gave him
19 land. And Hadad found great favour in the sight of Pharaoh,
so that he gave him to wife the sister of his own wife, the sister
20 of Tahpenes the queen. And the sister of Tahpenes bare him
Genubath his son, whom Tahpenes weaned in Pharaoh's house :
and Genubath was in Pharaoh's household among the sons of
21 Pharaoh. *x*And when Hadad heard in Egypt that David slept
with his fathers, and that Joab the captain of the host was dead,
Hadad said to Pharaoh, ¹Let me depart, that I may go to mine
22 own country. Then Pharaoh said unto him, But what hast thou
lacked with me, that, behold, thou seekest to go to thine own
country? And he answered, ²Nothing : howbeit let me go in
23 any wise. ¶And God stirred him up *another* adversary, Rezon
the son of Eliadah, which fled from his lord *y*Hadadezer king of
24 Zobah : and he gathered men unto him, and became captain
over a band, *z*when David slew them *of Zobah :* and they went
25 to Damascus, and dwelt therein, and reigned in Damascus. And
he was an adversary to Israel all the days of Solomon, beside the
mischief that Hadad *did :* and he abhorred Israel, and reigned
26 over Syria. ¶And *a*Jeroboam the son of Nebat, an Ephrathite
of Zereda, Solomon's servant, whose mother's name *was* Zeruah,
a widow woman, even he *b*lifted up *his* hand against the king.
27 And this *was* the cause that he lifted up *his* hand against the
king : *c*Solomon built Millo, *and* ³repaired the breaches of the
28 city of David his father. And the man Jeroboam *was* a mighty
man of valour : and Solomon seeing the young man that he ⁴was
industrious, he made him ruler over all the ⁵charge of the house

x 1 Kin. 2.
10, 34.

y 2 Sam. 8.3.

z 2 Sam. 8. 3.
& 10. 8, 18.

a ch. 12. 2.
2 Chr. 13. 6.

b 2 Sam. 20.
21.

c ch. 9. 15.

---

¹ Heb. *send me away.*   ³ Heb. *closed.*   ⁴ Heb. *did work.*
² Heb. *Not.*   ⁵ Heb. *burden.*

---

18. *Midian*] A town in the south of
Judah. Paran is the desert tract immediately to the south of Judæa, the modern
desert of et-Tih.

Pharaoh] King of the twenty-first (Tanite)
dynasty; probably he was Psusennes I.,
Manetho's second king. It appears to have
been the policy of the Pharaohs about this
time to make friends and contract alliances
with their eastern neighbours.

21. That Hadad should wait for the
death of Joab before requesting leave to
return to Idumæa shows how terrible an
impression had been made by the severe
measures which that commander had carried out twenty-five or thirty years previously (*v.* 16). The inability of refugees to
depart from an Oriental court without the
king's leave, and his unwillingness ordinarily to grant leave, are illustrated by
many passages in the history of Persia.

23. *Rezon*] Possibly the same as the
Hezion of xv. 18; but probably one who in-
terrupted the royal line of the Damascene
Hadads, which was restored after his death.

We may arrange the Damascus-kings of this
period as follows :—

Hadadezer (or Hadad I.), ab. B.C. 1040 (con-
quered by David).
Rezon (usurper) contemporary with Solomon.
Hezion (Hadad II.)   „   „   Rehoboam.
Tabrimon (Hadad III.) „   „   Abijam.
Ben-hadad (Hadad IV.) „   „   Asa.

24. *and* (*they*) *reigned*] A very slight
emendation gives the sense, "they made
him king at Damascus."

26. *Zereda*] See Judg. vii. 22.
lifted up his hand against the king] *i.e.*
"he rebelled." Cp. marg. ref.

27. Millo was probably fortified in Solomon's twenty-fourth or twenty-fifth year.

28. *a mighty man of valour*] Here " a man
of **strength and activity.**" It is a vague
term of commendation, the exact force of
which must be fixed by the context. See
Ruth ii. 1 ; 1 Sam. ix. 1, &c.

Solomon made Jeroboam superintendent
of all the forced labour ("the charge")
exacted from his tribe—the tribe of Ephraim
— during the time that he was building

29 of Joseph.   And it came to pass at that time when Jeroboam
went out of Jerusalem, that the prophet *d*Ahijah the Shilonite   *d*.ch. 14. 2.
found him in the way; and he had clad himself with a new
30 garment; and they two *were* alone in the field: and Ahijah
caught the new garment that *was* on him, and *e*rent it *in* twelve   *e* See
31 pieces: and he said to Jeroboam, Take thee ten pieces: for   1 Sam. 15.
*f*thus saith the LORD, the God of Israel, Behold, I will rend the   27.
kingdom out of the hand of Solomon, and will give ten tribes to   & 24. 5.
                                                                    f ver. 11, 13.
32 thee: (but he shall have one tribe for my servant David's sake,
and for Jerusalem's sake, the city which I have chosen out of all
33 the tribes of Israel:) *g*because that they have forsaken me, and   *g* ver. 5, 6, 7.
have worshipped Ashtoreth the goddess of the Zidonians, Che-
mosh the god of the Moabites, and Milcom the god of the
children of Ammon, and have not walked in my ways, to do *that*
which is right in mine eyes, and *to keep* my statutes and my
34 judgments, as *did* David his father.   Howbeit I will not take the
whole kingdom out of his hand: but I will make him prince all
the days of his life for David my servant's sake, whom I chose,
35 because he kept my commandments and my statutes: but *h*I   *h* ch. 12. 16,
will take the kingdom out of his son's hand, and will give it unto   17.
36 thee, *even* ten tribes.   And unto his son will I give one tribe,
that *i*David my servant may have a [1]light alway before me in   *i* ch. 15. 4.
Jerusalem, the city which I have chosen me to put my name   2 Kin. 8. 19.
                                                                    Ps. 132. 17.
37 there.   And I will take thee, and thou shalt reign according to
38 all that thy soul desireth, and shalt be king over Israel.   And
it shall be, if thou wilt hearken unto all that I command thee,
and wilt walk in my ways, and do *that is* right in my sight, to
keep my statutes and my commandments, as David my servant
did; that *k*I will be with thee, and *l*build thee a sure house, as   *k* ch. 1. 37.
39 I built for David, and will give Israel unto thee.   And I will   *l* 2 Sam. 7.
40 for this afflict the seed of David, but not for ever.   Solomon   11, 27.
sought therefore to kill Jeroboam.   And Jeroboam arose, and

[1] Heb. *lamp*, or, *candle*.

Millo and fortifying the city of Jerusalem
(ix. 15).

29. *at that time*] Probably after Jeroboam's return from Egypt (see *v.* 40).

the Shilonite] An inhabitant of Shiloh in
Mount Ephraim, the earliest and most
sacred of the Hebrew sanctuaries (Josh.
xviii. 10; Judg. xviii. 31; 1 Sam. iv. 3, &c.)

30. The first instance of the "acted
parable." Generally this mode was adopted
upon express divine command (see Jer. xiii.
1-11; Ezek. iii. 1-3).   A connexion may be
traced between the type selected and the
words of the announcement to Solomon (*vv.*
11-13.   Cp. 1 Sam. xv. 26–28).

34. Translate—"Howbeit I will not take
ought of the kingdom out of his hand."
The context requires this sense.

36. *that David may have a light*] Cp.
marg. reff.   The exact meaning of the expression is doubtful.   Perhaps the best explanation is, that "light" here is taken as
the essential feature of a continuing *home.*

38. See marg. reff.   To "build a sure
house," or "give a house," is to give a continuity of offspring, and so secure the per-

petuity of a family.   The promise, it will
be observed, is conditional; and as the
condition was not complied with, it did
not take effect (see xiv. 8-14).   The entire
house of Jeroboam was destroyed by Baasha
(xv. 29).

39. *but not for ever*] David had been distinctly promised that God should never
fail his seed, whatever their shortcomings
(Ps. lxxxix. 28-37).   The fulfilment of these
promises was seen, partly in the Providence
which maintained David's family in a royal
position till Zerubbabel, but mainly in the
preservation of his seed to the time fixed
for the coming of Christ, and in the birth
of Christ—the Eternal King—from one of
David's descendants.

40. Cp. *v.* 26.   The announcement of
Ahijah was followed within a little while
by rebellion on the part of Jeroboam.   As
Solomon's lustre faded, as his oppression
became greater and its objects more selfish,
and as a prospect of deliverance arose from
the personal qualities of Jeroboam (*v.* 28),
the tribe of Ephraim to which he belonged,
again aspired after its old position (see Josh.

fled into Egypt, unto Shishak king of Egypt, and was in Egypt

m 2 Chr. 9.
29.
41 until the death of Solomon. ¶And ᵐthe rest of the ¹acts of
Solomon, and all that he did, and his wisdom, *are* they not

n 2 Chr. 9.30.
42 written in the book of the acts of Solomon? ⁿAnd the ²time
that Solomon reigned in Jerusalem over all Israel *was* forty

o 2 Chr. 9.31.
43 years. ᵒAnd Solomon slept with his fathers, and was buried in

p Matt. 1. 7,
called
Roboam.
the city of David his father: and ᵖRehoboam his son reigned in
his stead.

a 2 Chr. 10.
1, &c.
CHAP. 12. AND ᵃRehoboam went to Shechem: for all Israel were
2 come to Shechem to make him king. ¶And it came to pass,

b ch. 11. 26.
c ch. 11. 40.
when ᵇJeroboam the son of Nebat, who was yet in ᶜEgypt,
heard *of it*, (for he was fled from the presence of king Solomon,
3 and Jeroboam dwelt in Egypt;) that they sent and called him.
And Jeroboam and all the congregation of Israel came, and

d 1 Sam. 8.
11—18.
ch. 4. 7.
4 spake unto Rehoboam, saying, Thy father made our ᵈyoke
grievous: now therefore make thou the grievous service of thy
father, and his heavy yoke which he put upon us, lighter, and

---

¹ Or, *words*, or, *things*.   ² Heb. *days*.

---

xvii. 14 note). Jeroboam, active, energetic, and ambitious, placed himself at their head. The step proved premature. The power of Solomon was too firmly fixed to be shaken; and the hopes of the Ephraimites had to be deferred till a fitter season.

The *exact* date of Jeroboam's flight into Egypt cannot be fixed. It was certainly not earlier than Solomon's twenty-fourth year, since it was after the building of Millo (*v.* 27). But it may have been several years later.

Shishak] This king is the first Pharaoh mentioned in Scripture who can be certainly identified with any known Egyptian monarch. He is the Sheshonk (Sheshonk I.) of the monuments, and the Sesonchosis of Manetho. The Egyptian date for his accession is B.C. 980 or 983, which synchronizes, according to the ordinary Hebrew reckoning, with Solomon's thirty-second or thirty-fifth year. Sheshonk I. has left a record of his expedition against Judah, which accords well with what is related of Shishak (xiv. 25, 26; 2 Chr. xii. 2-4).

41. *the book of the acts of Solomon*] See marg. ref. and Introd. p. 265.

42. Josephus gave Solomon a reign of eighty years, either because he wished to increase the glory of his country's greatest king, or through his having a false reading in his copy of the LXX. Version. It is, no doubt, remarkable that the three successive kings, Saul, David, and Solomon, should have each reigned forty years (Acts xiii. 21; 2 Sam. v. 4, 5); but such numerical coincidences occur from time to time in exact history.

XII. 1. The first step taken by the new king was a most judicious one. If anything could have removed the disaffection of the Ephraimites, and caused them to submit to the ascendancy of Judah, it would have been the honour done to their capital by its

selection as the scene of the coronation. Shechem (now *Nablous*) lay on the flank of Mount Gerizim, directly opposite to Mount Ebal, in a position second to none in all Palestine. Though Abimelech had destroyed the place (Judg. ix. 45), it had probably soon risen again, and was once more a chief city, or perhaps *the* chief city, of Ephraim. Its central position made it a convenient place for the general assembly of the tribes, as it had been in the days of Joshua (Josh. viii. 30-35, xxiv. 1-28); and this would furnish an additional reason for its selection.

2. *heard of it*] i.e. of the death of Solomon and accession of Rehoboam. This would be more clear without the division into chapters; which division, it must be remembered, is without authority.

dwelt in Egypt] By a change of the pointing of one word, and of one letter in another, the Hebrew text here will read as in 2 Chr. x. 2, "returned out of Egypt; and they sent and called him."

In the LXX. Version the story of Jeroboam is told in two different ways. The general narrative agrees closely with the Hebrew text; but an insertion into the body of ch. xii.—remarkable for its minuteness and circumstantiality—at once deranges the order of the events, and gives to the history in many respects a new aspect and colouring. This section of the Septuagint, though regarded by some as thoroughly authentic, absolutely conflicts with the Hebrew text in many important particulars. In its general outline it is wholly irreconcileable with the other narrative; and, if both stood on the same footing, and we were free to chose between them, there could be no question about preferring the history as given in our Version.

4. The complaint was probably twofold. The Israelites no doubt complained in part of the heavy weight of taxation laid upon

5 we will serve thee. And he said unto them, Depart yet *for* three days, then come again to me. And the people departed.
6 ¶And king Rehoboam consulted with the old men, that stood before Solomon his father while he yet lived, and said, How do
7 ye advise that I may answer this people? And they spake unto him, saying, *e* If thou wilt be a servant unto this people this day, and wilt serve them, and answer them, and speak good words to
8 them, then they will be thy servants for ever. But he forsook the counsel of the old men, which they had given him, and consulted with the young men that were grown up with him, *and*
9 which stood before him: and he said unto them, What counsel give ye that we may answer this people, who have spoken to me, saying, Make the yoke which thy father did put upon us lighter?
10 And the young men that were grown up with him spake unto him, saying, Thus shalt thou speak unto this people that spake unto thee, saying, Thy father made our yoke heavy, but make thou *it* lighter unto us; thus shalt thou say unto them, My little
11 *finger* shall be thicker than my father's loins. And now whereas my father did lade you with a heavy yoke, I will add to your yoke: my father hath chastised you with whips, but I will
12 chastise you with scorpions. ¶So Jeroboam and all the people came to Rehoboam the third day, as the king had appointed,
13 saying, Come to me again the third day. And the king answered the people ¹ roughly, and forsook the old men's counsel
14 that they gave him; and spake to them after the counsel of the young men, saying, My father made your yoke heavy, and I will add to your yoke: my father *also* chastised you with whips,
15 but I will chastise you with scorpions. Wherefore the king hearkened not unto the people; for *f* the cause was from the LORD, that he might perform his saying, which the LORD

e 2 Chr.10.7.
Prov. 15. 1.

f ver. 24.
Judg. 14. 4.
2 Chr. 10. 15.
& 22. 7.
& 25. 20.

¹ Heb. *hardly.*

---

them for the maintenance of the monarch and his court (iv. 19–23). But their chief grievance was the forced labour to which they had been subjected (v. 13, 14, xi. 28). Forced labour has been among the causes leading to insurrection in many ages and countries. It helped to bring about the French Revolution, and it was for many years one of the principal grievances of the Russian serfs. Jeroboam's position as superintendent of the forced labours of the tribe of Ephraim (xi. 28) revealed to him the large amount of dissatisfaction which Solomon's system had produced, and his contemplated rebellion in Solomon's reign may have been connected with this standing grievance.

6. *the old men, that stood before Solomon his father*] Perhaps "the princes" of iv. 2. Solomon placed great value upon good advisers (Prov. xi. 14, xv. 22, xxiv. 6).

7. The advice was not that the king should permanently resign the office of ruler, but that he should *for once* be ruled by his people.

8. The age of Rehoboam at his accession is an interesting and difficult question. According to the formal statement of the present text of xiv. 21, 2 Chr. xii. 13, he had

reached the mature age of forty-one years, and would therefore be unable to plead youth as an excuse for his conduct. The general narrative, however, seems to assume that he was quite a young man (cp. 2 Chr. xiii. 7). Perhaps the best way of removing the whole difficulty would be to read in the above text "twenty-one" for "forty-one." The corruption is one which might easily take place, if letters were used for numerals.

My little finger, &c.] *i.e.* "You shall find my hand heavier on you than my father's —as much heavier as if my little finger were thicker than his loins."

11. *scorpions*] By this word some understand whips having leaden balls at the ends of their lashes with hooks projecting from them; others the thorny stem of the eggplant, or "the scorpion plant." But it seems best to regard the expression as a figure of speech.

15. *The cause was from the* LORD] *i.e.* "the turn of events was from the Lord." Human passions, anger, pride, and insolence, worked out the accomplishment of the Divine designs. Without interfering with man's free will, God guides the course of events, and accomplishes His purposes.

g ch. 11. 11, 31.
h 2 Sam. 20. 1.
i ch. 11. 13, 36.
k ch. 4. 6. & 5. 14.
l 2 Kin. 17. 21.
m ch. 11. 13, 32.
n 2 Chr. 11. 1.

g spake by Ahijah the Shilonite unto Jeroboam the son of Nebat.
16 ¶ So when all Israel saw that the king hearkened not unto them, the people answered the king, saying, *h* What portion have we in David? neither *have we* inheritance in the son of Jesse: to your tents, O Israel: now see to thine own house, David. So Israel
17 departed unto their tents. But *i as for* the children of Israel which dwelt in the cities of Judah, Rehoboam reigned over
18 them. ¶ Then king Rehoboam *k* sent Adoram, who *was* over the tribute; and all Israel stoned him with stones, that he died. Therefore king Rehoboam *l* made speed to get him up to his
19 chariot, to flee to Jerusalem. So *l* Israel *2* rebelled against the
20 house of David unto this day. And it came to pass, when all Israel heard that Jeroboam was come again, that they sent and called him unto the congregation, and made him king over all Israel: there was none that followed the house of David, but the
21 tribe of Judah *m* only. ¶ And when *n* Rehoboam was come to Jerusalem, he assembled all the house of Judah, with the tribe of

1 Heb. *strengthened himself.*   *2* Or, *fell away.*

---

16. See marg. ref. The words breathe unmistakeably the spirit of tribal jealousy and dislike (xi. 40 note).

now see to thine own house, David] i.e. "Henceforth, house of David, look after thine own tribe, Judah, only." It is not a threat of war, but a warning against interference.

17. *Israel,* &c.] The Israelites proper, or members of the other tribes, who happened to be settled within the limits of the land of Judah. These Israelites quietly submitted to Rehoboam. "Israel" through this chapter, and throughout the rest of Kings," designates ordinarily " the ten tribes," and is antithetical to "Judah."

18. Adoram has been identified with Adoniram (marg. reff.), and even with the Adoram of 2 Sam. xx. 24. But it is highly improbable that the same person was chief superintendent of the forced labours during the whole of Solomon's long reign, and also during a part of David's and Rehoboam's. We may therefore conclude that the three names mark three distinct persons, perhaps of the same family, who were respectively contemporary with the three kings. Adoram was chosen, as best acquainted with the hardships whereof the rebels complained, to arrange some alleviation of their burthens.

19. *unto this day*] This expression shows that the writer, who lived during the Captivity, and consequently long after the rebellion of Israel had come to an end, is embodying in his history the exact words of an ancient document. His source, whatever it was, appears to have been also followed by the writer of Chronicles. (See 2 Chr. x. 19.)

20. The first act of the Israelites, on learning what had occurred at Shechem, was to bring together the great "congregation" of the people (cp. Judg. xx. 1), in

order that, regularly and in solemn form, the crown might be declared vacant, and a king elected in the room of the monarch whose authority had been thrown off. The congregation selected Jeroboam. The rank, the talent, and the known energy of the late exile, his natural hostility to the house of Solomon, his Ephraimitic descent, his acquaintance with the art of fortification, and the friendly relations subsisting between him and the great Egyptian king, pointed him out as the fittest man for the vacant post. If (according to the LXX.) Shishak had not only protected him against Solomon, but also given him an Egyptian princess, sister to his own queen, in marriage, his position must have been such that no other Israelite could have borne comparison with him. Again, the prophecy of Ahijah would have been remembered by the more religious part of the nation, and would have secured to Jeroboam their adhesion ; so that every motive, whether of policy or of religion, would have united to recommend the son of Nebat to the suffrages of his countrymen.

21. The adhesion of Benjamin to Judah at this time comes upon us as a surprise. By blood Benjamin was far more closely connected with Ephraim than with Judah. All the traditions of Benjamin were antagonistic to Judah, and hitherto the weak tribe had been accustomed to lean constantly on its strong northern neighbour. But it would seem that, in the half-century which had elapsed since the revolt of Sheba, the son of Bichri (2 Sam. xx. 1), the feelings of the Benjamites had undergone a complete change. This is best accounted for by the establishment of the religious and political capital at Jerusalem, on the border line of the two tribes (Josh. xv. 8, xviii. 16), whence it resulted that the new metropolis stood partly within the territory of either, and was in a

Benjamin, an hundred and fourscore thousand chosen men, which were warriors, to fignt against the house of Israel, to bring the kingdom again to Rehoboam the son of Solomon.

22 But °the word of God came unto Shemaiah the man of God, 23 saying, Speak unto Rehoboam, the son of Solomon, king of Judah, and unto all the house of Judah and Benjamin, and to 24 the remnant of the people, saying, Thus saith the LORD, Ye shall not go up, nor fight against your brethren the children of Israel: return every man to his house; ᵖfor this thing is from me. They hearkened therefore to the word of the LORD, and 25 returned to depart, according to the word of the LORD. ¶ Then Jeroboam ᑫbuilt Shechem in mount Ephraim, and dwelt therein; 26 and went out from thence, and built ʳPenuel. And Jeroboam said in his heart, Now shall the kingdom return to the house of 27 David: if this people ˢgo up to do sacrifice in the house of the LORD at Jerusalem, then shall the heart of this people turn again unto their lord, *even* unto Rehoboam king of Judah, and they shall kill me, and go again to Rehoboam king of Judah. 28 Whereupon the king took counsel, and ᵗmade two calves *of* gold, and said unto them, It is too much for you to go up to Jerusalem: ᵘbehold thy gods, O Israel, which brought thee up

° 2 Chr. 12. 5—8, 15.

ᵖ ver. 15.

ᑫ See Judg. 9. 45.
ʳ Judg. 8. 17.

ˢ Deut. 12. 5, 6.

ᵗ 2 Kin. 10. 29.

ᵘ Ex. 32. 4, 8.

---

certain sense common to both. One of the gates of Jerusalem was "the high gate of Benjamin" (Jer. xx. 2); and probably Benjamites formed a considerable part of the population. The whole tribe also, we may well believe, was sincerely attached to the Temple worship, in which they could participate far more freely and more constantly than the members of remoter tribes, and to which the habits of forty years had now accustomed them.

On the number of the Israelites, see notes on Ex. xii. 37, and 2 Sam. xxiv. 9. The number mentioned here is moderate, compared with the numbers given both previously and subsequently (2 Chr. xiii. 3, xvii. 14-18).

22. Shemaiah was the chief Prophet in Judah during the reign of Rehoboam, as Ahijah was in Israel. See marg. reff.

23. *the remnant*] *i.e.* "the children of Israel which dwelt in the cities of Judah" (*v.* 17 note).

25. *built Shechem*] In the sense of "enlarged and fortified." See Dan. iv. 30. The first intention of Jeroboam seems to have been to make Shechem his capital, and therefore he immediately set about its fortification. So also he seems to have fortified Penuel for the better security of his Trans-Jordanic possessions (marg. ref.).

26. Jeroboam's fear was lest a reaction should set in, and a desire for reunion manifest itself. He was not a man content to remain quiet, trusting simply to the promise made him (xi. 38). Hence he gave way to the temptation of helping forward the plans of Providence by the crooked devices of a merely human policy. His measures, like all measures which involve a dereliction of principle, brought certain

evils in their train, and drew down Divine judgment on himself. But they fully secured the object at which he aimed. They prevented all healing of the breach between the two kingdoms. They made the separation final. They produced the result that not only no reunion took place, but no symptoms of an inclination to reunite ever manifested themselves during the whole period of the double kingdom.

27. *kill me*] In case his subjects desired a reconciliation with Rehoboam, Jeroboam's death would at once facilitate the reestablishment of a single kingdom, and obtain favour with the legitimate monarch. (Cp. 2 Sam. iv. 7.)

28. The "calves of gold" were probably representations of the cherubic form, imitations of the two Cherubim which guarded the Ark of the Covenant in the Holy of Holies. But being unauthorised copies, set up in places which God had not chosen, and without any Divine sanction, the sacred writers call them "calves." They were not mere human figures with wings, but had at any rate the head of a calf or ox. [Hence, some attribute this calf-worship entirely to Assyrian and Phœnician influence.] Jeroboam, in setting them up, was probably not so much influenced by the Apis-worship of Egypt, as (1) by a conviction that the Israelites could not be brought to attach themselves to any worship which did not present them with sensible objects to venerate; (2) by the circumstance that he did not possess any of the old objects of reverence, which had been concentrated at Jerusalem; and (3) by the fact that he could plead for his "calves" the authority of so great a name as Aaron (marg. ref.).

x Gen. 28.19.
v Judg. 18.
29.
z ch. 13. 34.
2 Kin. 17. 21.
a ch. 13. 32.
b Num. 3. 10.
2 Kin. 17.32.
Ezek. 44.7,8.
c Lev. 23.
33, 34.
Num. 29. 12.
ch. 8. 2, 5.
d Amos 7.13.

e Num. 15.
39.

f ch. 13. 1.

a 2 Kin. 23.
17.
b ch. 12. 32,
33.

29 out of the land of Egypt. And he set the one in *x*Beth-el, and
30 the other put he in *v*Dan. And this thing became *z*a sin: for
31 the people went *to worship* before the one, *even* unto Dan. And
   he made an *a*house of high places, *b*and made priests of the
32 lowest of the people, which were not of the sons of Levi. And
   Jeroboam ordained a feast in the eighth month, on the fifteenth
   day of the month, like unto *c*the feast that *is* in Judah, and he
   ¹offered upon the altar. So did he in Beth-el, ²sacrificing unto
   the calves that he had made: *d*and he placed in Beth-el the
33 priests of the high places which he had made. So he ³offered
   upon the altar which he had made in Beth-el the fifteenth day of
   the eighth month, *even* in the month which he had *e*devised of
   his own heart; and ordained a feast unto the children of Israel:
   and he offered upon the altar, ⁴and *f*burnt incense.

CHAP. 13. AND, behold, there *a*came a man of God out of Judah
   by the word of the LORD unto Beth-el: *b*and Jeroboam stood by

---

¹ Or, *went up to the altar, &c.*   ³ Or, *went up to the altar, &c.*
² Or, *to sacrifice.*   ⁴ Heb. *to burn incense.*

---

29. In the first place, Jeroboam consulted the convenience of his subjects, who would thus in no case have very far to go in order to reach one or the other sanctuary. Further, he avoided the danger of reminding them continually that they had no ark—a danger which would have been imminent, had the two cherubs been placed together in one shrine.

He selected Bethel (in the south) for one of his seats of worship, on account of its pre-eminent sanctity. (See marg. ref.; Judg. xx. 26–28; 1 Sam. vii. 16.)

The north of Palestine did not furnish a spot possessing an equally sacred character, but still Dan had to some extent the character of a "holy city" (marg. ref.).

30. *this thing became a sin*] *i.e.* this act of Jeroboam's became an occasion of sin to the people. The author perhaps wrote the following words thus: "The people went to worship before the one to Bethel and before the other to Dan."

31. *he made an house of high places*] *i.e.* "He built a temple, or sanctuary, at each of the two cities where the calves were set up." The writer uses the expression "house of high places" in contempt, meaning that the buildings were not real temples, or houses of God, like that at Jerusalem, but only on a par with the temples upon high places which had long existed in various parts of the land.

made priests of the lowest of the people] More correctly, "**from all ranks of the people.**" That the Levites did not accept Jeroboam's innovations, and transfer their services to his two sanctuaries, must have been the consequence of their faithful attachment to the true worship of Jehovah. In all probability Jeroboam confiscated the Levitical lands within his dominions for the benefit of the new priestly order (2 Chr. xi. 13, 14).

32. *a feast*] Intended as a substitute for the Feast of Tabernacles (marg. ref. *c*). It *may* also have assumed the character of a feast of dedication, held at the same time, after the example of Solomon (viii. 2). His object in changing the month from the seventh to the eighth, and yet keeping the day of the month, is not clear. Perhaps it was on account of the later vintage of the more northern regions. It is remarkable that Josephus places the scene in the *seventh* month. He therefore was not aware that the people of Israel kept the feast of Tabernacles a month later than their brethren of Judah. The expression "he offered upon the altar" (see marg. and Ex. xx. 26) shows that Jeroboam himself officiated as priest, and offered this sacrifice—at Bethel, not at Dan; where it is possible that the priests descended from Jonathan, the son of Gershom and grandson of Moses, undertook the services (Judg. xviii. 30 note).

33. This verse belongs to ch. xiii. rather than to ch. xii., being intended as an introduction to what follows.

which he had devised of his own heart] The entire system of Jeroboam receives its condemnation in these words. His main fault was that he left a ritual and a worship where all was divinely authorised, for ceremonies and services which were wholly of his own devising. Not being a Prophet, he had no authority to introduce religious innovations. Not having received any commission to establish new forms, he had no right to expect that any religious benefit would accrue from them. (See *v.* 26 note.)

XIII. 1. Rather, "*in* the word of the Lord." The meaning seems to be, not merely that the Prophet was bid to come, but that he came in the strength and power of God's word, a divinely inspired messenger. (Cp. *vv.* 2, 5, 32.)

by the altar] "**On** the altar;" *i.e.* on the

2 the altar ¹to burn incense. And he cried against the altar in the word of the LORD, and said, O altar, altar, thus saith the LORD; Behold, a child shall be born unto the house of David, ᶜJosiah by name; and upon thee shall he offer the priests of the high places that burn incense upon thee, and men's bones 3 shall be burnt upon thee. And he gave ᵈa sign the same day, saying, This *is* the sign which the LORD hath spoken; Behold, the altar shall be rent, and the ashes that *are* upon it 4 shall be poured out. ¶And it came to pass, when king Jeroboam heard the saying of the man of God, which had cried against the altar in Beth-el, that he put forth his hand from the altar, saying, Lay hold on him. And his hand, which he put forth against him, dried up, so that he could not pull it in again 5 to him. The altar also was rent, and the ashes poured out from the altar, according to the sign which the man of God had given 6 by the word of the LORD. And the king answered and said unto the man of God, ᵉIntreat now the face of the LORD thy God, and pray for me, that my hand may be restored me again. And the man of God besought ²the LORD, and the king's hand 7 was restored him again, and became as *it was* before. And the king said unto the man of God, come home with me, and refresh 8 thyself, and ᶠI will give thee a reward. And the man of God said unto the king, ᵍIf thou wilt give me half thine house, I will not go in with thee, neither will I eat bread nor drink water in 9 this place: for so was it charged me by the word of the LORD, saying, ʰEat no bread, nor drink water, nor turn again by the 10 same way that thou camest. So he went another way, and re-

c 2 Kin. 23. 15—18.

d John 2. 18. 1 Cor. 1. 22.

e Ex. 8. 8. & 9. 28. & 10. 17. Num. 21. 7. Acts 8. 24. Jam. 5. 16.

f 1 Sam. 9. 7. 2 Kin. 5. 15. *g* So Num. 22. 18. & 24. 13.

h 1 Cor. 5. 11.

---

¹ Or, *to offer.*   ² Heb. *the face of the LORD.*

---

ledge, or platform, half-way up the Altar, whereupon the officiating priest always stood to sacrifice. Cp. xii. 32 note.

2. *a child shall be born...Josiah by name*] Divine predictions so seldom descend to such particularity as this, that doubts are entertained, even by orthodox theologians, with respect to the actual mention of Josiah's name by a Prophet living in the time of Jeroboam. Only one other instance that can be considered parallel occurs in the whole of Scripture—the mention of Cyrus by Isaiah. Of course no one who believes in the Divine foreknowledge can doubt that God could, if He chose, cause events to be foretold minutely by his Prophets; but certainly the general law of his Providence is, that He does not do so. If this law is to be at any time broken through, it will not be capriciously. Here it certainly does not appear what great effect was to be produced by the mention of Josiah's name so long before his birth ; and hence a doubt arises whether we have in our present copies the true original text. The sense is complete without the words "Josiah by name;" and these words, if originally a marginal note, may easily have crept into the text by the mistake of a copyist. It is remarkable that, where this narrative is again referred to in Kings (marg. ref.), there is no allusion to the fact that the man of God had prophesied of Josiah *by name.*

3. *he gave a sign*] A sign of this kind—an immediate prophecy to prove the Divine character of a remote prophecy — had scarcely been given before this. In the later history, however, such signs are not unfrequent (cp. 2 K. xix. 29; Is. vii. 14-16).

the ashes...shall be poured out] *i.e.* "The half-burnt remains of the offerings shall be ignominiously spilled upon the ground."

5. We need not suppose a complete shattering of the altar, but rather the appearance of a crack or fissure in the fabric, which, extending from top to bottom, caused the embers and the fragments of the victims to fall till they reached the ground.

7. *I will give thee a reward*] It was customary to honour a Prophet with a gift, if he performed any service that was requested at his hands (see marg. reff.).

9. *Eat no bread, nor drink water*] The reason of the command is evident. The man of God was not to accept the hospitality of any dweller at Bethel, in order to show in a marked way, which men generally could appreciate, God's abhorrence of the system which Jeroboam had "devised of his own heart."

nor turn again by the same way that thou camest] This command seems to have been given simply to test the obedience of the Prophet by laying him under a positive as well as a moral obligation.

11 turned not by the way that he came to Beth-el. ¶Now there dwelt an old prophet in Beth-el; and his [1]sons came and told him all the works that the man of God had done that day in Beth-el: the words which he had spoken unto the king, them
12 they told also to their father. And their father said unto them, What way went he? For his sons had seen what way the man
13 of God went, which came from Judah. And he said unto his sons, Saddle me the ass. So they saddled him the ass: and he
14 rode thereon, and went after the man of God, and found him sitting under an oak: and he said unto him, *Art* thou the man
15 of God that camest from Judah? And he said, I *am*. Then he
16 said unto him, Come home with me, and eat bread. And he said, *i* I may not return with thee, nor go in with thee: neither
17 will I eat bread nor drink water with thee in this place: for [2]it was said to me *k* by the word of the LORD, Thou shalt eat no bread nor drink water there, nor turn again to go by the way
18 that thou camest. He said unto him, I *am* a prophet also as thou *art;* and an angel spake unto me by the word of the LORD, saying, Bring him back with thee into thine house, that he may
19 eat bread and drink water. *But* he lied unto him. So he went back with him, and did eat bread in his house, and drank water.
20 ¶And it came to pass, as they sat at the table, that the word of
21 the LORD came unto the prophet that brought him back: and he cried unto the man of God that came from Judah, saying, Thus saith the LORD, Forasmuch as thou hast disobeyed the mouth of the LORD, and hast not kept the commandment which
22 the LORD thy God commanded thee, but camest back, and hast eaten bread and drunk water in the *l* place, of the which *the* LORD did say to thee, Eat no bread, and drink no water; thy
23 carcase shall not come unto the sepulchre of thy fathers. ¶And it came to pass, after he had eaten bread, and after he had drunk, that he saddled for him the ass, *to wit,* for the prophet
24 whom he had brought back. And when he was gone, *m* a lion met him by the way, and slew him: and his carcase was cast in the way, and the ass stood by it, the lion also stood by the
25 carcase. And, behold, men passed by, and saw the carcase cast in the way, and the lion standing by the carcase: and they

i ver. 8. 9.

k ch. 20. 35.
1 Thess. 4.
15.

ver. 9.

m ch. 20. 36.

---

[1] Heb. *son.*   [2] Heb. *a word was.*

---

11. The truly pious Israelites quitted their homes when Jeroboam made his religious changes, and, proceeding to Jerusalem, strengthened the kingdom of Rehoboam (2 Chr. x. 16, 17). This "old prophet" therefore, who, without being infirm in any way, had remained under Jeroboam, and was even content to dwell at Bethel—the chief seat of the new worship—was devoid of any deep and earnest religious feeling.

14. *under an oak*] Literally, "under the oak," or "the terebinth-tree." There was a single well-known tree of the kind, standing by itself in the vicinity of Bethel, which the author supposed his readers to be acquainted with.

18. *But he lied unto him*] It is always to be remembered that the prophetic gift

might co-exist with various degrees of moral imperfection in the person possessing it. Note especially the case of Balaam.

21. *Forasmuch as thou hast disobeyed the mouth of the* LORD] It was his duty not to have suffered himself to be persuaded. He should have felt that his obedience was being tried, and should have required, ere he considered himself released, *the same, or as strong, evidence,* as that on which he had received the obligation. Disobedience to certain positive commands of God, was one which it was at this time very important to punish signally, since it was exactly the sin of Jeroboam and his adherents.

22. On the anxiety of the Hebrews to be buried with their fathers, see Gen. xlvii. 30, xlix. 29, l. 25; 2 Sam. xix. 37, &c.

26 came and told *it* in the city where the old prophet dwelt. And
when the prophet that brought him back from the way heard
thereof, he said, It *is* the man of God, who was disobedient unto
the word of the LORD: therefore the LORD hath delivered him
unto the lion, which hath [1]torn him, and slain him, according to
27 the word of the LORD, which he spake unto him. And he spake
to his sons, saying, Saddle me the ass. And they saddled *him*.
28 And he went and found his carcase cast in the way, and the
ass and the lion standing by the carcase: the lion had not eaten
29 the carcase, nor [2]torn the ass. And the prophet took up the
carcase of the man of God, and laid it upon the ass, and brought
it back: and the old prophet came to the city, to mourn and to
30 bury him. And he laid his carcase in his own grave; and they
31 mourned over him, *saying*, [n]Alas, my brother! And it came to
pass, after he had buried him, that he spake to his sons, saying,
When I am dead, then bury me in the sepulchre wherein the
32 man of God *is* buried; [o]lay my bones beside his bones: [p]for the
saying which he cried by the word of the LORD against the altar
in Beth-el, and against all the houses of the high places which
33 *are* in the cities of [q]Samaria, shall surely come to pass. ¶ [r]After
this thing Jeroboam returned not from his evil way, but [3]made
again of the lowest of the people priests of the high places: whosoever would, he [4]consecrated him, and he became *one* of the
34 priests of the high places. [s]And this thing became sin unto the
house of Jeroboam, even [t]to cut *it* off, and to destroy *it* from off
the face of the earth.

n Jer. 22. 18.
o 2 Kin. 23. 17, 18.
p ver. 2. 2 Kin. 23. 16, 19.
q See ch. 16. 24.
r ch. 12. 31, 32. 2 Chr. 11. 15.
s ch. 12. 30.
t ch. 15. 29.

1 Heb. *broken*.
2 Heb. *broken*.
3 Heb. *returned and made*.
4 Heb. *filled his hand*, Lev. 8. 25.

---

28. *the lion had not eaten the carcase, nor torn the ass*] These strange circumstances were of a nature to call men's attention to the matter, and cause the whole story to be bruited abroad. By these means an incident, which Jeroboam would have wished hushed up, became no doubt the common talk of the whole people.

30. *he laid his carcase in his own grave*] As Joseph of Arimathæa did the body of our Lord (Matt. xxvii. 60). The possession of rock-hewn tombs by families, or individuals, was common among the Jews from their first entrance into the Holy Land to their final expulsion. A sepulchre usually consisted of an underground apartment, into which opened a number of long, narrow *loculi*, or cells, placed side by side, each adapted to receive one body. The cells were 6 or 7 feet long, 2 feet wide, and 3 feet high. They were commonly closed by a stone placed at the end of each. Many such tombs still exist in Palestine.

32. *against all the houses of the high places*] *i.e.* more than the two high places at Dan and Bethel. There were many lesser high places in the land, several of which would be likely to be in Israel (iii. 4).

in the cities of Samaria] The word Samaria cannot have been employed by the old prophet, in whose days Samaria did not exist (xvi. 24). The writer of Kings has substituted for the term used by him that whereby the country was known in his own day.

33. *whosoever would, he consecrated him*] *i.e.* he exercised no discretion, but allowed any one to become a priest, without regard to birth, character, or social position. We may suspect from this that the office was not greatly sought, since no civil governor who cared to set up a priesthood would wish to degrade it in public estimation. Jeroboam did impose one limitation, which would have excluded the very poorest class. The candidate for consecration was obliged to make an offering consisting of one young bullock and seven rams (2 Chr. xiii. 9).

34. This persistence in wrong, after the warning given him, brought a judgment, not only on Jeroboam himself, but on his family. Jeroboam's departure from the path of right forfeited the crown (xi. 38); and in that forfeiture was involved naturally the destruction of his family; for in the East, as already observed, when one dynasty supplants another, the ordinary practice is for the new king to destroy all the males belonging to the house of his predecessor. See xv. 29.

CHAP. 14. AT that time Abijah the son of Jeroboam fell sick. And
2 Jeroboam said to his wife, Arise, I pray thee, and disguise
thyself, that thou be not known to be the wife of Jeroboam;
and get thee to Shiloh: behold, there *is* Ahijah the prophet,
3 which told me that *^aI should be* king over this people. *^b*And
take ¹with thee ten loaves, and ²cracknels, and a ³cruse of honey,
and go to him: he shall tell thee what shall become of the child.
4 And Jeroboam's wife did so, and arose, *^c*and went to Shiloh,
and came to the house of Ahijah. ¶ But Ahijah could not see;
5 for his eyes ⁴were set by reason of his age. And the LORD said
unto Ahijah, Behold, the wife of Jeroboam cometh to ask *a*
thing of thee for her son; for he *is* sick: thus and thus shalt
thou say unto her: for it shall be, when she cometh in, that she
6 shall feign herself *to be* another *woman*. And it was *so*, when
Ahijah heard the sound of her feet, as she came in at the door,
that he said, Come in, thou wife of Jeroboam; why feignest
thou thyself *to be* another? for I *am* sent to thee *with* ⁵heavy
7 *tidings*. Go, tell Jeroboam, Thus saith the LORD God of Israel,
*^d*Forasmuch as I exalted thee from among the people, and made
8 thee prince over my people Israel, and *^e*rent the kingdom away
from the house of David, and gave it thee: and *yet* thou hast
not been as my servant David, *^f*who kept my commandments,
and who followed me with all his heart, to do *that* only *which*
9 *was* right in mine eyes; but hast done evil above all that were
before thee: *^g*for thou hast gone and made thee other gods, and

^a ch. 11. 31.
^b ch. 13. 7.
1 Sam. 9.7,8.

^c ch. 11. 29.

^d See
2 Sam. 12.
7, 8.
ch. 16. 2.
^e ch. 11. 31.
^f ch. 11. 33,
38.
& 15. 5.
^g ch. 12. 28.
2 Chr. 11.15.

¹ Heb. *in thine hand.*   ³ Or, *bottle.*   ⁴ Heb. *stood for his hoariness.*
² Or, *cakes.*   ⁵ Heb. *hard.*

XIV. 1. *at that time*] The phrase here
connects the narrative which follows with
Jeroboam's *persistence* in his evil courses.
The event related is the first judgment upon
him for his obduracy, the beginning of the
cutting off of his house from the face of the
earth.

Abijah] We see by this name that Jeroboam did not intend to desert the worship
of Jehovah, since its signification is "Jehovah is my father," or "Jehovah is my desire" (Job xxxiv. 36).

2. *disguise thyself*] Jeroboam fears that
even Ahijah the Shilonite, who in some
sort made him king, will scarcely give his
queen a favourable answer. The king's conscience tells him that he has not performed
the conditions on which he was promised
"a sure house" (xi. 38).

3. See marg. ref. The presents here
were selected for the purpose of deception,
being such as a poor country person would
have been likely to bring. Jeroboam
counted also on Ahijah's blindness (*v.* 4) as
favouring his plan of deception (cp. Gen.
xxvii. 1, 22).

cracknels] See margin. The Hebrew
word is thought to mean a kind of cake
which crumbled easily.

5. *feign herself to be another woman*] Lit.,
"she shall make herself strange," *i.e.,*
"she shall come in disguised." So *v.* 6.

6. *for I am sent to thee*] Rather, "I also

am sent to thee." As thou hast a message
to me from thy husband, so have I a message to thee from the Lord.

7. As Jeroboam's appointment to the
kingdom had been formally announced to
him by the Prophet Ahijah, so the same
Prophet is commissioned to acquaint him
with his forfeiture of it. Cp. 1 Sam. xv.
26-28.

9. *above all that were before thee*] *i.e.* above
all previous rulers of the people, whether
Judges or kings. Hitherto none of the
rulers of Israel had set up the idolatrous
worship of ephod, teraphim, and the like
(Judg. xviii. 17), as a substitute for the true
religion, or sought to impose an idolatrous
system on the nation. Gideon's ephod "*became* a snare" contrary to his intention
(Judg. viii. 27). Solomon's high places
were private—built for the use of his wives,
and not designed to attract the people.
Jeroboam was the first ruler who set himself to turn the Israelites away from the
true worship, and established a poor coun-
terfeit of it, which he strove to make, and
succeeded in making, the religion of the
great mass of his subjects.

and hast cast me behind thy back] A very
strong and very rare expression, occurring
again only in Ezek. xxiii. 35; where it is
said of the Jews generally, shortly before
the Captivity. The expressions in the marg.
reff. are similar but less fearful.

molten images, to provoke me to anger, and *hast cast me
10 behind thy back : therefore, behold, *I will bring evil upon the
house of Jeroboam, and *will cut off from Jeroboam him that
pisseth against the wall, *and him that is shut up and left in
Israel, and will take away the remnant of the house of Jero-
11 boam, as a man taketh away dung, till it be all gone. *Him
that dieth of Jeroboam in the city shall the dogs eat ; and him
that dieth in the field shall the fowls of the air eat : for the
12 Lord hath spoken *it. Arise thou therefore, get thee to thine
own house : and *when thy feet enter into the city, the child
13 shall die. And all Israel shall mourn for him, and bury him :
for he only of Jeroboam shall come to the grave, because in
him *there is found *some good thing toward the Lord God of
14 Israel in the house of Jeroboam. *Moreover the Lord shall
raise him up a king over Israel, who shall cut off the house of
15 Jeroboam that day : but what? even now. For the Lord shall
smite Israel, as a reed is shaken in the water, and he shall
*root up Israel out of this *good land, which he gave to their
fathers, and shall scatter them *beyond the river, *because they
16 have made their groves, provoking the Lord to anger. And he
shall give Israel up because of the sins of Jeroboam, *who did
17 sin, and who made Israel to sin. ¶And Jeroboam's wife arose,
and departed, and came to *Tirzah : and *when she came to the

h Neh. 9. 26.
Ps. 50. 17.
i ch. 15. 29.
k ch. 21. 21.
l Deut. 32. 36.
2 Kin. 14. 26.

m ch. 16. 4.
& 21. 21.

n ver. 17.

o 2 Chr. 12. 12.
& 19. 3.
p ch. 15. 27,
28, 29.
q Ps. 52. 5.
r Josh. 23.
15, 16.
s 2 Kin. 17. 23.
t Deut. 12.
3, 4.
u ch. 12. 30.
& 13. 34.
x ch. 16. 6,
8, 15, 23.
y ver. 12.

---

10. All the males of the family of Jeroboam were put to death by Baasha (xv.
28, 29). The phrase "will cut off," &c.,
appears to have been a common expression
among the Jews from the time of David
(1 Sam. xxv. 22) to that of Jehu (2 K. ix.
8), but scarcely either before or after. We
may suspect that, where the author of
Kings uses it, he found it in the documents
which he consulted.

him that is shut up and left in Israel]
See marg. ref. note.

and will take away the remnant, &c.] The
idea is, that the whole family is to be
cleared away at once, as men clear away
ordure or any vile refuse.

11. The dogs are the chief scavengers of
Oriental cities (cp. Ps. lix. 6, 14). And
the vulture is the chief scavenger in the
country districts, assisted sometimes by
kites and crows (see Job xxxix. 27-30,
where the vulture, not the eagle, is intended). Vultures are very abundant in
Palestine.

13. The child was evidently a prince of
some promise. It is probable that he was
heir to the throne.

14. The Hebrew text of this verse appears
to be defective in this place. No satisfactory
sense can be obtained from it. The true
meaning of the original passage is possibly :
—"Jehovah shall raise up a king who will
destroy the house of Jeroboam on the day
that he is raised up. What do I say? He
will destroy it even now."

15. The general prophecy of Moses (Deut.
xxix. 28), that the disobedient Israelites
would be rooted up out of their land, and
cast into another land, is here for the first

time repeated, and is definitively applied
to the ten tribes, which are to be removed
"beyond the river" (the Euphrates, iv. 21,
24), and "scattered." On the fulfilment of
this prophecy, and especially on the *scatter-
ing* of the ten tribes, see 2 K. xvii. 6
note.

groves] See Ex. xxxiv. 13 note. The grove-
(or, *asherah-*) worship, adopted from the
Canaanitish nations, appears to have died
away after the fierce onslaught which
Gideon made upon it (Judg. vi. 25-31). It
now revived, and became one of the most
popular of the idolatries both in Israel and
Judah (*v.* 23, and cp. marg. reff.).

.**17.** Jeroboam had by this time removed
from Shechem, and established a new capital in Tirzah, one of the old Canaanite
towns (Josh. xii. 24)—a town of great reputation for beauty, counted in that respect
on a par with Jerusalem (Cant. vi. 4).
Tirzah is perhaps to be identified with *Tel-
luzah*, a place in the mountains about
9 miles distant from Shechem (Nablous) [or
with Teiâsîr (Conder)]. It may have been
the palatial residence of the kings rather
than the actual capital of the country. It remained the capital till Omri built Samaria
(xvi. 23, 24). Towards the close of the
kingdom it appears again as the city of
Menahem, who murdered Shallum and succeeded him (2 K. xv. 14).

the threshold of the door] Lit., "the
threshold of the house." Cp. the prophecy
(*v.* 12). The child actually died as she
crossed the threshold of the palace. Probably the palace, like that of Sargon at
Khorsabad, lay at the outer edge of the
town.

z ver. 13.

a 2 Chr. 13. 2, &c.

b 2Chr.12.13.

c ch. 11. 36.

d ver. 31.
e 2 Chr. 12. 1.
f Deut.32.21.
Ps. 78. 58.
1 Cor. 10. 22.
g Deut. 12. 2.
h 2 Kin. 17. 9, 10.
i Isai. 57. 5.
k Deut.23.17.
ch. 15. 12.
& 22. 46.
2 Kin. 23. 7.
l ch. 11. 40.
2 Chr. 12. 2.
m 2 Chr. 12. 9, 10, 11.

18 threshold of the door, the child died; and they buried him; and all Israel mourned for him, ᶻaccording to the word of the LORD, which he spake by the hand of his servant Ahijah the prophet. 19 ¶And the rest of the acts of Jeroboam, how he ᵃwarred, and how he reigned, behold, they *are* written in the book of the 20 chronicles of the kings of Israel. And the days which Jeroboam reigned *were* two and twenty years: and he ¹slept with his 21 fathers, and Nadab his son reigned in his stead. ¶And Rehoboam the son of Solomon reigned in Judah. ᵇRehoboam *was* forty and one years old when he began to reign, and he reigned seventeen years in Jerusalem, the city ᶜwhich the LORD did choose out of all the tribes of Israel, to put his name there. 22 ᵈAnd his mother's name *was* Naamah an Ammonitess. ¶ ᵉAnd Judah did evil in the sight of the LORD, and they ᶠprovoked him to jealousy with their sins which they had committed, 23 above all that their fathers had done. For they also built them ᵍhigh places, and ²images, ʰand groves, on every high hill, and 24 ⁱunder every green tree. ᵏAnd there were also sodomites in the land: *and* they did according to all the abominations of the nations which the LORD cast out before the children of Israel. 25 ¶ˡAnd it came to pass in the fifth year of king Rehoboam, *that* 26 Shishak king of Egypt came up against Jerusalem: ᵐand he took away the treasures of the house of the LORD, and the trea-

¹ Heb. *lay down.*   ² Or, *standing images,* or, *statues.*

---

19. The wars of Jeroboam may be divided into—(1) his wars with Rehoboam (see *vv.* 25, 30); and (2) his war with Abijam (see marg. ref.).

the book of the chronicles of the kings of Israel...(of Judah, v. 29)] See the Introduction, p. 265.

21. On the age of Rehoboam at his accession, see xii. 8 note. The seventeen years of his reign must have been complete, or a little more than complete, if Abijam ascended the throne in the "eighteenth" year of Jeroboam (xv. 1).

22. This defection of Judah did not take place till Rehoboam's fourth year (marg. ref.).

they provoked him to jealousy] Cp. Ex. xx. 5; and on the force of the metaphor involved in the word, see Ex. xxxiv. 15 note.

23. The words "they also" are emphatic. Not only did the Israelites make themselves high places (xii. 31, xiii. 32), but the people of Judah also. The "high places," which are said to have been "built," were probably small shrines or tabernacles hung with bright-coloured tapestry (Ezek. xvi. 16), like the "sacred tent" of the Carthaginians.

The "images" were rather "pillars" (Gen. xxviii. 18 note).

groves] See *v.* 15, note. The "groves," it will be observed, were *built* on high hills and *under green trees.*

under every green tree] i.e. under all those remarkable trees which, standing singly about the land, were landmarks to their respective neighbourhoods, and places of re-

sort to travellers, who gladly rested under their shade (Deut. xii. 2).

24. *sodomites*] Literally, " (men) consecrated." The men in question were in fact "consecrated" to the mother of the gods, the famous "Dea Syra," whose priests, or rather devotees, they were considered to be. The nature of the ancient idolatries is best understood by recollecting that persons of this degraded class practised their abominable trade under a religious sanction.

25. The examination of the famous inscription of Shishak at Karnak has resulted in the proof that the expedition commemorated was directed against Palestine, and has further thrown a good deal of light on the relations of the two kingdoms at the period. Of the fifteen fenced cities fortified by Rehoboam in the early part of his reign (2 Chr. xi. 5-12), three, Shoco, Adoraim, and Aijalon are distinctly mentioned among Shishak's conquests. Other towns of Judah or Benjamin also occur. Further a considerable number of the captured cities are in the territory of Jeroboam: these cities are *either Canaanite or Levitical.* Hence we gather, that, during the four years which immediately followed the separation of the kingdoms, Rehoboam retained a powerful hold on the dominions of his rival, many Canaanite and Levitical towns acknowledging his sovereignty, and maintaining themselves against Jeroboam, who probably called in Shishak mainly to assist him in compelling these cities to submission. The campaign was completely successful.

26. The circumstances of Shishak's inva-

sures of the king's house; he even took away all: and he took
27 away all the shields of gold ⁿwhich Solomon had made. And
king Rehoboam made in their stead brasen shields, and committed *them* unto the hands of the chief of the ¹guard, which
28 kept the door of the king's house. And it was *so*, when the king
went into the house of the LORD, that the guard bare them, and
29 brought them back into the guard chamber. ¶ ^oNow the rest of
the acts of Rehoboam, and all that he did, *are* they not written
30 in the book of the chronicles of the kings of Judah? And there
31 was ^pwar between Rehoboam and Jeroboam all *their* days. ^qAnd
Rehoboam slept with his fathers, and was buried with his fathers
in the city of David. ^rAnd his mother's name *was* Naamah an
Ammonitess. And ^sAbijah his son reigned in his stead.

CHAP. 15. NOW ^ain the eighteenth year of king Jeroboam the son
2 of Nebat reigned Abijam over Judah. Three years reigned he in
Jerusalem. ^bAnd his mother's name *was* ^cMaachah, the daugh-
3 ter of ^dAbishalom. And he walked in all the sins of his father,
which he had done before him: and ^ehis heart was not perfect
4 with the LORD his God, as the heart of David his father. Nevertheless ^ffor David's sake did the LORD his God give him a ²lamp
in Jerusalem, to set up his son after him, and to establish Jeru-

Marginal references:
ⁿ ch. 10. 17.

^o 2Chr.12.15.
^p ch. 12. 24.
& 15. 6.
2 Chr. 12. 15.
^q 2Chr.12.16.
^r ver. 21.
^s 2 Chr. 12.
16, *Abijah*.
Matt. 1. 7,
Ab'a.
^a 2 Chr. 13.
1, 2.
^b 2 Chr. 11.
20, 21, 22.
^c 2 Chr. 13.
2, *Micha-
iah the
daughter of
Uriel.*
^d 2 Chr. 11.
21, *Absa-
lom.*
^e ch. 11. 4.
Ps. 119. 80.
^f ch. 11. 32,
36.
2 Chr. 21.7.

¹ Heb. *runners.*   ² Or, *candle*, ch. 11. 36.

---

sion, related here with extreme brevity, are
given with some fulness by the author of
Chronicles (marg. ref.). It is still a question whether the submission of the Jewish
king is or is not expressly recorded in the
Karnak inscription. Midway in the list of
cities and tribes occurs the entry "YUDeH-
MALK" which it has been proposed to
translate "Judah, king." Others regard it
as the name of a Palestinian town not
otherwise known to us.

28. It appears from this verse that Rehoboam, notwithstanding that he encouraged,
and perhaps secretly practised, idolatry (*vr.*
22-24, cp. xv. 3, 12; 2 Chr. xii. 1), maintained a public profession of faith in Jehovah, and attended in state the Temple services. Cp. the conduct of Solomon, ix. 25.

31. *slept with his fathers and was buried,*
&c.] Cp. xi. 43. The expression is a sort of
formula, and is used with respect to all the
kings of Judah, except two or three. The
writer probably regards the fact, which he
records so carefully, as a continuation of
God's mercy to David.

his mother's name, &c.] The mention of
the queen-mother so regularly in the account
of the kings of Judah is thought to indicate
that she had an important position in the
state. There are, however, only two instances where such a person seems to have
exercised any power (xv. 13; 2 K. xi. 1-20).

Abijam] Abijah (see marg. ref.) was probably his real name, while Abijam is a
form due to the religious feeling of the
Jews, who would not allow the word JAH to
be retained as an element in the name of so
bad a king. Instances of a similar feeling
are the change of Beth-*el* into Beth-*aven* in

Hosea (iv. 15), and perhaps of Jehoahaz
into Ahaz (2 K. xv. 38 note).

XV. 2. *Three years*] More strictly, not
much more than two years (cp. *vr.* 1, 9):
Any part of a year may, however, in Jewish reckoning, be taken as a year.

his mother's name was Maachah] Or Michaiah, according to the present reading of
marg. ref. ·

the daughter of Abishalom] Absalom seems
to have had but one daughter, Tamar (2
Sam. xiv. 27), so that Maachah must have
been, not his daughter, but his grand-daughter. Her father (see marg.) was Uriel of
Gibeah whom, therefore, Tamar married.
Maachah took her name from her great-
grandmother (2 Sam. iii. 3).

3. *he walked in all the sins of his father*]
Yet Abijam prepared precious offerings for
the Temple service (*v.* 15), probably to replace vessels which Shishak had carried off,
and in his war with Jeroboam professed
himself a faithful servant of Jehovah (2 Chr.
xiii. 10-12).

4. *to set up his son*] The idolatry of Abijam deserved the same punishment as that
of Jeroboam (xiv. 10-14), of Baasha (xvi. 2-
4), or of Zimri (xvi. 19), the cutting off of
his seed, and the transfer of the crown to another family. That these consequences did
not follow in the kingdom of Judah, was
owing to the "faithfulness" of David (see
marg. ref.), which brought a blessing on his
posterity. Few things are more remarkable
and more difficult to account for on mere
grounds of human reason, than the stability
of the succession in Judah, and its excessive
instability in the sister kingdom. One
family in Judah holds the throne from first

g ch. 14. 8.

h 2 Sam. 11.
4, 15.
& 12. 9.
i ch. 14. 30.
k 2 Chr. 13.
2—22.

l 2 Chr. 14. 1.

m 2 Chr. 14.
2.

n ch. 14. 24.
& 22. 46.
o 2 Chr. 15. 16.

p So Ex. 32.
20.
q ch. 22. 43.
2 Chr. 15.
17, 18.
r See ver. 3.

5 salem : because David *g*did *that which was* right in the eyes of the LORD, and turned not aside from any *thing* that he commanded him all the days of his life, *h*save only in the matter of
6 Uriah the Hittite. *i*And there was war between Rehoboam and
7 Jeroboam all the days of his life. ¶ *k*Now the rest of the acts of Abijam, and all that he did, *are* they not written in the book of the chronicles of the kings of Judah? And there was war
8 between Abijam and Jeroboam. *l*And Abijam slept with his fathers ; and they buried him in the city of David : and Asa his
9 son reigned in his stead. ¶ And in the twentieth year of Jero-
10 boam king of Israel reigned Asa over Judah. And forty and one years reigned he in Jerusalem. And his ¹mother's name
11 *was* Maachah, the daughter of Abishalom. *m*And Asa did *that which was* right in the eyes of the LORD, as *did* David his father.
12 *n* And he took away the sodomites out of the land, and removed
13 all the idols that his fathers had made. And also *o*Maachah his mother, even her he removed from *being* queen, because she had made an idol in a grove ; and Asa ²destroyed her idol, and
14 *p* burnt *it* by the brook Kidron. *q*But the high places were not removed : nevertheless Asa's *r*heart was perfect with the LORD
15 all his days. And he brought in the ³things which his father had dedicated, and the things which himself had dedicated, into
16 the house of the LORD, silver, and gold, and vessels. ¶ And there was war between Asa and Baasha king of Israel all their

---

¹ That is, *grandmother's,* ver. 2.   ² Heb. *cut off.*   ³ Heb. *holy.*

---

to last, during a space but little short of four centuries, while in Israel there are nine changes of dynasty within two hundred and fifty years.

6. The writer repeats what he had said in xiv. 30, in order to remind the reader that Abijam inherited this war from his father. Abijam's war is described in marg. ref. That the author of Kings gives none of its details is agreeable to his common practice in mere military matters. Thus he gives no details of Shishak's expedition, and omits Zerah's expedition altogether.

10. *mother's name*] Rather, *grandmother's.* The Jews call any male ancestor, however remote, a father, and any female ancestor a mother (cp. *v.* 2 ; Gen. iii. 20). This Maachah was the favourite wife of Rehoboam (2 Chr. xi. 21), and the mother of Abijam. The way in which she is here mentioned strongly favours the notion that the position of queen-mother was a definite one at the court, and could only be held by one person at a time.

13. Asa degraded Maachah from the rank and state of queen-mother.

The word translated "idol" both here and in the parallel passage (marg. ref.), does not occur elsewhere in Scripture. It is derived from a root signifying "fear" or "trembling," and may perhaps best be understood as "a fright, a horror." Such a name would seem best to apply to a grotesque and hideous image like the Phthah of the Egyptians. She made it to serve in lieu of the ordinary "grove" (*asherah*), or

idolatrous emblem of Astarte (Ex. xxxiv. 13 note). Asa cut it down, for like the usual *asherah,* Maachah's "horror" was fixed in the ground.

and burnt it at the brook Kidron] Similarly Josiah, when he removed Manasseh's "grove" (*asherah*) from the house of the Lord, brought it out to the brook Kidron, and burnt it there. The object probably was to prevent the pollution of the holy city by even the ashes from the burning.

14. 2 Chr. xiv. 3 would seem at first sight to imply that he entirely put down the worship. But idolatry, if at one time put down, crept back afterwards ; or while Asa endeavoured to sweep it wholly away, his subjects would not be controlled, but found a means of maintaining it in some places—not perhaps in the cities (see 2 Chr. xiv. 5), but in remote country districts, where the royal authority was weaker, and secrecy more practicable.

15. Abijam's dedications were made after his victory over Jeroboam, and probably consisted of a portion of the spoils which were the fruit of the battle (2 Chr. xiii. 16–19).

Asa's dedications may have been made from the spoils of Zerah the Ethiopian, who attacked him in his eleventh year (2 Chr. xiv. 9, &c.). They were not deposited in the temple till his fifteenth year (2 Chr. xv. 10, 18).

16. Baasha became king of Israel in the third year of Asa (*v.* 33). The petty warfare which ordinarily prevailed on the bor-

17 days. And [s]Baasha king of Israel went up against Judah, and built [t]Ramah, [u]that he might not suffer any to go out or come
18 in to Asa king of Judah. Then Asa took all the silver and the gold *that were* left in the treasures of the house of the LORD, and the treasures of the king's house, and delivered them into the hand of his servants : and king Asa sent them to [x]Benhadad, the son of Tabrimon, the son of Hezion, king of Syria,
19 that dwelt at [y]Damascus, saying, *There is* a league between me and thee, *and* between my father and thy father : behold, I have sent unto thee a present of silver and gold ; come and break thy league with Baasha king of Israel, that he may [1]depart from me.
20 So Ben-hadad hearkened unto king Asa, and sent the captains of the hosts which he had against the cities of Israel, and smote [z]Ijon, and [a]Dan, and [b]Abel-beth-maachah, and all Cinneroth,
21 with all the land of Naphtali. And it came to pass, when Baasha heard *thereof*, that he left off building of Ramah, and
22 dwelt in Tirzah. [c]Then king Asa made a proclamation throughout all Judah ; none *was* [2]exempted : and they took away the stones of Ramah, and the timber thereof, wherewith Baasha had builded ; and king Asa built with them [d]Geba of Benjamin, and

[s] 2 Chr. 16. 1, &c.
[t] Josh. 18. 25.
[u] See ch. 12. 27.

[x] 2 Chr. 16. 2.

[y] ch. 11. 23, 24.

[z] 2 Kin. 15. 29.
[a] Judg. 18. 29.
[b] 2 Sam. 20. 14.
[c] 2 Chr. 16. 6.

[d] Josh. 21. 17.

[1] Heb. *go up*.   [2] Heb. *free*.

---

ders of the two kingdoms continued "all the days" of Asa and Baasha. During the first ten years of Asa's reign he was little molested (2 Chr. xiv. 1, 6).

17. Ramah (perhaps *Er-Ram;* marg. ref.) was situated halfway between Bethel and Jerusalem. Its distance from Jerusalem was no more than five miles, so that its occupation was a menace to that capital. Baasha's seizure of Ramah implies a previous recovery of the towns taken by Abijam from Jeroboam, viz., Bethel, Jeshanah, and Ephrain (2 Chr. xiii. 19), and was a carrying of the war into the enemy's country. Could his conquest have been maintained, it would have crippled Judah seriously, and have almost compelled a transfer of the capital to Hebron.

that he might not suffer any to go out cr come in] Baasha, in seizing Ramah, professed to be acting on the defensive. His complaint seems to have been well founded (cp. 2 Chr. xv. 9); but it was more than a defensive measure—it was the first step towards a conquest of the southern kingdom.

18. *left*] Or, according to another reading, "found." The wealthy condition of the Temple treasury is sufficiently indicated in *v.* 15. Cp. 2 Chr. xv. 18.

Asa's conduct in calling Benhadad to his aid, condemned by the seer Hanani (2 Chr. xvi. 7), cannot, of course, be justified ; but there was much to excuse it. An alliance, it appears, had existed between Abijam and Tabrimon, Benhadad's father (*v.* 19)—an alliance which may have helped Abijam to gain his great victory over Jeroboam and achieve his subsequent conquests (2 Chr. xiii. 17-20). This had been brought to an end by Baasha, who had succeeded in in-

ducing Benhadad to enter into a league with him. It was only natural that Asa should endeavour to break up this league ; and, politically speaking, he had a full right to go further, and obtain, if he could, the support of the Syrian troops for himself. The Israelites had set the example of calling in a foreign power, when Jeroboam obtained the aid of Shishak.

to Benhadad] On the probable succession of the Damascene kings, and on the meaning of the name Hadad, see xi. 14, 23.

19. Rather, "**Let there be** a league between me and thee, **as there was** between my father and thy father."

20. Ijon is probably marked by the ruins called *Tel-Dibbin*, which are situated a few miles north-west of the site of Dan, in a fertile and beautiful little plain which bears the name of *Merj 'Ayûn* or "meadow of fountains." On Abel-beth-maachah, or Abel-maim ("Abel-on-the waters") and Dan, see marg. reff.

For Cinneroth or Genesareth see Josh. xi. 2.

22. Geba, situated opposite to Michmash (1 Sam. xiv. 5), is almost certainly *Jeba*, which stands picturesquely on the top of its steep terraced hill on the very edge of the *Wady Suweinit.* Its position was thus exceedingly strong ; and, as it lay further north than Ramah, Asa may have considered that to fortify and garrison it would be a better protection to his northern frontier than fortifying Ramah.

For Mizpah see marg. ref. From Jer. xli. 9 we learn that Asa, besides fortifying the place, sank a deep well there to secure his garrison from want of water if the town should be besieged.

e Josh.18.26.　23 *e*Mizpah. The rest of all the acts of Asa, and all his might, and all that he did, and the cities which he built, *are* they not written in the book of the chronicles of the kings of Judah?

f 2Chr.16.12.　Nevertheless *f*in the time of his old age he was diseased in his 24 feet. And Asa slept with his fathers, and was buried with his

g 2 Chr. 17.1.
h Matt. 1. 8, called Josap'iat.
fathers in the city of David his father: *g*and *h*Jehoshaphat his 25 son reigned in his stead. ¶ And Nadab the son of Jeroboam ¹began to reign over Israel in the second year of Asa king of 26 Judah, and reigned over Israel two years. And he did evil in the sight of the LORD, and walked in the way of his father, and

i ch. 12. 30.
& 14. 16.
k ch. 14. 14.
l Josh.19.44.
& 21. 23.
ch. 16. 15.
27 in *i*his sin wherewith he made Israel to sin. ¶ *k*And Baasha the son of Ahijah, of the house of Issachar, conspired against him; and Baasha smote him at *l*Gibbethon, which *belonged* to the Philistines; for Nadab and all Israel laid siege to Gibbethon. 28 Even in the third year of Asa king of Judah did Baasha slay 29 him, and reigned in his stead. And it came to pass, when he reigned, *that* he smote all the house of Jeroboam; he left not to Jeroboam any that breathed, until he had destroyed him, ac-

m ch. 14. 10, 14.
n ch. 14.9,16.
cording unto *m*the saying of the LORD, which he spake by his 30 servant Ahijah the Shilonite: *n*because of the sins of Jeroboam which he sinned, and which he made Israel sin, by his provocation wherewith he provoked the LORD God of Israel to anger.

¹ Heb. *reigned.*

---

23. *The rest of all the acts of Asa*] A few of these are preserved in 2 Chr. xv. 9-15, xvi. 7-12. From the whole narrative of Chronicles we gather that the character of Asa deteriorated as he grew old, and that, while he maintained the worship of Jehovah consistently from first to last, he failed to maintain the personal faith and piety which had been so conspicuous in his early youth.

the cities which he built] Asa, during the earlier part of his reign, before any serious attack had been made upon him, had the prudence to "build fenced cities in Judah," with "walls and towers, gates and bars," so strengthening himself against a possible evil day (2 Chr. xiv. 6, 7).

in the time of his old age] See marg. ref. If it has been rightly supposed that Rehoboam was a young man of twenty-one or twenty-two at his accession (xii. 8), Asa's age at this time must have been less than fifty. It may seem strange to speak of "old age" in such a case; but Solomon was regarded as "old" at about fifty (xi. 4 note).

24. Asa prepared his own sepulchre in his lifetime, as has been so often done by Oriental kings; and his funeral was conducted with great magnificence (2 Chr. xvi. 14).

25. The sacred historian now gives an account of the contemporary kings of Israel, beginning with Nadab, who ascended the throne in Asa's second year, and concluding with Ahab, in whose fourth year Asa died. This narrative occupies him almost to the close of the first Book of Kings.

CHRONOLOGY.

Year of the divided Kingdom.	Kings of Judah.	Years of Reign.	Kings of Israel.	Years of Reign.
1	REHOBOAM	17	JEROBOAM	22
5	(Invasion of Shishak).			
18	ABIJAM .	3		
20	ASA . .	41		
22	,,		NADAB .	2
23	,,		BAASHA .	24
31	(Invasion of Zerah).			
34	(Great feast at Jerusalem).			
46	,,		ELAH .	2
47	,,		{ ZIMRI . } { OMRI . }	12
53	,,		AHAB .	22
61	(Last year of Asa).		(4th year of AHAB).	

27. *Baasha...of the house of Issachar*] It is curious to find Issachar furnishing a king. Tola, its one very undistinguished Judge (Judg. x. 1), on obtaining office had at once settled himself in the territory of Ephraim. The tribe was as little famous as any that could be named. The "ass crouching between two burthens" was a true symbol of the patient, plodding cultivators of the plain of Esdraelon (Gen. xlix. 14,15). Baasha probably owed his rise neither to his tribe nor to his social position, but simply to his audacity, and his known valour and skill as a soldier (xvi. 2).

31 ¶ Now the rest of the acts of Nadab, and all that he did, *are*
they not written in the book of the chronicles of the kings of
32 Israel? *°* And there was war between Asa and Baasha king of
33 Israel all their days. ¶ In the third year of Asa king of Judah
began Baasha the son of Ahijah to reign over all Israel in
34 Tirzah, twenty and four years. And he did evil in the sight of
the LORD, and walked in *p* the way of Jeroboam, and in his sin
wherewith he made Israel to sin.

CHAP. 16. THEN the word of the LORD came to *a* Jehu the son of
2 Hanani against Baasha, saying, *b* Forasmuch as I exalted thee
out of the dust, and made thee prince over my people Israel;
and *c* thou hast walked in the way of Jeroboam, and hast made
my people Israel to sin, to provoke me to anger with their sins;
3 behold, I will *d* take away the posterity of Baasha, and the
posterity of his house; and will make thy house like *e* the house
4 of Jeroboam the son of Nebat. *f* Him that dieth of Baasha in
the city shall the dogs eat; and him that dieth of his in the
5 fields shall the fowls of the air eat. ¶ Now the rest of the acts
of Baasha, and what he did, and his might, *g* are they not written
6 in the book of the chronicles of the kings of Israel? So Baasha
slept with his fathers, and was buried in *h* Tirzah: and Elah his
7 son reigned in his stead. ¶ And also by the hand of the prophet
i Jehu the son of Hanani came the word of the LORD against
Baasha, and against his house, even for all the evil that he did
in the sight of the LORD, in provoking him to anger with the
work of his hands, in being like the house of Jeroboam; and
8 because *k* he killed him. ¶ In the twenty and sixth year of Asa
king of Judah began Elah the son of Baasha to reign over Israel
9 in Tirzah, two years. *l* And his servant Zimri, captain of half
his chariots, conspired against him, as he was in Tirzah, drinking himself drunk in the house of Arza *1* steward of *his* house in

o ver. 16.

p ch. 12. 28,
29.
& 13. 33.
& 14. 16.
a ver. 7.
2 Chr. 19. 2.
& 20. 34.
b ch. 14. 7..
c ch. 15. 34.

d ver. 11.
e ch. 14. 10.
& 15. 29.
f ch. 14. 11.

g 2 Chr. 16.1.

h ch. 14. 17.
& 15. 21.

i ver. 1.

k ch. 15. 27,
29.
See Hos.
1. 4.
l 2 Kin. 9.31.

1 Heb. *which* was *over.*

---

32. An exact repetition of *v.* 16. From
the book before him (*v.* 31) the writer extracts a passage which happens to correspond exactly with one which he has already extracted from the "Book of the
chronicles of the kings of Judah." He does
not object to repeating himself (cp. xiv. 21
and 31, xiv. 30 and xv. 6; 2 K. xvii. 6 and
xviii. 11).

XVI. 1. Hanani, the father of Jehu, was
seer to Asa in the kingdom of Judah (2 Chr.
xvi. 7-10). His son Jehu, who here dis-
charges the same office in the kingdom of
Israel, appears at a later date as an inhabitant of Jerusalem, where he prophesied under
Jehoshaphat, whom he rebuked on one occasion. He must have lived to a great age;
for he outlived Jehoshaphat, and wrote his
life (marg. reff.).

5. The "might" of Baasha is sufficiently
indicated by those successes which drove
Asa to call Ben-hadad to his aid. (xv. 17-21).

7. The natural position of this verse
would be after *v.* 4 and before *v.* 5. But it
may be regarded as added by the writer,
somewhat irregularly, as an afterthought;
its special force being to point out that the
sentence on Baasha was intended to punish,

not only his calf-worship, but emphatically
his murder of Jeroboam and his family.
Though the destruction of Jeroboam had
been foretold, and though Baasha may be
rightly regarded as God's instrument to
punish Jeroboam's sins, yet, as he received
no command to execute God's wrath on the
offender, and was instigated solely by am-
bition and self-interest, his guilt was just as
great as if no prophecy had been uttered.
Even Jehu's commission (2 K. ix. 5-10) was
not held to justify, altogether, his murder
of Jehoram and Jezebel.

8. *two years*] *i.e.* More than one year,
or, at any rate, some portion of two distinct
years (cp. *v.* 10).

9. The conspiracy of Zimri—Elah's "servant" (*i.e.* "subject")—was favoured by his
position, which probably gave him military
authority in the city, by the absence of a
great part of the people and of the officers
who might have checked him, at Gibbethon
(*v.* 15), and by the despicable character of
Elah, who, instead of going up to the war,
was continually reminding men of his low
origin by conduct unworthy of royalty.

steward] The office was evidently one of
considerable importance. In Solomon's

10 Tirzah. And Zimri went in and smote him, and killed him, in
the twenty and seventh year of Asa king of Judah, and reigned
11 in his stead. ¶ And it came to pass, when he began to reign, as
soon as he sat on his throne, *that* he slew all the house of

ᵐ 1 Sam. 25.
22.

Baasha : he left him ᵐnot one that pisseth against a wall,
12 ¹neither of his kinsfolks, nor of his friends. Thus did Zimri

ⁿ ver. 3.
ᵒ ver. 1.

destroy all the house of Baasha, ⁿaccording to the word of the
LORD, which he spake against Baasha ²ᵒby Jehu the prophet,
13 for all the sins of Baasha, and the sins of Elah his son, by which
they sinned, and by which they made Israel to sin, in provoking

ᵖ Deut. 32.
21.
1 Sam.12.21.
Isai. 41. 29.
Jonah 2. 8.
1 Cor. 8. 4.
& 10. 19.
q ch. 15. 27.

14 the LORD God of Israel to anger ᵖwith their vanities. Now
the rest of the acts of Elah, and all that he did, *are* they not
written in the book of the chronicles of the kings of Israel ?
15 ¶ In the twenty and seventh year of Asa king of Judah did Zimri
reign seven days in Tirzah. And the people *were* encamped
16 �q against Gibbethon, which *belonged* to the Philistines. And the
people *that were* encamped heard say, Zimri hath conspired, and
hath also slain the king: wherefore all Israel made Omri, the
17 captain of the host, king over Israel that day in the camp. And
Omri went up from Gibbethon, and all Israel with him, and they
18 besieged Tirzah. And it came to pass, when Zimri saw that the
city was taken, that he went into the palace of the king's house,
19 and burnt the king's house over him with fire, and died, for his

ʳ ch. 12. 28.
& 15. 26, 34.

sins which he sinned in doing evil in the sight of the LORD, ʳin
walking in the way of Jeroboam, and in his sin which he did, to
20 make Israel to sin. Now the rest of the acts of Zimri, and his
treason that he wrought, *are* they not written in the book of the
21 chronicles of the kings of Israel ? ¶ Then were the people of
Israel divided into two parts. half of the people followed Tibni
the son of Ginath, to make him king; and half followed Omri.
22 But the people that followed Omri prevailed against the people

---

¹ Or, *both his kinsmen and his friends.*   ² Heb. *by the hand of.*

---

court it gave the rank of *sar*, or prince. In
Persia the " steward of the household "
acted sometimes as a sort of regent during
the king's absence.

11. *neither of his kinsfolks, nor of his
friends*] Zimri's measures were of much
more than ordinary severity. Not only
was the royal family extirpated, but the
friends of the king, his councillors and
favourite officers, were put to death. Omri,
as having been in the confidence of the late
monarch, would naturally fear for himself,
and resolve to take the course which promised him at least a chance of safety.

13. *their vanities*] The "calves." The
Hebrews call an idol by terms signifying
" emptiness," " vapour," or " nothingness."
(Cp. marg. reff.)

16. *all Israel made Omri, the captain of
the host, king*] This passage of history recalls
the favourite practice of the Roman armies
under the Empire, which, when they heard
of the assassination of an emperor at Rome,
were wont to invest their own commander
with the purple.

17. *went up*] The expression " went up "
marks accurately the ascent of the army

from the Shephelah, where Gibbethon was
situated (Josh. xix. 44), to the hill country
of Israel, on the edge of which Tirzah stood
(xiv. 17).

18. *the palace of the king's house*] The
tower of the king's house. A particular
part of the palace—either the *harem*, or,
more probably, the keep or citadel, a tower
stronger and loftier than the rest of the
palace.

Zimri's desperate act has been repeated
more than once. That the last king of
Assyria, the Sardanapalus of the Greeks,
thus destroyed himself, is almost the only
fact which we know concerning him.

19. Zimri's death illustrates the general
moral which the writer of Kings draws from
the whole history of the Israelite monarchs,
that a curse was upon them on account of
their persistence in Jeroboam's sin, which,
sooner or later, brought each royal house to
a bloody end.

22. From a comparison of the dates given
in *vv*. 15, 23, and 29 it follows that the contest between the two pretenders lasted four
years.

Tibni's death can scarcely be supposed to

that followed Tibni the son of Ginath: so Tibni died, and Omri
23 reigned. ¶ In the thirty and first year of Asa king of Judah
began Omri to reign over Israel, twelve years: six years reigned
24 he in Tirzah. And he bought the hill Samaria of Shemer for
two talents of silver, and built on the hill, and called the name
of the city which he built, after the name of Shemer, owner of
25 the hill, ¹ˢSamaria. But ˢOmri wrought evil in the eyes of the
26 LORD, and did worse than all that *were* before him. For he
ᵘwalked in all the way of Jeroboam the son of Nebat, and in
his sin wherewith he made Israel to sin, to provoke the LORD
27 God of Israel to anger with their ˣvanities. Now the rest of
the acts of Omri which he did, and his might that he shewed,
are they not written in the book of the chronicles of the kings
28 of Israel? So Omri slept with his fathers, and was buried in
29 Samaria: and Ahab his son reigned in his stead. ¶ And in the
thirty and eighth year of Asa king of Judah began Ahab the
son of Omri to reign over Israel: and Ahab the son of Omri
30 reigned over Israel in Samaria twenty and two years. And
Ahab the son of Omri did evil in the sight of the LORD above all

ˢ See ch. 13.
32.
² Kin. 17.21.
John 4. 4.
ᵗ Mic. 6. 16.
ᵘ ver. 19.
ˣ ver. 13.

¹ Heb. *Shomeron.*

have been natural. Either he must have
been slain in battle against Omri, or have
fallen into his hands and been put to death.

There has probably been some derange-
ment of the text here. The passage may
have run thus :—"So Tibni died, and Omri
reigned in the thirty-first year of Asa, king
of Judah. Omri reigned over Israel twelve
years: six years reigned he in Tirzah."
Omri's reign of twelve years began in Asa's
27th (*vv.* 15 and 16), and terminated in his
38th (*v.* 29). The event belonging to Asa's
31st year was the death of Tibni, and the
consequent extension of Omri's kingdom.
The six years in Tirzah are probably made
up of the four years of contention with
Tibni, and two years afterwards, during
which enough of Samaria was built for the
king to transfer his residence there.

24. "Samaria" represents the Greek
form of the name (Σαμάρεια) ; the original is
Shomeron (marg.). The site is marked by the
modern *Sebustiyeh*, an Arabic corruption of
Sebaste, the name given by Herod to Samaria when he rebuilt it. Sebustiyeh is
situated on a very remarkable "hill." In
the heart of the mountains of Israel occurs
a deep basin-shaped depression, in the midst
of which rises an oblong hill, with steep but
not inaccessible sides, and a long flat top.
This was the site which Omri chose for his
new capital. Politically it was rather more
central than Shechem, and probably than
Tirzah. In a military point of view it was
admirably calculated for defence. The
country round it was peculiarly productive.
The hill itself possessed abundant springs of
water. The result is that we find no further
change. Shechem and Tirzah were each
tried and abandoned ; but through all the
later alterations of dynasty Samaria continued uninterruptedly, to the very close of

the independence, to be the capital of the
northern kingdom.

Omri *purchased* the right of property in
the hill, just as David purchased the threshing-floor (2 Sam. xxiv. 24; cp. 1 K. xxi. 2).
Two talents, or 6000 shekels (Ex. xxxviii.
24 note)—about 500*l.* (or perhaps 800*l.*) of our
money—may well have been the full value
of the ground. And while naming his city
after Shemer, Omri may.also have had in
view the appropriateness of such a name
to the situation of the place. Shomeron,
to a Hebrew ear, would have necessarily
conveyed the idea of a "watch-tower."
This name, however, appears not to have
been at first accepted by the surrounding
nations. The earlier Assyrian kings knew
the Israelite capital, not as Samaria, but as
Beth-Khumri,*i.e.* "the city (house) of Omri."
It is not till the time of Tiglath-pileser that
they exchange this designation for that of
Sammirin.

25. Omri outwent his idolatrous predecessors in his zeal, reducing the calf-
worship to a regular formal system, which
went down to posterity (cp. marg. ref.)

27. *his might*] Perhaps in the war between
Israel and Syria of Damascus (xx. 1, &c.),
during the reign of Omri. Its issue was very
disadvantageous to him (xx. 34, xxii. 2).

29. *twenty and two years*] Rather, from a
comparison between xv. 10 and xxii. 51, not
more than 21 years. Perhaps his reign did
not much exceed 20 years.

30. See *v.* 33. The great sin of Ahab—
that by which he differed from all his predecessors, and exceeded them in wickedness—
was his introduction of the worship of Baal,
consequent upon his marriage with Jezebel,
and his formal establishment of this gross
and palpable idolatry as the religion of the
state.

31 that *were* before him.   And it came to pass, [1]as if it had been a light thing for him to walk in the sins of Jeroboam the son of Nebat, *y*that he took to wife Jezebel the daughter of Ethbaal king of the *z*Zidonians, *a*and went and served Baal, and worshipped him. 32 And he reared up an altar for Baal in *b*the house of Baal, which 33 he had built in Samaria.   *c*And Ahab made a grove ; and Ahab *d*did more to provoke the LORD God of Israel to anger than all 34 the kings of Israel that were before him.   ¶ In his days did Hiel the Beth-elite build Jericho : he laid the foundation thereof in Abiram his firstborn, and set up the gates thereof in his youngest *son* Segub, *e*according to the word of the LORD, which he spake by Joshua the son of Nun.

CHAP. 17. AND [2]Elijah the Tishbite, *who was* of the inhabitants of Gilead, said unto Ahab, *a*As the LORD God of Israel liveth,

---

[1] Heb. *was it a light thing, &c.*

[2] Heb. *Eli'jahu.* Luke 1. 17. & 4. 25, he is called *El'as.*

---

31. *as if it had been a light thing for him to walk in the sins of Jeroboam*] Idolatries are not exclusive. Ahab, while he detested the pure worship of Jehovah, and allowed Jezebel to put to death every "prophet of the Lord" whom she could find (xviii. 4), readily tolerated the continued worship of the "calves," which had no doubt tended more and more to lose its symbolical character, and to become a thoroughly idolatrous image-worship.

Eth-baal] Identified with the Ithobalus of Menander, who reigned in Tyre, probably over all Phœnicia, within 50 years of the death of Hiram.   This Ithobalus, whose name means "With him is Baal," was originally priest of the great temple of Astarte, in Tyre.   At the age of 36 he conspired against the Tyrian king, Pheles (a usurping fratricide), slew him, and seized the throne.   His reign lasted 32 years, and he established a dynasty which continued on the throne at least 62 years longer.   The family-tree of the house may be thus exhibited :—

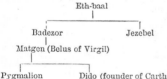

Eth-baal
    Badezor   Jezebel
    Matgen (Belus of Virgil)
Pygmalion   Dido (founder of Carthage).

Hence Jezebel was great-aunt to Pygmalion and his sister Dido.

served Baal] The worship of Baal by the Phœnicians is illustrated by such names as Ithobal, Hannibal, &c.   Abundant traces of it are found in the Phœnician monuments.

34. This seems to be adduced as a proof of the general impiety of Ahab's time. The curse of Joshua against the man who should rebuild Jericho had hitherto been believed and respected.   But now faith in the old religion had so decayed, that Joshua's malediction had lost its power. Hiel, a Bethelite of wealth and station, undertook to restore the long-ruined fortress.   But he suffered for his temerity.   In exact accordance with the words of Joshua's curse, he lost his firstborn son when he began to lay anew the foundations of the walls, and his youngest when he completed his work by setting up the gates.   We need not suppose that Jericho had been absolutely uninhabited up to this time.   But it was a ruined and desolate place without the necessary protection of walls, and containing probably but few houses (Judg. iii. 13 note). Hiel re-established it as a city, and it soon became once more a place of some importance (2 Chr. xxviii. 15).

XVII. 1. The name Elijah means "Jehovah is my God."   It is expressive of the truth which his whole life preached.

The two words rendered "Tishbite" and "inhabitant" are in the original (setting aside the vowel points) *exactly alike.*   The meaning consequently must either be "Elijah the stranger, of the strangers of Gilead," or (more probably) "Elijah the Tishbite, of Tishbi of Gilead."   Of Tishbi in Gilead there is no further trace in Scripture ; it is to be distinguished from another Tishbi in Galilee.   In forming to ourselves a conception of the great Israelite Prophet, we must always bear in mind that the wild and mountainous Gilead, which bordered on Arabia, and was half Arab in customs, was the country wherein he grew up.

His abrupt appearance may be compared with the similar appearances of Ahijah (xi. 29), Jehu (xvi. 1), Shemaiah (2 Chr. xi. 2), Azariah (do. xv. 1), and others.   It is clear that a succession of Prophets was raised up by God, both in faithful Judah and in idolatrous Israel, to witness of Him before the people of both countries, and leave them without excuse if they forsook His worship.   At this time, when a grosser and more deadly idolatry than had been practised before was

[b]before whom I stand, [c]there shall not be dew nor rain [d]these
2 years, but according to my word. ¶ And the word of the LORD
3 came unto him, saying, Get thee hence, and turn thee eastward,
and hide thyself by the brook Cherith, that *is* before Jordan.
4 And it shall be, *that* thou shalt drink of the brook; and I have
5 commanded the ravens to feed thee there. So he went and did
according unto the word of the LORD: for he went and dwelt
6 by the brook Cherith, that *is* before Jordan. And the ravens
brought him bread and flesh in the morning, and bread and
7 flesh in the evening; and he drank of the brook. And it came
to pass [1]after a while, that the brook dried up, because there had
8 been no rain in the land. ¶ And the word of the LORD came
9 unto him, saying, Arise, get thee to [e]Zarephath, which *belongeth*
to Zidon, and dwell there: behold, I have commanded a widow
10 woman there to sustain thee. So he arose and went to Zarephath.
And when he came to the gate of the city, behold, the widow
woman *was* there gathering of sticks: and he called to her, and
said, Fetch me, I pray thee, a little water in a vessel, that I may
11 drink. And as she was going to fetch *it*, he called to her, and
said, Bring me, I pray thee, a morsel of bread in thine hand.
12 And she said, *As* the LORD thy God liveth, I have not a cake,
but an handful of meal in a barrel, and a little oil in a cruse:
and, behold, I *am* gathering two sticks, that I may go in and
13 dress it for me and my son, that we may eat it, and die. And
Elijah said unto her, Fear not; go *and* do as thou hast said:
but make me thereof a little cake first, and bring *it* unto me,
14 and after make for thee and for thy son. For thus saith the
LORD God of Israel, The barrel of meal shall not waste, neither

[b] Deut. 10. 8
[c] Jam. 5. 17.
[d] Luke 4. 25.

[e] Obad. 2?.
Luke 4. 26,
called
Sarept 1.

[1] Heb. *at the end of days.*

introduced into Israel by the authority of
Ahab, and the total apostasy of the ten
tribes was consequently imminent, two
Prophets of unusual vigour and force of
character, endowed with miraculous powers
of an extraordinary kind, were successively
raised up, that the wickedness of the kings
might be boldly met and combated, and, if
possible, a remnant of faithful men preserved in the land. The unusual efflux of
miraculous energy at this time, is suitable to
the unusual emergency, and in very evident
proportion to the spiritual necessities of the
people.

as the LORD *God of Israel liveth, before
whom I stand*] This solemn formula, here
first used, was well adapted to impress the
king with the sacred character of the messenger, and the certain truth of his message.
Elisha adopted the phrase with very slight
modifications (2 K. iii. 14, v. 16).

Drought was one of the punishments
threatened by the Law, if Israel forsook
Jehovah and turned after other gods (Deut.
xi. 17, xxviii. 23; Lev. xxvi. 19, &c.).

3. *brook Cherith*] Rather, "the torrent
course," one of the many which carry the
winter rains from the highlands into that
stream.

4. *the ravens*] This is the translation of
most of the ancient Versions; others, omit-

ting the points, which are generally allowed
to have no authority, read "Arabians;"
others, retaining the present pointing,
translate either "merchants" (cp. the original of Ezek. xxvii. 9, 27), or "Orbites."
Jerome took it in this last sense, and so
does the Arabic Version.

9. The dependence of Zarephath (Sarepta)
on Sidon is indicated in the inscriptions
of Sennacherib, where it is mentioned as
belonging to Luliya (Elulæus), king of Sidon,
and as submitting to the Assyrian monarch
on Luliya's flight from his capital. Elijah
may have been sent to this place, so near
the city of Jezebel's father, as one which it
was most unlikely that he would visit.

12. *As the* LORD *thy God liveth*] The words
do not prove that the woman was an Israelite, or a worshipper of the true God; any
Phœnician, recognising in Elijah's appearance the garb and manner of a Jehovistic
Prophet, might have thus addressed him:
Baal-worshippers would have admitted Jehovah to be *a* living God. The woman does
not say "as the Lord *my* God liveth."

that we may eat it and die] Phœnicia always depended for its cereal supplies on the
harvests of Palestine (v. 9 note); and it is
evident that the famine was afflicting the
Phœnicians at this time no less than the
Israelites.

shall the cruse of oil fail, until the day *that* the LORD [1]sendeth
15 rain upon the earth. And she went and did according to the
saying of Elijah : and she, and he, and her house, did eat [2]*many*
16 days. *And* the barrel of meal wasted not, neither did the cruse
of oil fail, according to the word of the LORD, which he spake
17 [3]by Elijah. ¶ And it came to pass after these things, *that* the
son of the woman, the mistress of the house, fell sick ; and his
18 sickness was so sore, that there was no breath left in him. And

f See Luke
5. 8.

she said unto Elijah, *f*What have I to do with thee, O thou man
of God ? art thou come unto me to call my sin to remembrance,
19 and to slay my son ? And he said unto her, Give me thy son.
And he took him out of her bosom, and carried him up into a
20 loft, where he abode, and laid him upon his own bed. And he
cried unto the LORD, and said, O LORD my God, hast thou also
brought evil upon the widow with whom I sojourn, by slaying

g 2 Kin. 4.
34, 35.

21 her son ? *g*And he [4]stretched himself upon the child three times,
and cried unto the LORD, and said, O LORD my God, I pray
22 thee, let this child's soul come [5]into him again. And the LORD
heard the voice of Elijah ; and the soul of the child came into

h Heb. 11.35.

23 him again, and he *h*revived. And Elijah took the child, and
brought him down out of the chamber into the house, and delivered him unto his mother : and Elijah said, See, thy son liveth.

i John 3. 2.
& 16. 30.

24 And the woman said to Elijah, Now by this *i*I know that thou
art a man of God, *and* that the word of the LORD in thy mouth
is truth.

a Luke 4. 25.
Jam. 5. 17.

CHAP. 18. AND it came to pass *after* *a*many days, that the word of
the LORD came to Elijah in the third year, saying, Go, shew thy-

b ch. 17. 1.
Deut. 23. 12.

2 self unto Ahab ; and *b*I will send rain upon the earth. And
Elijah went to shew himself unto Ahab. And *there was* a sore

---

[1] Heb. *giveth.*   [3] Heb. *by the hand of.*   [5] Heb. *into his inward parts.*
[2] Or, *a full year.*   [4] Heb. *measured.*

---

16. This is the first recorded miracle of
its kind—a supernatural and inexplicable
multiplication of food (cp. 2 K. iv. 42
44 ; Matt. xiv. 15-21, xv. 32-38). The
sacred record does not explain these miracles ; but if the explanations sometimes
suggested—that there was a transforma-
tion of previously existing matter into
meal, oil, fish, and bread—be the true
one, the marvel of the thing would not
be much greater than that astonishing
natural chemistry by which, in the growth
of plants, particles of water, air, and earth
are transmuted into fruits and grains of
corn, and so fitted to be human food. There
would be a difference in the agency employed and in the time occupied in the
transmutation, but the thing done would
be almost the same.
17. *no breath*] Or, " no spirit," " no soul."
(Cp. Gen. ii. 7). The word used is translated " spirit " in Prov. xx. 27 ; Eccles. iii.
21 ; Job xxvi. 4 ; and elsewhere.
18. *What have I to do with thee ?*] *i.e.*
" What have we in common ? "—implying a
further question, " Why hast thou not left
me in peace ? " The woman imagines that
Elijah's visit had drawn God's attention to

her, and so to her sins, which (she feels) deserve a judgment—her son's death.
thou man of God] In the mouth of the
Phœnician woman this expression is remarkable. Among the Jews and Israelites (xii.
22 ; Judg. xiii. 6, 8) it seems to have become the ordinary designation of a Prophet.
We now see that it was understood in the
same sense beyond the borders of the Holy
Land.
19. *into a loft*] Rather, " into the upper
chamber ; " often the best apartment in an
Eastern house.
21. *he stretched himself upon the child three
times*] This action of Elijah is different from
that of Elisha (marg. ref.), and does not
imply the use of any natural means for the
restoration of suspended animation. It is
nearly parallel to the " touch," through
which our Lord wrought similar miracles
(Matt. ix. 25 ; Luke vii. 14).
XVIII. **1.** *the third year*] *i.e.* in the third
year of his sojourn with the widow. The
whole period of drought was three years and
a half (Luke iv. 25 ; Jam. v. 17) : of this,
probably about one year was passed by
Elijah in the torrent-course of Cherith, and
two years and a half at Sarepta.

3 famine in Samaria. ¶ And Ahab called [1]Obadiah, which *was* [2]the
governor of *his* house. (Now Obadiah feared the LORD greatly:
4 for it was *so*, when [3]Jezebel cut off the prophets of the LORD,
that Obadiah took an hundred prophets, and hid them by fifty
5 in a cave, and fed them with bread and water.) And Ahab said
unto Obadiah, Go into the land, unto all fountains of water,
and unto all brooks: peradventure we may find grass to save
the horses and mules alive, [4]that we lose not all the beasts.
6 So they divided the land between them to pass throughout it:
Ahab went one way by himself, and Obadiah went another way
7 by himself. ¶ And as Obadiah was in the way, behold, Elijah
met him: and he knew him, and fell on his face, and said, *Art*
8 thou that my lord Elijah? And he answered him, I *am:* go,
9 tell thy lord, Behold, Elijah *is here*. And he said, What have
I sinned, that thou wouldest deliver thy servant into the hand of
10 Ahab, to slay me? *As* the LORD thy God liveth, there is no
nation or kingdom, whither my lord hath not sent to seek thee:
and when they said, *He is* not *there;* he took an oath of the
11 kingdom and nation, that they found thee not. And now thou
12 sayest, Go, tell thy lord, Behold, Elijah *is here*. And it shall
come to pass, *as soon as* I am gone from thee, that *c*the Spirit of
the LORD shall carry thee whither I know not; and *so* when I
come and tell Ahab, and he cannot find thee, he shall slay me:
13 but I thy servant fear the LORD from my youth. Was it not
told my lord what I did when Jezebel slew the prophets of the
LORD, how I hid an hundred men of the LORD's prophets by
14 fifty in a cave, and fed them with bread and water? And now
thou sayest, Go, tell thy lord, Behold, Elijah *is here:* and he
15 shall slay me. And Elijah said, *As* the LORD of hosts liveth,
before whom I stand, I will surely shew myself unto him to day.
16 ¶ So Obadiah went to meet Ahab, and told him: and Ahab went

c 2 Kin.2. 16.
Ezek. 3.
12, 14.
Matt. 4. 1.
Acts 8. 39.

---

[1] Heb. *Obadiahu.*
[2] Heb. *over* his *house.*
[3] Heb. *Izebel.*
[4] Heb. *that we cut not off*
ourselves *from the beasts.*

---

3. Obadiah's name, "servant of Jehovah,"
indicates his religious character. It corresponds to the modern Arabic name Abdallah.
Ahab could scarcely have been ignorant of
Obadiah's faithfulness to Jehovah; and it
tells in favour of the monarch's tolerance
that he should have maintained an adherent
of the old religion in so important an
office. There seems to be no doubt that
the worst deeds of Ahab's reign sprang less
from his own free will and natural disposition than from the evil counsels, or rather
perhaps the imperious requirements, of his
wife.

4. We have no details of Jezebel's deed
of blood. Some have conjectured that it
was the answer of Jezebel to Elijah's threat,
and that the command given him to hide
in Cherith alone saved him from being one
of the victims. This view receives some
support from Obadiah's act and words (*v.*
13).

fifty in a cave] The limestone formation of
Judæa and Samaria abounds with large
natural caverns, the size of which is easily
increased by art. These "caves" play an
important part in the history of the country,

serving especially as refuges for political
offenders and other fugitives (Judg. vi. 2;
1 Sam. xiii. 6; Heb. xi. 38).

5. *unto all fountains of water and unto all
brooks*] Rather, "**to all springs of water
and to all torrent-courses.**" The former
are the perennial streams; the latter are
the torrent-courses which become dry in an
ordinary summer.

all the beasts] Rather, some, or, "**a portion of our beasts.**"

9. Obadiah thinks that to execute this
commission will be fatal to him (*v.* 12).

10. *there is no nation,* &c.] This is expressed in the style of Oriental hyperbole.
What Obadiah means is:—"there is no
nation nor kingdom, *of those over which he
has influence*, whither the king has not
sent." He could scarcely, for example,
have exacted an oath from such countries
as Egypt or Syria of Damascus. But Ahab
may have been powerful enough to exact an
oath from the neighbouring Hittite, Moabite, and Edomite tribes, perhaps even from
Ethbaal his father-in-law, and the kings of
Hamath and Arpad.

17 to meet Elijah.   ¶And it came to pass, when Ahab saw Elijah,

d ch. 21. 20.   that Ahab said unto him, *ᵈArt* thou he that *ᵉ*troubleth Israel ?
e Josh. 7. 25.
Acts 16. 20.   18 And he answered, I have not troubled Israel ; but thou, and thy
f 2 Chr. 15.2.   father's house, *ᶠ*in that ye have forsaken the commandments of

19 the LORD, and thou hast followed Baalim.   Now therefore send
g Josh.19.26.   *and* gather to me all Israel unto Mount *ᵍ*Carmel, and the pro-
h ch. 16. 33.   phets of Baal four hundred and fifty, *ʰ*and the prophets of the

20 groves four hundred, which eat at Jezebel's table.   So Ahab
ch. 22. 6.   sent unto all the children of Israel, and *ᶦ*gathered the prophets

21 together unto mount Carmel.   ¶And Elijah came unto all the
k 2 Kin. 17.   people, and said, *ᵏ*How long halt ye between two ¹opinions ? if
41.
Matt. 6. 24.   the LORD *be* God, follow him : but if Baal, *ˡthen* follow him.
l See Josh.
24. 15.   22 And the people answered him not a word.   Then said Elijah
m ch. 19. 10,   unto the people, *ᵐ*I, *even* I only, remain a prophet of the LORD ;
14.

¹ Or, *thoughts?*

---

17. *Art thou he,* &c.] Meaning, " Can it possibly be that thou dost venture to present thyself before me, thou that troublest Israel by means of this terrible drought ? " The charge of "troubling" had never before been brought against any one but Achan (marg. ref. *e*); it was one which must have called to the Prophet's recollection Achan's miserable fate.

18. Instead of apologies, and pleas for pardon, Elijah meets the charge with a countercharge, and makes a sudden demand. "Gather to me," &c. This boldness, this high tone, this absence of the slightest indication of alarm, seems to have completely discomfited Ahab, who ventured on no reply, made no attempt to arrest the Prophet, did not even press him to remove his curse and bring the drought to an end, but simply consented to do his bidding. There is no passage of Scripture which exhibits more forcibly the ascendancy that a Prophet of the Lord, armed with His spiritual powers, could, if he were firm and brave, exercise even over the most powerful and most unscrupulous of monarchs.

Baalim] *i.e.* the various aspects under which the god, Baal, was worshipped, Baal-shamin, Baal-zebub, Baal-Hamman, &c.

19. Carmel (Josh. xii. 22 note) was chosen by the Prophet as the scene of the gathering to which he invited, or rather summoned, Ahab.   Its thick jungles of copse and numerous dwarf-oaks and olives, would furnish abundant wood for his intended sacrifice.   Here was a perennial fountain ; and here again an ancient " altar of the LORD " (*v.* 30), belonging probably to the old times of non-idolatrous high-place worship —perhaps an erection of one of the Patriarchs.   On the one hand, there would be a view of the Mediterranean, whence the first sign of rain was likely to come, and on the other of Jezreel, the residence of the Court at the time, with its royal palace and its idol-temples, so that the intended trial would take place in the sight (so to speak) of the proud queen and her minions.

the prophets of Baal] The priests of Baal are so called not so much because they claimed a power of foretelling the future, as because they were *teachers* of the false religion, and more especially because they stand here in antagonism to the " Prophet of the LORD," with whom they are about to contend.

the prophets of the groves, four hundred] Rather, " of the **grove** "—the prophets, or priests, attached to the " grove " (*asherah*) which Ahab had made, probably at Jezreel (marg. ref.)   The number 400 seems to have been one especially affected by Ahab. We again find 400 prophets at the close of his reign (xxii. 6).   The number 40 entered largely into the religious system of the Jews (vi. 17; Ex. xxvi. 19; Deut. xxv. 3 ; Ezek. xli. 2).

which eat at Jezebel's table] Rather, "which eat from Jezebel's table." Oriental etiquette would not have allowed them to eat *at* the table of the queen, which was spread in the seraglio.   They were fed from the superfluity of her daily provision, which was no doubt on a sumptuous scale.   Cp. iv. 22, 23.

20. Local tradition places the site of Elijah's sacrifice, not on the highest point of the mountain (1728ft.), but at the south-eastern extremity (1600ft.) of the ridge, where a shapeless ruin, composed of great hewn stones, and standing amid thick bushes of dwarf-oak, in the near vicinity of a perennial spring, is known to the Arabs as " El-Maharrakah," " the burning," or " the sacrifice." All the circumstances of the locality adapt it for the scene of the contest.

21. The people were dumb.   They could not but feel the logical force of Elijah's argument ; but they were not prepared at once to act upon it.   They wished to unite the worship of Jehovah with that of Baal— to avoid breaking with the past and completely rejecting the old national worship, yet at the same time to have the enjoyment of the new rites, which were certainly sensuous, and probably impure.

22. *I, even I, only remain*] He means, "I

23 ⁿbut Baal's prophets *are* four hundred and fifty men. Let them
therefore give us two bullocks; and let them choose one bullock
for themselves, and cut it in pieces, and lay *it* on wood, and
put no fire *under:* and I will dress the other bullock, and lay *it*
24 on wood, and put no fire *under:* and call ye on the name of
your gods, and I will call on the name of the LORD: and the
God that ᵒanswereth by fire, let him be God. And all the people
25 answered and said, ¹It is well spoken. ¶And Elijah said unto
the prophets of Baal, Choose you one bullock for yourselves,
and dress *it* first; for ye *are* many; and call on the name of
26 your gods, but put no fire *under.* And they took the bullock
which was given them, and they dressed *it,* and called on the
name of Baal from morning even until noon, saying, O Baal,
²hear us. But *there was* ᵖno voice, nor any that ³answered.
27 And they ⁴leaped upon the altar which was made. And it came
to pass at noon, that Elijah mocked them, and said, Cry ⁵aloud:
for he *is* a god· either ⁶he is talking, or he ⁷is pursuing, or he
is in a journey, *or* peradventure he sleepeth, and must be
28 awaked. And they cried aloud, and ᑫcut themselves after

ⁿ ver. 19.

ᵒ ver. 38.
1 Chr. 21. 26.

ᵖ Ps. 115. 5.
Jer. 10. 5.
1 Cor. 8. 4.
& 12. 2.

ᑫ Lev. 19. 28.
Deut. 14. 1.

¹ Heb. *The word* is *good.*
² Or, *answer.*
³ Or, *heard.*

⁴ Or, *leaped up and down at the altar.*
⁵ Heb. *with a great voice.*

⁶ Or, *he meditateth.*
⁷ Heb. *hath a pursuit.*

only remain *in the exercise of the office* of a Prophet." The others (cp. *v.* 4) had been forced to fly and hide themselves in dens and caves of the earth; their voices were silenced; they had not ventured to come to Carmel. Elijah contrasts his solitary appearance on the side of Jehovah at the great gathering with the crowd of those opposed to him.

24. *the God that answereth by fire*] God had frequently before consumed offerings with supernatural fire (Lev. ix. 24; Judg. vi. 21). The Baal-worshippers were no doubt in the habit of attributing thunder and lightning to their god—the great Nature-power—and thus had no excuse for declining Elijah's challenge.

25. Elijah gives precedence in everything to the Baal-priests, to take away all ground for cavil in case of failure. It is his object to make an impression on king and people; and he feels rightly that the impression will depend greatly on the contrast between their inability and the power given to him.

26. *and called on the name of Baal from morning even until noon*] Cp. the parallel in the conduct of the Greeks of Ephesus. (Acts xix. 34). The words "O Baal, hear us," probably floated on the air as the refrain of a long and varied hymn of supplication.

they leaped upon the altar which was made] The marginal rendering is preferable to this. Wild dancing has always been a devotional exercise in the East, and remains so to this day; witness the dancing dervishes. It was practised especially in the worship of Nature-powers, like the Dea Phrygia (Cybele), the Dea Syra (Astarte?), and the like.

27. The object of Elijah's irony was twofold; (1) to stimulate the priests to greater exertions, and so to make their failure more complete, and (2) to suggest to the people that such failure would prove absolutely that Baal was no God.

The force of the expressions seems to be, "Cry on, only cry louder, and then you will make him hear; for surely he is a god; surely you are not mistaken in so regarding him." He is "talking," or "meditating;" the word used has both senses, for the Hebrews regarded "meditation" as "talking with oneself;" "or he is pursuing;" rather, perhaps, "he hath a *withdrawing*," *i.e.,* "he hath withdrawn himself into privacy for awhile," as a king does upon occasions. The drift of the whole passage is scornful ridicule of the anthropomorphic notions of God entertained by the Baal-priests and their followers (cp. Ps. l. 21). The heathen gods, as we know from the Greek and Latin classics, ate and drank, went on journeys, slept, conversed, quarrelled, fought. The explanations of many of these absurdities were unknown to the ordinary worshipper, and probably even the most enlightened, if his religion was not a mere vague Pantheism, had notions of the gods which were largely tainted with a false anthropomorphism.

28. Elijah's scorn roused the Baal-priests to greater exertions. At length, when the frenzy had reached its height, knives were drawn, and the blood spirted forth from hundreds of self-inflicted wounds, while an ecstasy of enthusiasm seized many, and they poured forth incoherent phrases, or perhaps an unintelligible jargon, which was believed to come from divine inspiration,

their manner with knives and lancets, till [1]the blood gushed
29 out upon them. And it came to pass, when midday was past,
r *and they prophesied until the *time* of the [2]offering of the
evening sacrifice, that *there was* [3]neither voice, nor any to an-
30 swer, nor any [3]that regarded. ¶And Elijah said unto all
the people, Come near unto me. And all the people came
near unto him. *t*And he repaired the altar of the LORD *that*
31 *was* broken down. And Elijah took twelve stones, according
to the number of the tribes of the sons of Jacob, unto whom
the word of the LORD came, saying, [u]Israel shall be thy name:
32 and with the stones he built an altar *x*in the name of the LORD:
and he made a trench about the altar, as great as would contain
33 two measures of seed. And he *y*put the wood in order, and
cut the bullock in pieces, and laid *him* on the wood, and said,
Fill four barrels with water, and *z*pour *it* on the burnt sacri-
34 fice, and on the wood. And he said, Do *it* the second time.
And they did *it* the second time. And he said, Do *it* the third
35 time. And they did *it* the third time. And the water [4]ran
round about the altar; and he filled *a*the trench also with water.
36 And it came to pass at *the time of* the offering of the *evening*
sacrifice, that Elijah the prophet came near, and said, LORD
*b*God of Abraham, Isaac, and of Israel, *c*let it be known this
day that thou *art* God in Israel, and *that* I *am* thy servant, and

r 1 Cor. 11.
4, 5.
s ver. 26.

t ch. 19. 10.

u Gen. 32. 28.
& 35. 10.
2 Kin. 17. 34.
x Col. 3. 17.
y Lev. 1. 6,
7, 8.

z See Judg.
6. 20.

a ver. 32. 38.

b Ex. 3. 6.
& 4. 5.
c ch. 8. 43.
2 Kin. 19. 19.
Ps. 83. 18.

[1] Heb. *poured out blood upon them.*
[2] Heb. *ascending.*
[3] Heb. *attention.*
[4] Heb. *went.*

---

and constituted one of their modes of
prophecy.

The practice of inflicting gashes on their
limbs, in their religious exercises, was common among the Carians, the Syrians, and
the Phrygians. We may regard it as a
modification of the idea of human sacrifice.
The gods were supposed to be pleased with
the shedding of human blood.

lancets] Lancets, in our modern sense of
the word, can scarcely have been intended
by our translators. The Hebrew word is
elsewhere always translated "spears," or
"lances;" and this is probably its meaning
here.

29. *and they prophesied*] Cp. xxii. 12.
The expression seems to be used of any case
where there was an utterance of words by
persons in a state of religious ecstasy.

until the time of the offering &c.] Rather,
"Until **towards** the time." Elijah had
built his altar by the actual time of the
offering (*v.* 36).

32. *he built an altar in the name of the
LORD*] *i.e.* calling, as he built it, on the
name of Jehovah, and so dedicating it to
His service.

two measures of seed] Literally, "two
seahs of seed." The *seah* contained about
three gallons.

33. *And he put the wood in order,* &c.] He
obeyed, that is, all the injunctions of the
Law with respect to the offering of a burnt
sacrifice (marg. ref.). He thus publicly

taught that the ordinances of the Law were
binding upon the kingdom of Israel.

barrels] Rather, "**pitchers**" or "water-
jars," such as the maidens used to carry on
their heads (Gen. xxiv. 14-20. Cp. Judg.
vii. 16, 19). The flooding the sacrifice and
the trench with water would at once do away
with any suspicion of fraud, and greatly
enhance in the eyes of the people the mar-
vellousness of the miracle. The unfailing
spring at the eastern end of Carmel (*v.* 19),
was capable of furnishing as much water as
he needed.

36. *at the time of the offering of the evening sacrifice*] *i.e.* probably "the ninth hour,"
or three o'clock. Thus there might still
remain about five hours of light, during
which the other events of the day were
accomplished.

LORD *God of Abraham, Isaac, and of
Israel*] This solemn address would carry
back the thoughts of the pious to the burning bush of Horeb, and the words there
spoken (marg. reff.); for there only had this
mysterious formula been used before. Its
use now was calculated to stir their faith
and prepare them in some degree for God's
answering *by fire.*

*that I have done all these things at thy
word*] *i.e.* "That I have been divinely
directed in all that I have done publicly as
a Prophet, in proclaiming the drought, in
gathering this assembly, and in proposing
this trial; that I have not done them of my
own mind" (marg. ref.).

37 *that* ^dI have done all these things at thy word. Hear me, O *d* Num. 16.
Lord, hear me, that this people may know that thou *art* the 28.
Lord God, and *that* thou hast turned their heart back again.
38 Then ^ethe fire of the Lord fell, and consumed the burnt sacri- *e* Lev. 9. 24.
fice, and the wood, and the stones, and the dust, and licked up Judg. 6. 21.
39 the water that *was* in the trench. And when all the people saw 2 Chr. 7. 1.
it, they fell on their faces: and they said, *f*The Lord, he *is* the *f* ver. 24.
40 God; the Lord, he *is* the God. And Elijah said unto them,
^{1g}Take the prophets of Baal; let not one of them escape. And *g* 2 Kin. 10.
they took them: and Elijah brought them down to the brook 25.
41 Kishon, and ^hslew them there. ¶ And Elijah said unto Ahab, *h* Deut. 13.5.
Get thee up, eat and drink; for *there is* ²a sound of abundance & 18. 20.
42 of rain. So Ahab went up to eat and to drink. And Elijah
went up to the top of Carmel; ⁱand he cast himself down upon *i* Jam. 5. 17,
43 the earth, and put his face between his knees, and said to his 18.
servant, Go up now, look toward the sea. And he went up,
and looked, and said, *There is* nothing. And he said, Go again
44 seven times. And it came to pass at the seventh time, that he
said, Behold, there ariseth a little cloud out of the sea, like a
man's hand. And he said, Go up, say unto Ahab, ³ Prepare *thy*
45 *chariot*, and get thee down, that the rain stop thee not. And
it came to pass in the mean while, that the heaven was black
with clouds and wind, and there was a great rain. And Ahab
46 rode, and went to Jezreel. And the hand of the Lord was on

---

¹ Or, *Apprehend.*   ² Or, *a sound of a noise of rain.*   ³ Heb. *Tie, or, Bind.*

---

37. *that thou hast turned their heart*] The
hearts of the people were turning. Elijah
speaks of them as already turned, anticipating the coming change, and helping
it on.
38. *the fire of the Lord fell*] This cannot
have been a flash of lightning. It was altogether, in its nature as well as in its oppor-
tuneness, miraculous. Cp. marg. reff. for
the conduct of the people.
39. *the Lord, he is the God*] The people
thus pronounced the matter to be clearly and
certainly decided. Baal was overthrown; he
was proved to be no god at all. The Lord
Jehovah, He, and He alone, is God. Him
would they henceforth acknowledge, and no
other.
40. Elijah required the people to show
their conviction by acts—acts which might
expose them to the anger of king or queen,
but which once committed would cause them
to break with Baal and his worshippers for
ever.
Elijah is said to have slain the "prophets of Baal," because the people slew
them by his orders. Why they were
brought down to the torrent-bed of Kishon
to be killed, is difficult to explain. Perhaps
the object of Elijah was to leave the bodies
in a place where they would not be found,
since the coming rain would, he knew, send
a flood down the Kishon ravine, and bear
off the corpses to the sea. Elijah's act is to
be justified by the express command of the
Law, that idolatrous Israelites were to be

put to death, and by the right of a Prophet
under the theocracy to step in and execute
the Law when the king failed in his duty.
41. *Get thee up, eat and drink*] Ahab had
descended the hill-side with Elijah, and
witnessed the slaughter of the priests. Elijah now bade him ascend the hill again, and
partake of the feast which was already prepared, and which always followed upon a
sacrifice.
there is a sound of abundance of rain]
Either the wind, which in the East usually
heralds rain, had begun to rise, and sighed
through the forests of Carmel—or perhaps
the sound was simply in the Prophet's ears,
a mysterious intimation to him that the
drought was to end, and rain to come that
day.
42. Ahab could feast; Elijah could not,
or would not. Ascending Carmel not quite
to the highest elevation (*v.* 43), but to a
point, a little below the highest, whence
the sea was not visible, he proceeded to
pray earnestly for rain, as he had prayed
formerly that it might not rain.
43. Tradition says that Elijah's servant
was the son of the widow of Sarepta (xvii.
23).
44. *a little cloud, &c.*] Sailors know full
well that such a cloud on the far horizon is
often the forerunner of a violent storm.
46. Divinely directed, and divinely up-
held, Elijah, instead of resting, ran in advance of the king's chariot the entire distance of at least 16 miles to the entrance of

k 2 Kin. 4.29.
& 9. 1.

a ch. 18. 40.

b Ruth 1. 17.
ch. 20. 10.
2 Kin. 6. 31.

c Num. 11.
15.
Jonah 4. 3, 8.

Elijah ; and he *k*girded up his loins, and ran before Ahab ¹to the entrance of Jezreel.

CHAP. 19. AND Ahab told Jezebel all that Elijah had done, and 2 withal how he had *a*slain all the prophets with the sword. Then Jezebel sent a messenger unto Elijah, saying, *b*So let the gods do *to me*, and more also, if I make not thy life as the life of one 3 of them by to morrow about this time. And when he saw *that*, he arose, and went for his life, and came to Beer-sheba, which 4 *belongeth* to Judah, and left his servant there. ¶ But he himself went a day's journey into the wilderness, and came and sat down under a juniper tree : and he *c*requested ²for himself that he might die; and said, It is enough; now, O LORD, take 5 away my life; for I *am* not better than my fathers. And as he lay and slept under a juniper tree, behold, then an angel

¹ Heb. *till thou come to Jezreel.*   ² Heb. *for his life.*

Jezreel. He thus showed himself ready to countenance and uphold the irresolute monarch, if he would turn from his evil courses, and proceed to carry out the religious reformation which the events of the day had inaugurated.

the entrance of Jezreel] Modern *Zerin*. Ahab had not removed the capital from Samaria (xxii. 10, 37); but he had built himself a palace at Jezreel (xxi. 1), and appears to have resided there ordinarily. A contemporary Assyrian inscription speaks of him as "Ahab of Jezreel."

Elijah's caution in accompanying Ahab only to "the entrance" is like that of the modern Arabs, who can seldom be induced to trust themselves within walls. He rested on the outskirts of the town, waiting to learn what Jezebel would say or do, knowing that it was she, and not Ahab, who really governed the country.

XIX. 2. The Prophet had not long to wait before learning the intentions of the queen. A priest's daughter herself, she would avenge the slaughtered priests; a king's wife and a king's child, she would not quail before a subject. That very night a messenger declared her determination to compass the Prophet's death within the space of a day.

so let the gods, &c.] A common oath about this time (marg. reff.). The Greek Version prefixes to this another clause, which makes the oath even more forcible, "As surely as thou art Elijah and I am Jezebel, so let the gods," &c.

3. The rapid movement of the original is very striking. "And he saw (or, *feared*, as some read), and he rose, and he went," &c." The fear and flight of Elijah are very remarkable. Jezebel's threat alone, had not, in all probability, produced the extraordinary change : but, partly, physical reaction from the over-excitement of the preceding day; and, partly, internal disquietude and doubt as to the wisdom of the course which he had adopted.

Beer-sheba is about 95 miles from Jezreel,

on the very borders of the desert et-Tih. Elijah cannot possibly have reached it until the close of the second day. It seems implied that he travelled both night and day, and did not rest till he arrived thus far on his way. It was one of the towns assigned to the tribe of Simeon (Josh. xix. 2). The Simeonites were, however, by this time absorbed into Judah.

4. Elijah did not feel himself safe till he was beyond the territory of Judah, for Ahab might demand him of Jehoshaphat (xviii. 10), with whom he was on terms of close alliance (xxii. 4). He therefore proceeds southward into the desert, simply to be out of the reach of his enemies.

a juniper-tree] The tree here mentioned (*rothem*) is not the juniper, but a species of broom (*Genista monosperma*), called *rethem* by the Arabs, which abounds in the Sinaitic peninsula. It grows to such a size as to afford shade and protection, both in heat and storm, to travellers.

requested for himself that he might die.] Like Moses and Jonah (marg. reff.). The Prophet's depression here reached its lowest point. He was still suffering from the reaction of overstrained feeling ; he was weary with nights and days of travel ; he was faint with the sun's heat ; he was exhausted for want of food ; he was for the first time alone —alone in the awful solitude and silence of the great white desert. Such solitude might brace the soul in certain moods ; but in others it must utterly overwhelm and crush. Thus the Prophet at length gave way completely—made his prayer that he might die —and, exhausted sank, to sleep.

I am not better than my fathers] i.e. "I am a mere weak man, no better nor stronger than they who have gone before me, no more able to revolutionize the world than they."

5. *an angel touched him*] The friendly ministration of Angels, common in the time of the Patriarchs (Gen. xviii. 2-16, xix. 1-22, xxviii. 12, xxxii. 1, 24-29), and known also under the Judges (Judg. vi. 11-21, xiii. 3-20), was now extended to Elijah.

6 touched him, and said unto him, Arise *and* eat. And he looked, and, behold, *there was* a cake baken on the coals, and a cruse of water at his ¹head. And he did eat and drink, and laid him
7 down again. And the angel of the LORD came again the second time, and touched him, and said, Arise *and* eat; because the
8 journey *is* too great for thee. And he arose, and did eat and drink, and went in the strength of that meat ᵈforty days and
9 forty nights unto ᵉHoreb the mount of God. ¶And he came thither unto a cave, and lodged there; and, behold, the word of the LORD *came* to him, and he said unto him, What doest thou
10 here, Elijah? And he said, ᶠI have been very ᵍjealous for the LORD God of hosts: for the children of Israel have forsaken thy covenant, thrown down thine altars, and ʰslain thy prophets with the sword; and ⁱI, *even* I only, am left; and they seek my
11 life, to take it away. And he said, Go forth, and stand ᵏupon the mount before the LORD. And, behold, the LORD passed by, and ˡa great and strong wind rent the mountains, and brake in pieces the rocks before the LORD; *but* the LORD *was* not in the
12 wind: and after the wind an earthquake; *but* the LORD *was* not in the earthquake: and after the earthquake a fire; *but* the LORD
13 *was* not in the fire: and after the fire a still small voice. And

d So Ex. 34. 28.
Deut. 9.9,18
Matt. 4. 2.
e Ex. 3. 1.

f Rom. 11. 3.
g Num. 25.
11, 13.
Ps. 69. 9.
h ch. 18. 4.
i Rom. 11. 3.
k Ex. 24. 12.

l Ezek. 1. 4.
& 37. 7.

¹ Heb. *bolster.*

Any other explanation of this passage does violence to the words. It is certainly not the intention of the writer to represent Elijah as relieved on this occasion by a human "messenger."

6. *a cake baken on the coals*] It is not implied that Elijah found a fire lighted and the cake on it, but only that he found one of the usual baked cakes of the desert, which form the ordinary food of the Arab at the present day.

at his head] The Hebrew word means simply "the place on which the head lies;" hence the marginal rendering, "bolster."

7. *Arise and eat, &c.*] i.e. "Eat a second time, for *otherwise* the journey will be beyond thy powers." "The journey" was not simply a pilgrimage to Horeb, which was less than 200 miles distant, and might have been reached in six or seven days. It was to be a wandering in the wilderness, not unlike that of the Israelites when they came out of Egypt; only it was to last forty days instead of forty years.

8. The old commentators generally understood this to mean that Elijah had no other food at all, and compared this long fast with that of Moses and that of our Lord (marg. reff.). But the words do not exclude the notion of the Prophet's having obtained such nourishment from roots and fruits as the desert offers to a wanderer, though these alone would not have sustained him.

9. *a cave*] Rather, "**the** cave." Some well-known cave must be intended—perhaps the "clift of the rock" (Ex. xxxiii. 22). The traditional "cave of Elijah" which is shown in the secluded plain immediately below the highest summit of the

Jebel Mousa, cannot, from its small size, be the real cavern.

10. *I, even I only, am left*] The same statement as in xviii. 22, but the sense is different. There Elijah merely said that he alone remained to execute the Prophet's office, which was true; here he implies that he is the only Prophet left alive, whereas a hundred had been saved by Obadiah (xviii. 4).

11. *and behold, the LORD passed by*] The remainder of this verse and the whole of the next are placed by the LXX., and by the Arabic translator, in the mouth of the Angel. But it seems best to regard the vision as ending with the words "before the Lord" —and the writer as then assuming that this was done, and proceeding to describe what followed.

12. *a still small voice*] Literally, "a sound of soft stillness." The teaching is a condemnation of that "zeal" which Elijah had gloried in, a zeal exhibiting itself in fierce and terrible vengeances, and an exaltation and recommendation of that mild and gentle temper, which "beareth all things, believeth all things, hopeth all things, endureth all things." But it was so contrary to the whole character of the stern, harsh, unsparing Tishbite, that it could have found no ready entrance into his heart. It may have for a while moderated his excessive zeal, and inclined him to gentler courses; but later in his life the old harshness recurred in a deed in reference to which our Lord himself drew the well-known contrast between the spirits of the two Dispensations (Luke ix. 51–56).

m So Ex.3.6.
Isai. 6. 2.

n ver. 9.
o ver. 10.

p 2 Kin. 8.
12, 13.
q 2 Kin. 9.
1—3.
r Luke 4.
27, called
Eliseus.
s 2 Kin. 8.12.
& 9. 14, &c.
& 10. 6, &c.
& 13. 3.
t See Hos.
6. 5.
u Rom. 11.4.
x See Hos.
13. 2.

it was *so*, when Elijah heard *it*, that *m*he wrapped his face in his mantle, and went out, and stood in the entering in of the cave. *n*And, behold, *there came* a voice unto him, and said, What doest 14 thou here, Elijah ? *o*And he said, I have been very jealous for the LORD God of hosts : because the children of Israel have forsaken thy covenant, thrown down thine altars, and slain thy prophets with the sword : and I, *even* I only, am left; and they 15 seek my life, to take it away. And the LORD said unto him, Go, return on thy way to the wilderness of Damascus : *p*and 16 when thou comest, anoint Hazael *to be* king over Syria : and *q*Jehu the son of Nimshi shalt thou anoint *to be* king over Israel : and *r*Elisha the son of Shaphat of Abel-meholah shalt thou 17 anoint *to be* prophet in thy room. And *s*it shall come to pass, *that* him that escapeth the sword of Hazael shall Jehu slay : and him that escapeth from the sword of Jehu *t*shall Elisha slay. 18 *u*Yet ¹I have left *me* seven thousand in Israel, all the knees which have not bowed unto Baal, *x*and every mouth which hath 19 not kissed him.   ¶ So he departed thence, and found Elisha the

¹ Or, *I will leave.*

---

13. *mantle*] The upper garment, a sort of short cloak or cape—perhaps made of untanned sheepskin, which was, besides the strip of leather round his loins, the sole apparel of the Prophet (cp. Matt. iii. 4). For the action cp. marg. reff.

there came a voice unto him, &c.] The question heard before in vision is now put again to the Prophet by the Lord Himself. Elijah gives no humbler and more gentle answer. He is still satisfied with his own statement of his case.

15. The answer is not a justification of the ways of God, nor a direct reproof of the Prophet's weakness and despondency, nor an explanation or application of what Elijah had seen. For the present, he is simply directed back into the path of practical duty. His mission is not yet over, there is still work for him to do. He receives special injunctions with respect to Hazael, Jehu, and Elisha; and he is comforted with a revelation well adapted to rouse him from his despondency : there are seven thousand who will sympathise with him in his trials, and who need his care and attention.

the wilderness of Damascus] Probably the district north of the Prophet's own country, between Bashan and Damascus itself, and which was known in later times as Iturea and Gaulanitis. Here the Prophet might be secure from Jezebel, while he could readily communicate with both Israel and Damascus, and execute the commissions with which he was intrusted.

when thou comest, anoint] Rather, "**and thou shalt go and anoint.**" Elijah performed one only of the three commissions given to him. He appears to have been left free to choose the time for executing his commissions, and it would seem that he thought the proper occasion had not arisen either for the first or the second before his

own translation. But he took care to communicate the divine commands to his successor, who performed them at the fitting moment (marg. reff.).

16. *Jehu, the son of Nimshi*] In reality the grandson of Nimshi. But he seems to have been commonly known by the above title (2 K. ix. 20 ; 2 Chr. xxii. 7), perhaps because his father had died and his grandfather had brought him up.

Abel-meholah] See Judg. vii. 22 note. [Conder identifies it with Ain Helweh.]

Elisha...shalt thou anoint] This is almost the only place where we hear of the anointing of Prophets (cp. 1 Chr. xvi. 22 and Ps. cv. 15).

17. Cp. marg. reff.

shall Elisha slay] *i.e.* With a spiritual slaying by the "word of the Lord," which is " sharper than any two-edged sword," and may be said to slay those whose doom it pronounces (cp. marg. ref. ; Jer. i. 10). Elisha does not seem, like Elijah, to have executed God's judgments on the guilty.

18. *Yet I have left me*, &c.] Rather, as in the margin. "Seven thousand" faithful Israelites shall survive all the persecutions of Ahab and Jezebel, and carry down the worship of Jehovah to another generation. Elijah is mistaken in supposing that he only is left. The number is manifestly a round number, not an exact estimate. Perhaps it is, moreover, a mystical or symbolic number. Cp. Rev. vii. 5-8. Of all the symbolical numbers used in Scripture, seven is the commonest.

every mouth which hath not kissed him] Idolaters sometimes kissed the hand to the object of their worship (Job xxxi. 26, 27) ; at other times they kissed the actual image (marg. ref.).

19. *plowing*] Elisha's occupation is an indication of his character. He is emphati-

son of Shaphat, who *was* plowing *with* twelve yoke *of oxen* before him, and he with the twelfth : and Elijah passed by him, 20 and cast his mantle upon him. And he left the oxen, and ran after Elijah, and said, *ʸ* Let me, I pray thee, kiss my father and my mother, and *then* I will follow thee. And he said unto him, 21 ¹Go back again : for what have I done to thee ? And he returned back from him, and took a yoke of oxen, and slew them, and *ᶻ* boiled their flesh with the instruments of the oxen, and gave unto the people, and they did eat. Then he arose, and went after Elijah, and ministered unto him.

CHAP. 20. AND Ben-hadad the king of Syria gathered all his host together : and *there were* thirty and two kings with him, and horses, and chariots : and he went up and besieged Samaria, 2 and warred against it. And he sent messengers to Ahab king of Israel into the city, and said unto him, Thus saith Ben-

ʸ Matt. 8. 21, 22.

ᶻ 2 Sam. 21.

¹ Heb. *Go return.*

---

cally a man of peace. He passes the year in those rural occupations which are natural to the son of a wealthy yeoman—superintending the field-labourers himself, and taking a share in their toils. He thus presents a strong contrast to the stern, harsh, rugged Gileadite, who is almost half an Arab, who seems to have no settled home, no quiet family circle, who avoids the haunts of men, and is content for months to dwell in a cavern instead of under a roof.

with twelve yoke of oxen] He was ploughing in a field with eleven other ploughs at work, each drawn by one yoke of oxen. Ploughing with a single pair of oxen was the practice in Egypt, in Assyria, in Palestine, and in modern times throughout Western Asia.

passed by him] Rather, " **crossed over to him.**" Perhaps it is meant that he crossed the stream of the Jordan.

cast his mantle upon him] The action is explained as constituting a species of adoption, because a father naturally clothes his children. The notion of fatherhood and sonship were evidently understood between them (2 K. ii. 9-12).

20. *let me, I pray thee, kiss my father,* &c.] Not an unnatural request before following his new spiritual father. Elijah sees in his address a divided heart, and will not give the permission or accept the service thus tendered. Hence his cold reply. See Luke ix. 61, 62.

go back again, &c.] *i.e.,* " Go, return to thy ploughing—why shouldest thou quit it ? Why take leave of thy friends and come with me ? What have I done to thee to require such a sacrifice ? for as a sacrifice thou evidently regardest it. Truly I have done nothing to thee. Thou canst remain as thou art."

21. Elisha returns to his oxen and labourers. He indicates his relinquishment of

his home and calling by the slaughter of the particular yoke of oxen with which he had himself been ploughing. probably the best beasts of the twelve, and by burning the "instruments," the ploughs and yokes, both made of wood. Next he feasts his people to show his gratitude for his call, Elijah apparently remaining the while ; and then, leaving father and mother, cattle and land, good position and comfortable home, Elisha became the " minister " to the wanderer. Cp. Ex. xxiv. 13 ; Josh. i. 1.

XX. **1.** *Ben-hadad, the king of Syria*] Probably the son of the Ben-hadad who assisted Asa against Baasha (xv. 18 note).

thirty and two kings with him] Not allies, but feudatories (*v.* 24). Damascus had in the reign of this Ben-hadad become the centre of an important monarchy, which may not improbably have extended from the Euphrates to the northern border of Israel. The Assyrian inscriptions show that this country was about the period in question parcelled out into a multitude of petty kingdoms, the chief tribes who possessed it being the Hittites, the Hamathites, and the Syrians of Damascus.

horses and chariots] The Assyrian inscriptions show us how very important an arm of the service the chariot force was reckoned by the Syrians. A king, who has been identified with this Ben-hadad, brought into the field against Assyria nearly four thousand chariots.

2. It may be supposed that a considerable time had passed in the siege, that the city had been reduced to an extremity, and that ambassadors had been sent by Ahab to ask terms of peace short of absolute surrender, before Ben-hadad would make such a demand. He would expect and intend his demand to be rejected, and this would have left him free to plunder the town, which was evidently what he desired and purposed.

3 hadad, thy silver and thy gold *is* mine ; thy wives also and thy
4 children, *even* the goodliest, *are* mine. And the king of Israel
answered and said, My lord, O king, according to thy saying, I
5 *am* thine, and all that I have. ¶ And the messengers came
again, and said, Thus speaketh Ben-hadad, saying, Although I
have sent unto thee, saying, Thou shalt deliver me thy silver,
6 and thy gold, and thy wives, and thy children ; yet I will send
my servants unto thee to morrow about this time, and they shall
search thine house, and the houses of thy servants ; and it shall
be, *that* whatsoever is [1]pleasant in thine eyes, they shall put *it*
7 in their hand, and take *it* away. Then the king of Israel called
all the elders of the land, and said, Mark, I pray you, and see
how this *man* seeketh mischief : for he sent unto me for my
wives, and for my children, and for my silver, and for my gold;
8 and [2]I denied him not. And all the elders and all the people
9 said unto him, Hearken not *unto him*, nor consent. Wherefore
he said unto the messengers of Ben-hadad, Tell my lord the
king, All that thou didst send for to thy servant at the first I
will do : but this thing I may not do. And the messengers de-
10 parted, and brought him word again. And Ben-hadad sent
unto him, and said, *a*The gods do so unto me, and more also, if
the dust of Samaria shall suffice for handfuls for all the people
11 that [3]follow me. And the king of Israel answered and said,
Tell *him*, Let not him that girdeth on *his harness* boast himself
12 as he that putteth it off. And it came to pass, when *Ben-hadad*
heard this [4]message, as he was *b*drinking. he and the kings in
the [5]pavilions, that he said unto his servants, [6]Set *yourselves in*
13 *array*. And they set *themselves in array* against the city. ¶ And,

a ch. 19. 2.

b ver. 16.

[1] Heb. *desirable*.
[2] Heb. *I kept not back from him*.
[3] Heb. *are at my feet*. So Ex. 11. 8. Judg. 4. 10.
[4] Heb. *word*.
[5] Or, *tents*.
[6] Or, *Place* the engines : *And they placed* engines.

---

6. Ben-hadad, disappointed by Ahab's consent to an indignity which he had thought no monarch could submit to, proceeds to put a fresh construction on his former demands.

7. The political institution of a Council of elders (Ex. iii. 16, &c.), which had belonged to the undivided nation from the sojourn in Egypt downwards, had therefore been continued among the ten tribes after their separation, and still held an important place in the system of Government. The Council was not merely called together when the king needed it, but held its regular sittings at the seat of government ; and hence "all the elders *of the land*" were now present in Samaria. On the "elders of towns," see xxi. *vv.* 8–14.

Apparently the king had not thought it necessary to summon the Council when the first terms were announced to him, inasmuch as they touched only himself. The fresh demands affected the people at large, and it became necessary, or at any rate fitting, that "the elders" should be consulted.

8. "The people" had no distinct place in the ordinary Jewish or Israelitish constitution ; but they were accustomed to signify their approbation or disapprobation of the decisions of the elders by acclamations or murmurs (Josh. ix. 18 ; Judg. xi. 11, &c.).

10. *if the dust of Samaria shall suffice for handfuls*, &c.] In its general sense this phrase is undoubtedly a boast that the number of Ben-hadad's troops was such as to make resistance vain and foolish. We may parallel it with the saying of the Trachinian at Thermopylæ, that the Persian arrows would darken the light of the sun. Probably the exact meaning is, "When your town is reduced to ruins, as it will be if you resist, the entire heap will not suffice to furnish a handful of dust to each soldier of my army, so many are they." There was a threat in the message as well as a boast.

11. Ahab's reply has the air of a proverb, with which Orientals always love to answer a foe.

12. *pavilions*] "Booths" (Gen. xxxiii. 17 marg. ; Lev. xxiii. 42 ; Jonah iv. 5). The term seems to be properly applied to a stationary "booth" or "hut," as distinguished from a moveable "tent." On military expeditions, and especially in the case of a siege, such "huts" were naturally constructed to shelter the king and his chief officers.

behold, there [1] came a prophet unto Ahab king of Israel, saying,
Thus saith the LORD, Hast thou seen all this great multitude?
behold, [c] I will deliver it into thine hand this day; and thou   [c] ver. 23.
14 shalt know that I *am* the LORD. And Ahab said, By whom?
And he said, Thus said the LORD, *Even* by the [2] young men of
the princes of the provinces. Then he said, Who shall [3] order
15 the battle? And he answered, Thou. ¶ Then he numbered
the young men of the princes of the provinces, and they were
two hundred and thirty two: and after them he numbered all
the people, *even* all the children of Israel, *being* seven thousand.
16 And they went out at noon. But Ben-hadad *was* [d] drinking   [d] ver. 12.
himself drunk in the pavilions, he and the kings, the thirty and   ch. 16. 9.
17 two kings that helped him. And the young men of the princes
of the provinces went out first; and Ben-hadad sent out, and
they told him, saying, There are men come out of Samaria.
18 And he said, Whether they be come out for peace, take them
alive; or whether they be come out for war, take them alive.
19 So these young men of the princes of the provinces came out of
20 the city, and the army which followed them. And they slew
every one his man: and the Syrians fled; and Israel pursued
them: and Ben-hadad the king of Syria escaped on an horse
21 with the horsemen. And the king of Israel went out, and smote
the horses and chariots, and slew the Syrians with a great
22 slaughter. ¶ And the prophet came to the king of Israel, and
said unto him, Go, strengthen thyself, and mark, and see what
thou doest: [e] for at the return of the year the king of Syria will   [e] 2 Sam 11.1.
23 come up against thee. ¶ And the servants of the king of Syria
said unto him, Their gods *are* gods of the hills; therefore they

---

[1] Heb. *approached.*   [2] Or, *servants.*   [3] Heb. *bind,* or, *tie.*

---

13. The Rabbinical commentators conjecture that this Prophet was Micaiah, the son of Imlah, who is mentioned below (xxii. 8).

hast thou seen all this great multitude?] The boast of Ben-hadad (*v.* 10), was not without a basis of truth; his force seems to have exceeded 130,000 (cp. *vv.* 25, 29, 30). In his wars with the Assyrians we find him sometimes at the head of 100,000 men.

14. The "princes of the provinces" are the governors of districts, many of whom may have fled to the capital, as the hostile army advanced through Galilee and northern Samaria. The "young men" are their attendants, youths unaccustomed to war.

Who shall order the battle?] *i.e.* "Who shall join battle, begin the attack? We or the enemy?" The reply was, that the Israelites were to attack.

15. *seven thousand*] Considering how populous Palestine was in the time of the earlier Israelite kings (see 2 Chr. xiii. 3, xiv. 8, xvii. 14-18), the smallness of this number is somewhat surprising. If the reading be sound, we must suppose, first, that Ben-hadad's attack was very sudden, and that Ahab had no time to collect forces from distant parts of the country; and secondly, that during the long siege the garrison of Samaria had been greatly reduced, till it now did not exceed 7,000 men fit for service.

16. *drinking himself drunk*] Ben-hadad meant probably to mark his utter contempt of his foe. Cp. the contempt of Belshazzar (Dan. v. 1-4).

17. *Ben-hadad sent out, and they told him*] The LXX. have a better reading—"they sent and told the king of Syria."

22. *Go, strengthen thyself,* &c.] That is, "collect troops, raise fortifications, obtain allies—take all the measures thou canst to increase thy military strength. Be not rash, but consider well every step—for a great danger is impending."

at the return of the year] *i.e.* "When the season for military operations again comes round." The wars of the Oriental monarchs at this time, like those of early Rome, were almost always of the nature of annual incursions into the territories of their neighbours, begun in spring and terminating in early autumn. Sustained invasions, lasting over the winter into a second or a third year, are not found till the time of Shalmaneser (2 K. xvii. 5, xviii. 9, 10), and do not become common till the Median and Babylonian period.

23. *Their gods are gods of the hills*] The local power and influence of deities was a fixed principle of the ancient polytheism. Each country was considered to have its own gods; and wars were regarded as being to a great extent struggles between the gods

were stronger than we; but let us fight against them in the
24 plain, and surely we shall be stronger than they. And do this
thing, Take the kings away, every man out of his place, and put
25 captains in their rooms: and number thee an army, like the
army [1]that thou hast lost, horse for horse, and chariot for chariot: and we will fight against them in the plain, *and* surely we
shall be stronger than they. And he hearkened unto their
26 voice, and did so. And it came to pass at the return of the
year, that Ben-hadad numbered the Syrians, and went up to

f Josh. 13. 4. 27 *f*Aphek, [2]to fight against Israel. And the children of Israel were
numbered, and [3]were all present, and went against them: and
the children of Israel pitched before them like two little flocks of
28 kids; but the Syrians filled the country. ¶And there came a
man of God, and spake unto the king of Israel, and said, Thus
saith the LORD, Because the Syrians have said, the LORD *is* God

g ver. 13. of the hills, but he *is* not God of the valleys, therefore *g*will I
deliver all this great multitude into thine hand, and ye shall
29 know that I *am* the LORD. ¶And they pitched one over against
the other seven days. And *so* it was, that in the seventh day the
battle was joined: and the children of Israel slew of the Syrians
30 an hundred thousand footmen in one day. But the rest fled to
Aphek, into the city; and *there* a wall fell upon twenty and seven
thousand of the men *that were* left. ¶And Ben-hadad fled, and
31 came into the city, [4,5]into an inner chamber. And his servants
said unto him, Behold now, we have heard that the kings of the

h Gen. 37. 34. house of Israel *are* merciful kings: let us, I pray thee, *h*put
sackcloth on our loins, and ropes upon our heads, and go out to

---

[1] Heb. *that was fallen.*
[2] Heb. *to the war with Israel.*
[3] Or, *were victualled.*
[4] Or, *from chamber to chamber.*
[5] Heb. *into a chamber within a chamber*, ch. 22, 25.

---

of the nations engaged in them. This is apparent throughout the Assyrian inscriptions. Cp. also 2 K. xviii. 33–35, xix. 12. The present passage gives an unusual modification of this view. The suggestion of the Syrian chiefs may have been a mere politic device—they being really anxious, *an military grounds*, to encounter their enemy on the plain, where alone their chariots would be of much service. In the plain the Israelites had always fought at a disadvantage, and had proved themselves weaker than on the hills (see Judg. i. 19, 27, 34).

24. The Syrian chiefs evidently thought that want of unity had weakened their army. They therefore proposed the deposition of the kings, and the substitution, in their place, of Syrian governors:—not "captains." The term used always denotes a civil office.

26. *Aphek*] There were several places of this name in Palestine (see marg. ref.). This Aphek has been almost certainly identified with the modern *Fik*, a large village on the present high road from Damascus to Nablous and Jerusalem. The expression "*went up* to Aphek" is appropriate; for *Fik*, though in a level country, is at a much higher elevation than Damascus.

27. *were all present*] The marginal rendering is adopted by almost all critics.

like two little flocks of kids] The word translated "little flocks" does not occur elsewhere in Scripture. It seems to mean simply "flocks." Compare the LXX., who render ὡσεὶ δύο ποίμνια αἰγῶν.

28. *a man of God*] Evidently not the Prophet who had spoken to Ahab the year before (*vv.* 13, 22). He probably dwelt in the neighbourhood of Samaria. Now that Ahab and his army had marched out into the Trans-Jordanic territory, another Prophet, a native probably of that region, announced God's will to them.

30. *a wall*] "The wall," *i.e.* the wall of the town. We may suppose a terrific earthquake during the siege of the place, while the Syrians were manning the defences in full force, which threw down the wall where they were most thickly crowded upon it, and buried them in its ruins. Ben-hadad fled from the wall, where he had been at the time of the disaster, into the inner parts of the city—probably to some massive stronghold—and there concealed himself.

31. *and ropes upon our heads*] "Ropes about our necks" is probably meant. They, as it were, put their lives at Ahab's disposal, who, if he pleased, might hang them at once.

32 the king of Israel : peradventure he will save thy life. So they girded sackcloth on their loins, and *put* ropes on their heads, and came to the king of Israel, and said, Thy servant Ben-hadad saith, I pray thee, let me live. And he said, *Is* he yet alive?

33 he *is* my brother. Now the men did diligently observe whether *any thing would come* from him, and did hastily catch *it :* and they said, Thy brother Ben-hadad. Then he said, Go ye, bring him. Then Ben-hadad came forth to him ; and he caused him

34 to come up into the chariot. And *Ben-hadad* said unto him, *i*The cities, which my father took from thy father, I will restore ; and thou shalt make streets for thee in Damascus, as my father made in Samaria. Then *said Ahab*, I will send thee away with this covenant. So he made a covenant with him, and sent

35 him away. ¶ And a certain man of *k*the sons of the prophets said unto his neighbour *l*in the word of the LORD, Smite me, I

36 pray thee. And the man refused to smite him. Then said he unto him, Because thou hast not obeyed the voice of the LORD, behold, as soon as thou art departed from me, a lion shall slay thee. And as soon as he was departed from him, *m*a lion found

37 him, and slew him. Then he found another man, and said, Smite me, I pray thee. And the man smote him, *1*so that in

i ch. 15. 20.

k 2 Kin. 2. 3, 5, 7, 15. *l* ch. 13. 17, 18.

m ch. 13. 24.

1 Heb. *smiting and wounding.*

32. Ben-hadad is now as humble as Ahab had been a year before (*v.* 9). He professes himself the mere *slave* of his conqueror.

33. The meaning of this verse is that the men from the first moment of their arrival were on the watch to note what Ahab would say ; and the moment he let fall the expression "He is my brother," they caught it up and repeated it, fixing him to it, as it were, and preventing his retreat. By the Oriental law of *dakheel* any one is at any time entitled to put himself under the protection of another, be that either his friend or his greatest enemy ; and if the man applied to does not at once reject him, if the slightest forms of friendly speech pass between the two, the bond is complete, and must not be broken. Ben-hadad's friends were on the watch to obtain for him *dakheel ;* and the single phrase "He is my brother," having been accepted by them on his part, was sufficient to complete the bond, and secure the life of the captive. Ahab having called Ben-hadad his brother, treated him as he would a brother ; he took him up into his chariot, than which there could not be a greater honour.

34. Ben-hadad, secure of his life, suggests terms of peace as the price of his freedom. He will restore to Ahab the Israelite cities taken from Omri by his father, among which Ramoth Gilead was probably the most important (xxii. 3) ; and he will allow Ahab the privilege of making for himself "streets," or rather squares, in Damascus, a privilege which his own father had possessed with respect to Samaria. Commercial advantages, rather than any other, were probably sought by this arrangement.

so he made a covenant with him, &c.] Ahab, without "inquiring of the Lord," at once agreed to the terms offered ; and, without even taking any security for their due observance, allowed the Syrian monarch to depart. Considered politically, the act was one of culpable carelessness and imprudence. Ben-hadad did not regard himself as bound by the terms of a covenant made when he was a prisoner—as his after conduct shows (xxii. 3). Ahab's conduct was even more unjustifiable in one who held his crown under a theocracy. "Inquiry at the word of the Lord" was still possible in Israel (xxii. 5, 8), and would seem to have been the course that ordinary gratitude might have suggested.

35. *the sons of the prophets*] The expression occurs here for the first time. It signifies (marg. reff.), the schools or colleges of Prophets which existed in several of the Israelite, and probably of the Jewish, towns, where young men were regularly educated for the prophetical office. These "schools" make their first appearance under Samuel (1 Sam. xix. 20). There is no distinct evidence that they continued later than the time of Elisha ; but it is on the whole most probable that the institution survived the Captivity, and that the bulk of the "Prophets," whose works have come down to us, belonged to them. Amos (vii. 14, 15) seems to speak as if his were an exceptional case.

said unto his neighbour] Rather, "to his friend" or "companion"—to one who was, like himself, "a Prophet's son," and who ought therefore to have perceived that his colleague spoke "in the word of the Lord."

n See
2 Sam. 12.
1, &c.

38 smiting he wounded *him*. So the prophet departed, and waited
for the king by the way, and disguised himself with ashes upon
39 his face. And *n* as the king passed by, he cried unto the king:
and he said, Thy servant went out into the midst of the battle ;
and, behold, a man turned aside, and brought a man unto me,
and said, Keep this man : if by any means he be missing, then

o 2 Kin. 10.
21.

o shall thy life be for his life, or else thou shalt [1] pay a talent of
40 silver. And as thy servant was busy here and there, [2] he was
gone. And the king of Israel said unto him, So *shall* thy judg-
41 ment *be ;* thyself hast decided *it*. And he hasted, and took the
ashes away from his face ; and the king of Israel discerned him
42 that he *was* of the prophets. And he said unto him, Thus saith

p ch. 22. 31
—37.

the LORD, *p* Because thou hast let go out of *thy* hand a man
whom I appointed to utter destruction, therefore thy life shall
43 go for his life, and thy people for his people. And the king of

q ch. 21. 1.

Israel *q* went to his house heavy and displeased, and came to
Samaria.

CHAP. 21. AND it came to pass after these things, *that* Naboth the
Jezreelite had a vineyard, which *was* in Jezreel, hard by the
2 palace of Ahab king of Samaria. And Ahab spake unto Naboth,

a 1Sam.8.14.

saying, Give me thy *a* vineyard, that I may have it for a garden
of herbs, because it *is* near unto my house : and I will give
thee for it a better vineyard than it; *or*, if it [3] seem good to thee,
3 I will give thee the worth of it in money. And Naboth said to

b Lev. 25. 23.
Num. 36. 7.
Ezek. 46. 18.

Ahab, The LORD forbid it me, *b* that I should give the inherit-
4 ance of my fathers unto thee. ¶ And Ahab came into his house
heavy and displeased because of the word which Naboth the
Jezreelite had spoken to him : for he had said, I will not give
thee the inheritance of my fathers. And he laid him down upon
his bed, and turned away his face, and would eat no bread.

[1] Heb. *weigh*.   [2] Heb. *he was not*.   [3] Heb. be *good in thine eyes*.

---

38. *ashes*] Rather, "**a bandage** " (and in
v. 41). The object of the wound and
bandage was double. Partly, it was to prevent Ahab from recognising the Prophet's
face ; partly, to induce him to believe that
the man had really been engaged in the
recent war.

41. *he was of the prophets*] Josephus and
others conjecture that this Prophet was
Micaiah, the son of Imlah (but cp. *v.* 13
note).

42. *a man whom I appointed to utter destruction*] or to *cherem, i.e.* a man on whom
My curse had been laid (Lev. xxvii. 28
note).

43. *heavy and displeased*] Rather, " **sul-
len and angry** " (and so marg. ref.), not
repentant, as after Elijah's warning (xxi.
27)—not acknowledging the justice of his
sentence—but full of sullenness and sup-
pressed anger.

XXI. 1. *a vineyard...in Jezreel*] The name
Jezreel is applied in Scripture, not merely
to the town (xviii. 46), but also to the valley
or plain which lies below it, between Mount
Gilboa and Little Hermon (2 Sam. ii. 9;
2 K. ix. 10; Hos. i. 5; &c.).

The palace of Ahab at Jezreel was on
the eastern side of the city, looking towards
the Jordan down the valley above described.
It abutted on the town wall (2 K. ix. 30,
31). Immediately below it was a dry moat.
Beyond, in the valley, either adjoining the
moat, or at any rate at no great distance,
was the plat of ground belonging to Naboth
(do. *v.* 21).

2. *I will give thee the worth of it in money*]
Lit., " I will give thee silver, the worth of
it." Money, in our sense of the word, that
is to say, coins of definite values, did not
yet exist. The first coin known to the Jews
was the Persian daric, with which they
became acquainted during the Captivity.
(1 Chr. xxix. 7 note).

3. *The* LORD *forbid it me*] Or, " Jehovah
forbid it me." Naboth, as a worshipper of
Jehovah, not of Baal, considers it would be
wrong for him to comply with the king's
request, as contrary to the Law (marg.).
His was not a mere refusal arising out of a
spirit of sturdy independence, or one based
upon the sentiment which attaches men to
ancestral estates.

4. *upon his bed*] That is, " upon his
couch." The Jews, like other Orientals,
reclined upon couches at their meals (Amos

5 ¶ But Jezebel his wife came to him, and said unto him, Why is
6 thy spirit so sad, that thou eatest no bread? And he said unto
her, Because I spake unto Naboth the Jezreelite, and said unto
him, Give me thy vineyard for money; or else, if it please thee,
I will give thee *another* vineyard for it: and he answered, I will
7 not give thee my vineyard. And Jezebel his wife said unto him,
Dost thou now govern the kingdom of Israel? arise, *and* eat
bread, and let thine heart be merry: I will give thee the vine-
8 yard of Naboth the Jezreelite. So she wrote letters in Ahab's
name, and sealed *them* with his seal, and sent the letters unto
the elders and to the nobles that *were* in his city, dwelling with
9 Naboth. And she wrote in the letters, saying, Proclaim a fast,
10 and set Naboth ¹on high among the people: and set two men,
sons of Belial, before him, to bear witness against him, saying,
Thou didst *c*blaspheme God and the king. And *then* carry him
11 out, and *d*stone him, that he may die. ¶ And the men of his
city, *even* the elders and the nobles who were the inhabitants in
his city, did as Jezebel had sent unto them, *and* as it *was* written
12 in the letters which she had sent unto them. *e*They proclaimed

c Ex. 22. 28.
Lev. 24. 15,
16.
Acts 6. 11.
d Lev. 24.14.

e Isai. 58. 4.

¹ Heb. *in the top of the people.*

---

vi. 4; Ezek. xxiii. 41, &c.). Ahab turns his face towards the back of the couch, rejecting all converse with others, and so remains, after the banquet is served, refusing to partake of it. Such an open manifestation of ill temper is thoroughly characteristic of an Oriental king.

7. The meaning is, "Art thou king, and yet sufferest thyself to be thwarted in this way by a mere subject? *I*, the queen, the weak woman, will give thee the vineyard, if thou, the king, the strong man, wilt do nothing."

8. *seal*] The seal is a very ancient invention. Judah's signet and Pharaoh's signet-ring are mentioned in Genesis (xxxviii. 18, xli. 42). Signets of Egyptian kings have been found which are referred to about B.C. 2000. Sennacherib's signet, and an impression of Sargon's, are still extant. There can be no doubt that in the East, from a very remote antiquity, kings had seals and appended them to all documents which they set forth under their authority. (Cp. also Esther iii. 12, viii. 8; Daniel vi. 17). The Hebrew mode of sealing seems to have been by attaching a lump of clay to the document, and impressing the seal thereupon (Job xxxviii. 14).

his city] i.e. Jezreel (*v.* 1). The mode in which it is spoken of here, and in *v.* 11, seems to imply that it was not the city from which Jezebel wrote. The court was evidently at this time residing at Samaria (xx. 43); and Ahab may either have met Naboth there, or have gone down (cp. *v.* 16) to Jezreel to make his request, and then, on being refused, have returned to Samaria. The distance is not more than seven miles.

9. The object of this fast was at once to raise a prejudice against Naboth, who was assumed by the elders to have disgraced the

town; and at the same time to give an air of religion to the proceedings, which might blind persons to their real injustice.

set Naboth on high among his people] This was not an order to do Naboth any, even apparent, honour; but simply a command to bring him forward before a court or assembly, where he might be seen by all, tried, and condemned.

10. *sons of Belial*] i.e. "worthless persons" (Deut. xiii. 13 note). Witnesses must be two in number according to the Law (Num. xxxv. 30; Deut. xvii. 6, xix. 15).

The word rendered "blaspheme" is that which commonly means "bless." The opposite sense of "cursing," seems, however, to be required here and in Job i. 5, 11, ii. 5. Perhaps the best explanation of the bad sense of the original word is to be found in the practice of blessing by way of salutation, not only on meeting, but also on taking leave (Gen. xlvii. 7, 10). From the latter custom the word came to mean "bidding farewell to," and so "renouncing," "casting off," "cursing."

carry him out and stone him] Naboth's offence would be twofold, and in both cases capital; blasphemy against God being punishable with death by the Law (marg. ref.), and blasphemy against the king being a capital offence by custom (ii. 8; 2 Sam. xvi. 9, xix. 21). The punishment would be stoning, since the greater crime would absorb the lesser, and the Law made stoning the punishment for blasphemy against God. As stoning always took place outside the city (see Acts vii. 58), Jezebel told the elders to "carry Naboth out."

11. The ready submission of the elders and nobles implies a deep moral degradation among the Israelites, the fruit of their lapse into idolatry.

13 a fast, and set Naboth on high among the people. And there came in two men, children of Belial, and sat before him : and the men of Belial witnessed against him, *even* against Naboth, in the presence of the people, saying, Naboth did blaspheme God

f See 2 Kin. 9. 26.

and the king. *f*Then they carried him forth out of the city, and 14 stoned him with stones, that he died. Then they sent to Jezebel, 15 saying, Naboth is stoned, and is dead. ¶And it came to pass, when Jezebel heard that Naboth was stoned, and was dead, that Jezebel said to Ahab, Arise, take possession of the vineyard of Naboth the Jezreelite, which he refused to give thee for money : 16 for Naboth is not alive, but dead. And it came to pass, when Ahab heard that Naboth was dead, that Ahab rose up to go down to the vineyard of Naboth the Jezreelite, to take possession of it.

g Ps. 9. 12.
h ch. 13. 32.
2 Chr. 22. 9.

17 ¶*g*And the word of the LORD came to Elijah the Tishbite, say-18 ing, Arise, go down to meet Ahab king of Israel, *h*which *is* in Samaria : behold, *he is* in the vineyard of Naboth, whither he is 19 gone down to possess it. And thou shalt speak unto him, saying, Thus saith the LORD, Hast thou killed, and also taken possession ? And thou shalt speak unto him, saying, Thus saith the

i ch. 22. 38.

LORD, *i*In the place where dogs licked the blood of Naboth shall 20 dogs lick thy blood, even thine. ¶And Ahab said to Elijah,

k ch. 18. 17.
l 2 Kin. 17. 17.
Rom. 7. 14.
m ch. 14. 10.
2 Kin. 9. 8.
n 1 Sam. 25. 22.
o ch. 14. 10.
p ch. 15. 29.
q ch. 16. 3, 11.

*k*Hast thou found me, O mine enemy ? And he answered, I have found *thee :* because *l*thou hast sold thyself to work evil in 21 the sight of the LORD. Behold, *m*I will bring evil upon thee, and will take away thy posterity, and will cut off from Ahab *n*him that pisseth against the wall, and *o*him that is shut up and 22 left in Israel, and will make thine house like the house of *p*Jeroboam the son of Nebat, and like the house of *q*Baasha the son of Ahijah, for the provocation wherewith thou hast provoked

r 2 Kin. 9. 36.

23 *me* to anger, and made Israel to sin. And *r*of Jezebel also spake

---

13. Naboth had sons who were also put to death at this time (marg. ref.). It is not improbable that they were stoned together with their parent (cp. Josh. vii. 24, 25). In the East a parent's guilt constantly involves the punishment of his children. Contrast 2 K. xiv. 6.

16. *to take possession of it*] The goods of traitors appear to have been forfeited to the Crown by the Jewish law as they still are almost universally throughout the East. Cp. 2 Sam. xvi. 4.

19. *Hast thou killed, and also taken possession ?*] These words rebuke especially Ahab's indecent haste. He went to Jezreel the very day after Naboth's execution (2 K. ix. 26).

The prophecy following had a double fulfilment. The main fulfilment was by the casting of the dead body of Jehoram into Naboth's plot of ground at Jezreel, where, like Naboth's, it was left for the dogs to eat (2 K. ix. 25). This spot, which was just outside the city-wall, and close to a gate (do. *v.* 31), was probably the actual scene of Naboth's execution. Here did dogs lick Ahab's blood, that is, his son's blood, the execution of the full retaliatory sentence having been deferred to the days of his son, formally and explicitly, on Ahab's repentance (*v.* 29). But, besides this, there was a

secondary fulfilment of the prophecy, when, not at Jezreel but at Samaria (marg. ref.), the actual blood of Ahab himself, was licked by dogs, only in a way that implied no disgrace. These two fulfilments are complementary to each other.

20. The words "O mine enemy," may refer partly to the old antagonism (marg. ref. ; xvii. 1, xix. 2, 3) ; but the feeling which it expresses is rather that of present opposition—the opposition between good and evil, light and darkness (John iii. 20.)

thou hast sold thyself to work evil] Cp. marg. reff. The metaphor is taken from the practice of men's selling themselves into slavery, and so giving themselves wholly up to work the will of their master. This was a wide-spread custom in the ancient world.

21. The Prophet changes, without warning, from speaking in his own person to speaking in the person of God. The transition is abrupt, probably because the compiler follows his materials closely, compressing by omission. One fragment omitted here is preserved in 2 K. ix. 26.

23. *And of Jezebel also spake the LORD, saying*] These are not the words of Elijah, but of the writer, who notes a special prophecy against Jezebel, whose guilt was at least equal to her husband's.

the LORD, saying, The dogs shall eat Jezebel by the [1] wall of
24 Jezreel. [s] Him that dieth of Ahab in the city the dogs shall eat; [s] ch. 14. 11.
and him that dieth in the field shall the fowls of the air eat. & 16. 4.
25 ¶ But [t] there was none like unto Ahab, which did sell himself to [t] ch. 16. 30,
work wickedness in the sight of the LORD, [u] whom Jezebel his &c.
26 wife [2] stirred up. And he did very abominably in following [u] ch. 16. 31.
idols, according to all *things* [x] as did the Amorites, whom the [x] 2 Kin. 21.
27 LORD cast out before the children of Israel. ¶ And it came to 11.
pass, when Ahab heard those words, that he rent his clothes,
and [y] put sackcloth upon his flesh, and fasted, and lay in sack- [y] Gen. 37.34,
28 cloth, and went softly. And the word of the LORD came to
29 Elijah the Tishbite, saying, Seest thou how Ahab humbleth
himself before me? because he humbleth himself before me,
I will not bring the evil in his days: *but* [z] in his son's days will [z] 2 Kin. 9.25.
I bring the evil upon his house.
CHAP. 22. AND they continued three years without war between
Syria and Israel. And it came to pass in the third year, that
2 [a] Jehoshaphat the king of Judah came down to the king of Israel. [a] 2 Chr. 18.
2, &c.

[1] Or, *ditch*.   [2] Or, *incited*.

---

wall] The marginal rendering "ditch," is
preferable. There is always in Oriental
towns a space outside the walls which lies
uncultivated, and which is naturally used
for the deposit of refuse of every kind.
Here the dogs prowl, and the kites and
vultures find many a feast.

25. *whom Jezebel stirred up*] The history of
Ahab's reign throughout exhibits him as
completely governed by his imperious wife.
Instances of her influence are seen in *vv.* 7,
15, marg. ref., xviii. 4, xix. 2.

26. The Amorites appear here as representatives of the old Canaanite nations
(Gen. xv. 16 note). It seems to be implied
here that their idolatries were in the main
identical with those of the Phœnicians
which Ahab had adopted.

27. The repentance of Ahab resembles
that of the Ninevites (Jonah iii. 5). It has the
same outward signs—fasting and sackcloth
—and it has much the same inward character. It springs, not from love, nor from
hatred of sin, but from fear of the consequences of sin. It is thus, although sincere
and real while it lasts, shallow and exceedingly short-lived. God, however, to mark
His readiness to receive the sinner who
turns to Him, accepted the imperfect offering
(as He likewise accepted the penitence of
the Ninevites), and allowed it to delay the
execution of the sentence (*v.* 29). So the
penitence of the Ninevites put off the fall of
Nineveh for a century.

and lay in sackcloth] In this particular he
seems to have gone beyond the usual practice. We do not read elsewhere of mourners
passing the night in sackcloth.

and went softly] "As if he had no heart
to go about any business" (Patrick).

29. *the evil*] *i.e.* the main evil. See
v. 19 note; and cp. xxii. 38 with marg.
ref.

XXII. 1. *three years*] These must be
counted from the close of the second campaign of Ben-hadad (xx. 34). They were
not full years, as is evident from the next
verse. Probably the first year is that of
Ben-hadad's dismissal after his defeat; the
second is a year of actual peace; while the
third is that in which Jehoshaphat paid his
visit, and the Ramoth-Gilead expedition
took place. The pause, here noticed, in the
war between Israel and Syria was perhaps
the result of a common danger. It was
probably in the year following Ben-hadad's
dismissal by Ahab, that the first great Assyrian expedition took place into these
parts. Shalmaneser II. relates that on his
first invasion of southern Syria, he was met
by the combined forces of Ben-hadad, Ahab,
the king of Hamath, the kings of the Hittites, and others, who gave him battle, but
suffered a defeat.

2. This visit indicates an entire change
in the relations which we have hitherto
found subsisting between the kingdoms of
Israel and Judah. The common danger to
which the two kingdoms were exposed from
the growing power of Syria had probably
induced them to forget their differences.
Jehoshaphat's eldest son, Jehoram, was
married to Athaliah, the daughter of Ahab;
but apparently the bond between the two
families had not hitherto led to any very
close intimacy, much less to any joint military expeditions. Jehoshaphat seems to
have taken no part in the former Syrian
wars of Ahab, nor did he join in the great
league against the Assyrians (*v.* 1 note).
His visit now was probably one of mere
friendliness, without any political object.
Ahab, however, turned the visit to political
advantage. From this time till the dis-
placement of Ahab's dynasty by Jehu, very
intimate relations subsisted between the

b Deut. 4. 43.	3 And the king of Israel said unto his servants, Know ye that
	*b*Ramoth in Gilead *is* our's, and we *be* ¹still, *and* take it not
	4 out of the hand of the king of Syria? And he said unto Je-
	hoshaphat, Wilt thou go with me to battle to Ramoth-gilead?
2 Kin. 3. 7.	And Jehoshaphat said to the king of Israel, *c*I *am* as thou *art*,
	5 my people as thy people, my horses as thy horses. ¶ And
	Jehoshaphat said unto the king of Israel, Enquire, I pray
	6 thee, at the word of the LORD to day. Then the king of Israel
d ch. 18. 19.	*d*gathered the prophets together, about four hundred men, and
	said unto them, Shall I go against Ramoth-gilead to battle, or
	shall I forbear? And they said, Go up; for the Lord shall
e 2 Kin. 3.11.	7 deliver *it* into the hand of the king. And *e*Jehoshaphat said,
	Is *there* not here a prophet of the LORD besides, that we might
	8 enquire of him? And the king of Israel said unto Jehoshaphat,
	There is yet one man, Micaiah the son of Imlah, by whom we
	may enquire of the LORD: but I hate him; for he doth not
	prophesy good concerning me, but evil. And Jehoshaphat said,
	9 Let not the king say so. ¶ Then the king of Israel called an

¹ Heb. *silent from taking it.*

two kingdoms (xxii. 49; 2 K. iii. 7, viii. 28, 29 ; 2 Chr. xx. 36, &c.).

3. By the terms of Ahab's covenant with Ben-hadad, Ramoth in Gilead ought, long ere this, to have been restored (xx. 34). Hence the claim "*is ours*," *i.e.* "it belongs to us of right though the Syrians still hold possession of it."

4. Ahab, well aware of the military strength of Syria, and feeling that he cannot now expect Divine aid (xx. 42, xxi. 21), asks the aid of Jehoshaphat, whose military resources were very great (2 Chr. xvii. 12-19). Jehoshaphat's answer is one of complete acquiescence, without reserve of any kind (cp. 2 Chr. xviii. 3). Jehoshaphat was afterwards rebuked for thus consenting to "help the ungodly" (2 Chr. xix. 2). He probably acted not merely from complaisance, but from a belief that the interests of his own kingdom would be advanced by the step which he agreed to take. The power of Syria was at this time very menacing.

5. Jehoshaphat, with characteristic piety (*v.* 43) takes advantage of his position as Ahab's friend and ally, to suggest inquiry of the Lord (Jehovah) before the expedition is undertaken. Lest Ahab should consent in word and put off the inquiry in act, he asks to have the Prophets called in at once : "*to-day.*"

6. *the prophets*] *i.e.* In all probability the prophets attached to the worship of the calves; not real Prophets of Jehovah. This seems evident both from Jehoshaphat's dissatisfaction (*v.* 7), and from the strong antagonism apparent between the true Jehovah-Prophet Micaiah, and these self-styled "prophets of the Lord" (*vv.* 22-25).

the Lord shall deliver it] In the Hebrew the word here used for "Lord" is "*Adonai.*" Later (*i.e.* in *vv.* 11, 12) LORD or "Jehovah"

is used. It would seem as if the idolatrous prophets shrank from employing the latter title until they found that Jehoshaphat insisted on learning the will of Jehovah in the matter.

7. Jehoshaphat was dissatisfied. These men—creatures of Ahab, tainted with the worship of calves if not with Baal-worship —had promised victory, but not in the name of Jehovah. Jehoshaphat, therefore, asked, "Is there not here a true Prophet of Jehovah besides these 400 professed prophets?"

8. *There is yet one man, Micaiah*] Elijah, it appears, had withdrawn again after the events of the last chapter, and there was no known Prophet of Jehovah within reach of Samaria except Micaiah.

he doth not prophesy good concerning me but evil] Whether the tradition in xx. 41 note be true or not, it is certain that Ahab had imprisoned him (*v.* 26), and probable that the imprisonment was on account of threatening prophecies. Ahab suggests to Jehoshaphat that Micaiah is one who allows his private feelings to determine the utterances which he delivers as if from Jehovah. Hence the force of Jehoshaphat's answer, "Let not the king say so ;" *i.e.* "Let not the king suppose that a Prophet would be guilty of such impiety,"—an impiety from which even Balaam shrank (Num. xxii. 18).

9. *an officer*] More properly, as in the margin, "a eunuch." Eunuchs seem to have been first introduced among the Israelites by David (1 Chr. xxviii. 1 note). They were a natural accompaniment of the seraglio of Solomon. The present passage is the first which shows that, after the separation of the kingdom, the kings of Israel employed them (cp. 2 K. viii. 6, ix. 32).

10 ¹officer, and said, Hasten *hither* Micaiah the son of Imlah. And
the king of Israel and Jehoshaphat the king of Judah sat
each on his throne, having put on their robes, in a ²void
place in the entrance of the gate of Samaria; and all the
11 prophets prophesied before them. And Zedekiah the son of
Chenaanah made him horns of iron: and he said, Thus saith
the LORD, With these shalt thou push the Syrians, until
12 thou have consumed them. And all the prophets prophesied
so, saying, Go up to Ramoth-gilead, and prosper: for the
13 LORD shall deliver *it* into the king's hand. ¶And the messenger that was gone to call Micaiah spake unto him, saying,
Behold now, the words of the prophets *declare* good unto the
king with one mouth: let thy word, I pray thee, be like the
14 word of one of them, and speak *that which is* good. And
Micaiah said, *As* the LORD liveth, *ᶠ*what the LORD saith unto   *ᶠ*Num.22.38.
15 me, that will I speak. So he came to the king. And the king
said unto him, Micaiah, shall we go against Ramoth-gilead to
battle, or shall we forbear? And he answered him, Go, and
prosper: for the LORD shall deliver *it* into the hand of the king.
16 And the king said unto him, How many times shall I adjure
thee that thou tell me nothing but *that which is* true in the name
17 of the LORD? And he said, I saw all Israel *ᵍ*scattered upon   *ᵍ* Matt. 9. 36.
the hills, as sheep that have not a shepherd: and the LORD said,
These have no master: let them return every man to his house
18 in peace. ¶And the king of Israel said unto Jehoshaphat, Did

<hr>

¹ Or, *eunuch*.   ² Heb. *floor*.

<hr>

10. *sat each on his throne*] Or, "were
sitting." They had removed from the banquet (2 Chr. xviii. 2) to the *void place*, or
empty space *at* the entrance of the gate
(Ruth iv. 1; 2 Sam. xv. 2), where Ahab
daily sat to hear complaints and decide
causes. Each was seated upon his throne,
the Oriental kings having portable thrones,
which they took with them upon their
journeys.

11. *horns of iron*] The horn in Scripture
is the favourite symbol of power; and
pushing with the horn is a common metaphor for attacking and conquering enemies
(see Deut. xxxiii. 17. Cp. Ps. xlv. 5; Dan.
viii. 4). Zedekiah, in employing a symbolical action, was following the example of a
former Israelite Prophet (xi. 30).

thus saith the LORD] Or, Jehovah. Zedekiah lays aside the unmeaning "lord"
(*adonai*) of the general company of Israelite
prophets (*v.* 6), and professes to have a
direct message from Jehovah to Ahab. He
may have believed his own words; for the
"lying spirit" (*v.* 22) may have seemed to
him a messenger from Jehovah. All the
rest followed his example (*v.* 12).

13. *And the messenger spake unto him*, &c.]
There seems to have been a wide-spread notion among the irreligious and the half-reli-
gious of the ancient world, that their prophets
were not the mere mouth-pieces of the god,
but that they were persons who had power
with the god, and could compel, or at least
induce, Him to work their will (cp. Num.

xxiv. 10; Is. xxx. 10). They saw that the
prophet's word was accomplished; they did
not understand that if he falsified his message
the accomplishment would no longer follow.

14. Micaiah, as a true Prophet of Jehovah, of course rejected the counsel offered
him, which he felt to be at once wicked
and foolish. Cp. also the resolution of Balaam, marg. ref.

15. *And he answered him*, &c.] Micaiah
speaks the exact words of the 400 in so
mocking and ironical a tone, that the king
cannot mistake his meaning, or regard his
answer as serious. The king's rejoinder implies that this mocking manner was familiar
to Micaiah, who had used it in some former
dealings with the Israelite monarch. Hence,
in part, the king's strong feeling of dislike
(cp. *v.* 8).

17. Thus adjured, Micaiah wholly changes
his tone. Ahab cannot possibly mistake
the meaning of his vision, especially as the
metaphor of "sheep and shepherd" for king
and people was familiar to the Israelites
from the prayer of Moses (Num. xxvii. 17).

18. See *v.* 8. Ahab implies that he believes Micaiah to have spoken out of pure
malevolence, without any authority for his
prediction from God. By implication he
invites Jehoshaphat to disregard this pseudo-
prophecy, and to put his trust in the unanimous declaration of the 400. Micaiah,
therefore, proceeds to explain the contradiction between himself and the 400, by re-
counting another vision.

I not tell thee that he would prophesy no good concerning me,
19 but evil? ¶And he said, Hear thou therefore the word of the
LORD: [h]I saw the LORD sitting on his throne, [i]and all the host
of heaven standing by him on his right hand and on his left.
20 And the LORD said, Who shall [1]persuade Ahab, that he may go
up and fall at Ramoth-gilead? And one said on this manner,
21 and another said on that manner. And there came forth a
spirit, and stood before the LORD, and said, I will persuade him.
22 And the LORD said unto him, Wherewith? And he said, I will
go forth, and I will be a lying spirit in the mouth of all his prophets. And he said, [k]Thou shalt persuade *him*, and prevail
23 also: go forth, and do so. [l]Now therefore, behold, the LORD
hath put a lying spirit in the mouth of all these thy prophets,
24 and the LORD hath spoken evil concerning thee. ¶But Zedekiah the son of Chenaanah went near, and smote Micaiah on the
cheek, and said, [m]Which way went the Spirit of the LORD from
25 me to speak unto thee? And Micaiah said, Behold, thou shalt
see in that day, when thou shalt go [2]into [3]an inner chamber
26 to hide thyself. ¶And the king of Israel said, Take Micaiah, and
carry him back unto Amon the governor of the city, and to

[h] Isai. 6. 1
Dan. 7. 9.
[i] Job 1. 6.
& 2. 1.
Dan. 7. 10.
Zech. 1. 10.
Matt. 18. 10.
Heb. 1. 7.

[k] Judg. 9. 23.
Job 12. 16.
Ezek. 14. 9.
2 Thes. 2. 11.
[l] Ezek. 14. 9.

[m] 2 Chr. 18.
23.

[1] Or, *deceive*.
[2] Or, *from chamber to chamber*.
[3] Heb. *a chamber in a chamber*, ch. 20. 30.

---

19. David's Psalms had familiarised the Israelites with Jehovah sitting upon a throne in the heavens (Ps. ix. 7, xi. 4, xlv. 6, ciii. 19, &c.); but to be allowed to see in vision the ineffable glory of the Almighty thus seated, was a rare favour. It was granted to Isaiah, to Daniel (marg. reff.), to Ezekiel (Ez. i. 26), and in Christian times to St. Stephen (Acts vii. 56), and St. John (Rev. iv. 2).

21. *a spirit*] "**The** spirit"—which some explain as "the evil spirit"—*i. e.* Satan; others as simply "the spirit" who should "persuade."

22. The difficulties which attach to this passage are considerable. On the one hand, it is hard to suppose one of the holy Angels a "lying spirit;" on the other, hard to find Satan, or an evil spirit, included among "the host of heaven" (*v.* 19) and acting as the minister of God. Still, Job i. 6, ii. 1 lend countenance to the latter point, and 2 Thess. ii. 11 to the former. But it may be doubted whether we ought to take literally, and seek to interpret exactly, each state-ment of the present narrative. Visions of the invisible world can only be a sort of parables; revelations, not of the truth as it actually is, but of so much of the truth as can be shown through such a medium. The details of a vision, therefore, cannot safely be pressed, any more than the details of a parable. Portions of each must be accom-modations to human modes of thought, and may very inadequately express the realities which they are employed to shadow forth to us.

24. *smote Micaiah on the cheek*] As Mi-caiah had been brought from prison (*v.* 26), it is probable that his hands were bound.

The Prophet, thus standing before the great ones of the earth, bound and helpless, bear-ing testimony to the truth, and for his testi-mony smitten on the face by an underling, whose blow he receives without either shame or anger, is a notable type of our Lord before Caiaphas suffering the same indignity.

Which way &c.] Zedekiah's meaning may perhaps be expounded as follows: "The Spirit of Jehovah *certainly* came to me, and inspired me with the answer which I gave. If He afterwards went to thee, as thou sayest that He did, perhaps thou canst tell us—as all the secrets of the invisible world are, thou pretendest, open to thee—which way He took."

25. Micaiah addresses himself not so much to Zedekiah's question, as to the main point which lies in dispute—which of them, namely, is a true Prophet. "When the news, *i.e.*, of Ahab's death, caused by his follow-ing thy counsels, reaches Samaria, and thou hast to hide thyself from the vengeance of Ahaziah or Jezebel, then, in that day, thou wilt know whether I or thou be the true Prophet."

26. *carry him back*] Lit. "cause him to *return*." Micaiah had been in custody before, and was brought by Ahab's mes-senger from his prison.

the governor of the city] This is one out of several notices respecting what may be called the "constitution" of the Israelite kingdom. The king consulted on important matters a Council of elders (xx. 7, 8). The general administration was carried on by means of the governors of provinces (xx. 14) and of cities (2 K. x. 5). The governors of cities, like the monarch, were assisted and checked by councils of elders, the wise

27 Joash the king's son: and say, Thus saith the king, Put this *fellow* in the prison, and feed him with bread of affliction and
28 with water of affliction, until I come in peace. And Micaiah said, If thou return at all in peace, [n]the LORD hath not spoken by me. And he said, Hearken, O people, every one of you.
29 ¶ So the king of Israel and Jehoshaphat the king of Judah went
30 up to Ramoth-gilead. And the king of Israel said unto Jehoshaphat, [1]I will disguise myself, and enter into the battle; but put thou on thy robes. And the king of Israel [o]disguised himself,
31 and went into the battle. But the king of Syria commanded his thirty and two captains that had rule over his chariots, saying, Fight neither with small nor great, save only with the king
32 of Israel. And it came to pass, when the captains of the chariots saw Jehoshaphat, that they said, Surely it *is* the king of Israel. And they turned aside to fight against him: and Je-
33 hoshaphat [p]cried out. And it came to pass, when the captains of the chariots perceived that it *was* not the king of Israel, that
34 they turned back from pursuing him. And a *certain* man drew a bow [2]at a venture, and smote the king of Israel between the [3]joints of the harness: wherefore he said unto the driver of his chariot, Turn thine hand, and carry me out of the host; for I
35 am [4]wounded. And the battle [5]increased that day: and the

[n] Num. 16. 29. Deut. 18. 20, 21, 22.	
[o] 2Chr.35.22.	
[p] 2 Chr. 18. 31. Prov. 13.20.	

[1] Or, *when he was to disguise himself, and enter into the battle.*

[2] Heb. *in his simplicity,* 2 Sam. 15. 11.

[3] Heb. *joints and the breast-plate.*

[4] Heb. *made sick.*

[5] Heb. *ascended.*

---

men of the several towns (xxi. 8–12; 2 K. x. 5). Thus Samaria, as we see from the present passage, was under a special governor, who, among his other duties, had the control of the public prison, and directed the treatment of the prisoners.

the king's son] The phrase seems to designate a state office, rather than relationship to the sovereign. Cp. 2 Chr. xxviii. 7.

27. *Feed him with bread of affliction,* &c.] Micaiah is to be once more put in prison, but, in order to punish him for his uncomplying spirit, upon a poorer and scantier diet than he had been previously allowed. This is to continue until Ahab returns *in peace.* Ahab introduces this expression purposely, in order to show his entire disbelief of Micaiah's prophecy.

29. It might have been expected that Jehoshaphat would have withdrawn from the expedition when he heard Micaiah denounce it. He had, however, rashly committed himself to take part in the war by a solemn promise, *before* he bethought himself of inquiring what was the will of God in the matter. Now he was ashamed to draw back, especially as Ahab, whom the prophecy chiefly threatened, was resolved to brave it. He may also have had a personal affection for Ahab, and so have been loth to desert him in his need. Cp. 2 Chr. xix. 2.

30. *I will disguise myself*] Ahab had probably heard of Ben-hadad's order to his captains (*v.* 31).

31. *commanded*] "Had commanded." Ben-hadad delivers his order in the hyper-

bolical style common in the East. His meaning is, "Make it your *chief* object to kill or take the king of Israel." Apparently, his own defeat and captivity were still rankling in his mind, and he wished to retaliate on Ahab the humiliation which he considered himself to have suffered. He shows small appreciation of the generosity which had spared his life and restored him to his kingdom.

32. *Surely it is the king of Israel*] This was a natural supposition, as Jehoshaphat alone wore royal robes.

and Jehoshaphat cried out] Jehoshaphat called to his men for help, using perhaps his own peculiar battle-cry, which would be distinct from that of Ahab, and would probably be known to the Syrians.

34. *at a venture*] Lit. as in margin, *i.e.* without intent to kill the king.

between the joints of the harness] Lit. as in the margin. The "joints" were probably pieces of armour which attached the breastplate to the helmet or to the greaves. The arrow entered between the breastplate and one of these "joints." Breastplates made of metal scales were common both in Egypt and Assyria.

Turn thine hand] Lit. "turn thy *hands.*" The driver of a chariot, both in Egypt and Assyria, held the reins with his two hands.

35. *the battle increased*] See margin; *i.e.* the tide of battle rose higher. Cp. Is. viii. 7, 8.

king was stayed up in his chariot against the Syrians, and died
at even : and the blood ran out of the wound into the ¹midst of
36 the chariot. And there went a proclamation throughout the
host about the going down of the sun, saying,. Every man to
37 his city, and every man to his own country. So the king died,
and ²was brought to Samaria ; and they buried the king in
38 Samaria. And *one* washed the chariot in the pool of Samaria ;
and the dogs licked up his blood ; and they washed his armour ;

q ch. 21. 19.   39 according *q*unto the word of the LORD which he spake. ¶Now
r Amos 3. 15.   the rest of the acts of Ahab, and all that he did, and *r*the ivory
house which he made, and all the cities that he built, *are* they
not written in the book of the chronicles of the kings of Israel ?
40 So Ahab slept with his fathers ; and Ahaziah his son reigned in

s 2 Chr. 20. 31.   41 his stead. ¶And *s*Jehoshaphat the son of Asa began to reign
42 over Judah in the fourth year of Ahab king of Israel. Jehoshaphat *was* thirty and five years old when he began to reign ;
and he reigned twenty and five years in Jerusalem. And his

t 2 Chr. 17. 3.   43 mother's name *was* Azubah the daughter of Shilhi. And *t*he
walked in all the ways of Asa his father ; he turned not aside
from it, doing *that which was* right in the eyes of the LORD :

u ch. 14. 23.
& 15. 14.
2 Kin. 12. 3.   nevertheless *u*the high places were not taken away ; *for* the
people offered and burnt incense yet in the high places. And

x 2 Chr. 19. 2.
2 Cor. 6. 14.   44 *x*Jehoshaphat made peace with the king of Israel. ¶ Now the

¹ Heb. *bosom.*   ² Heb. *came.*

---

the king was stayed up in his chariot] The
king's wound made it impossible for him to
remain standing without help ; he therefore
had himself supported in his chariot by
attendants, in order that his soldiers might
not lose heart, as they would be sure to do,
if they knew of his peril. Ahab must not
be denied the credit of right princely forti-
tude on this occasion.

the midst of the chariot] Lit., as in margin.
The " bosom " of the chariot is the rounded
front, with the portion of the standing
board that adjoined it. Here the blood
would naturally collect, forming a pool, in
which the king and his charioteer must
have stood.

36. *about the going down of the sun*] *i.e.*
as soon as Ahab was dead. The abandon-
ment of the expedition and dispersion of
the army on the death of the king is thoroughly Oriental.

The LXX. version reads *vv.* 36, 37,
" Every man to his city, and every man to
his own country ; for the king is dead : And
they came to Samaria," &c.

38. *they washed his armour*] Rather,
" **the harlots bathed in it.**" The " pool of
Samaria," which was stained with Ahab's
blood by the washing of his chariot in it,
was, according to Josephus, the usual bath-
ing-place of the Samaritan harlots. A large
tank or reservoir, probably identical with
this pool, still remains on the slope of the
hill of Samaria, immediately outside the
walls.

39. *the ivory house*] So called from the
character of its ornamentation. Ivory was

largely used in the ancient world as a covering of wood-work, and seems to have been
applied, not only to furniture, but to the
doors and walls of houses.

Nothing is known of the cities built by
Ahab ; but the fact is important as indicating the general prosperity of the country
in his time, and his own activity as a ruler.
Prosperity, it is plain, may for a while co-
exist with causes—such as, the decay of religion—which are sapping the vital power of
a nation, and leading it surely, if slowly, to
destruction.

the book of the chronicles, &c.] See above,
xiv. 19, xv. 31, xvi. 5, 14, 20, 27.

41. The writer returns to the history of
the kingdom of Judah (connect this verse
with xv. 24), sketching briefly a reign much
more fully given by the writer of Chronicles
(2 Chr. xvii.-xx). Cp. also the marg.
reff.

43. On the general piety of Asa, see
above, xv. 11-15 and reff. Jehoshaphat seems
to have been a still better king ; for he did
not, like Asa, fall away in his old age (2
Chr. xvi. 2-12).

the high places were not taken away] This
seems to contradict 2 Chr. xvii. 6. Probably the writer of Chronicles refers to the
desire and intention of the monarch, while
the author of Kings records the practical
failure of his efforts.

44. This refers probably to an early
period in Jehoshaphat's reign—about his
eighth or his ninth year—when he closed
the long series of wars between the two
kingdoms by a formal peace, perhaps at

45 rest of the acts of Jehoshaphat, and his might that he shewed,
and how he warred, *are* they not written in the book of the
46 chronicles of the kings of Judah? *y*And the remnant of the
sodomites, which remained in the days of his father Asa, he took
47 out of the land. *z*There was then no king in Edom: a deputy
48 *was* king.   ¶ *a*Jehoshaphat [1]*b*made ships of Tharshish to go to
Ophir for gold: *c*but they went not; for the ships were broken
49 at *d*Ezion-geber.   Then said Ahaziah the son of Ahab unto Jehoshaphat, Let my servants go with thy servants in the ships.
50 But Jehoshaphat would not.   ¶ And *e*Jehoshaphat slept with his
fathers, and was buried with his fathers in the city of David his
51 father: and Jehoram his son reigned in his stead.   ¶ *f*Ahaziah
the son of Ahab began to reign over Israel in Samaria the seventeenth year of Jehoshaphat king of Judah, and reigned two years
52 over Israel.   And he did evil in the sight of the LORD, and
*g*walked in the way of his father, and in the way of his mother,
and in the way of Jeroboam the son of Nebat, who made Israel
53 to sin: for *h*he served Baal, and worshipped him, and provoked to anger the LORD God of Israel, according to all that his
father had done.

[1] Or, had *ten ships*.

y ch. 14. 24.
& 15. 12.
z Gen. 25. 23.
2 Sam. 8. 14.
a 2 Chr. 20.
35, &c.
b ch. 10. 22.
c 2Chr.20.37.
d ch. 9. 26.
e 2 Chr. 21.1.

f ver. 40.

g ch. 15. 26.

h Judg.2.11.
ch. 16. 31.

---

once cemented by a marriage between Jehoram and Athaliah (*v.* 2 note).

45. *the book of the chronicles*, &c.] Cp.
v. 39 note. The biographer of Jehoshaphat
appears to have been Jehu, the son of
Hanani (2 Chr. xx. 34).

46. See marg. reff. notes.

47. In the time of Solomon, Hadad (xi.
14), according to the LXX., "reigned over
Edom." It appears by the present passage
that the country had been again reduced,
either by Jehoshaphat, or by an earlier
king, and was dependent on the kingdom
of Judah, being governed by a "deputy"
or viceroy, who, however, was allowed the
royal title (cp. 2 K. iii. 9, 12, 26). This
government of dependencies by means of
subject kings was the all but universal
practice in the East down to the time of
Cyrus (iv. 21 note).

48. The expression, "ships of Tharshish,"
probably designates ships of a particular
class, ships (*i.e.*) like those with which the
Phœnicians used to trade to Tharshish (Tartessus, x. 22 note). Cp. the use of "India-
man" for a vessel of a certain class. Jehoshaphat's fleet was constructed at Ezion-
Gaber, on the Red Sea (2 Chr. xx. 36),
where Solomon had previously built a navy
(ix. 26). Being lord-paramount of Edom,

Jehoshaphat had the right of using this
harbour.

49. 2 Chr. xx. 35, 36, explains that the
two kings conjointly built the fleet with
which the Ophir trade (ix. 28 note) was to
be reopened. Ahaziah had thus an interest
in the ships; and when they were wrecked,
attributing, as it would seem, the calamity
to the unskilfulness of his ally's mariners,
he proposed that the fleet should be manned
in part by Israelite sailors—men probably
accustomed to the sea, perhaps trained at
Tyre. This proposal Jehoshaphat refused,
either offended at the reflection on his subjects' skill, or accepting the wreck of the
ships, which Jehoshaphat had prophesied, as a
proof that God was against the entire undertaking.

51. *two years*] According to our reckoning, not much more than a twelvemonth.

52. *in the way of his mother*] In this
phrase, which does not occur anywhere
else, we see the strong feeling of the writer
as to the influence of Jezebel (cp. xvi. 31).

51-53. It would be of advantage if these
verses were transferred to the Second Book
of Kings, which would thus open with the
commencement of Ahaziah's reign. The
division of the Books does not proceed from
the author. See "Introd.," ɔ. 263.

THE SECOND BOOK

OF THE

KINGS,

COMMONLY CALLED, THE FOURTH BOOK OF THE KINGS.

a 2 Sam. 8. 2.
b ch. 3. 5.

CHAP. 1. THEN Moab *a*rebelled against Israel *b*after the death of
2 Ahab. And Ahaziah fell down through a lattice in his upper
chamber that *was* in Samaria, and was sick: and he sent messengers, and said unto them, Go, enquire of Baal-zebub the god

c Josh. 13. 3.

3 of *c*Ekron whether I shall recover of this disease. But the angel
of the LORD said to Elijah the Tishbite, Arise, go up to meet the
messengers of the king of Samaria, and say unto them, *Is it* not
because *there is* not a God in Israel, *that* ye go to enquire of
4 Baal-zebub the god of Ekron? Now therefore thus saith the
LORD, ¹Thou shalt not come down from that bed on which thou
5 art gone up, but shalt surely die. And Elijah departed. ¶ And
when the messengers turned back unto him, he said unto them,
6 Why are ye now turned back? And they said unto him, There
came a man up to meet us, and said unto us, Go, turn again
unto the king that sent you, and say unto him, Thus saith the
LORD, *Is it* not because *there is* not a God in Israel, *that* thou
sendest to enquire of Baal-zebub the god of Ekron? therefore
thou shalt not come down from that bed on which thou art gone
7 up, but shalt surely die. And he said unto them, ²What manner
of man *was he* which came up to meet you, and told you these

d See Zech.
13. 4.
Matt. 3. 4.

8 words? And they answered him, He *was* *d*an hairy man, and
girt with a girdle of leather about his loins. And he said, It *is*

---

¹ Heb. *The bed whither thou art gone up,*
thou shalt not come down from it.

² Heb. *What* was *the manner*
of the man.

I. 1. The Moabites, who had once lorded
over Israel (Judg. iii. 12–14), were reduced
to subjection by David, and treated with
extreme severity (marg. ref.). In the time
of Ahab they were dependent on the kingdom of Israel, to which it has been generally supposed that they fell at the
separation of Israel from Judah. The
Moabite monument (see iii. 4), discovered
in 1869, has now given reason to believe
that they then recovered their independence, but were again reduced by Omri,
who, with his son Ahab, is said (in round
numbers) to have "oppressed" them for
"forty years." Ahab's death was seized
upon as an occasion for revolt, and Moab
(perhaps owing to Ahaziah's sickness) easily
regained her independence.

2. *a lattice*] The "upper chamber" had
probably a single latticed window, through
which Ahaziah fell. Windows in the East
are to this day generally closed by lattices
of interlaced wood, which open outwards;
so that, if the fastening is not properly
secured, one who leans against them may
easily fall out.

Baal-zebub] Lit. "Lord (*i.e.*, averter) of

flies." Flies in the East constitute one of
the most terrible of plagues (Ps. cv. 31;
Ex. viii. 24); and Orientals would be as
likely to have a "god of flies" as a god of
storm and thunder. To enquire (*v.* 3) of
Baal-zebub was practically to deny Jehovah. Ahaziah cast aside the last remnant
of respect for the old religion, and consulted a foreign oracle, as if the voice
of God were wholly silent in his own
country.

For Ekron see marg. ref.

4. *therefore*, &c.] As a punishment for
this insult to Jehovah.

8. *an hairy man*] Either in allusion to his
shaggy cloak of untanned skin; or, more
probably, an expression descriptive of the
prophet's person, of his long flowing locks,
abundant beard, and general profusion of
hair. His costume was that of a thorough
ascetic. Generally the Jews wore girdles
of linen or cotton stuff, soft and comfortable. Under the girdle they wore one or
two long linen gowns or shirts, and over
these they had sometimes a large shawl.
Elijah had only his leathern girdle and his
sheepskin cape or "mantle."

9 Elijah the Tishbite.   ¶ Then the king sent unto him a captain of
  fifty with his fifty.   And he went up to him: and, behold, he
  sat on the top of an hill.   And he spake unto him, Thou man of
10 God, the king hath said, Come down.   And Elijah answered and
  said to the captain of fifty, If I *be* a man of God, then *e*let fire   *e* Luke 9. 51.
  come down from heaven, and consume thee and thy fifty.   And
  there came down fire from heaven, and consumed him and his
11 fifty.   Again also he sent unto him another captain of fifty with
  his fifty.   And he answered and said unto him, O man of God,
12 thus hath the king said, Come down quickly.   And Elijah
  answered and said unto them, If I *be* a man of God, let fire come
  down from heaven, and consume thee and thy fifty.   And the
  fire of God came down from heaven, and consumed him and his
13 fifty.   And he sent again a captain of the third fifty with his
  fifty.   And the third captain of fifty went up, and came and
  ¹fell on his knees before Elijah, and besought him, and said unto
  him, O man of God, I pray thee, let my life, and the life of these
14 fifty thy servants, *f*be precious in thy sight.   Behold, there came   *f* 1 Sam. 26.
  fire down from heaven, and burnt up the two captains of the   21.
  former fifties with their fifties: therefore let my life now be   Ps. 72. 14.
15 precious in thy sight.   And the angel of the LORD said unto
  Elijah, Go down with him: be not afraid of him.   And he arose,
16 and went down with him unto the king.   ¶ And he said unto
  him, Thus saith the LORD, Forasmuch as thou hast sent messengers to enquire of Baal-zebub the god of Ekron, *is it* not
  because *there is* no God in Israel to enquire of his word ? therefore thou shalt not come down off that bed on which thou art
17 gone up, but shalt surely die.   ¶ So he died according to the
  word of the LORD which Elijah had spoken.   And ²Jehoram
  reigned in his stead in the second year of Jehoram the son of
18 Jehoshaphat king of Judah; because he had no son.   Now the
  rest of the acts of Ahaziah which he did, *are* they not written in
  the book of the chronicles of the kings of Israel?

¹ Heb. *bowed*.   was *Prorex*, and the eighteenth of
² The second year that *Jehoram*   *Jehoshaphat*, ch. 3. 1.

---

9. *Then the king sent unto him*] *i.e.*, in
order to seize and punish him. Cp. 1 K.
xviii. 10, xxii. 27.
10. The charge of cruelty made against
Elijah makes it needful to consider the
question : What was Elijah's motive ?
And the answer is :—Simply to make a
signal example, to vindicate God's honour
in a striking way. Ahaziah had, as it
were, challenged Jehovah to a trial of
strength by sending a band of fifty to arrest one man. Elijah was not Jesus Christ,
able to reconcile mercy with truth, the
vindication of God's honour with the utmost tenderness for erring men, and awe
them merely by His Presence (cp. John
xviii. 6). In Elijah the spirit of the Law
was embodied in its full severity. His zeal
was fierce ; he was not shocked by blood ;
he had no softness and no relenting. He
did not permanently profit by the warning
at Horeb (1 K. xix. 12 note). He continued
the uncompromising avenger of sin, the
wielder of the terrors of the Lord, such

exactly as he had shown himself at Carmel. He is, consequently, no pattern for
Christian men (Luke. ix. 55) ; but his
character is the perfection of the purely legal
type. No true Christian after Pentecost
would have done what Elijah did. But
what he did, when he did it, was not sinful.
It was but executing strict, stern justice.
Elijah asked that fire should fall — God
made it fall ; and, by so doing, both vindicated His own honour, and justified th
prayer of His prophet.
17. The similarity of names in the two
royal houses of Israel and Judah at this
time, and at no other, seems to be the consequence of the close ties which united the
two reigning families, and is well noted
among the " undesigned coincidences " of
the Old Testament. The accession of the
Israelite Jehoram (Ahab's brother) took
place, according to iii. 1, in the eighteenth
year of Jehoshaphat. Jehoram of Judah
perhaps received the royal title from his
father as early as his father's sixteenth year,

a Gen. 5. 24.
b 1Kin.19.21.

c See Ruth
1. 15, 16.

d 1 Sam. 20.
3, 25, 26.
ch. 4. 30.
e 1Kin.20.35.
ver. 5, 7, 15.
ch. 4. 1, 38.
& 9. 1.

f So Ex. 14.
21.
Josh. 3. 16.
ver. 14.

CHAP. 2. AND it came to pass, when the LORD would *a* take up 2 Elijah into heaven by a whirlwind, that Elijah went with *b* Elisha from Gilgal. And Elijah said unto Elisha, *c* Tarry here, I pray thee; for the LORD hath sent me to Beth-el. And Elisha said unto him, *d* As the LORD liveth, and as thy soul liveth, I will not 3 leave thee. So they went down to Beth-el. And *e* the sons of the prophets that *were* at Beth-el came forth to Elisha, and said unto him, Knowest thou that the LORD will take away thy master from thy head to day? And he said, Yea, I know *it*; 4 hold ye your peace. And Elijah said unto him, Elisha, tarry here, I pray thee; for the LORD hath sent me to Jericho. And he said, *As* the LORD liveth, and as thy soul liveth, I will not 5 leave thee. So they came to Jericho. And the sons of the prophets that *were* at Jericho came to Elisha, and said unto him, Knowest thou that the LORD will take away thy master from thy head to day? And he answered, Yea, I know *it*; 6 hold ye your peace. And Elijah said unto him, Tarry, I pray thee, here; for the LORD hath sent me to Jordan. And he said, *As* the LORD liveth, and as thy soul liveth, I will not leave 7 thee. And they two went on. And fifty men of the sons of the prophets went, and stood [1] to view afar off: and they two stood 8 by Jordan. And Elijah took his mantle, and wrapped *it* together, and smote the waters, and *f* they were divided hither and

[1] Heb. *in sight*, or, *over against.*

---

when he was about to join Ahab against the Syrians; the same year might then be called either the eighteenth of Jehoshaphat or the second of Jehoram.

II. **1.** The events of this chapter are related out of their chronological order. Elijah's translation did not take place till after the accession of Jehoram in Judah (2 Chr. xxi. 12), which was not till the fifth year of Jehoram of Israel (viii. 16). The writer of Kings, having concluded his notices of the ministry of Elijah in ch. i., and being about to pass in ch. iii. to the ministry of Elisha, thought it best to insert at this point the final scene of Elijah's life, though it did not occur till several years later.

Gilgal] The modern *Jiljilieh*, on the high-land between Nablous and Beitin (Bethel), about eight and a half miles from the latter, is now commonly supposed to be the Gilgal here mentioned. Some regard it as the ordinary residence of Elisha (iv. 38).

2. *Tarry here*] Elijah's motive in making this request is not clear. Perhaps he thought that so awful and sacred a scene as that which he was led to expect (*v.* 9), should be kept as secret as possible.

the LORD *hath sent me to Bethel*] Elijah may have been directed to Bethel, because of the "School of the Prophets" there, that the sight of him—if not his words—might console and encourage them before they lost him for ever.

as the LORD *liveth*, &c.] This double oath, repeated three times (*vv.* 4, 6), is very re-

markable. The two clauses of it are separately used with some frequency (see Judg. viii. 19; Ruth iii. 13; 1 Sam. i. 26, &c.), but it is comparatively seldom that they are united (see marg. reff.).

3. *came forth to Elisha*] It does not appear that any interchange of speech took place between "the sons of the Prophets" (see marg. ref. note) and Elijah; but independent revelations had been made to the two "schools" at Bethel and Jericho (*v.* 5), and also to Elisha, with respect to Elijah's coming removal.

from thy head] i.e. from his position as teacher and master. The teacher sat on an elevated seat, so that his feet were level with the heads of his pupils (cp. Acts xxii. 3).

hold ye your peace] i.e. "Say nothing—disturb us not. The matter is too sacred for words."

7. *fifty men of the sons of the prophets*] We see by this how large were the prophetical schools. It is implied that the "fifty" were only a *portion* of the school of Jericho. They ascended the abrupt heights behind the town, whence they would command a view of the whole course of the river and of the opposite bank for many miles.

8. *they were divided*, &c.] The attestation to the divine mission of Elijah furnished by this miracle would tend to place him upon a par in the thoughts of men with the two great leaders of the nation named in the marg. reff.

9 thither, so that they two went over on dry ground. ¶ And
it came to pass, when they were gone over, that Elijah said
unto Elisha, Ask what I shall do for thee, before I be taken
away from thee. And Elisha said, I pray thee, let a double
10 portion of thy spirit be upon me. And he said, ¹Thou hast
asked a hard thing : *nevertheless*, if thou see me *when I am* taken
from thee, it shall be so unto thee; but if not, it shall not be *so*.
11 ¶ And it came to pass, as they still went on, and talked, that,
behold, *there appeared* ᵍa chariot of fire, and horses of fire, and
parted them both asunder; and Elijah went up by a whirlwind
12 into heaven. And Elisha saw *it*, and he cried, ʰMy father,
my father, the chariot of Israel, and the horsemen thereof.
And he saw him no more: and he took hold of his own
13 clothes, and rent them in two pieces. He took up also the
mantle of Elijah that fell from him, and went back, and stood
14 by the ²bank of Jordan ; and he took the mantle of Elijah that
fell from him, and smote the waters, and said, Where *is* the
LORD God of Elijah? and when he also had smitten the waters,
15 ⁱthey parted hither and thither: and Elisha went over. ¶ And
when the sons of the prophets which *were* ᵏto view at Jericho
saw him, they said, The spirit of Elijah doth rest on Elisha.
And they came to meet him, and bowed themselves to the
16 ground before him. And they said unto him, Behold now, there
be with thy servants fifty ³strong men; let them go, we pray
thee, and seek thy master: ⁱlest peradventure the Spirit of
the LORD hath taken him up, and cast him upon ⁴some mountain, or into some valley. And he said, Ye shall not send.
17 And when they urged him till he was ashamed, he said, Send.
They sent therefore fifty men ; and they sought three days, but -
18 found him not. And when they came again to him, (for he
tarried at Jericho,) he said unto them, Did I not say unto you,
19 Go not ? ¶ And the men of the city said unto Elisha, Behold, I

ᵍ ch. 6. 17.
Ps. 104. 4.

ʰ ch. 13. 14.

ⁱ ver. 8.
ᵏ ver. 7.

ⁱ See 1 Kin.
18. 12.
Ezek. 8. 3.
Acts 8. 39.

---

¹ Heb. *Thou hast done hard in asking.*   ² Heb. *lip.*   ³ Heb. *sons of strength.*
⁴ Heb. *one of the mountains.*

---

9. *let a double portion of thy spirit be upon me*] Like Solomon, Elisha asks for no worldly advantage, but for spiritual power to discharge his office aright. The "double portion" is that which denotes the proportion of a father's property which was the right of an eldest son (Deut. xxi. 17). Elisha therefore asked for twice as much of Elijah's spirit as should be inherited by any other of the "sons of the Prophets." He simply claimed, *i.e.*, to be acknowledged as Elijah's *firstborn* spiritual son.

10. It would be better to omit the words "when I am," which are not in the original. The sign was to be Elisha's seeing the actual translation, which he did (*v.* 12).

11. *Elijah went up*, &c.] No honest exegesis can explain this passage in any other sense than as teaching the translation of Elijah, who was taken from the earth, like Enoch (Gen. v. 24), without dying. Cp. Ecclus. xlviii. 9.

12. *the chariot of Israel and the horsemen thereof*] These difficult words are probably said of Elijah, whom Elisha addresses as

"the true defence of Israel, better than either the chariots or horsemen" which he saw. Hence his rending his clothes in token of his grief.

14. *Where*, &c.] Some prefer, "Where is the Lord God of Elijah, **even he**? And when he had smitten, &c." Or, according to others, "now when he, &c." Elisha's smiting of the waters seems to have been tentative. He was not sure of its result. Hence the form of his invocation—"Where is the Lord God of Elijah ? Is He here —*i.e.*—with me, or is He not ?" Answered by the event, he appears never subsequently to have doubted.

16. Cp. marg. reff. The words "cast him upon some mountain," rather imply that they expected. to find the Prophet alive.

17. *till he was ashamed*] *i.e.* to refuse them any longer.

19. *the water is naught*] *i.e.* "bad."

and the ground barren] Translate "**and the land apt to miscarry.**" The stream was thought to be the cause of untimely

m See Ex.
15. 25.
ch. 4. 41.
& 6. 6.
John 9. 6.

pray thee, the situation of this city *is* pleasant, as my lord
20 seeth : but the water *is* naught, and the ground ¹barren. And
he said, Bring me a new cruse, and put salt therein. And
21 they brought *it* to him. And he went forth unto the spring
of the waters, and ^mcast the salt in there, and said, Thus
saith the LORD, I have healed these waters; there shall not be
22 from thence any more death or barren *land*. So the waters
were healed unto this day, according to the saying of Elisha
23 which he spake. ¶And he went up from thence unto Beth-el :
and as he was going up by the way, there came forth little
children out of the city, and mocked him, and said unto him,
24 Go up, thou bald head; go up, thou bald head. And he
turned back, and looked on them, and cursed them in the
name of the LORD. And there came forth two she bears out of
25 the wood, and tare forty and two children of them. And he
went from thence to mount Carmel, and from thence he returned
to Samaria.

a ch. 1. 17.

CHAP. 3. NOW ^aJehoram the son of Ahab began to reign over
Israel in Samaria the eighteenth year of Jehoshaphat king of
2 Judah, and reigned twelve years. And he wrought evil in the
sight of the LORD, but not like his father, and like his mother :

b 1 Kin. 16.
31, 32.
c 1 Kin. 12.
28, 31, 32.

for he put away the ²image of Baal ^bthat his father had made.
3 Nevertheless he cleaved unto ^cthe sins of Jeroboam the son of
Nebat, which made Israel to sin ; he departed not therefrom.
4 ¶And Mesha king of Moab was a sheepmaster, and rendered

---

¹ Heb. *causing to miscarry.*   ² Heb. *statue.*

---

births, abortions, and the like, among the
cattle, perhaps also among the people, that
drank of it.
20. The "new cruse" and the "salt" are
evidently chosen from a regard to symbol-
ism. The foul stream represents sin, and to
cleanse it emblems of purity must be taken.
Hence the clean "new" dish previously un-
used, and thus untainted; and the salt, a
common Scriptural symbol of incorruption
(see Lev. ii. 13; Ezek. xliii. 24; Matt. v.
13, &c.).
21. *the spring of the waters*] The spring
intended is probably that now called Ain-
es-Sultan, which is not much more than a
mile from the site of the ancient town. It
is described as a large and beautiful fountain
of sweet and pleasant water. The springs
issuing from the eastern base of the highlands of Judah and Benjamin are to this
day generally brackish.
23. As Beth-el was the chief seat of the
calf-worship (1 K. xii. 32, 33, xiii. 1-32), a
Prophet of Jehovah was not unlikely to
meet with insult there.
by the way] *i.e.* "by the usual road," probably that which winds up the Wady Suweinit, under hills even now retaining some
trees, and in Elisha's time covered with a
dense forest, the haunt of savage animals.
Cp. 1 K. xiii. 24 ; and for the general prevalence of beasts of prey in the country,
both earlier and later than this, see Judg.
xiv. 5 ; 1 Sam. xvii. 34; 2 K. xvii. 25; Am.
v. 19, &c.

24. On this occasion only do we find Elisha a minister of vengeance. Perhaps it
was necessary to show, at the outset of his
career as a Prophet, that he too, so mild and
peaceful could, like Elijah, wield the terrors
of God's judgments (1 K. xix. 19 note). The
persons really punished were, not so much
the children, as the wicked parents (*v.* 23),
whose mouth-pieces the children were, and
who justly lost the gift of offspring of which
they had shown themselves unworthy.
25. *Carmel*] Where Elisha held gatherings
for religious purposes (iv. 23-25) during one
period of his life, if he did not actually reside
there.
III. 1. *in the eighteenth year of Jehoshaphat*] This date agrees exactly with the
statements that Jehoshaphat began to reign
in the fourth year of Ahab (1 K. xxii. 41),
and Ahaziah in the 17th of Jehoshaphat
(do. *v.* 51).
2. On the "evil" wrought by Ahab, see
especially 1 K. xvi. 30-34. Jehoram, warned
by the fate of his brother (i. 4 note), began
his reign by a formal abolition of the Phœnician state religion introduced by Ahab—
even if he connived at its continuance among
the people (x. 26, 27); and by a re-establishment of the old worship of the kingdom as
arranged by Jeroboam.
4. Moab, the region immediately east of
the Dead Sea and of the lower Jordan,
though in part suited for agriculture, is in
the main a great grazing country. Mesha
resembled a modern Arab Sheikh, whose

unto the king of Israel an hundred thousand ^dlambs, and an
5 hundred thousand rams, with the wool. But it came to pass,
when ^eAhab was dead, that the king of Moab rebelled against
6 the king of Israel. ¶And king Jehoram went out of Samaria
7 the same time, and numbered all Israel. And he went and sent
to Jehoshaphat the king of Judah, saying, The king of Moab
hath rebelled against me: wilt thou go with me against Moab
to battle? And he said, I will go up: ^fI *am* as thou *art*, my
8 people as thy people, *and* my horses as thy horses. And he said,
Which way shall we go up? And he answered, The way through
9 the wilderness of Edom. So the king of Israel went, and the
king of Judah, and the king of Edom: and they fetched a compass of seven days' journey: and there was no water for the
10 host, and for the cattle [1]that followed them. And the king of
Israel said, Alas! that the LORD hath called these three kings
11 together, to deliver them into the hand of Moab! But ^gJehosh-
aphat said, *Is there* not here a prophet of the LORD, that we may
enquire of the LORD by him? And one of the king of Israel's
servants answered and said, Here *is* Elisha the son of Shaphat,

d See Isa.16. 1.

e ch. 1. 1.

f 1 Kin. 22. 4.

g 1 Kin. 22. 7.

[1] Heb. *at their feet*, See Exod. 11. 8.

wealth is usually estimated by the number of his flocks and herds. His tribute of the wool of 100,000 lambs was a tribute in kind, the ordinary tribute at this time in the East.

Mesha is the monarch who wrote the in-scription on the "Moabite stone" (i. 1 note). The points established by the Inscription are—1. That Moab recovered from the blow dealt by David (2 Sam. viii. 2, 12), and be-came again an independent state in the in-terval between David's conquest and the accession of Omri; 2. That Omri recon-quered the country, and that it then became subject to the northern kingdom, and re-mained so throughout his reign and that of his son Ahab, and into the reign of Ahab's son and successor, Ahaziah; 3. That the in-dependence was regained by means of a war, in which Mesha took town after town from the Israelites, including in his conquests many of the towns which, at the original occupation of the Holy Land, had passed into the possession of the Reubenites or the Gadites, as Baal-Meon (Num. xxxii. 38), Kirjathaim (do. 37), Ataroth (do. 34), Nebo (do. 38), Jahaz (Josh. xiii. 18), &c. ; 4. That the name of Jehovah was well known to the Moabites as that of the God of the Is-raelites; and 5. That there was a sanctuary of Jehovah at Nebo, in the Trans-Jordanic territory, where "vessels" were used in His service.

7. The close alliance between the two kingdoms still subsisted. Jehoram there-fore sends confidently to make the same re-quest with respect to Moab that his father had made two years before with respect to Syria (marg. ref.). Jehoshaphat consented at once, notwithstanding that his former compliance had drawn upon him the rebuke of a Prophet (2 Chr. xix. 2). Perhaps Jeho-

ram's removal of the Baal-worship (*v.* 2) weighed with him. He had himself been attacked by the Moabites in the preceding year; and though the attempt had failed, Jehoshaphat would feel that it might be re-newed, and that it was important to seize the opportunity of weakening his enemy which now offered itself.

8. The readiest and most natural "way" was across the Jordan near Jericho into the Arboth-Moab, and then along the eastern shore of the Dead Sea to Moab proper, the tract south of the Arnon. But the way chosen was that which led to the Edomite country, viz., round the southern extremity of the Dead Sea, and across the Arabah, or continuation of the Jordan and Dead Sea valley. Thus would be effected a junction with the forces of Edom, which had re-sumed its dependence on Judah, though the year before it had been in alliance with Moab (2 Chr. xx. 22); and they would come upon the Moabites unprepared.

9. *seven days' journey*] The distance of the route probably followed is not much more than 100 miles. But the difficulties of the way are great; and the army might not be able to move along it at a faster rate than about 15 miles a day.

no water] The kings had probably ex-pected to find sufficient water for both men and baggage animals in the Wady-el-Ahsy, which divides Edom from Moab, and which has a stream that is now regarded as peren-nial. But it was dried up—quite a possible occurrence with any of the streams of this region.

11. *a prophet of the* LORD] *i.e.* of *Jehovah*. It was necessary to inquire thus definitely, as there were still plenty of prophets who were only prophets of Baal (*v.* 13).

h ch. 2. 25.
i Ezek. 14. 3.
k So Judg.
10. 14.
Ruth 1. 15.
l 1Kin.18.19.
m 1 Kin.17.1.
ch. 5. 16.

n See
1 Sam. 10. 5.
1 Chr. 25.1—
3.
o Ezek. 1. 3.
& 3. 14, 22.
& 8. 1.
p ch. 4. 3.

q Ex. 29. 39.
40.

12 which poured water on the hands of Elijah. And Jehoshaphat said, The word of the LORD is with him. So the king of Israel and Jehoshaphat and the king of Edom *h*went down to him. 13 And Elisha said unto the king of Israel, *i*What have I to do with thee ? *k*get thee to *l*the prophets of thy father, and to the prophets of thy mother. And the king of Israel said unto him, Nay: for the LORD hath called these three kings together, to 14 deliver them into the hand of Moab. And Elisha said, *m*As the LORD of hosts liveth, before whom I stand, surely, were it not that I regard the presence of Jehoshaphat the king of Judah, I 15 would not look toward thee, nor see thee. But now bring me *n*a minstrel. And it came to pass, when the minstrel played, 16 that *o*the hand of the LORD came upon him. And he said, Thus 17 saith the LORD, *p*Make this valley full of ditches. For thus saith the LORD, Ye shall not see wind, neither shall ye see rain; yet that valley shall be filled with water, that ye may drink, 18 both ye, and your cattle, and your beasts. And this is *but* a light thing in the sight of the LORD : he will deliver the Moab-19 ites also into your hand. And ye shall smite every fenced city, and every choice city, and shall fell every good tree, and stop all wells of water, and *l*mar every good piece of land with stones. 20 ¶ And it came to pass in the morning, when *q*the meat offering was offered, that, behold, there came water by the way of Edom,

---

l Heb. *grieve*.

Here is Elisha] Jehoram appears to have been ignorant of his presence with the host, and one of his "servants," or officers, answered Jehoshaphat's inquiry.

which poured water] An act signifying ministration or attendance (cp. John xiii. 5 seq.).

13. Jehoram's humility in seeking (*v.* 12) instead of summoning Elisha, does not save him from rebuke. His reformation (*v.* 2) had been but a half reformation—a compromise with idolatry.

Nay : for the LORD *hath called,* &c.] The force of this reply seems to be—"Nay, reproach me not, since I am in a sore strait—and not only I, but these two other kings also. The Lord — Jehovah — is about to deliver us into the hand of Moab. If thou canst not, or wilt not help, at least do not reproach."

15. Music seems to have been a regular accompaniment of prophecy in the "schools of the Prophets " (marg. ref.), and an occasional accompaniment of it elsewhere (Ex. xv. 20).

16. *ditches*] Or " pits " (Jer. xiv. 3). They were to dig pits in the broad valley or wady, wherein the water might remain, instead of flowing off down the torrent course.

17. No rain was to fall where the Israelites and their enemies were encamped ; there was not even to be that all but universal accompaniment of rain in the East, a sudden rise of wind (cp. 1 K. xviii. 45 ; Ps. cxlvii. 18 ; Matt. vii. 25).

cattle, and your beasts] The former are the

animals brought for food. The latter are the baggage animals.

19. *ye shall fell every good tree*] This is not an infringement of the rule laid down in Deut. xx. 19, 20. The Israelites were not forbidden to fell the fruit trees in an enemy's country, as a part of the ravage of war, when they had no thoughts of occupying the country. The plan of thus injuring an enemy was probably in general use among the nations of these parts at the time. We see the destruction represented frequently on the Assyrian monuments and mentioned in the inscriptions of Egypt.

and stop all wells of water] The stoppage of wells was a common feature of ancient, and especially Oriental, warfare (cp. Gen. xxvi. 15-18).

mar...with stones] The exact converse of that suggested in Isai. v. 2. The land in and about Palestine is so stony that the first work of the cultivator is to collect the surface stones together into heaps. An army marching through a land could easily undo this work, dispersing the stones thus gathered, and spreading them once more over the fields.

20. *when the meat offering was offered*] *i.e.* about sunrise, when the morning sacrifice was offered. Cp. 1 K. xviii. 29.

there came water by the way of Edom] The Wady-el-Ahsy drains a considerable portion of northern Edom. Heavy rain had fallen during the night in some part of this tract, and with the morning a freshet of water came down the valley, filling the pits.

21 and the country was filled with water. And when all the Moabites heard that the kings were come up to fight against them,
they ¹gathered all that were able to ²put on armour, and up-
22 ward, and stood in the border. And they rose up early in the
morning, and the sun shone upon the water, and the Moabites
23 saw the water on the other side *as* red as blood: and they said,
This *is* blood: the kings are surely ³slain, and they have smitten
24 one another: now therefore, Moab, to the spoil. And when
they came to the camp of Israel, the Israelites rose up and smote
the Moabites, so that they fled before them: but ⁴they went
25 forward smiting the Moabites, even in *their* country. And they
beat down the cities, and on every good piece of land cast every
man his stone, and filled it; and they stopped all the wells of
water, and felled all the good trees: ⁵only in ʳKir-haraseth left   *r* Isai. 16. 7,
they the stones thereof; howbeit the slingers went about *it*, and   11.
26 smote it. ¶And when the king of Moab saw that the battle
was too sore for him, he took with him seven hundred men
that drew swords, to break through *even* unto the king of Edom:
27 but they could not. Then ˢhe took his eldest son that should   *s* Mic. 6. 7.
have reigned in his stead, and offered him *for* a burnt offering upon the wall. And there was great indignation against
Israel: ᵗand they departed from him, and returned to *their own*   *t* ch. 8. 20.
land.

CHAP. 4. NOW there cried a certain woman of the wives of ᵃthe   *a* 1 Kin. 20.
sons of the prophets unto Elisha, saying, Thy servant my hus-   35.
band is dead; and thou knowest that thy servant did fear the
LORD: and the creditor is come ᵇto take unto him my two sons   *b* See Lev.
                                                                      25. 39.
                                                                      Matt. 18. 25.

¹ Heb. *were cried together.*   ³ Heb. *destroyed.*   ⁵ Heb. *until he left the*
² Heb. *gird himself with a*   ⁴ Or, *they smote in it even*   *stones thereof in Kir-*
   girdle.   *smiting.*   *haraseth.*

---

21. *and stood in the border*] On the north
side of the wady, ready to defend their
territory.

23. The sun had risen with a ruddy light,
as is frequently the case after a storm (cp.
Matt. xvi. 3), nearly over the Israelite camp,
and the pits, deep but with small mouths,
gleaming redly through the haze which
would lie along the newly moistened valley,
seemed to the Moabites like pools of blood.
The preceding year, they and their allies
had mutually destroyed each other (2 Chr.
xx. 23). It seemed to them, from their
knowledge of the jealousies between Judah,
Israel, and Edom, not unlikely that a
similar calamity had now befallen their
foes.

25. Kir-Haraseth, also Kir-Hareseth, is
identified almost certainly with the modern
Kerak, a strong city on the highland immediately east of the southern part of the Dead
Sea. It was the great fortress of Moab,
though not the capital, which was Rabbath
or Rabbah. It was an important stronghold at the time of the Crusades, and is
still a place of great strength. Kir seems
to have meant "fortress." It is found in
Cir-cesium, Car-chemish, &c.

Kir-Haraseth resisted all the attempts
to dismantle it; but the slingers found

places on the hills which surrounded it,
whence they could throw their stones into
it and harass the garrison, though they
could not take the town.

26. *to break through, even unto the king of
Edom*] Either because he thought that the
king of Edom would connive at his escape
or to take vengeance on him for having deserted his former allies (*v.* 8 note).

27. Cp. marg. ref. Mesha, when his
sally failed, took, as a last resource, his
first born son, and offered him as a burnt-
offering to appease the manifest anger of
his god Chemosh, and obtain his aid against
his enemies. This act was thoroughly in
accordance with Moabitish notions.

*and there was great indignation against
Israel*] Either the Israelites were indignant
with themselves, or the men of Judah and
the Edomites were indignant at the Israelites for having caused the pollution of this
sacrifice, and the siege was relinquished.

IV. 1. *the creditor is come, &c.*] The Law
of Moses, like the Athenian and the Roman
law, recognised servitude for debt, and
allowed that pledging of the debtor's person, which, in a rude state of society, is
regarded as the safest and the most natural
security (see marg. ref.). In the present
case it would seem that, so long as the

c See ch. 3. 16.

2 to be bondmen. And Elisha said unto her, What shall I do for thee ? tell me, what hast thou in the house ? And she said, Thine handmaid hath not any thing in the house, save a pot of 3 oil. Then he said, Go, borrow thee vessels abroad of all thy 4 neighbours, *even* empty vessels; *c*[1]borrow not a few. And when thou art come in, thou shalt shut the door upon thee and upon thy sons, and shalt pour out into all those vessels, and thou 5 shalt set aside that which is full. So she went from him, and shut the door upon her and upon her sons, who brought *the* 6 *vessels* to her; and she poured out. And it came to pass, when the vessels were full, that she said unto her son, Bring me yet a vessel. And he said unto her, *There is* not a vessel more. And 7 the oil stayed. Then she came and told the man of God. And he said, Go, sell the oil, and pay thy [2]debt, and live thou and 8 thy children of the rest. ¶And [3]it fell on a day, that Elisha

d Josh.19.18.

passed to *d*Shunem, where *was* a great woman; and she [4]constrained him to eat bread. And *so* it was, *that* as oft as he 9 passed by, he turned in thither to eat bread. And she said unto her husband, Behold now, I perceive that this *is* an holy man 10 of God, which passeth by us continually. Let us make a little chamber, I pray thee, on the wall; and let us set for him there bed, and a table, and a stool, and a candlestick : and it shall 11 be, when he cometh to us, that he shall turn in thither.　¶And it fell on a day, that he came thither, and he turned into the 12 chamber, and lay there. And he said to Gehazi his servant, Call this Shunammite. And when he had called her, she stood 13 before him. And he said unto him, Say now unto her, Behold, thou hast been careful for us with all this care ; what *is* to be done for thee ? wouldest thou be spoken for to the king, or to the captain of the host ? And she answered, I dwell among 14 mine own people. And he said, What then *is* to be done for her ? And Gehazi answered, Verily she hath no child, and her 15 husband is old. And he said, Call her. And when he had called

e Gen. 18.10. 14.

16 her, she stood in the door. And he said, *e*About this [5]season, according to the time of life, thou shalt embrace a son. And

---

[1] Or, *scant not.*　　　[3] Heb. *there was a day.*　　　[4] Heb. *laid hold on him.*
[2] Or, *creditor.*　　　　　　　　　　　　　　　　　　　　[5] Heb. *set time.*

---

debtor lived, the creditor had not enforced his right over his sons, but now on his death he claimed their services, to which he was by law entitled.

2. *a pot of oil*] Or, " an anointing of oil" —so much oil, *i.e.*, as would serve me for one anointing of my person. The word used occurs only in this passage.

8. *And it fell on a day*] The original of the expression here used, which occurs *three* times in the present narrative (*vv.* 11, 18), is also found in Job i. 6, 13, ii. 1. The character of the expression perhaps supports the view that the author of Kings has collected from various sources his account of the miracles of Elisha, and has kept in each case the words of the original writer.

a great woman] That is, " a *rich* woman." Cp. 1 Sam. xxv. 2 ; 2 Sam. xix. 32.

10. *a little chamber on the wall*] The room probably projected like a balcony beyond

the lower apartments — an arrangement common in the East.

a stool] Rather, " **a chair.**" The " chair " and " table," unusual in the sleeping-rooms of the East, indicate that the Prophet was expected to use his apartment for study and retirement, not only as a sleeping-chamber.

13. *thou hast been careful for us*] For the Prophet and his servant, who must have been lodged as well as his master.

I dwell among mine own people] The woman declines Elisha's offer. She has no wrong to complain of, no quarrel with any neighbour, in respect of which she might need the help of one in power. She "dwells among her own people"—her friends, and dependents, with whom she lives peaceably.

16. *do not lie*] Cp. a similar incredulity in Gen. xvii. 17, xviii. 12 ; Luke i. 20. The expression, " do not lie," which is harsh to us, accords with the plain, straightforward simplicity of ancient speech. It would

she said, Nay, my lord, *thou* man of God, *f*do not lie unto thine
17 handmaid. And the woman conceived, and bare a son at that
season that Elisha had said unto her, according to the time of
18 life. ¶ And when the child was grown, it fell on a day, that he
19 went out to his father to the reapers. And he said unto his
father, My head, my head. And he said to a lad, Carry him to
20 his mother. And when he had taken him, and brought him to
21 his mother, he sat on her knees till noon, and *then* died. And
she went up, and laid him on the bed of the man of God, and
22 shut *the door* upon him, and went out. And she called unto her
husband, and said, Send me, I pray thee, one of the young men,
and one of the asses, that I may run to the man of God, and
23 come again. And he said, Wherefore wilt thou go to him to
day? *it is* neither new moon, nor sabbath. And she said, *It*
24 *shall be* ¹well. Then she saddled an ass, and said to her servant,
Drive, and go forward; ²slack not *thy* riding for me, except I
25 bid thee. So she went and came unto the man of God *g*to mount
Carmel. ¶ And it came to pass, when the man of God saw her
afar off, that he said to Gehazi his servant, Behold, *yonder is*
26 that Shunammite: run now, I pray thee, to meet her, and say
unto her, *Is it* well with thee? *is it* well with thy husband? *is*
27 *it* well with the child? And she answered, *It is* well. And
when she came to the man of God to the hill, she caught ³him
by the feet: but Gehazi came near to thrust her away. And the
man of God said, Let her alone; for her soul *is* ⁴vexed within
her: and the LORD hath hid *it* from me, and hath not told me.
28 Then she said, Did I desire a son of my lord? *h*did I not say,
29 Do not deceive me? Then he said to Gehazi, *i*Gird up thy loins,
and take my staff in thine hand, and go thy way: if thou meet
any man, *k*salute him not; and if any salute thee, answer him

f ver. 23.

g ch. 2. 25.

h ver. 16.
i 1 Kin. 18. 46.
ch. 9. 1.
k Luke 10. 4.

¹ Heb. *peace.*
² Heb. *restrain not for me to ride.*
³ Heb. *by his feet*, Matt. 28. 9.
⁴ Heb. *bitter*, 1 Sam. 1. 10.

---

not mean more than "deceive" (cp. marg. ref.).

19. The child's malady was a sunstroke. The inhabitants of Palestine suffered from this (Ps. cxxi. 6; Isai. xlix. 10; Judith viii. 3).

22. *send me, I pray thee, one of the young men and one of the asses*] All the "young men" and all the "asses" were in the harvest field, the young men cutting and binding the sheaves, and placing them upon carts or wains, the asses drawing these vehicles fully laden, to the threshing-floor. Cp. Amos ii. 13.

23. Her husband did not connect the illness with his wife's demand, but thought she wished to attend one of the Prophet's devotional services. It is evident that such services were now held with something like regularity on Carmel for the benefit of the faithful in those parts.

new moon] By the Law the first day of each month was to be kept holy. Offerings were appointed for such occasions (Num. xxviii. 11-15), and they were among the days on which the silver trumpets were to be blown (Num. x. 10; Ps. lxxxi. 3). Hence "new moons" are frequently joined with

"sabbaths" (see Isai. i. 13; Ezek. xlv. 17; Hos. ii. 11; 1 Chr. xxiii. 31).

it shall be well] Rather, as in the margin, "**Peace**." *i.e.*, "Be quiet—trouble me not with inquiries—only let me do as I wish."

24. *slack not thy riding*] Translate, "**delay me not in my riding**, except I bid thee." The servant went on foot with the ass to urge it forward, as is the ordinary custom in the East.

25. The distance was about sixteen or seventeen miles.

27. *she caught him by the feet*] To lay hold of the knees or feet has always been thought in the East to add force to supplication, and is practised even at the present day. Cp. Matt. xviii. 29; John xi. 32.

28. Great grief shrinks from putting itself into words. The Shunammite cannot bring herself to say, "My son is dead;" but by reproaching the Prophet with having "deceived" her, she sufficiently indicates her loss.

29. *salute him not*] Cp. marg. ref. Salutation is the forerunner of conversation, and one bent on speed would avoid every temptation to loiter.

lay my staff upon the face of the child] Per-

l See Ex. 7.
19. & 14. 16.
ch. 2. 8. 14.
Acts 19. 12.
m ch. 2. 2.

n John 11. 11.

o ver. 4.
Matt. 6. 6.
p 1 Kin. 17.
20.
q 1 Kin. 17.
21.
Acts 20. 10.

r 1 Kin. 17.
21.
s ch. 8. 1, 5.

t 1 Kin. 17.
23.
u ch. 2. 1.
x ch. 8. 1.
y ch. 2. 3.
Luke 10. 39.
Acts 22. 3.

z Ex. 10. 17.
a See Ex. 15.
25.
ch. 2. 21.
& 5. 10.
John 9. 6.

30 not again: and *l*lay my staff upon the face of the child. And the mother of the child said, *m*As the LORD liveth, and *as* thy soul liveth, I will not leave thee. And he arose, and followed her.

31 ¶ And Gehazi passed on before them, and laid the staff upon the face of the child; but *there was* neither voice, nor [1]hearing. Wherefore he went again to meet him, and told him, saying,

32 The child is *n*not awakened. And when Elisha was come into the house, behold, the child was dead, *and* laid upon his bed.

33 He *o*went in therefore, and shut the door upon them twain,

34 *p*and prayed unto the LORD. And he went up, and lay upon the child, and put his mouth upon his mouth, and his eyes upon his eyes, and his hands upon his hands: and *q*he stretched himself

35 upon the child; and the flesh of the child waxed warm. Then he returned, and walked in the house [2]to and fro; and went up, *r*and stretched himself upon him: and *s*the child sneezed

36 seven times, and the child opened his eyes. And he called Gehazi, and said, Call this Shunammite. So he called her. And when she was come in unto him, he said, Take up thy son.

37 Then she went in, and fell at his feet, and bowed herself to the

38 ground, and *t*took up her son, and went out. ¶ And Elisha came again to *u*Gilgal: and *there was* a *x*dearth in the land; and the sons of the prophets *were* *y*sitting before him: and he said unto his servant, Set on the great pot, and seethe pottage

39 for the sons of the prophets. And one went out into the field to gather herbs, and found a wild vine, and gathered thereof wild gourds his lap full, and came and shred *them* into the pot of

40 pottage: for they knew *them* not. So they poured out for the men to eat. And it came to pass, as they were eating of the pottage, that they cried out, and said, O *thou* man of God, *there*

41 *is* *z*death in the pot. And they could not eat *thereof*. But he said, Then bring meal. And *a*he cast *it* into the pot; and he

[1] Heb. *attention.*   [2] Heb. *once hither, and once thither.*

---

haps Elisha's object in giving it was simply to assuage the grief of the mother, by letting her feel that something was being done for her child.

31. *there was neither voice nor hearing*] Cp. 1 K. xviii. 29.

the child is not awakened] See *v.* 20. The euphemism by which death is spoken of as a sleep was already familiar to the Jews (see 1 K. i. 21 note).

33. *prayed*] Prayer was the only remedy in such a case as this (cp. marg. ref. and Jam. v. 16), though it did not exclude the use of other means (*v.* 34).

34. *he stretched himself*] Or, " prostrated himself." The word is a different one from that used of Elijah, and expresses closer contact with the body. Warmth may have been actually communicated from the living body to the dead one; and Elisha's persistence (Heb. xi. 35), may have been a condition of the child's return to life.

36. *Take up thy son*] Compare Elijah's action (marg. ref. *t*) and our Blessed Lord's (Luke vii. 15).

38. *there was a dearth in the land*] Rather, " The famine was in the land." The seven

years' dearth of which Elisha had prophesied (marg. ref.) had begun.

the sons of the prophets] See 1 K. xx. 35 note. They were sitting before him as scholars before their master, hearing his instructions.

39. *a wild vine*] Not a real wild vine, the fruit of which, if not very palatable, is harmless; but some climbing plant with tendrils. The plant was probably either the *Ecbalium elaterium*, or "squirting cucumber," the fruit of which, egg-shaped, and of a very bitter taste, bursts at the slightest touch, when it is ripe, and squirts out sap and seed grains; or the *Colocynthis*, which belongs to the family of cucumbers, has a vine-shaped leaf, and bears a fruit as large as an orange, very bitter, from which is prepared the drug sold as colocynth. This latter plant grows abundantly in Palestine.

his lap full] Literally, " his shawl full." The prophet brought the fruit home in his " shawl " or " outer garment."

41. *Then bring meal*] The natural properties of meal would but slightly diminish either the bitterness or the unwholesome-

said, Pour out for the people, that they may eat. And there
42 was no ¹harm in the pot. ¶ And there came a man from ᵇBaal-
shalisha, ᶜand brought the man of God bread of the firstfruits,
twenty loaves of barley, and full ears of corn ²in the husk
thereof. And he said, Give unto the people, that they may eat.
43 And his servitor said, ᵈWhat, should I set this before an hundred men ? He said again, Give the people, that they may eat:
for thus saith the LORD, ᵉThey shall eat, and shall leave *thereof.*
44 So he set *it* before them, and they did eat, ᶠand left *thereof,* according to the word of the LORD.
CHAP. 5. NOW ᵃNaaman, captain of the host of the king of Syria,
was ᵇa great man ³with his master, and ⁴⁵honourable, because
by him the LORD had given ⁶deliverance unto Syria : he was
2 also a mighty man in valour, *but he was* a leper. And the
Syrians had gone out by companies, and had brought away captive out of the land of Israel a little maid ; and she ⁷waited on
3 Naaman's wife. And she said unto her mistress, Would God
my lord *were* ⁸with the prophet that *is* in Samaria ! for he would
4 ⁹recover him of his leprosy. And *one* went in, and told his lord,
saying, Thus and thus said the maid that *is* of the land of Israel.
5 ¶ And the king of Syria said, Go to, go, and I will send a letter

ᵇ 1 Sam. 9. 4.

ᶜ 1 Sam. 9. 7.
1 Cor. 9. 11.
Gal. 6. 6.

ᵈ Luke 9. 13.
John 6. 9.

ᵉ Luke 9. 17.
John 6. 11.
ᶠ Matt.14.20.
& 15. 37.

John 6. 13.
ᵃ Luke 4. 27.
ᵇ Ex. 11. 3.

---

¹ Heb. *evil thing.*
² Or, *in his scrip,* or, *gar-*
ment.
³ Heb. *before.*
⁴ Or, *gracious.*
⁵ Heb. *lifted up,* or, *ac-*
cepted in countenance.
⁶ Or, *victory.*
⁷ Heb. *was before.*
⁸ Heb. *before.*
⁹ Heb. *gather in.*

---

ness of a drink containing colocynth. It is
evident, therefore, that the conversion of
the food from a pernicious and unsavoury
mess into palatable and wholesome nourishment was by miracle.

42. *Baal-shalisha*] Fifteen Roman miles
north of Lydda, in the Sharon plain to the
west of the highlands of Ephraim. It was,
apparently, the chief city of the " land of
Shalisha" (marg. ref.).

bread of the first fruits] It appears by
this that the Levitical priests having withdrawn from the land of Israel (see 2 Chr. xi.
13, 14), pious Israelites transferred to the
Prophets, whom God raised up, the offerings
required by the Law to be given to the
priests (Num. xviii. 13 ; Deut. xviii. 4).

in the husk thereof] " In his bag." The
word does not occur elsewhere in Scripture.

43. This miracle was a faint foreshadow-
ing of our Lord's far more marvellous
feeding of thousands with even scantier
materials. The resemblance is not only in
the broad fact, but in various minute particulars, such as the distribution through the
hands of others ; the material, bread ; the
surprised question of the servant ; and the
evidence of superfluity in the fragments
that were left (see marg. reff.). As Elijah
was a type of the Baptist, so Elisha was in
many respects a type of our Blessed Lord.
In his peaceful, non-ascetic life, in his mild
and gentle character, in his constant cir-
cuits, in his many miracles of mercy, in the
healing virtue which abode in his bodily
frame (xiii. 21), he resembled, more than any

other Prophet, the Messiah, of Whom all
Prophets were more or less shadows and
figures.

V. 1. *by him the* LORD *had given deliver-*
ance unto Syria] An Assyrian monarch had
pushed his conquests as far as Syria exactly
at this period, bringing into subjection all
the kings of these parts. But Syria revolted
after a few years and once more made herself independent. It was probably in this
war of independence that Naaman had distinguished himself.

but he was a leper] Leprosy admitted of
various kinds and degrees (Lev. xiii. xiv.)
Some of the lighter forms would not incapa-
citate a man from discharging the duties of
a courtier and warrior.

2. No peace had been made on the failure
of Ahab's expedition (1 K. xxii. 1-36). The
relations of the two countries therefore continued to be hostile, and plundering inroads
naturally took place on the one side and on
the other.

4. *one went in*] Rather, "he went in," *i.e.*
Naaman went and told his lord, the king of
Syria.

5. *six thousand pieces of gold*] Rather, "six
thousand *shekels* of gold." Coined money
did not exist as yet, and was not introduced
into Judæa till the time of Cyrus. Gold
was carried in bars, from which portions
were cut when need arose, and the value was
ascertained by weighing. If the gold shekel
of the Jews corresponded, as some think,
to the daric of the Persians, the value of
the 6000 shekels would be about 6837*l*. If
the weight was the same as that of the silver

e 1 Sam. 9. 8.
ch. 8. 8, 9.

unto the king of Israel. And he departed, and *c*took [1]with him ten talents of silver, and six thousand *pieces* of gold, and ten
6 changes of raiment. And he brought the letter to the king of Israel, saying, Now when this letter is come unto thee, behold, I have *therewith* sent Naaman my servant to thee, that thou
7 mayest recover him of his leprosy. And it came to pass, when the king of Israel had read the letter, that he rent his clothes,

d Gen. 30. 2.
Deut. 32. 39.
1 Sam. 2. 6.

and said, *Am* I *d*God, to kill and to make alive, that this man doth send unto me to recover a man of his leprosy? wherefore consider, I pray you, and see how he seeketh a quarrel against
8 me. ¶ And it was *so*, when Elisha the man of God had heard that the king of Israel had rent his clothes, that he sent to the king, saying, Wherefore hast thou rent thy clothes? let him come now to me, and he shall know that there is a prophet in Israel.
9 So Naaman came with his horses and with his chariot, and
10 stood at the door of the house of Elisha. And Elisha sent a

e See ch. 4. 41.
John 9. 7.

messenger unto him, saying, Go and *e*wash in Jordan seven times, and thy flesh shall come again to thee, and thou shalt be
11 clean. But Naaman was wroth, and went away, and said, Behold, [2,3]I thought, He will surely come out to me, and stand, and call on the name of the LORD his God, and [4]strike his hand
12 over the place, and recover the leper. *Are* not [5]Abana and Pharpar, rivers of Damascus, better than all the waters of Israel ? may I not wash in them, and be clean ? So he turned
13 and went away in a rage. And his servants came near, and spake unto him, and said, My father, *if* the prophet had bid thee *do some* great thing, wouldest thou not have done *it* ? how much rather then, when he saith to thee, Wash, and be clean ?

[1] Heb. *in his hand*.   [3] Or, *I said with myself, He*   [4] Heb. *move up and down*.
[2] Heb. *I said*.   *will surely come out, &c.*   [5] Or, *Amana*.

---

shekel (see Ex. xxxviii. 24 note), the value would exceed 12,000*l*.

The ancient practice of including clothes among gifts of honour in the East (Gen. xli. 42; Esth. vi. 8; Dan. v. 7) continues to the present day.

6. *that thou mayest recover him*] Lit. "And thou shalt recover him." The Syrian king presumes that, if there is a cure for leprosy to be had in Israel, the mode of obtaining it will be well known to his royal brother.

7. *he rent his clothes*] The action indicated alarm and terror quite as much as sorrow (2 Sam. xiii. 19; Ezr. ix. 3; 2 Chr. xxxiv. 27; Jer. xxxvi. 22).

consider, I pray you] Jehoram speaks to his chief officers, and bids them mark the *animus* of the Syrian monarch. Compare the conduct of Ahab (1 K. xx. 7).

8. *he shall know...Israel*] viz. "That which *thou* (the king of Israel) appearest to have forgotten, that there is a Prophet—a real JehovahP-rophet—in Israel."

10. Elisha was not deterred from personally meeting Naaman because he was a leper. He sent a messenger because Naaman had over-estimated his own importance (v. 11), and needed rebuke.

go and wash in Jordan] Cp. marg. reff.

A command is given which tests the faith of the recipient, and the miracle is not wrought until such faith is openly evidenced.

11. *he will surely come out to me*] In the East a code of unwritten laws prescribes exactly how visits are to be paid, and how visitors are to be received, according to the worldly rank of the parties (cp. *v.* 21). No doubt, according to such a code, Elisha should have gone out to meet Naaman at the door of his house.

and call on the name of the LORD *his God*] Literally, "of Jehovah his God." Naaman is aware that *Jehovah* is the God of Elisha. Cp. the occurrence of the name of Jehovah on the "Moabite Stone" (iii. 4 note).

strike] Better, as in the margin, "pass the fingers up and down the place" at a short distance. It seems implied that the leprosy was partial.

12. The Abana is the Barada, or true river of Damascus, which, rising in the anti-Libanus, flows westward from its foot and forms the oasis within which Damascus is placed. The Pharpar is usually identified with the Awaaj.

Naaman thinks that, if washing is to cure him, his own rivers may serve the purpose. Their water was brighter, clearer, and colder than that of Jordan.

14 Then went he down, and dipped himself seven times in Jordan, according to the saying of the man of God: and *f*his flesh came again like unto the flesh of a little child, and *g*he was clean.

15 ¶ And he returned to the man of God, he and all his company, and came, and stood before him: and he said, Behold, now I know that *there is* *h*no God in all the earth, but in Israel: now

16 therefore, I pray thee, take *i*a blessing of thy servant. But he said, *k*As the LORD liveth, before whom I stand, *l*I will receive

17 none. And he urged him to take *it;* but he refused. And Naaman said, Shall there not then, I pray thee, be given to thy servant two mules' burden of earth? for thy servant will henceforth offer neither burnt offering nor sacrifice unto other gods,

18 but unto the LORD. In this thing the LORD pardon thy servant, *that* when my master goeth into the house of Rimmon to worship there, and *m*he leaneth on my hand, and I bow myself in the house of Rimmon: when I bow down myself in the house of

19 Rimmon, the LORD pardon thy servant in this thing. And he said unto him, Go in peace. So he departed from him *l*a little

20 way. ¶ But Gehazi, the servant of Elisha the man of God, said, Behold, my master hath spared Naaman this Syrian, in not receiving at his hands that which he brought: but, *as* the LORD

21 liveth, I will run after him, and take somewhat of him. So

f Job 33. 25.

g Luke 4. 27.

h Dan. 2. 47.
& 3. 29.
& 6. 26. 27.
i Gen. 33. 11.
k 1 Kin. 17. 1.
l Gen. 14. 23.
See Matt. 10. 8.

m ch. 7. 2, 17.

---

1 Heb. *a little piece of ground,* as Gen. 35. 16.

---

14. *seven times*] Cp. 1 K. xviii. 43. In both cases a somewhat severe trial was made of the individual's faith. Cp. the seven compassings of Jericho, and the sudden fall of the walls (Josh. vi. 3–20).

15. *he returned*] Naaman was grateful (cp. Luke xvii. 15). From the Jordan to Samaria was a distance of not less than thirty-two miles. Naaman further went to Damascus, far out of his way, lengthening his necessary journey by at least three days. His special object in returning seems to have been to relieve his feelings of obligation by inducing the Prophet to accept a "blessing," *i.e.* a gift.

there is no God, &c.] Cp. marg. reff. ; but in none of them are the expressions quite so strong as here. Naaman seems absolutely to renounce all belief in any other God but Jehovah.

16. *I will receive none*] The Prophets were in the habit of receiving presents from those who consulted them (1 Sam. ix. 7, 8 ; 1 K. xiv. 3), but Elisha refused. It was important that Naaman should not suppose that the Prophets of the true God acted from motives of self-interest, much less imagine that "the gift of God might be purchased with money" (Acts viii. 20).

17. *two mules' burden of earth*] This earth, Naaman thought, spread over a portion of Syrian ground, would hallow and render it suitable for the worship of Jehovah.

18. Rimmon is known to us as a god only by this passage. The name is connected with a root "to be high." Hadad-rimmon (Zech. xii. 11), the name of a place near

Megiddo, points to the identity of Rimmon with Hadad, who is known to have been the Sun, the chief object of worship to the Syrians.

when he leaneth on mine hand] The practice of a monarch's "leaning on the hand" of an attendant was not common in the East (cp. marg. ref.). It probably implied age or infirmity.

the LORD pardon thy servant in this thing] Naaman was not prepared to offend his master, either by refusing to enter with him into the temple of Rimmon, or by remaining erect when the king bowed down and worshipped the god. His conscience seems to have told him that such conduct was not right ; but he trusted that it might be pardoned, and he appealed to the Prophet in the hope of obtaining from him an assurance to this effect.

19. *so he departed,* &c.] This clause should not be separated from the succeeding verse. The meaning is, "So he departed from him, and had gone a little way, when Gehazi bethought himself of what he would do, and followed after him."

20. *this Syrian*] The words are emphatic. Gehazi persuades himself that it is right to spoil a *Syrian*—that is, a Gentile, and an enemy of Israel.

as the LORD liveth] These words are here a profane oath. Gehazi, anxious to make himself believe that he is acting in a proper, and, even, in a religious spirit, does not scruple to introduce one of the most solemn of religious phrases.

Gehazi followed after Naaman. And when Naaman saw *him*
running after him, he lighted down from the chariot to meet
22 him, and said, [1]*Is* all well? And he said, All *is* well. My master
hath sent me, saying, Behold, even now there be come to me
from mount Ephraim two young men of the sons of the prophets: give them, I pray thee, a talent of silver, and two changes
23 of garments. And Naaman said, Be content, take two talents.
And he urged him, and bound two talents of silver in two bags,
with two changes of garments, and laid *them* upon two of his
24 servants; and they bare *them* before him. And when he came
to the [2]tower, he took *them* from their hand, and bestowed *them*
25 in the house: and he let the men go, and they departed. But
he went in, and stood before his master. And Elisha said unto
him, Whence *comest thou*, Gehazi? And he said, Thy servant
26 went [3]no whither. And he said unto him, Went not mine heart
with thee, when the man turned again from his chariot to meet
thee? *Is it* a time to receive money, and to receive garments,
and oliveyards, and vineyards, and sheep, and oxen, and men-
27 servants, and maidservants? The leprosy therefore of Naaman
n shall cleave unto thee, and unto thy seed for ever. And he
went out from his presence *o* a leper *as white* as snow.

CHAP. 6. AND *a* the sons of the prophets said unto Elisha, Behold
2 now, the place where we dwell with thee is too strait for us. Let
us go, we pray thee, unto Jordan, and take thence every man a
beam, and let us make us a place there, where we may dwell.
3 And he answered, Go ye. And one said, Be content, I pray

n 1 Tim.6.10.
o Ex. 4. 6.
Num. 12. 10.
ch. 15. 5.
a ch. 4. 38.

---

[1] Heb. *Is there peace?*   [2] Or, *secret place.*   [3] Heb. *not hither or thither.*

---

21. *he lighted down from the chariot*] This
was an act of quite uncalled-for courtesy.
It indicates eagerness to honour the master
in the person of his servant.

22. *from mount Ephraim*] Bethel and
Gilgal (ii. 1), at both of which there were
"schools of the prophets," were situated on
Mount Ephraim.

a talent of silver] A large demand in respect of the pretended occasion; but small
compared with the amount which Naaman
had pressed on the Prophet (*v.* 4). Gehazi
had to balance between his own avarice,
on the one hand, and the fear of raising
suspicion on the other.

23. *Be content*] *i.e.* "consent."

24. *the tower*] Rather, "**the hill**," the
well-known hill by Elisha's house. The hill
interrupted the view in the direction taken
by Naaman, and Gehazi dismissed Naaman's servants at this point lest they should
be seen from his master's residence.

25. Lest his absence should be noticed,
Gehazi hastened, without being called, to
appear before his master. In the East it is
usual for servants to remain most of the day
in their lord's presence, only quitting it
when given some order to execute.

26. *Went not mine heart with thee?*] *i.e.*
"Was I not with thee in spirit—did I not
see the whole transaction, as if I had been
present at it?" He uses the verb "went,"
because Gehazi has just denied his "going."

Is it a time, &c.] *i.e.* "Was this a proper
occasion to indulge greed, when a Gentile
was to be favourably impressed, and made
to feel that the faith of the Israelites was
the only true religion? Was it not, on the
contrary, an occasion for the exhibition of
the greatest unselfishness, that so a heathen
might be won to the truth?"

and oliveyards and vineyards, &c.] Gehazi's thoughts had probably run on to the
disposition which he would make of his
wealth, and the Prophet here follows them,
enumerating his servant's intended pur-
chases.

VI. 1. The writer returns here to the
series of miracles which Elisha performed
for the benefit of the prophetical schools
under his care. The connexion, in this
point of view, is with iv. 44.

the place where we dwell with thee] Lit.
"the place where we **sit before** thee," *i.e.*
"the place where we assemble and sit to
hear thy teaching." Elisha visited the sons
of the Prophets in circuit, staying a short
time at each place where a "school" was
established. Perhaps he was now visiting
Jericho. Cp. ii. 5.

2. *take every man a beam*] Trees were rare
in most parts of Palestine, but plentiful in
the Jordan valley. Jericho was known in
early times as "the city of palms" (Deut.
xxxiv. 3; Judg. i. 16).

thee, and go with thy servants. And he answered, I will go.
4 So he went with them. And when they came to Jordan, they
5 cut down wood. But as one was felling a beam, the ¹axe head
fell into the water: and he cried, and said, Alas, master! for it
6 was borrowed. And the man of God said, Where fell it? And
he shewed him the place. And ᵇhe cut down a stick, and cast *it*   ᵇ ch. 2. 21.
7 in thither; and the iron did swim. Therefore said he, Take *it*
8 up to thee. And he put out his hand, and took it.   ¶ Then the
king of Syria warred against Israel, and took counsel with his
servants, saying, In such and such a place *shall be* my ²camp.
9 And the man of God sent unto the king of Israel, saying,
Beware that thou pass not such a place; for thither the Syrians
10 are come down. And the king of Israel sent to the place which
the man of God told him and warned him of, and saved him-
11 self there, not once nor twice. Therefore the heart of the king
of Syria was sore troubled for this thing; and he called his
servants, and said unto them, Will ye not shew me which of
12 us *is* for the king of Israel? And one of his servants said,
³None, my lord, O king: but Elisha, the prophet that *is* in
Israel, telleth the king of Israel the words that thou speakest in
13 thy bedchamber. And he said, Go and spy where he *is*, that I
may send and fetch him. And it was told him, saying, Behold,
14 *he is* in ᶜDothan. Therefore sent he thither horses, and chariots,   ᶜ Gen. 37. 17.
and a ⁴great host: and they came by night, and compassed the
15 city about. And when the ⁵servant of the man of God was
risen early, and gone forth, behold, an host compassed the city
both with horses and chariots. And his servant said unto him,
16 Alas, my master! how shall we do? And he answered, Fear
not: for ᵈthey that *be* with us *are* more than they that *be* with   ᵈ 2 Chr. 32. 7.
Ps. 55. 18.
Rom. 8. 31.

¹ Heb. *iron.*   ³ Heb. *No.*   ⁵ Or, *minister.*
² Or, *encamping.*   ⁴ Heb. *heavy.*

---

5. *the ax head*] Lit. as in margin. The
Jews used iron for the heads of axes at a
very early date (see Deut. xix. 5). They
probably acquired a knowledge of the
smelting process in Egypt, where iron was
employed at least from the time of the third
Rameses.

6. No doubt there is something startling
in the trivial character of this miracle, and
of the few others which resemble it. But,
inasmuch as we know very little as to the
laws which govern the exercise of miraculous powers, it is possible that they may be
so much under their possessor's control that
he can exercise them, or not exercise them,
at pleasure. And it may depend on his discretion whether they are exercised in important cases only, or in trivial cases also.
Elisha had evidently great kindness of
heart. He could not see a grief without
wishing to remedy it. And it seems as if
he had sometimes used his miraculous
power in pure good nature, when no natural way of remedying an evil presented
itself.

8. *the king of Syria*] Probably the great
Benhadad (see *v.* 24).

10. *saved himself*] Rather, he "**was**

ware." The verb used is the same which
is translated "beware" in the preceding
verse.

11. Benhadad supposed that there must
be a traitor in his camp. He asks therefore, "Will no one denounce him?"

12. *in thy bedchamber*] Lit. "in the secret place of thy bedchamber," *i.e.* "in the
greatest possible secrecy." The seclusion
of the harem must be taken into account for
the full appreciation of the force of the
phrase. Probably the Syrian lord who answered Benhadad had received his intelligence from some of the Israelites.

13. *Dothan*] See marg. ref. note. It was
at no great distance from Shechem. Its
ancient name still attaches to a Tel or hill
of a marked character (cp. *v.* 17), from the
foot of which arises a copious fountain.

16. *they that be with us,* &c.] Elisha gave
utterance to the conviction of all God's
Saints when the world persecutes them
(cp. marg. reff.). God—they know—is on
their side; they need "not fear what flesh
can do unto them." His Angels—an innumerable host—are ever guarding those who
love Him.

17 them. And Elisha prayed, and said, LORD, I pray thee, open his eyes, that he may see. And the LORD opened the eyes of the young man; and he saw: and, behold, the mountain *was* full of *c*horses and chariots of fire round about Elisha.

18 And when they came down to him, Elisha prayed unto the LORD, and said, Smite this people, I pray thee, with blindness. And *f*he smote them with blindness according to the word of

19 Elisha. And Elisha said unto them, This *is* not the way, neither *is* this the city: ¹follow me, and I will bring you to the man

20 whom ye seek. But he led them to Samaria. And it came to pass, when they were come into Samaria, that Elisha said, LORD, open the eyes of these *men*, that they may see. And the LORD opened their eyes, and they saw; and, behold, *they*

21 *were* in the midst of Samaria. And the king of Israel said unto Elisha, when he saw them, My father, shall I smite *them?*

22 shall I smite *them?* And he answered, Thou shalt not smite *them:* wouldest thou smite those whom thou hast taken captive with thy sword and with thy bow? *g*set bread and water before

23 them, that they may eat and drink, and go to their master. And he prepared great provision for them: and when they had eaten and drunk, he sent them away, and they went to their master. So *h*the bands of Syria came no more into the land of Israel.

24 ¶ And it came to pass after this, that Ben-hadad king of Syria

25 gathered all his host, and went up, and besieged Samaria. And there was a great famine in Samaria: and, behold, they besieged it, until an ass's head was *sold* for fourscore *pieces* of silver, and the fourth part of a cab of dove's dung for five *pieces* of silver.

c ch. 2. 11.
Ps. 34. 7.
& 68. 17.
Zech. 1. 8.
& 6. 1—7.,
f Gen. 19. 11.

g Rom.12.20.

h ch. 5. 2.
ver. 8, 9.

¹ Heb. *come ye after me.*

---

17. *open his eyes that he may see*] Elisha's servant lacked the faith of his master. Elisha therefore prays that he may be given a vision of the spiritual world, and see, as if with the bodily eye, the angelic host (marg. reff.) which he himself knows to be present.

18. *they came down to him*] The Syrians, who had been encamped on rising ground opposite the hill of Dothan, now descended and drew near to the city.

The blindness with which they were smitten was not real blindness—actual loss of sight—but a state of illusion in which a man sees things otherwise than as they are (cp. *v.* 20).

21. *My father*] A term of respect used by Jehoram in his joy at seeing an army of Syrians delivered up to him by the Prophet. That the king's character was not changed appears from *vv.* 31, 32.

shall I smite them? shall I smite them?] The repetition of the words mean, "Shall I **utterly** smite them?" Cp. similar repetitions with similar meanings in Gen. xxii. 17; Luke xxii. 15.

22. *wouldest thou smite, &c.*] It is doubtful whether this sentence is really interrogative. Others translate—"Smite those whom thou hast taken captive with thy sword," &c. A contrast is intended between ordinary captives—those made with the sword and bow—and these particular prisoners who have

been given into the king's hand by God. The former, Jehoram is told, he may slay, if he pleases (Deut. xx. 13), the latter, he is informed, he must not slay (cp. marg. ref.).

23. Jehoram did not merely follow the letter of the Prophet's direction, but understood its spirit, and acted accordingly. The plundering bands which had been in the habit of ravaging the territory (v. 2), ceased their incursions in consequence either of the miracle, or of the kind treatment which Elisha had recommended.

24. *after this*] Perhaps some years after —when the miracle and the kind treatment were alike forgotten.

25. As the ass was "unclean," it would not be eaten except in the last resort; and its head would be its worst and cheapest part.

cab] This measure is not mentioned elsewhere in Scripture. According to the Rabbinical writers it was the smallest of all the dry measures in use among the Jews, being the sixth part of a *seah*, which was the third part of an *ephah*. If it was about equal to two of our quarts, the "fourth part of a cab" would be about a pint.

dove's dung] Most commentators understand by this expression a sort of pulse, which is called "dove's dung," or "sparrow's dung" in Arabic. But it is possible that the actual excrement of pigeons is

26 And as the king of Israel was passing by upon the wall, there
27 cried a woman unto him, saying, Help, my lord, O king. And
he said, [1]If the LORD do not help thee, whence shall I help thee?
28 out of the barnfloor, or out of the winepress? And the king
said unto her, What aileth thee? And she answered, This woman
said unto me, Give thy son, that we may eat him to day, and we
29 will eat my son to-morrow. So [i]we boiled my son, and did
eat him: and I said unto her on the [2]next day, Give thy son, that
30 we may eat him: and she hath hid her son. And it came to
pass, when the king heard the words of the woman, that he [k]rent
his clothes; and he passed by upon the wall, and the people
looked, and, behold, *he had* sackcloth within upon his flesh.
31 Then he said, [l]God do so and more also to me, if the head of
32 Elisha the son of Shaphat shall stand on him this day. But
Elisha sat in his house, and [m]the elders sat with him; and *the
king* sent a man from before him: but ere the messenger came
to him, he said to the elders, [n]See ye how this son of [o]a murderer hath sent to take away mine head? look, when the messenger cometh, shut the door, and hold him fast at the door: *is*
33 not the sound of his master's feet behind him? And while

[i] Lev. 26. 29.
Deut. 28. 53, 57.

[k] 1 Kin. 21. 27.

[l] 1 Kin. 19. 2.

[m] Ezek. 8. 1. & 20. 1.

[n] Luke 13. 32.
[o] 1 Kin. 18. 4.

[1] Or, *Let not the LORD save thee.*   [2] Heb. *other.*

---

meant. The records of sieges show that both animal and human excrement have been used as food—under circumstances of extreme necessity.

26. The walls of fortified towns had a broad space at the top, protected towards the exterior by battlements, along which the bulk of the defenders were disposed, and from which they hurled their missiles and shot their arrows. The king seems to have been going his rounds, to inspect the state of the garrison and the defences.

27. *If the LORD do not help*] The translation in the text is decidedly better than the marginal rendering. Some prefer to render —"Nay—let Jehovah help thee. Whence shall I help thee?"

out of the barnfloor, &c.] The king means that both were empty—that he had no longer any food in store; and therefore could not help the woman. Cp. Hos. ix. 2.

28. The king had assumed that the cry of the woman was for food. Her manner indicated that it was not so. He therefore proceeded to inquire what she wanted of him.

this woman] Both women, it would seem, were present; and the aggrieved one pointed to the other.

29. The prophecy alluded to in the marg. reff. was now fulfilled, probably for the first time. It had a second accomplishment when Jerusalem was besieged by Nebuchadnezzar (Lam. iv. 10), and a third in the final siege of the same city by Titus.

30. *sackcloth*] Jehoram hoped perhaps to avert Jehovah's anger, as his father had done (1 K. xxi. 29). But there was no spirit of self-humiliation, or of true penitence in his heart (v. 7). See the next verse.

31. *God do so,* &c.] Jehoram uses almost the very words of his wicked mother, when she sought the life of Elijah (marg. ref.).

the head of Elisha] Beheading was not an ordinary Jewish punishment. The Law did not sanction it. But in Assyria, Babylonia, and generally through the East, it was the most common form of capital punishment. It is not quite clear why Elisha was to be punished. Perhaps Jehoram argued from his other miracles that he could give deliverance from the present peril, if he liked.

32. *But Elisha sat,* &c.] Translate, "And Elisha was sitting in his house, and all the elders were sitting with him, when the king sent, &c."

The "elders,"—either "the elders of the city" or "the elders of the land,"—who may have been in session at Samaria now, as they had been at the time of a former siege (1 K. xx. 7)—had gone to Elisha for his advice or assistance. Their imminent peril drove them to acknowledge the power of Jehovah, and to consult with His Prophet.

this son of a murderer] *i.e.* of Ahab, the murderer, not only of Naboth, but also of all the Prophets of the Lord (marg. ref.), whom he allowed Jezebel to slay.

hold him fast at the door] The elders, public officials, not private friends of Elisha, could not have been expected to resist the entrance of the executioner at the *mere* request of the Prophet. He therefore assigns a reason for his request—"the king is coming in person, either to confirm or revoke his order—will they detain the headsman until his arrival?"

33. *the messenger*] It has been proposed to change "messenger" into "king," the two words being in Hebrew nearly alike, and the speech with which the chapter ends being considered only suitable in the mouth of the

he yet talked with them, behold, the messenger came down unto

p Job 2. 9.   him : and he said, Behold, this evil *is* of the LORD ; *p*what
should I wait for the LORD any longer ?

CHAP. 7. THEN Elisha said, Hear ye the word of the LORD ; Thus

a ver. 18, 19.   saith the LORD, *a*To morrow about this time *shall* a measure of
fine flour *be sold* for a shekel, and two measures of barley for a

b ver. 17.   2 shekel, in the gate of Samaria. *b*Then *1*a lord on whose hand
ch. 5. 18.
c Mal. 3. 10.   the king leaned answered the man of God, and said, Behold, *c*if
the LORD would make windows in heaven, might this thing be ?
And he said, Behold, thou shalt see *it* with thine eyes, but shalt

d Lev. 13. 46.   3 not eat thereof. ¶ And there were four leprous men *d*at the
entering in of the gate : and they said one to another, Why sit
4 we here until we die ? If we say, We will enter into the city,
then the famine *is* in the city, and we shall die there : and if
we sit still here, we die also. Now therefore come, and let us
fall unto the host of the Syrians : if they save us alive, we shall
5 live ; and if they kill us, we shall but die. And they rose up
in the twilight, to go unto the camp of the Syrians : and when
they were come to the uttermost part of the camp of Syria,
6 behold, *there was* no man there. For the Lord had made the

e 2 Sam.5.21.   host of the Syrians *e*to hear a noise of chariots, and a noise
ch. 19. 7.
Job 15. 21.   of horses, *even* the noise of a great host : and they said one to
f 1 Kin.10.29.   another, Lo, the king of Israel hath hired against us *f*the kings

1 Heb. *a lord which* belonged *to the king leaning upon his hand,* ch. 5. 18.

---

king, whose presence is indicated in vii. 2,
17. Others think that the words "and the
king after him" have fallen out of the text.
came down] The messenger came *down*
from off the wall to the level of the streets.
Behold this evil, &c.] Jehoram bursts into
the Prophet's presence with a justification
of the sentence (*v.* 31) he has pronounced
against him. "Behold this evil—this siege
with all its horrors—is from Jehovah—from
Jehovah, Whose Prophet thou art. Why
should I wait for Jehovah—temporise with
Him—keep, as it were, on terms with Him
by suffering thee to live—any longer ? What
hast thou to say in arrest of judgment ?"
VII. 1. The division between the chapters is most awkward here. Elisha, in this
verse, replies to the king's challenge in vi.
33—that his God, Jehovah, will give deliverance in the space of a day. On the
morrow, by the same time in the day, the
famine will have ceased, and food will be
even cheaper than usual.
a measure of fine flour] Lit. "*a seah* of
fine flour ;" about a peck and a half.
for a shekel] About 2s. 8½d.
two measures of barley] Or, "two *seahs* of
barley ;" about three pecks.
in the gate] The "gates," or "gateways,"
of Eastern towns are favourite places for the
despatch of various kinds of business. It
would seem that at Samaria one of the
gates was used for the corn market.
2. *a lord*] Rather, "**the captain,**" as in
Ex. xiv. 7 ; 1 K. ix. 22 ; &c. The term itself,
shalish (derived from *shalosh,* "three,") may
be compared with the Latin "tribunus."

windows] Rather, "sluices" (cp. Gen. vii.
11). The "lord" means to say—"If Jehovah were to open sluices in heaven, and pour
down corn as He poured down rain in the
time of the Deluge, even then could there
be such abundance as thou speakest of ?"
3. The position of the lepers is in accordance with the Law of Moses (marg. reff.) ;
and shows that the Law was still observed
to some extent in the kingdom of Israel.
5. *the twilight*] The *evening* twilight (see
v. 9).
the uttermost part of the camp] The extreme boundary of the camp *towards the
city,* not its furthest or most distant portion.
Cp. *v.* 8.
6. It is a matter of no importance whether
we say that the miracle by which God now
wrought deliverance for Samaria consisted
in a mere illusion of the sense of hearing
(cp. vi. 19, 20) ; or whether there was any
objective reality in the sound (cp. marg.
reff.).
the king of Israel hath hired] The swords
of mercenaries had been employed by the
nations bordering on Palestine as early as
the time of David (2 Sam. x. 6 ; 1 Chr. xix.
6, 7). Hence the supposition of the Syrians
was far from improbable.
the kings of the Hittites] The Hittites, who
are found first in the south (Gen. xxiii. 7),
then in the centre of Judæa (Josh. xi. 3),
seem to have retired northwards after the
occupation of Palestine by the Israelites.
They are found among the Syrian enemies
of the Egyptians in the monuments of the
19th dynasty (about B.C. 1300), and appear at

of the Hittites, and the kings of the Egyptians, to come upon
7 us. Wherefore they *arose and fled in the twilight, and left
their tents, and their horses, and their asses, even the camp as it
8 *was*, and fled for their life. And when these lepers came to the
uttermost part of the camp, they went into one tent, and did eat
and drink, and carried thence silver, and gold, and raiment,
and went and hid *it;* and came again, and entered into another
9 tent, and carried thence *also*, and went and hid *it*. Then they
said one to another, We do not well : this day *is* a day of good
tidings, and we hold our peace: if we tarry till the morning
light, [1]some mischief will come upon us : now therefore come,
10 that we may go and tell the king's household. So they came
and called unto the porter of the city: and they told them,
saying, We came to the camp of the Syrians, and, behold, *there
was* no man there, neither voice of man, but horses tied, and
11 asses tied, and the tents as they *were*. And he called the porters;
12 and they told *it* to the king's house within. ¶ And the king
arose in the night, and said unto his servants, I will now shew
you what the Syrians have done to us. They know that we *be*
hungry; therefore are they gone out of the camp to hide themselves in the field, saying, When they come out of the city, we
13 shall catch them alive, and get into the city. And one of his
servants answered and said, Let *some* take, I pray thee, five of
the horses that remain, which are left [2]in the city, (behold, they
are as all the multitude of Israel that are left in it : behold, *I
say*, they *are* even as all the multitude of the Israelites that are
14 consumed :) and let us send and see. They took therefore two

g Ps. 48. 4,
5, 6.
Prov. 28. 1.

---

[1] Heb. *we shall find punishment.*   [2] Heb. *in it.*

---

that time to have inhabited the valley of
the Upper Orontes. In the early Assyrian
monuments they form a great confederacy,
as the most powerful people of northern
Syria, dwelling on both banks of the
Euphrates, while at the same time there is
a second confederacy of their race further
to the south, which seems to inhabit the
anti-Lebanon between Hamath and Damascus. These southern Hittites are in the
time of Benhadad and Hazael a powerful
people, especially strong in *chariots ;* and
generally assist the Syrians against the
Assyrians. The Syrians seem now to have
imagined that these southern Hittites had
been hired by Jehoram.

the kings of the Egyptians] This is a remarkable expression, since Egypt elsewhere
throughout Scripture appears always as·a
centralised monarchy under a single ruler.
The probability is that the principal Pharaoh had a prince or princes associated
with him on the throne, a practice not uncommon in Egypt. The period, which is
that of the 22nd dynasty, is an obscure one,
on which the monuments throw but little
light.

9. The lepers began to think that if they
kept this important matter secret during
the whole night for their own private
advantage, when the morning came they
would be found out, accused, and punished
(see marg.).

10. *they called unto the porter...and told
them*] The word "porter" is used like our
"guard," and the meaning here is, not that
the lepers called to any particular individual,
but that they roused the body of men who
were keeping guard at one of the gates.

12. *his servants*] *i.e.*, "high officers of the
household," not mere domestics.

I will shew you what the Syrians have done]
Jehoram sees in the deserted camp a stra-
tagem like that connected with the taking
of Ai (Josh. viii. 3-19). The suspicion was
a very natural one, since the Israelites
knew of no reason why the Syrians should
have raised the siege.

13. *behold*, &c.] The LXX. and a large
number of the Hebrew MSS. omit the
clause, "behold, they are as all the multitude of Israel that are left in it." But the
text followed by our translators, which is
that of the best MSS., is intelligible and
needs no alteration. It is merely a prolix
way of stating that the horsemen will incur
no greater danger by going to reconnoitre
than the rest of their countrymen by remaining in the city, since the whole multitude is perishing.

14. *two chariot horses*] Translate, "**two
horse-chariots.**" They dispatched *i.e.* two

chariot horses; and the king sent after the host of the Syrians,
15 saying, Go and see. And they went after them unto Jordan:
and, lo, all the way *was* full of garments and vessels, which the
Syrians had cast away in their haste. And the messengers
16 returned, and told the king. ¶And the people went out, and
spoiled the tents of the Syrians. So a measure of fine flour was

h ver. 1.

sold for a shekel, and two measures of barley for a shekel, *h*ac-
17 cording to the word of the LORD. And the king appointed the
lord on whose hand he leaned to have the charge of the gate:

i ch. 6. 32.
ver. 2.

and the people trode upon him in the gate, and he died, *i*as the
man of God had said, who spake when the king came down to
18 him. And it came to pass as the man of God had spoken to the

k ver. 1.

king, saying, *k*Two measures of barley for a shekel, and a
measure of fine flour for a shekel, shall be to morrow about
19 this time in the gate of Samaria: and that lord answered the
man of God, and said, Now, behold, *if* the LORD should make
windows in heaven, might such a thing be? And he said,
Behold, thou shalt see it with thine eyes, but shalt not eat
20 thereof. And so it fell out unto him: for the people trode upon
him in the gate, and he died.

a ch. 4. 35.

CHAP. 8. THEN spake Elisha unto the woman, *a*whose son he had
restored to life, saying, Arise, and go thou and thine household,
and sojourn wheresoever thou canst sojourn: for the LORD

b Ps. 105. 16.
Hag. 1. 11.

*b*hath called for a famine; and it shall also come upon the land
2 seven years. And the woman arose, and did after the saying of
the man of God: and she went with her household, and sojourned
3 in the land of the Philistines seven years. And it came to pass
at the seven years' end, that the woman returned out of the
land of the Philistines: and she went forth to cry unto the king
4 for her house and for her land. And the king talked with

c ch. 5. 27.

*c*Gehazi the servant of the man of God, saying, Tell me, I pray
5 thee, all the great things that Elisha hath done. And it came

d ch. 4. 35.

to pass, as he was telling the king how he had *d*restored a dead
body to life, that, behold, the woman, whose son he had restored
to life, cried to the king for her house and for her land. And
Gehazi said, My lord, O king, this *is* the woman, and this *is* her

---

war-chariots, with their proper complement
of horses and men, to see whether the retreat was a reality or only a feint. The
" horses " sent would be four or six, since
chariots were drawn by either two or three
horses.

15. The Syrians had fled probably by the
great road which led from Samaria to
Damascus through Geba, En-gannim, Beth-
shean, and Aphek. It crosses the Jordan at
the *Jisr Mejamia*, about thirty-five miles
north-east of Samaria.

VIII. 1. The famine here recorded, and
the conversation of the monarch with
Gehazi, must have been anterior to the
events related in ch. v.—since we may be
sure that a king of Israel would not have
entered into familiar conversation with a
confirmed leper. The writer of Kings probably collected the miracles of Elisha from
various sources, and did not always arrange
them chronologically. Here the link of
connexion is to be found in the nature of

the miracle. As Elisha on one occasion
prophesied plenty, so on another he had
prophesied a famine.

called for a famine] A frequent expression
(cp. marg. reff.). God's " calling for " anything is the same as His producing it (see
Ezek. xxxvi. 29 ; Rom. iv. 17).

2. The country of the Philistines—the
rich low corn-growing plain along the sea-
coast of Judah—was always a land of plenty
compared with the highlands of Palestine.
Moreover, if food failed there, it was easily
imported by sea from the neighbouring
Egypt.

3. During the Shunammite's absence in
Philistia, her dwelling and her corn-fields
had been appropriated by some one who
refused to restore them. She therefore
determined to appeal to the king. Such
direct appeals are common in Oriental
countries. Cp. vi. 26; 2 Sam. xiv. 4; 1
K. iii. 16.

6 son, whom Elisha restored to life. And when the king asked the woman, she told him. So the king appointed unto her a certain ¹officer, saying, Restore all that *was* her's, and all the fruits of the field since the day that she left the land, even until
7 now. ¶ And Elisha came to Damascus; and Ben-hadad the king of Syria was sick; and it was told him, saying, The man of
8 God is come hither. And the king said unto *ᵉ*Hazael, *ᶠ*Take a present in thine hand, and go, meet the man of God, and *ᵍ*enquire
9 of the LORD by him, saying, Shall I recover of this disease? So Hazael went to meet him, and took a present ²with him, even of every good thing of Damascus, forty camels' burden, and came and stood before him, and said, Thy son Ben-hadad king of Syria hath sent me to thee, saying, Shall I recover of this
10 disease? And Elisha said unto him, Go, say unto him, Thou mayest certainly recover: howbeit the LORD hath shewed me
11 that *ʰ*he shall surely die. And he settled his countenance ³stedfastly, until he was ashamed: and the man of God *ⁱ*wept.
12 And Hazael said, Why weepeth my lord? And he answered, Because I know *ᵏ*the evil that thou wilt do unto the children of

ᵉ 1 Kin. 19. 15.
ᶠ 1 Sam. 9. 7.
1 Kin. 14. 3.
ch. 5. 5.
ᵍ ch. 1. 2.

ʰ ver. 15.

ⁱ Luke 19. 11.

ᵏ ch. 10. 32.
& 12. 17.
& 13. 3, 7.
Amos 1. 3.

¹ Or, *eunuch.*   ² Heb. *in his hand.*   ³ Heb. *and set it.*

---

6. *a certain officer*] Lit., "a certain eunuch" (marg.). Eunuchs were now in common use at the Samaritan Court (cp. ix. 32). They are ascribed to the Court of David in Chronicles (1 Chr. xxviii. 1); and we may conjecture that they were maintained by Solomon. But otherwise we do not find them in the kingdom of Judah till the time of Hezekiah (Isai. lvi. 3, 4).

7. The hour had come for carrying out the command given by God to Elijah (marg. ref. *e*), and by him probably passed on to his successor. Elisha, careless of his own safety, quitted the land of Israel, and proceeded into the enemy's country, thus putting into the power of the Syrian king that life which he had lately sought so eagerly (vi. 13-19).

the man of God] The Damascenes had perhaps known Elisha by this title from the time of his curing Naaman. Or the phrase may be used as equivalent to "Prophet," which is the title commonly given to Elisha by the Syrians. See vi. 12. Cp. v. 13.

8. Hazael was no doubt a high officer of the court. The names of Hazael and Benhadad occur in the Assyrian inscription on the Black Obelisk now in the British Museum. Both are mentioned as kings of Damascus, who contended with a certain Shalmaneser, king of Assyria, and suffered defeat at his hands. In one of the battles between this king and Benhadad, "Ahab of Jezreel" is mentioned among the allies of the latter. This same Shalmaneser took tribute from Jehu. This is the point at which the Assyrian records first come in direct contact with those of the Jews.

9. *every good thing of Damascus*] Probably, besides rich robes and precious metals, the luscious wine of Helbon, which was the drink of the Persian kings, the soft white wool of the anti-Libanus (Ezek. xxvii. 18), *damask* coverings of couches (Am. iii. 12), and numerous manufactured articles of luxury, which the Syrian capital imported from Tyre, Egypt, Nineveh, and Babylon. Forty camels were laden with it, and this goodly caravan paraded the streets of the town, conveying to the prophet the splendid gift designed for him. Eastern ostentation induces donors to make the greatest possible show of their gifts, and each camel would probably bear only one or two articles.

thy son Ben-hadad] A phrase indicative of the greatest respect, no doubt used at the command of Benhadad in order to dispose the Prophet favourably towards him. Cp. vi. 21.

10. Translate—"Go, say unto him, Thou shalt certainly live: howbeit the Lord hath showed me that he shall certainly die." *i.e.* "Say to him, what thou hast already determined to say, what a courtier is sure to say (cp. 1 K. xxii. 15), but know that the *fact* will be otherwise."

11. That is, "And he (Elisha) settled his countenance, and set it (towards Hazael), till he (Hazael) was ashamed." Elisha fixed on Hazael a long and meaning look, till the latter's eyes fell before his, and his cheek flushed. Elisha, it would seem, had detected the guilty thought that was in Hazael's heart, and Hazael perceived that he had detected it. Hence the "shame."

12. *the evil that thou wilt do*] The intention is not to tax Hazael with special cruelty, but only to enumerate the ordinary horrors of war, as it was conducted among the Oriental nations of the time. Cp. marg. reff.

Israel: their strong holds wilt thou set on fire, and their young

t ch. 15. 16.
Hos. 13. 16.
Amos 1. 13.
m 1 Sam. 17.
43.
n 1Kin.19.15.

men wilt thou slay with the sword, and *l* wilt dash their children,
13 and rip up their women with child. And Hazael said, But
what, *m is* thy servant a dog, that he should do this great thing?
And Elisha answered, *n*The LORD hath shewed me that thou
14 *shalt be* king over Syria. So he departed from Elisha, and came
to his master; who said to him, What said Elisha to thee? And
he answered, He told me *that* thou shouldest surely recover.
15 And it came to pass on the morrow, that he took a thick cloth,
and dipped *it* in water, and spread *it* on his face, so that he died:
16 and Hazael reigned in his stead. ¶ And in the fifth year of
Joram, the son of Ahab king of Israel, Jehoshaphat *being* then

o 2 Chr. 21.3,
4.
p 2 Chr. 21.
5, &c.

king of Judah, *o*Jehoram the son of Jehoshaphat king of Judah
17 ¹began to reign. *p*Thirty and two years old was he when he
18 began to reign; and he reigned eight years in Jerusalem. And
he walked in the way of the kings of Israel, as did the house of

q ver. 26.
r 2Sam.7.13.
1 Kin. 11. 36.
& 15. 4.
2 Chr. 21. 7.

Ahab: for *q*the daughter of Ahab was his wife: and he did evil
19 in the sight of the LORD. Yet the LORD would not destroy
Judah for David his servant's sake, *r* as he promised him to give

¹ Heb. *reigned.* Began to reign in consort with his father.

---

13. *But what, is thy servant a dog?*] This
is a mistranslation, and conveys to the English reader a sense quite different from that
of the original. Hazael's speech runs thus—
"**But what is thy servant, this dog, that
he should do this great thing?**" He does
not shrink from Elisha's words, or mean to
say that he would be a dog, could he act so
cruelly as Elisha predicts he will. On the
contrary, Elisha's prediction has raised his
hopes, and his only doubt is whether so
much good fortune ("this great thing")
can be in store for one so mean. "Dog"
here, as generally (though not always) in
Scripture, has the sense of "mean," "low,"
"contemptible."

14. Hazael omitted the clause by which
Elisha had shown how those words were to
be understood. He thus deceived his master, while he could flatter himself that he
had not uttered a lie.

15. *a thick cloth*] Probably, a cloth or
mat placed between the head and the upper
part of the bedstead, which in Egypt and
Assyria was often so shaped that pillows (in
our sense) were unnecessary.

The objection that Elisha is involved in
the guilt of having suggested the deed, has
no real force or value. Hazael was no more
obliged to murder Benhadad because a Prophet announced to him that he would one
day be king of Syria, than David was obliged to murder Saul because another Prophet anointed him king in Saul's room (1
Sam. xvi. 1-13).

16-19. The passage is parenthetic, re-
suming the history of the kingdom of Judah
from 1 K. xxii. 50.

16. The opening words are — "**In the
fifth year of Joram, son of Ahab, king of
Israel, and of Jehoshaphat, king of Ju-**

dah;" but they contradict all the other
chronological notices of Jehoshaphat (1 K.
xxii. 42, 51; 2 K. iii. 1; 2 Chr. xx. 31),
which give him a reign of at least twenty-
three years. Hence some have supposed
that the words "Jehoshaphat being then
king of Judah," are accidentally repeated.
Those, however, who regard them and i. 17
as sound, suppose that Jehoshaphat gave
his son the royal title in his sixteenth year,
while he advanced him to a real association
in the empire seven years later, in his
twenty-third year. Two years afterwards,
Jehoshaphat died, and Jehoram became sole
king.

17. The "eight years" are counted from
his association in the kingdom. They ter-
minate in the twelfth year of Jehoram of
Israel.

18. Jehoshaphat's alliance, political and
social, with Ahab and Ahab's family had
not been allowed to affect the purity of
his faith. Jehoram his son, influenced by
his wife, Athaliah, the daughter of Ahab,
"walked in the way of the kings of Israel;"
he allowed, *i.e.,* the introduction of the
Baal-worship into Judæa.

Among the worst of Jehoram's evil doings must be reckoned the cruel murder of
his six brothers (2 Chr. xxi. 4), whom he
slew to obtain their wealth.

19. The natural consequence of Jehoram's
apostasy would have been the destruction
of his house, and the transfer of the throne
of Judah to another family. Cp. the
punishments of Jeroboam (1 K. xiv. 10),
Baasha (do. xvi. 2-4), and Ahab (do. xxi.
20-22). But the promises to David (marg.
reff.) prevented this removal of the dynasty; and so Jehoram was punished in
other ways (*v.* 22; 2 Chr. xxi. 12-19).

20 him alway a ¹light, *and* to his children. In his days ˢEdom
revolted from under the hand of Judah, ᵗand made a king over
21 themselves. So Joram went over to Zair, and all the chariots
with him: and he rose by night, and smote the Edomites which
compassed him about, and the captains of the chariots: and the
22 people fled into their tents. ²Yet Edom revolted from under
the hand of Judah unto this day. ᵘThen Libnah revolted at
23 the same time. ¶ And the rest of the acts of Joram, and all
that he did, *are* they not written in the book of the chronicles
24 of the kings of Judah? And Joram slept with his fathers, and
was buried with his fathers in the city of David: and ˣ³Ahaziah
25 his son reigned in his stead. ¶ In the twelfth year of Joram
the son of Ahab king of Israel did Ahaziah the son of Jehoram
26 king of Judah begin to reign. ᵛTwo and twenty years old *was*
Ahaziah when he began to reign; and he reigned one year in
Jerusalem. And his mother's name *was* Athaliah, the ⁴daughter
27 of Omri king of Israel. ᶻAnd he walked in the way of the
house of Ahab, and did evil in the sight of the LORD, as *did*
the house of Ahab: for he *was* the son in law of the house of
28 Ahab. And he went ᵃwith Joram the son of Ahab to the war
against Hazael king of Syria in Ramoth-gilead; and the Syrians

ˢ 2 Chr. 21.8,
9, 10.
ᵗ 1 Kin. 22.
47.

ᵘ 2 Chr. 21.
10.

ˣ 2 Chr.22.1.

ᵛ See 2 Chr.
22. 2.

ᶻ 2 Chr. 22.
3, 4.

ᵃ 2 Chr. 22.5.

---

¹ Heb. *candle*, or, *lamp*.
² And so fulfilled, Gen. 27.
40.

⁶ Called, *Azariah*, 2 Chr.
22. 6, and *Jehoahaz*, 2
Chr. 21. 17. & 25. 23.

⁴ Or, *granddaughter:* See
ver. 18.

---

20. Edom, which had been reduced by
David (2 Sam. viii. 14; 1 K. xi. 15, 16), but
had apparently revolted from Solomon (1 K.
xi. 14), was again subjected to Judah in the
reign of Jehoshaphat (iii. 8–26). The Edomites had, however, retained their native
kings, and with them the spirit of independence. They now rose in revolt, and fulfilled the prophecy (Gen. xxvii. 40), remaining from henceforth a separate and independent people (Jer. xxv. 21, xxvii. 3;
Am. i. 11, &c.). Kings of Edom, who seem
to be independent monarchs, are often mentioned in the Assyrian inscriptions.

21. *Zair*] Perhaps Seir, the famous mountain of Edom (Gen. xiv. 6).

the people] *i.e.* The Edomites. Yet, notwithstanding his success, Joram was forced
to withdraw from the country, and to
leave the natives to enjoy that independence (*v.* 22), which continued till the time
of John Hyrcanus, who once more reduced
them.

Libnah revolted] Libnah being towards•
the south-*west* of Palestine (Josh. xv. 42), its
revolt cannot well have had any direct connexion with that of Edom. It had been
the capital of a small Canaanite state
under a separate king before its conquest
by Joshua (Josh. x. 30, xii. 15), and may
perhaps always have retained a considerable
Canaanitish population. Or its loss may
have been connected with the attacks made
by the Philistines on Jehoram's territories
(2 Chr. xxi. 16, 17).

24. On the death of Jehoram, see 2 Chr.
xxi. 12-19. His son is also called Jehoahaz

(margin) by a transposition of the two elements of the name.

26. Such names as Athaliah, Jehoram,
and Ahaziah, indicate that the Baal-wor-
shipping kings of Israel did not openly renounce the service of Jehovah. Athaliah is
"the time for Jehovah;" Ahaziah "the
possession of Jehovah;" Jehoram, or Joram, "exalted by Jehovah."

the daughter of Omri] "Son" and "daughter" were used by the Jews of any descendants (cp. Matt. i. 1). The whole race were
"the children of Israel." Athaliah was
the *grand-daughter* of Omri (see marg.). Her
being called "the daughter of Omri" implies that an idea of special greatness was
regarded as attaching to him, so·that his
name prevailed over that of Ahab. Indications of this ideal greatness are found in
the Assyrian inscriptions, where the early
name for Samaria is Beth-Omri, and where
even Jehu has the title of "the son of
Omri."

28. This war of the two kings against
Hazael seems to have had for its object the
recovery of Ramoth-gilead, which Ahab
and Jehoshaphat had vainly attempted
fourteen years earlier (1 K. xxii. 3-36).
Joram probably thought that the accession
of a new and usurping monarch presented a
favourable opportunity for a renewal of the
war. It may also have happened that Hazael was engaged at the time upon his
northern frontier with repelling one of those
Assyrian attacks which seem by the inscriptions to have fallen upon him in quick succession during his earlier years. At any

b ch. 9. 15.

c ch. 9. 16.
2 Chr.22.6,7.

a 1 Kin. 20.
35.
b ch. 4. 29.
Jer. 1. 17.
c ch. 8. 28,29.

d ver. 5, 11.
e 1 Kin.19.16.

f 1 Kin.19.16.
2 Chr. 22. 7.

g 1 Kin.18.4.
& 21. 15.

h 1Kin.14.10.
& 21. 21.
i 1 Sam. 25.
22.
k Deut.32.36.
l 1 Kin. 14.
10.
& 15. 29.
& 21. 22.
m 1 Kin.16.3,
11.
n 1 Kin. 21.
23.
ver. 35. 36.
o Jer. 29. 26.
John 10. 20.
Acts 26. 24.
1 Cor. 4. 10.
p Matt. 21. 7.

29 wounded Joram. And *b*king Joram went back to be healed in Jezreel of the wounds ¹which the Syrians had given him at ²Ramah, when he fought against Hazael king of Syria. *c*And Ahaziah the son of Jehoram king of Judah went down to see Joram the son of Ahab in Jezreel, because he was ³sick.

CHAP. 9. AND Elisha the prophet called one of *a*the children of the prophets, and said unto him, *b*Gird up thy loins, and take 2 this box of oil in thine hand, *c*and go to Ramoth-gilead: and when thou comest thither, look out there Jehu the son of Jehoshaphat the son of Nimshi, and go in, and make him arise up from among *d*his brethren, and carry him to an ⁴inner chamber; 3 then *e*take the box of oil, and pour *it* on his head, and say, Thus saith the LORD, I have anointed thee king over Israel. 4 Then open the door, and flee, and tarry not. So the young man, *even* the young man the prophet, went to Ramoth-gilead. 5 ¶And when he came, behold, the captains of the host *were* sitting; and he said, I have an errand to thee, O captain. And Jehu said, Unto which of all us? And he said, To thee, O 6 captain. And he arose, and went into the house; and he poured the oil on his head, and said unto him, *f*Thus saith the LORD God of Israel, I have anointed thee king over the people of the 7 LORD, *even* over Israel. And thou shalt smite the house of Ahab thy master, that I may avenge the blood of my servants the prophets, and the blood of all the servants of the LORD, *g*at 8 the hand of Jezebel. For the whole house of Ahab shall perish: and *h*I will cut off from Ahab *i*him that pisseth against the 9 wall, and *k*him that is shut up and left in Israel: and I will make the house of Ahab like the house of *l*Jeroboam the son of Nebat, and like the house of *m*Baasha the son of Ahijah: 10 *n*and the dogs shall eat Jezebel in the portion of Jezreel, and *there shall be* none to bury *her.* And he opened the door, and 11 fled. ¶Then Jehu came forth to the servants of his lord: and *one* said unto him, *Is* all well? wherefore came *o*this mad *fellow* to thee? And he said unto them, Ye know the man, and his 12 communication. And they said, *It is* false; tell us now. And he said, Thus and thus spake he to me, saying, Thus saith the 13 LORD, I have anointed thee king over Israel. Then they hasted, and *p*took every man his garment, and put *it* under him on the

---

¹ Heb. *wherewith the Syrians had wounded.*　² Called, *Ramoth,* ver. 28.　³ Heb. *wounded.*　⁴ Heb. *chamber in a chamber.*

---

rate, the war appears to have been successful. Ramoth-gilead was recovered (ix. 14), and remained probably thenceforth in the hands of the Israelites.

the Syrians wounded Joram] According to Josephus, Joram was struck by an arrow in the course of the siege, but remained till the place was taken. He then withdrew to Jezreel (1 K. xviii. 45, xxi. 1), leaving his army under Jehu within the walls of the town.

IX. 1. *box*] Rather, "**flask**," or "**vial**" (1 Sam. x. 1). Oil and ointment were commonly kept in open-mouthed jars, vases, or bottles made of glass, alabaster, or earthenware. Many such vessels have been found both in Egypt and Assyria. The "oil" was the holy oil, compounded after the receipt given in Exodus (xxx. 23–25).

3. *flee, and tarry not*] The probable object of these directions was at once to prevent questioning, and to render the whole thing more striking.

5. The chief officers—the generals—were assembled together in Jehu's quarters, perhaps holding a council of war. The place of assembly seems to have been the great court. Hence, Jehu "went into the house" (*v.* 6)—entered, that is, one of the rooms opening into the court.

11. *this mad fellow*] The captains, seeing his excited look, his strange action, and his extreme haste, call him (as soldiers would) "this wild fellow."

13. *took every man his garment, and put it under him*] The outer cloak of the Jews was a sort of large shawl or blanket, which might well serve for a carpet of state. Such

top of the stairs, and blew with trumpets, saying, Jehu [1]is king.
14 So Jehu the son of Jehoshaphat the son of Nimshi conspired
against Joram. (Now Joram had kept Ramoth-gilead, he and
15 all Israel, because of Hazael king of Syria. But *king [2]Joram   *q* ch. 8. 29.
was returned to be healed in Jezreel of the wounds which the
Syrians [3]had given him, when he fought with Hazael king of
Syria.) ¶ And Jehu said, If it be your minds, *then* [4]let none go
16 forth *nor* escape out of the city to go to tell *it* in Jezreel. So
Jehu rode in a chariot, and went to Jezreel; for Joram lay there.
17 *r* And Ahaziah king of Judah was come down to see Joram. And   *r* ch. 8. 29.
there stood a watchman on the tower in Jezreel, and he spied
the company of Jehu as he came, and said, I see a company.
And Joram said, Take an horseman, and send to meet them,
18 and let him say, *Is it* peace? So there went one on horseback
to meet him, and said, Thus saith the king, *Is it* peace? And
Jehu said, What hast thou to do with peace? turn thee behind
me. And the watchman told, saying, The messenger came to
19 them, but he cometh not again. Then he sent out a second on
horseback, which came to them, and said, Thus saith the king,
Is it peace? And Jehu answered, What hast thou to do with
20 peace? turn thee behind me. And the watchman told, saying,
He came even unto them, and cometh not again: and the
[5]driving *is* like the driving of Jehu the son of Nimshi; for he
21 driveth [6]furiously. And Joram said, [7]Make ready. And his
chariot was made ready. And *s* Joram king of Israel and Aha-   *s* 2 Chr. 22.7.
ziah king of Judah went out, each in his chariot, and they went
out against Jehu, and [8]met him in the portion of Naboth the
22 Jezreelite. ¶ And it came to pass, when Joram saw Jehu, that
he said, *Is it* peace, Jehu? And he answered, What peace, so
long as the whoredoms of thy mother Jezebel and her witch-

---

[1] Heb. *reigneth.*
[2] Heb. *Jehoram.*
[3] Heb. *smote.*
[4] Heb. *let no escaper go,* &c.
[5] Or, *marching.*
[6] Heb. *in madness.*
[7] Heb. *Bind.*
[8] Heb. *found.*

---

a carpet is commonly represented on the seat of an Assyrian throne in the Nineveh sculptures.

The stairs rose against the wall of the house from the pavement of the court to the level of the upper story, or of the roof. At the top of the stairs would be a flat platform, and this would form a throne, on which the new king could exhibit himself to his subjects.

blew with trumpets] On this recognised part of the ceremony of a coronation, see xi. 14; 2 Sam. xv. 10; 1 K. i. 39.

14. *had kept*] Rather, "**was keeping watch.**" The city had been taken: but the war continuing, and there being a danger of the Syrians recovering it, Joram and all Israel (*i.e.* the whole military force) were guarding the recent conquest, while Hazael threatened it.

18. *What hast thou to do with peace?*] *i.e.*, "What does it matter to *thee* whether my errand is one of peace or not?"

20. *the driving ... furiously*] The word translated "driving" means "leading" or "conducting" a band. The watchman observed that the "company" (or, multitude)

was led forward madly, and associated this strange procedure with the known character of Jehu. It is curious that some Versions, as well as Josephus, give an opposite sense :— "he driveth quietly."

Jehu was properly "the grandson" of Nimshi, who was probably a more famous person than Jehoshaphat (*v.* 2).

21. *Make ready*] Lit. (as in marg.) "Bind," *i.e.* "Harness the horses to the chariot." The king had no suspicion of Jehu's treason. Probably he imagined that he was bringing him important news from the seat of war. Ahaziah's accompanying him is significant of the close friendship which united the uncle and the nephew. They went out not "against" Jehu, but rather "to meet him."

in the portion of Naboth] This is no longer called a "vineyard" (1 K. xxi. 1-18); probably because it had been thrown into the palace garden, and applied to the purpose for which Ahab originally wanted it. The approach to the city on this side must have lain either through it, or close by it.

22. Joram had asked the usual question, "Is it peace?"—meaning simply, "Is all

23 crafts *are so* many ? And Joram turned his hands, and fled, and
24 said to Ahaziah, *There is* treachery, O Ahaziah. And Jehu ¹drew
a bow with his full strength, and smote Jehoram between his
arms, and the arrow went out at his heart, and he ²sunk down
25 in his chariot. Then said *Jehu* to Bidkar his captain, Take up,
and cast him in the portion of the field of Naboth the Jezreelite:
for remember how that, when I and thou rode together after

ᵗ 1 Kin. 21. 29.   26 Ahab his father, *ᵗ*the LORD laid this burden upon him ; surely
I have seen yesterday the ³blood of Naboth, and the blood of

ᵘ 1 Kin. 21.   his sons, saith the LORD ; and *ᵘ*I will requite thee in this ⁴plat,
19.   saith the LORD. Now therefore take *and* cast him into the plat
27 *of ground*, according to the word of the LORD. ¶But when
Ahaziah the king of Judah saw *this*, he fled by the way of the
garden house. And Jehu followed after him, and said, Smite
him also in the chariot. *And they did so* at the going up to

ˣ In the   Gur, which *is* by Ibleam. And he fled to *ˣ*Megiddo, and died
kingdom of   28 there. And his servants carried ˙him in a chariot to Jerusalem,
Samaria,
2 Chr. 22. 9.   and buried him in his sepulchre with his fathers in the city of
29 David. And in the eleventh year of Joram the son of Ahab
30 began Ahaziah to reign over Judah. ¶And when Jehu was

ʸ Ezek. 23.   come to Jezreel, Jezebel heard *of it ;* *ʸ*and she ⁵painted her face,
40.

¹ Heb. *filled his hand with*	² Heb. *bowed.*	⁵ Heb. *put her eyes in*
a bow.	³ Heb. *bloods.*	*painting.*
	⁴ Or, *portion.*	

---

well ? ” In Jehu's reply, by “whoredoms”
we are probably to understand “idolatries,”
acts of spiritual unfaithfulness; by “witch-
crafts,” dealings with the Baal prophets
and oracles. Cp. i. 2 note.

23. *turned his hands*] The meaning is
that Joram *ordered his charioteer* to turn
round and drive back to the town.

24. *Jehu drew a bow*, &c.] Lit. as in margin, *i.e.* “Jehu took a bow in his hand.”
The arrow struck Jehoram's back, between
his two shoulders, as he fled.

25. *rode together after Ahab*] The Assyrian
sculptures make it probable that Josephus
was right in interpreting this “rode side
by side *behind Ahab in his chariot.*” The
Assyrian monarchs, when they go out to
war, are frequently attended by two guards,
who stand behind them in the same
chariot.

burden] Cp. the use of the same word in
Isaiah (xiii. 1, xv. 1, &c.), and in Lamentations (ii. 14), for a denunciation of woe.

26. The passage from “Surely I have
seen” to “Saith the Lord,” is exegetical
of *v.* 25, containing the “burden” there
spoken of.

and the blood of his sons] The murder of
Naboth's sons is here for the first time
mentioned ; but as the removal of the sons
was necessary, if the vineyard was to pass
to Ahab, we can well understand that Jezebel would take care to clear them out of the
way.

27. *by the way of the garden-house*] Or,
“by the way of Beth-Gan,” which has been
conjectured to be another name for En-

Gannim, “the spring of the gardens.” Both
are considered identical with Ginæa, the
modern *Jenin*, which lies due south of
Jezreel. The road from Jezreel (*Zerin*) to
Jenin passes at first along the plain of
Esdraelon, but after a while begins to rise
over the Samaritan hills. Here probably
was “the ascent of Gur, by Ibleam,” which
may have occupied the site of the modern
Jelama. Whether the soldiers attacked
him there or not is uncertain. The words,
“*And they did so,*” are not in the original.

Megiddo] On its situation, see Josh. xii.
21 note ; and on the possible reconcilement
of this passage with 2 Chr. xxii. 9, see the
note there.

29. *in the eleventh year*] The twelfth according to viii. 25. The discrepancy may
be best explained from two ways of reckoning the accession of Ahaziah, who is likely
to have been regent for his father during at
least one year. See 2 Chr. xxi. 19.

30. *painted her face*] Lit. “put her eyes
in antimony”—*i.e.* dyed the upper and
under eyelids, a common practice in the
East, even at the present day. The effect
is at once to increase the apparent size of
the eye, and to give it unnatural brilliancy.
Representations of eyes thus embellished
occur on the Assyrian sculptures, and the
practice existed among the Jews (marg.
ref.; and Jer. iv. 30).

tired her head] Dressed (attired) her head,
and no doubt put on her royal robes, that
she might die as became a queen, in true
royal array.

31 and tired her head, and looked out at a window. And as Jehu
entered in at the gate, she said, *Had Zimri peace, who slew his
32 master? And he lifted up his face to the window, and said,
Who *is* on my side? who? And there looked out to him two
33 *or* three ¹eunuchs. And he said, Throw her down. So they
threw her down: and *some* of her blood was sprinkled on the
34 wall, and on the horses: and he trode her under foot. And
when he was come in, he did eat and drink, and said, Go, see
now this cursed *woman*, and bury her: for ᵃshe *is* a king's
35 daughter. And they went to bury her: but they found no more
of her than the skull, and the feet, and the palms of *her* hands.
36 Wherefore they came again, and told him. And he said, This
is the word of the LORD, which he spake ²by his servant Elijah
the Tishbite, saying, ᵇIn the portion of Jezreel shall dogs eat
37 the flesh of Jezebel: and the carcase of Jezebel shall be ᶜas dung
upon the face of the field in the portion of Jezreel; *so* that they
shall not say, This *is* Jezebel.

CHAP. 10. AND Ahab had seventy sons in Samaria. And Jehu
wrote letters, and sent to Samaria, unto the rulers of Jezreel,
to the elders, and to ³them that brought up Ahab's *children*,
2 saying, Now as soon as this letter cometh to you, seeing your
master's sons *are* with you, and *there are* with you chariots and
3 horses, a fenced city also, and armour; look even out the best
and meetest of your master's sons, and set *him* on his father's
4 throne, and fight for your master's house. But they were exceedingly afraid, and said, Behold, two kings stood not before
5 him: how then shall we stand? And he that *was* over the
house, and he that *was* over the city, the elders also, and the
bringers up *of the children*, sent to Jehu, saying, We *are* thy
servants, and will do all that thou shalt bid us; we will not
make any king: do thou *that which is* good in thine eyes.
6 ¶ Then he wrote a letter the second time to them, saying, If ye
be ⁴mine, and *if* ye will hearken unto my voice, take ye the

ᵃ 1 Kin. 16.
9—20.

ᵃ 1 Kin. 16.
31.

ᵇ 1 Kin. 21.
23.
ᶜ Ps. 83. 10.

¹ Or, *chamberlains.*   ² Heb. *by the hand of.*   ⁴ Heb. *for me.*
³ Heb. *nourishers.*

a window] Rather, "the window." The
gate-tower had probably, as many of those
in the Assyrian sculptures, one window
only.

34. Leaving the mangled body on the
bare earth, Jehu went to the banquet. It
was, no doubt, important that he should at
once show himself to the Court as king. In
calling Jezebel "this cursed one," Jehu
means to remind his hearers that the curse
of God had been pronounced upon her by
Elijah (*v.* 36), and so to justify his own conduct.

a king's daughter] Merely as the widow of
Ahab and mother of Jehoram, Jehu would
not have considered Jezebel entitled to
burial. But she was the daughter of Eth-
baal, king of the Sidonians (marg. ref.),
and so a princess born. This would entitle
her to greater respect. Wilfully to have
denied her burial would have been regarded
as an unpardonable insult by the reigning
Sidonian monarch.

X. 1. *seventy sons*] *i.e.* descendants; there

were included among them children of Jehoram (*vv.* 2, 3, &c.).

2. *a fenced city*] Or, "fenced cities." If
Samaria had refused to acknowledge Jehu,
many other Israelite towns would have been
sure to follow the example.

3. Jehu, placing his adversaries' advantages before them in the most favourable
light, called upon them to decide what they
would do. The unscrupulous soldier shows
shrewdness as well as courage, a sharp wit
as well as a bold heart.

4. *two kings*] Lit. "the two kings," *i.e.*
Jehoram and Ahaziah (ix. 21—28).

5. The officer who had the charge of the
palace (1 K. iv. 6 note) and the governor
of the town (1 K. xxii. 26 note) seem to correspond to the "rulers" of *v.* 1.

6. The heads of rivals, pretenders, and
other obnoxious persons are commonly
struck off in the East, and conveyed to the
chief ruler, in order that he may be posi-
tively certified that his enemies have ceased
to live. In the Assyrian sculptures we

heads of the men your master's sons, and come to me to Jezreel by to morrow this time. Now the king's sons, *being* seventy persons, *were* with the great men of the city, which brought them
7 up. And it came to pass, when the letter came to them, that they took the king's sons, and *a*slew seventy persons, and put
8 their heads in baskets, and sent him *them* to Jezreel. And there came a messenger, and told him, saying, They have brought the heads of the king's sons. And he said, Lay ye them in two
9 heaps at the entering in of the gate until the morning. And it came to pass in the morning, that he went out, and stood, and said to all the people, Ye *be* righteous : behold, *b*I conspired against my master, and slew him : but who slew all these ?
10 Know now that there shall *c*fall unto the earth nothing of the word of the LORD, which the LORD spake concerning the house of Ahab : for the LORD hath done *that* which he spake *d*1by his
11 servant Elijah. So Jehu slew all that remained of the house of Ahab in Jezreel, and all his great men, and his 2kinsfolks,
12 and his priests, until he left him none remaining. ¶And he arose and departed, and came to Samaria. *And* as he *was* at
13 the 3shearing house in the way, *e*Jehu 4met with the brethren of Ahaziah king of Judah, and said, Who *are* ye ? And they answered, We *are* the brethren of Ahaziah ; and we go down 5to salute the children of the king and the children of the queen.
14 And he said, Take them-alive. And they took them alive, and slew them at the pit of the shearing house, *even* two and forty
15 men ; neither left he any of them. ¶And when he was departed thence, he 6lighted on *f*Jehonadab the son of *g*Rechab *coming* to meet him : and he 7saluted him, and said to him, Is thine heart right, as my heart *is* with thy heart ? And Jeho-

a 1 Kin. 21. 21.

b ch. 9.14,24.

c 1 Sam. 3.19.

d 1 Kin. 21. 19, 21, 29.

e ch. 8. 29. 2 Chr. 22. 8.

f Jer. 35. 6, &c.
g 1 Chr. 2. 55.

---

1 Heb. *by the hand of.*
2 Or, *acquaintance.*
3 Heb. *house of shepherds binding sheep.*
4 Heb. *found.*
5 Heb. *to the peace of, &c.*
6 Heb. *found.*
7 Heb. *blessed.*

---

constantly see soldiers conveying heads from place to place, not, however, in baskets, but in their hands, holding the head by the hair.

8. *two heaps*] Probably placed one on either side of the gateway, to strike terror into the partisans of the late dynasty as they passed in and out of the town.

9. *Ye be righteous*] i.e. "Ye are just, and can judge aright." Jehu unfairly keeps back the fact that he had commanded the execution.

10. *shall fall to the earth*] i.e. "Shall remain unfulfilled' (cp. marg. ref.). Jehu and others were but executing the word of the Lord.

11. *So Jehu slew*] Rather, "**And** Jehu slew." The reference is to fresh executions (cp. *v.* 17). He proceeded on his bloody course, not merely destroying the remainder of the kindred of Ahab, but further putting to death all the most powerful of Ahab's partisans.

his priests] Not the Baal priests generally, whose persecution came afterwards (*v.* 19), but only such of them as were attached to the Court.

12. *the shearing-house*] Lit. as in marg.

Perhaps already a proper name, Beth-eked, identical with the Beth-akad of Jerome, which is described as between Jezreel and Samaria ; but not yet identified.

13. *the brethren of Ahaziah*] Not the actual brothers of Ahaziah, who had all been slain by the Arabs before his accession to the throne (2 Chr. xxi. 17, xxii. 1) ; but his nephews, the sons of his brothers (marg. ref.). It is remarkable that they should have penetrated so far into the kingdom of Israel without having heard of the revolution.

the children of the king, &c.] i.e. "the sons of Jehoram, and the children (sons and grandsons) of the queen-mother, Jezebel." Some of both may well have been at Jezreel, though the younger branches of the royal family were at Samaria (*v.* 1).

15. Jehonadab (cp. margin) belonged to the tribe of the Kenites, one of the most ancient in Palestine (Gen. xv. 19). Their origin is unknown, but their habits were certainly those of Arabs. Owing to their connexion with Moses (Num. xxiv. 21 note), they formed a friendship with the Israelites, accompanied them in their wanderings, and finally received a location in the wilderness of Judah (Judg. i. 16). The character of this chief,

nadab answered, It is. If it be, *h* give *me* thine hand. And he
gave *him* his hand; and he took him up to him into the chariot.
16 And he said, Come with me, and see my *i* zeal for the LORD. So
17 they made him ride in his chariot. And when he came to
Samaria, *k* he slew all that remained unto Ahab in Samaria, till
he had destroyed him, according to the saying of the LORD,
18 *l* which he spake to Elijah. ¶ And Jehu gathered all the people
together, and said unto them, *m* Ahab served Baal a little; *but*
19 Jehu shall serve him much. Now therefore call unto me all the
n prophets of Baal, all his servants, and all his priests; let none
be wanting: for I have a great sacrifice *to do* to Baal; whosoever
shall be wanting, he shall not live. But Jehu did *it* in subtilty,
to the intent that he might destroy the worshippers of Baal.
20 And Jehu said, ¹ Proclaim a solemn assembly for Baal. And
21 they proclaimed *it*. And Jehu sent through all Israel: and all
the worshippers of Baal came, so that there was not a man left
that came not. And they came into the *o* house of Baal; and
22 the house of Baal was ² full from one end to another. And he
said unto him that *was* over the vestry, Bring forth vestments

h Ezra 10.19.

i 1Kin.19.10.

k ch. 9. 8.
2 Chr. 22. 8.

l 1Kin.21.21.
m 1 Kin. 16.
31, 32.

n 1 Kin.22.6.

o 1 Kin. 16.
32.

---

¹ Heb. *Sanctify.* ² Or, so *full*, that they stood *mouth to mouth.*

Jonadab, is best seen in the rule which he
established for his descendants (Jer. xxxv.
6, 7)—a rule said to be still observed at the
present day. It would seem that he sym-
pathised strongly with Jehu's proceedings,
and desired to give the countenance of his
authority, such as it was, to the new reign.
According to the Hebrew text, Jehu "saluted" (or blessed) Jehonadab. According
to the LXX. and Josephus, Jehonadab
"saluted" (or blessed) the king. Further,
the Hebrew text runs—"And Jehonadab
answered, It is, it is. Give (me) thy hand.
And he gave (him) his hand, and took him
up to him into the chariot." Our translators appear to have preferred the LXX.;
but the Hebrew is more graphic. Jehu was
no doubt glad to have the countenance of
Jehonadab on his public entrance into Samaria. The ascetic had a reputation for
sanctity, which could not fail to make his
companionship an advantage to the but
half-established monarch.

17. Cp. *v.* 11. Thus was finally completed the political revolution which transferred the throne from the house of Omri to
that of Nimshi, the fifth of the royal families of Israel.

according to the saying of the LORD]
This emphatic reiteration (cp. *v.* 10) marks,
first, how in the mind of the writer all this
history is viewed as deriving its special interest from its being so full and complete
an accomplishment of Elijah's prophecies;
and, secondly, how at the time Jehu carefully put forward the plea that what he did
had this object. It does not indicate that a
single-minded wish to execute God's will
was Jehu's predominate motive. Probably,
even where he most strictly fulfilled the
letter of prophecies, he was working for

himself, not for God; and hence vengeance
was denounced upon his house even for the
very "blood of Jezreel" (Hos. i. 4).

18. Though we cannot ascribe to Jehu a
spirit of true piety (see *v.* 29), we can well
enough understand how the soldier, trained
in the Syrian wars, revolted against the
unmanly and voluptuous worship of the
Dea Syra, and wished to go back to the
simple solemn service of Jehovah. These
views and feelings it would have been dangerous to declare during the lifetime of Jezebel. Even after her death it was prudent
to temporise, to wait until the party of
Ahab was crushed politically, before broach-
ing the religious question. Having now
slain all the issue of Ahab in the kingdom
of Israel, and all the influential men of the
party (*vv.* 7, 11, and 17), Jehu felt that he
might begin his reformation of religion.
But even now he uses "subtilty" rather
than open violence. "Ahab served Baal a
little; but Jehu shall serve him much."

19. It appears from this verse that the
"prophets" and "priests" of Baal were
not identical. The former would correspond
to the dervishes, the latter to the mollahs, of
Mahometan countries. By the "servants"
of Baal are meant the ordinary worshippers.

20. *a solemn assembly*] Jehu applies to
his proposed gathering the sacred name assigned in the Law to the chiefest Festivals
of Jehovah (see Lev. xxiii. 36; Num. xxix.
35; Deut. xvi. 8).

21. In order to understand how such
numbers could find room, we must remember that the ancient temples had vast courts
around them, which could contain many
thousands.

22. *the vestry*] The sacred robes of the

for all the worshippers of Baal. And he brought them forth
23 vestments. And Jehu went, and Jehonadab the son of Rechab,
into the house of Baal, and said unto the worshippers of Baal,
Search, and look that there be here with you none of the ser-
24 vants of the LORD, but the worshippers of Baal only. And
when they went in to offer sacrifices and burnt offerings, Jehu
appointed fourscore men without, and said, *If* any of the men
whom I have brought into your hands escape, *he that letteth him*
25 *go,* *p*his life *shall be* for the life of him. And it came to pass, as
soon as he had made an end of offering the burnt offering, that
Jehu said to the guard and to the captains, Go in, *and* slay them;
let none come forth. And they smote them with ¹the edge of
the sword; and the guard and the captains cast *them* out, and
26 went to the city of the house of Baal. And they brought forth
27 the ²*q*images out of the house of Baal, and burned them. And
they brake down the image of Baal, and brake down the house
28 of Baal, *r*and made it a draught house unto this day. ¶ Thus
29 Jehu destroyed Baal out of Israel. Howbeit *from* the sins of
Jeroboam the son of Nebat, who made Israel to sin, Jehu departed not from after them, *to wit,* *s*the golden calves that *were*
30 in Beth-el, and that *were* in Dan. ¶ And the LORD said unto
Jehu, Because thou hast done well in executing *that which is*
right in mine eyes, *and* hast done unto the house of Ahab according to all that *was* in mine heart, *t*thy children of the fourth

p 1 Kin. 20.
39.

q 1 Kin. 14.
23.

r Ezra 6. 11.
Dan. 2. 5.
& 3. 29.

s 1 Kin. 12.
28, 29.

t See ver. 35.
ch. 13. 1, 10.
& 14. 23.
& 15. 8, 12.

¹ Heb. *the mouth.*   ² Heb. *statues.*

Baal priests seem to have been of linen, and
were probably white. The vestry here mentioned may, probably, be the robe-chamber
of the royal palace, from which the king
gave a festal garment to each worshipper.

23. The presence of persons belonging to
another religion was usually regarded by
the ancients as a profanation of the rites.
In the case of the Greek mysteries such in-
trusion is said to have been punished by
death. Consequently Jehu could give these
injunctions without arousing any suspicion.

25. *as soon as he had made an end of offering*] The actual sacrificers were no doubt
the priests of Baal : but Jehu is considered
to have made the offering, since he furnished
the victims. Cp. 1 K. viii. 62, 63.

the guard] Lit. "the runners." This
name seems to have been given to the royal
body-guard as early as the time of Saul
(1 Sam. xxii. 17, marg.). It was their duty
to *run* by the side of the king's chariot as
he moved from place to place.

cast them out, and went] Rather, "the captains *hasted* and went," or "went *hastily ;*"
which gives a satisfactory sense. That the
soldiers should have troubled themselves to
cast the bodies of the slain out of the temple
enclosure is very unlikely.

the city of the house of Baal] i.e. the temple
itself, as distinguished from the court in
which it stood, is intended. The guard
having slain all who were in the court,
rushed on and entered the sanctuary, there
no doubt completing the massacre, and further tearing down and bringing out the

sacred objects mentioned in the next
verse.

26. *the images*] Or "pillars" of wood.
The Phœnician pillar idols were mere columns, obelisks, or posts, destitute of any
shaping into the semblance of humanity
(cp. 1 K. xiv. 23 note).

27. *And they brake down the image of Baal*]
The other images, it appears, were not
images of Baal, but of inferior deities. The
image of Baal, which was "broken down,"
and not burnt, would seem to have been of
stone, perhaps erected in front of the temple.

29. To abolish the calf-worship was a
thought which had probably never occurred
to Jehu. He had religious feeling enough,
and patriotism enough, to detest the utterly
debasing Astarte worship ; but the pure
worship of Jehovah was altogether beyond
and above him.

30. *And the LORD said unto Jehu*] Probably by the mouth of Elisha. To a certain
extent Jehu's measures were acts of obedience, for which God might see fit to assign
him a temporal reward.

thy children, &c.] This was accomplished
in the persons of Jehoahaz, Joash, Jeroboam, and Zachariah, the son, grandson,
great-grandson, and great-great-grandson of
Jehu (cp. marg. reff.). No other family sat
upon the throne of Israel so long. The
house of Omri, which furnished four kings,
held the crown for three generations only
and for less than fifty years—that of Jehu
reigned for five generations and for above a
hundred years.

31 *generation* shall sit on the throne of Israel. But Jehu ¹took no
heed to walk in the law of the LORD God of Israel with all his
heart : for he departed not from ᵘthe sins of Jeroboam, which
32 made Israel to sin. ¶ In those days the LORD began ²to cut
Israel short : and ˣHazael smote them in all the coasts of Israel ;
33 from Jordan ³eastward, all the land of Gilead, the Gadites, and
the Reubenites, and the Manassites, from Aroer, which *is* by
34 the river Arnon, ⁴even ᵛGilead and Bashan. ¶ Now the rest of
the acts of Jehu, and all that he did, and all his might, *are* they
not written in the book of the chronicles of the kings of Israel ?
35 And Jehu slept with his fathers : and they buried him in Sa-
36 maria. And Jehoahaz his son reigned in his stead. And ⁵the
time that Jehu reigned over Israel in Samaria *was* twenty and
eight years.

CHAP. **11**. AND when ᵃAthaliah ᵇthe mother of Ahaziah saw that
her son was dead, she arose and destroyed all the ⁶seed royal.
2 But ⁷Jehosheba, the daughter of king Joram, sister of Ahaziah,
took ⁸Joash the son of Ahaziah, and stole him from among the
king's sons *which were* slain ; and they hid him, *even* him and
his nurse, in the bedchamber from Athaliah, so that he was not

ᵘ 1 Kin. 14.
16.

ˣ ch. 8. 12.

ᵛ Amos 1. 3.

ᵃ 2 Chr. 22.
10.
ᵇ ch. 8. 26.

---

¹ Heb. *observed not.*
² Heb. *to cut off the ends.*
³ Heb. *toward the rising of the sun.*
⁴ Or, *even to Gilead and Bashan.*
⁵ Heb. *the days* were.
⁶ Heb. *seed of the kingdom.*
⁷ 2 Chr. 22. 11, *Jehosha-beath.*
⁸ Or, *Jehoash.*

---

32. *to cut Israel short*] Lit. "to cut off in
Israel," *i.e.* to take away from Israel portions of its territory (see marg. ref.).

33. The loss of the entire trans-Jordanic
territory seems to be intended, or at any
rate its complete ruin and devastation (cp.
marg. ref. *y*). This was the home of the
tribes of Reuben and Gad, and of the half
tribe of Manasseh (Josh. xxii. 1-9). It was
more accessible from Damascus than the region west of the river.

Aroer] There were several places of this
name. The one here mentioned is the most
famous (cp. Deut. ii. 36 note).

even Gilead and Bashan] The writer
had previously called the whole territory
"Gilead ;" now he distinguishes it, more
accurately, into Gilead, the southern, and
Bashan, the northern region (1 K. iv. 13,
19).

34. *all his might*] It is remarkable that
this expression, which is not used by the
author of Kings in connexion with any
other king of *Israel*, should be applied to
Jehu, whose ill success in his struggle with
Hazael has just been noted, and who submitted to the Assyrians and consented to
become a tributary. Perhaps the word is
used here in the sense of "personal courage"
rather than of "power."

36. *in Samaria*] The family of Ahab had
made Jezreel a sort of second capital, and
had reigned there, at least in part (ix. 15-
30). Jehu and his descendants seem to
have fixed their residence wholly in Samaria
(xiii. 1, 10, xiv. 23, xv. 8).

XI. **1.** Athaliah, as wife of Joram and

mother of Ahaziah, had guided both the internal and the external policy of the Jewish
kingdom ; she had procured the establishment of the worship of Baal in Judæa (viii.
18, 27), and had maintained a close alliance
with the sister kingdom (do. *v.* 29, x. 13).
The revolution effected by Jehu touched
her nearly. It struck away from her the
support of her relatives ; it isolated her religious system, severing the communication
with Phœnicia ; and the death of Ahaziah
deprived her of her legal status in Judæa,
which was that of queen-mother (1 K. xv.
13 note), and transferred that position to
the chief wife of her deceased son. Athaliah, instead of yielding to the storm, or
merely standing on the defensive, resolved
to become the assailant, and strike before
any plans could be formed against her.
In the absence of her son, hers was probably the chief authority at Jerusalem.
She used it to command the immediate
destruction of all the family of David,
already thinned by previous massacres (x.
14 ; 2 Chr. xxi. 4, 17), and then seized the
throne.

2. *Jehosheba...sister of Ahaziah*] "Half-
sister," according to Josephus—daughter of
Joram, not by Athaliah, but by another
wife. She was married to Jehoiada the
High-Priest, and was thus in a position to
save and conceal her nephew, Joash, who
was only one year old (cp. *vv.* 3, 21).

in the bedchamber] Lit. "in the chamber
of mattresses "—probably a store-room in
the palace in which mattresses were kept.

3 slain. And he was with her hid in the house of the LORD six
4 years. And Athaliah did reign over the land. ¶ And ^cthe
seventh year Jehoiada sent and fetched the rulers over hundreds,
with the captains and the guard, and brought them to him into
the house of the LORD, and made a covenant with them, and
took an oath of them in the house of the LORD, and shewed them
5 the king's son. And he commanded them, saying, This *is* the
thing that ye shall do; A third part of you that enter in ^don
the sabbath shall even be keepers of the watch of the king's
6 house; and a third part *shall be* at the gate of Sur; and a third
part at the gate behind the guard: so shall ye keep the watch
7 of the house, ¹that it be not broken down. And two ^{2 3}parts of
all you that go forth on the sabbath, even they shall keep the
8 watch of the house of the LORD about the king. And ye shall
compass the king round about, every man with his weapons in
his hand: and he that cometh within the ranges, let him be
slain: and be ye with the king as he goeth out and as he cometh
9 in. ¶ ^eAnd the captains over the hundreds did according to all
things that Jehoiada the priest commanded: and they took every
man his men that were to come in on the sabbath, with them
that should go out on the sabbath, and came to Jehoiada the
10 priest. And to the captains over hundreds did the priest give
king David's spears and shields, that *were* in the temple of the
11 LORD. And the guard stood, every man with his weapons in
his hand, round about the king, from the right ⁴corner of the

Margin notes (left):
c 2 Chr. 23.1, &c.

d 1 Chr. 9. 25.

e 2 Chr. 23. 8.

---

¹ Or, *from breaking up.*   ³ Heb. *hands.*
² Or, *companies.*   ⁴ Heb. *shoulder.*

---

3. *and Athaliah did reign over the land*] In these words the writer dismisses the entire reign of Athaliah, whereof he scorns to speak. We gather incidentally from xii. 5–12, compared with 2 Chr. xxiv. 7, that Athaliah used her power to establish the *exclusive* worship of Baal through the kingdom of Judah, and to crush that of Jehovah. She stopped the Temple service, gave over the sacred vessels of the Sanctuary to the use of the Baal priests, and employed the Temple itself as a quarry from which materials might be taken for the construction of a great temple to Baal, which rose in the immediate neighbourhood.

4. See marg. ref.

the captains] The word used here and in *v.* 19, *hak-kari*, designates a certain part of the royal guard, probably that which in the earlier times was known under the name of Cherethites (1 K. i. 38). Others see in the term an ethnic name—"Carians," who seem certainly to have been much inclined to take service as mercenaries from an early date. Render the whole passage thus—"And in the seventh year Jehoiada sent and fetched **the centurions of the Carians and the guardsmen** (lit. 'runners,' x. 25), &c."

5–8. Five divisions of the guard under their five captains are distinguished here. Three of the five divisions "enter in" on the Sabbath; the other two "go forth" on the Sabbath (*v.* 7). By the former phrase

seems to be meant the mounting guard at the royal palace (the "king's house," where Athaliah then was); by the latter the serving of escort to the sovereign beyond the palace bounds. Jehoiada orders that of those whose business it would be to guard the palace on the ensuing Sabbath, one company or cohort should perform that task in the ordinary way, while another should watch the gate of Sur,—or better, "the gate of the foundation" (2 Chr. xxiii. 5)—that by which the palace was usually quitted for the Temple, and a third should watch another of the palace gates, called "the gate of the guard" (see *v.* 19). The two companies whose proper business it would be to serve as the royal escort beyond the palace walls, he orders to enter the Temple, and surround the person of the young king.

6. *that it be not broken down*] The one word in the original text of which this is a translation occurs nowhere else; and its meaning is very doubtful.

8. *within the ranges*] Rather, "within **the ranks.**" If any one tried to break through the soldiers' ranks to the king, or even to disturb their order, he was to be immediately slain.

11. *From the right corner,* &c.] Rather, "from the right **side** of the Temple buildings to the left **side**"—*i.e.* right across the Temple court from the one side to the other, by the Altar of Burnt offerings, &c.

temple to the left corner of the temple, *along* by the altar and
12 the temple. And he brought forth the king's son, and put the
crown upon him, and *gave him* the testimony; and they made
him king, and anointed him; and they clapped their hands, and
13 said, [1]*God save the king.* ¶[g]And when Athaliah heard the
noise of the guard *and* of the people, she came to the people
14 into the temple of the LORD. And when she looked, behold, the
king stood by [h]a pillar, as the manner *was*, and the princes and
the trumpeters by the king, and all the people of the land rejoiced, and blew with trumpets: and Athaliah rent her clothes,
15 and cried, Treason, Treason. But Jehoiada the priest commanded the captains of the hundreds, the officers of the host,
and said unto them, Have her forth without the ranges: and
him that followeth her kill with the sword. For the priest had
16 said, Let her not be slain in the house of the LORD. And they
laid hands on her; and she went by the way by the which the
horses came into the king's house: and there was she slain.
17 ¶[i]And Jehoiada made a covenant between the LORD and the
king and the people, that they should be the LORD's people;
18 [k]between the king also and the people. And all the people of
the land went into the [l]house of Baal, and brake it down; his
altars and his images [m]brake they in pieces thoroughly, and
slew Mattan the priest of Baal before the altars. And [n]the
19 priest appointed [2]officers over the house of the LORD. And he
took the rulers over hundreds, and the captains, and the guard,
and all the people of the land; and they brought down the
king from the house of the LORD, and came by the way of the

[f]1 Sam. 10.
24.
[g]2 Chr. 23.
12, &c.
[h]ch. 23. 3.
2 Chr. 34.21.

[i]2 Chr.23.16.
[k]2 Sam. 5.3.
[l]ch. 10. 26.
[m]Deut.12.3.
2 Chr. 23. 17.
[n]2 Chr. 23.
18, &c.

---

[1] Heb. *Let the king live.*   [2] Heb. *offices.*

This Altar stood exactly in front of the Temple-porch. Here the king was stationed; and before him and behind him, ("round about" him) stood the soldiers, drawn up several ranks deep across the entire court, just in front of the sacred building.

12. *the testimony*] *i.e.* "The Book of the Law" which was kept in the Ark of the Covenant (Deut. xxxi. 26). This Jehoiada placed on the king's head at the moment of coronation, perhaps to indicate that the king was not to be above, but under, the direction of the Law of his country.

14. *by a pillar*] Rather, "**upon the pillar**," probably a sort of stand, or pulpit, raised on a pillar. Under the later monarchy the Jewish king seems to have had a special place assigned him in the Temple-court, from which on occasions he addressed the people (marg. reff.).

15. *Have her forth without the ranges*] Rather, "**Conduct her out between your ranks.**" Guard her, *i.e.* on all sides, that the people may not fall upon her and kill her as she passes through the court, thereby polluting the Temple.

16. *And they laid hands on her*] Most modern critics render—"and they **gave her space**," *i.e.* they cleared a way for her, and allowed her to walk out of the Temple not only unharmed but untouched.

17. *a covenant*] Rather, "*the* covenant," which either was already an established part of a coronation (marg. ref. k), or at least became such afterwards.

18. A temple had been built to Baal at Jerusalem itself by Athaliah, Ahaziah, or Jehoram. According to Josephus, it was constructed in the reign of Jehoram. Its exact position is uncertain.

images] The word used here is not the same as in x. 26, but a word which implies likeness. The Phœnicians had fashioned images, besides their unfashioned pillar-idols.

the priest appointed, &c.] The Temple worship having been discontinued during Athaliah's rule, it devolved on Jehoiada now to re-establish it (see marg. ref.). He had already summoned the Levites out of all the cities of Judah (2 Chr. xxiii. 2), and had made use of them in the events of the day. He therefore proceeded at once to assign the custody of the Temple to a particular course, before conducting the young king to the palace.

19. They conducted the king *down* from the Temple hill, across the valley of the Tyropœum, and up the opposite hill to the royal palace, entering it not by the "horse-gate" (*v.* 16), where Athaliah had just been slain, but by the "gate of the guard" (*v.* 6), which was probably the main gate of the

gate of the guard to the king's house. And he sat on the throne 20 of the kings. And all the people of the land rejoiced, and the city was in quiet : and they slew Athaliah with the sword *beside*

o 2 Chr. 24. 1.   21 the king's house. ¶ *o*Seven years old *was* Jehoash when he

a 2 Chr. 24. 1.   12 began to reign. IN the seventh year of Jehu *a*Jehoash began to reign ; and forty years reigned he in Jerusalem. And his 2 mother's name *was* Zibiah of Beer-sheba. And Jehoash did *that which was* right in the sight of the LORD all his days wherein

b 1 Kin. 15. 14.   3 Jehoiada the priest instructed him. But *b*the high places were
& 22. 3.
ch. 14. 4.   not taken away : the people still sacrificed and burnt incense in
c ch. 22. 4.   4 the high places. ¶ And Jehoash said to the priests, *c*All the money of the ^{12}dedicated things that is brought into the house

d Ex. 30. 13.   of the LORD, *even* *d*the money of every one that passeth *the account,* ^{3}the money that every man is set at, *and* all the money

e Ex. 35. 5.   that ^{4e}cometh into any man's heart to bring into the house of
1 Chr. 29. 9.   5 the LORD, let the priests take *it* to them, every man of his acquaintance : and let them repair the breaches of the house, 6 wheresoever any breach shall be found. ¶ But it was *so, that*

f 2 Chr. 24. 5. ^{5}in the three and twentieth year of king Jehoash *f*the priests
g 2 Chr. 24. 6.   7 had not repaired the breaches of the house. *g*Then king Jehoash called for Jehoiada the priest, and the *other* priests, and said unto them, Why repair ye not the breaches of the house ? now therefore receive no *more* money of your acquaintance, but de-8 liver it for the breaches of the house. And the priests consented to receive no *more* money of the people, neither to repair the

---

^{1} Or, *holy things.*   *souls of his estimation,*   *heart of a man.*
^{2} Heb. *holinesses.*   Lev. 27. 2. ^{5} Heb. *in the twentieth year*
^{3} Heb. *the money of the* ^{4} Heb. *ascendeth upon the*   *and third year.*

---

palace on the eastern side (see 2 Chr. xxiii. 20).

20. *they slew Athaliah with the sword*] This **is** one of the many little repetitions which mark the manner of the writer, and which generally contain some *little* point which has not been mentioned before (cp. *v.* 16).

XII. 2. *all his days,* &c.] *i.e.* " so long as Jehoiada was his adviser " (cp. 2 Chr. xxiv. 15–22). Jehoiada was, practically speaking, regent during the minority of Jehoash, *i.e.* 10 or 12 years. An increase of power to the priestly order was the natural consequence. Jehoiada bore the title of " High-Priest " (*v.* 10), which had been dropped since the time of Eleazar (Josh. xx. 6), and the Levitical order from this time became more mixed up with public affairs and possessed greater influence than previously. Jehoiada's successors traced their office to him rather than to Aaron (Jer. xxix. 26).

3. The worship on the " high places " seems to have continued uninterruptedly to the time of Hezekiah, who abolished it (xviii. 4). It was, however, again established by Manasseh, his son (xxi. 3). The priests at this time cannot have regarded it as idolatrous, or Jehoiada would have put it down during his regency.

4. It is remarkable that the first movement towards restoring the fabric of the

Temple should have come, not from Jehoiada, but from Jehoash (cp. 2 Chr. xxiv. 4). Jehoiada had, it seems, allowed the mischief done in Athaliah's time to remain unrepaired during the whole term of his government.

the money of every one, &c.] Three kinds of sacred money are here distinguished— first, the half shekel required in the Law (Ex. xxx. 13) to be paid by every one above twenty years of age when he passed the numbering ; secondly, the money to be paid by such as had devoted themselves, or those belonging to them, by vow to Jehovah, which was a variable sum dependent on age, sex, and property (Lev. xxvii. 2–8) ; and thirdly, the money offered in the way of free-will offerings.

5. The collection was not to be made at Jerusalem only, but in all "the cities of Judah " (2 Chr. xxiv. 5) ; the various priests and Levites being collectors in their own neighbourhoods.

breaches] The word in the original includes every kind and degree of ruin or dilapidation.

6. No money had for some time been brought in (marg. ref. *g*). Perhaps it was difficult for the priests and Levites to know exactly what proportion of the money paid to them was fairly applicable to the Temple service and to their own sup-

9 breaches of the house. But Jehoiada the priest took *a chest, *2 Chr. 24. 8, &c.
and bored a hole in the lid of it, and set it beside the altar, on
the right side as one cometh into the house of the LORD : and
the priests that kept the ¹door put therein all the money *that*
10 *was* brought into the house of the LORD. And it was *so*, when
they saw that *there was* much money in the chest, that the king's
²scribe and the high priest came up, and they ³put up in bags,
and told the money that was found in the house of the LORD.
11 And they gave the money, being told, into the hands of them
that did the work, that had the oversight of the house of the
LORD : and they ⁴laid it out to the carpenters and builders, that
12 wrought upon the house of the LORD, and to masons, and hewers
of stone, and to buy timber and hewed stone to repair the
breaches of the house of the LORD, and for all that ⁵was laid
13 out for the house to repair *it*. Howbeit *there were not made *See 2 Chr. 24. 14.
for the house of the LORD bowls of silver, snuffers, basons,
trumpets, any vessels of gold, or vessels of silver, of the money
14 *that was* brought into the house of the LORD : but they gave
that to the workmen, and repaired therewith the house of the
15 LORD. Moreover *they reckoned not with the men, into whose *ch. 22. 7.
hand they delivered the money to be bestowed on workmen :
16 for they dealt faithfully. *The trespass money and sin money *Lev. 5. 15, 18.
was not brought into the house of the LORD : *it was the priests'. *Lev. 7. 7.
17 ¶ Then *Hazael king of Syria went up, and fought against Gath, Num. 18. 9.
and took it : and *Hazael set his face to go up to Jerusalem. *ch. 8. 12.
*See 2 Chr. 24. 23.

¹ Heb. *threshold.*   ³ Heb. *bound up.*   ⁵ Heb. *went forth.*
² Or, *secretary.*   ⁴ Heb. *brought it forth.*

port ; and what, consequently, was the
balance which they ought to apply to the
repairs.

9. *the priests that kept the door*] The north
door into the priests' court (Ezek. xl. 35-43)
seems to be intended, not the door of the
Temple building. The chest must have
been placed a little to the right of this
north door, between it and the Altar of
Burnt-offering, so that the people could see
it from the doorway. The people were not
ordinarily allowed to go within the doorway into this court, which belonged to the
priests and Levites only.

10. *the king's scribe*] Or "secretary"
(1 K. iv. 3 note). Such persons are often
seen in the Assyrian sculptures, with a
roll, apparently of parchment, in one hand
and a pen in the other, taking account for
the king of the spoil brought in from
foreign expeditions.

13. Comparing this verse with the marg.
ref., it will be seen that the author of
Kings desires to point out, that the repairs
were not delayed by any deductions from
the money that flowed in. The writer of
Chronicles describes what became of the
surplus in the chest after the last repairs
were completed.

The need of supplying fresh bowls,
snuffers, &c., arose from the pollution of
those previously used in the Temple service
by their application to the Baal worship

during the reigns of Ahaziah and Athaliah
(see 2 Chr. xxiv. 7).

16. *The trespass money and the sin money*]
In all cases of injury done to another, a
man was bound by the Law to make compensation, to the sufferer, if possible ; if not,
to his nearest kinsman. If the man was
dead and had left no kinsman, then the
compensation was to be made to the priest
(Num. v. 8). This would form a part of
the trespass and sin money. The remainder
would accrue from the voluntary gifts made
to the priests by those who came to make
atonement for sins or trespasses (do. *v.* 10).
On the difference between "sins" and
"trespasses," see Lev. v. 14 note.

17, 18. There was probably a considerable interval between the conclusion of the
arrangement for the repairs and the Syrian
expedition related in these verses. For the
events which had happened, see 2 Chr.
xxiv. 15-22.

17. This is the first and last time that we
hear of the Damascene Syrians undertaking so distant an expedition. Gath (see
Josh. xiii. 3 note) could only be reached from
Syria through Israel or Judah. It was not
more than 25 or 30 miles from Jerusalem.
It is uncertain whether the city belonged at
this time to Judah or to the Philistines.

Hazael set his face, &c.] This is a phrase
for determination generally, but especially
for determination to proceed somewhere

<table>
<tr><td>p 1Kin.15.18.
ch. 13. 15,16.</td><td>18 And Jehoash king of Judah *p*took all the hallowed things that Jehoshaphat, and Jehoram, and Ahaziah, his fathers, kings of Judah, had dedicated, and his own hallowed things, and all the gold *that was* found in the treasures of the house of the LORD, and in the king's house, and sent *it* to Hazael king of Syria:</td></tr>
</table>

p 1Kin.15.18.
ch. 13. 15,16.

18 And Jehoash king of Judah *p*took all the hallowed things that Jehoshaphat, and Jehoram, and Ahaziah, his fathers, kings of Judah, had dedicated, and his own hallowed things, and all the gold *that was* found in the treasures of the house of the LORD, and in the king's house, and sent *it* to Hazael king of Syria:
19 and he [1]went away from Jerusalem. ¶And the rest of the acts of Joash, and all that he did, *are* they not written in the book

q ch. 14. 5.
2 Chr. 24. 25.

20 of the chronicles of the kings of Judah? And *q*his servants arose, and made a conspiracy, and slew Joash in [2]the house of

r 2 Chr. 24.
26, Zabaa.

21 Millo, which goeth down to Silla. For *r*Jozachar the son of Shimeath, and Jehozabad the son of [3]Shomer, his servants, smote him, and he died; and they buried him with his fathers

s 2Chr.24.27.

in the city of David: and *s*Amaziah his son reigned in his stead.

CHAP. 13. IN [4]the three and twentieth year of Joash the son of Ahaziah king of Judah Jehoahaz the son of Jehu began to reign
2 over Israel in Samaria, *and reigned* seventeen years. And he did *that which was* evil in the sight of the LORD, and [5]followed the sins of Jeroboam the son of Nebat, which made Israel to

a Judg. 2.14.

3 sin; he departed not therefrom. And *a*the anger of the LORD was kindled against Israel, and he delivered them into the hand

b ch. 8. 12.
c Ps. 78. 34.

of *b*Hazael king of Syria, and into the hand of Ben-hadad the
4 son of Hazael, all *their* days. And Jehoahaz *c*besought the

d Ex. 3. 7.
ch. 14. 26.

LORD, and the LORD hearkened unto him: for *d*he saw the oppression of Israel, because the king of Syria oppressed them.

e ch.14.25,27.

5 (*e*And the LORD gave Israel a saviour, so that they went out

---

[1] Heb. *went up.*   [3] Or, *Shimrith.*   and third year.
[2] Or, *Beth-millo.*   [4] Heb. *the twentieth year*   [5] Heb. *walked after.*

(cp. Jer. xlii. 15 ; Luke ix. 51). Jerusalem can scarcely have been the primary object of this expedition, or it would have been attacked by a less circuitous route. Perhaps the Syrians were induced to make a sudden march against the Jewish capital, by learning, while at Gath, that a revolution had occurred there (cp. 2 Chr. xxiv. 18–23).

18. Jehoash did not submit without a struggle. See the details in Chronicles. It was not till his army was defeated that he followed the example of his ancestor, Asa, and bought the friendship of the Syrians with the Temple treasures (1 K. xv. 18. Cp. the conduct of Hezekiah, xviii. 15, 16).

Jehoram and Ahaziah] Though these two monarchs had been worshippers of Baal, yet they had combined with that idolatrous cult a certain amount of decent respect for the old religion. It is evident from this passage that they had made costly offerings to the Temple.

20. *a conspiracy*] Cp. marg. ref. Joash, either from a suspicion of intended treason, or from some other unknown cause, took up his abode in the fortress of Millo (1 K. ix. 24). This conspiracy was connected with religion. Soon after the death of Jehoiada, Joash had apostatised; had renewed the worship of Baal ; and, despite of many prophetic warnings, had persisted

in his evil courses, even commanding Zechariah ·to be slain when he rebuked them (2 Chr. xxiv. 18–27). The conspirators, who wished to avenge Zechariah, no doubt wished also to put down the Baal worship. In this it appears that they succeeded. For, though Amaziah punished the actual murderers after a while (xiv. 5), yet he appears not to have been a Baal-worshipper. The only idolatries laid to his charge are the maintenance of the high places (xiv. 4), and a worship of the gods of Edom (2 Chr. xxv. 14–20).

Silla] This place is quite unknown.

XIII. In this chapter the history of the kingdom of Israel is traced through the two reigns of Jehoahaz and Jehoash. In ch. xiv. the history of Judah is resumed.

in the three and twentieth year] Rather, the "one and twentieth year." See *v.* 10.

3. *all their days*] Lit. "all the days." Not "all the days" of the two Syrian kings, for Ben-hadad lost to Joash all the cities which he had gained from Jehoahaz (*v.* 25) ; but either "all the days of Jehoahaz" (*v.* 22), or "all the days of Hazael "— both while he led his own armies, and while they were led by his son.

5. *the* LORD *gave Israel a saviour*] Not immediately on the repentance of Jehoahaz, but after his death (see *v.* 25).

from under the hand of the Syrians : and the children of Israel
6 dwelt in their tents, ¹as beforetime. Nevertheless they departed
not from the sins of the house of Jeroboam, who made Israel
sin, *but* ²walked therein : *f*and there ³remained the grove also in
7 Samaria.) Neither did he leave of the people to Jehoahaz but
fifty horsemen, and ten chariots, and ten thousand footmen ;
for the king of Syria had destroyed them, *g*and had made them
8 like the dust by threshing. ¶Now the rest of the acts of Jehoahaz, and all that he did, and his might, *are* they not written in
9 the book of the chronicles of the kings of Israel ? And Jehoahaz
slept with his fathers ; and they buried him in Samaria : and
10 ⁴Joash his son reigned in his stead.⁵ ¶In the thirty and seventh
year of Joash king of Judah began ⁶Jehoash the son of Jehoahaz
11 to reign over Israel in Samaria, *and reigned* sixteen years. And
he did *that which was* evil in the sight of the LORD ; he departed
not from all the sins of Jeroboam the son of Nebat, who made
12 Israel sin : *but* he walked therein. *h*And the rest of the acts of
Joash, and *i*all that he did, and *k*his might wherewith he fought
against Amaziah king of Judah, *are* they not written in the book
13 of the chronicles of the kings of Israel ? And Joash slept with
his fathers ; and Jeroboam sat upon his throne : and Joash was
14 buried in Samaria with the kings of Israel. ¶Now Elisha was
fallen sick of his sickness whereof he died. And Joash the king
of Israel came down unto him, and wept over his face, and said,
O my father, my father, *l*the chariot of Israel, and the horse-
15 men thereof. And Elisha said unto him, Take bow and arrows.
16 And he took unto him bow and arrows. And he said to the
king of Israel, ⁷Put thine hand upon the bow. And he put his
hand *upon it :* and Elisha put his hands upon the king's hands.

f 1Kin.16.33.

g Amos 1. 3.

h ch. 14. 15.
i See ver. 14.
& 25.
k ch.14.9,&c.
2 Chr. 25.17,
&c.

l ch. 2. 12.

¹ Heb. *as yesterday,* and   ³ Heb. *stood.*   ⁶ In consort with his father,
    third day.   ⁴ ver. 10, *Jehoash.*   ch. 14. 1.
² Heb. *he walked.*   ⁵ Alone.   ⁷ Heb. *Make thine hand to ride.*

they went out from under the hand of the
Syrians] *i.e.* they ceased to be oppressed by
the Syrians ; they shook off their yoke, and
became once more perfectly independent.

tents] See 1 K. viii. 66 note.

6. *but walked therein*] Rather, "**he** walked
therein," meaning Joash, the "saviour" of
the preceding verse.

there remained the grove also in Samaria]
It seems strange that Jehu had not destroyed this when he put down the worship
of Baal (x. 26-28). Perhaps the "grove"
or "Asherah" worship was too closely connected with the old worship in high places
to be set aside with the same ease as the
rites newly introduced from Phœnicia.

7. The meaning is that "he, the king of
Syria" (*v.* 4 Hazael) limited the standing
army of Jehoahaz.

like the dust by threshing] An expression
not only employed metaphorically, and im-
porting defeat, conquest, and grinding oppression (Jer. li. 33 ; Mic. iv. 12), but implying also the literal use of threshing-
instruments in the execution of prisoners of
war (marg. ref., and cp. 2 Sam. xii. 31).

12, 13. According to ordinary laws of
historical composition, these verses should

form the closing paragraph of the present
chapter.

14. The closing scene of Elisha's life. It
was now at least sixty-three years since his
call, so that he was at this time very possibly above ninety. He seems to have lived
in almost complete retirement from the
time he sent the young Prophet to anoint
Jehu king (ix. 1). And now it was not he
who sought the king, but the king who
sought him. Apparently, the special func-
tion of the two great Israelite Prophets
(Elijah and Elisha) was to counteract the
noxious influence of the Baalistic rites ;
and, when these ceased, their extraordinary
ministry came to an end.

the chariot of Israel, &c.] See marg. ref.
Joash must have known the circumstances
of Elijah's removal, which were perhaps already entered in the "book of the Chronicles
of the kings of Israel ;" and he must have
intended to apply to Elisha his own words
on that solemn occasion ; "Thou too art
about to leave us, and to follow Elijah—
thou who hast been since his departure,
that which he was while he remained on
earth, the true defence of Israel."

16. *Elisha put his hands upon the king's*

17 And he said, Open the window eastward. And he opened *it*.
Then Elisha said, Shoot. And he shot. And he said, The
arrow of the LORD's deliverance, and the arrow of deliverance
^m 1 Kin. 20. 26. from Syria : for thou shalt smite the Syrians in ^mAphek, till
18 thou have consumed *them*. And he said, Take the arrows. And
he took *them*. And he said unto the king of Israel, Smite upon
19 the ground. And he smote thrice, and stayed. And the man
of God was wroth with him, and said, Thou shouldest have
smitten five or six times ; then hadst thou smitten Syria till thou
ⁿ ver. 25. hadst consumed *it* : ⁿwhereas now thou shalt smite Syria *but*
20 thrice. ¶ And Elisha died, and they buried him. And the
bands of the Moabites invaded the land at the coming in of the
21 year. And it came to pass, as they were burying a man, that,
behold, they spied a band *of men;* and they cast the man into
the sepulchre of Elisha : and when the man ¹was let down, and
touched the bones of Elisha, he revived, and stood up on his feet.
^o ch. 8. 12. 22 ¶ But ^oHazael king of Syria oppressed Israel all the days of
^p ch. 14. 27. 23 Jehoahaz. ^pAnd the LORD was gracious unto them, and had
^q Ex.2.24,25. compassion on them, and ^qhad respect unto them, ^rbecause of
^r Ex. 32. 13.

¹ Heb. *went* down.

---

hands] A symbolical act, indicating that
the successes, which the shooting typified,
were to come, not from human skill, or
strength, or daring, but from the Presence
and the power of God.

17. *eastward*] Syria of Damascus lay
partly east, but still more north, of the
Holy Land. The arrow was to be shot,
eastward, not so much against Syria itself
as against the scene of the recent Syrian
successes, Gilead (x. 33), which was also to
be the scene of Joash's victories over them.
Aphek is almost due east from Shunem,
where it is not unlikely that Elisha now
was.

the arrow, &c.] Lit. "An arrow of deliverance from the Lord, and an arrow of
deliverance against Syria ; and thou shalt
smite the Syrians in Aphek, even to con-
suming."

18. *Smite upon the ground*] Some prefer
to render—"**Shoot to the ground** ;" *i.e.*
"Shoot arrows from the window into the
ground outside, as if thou wert shooting
against an enemy."

19. The unfaithfulness of man limits the
goodness of God. Though Joash did the
Prophet's bidding, it was without any zeal
or fervour ; and probably without any
earnest belief in the efficacy of what he was
doing. Cp. Mark vi. 5, 6. God had been
willing to give the Israelites complete victory over Syria (*v.* 17) ; but Joash by his
non-acceptance of the divine promise in its
fulness had checked the outflow of mercy ;
and the result was that the original promise
could not be fulfilled.

20. *the bands of the Moabites invaded the
land*] The Moabites had been increasing in
strength ever since their revolt from Ahaziah (i. 1). The defeat which they suffered
at the hands of Jehoram and Jehoshaphat

(iii. 24) did not affect their subjugation.
They spread themselves into the country
north of the Arnon (Isai. xvi. 2), and thence
proceeded to make plundering expeditions
year by year into Samaria, in Spring. This
was the natural season for incursions, as
then in Palestine the crops began to be
ripe.

21. *they cast the man*] Rather, "they thrust
the man." The graves of the Jews were
not pits dug in the ground, like ours, but
caves or cells excavated in the side of a
rock, the mouth of the cave being ordinarily shut by a heavy stone.

stood up on his feet] Coffins were not used
by the Jews. The body was simply wrapped
or swathed in grave-clothes (cp. Luke vii.
15 ; John xi. 44).

This miracle of Elisha's after his death
is more surprising than any of those which
he performed during his lifetime. The Jews
regarded it as his highest glory (cp. Ecclus.
xlviii. 13, 14). It may be said to belong to
a class of Scriptural miracles, cases, *i.e.*
where the miracle was not wrought through
the agency of a living miracle-worker, but
by a material object in which, by God's
will, "virtue" for the time resided (cp.
Acts xix. 12). The primary effect of the
miracle was, no doubt, greatly to increase
the reverence of the Israelites for the memory of Elisha, to lend force to his teaching, and especially to add weight to his unfulfilled prophecies, as to that concerning
the coming triumphs of Israel over Syria.
In the extreme state of depression to which
the Israelites were now reduced, a very
signal miracle may have been needed to encourage and reassure them.

23. The writer regards the Captivity of
Israel as God's "casting them out of His
sight" (see xvii. 18, 20) ; and notes that this

his covenant with Abraham, Isaac, and Jacob, and would not destroy them, neither cast he them from his [1]presence as yet.

24 So Hazael king of Syria died; and Ben-hadad his son reigned in 25 his stead. And Jehoash the son of Jehoahaz [2]took again out of the hand of Ben-hadad the son of Hazael the cities, which he had taken out of the hand of Jehoahaz his father by war. *Three times did Joash beat him, and recovered the cities of Israel.   *ver. 18, 19.

CHAP. 14. IN *the second year of Joash son of Jehoahaz king of 2 Israel reigned *Amaziah the son of Joash king of Judah. He was twenty and five years old when he began to reign, and reigned twenty and nine years in Jerusalem. And his mother's 3 name was Jehoaddan of Jerusalem. And he did that which was right in the sight of the LORD, yet not like David his father: he 4 did according to all things as Joash his father did. *Howbeit the high places were not taken away: as yet the people did 5 sacrifice and burnt incense on the high places. And it came to pass, as soon as the kingdom was confirmed in his hand, that he 6 slew his servants *which had slain the king his father. But the children of the murderers he slew not: according unto that which is written in the book of the law of Moses, wherein the LORD commanded, saying, *The fathers shall not be put to death for the children, nor the children be put to death for the fathers; 7 but every man shall be put to death for his own sin. *He slew of Edom in *the valley of salt ten thousand, and took [3]Selah

a ch. 13. 10.
b 2 Chr. 25. 1.

c ch. 12. 3.

d ch. 12. 20.

e Deut. 24. 16.
Ezek. 18. 4, 20.
f 2 Chr. 25. 5—13.
g 2 Sam. 8. 13.
Ps. 60, title.

[1] Heb. face.   [2] Heb. returned and took.   [3] Or, The rock.

---

extreme punishment, though deserved, was by God's mercy not allowed to fall on them as yet.

24. *So Hazael...died*] Literally, "*And* Hazael died," a fact not mentioned before.

25. *the cities which*, &c.] Probably cities west of the Jordan, since the tract east of that river was conquered, mainly if not wholly, in the reign of Jehu (x. 33).

XIV. The history of Judah is resumed (1–22), followed by a brief account of the contemporary history of Israel under Jeroboam II. (*vv.* 23-29). The earlier narrative runs parallel with 2 Chr. xxv.

2. Joash of Judah reigned forty years (xii. 1), and Joash of Israel ascended the throne in his namesake's thirty-seventh year (xiii. 10); hence we should have expected to hear that Amaziah succeeded his father in the fourth rather than in the second year of Joash (of Israel). The usual explanation of the discrepancy is to suppose a double accession of the Israelitish Joash —as co-partner with his father in the thirty-seventh year of his namesake, as sole king two years afterwards.

3. *he did...as Joash*] There is a curious parity between the lives of Joash and Amaziah. Both were zealous for Jehovah in the earlier portion of their reigns, but in the latter part fell away; both disregarded the rebukes of Prophets; and both, having forsaken God, were in the end conspired against and slain (cp. 2 Chr. xxiv. 25, xxv. 27).

5. The phrase, "confirmed in his hand"

(xv. 19), usually expresses the authorisation of a new reign by an imperial superior (see xv. 19 note); but here it describes the result when the troubles consequent upon the murder of Joash had passed away. The new king's authority was generally recognised by his subjects.

6. *the children of the murderers he slew not*] This seems to be noted as a rare instance of clemency (cp. ix. 26 note). It is strange at first sight, that, when the Law contained so very plain a prohibition (marg. reff.), the contrary practice should have established itself. But we must remember, first, that the custom was that of the East generally (see Dan. vi. 24); and secondly, that it had the sanction of one who might be thought to have known thoroughly the mind of the legislator, viz. Joshua (see Josh. vii. 24, 25).

7. Amaziah's Idumæan war is treated at length by the writer of Chronicles (marg. ref.).

The "Valley of Salt" is usually identified with the broad open plain called the Sabkah, at the southern end of the Dead Sea—the continuation of the *Ghor* or Jordan gorge. At the north-western corner of this plain stands a mountain of rock-salt, and the tract between this mountain and the sea is a salt-marsh. Salt springs also abound in the plain itself, so that the name would be fully accounted for. It is doubted, however, whether the original of the word "valley," commonly used of clefts and ra-

by war, [h]and called the name of it Joktheel unto this day.
8 ¶ [i]Then Amaziah sent messengers to Jehoash, the son of Jehoahaz son of Jehu, king of Israel, saying, Come, let us look one
9 another in the face. And Jehoash the king of Israel sent to
Amaziah king of Judah, saying, [k]The thistle that *was* in Lebanon sent to the [l]cedar that *was* in Lebanon, saying, Give thy
daughter to my son to wife: and there passed by a wild beast
10 that *was* in Lebanon, and trode down the thistle. Thou hast
indeed smitten Edom, and [m]thine heart hath lifted thee up:
glory *of this*, and tarry [1]at home: for why shouldest thou meddle
to *thy* hurt, that thou shouldest fall, *even* thou, and Judah with
11 thee? But Amaziah would not hear. Therefore Jehoash king
of Israel went up; and he and Amaziah king of Judah looked
one another in the face at [n]Beth-shemesh, which *belongeth* to
12 Judah. And Judah [2]was put to the worse before Israel; and
13 they fled every man to their tents. And Jehoash king of Israel
took Amaziah king of Judah, the son of Jehoash the son of
Ahaziah, at Beth-shemesh, and came to Jerusalem, and brake
down the wall of Jerusalem from [o]the gate of Ephraim unto
14 [p]the corner gate, four hundred cubits. And he took all [q]the

[h] Josh. 15. 38.
[i] 2 Chr. 25. 17, 18, &c.
[k] See Judg. 9. 8.
[l] 1 Kin. 4. 33.
[m] Deut. 8. 14. 2 Chr. 32. 25. Ezek. 28. 2, 5, 17. Hab. 2. 4.
[n] Josh. 19. 38. & 21. 16.
[o] Neh. 8. 16. & 12. 39.
[p] Jer. 31. 38. Zech. 14. 10.
[q] 1 Kin. 7. 51.

[1] Heb. *at thy house.*
[2] Heb. *was smitten.*

vines, can be applied to such a sunk plain as the Sabkah; and it is certainly most unlikely that 10,000 prisoners would have been conveyed upwards of eighty miles (the distance of the Sabkah from Petra), through a rough and difficult country, only in order to be massacred. On the whole, it is perhaps most probable that the "Valley of Salt" yet remains to be discovered, and that its true position was near Selah or Petra (see Judg. i. 36 note). Amaziah gave to Petra the name Joktheel, "subdued by God," in a religious spirit, as an acknowledgment of the divine aid by which his victory was gained. The name failed to take permanent hold on the place, because the Edomites, on not long afterwards recovering their city, restored the old appellation (2 Chr. xxviii. 17; cp. Isai. xvi. 1, and Am. i. 11).

unto this day] The writer of Kings evidently gives the exact words of his document, composed not later than the reign of Ahaz, before whose death the Edomites had recovered Petra.

8. Amaziah's success against Edom had so elated him that he thought himself more than a match for his northern neighbour. The grounds of the quarrel between them were furnished by the conduct of the hired, but dismissed, Israelite soldiers (see marg. ref.).

let us look one another in the face] *i.e.* "let us meet face to face in arms, and try each other's strength" (*vv.* 11, 12).

9. The Oriental use of apologues on the most solemn and serious occasions is well known to all, and scarcely needs illustration (cp. marg. ref.). It is a common feature of such apologues that they are not exact parallels to the case whereto they are applied, but only general or partial resemblances. Hence there is need of caution in applying the several points of the illustration.

10. *glory of this*, &c.] Lit. "Be honoured;" *i.e.* "Enjoy thy honour—be content with it." "Why wilt thou meddle **with misfortune?**"

11. Jehoash did not wait to be attacked. Invading Judæa from the west, and so *ascending* out of the low coast tract, he met the army of Amaziah at Beth-shemesh (see Josh. xix. 21 note), about 15 miles from Jerusalem.

12. The author of Chronicles notes that Amaziah's obstinacy, and his consequent defeat and captivity, were judgments upon him for an idolatry into which he had fallen after his conquest of Edom (2 Chr. xxv. 14, 20).

13. The object of breaking down the wall was to leave Jerusalem at the mercy of her rival; and it must have been among the conditions of the peace that the breach thus made should not be repaired.

Gates in Oriental cities are named from the places to which they lead. The gate of Ephraim must therefore have been a north gate: perhaps also known, later on, by the name of the "gate of Benjamin" (Jer. xxxvii. 13; Zech. xiv. 10). The corner gate was probably a gate at the north-west angle of the city, where the north wall approached the Valley of Hinnom. The entire breach was thus in the north wall, on the side where Jerusalem was naturally the weakest. Josephus says that Joash drove his chariot through the breach into the town, a practice not unusual with conquerors.

14. This is the only distinct mention of "hostages" in the Old Testament. It would seem that the Oriental conquerors generally regarded the terror of their arms as sufficient

gold and silver, and all the vessels that were found in the house of the LORD, and in the treasures of the king's house, and hos- 15 tages, and returned to Samaria. ¶ʳNow the rest of the acts of Jehoash which he did, and his might, and how he fought with Amaziah king of Judah, *are* they not written in the book of the 16 chronicles of the kings of Israel? And Jehoash slept with his fathers, and was buried in Samaria with the kings of Israel; 17 and Jeroboam his son reigned in his stead. ¶ˢAnd Amaziah the son of Joash king of Judah lived after the death of Jehoash 18 son of Jehoahaz king of Israel fifteen years. And the rest of the acts of Amaziah, *are* they not written in the book of the 19 chronicles of the kings of Judah? Now ᵗthey made a conspiracy against him in Jerusalem: and he fled to ᵘLachish; but they 20 sent after him to Lachish, and slew him there. And they brought him on horses: and he was buried at Jerusalem with 21 his fathers in the city of David. And all the people of Judah took ˣAzariah, which *was* sixteen years old, and made him king 22 instead of his father Amaziah. He built ʸElath, and restored 23 it to Judah, after that the king slept with his fathers. ¶In the fifteenth year of Amaziah the son of Joash king of Judah Jero- boam the son of Joash king of Israel began to reign in Samaria, 24 *and reigned* forty and one years. And he did *that which was* evil in the sight of the LORD: he departed not from all the sins 25 of Jeroboam the son of Nebat, who made Israel to sin. He re- stored the coast of Israel ᶻfrom the entering of Hamath unto ᵃthe sea of the plain, according to the word of the LORD God of Israel, which he spake by the hand of his servant ᵇJonah, the

ʳ ch. 13. 12

ˢ 2 Chr. 25. 25, &c.

ᵗ 2 Chr. 25. 27.
ᵘ Josh. 10. 3.

ˣ ch. 15. 13. & 2 Chr. 26. 1, he is called *Uzziah.*
ʸ ch. 16. 6. 2 Chr. 26. 2.

ᶻ Num. 13. 21. & 34. 8.
ᵃ Deut. 3. 17.
ᵇ Jonah 1. 1. Matt. 12. 39, 40, called *Jonas.*

---

to secure the performance of the engage- ments contracted towards them.

15, 16. These two verses (repeated from xiii. 12, 13) are out of place here, where they interrupt the history of Amaziah's reign.

20. *they brought him on horses*] *i.e.* they conveyed his body back to Jerusalem in the royal chariot. The combination of relent- less animosity against the living prince with the deepest respect for his dead remains is very characteristic of an Oriental people.

21. *all the people of Judah*] The words imply that the conspiracy was one in which the general mass of the people did not par- ticipate. There was no confusion and trou- ble as on the occasion of the murder of Joash. Azariah ("the strength of Jeho- vah"), and Uzziah ("whom Jehovah as- sists"), were mere variants of one name.

22. Elath, or Eloth (marg. ref. 1 K. ix. 26), was near Ezion-Geber, in the Gulf of Akabah. It had been lost to the Jews on the revolt of Edom from Joram (viii. 22). Uzziah's re-establishment of the place, ren- dered possible by his father's successes (*v.* 7), was one of his first acts, and seems to imply a desire to renew the commercial projects which Solomon had successfully carried out, and which Jehoshaphat had vainly at- tempted (1 K. xxii. 48).

23. *Jeroboam*] This is the only instance, in the history of either kingdom, of a recur- rent royal appellation. We can scarcely

doubt that Jeroboam II. was named after the great founder of the Israelite kingdom by a father who trusted that he might prove a sort of second founder. Perhaps the pro- phecy of Jonah (see *v.* 25) had been already given, and it was known that a great deli- verance was approaching.

25. *He restored the coast of Israel*] Jero- boam, in the course of his long reign, reco- vered the old boundaries of the Holy Land to the north, the east, and the south-east. The "entering in of Hamath" is spoken of as the northern boundary; the "sea of the plain," or the Dead Sea, is the southern boundary (see marg. reff.): here Israel ad- joined on Moab. The entire tract east of Jordan had been lost to Israel in the reign of Jehu and that of Jehoahaz (x. 33, xiii. 3, 25). All this was now recovered: and not only so, but Moab was reduced (Amos vi. 14), and the Syrians were in their turn forced to submit to the Jews (*v.* 28). The northern conquests were perhaps little less important than the eastern (do.).

the word of the LORD...*which he spake*] Some have found the prophecy of Jonah here alluded to, or a portion of it, in Isaiah xv. and xvi. (see xvi. 13); but without suffi- cient grounds.

This passage tends to fix Jonah's date to some period not very late in the reign of Jeroboam II., *i.e.* (according to the ordinary chronology) from B.C. 823 to B.C. 782. On Gath-hepher, see marg. ref. and note.

e Josh. 19. 13.
d ch. 13. 4.
e Deut. 32. 36.
f ch. 13. 5.

g 2 Sam. 8. 6.
1 Kin. 11. 24.
2 Chr. 8. 3.

h After an interregnum of 11 years,
ch. 15. 8.
a ch. 14. 21.
2 Chr. 26. 1, 3, 4.
b called *Uzziah*, ver. 13. 30, &c.
& 2 Chr. 26. 1.
c ver. 35.
ch. 12. 3.
& 14. 4.
d 2 Chr. 26. 19—21.
e Lev. 13. 46.

f 2 Chr. 26. 23.

26 son of Amittai, the prophet, which was of *c*Gath-hepher. For the LORD *d*saw the affliction of Israel, that it was very bitter: for *e*there was not any shut up, nor any left, nor any helper for 27 Israel. *f*And the LORD said not that he would blot out the name of Israel from under heaven : but he saved them by the 28 hand of Jeroboam the son of Joash. ¶ Now the rest of the acts of Jeroboam, and all that he did, and his might, how he warred, and how he recovered Damascus, and Hamath, *g*which belonged to Judah, for Israel, are they not written in the book of the 29 chronicles of the kings of Israel ? . And Jeroboam slept with his fathers, even with the kings of Israel; and *h*Zachariah his son reigned in his stead.

CHAP. 15. IN the twenty and seventh year of Jeroboam king of Israel *a*began *b*Azariah son of Amaziah king of Judah to reign. 2 Sixteen years old was he when he began to reign, and he reigned two and fifty years in Jerusalem. And his mother's name was 3 Jecholiah of Jerusalem. And he did that which was right in the sight of the LORD, according to all that his father Amaziah 4 had done; *c*save that the high places were not removed: the people sacrificed and burnt incense still on the high places. 5 ¶ And the LORD *d*smote the king, so that he was a leper unto the day of his death, and *e*dwelt in a several house. And Jotham the king's son was over the house, judging the people of the 6 land. And the rest of the acts of Azariah, and all that he did, are they not written in the book of the chronicles of the kings 7 of Judah? So Azariah slept with his fathers; and *f*they buried him with his fathers in the city of David: and Jotham his son 8 reigned in his stead. ¶ In the thirty and eighth year of Azariah king of Judah did Zachariah the son of Jeroboam reign over

---

26. *the affliction of Israel*] That which the Israelites had suffered for two reigns at the hands of the Syrians (x. 32, 33, xiii. 3, 7, 22).

there was not any shut up, nor any left] A phrase implying complete depopulation (see marg. ref. note ; 1 K. xiv. 10), but here meaning no more than extreme depression and weakness.

27. *And the LORD said not*] Though the Israelites were brought thus low, yet the fiat did not as yet go forth for their destruction. God did not send a Prophet to say that He would blot out the name of Israel from under heaven ; but on the contrary sent two to announce that they should be delivered from their present enemies, and obtain triumphs over them (see v. 25, xiii. 17–19).

that he would blot out, &c.] This is a Mosaic phrase, found only here and in Deuteronomy (ix. 14, xxix. 20).

28. *he recovered Damascus*] Jeroboam probably gained certain advantages over Ben-hadad, which induced the latter to make his submission and consent to such terms as those extorted by Ahab (1 K. xx. 34).

Hamath was probably among the actual conquests of Jeroboam. It was brought so low in his reign, as to have become almost a by-word for calamity (cp. Amos vi. 2).

which belonged to Judah, for Israel] i.e.

these cities were recovered to Judah, i.e. to the people of God generally, through or by means of being added to Israel, i.e. to the northern kingdom.

A few further facts in the history of Jeroboam II. are recorded by the prophet Amos (cp. ch. vii. 10 &c.).

XV. 5. *the* LORD *smote the king, so that he was a leper*] The circumstances under which this terrible affliction befel one of the greatest of the Jewish kings, are given at some length by the author of Chronicles (marg. ref.), who supplies us with a tolerably full account of this important reign, which the writer of Kings dismisses in half-a-dozen verses.

a several house] "A house of liberation," or, freedom. On the necessity, under which the Law placed lepers, of living apart from other men, see marg. ref. Jotham became regent in his father's room, and exercised the functions of judge (1 K. iii. 9 note), from the time that his father became a leper.

8. *In the thirty and eighth year*] Rather, according to the previous numbers (xiv. 23, xv. 2), the 27th year of Azariah. Some suppose an interregnum between Jeroboam and Zachariah, which, however, is very improbable.

9 Israel in Samaria six months. And he did *that which was* evil in the sight of the LORD, as his fathers had done: he departed not from the sins of Jeroboam the son of Nebat, who made
10 Israel to sin. And Shallum the son of Jabesh conspired against him, and *g*smote him before the people, and slew him, and
11 reigned in his stead. And the rest of the ácts of Zachariah, behold, they *are* written in the book of the chronicles of the
12 kings of Israel. This *was* *h*the word of the LORD which he spake unto Jehu, saying, Thy sons shall sit on the throne of Israel unto the fourth *generation*. And so it came to pass.
13 ¶ Shallum the son of Jabesh began to reign in the nine and thirtieth year of *i*Uzziah king of Judah; and he reigned *l*a full
14 month in Samaria. For Menahem the son of Gadi went up from *k*Tirzah, and came to Samaria, and smote Shallum the son of Jabesh in Samaria, and slew him, and reigned in his stead.
15 And the rest of the acts of Shallum, and his conspiracy which he made, behold, they *are* written in the book of the chronicles
16 of the kings of Israel. ¶ Then Menahem smote *l*Tiphsah, and all that *were* therein, and the coasts thereof from Tirzah: because they opened not *to him*, therefore he smote *it;* and all *m*the
17 women therein that were with child he ripped up. In the nine and thirtieth year of Azariah king of Judah began Menahem the son of Gadi to reign over Israel, *and reigned* ten years in
18 Samaria. And he did *that which was* evil in the sight of the LORD: he departed not all his days from the sins of Jeroboam
19 the son of Nebat, who made Israel to sin. *And* *n*Pul the king of Assyria came against the land: and Menahem gave Pul a

g As prophesied, Amos 7. 9.

h ch. 10. 30.

i Matt. 1. 8, 9, called *Ozias,* and ver. 1. *Azariah.*
k 1 Kin. 14. 17.

l 1 Kin. 4. 24.

ⁱ¹ ch. 8. 12.

n 1 Chr. 5. 26. Isai. 9. 1. Hos. 8. 9.

Heb. *a month of days.*

---

10. *before the people*] *i.e.* openly and publicly. The LXX. turns the original of the above words into a proper name, Keblaam, and makes him the actual assassin, but without much ground.

14. Tirzah, the old capital, once more appears as a place of importance, giving birth to the pretender, who alone of all these later kings died a natural death, and left the crown to his son (*v.* 22). It would seem from the present passage to have been on lower ground than Samaria.

16. With respect to the supposed inability of Menahem to lead an expedition to Tiphsah (Thapsacus, see marg. ref.) on the Euphrates, we may note in the first place that such an expedition was a natural sequel to Jeroboam's occupation of Hamath (xiv. 28); and further, that it would have been greatly facilitated by the weakness of Assyria at this time, that empire having fallen into a state of depression about B.C. 780.

19. This is the first distinct mention which we find in Scripture of Assyria as an aggressive power. From the native monuments we learn that she had been for above a century pushing her conquests beyond the Euphrates, and seeking to reduce under her dominion the entire tract between that river and Egypt. Jehu had paid tribute. Some—arguing from the use of the phrase "confirmed the kingdom"

(here, and in xiv. 5)—think that Jehoahaz had acknowledged Assyrian suzerainty, and consented that her monarchs should receive their investiture from the hands of the Ninevite king. But hitherto there had been no hostile invasion of Jewish or Israelite soil by an Assyrian army. Now, however, the Assyrians are at last formally introduced into the history. A series of aggressions is related in this and the four following chapters, culminating, on the one hand, in the destruction of the northern kingdom, on the other, in the complete failure of Sennacherib's attempt upon Judæa and Egypt.

With respect to the present expedition, there are certain difficulties. The name of Pul does not appear among the Assyrian monumental kings, and it is absent from the copies of the Assyrian Canon, containing the entire list of monarchs from about B.C. 910 to B.C. 670. Assyria Proper, moreover, appears to have been in a state of depression for some forty years before the accession of Tiglath-Pileser (*v.* 29). It is probable that, during the depression of the Ninevite line, Pul, a *Chaldæan* and not an Assyrian king, established a second monarchy upon the Euphrates, which claimed to be the true Assyria, and was recognised as such by the nations of Syria and Palestine. His invasion was probably provoked by Menahem's conquest of Thapsacus,

thousand talents of silver, that his hand might be with him to
20 °confirm the kingdom in his hand. And Menahem [1]exacted the
money of Israel, *even* of all the mighty men of wealth, of
each man fifty shekels of silver, to give to the king of Assyria.
So the king of Assyria turned back, and stayed not there
21 in the land. ¶ And the rest of the acts of Menahem, and all
that he did, *are* they not written in the book of the chronicles
22 of the kings of Israel? And Menahem slept with his fathers;
23 and Pekahiah his son reigned in his stead. ¶ In the fiftieth
year of Azariah king of Judah Pekahiah the son of Menahem
began to reign over Israel in Samaria, *and reigned* two years.
24 And he did *that which was* evil in the sight of the LORD: he
departed not from the sins of Jeroboam the son of Nebat, who
25 made Israel to sin. But Pekah the son of Remaliah, a captain
of his, conspired against him, and smote him in Samaria, in the
palace of the king's house, with Argob and Arieh, and with him
fifty men of the Gileadites: and he killed him, and reigned in
26 his room. And the rest of the acts of Pekahiah, and all that
he did, behold, they *are* written in the book of the chronicles
27 of the kings of Israel. ¶ In the two and fiftieth year of Azariah

king of Judah *p* Pekah the son of Remaliah began to reign over
28 Israel in Samaria, *and reigned* twenty years. And he did *that
which was* evil in the sight of the LORD: he departed not from
the sins of Jeroboam the son of Nebat, who made Israel to sin.

29 In the days of Pekah king of Israel *q* came Tiglath-pileser king
of Assyria, and took *r* Ijon, and Abel-beth-maachah, and Janoah,

---

[1] Heb. *caused to come forth.*

---

which he would view as a wanton aggression upon his territory.

a thousand talents of silver] Compared with the tribute of Hezekiah soon afterwards (xviii. 14), this seems a large sum; but it is not beyond the resources of such a State as Samaria at the period. The tie which had bound Samaria to Assyria from the reign of Jehu to that of Jeroboam II., had ceased to exist during the period of Assyrian depression. Menahem now renewed it, undertaking the duties of a tributary, and expecting the support which Assyria was accustomed to lend to her dependencies in their struggles with their neighbours. Hence the reproaches of Hosea (marg. ref. *n*).

20. *Menahem exacted the money*] The kings of Israel had no such ready resource in difficulties as that possessed by the kings of Judah in the Temple treasury (xii. 18, xvi. 8). Hence, the forced contribution from the people, the odium of which was diminished by confining the levy to the comparatively rich.

each man fifty shekels] As the silver talent contained 3000 shekels, the levy of fifty shekels a head must have extended to 60,000 persons.

21. Assyrian inscriptions show that Menahem was subsequently reduced to subjection by Tiglath-Pileser (*v.* 29).

25. *a captain of his*] A mere "captain," a person, therefore, of very moderate rank.

The low birth of Pekah is probably glanced at in Isaiah's favourite designation of him as "Remaliah's son" (Isai. vii. 4, 5, 9, viii. 6).

From the fact that Pekah employed Gileadites to carry out his designs, it has been conjectured that he himself belonged to the trans-Jordanic region.

in the palace of the king's house] Rather, "In the tower of the king's palace;" or possibly "in the *harem* of the king's palace" (1 K. xvi. 18 note).

29. Tiglath-Pileser is the first among the Assyrian monarchs of Scripture whom we can certainly identify with a king mentioned in the monuments. According to the Assyrian Canon he reigned from B.C. 745 to B.C. 727; and the monuments show us this energetic and powerful prince (though, probably, an usurper); building and repairing palaces, levying armies, and carrying on successful wars against Merodach-Baladan in Babylonia, Rezin at Damascus, Hiram at Tyre, the Medes, the Armenians, the natives of Northern Mesopotamia, and the Arabs who bordered upon Egypt. His Assyrian name, Tiglat-pal-zira, is composed of the elements *tiglat*, "adoration," *pal*, "son," and *zira*, a word of uncertain meaning.

Ijon and Abel-beth-maachah] On the position of some of the towns mentioned in this verse see marg. ref. and Josh. xix. 36. Janoah is not the Janohah of Josh. xvi. 6

and Kedesh, and Hazor, and Gilead, and Galilee, all the land
30 of Naphtali, and carried them captive to Assyria. ¶And
Hoshea the son of Elah made a conspiracy against Pekah the
son of Remaliah, and smote him, and slew him, and *reigned in
his stead, *in the twentieth year of Jotham the son of Uzziah.
31 And the rest of the acts of Pekah, and all that he did, behold,
they *are* written in the book of the chronicles of the kings of
32 Israel. ¶In the second year of Pekah the son of Remaliah king of
Israel began *Jotham the son of Uzziah king of Judah to reign.
33 Five and twenty years old was he when he began to reign, and
he reigned sixteen years in Jerusalem. And his mother's name
34 *was* Jerusha, the daughter of Zadok. And he did *that which
was* right in the sight of the LORD : he did *according to all that
35 his father Uzziah had done. *Howbeit the high places were
not removed : the people sacrificed and burned incense still in
the high places. *He built the higher gate of the house of the
36 LORD. Now the rest of the acts of Jotham, and all that he
did, *are* they not written in the book of the chronicles of the
37 kings of Judah? ¶In those days the LORD began to send
against Judah *Rezin the king of Syria, and *Pekah the son
38 of Remaliah. And Jotham slept with his fathers, and was
buried with his fathers in the city of David his father : and
Ahaz his son reigned in his stead.

CHAP. 16. IN the seventeenth year of Pekah the son of Remaliah
2 *Ahaz the son of Jotham king of Judah began to reign. Twenty
years old *was* Ahaz when he began to reign, and reigned sixteen
years in Jerusalem, and did not *that which was* right in the
3 sight of the LORD his God, like David his father. But he
walked in the way of the kings of Israel, yea, *and made his

* After an
anarchy for
some years,
ch. 17. 1.
Hos. 10. 3,
7, 15.
t In the
fourth year
of Ahaz, in
the twen-
tieth year
after Jo-
tham had
begun to
reign : *Ush.*
u 2 Chr. 27.1.
x ver. 3.
y ver. 4.
z 2 Chr. 27.
3, &c.

a ch. 16. 5.
b ver. 27.

a 2 Chr. 28.
1, &c.

b Lev. 18. 21.
2 Chr. 28. ?.

(modern *Yanûn*, S.E. of Nablous), but a
city (? *Hunîn*) near the Sea of Merom.
Gilead is, probably, to be limited here to a
small district of Peræa, lying to the east of
Lake Merom, and in later times known as
Gaulanitis (the reading of LXX. here). If so,
we must suppose two expeditions of Tiglath-
Pileser against Pekah, the first mentioned
here, and the second recorded in Chronicles
and Isaiah (see marg. ref. *q* ; xvi. 9 note).

30. *Hoshea, the son of Elah*] One of Pekah's friends, according to Josephus.

the twentieth year of Jotham] According to
v. 33 and 2 Chr. xxvii. 1, Jotham reigned only
sixteen years. See also the suggestion in the
margin. Strangely enough, this first year
of Hoshea is also called, not the fourth, but
the twelfth of Ahaz (xvii. 1). The chronological confusion of the history, as it stands,
is striking.

Uzziah] *i.e.* Azariah. See *vv.* 1-4.

31. *the rest of the acts of Pekah*] On these,
see xvi. 5 note.

32. The writer here resumes the history
of Judah from *v.* 7, to resume and conclude
the history of Israel in ch. xvii.

34. Jotham imitated his father in all respects, excepting in his impious usurpation
of the priestly functions (*v.* 5 note ; 2 Chr.
xxvii. 2).

35. *He built the higher gate*] Jotham

followed the example of his father in military, no less than in religious, matters (cp.
marg. ref. with 2 Chr. xxvi. 9). The
"higher" or "upper gate" of the Temple
is thought to have been that towards the
north ; and its fortification would seem to
indicate fear of an attack from that
quarter.

37. The recent invasions of Pul and Tiglath-Pileser had effectually alarmed Pekah
and Rezin, and had induced them to put
aside the traditional jealousies which naturally kept them apart, and to make a
league offensive and defensive. Into this
league they were anxious that Judæa should
enter ; but they distrusted the house of David, which had been so long hostile both to
Damascus and to Samaria. They consequently formed the design of transferring
the Jewish crown to a certain Ben-Tabeal
(Isai. vii. 6), probably a Jewish noble, perhaps a refugee at one of their courts, whom
they could trust to join heartily in their
schemes (xvi. 5 note).

XVI. 3. Ahaz was the worst of all the
kings of Judah. He imitated the worst of
the Israelite kings—Ahab and Ahaziah,—
by a re-introduction of the Baal worship,
which had been rooted out of Israel by
Jehu and out of Judah by Jehoiada.

and made his son to pass through the fire]

e Deut. 12. 31.

d Deut. 12. 2.
1 Kin. 14. 23.
e Isai. 7. 1,
4, &c.

f ch. 14. 22.

g ch. 15. 29.

h ch. 12. 18.
See 2 Chr.
28. 21.

i Foretold,
Amos 1. 5.

son to pass through the fire, according to the ᶜabominations of the heathen, whom the LORD cast out from before the children 4 of Israel. And he sacrificed and burnt incense in the high 5 places, and ᵈon the hills, and under every green tree. ¶ ᵉThen Rezin king of Syria and Pekah son of Remaliah king of Israel came up to Jerusalem to war: and they besieged Ahaz, but 6 could not overcome *him*. At that time Rezin king of Syria ᶠrecovered Elath to Syria, and drave the Jews from ¹Elath: and 7 the Syrians came to Elath, and dwelt there unto this day. So Ahaz sent messengers ᵍto ²Tiglath-pileser king of Assyria, saying, I *am* thy servant and thy son: come up, and save me out of the hand of the king of Syria, and out of the hand of the king 8 of Israel, which rise up against me. And Ahaz ʰtook the silver and gold that was found in the house of the LORD, and in the treasures of the king's house, and sent *it for* a present to the 9 king of Assyria. And the king of Assyria hearkened unto him: for the king of Assyria went up against ³Damascus, and ⁱtook it, and carried *the people of* it captive to Kir, and slew Rezin.

---

¹ Heb. *Eloth.*　　　　1 Chr. 5. 26. & 2 Chr. 28.　　³ Heb. *Dammesek.*
² Heb. *Tilgath-pileser,*　20, *Tilgath-pilneser.*

---

i.e. Ahaz adopted the Moloch worship of the Ammonites and Moabites (iii. 27 ; Mic. vi. 7), and sacrificed at least one son, probably his firstborn, according to the horrid rites of those nations, and the Canaanite tribes (Deut. xii. 31 ; Ps. cvi. 37, 38). Hitherto, apparently, the Jews had been guiltless of this abomination. They had been warned against it by Moses (marg. ref. ; Deut. xviii. 10) ; and if (as some think) they had practised it in the wilderness (Ezek. xx. 26 ; Am. v. 26), the sin must have been rare and exceptional ; from the date of their entrance into the Promised Land they had wholly put it away. Now, however, it became so frequent (cp. xvii. 17, xxi. 6) as to meet with the strongest protest from Jeremiah and Ezekiel (Jer. vii. 31, 32, xix. 2-6 ; xxxii. 35 ; Ezek. xvi. 20, xx. 26, xxiii. 37, &c.).

4. *he sacrificed,* &c.] Other kings of Judah had allowed their people to do so. Ahaz was the first, so far as we know, to countenance the practice by his own example.

5. Rezin and Pekah, who had already begun their attacks upon Judæa in the reign of Jotham (xv. 37), regarded the accession of a boy-king, only sixteen years of age, as peculiarly favourable to their projects, and proceeded without loss of time to carry them out. The earlier scenes of the war, omitted by the writer of Kings, are given at some length in 2 Chr. xxviii. 5-15.

6. Either during the siege, or on breaking up from before Jerusalem, Rezin made an expedition to the Red Sea coast, and became master of the city which had belonged to Judæa about seventy years (marg. ref.). Most moderns render this verse, "Rezin recovered (or restored) Elath to Edom,...and the **Edomites** came to Elath."

On the resemblance of the words Aram and Edom in the original, see 2 Sam. viii. 12 note.

7. Ahaz was threatened on all sides, on the north by Rezin and Pekah ; on the south-east by Edom (2 Chr. xxviii. 17) ; and on the south-west by the Philistines (do. 18). To these external dangers was added the still greater peril of disaffection at home. A large party in Judah was "weary" of the house of David (Is. vii. 13), ready to join the confederacy (do. viii. 6, 12), and to accept for king "the son of Tabeal." Ahaz saw no hope of safety unless he could obtain a powerful protector ; and, Egypt being particularly weak at this time, he turned to Assyria.

8. Cp. marg. ref. and 1 K. xv. 18. Political necessity was always held to justify the devotion of the Temple treasure to secular purposes.

9. The submission of Judah, which Ahaz proffered, would be of the utmost importance in connexion with any projects that might be entertained of Egyptian conquests. Naturally, Damascus was the first object of attack. It was the head of the confederacy, and it lay nearest to an army descending upon Lower Syria, as all Asiatic armies would descend, from the north. It appears from an inscription of Tiglath-pileser's, that Rezin met him in the field, was defeated, and slain. An attack upon Pekah followed. Now probably it was that the entire trans-Jordanic region was overrun ; and that the Reubenites, the Gadites, and the half-tribe of Manasseh, were carried into captivity (1 Chr. v. 26). Megiddo and Dor appear also to have been occupied, and the Arabs of the south chastised. Tiglath-pileser then returned to Damascus, where a son of Rezin had assumed the crown ; he besieged and took the city, and punished

10 ¶ And king Ahaz went to Damascus to meet Tiglath-pileser king of Assyria, and saw an altar that *was* at Damascus: and king Ahaz sent to Urijah the priest the fashion of the altar, and the 11 pattern of it, according to all the workmanship thereof. And Urijah the priest built an altar according to all that king Ahaz had sent from Damascus: so Urijah the priest made *it* against 12 king Ahaz came from Damascus. And when the king was come from Damascus, the king saw the altar: and *k* the king 13 approached to the altar, and offered thereon. And he burnt his burnt offering and his meat offering, and poured his drink offering, and sprinkled the blood of [1] his peace offerings upon the 14 altar. And he brought also *l* the brasen altar, which *was* before the LORD, from the forefront of the house, from between the altar and the house of the LORD, and put it on the north side of 15 the altar. And king Ahaz commanded Urijah the priest, saying, Upon the great altar burn *m* the morning burnt offering, and the evening meat offering, and the king's burnt sacrifice, and his meat offering, with the burnt offering of all the people of the land, and their meat offering, and their drink offerings; and sprinkle upon it all the blood of the burnt offering, and all the blood of the sacrifice: and the brasen altar shall be for me to 16 enquire *by*. Thus did Urijah the priest, according to all that 17 king Ahaz commanded. ¶ *n* And king Ahaz cut off *o* the borders of the bases, and removed the laver from off them; and took down *p* the sea from off the brasen oxen that *were* under it, and

k 2 Chr. 26. 16, 19.

l 2 Chr. 4. 1.

m Ex. 20. 39, 40, 41.

n 2Chr. 23. 24.
o 1 Kin. 7. 27, 28.
p 1 Kin. 7. 23, 25.

[1] Heb. *which were his.*

Rezin's son with death. Tiglath-pileser appears by one of his inscriptions to have held a court at Damascus, to which it is probable that the tributary kings of the neighbourhood were summoned to pay their tributes and do homage for their kingdoms. Among the tributes brought to him at this time, those of Judæa, Edom, Ammon, Moab, Gaza, Ascalon, and Tyre, are mentioned.

Kir] Kir is mentioned by Amos (ix. 7) as the country from which the Syrians came. It is joined by Isaiah (xxii. 6) with Elam or Elymais. Its position can only be conjectured. Perhaps the word designates a region adjoining Elymais, in the extreme south-eastern limits of Assyria.

10. *and saw an altar*] Rather, "The altar," *i.e.* an Assyrian altar, and connected with that formal recognition of the Assyrian deities which the Ninevite monarchs appear to have required of all the nations whom they received into their empire.

the fashion of the altar] Assyrian altars were not very elaborate, but they were very different from the Jewish. They were comparatively small, and scarcely suited for "whole burnt-offerings." One type was square, about half the height of a man, and ornamented round the top with a sort of battlement. Another had a triangular base and a circular top consisting of a single flat stone. A third was a sort of portable stand, narrow, and about the height of a man.

This last was of the kind which the kings took with them in their expeditions.

14. Hitherto the "Brasen Altar" (marg. ref.) had, it would seem, occupied a position directly in front of the Temple porch, which it exactly equalled in width. Now Ahaz removed it from this place, and gave the honourable position to his new altar, which he designed to supersede the old for all ordinary purposes (*v.* 15).

from between the altar, &c.] Urijah, having received no official directions, had placed the new altar in front of the old, between it and the eastern gate of the court. Ahaz consequently on his arrival found the brasen altar "between the (new) altar and the house of the Lord."

15. *the brasen altar shall be for me to enquire by*] The bulk of modern commentators translate—"As for the Brasen Altar, it will be for me to enquire (or consider) what I shall do with it."

16. The writer condemns the obsequiousness of Urijah, whose conduct was the more inexcusable after the noble example of his predecessor Azariah (2 Chr. xxvi. 17-20).

17. See marg. reff. The acts recorded here, were probably not mere wanton acts of mutilation, but steps in the conversion of these sacred objects to other uses, as to the ornamentation of a palace or of an idol temple. The bases, the oxen, and the sea were not destroyed—they remained at Jerusalem till its final capture (Jer. lii.

18 put it upon a pavement of stones. And the covert for the sabbath that they had built in the house, and the king's entry without, turned he from the house of the LORD for the king of
19 Assyria. ¶ Now the rest of the acts of Ahaz which he did, *are* they not written in the book of the chronicles of the kings of
20 Judah? And Ahaz slept with his fathers, and *ᵍwas buried with his fathers in the city of David: and Hezekiah his son reigned in his stead.

q 2Chr.28.27.

CHAP. 17. IN the twelfth year of Ahaz king of Judah began
*ᵃHoshea the son of Elah to reign in Samaria over Israel nine
2 years. And he did *that which was* evil in the sight of the LORD,
3 but not as the kings of Israel that weᵣₑ before him. Against him came up *ᵇShalmaneser king of Assyria; and Hoshea became
4 his servant, and ¹gave him ²presents. And the king of Assyria found conspiracy in Hoshea: for he had sent messengers to So king of Egypt, and brought no present to the king of Assyria, as *he had done* year by year · therefore the king of Assyria shut

ᵃ After an interregnum, ch. 15. 30.
ᵇ ch. 18. 9.

¹ Heb. *rendered,* 2 Sam. 8. 2.   ² Or, *tribute.*

17, 20). Probably they were restored to their original uses by Hezekiah (2 Chr. xxix. 19).

a pavement of stones] Probably a pavement made expressly, for the stones of the court seem to have been covered with a planking of cedar (1 K. vi. 36, vii. 12).

18. *the covert...in the house*] A canopied seat in the Temple for the king and his family when they attended public worship on the sabbath. It stood no doubt in the inner court of the Temple.

the king's entry without] This would seem to have been a private passage by which the king crossed the outer court to the east gate of the inner court when he visited the Temple (Ezek. xlvi. 1, 2).

turned he from the house of the LORD for the king of Assyria] This passage is very obscure. Some translate—"altered he in the house of the Lord, because of the king of Assyria," supposing the "covert" and the "passage" to have been of rich materials, and Ahaz to have taken them to eke out his "presents to the king of Assyria." Others render, "removed he into the house of the Lord from fear of the king of Assyria."

19. *the rest of the acts of Ahaz*] Such as are described in Isai. vii. 10-13; 2 Chr. xxviii. 23-25, xxix. 3, 7.

XVII. 1. *In the twelfth year*] Cp. xv. 30 note. The history of the kingdom of Israel is in this chapter brought to a close.

2. *not as the kings of Israel that were before him*] The repentance of a nation, like that of an individual, may be "too late." God is long-suffering; but after national sins have reached a certain height, after admonitions and warnings have been repeatedly rejected, after lesser punishments have failed,—judgment begins to fall. Forces have been set in motion, which nothing but a miracle could stop; and God does not see fit to work a miracle in such a case. Cp. Butler, 'Analogy,' Pt. I. ch. ii. end.

3. Of Shalmaneser, the successor of Tiglath-pileser in the Assyrian Canon, we know little from Assyrian sources, since his records have been mutilated by his successors, the Sargonids, who were of a wholly different family. The archives of Tyre mention him as contemporary with, and warring against, a Tyrian king named Elulæus.

The expedition, referred to here, was probably in the first year of Shalmaneser (B.C. 727). Its main object was the reduction of Phœnicia, which had re-asserted its independence, but (except Tyre) was once more completely reduced. Shalmaneser probably passed on from Phœnicia into Galilee, where he attacked and took Beth-arbel (Arbela of Josephus, now *Irbid*), treating it with great severity (Hos. x. 14), in order to alarm Hoshea, who forthwith submitted, and became tributary (see marg. rendering and 1 K. iv. 21 note). Shalmaneser then returned into Assyria.

4. So, king of Egypt, is generally identified with Shebek (B.C. 730), the Sabaco of Herodotus. Hoshea's application to him was a return to a policy which had been successful in the reign of Jeroboam I. (1 K. xii. 20 note), but had not been resorted to by any other Israelite monarch. Egypt had for many years been weak, but Sabaco was a conqueror, who at the head of the swarthy hordes of Ethiopia had invaded Egypt and made himself master of the country. In the inscriptions of Shebek he boasts to have received tribute from "the king of *Shara*" (Syria), which is probably his mode of noticing Hoshea's application. References to the Egyptian proclivities of Hoshea are frequent in the Prophet Hosea (vii. 11, xi. 1, 5, xii. 4). King Hoshea, simultaneously with his reception as a vassal by Sabaco, ceased to pay tribute to Shalmaneser, thus openly rebelling, and provoking the chastisement which followed.

5 him up, and bound him in prison. ¶ Then *e* the king of Assyria   *e* ch. 18. 9.
came up throughout all the land, and went up to Samaria, and
6 besieged it three years.   *d* In the ninth year of Hoshea the king   *d* ch. 18. 10.
of Assyria took Samaria, and *e* carried Israel away into Assyria,   Hos. 13. 16,
f and placed them in Halah and in Habor *by* the river of Gozan,   *e* Lev. 26. 32,
7 and in the cities of the Medes.   For *so* it was, that the children   33.
of Israel had sinned against the LORD their God, which had   Deut. 28. 36,
brought them up out of the land of Egypt, from under the hand   *f* 1 Chr. 5.26.
8 of Pharaoh king of Egypt, and had feared other gods, and
g walked in the statutes of the heathen, whom the LORD cast out   *g* Lev. 18. 3.
from before the children of Israel, and of the kings of Israel,   ch. 16. 3.
9 which they had made.   And the children of Israel did secretly   *h* ch. 18. 8.
those things that *were* not right against the LORD their God, and   *i* 1Kin.14.23.
they built them high places in all their cities, *h* from the tower of   Isai. 57. 5.
10 the watchmen to the fenced city.   *i* And they set them up *1* images   Deut. 16. 21.
and *k* groves *l* in every high hill, and under every green tree :   Mic. 5. 14.
l Deut. 12. 2.
ch. 16. 4.

1 Heb. *statues.*

---

5. *all the land*] The second invasion of
Shalmaneser (B.C. 723, his fifth year), is
here contrasted with the first, as extending
to the *whole* country, whereas the first had
afflicted only a part.

three years] From the fourth to the sixth
of Hezekiah, and from the seventh to the
ninth of Hoshea; two years, therefore, according to our reckoning, but three, according to that of the Hebrews.   This was a
long time for so small a place to resist the
Assyrians but Samaria was favourably
situated on a steep hill; probably Sabaco
made some attempts to relieve his vassal;
the war with Tyre must have distracted Shalmaneser ; and there is reason to believe
that before the capture was effected a revolt
had broken out at Nineveh which must
have claimed Shalmaneser's chief attention,
though it did not induce him to abandon
his enterprise.

6. *the king of Assyria took Samaria*] i.e.,
from the Assyrian inscriptions, not Shalmaneser but Sargon, who claims to have
captured the city in the first year of his
reign (B.C. 721).   At first Sargon carried off
from Samaria no more than 27,280 prisoners
and was so far from depopulating the
country that he assessed the tribute on the
remaining inhabitants at the same rate as
before the conquest.   But later in his reign
he effected the wholesale deportation here
mentioned.

Halah and in Habor by the river of Gozan]
Rather, " **on the** Habor, the river of Gozan."   Halah is the tract which Ptolemy
calls Chalcitis, on the borders of Gauzanitis
(Gozan) in the vicinity of the Chaboras, or
Khabour (Habor, the great affluent of the
Euphrates).   In this region is a remarkable
mound called *Gla*, which probably marks
the site, and represents the name, of the
city of Chalach, whence the district Chalcitis
was so called.

in the cities of the Medes] Sargon relates
that he overran Media, seized and " an-

nexed to Assyria " a number of the towns,
and also established in the country a set of
fortified posts or colonies.

7. The reasons for which God suffered the
Israelites to be deprived of their land and
carried into captivity were—1, their idolatries; 2, their rejection of the Law; 3, their
disregard of the warning voices of Prophets
and seers.

8. Idolatry was worse in the Israelites
than in other nations, since it argued not
merely folly and a gross carnal spirit,
but also black ingratitude (Ex. xx. 2, 3).
The writer subdivides the idolatries of the
Israelites into two classes, heathen and native—those which they adopted from the nations whom they drove out, and those which
their own kings imposed on them.   Under
the former head would come the great mass
of the idolatrous usages described in *vv.* 9,
10, 11, 17 ; " the high places " (*vv.* 9 and 11);
the " images " and " groves " (*v.* 10) ; the
causing of their children to " pass through
the fire" (*v.* 17); and the "worship of the host
of heaven " (*v.* 16) : under the latter would
fall the principal points in *vv.* 12, 16, 21.

which they had made] "Which" refers to
" statutes."   The Israelites had "walked in
the statutes of the heathen, and in those of
the kings of Israel, which (statutes) they
(the kings) had made."

9. Lit., the words run thus—" And the
children of Israel concealed (or 'dissembled')
words which were not so concerning the
Lord their God ;" the true meaning of
which probably is, the Israelites cloaked or
covered their idolatry with the pretence that
it was a worship of Jehovah : they glossed
it over and dissembled towards God, instead
of openly acknowledging their apostasy.

*from the tower of the watchmen to the fenced
city*] This phrase was probably a proverbial
expression for universality, meaning strictly;
—" alike in the most populous and in the
most desolate regions."   "Towers of watchmen " were built for the protection of the

m Ex. 20. 3.
Lev. 26. 1.
Deut. 5. 7.
n Deut. 4. 19.
o 1 Sam. 9.9.
p Hos. 12. 6.
Joel 2. 12.
Am. 5. 4.
Is. 1. 16.
Jer. 18. 11.
q Deut. 31.27.
Prov. 29. 1.
r Deut. 29.25.
s Deut. 32.21.
1 Kin. 16.13.
1 Cor. 8. 4.
t Ps. 115. 8.
Rom. 1. 21.
u Deut. 12.
30, 31.
x Ex. 32. 8.
1 Kin. 12.28.
y 1 Kin.16.33.
z 1 Kin.16.31.
& 22. 53.
ch. 11. 18.
a Lev. 18. 21.
Ezek. 23. 37.

11 and there they burnt incense in all the high places, as *did* the heathen whom the LORD carried away before them; and wrought 12 wicked things to provoke the LORD to anger: for they served idols, *m* whereof the LORD had said unto them, *n* Ye shall not do 13 this thing. ¶ Yet the LORD testified against Israel, and against Judah, ¹ by all the prophets, *and by* all *o* the seers, saying, *p* Turn ye from your evil ways, and keep my commandments *and* my statutes, according to all the law which I commanded your fathers, and which I sent to you by my servants the prophets. 14 Notwithstanding they would not hear, but *q* hardened their necks, like to the neck of their fathers, that did not believe in 15 the LORD their God. And they rejected his statutes, *r* and his covenant that he made with their fathers, and his testimonies which he testified against them; and they followed *s* vanity, and *t* became vain, and went after the heathen that *were* round about them, *concerning* whom the LORD had charged them, that they 16 should *u* not do like them. And they left all the commandments of the LORD their God, and *x* made them molten images, *even* two calves, *y* and made a grove, and worshipped all the host of 17 heaven, *z* and served Baal. *a* And they caused their sons and

¹ Heb. *by the hand of all.*

---

flocks and herds which were pastured in waste and desert places (2 Chr. xxvi. 10, xxvii. 4).

11. The burning of incense was a common religious practice among the Egyptians and the Babylonians; and from the present passage we gather that the Canaanitish nations practised it as one of their ordinary sacred rites. The Israelites are frequently reproached with it (Hos. ii. 13, iv. 13; Isai. lxv. 3).

13. God raised up a succession of Prophets and seers, who repeated and enforced the warnings of the Law, and breathed into the old words a new life. Among this succession were, in Israel, Ahijah the Shilonite (1 K. xiv. 2), Jehu the son of Hanani (do. xvi. 1), Elijah, Micaiah the son of Imlah (do. xxii. 8), Elisha, Jonah the son of Amittai (2 K. xiv. 25), Oded (2 Chr. xxviii. 9), Amos, and Hosea; in Judah, up to this time, Shemaiah (2 Chr. xi. 2, xii. 5), Iddo (do. xii. 15, xiii. 22), Azariah the son of Oded (do. xv. 1), Hanani (do. xvi. 7), Jehu his son (do. xix. 2), Jahaziel the son of Zechariah (do. xx. 14), Eliezer the son of Dodavah (do. v. 37), Zechariah the son of Jehoiada (do. xxiv. 20), another Zechariah (do. xxvi. 5), Joel, Micah, and Isaiah, besides several whose names are not known. Some of these persons are called "prophets," others "seers." Occasionally the same person has both titles (as Iddo and Jehu the son of Hanani), which seems to show that there was no very important distinction between them.

Probably the conjecture is right that "prophet" (*nâbi*) in strictness designates the official members of the prophetical order only, while "seer" (*chôzeh*) is applicable to all, whether members of the order or not, who receive a prophetical revelation.

14. To "harden" or "stiffen the neck" is a common Hebrew expression significative of unbending obstinacy and determined self-will. See marg. reff.

15. As idols are "vanity" and "nothingness," mere weakness and impotence, so idolators are "vain" and impotent. Their energies have been wasted, their time misspent; they have missed the real object of their existence; their whole life has been a mistake; and the result is utter powerlessness. Lit., the word rendered "vanity" seems to mean "breath" or "vapour"—a familiar image for nonentity. It occurs frequently in the Prophets, and especially in Jeremiah (*e.g.* ii. 5, viii. 19, xiv. 22, &c.).

16. In *v.* 10 there is a reference to the old high-place worship, which was professedly a worship of Jehovah, but with unauthorised rites and emblems; here the reference is to Ahab's setting up a grove to Baal in the city of Samaria (marg. ref.).

and worshipped all the host of heaven] Astral worship has not hitherto been mentioned as practised by the Israelites. Moses had warned against it (Deut. iv. 19, xvii. 3), so that it no doubt existed in his day, either among the Canaanitish nations or among the Arabians (Job xxxi. 26–28). Perhaps it was involved to some extent in the Baal worship of the Phœnicians, for Baal and Astarte were probably associated in the minds of their worshippers with the Sun and Moon. Later in the history we shall find a very decided and well-developed astral worship prevalent among the Jews, which is probably Assyro-Babylonian (xxi. 3 note).

17. Cp. xvi. 3 note, and see Lev. xx. 2–5 note.

their daughters to pass through the fire, and *b*used divination *b* Deut. 18. 10.
and enchantments, and *c*sold themselves to do evil in the sight *c* 1 Kin. 21.
18 of the LORD, to provoke him to anger. ¶ Therefore the LORD 20.
was very angry with Israel, and removed them out of his sight:
19 there was none left *d*but the tribe of Judah only. Also *e*Judah *d* 1 Kin. 11.
kept not the commandments of the LORD their God, but walked 13, 32.
20 in the statutes of Israel which they made. And the LORD re- *e* Jer. 3. 8.
jected all the seed of Israel, and afflicted them, and *f*delivered *f* ch. 13. 3.
them into the hand of spoilers, until he had cast them out of & 15. 29.
21 his sight. For *g*he rent Israel from the house of David; and *g* 1 Kin. 11.
*h*they made Jeroboam the son of Nebat king: and Jeroboam 11, 31.
drave Israel from following the LORD, and made them sin a *h* 1 Kin. 12.
22 great sin. For the children of Israel walked in all the sins of 20, 28.
23 Jeroboam which he did; they departed not from them; until
the LORD removed Israel out of his sight, *i*as he had said by all *i* 1 Kin. 14. 16.
his servants the prophets. *k*So was Israel carried away out of *k* ver. 6.
24 their own land to Assyria unto this day. ¶ *l*And the king of *l* Ezra 4. 2,
Assyria brought *men* *m*from Babylon, and from Cuthah, and 10.
from *n*Ava, and from Hamath, and from Sepharvaim, and placed *m* See ver. 30.
                                                                  n ch. 18. 34,
                                                                  Ivah.

---

19. This verse and the next are parenthe-
tical. Here again, as in *v.* 13, the writer is led
on from his account of the sins and punishment of the Israelites to glance at the
similar sins and similar punishment of the
Jews.

It was the worst reproach which could be
urged against any Jewish king, that he
"walked in the way of the kings of Israel"
(viii. 18, xvi. 3; 2 Chr. xxi. 6, xxviii. 2).
The Baal worship is generally the special
sin at which the phrase is levelled; but the
meaning here seems to be wider. Cp. Mic.
vi. 16.

20. *all the seed of Israel*] The Jews, *i.e.*
as well as the Israelites. God's dealings
with both kingdoms were alike. "Spoilers" were sent against each, time after
time, before the final ruin came on them—
against Israel, Pul and Tiglath-pileser (xv.
19, 29; 1 Chr. v. 26); against Judah, Sennacherib (xviii. 13-16), Esar-haddon (2 Chr.
xxxiii. 11), and Nebuchadnezzar thrice.

21. The strong expression "drave Israel"
is an allusion to the violent measures whereto Jeroboam had recourse in order to stop
the efflux into Judæa of the more religious
portion of his subjects (2 Chr. xi. 13-16),
the calling in of Shishak, and the permanent assumption of a hostile attitude towards the southern kingdom.

23. *as he had said by all his servants the
prophets*] The writer refers not only to the
extant prophecies of Moses (Lev. xxvi. 33;
Deut. iv. 26, 27, xxviii. 36, &c.), Ahijah
the Shilonite (marg. ref.), Hosea (ix. 3,
17), and Amos (vii. 17), but also to the entire series of warnings and predictions which
Prophet after Prophet in a long unbroken
succession had addressed to the disobedient
Israelites (*v.* 13) on their apostasy, and so
leaving them wholly "without excuse"
(see *v.* 13 note).

unto this day] The words, taken in combination with the rest of the chapter,
distinctly show that the Israelites had
not returned to their land by the time of
the composition of the Books of Kings.
They show nothing as to their ultimate
fate. But on the whole, it would seem
probable (1) that the ten tribes never
formed a community in their exile, but were
scattered from the first; and (2) that their
descendants either blended with the heathen
and were absorbed, or returned to Palestine
with Zerubbabel and Ezra, or became inse-
parably united with the dispersed Jews in
Mesopotamia and the adjacent countries.
No discovery, therefore, of the ten tribes
is to be expected, nor can works written to
prove their identity with any existing race
or body of persons be regarded as anything
more than ingenious exercitations.

24. Sargon is probably the king of Assyria intended, not (as generally supposed)
either Shalmaneser or Esar-haddon.

The ruins of Cutha have been discovered
about 15 miles north-east of Babylon, at a
place which is called Ibrahim, because it is
the traditional site of a contest between
Abraham and Nimrod. The name of Cutha is found on the bricks of this place,
which are mostly of the era of Nebuchadnezzar. The Assyrian inscriptions show that
the special god of Cutha was Nergal (*v.* 30
note).

Ava or Ivah or Ahava (Ezra viii. 15) was
on the Euphrates; perhaps the city in ancient times called Ihi or Aia, between Sippara (Sepharvaim) and Hena (Anab).

On Hamath, see 1 K. viii. 65 note.

Sepharvaim or Sippara is frequently mentioned in the Assyrian inscriptions under
the name of *Tsipar* (*v.* 31 note). The dual
form of the Hebrew name is explained by
the fact that the town lay on both sides of

them in the cities of Samaria instead of the children of Israel:
and they possessed Samaria, and dwelt in the cities thereof.
25 And *so* it was at the beginning of their dwelling there, *that* they
feared not the LORD: therefore the LORD sent lions among them,
26 which slew *some* of them. Wherefore they spake to the king of
Assyria, saying, The nations which thou hast removed, and placed
in the cities of Samaria, know not the manner of the God of the
land: therefore he hath sent lions among them, and, behold,
they slay them, because they know not the manner of the God
27 of the land. Then the king of Assyria commanded, saying,
Carry thither one of the priests whom ye brought from thence;
and let them go and dwell there, and let him teach them the
28 manner of the God of the land. Then one of the priests whom
they had carried away from Samaria came and dwelt in Beth-el,
29 and taught them how they should fear the LORD. ¶ Howbeit
every nation made gods of their own, and put *them* in the houses
of the high places which the Samaritans had made, every nation
30 in their cities wherein they dwelt. And the men of [o] Babylon
made Succoth-benoth, and the men of Cuth made Nergal, and
31 the men of Hamath made Ashima, [p] and the Avites made Nibhaz
and Tartak, and the Sepharvites [q] burnt their children in fire to

[o] ver. 24.
[p] Ezra 4. 9.
[q] Lev. 18. 21. Deut. 12. 31.

the river. Its position is marked by the modern village of *Mosaib*, about 20 miles from the ruins of Babylon up the course of the stream.

The towns mentioned in this verse were, excepting Hamath, conquered by Sargon in his twelfth year, B.C. 709; and it cannot have been until this time, or a little later, that the transplantation here recorded took place. Hamath had revolted, and been conquered by Sargon in his first year, shortly after the conquest of Samaria.

instead of the children of Israel] This does not mean that the *whole* population of Samaria was carried off (cp. 2 Chr. xxxiv. 9). The writer here, by expressly confining the new comers to the "*cities* of Samaria," seems to imply that the country districts were in other hands.

25. The depopulation of the country, insufficiently remedied by the influx of foreigners, had the natural consequence of multiplying the wild beasts and making them bolder. Probably a certain number had always lurked in the jungle along the course of the Jordan (Jer. xlix. 19, l. 44); and these now ventured into the hill country, and perhaps even into the cities. The colonists regarded their sufferings from the lions as a judgment upon them from "the god of the land" (*v.* 26; cp. 1 K. xx. 23 note).

27. *Carry one of the priests...; let them go and dwell there, and let him teach*] The double change of number is curious; but the text needs no emendation. The priest would require to be accompanied by assistants, who would "go and dwell," but would not be qualified to "teach." The *arcana* of the worship would be known to none excepting the priests who had ministered at the two national sanctuaries of Dan and Bethel.

28. The priest sent to the colonists was not a true Jehovah-priest, but one of those who had been attached to the calf-worship, probably at Bethel. Hence, he would be willing to tolerate the mixed religion, which a true Jehovah-priest would have unsparingly condemned.

29. The "Samaritans" here are the Israelites. The temples built by them at the high places (1 K. xii. 31, xiii. 32) had remained standing at the time of their departure. They were now occupied by the new comers, who set up their own worship in the old sanctuaries.

30. Succoth-benoth probably represents a Babylonian goddess called Zir-banit, the wife of Merodach. She and her husband were, next to Bel and Beltis, the favourite divinities of the Babylonians.

Nergal, etymologically "the great man," or "the great hero," was the Babylonian god of war and hunting. His name forms an element in the Babylonian royal appellation, Nergal-shar-ezar or Neriglissar. The Assyrian inscriptions connect Nergal in a very special way with Cutha, of which he was evidently the tutelary deity.

Ashima is ingeniously conjectured to be the same as Esmûn, the Æsculapius of the Cabiri or "great gods" of the Phœnicians.

31. Nibhaz and Tartak are either gods of whom no other notice has come down to us, or intentional corruptions of the Babylonian names Nebo and Tir, the great god of Borsippa, who was the tutelar deity of so many Babylonian kings. The Jews, in their scorn and contempt of polytheism, occasionally and purposely altered, by way of derision, the names of the heathen deities.

32 Adrammelech and Anammelech, the gods of Sepharvaim. So
    they feared the LORD, *r*and made unto themselves of the lowest
    of them priests of the high places, which sacrificed for them in
33 the houses of the high places. *s*They feared the LORD, and
    served their own gods, after the manner of the nations ¹whom
34 they carried away from thence. Unto this day they do after
    the former manners: they fear not the LORD, neither do they
    after their statutes, or after their ordinances, or after the law
    and commandment which the LORD commanded the children of
35 Jacob, *t*whom he named Israel; with whom the LORD had made
    a covenant, and charged them, saying, *u*Ye shall not fear other
    gods, nor *x*bow yourselves to them, nor serve them, nor sacri-
36 fice to them: but the LORD, who brought you up out of the
    land of Egypt with great power and *y*a stretched out arm, *z*him
    shall ye fear, and him shall ye worship, and to him shall ye do
37 sacrifice. And the statutes, and the ordinances, and the law,
    and the commandment, which he wrote for you, *a*ye shall ob-
    serve to do for evermore; and ye shall not fear other gods.
38 And the covenant that I have made with you *b*ye shall not
39 forget; neither shall ye fear other gods. But the LORD your
    God ye shall fear; and he shall deliver you out of the hand of
40 all your enemies. Howbeit they did not hearken, but they did
41 after their former manner. *c*So these nations feared the
    LORD, and served their graven images, both their children, and
    their children's children : as did their fathers, so do they unto
    this day.

r 1 Kin. 12.
31.

s Zeph. 1. 5.

t Gen. 32. 28.
& 35. 10.
1 Kin. 11. 31.
u Judg. 6. 10.
x Ex. 20. 5.
& 34. 15.
y Ex. 6. 6.
z Deut. 10. 20.

a Deut. 5. 32.

b Deut. 4. 23.

c ver. 32, 33.

¹ Or, *who carried them away from thence.*

Anammelech is possibly an instance of the
same contemptuous play upon words.

Adrammelech, "the glorious king," signifies the sun. The Assyrian inscriptions commonly designate *Tsipar*, or Sepharvaim
(*v.* 24), "Sippara of the Sun." The title
"Adrammelech" has not yet been found
in the inscriptions hitherto; but it would
plainly be a fitting epithet of the great
luminary.

The sun-god of the Babylonians, Shamas,
was united at Sippara and elsewhere with
a sun-goddess, Anunit, whose name may
be represented in the Anammelech of the
text. The Hebrews, taking enough of this
name to show what they meant, assimi-
lated the termination to that of the male
deity, thus producing a ridiculous effect, regarded as insulting to the gods in question.

32. *of the lowest of them*] Rather, "from
all ranks." See marg. ref. note.

33. Understand the passage thus: "They
(the colonists) served their own gods after
the manner of the nations from which they
(the government) removed them," *i.e.*, after
the manner of their own countrymen at
home.

34. *they fear not the LORD*] The new
comers in one sense feared Jehovah (*vv.* 33,
41). They acknowledged His name, admitted Him among their gods, and kept up
His worship at the high place at Bethel
according to the rites instituted by Jeroboam (*v.* 28). But in another sense they did

not fear Him. To acknowledge Jehovah
together with other gods is not really to acknowledge H m at all.

37. *which he wrote for you*] It is worth
observing here, first, that the author regards the whole Law as given to the Israelites in a written form; and secondly, that
he looks on the real writer as God.

41. *their graver images*] The Babylonians
appear to have made a very sparing use of
animal forms among their religious emblems. They represented the male Sun,
Shamas, by a circle, plain or crossed; the
female Sun, Anunit, by a six-rayed or
eight-rayed star; Nebo by a single wedge
or arrow-head, the fundamental element of
their writing; the god of the atmosphere
by a double or triple thunderbolt. The
gods generally were represented under human forms. A few of them had, in addition,
animal emblems—the lion, the bull, the
eagle, or the serpent; but these seem never
to have been set up for worship in temples.
There was nothing intentionally grotesque
in the Babylonian religion, as there was in
the Egyptian and Phoenician.

so do they unto this day] The mixed worship, the union of professed reverence for
Jehovah with the grossest idolatry, continued to the time of the composition of this
Book, which must have been as late as B.C.
561, or, at any rate, as late as B.C. 580
(xxv. 27). It did not, however, continue
much longer. When the Samaritans wished

CHAP. 18. NOW it came to pass in the third year of Hoshea son of Elah king of Israel, *that* *ᵃHezekiah* the son of Ahaz king of 2 Judah began to reign. Twenty and five years old was he when he began to reign; and he reigned twenty and nine years in Jerusalem. His mother's name also *was* ᵇAbi, the daughter of 3 Zachariah. And he did *that which was* right in the sight of the 4 LORD, according to all that David his father did. ᶜHe removed the high places, and brake the ¹images, and cut down the groves, and brake in pieces the ᵈbrasen serpent that Moses had made: for unto those days the children of Israel did burn incense to it: 5 and he called it ²Nehushtan. He ᵉtrusted in the LORD God of Israel; ᶠso that after him was none like him among all the 6 kings of Judah, nor *any* that were before him. For he ᵍclave to .the LORD, and departed not ³from following him, but kept

Marginal references:
ᵃ 2 Chr. 28. 27.
& 29. 1.
He is called *Ezekias*, Matt. 1. 9.
ᵇ 2 Chr. 29.
1, *Abijah*.
ᶜ 2 Chr. 31. 1.
ᵈ Num. 21. 9.
ᵉ ch. 19. 10.
Job 13. 15
Ps. 13. 5.
ᶠ ch. 23. 25.
ᵍ Deut. 10. 20.
Josh. 23. 8.

¹ Heb. *statues.*   ² That is, *A piece of brass.*   ³ Heb. *from after him.*

---

to join the Jews in rebuilding the Temple (about B.C. 537), they showed that inclination to draw nearer to the Jewish cult which henceforth marked their religious progress. Long before the erection of a temple to Jehovah on Mount Gerizim (B.C. 409) they had laid aside all their idolatrous rites, and, admitting the binding authority of the Pentateuch, had taken upon them the observance of the entire Law.

XVIII. The sacred writer, having now completed the history of the joint kingdom, and having cast his glance forward over the religious history of the mixed race which replaced the Israelites in Samaria, proceeds to apply himself uninterruptedly to the remaining history of the Jewish kingdom.

1. *in the third year*] If Hoshea ascended the throne towards the close of the twelfth year of Ahaz (xvii. 1), and if Ahaz reigned not much more than fifteen years (xvi. 2), the first of Hezekiah might synchronise *in part* with Hoshea's third year.

Hezekiah] The name given by our translators follows the Greek form, 'Εξεκίας, rather than the Hebrew, which is *Hizkiah.* Its meaning is "strength of Jehovah."

2. *Twenty and five years old was he*] This statement, combined with that of xvi. 2, would make it necessary that his father Ahaz should have married at the age of ten, and have had a child born to him when he was eleven. This is not impossible; but its improbability is so great, that most commentators suggest a corruption in some of the numbers.

The Zachariah here mentioned was perhaps one of the "faithful witnesses" of Isaiah (viii. 2).

3. *he did that which was right*, &c.] This is said without qualification of only three kings of Judah, Asa (1 K. xv. 11), Hezekiah, and Josiah (2 K. xxii. 2). See some details of Hezekiah's acts at the commencement of his reign in 2 Chr. xxix. &c. It is thought that his reformation was preceded, and perhaps caused, by the prophecy of Micah recorded in Jer. xxvi. 18; Mic. iii. 12.

4. *He removed the high places*] This religious reformation was effected in a violent and tumultuous manner (marg. ref.). The "high places," though forbidden in the Law (Deut. xii. 2–4, 11–14; cp. Lev. xxvi. 30), had practically received the sanction of Samuel (1 Sam. vii. 10; ix. 12–14), David (2 Sam. xv. 32), Solomon (1 K. iii. 4), and others, and had long been the favourite resorts of the mass of the people (see 1 K. iii. 2 note). They were the rural centres for the worship of Jehovah, standing in the place of the later synagogues, and had hitherto been winked at, or rather regarded as legitimate, even by the best kings. Hezekiah's desecration of these time-honoured sanctuaries must have been a rude shock to the feelings of numbers; and indications of the popular discontent may be traced in the appeal of Rab-shakeh (*v.* 22), and in the strength of the reaction under Manasseh (xxi. 2-9; 2 Chr. xxxiii. 3–17).

the brasen serpent] See marg. ref. Its history from the time when it was set up to the date of Hezekiah's reformation is a blank. The present passage favours the supposition that it had been brought by Solomon from Gibeon and placed in the Temple; for it implies a long continued worship of the serpent by the Israelites generally, and not a mere recent worship of it by the Jews.

and he called it Nehushtan] Rather, "And it was called Nehushtan." The people called it, not "the serpent" (*nachash*), but "the brass," or "the brass thing" (*nechushtan*). Probably they did not like to call it "the serpent," on account of the dark associations which were attached to that reptile (Gen. iii. 1–15; Is. xxvii. 1; Ps. xci. 13; &c).

5. *after him was none like him*] The same is said of Josiah (marg. ref.). The phrase was probably proverbial, and was not taken to mean more than we mean when we say that such and such a king was one of *singular* piety.

6. Other good kings, as Solomon, Jehosh-

7 his commandments, which the LORD commanded Moses. And the LORD [h]was with him; *and* he [i]prospered whithersoever he went forth: and he [k]rebelled against the king of Assyria, and

8 served him not. [l]He smote the Philistines, *even* unto [1]Gaza, and the borders thereof, [m]from the tower of the watchmen to

9 the fenced city. ¶And [n]it came to pass in the fourth year of king Hezekiah, which *was* the seventh year of Hoshea son of Elah king of Israel, *that* Shalmaneser king of Assyria came up

10 against Samaria, and besieged it. And at the end of three years they took it: *even* in the sixth year of Hezekiah, that *is* [o]the

11 ninth year of Hoshea king of Israel, Samaria was taken. [p]And the king of Assyria did carry away Israel unto Assyria, and put them [q]in Halah and in Habor *by* the river of Gozan, and in the

12 cities of the Medes: [r]because they obeyed not the voice of the LORD their God, but transgressed his covenant, *and* all that Moses the servant of the LORD commanded, and would not hear

13 *them*, nor do *them*. ¶Now [s]in the fourteenth year of king Hezekiah did [2]Sennacherib king of Assyria come up against all

14 the fenced cities of Judah, and took them. And Hezekiah king of Judah sent to the king of Assyria to Lachish, saying, I have

[h] 2 Sam. 5. 10.
[i] 1 Sam. 18. 5, 14.
Ps. 60. 12.
[k] ch. 16. 7.
[l] 1 Chr. 4. 41.
Isai. 14. 29.
[m] ch. 17. 9.
[n] ch. 17. 3.

[o] ch. 17. 6.
[p] ch. 17. 6.

[q] 1 Chr. 5. 26.

[r] ch. 17. 7.
Dan. 9. 6, 10.

[s] 2 Chr. 32. 1, &c.
Isai. 36. 1, &c.

---

[1] Heb. *Azzah*.   [2] Heb. *Sanherib*.

---

aphat, Joash, and Amaziah, had fallen away in their later years. Hezekiah remained firm to the last. The phrase "cleaving to God" is frequent in Deuteronomy, but rare elsewhere.

7. *the* LORD *was with him*] This had been said of no king since David (marg. ref.). The phrase is very emphatic. The general prosperity of Hezekiah is set forth at some length by the author of Chronicles (2 Chr. xxxii. 23, 27–29). His great influence among the nations bordering on the northern kingdom, was the cause of the first expedition of Sennacherib against him, the Ekronites having expelled an Assyrian viceroy from their city, and delivered him to Hezekiah for safe keeping: an expedition which did not very long precede that of *v.* 13, which fell towards the close of Hezekiah's long reign.

8. Sargon had established the complete dominion of Assyria over the Philistines. Hence the object of Hezekiah's Philistine campaign was not so much conquest as opposition to the Assyrian power. How successful it was is indicated in the Assyrian records by the number of towns in this quarter which Sennacherib recovered before he proceeded against Jerusalem.

9–12. These verses repeat the account given in the marg. ref. The extreme importance of the event may account for the double insertion.

13. *in the fourteenth year*] This note of time, which places the invasion of Sennacherib eight years only after the capture of Samaria, is hopelessly at variance with the Assyrian dates for the two events, the first of which falls into the first of Sargon, and the second into the fourth of Sennacherib,

twenty-one years later. We have therefore to choose between an entire rejection of the Assyrian chronological data, and an emendation of the present passage. Of the emendations proposed the simplest is to remove the note of time altogether, regarding it as having crept in from the margin.

Sennacherib] This is the Greek form of the Sinakhirib of the inscriptions, the son of Sargon, and his immediate successor in the monarchy. The death of Sargon (B.C. 705) had been followed by a number of revolts. Hezekiah also rebelled, invaded Philistia, and helped the national party in that country to throw off the Assyrian yoke.

From Sennacherib's inscriptions we learn that, having reduced Phœnicia, recovered Ascalon, and defeated an army of Egyptians and Ethiopians at Ekron, he marched against Jerusalem.

the fenced cities] Sennacherib reckons the number taken by him at "forty-six." He seems to have captured on his way to the Holy City a vast number of small towns and villages, whose inhabitants he carried off to the number of 200,000. Cp. Is. xxiv. 1–12. The ground occupied by his main host outside the modern Damascus gate was thenceforth known to the Jews as "the camp of the Assyrians." Details connected with the siege may be gathered from Isai. xxii. and Chronicles (marg. ref. *s*). After a while Hezekiah resolved on submission. Sennacherib (*v.* 14) had left his army to continue the siege, and gone in person to Lachish. The Jewish monarch sent his embassy to that town.

14. *return from me*] Or "retire from me," *i.e.*, "withdraw thy troops."

offended; return from me : that which thou puttest on me will I bear. And the king of Assyria appointed unto Hezekiah king of Judah three hundred talents of silver and thirty talents of

t ch. 16. 8.   15 gold. And Hezekiah *t*gave *him* all the silver that was found in the house of the LORD, and in the treasures of the king's house.

16 At that time did Hezekiah cut off *the gold from* the doors of the temple of the LORD, and *from* the pillars which Hezekiah king of Judah had overlaid, and gave [1]it to the king of Assyria.

17 ¶ And the king of Assyria sent Tartan and Rabsaris and Rab-shakeh from Lachish to king Hezekiah with a [2]great host against Jerusalem. And they went up and came to Jerusalem. And when they were come up, they came and stood by the con-

u Isai. 7. 3   duit of the upper pool, *u*which *is* in the highway of the fuller's
18 field. And when they had called to the king, there came out to them Eliakim the son of Hilkiah, which *was* over the household, and Shebna and Joah the son of Asaph the recorder.

19 ¶ And Rab-shakeh said unto them, Speak ye now to Hezekiah,

x 2 Chr. 32.   Thus saith the great king, the king of Assyria, *x*What confidence
10, &c.   20 *is* this wherein thou trustest? Thou [4]sayest, (but *they are but* [5]vain words,) [6]*I have* counsel and strength for the war. Now on

---

[1] Heb. *them.*	[3] Or, *secretary.*	[6] Or, *But counsel and*
[2] Heb. *heavy.*	[4] Or, *talkest.*	*strength* are *for the war.*
	[5] Heb. *word of the lips.*	

---

three hundred talents, &c.] According to Sennacherib's own account, the terms of peace were as follows :—(1) A money payment to the amount of 800 talents of silver and 30 talents of gold. (2) The surrender of the Ekronite king. (3) A cession of territory towards the west and the south-west, which was apportioned between the kings of Ekron, Ashdod, and Gaza.

16. Ahaz had already exhausted the treasuries (xvi. 8) ; Hezekiah was therefore compelled to undo his own work.

17. An interval of time must be placed between this verse and the last. Sennacherib, content with his successes, had returned to Nineveh with his spoil and his numerous captives. Hezekiah, left to himself, repented of his submission, and commenced negotiations with Egypt (*vv.* 21, 24; Isai. xxx. 2-6, xxxi. 1), which implied treason against his Assyrian suzerain. It was under these circumstances that Sennacherib appears to have made his second expedition into Palestine very soon after the first. Following the usual coast route he passed through Philistia on his way to Egypt, leaving Jerusalem on one side, despising so puny a state, and knowing that the submission of Egypt would involve that of her hangers-on. While, however, he was besieging Lachish on his way to encounter his main enemy, he determined to try the temper of the Jews by means of an embassy, which he accordingly sent.

Tartan and Rabsaris and Rab-shakeh] None of these are proper names. "Tartan" was the ordinary title of an Assyrian general ; "Rab-saris" is "chief eunuch," always a high officer of the Assyrian court ;

Rab-shakeh is probably "chief cup-bearer."

by the conduit of the upper pool] Possibly a conduit on the north side of the city, near the "camp of the Assyrians." The spot was the same as that on which Isaiah had met Ahaz (Isai. vii. 3).

18. *when they had called to the king*] The ambassadors summoned Hezekiah, as if their rank were equal to his. Careful of his dignity, he responds by sending officers of his court.

Eliakim...which was over the household] Eliakim had been promoted to fill the place of Shebna (Isai. xxii. 20-22). He was a man of very high character. The comptroller of the household, whose position (1 K. iv. 6) must have been a subordinate one in the time of Solomon, appears to have now become the chief minister of the crown. On the "scribe" or secretary, and the "recorder," see 1 K. iv. 3 note.

19. The Rab-shakeh, the *third* in rank of the three Assyrian ambassadors, probably took the prominent part in the conference because he could speak Hebrew (*v.* 26), whereas the Tartan and the Rabsaris could not do so.

the great king] This title of the monarchs of Assyria is found in use as early as B.C. 1120. Like the title, "king of kings," the distinctive epithet "great" served to mark emphatically the vast difference between the numerous vassal monarchs and the suzerain of whom they held their crowns.

20. Hezekiah no doubt believed that in the "counsel" of Eliakim and Isaiah, and in the "strength" promised him by Egypt, he had resources which justified him in provoking a war.

21 whom dost thou trust, that thou rebellest against me ?   *Now,   *Ezek. 29.
behold, thou ¹trustest upon the staff of this bruised reed, *even*   6, 7.
upon Egypt, on which if a man lean, it will go into his hand,
and pierce it: so *is* Pharaoh king of Egypt unto all that trust
22 on him. But if ye say unto me, We trust in the LORD our God:
is not that he, ²whose high places and whose altars Hezekiah   *ver. 4.
hath taken away, and hath said to Judah and Jerusalem, Ye   2 Chr. 31. 1.
23 shall worship before this altar in Jerusalem ?   Now therefore, I   & 32. 12.
pray thee, give ²pledges to my lord the king of Assyria, and I
will deliver thee two thousand horses, if thou be able on thy
24 part to set riders upon them. How then wilt thou turn away
the face of one captain of the least of my master's servants, and
25 put thy trust on Egypt for chariots and for horsemen ? Am I
now come up without the LORD against this place to destroy it ?
The LORD said to me, Go up against this land, and destroy it.
26 ¶Then said Eliakim the son of Hilkiah, and Shebna, and Joah,
unto Rab-shakeh, Speak, I pray thee, to thy servants in the
Syrian language ; for we understand *it :* and talk not with us
in the Jews' language in the ears of the people that *are* on the
27 wall. But Rab-shakeh said unto them, Hath my master sent
me to thy master, and to thee, to speak these words ? *hath he*
not *sent me* to the men which sit on the wall, that they may eat
28 their own dung, and drink ³their own piss with you ? Then
Rab-shakeh stood and cried with a loud voice in the Jews' language, and spake, saying, Hear the word of the great king, the
29 king of Assyria : thus saith the king, ªLet not Hezekiah deceive   ª 2 Chr. 32.
you : for he shall not be able to deliver you out of his hand :   15.
30 neither let Hezekiah make you trust in the LORD, saying, The
LORD will surely deliver us, and this city shall not be delivered

¹ Heb. *trustest thee.*   ² Or, *hostages.*   ³ Heb. *the water of their feet.*

rain words] Lit. as in marg., *i.e.* a *mere*
word, to which the facts do not correspond.
   21. *this bruised reed*] The "tall reed of
the Nile bulrush" fitly symbolised the land
where it grew. Apparently strong and firm,
it was quite unworthy of trust. Let a man
lean upon it, and the rotten support instantly gave way, wounding the hand that
stayed itself so insecurely. So it was with
Egypt throughout the whole period of
Jewish history (cp. xvii. 4-6). Her actual
practice was to pretend friendship, to hold
out hopes of support, and then to fail in
time of need.
   22. The destruction of numerous shrines
and altars where Jehovah had been worshipped (*v.* 4) seemed to the Rab-shakeh
conduct calculated not to secure the favour,
but to call forth the anger, of the god. At
any rate, it was conduct which he knew
had been distasteful to many of Hezekiah's
subjects.
   23. The phrase translated "give pledges,"
or "hostages" (marg.) may perhaps be
best understood as meaning "make an agreement." If you will "bind yourself to find
the riders" (*i.e.* trained horsemen), we will
"bind ourselves to furnish the horses."
The suggestion implied that in all Judæa

there were not 2000 men accustomed to
serve as cavalry.
   25. The Rab-shakeh probably tries the
effect of a bold assertion, which had no
basis of fact to rest upon.
   26. *the Syrian language*] *i.e.* Aramaic ;
probably the dialect of Damascus, a Semitic
language nearly akin to their own, but suff-
ciently different to be unintelligible to ordinary Jews
   the people that are on the wall] The conference must have been held immediately
outside the wall for the words of the speakers
to have been audible.
   27. *that they may eat, &c.*] "My master
hath sent me," the Rab-shakeh seems to
say, " to these men, whom I see stationed
on the wall to defend the place and bear
the last extremities of a prolonged siege—
these men on whom its worst evils will fall,
and who have therefore the greatest interest
in avoiding it by a timely surrender." He
expresses the evils by a strong coarse
phrase, suited to the rude soldiery, and
well calculated to rouse their feelings. The
author of Chronicles has softened down the
words (2 Chr. xxxii. 11).
   29, 30. There were two grounds, and two
only, on which Hezekiah could rest his
refusal to surrender, (1) ability to resist by

31 into the hand of the king of Assyria. Hearken not to Hezekiah:
for thus saith the king of Assyria, ¹²Make *an agreement* with
me by a present, and come out to me, and *then* eat ye every
man of his own vine, and every one of his fig tree, and drink ye
32 every one the waters of his ³cistern: until I come and take you

b Deut. 8.7,8.

away to a land like your own land, *b*a land of corn and wine, a
land of bread and vineyards, a land of oil olive and of honey,
that ye may live, and not die: and hearken not unto Hezekiah,
when he ⁴persuadeth you, saying, The LORD will deliver us.

c ch. 19. 12.
2 Chr. 32. 14.
Isai. 10. 10,
11.
d ch. 19. 13.
e ch. 17. 24,
Ava?
f Dan. 3. 15.

33 *c*Hath any of the gods of the nations delivered at all his land out
34 of the hand of the king of Assyria? *d*Where *are* the gods of
Hamath, and of Arpad? where *are* the gods of Sepharvaim,
Hena, and *e*Ivah? have they delivered Samaria out of mine
35 hand? Who *are* they among all the gods of the countries, that
have delivered their country out of mine hand, *f*that the LORD
36 should deliver Jerusalem out of mine hand? ¶But the people
held their peace, and answered him not a word: for the king's
37 commandment was, saying, Answer him not. Then came
Eliakim the son of Hilkiah, which *was* over the household, and
Shebna the scribe, and Joah the son of Asaph the recorder, to

g Isai. 33. 7.

Hezekiah *g*with *their* clothes rent, and told him the words of

a Isai. 37. 1,
&c.

19 Rab-shakeh. AND *a*it came to pass, when king Hezekiah
heard *it*, that he rent his clothes, and covered himself with sack-
2 cloth, and went into the house of the LORD. And he sent
Eliakim, which *was* over the household, and Shebna the scribe,
and the elders of the priests, covered with sackcloth, to *b*Isaiah

b Luke 3, 4,
called
Esaias.

¹ Or, *Seek my favour.*   *blessing,* Gen. 32. 20. &   ³ Or, *pit.*
² Heb. *Make with me a*   33. 11. Prov. 18. 16.   ⁴ Or, *deceiveth.*

---

his own natural military strength and that
of his allies; and (2) expectation based upon
the language of Isaiah (xxx. 31, xxxi. 4-9),
of supernatural assistance from Jehovah.
The Rab-shakeh argues that both grounds
of confidence are equally fallacious.

31. *Make an agreement,*&c.] Rather, "Make
peace with me." The word, which primarily means "blessing," and secondarily "a
gift," has also the meaning, though more
rarely, of "peace." Probably it acquired
this meaning from the fact that a peace
was commonly purchased by presents.

eat...drink] A picture of a time of quiet
and prosperity, a time when each man might
enjoy the fruits of his land, without any
fear of the spoiler's violence. The words
are in contrast with the latter part of *v.* 27.

cistern] Rather, "**well**" (Deut. vi. 11).
Each cultivator in Palestine has a "well"
dug in some part of his ground, from which
he draws water for his own use. "Cisterns,"
or reservoirs for rain-water, are comparatively rare.

33. The boast is natural. The Assyrians
had had an uninterrupted career of success,
and might well believe that their gods were
more powerful than those of the nations
with whom they had warred. It is not surprising that they did not understand that
their successes hitherto had been allowed by
the very God, Jehovah, against Whom they
were now boasting themselves.

34. Arpad was situated somewhere in
southern Syria; but it is impossible to fix
its exact position. Sargon mentions it in
an inscription as joining with Hamath in
an act of rebellion, which he chastised. It
was probably the capture and destruction
of these two cities on this occasion which
caused them to be mentioned together here
(and in xix. 13, and again in Isaiah x. 9).
Sennacherib adduces late examples of the
inability of the nations' gods to protect their
cities. On the other cities mentioned in this
verse, see xvii. 24 notes.

XIX. 1. Hezekiah, like his officers, probably rent his clothes on account of Rab-
shakeh's blasphemies: and he put on sackcloth in self-humiliation and in grief. The
only hope left was in Jehovah; for Egypt
could not be trusted to effect anything of
importance. Rab-shakeh's boldness had
told upon Hezekiah. He was dispirited
and dejected. He perhaps began to doubt
whether he had done right in yielding to the
bolder counsels of Eliakim and Isaiah. He
had not lost his faith in God; but his faith
was being severely tried. He wisely went
and strove by prayer to strengthen it.

2. Isaiah is here for the first time introduced into the history. His own writings
show us how active a part he had taken in
it for many years previously. This was the
fourth reign since he began his prophesyings; and during two reigns at least, those

3 the prophet the son of Amoz. And they said unto him, Thus
saith Hezekiah, This day *is* a day of trouble, and of rebuke, and
¹blasphemy : for the children are come to the birth, and *there is*
4 not strength to bring forth. *c*It may be the LORD thy God   *c* 2 Sam. 16.
will hear all the words of Rab-shakeh, *d*whom the king of   12.
Assyria his master hath sent to reproach the living God ; and   *d* ch. 18. 35.
will *e*reprove the words which the LORD thy God hath heard :   *e* Ps. 50. 21.
wherefore lift up *thy* prayer for the remnant that are ²left.
5, 6 ¶ So the servants of king Hezekiah came to Isaiah. *f*And Isaiah   *f* Isai. 37. 6,
said unto them, Thus shall ye say to your master, Thus saith   &c.
the LORD, Be not afraid of the words which thou hast heard,
with which the *g*servants of the king of Assyria have blasphemed   *g* ch. 18. 17.
7 me. Behold, I will send *h*a blast upon him, and he shall hear   *h* ver. 35, 36,
a rumour, and shall return to his own land ; and I will cause   37.
8 him to fall by the sword in his own land. ¶ So Rab-shakeh re-   Jer. 51. 1.
turned, and found the king of Assyria warring against Libnah :
9 for he had heard that he was departed *i*from Lachish. And   *i* ch. 18. 14.
*k*when he heard say of Tirhakah king of Ethiopia, Behold, he is   *k* See 1 Sam.
come out to fight against thee : he sent messengers again unto   23. 27.
10 Hezekiah, saying, Thus shall ye speak to Hezekiah king of
Judah, saying, Let not thy God *l*in whom thou trustest deceive   *l* ch. 18. 5.
thee, saying, Jerusalem shall not be delivered into the hand of
11 the king of Assyria. Behold, thou hast heard what the kings
of Assyria have done to all lands, by destroying them utterly :

---

¹ Or, *provocation.*   ² Heb. *found.*

---

of Ahaz and Hezekiah, he had been a
familiar counsellor of the monarch. He
had probably counselled the revolt from
Assyria, and had encouraged the king and
people to persevere in their resistance. The
exact date of prophecies can seldom be
fixed with any certainty ; but we can
scarcely be mistaken in regarding chs. x.
xxx. and xxxi. as written about the time of
Hezekiah's second revolt.

3. The "trouble" consisted in "rebuke"
(rather, "**chastisement**,") for sins at the
hand of God, and " blasphemy " (rather,
"**reproach**,") at the hands of man.

the children, &c.] *i.e.* " we are in a fearful
extremity—at the last gasp—and lack the
strength that might carry us through the
danger."

4. *will hear*] *i.e.* " will show that he has
heard—will notice and punish."

the living God] See 1 Sam. xvii. 26 note.

and will reprove the words] Rather, "will
reprove **him for** the words."

the remnant] *i.e.* for the kingdom of
Judah, the only remnant of God's people
that was now left, after Galilee and Gilead
and Samaria had all been carried away
captive.

7. *I will send a blast upon him*] Rather,
" I will **put a spirit in** him "—*i.e.* " I will
take from him his present pride and will
put in him a new spirit, a spirit of craven
fear." Men shall tell him of the destruction that has come upon his host (*v.* 35), and
he shall straightway return, &c.

8. On Lachish and Libnah, see Josh. x. 3,
29 notes. The phrase, "he was departed
from Lachish " is suggestive of successful
resistance.

9. *Tirhakah king of Ethiopia*] The *Tehrak*
or *Teharka* of the hieroglyphics. He was
the last king of the 25th or Ethiopian
dynasty, which commenced with Shebek or
Sabaco, and he reigned upwards of 26 years.
The Assyrian inscriptions show that he still
ruled in Egypt as late as B.C. 667, when
Esarhaddon (*v.* 37) died, and his son Asshur-
bani-pal succeeded him. He probably ascended the Egyptian throne about B.C. 692,
having previously ruled over Ethiopia before
he became king of Egypt (cp. Isai. xxxvii. 9).
Thus he was probably reigning in Ethiopia
at the time of Sennacherib's expedition, while
Sethos and perhaps other secondary monarchs bore rule over Egypt. His movements
caused Sennacherib to send a second embassy,
instead of marching in person against the
Jewish king.

11. *all lands*] This boast is in strict accordance with the general tenor of the
Assyrian inscriptions. Hyperbole is the
general language of the East ; but in this
instance it was not so extreme as in some
others. The Assyrians under Sargon and
Sennacherib had enjoyed an uninterrupted
series of military successes : they had succeeded in establishing their pre-eminence
from the Median desert to the banks of the
Nile, and from the shores of Lake Van to
those of the Persian Gulf.

m ch. 18. 33.

n Ezek. 27.
23.
o ch. 18. 34.

p Isai. 37.
14, &c.

q 1 Sam. 4.4.
Ps. 80. 1.
r 1 Kin. 18.
39.
Isai. 44. 6.
Jer. 10. 10,
11, 12.
s Ps. 31. 2.
t 2 Chr. 6. 40.
u ver. 4.

x Ps. 115. 4.
Jer. 10. 3.

y Ps. 83. 18.

z Isai. 37. 21,
&c.
a Ps. 65. 2.

12 and shalt thou be delivered? *m* Have the gods of the nations delivered them which my fathers have destroyed; *as* Gozan, and Haran, and Rezeph, and the children of *n* Eden which *were* 13 in Thelasar? *o* Where *is* the king of Hamath, and the king of Arpad, and the king of the city of Sepharvaim, of Hena, and 14 Ivah? ¶*p* And Hezekiah received the letter of the hand of the messengers, and read it: and Hezekiah went up into the house 15 of the LORD, and spread it before the LORD. And Hezekiah prayed before the LORD, and said, O LORD God of Israel, *q* which dwellest *between* the cherubims, *r* thou art the God, *even* thou alone, of all the kingdoms of the earth; thou hast made heaven 16 and earth. LORD, *s* bow down thine ear, and hear: *t* open, LORD, thine eyes, and see: and hear the words of Sennacherib, *u* which 17 hath sent him to reproach the living God. Of a truth, LORD, the kings of Assyria have destroyed the nations and their lands, 18 and have ¹ cast their gods into the fire: for they *were* no gods, but *x* the work of men's hands, wood and stone: therefore they 19 have destroyed them. Now therefore, O LORD our God, I beseech thee, save thou us out of his hand, *y* that all the kingdoms of the earth may know that thou *art* the LORD God, *even* thou 20 only. ¶ Then Isaiah the son of Amoz sent to Hezekiah, saying, Thus saith the LORD God of Israel, *z* That* which thou hast prayed to me against Sennacherib king of Assyria *a* I have heard. 21 This *is* the word that the LORD hath spoken concerning him;

¹ Heb. *given.*

---

12. *Haran*] Harrán, the Carrhæ of the Greeks and Romans (Gen. xi. 31), was among the earliest conquests of the Assyrians; being subject to them from the 12th century. Its conquest would have naturally followed that of Gozan (Gauzanitis, xvii. 6), which lay between it and Assyria proper.

Rezeph] Probably the Rozappa of the Assyrian inscriptions, a city in the neighbourhood of Haran.

the children of Eden] Or, "the Beni-Eden," who appear from the Assyrian inscriptions to have inhabited the country on the east bank of the Euphrates, about the modern Balis. Here they had a city called Beth-Adina, taken by the Assyrians about B.C. 880. This is probably the "Eden" of marg. ref.

Thelasar] Or Telassar. Probably a city on the Euphrates, near Beth-Adina, called after the name of the god Asshur. The name would signify "the Hill of Asshur."

13. Cp. marg. ref. xvii. 24. Verse 12 refers to former Assyrian successes, verse 13 to comparatively recent ones.

14. *Hezekiah received the letter*] The inscriptions show that scribes accompanied the Assyrian armies, with the materials of their craft, so that such a dispatch might be easily drawn up. As Hezekiah himself "read" it, we may presume that it was in the Hebrew tongue.

15. *which dwellest between the cherubims*] The reference is to the *shechinah*, or miraculous glory, which from time to time appeared above the Mercy-seat from between the two Cherubims, whose wings over-

shadowed the Ark of the Covenant (1 K. vi. 23–27; cp. Ex. xxv. 22; Lev. xvi. 2, &c.).

thou art the God, even thou alone] This is the protest of the pure theist against the intense polytheism of Sennacherib's letter, which assumes that gods are only gods of particular nations, and that Hezekiah's God is but one out of an indefinite number, no stronger or more formidable than the rest.

18. *have cast their gods into the fire*] In general the Assyrians carried off the images of the gods from the temples of the conquered nations, and deposited them in their own shrines, as at once trophies of victory and proof of the superiority of the Assyrian deities over those of their enemies. But sometimes the gods are said to have been "destroyed" or "burnt with fire;" which was probably done when the idols were of rude workmanship or coarse material; and when it was inconvenient to encumber an army with spoils so weighty and difficult of transport.

19. If the mighty army of the great Assyrian king were successfully defied by a petty monarch like Hezekiah, it would force the surrounding nations to confess that the escape was owing to the protecting hand of Jehovah. They would thus be taught, in spite of themselves, that He, and He alone, was the true God.

21. *concerning him*] i.e. "concerning Sennacherib." Verses 21–28 are addressed to the great Assyrian monarch himself, and are God's reply to his proud boastings.

The virgin, the daughter of Zion] Rather, "the virgin daughter, Zion." Zion, the

The virgin [b]the daughter of Zion hath despised thee, *and*   [b] Is. 23. 10.
     laughed thee to scorn;   Lam. 2. 13.
The daughter of Jerusalem [c]hath shaken her head at thee.   [c] Job 16. 4.
22   Whom hast thou reproached and blasphemed?   Ps. 22. 7, 8.
And against whom hast thou exalted *thy* voice,   Lam. 2. 15.
And lifted up thine eyes on high?
Even against [d]the Holy *One* of Israel.   [d] Isai. 5. 24.
23   [1][e]By thy messengers thou hast reproached the LORD, and [e] ch. 18. 17.
     hast said,
     [f]With the multitude of my chariots I am come up to the   [f] Ps. 20. 7.
     height of the mountains, to the sides of Lebanon,
And will cut down [2]the tall cedar trees thereof, *and* the choice
     fir trees thereof:
And I will enter into the lodgings of his borders, *and into*
     [3]the forest of his Carmel.
24   I have digged and drunk strange waters,
And with the sole of my feet have I dried up all the rivers
     of [4]besieged places.
25   ¶ [5]Hast thou not heard long ago *how* [g]I have done it, [g] Isai. 45. 7.

[1] Heb. *By the hand of.*   [4] Or, *fenced.*   *ancient times? should I*
[2] Heb. *the tallness, &c.*   [5] Or, *Hast thou not heard* *now bring it to be laid*
[3] Or, *the forest* and *his*   *how I have made it long*   *waste,* and *fenced cities*
fruitful field, Isai. 10. 18.   *ago, and formed it of*   to be *ruinous heaps?*

holy eastern city, is here distinguished from Jerusalem, the western one, and is given the remarkable epithet "virgin," which is not applied to her sister; probably because the true Zion, the city of David, had remained inviolable from David's time, having never been entered by an enemy. Jerusalem, on the other hand, had been taken, both by Shishak (1 K. xiv. 26) and by Jehoash (xiv. 13). The personification of cities as females is a common figure (cp. marg. reff.).

hath shaken her head at thee] This was a gesture of scorn with the Hebrews (cp. marg. reff.; Matt. xxvii. 39).

22. *the Holy One of Israel*] This is a favourite phrase with Isaiah, in whose prophecies it is found twenty-seven times, while it occurs five times only in the rest of Scripture (Pss. lxxi. 22, lxxviii. 41, lxxxix. 18; Jer. l. 29, li. 5). Its occurrence here is a strong proof—one among many—of the genuineness of the present passage, which is not the composition of the writer of Kings, but an actual prophecy delivered at this time by Isaiah.

23. *and hast said*] Isaiah clothes in words the thoughts of Sennacherib's heart—thoughts of the extremest self-confidence. Cp. Isai. x. 7-14, where, probably at an earlier date, the same overweening pride is ascribed to this king.

with the multitude of my chariots] There are two readings here, which give, however, nearly the same sense. The more difficult and more poetical of the two is to be preferred. Literally translated it runs—"With **chariots upon** chariots am I come up, &c."

to the sides of Lebanon] "Lebanon," with

its "cedars" and its "fir-trees," is to be understood here both literally and figuratively. Literally, the hewing of timber in Lebanon was an ordinary feature of an Assyrian expedition into Syria. Figuratively, the mountain represents all the more inaccessible parts of Palestine, and the destruction of its firs and cedars denotes the complete devastation of the entire country from one end to the other.

the lodgings of his borders] Lit., "the lodge of its (Lebanon's) end;" either an actual habitation situated on the highest point of the mountain-range, or a poetical periphrasis for the highest point itself.

the forest of his Carmel] Or, "the forest of its garden"—*i.e.* "its forest which is like a garden," &c.

24. *have digged and drunk ... and dried up*] The meaning seems to be—"Mountains do not stop me—I cross them even in my chariots. Deserts do not stop me—I dig wells there, and drink the water. Rivers do not stop me—I pass them as easily as if they were dry land."

the rivers of besieged places] Rather, "the rivers of **Egypt.**" The singular form, *Mazor* (compare the modern *Misr* and the Assyrian *Muzr*), is here used instead of the ordinary dual form, *Mizraim*, perhaps because "Lower Egypt" only is intended. This was so cut up with canals and branches of the Nile, natural and artificial, that it was regarded as impassable for chariots and horses. Sennacherib, however, thought that these many streams would prove no impediments to him; he would advance as fast as if they were "dried up."

25. *Hast thou not heard long ago, &c.*]

And of ancient times that I have formed it?
Now have I brought it to pass,

h Isai. 10. 5.

That *h*thou shouldest be to lay waste fenced cities *into* ruinous heaps.

26   Therefore their inhabitants were [1]of small power,
They were dismayed and confounded;
They were *as* the grass of the field, and *as* the green herb,

i Ps. 129. 6.

As *i*the grass on the house tops, and *as* corn blasted before it be grown up.

k Ps. 139. 1, &c.

27   But *k*I know thy [2]abode,
And thy going out, and thy coming in,
And thy rage against me.

28   Because thy rage against me and thy tumult is come up into mine ears,

l Job 41. 2.
Ezek. 29. 4.
& 38. 4.
Amos 4. 2.
m ver. 33, 36, 37.
n 1 Sam. 2. 34.
ch. 20. 8, 9.
Isai. 7. 11, 14.
Luke 2. 12.

Therefore *l*I will put my hook in thy nose, and my bridle in thy lips,
And I will turn thee back *m*by the way by which thou camest.

29   ¶ And this *shall be* *n*a sign unto thee,
Ye shall eat this year such things as grow of themselves,
And in the second year that which springeth of the same;
And in the third year sow ye, and reap,
And plant vineyards, and eat the fruits thereof.

o 2 Chr. 32. 22, 23.

30   *o*And [3]the remnant that is escaped of the house of Judah
Shall yet again take root downward, and bear fruit upward.

31   For out of Jerusalem shall go forth a remnant,
And [4]they that escape out of Mount Zion:

p Isai. 9. 7.

*p*The zeal of the LORD *of hosts* shall do this.

---

[1] Heb. *short of hand.*
[2] Or, *sitting.*
[3] Heb. *the escaping of the house of Judah that remaineth.*
[4] Heb. *the escaping.*

Rather, "Hast thou not heard, **that from long ago I did** this, from ancient times I fashioned it? &c." The former part of the verse refers to the secret Divine decrees, whereby the affairs of this world are determined and ordered from the very beginning of things. Sennacherib's boasting, however, proved that he did not know this, that he did not recognise himself simply as God's instrument—"the rod of His anger" (Isai. x. 5)—but regarded his victories as gained by his own "strength and wisdom" (do. v. 13).

26. The weakness of the nations exposed to the Assyrian attacks was as much owing to the Divine decrees as was the strength of the Assyrians themselves.

the grass on the house tops] Cp. marg. ref. The vegetation on the flat roofs of Oriental houses is the first to spring up and the first to fade away.

27. See 1 K. iii. 7 note.

28. *thy tumult*] Rather, "thy **arrogance.**"

I will put my hook in thy nose] Rather, "my **ring.**" The sculptures show that the kings of Babylon and Assyria were in the habit of actually passing a ring through the flesh of their more distinguished prisoners,

of attaching a thong or a rope to it, and of thus leading them about as with a "bridle." In Assyria the ring was, at least ordinarily, passed through the lower lip; while in Babylonia it appears to have been inserted into the membrane of the *nose.* Thus Sennacherib would be here threatened with a punishment which he was perhaps in the habit of inflicting.

29. The prophet now once more addresses Hezekiah, and gives him a "sign," or token, whereby he and his may be assured that Sennacherib is indeed bridled, and will not trouble Judæa any more. It was a sign of the continued freedom of the land from attack during the whole of the remainder of Sennacherib's reign—a space of seventeen years.

30. *the remnant that is escaped*] Terrible ravages seem to have been committed in the first attack (xviii. 13 note). And though the second invasion was comparatively harmless, yet it probably fell heavily on the cities of the west and the south-west. Thus the "escaped" were but "a remnant."

bear fruit upward] The flourishing time of Josiah is the special fulfilment of this prophecy (xxiii. 15-20).

32 ¶ Therefore thus saith the LORD concerning the king of Assyria, He shall not come into this city, nor shoot an
arrow there,
Nor come before it with shield, nor cast a bank against it.
33 By the way that he came, by the same shall he return,
And shall not come into this city, saith the LORD.
34 For *q*I will defend this city, to save it,
For mine own sake, and *r*for my servant David's sake.
35 ¶ And *s*it came to pass that night, that the angel of the LORD
went out, and smote in the camp of the Assyrians an hundred
fourscore and five thousand: and when they arose early in the
36 morning, behold, they *were* all dead corpses. So Sennacherib
king of Assyria departed, and went and returned, and dwelt at

z ch. 20. 6.
r 1 Kin. 11.
12, 13.
s 2Chr.32.21.
Isai. 37. 36.

---

32. *nor come before it with shield*] The
"shields" of the Assyrians are very conspicuous in the sculptures, and were of great
importance in a siege, since the assailing
archers were in most instances defended, as
they shot their weapons, by a comrade,
who held before himself and his friend a
shield of an enormous size. It was made
of a framework of wood, filled in with
wattling, and perhaps lined with skin; it
was rested upon the ground, and it generally curved backward towards the top;
ordinarily it somewhat exceeded the height
of a man. From the safe covert afforded
by these large defences the archers were
able to take deliberate aim, and deliver
their volleys with effect.

nor cast a bank against it] "Mounds" or
"banks" were among the most common of
the means used by the Assyrians against a
besieged town. They were thrown up
against the walls, and consisted of loose
earth, trees, brushwood, stones, and rubbish. Sometimes the surface of the mound
was regularly paved with several layers of
stone or brick, which formed a solid road or
causeway capable of bearing a great weight.
The intention was not so much to bring the
mounds to a level with the top of the walls,
as to carry them to such a height as should
enable the battering-ram to work effectively.
Walls were made very solid towards their
base, for the purpose of resisting the ram;
half-way up their structure was comparatively weak and slight. The engines of the
assailants, rams and catapults, where therefore far more serviceable if they could
attack the upper and weaker portion of the
defences; and it was to enable them to
reach these portions that the "mounds"
were raised.

33. *By the way that he came*] *i.e.* through
the low country of the Shephelah, thus
avoiding not only Jerusalem, but even
Judæa.

34. *for mine own sake*] God's honour was
concerned to defend His own city against
one who denied His power in direct terms,
as did Sennacherib (xviii. 35, xix. 10–12).
His faithfulness was also concerned to keep

the promise made to David (Ps. cxxxii.
12-18).

35. *the camp of the Assyrians*] Which
was now moved to Pelusium, if we may
trust Herodotus; or which, at any rate,
was at some considerable distance from
Jerusalem.

*when they arose early in the morning, be-
hold, &c.*] These words form the only trustworthy data that we possess for determining
to any extent the *manner* of the destruction
now wrought. They imply that there was
no disturbance during the night, no alarm,
no knowledge on the part of the living that
their comrades were dying all around them
by thousands. All mere natural causes
must be rejected, and God must be regarded as having slain the men in their
sleep without causing disturbance, either
by pestilence or by that "visitation" of
which English Law speaks. The most
nearly parallel case is the destruction of
the first-born (Ex. xii. 29).

The Egyptian version of this event recorded in Herodotus is that, during the
night, silently and secretly, an innumerable
multitude of field-mice spread themselves
through the Assyrian host, and gnawed
their quivers, bows, and shield-straps, so as
to render them useless. When morning
broke, the Assyrians fled hastily, and the
Egyptians pursuing put a vast number to
the sword.

36. *dwelt at Nineveh*] The meaning is
not that Sennacherib made no more expeditions at all, which would be untrue, for
his annals show us that he warred in Armenia, Babylonia, Susiana, and Cilicia,
during his later years; but that he confined
himself to his own part of Asia, and did not
invade Palestine or threaten Jerusalem any
more. Nineveh, marked by some ruins
opposite Mosul, appears here unmistakably
as the Assyrian capital, which it became towards the close of the ninth century B.C.
It has previously been mentioned only in
Genesis (marg. ref.). Sennacherib was the
first king who made it his permanent residence. Its great size and large population
are marked in the description of Jonah

t Gen. 10. 11.
u 2 Chr. 32. 21.
x ver. 7.
v Ezra 4. 2.

37 *t*Nineveh. And it came to pass, as he was worshipping in the house of Nisroch his god, that *u*Adrammelech and Sharezer his sons *x*smote him with the sword: and they escaped into the land of ¹Armenia. And *v*Esarhaddon his son reigned in his stead.

a 2 Chr. 32. 24, &c.
Isai. 38. 1, &c.

CHAP. 20. IN *a*those days was Hezekiah sick unto death. And the prophet Isaiah the son of Amoz came to him, and said unto him, Thus saith the LORD, ²Set thine house in order; for thou 2 shalt die, and not live. Then he turned his face to the wall, and

b Neh. 13. 22.
c Gen. 17. 1.
1 Kin. 3. 6.

3 prayed unto the LORD, saying, I beseech thee, O LORD, *b*remember now how I have *c*walked before thee in truth and with a perfect heart, and have done *that which is* good in thy sight.
4 And Hezekiah wept ³sore. And it came to pass, afore Isaiah was gone out into the middle ⁴court, that the word of the LORD

d 1 Sam. 9. 16. & 10. 1.

5 came to him, saying, Turn again, and tell Hezekiah *d*the captain of my people, Thus saith the LORD, the God of David thy

e ch. 19. 20.
Ps. 65. 2.
f Ps. 39. 12. & 56. 8.

father, *e*I have heard thy prayer, I have seen *f*thy tears: behold, I will heal thee: on the third day thou shalt go up unto the

¹ Heb. *Ararat.*
² Heb. *Give charge con-*
cerning thine house, 2 Sam. 17. 23.
³ Heb. *with a great weeping.*
⁴ Or, *city.*

(iii. 2, 3, iv. 11), whose visit probably fell about B.C. 760.

37. The death of Sennacherib, which took place many years afterwards (B.C. 680), is related here, as, from the divine point of view, the sequel to his Syrian expeditions.

Nisroch his god.] Nisroch has not been as yet identified with any known Assyrian deity. The word *may* not be the name of a god at all but the name of the temple, as Josephus understood it. Assyrian temples were almost all distinguished by special names. If this be the true solution, the translation should run—"As he was worshipping his god in the house Nisroch."

they escaped into the land of Armenia] Lit. "the land of Ararat," or the north-eastern portion of Armenia, where it adjoined Media. The Assyrian inscriptions show that Armenia was at this time independent of Assyria, and might thus afford a safe refuge to the rebels.

Esar-haddon (or Esar-chaddon), is beyond a doubt the Asshur-akh-iddin of the inscriptions, who calls himself the son, and appears to be the successor of Sin-akh-irib. He commenced his reign by a struggle with his brother Adrammelech, and occupied the throne for only thirteen years, when he was succeeded by his son, Sardanapalus or Asshur-bani-pal. He warred with Phœnicia, Syria, Arabia, Egypt, and Media, and built three palaces, one at Nineveh, and the others at Calah and Babylon.

XX. 1. *In those days*] Hezekiah seems to have died B.C. 697; and his illness must belong to B.C. 713 or 714 (cp. *v.* 6), a date which falls early in the reign of Sargon. The true chronological place of this narrative is therefore prior to all the other facts related of Hezekiah except his religious reforms.

the prophet Isaiah the son of Amoz] This full description of Isaiah (cp. xix. 2), by the addition of his father's name and of his office, marks the original independence of this narrative. The writer of Kings may have found it altogether separate from the other records of Hezekiah, and added it in the state in which he found it.

This history (cp. Jon. iii. 4–10) shows that the prophetic denunciations were often not absolute predictions of what was certainly about to happen, but designed primarily to prove, or to lead to repentance, those against whom they were uttered, and only obtaining accomplishment if this primary design failed.

2. *he turned his face to the wall*] Contrast 1 K. xxi. 4. Ahab turned in sullenness, because he was too angry to converse; Hezekiah in devotion, because he wished to pray undisturbed.

3. *remember now*] The old Covenant promised temporal prosperity, including length of days, to the righteous. Hezekiah, conscious of his faithfulness and integrity (xviii. 3–6), ventures to expostulate (cp. also xxi. 1 note). According to the highest standard of morality revealed up to this time, there was nothing unseemly in the self-vindication of the monarch, which has many parallels in the Psalms of David (Pss. vii. 3–10, xviii. 19–26, xxvi. 1–8, &c.).

4. *the middle court*] i.e. of the royal palace. This is preferable to the marg. reading.

5. *the captain of my people*] This phrase (which does not occur elsewhere in Kings) is remarkable, and speaks for the authenticity of this full report of the actual words of the Prophet's message (abbreviated in Isai. xxxviii. 1, &c.). The title, "Captain (*negid*) of God's people," commonly used of David,

6 house of the LORD. And I will add unto thy days fifteen years; and I will deliver thee and this city out of the hand of the king of Assyria; and *a* I will defend this city for mine own sake, and
7 for my servant David's sake. And *h* Isaiah said, Take a lump of figs. And they took and laid *it* on the boil, and he recovered.
8 ¶ And Hezekiah said unto Isaiah, *i* What *shall be* the sign that the LORD will heal me, and that I shall go up into the house of
9 the LORD the third day? And Isaiah said, *k* This sign shalt thou have of the LORD, that the LORD will do the thing that he hath spoken: shall the shadow go forward ten degrees, or go
10 back ten degrees? And Hezekiah answered, It is a light thing for the shadow to go down ten degrees: nay, but let the shadow
11 return backward ten degrees. And Isaiah the prophet cried unto the LORD: and *l* he brought the shadow ten degrees back-
12 ward, by which it had gone down in the ¹dial of Ahaz. ¶ *m* At that time ²Berodach-baladan, the son of Baladan, king of

a ch. 19. 34.
h Isai. 38. 21.

i See Isai. 7. 11, 14. & 38. 22.
k See Isai. 38. 7, 8.

l See Josh. 10. 12, 14. Isai. 38. 8.
m Isai. 39. 1, &c.

¹ Heb. *degrees*.   ² Or, *Merodach-baladan*.

---

is applied to Hezekiah, as David's true follower (xviii. 3).

6. The king of Assyria in B.C. 714 and 713 was Sargon (B.C. 721-705). If then the Biblical and Assyrian chronologies *which agree exactly in the year of the taking of Samaria* (B.C. 721), are to be depended on, the king of Assyria here must have been Sargon. It may be conjectured that he had taken offence at something in the conduct of Hezekiah, and have threatened Jerusalem about this time (cp. Isai. xx. 6). There is, however, no evidence of actual hostilities between Judæa and Assyria in Sargon's reign.

7. *a lump of figs*] The usual remedy in the East, even at the present day, for ordinary boils. But such a remedy would not *naturally* cure the dangerous tumour or carbuncle from which Hezekiah suffered. Thus the means used in this miracle were means having a tendency towards the result wrought by them, but insufficient of themselves to produce that result (cp. iv. 34 note).

8. *And Hezekiah said*] Previous to the actual recovery Hezekiah, who at first may have felt himself no better, asked for a "sign" that he would indeed be restored to health.

Asking for a sign is a pious or a wicked act according to the spirit in which it is done. No blame is attached to the requests of Gideon (Judg. vi. 17, 37, 39), or to this of Hezekiah, because they were real wishes of the heart expressed humbly. The "evil generation" that "sought for a sign" in our Lord's days did not really want one, but made the demand captiously, neither expecting nor wishing that it should be granted.

9. *ten degrees*] Lit. "ten steps." It is not, perhaps, altogether certain whether the "dial of Ahaz" (*v.* 11) was really a dial with a gnomon in the centre, and "degrees"

marked round it, or a construction for marking time by means of "steps." Sundials proper had been invented by the Babylonians before the time of Herodotus; but the instrument here was probably an instrument consisting of a set of steps, or stairs, with an obelisk at the top, the shadow of which descended or ascended the steps according as the sun rose higher in the heavens or declined.

The question as to the mode whereby the return of the shadow was produced is one on which many opinions have been held. Recently, it has been urged that the true cause of the phenomenon was a solar eclipse, in which the moon obscured the entire upper limb of the sun; and it has been clearly shown that if such an occurrence took place a little before midday, it would have had the effect described as having taken place— *i.e.* during the obscuration of the sun's upper limb shadows would be sensibly lengthened, and that of the obelisk would descend the stairs; as the obscuration passed off the reverse would take place, shadows would shorten, and that of the obelisk would once more retire up the steps. If this be the true account, the *miracle* would consist in Isaiah's supernatural foreknowledge of an event which the astronomy of the age was quite incapable of predicting, and in the providential guidance of Hezekiah's will, so that he chose the "sign" which in the natural course of things was about to be manifested.

10. *It is a light thing*] It seemed to Hezekiah comparatively easy that the shadow, which had already begun to lengthen, should merely make a sudden jump *in the same direction;* but, wholly contrary to all experience that it should change its direction, advancing up the steps again when it had once begun to descend them.

12. *Berodach-baladan*] The correct form of this name, Merodach-baladan, is given

Babylon, sent letters and a present unto Hezekiah : for he had
13 heard that Hezekiah had been sick. And *n* Hezekiah hearkened
unto them, and shewed them all the house of his ¹precious
things, the silver, and the gold, and the spices, and the precious
ointment, and *all* the house of his ²³armour, and all that was
found in his treasures : there was nothing in his house, nor in
14 all his dominion, that Hezekiah shewed them not. Then came
Isaiah the prophet unto king Hezekiah, and said unto him,
What said these men ? and from whence came they unto thee ?
And Hezekiah said, They are come from a far country, *even*
15 from Babylon. And he said, What have they seen in thine
house ? And Hezekiah answered, *o* All *the things* that *are* in
mine house have they seen : there is nothing among my trea-
16 sures that I have not shewed them. And Isaiah said unto Heze-
17 kiah, Hear the word of the LORD. Behold, the days come, that
all that *is* in thine house, and that which thy fathers have laid
up in store unto this day, *p* shall be carried into Babylon : no-
18 thing shall be left, saith the LORD. And of thy sons that shall
issue from thee, which thou shalt beget, *q* shall they take away ;

n 2 Chr. 32.
27.

o ver. 13.

p ch. 24. 13.
& 25. 13.
Jer.27.21,22.
& 52. 17.
q ch. 24. 12.

¹ Or, *spicery*.   ² Or, *jewels*.   ³ Heb. *vessels*.

---

in Isaiah (xxxix. 1). It is a name composed of three elements, *Merodach*, the
well-known Babylonian god (Jer. l. 2), *bal*
(=*pal*) "a son ;" and *iddin*, or *iddina*, "has
given ;" or *Baladan* may be a form of *Bel-
iddin*. This king of Babylon is mentioned
frequently in the Assyrian inscriptions, and
he was not unknown to the Greeks. He
had two reigns in Babylon. First of all, he
seized the throne in the same year in which
Sargon became king of Assyria, B.C. 721,
and held it for 12 years, from B.C. 721 to
B.C. 709, when Sargon defeated him, and
took him prisoner. Secondly, on the death
of Sargon and the accession of Sennacherib,
when troubles once more arose in Babylonia,
he returned thither, and had another reign,
which lasted six months, during a part of
the year B.C. 703. As the embassy of Merodach-Baladan followed closely on the illness of Hezekiah, it would probably be in
B.C. 713.

the son of Baladan] In the inscriptions
Merodach-Baladan is repeatedly called the
son of Yakin or Yagin. This, however, is
a discrepancy which admits of easy explanation. The Assyrians are not accurate in
their accounts of the parentage of foreign
kings. With them Jehu is "the son of
Omri." Yakin was a prince of some repute,
to whose dominions Merodach-baladan had
succeeded. The Assyrians would call him
Yakin's son, though he might have been
his son-in-law, or his grandson.

The embassy was not merely one of congratulation. Its chief object was to inquire
with respect to the going back of the shadow,
an astronomical marvel in which the Chal-
dæans of Babylon would feel a keen interest
(2 Chr. xxxii. 31). A political purpose is
moreover implied in the next verse. Merodach-baladan was probably desirous of

strengthening himself against Assyria by an
alliance with Judæa and with Egypt.

13. *Hezekiah hearkened unto them, and
shewed them*] The Jewish king lent a favourable ear to the proposals of the ambassadors, and exhibited to them the resources
which he possessed, in order to induce them
to report well of him to their master.

all the house of his precious things] Lit.
the "spice-house;" the phrase had acquired the more generic sense of "treasure-
house" from the fact that the gold, the
silver, and the spices were all stored together.

14. Hezekiah did not answer Isaiah's first
question, "What said these men?" but
only his second. Probably he knew that
Isaiah would oppose reliance on an "arm of
flesh."

Babylon now for the first time became
revealed to the Jews as an actual power in
the world, which might effect them politically. As yet even the Prophets had
spoken but little of the great southern city;
up to this time she had been little more
to them than Tyre, or Tarshish, or any
other rich and powerful idolatrous city.
Henceforth all this was wholly changed.
The prophetic utterance of Isaiah on this
occasion (*rv.* 16-18) never was, never could
be, forgotten. He followed it up with a
burst of prophecy (Is. xl.-lxvi.), in which
Babylon usurps altogether the place of Assyria as Israel's enemy, and the Captivity
being assumed as a matter of certainty, the
hopes of the people are directed onward
beyond it to the Return. Other Prophets
took up the strain and repeated it (Habak.
i. 6-11, ii. 5-8 ; Mic. iv. 10). Babylon thus
became henceforth, in lieu of Assyria, the
great object of the nation's fear and hatred.

18. This prophecy had two fulfilments,

and they shall be eunuchs in the palace of the king of Babylon.
19 Then said Hezekiah unto Isaiah, *Good *is* the word of the LORD
  which thou hast spoken. And he said, ¹*Is it* not *good*, if peace
20 and truth be in my days? ¶ *And the rest of the acts of Hezekiah, and all his might, and how he *made a pool, and a conduit,
  and *brought water into the city, *are* they not written in the
21 book of the chronicles of the kings of Judah? And *Hezekiah
  slept with his fathers: and Manasseh his son reigned in his
  stead.

CHAP. 21. MANASSEH *was* twelve years old when he began to
  reign, and reigned fifty and five years in Jerusalem. And his
2 mother's name *was* Hephzi-bah. And he did *that which was* evil
  in the sight of the LORD, *after the abominations of the heathen,
3 whom the LORD cast out before the children of Israel. For he
  built up again the high places *which Hezekiah his father had
  destroyed; and he reared up altars for Baal, and made a grove,

r 1Sam.3.18.
Job 1. 21.
Ps. 39. 9.
s 2Chr.32.32.
t Neh. 3. 16.
u 2 Chr. 32.
30.
x 2 Chr. 32.
33.

a 2 Chr. 33.
1, &c.

b ch. 16. 3.

c ch. 18. 4.

---

¹ Or, *Shall there not be peace and truth, &c.*

---

each complementary to the other. Manasseh, Hezekiah's *actual son*, was "carried to Babylon" (2 Chr. xxxiii. 11), but did not become a eunuch in the palace. Daniel and others, not his actual sons, but of the royal seed (Dan. i. 3), and therefore Hezekiah's descendants, are thought by some to have literally fulfilled the latter part of the prophecy, being eunuchs in the palace of Nebuchadnezzar.

19. *Good is the word*, &c.] The language is, according to some, that of a true spirit of resignation and humility; according to others, that of a feeling of relief and satisfaction that the evil was not to come in his day. Such a feeling would be but natural, and though not according to the standard of Christian perfectness, would imply no very great defect of character in one who lived under the old Dispensation.

peace and truth] Rather, "peace and **continuance.**" The evils threatened were war and the dissolution of the kingdom.

20, 21. Consult the marg. reff.

XXI. 1. *Manasseh was twelve years old*] Manasseh, therefore, was not born at the time of Hezekiah's dangerous illness; and it is probable that Hezekiah had at that time no son to succeed him. According to Josephus, this was the principal cause of his grief.

Hephzibah] Jewish tradition makes Hephzibah, Hezekiah's wife, the daughter of Isaiah; but this is scarcely probable. She was, however, no doubt, known to the Prophet, and it may well have been in special compliment to her that Isaiah introduced her name (lxii. 4) as one that Jerusalem would bear after her restoration to God's favour. The name means, "My delight (is) in her."

2. Manasseh during his minority naturally fell under the influence of the chief Jewish nobles, with whom the pure religion of Jehovah was always unpopular (cp.

2 Chr. xxiv. 17, 18; Jer. viii. 1, 2). They seem to have persuaded him, not only to undo Hezekiah's work, but to proceed to lengths in polytheism, magic, and idolatry, unknown before. The sins of Manasseh's reign appear to have been those which filled up the measure of Judah's iniquity, and brought down the final sentence of doom on the last remnant of the chosen people (xxiii. 26; cp. Jer. xv. 4).

3. The first step in the re-establishment of idolatry seems to have been the restoration of the high places where Jehovah was professedly worshipped (xviii. 22), but with idolatrous rites (1 K. xiv. 23). The next was to re-introduce the favourite idolatry of Israel, Baal-worship, which had formerly flourished in Judæa under Athaliah (xi. 18), and Ahaz (2 Chr. xxviii. 2). After this, Manasseh seems to have specially affected Sabaism, which had been previously unknown in Judæa (cp. xvii. 16 and note).

worshipped all the host of heaven] Sabaism, or pure star-worship, without images, and without astrological superstitions, included a reverence for the sun, the moon, the chief stars, and the twelve signs of the Zodiac (xxiii. 5 note). The main worship was by altars, on which incense was burnt (Jer. xix. 13). These altars were placed either upon the ground (*v.* 5), or upon the house-tops (xxiii. 12; Zeph. i. 5). The sun was worshipped with the face towards the east (Ezek. viii. 16); chariots and horses were dedicated to him (xxiii. 11). The star-worship of the Jews has far more the character of an Arabian than an Assyrian or Chaldæan cult. It obtained its hold at a time when Assyria and Babylonia had but little communication with Judæa—*i.e.* during the reign of Manasseh. It crept in probably from the same quarter as the Molech worship, with which it is here (and in 2 Chr. xxxiii. 3-6) conjoined.

d 1 Kin. 16.
32, 33.
e Deut. 4. 19.
& 17. 3.
ch. 17. 16.
f Jer. 32. 34.
g 2 Sam. 7. 13.
1 Kin. 8. 29.
& 9. 3.
h Lev. 18. 21.
& 20. 2.
ch. 16. 3.
& 17. 17.
i Lev. 19. 26,
31.
Deut. 18. 10,
11.
ch. 17. 17.
k 2 Sam. 7. 13.
1 Kin. 8. 29.
& 9. 3.
ch. 23. 27.
Ps. 132. 13,
14.
Jer. 32. 34.
l 2 Sam. 7. 10.
m Prov. 20.
12.
n ch. 23. 26,
27.
& 24. 3, 4.
Jer. 15. 4.
o 1 Kin. 21. 26.
p ver. 9.
q 1 Sam. 3. 11.
Jer. 19. 3.
r See Isai.
34. 11.
Lam. 2. 8.
Amos 7. 7, 8.

^das did Ahab king of Israel; and ^eworshipped all the host of
4 heaven, and served them. And ^fhe built altars in the house of
the LORD, of which the LORD said, ^gIn Jerusalem will I put my
5 name. And he built altars for all the host of heaven in the two
6 courts of the house of the LORD. ^hAnd he made his son pass
through the fire, and observed ⁱtimes, and used enchantments,
and dealt with familiar spirits and wizards: he wrought much
wickedness in the sight of the LORD, to provoke *him* to anger.
7 And he set a graven image of the grove that he had made in the
house, of which the LORD said to David, and to Solomon his son,
^kIn this house, and in Jerusalem, which I have chosen out of
8 all tribes of Israel, will I put my name for ever: ^lneither will I
make the feet of Israel move any more out of the land which I
gave their fathers; only if they will observe to do according to
all that I have commanded them, and according to all the law
9 that my servant Moses commanded them. But they hearkened
not: and Manasseh ^mseduced them to do more evil than did the
nations whom the LORD destroyed before the children of Israel.
10 ¶ And the LORD spake by his servants the prophets, saying, ⁿBe-
11 cause Manasseh king of Judah hath done these abominations,
^o*and* hath done wickedly above all that the Amorites did, which
were before him, and ^phath made Judah also to sin with his
12 idols: therefore thus saith the LORD God of Israel, Behold, I *am*
bringing *such* evil upon Jerusalem and Judah, that whosoever
13 heareth of it, both ^qhis ears shall tingle. And I will stretch
over Jerusalem ^rthe line of Samaria, and the plummet of the
house of Ahab: and I will wipe Jerusalem as *a man* wipeth a
14 dish, ¹wiping *it*, and turning *it* upside down. And I will forsake
the remnant of mine inheritance, and deliver them into the
hand of their enemies; and they shall become a prey and a
15 spoil to all their enemies; because they have done *that which*

---

¹ Heb. *he wipeth and turneth* it *upon the face thereof.*

---

4. The "altars" of this verse seem to be
the same with those of *v.* 5, and consequently were not in the Temple building,
but in the outer and inner courts.

6. On the meaning of the phrase "passing
through the fire," see xvi. 3, and Lev. xx.
2–5.

To "observe times" was forbidden in the
Law (marg. reff.), and was no doubt among
the modes of divination practised by the
Canaanitish nations. It has been explained
as, (1) Predicting from the state of the
clouds and atmosphere; (2) Fascination with
the eye; (3) Watching and catching at
chance words as ominous.

dealt with familiar spirits] This practice
was forbidden by Moses (Lev. xix. 31) under
the penalty of death (do. xx. 27). Its nature
is best learnt from Saul's visit to the witch
of Endor (1 Sam. xxviii. 7, &c.).

wizards] "Wizards" — literally, "wise
men"—are always joined with those who
have familiar spirits. Probably they were
a sort of necromancers.

7. *a graven image of the grove*] Rather,
" **the carved work** of the Asherah." This
Asherah Manasseh placed in the very Tem-

ple itself, whence it was afterwards taken
by Josiah to be destroyed (xxiii. 6). Such
a profanation was beyond anything that
had been done either by Athaliah (xi. 18),
or by Ahaz (xvi. 14–18; 2 Chr. xxix. 5–7).

9. During the long reign of Manasseh
idolatry in all manner of varied forms took
a hold upon the Jewish people such as had
never been known before. Cp. Jer. vii. 18,
31; Ezek. xxiii. 37; Zeph. i. 5. The corruption of morals kept pace with the degradation of religion. Cp. xxiii. 7; Zeph. iii.
1–3; Jer. ii. 8, v. 1.

10. *the prophets*] None of the Prophets of
this reign are certainly known. One may
possibly have been Hosai or Hozai (2 Chr.
xxxiii. 19, marg.), who perhaps wrote a life
of Manasseh.

13. The general meaning is plain, but
the exact force of the metaphor used is not
so clear. If the "line" and the "plummet"
be "symbols of rule" or law, the meaning
will be—"I will apply exactly the same
measure and rule to Jerusalem as to Samaria—I will treat both alike with strict and
even justice."

was evil in my sight, and have provoked me to anger, since the day their fathers came forth out of Egypt, even unto this day.

16 ¶ *ˢ*Moreover Manasseh shed innocent blood very much, till he had filled Jerusalem ¹from one end to another; beside his sin wherewith he made Judah to sin, in doing *that which was* evil

17 in the sight of the LORD. Now *ᵗ*the rest of the acts of Manasseh, and all that he did, and his sin that he sinned, *are* they not written in the book of the chronicles of the kings of Judah?

18 And *ᵘ*Manasseh slept with his fathers, and was buried in the garden of his own house, in the garden of Uzza: and Amon his

19 son reigned in his stead. ¶ *ˣ*Amon *was* twenty and two years old when he began to reign, and he reigned two years in Jerusalem. And his mother's name *was* Meshullemeth, the daughter

20 of Haruz of Jotbah. And he did *that which was* evil in the sight

21 of the LORD, *ʸ*as his father Manasseh did. And he walked in all the way that his father walked in, and served the idols that

22 his father served, and worshipped them: and he *ᶻ*forsook the LORD God of his fathers, and walked not in the way of the LORD.

23 *ᵃ*And the servants of Amon conspired against him, and slew the

24 king in his own house. And the people of the land slew all them that had conspired against king Amon; and the people of

25 the land made Josiah his son king in his stead. Now the rest of the acts of Amon which he did, *are* they not written in the

26 book of the chronicles of the kings of Judah? And he was buried in his sepulchre in the garden of Uzza: and *ᵇ*Josiah his son reigned in his stead.

ˢ ch. 24. 4.

ᵗ 2 Chr. 33. 11—19.

ᵘ 2Chr.33.20.

ˣ 2 Chr. 33. 21—23.

ʸ ver. 2, &c.

ᶻ 1Kin.11.33.

ᵃ 2 Chr. 33. 24, 25.

ᵇ Matt. 1. 10, called *Josias.*

---

¹ Heb. *from mouth to mouth.*

---

16. Cp. Jer. ii. 30; Heb. xi. 37; Isai. lvii. 1–4. According to tradition, Isaiah was among the first to perish. More than a century afterwards, the final judgment upon Jerusalem was felt to be in an especial way the punishment of Manasseh's bloody persecution of God's people (marg. ref.).

17. The writer of Kings relates in eighteen verses the history of fifty-five years, and consequently omits numerous facts of great importance in the life of Manasseh. Among the most remarkable of the facts omitted are the capture of Manasseh by the king of Assyria, his removal to Babylon, his repentance there, his restoration to his kingdom, and his religious reforms upon his return to it. These are recorded only in Chronicles (marg. ref., see note). The writer of Kings probably considered the repentance of Manasseh but a half-repentance, followed by a half-reformation, which left untouched the root of the evil.

18. *was buried*] The catacomb of David was probably full, and the later kings, from Ahaz downwards, had to find sepulture elsewhere. Ahaz was buried in Jerusalem, but not in the sepulchres of the kings (2 Chr. xxviii. 27). Hezekiah found a resting-place on the way that led up to David's catacomb (do. xxxii. 33). Manasseh and Amon were interred in "the garden of Uzza," a portion (apparently) of the royal palace-garden; perhaps so called after the name of the previous owner. Josiah

was buried in "his own sepulchre" (xxiii. 30).

Amon his son] This name, which occurs only at this time and in the reign of the idolatrous Ahab (1 K. xxii. 26), is identical in form with the Hebrew representative of the great Egyptian god, Amen or Amun (Nahum iii. 8 marg.); and it is therefore probable that Manasseh selected it and gave it to his son in compliment to the Egyptians.

21. At Manasseh's death, the idolatrous party, held in some check during his later years (2 Chr. xxxiii. 15–17), recovered the entire direction of affairs, and obtained authority from Amon to make once more all the changes which Manasseh had made in the early part of his reign. Hence we find the state of things at Josiah's accession (xxiii. 4–14; Zeph. i. 4–12, iii. 1–7), the exact counterpart of that which had existed under Manasseh.

23. This conspiracy may have been due to the popular reaction against the extreme idolatry which the young king had established.

24. The intention of the conspirators had perhaps been to declare a forfeiture of the crown by the existing line, and to place a new dynasty on the throne. This the people would not suffer. They arrested them and put them to death; and insisted on investing with the royal authority the true heir of David, the eldest son of Amon, though he was a boy only eight years old.

CHAP. 22. JOSIAH *a was* eight years old when he began to reign, and he reigned thirty and one years in Jerusalem. And his mother's name *was* Jedidah, the daughter of Adaiah of *b* Boscath.

2 And he did *that which was* right in the sight of the LORD, and walked in all the way of David his father, and *c* turned not aside 3 to the right hand or to the left. ¶ *d* And it came to pass in the eighteenth year of king Josiah, *that* the king sent Shaphan the son of Azaliah, the son of Meshullam, the scribe, to the house 4 of the LORD, saying, Go up to Hilkiah the high priest, that he may sum the silver which is *e* brought into the house of the LORD, which *f* the keepers of the ¹door have gathered of the 5 people : and let them *g* deliver it into the hand of the doers of the work, that have the oversight of the house of the LORD : and let them give it to the doers of the work which *is* in the 6 house of the LORD, to repair the breaches of the house, unto carpenters, and builders, and masons, and to buy timber and 7 hewn stone to repair the house. Howbeit *h* there was no reckoning made with them of the money that was delivered into their 8 hand, because they dealt faithfully. ¶ And Hilkiah the high priest said unto Shaphan the scribe, *i* I have found the book of

¹ Heb. *threshold.*

XXII. **3.** *in the eighteenth year*] This is the date of the finding of the Book of the Law and of the Passover (marg. ref., and xxiii. 23), but is not meant to apply to all the various reforms of Josiah as related in xxiii. 4–20. The true chronology of Josiah's reign is to be learnt from 2 Chr. xxxiv. 3–8, xxxv. 1. From these places it appear that at least the greater part of his reforms preceded the finding of the Book of the Law. He began them in the twelfth year of his reign, at the age of twenty, and had accomplished all, or the greater part, by his eighteenth year, when the Book of the Law was found.

Shaphan is mentioned frequently by Jeremiah. He was the father of Ahikam, Jeremiah's friend and protector at the court of Jehoiakim (Jer. xxvi. 24), and the grandfather of Gedaliah, who was made governor of Judæa by the Babylonians after the destruction of Jerusalem (xxv. 22). Several others of his sons and grandsons were in favour with the later Jewish kings (Jer. xxix. 3, xxxvi. 10–12, 25; Ezek. viii. 11). Shaphan's office was one of great importance, involving very confidential relations with the king (1 K. iv. 3).

4. *Hilkiah*] Hilkiah was the father (or grandfather) of Seraiah (cp. 1 Chr. vi. 13, 14, with Neh. xi. 11), High-Priest at the time of the Captivity (xxv. 18), and ancestor of Ezra the scribe (Ezr. vii. 1).

It is evident from the expressions of this verse that a collection for the repairs of the Temple, similar to that established in the reign of Joash (xii. 9, 10), had been for some considerable time in progress (cp. 2 Chr. xxxiv. 3), and the king now sent to know the result.

5. See marg. ref. The "doers" of the first part of the verse are the contractors, or overseers, who undertook the general superintendence; they are to be distinguished from a lower class of "doers," the actual labourers, carpenters, and masons of the latter portion of the verse.

which is in the house of the LORD] Rather, "who are," &c. ; *i.e.* the persons who were actually employed in the Temple.

7. *they dealt faithfully*] Cp. marg. ref. The names of these honest overseers are given in Chronicles (2 Chr. xxxiv. 12).

8. Some have concluded from this discovery, either that no "book of the law" had ever existed before, the work now said to have been "found" having been forged for the occasion by Hilkiah ; or that all knowledge of the old "book" had been lost, and that a work of unknown date and authorship having been at this time found was accepted as the Law of Moses on account of its contents, and has thus come down to us under his name. But this is to see in the narrative far more than it naturally implies. If Hilkiah had been bold enough and wicked enough to forge, or if he had been foolish enough to accept hastily as the real "book of the law" a composition of which he really knew nothing, there were four means of detecting his error or his fraud :— (1) The Jewish Liturgies, which embodied large portions of the Law ; (2) The memory of living men, which in many instances may have extended to the entire Five Books, as it does now with the modern Samaritans ; (3) Other copies, entire or fragmentary, existing among the more learned Jews, or in the Schools of the Prophets; and (4) Quotations from the Law in other works, especially in the Psalmists and Prophets, who refer to it on almost every page.

The copy of the Book of the Law found

the law in the house of the LORD. And Hilkiah gave the book
9 to Shaphan, and he read it. And Shaphan the scribe came to
the king, and brought the king word again, and said, Thy servants have ¹gathered the money that was found in the house,
and have delivered it into the hand of them that do the work,
10 that have the oversight of the house of the LORD. And Shaphan the scribe shewed the king, saying, Hilkiah the priest hath
delivered me a book. And Shaphan read it before the king.
11 And it came to pass, when the king had heard the words of the
12 book of the law, that he rent his clothes. And the king commanded Hilkiah the priest, and Ahikam the son of Shaphan,
and ᵏAchbor the son of ²Michaiah, and Shaphan the scribe, and
13 Asahiah a servant of the king's, saying, Go ye, enquire of the
LORD for me, and for the people, and for all Judah, concerning
the words of this book that is found: for great *is* ˡthe wrath of
the LORD that is kindled against us, because our fathers have
not hearkened unto the words of this book, to do according unto
14 all that which is written concerning us. ¶ So Hilkiah the priest,
and Ahikam, and Achbor, and Shaphan, and Asahiah, went unto
Huldah the prophetess, the wife of Shallum the son of ᵐTikvah,
the son of ³Harhas, keeper of the ⁴wardrobe; (now she dwelt
in Jerusalem ⁵in the college;) and they communed with her.
15 And she said unto them, Thus saith the LORD God of Israel,
16 Tell the man that sent you to me, Thus saith the LORD, Behold,
ⁿI will bring evil upon this place, and upon the inhabitants
thereof, *even* all the words of the book which the king of Judah

k Abdon,
2 Chr. 34. 20.

l Deut. 29. 27.

m Tikvath,
2 Chr. 34. 22.

*n Deut. 29. 27.
Dan. 9. 11.
12, 13, 14.*

---

¹ Heb. *melted.*
² Or, *Micah.*
³ Or, *Hasrah.*
⁴ Heb. *garments.*
⁵ Or, *in the second part.*

---

by Hilkiah was no doubt that deposited, in
accordance with the command of God, by
Moses, by the side of the Ark of the Covenant, and kept ordinarily in the Holy of
Holies (marg. ref.). It had been lost, or
secreted, during the desecration of the
Temple by Manasseh, but had not been
removed out of the Temple building.

9. *have gathered*] Rather, "have poured
out" or "**emptied out.**" The allusion probably is to the emptying of the chest in
which all the money collected had been
placed (xii. 9).

11. *he rent his clothes*] Partly in grief and
horror, like Reuben (Gen. xxxvii. 29) and
Job (i. 20), partly in repentance, like Ahab
(1 K. xxi. 27).

13. *enquire of the* LORD] As inquiry by
Urim and Thummim had ceased—apparently because superseded by prophecy—
this order was equivalent to an injunction
to seek the presence of a Prophet (cp. iii.
11; 1 K. xxii. 5).

because our fathers have not hearkened]
Josiah, it will be observed, assumes that
preceding generations had had full opportunity of hearing and knowing the Law. He
thus regards the loss as comparatively recent (cp. *v.* 8 note).

14. *went unto Huldah*] It might have
been expected that the royal commissioners
would have gone to Jeremiah, on whom the

prophetic spirit had descended in Josiah's
thirteenth year (Jer. i. 2), or five years previous to the finding of the Law. Perhaps
he was at some distance from Jerusalem at
the time; or his office may not yet have
been fully recognized.

the prophetess] Cp. the cases of Miriam
(Ex. xv. 20; Num. xii. 2) and Deborah
(Judg. iv. 4).

keeper of the wardrobe] Lit. "of the
robes." Shallum had the superintendenc·,
either of the vestments of the priests who
served in the Temple, or of the royal robe-
room in which dresses of honour were stored,
in case of their being needed for presents
(see *v.* 5 note).

in the college] The marginal translation
"in the second part" is preferable; and
probably refers to the new or outer city—
that which had been enclosed by the wall of
Manasseh, to the north of the old city (2
Chr. xxxiii. 14).

16. *all the words of the book*] The "words"
here intended are no doubt the threatenings
of the Law, particularly those of Lev. xxvi.
16-39 and Deut. xxviii. 15-68. Josiah had
probably only heard a portion of the Book
of the Law; but that portion had contained those awful denunciations of coming
woe. Hence Josiah's rending of his clothes
(*v.* 11), and his hurried message to Huldah.

o Deut. 29.
25, 26, 27.

17 hath read: °because they have forsaken me, and have burned
incense unto other gods, that they might provoke me to anger
with all the works of their hands; therefore my wrath shall be
18 kindled against this place, and shall not be quenched. But to

p 2 Chr. 34.
26, &c.

ᵖthe king of Judah which sent you to enquire of the LORD, thus
shall ye say to him, Thus saith the LORD God of Israel, *As*

q Ps. 51. 17.
Isai. 57. 15.
r 1 Kin.21.29.

19 *touching* the words which thou hast heard; because thine ᑫheart
was tender, and thou hast ʳhumbled thyself before the LORD,
when thou heardest what I spake against this place, and against

s Lev. 26.
31, 32.
t Jer. 26. 6.
& 44. 22.

the inhabitants thereof, that they should become ˢa desolation
and ᵗa curse, and hast rent thy clothes, and wept before me;
20 I also have heard *thee*, saith the LORD. Behold therefore, I

u Ps. 37. 37.
Isai. 57. 1, 2.

will gather thee unto thy fathers, and thou ᵘshalt be gathered
into thy grave in peace; and thine eyes shall not see all the
evil which I will bring upon this place. And they brought the
king word again.

a 2 Chr. 34.
29, 30, &c.

CHAP. 23. AND ᵃthe king sent, and they gathered unto him all
2 the elders of Judah and of Jerusalem. And the king went up
into the house of the LORD, and all the men of Judah and all
the inhabitants of Jerusalem with him, and the priests, and the
prophets, and all the people, ¹both small and great: and he
read in their ears all the words of the book of the covenant

b ch. 22. 8.
c ch.11.14,17.

3 ᵇwhich was found in the house of the LORD. And the king
ᶜstood by a pillar, and made a covenant before the LORD, to
walk after the LORD, and to keep his commandments and his
testimonies and his statutes with all *their* heart and all *their*
soul, to perform the words of this covenant that were written in
4 this book. And all the people stood to the covenant. ¶And
the king commanded Hilkiah the high priest, and the priests of

¹ Heb. *from small even unto great.*

---

17. *have burned incense*] In the marg.
ref. the corresponding phrase is:—" have
served other gods, and worshipped them."
Its alteration to "have burned incense"
points to the fact that the favourite existing
idolatry was burning incense on the house-
tops to Baal (Jer. xix. 13, xxxii. 29) and to
the host of heaven (xxi. 3).

19. See marg. reff.

20. *in peace*] The death of Josiah *in battle*
(xxiii. 29) is in verbal contradiction to this
prophecy, but not in real opposition to its
spirit, which is simply that the pious prince
who has sent to inquire of the Lord, shall
be gathered to his fathers before the troubles
come upon the land which are to result in
her utter desolation. Now those troubles
were to come, not from Egypt, but from
Babylon; and their commencement was
not the invasion of Necho in B.C. 608, but
that of Nebuchadnezzar three years later.
Thus was Josiah "taken away from the
evil to come," and died "in peace" before
his city had suffered attack from the really
formidable enemy.

XXIII. 2. *the prophets*] The suggestion
to regard this word an error of the pen
for "Levites," which occurs in Chronicles
(marg. ref.), is unnecessary. For though
Zephaniah, Urijah, and Jeremiah are all

that we can *name* as belonging to the Order
at the time, there is no reason to doubt that
Judæa contained others whom we cannot
name. "Schools of the Prophets" were as
common in Judah as in Israel.

he read] The present passage is strong
evidence that the Jewish kings could read.
The solemn reading of the Law—a practice
commanded in the Law itself once in seven
years (Deut. xxxi. 10-13),—had been inter-
mitted, at least for the last seventy-five
years, from the date of the accession of
Manasseh.

3. *by a pillar*] Rather, "upon the pillar "
(see xi. 14, note).

made a covenant] " The covenant." Josiah
renewed *the old* Covenant made between
God and His people in Horeb (Deut. v. 2),
so far at least as such renewal was possible
by the mere act of an individual. He bound
himself by a solemn promise to the faithful
performance of the entire Law.

with all their heart] " Their " rather than
" his," because the king was considered as
pledging the whole nation to obedience with
himself. He and they "stood to it," *i.e.*
" accepted it, came into the Covenant."

4-20. A parenthesis giving the earlier
reforms of Josiah.

4. *the priests of the second order*] This is a

the second order, and the keepers of the door, to bring forth out of the temple of the LORD all the vessels that were made for Baal, and for ^dthe grove, and for all the host of heaven: and he burned them without Jerusalem in the fields of Kidron, and 5 carried the ashes of them unto Beth-el. And he ¹put down the ²idolatrous priests, whom the kings of Judah had ordained to burn incense in the high places in the cities of Judah, and in the places round about Jerusalem; them also that burned incense unto Baal, to the sun, and to the moon, and to the four ³planets, 6 and to ^eall the host of heaven. And he brought out the ^fgrove from the house of the LORD, without Jerusalem, unto the brook Kidron, and burned it at the brook Kidron, and stamped *it* small to powder, and cast the powder thereof upon ^gthe graves 7 of the children of the people. And he brake down the houses ^hof the sodomites, that *were* by the house of the LORD, ⁱwhere 8 the women wove ⁴hangings for the grove. ¶ And he brought all the priests out of the cities of Judah, and defiled the high places where the priests had burned incense, from ^kGeba to Beer-sheba, and brake down the high places of the gates that

d ch. 21. 3, 7.

e ch. 21. 3.
f ch. 21. 7.

g 2 Chr. 34. 4.

h 1 Kin. 14, 24.
& 15. 12.
i Ezek. 16. 16.

k 1 Kin. 15. 22.

---

¹ Heb. *caused to cease.*
² Heb. *Chemarim,* Hos. 10.
³ Or, *twelve signs,* or, *con-*
5. Foretold, Zeph. 1. 4.
stellat'ons.
⁴ Heb. *houses.*

---

new expression; and probably refers to the ordinary priests, called here " priests of the second order," in contrast with the High-Priest, whose dignity was reviving (xii. 2 note).

the vessels] This would include the whole apparatus of worship, altars, images, dresses, utensils, &c., for Baal, &c. (xxi. 3–5 notes). The ashes of the idolatrous objects burnt in the first instance in the "fields of Kidron" (*i.e.* in the part of the valley which lies north-east of the city, a part much broader than that between the Temple Hill and the Mount of Olives) were actually taken to Bethel, as to an accursed place, and one just beyond the borders of Judah ; while those of other objects burnt afterwards were not carried so far, the trouble being great and the need not absolute, but were thrown into the Kidron (v. 12), when there happened to be water to carry them away, or scattered on graves which were already unclean (v. 6). Cp. 1 K. xv. 13.

5. *he put down,* &c.] or, "He caused to cease the idolatrous priests " (marg.) ; *i.e.* he stopped them. The word translated "idolatrous priests" (see marg.) is a rare one, occurring only here and in marg. reff. Here and in Zephaniah it is contrasted with *cohanim,* another class of high-place priests. The *cohanim* were probably " Levitical," the *chemarim* "non-Levitical priests of the high-places." *Chemarim* appears to have been a foreign term, perhaps derived from the Syriac *cûmrô,* which means a priest of any kind.

whom the kings of Judah had ordained] The consecration of non-Levitical priests by the kings of Judah (cp. 1 K. xii. 31) had not been previously mentioned ; but it is quite

in accordance with the other proceedings cf Manasseh and Amon.

the planets] See marginal note, *i.e.* the " signs of the Zodiac." Cp. Job xxxviii. 32 marg. The word in the original probably means primarily "houses" or "stations," which was the name applied by the Babylonians to their divisions of the Zodiac.

6. The ashes, being polluted and polluting, were thrown upon graves, because there no one could come into contact with them, since graves were avoided as unclean places.

7. *by the house of the* LORD] This did not arise from intentional desecration, but from the fact that the practices in question were a part of the idolatrous ceremonial, being regarded as pleasing to the gods, and, indeed, as positive acts of worship (cp. marg. ref.).

The " women " were probably the priestesses attached to the worship of Astarte, which was intimately connected with that of the Asherah or " grove." Among their occupations one was the weaving of coverings (lit. "houses " marg.) for the Asherah, which seem to have been of various colours (marg. ref.).

8. Josiah removed the Levitical priests, who had officiated at the various high-places, from the scenes of their idolatries, and brought them to Jerusalem, where their conduct might be watched.

from Geba to Beer-sheba] *i.e.* from the extreme north to the extreme south of the kingdom of Judah. On Geba see marg. ref. note. The high-place of Beer-sheba had obtained an evil celebrity (Am. v. 5, viii. 14).

the high places of the gates, &c.] Render,

l See Ezek.
44. 10—14.
m 1 Sam. 2.
36.
n Isai. 30.33.
Jer. 7. 31.
& 19. 6, 11,
12, 13.
o Josh. 15. 8.
p Lev. 18. 21.
Deut. 18. 10.
Ezek. 23. 37,
39.
q See Jer.
19. 13.
Zeph. 1. 5.
r ch. 21. 5.

were in the entering in of the gate of Joshua the governor of the city, which *were* on a man's left hand at the gate of the city. 9 *l*Nevertheless the priests of the high places came not up to the altar of the LORD in Jerusalem, *m*but they did eat of the un- 10 leavened bread among their brethren. ¶ And he defiled *n*To- pheth, which *is* in *o*the valley of the children of Hinnom, *p*that no man might make his son or his daughter to pass through the 11 fire to Molech. And he took away the horses that the kings of Judah had given to the sun, at the entering in of the house of the LORD, by the chamber of Nathan-melech the [1] chamberlain, which *was* in the suburbs, and burned the chariots of the sun 12 with fire. And the altars that *were* *q*on the top of the upper chamber of Ahaz, which the kings of Judah had made, and the altars which *r*Manasseh had made in the two courts of the house of the LORD, did the king beat down, and [2]brake *them* down from thence, and cast the dust of them into the brook Kidron. 13 And the high places that *were* before Jerusalem, which *were* on

---

[1] Or, *eunuch*, or, *officer*.   [2] Or, *ran from thence*.

"He brake down the high-places of the gates, **both that which was** at the entering in of the gate of Joshua, the governor of the city (1 K. xxii. 26 note), **and also that** which was on a man's left hand at the gate of the city." According to this, there were only two "high-places of the gates" (or idolatrous shrines erected in the city at gate-towers) at Jerusalem. The "gate of Joshua" is conjectured to have been a gate in the inner wall; and the "gate of the city," the Valley-gate (modern "Jaffa-gate").

9. *Nevertheless*] Connect this verse with the first clause of *v.* 8. The priests were treated as if they had been disqualified from serving at the Altar by a bodily blemish (Lev. xxi. 21-23). They were not secularised, but remained in the priestly order and received a maintenance from the ecclesiastical revenues. Contrast with this treatment Josiah's severity towards the priests of the high-places in Samaria, who were sacrificed upon their own altars (*v.* 20). Probably the high-place worship in Judæa had continued in the main a worship of Jehovah with idolatrous rites, while in Samaria it had degenerated into an actual worship of other gods.

10. The word Topheth, or Tophet—vari- ously derived from *tôph*, "a drum" or "tabour," because the cries of the sacrificed children were drowned by the noise of such instruments; or, from a root *taph* or *toph*, meaning "to burn"—was a spot in the valley of Hinnom (marg. ref. note). The later Jewish kings, Manasseh and Amon (or, perhaps, Ahaz, 2 Chr. xxviii. 3), had given it over to the Moloch priests for their worship; and here, ever since, the Moloch service had maintained its ground and flourished (marg. reff.).

11. The custom of dedicating a chariot and horses to the Sun is a Persian practice.

There are no traces of it in Assyria; and it is extremely curious to find that it was known to the Jews as early as the reign of Manasseh. The idea of regarding the Sun as a charioteer who drove his horses daily across the sky, so familiar to the Greeks and Romans, may not improbably have been imported from Asia, and may have been at the root of the custom in question. The chariot, or chariots, of the Sun appear to have been used, chiefly if not solely, for sacred processions. They were white, and were drawn probably by white horses. The kings of Judah who gave them were Ma- nasseh and Amon certainly; perhaps Ahaz; perhaps even earlier monarchs, as Joash and Amaziah.

in the suburbs] The expression used here (*parvârim*) is of unknown derivation and occurs nowhere else. A somewhat similar word occurs in 1 Chr. xxvi. 18, viz. *parbar*, which seems to have been a place just out- side the western wall of the Temple, and therefore a sort of "purlieu" or "suburb." The *parvârim* of this passage *may* mean the same place, or it may signify some other "suburb" of the Temple.

12. *the upper chamber of Ahaz*] Con- jectured to be a chamber erected on the flat roof of one of the gateways which led into the Temple Court. It was probably built in order that its roof might be used for the worship of the host of heaven, for which house-tops were considered specially appro- priate (cp. marg. reff.).

brake them down from thence] Rather as in margin, *i.e.* he "hasted and cast the dust into Kidron."

13. On the position of these high-places see 1 K. xi. 7 note. As they were allowed to remain under such kings as Asa, Jehosh- aphat, and Hezekiah, they were probably among the old high-places where Jehovah had been worshipped blamelessly, or at

the right hand of ¹the mount of corruption, which ˢSolomon
the king of Israel had builded for Ashtoreth the abomination of
the Zidonians, and for Chemosh the abomination of the Moabites,
and for Milcom the abomination of the children of Ammon, did
14 the king defile. And he ᵗbrake in pieces the ²images, and cut
down the groves, and filled their places with the bones of men.
15 ¶ Moreover the altar that *was* at Beth-el, *and* the high place
ᵘwhich Jeroboam the son of Nebat, who made Israel to sin,
had made, both that altar and the high place he brake down,
and burned the high place, *and* stamped *it* small to powder,
16 and burned the grove. And as Josiah turned himself, he spied
the sepulchres that *were* there in the mount, and sent, and took
the bones out of the sepulchres, and burned *them* upon the
altar, and polluted it, according to the ˣword of the LORD which
17 the man of God proclaimed, who proclaimed these words. Then
he said, What title *is* that that I see ? And the men of the city
told him, It *is* ʸthe sepulchre of the man of God, which came
from Judah, and proclaimed these things that thou hast done
18 against the altar of Beth-el. And he said, Let him alone; let
no man move his bones. So they let his bones ³alone, with the
19 bones of ᶻthe prophet that came out of Samaria. ¶ And all the
houses also of the high places that *were* ᵃin the cities of Samaria,
which the kings of Israel had made to provoke *the* LORD to
anger, Josiah took away, and did to them according to all the

s 1 Kin.]1.7.

t Ex. 23. 2*t*.
Deut. 7.5,25.

u 1 Kin. 12.
28, 33.

x 1 Kin. 13.2.

y 1 Kin. 13.
1, 30.

z 1Kin.13.31.
a See 2 Chr.
3*t*. 6, 7.

---

¹ That is, the mount of Olives.　　² Heb. *statues*.　　³ Heb. *to escape*.

---

least without any consciousness of guilt (see
1 K. iii. 2 note). Manasseh or Amon had
however restored them to the condition
which they had held in the reign of Solomon, and therefore Josiah would condemn
them to a special defilement.

the mount of corruption] See marg. It is
suspected that the original name was *Har
ham-mishcah*, "mount of anointing," and
that this was changed afterwards, by way of
contempt, into *Har ham-mashchith*, "mount
of corruption."

14. The Law attached uncleanness to the
"bones of men," no less than to actual
corpses (Num. xix. 16). We may gather
from this and other passages (*v.* 20 ; 1 K.
xiii. 2), that the Jews who rejected the
Law were as firm believers in the defilement
as those who adhered to the Law.

15. *and burned the high place*] This "high
place " is to be distinguished from the altar
and the grove (Asherah). It may have been
a shrine or tabernacle, either standing by
itself or else covering the "grove" (*v.* 7 note ;
1 K. xiv. 23 note). As it was "stamped
small to powder," it must have been made
either of metal or stone.

16. To burn human bones was contrary
to all the ordinary Jewish feelings with
respect to the sanctity of the sepulchre, and
had even been denounced as a sin of a
heinous character when committed by a
king of Moab (Am. ii. 1). Joshua did it,
because justified by the Divine command
(marg. ref.).

17. *What title is that ?*] Rather, "What
pillar is that ?" The word in the original indicates a short stone pillar, which was set up
either as a way-mark (Jer. xxxi. 21), or as
a sepulchral monument (Gen. xxxv. 20 ;
Ezek. xxxix. 15).

19. *the cities of Samaria*] The reformation
which Josiah effected in Samaria, is narrated in Chronicles. It implies sovereignty
to the furthest northern limits of Galilee,
and is explained by the general political
history of the East during his reign. Between B.C. 632-626 the Scythians ravaged
the more northern countries of Armenia,
Media, and Cappadocia, and found their
way across Mesopotamia to Syria, and
thence made an attempt to invade Egypt.
As they were neither the fated enemy of
Judah, nor had any hand in bringing that
enemy into the country, no mention is
made of them in the Historical Books of
Scripture. It is only in the Prophets that
we catch glimpses of the fearful sufferings
of the time (Zeph. ii. 4-6 ; Jer. i. 13-15, vi.
2-5 ; Ezek. xxxviii. and xxxix.). The invasion had scarcely gone by, and matters
settled into their former position, when the
astounding intelligence must have reached
Jerusalem that the Assyrian monarchy had
fallen ; that Nineveh was destroyed, and
that her place was to be taken, so far as
Syria and Palestine were concerned, by
Babylon. This event is fixed about B.C.
625, which seems to be exactly the time
during which Josiah was occupied in carry-

b 1 Kin. 13.
2, 32.
c Ex. 22. 20.
1 Kin. 18. 40.
ch. 11. 18.
d 2 Chr. 34.5.
e 2 Chr. 35. 1.
f Ex. 12. 3.
Lev. 23. 5.
Num. 9. 2.
Deut. 16. 2.
g 2 Chr. 35.
18, 19.
h ch. 21. 6.

i Lev. 19. 31.
& 20. 27.
Deut. 18. 11.
k ch. 18. 5.

l ch. 21. 11, 12.
& 24. 3, 4.
Jer. 15. 4.
m ch. 17. 18,
20.
& 18. 11.
& 21. 13.
n 1 Kin. 8. 29.
& 9. 3.
ch. 21. 4, 7.

20 acts that he had done in Beth-el. And b he 1 c slew all the priests of the high places that were there upon the altars, and d burned 21 men's bones upon them, and returned to Jerusalem. ¶ And the king commanded all the people, saying, e Keep the passover unto the LORD your God, f as it is written in the book of this 22 covenant. Surely g there was not holden such a passover from the days of the judges that judged Israel, nor in all the days 23 of the kings of Israel, nor of the kings of Judah; but in the eighteenth year of king Josiah, wherein this passover was holden 24 to the LORD in Jerusalem. ¶ Moreover h the workers with familiar spirits, and the wizards, and the 2 images, and the idols, and all the abominations that were spied in the land of Judah and in Jerusalem, did Josiah put away, that he might perform the words of i the law which were written in the book that 25 Hilkiah the priest found in the house of the LORD. k And like unto him was there no king before him, that turned to the LORD with all his heart, and with all his soul, and with all his might, according to all the law of Moses; neither after him arose there 26 any like him. ¶ Notwithstanding the LORD turned not from the fierceness of his great wrath, wherewith his anger was kindled against Judah, l because of all the 3 provocations that 27 Manasseh had provoked him withal. And the LORD said, I will remove Judah also out of my sight, as m I have removed Israel, and will cast off this city Jerusalem which I have chosen, and 28 the house of which I said, n My name shall be there. ¶ Now

1 Or, sacrificed.   2 Or, teraphim, Gen. 31. 19 note.   3 Heb. angers.

---

ing out his reformation in Samaria. The confusion arising in these provinces from the Scythian invasion and the troubles in Assyria was taken advantage of by Josiah to enlarge his own sovereignty. There is every indication that Josiah did, in fact, unite under his rule all the old "land of Israel" except the trans-Jordanic region, and regarded himself as subject to Nabopolassar of Babylon.

20. Here, as in v. 16, Josiah may have regarded himself as bound to act as he did (marg. ref. b). Excepting on account of the prophecy, he would scarcely have slain the priests upon the altars.

21. See v. 4 note. With this verse the author returns to the narrative of what was done in Josiah's 18th year. The need of the injunction, "as it was written in the book of this covenant," was owing to the fact—not that Josiah had as yet held no Passover—but that the reading of the Book had shown him differences between the existing practice and the letter of the Law —differences consequent upon negligence, or upon the fact that tradition had been allowed in various points to override the Law.

22. The details of the Passover are given by the author of Chronicles (marg. ref.). Its superiority to other Passovers seems to have consisted—(1) in the multitudes that attended it; and (2) in the completeness with which all the directions of the Law

were observed in the celebration. Cp. Neh. viii. 17.

24. perform] Rather, establish. Josiah saw that it was necessary, not only to put down open idolatry, but also to root out the secret practices of a similar character which were sometimes combined with the worship of Jehovah, notwithstanding that the Law forbade them (marg. reff.), and which probably formed, with many, practically almost the whole of their religion.

25. And like unto him, &c.] See xviii. 5 note. We must not press the letter of either passage, but regard both kings as placed among the very best of the kings of Judah.

26. See marg. reff. True repentance might have averted God's anger. But the people had sunk into a condition in which a true repentance was no longer possible. Individuals, like Josiah, were sincere, but the mass of the nation, despite their formal renewal of the Covenant (v. 3), and their outward perseverance in Jehovah-worship (2 Chr. xxxiv. 33), had feigned rather than felt repentance. The earlier chapters of Jeremiah are full at once of reproaches which he directs against the people for their insincerity, and of promises if they would repent in earnest.

27. It added to the guilt of Judah that she had had the warning of her sister Israel's example, and had failed to profit by it.

28. Josiah lived 13 years after the celebration of his great Passover. Of this

the rest of the acts of Josiah, and all that he did, *are* they not
written in the book of the chronicles of the kings of Judah?
29 [o]In his days Pharaoh-nechoh king of Egypt went up against
the king of Assyria to the river Euphrates: and king Josiah
went against him; and he slew him at [p]Megiddo, when he [q]had
30 seen him. [r]And his servants carried him in a chariot dead from
Megiddo, and brought him to Jerusalem, and buried him in his
own sepulchre. And [s]the people of the land took Jehoahaz the
son of Josiah, and anointed him, and made him king in his
31 father's stead. ¶ [1]Jehoahaz *was* twenty and three years old
when he began to reign; and he reigned three months in Jerusalem.
And his mother's name *was* [t]Hamutal, the daughter of
32 Jeremiah of Libnah. And he did *that which was* evil in the
sight of the LORD, according to all that his fathers had done.
33 And Pharaoh-nechoh put him in bands [u]at Riblah in the land
of Hamath, [2]that he might not reign in Jerusalem; and [3]put
the land to a tribute of an hundred talents of silver, and a talent

o 2 Chr. 35. 20.
p Zech. 12. 11.
q ch. 14. 8.
r 2 Chr. 35. 24.
s 2 Chr. 36
t ch. 24. 18.
u ch. 25. 6. Jer. 52. 27.

1 Called *Shallum*, 1 Chr. 3. 15. Jer. 22. 11.
2 Or, *because he reigned.*
3 Heb. *set a mulct upon the land*, 2 Chr. 36. 3.

period we know absolutely nothing, except that in the course of it he seems to have submitted himself to Nabopolassar; who, after the fall of Nineveh, was accepted as the legitimate successor of the Assyrian monarchs by all the nations of the western coast. Josiah, after perhaps a little hesitation (see Jer. ii. 18, 36), followed the example of his neighbours, and frankly accepted the position of an Assyro-Babylonian tributary. In this state matters remained till B.C. 608, when the great events happened which are narrated in *v.* 29.

29. *Pharaoh-Nechoh*] This king is well known to us both from profane historians, and from the Egyptian monuments. He succeeded his father Psammetichus (Psamatik) in the year B.C. 610, and was king of Egypt for 16 years. He was an enlightened and enterprising monarch. The great expedition here mentioned was an attempt to detach from the newly-formed Babylonian empire the important tract of country extending from Egypt to the Euphrates at Carchemish. Calculating probably on the friendship or neutrality of most of the native powers, the Egyptian monarch, having made preparations for the space of two years, set out on his march, probably following the (usual) coast route through Philistia and Sharon, from thence intending to cross by Megiddo into the Jezreel (Esdraelon) plain.

the king of Assyria] This expression does not imply that Nineveh had not yet fallen. The Jews, accustomed to Assyrian monarchs, who held their courts alternately at Nineveh and Babylon (xix. 36; 2 Chr. xxxiii. 11), *at first* regarded the change as merely dynastic, and transferred to the new king, Nabopolassar, the title which they had been accustomed to give to their former suzerains. When, later on, Nebuchadnezzar invaded their country they found that he did not call himself "King of Assyria," but "King of Babylon," and thenceforth that title came into use; but the annalist who wrote the life of Josiah immediately upon his death, and whom the author of Kings copied, used, not unnaturally, the more familiar, though less correct, designation.

Josiah went against him] Josiah probably regarded himself as in duty bound to oppose the march of a hostile force through his territory to attack his suzerain. For further details see the account in Chronicles (marg. ref.). On Megiddo, see Josh. xii. 21 note.

30. *dead*] It appears from a comparison of this passage with 2 Chronicles (marg. ref.) that Josiah was not actually killed in the battle.

Jehoahaz] Or Shallum (marg. note). He may have taken the name of Jehoahaz (="the Lord possesses") on his accession. He was not the eldest son of Josiah (see *v.* 36 note). The mention of "anointing" here favours the view that there was some irregularity in the succession (see 1 K. i. 34 note).

33. Pharaoh-Nechoh, after bringing Phœnicia and Syria under his rule, and penetrating as far as Carchemish, returned to Southern Syria, and learnt what had occurred at Jerusalem in his absence. He sent orders to Jehoahaz to attend the court which he was holding at Riblah, and Jehoahaz fell into the trap (Ezek. xix. 4).

Riblah still retains its name. It is situated on the Orontes, in the Cœle-Syrian valley, near the point where the valley opens into a wide and fertile plain. Neco seems to have been the first to perceive its importance. Afterwards Nebuchadnezzar made it his head-quarters during his sieges of Jerusalem and Tyre (xxv. 21; Jer. xxxix. 5, lii. 9, 10, 26).

ᵉ 2 Chr. 36.4.
ʸ See ch. 24. 17.
Dan. 1. 7.
ᶻ Matt. 1. 11, called *Jakim*.
ᵃ Jer. 22. 11, 12.
Ezek. 19.3,4.
ᵇ ver. 33.
ᶜ 2 Chr. 36. 5.

34 of gold. And ˣPharaoh-nechoh made Eliakim the son of Josiah king in the room of Josiah his father, and ʸturned his name to ᶻJehoiakim, and took Jehoahaz away: ᵃand he came to Egypt, 35 and died there. And Jehoiakim gave ᵇthe silver and the gold to Pharaoh; but he taxed the land to give the money according to the commandment of Pharaoh: he exacted the silver and the gold of the people of the land, of every one according 36 to his taxation, to give *it* unto Pharaoh-nechoh. ¶ ᶜJehoiakim *was* twenty and five years old when he began to reign; and he reigned eleven years in Jerusalem. And his mother's name 37 *was* Zebudah, the daughter of Pedaiah of Rumah. And he did *that which was* evil in the sight of the LORD, according to all that his fathers had done.

ᵃ 2 Chr. 36.6.

CHAP. 24. IN ᵃhis days Nebuchadnezzar king of Babylon came up, and Jehoiakim became his servant three years: then he

ᵇ Jer. 25. 9. & 32. 28. Ezek. 19. 8.

2 turned and rebelled against him. ᵇAnd the LORD sent against him bands of the Chaldees, and bands of the Syrians, and bands of the Moabites, and bands of the children of Ammon, and sent them against Judah to destroy it, ᶜaccording to the word of the

ᶜ ch. 20. 17. & 21. 12, 13, 14. & 23. 27.
ᵈ ch. 21.2,11. & 23. 26.
ᵉ ch. 21. 16.

3 LORD, which he spake ¹by his servants the prophets. Surely at the commandment of the LORD came *this* upon Judah, to remove *them* out of his sight, ᵈfor the sins of Manasseh, according to 4 all that he did; ᵉand also for the innocent blood that he shed:

---

¹ Heb. *by the hand of.*

---

34. *in the room of Josiah his father*] Not "in the room of Jehoahaz his brother;" the phrase is intended to mark the fact, that Neco did not acknowledge that Jehoahaz had ever been king.

turned his name to Jehoiakim] Cp. *v.* 30 and xxiv. 17. It seems likely, from their purely Jewish character, that the new names of the Jewish kings, though formally imposed by the suzerain, were selected by the individuals themselves. The change now made consisted merely in the substitution of Jehovah for El ("God, Jehovah, will set up"). Both names alike refer to the promise which God made to David (2 Sam. vii. 12) and imply a hope that, notwithstanding the threats of the Prophets, the seed of David would still be allowed to remain upon the throne.

36. *twenty and five years old*] Jehoiakim was therefore two years older than his half-brother, Jehoahaz (*v.* 31). See his character in *v.* 37; 2 Chr. xxxvi. 8; Ezek. xix. 5-7; Jer. xxii. 13-17, xxvi. 20-23, xxxvi.

XXIV. 1. *In his days*] *i.e.* B.C. 605, which was the third completed (Dan. i. 1), and fourth commencing (Jer. xxv. 1), year of Jehoiakim.

Nebuchadnezzar] or Nebuchadrezzar, which is closer to the original, *Nabu-kudurri-uzur*. This name, like most Babylonian names, is made up of three elements, *Nebo*, the well-known god (Isai. xlvi. 1), *kudur*, of doubtful signification (perhaps "crown," perhaps "landmark"), and *uzur* "protects." Nebuchadnezzar, the son of Nabopolassar, and second monarch of the Babylonian empire,

ascended the throne, B.C. 604, and reigned forty-three years, dying B.C. 561. He married Amuhia (or Amyitis), daughter of Cyaxares, king of the Medes, and was the most celebrated of all the Babylonian sovereigns. No other heathen king occupies so much space in Scripture. He was not actual king at this time, but only Crown Prince and leader of the army under his father. As he would be surrounded with all the state and magnificence of a monarch, the Jews would naturally look upon him as actual king.

came up] Nebuchadnezzar began his campaign by attacking and defeating Neco's Egyptians at Carchemish (Jer. xlvi. 2). He then pressed forward towards the south, overran Syria, Phœnicia, and Judæa, took Jerusalem, and carried off a portion of the inhabitants as prisoners (Dan. i. 1-4): after which he proceeded southwards, and had reached the borders of Egypt when he was suddenly recalled to Babylon by the death of his father.

three years] Probably from B.C. 605 to B.C. 602. Jehoiakim rebelled because he knew Nebuchadnezzar to be engaged in important wars in some other part of Asia.

2. See marg. reff. Instead of coming up in person Nebuchadnezzar sent against Jehoiakim his own troops and those of the neighbouring nations.

The ravages of the Moabites and the Ammonites are specially alluded to in the following passages: Jer. xlviii. 26, 27, xlix. 1; Ezek. xxv. 3-6; Zeph. ii. 8.

for he filled Jerusalem with innocent blood; which the LORD
5 would not pardon. ¶Now the rest of the acts of Jehoiakim,
and all that he did, *are* they not written in the book of the
6 chronicles of the kings of Judah? *f*So Jehoiakim slept with
7 his fathers: and Jehoiachin his son reigned in his stead. And
*g*the king of Egypt came not again any more out of his land:
for *h*the king of Babylon had taken from the river of Egypt
unto the river Euphrates all that pertained to the king of Egypt.
8 ¶ [1]*i*Jehoiachin *was* eighteen years old when he began to reign,
and he reigned in Jerusalem three months. And his mother's
name *was* Nehushta, the daughter of Elnathan of Jerusalem.
9 And he did *that which was* evil in the sight of the LORD, accord-
10 ing to all that his father had done. ¶ *k*At that time the servants of Nebuchadnezzar king of Babylon came up against
11 Jerusalem, and the city [2]was besieged. And Nebuchadnezzar
king of Babylon came against the city, and his servants did
12 besiege it. *l*And Jehoiachin the king of Judah went out to the
king of Babylon, he, and his mother, and his servants, and his
princes, and his [3]officers: *m*and the king of Babylon *n*took him
13 *o*in the eighth year of his reign. *p*And he carried out thence all
the treasures of the house of the LORD, and the treasures of the
king's house, and *q*cut in pieces all the vessels of gold which
Solomon king of Israel had made in the temple of the LORD, *r*as
14 the LORD had said. And *s*he carried away all Jerusalem, and
all the princes, and all the mighty men of valour, *t even* ten

Right margin notes:
f See 2 Chr.
36. 6, 8.
Jer. 22. 18,19.
& 36. 30.
g See Jer.
37. 5, 7.
h Jer. 46. 2.
i 2 Chr. 36. 9.

k Dan. 1. 1.

l Jer. 24. 1.
Ezek. 17. 12.
m Nebuchad-
nezzar's
eighth year,
Jer. 25. 1.
n See ch. 25.
27.
o See Jer.
52. 28.
p ch. 20. 17.
Isai. 39. 6.
q See Dan.
5. 2, 3.
r Jer. 20. 5.
s Jer. 24. 1.
t See Jer. 52.
28.

---

[1] Called *Jeconiah*, 1 Chr. 3.
16. Jer. 24. 1, and Co-
niah, Jer. 22. 24, 28.
[2] Heb. *came into siege.*
[3] Or, *eunuchs*

---

5. Comparing Jer. xxii. 19, xxxvi. 6,
30, and Ezek. xix. 8, 9, it would seem that
Nebuchadnezzar must in the fifth or sixth
year after Jehoiakim's revolt have determined to go in person to Riblah, to direct
operations, first against Tyre and then
against Jerusalem. Jehoiakim was taken
prisoner, and brought in chains to Nebuchadnezzar, who at first designed to convey him
to Babylon, but afterwards had him taken
to Jerusalem, where he was executed.
Afterwards, when the Babylonians had
withdrawn, the remains were collected and
interred in the burying-place of Manasseh,
so that the king ultimately "slept with his
fathers" (*v.* 6).

6. *Jehoiachin*] Also called Jeconiah and
Coniah. Jehoiachin and Jeconiah both
mean "Jehovah will establish," Coniah,
"Jehovah establishes." Probably his original name was Jehoiachin. When he ascended the throne, and was required to take
a new name, anxious not to lose the good
omen contained in his old one, he simply
transposed the two elements. Jeremiah
shortened this new name from Jeconiah to
Coniah, thus cutting off from it the notion
of futurity, to imply that that would not be
which the name declared would be. In
other words, "Jehovah establishes," but
this prince he will not establish.

7. Neco, from the year of the battle of Carchemish, confined himself to his own country
and made no efforts to recover Syria or Judæa.

8. *his mother's name*] On the position of
the "queen mother" see 1 K. xv. 10
note. Nehushta's rank and dignity are
strongly marked by the distinct and express mention which is made of her in
almost every place where her son's history is touched (*v.* 12; cp. Jer. xxii. 26,
xxix. 2).

10. *came up against Jerusalem*] The cause
and circumstances of this siege are equally
obscure. Perhaps Nebuchadnezzar detected
Jehoiachin in some attempt to open communications with Egypt.

12. *the eighth year*] Jeremiah calls it the
seventh year (Jer. lii. 28), a statement which
implies only a different manner of counting
regnal years.

13. On the first capture of the city in the
fourth (third) year of Jehoiakim (Dan. i. 2;
2 Chr. xxxvi. 7), the vessels carried off consisted of smaller and lighter articles; while
now the heavier articles, as the Table of
Shewbread, the Altar of Incense, the Ark
of the Covenant were stripped of their gold,
which was carried away by the conquerors.
Little remained more precious than brass at
the time of the final capture in the reign of
Zedekiah (xxv. 13-17).

14. The entire number of the captives
was not more than 11,000. They consisted
of three classes: (1) the "princes" or
"mighty of the land," *i.e.* courtiers,
priests, elders, and all who had any position or dignity—in number 3000 (cp. *vv.*

u So 1 Sam. 13. 19, 22.
x ch. 25. 12. Jer. 40. 7.
y 2Chr.36.10. ch. 20. 18. Jer. 22. 24, &c.
z See Jer. 52. 28.

a Jer. 37. 1.
b 1 Chr. 3.15. 2 Chr. 36. 10.
c 2 Chr. 36.4.
d 2 Chr. 36.11 Jer. 37. 1. & 52. 1.
e ch. 23. 31.
f 2Chr.36.12.

g 2Chr.36.13. Ezek. 17. 15.

thousand captives, and *u*all the craftsmen and smiths: none 15 remained, save *x*the poorest sort of the people of the land. And *y*he carried away Jehoiachin to Babylon, and the king's mother, and the king's wives, and his [1]officers, and the mighty of the land, *those* carried he into captivity from Jerusalem to Babylon. 16 And *z*all the men of might, *even* seven thousand, and craftsmen and smiths a thousand, all *that were* strong *and* apt for war, even them the king of Babylon brought captive to Babylon. 17 ¶ And *a*the king of Babylon made Mattaniah *b*his father's brother king in his stead, and *c*changed his name to Zedekiah. 18 *d*Zedekiah *was* twenty and one years old when he began to reign, and he reigned eleven years in Jerusalem. And his mother's name *was* *e*Hamutal, the daughter of Jeremiah of 19 Libnah. *f*And he did *that which was* evil in the sight of the 20 LORD, according to all that Jehoiakim had done. For through the anger of the LORD it came to pass in Jerusalem and Judah, until he had cast them out from his presence, *g*that Zedekiah rebelled against the king of Babylon.

[1] Or, *eunuchs.*

14, 16). (2) The "mighty men of valour" or "men of might," *i.e.* the soldier class, who were 7000. And (3) craftsmen or artisans, who numbered 1000. The word here translated "craftsmen" denotes artisans in stone, wood, or metal, and thus includes our "masons, carpenters, and smiths." The word translated "smiths" means strictly "lock-smiths." The object of carrying off these persons was twofold : (1) it deprived the conquered city of those artisans who were of most service in war ; and (2) it gave the conqueror a number of valuable assistants in the construction of his buildings and other great works. The Assyrian monarchs frequently record their removal of the skilled artisans from a conquered country. The population of the ancient city has been calculated, from its area, at 15,000. The remnant left was therefore about 5000 or 6000.

15. *the mighty of the land*] Or "the great," "the powerful." The word used is quite distinct from that in *vv.* 14 and 16. It refers, not to bodily strength or fitness for war, but to civil rank or dignity. The term would include all civil and all ecclesiastical functionaries — the nobles, courtiers, and elders of the city on the one hand, the priests, Prophets (among them, Ezekiel), and Levites on the other.

17. Mattaniah, son of Josiah and brother of Jehoahaz, but thirteen years his junior, adopted a name significant of the blessings promised by Jeremiah to the reign of a king whose name should be "Jehovah, our righteousness" (Jer. xxiii. 5-8).

19. *he did that which was evil*] The character of Zedekiah seems to have been weak rather than wicked. Consult Jer. xxxiv., xxxvii. His chief recorded sins were : (1) his refusal to be guided in his political conduct by Jeremiah's counsels, while never-

theless he admitted him to be a true Jehovah-Prophet ; and (2) his infraction of the allegiance which he had sworn to Nebuchadnezzar.

20. *it came to pass*] Some prefer "came this to pass :" in the sense, "Through the anger of the Lord was it that another bad king ruled in Jerusalem and in Judah:" concluding the chapter with the word "presence ;" and beginning the next chapter with the words, "And Zedekiah rebelled against the king of Babylon."

rebelled] The Book of Jeremiah explains the causes of rebellion. In Zedekiah's early years there was an impression, both at Jerusalem (Jer. xxviii. 1-11) and at Babylon (do. xxix. 5-28), that Nebuchadnezzar was inclined to relent. By embassy to Babylon (do. xxix. 3), and a personal visit (do. li. 59), Zedekiah strove hard to obtain the restoration of the captives and the holy vessels. But he found Nebuchadnezzar obdurate. Zedekiah returned to his own country greatly angered against his suzerain, and immediately proceeded to plot a rebellion. He sought the alliance of the kings of Tyre, Sidon, Moab, Ammon, and Edom (do. xxvii. 3), and made overtures to Hophra, in Egypt, which were favourably received (Ezek. xvii. 15), whereupon he openly revolted, apparently in his ninth year, B.C. 588. Tyre, it must be remembered, was all this time defying the power of Nebuchadnezzar, and thus setting an example of successful revolt very encouraging to the neighbouring states. Nebuchadnezzar, while constantly maintaining an army in Syria, and continuing year after year his attempts to reduce Tyre (cp. Ezek. xxix. 18) was, it would seem, too much occupied with other matters, such, probably, as the reduction of Susiana (Jer. xlix. 34-38), to devote more than a small share of his attention to his extreme western

Chap. 25. AND it came to pass *a*in the ninth year of his reign, in the tenth month, in the tenth *day* of the month, *that* Nebuchadnezzar king of Babylon came, he, and all his host, against Jerusalem, and pitched against it ; and they built forts against it 2 round about. And the city was besieged unto the eleventh year 3 of king Zedekiah. And on the ninth *day* of the *b*fourth month the famine prevailed in the city, and there was no bread for the 4 people of the land. And *c*the city was broken up, and all the men of war *fled* by night by the way of the gate between two walls, which *is* by the king's garden : (now the Chaldees *were* against the city round about :) and *d*the king went the way 5 toward the plain. And the army of the Chaldees pursued after the king, and overtook him in the plains of Jericho : and all his 6 army were scattered from him. So they took the king, and brought him up to the king of Babylon *e*to Riblah ; and they 7 *1*gave judgment upon him. And they slew the sons of Zedekiah before his eyes, and *2f*put out the eyes of Zedekiah, and

a 2Chr.33.17.
Jer. 34. 2.
& 39. 1.
& 52. 4, 5.

b Jer. 39. 2.
& 52. 6.

c Jer. 39. 2.
& 52. 7, &c.

d Jer. 39.
4—7.
& 52. 7.
Ezek. 12.12.

e Jer. 52. 9.

f Jer. 39. 7.

---

¹ Heb. *spake judgment with him.*   ² Heb. *made blind.*

---

frontier. In that same year, however (B.C. 588), the new attitude taken by Egypt induced him to direct to that quarter the main force of the Empire, and to take the field in person.

XXV. 1. *in the ninth year*, &c.] As the final catastrophe approaches, the historian becomes more close and exact in his dates, marking not only the year, but the *month* and the *day*, on which the siege began, no less than those on which it closed (*v.* 3). From Ezek. xxiv. 1 we find that on the very day when the host of Nebuchadnezzar made its appearance before Jerusalem the fact was revealed to Ezekiel in Babylonia, and the fate of the city announced to him (do. *vv.* 6–14). The army seems to have at first spread itself over all Judæa. It fought, not only against Jerusalem, but especially against Lachish and Azekah (Jer. xxxiv. 7), two cities of the south (2 Chr. xi. 9), which had probably been strongly garrisoned in order to maintain the communication with Egypt. This division of the Babylonian forces encouraged Hophra to put his troops in motion and advance to the relief of his Jewish allies (Jer. xxxvii. 5). On hearing this, Nebuchadnezzar broke up from before Jerusalem and marched probably to Azekah and Lachish. The Egyptians shrank back, returned into their own country (Jer. xxxvii. 7 ; Ezek. xvii. 17), and took no further part in the war. Nebuchadnezzar then led back his army, and once more invested the city. (It is uncertain whether the date at the beginning of this verse refers to the first or to the second investment.)

forts] Probably moveable towers, sometimes provided with battering-rams, which the besiegers advanced against the walls, thus bringing their fighting men on a level with their antagonists. Such towers are seen in the Assyrian sculptures.

2. The siege lasted almost exactly a year

and a half. Its calamities—famine, pestilence, and intense suffering—are best understood from the Lamentations of Jeremiah, written probably almost immediately after the capture.

4. *the city was broken up*] Rather, "broken **into**," *i.e.* A breach was made about midnight in the northern wall (Ezek. ix. 2), and an entry effected into the second or lower city (xxii. 14 note), which was protected by the wall of Manasseh (2 Chr. xxxiii. 14).

Precipitate flight followed on the advance of the Babylonians to the "middle gate," or gate of communication between the upper and the lower cities. This position was only a little north of the royal palace, which the king therefore quitted. He escaped by the royal garden at the junction of the Hinnom and Kidron valleys, passing between **the** two walls which skirted on either side the valley of the Tyropœon.

toward the plain] "The Arabah" or the great depression which bounds Palestine Proper on the east (Num. xxi. 4 note). The "way toward the Arabah" is here the road leading eastward over Olivet to Bethany and Jericho.

5. Jeremiah (xxxviii. 23) and Ezekiel (xii. 13) had prophesied this capture ; and the latter had also prophesied the dispersion of the troops (*v.* 14).

6. *to Riblah*] See xxiii. 33 note. A position whence Nebuchadnezzar could most conveniently superintend the operations against Tyre and Jerusalem. In the absence of the monarch, the siege of Jerusalem was conducted by a number of his officers, the chief of whom were Nebuzar-adan, the captain of the guard, and Nergal-shar-ezer (Neriglissar), the Rab-mag (Jer. xxxix. 3, 13).

7. *before his eyes*] This refinement of cruelty seems to have especially shocked the Jews, whose manners were less bar-

v See Jer.
52. 12–14.
h See ch. 24.
12.
& ver. 27.
i Jer. 39. 9.
k 2 Chr.36.19.
l Jer. 39. 8.
Amos 2. 5.

m Neh. 1. 3.
Jer. 52. 14.
n Jer. 39. 9.
& 52. 15.

o ch. 24. 14.
Jer. 39. 10.
& 40. 7.
& 52. 16.
p ch. 20. 17.
Jer.27.19,22.
q 1 Kin. 7.15.
r 1 Kin. 7.27.
s 1 Kin. 7.23.
t Ex. 27. 3.
1 Kin. 7. 45,
50.

v 1 Kin. 7.47.
x 1 Kin. 7.15.
Jer. 52. 21.

bound him with fetters of brass, and carried him to Babylon.
8 ¶ And in the fifth month, *v* on the seventh *day* of the month,
which is *h* the nineteenth year of king Nebuchadnezzar king of
Babylon, *i* came Nebuzar-adan, ¹ captain of the guard, a servant
9 of the king of Babylon, unto Jerusalem : *k* and he burnt the
house of the LORD, *l* and the king's house, and all the houses of
Jerusalem, and every great *man's* house burnt he with fire.
10 And all the army of the Chaldees, that *were with* the captain of
the guard, *m* brake down the walls of Jerusalem round about.
11 *n* Now the rest of the people *that were* left in the city, and the
² fugitives that fell away to the king of Babylon, with the remnant of the multitude, did Nebuzar-adan the captain of the
12 guard carry away. But the captain of the guard *o* left of the
13 poor of the land *to be* vinedressers and husbandmen. ¶ And *p* the
q pillars of brass that *were* in the house of the LORD, and *r* the
bases, and *s* the brasen sea that *was* in the house of the LORD,
did the Chaldees break in pieces, and carried the brass of them
14 to Babylon. And *t* the pots, and the shovels, and the snuffers,
and the spoons, and all the vessels of brass wherewith they
15 ministered, took they away. And the firepans, and the bowls,
and such things as *were* of gold, *in* gold, and of silver, *in* silver,
16 the captain of the guard took away. The two pillars, ³ one sea,
and the bases which Solomon had made for the house of the
17 LORD ; *x* the brass of all these vessels was without weight. *x* The

---

¹ Or, *chief marshal.*   ² Heb. *fallen away.*   ³ Heb. *the one sea.*

---

barous than those of most Orientals. It is
noted by Jeremiah in two places (xxxix. 6,
lii. 10).

and put out the eyes of Zedekiah] Blinding
has always been among the most common
of secondary punishments in the East (cp.
Judg. xvi. 21). The blinding of Zedekiah
reconciled in a very remarkable way prophecies, apparently contradictory, which
had been made concerning him. Jeremiah
had prophesied distinctly that he would be
carried to Babylon (xxxii. 5, xxxiv. 3). Ezekiel had said that he should not "see Babylon" (xii. 13). His deprivation of sight
before he was carried to the conqueror's
capital fulfilled the predictions of both
Prophets.

with fetters of brass] Lit. (see Jer. xxxix.
7 marg.), "with **two chains** of brass."
The Assyrians' captives are usually represented as bound hand and foot—the two
hands secured by one chain, the two feet by
another. According to Jewish tradition
Zedekiah was, like other slaves, forced to
work in a mill at Babylon. Jeremiah tells us
that he was kept in prison till he died (lii. 11).

8. *the nineteenth year of king N.*] B.C. 586,
if we count from the real date of his accession (B.C. 604) ; but B.C. 587, if, with the
Jews, we regard him as beginning to reign
when he was sent by his father to recover
Syria and gained the battle of Carchemish
(in B.C. 605).

captain of the guard] Lit., "the chief of
the executioners" (Gen. xxxvii. 36).

9. *he burnt the house of the* LORD] Cp. the

prophecies of Jeremiah (xxi. 10, xxxiv. 2,
xxxviii. 18, 23). Psalm lxxix. is thought to
have been written soon after this destruction of the Temple.

11. *the fugitives* &c.] It was from a fear
of the treatment which he would receive at
the hands of these deserters that Zedekiah
persisted in defending the city to the last
(Jer. xxxviii. 19).

12. There was probably an intention of
sending colonists into the country from some
other part of the Empire, as the Assyrians
had done in Samaria (xvii. 24).

13. *the pillars of brass,* &c.] All the more
precious treasures had been already removed from the Temple (xxiv. 13). But
there still remained many things, the list of
which is given in Jer. lii. 17–23 much more
fully than in this place. Objects in brass,
or rather bronze, were frequently carried off
by the Assyrians from the conquered nations. Bronze was highly valued, being
the chief material both for arms and imple-
ments. The breaking up of the pillars,
bases, &c., shews that it was for the material, and not for the workmanship, that
they were valued. On the various articles
consult the marg. reff.

16. *without weight*] The Babylonians did
not take the trouble to weigh the brass as
they did the gold and silver. In the Assyrian
monuments there are representations of the
weighing of captured articles in gold and
silver in the presence of the royal scribes.

17. Compare with this description the
accounts in marg. reff. The height of the

height of the one pillar *was* eighteen cubits, and the chapiter
upon it *was* brass: and the height of the chapiter three cubits;
and the wreathen work, and pomegranates upon the chapiter
round about, all of brass: and like unto these had the second
18 pillar with wreathen work. ¶ *v*And the captain of the guard
took *z*Seraiah the chief priest, and *a*Zephaniah the second
19 priest, and the three keepers of the ¹door: and out of the city
he took an ²officer that was set over the men of war, and *b*five
men of them that ³were in the king's presence, which were found
in the city, and the ⁴principal scribe of the host, which mustered
the people of the land, and threescore men of the people of
20 the land *that were* found in the city: and Nebuzar-adan captain of the guard took these, and brought them to the king of
21 Babylon to Riblah: and the king of Babylon smote them, and
slew them at Riblah in the land of Hamath. *c*So Judah was
22 carried away out of their land. ¶ *d*And *as for* the people that
remained in the land of Judah, whom Nebuchadnezzar king of
Babylon had left, even over them he made Gedaliah the son of
23 Ahikam, the son of Shaphan, ruler. And when all the *c*captains of the armies, they and their men, heard that the king of
Babylon had made Gedaliah governor, there came to Gedaliah
to Mizpah, even Ishmael the son of Nethaniah, and Johanan the
son of Careah, and Seraiah the son of Tanhumeth the Netopha-

v Jer. 52. 2¹,
&c.
z 1 Chr. 6. 14.
Ezra 7. 1.
a Jer. 21. 1.
& 29. 25.
b See Jer.
52. 25.

c Lev. 26. 33.
Deut. 28. 36,
64.
ch. 23. 27.
d Jer. 40. 5.
e Jer. 40. 7,
8, 9.

---

¹ Heb. *threshold.*
² Or, *eunuch.*
³ Heb. *saw the king's face,*
Esth. 1. 14.
⁴ Or, *scribe of the captain of the host.*

---

capital ("*three* cubits") must be corrected,
in accordance with those passages, to "*five*
cubits."
  18. It devolved on Nebuzaradan to select
for exemplary punishment the persons
whom he regarded as most guilty, either in
respect of the original rebellion or of the
protracted resistance. Instead of taking
indiscriminately the first comers, he first
selected those who by their offices would be
likely to have had most authority—the High-
Priest; the second priest (xxiii. 4 note);
three of the Temple Levites; the commandant of the city; five members of the king's
Privy Council (or seven, see *r.* 19 note); and
the secretary (or adjutant) of the captain of
the host. To these he added sixty others, who
were accounted "princes." Compared with
the many occasions on which Assyrian and
Persian conquerors put to death hundreds
or thousands after taking a revolted town,
Nebuzaradan (and Nebuchadnezzar) must
be regarded as moderate, or even merciful,
in their vengeance. Cp. Jer. xl. 2-5.
  the three keepers of the door] Rather,
"three keepers.". The Hebrew has no
article. The Temple "door-keepers" in
the time of Solomon numbered twenty-four
(1 Chr. xxvi. 17, 18), who were probably
under six chiefs. After the Captivity the
chiefs are either six (Ez. ii. 42; Neh. vii.
45) or four (1 Chr. ix. 17).
  19. *out of the city*] This clause shows that
the five persons mentioned in *r.* 18 were
taken out of the Temple.
  five men] Or, "seven men," according to

Jer. lii. 25. It is impossible to say which of
the two numbers is correct.
  of them that were in the king's presence] See
marg. A mode of speech arising from the custom of Eastern rulers to withdraw themselves as much as possible from the view of
their subjects.
  21. *So Judah was carried away*] The kingdom of the two tribes was at an end; and
the task of the historian might seem to be
accomplished. He still, however, desires to
notice two things: (1) the fate of the remnant (*rr.* 22-26) left in the land by Nebuzaradan; and (2) the fate of Jehoiachin,
who, of all those led into captivity, was the
least to blame (*rr.* 27-30).
  22. We may be allowed to conjecture that
Jeremiah, in gratitude for Ahikam's service
to himself (Jer. xxvi. 24), recommended his
son Gedaliah to Nebuzaradan, and through
him to Nebuchadnezzar, for the office of
governor.
  23. *the captains of the armies*] *i.e.* the officers of the troops who had fled from Jerusalem with Zedekiah (*r.* 4), and had then
dispersed and gone into hiding (*v.* 5).
  For Mizpah, see Josh. xviii. 26 note.
  the Netophathite] Netophah, the city of
Ephai (cp. Jer. xl. 8), appears to have been
in the neighbourhood of Bethlehem (Neh.
vii. 26; Ezr. ii. 21, 22). The name is perhaps continued in the modern *Antubeh,*
about 2½ miles S.S.E. of Jerusalem.
  a Maachathite] Maachah lay in the stony
country east of the upper Jordan, bordering
upon Bashan (Deut. iii. 14).

thite, and Jaazaniah the son of a Maachathite, they and their
24 men.   And Gedaliah sware to them, and to their men, and said
unto them, Fear not to be the servants of the Chaldees: dwell
in the land, and serve the king of Babylon; and it shall be well
f Jer. 41. 1, 2.   25 with you.   But *f* it came to pass in the seventh month, that
Ishmael the son of Nethaniah, the son of Elishama, of the seed
[1] royal, came, and ten men with him, and smote Gedaliah, that
he died, and the Jews and the Chaldees that were with him at
26 Mizpah.   And all the people, both small and great, and the
g Jer. 43. 4, 7.   captains of the armies, arose, *g* and came to Egypt: for they
h Jer. 52. 31,   27 were afraid of the Chaldees.   ¶ *h* And it came to pass in the
&c.   seven and thirtieth year of the captivity of Jehoiachin king of
Judah, in the twelfth month, on the seven and twentieth *day* of
the month, *that* Evil-merodach king of Babylon in the year that
i See Gen.   he began to reign *i* did lift up the head of Jehoiachin king of
40. 13, 20.   28 Judah out of prison; and he spake [2] kindly to him, and set his
throne above the throne of the kings that *were* with him in
k 2 Sam. 9.7.   29 Babylon; and changed his prison garments: and he did *k* eat
30 bread continually before him all the days of his life.   And his
allowance *was* a continual allowance given him of the king, a
daily rate for every day, all the days of his life.

[1] Heb. *of the kingdom.*   [2] Heb. *good things with him.*

---

24. As rebels against the Babylonian
king, their lives were forfeit.   Gedaliah
pledged himself to them by oath, that, if
they gave no further cause of complaint,
their past offences should be forgiven.

25, 26. Jeremiah gives this history with
much fulness of detail (xli–xliii).

27. The captivity of Jehoiachin commenced in the year B.C. 597—the eighth
year of Nebuchadnezzar.   It terminated
B.C. 561—the first year of Evil-merodach,
the son and successor of Nebuchadnezzar.
He reigned only two years, being murdered
by his brother-in-law, Neriglissar, or Nergal-
shar-ezer.   He is said to have provoked his
fate by lawless government and intemperance.

28. *the kings that were with him*] Probably
captive kings, like Jehoiachin himself.   Cp.
Judg. i. 7.

29. Evil-merodach gave him garments
befitting his rank.   To dress a man suitably
to his position was the first thought of an
Oriental (Gen. xli. 42; Esth. viii. 15;
Dan. v. 29; Luke xv. 22).   So again,
Oriental kings regarded it as a part of their
greatness to feed daily a vast multitude of
persons at their Courts (see 1 K. iv. 22, 23).
Of these, as here, a certain number had
the special privilege of sitting actually at
the royal board, while the others ate separately, generally at a lower level.   See
Judg. i. 7; 2 Sam. ix. 13; 1 K. ii. 7; Ps.
xli. 9.

30. *allowance*] From the treasury, in order
to enable him to maintain the state proper
to his rank, and in addition to his food at
the royal table.   Jehoiachin, to the day of
his death, lived in peace and comfort at the
court of Babylon (cp. Jer. lii. 34).

CHRONICLES.

INTRODUCTION TO BOOKS I. AND II.

1. LIKE the two Books of Kings, the two Books of Chronicles formed originally a single work, the separation of which into two "Books" is referable to the Septuagint translators, whose division was adopted by Jerome, and from whom it passed to the various branches of the Western Church. In the Hebrew Bibles the title of the work means literally "the daily acts" or "occurrences,"[1] a title originally applied to the accounts of the reigns of the several kings, but afterwards applied to general works made up from these particular narratives.

The Septuagint translators substituted one which they regarded as more suitable to the contents of the work and the position that it occupies among the Historical Books of the Bible. This was *Paraleipomena*, or "the things omitted"—a name intended to imply that Chronicles was *supplementary* to Samuel and Kings, written, *i.e.*, mainly for the purpose of supplying the omissions of the earlier history.

The English title, "Chronicles," (derived from the Vulgate) is a term primarily significative of time; but in practical use it designates a simple and primitive style of history rather than one in which the chronological element is peculiarly prominent.

2. The "Book of Chronicles" stands in a position unlike that occupied by any other Book of the Old Testament. It is historical, yet not new history. The writer traverses ground that has been already trodden by others.[2]

His purpose in so doing is sufficiently indicated by the practical object he had in view, viz., that of meeting the peculiar difficulties of his own day. The people had lately returned from the Captivity[3] and had rebuilt the Temple;[4] but they had not yet gathered up the threads of the old national life, broken by the Captivity. They were therefore reminded, in the first place, of their entire history, of the whole past course of mundane events, and of the position which they themselves held among the nations of the earth. This was done, curtly and drily, but sufficiently, by genealogies,[5] which have always possessed a peculiar attraction for Orientals. They were then more especially reminded of their own past as an

---

[1] 1 K. xi. 41; 2 Chr. xii. 15, xxxiii. 19, &c.

[2] The author of Kings wrote, as has been already shown (Introduction to Kings, p. 264), before the return from the Captivity. The author of Chronicles writes after the return.

[3] See 1 Chr. ix. 1–34; 2 Chr. xxxvi. 20–23. See p. 446, note 6.

[4] 1 Chr. ix. 11, 13, 19, &c.

[5] 1 Chr. i.–viii.

organised nation—a settled people with a religion which has a fixed home in the centre of the nation's life. It was the strong conviction of the writer that the whole future prosperity of his countrymen was bound up with the preservation of the Temple service, with the proper maintenance of the priests and Levites, the regular establishment of the "courses," and the rightful distribution of the several ministrations of the Temple among the Levitical families. He therefore drew the attention of his countrymen to the past history of the Temple, under David, Solomon, and the later kings of Judah; pointing out that in almost every instance temporal rewards and punishments followed in exact accordance with the attitude in which the king placed himself towards the national religion. Such a picture of the past, a sort of condensed view of the entire previous history, written in the idiom of the day, with frequent allusions to recent events, and with constant reiteration of the moral intended to be taught, was calculated to affect the newly returned and still unsettled people far more strongly and deeply than the old narratives. The Book of Chronicles bridged over, so to speak, the gulf which separated the nation after, from the nation before, the Captivity: it must have helped greatly to restore the national life, to revive hope and encourage high aspirations by showing to the nation that its fate was in its own hands, and that religious faithfulness would be certain to secure the Divine blessing.

3. That the Book of Chronicles was composed after the return from the Captivity is evident, not only from its closing passage, but from other portions of it.[6]

The evidence of style accords with the evidence furnished by the contents. The phraseology is similar to that of Ezra, Nehemiah, and Esther, all books written after the exile. It has numerous Aramæan forms,[7] and at least one word derived from the Persian.[8] The date cannot therefore well be earlier than B.C. 538, but may be very considerably later. The very close connexion of style between Chronicles and Ezra, makes it probable that they were composed at the same time, if not even by the same person. If Ezra was the author, as so many think, the date could not well be much later than B.C. 435, for Ezra probably died about that time. There is nothing in the contents or style of the work to make the date B.C. 450-435 improbable; for the genealogy in iii. 23, 24, which appears to be later than this, may be a subsequent addition.[9]

4. The writer of Chronicles cites, as his authorities, works of two distinct classes.

(a) His most frequent reference is to a *general* history—the "Book of the Kings of Israel and Judah,"[10] This was a compilation

---

[6] A comparison of 1 Chr. ix. 10-16 with Nehem. xi. 10-17 will show that almost the whole of 1 Chr ix. belongs to the period after the Captivity. Ch. iii. contains a genealogy of the descendants of Zerubbabel (19-24), which is continued down to, at least, the third generation.

[7] *e.g.* 1 Chr. xviii. 5 (Darmesek).
[8] See 1 Chr. xxix. 7 note. The other supposed Persian words in Chronicles are somewhat doubtful.
[9] See p. 449, note 3.
[10] See 2 Chr. xvi. 11, xxv. 26, xxvii. 7, xxviii. 26, xxxv. 27, xxxvi. 8.

from the two histories constantly mentioned in Kings—the "Book of the Chronicles of the Kings of Israel," and the "Book of the Chronicles of the Kings of Judah,"[1] which it had been found convenient to unite into one. (*b*) The other works cited by him were 12 or 13 part-histories, the works of Prophets who dealt with particular portions of the national annals.[2] Of none of these works is the exact character known to us ; but the manner in which they are cited makes it probable that for the most part they treated with some fulness the history—especially the religious history—of the times of their authors. They may be regarded as independent compositions — monographs upon the events of their times, written by individual Prophets, of which occasionally one was transferred, not into our "Books of Kings," but into the "Book of the Kings of Israel and Judah ; " while the remainder existed for some centuries side by side with the "Book of the Kings," and furnished to the writer of Chronicles much of the special information which he conveys to us.

There is also ample proof that the writer made use of the whole of the earlier historical Scriptures, and especially of the Books of Samuel and Kings, such as we have them. The main sources of 1 Chr. i.–viii., are the earlier Scriptures from Genesis to Ruth, supplemented by statements drawn from *private* sources, such as the genealogies of families, and numerous important points of family history, carefully preserved by the "chiefs of the fathers" in almost all the Israelite tribes ; a main source of 1 Chr. x.–xxvii. is Samuel ; and a source, though scarcely a main source, of 2 Chr. i.–xxxvi. is Kings (cp. the marg. reff. and notes). But the writer has always some further authority besides these; and there is no section of the Jewish history, from the death of Saul to the fall of Jerusalem, which he has not illustrated with new facts, drawn from some source which has perished.

5. The indications of unity in the authorship preponderate over those of diversity, and lead to the conclusion that the entire work is from one and the same writer. The genealogical tendency, which shows itself so strongly in the introductory section (1 Chr. i.–ix.), is remarkably characteristic of the writer, and continually thrusts itself into notice in the more purely historical portions of his narrative.[3] Conversely, the mere genealogical portion of the work is penetrated by the same spirit as animates the historical chapters,[4]

---

[1] See Introduction to Kings, p. 265.

[2] *e.g.* "The Chronicles of King David" (1 Chr. xxvii. 24), "The Acts of Samuel the Seer," "The Acts of Nathan the Prophet," "The Acts of Gad the Seer" (xxix. 29), "The Prophecy of Ahijah the Shilonite," "The Visions of Iddo the Seer" (2 Chr. ix. 29), "The Acts of Shemaiah the Prophet," "Iddo the Seer on Genealogies" (xii. 15), "The Commentary of the Prophet Iddo" (xiii. 22), "The Acts of Jehu the son of Hanani" (xx. 34),

"The Commentary of the Book of the Kings" (xxiv. 27), "Isaiah's Acts of Uzziah" (xxvi. 22), "The Vision of Isaiah" (xxxii. 32), and "The Acts of Hosai" (xxxiii. 19 ; see note).

[3] See 2 Chr. xi. 18-20, xx. 14, xxi. 2, xxiii. 1, xxix. 12-14, and xxxiv. 12.

[4] *e.g.* (*a*) The Levitical spirit, as it has been called ; the sense, *i.e.*, of the importance of the Levitical order and its various divisions, offices, and arrangements, which so markedly characterises the his-

and moreover abounds with phrases, characteristic of the writer.[5]

That the historical narrative (1 Chr. x.—2 Chr. xxxvi.) is from one hand, can scarcely be doubted. One pointedly didactic tone pervades the whole—each signal calamity and success being ascribed in the most direct manner to the action of Divine Providence, rewarding the righteous and punishing the evil-doers.[6] There is everywhere the same method of composition—a primary use of Samuel and Kings as bases of the narrative, the abbreviation of what has been narrated before, the omission of important facts, otherwise known to the reader;[7] and the addition of new facts, sometimes minute, and less important than curious,[8] at other times so striking that it is surprising that the earlier historians should have passed them over.[9]

6. The abrupt termination of Chronicles, in the middle of a sentence,[1] is an unanswerable argument against its having come down to us in the form in which it was originally written.

And the recurrence of the final passage of our present copies of Chronicles at the commencement of Ezra, taken in conjunction with the undoubted fact, that there is a very close resemblance of style and tone between the two Books, suggests naturally the explanation, which has been accepted by some of the best critics, that the two works, Chronicles and Ezra, were originally one, and were afterwards separated:[2] that separation having probably arisen out of a desire to arrange the history of the post-Captivity period in chronological sequence.

7. The condition of the text of Chronicles is far from satisfactory. Various readings are frequent, particularly in the names of persons and places; omissions are found, especially in the genealogies; and the numbers are sometimes self-contradictory, sometimes contradict-

---

torical portion of Chronicles, appears in the genealogical section by the large space assigned to the account of the sons of Levi, who occupy not only the whole of 1 Chr. vi. but also the greater part of ch. ix. (b) The strong feeling with respect to Divine Providence, and the very plain and direct teaching on the subject, which is the most striking feature of the general narrative appears also in the genealogical chapters, as in 1 Chr. iv. 10, v. 20, 22, 25-26, and ix. 1.

[5] e.g. "Moses the servant of God," 1 Chr. vi. 49; cp. 2 Chr. i. 3, xxiv. 6. "Samuel the seer," 1 Chr. ix. 22; cp. xxvi. 28. "The ruler of the house of God," 1 Chr. ix. 11; cp. 2 Chr. xxxi. 13.

[6] Cp. 1 Chr. x. 13, xi. 9; 2 Chr. xii. 2, xiii. 18, &c. Cp. note 4 (b).

[7] e.g. The burning of Saul's body (1 Sam. xxxi. 12), omitted in 1 Chr. x. yet implied in v. 12; the cession of certain cities to Hiram (1 K. ix. 12), omitted but implied in 2 Chr. viii. 2; the destruction

of the kingdom of Israel by the Assyrians (2 K. xvii. 3-6), omitted in Chronicles but implied in the words of Hezekiah (2 Chr. xxx. 6-7, &c.).

[8] e.g. 1 Chr. xxi. 27.

[9] e.g. The solemn addresses of David (1 Chr. xxviii. and xxix. 1-20); the letters from Solomon to Hiram and from Hiram to Solomon (2 Chr. ii. 3-16); the religious and other reforms of Jehoshaphat (xvii. 6-9, xix. 4-11); the religious reformation of Hezekiah (xxix.-xxxi.); the captivity of Manasseh, his repentance, and his restoration to his kingdom (xxxiii. 11-13); and the establishment by Josiah of his authority in the old kingdom of Israel (xxxiv. 6-7, 9, xxxv. 17-18).

[1] 2 Chr. xxxvi. 23, "Who is there among you of all his people? [The Lord] his God be with him, and let him go up ——." Every reader naturally asks, whither? Cp. Ezra i. 3.

[2] This is more satisfactory than to consider that the Books of Chronicles closed with 2 Chr. xxxvi. 21.

ory of more probable numbers in Samuel or Kings, sometimes unreasonably large, and therefore justly suspected.

The work is, however, free from defects of a more serious character.[3] The unity is unbroken, and there is every reason to believe that we have the work, in almost all respects, exactly as it came from the hand of the author.

8. As compared with the parallel histories of Samuel and Kings, the history of Chronicles is characterised by three principal features : (a) A greater tendency to dwell on the externals of religion, on the details of the Temple worship, the various functions of the Priests and Levites, the arrangement of the courses, and the like. Hence the history of Chronicles has been called " ecclesiastical," that of Samuel and Kings " political."[4] This tendency does not detract from the credibility, or render the history undeserving of confidence. (b) A marked genealogical bias and desire to put on record the names of persons engaged in any of the events narrated ; and (c) A more constant, open, and direct ascription of all the events of the history to the Divine agency, and especially a

more plain reference of every great calamity or deliverance to the good or evil deeds of the monarch, or the nation, which Divine Providence so punished or rewarded.[5]

There is no reason to regard Chronicles as less trustworthy than Samuel or Kings. A due consideration of disputed points, the " Levitical spirit," contradictions, alleged mistakes, &c., does not, speaking generally, impugn the honesty of the writer or the authenticity of his work. The Book may fairly be regarded as authentic in all its parts, with the exception of some of its numbers. These appear to have occasionally suffered corruption, though scarcely to a greater extent than those of other Books of equal antiquity. From blemishes of this kind it has not pleased God to keep His Word free. It will scarcely be maintained at the present day that their occurrence affects in the very slightest degree the authenticity of the rest of the narrative.

The style of Chronicles is simpler and less elevated than that of Kings. Excepting the psalm of David in 1 Chr. xvi. and the prayer of Solomon in 2 Chr. vi., the whole is prosaic, level, and uniform. There are no especially

---

[3] One interpolation into the text is to be noted (1 Chr. iii. 22-24 ; see v. 19 note) —an authorised addition, probably, by a later Prophet, such as Malachi.

[4] The reign of Hezekiah may be taken as a crucial instance of the difference between the modes of treatment pursued by the writers of Chronicles and Kings. The writer of Kings devotes three, the writer of Chronicles four, chapters to the subject. Both represent the reign as remarkable : (1) for a religious reformation ; and (2) for striking events of secular history, in which Judæa was brought into

connexion with the great monarchies of the time, Babylonia and Assyria. But while the writer of Kings thinks it enough to relate the religious reformation in three verses (1 K. xviii. 4-6), and devotes to the secular history, treated indeed from a religious point of view, the whole remainder of his three chapters, the writer of Chronicles gives the heads of the secular history in one chapter, while he devotes to the religious reformation the remaining three chapters of his four.

[5] See p. 448.

striking chapters, as in Kings; but it is less gloomy, being addressed to the restored nation, which it seeks to animate and inspirit. The captive people, weeping by the waters of Babylon, fitly read their mournful history in Kings: the liberated nation, entering hopefully upon a new life, found in Chronicles a review of its past, calculated to help it forward on the path of progress, upon which it was entering.

THE FIRST BOOK

OF THE

CHRONICLES.

Chap. 1. ADAM, *a*Sheth, Enosh, Kenan, Mahalaleel, Jered, He-
4 noch, Methuselah, Lamech, Noah, Shem, Ham, and Japheth.
5 ¶ *b*The sons of Japheth; Gomer, and Magog, and Madai, and
6 Javan, and Tubal, and Meshech, and Tiras. And the sons of
7 Gomer; Ashchenaz, and [1]Riphath, and Togarmah. And the
sons of Javan; Elishah, and Tarshish, Kittim, and [2]Dodanim.
8 ¶ *c*The sons of Ham; Cush, and Mizraim, Put, and Canaan.
9 And the sons of Cush; Seba, and Havilah, and Sabta, and Raamah, and Sabtecha. And the sons of Raamah; Sheba, and
10 Dedan. And Cush *d*begat Nimrod: he began to be mighty upon
11 the earth. And Mizraim begat Ludim, and Anamim, and Leha-
12 bim, and Naphtuhim, and Pathrusim, and Casluhim, (of whom
13 came the Philistines,) and *e*Caphthorim. And *f*Canaan begat
14 Zidon his firstborn, and Heth, the Jebusite also, and the Amo-
15 rite, and the Girgashite, and the Hivite, and the Arkite, and the
16 Sinite, and the Arvadite, and the Zemarite, and the Hamathite.
17 ¶ The sons of *g*Shem; Elam, and Asshur, and Arphaxad, and
Lud, and Aram, and Uz, and Hul, and Gether, and [3]Meshech.
18, 19 And Arphaxad begat Shelah, and Shelah begat Eber. And
unto Eber were born two sons: the name of the one *was* [4]Peleg;
because in his days the earth was divided: and his brother's
20 name *was* Joktan. And *h*Joktan begat Almodad, and Sheleph,
21 and Hazarmaveth, and Jerah, Hadoram also, and Uzal, and
22, 23 Diklah, and Ebal, and Abimael, and Sheba, and Ophir, and
Havilah, and Jobab. All these *were* the sons of Joktan.
24, 25, 26 ¶ *i*Shem, Arphaxad, Shelah, *k*Eber, Peleg, Reu, Serug,
27, 28 Nahor, Terah, *l*Abram; the same *is* Abraham. The sons of
29 Abraham; *m*Isaac, and *n*Ishmael. ¶ These *are* their generations:
the *o*firstborn of Ishmael, Nebaioth; then Kedar, and Adbeel, and

a Gen. 4. 25,
26.
& 5. 3, 9.
b Gen. 10. 2,
&c.

c Gen. 10. 6,
&c.

d Gen. 10. 8,
13, &c.

e Deut. 2. 23.
f Gen. 10. 15,
&c.

g Gen. 10. 22.
& 11. 10.

h Gen. 10. 23.

i Gen. 11. 10,
&c.
Luke 3. 34,
&c.
k Gen. 11. 15.
l Gen. 17. 5.
m Gen. 21. 2,
3.
n Gen. 16.
o Gen. 25.
13–16.

[1] Or, *Diphath,* as it is in
some copies.

[2] Or, *Rodanim,* according
to some copies.

[3] Or, *Mash,* Gen. 10. 23.

[4] That is, *Division,* Gen.
10. 25.
11, 15.

I. 1. Cp. marg. reff. and notes.
7. *Dodanim*] See Gen. x. 4 note.
16. *the Zemarite*] See Gen. x. 18 note. The
inscriptions of the Assyrian monarch, Sargon, (B.C. 720) mention Zimira, which is
joined with Arpad (Arvad); and there can
be little doubt that it is the city indicated
by the term "Zemarite."
17. *The sons of Shem*] i.e., descendants.
Uz, Hul, Gether, and Meshech (or Mash),
are stated to have been "sons of Aram"
(Gen. x. 23). Meshech is the reading of all
the MSS., and is supported by the LXX.
here and in Gen. x. 23. It seems preferable
to "Mash," which admits of no very probable explanation. Just as Hamites and
Semites were intermingled in Arabia (Gen.
x. 7, 29 notes), so Semites and Japhethites
may have been intermingled in Cappadocia

—the country of the Meshech or Moschi
(Gen. x. 2 note); and this Aramæan ad-
mixture may have been the origin of the
notion, so prevalent among the Greeks, that
the Cappadocians were Syrians.
28. *Isaac and Ishmael*] Isaac, though
younger than Ishmael, is placed first, as
the legitimate heir, since Sarah alone was
Abraham's true wife (cp. v. 35 note).
29. *These are their generations*] As Shem
was reserved till after Japheth and Ham
(*vv.* 5-16), because in him the genealogy was
to be continued (Gen. x. 2 note), so Isaac is
now reserved till the other lines of descent
from Abraham have been completed. The
same principle gives the descendants of
Esau a prior place to those of Jacob (*vv.* 35–
54; ii. 1).

30 Mibsam, Mishma, and Dumah, Massa, [1]Hadad, and Tema,
31 Jetur, Naphish, and Kedemah. These are the sons of Ishmael.

p Gen.25.1,2.

32 ¶ Now *p* the sons of Keturah, Abraham's concubine: she bare
Zimran, and Jokshan, and Medan, and Midian, and Ishbak,
33 and Shuah. And the sons of Jokshan; Sheba, and Dedan.
And the sons of Midian; Ephah, and Epher, and Henoch, and
34 Abida, and Eldaah. All these are the sons of Keturah. ¶ And

q Gen.21.2,3
r Gen. 25.
25, 26.
s Gen. 36. 9,
10.

q Abraham begat Isaac. *r* The sons of Isaac; Esau and Israel.
35 ¶ The sons of *s* Esau; Eliphaz, Reuel, and Jeush, and Jaalam,
36 and Korah. The sons of Eliphaz; Teman, and Omar, [2]Zephi,
37 and Gatam, Kenaz, and Timna, and Amalek. The sons of

t Gen. 36. 20.

38 Reuel; Nahath, Zerah, Shammah, and Mizzah. ¶ And *t* the
sons of Seir; Lotan, and Shobal, and Zibeon, and Anah, and
39 Dishon, and Ezar, and Dishan. And the sons of Lotan; Hori,
40 and [3]Homam: and Timna was Lotan's sister. The sons of
Shobal; [4]Alian, and Manahath, and Ebal, [5]Shephi, and Onam.
41 And the sons of Zibeon; Aiah, and Anah. The sons of Anah;

u Gen. 36.25.

u Dishon. And the sons of Dishon; [6]Amram, and Eshban, and
42 Ithran, and Cheran. The sons of Ezer; Bilhan, and Zavan,
43 and [7]Jakan. The sons of Dishan; Uz, and Aran. ¶ Now

x Gen. 36.31,
&c.

these are the *x* kings that reigned in the land of Edom before
any king reigned over the children of Israel; Bela the son of
44 Beor: and the name of his city was Dinhabah. And when Bela
was dead, Jobab the son of Zerah of Bozrah reigned in his
45 stead. And when Jobab was dead, Husham of the land of the
46 Temanites reigned in his stead. And when Husham was dead,
Hadad the son of Bedad, which smote Midian in the field of
Moab, reigned in his stead: and the name of his city was Avith.
47 And when Hadad was dead, Samlah of Masrekah reigned in his

y Gen. 36.37.

48 stead. *y* And when Samlah was dead, Shaul of Rehoboth by the
49 river reigned in his stead. And when Shaul was dead, Baal-
50 hanan the son of Achbor reigned in his stead. And when Baal-
hanan was dead, [8]Hadad reigned in his stead: and the name of
his city was [9]Pai; and his wife's name was Mehetabel, the
51 daughter of Matred, the daughter of Mezahab. Hadad died

z Gen. 36. 40.

also. And the *z* dukes of Edom were; duke Timnah, duke
52 [1]Aliah, duke Jetheth, duke Aholibamah, duke Elah, duke
53, 54 Pinon, duke Kenaz, duke Teman, duke Mibzar, duke Magdiel,
duke Iram. These are the dukes of Edom.

---

[1] Or, Hadar, Gen. 25. 15.
[2] Or, Zepho, Gen. 36. 11.
[3] Or, Heman, Gen. 36. 22.
[4] Or, Alvan, Gen. 36. 23.
[5] Or, Shepho, Gen. 36. 23.
[6] Or, Hemdan, Gen. 36. 26.
[7] Or, Akan, Gen. 36. 27.
[8] Or, Hadar, Gen. 36. 39.
[9] Or, Pau, Gen. 36. 39.
[1] Or, Alvah.

---

30. Hadad here and in *v*. 50 is the well-known Syrian name, of which Hadar (marg.) is an accidental corruption, consequent on the close resemblance between *d* and *r* in Hebrew, the final letters of the two names.

32. *Keturah, Abraham's concubine*] This passage, and Gen. xxv. 6, sufficiently prove that the position of Keturah was not that of the full wife, but of the "secondary" or "concubine wife" (Jud. xix. 1) so common among Orientals.

36. *Timna*] In Gen. xxxvi. 11, Eliphaz has no son Timna; but he has a concubine of the name, who is the mother of Amalek,

and conjectured to be Lotan's sister (*v*. 39). The best explanation is, that the writer has in his mind rather the tribes descended from Eliphaz than his actual children, and as there was a place, Timna, inhabited by his "dukes" (*v*. 51; cp. Gen. xxxv. 40), he puts the race which lived there among his "sons."

41. Amram (rather **Hamran**), and Hemdan (marg.), differ in the original by the same letter only which marks the difference in *v*. 30.

43-54. The slight differences favour the view, that the writer of Chronicles has here, as elsewhere, abridged from Genesis (see marg. reff.).

Chap. 2. THESE *are* the sons of [1]Israel; [a]Reuben, Simeon, Levi,
2 and Judah, Issachar, and Zebulun, Dan, Joseph, and Benjamin,
3 Naphtali, Gad, and Asher. ¶The sons of [b]Judah; Er, and
Onan, and Shelah : *which* three were born unto him of the
daughter of [c]Shua the Canaanitess. And [d]Er, the firstborn of
Judah, was evil in the sight of the LORD; and he slew him.
4 And [e]Tamar his daughter in law bare him Pharez and Zerah.
5 All the sons of Judah *were* five. The sons of [f]Pharez; Hezron,
6 and Hamul. ¶And the sons of Zerah ; [2]Zimri, [g]and Ethan, and
7 Heman, and Calcol, and [3]Dara : five of them in all. And the
sons of [h]Carmi ; [4]Achar, the troubler of Israel, who trans-
8 gressed in the thing [i]accursed. And the sons of Ethan; Aza-
9 riah. ¶The sons also of Hezron, that were born unto him ;
10 Jerahmeel, and [5]Ram, and [6]Chelubai. And Ram [k]begat Amminadab ; and Amminadab begat Nahshon, [l]prince of the
11 children of Judah ; and Nahshon begat [7]Salma, and Salma
12 begat Boaz, and Boaz begat Obed, and Obed begat Jesse, [m]and
13 Jesse begat his firstborn Eliab, and Abinadab the second, and
14 [8]Shimma the third, Nethaneel the fourth, Raddai the fifth,
15, 16 Ozem the sixth, David the seventh: whose sisters *were* Zeruiah, and Abigail. [n]And the sons of Zeruiah ; Abishai, and Joab,
17 and Asahel, three. And [o]Abigail bare Amasa : and the father
18 of Amasa *was* [9]Jether the Ishmeelite. ¶And Caleb the son of
Hezron begat *children* of Azubah *his* wife, and of Jerioth : her
19 sons *are* these ; Jesher, and Shobab, and Ardon. And when
Azubah was dead, Caleb took unto him [p]Ephrath, which bare
20 him Hur. And Hur begat Uri, and Uri begat [q]Bezaleel.

Right margin references:
a Gen. 29. 32.
& 30. 5, &c.
& 35. 18, 22.
& 46. 8, &c.
b Gen. 38. 3.
& 46. 12.
Num. 26. 19.
c Gen. 38. 2.
d Gen. 38. 7.
e Gen. 38.
29, 30.
Matt. 1. 3.
f Gen. 46. 12.
Ruth 4. 18.
g 1 Kin. 4.31.
h See ch.4.1.
i Josh. 6. 18.
& 7. 1.
k Ruth 4. 19,
20.
Matt. 1. 4.
l Num. 1. 7.
& 2. 3.
m 1Sam.16.6.

n 2Sam.2.18.
o 2 Sam. 17
25.

p ver. 50.

q Ex. 31. 2.

---

1 Or, *Jacob.*
2 Or, *Zabdi,* Josh. 7. 1.
3 Or, *Darda.*
4 Or, *Achan.*
5 Or, *Aram,* Matt. 1. 3, 4.
6 Or, *Caleb,* ver. 18, 42.
7 Or, *Salmon,* Ruth 4. 21.
Matt. 1. 4.
8 Or, *Shammah,* 1 Sam.
16. 9.
9 2 Sam. 17. 25, *Ithra an
Israelite.*

II. 1. *the sons of Israel*] The order of the
names here approximates to an order determined by legitimacy of birth. A single
change—the removal of Dan to the place
after Benjamin—would give the following
result :—
(1) The six sons of the first wife, Leah.
(2) The two sons of the second wife,
Rachel.
(3) The two sons of the first concubine,
Bilhah.
(4) The two sons of the second concubine,
Zilpah.
Dan's undue prominency may, perhaps,
be accounted for by his occupying the
seventh place in the "blessing of Jacob"
(Gen. xlix. 16).
6. *the sons of Zerah*] Here, for the first
time, the writer of Chronicles draws from
sources not otherwise known to us, recording facts not mentioned in the earlier Scriptures. Ethan, Heman, Calcol, and Dara,
sons of Zerah, are only known to us from
this passage, since there are no sufficient
grounds for identifying them with the "sons
of Mahol" (marg. ref.).
7. "Achan" (Josh. vii. 1) seems to have
become "Achar," in order to assimilate the
word more closely to the Hebrew term for

"troubler," which was from the time of
Achan's sin regarded as the true meaning
of his name (Josh. vii. 25, 26).
15. *David the seventh*] Jesse had eight
sons, of whom David was the youngest
(1 Sam. xvi. 10, 11, xvii. 12). Probably one
of the sons shown to Samuel at Bethlehem
did not grow up.
16. *sisters*] *i.e.* half-sisters. Abigail and
Zeruiah were daughters not of Jesse, but of
a certain Nahash, whose widow Jesse took
to wife (2 Sam. xvii. 25).
From the present passage, and from the
fact that Abishai joined David as a comrade
in arms before Joab (1 Sam. xxvi. 6), it
would seem that, although Joab was pre-
eminent among the three (2 Sam. ii. 13, 16),
Abishai was the eldest.
17. *Jether the Ishmeelite*] See marg. note
and ref.
18. In the remainder of this chapter the
writer obtains scarcely any assistance from
the earlier Scriptures, and must have drawn
almost entirely from genealogical sources,
accessible to him, which have since perished.
Azubah was Caleb's wife ; Jerioth his
concubine. He had children by both ; but
those of Azubah are alone recorded.

r Num. 27. 1.
21 ¶ And afterward Hezron went in to the daughter of r Machir the father of Gilead, whom he ¹ married when he was threescore
22 years old ; and she bare him Segub. And Segub begat Jair,

s Num 32. 41.
Deut. 3. 14.
Josh. 13. 30.
23 who had three and twenty cities in the land of Gilead. s And he took Geshur, and Aram, with the towns of Jair, from them, with Kenath, and the towns thereof, even threescore cities. All
24 these belonged to the sons of Machir the father of Gilead. And after that Hezron was dead in Caleb-ephratah, then Abiah

t ch. 4. 5.
25 Hezron's wife bare him t Ashur the father of Tekoa. ¶ And the sons of Jerahmeel the firstborn of Hezron were, Ram the first-
26 born, and Bunah, and Oren, and Ozem, and Ahijah. Jerah-meel had also another wife, whose name was Atarah; she was
27 the mother of Onam. And the sons of Ram the firstborn of
28 Jerahmeel were, Maaz, and Jamin, and Eker. And the sons of Onam were, Shammai, and Jada. And the sons of Shammai;
29 Nadab, and Abishur. And the name of the wife of Abishur was
30 Abihail, and she bare him Ahban, and Molid. And the sons of Nadab; Seled, and Appaim : but Seled died without children.
31 And the sons of Appaim; Ishi. And the sons of Ishi; Sheshan.

u See ver.
34, 35.
32 And u the children of Sheshan ; Ahlai. And the sons of Jada the brother of Shammai ; Jether, and Jonathan : and Jether
33 died without children. And the sons of Jonathan ; Peleth, and
34 Zaza. These were the sons of Jerahmeel. ¶ Now Sheshan had no sons, but daughters. And Sheshan had a servant, an
35 Egyptian, whose name was Jarha. And Sheshan gave his daughter to Jarha his servant to wife ; and she bare him Attai.

x ch. 11. 41.
36, 37 And Attai begat Nathan, and Nathan begat x Zabad, and Za-
38 bad begat Ephlal, and Ephlal begat Obed, and Obed begat Jehu,
39 and Jehu begat Azariah, and Azariah begat Helez, and Helez
40 begat Eleasah, and Eleasah begat Sisamai, and Sisamai begat
41 Shallum, and Shallum begat Jekamiah, and Jekamiah begat
42 Elishama. ¶ Now the sons of Caleb the brother of Jerahmeel were, Mesha his firstborn, which was the father of Ziph ; and
43 the sons of Mareshah the father of Hebron. And the sons of
44 Hebron ; Korah, and Tappuah, and Rekem, and Shema. And Shema begat Raham, the father of Jorkoam : and Rekem begat

---

¹ Heb. took.

---

22. Jair, who had three and twenty cities] The places called "Havoth-Jair" in the earlier Scriptures (see Num. xxxii. 41 note), which appear to have been a number of "small towns," or villages, in the Ledjah, the classical "Trachonitis."

23. Rather, "And Geshur and Aram (i.e. the Geshurites (Deut. iii. 14) and Syrians) **took the villages of Jair from them**:" re-covered, that is, from the new settlers the places which Jair had conquered.

all these belonged to the sons of Machir] Rather, "All these **were sons** of Machir," i.e. Segub and Jair, with their descendants, were reckoned sons of Machir, rather than sons of Hezron, although only descended from Machir on the mother's side. The reason of this seems to have been that they cast in their lot with the Manassites, and remained in their portion of the trans-Jor-danic region.

25. and Ahijah] There is no "and" in

the original. Hence some would read : "the sons" were born "of" or "from Ahijah," the first wife of Jerahmeel (see next verse).

42. A third line of descent from Caleb, the son of Hezron, the issue probably of a different mother, perhaps Jerioth (v. 18). The supposed omissions in this verse have been supplied as follows : (1) "Mesha, the father of Ziph ; and the sons of Ziph, Mare-shah, the father of Hebron ;" or (2) "Mare-shah, the father of Ziph ; and the sons of Mareshah, the father of Ziph, Hebron."

Ziph, like Jorkoam (v. 44) and Beth-zur (v. 45), is the name of a place where the re-spective chiefs ("fathers") settled. Similarly Madmannah, Machbenah, and Gibea (v. 49), Kirjath-jearim (Josh. ix. 17 note), Beth-lehem and Beth-gader (Jedur, v. 51) are unmistakeable names of places in the list, names which it is not probable were ever borne by persons.

45 Shammai. And the son of Shammai *was* Maon : and Maon *was*
46 the father of Beth-zur. And Ephah, Caleb's concubine, bare
47 Haran, and Moza, and Gazez: and Haran begat Gazez. And
the sons of Jahdai; Regem, and Jotham, and Gesham, and
48 Pelet, and Ephah, and Shaaph. Maachah, Caleb's concubine,
49 bare Sheber, and Tirhanah. She bare also Shaaph the father
of Madmannah, Sheva the father of Machbenah, and the father
50 of Gibea : and the daughter of Caleb *was* ʸAchsa. ¶ These were
the sons of Caleb the son of Hur, the firstborn of ¹Ephratah ;
51 Shobal the father of Kirjath-jearim. Salma the father of
52 Beth-lehem, Hareph the father of Beth-gader. And Shobal the
father of Kirjath-jearim had sons ; ²Haroeh, *and* ³half of the
53 Manahethites. And the families of Kirjath-jearim; the Ithrites,
and the Puhites, and the Shumathites, and the Mishraites; of
54 them came the Zareathites, and the Eshtaulites. The sons
of Salma; Beth-lehem, and the Netophathites, ⁴Ataroth, the
55 house of Joab, and half of the Manahethites, the Zorites. And
the families of the scribes which dwelt at Jabez; the Tirathites,
the Shimeathites, *and* Suchathites. These *are* the ᶻKenites that
came of Hemath, the father of the house of ᵃRechab.

CHAP. 3. NOW these were the sons of David, which were born
unto him in Hebron ; the firstborn ᵃAmnon, of Ahinoam the
ᵇJezreelitess; the second ⁵Daniel, of Abigail the Carmelitess:
2 the third, Absalom the son of Maachah the daughter of Talmai
3 king of Geshur: the fourth, Adonijah the son of Haggith: the
fifth, Shephatiah of Abital: the sixth, Ithream by ᶜEglah his
4 wife. *These* six were born unto him in Hebron; and ᵈthere he
reigned seven years and six months: and ᵉin Jerusalem he
5 reigned thirty and three years. ᶠAnd these were born unto him
in Jerusalem; ⁶Shimea, and Shobab, and Nathan, and ᵍSolomon,

ʸ Josh.15.17.

ᶻ Judg. 1. 16.
ᵃ Jer. 35. 2.

ᵃ 2 Sam. 3.2.
ᵇ Josh.15.56.

ᶜ 2 Sam. 3. 5.
ᵈ 2 Sam. 2. 11.
ᵉ 2 Sam. 5 5.
ᶠ 2 Sam.5.14. ch. 14. 4.
ᵍ 2 Sam. 12. 24.

¹ Or, *Ephrath*, ver. 19.
² Or, *Reaiah*, ch. 4. 2.
³ Or, *half of the Menu-*
chites, or, *Hatsi-ham-
menuchoth.*
⁴ Or, *Atarites*, or, *crowns of
the house of Joab.*
⁵ Or, *Chileab*, 2 Sam. 3. 3.
⁶ Or, *Shammua*, 2 Sam. 5. 14.

---

50. *Caleb the son of Hur*] Hur was the son, not the father, of Caleb (*v.* 19). The text should perhaps be read : " These (the list in *vv.* 42-49) were the sons of Caleb. The sons of Hur, the first-born of Ephratah, were Shobal, &c."

54. *Ataroth, the house of Joab*] Rather, "Ataroth-beth-Joab," probably so called, to distinguish it from Ataroth-Adar, a city of Benjamin (Josh. xviii. 13). It is uncertain from what Joab it derived its distinctive appellation.

55. *Kenites*] It is remarkable that Kenites—people of a race quite distinct from the Israelites (Gen. xv. 19)—should be attached to, and, as it were, included in the descendants of Judah. It seems, however, that the friendly feeling between the two tribes—based on the conduct of the Kenites at the time of the Exodus (Ex. xviii. 10-19; Num. x. 29-32 ; 1 Sam. xv. 6)—led to their intermixture and almost amalgamation with the Israelites, Kenite families not only dwelling among them but being actually regarded as of one blood with them.

III. 1. *the sons of David*] The writer re-turns to the point at which he had left the posterity of Ram (ii. 9, 15), and traces out the family of David—the royal house of the tribe of Judah.

Daniel] See marg. note and ref.
There are three lists of the sons of David, born in Jerusalem.

	I.	II.	III.
	2 S. v. 14-16.	1 Chr. iii. 5-8.	1 Chr. xiv. 4-7.
1.	Shammuah . .	Shimeah* .	Shammuah.
2.	Shobab . .	Shobab .	Shobab.
3.	Nathan . .	Nathan .	Nathan.
4.	Solomon .	Solomon .	Solomon.
5.	Ibhar . .	Ibhar .	Ibhar.
6.	Elishua .	Elishama* .	Elishua.
7.		Eliphelet* .	Elpalet.*
8.		Nogah . .	Nogah.
9.	Nepheg .	Nepheg .	Nepheg.
10.	Japhia . .	Japhia .	Japhia.
11.	Elishama .	Elishama .	Elishama.
12.	Eliada . .	Eliada . .	Beeliada.*
13.	Eliphelet .	Eliphelet .	Eliphelet.

(Differences are marked with an asterisk).

A comparison of the three lists serves to show—(1) That "Shimeah" and the first "Elishama" in the list of this chapter are

6 four, of [1]Bath-shua the daughter of [2]Ammiel: Ibhar also, and
7 [3]Elishama, and Eliphelet, and Nogah, and Nepheg, and Japhia,
8, 9 and Elishama, and [4]Eliada, and Eliphelet, [h]nine. *These were*
all the sons of David, beside the sons of the concubines, and
10 [i]Tamar their sister. ¶ And Solomon's son *was* [k]Rehoboam, [5]Abia
11 his son, Asa his son, Jehoshaphat his son, Joram his son,
12 [6]Ahaziah his son, Joash his son, Amaziah his son, [7]Azariah his
13 son, Jotham his son, Ahaz his son, Hezekiah his son, Manasseh
14, 15 his son, Amon his son, Josiah his son. And the sons of Josiah
were, the firstborn [8]Johanan, the second [9]Jehoiakim, the third
16 [l]Zedekiah, the fourth Shallum. And the sons of [l]Jehoiakim:
17 [2]Jeconiah his son, Zedekiah [m]his son. ¶ And the sons of Jeco-
18 niah; Assir, [3]Salathiel [n]his son, Malchiram also, and Pedaiah,
19 and Shenazar, Jecamiah, Hoshama, and Nedabiah. And the
sons of Pedaiah *were*, Zerubbabel, and Shimei: and the sons of
Zerubbabel; Meshullam, and Hananiah, and Shelomith their
20 sister: and Hashubah, and Ohel, and Berechiah, and Hasadiah,

h See
2 Sam. 5. 14,
15, 16.
i 2 Sam.13.1.
k 1Kin.11.43.
& 15. 6.

l Matt. 1. 11.
m 2 Kin. 24.
17,
being his
uncle.
n Matt. 1. 12.

1 Or, *Bath-sheba*, 2 Sam.
11. 3.
2 Or, *Eliam*, 2 Sam. 11. 3.
3 Or, *Elishua*, 2 Sam. 5.
15.
4 Or, *Beeliada*, ch. 14. 7.
5 Or, *Abijam*, 1 Kin. 15. 1.

6 Or, *Azariah*, 2 Chr. 22.
6. or, *Jehoahaz*, 2 Chr.
21. 17.
7 Or, *Uzziah*, 2 Kin. 15.
30.
8 Or, *Jehoahaz*, 2 Kin. 23.
30.

9 Or, *Eliakim*, 2 Kin.23.34.
1 Or, *Mattaniah*, 2 Kin.
24. 17.
2 Or, *Jehoiachin*, 2 Kin.
24. 6. or, *Coniah*, Jer.
22. 24.
3 Heb. *Shealtiel*.

---

corruptions; (2) That David had really
13 sons born in Jerusalem, of whom two
— the first Eliphelet and Nogah—probably
died in their childhood; and (3) That Eliada,
the twelfth son, was also called Beeliada,
the term *Baal*, "lord," not having (previous
to the introduction of the Baal worship) a
bad sense, but being regarded as an equivalent with *El*, "God."

Bathshua, the daughter of Ammiel] Both
names are here given in an unusual form,
but it may be doubted whether in either
case there has been any corruption. In
"Bathshua," for "Bathsheba," a *vau* (*v*)
replaces the *beth* (*b*) of the earlier writer, *v*
and *b* having nearly the same sound. In
"Ammiel," for "Eliam," the two elements
which form the name are inverted, as in
Jehoiachin = Jechoniah, and the like.

10. *Abia*] Rather, "Abijah," as in 2 Chr.
xi.-xiv., where the Hebrew word is exactly
the same.

11. *Ahaziah*] Called "Jehoahaz" by a
transposition of the elements composing the
name, and "Azariah," probably by a transcriber's error (see marg. notes and reff.).

12. *Azariah*] Elsewhere in Chronicles
called uniformly "Uzziah" (2 Chr. xxvi. 1,
3, 9, 11, &c.), but called indifferently "Azariah" and "Uzziah" in Kings ("Azariah"
in 2 K. xiv. 21, xv. 1, 6, 17, 23, 27, &c.;
"Uzziah" in xv. 13, 32, and 34).

15. Of the sons of Josiah, Johanan, "the
first-born," who is mentioned in this place
only, must, it would seem, have died before
his father, or with him at Megiddo; and
Shallum (also called Jehoahaz, marg. note
and ref.) was considerably older than Zedekiah, and was consequently the *third*, and

not the *fourth*, son. He is perhaps assigned
the fourth place here by way of intentional
degradation. Cp. Jer. xxii. 10-12; Ezek.
xix. 3, 4.

17. *Assir*] Perhaps born in the captivity,
and therefore so named, who either died
young, or was made a eunuch (Isai. xxxix.
7; cp. Jer. xxii. 30). After Assir's decease,
or mutilation, the line of Solomon became
extinct, and according to the principles of
the Jewish law (Num. xxvii. 8-11) the inheritance passed to the next of kin, who
were Salathiel and his brethren, descendants from David by the line of Nathan.
St. Luke in calling Salathiel "the son of
Neri" (iii. 27), gives his real, or natural, descent; since no genealogy would assign to
the true son and heir of a king any inferior
and private parentage. Hence, "Malchiram," &c., *i.e.* not Salathiel only, but his
brothers also were reckoned "sons" of
Jeconiah.

19. Zerubbabel, elsewhere always called
"the son of Salathiel," was only Salathiel's
heir and legal son, being naturally his
nephew, the son of his brother, Pedaiah.

six] There are only five names in the Hebrew text. The Syriac and Arabic Versions supply "Azariah" between Neariah
and Shaphat.

The question of the proper arrangement
of the genealogy of the descendants of Zerubbabel (*vv.* 19-24) is important in its bearing
on the interesting point of the time at
which the Canon of the Old Testament was
closed. Assuming the average of a generation to be in the East twenty years, the
genealogy of the present chapter, drawn
out according to the Hebrew text, does not

21 Jushab-hesed, five. And the sons of Hananiah; Pelatiah, and
Jesaiah: the sons of Rephaiah, the sons of Arnan, the sons of
22 Obadiah, the sons of Shechaniah. And the sons of Shechaniah;
Shemaiah: and the sons of Shemaiah; ^oHattush, and Igeal, and   *o* Ezra 8. 2.
23 Bariah, and Neariah, and Shaphat, six. And the sons of
24 Neariah; Elioenai, and ¹Hezekiah, and Azrikam, three. And
the sons of Elioenai *were*, Hodaiah, and Eliashib, and Pelaiah,
and Akkub, and Johanan, and Dalaiah, and Anani, seven.

CHAP. 4. THE sons of Judah; ^aPharez, Hezron, and ²Carmi, and   *a* Gen. 38.29.
2 Hur, and Shobal. And ³Reaiah the son of Shobal begat Jahath;   & 46. 12.
and Jahath begat Ahumai, and Lahad. These *are* the families
3 of the Zorathites. And these *were of* the father of Etam; Jezreel, and Ishma, and Idbash: and the name of their sister *was*
4 Hazelelponi: and Penuel the father of Gedor, and Ezer the
father of Hushah. These *are* the sons of ^bHur, the firstborn of   *b* ch. 2. 50.
5 Ephratah, the father of Beth-lehem. ¶And ^cAshur the father   *c* ch. 2. 24.
6 of Tekoa had two wives, Helah and Naarah. And Naarah bare
him Ahuzam, and Hepher, and Temeni, and Haahashtari. These
7 *were* the sons of Naarah. And the sons of Helah *were*, Zereth,
8 and Jezoar, and Ethnan. And Coz begat Anub, and Zobebah,
9 and the families of Aharhel the son of Harum. ¶And Jabez
was ^dmore honourable than his brethren: and his mother called   *d* Gen. 34. 19.
10 his name ⁴Jabez, saying, Because I bare him with sorrow. And
Jabez called on the God of Israel, saying, ⁵Oh that thou wouldest
bless me indeed, and enlarge my coast, and that thine hand
might be with me, and that thou wouldest ⁶keep *me* from evil,
that it may not grieve me! And God granted him that which
11 he requested. ¶And Chelub the brother of Shuah begat Mehir,
12 which *was* the father of Eshton. And Eshton begat Beth-rapha,
and Paseah, and Tehinnah the father of ⁷Ir-nahash. These *are*
13 the men of Rechah. And the sons of Kenaz; ^eOthniel, and   *e* Josh. 15.17.
14 Seraiah: and the sons of Othniel; ⁸Hathath. And Meonothai
begat Ophrah: and Seraiah begat Joab, the father of ^fthe   *f* Neh. 11.35.

---

¹ Heb. *Hiskijahu.*
² Or, *Chelubai,* ch. 2.9. or,
   Caleb, ch. 2. 18.
³ Or, *Haroeh,* ch. 2. 52.
⁴ That is, *Sorrowful.*
⁵ Heb. *If thou wilt, &c.*
⁶ Heb. *do me.*
⁷ Or, *the city of Nahash.*
⁸ Or, *Hathath,* and *Meo-*
   nothai, who begat, &c.

---

descend below about B.C. 410, and thus
falls within the probable lifetime of Nehemiah.

If, further, we regard it as most probable
that Ezra died before B.C. 431, and that this
passage in question was not wholly written
by him, this does not disprove the theory
(Introd. p. 446), that Ezra was the author
of Chronicles. Deuteronomy is by Moses,
though the last chapter cannot be from his
hand. The "dukes of Edom" might be
an insertion into the text of Genesis (xxxvi.
40–43) without the authorship of the remainder of the work being affected by it.
So here; Nehemiah, or Malachi, may have
carried on the descent of the "sons of David"
as far as it had reached in their time, adding
to the account given by Ezra one, or at the
most two verses.

IV. 3. Read, "These are the sons of the
father (*i.e.* chief) of Etam" (2 Chr. xi. 6), a
city of Judah, not far from Bethlehem.

9. It is remarkable that Jabez should be
introduced without description, or patro-
nymic, as if a well-known personage. We
can only suppose that he was known to
those for whom Chronicles was written,
either by tradition, or by writings which
have perished. In *v.* 10 Jabez alludes to his
name, "sorrowful" (marg.): "Grant that
the grief implied in my name may not come
upon me!"

11, 12. It has been conjectured from the
strangeness of all the names in this list,
that we have here a fragment of Canaanite
record, connected with the family of the
"Shua," whose daughter Judah took to
wife (ii. 3; Gen. xxxviii. 2), and whose
family thus became related to the tribe of
Judah.

14. The words "and Meonothai" should
be added to the end of *v.* 13; but they
should be retained also at the commencement of *v.* 14. Or, see marg. note.

15 ¹valley of ²Charashim; for they were craftsmen. And the sons
of Caleb the son of Jephunneh; Iru, Elah, and Naam: and the
16 sons of Elah, ³even Kenaz. And the sons of Jehaleleel; Ziph,
17 and Ziphah, Tiria, and Asareel. And the sons of Ezra *were*,
Jether, and Mered, and Epher, and Jalon: and she bare Miriam,
18 and Shammai, and Ishbah the father of Eshtemoa. And his
wife ⁴Jehudijah bare Jered the father of Gedor, and Heber the
father of Socho, and Jekuthiel the father of Zanoah. And these
are the sons of Bithiah the daughter of Pharaoh, which Mered
19 took. And the sons of *his* wife ⁵Hodiah the sister of Naham,
the father of Keilah the Garmite, and Eshtemoa the Maacha-
20 thite. And the sons of Shimon *were*, Amnon, and Rinnah,
Ben-hanan, and Tilon. And the sons of Ishi *were*, Zoheth, and

g Gen. 38. 1, 21 Ben-zoheth. ¶ The sons of Shelah *g*the son of Judah *were*, Er
5.   the father of Lecah, and Laadah the father of Mareshah, and
& 43. 12. the families of the house of them that wrought fine linen, of the
22 house of Ashbea, and Jokim, and the men of Chozeba, and Joash,
and Saraph, who had the dominion in Moab, and Jashubi-lehem.
23 And *these are* ancient things. These *were* the potters, and those
that dwelt among plants and hedges: there they dwelt with the
24 king for his work. ¶ The sons of Simeon *were*, ⁶Nemuel, and
25 Jamin, ⁷Jarib, Zerah, *and* Shaul: Shallum his son, Mibsam his
26 son, Mishma his son. And the sons of Mishma; Hamuel his
27 son, Zacchur his son, Shimei his son. And Shimei had sixteen
sons and six daughters; but his brethren had not many children,
neither did all their family multiply, ⁸like to the children of

h Josh. 19. 2. 28 Judah. And they dwelt at ʰBeer-sheba, and Moladah, and
29, 30 Hazar-shual, and at ⁹Bilhah, and at Ezem, and at ¹Tolad, and
31 at Bethuel, and at Hormah, and at Ziklag, and at Beth-marca-
both, and ²Hazarsusim, and at Beth-birei, and at Shaaraim.
32 These *were* their cities unto the reign of David. And their
villages *were*, ³Etam, and Ain, Rimmon, and Tochen, and

¹ Or, inhabitants *of the*   ⁵ Or, *Jehudijah*, mentioned   ⁹ Or, *Baluh*, Josh. 19. 3.
  valley.   before.   ¹ Or, *Eltolad*, Josh. 19. 4.
² That is, *Craftsmen*.   ⁶ Or, *Jemuel*, Gen. 46. 10.   ² Or, *Hazar-susah*, Josh.
³ Or, *Uknaz*.   Ex. 6. 15. Num. 26. 12.   19. 5.
⁴ Or, *the Jewess*.   ⁷ Or, *Jachin, Zohar*.   ³ Or, *Ether*, Josh. 19. 7.
                               ⁸ Heb. *unto*.

---

17. *she bare Miriam*] Rather, "she conceived." The mother is not mentioned, and
it seems impossible to restore the original
text with any certainty.
18. *his wife*] *i.e.* Mered's. Mered, it
would seem, had two wives, Bithiah, an
Egyptian woman, and a Jewish wife (see
marg.), whose name is not given. If Mered
was a chief of rank, Bithiah may have
been married to him with the consent of her
father; for the Egyptian kings often gave
their daughters in marriage to foreigners.
Or she may have elected to forsake her
countrymen and cleave to a Jewish husband, becoming a convert to his religion.
Her name, Bithiah, "daughter of Jehovah,"
is like that of a convert.
19. *his wife Hodiah*] Not as in marg., but
rather, "the sons of the wife of Hodiah."
Hodiah is elsewhere always a man's name
(Neh. viii. 7, ix. 5, x. 10, 13, 18).
22. *who had the dominion in Moab*] Moab

was conquered by David (2 Sam. viii. 2),
and again by Omri, after which it remained
subject until the death of Ahab (2 K. iii. 5).
But a more ancient rule, in times of which
we have no further record, is probably intended.
23. *among plants and hedges*] Rather,
"in Netaim and Gederah" (Josh. xv.
36).
with the king] Or, probably, "on the
king's property." Both David and several
of the later kings had large territorial possessions in various parts of Judæa (1 Chr.
xxvii. 25-31; 2 Chr. xxvi.10, xxvii. 4, xxxii.
28, 29).
31. *unto the reign of David*] It is not
quite clear why this clause is added. Perhaps the writer is quoting from a document
belonging to David's reign. Or, he may
mean that some of the cities, as Ziklag (1
Sam. xxvii. 6), were lost to Simeon about
David's time.

33 Ashan, five cities: and all their villages that *were* round about the same cities, unto [1]Baal. These *were* their habitations, and
34 [2]their genealogy. And Meshobab, and Jamlech, and Joshah
35 the son of Amaziah, and Joel, and Jehu the son of Josibiah, the
36 son of Seraiah, the son of Asiel, and Elioenai, and Jaakobah, and Jeshohaiah, and Asaiah, and Adiel, and Jesimiel, and
37 Benaiah, and Ziza the son of Shiphi, the son of Allon, the son
38 of Jedaiah, the son of Shimri, the son of Shemaiah; these [3]mentioned by *their* names *were* princes in their families: and the
39 house of their fathers increased greatly. ¶And they went to the entrance of Gedor, *even* unto the east side of the valley, to
40 seek pasture for their flocks. And they found fat pasture and good, and the land *was* wide, and quiet, and peaceable; for *they*
41 of Ham had dwelt there of old. And these written by name came in the days of Hezekiah king of Judah, and [i]smote their tents, and the habitations that were found there, and destroyed them utterly unto this day, and dwelt in their rooms: because
42 *there was* pasture there for their flocks. And *some* of them, *even* of the sons of Simeon, five hundred men, went to mount Seir, having for their captains Pelatiah, and Neariah, and
43 Rephaiah, and Uzziel, the sons of Ishi. And they smote [k]the rest of the Amalekites that were escaped, and dwelt there unto this day.

CHAP. 5. NOW the sons of Reuben the firstborn of Israel, (for [a]he *was* the firstborn; but, forasmuch as he [b]defiled his father's bed, [c]his birthright was given unto the sons of Joseph the son of Israel: and the genealogy is not to be reckoned after the birth-
2 right. For [d]Judah prevailed above his brethren, and of him
3 *came* the [e]chief [4]ruler; but the birthright *was* Joseph's:) the sons, *I say,* of [f]Reuben the firstborn of Israel *were*, Hanoch,
4 and Pallu, Hezron, and Carmi. The sons of Joel; Shemaiah
5 his son, Gog his son, Shimei his son, Micah his son, Reaia his
6 son, Baal his son, Beerah his son, whom [5]Tilgath-pilneser king of Assyria carried away *captive:* he *was* prince of the Reuben-
7 ites. And his brethren by their families, [g]when the genealogy of their generations was reckoned, *were* the chief, Jeiel, and

i 2 Kin. 18. 8.

k See
1 Sam. 15. 8.
& 30. 17.
2 Sam. 8. 12.
a Gen. 29. 32.
& 49. 3.
b Gen. 35. 22.
& 49. 4.
c Gen. 48. 15.
d Gen. 49. 8, 10.
Ps. 60. 7.
& 108. 8.
e Mic. 5. 2.
Matt. 2. 6.
f Gen. 46. 9.
Ex. 6. 14.
Num.,26. 5.
g See ver.17.

[1] Or, *Baalath-beer*, Josh. 19. 8.
[2] Or, *as they divided them-*
selves by nations among them.
[3] Heb. *coming.*
[4] Or, *prince.*
[5] Or, *Tiglath-pileser,* 2 Kin. 15. 29. & 16. 7.

---

33. *and their genealogy*] Rather, "**and their register was according thereto**"—they were registered, *i.e.* according to the places where they dwelt.

38. *these mentioned by their names were princes*] The registered chiefs of the cities in the first list (*rr.* 28-31), in the time of Hezekiah (*v.* 41).

39. *Gedor*] Rather read, "Gerar" (LXX.) a fertile district (Gen. xxvi. 6-12; 2 Chr. xiv. 14, 15) in Philistine country.

41. *the habitations*] Rather, "**the Mehunim**" (cp. 2 Chr. xxxvi. 7), called also "Maonites" (see Judg. x. 12 note).

43. *unto this day*] These words are probably taken from the record which the writer of Chronicles had before him, and do not imply that the Simeonites remained undisturbed in their conquests till after the return from the Captivity. So *v.* 41.

V. 1. *his birthright was given* &c.] In particular, the right of the first-born to a double inheritance (Deut. xxi. 17) was conferred on Joseph, both by the expressed will of Jacob (Gen. xlviii. 22) and in the actual partition of Canaan (Josh. xvi. and xvii.). But though the birthright, as respecting its material privileges, passed to Joseph, its other rights, those of dignity and pre-eminence, fell to Judah; of whom came the chief ruler, an allusion especially to David, though it may reach further, and include a glance at the Messiah, the true "Ruler" of Israel (Micah v. 2).

4. *The sons of Joel*] The line of succession here given must be broken by one great gap or several smaller ones, since nine generations before Tiglath-pileser would carry us back no further than the reign of Rehoboam.

8 Zechariah, and Bela the son of Azaz, the son of [1]Shema, the son
of Joel, who dwelt in [h]Aroer, even unto Nebo and Baal-meon:
9 and eastward he inhabited unto the entering in of the wilderness from the river Euphrates: because their cattle were mul-
10 tiplied [i]in the land of Gilead. And in the days of Saul they
made war [k]with the Hagarites, who fell by their hand: and
they dwelt in their tents [2]throughout all the east *land* of Gilead.
11 ¶ And the children of Gad dwelt over against them, in the land
12 of [l]Bashan unto Salcah: Joel the chief, and Shapham the next,
13 and Jaanai, and Shaphat in Bashan. And their brethren of the
house of their fathers *were*, Michael, and Meshullam, and Sheba,
14 and Jorai, and Jachan, and Zia, and Heber, seven. These *are*
the children of Abihail the son of Huri, the son of Jaroah, the
15 son of Gilead, the son of Michael, the son of Jeshishai, the son
of Jahdo, the son of Buz; Ahi the son of Abdiel, the son of
16 Guni, chief of the house of their fathers. And they dwelt in
Gilead in Bashan, and in her towns, and in all the suburbs of
17 [m]Sharon, upon [3]their borders. All these were reckoned by
genealogies in the days of [n]Jotham king of Judah, and in the
18 days of [o]Jeroboam king of Israel. ¶ The sons of Reuben, and
the Gadites, and half the tribe of Manasseh, [4]of valiant men,
men able to bear buckler and sword, and to shoot with bow, and
skilful in war, *were* four and forty thousand seven hundred and
19 threescore, that went out to the war. And they made war with
20 the Hagarites, with [p]Jetur, and Nephish, and Nodab. And
[q]they were helped against them, and the Hagarites were delivered into their hand, and all that *were* with them: for they
cried to God in the battle, and he was intreated of them; because
21 they [r]put their trust in him. And they [5]took away their cattle;
of their camels fifty thousand, and of sheep two hundred and
fifty thousand, and of asses two thousand, and of [6]men an hun-
22 dred thousand. For there fell down many slain, because the
war *was* of God. And they dwelt in their steads until [s]the cap-

Marginal notes:
[h] Josh. 13. 15—17.
[i] Josh. 22. 9.
[k] Gen. 25. 12.
[l] Josh. 13. 11, 24.
[m] ch. 27. 29.
[n] 2 Kin. 15. 5, 32.
[o] 2 Kin. 14. 16, 28.
[p] Gen. 25. 15. ch. 1. 31.
[q] See ver. 22.
[r] Ps. 22. 4, 5.
[s] 2 Kin. 15. 29. & 17. 6.

---

[1] Or, *Shemaiah*, ver. 4.
[2] Heb. *upon all the face of the east.*
[3] Heb. *their goings forth.*
[4] Heb. *sons of valour.*
[5] Heb. *led captive.*
[6] Heb. *souls of men:* as Num. 31. 35.

---

9. *he inhabited*] i.e. Reuben. Eastward
the Reubenites inhabited as far as the commencement of the great Syrian Desert,
which extended all the way from the river
Euphrates to their borders.

10. The "Hagarites" or "Hagarenes"
are generally regarded as descendants of
Hagar, and a distinct branch of the Ish-
maelites (1 Chr. xxvii. 30, 31; Ps. lxxxiii.
6). They appear to have been one of
the most wealthy (v. 21) and widely-
spread tribes of the Syrian Desert, being
found on the side of the Euphrates in contact with the Assyrians, and also in the
Hauran, in the neighbourhood of Palestine,
in contact with the Moabites and Israelites. If identical with the Agræi of the
classical writers, their name may be considered as still surviving in that of the
district called *Hejer* or *Hejera* in north-
eastern Arabia, on the borders of the Persian Gulf. A full account of the war is
given in *vv.* 18-22.

11. From this passage and from the sub-

sequent account of the Manassites (*vv.* 23,
24), the Gadites extended themselves to the
north at the expense of their brethren,
gradually occupying a considerable portion
of the tract originally allotted to the "half
tribe."

17. The writer refers here to two registra-
tions, one made under the authority of
Jeroboam II. when he was king and Israel
flourishing, the other made under the authority of Jotham, king of Judah, during the
troublous time which followed on the great
invasion of Tiglath-pileser. There is nothing
surprising in a king of Judah having exercised a species of lordship over the trans-
Jordanic territory at this period.

19. Jetur no doubt gave his name to the
important tribe of the Ituræans who inhabited the region south-west of the Damascene plain, between Gaulonitis (*Jaulan*) and
the Ledjah. This tribe was noted for its
thievish habits, and was regarded as savage
and warlike.

23 tivity. ¶ And the children of the half tribe of Manasseh dwelt in the land: they increased from Bashan unto Baal-hermon
24 and Senir, and unto mount Hermon. And these *were* the heads of the house of their fathers, even Epher, and Ishi, and Eliel, and Azriel, and Jeremiah, and Hodaviah, and Jahdiel, mighty men of valour, [1]famous men, *and* heads of the house of their
25 fathers. And they transgressed against the God of their fathers, and went a *whoring after the gods of the people of the land, *t* 2 Kin. 17.7.*
26 whom God destroyed before them. And the God of Israel stirred up the spirit of *u*Pul king of Assyria, and the spirit of *u* 2 Kin. 15. 19. *x*Tilgath-pilneser king of Assyria, and he carried them away, *x* 2 Kin. 15. 29. even the Reubenites, and the Gadites and the half tribe of *y*Halah, and Habor, and *y* 2 Kin. 17.6. Manasseh, and brought them unto *y*Halah, and Habor, and & 18. 11. Hara, and to the river Gozan, unto this day.

CHAP. 6. THE sons of Levi; *a[2]*Gershon, Kohath, and Merari. And *a* Gen. 46.11.
2 the sons of Kohath; Amram, *b*Izhar, and Hebron, and Uzziel. Ex. 6. 16. Num. 26. 57.
3 And the children of Amram; Aaron, and Moses, and Miriam. ch. 23. 6. The sons also of Aaron; *c*Nadab, and Abihu, Eleazar, and *b* See ver. 22.
4 Ithamar. Eleazar begat Phinehas, Phinehas begat Abishua, *c* Lev. 10. 1.
5, 6 and Abishua begat Bukki, and Bukki begat Uzzi, and Uzzi
7 begat Zerahiah, and Zerahiah begat Meraioth, Meraioth begat
8 Amariah, and Amariah begat Ahitub, and *d*Ahitub begat Zadok, *d* 2Sam.8.17.
9 and *e*Zadok begat Ahimaaz, and Ahimaaz begat Azariah, and *e* 2 Sam. 15.
10 Azariah begat Johanan, and Johanan begat Azariah, (he *it is* 27. *f*that executed the priest's office [3]in the *g*temple that Solomon *f* See
11 built in Jerusalem:) and *h*Azariah begat Amariah, and Amariah 2 Chr. 26.
12 begat Ahitub, and Ahitub begat Zadok, and Zadok begat [4]Shal- 17, 18. *g* 1 Kin. 6.
13 lum, and Shallum begat Hilkiah, and Hilkiah begat Azariah, 2 Chr. 3.
14 and Azariah begat *i*Seraiah, and Seraiah begat Jehozadak, and *h* See Ezra 7. 3.
15 Jehozadak went *into captivity,* *k*when the LORD carried away *i* Neh. 11.11. *k* 2 Kin. 25. 18.

[1] Heb. *men of names.*
[2] Or, *Gershom,* ver. 16.
[3] Heb. *in the house.*
[4] Or, *Meshullam,* ch. 9. 11.

---

23. "Baal-Hermon," "Senir" (Deut. iii. 9), and "Mount Hermon," are here not so much three names of the one great snow-clad eminence in which the Anti-Lebanon terminates towards the south, as three parts of the mountain—perhaps the "three summits" in which it terminates.

26. "Habor" here seems to be a city or a district, and not a river, as in marg. ref. There is some reason to believe that districts among the Assyrians were occasionally named from streams.

Hara is probably the same as "Haran" (Gen. xi. 31: 2 K. xix. 12; Ezek. xxvii. 23), being a softening down of the rugged original "Kharan."

VI. 1–15. The genealogy of the High-priestly stem to the Captivity.

9. *Ahimaaz begat Azariah*] It must, apparently, be this Azariah, and not the son of Johanan (*v.* 10), who was High-Priest at the dedication of Solomon's Temple. For Zadok, who lived into the reign of Solomon (1 K. iv. 4) cannot have been succeeded by a great-great-grandson. The notice in *v.* 10, which is attached to the second Azariah, must, beyond a doubt, belong properly to the first.

11. *Ahitub*] Between Amariah and Hilkiah (*v.* 13) this genealogy is most certainly defective, as it gives three generations only for a period for which nine generations are furnished by the list of the kings of Judah, and which cannot be estimated as much short of 200 years. Further, no one of the names in this part of the list occurs among the High-Priests of the period, several of whom are mentioned both in the Second Book of Chronicles and in Kings; the explanation of which seems to be that the present is not a list of High-Priests, but the genealogy of Jozadak or Jehozadak, whose line of descent partly coincided with the list of High-Priests, partly differed from it. Where it coincided, all the names are given; where it differed, some are omitted, in order (probably) to render the entire list from Phinehas a multiple of seven. See note on *v.* 20.

15. *Jehozadak*] The meaning of the name is "Jehovah is righteous." It has been noted as remarkable that the heads of both the priestly and the royal stock carried to Babylon should have had names (Zedekiah and Jehozadak) composed of the same elements, and assertive of the "justice of

16 Judah and Jerusalem by the hand of Nebuchadnezzar. ¶ The

l Ex. 6. 16.

17 sons of Levi; [11]Gershom, Kohath, and Merari. And these *be*
18 the names of the sons of Gershom; Libni, and Shimei. And
the sons of Kohath *were*, Amram, and Izhar, and Hebron, and
19 Uzziel. The sons of Merari; Mahli, and Mushi. ¶ And these
20 *are* the families of the Levites according to their fathers. ¶ Of

m ver. 42.

Gershom; Libni his son, Jahath his son, [m]Zimmah his son,
21 [2]Joah his son, [3]Iddo his son, Zerah his son [4]Jeaterai his son.
22 ¶ The sons of Kohath; [5]Amminadab his son, Korah his son,
23 Assir his son, Elkanah his son, and Ebiasaph his son, and Assir
24 his son, Tahath his son, [6]Uriel his son, Uzziah his son, and

n See ver. 35, 36.

25 Shaul his son. And the sons of Elkanah; [n]Amasai, and Ahi-
26 moth. *As for* Elkanah: the sons of Elkanah; [7]Zophai his

o ver. 34, *Toah.*
p ver. 34, *Eliel.*

27 son, and [o]Nahath his son, [p]Eliab his son, Jeroham his son,
28 Elkanah his son. And the sons of Samuel; the firstborn [8]Vashni,
29 and Abiah. ¶ The sons of Merari; Mahli, Libni his son, Shimei
30 his son, Uzza his son, Shimea his son, Haggiah his son, Asaiah
31 his son. ¶ And these *are they* whom David set over the service

q ch. 16. 1.

of song in the house of the LORD, after that the [q]ark had rest.
32 And they ministered before the dwelling place of the tabernacle
of the congregation with singing, until Solomon had built the
house of the LORD in Jerusalem: and *then* they waited on their
33 office according to their order. ¶ And these *are* they that [9]waited
with their children. Of the sons of the Kohathites: Heman a
34 singer, the son of Joel, the son of Shemuel, the son of Elkanah,
35 the son of Jeroham, the son of Eliel, the son of [1]Toah, the son of
36 [2]Zuph, the son of Elkanah, the son of Mahath, the son of Amasai,
the son of Elkanah, the son of [3]Joel, the son of Azariah, the son
37 of Zephaniah, the son of Tahath, the son of Assir, the son of

r Ex 6. 24

38 [r]Ebiasaph, the son of Korah, the son of Izhar, the son of Ko-
39 hath, the son of Levi, the son of Israel. ¶ And his brother
Asaph, who stood on his right hand, *even* Asaph the son of

---

[1] Or, *Gershon*, ver. 1.
[2] Or, *Ethan*, ver. 42.
[3] Or, *Adaiah*, ver. 41.
[4] Or, *Ethni*, ver. 41.
[5] Or, *Izhar*, ver. 2, 18.

[6] Or, *Zephaniah, Azariah, Joel*, ver. 36.
[7] Or, *Zuph*, ver. 35. 1 Sam. 1. 1.
[8] Called also *Joel*, ver. 33. & 1 Sam. 8. 2.

[9] Heb. *stood.*
[1] ver. 26, *Nahath.*
[2] Or, *Zophai.*
[3] ver. 24, *Shaul, Uzziah, Uriel.*

God," which their sufferings showed forth so signally.

16, &c.] A general account of the several branches of the tribe of Levi.

20. *Of Gershom*] The names in this list are curiously different from those in *vv.* 41–43, which yet appear to represent the same line reversed. Probably both lists are more or less corrupted, and, as in many genealogies, omission is made, to reduce the number of the names to seven. Cp. *e.g. vv.* 22–28 with *vv.* 33–38. Cp. the other genealogies of this chapter; and see also Matt. i. 1–17.

28. *Vashni*] The true name of Samuel's first-born, which was "Joel" (see marg. and reff.), has here dropped out; and the word properly meaning "and his second [son]" has been taken as the name of the first.

31–48. The genealogies of David's three chief singers, Heman, Asaph, and Ethan or Jeduthun.

32. *they waited on their office*] On the establishment and continuance of the choral service in the Temple, see 2 Chr. v. 12, xxix. 27–30, xxxv. 15.

33. *Heman*] In general Asaph takes precedence of Heman and Jeduthun, but here Heman is placed first, because his family, that of the Kohathites, had the highest priestly rank, being the family which furnished the High-Priests (see *vv.* 2–15).

Shemuel] *i.e.* "Samuel." Our translators have here given the Hebrew, while elsewhere they give uniformly the Greek, form of the name. We learn by this genealogy that Heman was Samuel's grandson.

39. *his brother Asaph*] Not "brother" in the ordinary sense of the term, since Asaph was the son of Berachiah, and a Gershonite, not a Kohathite. "Brother" here may mean "fellow-craftsman" (cp. xxv. 7).

40 Berachiah, the son of Shimea, the son of Michael, the son of
41 Baaseiah, the son of Malchiah, the son of *Ethni, the son of   *See ver. 21.
42 Zerah, the son of Adaiah, the son of Ethan, the son of Zimmah,
43 the son of Shimei, the son of Jahath, the son of Gershom, the
44 son of Levi. ¶And their brethren the sons of Merari *stood* on
   the left hand: ¹Ethan the son of ²Kishi, the son of Abdi, the
45 son of Malluch, the son of Hashabiah, the son of Amaziah, the
46 son of Hilkiah, the son of Amzi, the son of Bani, the son of
47 Shamer, the son of Mahli, the son of Mushi, the son of Merari,
48 the son of Levi. Their brethren also the Levites *were* appointed
   unto all manner of service of the tabernacle of the house of God.
49 ¶But Aaron and his sons offered *upon the altar of the burnt   *Lev. 1. 9.
   offering, and "on the altar of incense, *and were appointed* for "Ex. 30. 7.
   all the work of the *place* most holy, and to make an atonement
   for Israel, according to all that Moses the servant of God had
50 commanded. And these *are* the sons of Aaron; Eleazar his
51 son, Phinehas his son, Abishua his son, Bukki his son, Uzzi his
52 son, Zerahiah his son, Meraioth his son, Amariah his son, Ahitub
53, 54 his son, Zadok his son, Ahimaaz his son. ¶ˣNow these *are*   ˣJosh. 21.
   their dwelling places throughout their castles in their coasts, of
   the sons of Aaron, of the families of the Kohathites: for their's
55 was the lot. ʸAnd they gave them Hebron in the land of Judah,   ʸJosh. 21.
56 and the suburbs thereof round it. ᶻBut the fields of the city,   11, 12.
   and the villages thereof, they gave to Caleb the son of Jephun-   ᶻJosh. 14.13.
                                                                     & 15. 13.
57 neh. And ᵃto the sons of Aaron they gave the cities of Judah,   ᵃJosh.21.13.
   namely, Hebron, *the city* of refuge, and Libnah with her suburbs,
58 and Jattir, and Eshtemoa, with their suburbs, and ³Hilen with
59 her suburbs, Debir with her suburbs, and ⁴Ashan with her
60 suburbs, and Beth-shemesh with her suburbs: and out of the
   tribe of Benjamin; Geba with her suburbs, and ⁵Alemeth with

¹ Called *Jeduthun*, ch. 9.   ² Or, *Kushaiah*, ch. 15. 17.   ⁴ Or, *Ain*, Josh. 21. 16.
16. & 25. 1, 3, 6.   ³ Or, *Holon*, Josh. 21. 15.   ⁵ Or, *Almon*, Josh. 21. 18.

---

44. *Ethan*] Or Jeduthun (see marg.).
Corruption will scarcely account for the
two forms of the name, since Ethan is used
persistently up to a certain point (xv. 19),
after which we have uniformly "Jeduthun."
The case seems to be rather one in which
a new name was taken after a while, which
thenceforth superseded the old. Compare
Abraham, Sarah, Joshua, Jehoiakim, Zedekiah, &c.

50. *the sons of Aaron*] This list, a mere
repetition of that in *vv*. 3–8, came, probably,
from a different source—a source belonging
to the time of David, with whom Ahimaaz
(the last name on the list) was contemporary. The other list (*vv*. 4–15) came, no
doubt, from a document belonging to the
time of the Captivity (see *v*. 15).

54. *their's was the lot*] *i.e.* "the *first* lot."
The Kohathites had the *first* lot among the
Levitical families, as being the family
whereto the High-priesthood was attached
(cp. Josh. xxi. 10).

56–81. The writer evidently had before
him Josh. xxi., which he followed, as to its
matter, closely. In some cases he perhaps
modernised the ancient names (*vv*. 58, 60,
72, &c.); in a few he substituted for the old

an entirely new name, the modern appellation, probably, of the ancient site (*vv*. 70,
77). At one time, it would seem, his intention was to give the cities of the priests
only, and to content himself with stating
the mere number of the rest. His account
of the matter was then brought to a conclusion, and summed up, in *v*. 64. But,
afterwards, either he or a later writer
thought it best to add to the list of the
priestly cities the information contained in
Judges as to those which were not priestly,
but merely Levitical. The passage *vv*. 65–
81 was then added.

The entire account has suffered much
from corruption. In the first list two
names, those of Juttah and Gideon, have
dropped out. It is necessary to restore
them in order to complete the number of
thirteen cities (*v*. 60). In the second list
(*vv*. 67–70) there is likewise an omission of
two cities, Eltekeh and Gibbethon, which
are wanted to make up the number ten (*v*.
61). The third list is complete, though some
of the names are very different from those
of Joshua. In the fourth, two names are
again wanting, those of Jokneam and
Kartah.

her suburbs, and Anathoth with her suburbs.   All their cities
61 throughout their families *were* thirteen cities.   ¶ And unto the

a ver. 66.

sons of Kohath *b which were* left of the family of that tribe, *were
cities given* out of the half tribe, *namely, out of* the half *tribe* of

c Josh. 21. 5.

62 Manasseh, *c* by lot, ten cities.   ¶ And to the sons of Gershom
throughout their families out of the tribe of Issachar, and out
of the tribe of Asher, and out of the tribe of Naphtali, and out
63 of the tribe of Manasseh in Bashan, thirteen cities.   ¶ Unto the
sons of Merari *were given* by lot, throughout their families, out
of the tribe of Reuben, and out of the tribe of Gad, and out of

d Josh. 21. 7, 34.

64 the tribe of Zebulun, *d* twelve cities.   And the children of Israel
65 gave to the Levites *these* cities with their suburbs.   And they
gave by lot out of the tribe of the children of Judah, and out of
the tribe of the children of Simeon, and out of the tribe of the
children of Benjamin, these cities, which are called by *their*

e ver. 61.

66 names.   ¶ And *e the residue* of the families of the sons of Kohath

f Josh. 21.21.

67 had cities of their coasts out of the tribe of Ephraim.   *f* And
they gave unto them, *of* the cities of refuge, Shechem in mount
Ephraim with her suburbs; *they gave* also Gezer with her sub-

g See Josh.
21. 22—35,
where many
of these
cities have
other
names.

68 urbs, and *g* Jokmeam with her suburbs, and Beth-horon with her
69 suburbs, and Aijalon with her suburbs, and Gath-rimmon with
70 her suburbs : and out of the half tribe of Manasseh ; Aner with
her suburbs, and Bileam with her suburbs, for the family of the
71 remnant of the sons of Kohath.   ¶ Unto the sons of Gershom
were given out of the family of the half tribe of Manasseh,
Golan in Bashan with her suburbs, and Ashtaroth with her
72 suburbs : and out of the tribe of Issachar ; Kedesh with her
73 suburbs, Daberath with her suburbs, and Ramoth with her sub-
74 urbs, and Anem with her suburbs : and out of the tribe of Asher ;
Mashal with her suburbs, and Abdon with her suburbs, and
75, 76 Hukok with her suburbs, and Rehob with her suburbs : and
out of the tribe of Naphtali ; Kedesh in Galilee with her suburbs, and Hammon with her suburbs, and Kirjathaim with her
77 suburbs.   ¶ Unto the rest of the children of Merari *were given*
out of the tribe of Zebulun, Rimmon with her suburbs, Tabor
78 with her suburbs : and on the other side Jordan by Jericho, on
the east side of Jordan, *were given them* out of the tribe of
Reuben, Bezer in the wilderness with her suburbs, and Jahzah
79 with her suburbs, Kedemoth also with her suburbs, and Me-
80 phaath with her suburbs : and out of the tribe of Gad ; Ramoth
in Gilead with her suburbs, and Mahanaim with her suburbs,
81 and Heshbon with her suburbs, and Jazer with her suburbs.

a Gen. 46. 13.
Num. 26. 23.

CHAP. 7. NOW the sons of Issachar *were*, *a* Tola, and [1] Puah, Ja-
2 shub, and Shimrom, four.   And the sons of Tola ; Uzzi, and
Rephaiah, and Jeriel, and Jahmai, and Jibsam, and Shemuel,
heads of their father's house, *to wit*, of Tola : they *were* valiant

[1] *Phuvah, Job.*

---

61. *unto the sons of Kohath which were left*]
i.e. to such of them as were not priests.

out of the half tribe ... ten cities] The half
tribe furnished two cities only (*v.* 70, and
cp. Josh. xxi. 25).   It is evident therefore
that something has fallen out.   We may
supply from Joshua the words "**out of
Ephraim and out of Dan, and**" before
"out of the half tribe."

77. *Unto the rest of the children of Merari*]

Rather, "Unto the rest, the children of
Merari"—that is to say, "unto the remainder of the Levites, who were descendants of Merari :"—the two other branches,
the Kohathites and the Gershomites, having
been treated of previously.

VII. **2.** *whose number was in the days of
David*, &c.] The writer would seem by this
passage to have had access to the statistics
of the tribes collected by David, when he

men of might in their generations; [b]whose number *was* in the
3 days of David two and twenty thousand and six hundred. And
the sons of Uzzi; Izrahiah: and the sons of Izrahiah; Michael,
4 and Obadiah, and Joel, Ishiah, five: all of them chief men. And
with them, by their generations, after the house of their fathers,
were bands of soldiers for war, six and thirty thousand *men*: for
5 they had many wives and sons. And their brethren among all
the families of Issachar *were* valiant men of might, reckoned in
6 all by their genealogies fourscore and seven thousand. ¶ *The*
7 *sons* of [c]Benjamin; Bela, and Becher, and Jediael, three. And
the sons of Bela; Ezbon, and Uzzi, and Uzziel, and Jerimoth, and
Iri, five; heads of the house of *their* fathers, mighty men of
valour; and were reckoned by their genealogies twenty and two
8 thousand and thirty and four. And the sons of Becher; Zemira,
and Joash, and Eliezer, and Elioenai, and Omri, and Jerimoth,
and Abiah, and Anathoth, and Alameth. All these *are* the sons
9 of Becher. And the number of them, after their genealogy by
their generations, heads of the house of their fathers, mighty
10 men of valour, *was* twenty thousand and two hundred. The
sons also of Jediael; Bilhan: and the sons of Bilhan; Jeush,
and Benjamin, and Ehud, and Chenaanah, and Zethan, and
11 Tharshish, and Ahishahar. All these the sons of Jediael, by the
heads of their fathers, mighty men of valour, *were* seventeen
thousand and two hundred *soldiers*, fit to go out for war *and*
12 battle. [d]Shuppim also, and Huppim, the children of [1]Ir, *and*
13 Hushim, the sons of [2]Aher. ¶ The sons of Naphtali; Jahziel,
14 and Guni, and Jezer, and [e]Shallum, the sons of Bilhah. ¶ The
sons of Manasseh; Ashriel, whom she bare: (*but* his concubine
15 the Aramitess bare Machir the father of Gilead: and Machir
took to wife *the sister* of Huppim and Shuppim, whose sister's
name *was* Maachah;) and the name of the second *was* Zelo-
16 phehad: and Zelophehad had daughters. And Maachah the
wife of Machir bare a son, and she called his name Peresh; and
the name of his brother *was* Sheresh; and his sons *were* Ulam
17 and Rakem. And the sons of Ulam; [f]Bedan. These *were* the
18 sons of Gilead, the son of Machir, the son of Manasseh. And
his sister Hammoleketh bare Ishod, and [g]Abiezer, and Mahalah.
19 And the sons of Shemidah *were*, Ahian, and Shechem, and

[b] 2 Sam. 24.
1, 2.
ch. 27. 1.

[c] Gen. 46. 21.
Num. 26. 38.
ch. 8. 1, &c.

[d] Num. 26.
39, *Shupham,*
and *Hu-
pham.*
[e] Gen. 46. 24,
Shillem.

[f] 1 Sam. 12.
11:

[g] Num. 23.
30, *Jeezer.*

---

[1] Or, *Iri*, ver. 7.   [2] Or, *Ahiram*, Num. 26. 38.

---

sinfully "numbered the people" (marg.
ref.). The numbers given in *vv.* 4, 5 probably came from the same source.

6. *three*] In Genesis, *ten* "sons" of Benjamin are mentioned; in Numbers, *five*
(marg. reff.). Neither list, however, contains Jediael who was perhaps a later chieftain. If so, "son" as applied to him means
only "descendant."

It is conjectured that Becher has disap-
peared from the lists in ch. viii. and in
Numbers, because he, or his heir, married
an Ephraimite heiress, and that his house
thus passed over in a certain sense into the
tribe of Ephraim, in which the "Bachrites"
are placed in Numbers (xxvi. 35). He retains, however, his place here, because, by
right of blood, he really belonged to Benjamin.

7, 8, 10. The lists here are remarkably
different from those in marg. reff. Probably
the persons here mentioned were not literally "sons," but were among the later
descendants of the founders, being the chief
men of the family at the time of David's
census.

17. *These were the sons of Gilead*] *i.e.*
these descendants of Machir were reckoned to the family of Gilead. The name
"Gilead" prevailed above all others in the
line of Manasseh, the term "Gileadite"
almost taking the place of "Manassite."

18. *Abiezer*] His descendants formed one
of the most important branches of the
Manassites. They furnished to Israel the
greatest of the Judges, Gideon (Jud. vi. 11,
24, 34), and were regarded as the leading
family among the so-called "sons of Gilead.

Num.26.35.   20 Likhi, and Aniam. ¶And *ʰ*the sons of Ephraim; Shuthelah, and Bered his son, and Tahath his son, and Eladah his son, and
21 Tahath his son, and Zabad his son, and Shuthelah his son, and Ezer, and Elead, whom the men of Gath *that were* born in *that* land slew, because they came down to take away their cattle.
22 And Ephraim their father mourned many days, and his brethren
23 came to comfort him. And when he went in to his wife, she conceived, and bare a son, and he called his name Beriah, because
24 it went evil with his house. (And his daughter *was* Sherah, who built Beth-horon the nether, and the upper, and Uzzen-sherah.)
25 And Rephah *was* his son, also Resheph, and Telah his son, and
26 Tahan his son, Laadan his son, Ammihud his son, Elishama his
27, 28 son, ¹Non his son, Jehoshuah his son. And their possessions and habitations *were*, Beth-el and the towns thereof, and

ⁱ Josh. 16. 7,   eastward *ⁱ*Naaran, and westward Gezer, with the ²towns thereof;
Naarath.   Shechem also and the towns thereof, unto Gaza and the towns
ᵏ Josh. 17. 7.   29 thereof : and by the borders of the children of *ᵏ*Manasseh, Beth-
ˡ 1 Kin. 4.   shean and her towns, Taanach and her towns, *ˡ*Megiddo and her
11, 12.   towns, Dor and her towns. In these dwelt the children of
ᵐ Gen.46.17.   30 Joseph the son of Israel. ¶*ᵐ*The sons of Asher; Imnah, and
Num. 26. 44.   31 Isuah, and Ishuai, and Beriah, and Serah their sister. And the sons of Beriah; Heber, and Malchiel, who *is* the father of Bir-
ⁿ ver. 34,   32 zavith. And Heber begat Japhlet, and *ⁿ*Shomer, and Hotham,
Shamer.   33 and Shua their sister. And the sons of Japhlet; Pasach, and
34 Bimhal, and Ashvath. These *are* the children of Japhlet. And
ᵒ ver. 32,   the sons of *ᵒ*Shamer; Ahi, and Rohgah, Jehubbah, and Aram.
Shomer.   35 And the sons of his brother Helem; Zophah, and Imna, and
36 Shelesh, and Amal. The sons of Zophah; Suah, and Harne-
37 pher, and Shual, and Beri, and Imrah, Bezer, and Hod, and
38 Shamma, and Shilshah, and Ithran, and Beera. And the sons
39 of Jether; Jephunneh, and Pispah, and Ara. And the sons of
40 Ulla; Arah, and Haniel, and Rezia. All these *were* the children of Asher, heads of *their* father's house, choice *and* mighty men of valour, chief of the princes. And the number throughout the genealogy of them that were apt to the war *and* to battle *was* twenty and six thousand men.

ᵃ Gen. 46. 21.   **CHAP. 8.** NOW Benjamin begat *ᵃ*Bela his first-born, Ashbel the
Num. 26. 33.   2 second, and Aharah the third, Nohah the fourth, and Rapha
ch. 7. 6.   3 the fifth. And the sons of Bela were, ³Addar, and Gera, and
4, 5 Abihud, and Abishua, and Naaman, and Ahoah, and Gera,
6 and ⁴Shephuphan, and Huram. And these *are* the sons of

---

¹ Or, *Nun,* Num. 13. 8, 16.   ³ Or, *Ard,* Gen. 46. 21.   ⁴ Or, *Shupham,* Num. 26.
² Heb. *daughters.*   39. See ch. 7. 12.

---

20. *the sons of Ephraim*] The genealogy is difficult. It is perhaps best to consider Ezer and Elead (*v.* 21) as not sons of Zabad and brothers of the second Shuthelah, but natural sons of Ephraim. The passage would then run—
"And the sons of Ephraim, Shuthelah (and Bered *was* his son, and Tahath his son and Eladah his son, and Tahath his son, and Zabad his son, and Shuthelah his son) and Ezer and Elead, whom the men of Gath slew" (*i.e.* the settled inhabitants, as contrasted with the nomadic Hebrews, Amalekites, &c.).
24. Sherah could scarcely herself have built the Palestinian cities here mentioned,

which must belong to a time not earlier than Joshua. By "she built" we must understand "her descendants built."
34. *Shamer; Ahi, and Rohgah*] Translate —"The sons of Shamer (*v.* 32), **his brother,** Rohgah, &c."
VIII. 1. The reason of this return to the genealogy of the Benjamites seems to be the desire to connect the genealogical introduction with the historical body of the work. As the history is to begin with Saul, the genealogical portion is made to end with an account of the family of this Benjamite monarch.
6. *and they removed them to Manahath*]

Ehud : these are the heads of the fathers of the inhabitants of
7 Geba, and they removed them to ^bManahath : and Naaman, and
Ahiah, and Gera, he removed them, and begat Uzza, and Ahihud.
8 And Shaharaim begat *children* in the country of Moab, after he
9 had sent them away; Hushim and Baara *were* his wives. And
he begat of Hodesh his wife, Jobab, and Zibia, and Mesha, and
10 Malcham, and Jeuz, and Shachia, and Mirma. These *were* his
11 sons, heads of the fathers. And of Hushim he begat Abitub,
12 and Elpaal. The sons of Elpaal; Eber, and Misham, and
13 Shamed, who built Ono, and Lod, with the towns thereof : Beriah also, and ^cShema, who *were* heads of the fathers of the
inhabitants of Aijalon, who drove away the inhabitants of Gath :
14, 15 and Ahio, Shashak, and Jeremoth, and Zebadiah, and Arad,
16 and Ader, and Michael, and Ispah, and Joha, the sons of Be-
17 riah ; and Zebadiah, and Meshullam, and Hezeki, and Heber,
18 Ishmerai also, and Jezliah, and Jobab, the sons of Elpaal ;
19, 20 and Jakim, and Zichri, and Zabdi, and Elienai, and Zilthai,
21 and Eliel, and Adaiah, and Beraiah, and Shimrath, the sons of
22, 23 ¹Shimhi; and Ishpan, and Heber, and Eliel, and Abdon,
24 and Zichri, and Hanan, and Hananiah, and Elam, and Anto-
25, 26 thijah, and Iphedeiah, and Penuel, the sons of Shashak; and
27 Shamsherai, and Shehariah, and Athaliah, and Jaresiah, and
28 Eliah, and Zichri, the sons of Jeroham. These *were* heads of
the fathers, by their generations, chief *men*. These dwelt in
29 Jerusalem. ¶And at Gibeon dwelt the ²father of Gibeon ;
30 whose ^dwife's name *was* Maachah : and his firstborn son Abdon,
31 and Zur, and Kish, and Baal, and Nadab, and Gedor, and
32 Ahio, and ³Zacher. And Mikloth begat ⁴Shimeah. And these
also dwelt with their brethren in Jerusalem, over against them.
33 ¶And ^eNer begat Kish, and Kish begat Saul, and Saul begat
Jonathan, and Malchi-shua, and ^fAbinadab, and ⁵Esh-baal.
34 And the son of Jonathan *was* ^gMerib-baal ; and Merib-baal
35 begat ^gMicah. And the sons of Micah *were*, Pithon, and Me-
36 lech, and ⁷Tarea, and Ahaz. And Ahaz begat ^hJehoadah ; and
Jehcadah begat Alemeth, and Azmaveth, and Zimri ; and Zimri
37 begat Moza, and Moza begat Binea : ⁱRapha *was* his son,

Marginal references:
^b ch. 2. 52.

^c ver. 21.

^d ch. 9. 35.

^e 1 Sam. 14. 51.
^f 1 Sam. 14. 49, *Ishui.*
^g 2 Sam.9.12.
^h *Jarah,* ch. 9. 42.
ⁱ ch. 9. 43, *Rephaiah.*

¹ Or, *Shema,* ver. 13.
² Called *Jehiel,* ch. 9. 35.
³ Or, *Zechariah,* ch. 9. 37.
⁴ Or, *Shimeam,* ch. 9. 38.
⁵ Or, *Ish-bosheth,* 2 Sam. 2. 8.
⁶ Or, *Mephibosheth,* 2 Sam. 4. 4. & 9. 6, 10.
⁷ Or, *Tahrea,* ch. 9. 41.

" They " has no antecedent ; and it is difficult to supply one. Almost all commentators suppose that there has been some
corruption here, from which, however, we
may gather that the " sons of Ehud "
(or, perhaps, of Ahoah, *v.* 4) were originally
settled at Geba (Josh. xviii. 24 note), but
afterwards removed to a place called Manahath, probably a town in the vicinity. Gera
(*v.* 7) directed the movement.

8. *after he had sent them away*] Translate,
" after he had **divorced his wives,** Hushim
and Baara."

28. *These dwelt in Jerusalem*] Jerusalem
was partly within the limits of the tribe of
Benjamin (Josh. xviii. 28) ; but we do not
hear of Benjamites inhabiting it until after
the return from the Captivity (ix. 3 ; Neh.
xi. 4).

33. This verse combined with ix. 35-39,

seems to show that the genealogy of **Saul**
was

rather than that to be inferred from 1 Sam.
ix. 1, xiv. 50, 51.

In 1 Sam. xiv. 49 note, it is concluded
that Saul's second son bore the two names
of " Ishui " and " Abinadab." But the
order of the names here—(1) Jonathan ; (2)
Malchi-shua ; and (3) Abinadab—suggests
another explanation, viz., that Ishui, the
second son, died young, and that Abinadab
was really the fourth son.

Esh-baal] Previous to the introduction

38 Eleasah his son, Azel his son: and Azel had six sons, whose
names *are* these, Azrikam, Bocheru, and Ishmael, and Sheariah,
and Obadiah, and Hanan. All these *were* the sons of Azel.

39 And the sons of Eshek his brother *were*, Ulam his firstborn,
40 Jehush the second, and Eliphelet the third. And the sons of
Ulam were mighty men of valour, archers, and had many sons,
and sons' sons, an hundred and fifty. All these *are* of the sons
of Benjamin.

a Ezra 2. 59.

CHAP. 9. SO *a*all Israel were reckoned by genealogies; and, behold, they *were* written in the book of the kings of Israel and
Judah, *who* were carried away to Babylon for their transgression.

b Ezra 2. 70.
Neh. 7. 73.
c Josh. 9. 27.
Ezra 2. 43.
& 8. 20.
d Neh. 11. 1.

2 ¶ *b*Now the first inhabitants that *dwelt* in their possessions in
their cities *were*, the Israelites, the priests, Levites, and *c*the
3 Nethinims.   ¶And in *d*Jerusalem dwelt of the children of
Judah, and of the children of Benjamin, and of the children of
4 Ephraim, and Manasseh; Uthai the son of Ammihud, the son
of Omri, the son of Imri, the son of Bani, of the children of
5 Pharez the son of Judah. And of the Shilonites; Asaiah the
6 firstborn, and his sons. And of the sons of Zerah; Jeuel, and
7 their brethren, six hundred and ninety. And of the sons of
Benjamin; Sallu the son of Meshullam, the son of Hodaviah,
8 the son of Hasenuah, and Ibneiah the son of Jeroham, and Elah
the son of Uzzi, the son of Michri, and Meshullam the son of
9 Shephathiah, the son of Reuel, the son of Ibnijah; and their
brethren, according to their generations, nine hundred and fifty

e Neh. 11.
10, &c.

and six. All these men *were* chief of the fathers in the house
10 of their fathers.   ¶*e*And of the priests; Jedaiah, and Jehoiarib,

---

of the Phœnician Baal-worship into Israel
by Ahab, the word "Baal" had no bad
sense in Hebrew, but was simply an equivalent of the more ordinary *El*, "God"
(1 Chr. iii. 1 note). Hence, there is nothing
strange in the use at this time of the names,
"Esh-baal" ("man of God"), "Baal,"
"Beel-iada," "Merib-baal," &c. Later on
such names became offensive to pious ears,
and were changed for the better, or for the
worse, "Beel-iada" becoming "El-iada"
("let God aid") — "Esh-baal," "Ish-bosheth" ("man of shame")—"Merib-baal,"
"Mephi-bosheth"; and the like.

40. *sons, and sons' sons*] This genealogy
of the house of Saul appears by the number
of the generations to belong probably to
the time of Hezekiah (cp. iv. 41). Ulam's
"sons' sons" ,are in the 13th generation
from Jonathan, as Hezekiah is in the 13th
generation from David.

IX. 1. Rather, "So all Israel were reckoned...the kings of Israel. **And Judah was**
carried away captive to Babylon for .their
transgressions."

2. *the first inhabitants*] i.e. the first inhabitants of the Holy Land after the return
from the Captivity. They are enumerated
under four heads: (1) Israelites, *i.e.* the
mass of the laity, whether belonging to the
ten tribes or the two; (2) priests; (3) Levites; and (4) the lowest order of the ministry, the Nethinims. These last, whose
name is derived from a root "to give," were

a sort of sacred slaves—persons "given"
to the Levites to perform the more laborious
duties of the Sanctuary. Some had been
"given" as early as the time of Moses
(Num. xxxi. 47); and the number afterwards increased (Josh. ix. 23; Ezr. viii. 20).
At the time of the return from the Captivity, owing to the small number of Levites
who came back (Ezr. ii. 40-42), the services
of the Nethinims became very important.
They are mentioned under the name of
Nethinims only in Chronicles, Ezra, and
Nehemiah.

3. The correspondence and the diversity
between the account here and in Nehemiah
(xi. 4-19) are explained by the probability
that both writers drew from a common and
fuller document. They selected, in some
instances, different names, or names which
are now different through corruption; and
they frequently expressed the genealogies
of the same persons differently, both going
on the principle of compression by means
of omissions, but omitting from their lists
different links of the chain.

9. The discrepancy between the numbers
here and in Nehemiah (xi. 8) may arise from
corruption. So in *vv.* 13, 22.

10. "Jedaiah," "Jehoiarib," and "Jachin," are not here names of individuals
but of priestly families. From xxiv. 7-17,
it appears that Jehoiarib was the original
head of the first "course," Jedaiah of the
second, and Jachin of the twenty-first.

11 and Jachin, and [1]Azariah the son of Hilkiah, the son of Meshullam, the son of Zadok, the son of Meraioth, the son of
12 Ahitub, the ruler of the house of God; and Adaiah the son of
Jeroham, the son of Pashur, the son of Malchijah, and Maasiai
the son of Adiel, the son of Jahzerah, the son of Meshullam, the
13 son of Meshillemith, the son of Immer; and their brethren,
heads of the house of their fathers, a thousand and seven hundred and threescore; [2]very able men for the work of the service
14 of the house of God.   ¶ And of the Levites; Shemaiah the son of
Hasshub, the son of Azrikam, the son of Hashabiah, of the sons
15 of Merari; and Bakbakkar, Heresh, and Galal, and Mattaniah
16 the son of Micah, the son of Zichri, the son of Asaph; and
Obadiah the son of Shemaiah, the son of Galal, the son of
Jeduthun, and Berechiah the son of Asa, the son of Elkanah,
17 that dwelt in the villages of the Netophathites. And the porters
were, Shallum, and Akkub, and Talmon, and Ahiman, and their
18 brethren: Shallum *was* the chief; who hitherto *waited* in the
king's gate eastward: they *were* porters in the companies of the
19 children of Levi. And Shallum the son of Kore, the son of
Ebiasaph, the son of Korah, and his brethren, of the house of
his father, the Korahites, *were* over the work of the service,
keepers of the [3]gates of the tabernacle: and their fathers, *being*
20 over the host of the LORD, *were* keepers of the entry.   And
*f*Phinehas the son of Eleazar was the ruler over them in time
21 past, *and* the LORD *was* with him.   *And* Zechariah the son of
Meshelemiah *was* porter of the door of the tabernacle of the
22 congregation.   ¶ All these *which were* chosen to be porters in the
gates *were* two hundred and twelve.   These were reckoned by
their genealogy in their villages, whom *g*David and Samuel *h*the
23 seer [4]did ordain in their [5]set office.   So they and their children
had the oversight of the gates of the house of the LORD, *namely*,
24 the house of the tabernacle, by wards.   In four quarters were
25 the porters, toward the east, west, north, and south.   And their
brethren, *which were* in their villages, *were* to come [6]after seven
26 days from time to time with them.   For these Levites, the four

f Num. 31. 6.

g ch. 26. 1, 2.
h 1 Sam. 9. 9.

i 2 Kin. 11. 5.
2 Chr. 23. 4.

---

[1] Neh. 11. 11, *Seraiah.*
[2] Heb. *mighty men of valour.*
[3] Heb. *thresholds.*
[4] Heb. *founded.*
[5] Or, *trust.*

---

18. *who hitherto waited*] Translate, "Who
to this day waits. These were the porters in the **stations** of the sons of Levi."
The words of the first clause refer to
Shallum, and imply that, whereas Shallum (or his house) had originally the general
superintendence of the Temple gates, a
change had been made when the author
wrote, and Shallum's charge had become
the east gate only.   The second clause
means; "these were the porters in those
fixed stations at the outer gates of the
Temple, which corresponded to the camp
stations of the Levites who guarded the
Tabernacle in the early times."

19. *Shallum the son of Kore*] A different
person from the Shallum of *v.* 17, and
with a different office, viz., the guarding
the inner doors of the Temple.   The original
Shallum, Shelemaiah, or Meshelemaiah,
was a Levite of the time of David (xxvi. 14).
His descendants were still called by his
name, but had now a more important charge
assigned to them.

22. The porters, like the singers (Neh.
xii. 29), dwelt for the most part in the villages round Jerusalem.   They were the
descendants of those originally selected
for the work by David.   David's arrangements are here regarded as having had
the sanction of Samuel—which would imply that he planned them in the lifetime
of Saul, while he was still a fugitive and
an outlaw.

25. See marg. reff.   If the number of
warders was, as stated in Nehemiah (xi. 19)
172 (*i.e.* 168 besides the four chief warders),
and the number employed at any one time
was, as under David (xxvi. 17, 18), twenty-
four, then the turn of the courses to keep
ward came every seven weeks.

26. Rather, "For the four chief porters,
**who were themselves Levites, were in
trust, who also** had the charge of the

chief porters, were in *their* [1]set office, and were over the [2]cham-
27 bers and treasuries of the house of God. And they lodged round
about the house of God, because the charge *was* upon them, and
28 the opening thereof every morning *pertained* to them. And
certain of them had the charge of the ministering vessels, that
29 they should [3]bring them in and out by tale. *Some* of them also
were appointed to oversee the vessels, and all the [4]instruments
of the sanctuary, and the fine flour, and the wine, and the oil,
30 and the frankincense, and the spices. And *some* of the sons cf

k Ex. 30. 23.
31 the priests made [k] the ointment of the spices. And Mattithiah,
one of the Levites, who *was* the firstborn of Shallum the Ko-

l Lev. 2. 5.
& 6. 21.
rahite, had the [5]set office *l* over the things that were made [6]in
32 the pans. And *other* of their brethren, of the sons of the Koha-

m Lev. 21. 8.
thites, *m were* over the [7]shewbread, to prepare *it* every sabbath.

n ch. 6. 31.
& 25. 1.
33 And these *are* *n* the singers, chief of the fathers of the Levites,
who remaining in the chambers *were* free: for [8]they were em-
34 ployed in *that* work day and night. These chief fathers of the
Levites *were* chief throughout their generations; these dwelt at
35 Jerusalem. ¶ And in Gibeon dwelt the father of Gibeon, Jehiel,

o ch. 8. 29.
36 whose wife's name *was* *o* Maachah: and his firstborn son Abdon,
37 then Zur, and Kish, and Baal, and Ner, and Nadab, and Gedor,
38 and Ahio, and Zechariah, and Mikloth. And Mikloth begat
Shimeam. And they also dwelt with their brethren at Jeru-

p ch. 8. 33.
39 salem, over against their brethren. *p* And Ner begat Kish; and
Kish begat Saul; and Saul begat Jonathan, and Malchi-shua,
40 and Abinadab, and Esh-baal. And the son of Jonathan *was*
41 Merib-baal: and Merib-baal begat Micah. And the sons of

q ch. 8. 35.
42 Micah *were*, Pithon, and Melech, and Tahrea, *q and Ahaz*. And
Ahaz begat Jarah; and Jarah begat Alemeth, and Azmaveth,
43 and Zimri; and Zimri begat Moza; and Moza begat Binea;
44 and Rephaiah his son, Eleasah his son, Azel his son. And Azel
had six sons, whose names *are* these, Azrikam, Bocheru, and
Ishmael, and Sheariah, and Obadiah, and Hanan: these *were*
the sons of Azel.

a 1 Sam. 31.
1, 2.
CHAP. 10. NOW *a* the Philistines fought against Israel; and the
men of Israel fled from before the Philistines, and fell down

[1] Or, *trust.*
[2] Or, *storehouses.*
[3] Heb. *bring them in by tale,*
and carry them out by tale.
[4] Or, *vessels.*
[5] Or, *trust.*
[6] Or, *on flat plates*, or, *slices.*
[7] Heb. *bread of ordering.*
[8] Heb. *upon them.*

---

chambers, &c." A contrast seems intended
between the four chief porters, whose charge
was constant, and the remainder, who kept
watch by turns.

28. *by tale*] Lit., "by number." The
vessels for service taken out of the treasury
were counted, that the same number should
be returned to the treasury after the service
was over.

31. *Mattithiah...the first-born of Shallum
the Korahite*] This Shallum would seem to
be the person mentioned in *v.* 19, whose
actual first-born was Zechariah (xxvi. 2).
Mattithiah may have been his eldest lineal
descendant at the time here spoken of.

33. *the singers*] No names follow, and it
is thought that they have fallen out.

were free] "Free," *i.e.* from any special
duties besides those of supervision, which
was so arranged among the overseers that

some one exercised it during every part of
both day and night.

34. *chief throughout their generations*] The
superintendents, that is, were the genealogical head of the different Levitical divisions, and bore special rule, each over those
of his own blood and race. The hereditary
principle prevailed, not only in the High-
priesthood, but also in the priestly offices of
the second rank.

35–44. An almost exact repetition of viii.
29–38; and probably intentionally made by
the author. In order to connect the genealogical section of his work with the historical, he re-introduces the genealogy of the
person with whose death his historical section opens.

X. The present chapter contains two
facts not found in 1 Sam. xxxi.—the fastening of Saul's head in the temple of Dagon

2 ¹slain in Mount Gilboa. And the Philistines followed hard after
Saul, and after his sons; and the Philistines slew Jonathan, and
3 ²Abinadab, and Malchi-shua, the sons of Saul. And the battle
went sore against Saul, and the ³archers ⁴hit him, and he was
4 wounded of the archers. Then said Saul to his armourbearer,
Draw thy sword, and thrust me through therewith; lest these
uncircumcised come and ⁵abuse me. But his armourbearer
would not; for he was sore afraid. So Saul took a sword, and
5 fell upon it. And when his armourbearer saw that Saul was
6 dead, he fell likewise on the sword, and died. So Saul died, and
7 his three sons, and all his house died together. And when all
the men of Israel that *were* in the valley saw that they fled, and
that Saul and his sons were dead, then they forsook their cities,
8 and fled: and the Philistines came and dwelt in them. And it
came to pass on the morrow, when the Philistines came to strip
the slain, that they found Saul and his sons fallen in mount
9 Gilboa. And when they had stripped him, they took his head,
and his armour, and sent into the land of the Philistines round
about, to carry tidings unto their idols, and to the people.
10 ᵇAnd they put his armour in the house of their gods, and
11 fastened his head in the temple of Dagon. ¶And when all
Jabesh-gilead heard all that the Philistines had done to Saul,
12 they arose, all the valiant men, and took away the body of Saul,
and the bodies of his sons, and brought them to Jabesh, and
buried their bones under the oak in Jabesh, and fasted seven
13 days. ¶So Saul died for his transgression which he ⁶committed
against the LORD, ᶜeven against the word of the LORD, which he
kept not, and also for asking *counsel* of *one that had* a familiar
14 spirit, ᵈto enquire *of it*; and enquired not of the LORD: therefore he slew him, and ᵉturned the kingdom unto David the son
of ⁷Jesse.

CHAP. 11. THEN ᵃall Israel gathered themselves to David unto
2 Hebron, saying, Behold, *we are* thy bone and thy flesh. And
moreover ⁸in time past, even when Saul was king, thou *wast* he
that leddest out and broughtest in Israel: and the LORD thy
God said unto thee, Thou shalt ⁹ᵇfeed my people Israel, and
3 thou shalt be ruler over my people Israel. Therefore came all
the elders of Israel to the king to Hebron; and David made a
covenant with them in Hebron before the LORD; and ᶜthey
anointed David king over Israel, according to the word of the
4 LORD ¹by ᵈSamuel. ¶And David and all Israel ᵉwent to Jerusalem, which is Jebus; ᶠwhere the Jebusites *were*, the inhabit-

ᵇ 1 Sam. 31. 10.

ᶜ 1 Sam. 13. 13.
& 15. 23.
ᵈ 1 Sam. 28. 7.
ᵉ 1 Sam. 15. 28.
2 Sam. 3. 9, 10.
& 5. 3.
ᵃ 2 Sam. 5. 1.

ᵇ Ps. 78. 71.

ᶜ 2 Sam. 5. 3.
ᵈ 1 Sam. 16. 1, 12, 13.
ᵉ 2 Sam. 5. 6.
ᶠ Judg. 1. 21.
& 19. 10.

---

¹ Or, *wounded.*
² Or, *Ishui,* 1 Sam. 14. 49.
³ Heb. *shooters with bows.*
⁴ Heb. *found him.*
⁵ Or, *mock me.*
⁶ Heb. *transgressed.*
⁷ Heb. *Isai.*
⁸ Heb. *both yesterday and the third day.*
⁹ Or, *rule.*
¹ Heb. *by the hand of.*

(*v.* 10), and the burial of his bones, and
those of his sons, under an *oak* (*v.* 12).
Otherwise the narrative differs from 1 Sam.
xxxi. only by being abbreviated (see especially *vv.* 6, 7, 11, and 12), and by having
some moral reflections attached to it (*vv.* 13
and 14).

6. *all his house died together*] Not the
whole of his family, nor even "all his sons"
(see 2 Sam. ii. 8–15, iii. 6–15, iv. 1–12).
The phrase is perhaps an abbreviation of
the expression in the parallel passage of
Samuel (1 Sam. xxxi. 6).

13. *for his transgression*] Cp. ix. 1. The
"transgression" intended is probably the
disobedience with respect to Amalek, recorded in 1 Sam. xv. 1–9 (cp. 1 Sam. xxviii.
17, 18).

XI. This chapter runs parallel with 2
Sam. v. as far as *v.* 9, after which it is to be
compared with 2 Sam. (xxiii. 8–39) as far
as *v.* 40, the remainder (*vv.* 41–47) being
an addition, to which Samuel has nothing
corresponding. Cp. throughout the notes
in Samuel.

5 ants of the land. And the inhabitants of Jebus said to David, Thou shalt not come hither. Nevertheless David took the castle
6 of Zion, which *is* the city of David. And David said, Whosoever smiteth the Jebusites first shall be ¹chief and captain. So Joab
7 the son of Zeruiah went first up, and was chief. And David dwelt in the castle; therefore they called ²it the city of David.
8 And he built the city round about, even from Millo round
9 about: and Joab ³repaired the rest of the city. So David ⁴waxed greater and greater: for the LORD of hosts *was* with him.

g 2 Sam.23.8.

10 ¶ ᵍThese also *are* the chief of the mighty men whom David had, who ⁵strengthened themselves with him in his kingdom, *and*

h 1 Sam. 16. 1, 12.

with all Israel, to make him king, according to ʰthe word of the
11 LORD concerning Israel. And this *is* the number of the mighty men whom David had; Jashobeam, ⁶an Hachmonite, the chief of the captains: he lifted up his spear against three hundred
12 slain *by him* at one time. And after him *was* Eleazar the son
13 of Dodo, the Ahohite, who *was one* of the three mighties. He was with David at ⁷Pas-dammim, and there the Philistines were gathered together to battle, where was a parcel of ground full
14 of barley; and the people fled from before the Philistines. And they ⁸set themselves in the midst of *that* parcel, and delivered it, and slew the Philistines; and the LORD saved *them* by a great

i 2 Sam. 23. 13.

15 ⁹deliverance. ¶Now ¹three of the thirty captains ⁱwent down to the rock to David, into the cave of Adullam; and the host of

k ch. 14. 9.

16 the Philistines encamped ᵏin the valley of Rephaim. And David *was* then in the hold, and the Philistines' garrison *was* then at
17 Beth-lehem. And David longed, and said, Oh that one would give me drink of the water of the well of Beth-lehem, that *is* at
18 the gate! And the three brake through the host of the Philistines, and drew water out of the well of Beth-lehem, that *was* by the gate, and took *it*, and brought *it* to David: but David
19 would not drink *of* it, but poured it out to the LORD, and said, My God forbid it me, that I should do this thing: shall I drink the blood of these men ²that have put their lives in jeopardy? for with *the jeopardy of* their lives they brought it. Therefore he would not drink it. These things did these three mightiest.

l 2 Sam. 23. 18.

20 ¶ ˡAnd Abishai the brother of Joab, he was chief of the three: for lifting up his spear against three hundred, he slew *them*, and

m 2 Sam. 23. 19.

21 had a name among the three. ᵐOf the three, he was more

---

¹ Heb. *head*.	⁵ Or, *held strongly with*
² That is, *Zion*, 2 Sam. 5.7.	*him*.
³ Heb. *revived*.	⁶ Or, *son of Hachmoni*.
⁴ Heb. *went in going and*	⁷ Or, *Ephes-dammim*,
increasing.	1 Sam. 17. 1.

⁸ Or, *stood*.
⁹ Or, *salvation*.
ˡ Or, *three captains over the thirty*.
² Heb. *with their lives?*

6-8. The narrative here given fills out a manifest defect in 2 Sam. v. 8, where something has evidently dropped out of the text.

The prowess of Joab on this occasion, and the part which he took in the building of the city of David (*v.* 8), are known to us only from this passage of Chronicles.

10. *strengthened themselves*] Or "*exerted* themselves"—"strenuously assisted with all Israel in making David king." This list of David's principal heroes belongs, therefore, to his reign at Hebron. In Samuel the list is not given till nearly the end of David's reign (2 Sam. xxiii. 8–39).

11. *chief of the captains*] Or, "of the thirty," according to another and better reading (see *vv.* 15, 25; cp. 2 Sam. xxiii. 8 note). Jashobeam was the commander of the first monthly course of 24,000 soldiers (xxvii. 2). He is probably the warrior of the name who joined David at Ziklag (xii. 6).

13. Cp. this passage with 2 Sam. xxiii. 9, 10.

barley] In 2 Sam. xxiii. 11, "lentiles." The words for barley and lentils are so similar in the Hebrew that we may fairly explain the diversity by an accidental corruption.

honourable than the two; for he was their captain: howbeit he
22 attained not to the *first* three. ¶ Benaiah the son of Jehoiada,
the son of a valiant man of Kabzeel, [1] who had done many acts;
n he slew two lionlike men of Moab: also he went down and   *n* 2 Sam. 23.
23 slew a lion in a pit in a snowy day. And he slew an Egyptian,   20.
[2] a man of *great* stature, five cubits high; and in the Egyptian's
hand *was* a spear like a weaver's beam; and he went down to
him with a staff, and plucked the spear out of the Egyptian's
24 hand, and slew him with his own spear. These *things* did
Benaiah the son of Jehoiada, and had the name among the three
25 mightiest. Behold, he was honourable among the thirty, but
attained not to the *first* three: and David set him over his
26 guard. ¶ Also the valiant men of the armies *were*, *o* Asahel the   *o* 2 Sam. 23.
27 brother of Joab, Elhanan the son of Dodo of Beth-lehem, [3] Sham-   21.
28 moth the [4] Harorite, Helez the [5] Pelonite, Ira the son of Ikkesh
29 the Tekoite, Abi-ezer the Antothite, [6] Sibbecai the Hushathite,
30 [7] Ilai the Ahohite, Maharai the Netophathite, [8] Heled the son of
31 Baanah the Netophathite, Ithai the son of Ribai of Gibeah, *that*
pertained to the children of Benjamin, Benaiah the Pirathonite,
32, 33 [9] Hurai of the brooks of Gaash, [1] Abiel the Arbathite, Azma-
34 veth the Baharumite, Eliahba the Shaalbonite, the sons of [2] Hashem the Gizonite, Jonathan the son of Shage the Hararite,
35 Ahiam the son of [3] Sacar the Hararite, [4] Eliphal the son of [5] Ur,
36, 37 Hepher the Mecherathite, Ahijah the Pelonite, [6] Hezro the
38 Carmelite, [7] Naarai the son of Ezbai, Joel the brother of Nathan,
39 Mibhar [8] the son of Haggeri, Zelek the Ammonite, Naharai the
40 Berothite, the armourbearer of Joab the son of Zeruiah, Ira the
41 Ithrite, Gareb the Ithrite, Uriah the Hittite, Zabad the son of
42 Ahlai, Adina the son of Shiza the Reubenite, a captain of the
43 Reubenites, and thirty with him, Hanan the son of Maachah,
44 and Joshaphat the Mithnite, Uzzia the Ashterathite, Shama
45 and Jehiel the sons of Hothan the Aroerite, Jediael the [9] son of
46 Shimri, and Joha his brother, the Tizite, Eliel the Mahavite,
and Jeribai, and Joshaviah, the sons of Elnaam, and Ithmah the
47 Moabite, Eliel, and Obed, and Jasiel the Mesobaite.

---

[1] Heb. *great of deeds.*
[2] Heb. *a man of measure.*
[3] Or, *Shammah.*
[4] Or, *Harodite*, 2 Sam. 23.
25.
[5] Or, *Paltite*, 2 Sam. 23.
26.

[6] Or, *Mebunnai.*
[7] Or, *Zalmon.*
[8] Or, *Heleb.*
[9] Or, *Hiddai.*
[1] Or, *Abi-allon.*
[2] Or, *Jashen*, See 2 Sam.
23. 32, 33.

[3] Or, *Sharar.*
[4] Or, *Eliphelet.*
[5] Or, *Ahasbai.*
[6] Or, *Hezrai.*
[7] Or, *Paarai the Arbite.*
[8] Or, *the Haggerite.*
[9] Or, *Shimrite.*

---

23. *five cubits high*] About 7 ft. 6 in. high. The height is not so great as that recorded of other giants.

26., &c. The list of names here given corresponds generally with that in 2 Sam. xxiii. 24–39, but presents several remarkable differences. (1) The number in Chronicles is 47; in Samuel 31. (2) Four names in the list of Chronicles are not in Samuel. (3) Five names in Samuel are not in Chronicles. (4) Many of the other names, both personal and local, vary in the two lists. It is quite possible that the two lists varied to some extent originally. The writer of Chronicles distinctly states that he gives the list as it stood at the time of David's becoming king over all Israel (*v.* 10). The writer of Samuel does not assign his list to any definite period

of David's reign, but probably delivers it to us as it was constituted at a later date. It is quite possible therefore that the names which occur only in Chronicles are those of persons who had died or quitted the army before the other list was made out, and that the new names in Samuel are the names of those who had taken their places. See 2 Sam. xxiii. 39 note.

34. *The sons of Hashem*] It is impossible that this can be the true reading, since an individual warrior must be spoken of. Comparing 2 Sam. xxiii. 32, perhaps the most probable conjecture is that the " Beni Hashem " of Chronicles and the " Beni Jashen " of Samuel alike conceal some single name of a man which cannot now be recovered.

CHAP. 12. NOW [a]these *are* they that came to David to [b]Ziklag, [1]while he yet kept himself close because of Saul the son of Kish: and they *were* among the mighty men, helpers of the 2 war. *They were* armed with bows, and could use both the right hand and [c]the left in *hurling* stones and *shooting* arrows out of a 3 bow, *even* of Saul's brethren of Benjamin. The chief *was* Ahiezer, then Joash, the sons of [2]Shemaah the Gibeathite; and Jeziel, and Pelet, the sons of Azmaveth; and Berachah, and Jehu the 4 Antothite, and Ismaiah the Gibeonite, a mighty man among the thirty, and over the thirty; and Jeremiah, and Jahaziel, and 5 Johanan, and Josabad the Gederathite, Eluzai, and Jerimoth, and Bealiah, and Shemariah, and Shephatiah the Haruphite, 6 Elkanah, and Jesiah, and Azareel, and Joezer, and Jashobeam, 7 the Korhites, and Joelah, and Zebadiah, the sons of Jeroham of 8 Gedor. ¶ And of the Gadites there separated themselves unto David into the hold to the wilderness men of might, *and* men [3]of war *fit* for the battle, that could handle shield and buckler, whose faces *were like* the faces of lions, and *were* [d][4]as swift as 9 the roes upon the mountains; Ezer the first, Obadiah the second, 10 Eliab the third, Mishmannah the fourth, Jeremiah the fifth, 11, 12 Attai the sixth, Eliel the seventh, Johanan the eighth, Elza- 13 bad the ninth, Jeremiah the tenth, Machbanai the eleventh. 14 These *were* of the sons of Gad, captains of the host: [5]one of the least *was* over an hundred, and the greatest over a thousand. 15 These *are* they that went over Jordan in the first month, when it had [6]overflown all his [e]banks; and they put to flight all *them* 16 of the valleys, *both* toward the east, and toward the west. ¶ And there came of the children of Benjamin and Judah to the hold 17 unto David. And David went out [7]to meet them, and answered and said unto them, If ye be come peaceably unto me to help me, mine heart shall [8]be knit unto you: but if *ye be come* to betray me to mine enemies, seeing *there is* no [9]wrong in mine hands, the 18 God of our fathers look *thereon*, and rebuke *it*. Then [1]the spirit came upon [f]Amasai, who was chief of the captains *and he said,*

Thine *are* we, David,
And on thy side, thou son of Jesse:

Marginal references (left):
[a] 1 Sam. 27. 2.
[b] 1 Sam. 27. 6.
[2] Judg. 20. 16.
[d] 2 Sam. 2. 18.
[e] Josh. 3. 15.
[f] 2 Sam. 17. 25.

---

[1] Heb. *being yet shut up.*	[5] Or, *one that was least could resist an hundred, and the greatest a thousand.*	[7] Heb. *before them.*
[2] Or, *Hasmaah.*		[8] Heb. *be one.*
[3] Heb. *of the host.*		[9] Or, *violence.*
[4] Heb. *as the roes upon the mountains to make haste.*	[6] Heb. *filled over.*	[1] Heb. *the spirit clothed Amasai:* So Judg. 6. 34.

XII. This chapter is composed wholly of matter that is new to us, no corresponding accounts occurring in Samuel. It comprises four lists,—(1) One of men, chiefly Benjamites, who joined David at Ziklag (*vv.* 1–7); (2) A second of Gadites who united themselves to him when he was in a stronghold near the desert (*vv.* 8–15); (3) A third of Manassites who came to him when he was dismissed by the Philistines upon suspicion (*vv.* 19–22); and (4) A fourth of the numbers from the different tribes who attended and made him king at Hebron (*vv.* 23–40).

2. The skill of the Benjamites as archers is noted in viii. 40, and 2 Chr. xiv. 8. Their proficiency in using the left hand appears in the narrative of Judges (iii. 15, and marg. ref.) where their peculiar excellency as slingers is also noticed.

even of Saul's brethren] Cp. *v.* 29. Even of Saul's own tribe there were some who separated themselves from his cause, and threw in their lot with David.

8. *into the hold to the wilderness*] Rather, "into the hold **towards** the wilderness." Some understand by this Ziklag, some Engedi (1 Sam. xxiv. 1, 2); but it seems most probable that here and in *v.* 16 the stronghold of Adullam is intended (xi. 15, 16).

14. The marginal rendering is preferable. (Cp. Lev. xxvi. 8).

15. On the danger of the exploit, see marg. ref. note.

This passage (*vv.* 8–15) seems to be taken *verbatim* from an ancient source, the poetical expressions in *vv.* 8, 14, being especially unlike the usual style of our author.

18. *Amasai*] The marg. ref. identifies him

Peace, peace *be* unto thee,
And peace *be* to thine helpers;
For thy God helpeth thee.

Then David received them, and made them captains of the band.

19 ¶ And there fell *some* of Manasseh to David, *g*when he came with *g* 1Sam.29.2.
the Philistines against Saul to battle: but they helped them
not: for the lords of the Philistines upon advisement sent him
away, saying, *h*He will fall to his master Saul ¹to *the jeopardy* *h* 1Sam.29.4.

20 *of* our heads. As he went to Ziklag, there fell to him of Manasseh, Adnah, and Jozabad, and Jediael, and Michael, and
Jozabad, and Elihu, and Zilthai, captains of the thousands that

21 *were* of Manasseh. And they helped David ²against *i*the band *i* 1 Sam. 30.
- *of the rovers :* for they *were* all mighty men of valour, and were 1, 9, 10.

22 captains in the host. For at *that* time day by day there came
to David to help him, until *it was* a great host, like the host of

23 God. ¶ And these *are* the numbers of the ³ ⁴bands *that were*
ready armed to the war, *and* *k*came to David to Hebron, to *l*turn *k* 2 Sam. 2.
the kingdom of Saul to him, *m*according to the word of the 3, 4.
& 5. 1.
24 LORD. The children of Judah that bare shield and spear *were* ch. 11. 1.
25 six thousand and eight hundred, ready ⁵armed to the war. Of *l* ch. 10. 14.
the children of Simeon, mighty men of valour for the war, seven *m* 1 Sam. 16.
26 thousand and one hundred. Of the children of Levi four thou- 1, 3.
27 sand and six hundred. And Jehoiada *was* the leader of the
Aaronites, and with him *were* three thousand and seven hundred;

28 and *n*Zadok, a young man mighty of valour, and of his father's *n* 2Sam.8.17.
29 house twenty and two captains. And of the children of Benjamin, the ⁶kindred of Saul, three thousand: for hitherto ⁷*o*the *o* 2 Sam. 2.
greatest part of them had kept the ward of the house of Saul. 8, 9.

30 And of the children of Ephraim twenty thousand and eight
hundred, mighty men of valour, ⁸famous throughout the house

31 of their fathers. And of the half tribe of Manasseh eighteen
thousand, which were expressed by name, to come and make

32 David king. And of the children of Issachar, *p which were men* *p* Esth. 1. 13.
that had understanding of the times, to know what Israel ought
to do; the heads of them *were* two hundred; and all their

33 brethren *were* at their commandment. Of Zebulun, such as

---

¹ Heb. *on our heads.*   ⁴ Heb. *heads.*   ⁷ Heb. *a multitude of them.*
² Or, *with a band.*   ⁵ Or, *prepared.*   ⁸ Heb. *men of names.*
³ Or, *captains,* or, *men.*   ⁶ Heb. *brethren,* Gen. 31. 23.

---

with Amasa, David's nephew, but it seems
unlikely that David would have misdoubted
a band led by his own nephew.

The passionate earnestness of Amasai's
speech is strongly marked in the original,
and will be better seen by omitting the
words which our Version adds in italics.
Here, as in *vv.* 8-15, we have manifestly
the actual words of a very ancient record.

21. *the band of the rovers*] See marg. ref.

23. Rather, "These are the numbers of
the **men**, ready equipped **for the host**, that
came to David, &c."

In the list which follows such points as
(1) The large number sent by the trans-
Jordanic tribes; (2) The large numbers
from Zebulon, Asher, Naphtali, and Dan,
all tribes somewhat remote, and generally
speaking undistinguished; (3) The small
size of the contingent from Judah, which is

generally represented as numerically superior to every other tribe, and which might
have been expected to be especially zealous
on behalf of its own prince and tribesman;
—throw some doubt upon the numbers,
which may be suspected of having in some
instances undergone corruption.

29. *for hitherto* &c.] Rather, "For still
the greatest part of them **maintained their
allegiance to** the house of Saul." This is
given as the reason for so few coming to
Hebron. It shows us that, even after the
death of Ishbosheth, the Benjamites had
hopes of furnishing a third king to the
nation.

32. *men that had understanding of the
times*] This is best interpreted politically.
Cp. marg. ref.

33. *expert in war,* &c.] Rather "**arrayed
for battle** with all harness of battle, who

went forth to battle, [1]expert in war, with all instruments of war,
fifty thousand, which could [2]keep rank: *they were* [3]not of dou-
34 ble heart.   And of Naphtali a thousand captains, and with them
35 with shield and spear thirty and seven thousand.   And of the
Danites expert in war twenty and eight thousand and six hun-
36 dred.   And of Asher, such as went forth to battle, [4]expert in
37 war, forty thousand.   And on the other side of Jordan, of the
Reubenites, and the Gadites, and of the half tribe of Manasseh,
with all manner of instruments of war for the battle, an hundred
38 and twenty thousand.   ¶ All these men of war, that could keep
rank, came with a perfect heart to Hebron, to make David king
over all Israel: and all the rest also of Israel *were* of one heart
39 to make David king.   And there they were with David three
days, eating and drinking: for their brethren had prepared for
40 them.   Moreover they that were nigh them, *even* unto Issachar
and Zebulun and Naphtali, brought bread on asses, and on
camels, and on mules, and on oxen, *and* [5]meat, meal, cakes of
figs, and bunches of raisins, and wine, and oil, and oxen, and
sheep abundantly: for *there was* joy in Israel.

CHAP. 13. AND David consulted with the captains of thousands
2 and hundreds, *and* with every leader.   And David said unto all
the congregation of Israel, If *it seem* good unto you, and *that it
be* of the LORD our God, [6]let us send abroad unto our brethren
every where, *that are* [a]left in all the land of Israel, and with
them *also* to the priests and Levites *which are* [7]in their cities
3 *and* suburbs, that they may gather themselves unto us: and
let us [8]bring again the ark of our God to us: [b]for we enquired
4 not at it in the days of Saul.   And all the congregation said that
they would do so: for the thing was right in the eyes of all the
5 people.   ¶ So [c]David gathered all Israel together, from [d]Shihor
of Egypt even unto the entering of Hemath, to bring the ark of
6 God [e]from Kirjath-jearim.   And David went up, and all Israel,
to [f]Baalah, *that is,* to Kirjath-jearim, which *belonged* to Judah,
to bring up thence the ark of God the LORD, [g]that dwelleth
7 *between* the cherubims, whose name is called *on it.*   And they
[9]carried the ark of God [h]in a new cart [i]out of the house of
8 Abinadab: and Uzza and Ahio drave the cart.   [k]And David
and all Israel played before God with all *their* might, and with
[l]singing, and with harps, and with psalteries, and with timbrels,
9 and with cymbals, and with trumpets.   And when they came
unto the threshingfloor of [2]Chidon, Uzza put forth his hand to
10 hold the ark; for the oxen [3]stumbled.   And the anger of the
LORD was kindled against Uzza, and he smote him, [l]because he
11 put his hand to the ark: and there he [m]died before God.   And

Marginal references (left):

[a] 1 Sam. 31. 1.
Isai. 37. 4.

[b] 1 Sam. 7. 1, 2.

[c] 1 Sam. 7. 5.
2 Sam. 6. 1.
[d] Josh. 13. 3.
[e] 1 Sam. 6. 21.
& 7. 1.
[f] Josh. 15. 9,
60.
[g] 1 Sam. 4. 4.
2 Sam. 6. 2.
[h] See Num.
4. 15.
ch. 15. 2, 13.
[i] 1 Sam. 7. 1.
[k] 2 Sam. 6. 5.

[l] Num. 4. 15.
ch. 15. 13, 15.
[m] Lev. 10. 2.

Footnotes:

[1] Or, *rangers of battle,* or, *ranged in battle.*
[2] Or, *set the battle in array.*
[3] Heb. *without a heart and a heart,* Ps. 12. 2.
[4] Or, *keeping their rank.*
[5] Or, *victual of meal.*
[6] Heb. *let us break forth* and *send.*
[7] Heb. *in the cities of their suburbs.*
[8] Heb. *bring about.*
[9] Heb. *made the ark to ride.*
[1] Heb. *songs.*
[2] Called *Nachon,* 2 Sam. 6. 6.
[3] Heb. *shook it.*

set the battle in array with no double
heart,"—excelling, that is, in the matter of
their arms and accoutrements.   The writer
notes in each tribe the point in which it was
most admirable.

XIII. Cp. 2 Sam. vi. 1–11 and notes.

1. *the captains* &c.] Such an organisation
had probably been established generally

through the tribes prior to the time of David: but David seems to have been the first
to recognise in these officers of the host representatives of the people, to consult them
on public affairs, and to give them a certain
political position.

5. *Shihor*] See marg. ref. and 1 K. viii.
65 note.

David was displeased, because the LORD had made a breach upon Uzza: wherefore that place is called [1]Perez-uzza to this 12 day. And David was afraid of God that day, saying, How shall 13 I bring the ark of God *home* to me? So David [2]brought not the ark *home* to himself to the city of David, but carried it aside 14 into the house of Obed-edom the Gittite. ¶ [n]And the ark of God remained with the family of Obed-edom in his house three months. And the LORD blessed [o]the house of Obed-edom, and all that he had.

[n] 2 Sam. 6. 11.
[o] As Gen. 30. 27.
ch. 26. 5.

CHAP. 14. NOW [a]Hiram king of Tyre sent messengers to David, and timber of cedars, with masons and carpenters, to build him 2 an house. And David perceived that the LORD had confirmed him king over Israel, for his kingdom was lifted up on high, 3 because of his people Israel. ¶ And David took [3]more wives at 4 Jerusalem: and David begat more sons and daughters. Now [b]these *are* the names of *his* children which he had in Jerusalem; 5 Shammua, and Shobab, Nathan, and Solomon, and Ibhar, and 6 Elishua, and Elpalet, and Nogah, and Nepheg, and Japhia, 7, 8 and Elishama, and [4]Beeliada, and Eliphalet. ¶ And when the Philistines heard that [c]David was anointed king over all Israel, all the Philistines went up to seek David. And David 9 heard *of it*, and went out against them. And the Philistines 10 came and spread themselves [d]in the valley of Rephaim. And David enquired of God, saying, Shall I go up against the Philistines? and wilt thou deliver them into mine hand? And the LORD said unto him, Go up; for I will deliver them into thine 11 hand. So they came up to Baal-perazim; and David smote them there. Then David said, God hath broken in upon mine enemies by mine hand like the breaking forth of waters: there-12 fore they called the name of that place [5]Baal-perazim. And when they had left their gods there, David gave a command-13 ment, and they were burned with fire. ¶ [e]And the Philistines 14 yet again spread themselves abroad in the valley. Therefore David enquired again of God; and God said unto him, Go not up after them; turn away from them, [f]and come upon them 15 over against the mulberry trees. And it shall be, when thou shalt hear a sound of going in the tops of the mulberry trees, *that* then thou shalt go out to battle: for God is gone forth 16 before thee to smite the host of the Philistines. David therefore did as God commanded him: and they smote the host of 17 the Philistines from [g]Gibeon even to Gazer. ¶ And [h]the fame of David went out into all lands; and the LORD [i]brought the fear of him upon all nations.

[a] 2 Sam. 5.
11, &c.

[b] ch. 3. 5.

[c] 2 Sam. 5. 17.

[d] ch. 11. 15.

[e] 2 Sam. 5. 22.

[f] 2 Sam. 5. 23.

[g] 2 Sam. 5.
25, *Geba*.
[h] Josh 6. 27.
2 Chr. 26. 8.
[i] Deut. 2. 25.
& 11. 25.

CHAP. 15. AND *David* made him houses in the city of David, and prepared a place for the ark of God, [a]and pitched for it a tent.

[a] ch. 16. 1.

---

[1] That is, *The breach of Uzza*.   [3] Heb. *yet*.   [5] That is, *A place of*
[2] Heb. *removed*.   [4] Or, *Eliada*, 2 Sam. 5. 16.   *breaches*.

XIV. Cp. 2 Sam. v. 11-25, the only important variations from which are in *vv.* 4-7, the list of the sons of David (see iii. 1 note), and in *v.* 12, where the fact is added that the idols taken from the Philistines were burned.

12. *when they had left their gods there*] The practice of carrying images of the gods to battle was common among the nations of antiquity, and arose from the belief that there was virtue in the images themselves,

and that military success would be obtained by means of them.

XV. The bulk of this chapter consists of new matter, which the writer of Chronicles found in his authorities.

1. *and pitched for it a tent*] The old "Tent" or "Tabernacle" was still in existence at Gibeon (xvi. 39; 2 Chr. i. 3); but the Ark had long been separated from it, and David probably thought that something newer and more magnificent was requisite.

⁵ Num. 4. 2,
15.
Deut. 10. 8.
& 31. 9.
ᶜ 1 Kin. 8. 1.
ch. 13. 5.

ᵈ 3x. 6: 22.
ᵉ Ex. 6. 13.

ƒ 2 Sam. 6. 3.
ch. 13. 7.
ᵍ ch. 13. 10,
11.

ʰ Ex. 25. 14.
Num. 4. 15.
& 7. 9.

ᶦ ch. 6. 33.
ᵏ ch. 6. 30.
ˡ ch. 6. 44.

2 Then David said, ¹None ought to carry the ᵇark of God but the Levites: for them hath the LORD chosen to carry the ark of 3 God, and to minister unto him for ever. And David ᶜgathered all Israel together to Jerusalem, to bring up the ark of the 4 LORD unto his place, which he had prepared for it. And David 5 assembled the children of Aaron, and the Levites: of the sons of Kohath; Uriel the chief, and his ²brethren an hundred and 6 twenty: of the sons of Merari; Asaiah the chief, and his brethren 7 two hundred and twenty; of the sons of Gershom; Joel the 8 chief, and his brethren an hundred and thirty: of the sons of ᵈElizaphan; Shemaiah the chief, and his brethren two hundred: 9 of the sons of ᵉHebron; Eliel the chief, and his brethren four- 10 score: of the sons of Uzziel; Amminadab the chief, and his 11 brethren an hundred and twelve. ¶And David called for Zadok and Abiathar the priests, and for the Levites, for Uriel, Asaiah, 12 and Joel, Shemaiah, and Eliel, and Amminadab, and said unto them, Ye *are* the chief of the fathers of the Levites: sanctify yourselves, *both* ye and your brethren, that ye may bring up the ark of the LORD God of Israel unto *the place that* I have pre- 13 pared for it. For ƒbecause ye *did it* not at the first, ᵍthe LORD our God made a breach upon us, for that we sought him not 14 after the due order. So the priests and the Levites sanctified 15 themselves to bring up the ark of the LORD God of Israel. And the children of the Levites bare the ark of God upon their shoulders with the staves thereon, as ʰMoses commanded ac- 16 cording to the word of the LORD. ¶And David spake to the chief of the Levites to appoint their brethren *to be* the singers with instruments of musick, psalteries and harps and cymbals, 17 sounding, by lifting up the voice with joy. So the Levites appointed ᶦHeman the son of Joel; and of his brethren, ᵏAsaph the son of Berechiah; and of the sons of Merari their brethren, 18 ˡEthan the son of Kushaiah; and with them their brethren of the second *degree*, Zechariah, Ben, and Jaaziel, and Shemira- moth, and Jehiel, and Unni, Eliab, and Benaiah, and Maaseiah, and Mattithiah, and Elipheleh, and Mikneiah, and Obed-edom, 19 and Jeiel, the porters. So the singers, Heman, Asaph, and

---

¹ Heb. It is *not to carry the ark of God, but for the Levites.*

² Or, *kinsmen.*

He therefore allowed the former Tabernacle to keep its place, and had another made and erected.

2. *None ought to carry the ark of God but the Levites*] Cp. marg. reff. We can easily understand that David, after the "breach upon Uzza" (xiii. 11), had carefully considered all the legal requirements with respect to moving the Ark, and was anxious that they should be strictly observed (cp. *v.* 13).

3. *all Israel*] Chosen men probably, like the 30,000 of 2 Sam. vi. 1. See *v.* 25.

4. *the children of Aaron*] i.e. the priests.

5. *the sons of Kohath*] The order of the sons of Levi according to primogeniture is, Gershom, Kohath, Merari (Gen. xlvi. 11; Ex. vi. 16). But the Kohathites, of whom came the priestly family of the Aaronites, had precedence in all respects. To them especially was committed the attendance

upon the Ark and the bearing of it. Of the six Levitical families mentioned (*vv.* 5-10) one only was descended from Gershom, one from Merari, and four (Uriel, Elizaphan, Hebron, and Uzziel) from Kohath.

13. The "due order" was that the Ark should be borne on the shoulders of Kohathite Levites—not that it should be placed upon a cart, drawn by oxen, and rudely shaken.

16. *the singers*] Singing had long been recognised as appropriate to religious cere- monies (Ex. xv. 21; Judg. v. 1; 1 Chr. xiii. 8); but this is the first occasion on which we find the duty of conducting musical services expressly laid on the Levites. Henceforth the services of the Tabernacle and the Temple were regularly choral, and a considerable section of the Levites was trained in musical knowledge, and set apart to conduct this portion of the national worship.

20 Ethan, *were appointed* to sound with cymbals of brass; and
Zechariah, and [1]Aziel, and Shemiramoth, and Jehiel, and Unni,
and Eliab, and Maaseiah, and Benaiah, with psalteries [m]on   *m* Ps. 45,
21 Alamoth; and Mattithiah, and Elipheleh, and Miknciah, and   title.
Obed-edom, and Jeiel, and Azaziah, with harps [2]on the Shemi-
22 nith to excel. And Chenaniah, chief of the Levites, [3]*was* for
[4]song: he instructed about the song, because he *was* skilful.
23 And Berechiah and Elkanah *were* doorkeepers for the ark.
24 And Shebaniah, and Jehoshaphat, and Nethaneel, and Amasai,
and Zechariah, and Benaiah, and Eliezer, the priests, [n]did blow   *n* Num. 10. 8.
with the trumpets before the ark of God: and Obed-edom and   Ps. 81. 3.
25 Jehiah *were* doorkeepers for the ark. ¶ So [o]David, and the   *o* 2 Sam. 6.
elders of Israel, and the captains over thousands, went to bring   12, 13, &c.
up the ark of the covenant of the LORD out of the house of   1 Kin. 8. 1.
26 Obed-edom with joy. And it came to pass, when God helped
the Levites that bare the ark of the covenant of the LORD, that
27 they offered seven bullocks and seven rams. And David *was*
clothed with a robe of fine linen, and all the Levites that bare
the ark, and the singers, and Chenaniah the master of the [5]song
with the singers: David also *had* upon him an ephod of linen.
28 [p]Thus all Israel brought up the ark of the covenant of the LORD   *p* ch. 13. 8.
with shouting, and with sound of the cornet, and with trumpets,
and with cymbals, making a noise with psalteries and harps.
29 And it came to pass, [q]*as* the ark of the covenant of the LORD   *q* 2 Sam. 6. 16.
came to the city of David, that Michal the daughter of Saul
looking out at a window saw king David dancing and playing:
and she despised him in her heart.

CHAP. 16. SO [a]they brought the ark of God, and set it in the midst   *a* 2 Sam. 6.
of the tent that David had pitched for it: and they offered burnt   17—19.
2 sacrifices and peace offerings before God. And when David had
made an end of offering the burnt offerings and the peace offer-
3 ings, he blessed the people in the name of the LORD. And he
dealt to every one of Israel, both man and woman, to every one
a loaf of bread, and a good piece of flesh, and a flagon *of wine*.

---

[1] ver. 18, *Jaaz'el*.
[2] Or, *on the eighth to over-see*, Ps. 6, title.
[3] Or, was *for the carriage: he instructed about the carriage*.
[4] Heb. *lifting up*.
[5] Or, *carriage*.

---

20. *psalteries on Alamoth*] Probably, psalteries whose tone resembled the voices of girls (*alamoth*). Cp. the "female flutes" of the Lydians.

21. *harps on the Sheminith*] "Sheminith" means properly "the eighth," and has been compared with the modern musical term "octave." Further, "Sheminith" and "Alamoth" are regarded as contrasted, and the harps of Mattithiah and his companions are supposed to have been pitched an octave below the psalteries of Zechariah and his brethren.

The word translated "to excel," is taken as meaning "to lead," and Mattithiah, &c., as leaders of the singers.

22. *for song*] See marg. Hebraists are still at variance as to the meaning of this passage, some supposing elevation [or, delivery] of the voice, others elevation of the Ark, to be intended.

26. *when God helped the Levites*] The death of Uzza had deeply impressed both David and the Levites, and it was doubted whether God would allow the Ark to be moved any more. Sacrificial animals were held ready; and when it appeared—by the movement of the Ark six paces (2 Sam. vi. 13), without any manifestation of the Divine displeasure—that God was not opposing but rather helping the Levites in their task, the victims were at once offered.

27. "Fine linen" (*byssus*) is here first spoken of as used for dress. It seems to have been reserved for nobles of the highest rank (Esth. viii. 15), for kings, and for priests (2 Chr. v. 12). David's robe was probably worn, like that of the High-Priest, immediately under the ephod, and may, like that, have reached the feet.

XVI. The first three verses form part of the narrative commenced at xv. 25. Cp. 2 Sam. vi. 17-19, where the passage is not torn from its proper context.

b Ps. 33,
& 70, title.

4 ¶ And he appointed *certain* of the Levites to minister before the ark of the LORD, and to *b*record, and to thank and praise the
5 LORD God of Israel: Asaph the chief, and next to him Zechariah, Jeiel, and Shemiramoth, and Jehiel, and Mattithiah, and Eliab, and Benaiah, and Obed-edom: and Jeiel ¹with psalteries and with harps; but Asaph made a sound with cymbals;
6 Benaiah also and Jahaziel the priests with trumpets continually
7 before the ark of the covenant of God. ¶ Then on that day

c See
2 Sam. 23. 1.

David delivered *c*first *this psalm* to thank the LORD into the hand of Asaph and his brethren.

d Ps. 105.
1—15.

8   *d*Give thanks unto the LORD, call upon his name,
       Make known his deeds among the people.

9   Sing unto him, sing psalms unto him,
       Talk ye of all his wondrous works.

10   Glory ye in his holy name:
      Let the heart of them rejoice that seek the LORD.

11   Seek the LORD and his strength,
      Seek his face continually.

12   Remember his marvellous works that he hath done,
      His wonders, and the judgments of his mouth;

13   O ye seed of Israel his servant,
      Ye children of Jacob, his chosen ones.

14   He *is* the LORD our God;
      His judgments *are* in all the earth.

15   Be ye mindful always of his covenant;
      The word *which* he commanded to a thousand generations;

e Gen. 17. 2.
& 26. 3.
& 28. 13.
& 35. 11.

16   *Even of the* *e*covenant which he made with Abraham,
      And of his oath unto Isaac;

17   And hath confirmed the same to Jacob for a law,
      And to Israel *for* an everlasting covenant,

18   Saying, Unto thee will I give the land of Canaan,
      ²The lot of your inheritance;

19   When ye were but ³few,

f Gen. 34. 30.

20   *f*Even a few, and strangers in it.
      And *when* they went from nation to nation,
      And from *one* kingdom to another people;

21   He suffered no man to do them wrong:

g Gen. 12. 17.
& 20. 3.
Exod. 7. 15
—18.
h Ps. 105. 15.
i Ps. 96.1,&c.

22   Yea, he *g*reproved kings for their sakes,
      Saying, *h*Touch not mine anointed,
      And do my prophets no harm.

23   *i*Sing unto the LORD, all the earth;
      Shew forth from day to day his salvation.

24   Declare his glory among the heathen;
      His marvellous works among all nations.

¹ Heb. *with instruments of psalteries and harps.*   ² Heb. *the cord.*   ³ Heb. *men of number.*

4–42. This passage is interposed by the writer of Chronicles between two sentences of the parallel passage in Samuel. It contains a detailed account of the service which David instituted at this time, a service out of which grew the more elaborate service of the Temple. The language of much of the passage is remarkably archaic, and there can be no reasonable doubt that it is in the main an extract from a record of the time of David.

5. The occurrence of the name "Jeiel" twice in this list is considered suspicious.

Hence the first "Jeiel" is thought to be a corrupt reading for "Aziel" (xv. 20), or "Jaaziel" (xv. 18).

8. The Psalm here put before us by the Chronicler, as sung liturgically by Asaph and his brethren on the day of the Ark's entrance into Jerusalem, accords closely with the passages in the present Book of Psalms noted in the marg. reff.

It is, apparently, a thanksgiving service composed for the occasion out of Psalms previously existing.

25 For great *is* the LORD, and greatly to be praised:
    He also *is* to be feared above all gods.
26 For all the gods *k*of the people *are* idols: *k* Lev. 19. 4
    But the LORD made the heavens.
27 Glory and honour *are* in his presence;
    Strength and gladness *are* in his place.
28 Give unto the LORD, ye kindreds of the people,
    Give unto the LORD glory and strength.
29 Give unto the LORD the glory *due* unto his name:
    Bring an offering, and come before him:
    Worship the LORD in the beauty of holiness.
30 Fear before him, all the earth:
    The world also shall be stable, that it be not moved.
31 Let the heavens be glad, and let the earth rejoice:
    And let *men* say among the nations, The LORD reigneth.
32 Let the sea roar, and the fulness thereof:
    Let the fields rejoice, and all that *is* therein.
33 Then shall the trees of the wood sing out at the presence
        of the LORD,
    Because he cometh to judge the earth.
34 *l*O give thanks unto the LORD; for *he is* good;   *l* Ps. 106. 1.
    For his mercy *endureth* for ever.   & 107. 1.
                                                                & 118. 1.
35 *m*And say ye, Save us, O God of our salvation,   & 136. 1.
    And gather us together, and deliver us from the heathen,   *m* Ps. 106.
    That we may give thanks to thy holy name, *and* glory in   47, 48.
        thy praise.
36 *n*Blessed *be* the LORD God of Israel for ever and ever.   *n* 1 Kin. 8.15.
37 And all *o*the people said, Amen, and praised the LORD. ¶ So   *o* Deut. 27. 15.
    he left there before the ark of the covenant of the LORD Asaph
    and his brethren, to minister before the ark continually, as every
38 day's work required: and Obed-edom with their brethren, three-
    score and eight; Obed-edom also the son of Jeduthun and
39 Hosah *to be* porters: and Zadok the priest, and his brethren the
    priests, *p*before the tabernacle of the LORD *q*in the high place   *p* ch. 21. 29.
40 that *was* at Gibeon, to offer burnt offerings unto the LORD   2 Chr. 1. 3.
    upon the altar of the burnt offering continually *r 1*morning and   *q* 1 Kin. 3. 4.
    evening, and *to do* according to all that is written in the law of   *r* Ex. 29. 38.
41 the LORD, which he commanded Israel; and with them Heman   Num. 28. 3.
    and Jeduthun, and the rest that were chosen, who were ex-
    pressed by name, to give thanks to the LORD, *s*because his   *s* ver. 34.
42 mercy *endureth* for ever; and with them Heman and Jeduthun   2 Chr. 5. 13.
                                                                & 7. 3.
                                                                Ezra 3. 11.
                                                                Jer. 33. 11.

¹ Heb. *in the morning, and in the evening.*

---

39. This is the first mention that we have of Gibeon as the place at which the Tabernacle of the congregation now rested. Previously it had been at Nob (1 Sam. xxi. 1–6), whence it was removed probably at the time of the slaughter of the priests by Doeg (1 Sam. xxii. 18, 19). It is uncertain whether Gibeon was regarded as a "high place" before the transfer to it of the Tabernacle: but thenceforth, till the completion of Solomon's Temple, it was the "great high place" (1 K. iii. 4)—a second centre of the national worship which for above 50 years was divided between Gibeon and Jerusalem.

40. *upon the altar of the burnt offering*]

The original Altar of Burnt-offering (Ex. xxvii. 1–8) continued at Gibeon with the Tabernacle (2 Chr. i. 3, 5). David must have erected a new Altar for sacrifice at Jerusalem (xvi. 1). The sacrifices commanded by the Law were, it appears, offered at the former place; at the latter were offered voluntary additional sacrifices.

41. *the rest* &c.] Rather, "**the rest of the chosen ones, who were mentioned by name.**" The "chosen ones" were "mentioned by name" in xv. 17–24. A portion of them, viz., those named in xvi. 5, 6, conducted the service in Jerusalem; the remainder were employed in the worship at Gibeon.

with trumpets and cymbals for those that should make a sound, and with musical instruments of God. And the sons of Jedu-

t 2 Sam. 6. 19, 20.

43 thun *were* [1]porters. *t*And all the people departed every man to his house: and David returned to bless his house.

a 2 Sam. 7. 1, &c.

CHAP. 17. NOW *a*it came to pass, as David sat in his house, that David said to Nathan the prophet, Lo, I dwell in an house of cedars, but the ark of the covenant of the LORD *remaineth* under
2 curtains. Then Nathan said unto David, Do all that *is* in thine
3 heart; for God *is* with thee. ¶ And it came to pass the same
4 night, that the word of God came to Nathan, saying, Go and tell David my servant, Thus saith the LORD, Thou shalt not build
5 me an house to dwell in: for I have not dwelt in an house since the day that I brought up Israel unto this day; but [2]have gone
6 from tent to tent, and from *one* tabernacle *to another*. Where-soever I have walked with all Israel, spake I a word to any of the judges of Israel, whom I commanded to feed my people,
7 saying, Why have ye not built me an house of cedars? Now therefore thus shalt thou say unto my servant David, Thus saith the LORD of hosts, I took thee from the sheepcote, *even* [3]from following the sheep, that thou shouldest be ruler over my
8 people Israel: and I have been with thee whithersoever thou hast walked, and have cut off all thine enemies from before thee, and have made thee a name like the name of the great men that
9 *are* in the earth. Also I will ordain a place for my people Israel, and will plant them, and they shall dwell in their place, and shall be moved no more; neither shall the children of
10 wickedness waste them any more, as at the beginning, and since the time that I commanded judges *to be* over my people Israel. Moreover I will subdue all thine enemies. Furthermore I tell
11 thee that the LORD will build thee an house. And it shall come to pass, when thy days be expired that thou must go *to be* with thy fathers, that I will raise up thy seed after thee, which shall
12 be of thy sons; and I will establish his kingdom. He shall build me an house, and I will stablish his throne for ever.

b 2 Sam. 7. 14, 15.

13 *b*I will be his father, and he shall be my son: and I will not take my mercy away from him, as I took *it* from *him* that was

c Luke 1. 33.

14 before thee: but *c*I will settle him in mine house and in my kingdom for ever: and his throne shall be established for ever-
15 more. According to all these words, and according to all this

d 2Sam.7.18.

16 vision, so did Nathan speak unto David. ¶ *d*And David the king came and sat before the LORD, and said, Who *am* I, O LORD God, and what *is* mine house, that thou hast brought me
17 hitherto? And *yet* this was a small thing in thine eyes, O God; for thou hast *also* spoken of thy servant's house for a great while to come, and hast regarded me according to the estate of a
18 man of high degree, O LORD God. What can David *speak* more to thee for the honour of thy servant? for thou knowest thy

---

[1] Heb. *for the gate.*   [2] Heb. *have been.*   [3] Heb. *from after.*

XVII. Cp. throughout 2 Sam. vii. and notes.

13. *my son*] The minatory clause which occurs after this in Samuel is here omitted, because the writer is not about to record the sins of Solomon, or the sufferings (1 K. xi. 9-40) which he thereby brought upon himself.

17. *hast regarded me* &c.] *i.e.* "Thou hast elevated me above other men, by making my

kingdom perpetual, regarding me as if I were a man of high degree." Cp. 2 Sam. vii. 19 note.

18. *for the honour of thy servant*] *i.e.* "for the honour which Thou hast done for Thy servant." The LXX. omits "Thy servant," and renders, "What can David say more to Thee to glorify Thee? For Thou knowest," &c.

19 servant. O LORD, for thy servant's sake, and according to
thine own heart, hast thou done all this greatness, in making
20 known all *these* [1]great things. O LORD, *there is* none like thee,
neither *is there any* God beside thee, according to all that we
21 have heard with our ears. And what one nation in the earth *is*
like thy people Israel, whom God went to redeem *to be* his own
people, to make thee a name of greatness and terribleness, by
driving out nations from before thy people, whom thou hast
22 redeemed out of Egypt? For thy people Israel didst thou make
thine own people for ever; and thou, LORD, becamest their
23 God. Therefore now, LORD, let the thing that thou hast spoken
concerning thy servant and concerning his house be established
24 for ever, and do as thou hast said. Let it even be established,
that thy name may be magnified for ever, saying, The LORD of
hosts *is* the God of Israel, *even* a God to Israel: and *let* the
25 house of David thy servant *be* established before thee. For
thou, O my God, [2]hast told thy servant that thou wilt build
him an house: therefore thy servant hath found *in his heart* to
26 pray before thee. And now, LORD, thou art God, and hast pro-
27 mised this goodness unto thy servant: now therefore [3]let it
please thee to bless the house of thy servant, that it may be
before thee for ever: for thou blessest, O LORD, and *it shall be*
blessed for ever.

CHAP. 18. NOW after this [a]it came to pass, that David smote the
Philistines, and subdued them, and took Gath and her towns
2 out of the hand of the Philistines. And he smote Moab; and
3 the Moabites became David's servants, *and* brought gifts. And
David smote [4]Hadarezer king of Zobah unto Hamath, as he
4 went to stablish his dominion by the river Euphrates. And
David took from him a thousand chariots, and [b]seven thousand
horsemen, and twenty thousand footmen: David also houghed
all the chariot *horses*, but reserved of them an hundred chariots.
5 And when the Syrians of [5]Damascus came to help Hadarezer
king of Zobah, David slew of the Syrians two and twenty thou-
6 sand men. Then David put *garrisons* in Syria-damascus; and
the Syrians became David's servants, *and* brought gifts. Thus
7 the LORD preserved David whithersoever he went. And David
took the shields of gold that were on the servants of Hadarezer,
8 and brought them to Jerusalem. Likewise from [6]Tibhath, and
from Chun, cities of Hadarezer, brought David very much brass,
wherewith [c]Solomon made the brasen sea, and the pillars, and
9 the vessels of brass. ¶ Now when [7]Tou king of Hamath heard
how David had smitten all the host of Hadarezer king of Zobah;
10 he sent [8]Hadoram his son to king David, [9]to enquire of his
welfare, and [1]to congratulate him, because he had fought against
Hadarezer, and smitten him; (for Hadarezer [2]had war with

a 2 Sam. 8.
1, &c.

b 2 Sam. 8.
4, *seven
hundred.*

c 1 Kin. 7.
15, 23.
2 Chr. 4. 12,
15, 16.

---

[1] Heb. *greatnesses.*
[2] Heb. *hast revealed the ear
of thy servant.*
[3] Or, *it hath pleased thee.*
[4] Or, *Hadadezer,* 2 Sam.
8. 3.
[5] Heb. *Darmesek.*
[6] Called in the book of
Samuel *Betah,* and *Be-
rothai.*
[7] Or, *Toi,* 2 Sam. 8. 9.
[8] Or, *Joram,* 2 Sam. 8. 10.
[9] Or, *to salute.*
[1] Heb. *to bless.*
[2] Heb. *was the man of
wars.*

---

24. Some prefer, "And let **Thy name be
established** and magnified for ever:" *i.e.*
"Let not only Thy promise stand firm, but
let Thy Name also stand firm (continue to
be held in honour) and be magnified," &c.

27. The marg. rendering is preferable.
XVIII. This chapter is closely parallel
with 2 Sam. viii.
  1. *Gath and her towns*] In Samuel, Metheg-
ammah (see marg. ref. note).

Tou;) and *with him* all manner of vessels of gold and silver and
11 brass. Them also king David dedicated unto the LORD, with
the silver and the gold that he brought from all *these* nations;
from Edom, and from Moab, and from the children of Ammon,
12 and from the Philistines, and from Amalek. Moreover [1]Abishai
the son of Zeruiah slew of the Edomites in the valley of salt

d 2Sam.8.13.
e 2 Sam. 8.
14, &c.

13 *d*eighteen thousand. *e*And he put garrisons in Edom; and all
the Edomites became David's servants. Thus the LORD pre-
14 served David whithersoever he went. ¶So David reigned over
all Israel, and executed judgment and justice among all his
15 people. And Joab the son of Zeruiah *was* over the host; and
16 Jehoshaphat the son of Ahilud, [2]recorder. And Zadok the son
of Ahitub, and [3]Abimelech the son of Abiathar, *were* the priests;

f 2 Sam.8.18.

17 and [4]Shavsha was scribe; *f*and Benaiah the son of Jehoiada
was over the Cherethites and the Pelethites; and the sons of
David *were* chief [5]about the king.

a 2 Sam. 10.
1, &c.

CHAP. 19. NOW *a*it came to pass after this, that Nahash the king
of the children of Ammon died, and his son reigned in his stead.
2 And David said, I will shew kindness unto Hanun the son of
Nahash, because his father shewed kindness to me. And David
sent messengers to comfort him concerning his father. So the
servants of David came into the land of the children of Ammon
3 to Hanun, to comfort him. But the princes of the children of
Ammon said to Hanun, [6]Thinkest thou that David doth honour
thy father, that he hath sent comforters unto thee? are not his
servants come unto thee for to search, and to overthrow, and to
4 spy out the land? Wherefore Hanun took David's servants,
and shaved them, and cut off their garments in the midst hard
5 by their buttocks, and sent them away. Then there went *certain*,
and told David how the men were served. And he sent to meet
them: for the men were greatly ashamed. And the king said,
Tarry at Jericho until your beards be grown, and *then* return.
6 ¶And when the children of Ammon saw that they had made
themselves [7]odious to David, Hanun and the children of Ammon
sent a thousand talents of silver to hire them chariots and

b ch. 18. 5, 9.

horsemen out of Mesopotamia, and out of Syria-maachah, *b*and
7 out of Zobah. So they hired thirty and two thousand chariots,

---

[1] Heb. *Abshai.*
[2] Or, *remembrancer.*
[3] Called *Ahimelech*, 2 Sam.
8. 17.

[4] Called *Seraiah*, 2 Sam.
8. 17, and *Shisha*, 1 Kin.
4. 3.
[5] Heb. *at the hand of the king.*

[6] Heb. *In thine eyes doth
David, &c.*
[7] Heb. *to stink.*

XIX. Cp. marg. reff. and notes. The
writer here adds one or two touches, and
varies in one or two of the numbers.

2. *Hanun*] A Philistine king of this name
is mentioned in the Assyrian inscriptions as
paying tribute to Tiglath-pileser and warring
with Sargon.

6. *a thousand talents of silver*] The price
is not given in Samuel. On the practice of hiring troops about this time in
western Asia, see 1 K. xv. 18; 2 K. vii. 6;
2 Chr. xxv. 6.

7. *they hired thirty and two thousand
chariots*] The reading is corrupt. Such a
number as 32,000 chariots alone was never
brought into battle on any occasion. Cp.
the numbers in Ex. xiv. 7; 1 K. x. 26; 2
Chr. xii. 3. The largest force which an

Assyrian king ever speaks of encountering
is 3,940. The words " and horsemen " have
probably fallen out of the text after the
word "chariots" (cp. *v.* 6). The 32,000
would be the number of the warriors serving
on horseback or in chariots; and this number would agree closely with 2 Sam. x. 6, as
the following table shows:—

2 Sam. x. 6:—

		MEN.
Syrians of Beth-rehob and Zobah	.	20,000
Syrians of Ish-tob	. . . .	12,000
Syrians of Maachah.	. . . .	1,000
		33,000

1 Chr. xix. 7:—

Syrians of Zobah, &c.	. . .	32,000
Syrians of Maachah (number not given)	}	[1,000]
		33,000

and the king of Maachah and his people; who came and pitched
before Medeba. And the children of Ammon gathered them-
8 selves together from their cities, and came to battle. And when
David heard *of it*, he sent Joab, and all the host of the mighty
9 men. And the children of Ammon came out, and put the battle
in array before the gate of the city: and the kings that were
10 come *were* by themselves in the field. Now when Joab saw that
¹the battle was set against him before and behind, he chose out
of all the ²choice of Israel, and put *them* in array against the
11 Syrians. And the rest of the people he delivered unto the hand
of ³Abishai his brother, and they set *themselves* in array against
12 the children of Ammon. And he said, If the Syrians be too
strong for me, then thou shalt help me: but if the children of
13 Ammon be too strong for thee, then I will help thee. Be of
good courage, and let us behave ourselves valiantly for our
people, and for the cities of our God: and let the LORD do *that*
14 *which is* good in his sight. ¶ So Joab and the people that *were*
with him drew nigh before the Syrians unto the battle; and
15 they fled before him. And when the children of Ammon saw
that the Syrians were fled, they likewise fled before Abishai his
brother, and entered into the city. Then Joab came to Jeru-
16 salem. ¶ And when the Syrians saw that they were put to the
worse before Israel, they sent messengers, and drew forth the
Syrians that *were* beyond the ⁴river: and ⁵Shophach the captain
17 of the host of Hadarezer *went* before them. And it was told
David; and he gathered all Israel, and passed over Jordan, and
came upon them, and set *the battle* in array against them. So
when David had put the battle in array against the Syrians,
18 they fought with him. But the Syrians fled before Israel; and
David slew of the Syrians seven thousand *men which fought in*
chariots, and forty thousand footmen, and killed Shophach the
19 captain of the host. And when the servants of Hadarezer saw
that they were put to the worse before Israel, they made peace
with David, and became his servants: neither would the Syrians
help the children of Ammon any more.

CHAP. 20. AND ᵃit came to pass, that ⁶after the year was expired, at the time that kings go out *to battle*, Joab led forth the
power of the army, and wasted the country of the children of
Ammon, and came and besieged Rabbah. But David tarried
at Jerusalem. And ᵇJoab smote Rabbah, and destroyed it.
2 And David ᶜtook the crown of their king from off his head, and
found ⁷to weigh a talent of gold, and *there were* precious
stones in it; and it was set upon David's head: and he brought
3 also exceeding much spoil out of the city. And he brought out
the people that *were* in it, and cut *them* with saws, and with
harrows of iron, and with axes. Even so dealt David with all
the cities of the children of Ammon. And David and all the
4 people returned to Jerusalem. ¶ And it came to pass after this,
ᵈthat there ⁸⁹arose war at ¹Gezer with the Philistines; at which

a 2Sam.11.1.

b 2 Sam. 12. 26.
c 2 Sam. 12. 30, 31.

d 2 Sam. 21. 18.

---

¹ Heb. *the face of the battle was.*
² Or, *young men.*
³ Heb. *Abishai.*
⁴ That is. *Euphrates.*
⁵ Or, *Shobach,* 2 Sam. 10. 16.
⁶ Heb. *at the return of the year.*
⁷ Heb. *the weight of.*
⁸ Or, *continued.*
⁹ Heb. *stood.*
¹ Or, *Gob.*

XX. This chapter, containing such other warlike exploits belonging to David's reign as the writer of Chronicles thinks it important to put on record, is to be compared with the passages of Samuel noted in the marginal reff.
4, 5. See marg. ref. and notes.

c ch. 11. 29.

time *e*Sibbechai the Hushathite slew [1]Sippai, *that was* of the 5 children of [2]the giant: and they were subdued. And there was war again with the Philistines; and Elhanan the son of [3]Jair slew Lahmi the brother of Goliath the Gittite, whose spear staff

f 2 Sam. 21. 20.

6 *was* like a weaver's beam. And yet again *f* there was war at Gath, where was [4]a man of *great* stature, whose fingers and toes *were* four and twenty, six *on each hand*, and six *on each foot*: 7 and he also was [5]the son of the giant. But when he [6]defied Israel, Jonathan the son of [7]Shimea David's brother slew him. 8 These were born unto the giant in Gath; and they fell by the hand of David, and by the hand of his servants.

a 2 Sam. 24. 1, &c.

CHAP. 21. AND *a*Satan stood up against Israel, and provoked 2 David to number Israel. And David said to Joab and to the rulers of the people, Go, number Israel from Beer-sheba even

b ch. 27. 23.

to Dan; *b*and bring the number of them to me, that I may know 3 *it.* And Joab answered, The LORD make his people an hundred times so many more as they *be:* but, my lord the king, *are they* not all my lord's servants? why then doth my lord require this 4 thing? why will he be a cause of trespass to Israel? Nevertheless the king's word prevailed against Joab. Wherefore Joab departed, and went throughout all Israel, and came to Jeru-5 salem. And Joab gave the sum of the number of the people unto David. And all *they of* Israel were a thousand thousand and an hundred thousand men that drew sword: and Judah *was* four hundred threescore and ten thousand men that drew sword.

c ch. 27. 24.

6 *c*But Levi and Benjamin counted he not among them: for the 7 king's word was abominable to Joab. ¶[8] And God was dis-8 pleased with this thing; therefore he smote Israel. And David

d 2 Sam. 24. 10.
e 2 Sam. 12. 13.

said unto God, *d*I have sinned greatly, because I have done this thing: *e*but now, I beseech thee, do away the iniquity of thy 9 servant; for I have done very foolishly. ¶ And the LORD spake

f See 1 Sam. 9. 9.

10 unto Gad, David's *f*seer, saying, Go and tell David, saying, Thus saith the LORD, I [9]offer thee three *things:* choose thee one

---

[1] Or, *Saph*, 2 Sam. 21. 18.
[2] Or, *Rapha.*
[3] Called also *Jaare-ore-gim*, 2 Sam. 21. 19.
[4] Heb. *a man of measure.*

[5] Heb. *born to the giant*, or, *Rapha.*
[6] Or, *reproached.*
[7] Called *Shammah*, 1 Sam. 16. 9.

[8] Heb. *And it was evil in the eyes of the LORD concerning this thing.*
[9] Heb. *stretch out.*

XXI. The resemblance to the parallel passage in Samuel is throughout less close than usual; the additions are more numerous, the supernatural circumstances of the narrative being brought out into greater prominence. The history is evidently not drawn from Samuel, but from some quite separate document, probably a contemporary account of the occurrence drawn up by Gad.

1. As the books of Scripture are arranged in our Version, Satan is here for the first time by name introduced to us. He appears not merely as an " adversary " who seeks to injure man from without, but as a Tempter able to ruin him by suggesting sinful acts and thoughts from within. In this point of view, the revelation made of him here is the most advanced that we find in the Old Testament.

The difficulty in reconciling the statement here, "Satan provoked David," &c., with that of Samuel, "the Lord moved

David," &c. (2 Sam. xxiv. 1) is not serious. All temptation is permitted by God. When evil spirits tempt us, they do so by permission (Job i. 12, ii. 6 ; Luke xxii. 31, &c.). If Satan therefore provoked David to number the people, God allowed him. And what God allows, He may be said to do. [Another view is maintained in 2 Sam. xxiv. 1 note].

5. In 2 Sam. xxiv. 9 the numbers are different. The explanation there given is not so generally accepted as the supposition that the numbers have, in one passage or the other (or possibly in both), suffered corruption.

6. To omit the Levites would be to follow the precedent recorded in Num. i. 47-49. The omission of Benjamin must be ascribed to a determination on the part of Joab to frustrate the king's intention, whereby he might hope to avert God's wrath from the people.

11 of them, that I may do *it* unto thee. So Gad came to David,
12 and said unto him, Thus saith the LORD, [1]Choose thee [g]either
three years' famine; or three months to be destroyed before thy
foes, while that the sword of thine enemies overtaketh *thee;* or
else three days the sword of the LORD, even the pestilence, in
the land, and the angel of the LORD destroying throughout all
the coasts of Israel. Now therefore advise thyself what word I
13 shall bring again to him that sent me. And David said unto
Gad, I am in a great strait: let me fall now into the hand of the
LORD; for very [2]great *are* his mercies: but let me not fall into
14 the hand of man. So the LORD sent pestilence upon Israel:
15 and there fell of Israel seventy thousand men. ¶ And God
sent an [h]angel unto Jerusalem to destroy it: and as he was
destroying, the LORD beheld, and [i]he repented him of the evil,
and said to the angel that destroyed, It is enough, stay now
thine hand. And the angel of the LORD stood by the threshing-
16 floor of [3]Ornan the Jebusite. And David lifted up his eyes,
and [k]saw the angel of the LORD stand between the earth and
the heaven, having a drawn sword in his hand stretched out
over Jerusalem. Then David and the elders *of Israel, who were*
17 clothed in sackcloth, fell upon their faces. And David said unto
God, *Is it* not I *that* commanded the people to be numbered?
even I it is that have sinned and done evil indeed; but *as for*
these sheep, what have they done? let thine hand, I pray thee,
O LORD my God, be on me, and on my father's house; but not
18 on thy people, that they should be plagued. ¶ Then the [l]angel
of the LORD commanded Gad to say to David, that David should
go up, and set up an altar unto the LORD in the threshingfloor of
19 Ornan the Jebusite. And David went up at the saying of Gad,
20 which he spake in the name of the LORD. [4]And Ornan turned
back, and saw the angel; and his four sons with him hid them-
21 selves. Now Ornan was threshing wheat. And as David came to
Ornan, Ornan looked and saw David, and went out of the thresh-

g 2 Sam. 24.
13.

h 2 Sam. 24.
16.
i See Gen. 6.
6.

k 2 Chr. 3. 1.

l 2 Chr. 2. 1.

---

[1] Heb. *Take to thee.*
[2] Or, *many.*
[3] Or, *Araunah,* 2 Sam. 24. 18.

[4] Or, *When Ornan turned
back and saw the angel,*
then he *and his four*

*sons with him hid them-
selves.*

---

12. *and the angel of the* LORD *destroying*
&c.] These words are not in Samuel, which
puts the third alternative briefly. They
prepare the way for the angelic appearance
(*v.* 16), on which the author is about to lay
so much stress.

16. Here a picture of awful grandeur
takes the place of the bare statement of the
earlier historian (2 Sam. xxiv. 17). And here,
as elsewhere, the author probably extracts
from the ancient documents such circumstances as harmonise with his general plan.
As the sanctity of the Temple was among
the points whereon he was most anxious to
lay stress, he gives in full all the miraculous
circumstances attending this first designation of what became the Temple site (marg.
ref. *k*) as a place "holy to the Lord."

*David and the elders…clothed in sackcloth,
fell upon their faces*] Facts additional to the
narrative of Samuel; but facts natural in
themselves, and in harmony with that narrative. Similarly the narrative in *v.* 20 is

additional to the account in Samuel; but
its parts hang together; and there is no
sufficient ground for suspecting it.

18. It has been observed that it is only
in books of a late period that Angels are
brought forward as intermediaries between
God and the prophets. This, no doubt, is
true; and it is certainly unlikely that the
records, from which the author of Chronicles drew, spoke of Gad as receiving his
knowledge of God's will from an Angel.
The touch may be regarded as coming from
the writer of Chronicles himself, who expresses the fact related by his authorities in
the language of his own day (see Zech. i. 9,
14, 19, ii. 3, iv. 1, v. 5, &c.); language, however, which we are not to regard as rhetori-
cal, but as strictly in accordance with truth,
since Angels were doubtless employed as
media between God and the prophets as
much in the time of David as in that of
Zechariah.

ingfloor, and bowed himself to David with *his* face to the ground.

22 Then David said to Ornan, [1]Grant me the place of *this* threshing-floor, that I may build an altar therein unto the LORD: thou shalt grant it me for the full price: that the plague may be stayed

23 from the people. And Ornan said unto David, Take *it* to thee, and let my lord the king do *that which is* good in his eyes: lo, I give *thee* the oxen *also* for burnt offerings, and the threshing instruments for wood, and the wheat for the meat offering; I

24 give it all. And king David said to Ornan, Nay; but I will verily buy it for the full price: for I will not take *that* which *is* thine for the LORD, nor offer burnt offerings without cost.

m 2 Sam. 24.
24.

25 So *m*David gave to Ornan for the place six hundred shekels of

26 gold by weight. And David built there an altar unto the LORD, and offered burnt offerings and peace offerings, and called upon

n Lev. 9. 24.
2 Chr. 3. 1.
& 7. 1.

the LORD; and *n*he answered him from heaven by fire upon

27 the altar of burnt offering. And the LORD commanded the angel; and he put up his sword again into the sheath thereof.

28 ¶At that time when David saw that the LORD had answered him in the threshingfloor of Ornan the Jebusite, then he sacri-

o ch. 16. 39.

29 ficed there. *o*For the tabernacle of the LORD, which Moses made in the wilderness, and the altar of the burnt offering, *were*

p 1 Kin. 3. 4.
ch. 16. 39.
2 Chr. 1. 3.
a Deut. 12. 5.
2 Sam. 24. 18.
ch. 21. 18,
19, 26, 28.
2 Chr. 3. 1.
b 1 Kin. 9. 21.

30 at that season in the high place at *p*Gibeon. But David could not go before it to enquire of God: for he was afraid because of

22 the sword of the angel of the LORD. THEN David said, *a*This *is* the house of the LORD God, and this *is* the altar of the burnt

2 offering for Israel. ¶And David commanded to gather together *b*the strangers that *were* in the land of Israel; and he set masons

3 to hew wrought stones to build the house of God. And David prepared iron in abundance for the nails for the doors of the

c ver. 14.
1 Kin. 7. 47.
d 1 Kin. 5. 6,
16.
e ch. 29. 1.

gates, and for the joinings; and brass in abundance *c*without

4 weight; also cedar trees in abundance: for the *d*Zidonians and

5 they of Tyre brought much cedar wood to David. And David said, *e*Solomon my son *is* young and tender, and the house *that*

[1] Heb. *Give.*

---

25. Cp. marg. ref. and note. It may also be conjectured that we should read " six " for " six hundred " here; since, according to the later Jewish system, six gold shekels were nearly equal in value to fifty silver ones.

26. *he answered him from heaven by fire*] This fact is not mentioned by the author of Samuel, since his object is to give an account of the sin of David, its punishment, and the circumstances by which that punishment was brought to a close, not to connect those circumstances with anything further in the history. With the writer of Chronicles the case is different. He would probably have omitted the whole narrative, as he did the sin of David in the matter of Uriah, but for its connexion with the fixing of the Temple site (xxii.). It was no doubt mainly the fact that God answered him by fire from heaven on this altar, which determined David, and Solomon after him, to build the Temple on the spot so consecrated.

30. David, knowing that by sacrifice on this altar he had caused the angel to stay his hand, was afraid to transfer his offerings

elsewhere, lest the Angel should resume his task and pestilence again break out.

XXII. This chapter, which consists entirely of new matter, helps to fill up the gap which had been left by the earlier authors between 2 Sam. xxiv. and 1 K. i.

1. *This is the house of the LORD God*] The double miracle—that of the angelic appearance and that of the fire from heaven—had convinced David that here he had found the destined site of that "house" which it had been told him that his son should build (*v.* 10). Hence, this public announcement.

2. *the strangers*] *i.e.* the aliens—the non-Israelite population of the land. Cp. 2 Chr. ii. 17.

3. *for the joinings*] *i.e.* the girders, or cramps—pieces of iron to be used in joining beams or stones together.

4. See marg. reff. and notes; xiv. 1.

5. *young and tender*] The exact age of Solomon at this time is uncertain; but it cannot have been more than twenty-four or twenty-five. It may have been as little as fourteen or fifteen. Cp. 1 K. ii. 2 note.

is to be builded for the LORD *must be* exceedingly magnifical, of fame and of glory throughout all countries: I will *therefore* now make preparation for it. So David prepared abundantly before
6 his death. ¶ Then he called for Solomon his son, and charged
7 him to build an house for the LORD God of Israel. And David said to Solomon, My son, as for me, *f*it was in my mind to build
8 an house *g*unto the name of the LORD my God: but the word of the LORD came to me, saying, *h*Thou hast shed blood abundantly, and hast made great wars: thou shalt not build an house unto my name, because thou hast shed much blood upon the earth in
9 my sight. *i*Behold, a son shall be born to thee, who shall be a man of rest; and I will give him *k*rest from all his enemies round about: for his name shall be *1*Solomon, and I will give
10 peace and quietness unto Israel in his days. *l*He shall build an house for my name; and *m*he shall be my son, and I *will be* his father; and I will establish the throne of his kingdom over
11 Israel for ever. Now, my son, *n*the LORD be with thee; and prosper thou, and build the house of the LORD thy God, as he
12 hath said of thee. Only the LORD *o*give thee wisdom and understanding, and give thee charge concerning Israel, that thou
13 mayest keep the law of the LORD thy God. *p*Then shalt thou prosper, if thou takest heed to fulfil the statutes and judgments which the LORD charged Moses with concerning Israel: *q*be strong, and of good courage; dread not, nor be dismayed.
14 Now, behold, *2*in my trouble I have prepared for the house of the LORD an hundred thousand talents of gold, and a thousand thousand talents of silver; and of brass and iron *r*without weight; for it is in abundance: timber also and stone have I
15 prepared; and thou mayest add thereto. Moreover *there are* workmen with thee in abundance, hewers and *3*workers of stone and timber, and all manner of cunning men for every manner
16 of work. Of the gold, the silver, and the brass, and the iron, *there is* no number. Arise *therefore*, and be doing, and *s*the LORD
17 be with thee. ¶ David also commanded all the princes of Israel
18 to help Solomon his son, *saying, Is* not the LORD your God with you? *t*and hath he *not* given you rest on every side? for he hath given the inhabitants of the land into mine hand; and the land is
19 subdued before the LORD, and before his people. Now *u*set your

	f 2 Sam. 7. 2. 1 Kin. 8. 17. ch. 17. 1. & 28. 2.
	g Deut. 12. 5, 11.
	h 1 Kin. 5. 3.
	i ch. 28. 5.
	k 1 Kin. 4. 25. & 5. 4.
	l 2 Sam. 7.13. 1 Kin. 5. 5, ch. 17. 12, 13. & 28. 6.
	m Heb. 1. 5.
	n ver. 16.
	o 1 Kin. 3. 9, 12. Ps. 72. 1.
	p Josh.1.7,8. ch. 28. 7.
	q Deut. 31. 6 −8. Josh. 1.6,7,9. ch. 28. 20.
	r As ver. 3.
	s ver. 11.
	t Deut. 12.10. Josh. 22. 4. 2 Sam. 7. 1. ch. 23. 25. *u* 2 Chr. 20.3.

---

1 That is, *Peaceable.*   *2* Or, *in my poverty.*   *3* That is, *masons and carpenters.*

---

8. *the word of the* LORD *came to me,* &c.] Not by Nathan (xvii. 4–15), but on some other occasion (xxviii. 3). On the bloody character of David's wars, see 2 Sam. viii. 2, 5, x. 18, xii. 31 ; and 1 K. xi. 16.

9. For the names of Solomon, cp. 2 Sam. xii. 24 note. The former name prevailed, probably on account of this prophecy, which attached to the name the promise of a blessing.

13. *be strong,* &c.] David adopts the words of Moses to the Israelites (cp. marg. reff.) and to Joshua.

14. *in my trouble*] See marg. David refers to the manifold troubles of his reign, which had prevented him from accumulating very much treasure.

an hundred thousand talents of gold, &c.] We do not know the value of the Hebrew talent at this period, and therefore these numbers may be sound. But in that case we must suppose an enormous difference between the pre-Babylonian and the post-Babylonian talents. According to the value of the post-Babylonian Hebrew talent, the gold here spoken of would be worth more than 1000 millions of our pounds sterling, while the silver would be worth above 400 millions. Accumulations to anything like this amount are inconceivable under the circumstances, and we must therefore either suppose the talents of David's time to have been little more than the hundredth part of the later talents, or regard the numbers of this verse as augmented at least a hundredfold by corruption. Of the two the latter is certainly the more probable supposition.

x 1 Kin. 8. 6,
21.
2 Chr. 5. 7.
& 6. 11.
y ver. 7.
1 Kin. 5. 3.
a 1 Kin. 1.
33—39.
ch. 28. 5.
b Num. 4. 3,
47.

c Deut.16.18.
ch. 26. 29.
2 Chr. 19. 8.
d See 2 Chr.
29. 25, 26.
Amos 6. 5.
e Ex. 6. 16.
Num. 26. 57.
ch. 6. 1, &c.
2 Chr. 8. 14.
& 29. 25.
f ch. 26. 21.

g Ex. 6. 18.

h Ex. 6. 20.
i Ex. 28. 1.
Heb. 5. 4.
k Ex. 30. 7.
Num. 16. 40.
1 Sam. 2. 28.
l Deut. 21. 5.
m Num.6.23.
n See ch. 26.
23, 24, 25.
o Ex. 2. 22.
& 18. 3, 4.
p ch. 26. 24.
q ch. 26. 25.
r ch. 24. 23.

s ch. 24. 26.
t ch. 24. 29.
u ch. 24. 28.
x See Num.
36. 6, 8.
y ch. 24. 30.
z Num. 10.
17, 21.

a See Num.
1. 3. & 4. 3.

heart and your soul to seek the LORD your God; arise therefore, and build ye the sanctuary of the LORD God, to *x* bring the ark of the covenant of the LORD, and the holy vessels of God, into the

23 house that is to be built *y* to the name of the LORD. SO when David was old and full of days, he made *a* Solomon his son king

2 over Israel. ¶ And he gathered together all the princes of Israel,

3 with the priests and the Levites. Now the Levites were numbered from the age of *b* thirty years and upward: and their number by their polls, man by man, was thirty and eight

4 thousand. Of which, twenty and four thousand *were* [1] to set forward the work of the house of the LORD; and six thousand

5 *were* *c* officers and judges: moreover four thousand *were* porters; and four thousand praised the LORD with the instruments

6 *d* which I made, *said David*, to praise *therewith*. ¶ And *e* David divided them into [2] courses among the sons of Levi, *namely*,

7 Gershon, Kohath and Merari. ¶ Of the *f* Gershonites *were*,

8 [3] Laadan, and Shimei. The sons of Laadan; the chief *was*

9 Jehiel, and Zetham, and Joel, three. The sons of Shimei; Shelomith, and Haziel, and Haran, three. These *were* the chief

10 of the fathers of Laadan. And the sons of Shimei *were*, Jahath, [4] Zina, and Jeush, and Beriah. These four *were* the sons of

11 Shimei. And Jahath was the chief, and Zizah the second: but Jeush and Beriah [5] had not many sons; therefore they were in

12 one reckoning, according to *their* father's house. ¶ *g* The sons of

13 Kohath; Amram, Izhar, Hebron, and Uzziel, four. The sons of *h* Amram; Aaron and Moses: and *i* Aaron was separated, that he should sanctify the most holy things, he and his sons for ever, *k* to burn incense before the LORD, *l* to minister unto him, and *m* to

14 bless in his name for ever. Now *concerning* Moses the man of

15 God, *n* his sons were named of the tribe of Levi. *o* The sons of

16 Moses *were*, Gershom, and Eliezer. Of the sons of Gershom,

17 *p* [6] Shebuel *was* the chief. And the sons of Eliezer *were*, *q* Rehabiah [7] the chief. And Eliezer had none other sons; but the

18 sons of Rehabiah [8] were very many. Of the sons of Izhar;

19 [9] Shelomith the chief. *r* Of the sons of Hebron; Jeriah the first, Amariah the second, Jahaziel the third, and Jekameam the

20 fourth. Of the sons of Uzziel; Micah the first, and Jesiah the

21 second. ¶ *s* The sons of Merari; Mahli, and Mushi. The sons

22 of Mahli; Eleazar, and *t* Kish. And Eleazar died, and *u* had no sons, but daughters: and their [1] brethren the sons of Kish *x* took

23 them. *y* The sons of Mushi; Mahli, and Eder, and Jeremoth,

24 three. ¶ These *were* the sons of *z* Levi after the house of their fathers; *even* the chief of the fathers, as they were counted by number of names by their polls, that did the work for the service of the house of the LORD, from the age of *a* twenty years

---

[1] Or, *to oversee.*
[2] Heb. *divisions.*
[3] Or, *Libni,* ch. 6. 17.
[4] Or, *Zizah,* ver. 11.
[5] Heb. *did not multiply sons.*
[6] *Shubael,* ch. 24. 20.
[7] Or, *the first.*
[8] Heb. *were highly multiplied.*
[9] *Shelomoth,* ch. 24. 22.
[1] Or, *kinsmen.*

XXIII. See marg. reff. and notes. Verses 28–32 give the most complete account in Scripture of the nature of the Levitical office.

24. *from the age of twenty years*] The Levites had hitherto not entered upon their regular functions until the age of thirty (*v.* 3). Certain lighter duties were by the

Law imposed on them at twenty-five (Num. viii. 24); but it was not until they were five years older that they became liable to the full service of the Sanctuary. David appears now to have made a change. By his "last words" (*v.* 27) the time for the Levites to enter on the full duties of their office was advanced from thirty to twenty. This

25 and upward. For David said, The LORD God of Israel [b]hath given rest unto his people, [1]that they may dwell in Jerusalem
26 for ever : and also unto the Levites ; they shall no *more* [c]carry
27 the tabernacle, nor any vessels of it for the service thereof. For by the last words of David the Levites *were* [2]numbered from
28 twenty years old and above : because [3]their office *was* to wait on the sons of Aaron for the service of the house of the LORD, in the courts, and in the chambers, and in the purifying of all holy
29 things, and the work of the service of the house of God ; both for [d]the shewbread, and for [e]the fine flour for meat offering, and for [f]the unleavened cakes, and for [g]*that which is baked in* the [4]pan, and for that which is fried, and for all manner of [h]mea-
30 sure and size ; and to stand every morning to thank and praise
31 the LORD, and likewise at even ; and to offer all burnt sacrifices unto the LORD [i]in the sabbaths, in the new moons, and on the [k]set feasts, by number, according to the order commanded unto
32 them, continually before the LORD : and that they should [l]keep the charge of the tabernacle of the congregation, and the charge of the holy *place*, and [m]the charge of the sons of Aaron their brethren, in the service of the house of the LORD.

CHAP. 24 NOW *these are* the divisions of the sons of Aaron. [a]The
2 sons of Aaron ; Nadab, and Abihu, Eleazar, and Ithamar. But [b]Nadab and Abihu died before their father, and had no children :
3 therefore Eleazar and Ithamar executed the priest's office. And David distributed them, both Zadok of the sons of Eleazar, and Ahimelech of the sons of Ithamar, according to their offices in
4 their service. And there were more chief men found of the sons of Eleazar than of the sons of Ithamar ; and *thus* were they divided. Among the sons of Eleazar *there were* sixteen chief men of the house of *their* fathers, and eight among the sons of
5 Ithamar according to the house of their fathers. Thus were they divided by lot, one sort with another ; for the governors of the sanctuary, and governors *of the house* of God, were of the sons
6 of Eleazar, and of the sons of Ithamar. And Shemaiah the son of Nethaneel the scribe, *one* of the Levites, wrote them before the king, and the princes, and Zadok the priest, and Ahimelech the

Side notes:
[b] ch. 22. 18.

[c] Num. 4. 5, &c.

[d] Ex. 25. 30.
[e] Lev. 6. 20.
ch. 9. 29, &c.
[f] Lev. 2. 4.
[g] Lev. 2. 5, 7.
[h] Lev. 19. 35.
[i] Num. 10. 10.
Ps. 81. 3.
[k] Lev. 23. 4.
[l] Num. 1. 53.

[m] Num. 3.
6—9.

[a] Lev. 10. 1, 6.
Num. 26. 60.

[b] Num. 3. 4.
& 26. 61.

---

[1] Or, *and he dwelleth in Jerusalem, &c.*
[2] Heb. *number.*
[3] Heb. *their station* was at the hand of the *sons of Aaron*, Neh. 11. 24.
[4] Or, *flat plate.*

---

change was based upon the lighter character of the labours imposed on them now that the Ark had ceased to be carried from place to place and obtained a permanent habitation (*v.* 26). The limit of age continued in after times where David had fixed it (see Ezra iii. 8).

27. By the "last words of David" some understand an historical work on the latter part of his reign, drawn up probably by Gad or Nathan (cp. xxvii. 24, xxix. 29). Others suppose that he left behind him a work containing directions for the service of the Sanctuary.

31. Though the Levites were not allowed by themselves to offer sacrifice, yet there were many respects in which they assisted the priests when sacrifice was offered. See 2 Chr. xxix. 34, xxxv. 11, 12.

the set feasts] The Passover, Feast of Pen-

tecost, and Feast of Tabernacles (marg. ref.).

XXIV. 3. Zadok and Ahimelech (rather Abiathar, see *v.* 6) assisted David in drawing up the priestly courses, as the "captains of the host" assisted him in making the divisions of the singers (xxv. 1).

5. *one sort with another*] *i.e.* "the assignment of their order in the courses was made by lot to the families belonging to Eleazar, and to the families belonging to Ithamar, equally." Both houses had furnished functionaries of the highest class, and therefore no preference was now given to either over the other.

6. *wrote them before the king*] *i.e.* "wrote down their names as the lots were drawn forth."

Ahimelech the son of Abiathar] A wrong reading. It should be "Abiathar, the son of Ahimelech." See 2 Sam. viii. 17 note.

son of Abiathar, and *before* the chief of the fathers of the priests
and Levites : one ¹principal household being taken for Eleazar,
7 and *one* taken for Ithamar.   ¶ Now the first lot came forth to
8 Jehoiarib, the second to Jedaiah, the third to Harim, the fourth
9, 10 to Seorim, the fifth to Malchijah, the sixth to Mijamin, the
11 seventh to Hakkoz, the eighth to ᶜAbijah, the ninth to Jeshuah,
12 the tenth to Shecaniah, the eleventh to Eliashib, the twelfth to
13 Jakim, the thirteenth to Huppah, the fourteenth to Jeshebeab,
14, 15 the fifteenth to Bilgah, the sixteenth to Immer, the seven-
16 teenth to Hezir, the eighteenth to Aphses, the nineteenth to
17 Pethahiah, the twentieth to Jehezekel, the one and twentieth to
18 Jachin, the two and twentieth to Gamul, the three and twentieth
19 to Delaiah, the four and twentieth to Maaziah.   ¶ These *were*
the orderings of them in their service ᵈto come into the house of
the LORD, according to their manner, under Aaron their father,
20 as the LORD God of Israel had commanded him.   ¶ And the rest
of the sons of Levi *were these :* Of the sons of Amram ; ᵉShubael :
21 of the sons of Shubael ; Jehdeiah.   Concerning ᶠRehabiah : of
22 the sons of Rehabiah, the first *was* Isshiah.   Of the Izharites ;
23 ᵍShelomoth : of the sons of Shelomoth ; Jahath.   And the sons
of ʰHebron ; Jeriah *the first*, Amariah the second, Jahaziel the
24 third, Jekameam the fourth.   Of the sons of Uzziel ; Michah :
25 of the sons of Michah ; Shamir.   The brother of Michah *was*
26 Isshiah : of the sons of Isshiah ; Zechariah.   ⁱThe sons of Merari
27 *were* Mahli and Mushi : the sons of Jaaziah ; Beno.   The sons
of Merari by Jaaziah ; Beno, and Shoham, and Zaccur, and Ibri.
28, 29 Of Mahli *came* Eleazar, ᵏwho had no sons.   Concerning Kish :
30 the son of Kish *was* Jerahmeel.   ˡThe sons also of Mushi ; Mahli,
and Eder, and Jerimoth. These *were* the sons of the Levites after
31 the house of their fathers.   These likewise cast lots over against
their brethren the sons of Aaron in the presence of David the
king, and Zadok, and Ahimelech, and the chief of the fathers of
the priests and Levites, even the principal fathers over against
their younger brethren.

ᶜ Neh. 12. 4, 17.
Luke 1. 5.

ᵈ ch. 9. 25.

ᵉ ch. 23. 16, Shebuel.
ᶠ ch. 23. 17.

ᵍ ch. 23. 18, Shelomith.
ʰ ch. 26. 31.

ⁱ Ex. 6. 19. ch. 23. 21.

ᵏ ch. 23. 22.
ˡ ch. 23. 23.

¹ Heb. *house of the father.*

---

19. *These were the orderings* &c.] *i.e.*
" this was the numerical order fixed for
their ministerial attendance in the house of
the Lord —an attendance which was after the
manner determined for them by their fore-
father Aaron, according to instructions
which he received from God."

20. The object of this second enumeration
of the Levitical families (cp. xxiii. 7-23)
seems to be the designation of the *heads* of
the families in David's time.   The omission
of the Gershonites is curious, and can only
be accounted for by supposing that the
author did not find any account of their
heads in his authorities.   The addition to
the Merarites (*vv.* 26, 27) is also curious.   It
brings the number of families up to twenty-
five, which is one more than we should have
expected.

23. Neither " Hebron " nor " the first "
is found in the present Hebrew text ; but
they seem to have been rightly supplied by
our translators from xxiii. 19.   The four
persons named appear to have been con-

temporaries of David, the heads of the
Hebronite houses in his time (cp. xxvi.
31).

26, 27. *The sons of Jaaziah, Beno*] Beno is
not really a name.   It is the Hebrew for
" his son," and is to be attached to Jaaziah.
Translate *v.* 27, " and the sons of Merari by
Jaaziah his son [were] Shoham and Zaccur,
and Ibri."   The meaning of the whole passage (*vv.* 26-30) seems to be that there were
three branches of the Merarites—the Beni-
Mahli, the Beni-Mushi, and the Beni-Jaa-
ziah.

31. *the principal fathers over against their
younger brethren*] *i.e.* " all the Levitical
houses enumerated drew lots in their courses
on equal terms, the elder families having no
advantage over the younger ones."   As there
were twenty-four courses of the priests, so
we must suppose that there were twenty-four
of the Levites, though the number of the
families as given in the text (xxiii. 7-23,
xxiv. 20-30) is twenty-*five*.

Chap. 25 MOREOVER David and the captains of the host separated to the service of the sons of ^aAsaph, and of Heman, and of Jeduthun, who should prophesy with harps, with psalteries, and with cymbals : and the number of the workmen according to
2 their service was : of the sons of Asaph ; Zaccur, and Joseph, and Nethaniah, and ¹Asarelah, the sons of Asaph under the hands of Asaph, which prophesied ²according to the order of
3 the king.   Of Jeduthun : the sons of Jeduthun ; Gedaliah, and ³Zeri, and Jeshaiah, Hashabiah, and Mattithiah, ⁴six, under the hands of their father Jeduthun, who prophesied with a harp,
4 to give thanks and to praise the LORD.   Of Heman : the sons of Heman ; Bukkiah, Mattaniah, ⁵Uzziel, ⁶Shebuel, and Jerimoth, Hananiah, Hanani, Eliathah, Giddalti, and Romamti-ezer, Josh-
5 bekashah, Mallothi, Hothir, *and* Mahazioth : all these *were* the sons of Heman the king's seer in the ⁷words of God, to lift up the horn.   And God gave to Heman fourteen sons and three
6 daughters.   All these *were* under the hands of their father for song *in* the house of the LORD, with cymbals, psalteries, and harps, for the service of the house of God, ^{b 8}according to the
7 king's order to Asaph, Jeduthun, and Heman.   So the number of them, with their brethren that were instructed in the songs of the LORD, *even* all that were cunning, was two hundred fourscore
8 and eight.   ¶ And they cast lots, ward against *ward*, as well the
9 small as the great, ^cthe teacher as the scholar.   Now the first lot came forth for Asaph to Joseph : the second to Gedaliah, who
10 with his brethren and sons *were* twelve : the third to Zaccur, *he*,
11 his sons, and his brethren, *were* twelve : the fourth to Izri, *he*,
12 his sons, and his brethren, *were* twelve : the fifth to Nethaniah,
13 *he*, his sons, and his brethren, *were* twelve : the sixth to Bukkiah,
14 *he*, his sons, and his brethren, *were* twelve : the seventh to Je-
15 sharelah, *he*, his sons, and his brethren, *were* twelve : the eighth
16 to Jeshaiah, *he*, his sons, and his brethren, *were* twelve : the ninth to Mattaniah, *he*, his sons, and his brethren, *were* twelve :

a ch. 6. 33, 30, 44.

b ver. 2.

c 2Chr.23.13.

¹ Otherwise called *Jesha-relah*, ver. 14.
² Heb. *by the hands of the king :* So ver. 6.
³ Or, *Izri*, ver. 11.
⁴ With Shimei mentioned, ver. 17.
⁵ Or, *Azareel*, ver. 18.
⁶ Or, *Shubael*, ver. 20.
⁷ Or, *matters*.
⁸ Heb. *by the hands of the king*.

XXV. 1. *the captains of the host*] Rather, "**the princes**" of xxiii. 2, and xxiv. 6.

2. *under the hands of Asaph*, &c.] That is to say, "under the direction of Asaph"—who himself "prophesied," or performed the sacred services, "under the direction of the king."

5. *to lift up the horn*] Some take this literally, and consider that Heman and his sons played on the horn in the musical services ; but there is no other evidence that the horn was so employed.   Perhaps the most probable explanation is that it has been transferred from the next clause, where (as here) it followed the word "God," with the sense that "God, to exalt Heman's horn (or, increase his dignity), gave him fourteen sons and three daughters."

7. *with their brethren*] *i.e.* "with others of the tribe of Levi."   Each son of Asaph, Jeduthun, and Heman, was at the head of a band of twelve skilled musicians, consisting partly of his own sons, partly of Levites belonging to other families (*vv.* 9-31).   The 24 band-leaders, together with their bands, formed a body of 288 persons (24 × 12 = 288)   Besides these, we hear of there being above 3,700 singers, who were probably divided, like the trained musicians, into 24 courses, which must have contained about 155 each (xxiii. 5).

8. *as well the small as the great*] Cp. xxiv. 31.   The lot was not applied indiscriminately to all the twenty-four courses, but was only used to settle which course of Asaph, which of Jeduthun, and which of Heman, should on each occasion be taken.   Asaph was given the precedence over his brethren, and his four courses were assigned the first, and then each alternate place.   Jeduthun took rank next, and received alternate places, first with Asaph, and then with Heman, until his courses were exhausted.   After this all the later places fel necessarily to Heman, whose courses continue without interruption from the 15th.

17 the tenth to Shimei, *he*, his sons, and his brethren, *were* twelve:
18 the eleventh to Azareel, *he*, his sons, and his brethren, *were*
19 twelve: the twelfth to Hashabiah, *he*, his sons, and his brethren,
20 *were* twelve: the thirteenth to Shubael, *he*, his sons, and his
21 brethren, *were* twelve: the fourteenth to Mattithiah, *he*, his
22 sons, and his brethren, *were* twelve: the fifteenth to Jeremoth,
23 *he*, his sons, and his brethren, *were* twelve: the sixteenth to
24 Hananiah, *he*, his sons, and his brethren, *were* twelve: the
seventeenth to Joshbekashah, *he*, his sons, and his brethren,
25 *were* twelve: the eighteenth to Hanani, *he*, his sons, and his
26 brethren, *were* twelve: the nineteenth to Mallothi, *he*, his sons,
27 and his brethren, *were* twelve: the twentieth to Eliathah, *he*, his
28 sons, and his brethren, *were* twelve: the one and twentieth to
29 Hothir, *he*, his sons, and his brethren, *were* twelve: the two and
twentieth to Giddalti, *he*, his sons, and his brethren, *were* twelve:
30 the three and twentieth to Mahazioth, *he*, his sons, and his
31 brethren, *were* twelve: the four and twentieth to Romamti-ezer,
he, his sons, and his brethren, *were* twelve.

CHAP. 26. CONCERNING the divisions of the porters: of the
Korhites *was* [1]Meshelemiah the son of Kore, of the sons of
2 [2]Asaph. And the sons of Meshelemiah *were*, Zechariah the firstborn, Jediael the second, Zebadiah the third, Jathniel the fourth,
3 Elam the fifth, Jehohanan the sixth, Elioenai the seventh.
4 Moreover the sons of Obed-edom *were*, Shemaiah the firstborn,
Jehozabad the second, Joah the third, and Sacar the fourth, and
5 Nethaneel the fifth, Ammiel the sixth, Issachar the seventh,
6 Peulthai the eighth: for God blessed [3]him. Also unto Shemaiah
his son were sons born, that ruled throughout the house of their
7 father: for they *were* mighty men of valour. The sons of Shemaiah;
Othni, and Rephael, and Obed, Elzabad, whose brethren *were*
8 strong men, Elihu, and Semachiah. All these of the sons of
Obed-edom: they and their sons and their brethren, able men
for strength for the service, *were* threescore and two of Obed-
9 edom. And Meshelemiah had sons and brethren, strong men,
10 eighteen. Also [a]Hosah, of the children of Merari, had sons;
Simri the chief, (for *though* he was not the firstborn, yet his
11 father made him the chief;) Hilkiah the second, Tebaliah the
third, Zechariah the fourth: all the sons and brethren of Hosah
12 *were* thirteen. Among these *were* the divisions of the porters,
even among the chief men, *having* wards one against another,
13 to minister in the house of the LORD. ¶And they cast lots,
[4]as well the small as the great, according to the house of their
14 fathers, for every gate. And the lot eastward fell to [5]Shele-
miah. Then for Zechariah his son, a wise counsellor, they cast
15 lots; and his lot came out northward. To Obed-edom south-

[a] ch. 16. 38.

---

[1] Or, *Shelemiah*, ver. 14.
[2] Or, *Ebiasaph*, ch. 6. 37. & 9. 19.
[3] That is, Obed-edom, as ch. 13. 14.
[4] Or, *as well for the small*
as for the great.
[5] Called *Meshelemiah*, ver. 1.

XXVI. 1. *the porters*] See ix. 17–27, xxiii. 5.

4. Obed-edom and Hosah (*v.* 10) had been "porters," or door-keepers, from the time of the bringing up of the Ark into Jerusalem (xv. 24, xvi. 38).

12. This verse is obscure, but its probable meaning is the following: " To these divisions of the porters, principal men, [were

assigned[1] the watches, together with their brethren, for service in the house of the Lord ; " *i.e.* the " chief men " (*vv.* 1–11), amounting to no more than 93, kept the watch and ward of the house, together with a further number of their brethren (4000, xxiii. 5), who assisted them from time to time.

15. *the house of Asuppim*] Lit. " the house

16 ward; and to his sons the house of ¹Asuppim. To Shuppim
and Hosah *the lot came forth* westward, with the gate Shallecheth,
17 by the causeway of the going ²up, ward against ward. Eastward *were* six Levites, northward four a day, southward four a
18 day, and toward Asuppim two *and* two. At Parbar westward,
19 four at the causeway, *and* two at Parbar. These *are* the divisions of the porters among the sons of Kore, and among the sons
20 of Merari. ¶ And of the Levites, Ahijah *was* ᵇover the treasures
of the house of God, and over the treasures of the ³dedicated
21 things. *As concerning* the sons of ⁴Laadan; the sons of the Gershonite Laadan, chief fathers, *even* of Laadan the Gershonite,
22 *were* ⁵Jehieli. The sons of Jehieli; Zetham, and Joel his brother,
23 *which were* over the treasures of the house of the LORD. Of the
Amramites, *and* the Izharites, the Hebronites, *and* the Uzzielites:
24 and ᶜShebuel the son of Gershom, the son of Moses, *was* ruler
25 of the treasures. And his brethren by Eliezer; Rehabiah his
son, and Jeshaiah his son, and Joram his son, and Zichri his son,
26 and ᵈShelomith his son. Which Shelomith and his brethren
were over all the treasures of the dedicated things, which David
the king, and the chief fathers, the captains over thousands and
27 hundreds, and the captains of the hosts, had dedicated. ⁶Out
of the spoils won in battles did they dedicate to maintain the
28 house of the LORD. And all that Samuel ᵉthe seer, and Saul
the son of Kish, and Abner the son of Ner, and Joab the son of
Zeruiah, had dedicated; *and* whosoever had dedicated *any thing*,
29 *it was* under the hand of Shelomith, and of his brethren. ¶ Of
the Izharites, Chenaniah and his sons *were* for the outward

ᵇ ch. 28. 12.
Mal. 3. 10.

ᶜ ch. 23. 16.

ᵈ ch. 23. 18.

ᵉ 1 Sam. 9. 9.

---

¹ Heb. *Gatherings.*
² See 1 Kings 10. 5.
  2 Chr. 9. 4.
³ Heb. *holy things.*
⁴ Or, *Libni,* ch. 6. 17.
⁵ Or, *Jehiel,* ch. 23. 8. & 29. 8.
⁶ Heb. *Out of ͵the battles and spoils.*

---

of collections" (see marg. and cp. Neh. xii.
25 marg.). A treasure-house of some kind
or other is probably intended.

16. All recent commentators seem to be
agreed that the words "to Shuppim" ought
to be cancelled, the name having arisen
from an accidental repetition of the preceding word, "Asuppim."

the gate Shallecheth] Lit. "the gate *of pro-
jection*"—the gate, *i.e.* through which were
"thrown out" the sweepings of the Temple,
the ashes, the offal of the victims, and the
like.

the causeway of the going up] Cp. marg.
ref. note.

ward against ward] Or, "watch opposite
to watch." Hosah had in charge both the
western gate of the Temple, and also the
gate Shallecheth, which was in the outer
wall, opposite. Hence he had to keep two
watches, one over against the other.

17. *toward Asuppim two and two*] It is
conjectured that the "store-house" in
question (*v.* 15 note) had two doors, to each
of which two porters were appointed.

18. "Parbar" must designate here the
space between the western wall of the
Temple building and the wall of the court,
which would be a sort of "precinct" or
"purlieu" of the Temple (2 K. xxiii. 11

note). Here were two gates, at one of
which two guards were stationed; while
at the Shallecheth, which gave upon the
causeway, there were four. In this whole
account, the Temple is spoken of as if
it were existing, when it was not as yet
built. We must suppose that David formed
the whole plan of the Temple, and fixed
the stations and numbers of the porters,
though it was left for Solomon to carry out
his instructions.

19. *the divisions of the porters*] The account of the porters here given makes them
only twenty-four in number at any one
time; xxiii. 5 states that the duty was discharged by 4000 persons. Perhaps of the
ninety-three *chief* porters spoken of
(*vv.* 8. 9, and 11), twenty-four were always
on guard *as officers*, while of the remaining
3907, a certain proportion were each day on
duty as their subordinates.

28. The foundations of a sacred treasury
had therefore been laid as far back as the
time of Samuel, when the Israelites began
to recover from their last servitude. Such
a treasury had been once before established,
viz., under Joshua (Josh. vi. 24); but it appears to have been soon exhausted, and we
hear nothing of it under any of the later
judges until Samuel,

30 business over Israel, for *f*officers and judges. *And* of the Hebronites, Hashabiah and his brethren, men of valour, a thousand and seven hundred, *were* [1]officers among them of Israel on this side Jordan westward in all the business of the LORD, and in
31 the service of the king. Among the Hebronites *was* *g*Jerijah the chief, *even* among the Hebronites, according to the generations of his fathers. In the fortieth year of the reign of David they were sought for, and there were found among them mighty
32 men of valour *h*at Jazer of Gilead. And his brethren, men of valour, *were* two thousand and seven hundred chief fathers, whom king David made rulers over the Reubenites, the Gadites, and the half tribe of Manasseh, for every matter pertaining to
God, and [2]*i*affairs of the king.

CHAP. 27. NOW the children of Israel after their number, *to wit*, the chief fathers and captains of thousands and hundreds, and their officers that served the king in any matter of the courses, which came in and went out month by month throughout all the months of the year, of every course *were* twenty and four thou-
2 sand. ¶ Over the first course for the first month *was* *a*Jashobeam the son of Zabdiel: and in his course *were* twenty and four thou-
3 sand. Of the children of Perez *was* the chief of all the captains
4 of the host for the first month. And over the course of the second month *was* [3]Dodai an Ahohite, and of his course *was* Mikloth also the ruler: in his course likewise *were* twenty and
5 four thousand. The third captain of the host for the third month *was* Benaiah the son of Jehoiada, a [4]chief priest: and
6 in his course *were* twenty and four thousand. This *is that*
Benaiah, who *was* *b*mighty *among* the thirty, and above the
7 thirty: and in his course *was* Ammizabad his son. The fourth *captain* for the fourth month *was* *c*Asahel the brother of Joab, and Zebadiah his son after him: and in his course *were* twenty
8 and four thousand. The fifth captain for the fifth month *was*

---

[1] Heb. *over the charge.*   [3] Or, *Dodo,* 2 Sam. 23. 9.   [4] Or, *principal officer,* 1 Kin. 4. 5.
[2] Heb. *thing.*

---

30. The "business of the Lord" in the provinces would consist especially in the collection of the tithes, the redemption-money, and the free-will offerings of the people. It may perhaps have included some religious teaching. Cp. 2 Chr. xvii. 7-9.

32. *rulers*] This term is somewhat too strong. The same kind of office was assigned to Jerijah and his brethren in the trans-Jordanic region as to Hashabiah and his brethren in western Palestine (*v.* 30), viz., a superintendence over religious matters and over the interests of the king.

XXVII. **1.** This verse is a general heading to the list (*vv.* 2-15). The heading has been taken from some fuller and more elaborate description of David's army, whereof the writer of Chronicles gives us only an abridgement. Omitting the captains of thousands, the captains of hundreds, and the officers (probably "scribes") who served the king, he contents himself with recording the "chief fathers" or heads of the divisions (xxviii. 1), and the number of Israelites in each course.

2. *Jashobeam*] Jashobeam is mentioned in marg. reff. as the chief of David's mighty men. He is called in xi. 11 "the son of Hachmoni." We learn from *v.* 3 that he was of the tribe of Judah, being descended from Perez (or Pharez), the son of Judah, from whom David himself sprang. See ii. 3-15.

4. *Dodai*] The words "**Eleazar, son of,**" have probably fallen out before Dodai (or Dodo). According to Jewish tradition, Eleazar (xi. 12) was cousin to David; his father, Dodai, being Jesse's brother. Mikloth was probably second in command to Eleazar.

5. *a chief priest*] Rather, "*the* chief priest"—an expression by which is meant, not the high-priest, but probably the high-priest's deputy, who is sometimes called "the second priest" (2 K. xxv. 18).

7. Asahel died before the courses, as here described, could have been instituted. Perhaps the arrangements of David in his later years were based upon institutions belonging to the period of his reign at Hebron.

Shamhuth the Izrahite: and in his course *were* twenty and four
9 thousand. The sixth *captain* for the sixth month *was* ^dIra the   ^d ch. 11. 28.
son of Ikkesh the Tekoite: and in his course *were* twenty and
10 four thousand. The seventh *captain* for the seventh month *was*
^eHelez the Pelonite, of the children of Ephraim: and in his   ^e ch. 11. 27.
11 course *were* twenty and four thousand. The eighth *captain* for
the eighth month *was* ^fSibbecai the Hushathite, of the Zarhites: ^f 2 Sam. 21.
12 and in his course *were* twenty and four thousand. The ninth   18.
captain for the ninth month *was* ^gAbiezer the Anetothite, of the   ch. 11. 29.
Benjamites: and in his course *were* twenty and four thousand.   ^g ch. 11. 28.
13 The tenth *captain*, for the tenth month *was* ^hMaharai the Neto-   ^h 2 Sam. 23.
phathite, of the Zarhites: and in his course *were* twenty and   28.
14 four thousand. The eleventh *captain* for the eleventh month   ch. 11. 30.
was ⁱBenaiah the Pirathonite, of the children of Ephraim: and   ⁱ ch. 11. 31.
15 in his course *were* twenty and four thousand. The twelfth
capt tin for the twelfth month *was* ¹Heldai the Netophathite, of
Othniel: and in his course *were* twenty and four thousand.
16 ¶ Furthermore over the tribes of Israel: the ruler of the Reubenites *was* Eliezer the son of Zichri: of the Simeonites, Shepha-
17 tiah the son of Maachah: of the Levites, ^kHashabiah the son of   ^k ch. 26. 30.
18 Kemuel: of the Aaronites, Zadok: of Judah, ^lElihu, one of the   ^l 1 Sam. 16.
19 brethren of David: of Issachar, Omri the son of Michael: of   6, *Eliab.*
Zebulun, Ishmaiah the son of Obadiah: of Naphtali, Jerimoth
20 the son of Azriel: of the children of Ephraim, Hoshea the son
of Azaziah: of the half tribe of Manasseh, Joel the son of
21 Pedaiah: of the half *tribe* of Manasseh in Gilead, Iddo the son
22 of Zechariah: of Benjamin, Jaasiel the son of Abner: of Dan,
Azareel the son of Jeroham. These *were* the princes of the tribes
23 of Israel. ¶ But David took not the number of them from
twenty years old and under: because ^mthe LORD had said he   ^m Gen. 15. 5.
24 would increase Israel like to the stars of the heavens. Joab the
son of Zeruiah began to number, but he finished not, because
ⁿthere fell wrath for it against Israel; neither ²was the number   ⁿ 2 Sam. 24.
25 put in the account of the chronicles of king David. ¶ And over   15.
   ch. 21. 7.

¹ Or, *Heled,* ch. 11. 30.   ² Heb. *ascended.*

16-22. Gad and Asher are omitted from
this list of the tribes. Similarly, Dan and
Zebulon are omitted from the genealogical
survey of the tribes (iv.-viii). We can
only suppose that the lists, as they came
down to the writer of Chronicles, were incomplete. The "rulers" or "princes" of
the tribes appear to have been the eldest
lineal descendants of the patriarchs according to the law of primogeniture.

23. David's numbering of the people was
therefore a military arrangement in order to
fix the amount of his standing army. To
the general Oriental prejudice against numbering possessions, &c., there was added in
the case of the Jews a special objection—a
feeling that it would be irreverent to attempt to count what God had promised
should be countless.

24. *because there fell wrath*] Lit. "*And
there fell wrath.*" The falling of God's
wrath was not the cause of Joab's ceasing.

His motive is clearly stated in xxi. 6. See
also marg. reff.

neither was the number &c.] The meaning
is, that in the portion of the Chronicles of
king David which treated of numbers—
the number of the standing army, of the
Levitical and priestly courses, the singers,
&c.—the return of the number of the
people made by Joab was not entered.
The disastrous circumstances which followed on the taking of the census perhaps
produced a feeling that God might be further provoked by its being put on record in
the state archives. The numbers which
have come down to us must therefore have
been derived from private sources.

25-31. This section is important as showing that David, the younger son of a not
very opulent family (1 Sam. xvi. 11, 20),
had now become a large landed proprietor,
as well as a capitalist, possessed of much
moveable wealth. We may perhaps see

the king's treasures *was* Azmaveth the son of Adiel: and over
the storehouses in the fields, in the cities, and in the villages,
26 and in the castles, *was* Jehonathan the son of Uzziah: and
over them that did the work of the field for tillage of the ground
27 *was* Ezri the son of Chelub: and over the vineyards *was* Shimei
the Ramathite: [1]over the increase of the vineyards for the wine
28 cellars *was* Zabdi the Shiphmite: and over the olive trees and
the sycomore trees that *were* in the low plains *was* Baal-hanan
29 the Gederite: and over the cellars of oil *was* Joash: and over
the herds that fed in Sharon *was* Shitrai the Sharonite: and
over the herds *that were* in the valleys *was* Shaphat the son of
30 Adlai: over the camels also *was* Obil the Ishmaelite: and over
31 the asses *was* Jehdeiah the Meronothite: and over the flocks
was Jaziz the Hagerite. All these *were* the rulers of the sub-
32 stance which *was* king David's. ¶ Also Jonathan David's uncle
was a counsellor, a wise man, and a [2]scribe: and Jehiel the
33 [3]son of Hachmoni *was* with the king's sons: and [o]Ahithophel
was the king's counsellor: and [p]Hushai the Archite *was* the
34 king's companion: and after Ahithophel *was* Jehoiada the son of
Benaiah, and [q]Abiathar: and the general of the king's army
was [r]Joab.

Chap. 28. AND David assembled all the princes of Israel, [a]the
princes of the tribes, and [b]the captains of the companies that
ministered to the king by course, and the captains over the
thousands, and captains over the hundreds, and [c]the stewards
over all the substance and [4]possession of the king, [5]and of his
sons, with the [6]officers, and with [d]the mighty men, and with all
2 the valiant men, unto Jerusalem. ¶ Then David the king stood
up upon his feet, and said, Hear me, my brethren, and my
people: *As for me*, [e]*I had* in mine heart to build an house of

[o] 2 Sam. 15. 12.
[p] 2 Sam. 15. 37. & 16. 16.
[q] 1 Kin. 1. 7.
[r] ch. 11. 6.
[a] ch. 27. 16.
[b] ch. 27. 1, 2.
[c] ch. 27. 25.
[d] ch. 11. 10.
[e] 2 Sam. 7. 2. Ps. 132. 3, 4, 5.

[1] Heb. *over that which was of the vineyards.*
[2] Or, *secretary.*
[3] Or, *Hachmonite.*
[4] Or, *cattle.*
[5] Or, *and his sons.*
[6] Or, *eunuchs.*

---

the sources of both these kinds of property, in the successful wars which he had waged (1 Sam. xxvii. 8, 9, xxx. 20; 2 Sam. viii. 4, 7, 8, 12); in the revenue derived from subject kings (1 Sam. viii. 2, 14, x. 19); and in the purchase and occupation of lands in different places. Further, he enjoyed, of course, the usual rights of a Jewish king over the landed property of his subjects, and was thus entitled to receive a tithe of the produce in tithes (1 Sam. viii. 15, 17) and in "benevolences." Cp. 1 Sam. x. 27, xvi. 20, &c.

25. *the castles*] Probably the watch-towers in the border districts, exposed to raids from the plundering tribes of the desert (2 Chr. xxvi. 10, xxvii. 4).

28. *in the low plains*] Rather, "in the Shephelah," the proper name of the low tract between the hill country of Judæa and the Mediterranean.

32-34. A list—supplemental in character—of some chief officers of David, not mentioned before. The list cannot belong to a very late part of David's reign, since it contains the name of Ahithophel, who slew himself during Absalom's rebellion (2 Sam. xvii. 23).

33. *was the king's companion*] Or, "king's friend," as in 1 K. iv. 5. Cp. also 2 Sam. xvi. 17.

34. *after Ahithophel*] *i.e.* next in counsel to Ahithophel: inferior to him, but superior to all others.

XXVIII. **1.** *officers*] Lit. as in margin. This is the only occasion in which eunuchs are mentioned in connexion with David's reign; and it is to be remarked that they occupy, during the earlier period of the Jewish kingdom, a very subordinate position.

2. *my brethren*] David retains the modest phrase of a king not born in the purple, but raised from the ranks of the people (see 1 Sam. xxx. 23; 2 Sam. xix. 12). No later Jewish monarch would have thus addressed his subjects.

the footstool of our God] David views the Ark as God's "footstool," because He was enthroned above it visibly in the Shechinah, or luminous cloud, present from time to

rest for the ark of the covenant of the LORD, and for *f* the foot-
3 stool of our God, and had made ready for the building : but
God said unto me, *g* Thou shalt not build an house for my name,
because thou *hast been* a man of war, and hast shed [1] blood.
4 Howbeit the LORD God of Israel *h* chose me before all the house
of my father to be king over Israel for ever : for he hath chosen
i Judah *to be* the ruler ; and of the house of Judah, *k* the house
of my father ; and *l* among the sons of my father he liked me to
5 make *me* king over all Israel : *m* and of all my sons, (for the
LORD hath given me many sons,) *n* he hath chosen Solomon my
son to sit upon the throne of the kingdom of the LORD over Israel.
6 And he said unto me, *o* Solomon thy son, he shall build my house
and my courts : for I have chosen him *to be* my son, and I will
7 be his father. Moreover I will establish his kingdom for ever,
p if he be [2] constant to do my commandments and my judgments,
8 as at this day. Now therefore in the sight of all Israel the congregation of the LORD, and in the audience of our God, keep
and seek for all the commandments of the LORD your God :
that ye may possess this good land, and leave *it* for an inherit-
9 ance for your children after you for ever. And thou, Solomon
my son, *q* know thou the God of thy father, and serve him *r* with a
perfect heart and with a willing mind : for *s* the LORD searcheth all
hearts, and understandeth all the imaginations of the thoughts :
t if thou seek him, he will be found of thee, but if thou forsake
10 him, he will cast thee off for ever. Take heed now ; *u* for the
LORD hath chosen thee to build an house for the sanctuary : be
11 strong, and do *it*. ¶ Then David gave to Solomon his son *x* the
pattern of the porch, and of the houses thereof, and of the
treasures thereof, and of the upper chambers thereof, and of
the inner parlours thereof, and of the place of the mercy seat,
12 and the pattern [3] of all that he had by the spirit, of the courts

f Ps. 99. 5.
& 132. 7.
g 2 Sam. 7.
5, 13.
1 Kin. 5. 3.
ch. 17. 4.
& 22. 8.
h 1 Sam. 16.
7—13.
i Gen. 49. 8.
ch. 5. 2.
Ps. 60. 7.
& 78. 68.
k 1 Sam.16.1.
l 1 Sam. 16.
12, 13.
m ch. 3.1,&c.
& 23. 1.
n ch. 22. 9.
o 2 Sam. 7.
13, 14.
ch. 22. 9, 10.
2 Chr. 1. 9.
p ch. 22. 13.

q Jer. 9. 24.
Hos. 4. 1.
John 17. 3.
r 2 Kin. 20.3.
Ps. 101. 2.
s 1 Sam.16.7.
1 Kin. 8. 39.
ch. 29. 17.
Ps. 7. 9.
& 139. 2.
Prov. 17. 3.
Jer. 11. 20.
& 17. 10.
& 20. 12.
Rev. 2. 2?.
t 2 Chr. 15. 2.
u ver. 6.
x See Ex. 25.
40.

[1] Heb. *bloods*.   [2] Heb. *strong*.   [3] Heb. *of all that was with him*.

---

time above the Mercy Seat and between the
Cherubim (cp. marg. reff.).

6. Besides the message sent to David
through Nathan, he had a revelation, of
which we have only the indirect account
given here and in xxii. 8-10 (see note). He
was told that one of his sons should be
raised up to fill his throne after him, and
should build the Temple. In the second
revelation it was distinctly declared to him
that the son intended was Solomon.

my house and my courts] *i.e.* the Temple
and the courts of the Temple (see 2 Chr.
iv. 9).

7. *if he be constant*] The conditional character of the promise made to David, as to
the continuance of his posterity on the
Jewish throne (marg. ref. ; 2 Sam. vii. 14),
is now clearly declared.

9. *know thou the God of thy father*]
"Knowing God," in the sense of having a
religious trust in Him, is an unusual phrase
in the earlier Scriptures. It scarcely occurs
elsewhere in the Historical Books. David,
however, uses the phrase in his Psalms (Ps.
xxxvi. 10) ; and its occurrence here may be

accepted as evidence that the entire speech
is recorded in the actual words of the
monarch.

11. Cp. *v.* 19. As God had revealed to
Moses the pattern of the Tabernacle (Ex.
xxvi. xxvii.), so He had made known by
revelation to David the pattern of the
Temple and its furniture. This pattern,
which consisted of a set of directions in
writing, David now handed over to Solomon.

the houses] The "Holy Place" and the
"Holy of Holies"—called respectively "the
house" and the "inner house" (1 K. vi.
17, 27), and (2 Chr. iii. 5, 8) "the greater
house" and "the most holy house."

the upper chambers] Cp. 2 Chr. iii. 9 note.

the inner parlours] The small rooms of
the "lean-to" (1 K. vi. 5 note), entered one
from another.

12. *the pattern* &c.] Lit. "the pattern of
all that was with him in the spirit ;" perhaps to be paraphrased, "the form of all
that floated before his mind." It seems to
be David's spirit, not God's Spirit, that is
here spoken of.

of the house of the LORD, and of all the chambers round about,

y ch. 26. 20.

y of the treasuries of the house of God, and of the treasuries of
13 the dedicated things: also for the courses of the priests and the
Levites, and for all the work of the service of the house of the
LORD, and for all the vessels of service in the house of the
14 LORD. *He gave* of gold by weight for *things* of gold, for all
instruments of all manner of service; *silver also* for all instruments of silver by weight, for all instruments of every kind of
15 service: even the weight for the candlesticks of gold, and for
their lamps of gold, by weight for every candlestick, and for
the lamps thereof: and for the candlesticks of silver by weight,
both for the candlestick, and *also* for the lamps thereof, according
16 to the use of every candlestick. And by weight *he gave* gold for
the tables of shewbread, for every table; and *likewise* silver for
17 the tables of silver: also pure gold for the fleshhooks, and the
bowls, and the cups: and for the golden basons *he gave gold* by
weight for every bason; and *likewise silver* by weight for every
18 bason of silver: and for the altar of incense refined gold by

z Ex. 25. 19
—22.
1 Sam. 4. 4.
1 Kin. 6. 23,
&c.

weight; and gold for the pattern of the chariot of the *z*cherubims, that spread out *their wings*, and covered the ark of the
19 covenant of the LORD. All *this, said David, a*the LORD made

a See Ex. 25.
40.

me understand in writing by *his* hand upon me, *even* all the
20 works of this pattern. ¶ And David said to Solomon his son,

ver. 11, 12.
b Deut. 31. 7.
8.
Josh.1.6,7,9.
ch. 22. 13.

*b*Be strong and of good courage, and do *it:* fear not, nor be dismayed: for the LORD God, *even* my God, *will be* with thee; *c*he
will not fail thee, nor forsake thee, until thou hast finished all

c Josh. 1. 5.
d ch. 24, &
25, & 26.

21 the work for the service of the house of the LORD. And, behold,
*d*the courses of the priests and the Levites, *even they shall be
with thee* for all the service of the house of God: and *there shall
be* with thee for all manner of workmanship *e*every willing

e Ex. 35. 25,
26.
& 36. 1, 2.

skilful man, for any manner of service: also the princes and all
the people *will be* wholly at thy commandment.
CHAP. 29. FURTHERMORE David the king said unto all the
congregation, Solomon my son, whom alone God hath chosen,

a 1 Kin.3. 7.
ch. 22. 5.
Prov. 4. 3.

*is yet a*young and tender, and the work *is* great: for the palace
2 *is* not for man, but for the LORD God. Now I have prepared
with all my might for the house of my God the gold for *things
to be made* of gold, and the silver for *things* of silver, and the
brass for *things* of brass, the iron for *things* of iron, and wood
for *things* of wood; *b*onyx stones, and *stones* to be set, glistering

b See Isai.
54. 11, 12.
Rev. 21. 18,
&c.

stones, and of divers colours, and all manner of precious stones,
3 and marble stones in abundance. Moreover, because I have set
my affection to the house of my God, I have of mine own proper
good, of gold and silver, *which* I have given to the house of my

---

18. *the chariot of the cherubims*] The
Cherubim are themselves the chariot on
which Jehovah rides (Ps. xviii. 10, xcix.
1).

XXIX. 1. *the palace*] The original word
here used is the Hebrew form of a Persian
word, and generally designates the residence
of the Persian monarch (Esth. i. 2, 5, ii. 3,
8; Neh. i. 1; Dan. viii. 2). It is only here
and in *v.* 19 that it is applied to the Temple.

2. *glistering stones*] Rather, ' coloured
stones;' or, " *dark* stones "—stones of a

hue like that of the antimony wherewith
women painted their eyes.

marble stones] Or, " *white* stones"—perhaps " alabaster," which is found near Damascus. On the use made of the " stones "
in building the Temple, see 2 Chr. iii. 6
note.

3. *of mine own proper good*] i.e. from his
own private estate. He makes the offering
publicly in order to provoke others by his
example (*v.* 5).

God, over and above all that I have prepared for the holy house,
4 *even* three thousand talents of gold, of the gold of *c*Ophir, and
seven thousand talents of refined silver, to overlay the walls of
5 the houses *withal :* the gold for *things* of gold, and the silver for
things of silver, and for all manner of work *to be made* by the
hands of artificers. And who *then* is willing ¹to consecrate his
6 service this day unto the LORD ? ¶Then *d*the chief of the fathers
and princes of the tribes of Israel, and the captains of thousands
and of hundreds, with *e*the rulers of the king's work, offered
7 willingly, and gave for the service of the house of God of gold
five thousand talents and ten thousand drams, and of silver ten
thousand talents, and of brass eighteen thousand talents, and
8 one hundred thousand talents of iron. And they with whom
precious stones were found gave *them* to the treasure of the house
9 of the LORD, by the hand of *f* Jehiel the Gershonite. Then the
people rejoiced, for that they offered willingly, because with
perfect heart they *g*offered willingly to the LORD : and David
10 the king also rejoiced with great joy. ¶Wherefore David blessed
the LORD before all the congregation : and David said, Blessed
be thou, LORD God of Israel our father, for ever and ever.
11 *h*Thine, O LORD, *is* the greatness, and the power, and the glory,
and the victory, and the majesty : for all *that is* in the heaven
and in the earth *is thine ;* thine *is* the kingdom, O LORD, and thou
12 art exalted as head above all. *i*Both riches and honour *come* of
thee, and thou reignest over all ; and in thine hand *is* power
and might ; and in thine hand *it is* to make great, and to give
13 strength unto all. Now therefore, our God, we thank thee,
14 and praise thy glorious name. But who *am* I, and what *is* my
people, that we should ²be able to offer so willingly after this
sort ? for all things *come* of thee, and ³of thine own have we
15 given thee. For *k*we *are* strangers before thee, and sojourners,
as *were* all our fathers : *l*our days on the earth *are* as a shadow,
16 and *there is* none ⁴abiding. O LORD our God, all this store that
we have prepared to build thee an house for thine holy name
17 *cometh* of thine hand, and *is* all thine own. I know also, my
God, that thou *m*triest the heart, and *n*hast pleasure in uprightness. As for me, in the uprightness of mine heart I have wil-

c 1 Kin. 9. 28.

d ch. 27. 1.

e ch. 27. 25, &c.

f ch. 26. 21.

g 2 Cor. 9. 7.

h Matt. 6. 13.
1 Tim. 1. 17.
Rev. 5. 13.

i Rom. 11. 36.

k Ps. 39. 12.
Heb. 11. 13.
1 Pet. 2. 11.
l Job 14. 2.
Ps. 90. 9.
& 102. 11.
& 144. 4.
m 1 Sam. 16. 7.
ch. 28. 9.
*n*Prov. 11. 20.

---

¹ Heb. *to fill his hand.* ² Heb. *retain,* or, *obtain*   ³ Heb. *of thine hand.*
strength.   ⁴ Heb. *expectation.*

---

4. The numbers here have also suffered to
some extent from the carelessness of copyists
(cp. xxii. 14 note). The amount of silver
is not indeed improbable, since its value
would not exceed three millions of our
money ; but as the gold would probably
exceed in value thirty millions, we may
suspect an error in the words "three
thousand."

5. *to consecrate his service*] Lit. as in the
margin, "to fill his hand," *i.e.* "to come
with full hands to Jehovah." The words
contain an appeal to the assembly for voluntary offerings.

7. The word here translated "dram" is
regarded by most critics as the Hebrew
equivalent of the Persian "daric," or ordinary gold coin, worth about 22 shillings of
our money. Not, however, that the Jews

possessed darics in David's time : the writer
wished to express, in language that would
be intelligible to his readers, the value of
the gold subscribed, and therefore he translated the terms employed in his documents,
whatever they were, into terms that were
in use in his own day. The daric became
current in Palestine soon after the return
from the Captivity (Ezra ii. 69, viii. 27 ;
Neh. vii. 70—72).

8. Cp. Ex. xxxv. 27. The same spirit
prevailed now as at the setting up of the
Tabernacle. Each offered what he had that
was most precious.

9. *the people rejoiced for that they offered
willingly*] *i.e.* the munificence of the princes
and officers (*v.* 6) caused general joy among
the people.

lingly offered all these things: and now have I seen with joy
thy people, which are [1]present here, to offer willingly unto thee.
18 O LORD God of Abraham, Isaac, and of Israel, our fathers, keep
this for ever in the imagination of the thoughts of the heart of
[o] Ps. 72. 1. 19 thy people, and [2]prepare their heart unto thee: and [o]give unto
Solomon my son a perfect heart, to keep thy commandments,
thy testimonies, and thy statutes, and to do all *these things*, and
[p] ver. 2. ch. 22. 14. to build the palace, *for* the which [p]I have made provision.
20 ¶ And David said to all the congregation, Now bless the LORD
your God. And all the congregation blessed the LORD God of
their fathers, and bowed down their heads, and worshipped the
21 LORD, and the king. And they sacrificed sacrifices unto the
LORD, and offered burnt offerings unto the LORD, on the morrow
after that day, *even* a thousand bullocks, a thousand rams, *and*
a thousand lambs, with their drink offerings, and sacrifices in
22 abundance for all Israel: and did eat and drink before the LORD
on that day with great gladness. And they made Solomon the
[q] 1 Kin. 1. 35, 39. son of David king the second time, and [q]anointed *him* unto the
23 LORD *to be* the chief governor, and Zadok *to be* priest. Then
Solomon sat on the throne of the LORD as king instead of David
24 his father, and prospered; and all Israel obeyed him. And all
the princes, and the mighty men, and all the sons likewise of
[r] Eccles. 8. 2. king David, [r] [3]submitted themselves unto Solomon the king.
25 And the LORD magnified Solomon exceedingly in the sight of all
[s] 1 Kin. 3. 13. 2 Chr. 1. 12. Eccles. 2. 9. Israel, and [s]bestowed upon him *such* royal majesty as had not
26 been on any king before him in Israel. ¶ Thus David the son
[t] 2 Sam. 5. 4. 1 Kin. 2. 11. 27 of Jesse reigned over all Israel. [t]And the time that he reigned
[u] 2 Sam. 5. 5. over Israel *was* forty years; [u]seven years reigned he in Hebron,
28 and thirty and three *years* reigned he in Jerusalem. And he
[x] Gen. 25. 8. [x]died in a good old age, [y]full of days, riches, and honour: and
[y] ch. 23. 1. 29 Solomon his son reigned in his stead. ¶ Now the acts of David

[1] Or, *found.*
[2] Or, *stablish,* Ps. 10. 17.
[3] Heb. *gave the hand under Solomon:* See Gen. 24. 2. & 47. 29. 2 Chr. 30. 8. Ezek. 17. 18.

---

18. *keep this for ever* &c.] *i.e.* "Preserve for ever this spirit of liberal and spontaneous giving in the hearts of Thy people, and **establish** their hearts toward Thee."

20. *worshipped the* LORD, *and the king*] The same outward signs of reverence were accorded by the customs of the Jews (as of the Oriental nations generally) to God and to their monarchs (see 1 K. i. 31). But the application of the terms to both in the same passage, which occurs nowhere in Scripture but here, is thought to indicate a time when a long servitude under despotic lords had orientalised men's mode of speech.

21. *with their drink offerings*] *i.e.* with the drink offerings appropriate to each kind of Burnt offering, and required by the Law to accompany them (see Num. xv. 5, 7, 10, &c.).

sacrifices] Or, "thank-offerings," as the same word is translated in 2 Chr. xxix. 31, xxxiii. 16. Of "peace-offerings for thanksgivings" only a small part was the priest's; the sacrificer and his friends feasted on the remainder (Lev. vii. 15, 29-34).

22. *king the second time*] Solomon's first appointment was at the time of Adonijah's rebellion (marg. ref.). As that appointment was hurried and, comparatively speaking, private, David now thought it best formally to invest Solomon a second time with the sovereignty, in the face of all Israel. For a similar reason a second and public appointment of Zadok alone to the High-Priest's office took place. Abiathar was not as yet absolutely thrust out; but it may be doubtful whether he was ever allowed to perform High-priestly functions after his rebellion (1 K. i. 7, ii. 27).

23. The throne of David is called here "the throne of the Lord," as in xxviii. 5 it is called "the throne of the kingdom of the Lord," because God had set it up and had promised to establish it.

28. See 1 K. i. 1 note.

29. On the character of the works alluded to, see Introduction to Chronicles, p. 447.

Gad the seer] Gad is not given here the same title as Samuel. Samuel's title is one, apparently, of higher dignity, applied only to him and to Hanani (2 Chr. xvi. 7, 10). Gad's is a far commoner title; it is applied

the king, first and last, behold, they *are* written in the [1][2]book
of Samuel the seer, and in the book of Nathan the prophet, and
30 in the book of Gad the seer, with all his reign and his might,
[z]and the times that went over him, and over Israel, and over all
the kingdoms of the countries.

[z] Dan. 2. 21.

[1] Or, *history.*   [2] Heb. *words.*

---

to his contemporaries Asaph (2 Chr. xxix.
30), Heman (1 Chr. xxv. 5), and Jeduthun
(2 Chr. xxxv. 15), to Iddo (2 Chr. ix. 29,
xii. 15), to Jehu the son of Hanani (2 Chr.
xix. 2), and to the prophet Amos (Am. vii.
12). When "seers" are spoken of in the
plural, it is the term almost universally
used, only one instance (Is. xxx. 10) occurring to the contrary.

30. *the times that went over him*] *i.e.* the
events that happened to him. Cp.Ps.xxxi.15.
  all the kingdoms of the countries] The
kingdoms, *i.e.* of Moab, Ammon, Damascus, Zobah, &c. See the full phrase in 2
Chr. xvii. 10. Some account of these kingdoms would necessarily have been given in
any history of David's reign.

CHAP. 1. AND ^a Solomon the son of David was strengthened in his kingdom, and ^bthe LORD his God *was* with him, and ^cmagnified
2 him exceedingly. Then Solomon spake unto all Israel, to ^dthe captains of thousands and of hundreds, and to the judges, and
3 to every governor in all Israel, the chief of the fathers. So Solomon, and all the congregation with him, went to the high place that *was* at ^eGibeon; for there was the tabernacle of the congregation of God, which Moses the servant of the LORD had
4 made in the wilderness. ^fBut the ark of God had David brought up from Kirjath-jearim to *the place which* David had prepared for it: for he had pitched a tent for it at Jerusalem.
5 Moreover ^gthe brasen altar, that ^hBezaleel the son of Uri, the son of Hur, had made, ¹he put before the tabernacle of the
6 LORD: and Solomon and the congregation sought unto it. And Solomon went up thither to the brasen altar before the LORD, which *was* at the tabernacle of the congregation, and ⁱoffered a
7 thousand burnt offerings upon it. ¶ ^kIn that night did God appear unto Solomon, and said unto him, Ask what I shall give
8 thee. And Solomon said unto God, Thou hast shewed great mercy unto David my father, and hast made me ^lto reign in his
9 stead. Now, O LORD God, let thy promise unto David my father be established: ^mfor thou hast made me king over a
10 people ²like the dust of the earth in multitude. ⁿGive me now wisdom and knowledge, that I may ^ogo out and come in before this people: for who can judge this thy people, *that is so* great?
11 ^pAnd God said to Solomon, Because this was in thine heart, and thou hast not asked riches, wealth, or honour, nor the life of thine enemies, neither yet hast asked long life; but hast asked wisdom and knowledge for thyself, that thou mayest
12 judge my people, over whom I have made thee king: wisdom and knowledge *is* granted unto thee; and I will give thee riches, and wealth, and honour, such as ^qnone of the kings have

Marginal references:
- ^a 1 Kin. 2.46.
- ^b Gen. 39. 2.
- ^c 1Chr.29.25.
- ^d 1 Chr. 27.1.
- ^e 1Chr.16.39. & 21. 29.
- ^f 2 Sam. 6. 2, 17. 1 Chr. 15. 1.
- ^g Ex. 27. 1, 2. & 38. 1, 2.
- ^h Ex. 31. 2.
- ⁱ 1 Kin. 3. 4.
- ^k 1Kin.3.5,6.
- ^l 1Chr. 28. 5.
- ^m 1 Kin. 3. 7, 8.
- ⁿ 1 Kin. 3.9.
- ^o Num.27.17. Deut. 31. 2.
- ^p 1 Kin. 3. 11, 12, 13.
- ^q 1Chr.29.25. ch. 9. 22. Eccles. 2. 9.

¹ Or, was *there*.　　　　² Heb. *much as the dust of the earth.*

I. 2–7. The narrative here corresponds with 1 K. iii. 4; but is very much fuller. We learn from the present passage, (1) that Solomon's sacrifice at Gibeon was a great public festivity, to which he collected vast numbers of the people; (2) that it was made upon the Brazen Altar of Bezaleel, which (3) stood before the Tabernacle; and (4) that Solomon's vision was on the night of his sacrifice. Consult the marg. reff.

5. *sought unto it*] i.e. "frequented it"— "were in the habit of making use of it."

7–12. The verbal differences between this passage and the corresponding one of Kings (1 K. iii. 5–14) are very considerable, and indicate the general truth that the object of the sacred historians is to give a true account of the real bearing of what was said:

not ordinarily to furnish us with all or the exact words that were uttered. The most important point omitted in Chronicles, and supplied by Kings, is the *conditional* promise of long life made to Solomon (1 K. iii. 14); while the chief point absent from Kings, and recorded by our author, is the solemn appeal made by Solomon to the promise of God to David his father (*v.* 9), which he now called upon God to "establish," or perform.

12. *I will give thee riches, and wealth, and honour*] Remark that the writer says nothing of any promise to Solomon of "long life," which, however, had been mentioned in *v.* 11 among the blessings which he might have been expected to ask. The reason for the omission would seem to lie in the writer's

had that *have been* before thee, neither shall there any after thee
13 have the like. ¶ Then Solomon came *from his journey* to the
high place that *was* at Gibeon to Jerusalem, from before the
14 tabernacle of the congregation, and reigned over Israel. *r* And
Solomon gathered chariots and horsemen: and he had a thousand and four hundred chariots, and twelve thousand horsemen,
which he placed in the chariot cities, and with the king at
15 Jerusalem. *s* And the king [1]made silver and gold at Jerusalem
as plenteous as stones, and cedar trees made he as the syco-
16 more trees that *are* in the vale for abundance. *t* And [2]Solomon
had horses brought out of Egypt, and linen yarn: the king's
17 merchants received the linen yarn at a price. And they fetched
up, and brought forth out of Egypt a chariot for six hundred
shekels of silver, and an horse for an hundred and fifty: and so
brought they out *horses* for all the kings of the Hittites, and for
the kings of Syria, [3]by their means.

CHAP. 2. AND Solomon *a* determined to build an house for the
2 name of the LORD, and an house for his kingdom. And *b* Solomon told out threescore and ten thousand men to bear burdens,
and fourscore thousand to hew in the mountain, and three thou-
3 sand and six hundred to oversee them. ¶ And Solomon sent to
[4]Huram the king of Tyre, saying, *c* As thou didst deal with
David my father, and didst send him cedars to build him an
4 house to dwell therein, *even so deal with me.* Behold, *d* I build
an house to the name of the LORD my God, to dedicate *it* to
him, *and* *e* to burn before him [5]sweet incense, and for *f* the continual shewbread, and for *g* the burnt offerings morning and
evening, on the sabbaths, and on the new moons, and on the
solemn feasts of the LORD our God. This *is an ordinance for*
5 ever to Israel. And the house which I build *is* great: for *h* great
6 *is* our God above all gods. *i* But who [6]is able to build him an
house, seeing the heaven and heaven of heavens cannot contain
him? who *am* I then, that I should build him an house, save

r	1 Kin. 4.26. ch. 9. 25.
s	ch. 9. 27. Job 22. 24.
t	ch. 9. 28.
a	1 Kin. 5. 5.
b	1 Kin. 5.15. ver. 18.
c	1 Chr. 14. 1.
d	ver. 1.
e	Ex. 30. 7.
f	Ex. 25. 30. Lev. 24. 8.
g	Num. 28. 3, 9, 11.
h	Ps. 135. 5.
i	1 Kin. 8. 27. ch. 6. 18. Isai. 66. 1.

---

[1] Heb. *gave.*
[2] Heb. *the going forth of the horses which* was *Solomon's.*
[3] Heb. *by their hand.*
[4] Or, *Hiram,* 1 Kin. 5. 1.
[5] Heb. *incense of spices.*
[6] Heb. *hath retained,* or, *obtained strength.*

---

desire to record only what is good of this
great king. Long life was included in the
promises made to him; but it was granted
conditionally; and Solomon not fulfilling
the conditions, it did not take effect (1 K.
iii. 14 note).

13. *from his journey*] These words are not
in the original text, which is thought to be
corrupt. It is best to correct the text, and
then simply to translate: "And Solomon
came from the high place that was at
Gibeon to Jerusalem."

14–17. This passage is very nearly identical with 1 K. x. 26–29.

II. 3. Huram, the form used throughout
Chronicles (except 1 Chr. xiv. 1) for the
name both of the king and of the artisan
whom he lent to Solomon (*v.* 13, iv. 11, 16),
is a late corruption of the true native word,
Hiram (marg. note and ref.).

4. The symbolical meaning of "burning
incense" is indicated in Rev. viii. 3, 4.
Consult the marg. reff. to this verse.

the solemn feasts] The three great annual
festivals, the Passover, the Feast of Weeks
(Pentecost), and the Feast of Tabernacles
(Lev. xxiii. 4–44; Deut. xvi. 1–17).

5. See 1 K. vi. 2 note. In Jewish eyes, at
the time that the Temple was built, it may
have been "great," that is to say, it may
have exceeded the dimensions of any single
separate building existing in Palestine up
to the time of its erection.

great is our God &c.] This may seem inappropriate as addressed to a heathen king.
But it appears (*vv.* 11, 12) that Hiram acknowledged Jehovah as the supreme deity,
probably identifying Him with his own
Melkarth.

6. *save only to burn sacrifice before him*]
Solomon seems to mean that to build the
Temple can only be justified on the human—
not on the divine—side. "God dwelleth not
in temples made with hands;" He cannot be
confined to them; He does in no sort need
them. The sole reason for building a Temple

7 only to burn sacrifice before him ? Send me now therefore a
man cunning to work in gold, and in silver, and in brass, and
in iron, and in purple, and crimson, and blue, and that can skill
¹to grave with the cunning men that *are* with me in Judah

k 1Chr.22.15. 8 and in Jerusalem, *k* whom David my father did provide. *l* Send
l 1 Kin. 5. 6.   me also cedar trees, fir trees, and ²algum trees, out of Lebanon: for I know that thy servants can skill to cut timber in
Lebanon ; and, behold, my servants *shall be* with thy servants,
9 even to prepare me timber in abundance : for the house which I

m 1Kin.5.11. 10 am about to build *shall be* ³wonderful great. *m* And, behold, I
will give to thy servants, the hewers that cut timber, twenty
thousand measures of beaten wheat, and twenty thousand measures of barley, and twenty thousand baths of wine, and twenty

11 thousand baths of oil. ¶ Then Huram the king of Tyre an-
n 1 Kin. 10.9.   swered in writing, which he sent to Solomon, *n* Because the LORD
ch. 9. 8.   hath loved his people, he hath made thee king over them.

o 1 Kin. 5. 7. 12 Huram said moreover, *o* Blessed *be* the LORD God of Israel.
p Gen. 1. & 2.   *p* that made heaven and earth, who hath given to David the
Ps. 33. 6.   king a wise son, ⁴endued with prudence and understanding,
& 102. 25.
& 124. 8.   that might build an house for the LORD, and an house for his
& 136. 5, 6. 13 kingdom. And now I have sent a cunning man, endued with
Acts 4. 24.   14 understanding, of Huram my father's, *q* the son of a woman of
& 14. 15.
Rev. 10. 6.   the daughters of Dan, and his father *was* a man of Tyre, skilful
q 1 Kin. 7.
13, 14.

¹ Heb. *to grave gravings.*   ³ Heb. *great and wonder-* ⁴ Heb. *knowing prudence*
² Or, *almuggim,* 1 Kin. 10. 11.   *ful.*   *and understanding.*

---

lies in the needs of man : his worship must
be local ; the sacrifices commanded in the
Law had of necessity to be offered somewhere.

7. See 1 K. v. 6, vii. 13 notes.

purple &c.] " Purple, crimson, and blue,"
would be needed for the hangings of the
Temple, which, in this respect, as in others,
was conformed to the pattern of the Tabernacle (see Ex. xxv. 4, xxvi. 1, &c.). Hiram's
power of " working in purple, crimson,"
&c., was probably a knowledge of the best
modes of dyeing cloth these colours. The
Phœnicians, off whose coast the *murex* was
commonly taken, were famous as purple
dyers from a very remote period.

crimson] *Karmil,* the word here and elsewhere translated " crimson," is peculiar to
Chronicles [and probably of Persian origin].
The famous red dye of Persia and India,
the dye known to the Greeks as κόκκος,
and to the Romans as *coccum,* is obtained
from an insect. Whether the " scarlet "
(*shani*) of Exodus (xxv. 4, &c.) is the same
or a different red, cannot be certainly determined.

10. *beaten wheat*] The Hebrew text is
probably corrupt here. The true original
may be restored from marg. ref., where the
wheat is said to have been given " for food."
The barley and the wine are omitted in
Kings. The author of Chronicles probably
filled out the statement which the writer of
Kings has given in brief ; the barley, wine,
and ordinary oil, would be applied to the
sustenance of the foreign labourers.

11. Josephus and others professed to give
Greek versions of the correspondence, which
(they said) had taken place between Hiram
and Solomon. No value attaches to those
letters, which are evidently forgeries.

Because the LORD *hath loved his people*]
Cp. marg. reff. The neighbouring sovereigns, in their communications with the
Jewish monarchs, seem to have adopted the
Jewish name for the Supreme Being (Jehovah), either identifying Him (as did Hiram)
with their own chief god or (sometimes)
meaning merely to acknowledge Him as
the special God of the Jewish nation and
country.

12. *the* LORD...*that made heaven and earth*]
This appears to have been a formula designating the Supreme God with several of
the Asiatic nations. In the Persian inscriptions Ormazd is constantly called " the
great god, who gave " (or made) " heaven
and earth."

13. *of Huram my father's*] A wrong translation. Huram here is the workman sent
by the king of Tyre and not the king of
Tyre's father (see 1 K. v. 1 note). The
words in the original are Huram Abi, and
the latter word is now commonly thought to
be either a proper name or an epithet of
honour, *e.g.* my master-workman.

14. *to find out every device*] Cp. Ex. xxxi.
4. The " devices " intended are plans or
designs connected with art, which Huram
could invent on any subject that was " put
to him."

to work in gold, and in silver, in brass, in iron, in stone, and in timber, in purple, in blue, and in fine linen, and in crimson; also to grave any manner of graving, and to find out every device which shall be put to him, with thy cunning men, and 15 with the cunning men of my lord David thy father. Now therefore the wheat, and the barley, the oil, and the wine, which 16 ʳmy lord hath spoken of, let him send unto his servants: ˢand we will cut wood out of Lebanon, ¹as much as thou shalt need: and we will bring it to thee in flotes by sea to ²Joppa; and thou 17 shalt carry it up to Jerusalem.   ¶ ᵗAnd Solomon numbered all ³the strangers that *were* in the land of Israel, after the numbering wherewith ᵘDavid his father had numbered them; and they were found an hundred and fifty thousand and three thousand 18 and six hundred.   And he set ˣthreescore and ten thousand of them *to be* bearers of burdens, and fourscore thousand *to be* hewers in the mountain, and three thousand and six hundred overseers to set the people a work.

Chap. 3. THEN ᵃSolomon began to build the house of the Lord at ᵇJerusalem in mount Moriah, ⁴where *the Lord* appeared unto David his father, in the place that David had prepared in the thresh-2 ingfloor of ᶜ⁵Ornan the Jebusite.   And he began to build in the second *day* of the second month, in the fourth year of his reign. 3 ¶ Now these *are the things* ᵈ*wherein* Solomon was ⁶instructed for the building of the house of God.   The length by cubits after the first measure *was* threescore cubits, and the breadth twenty 4 cubits.   And the ᵉporch that *was* in the front *of the house*, the length *of it was* according to the breadth of the house, twenty cubits, and the height *was* an hundred and twenty: and he over-5 laid it within with pure gold.   And ᶠthe greater house he cieled

Right margin references:
ʳ ver. 10.
ˢ 1 Kin.5.8,9.

ᵗ As ver. 2.
1 Kin. 5. 13, 15, 16.
& 9. 20, 21.
ch. 8. 7, 8.
ᵘ 1 Chr. 22.2.
ˣ As it is
ver. 2.

ᵃ 1 Kin. 6. 1, &c.
ᵇ Gen. 22. 2, 14.

ᶜ 1 Chr. 22. 1.

ᵈ 1 Kin. 6. 2.

ᵉ 1 Kin. 6. 3.

ᶠ 1 Kin. 6. 15—18.

---

¹ Heb. *according to all thy need.*
² Heb. *Japho*, Josh. 19. 46. Acts 9. 36.
³ Heb. *the men the strangers.*
⁴ Or, *which was seen of David his father.*
⁵ Or, *Araunah*, 2 Sam. 24. 18.
⁶ Heb. *founded.*

---

17. The strangers are the non-Israelite population of the Holy Land, the descendants (chiefly) of those Canaanites whom the children of Israel did not drive out. The reimposition of the bond-service imposed on the Canaanites at the time of the conquest (Judg. i. 28, 30, 33, 35), but discontinued in the period of depression between Joshua and Saul, was (it is clear) due to David, whom Solomon merely imitated in the arrangements described in these verses.

18. On the numbers, see 1 K. v. 16 note.

to set the people a work] Or, "to set the people *to* work"—*i.e.* to compel them to labour. Probably, like the Egyptian and Assyrian overseers of forced labour, these officers carried whips or sticks, wherewith they quickened the movements of the sluggish.

III. 1. *where the Lord appeared unto David*] The marg. rendering, or "which was shown to David," is preferred by some; and the expression is understood to point out to David the proper site for the Temple by the appearance of the Angels and the command to build an altar (2 Sam. xxiv. 17-25; 1 Chr. xxi. 16-26).

in the place that David had prepared] This seems to be the true meaning of the passage, though the order of the words in the original has been accidentally deranged.

3. The marginal "founded" gives a clue to another meaning of this passage, which may be translated: "Now **this is the ground-plan** of Solomon for the building, &c."

cubits after the first measure] *i.e.* cubits according to the ancient standard. The Jews, it is probable, adopted the Babylonian measures during the Captivity, and carried them back into their own country. The writer notes that the cubit of which he here speaks is the old (Mosaic) cubit.

4. *the height was an hundred and twenty cubits*] This height, which so much exceeds that of the main building (1 K. vi. 2), is probably to be corrected by the reading of the Arabic Version and the Alexandrian Septuagint, "twenty cubits." But see *v.* 9.

5. *the greater house*] *i.e.* the Holy Place, or main chamber of the Temple, intervening between the porch and the Holy of Holies (so in *v.* 7).

he cieled with fir tree] Rather, "he

with fir tree, which he overlaid with fine gold, and set thereon
6 palm trees and chains. And he [1]garnished the house with
precious stones for beauty: and the gold *was* gold of Parvaim.,
7 He overlaid also the house, the beams, the posts, and the walls
thereof, and the doors thereof, with gold; and graved cherubims
8 on the walls. And he made the most holy house, the length
whereof *was* according to the breadth of the house, twenty
cubits, and the breadth thereof twenty cubits: and he overlaid
9 it with fine gold, *amounting* to six hundred talents. And the
weight of the nails *was* fifty shekels of gold. And he overlaid
10 the upper chambers with gold. ¶ [g]And in the most holy house
he made two cherubims [2]of image work, and overlaid them with
11 gold. And the wings of the cherubims *were* twenty cubits long:
one wing *of the one cherub was* five cubits, reaching to the wall
of the house: and the other wing *was likewise* five cubits,
12 reaching to the wing of the other cherub. And *one* wing of the
other cherub *was* five cubits, reaching to the wall of the house:
and the other wing *was* five cubits *also*, joining to the wing of
13 the other cherub. The wings of these cherubims spread themselves forth twenty cubits: and they stood on their feet, and
14 their faces *were* [3]inward. ¶ And he made the [h]vail *of* blue, and
purple, and crimson, and fine linen, and [4]wrought cherubims
15 thereon. ¶ Also he made before the house [i]two pillars of thirty
and five cubits [5]high, and the chapiter that *was* on the top of
16 each of them *was* five cubits. And he made chains, *as* in the

g 1 Kin. G
23, &c.

h Matt 27.51.
Heb. 9. 3.
i 1 Kin. 7.
15—21.
Jer. 52. 21.

---

[1] Heb. *covered.*
[2] Or, (as some think) *of*   *moveable work.*
[3] Or, *toward the house.*
[4] Heb. *caused to ascend.*
[5] Heb. *long.*

---

covered," or **"lined."** The reference is not
to the ceiling, which was entirely of wood,
but to the walls and floor, which were of
stone, with a covering of planks (marg.
ref.). The word translated " fir ·" bears
probably in this place, not the narrow
meaning which it has in ii. 8, where it is
opposed to cedar, but a wider one, in which
cedar is included.

palm trees and chains] See 1 K. vi. 29.
The "chains" are supposed to be garlands
or festoons.

6. *precious stones for beauty*] Not marbles
but gems (cp. 1 Chr. xxix. 2). The phrase
translated "for beauty" means "for its
beautification," "**to beautify it.**"

Parvaim is probably the name of a place,
but what is quite uncertain.

8. *the most holy house*]. *i.e.* the sanctuary,
or Holy of Holies. On the probable value
of the gold, see 1 K. x. 14 note.

9. *the upper chambers*] Cp. 1 Chr. xxviii.
11. Their position is uncertain. Some
place them above the Holy of Holies,
which was ten cubits, or fifteen feet lower
than the main building (cp. 1 K. vi. 2;
20); others, accepting the height of the
porch 120 cubits (*v.* 4), regard the "upper
chambers" or "chamber" (ὑπερῷον, LXX.),
as having been a lofty building erected over
the entrance to the Temple; others suggest that the chambers intended are simply
the uppermost of the three sets of chambers
which on three sides surrounded the Tem-

ple (see 1 K. vi. 5-10). This would seem to
be the simplest and best explanation, though
we cannot see any reason for the rich ornamentation of these apartments, or for David's special directions concerning them.

10. The word translated "image work,"
or, in the margin, "moveable work," occurs
only in this passage, and has not even a
Hebrew derivation. Modern Hebraists find
an Arabic derivation, and explain the word
to mean "carved work."

11, 12. *the wings of the cherubims*] Compare 1 K. vi. 24–27.

13. *their faces were inward*] Lit. as in
marg. Instead of looking towards one another, with heads bent downward over the
Mercy Seat, like the Cherubim of Moses
(Ex. xxxvii. 9), these of Solomon looked out
from the sanctuary into the great chamber
("*the* house"). The Cherubim thus stood
upright on either side of the Ark, like two
sentinels guarding it.

14. This is an important addition to the
description in Kings, where the vail is not
mentioned. It was made of exactly the
same colours as the vail of the Tabernacle
(Ex. xxvi. 31).

15. *of thirty and five cubits*] See 1 K. vii.
15 note. Some suppose that there has been
a corruption of the number in the present
passage.

16. *as in the oracle*] This passage is probably corrupt. Our translators supposing
that a single letter had fallen out at the be-

oracle, and put *them* on the heads of the pillars; and made [k]an
17 hundred pomegranates, and put *them* on the chains. And he
[l]reared up the pillars before the temple, one on the right hand,
and the other on the left; and called the name of that on the
right hand [1]Jachin, and the name of that on the left [2]Boaz.

CHAP. 4. MOREOVER he made [a]an altar of brass, twenty cubits
the length thereof, and twenty cubits the breadth thereof, and
2 ten cubits the height thereof. ¶[b]Also he made a molten
sea of ten cubits [3]from brim to brim, round in compass,
and five cubits the height thereof; and a line of thirty cubits
3 did compass it round about. [c]And under it *was* the similitude
of oxen, which did compass it round about: ten in a cubit,
compassing the sea round about. Two rows of oxen *were* cast,
4 when it was cast. It stood upon twelve oxen, three looking
toward the north, and three looking toward the west, and three
looking toward the south, and three looking toward the east: and
the sea *was set* above upon them, and all their hinder parts *were*
5 inward. And the thickness of it *was* an handbreadth, and the
brim of it like the work of the brim of a cup, [4]with flowers of
6 lilies; *and* it received and held [d]three thousand baths. ¶He
made also [e]ten lavers, and put five on the right hand, and five
on the left, to wash in them: [5]such things as they offered for
the burnt offering they washed in them; but the sea *was* for the
7 priests to wash in. [f]And he made ten candlesticks of gold
[g]according to their form, and set *them* in the temple, five on the
8 right hand, and five on the left. [h]He made also ten tables, and
placed *them* in the temple, five on the right side, and five on the
9 left. And he made a hundred [6]basons of gold. ¶Furthermore
[i]he made the court of the priests, and the great court, and doors
10 for the court, and overlaid the doors of them with brass. And
[k]he set the sea on the right side of the east end, over against the
11 south. ¶And [l]Huram made the pots, and the shovels, and the
[7]basons. And Huram [8]finished the work that he was to make
12 for king Solomon for the house of God; *to wit*, the two pillars,
and [m]the pommels, and the chapiters *which were* on the top of the
two pillars, and the two wreaths to cover the two pommels of the
13 chapiters which *were* on the top of the pillars; and [n]four hundred pomegranates on the two wreaths; two rows of pomegranates on each wreath, to cover the two pommels of the chapiters
14 which *were* [9]upon the pillars. He made also [o]bases, and [1]lavers
15 made he upon the bases; one sea, and twelve oxen under it.

Side notes:
[k] 1 Kin. 7. 20.
[l] 1 Kin. 7. 21.
[a] Ex. 27. 1, 2. 2 Kin. 16. 14. Ezek. 43. 13, 16.
[b] 1 Kin. 7. 23.
[c] 1 Kin. 7. 24, 25, 26.
[d] See 1 Kin. 7. 26.
[e] 1 Kin. 7. 38.
[f] 1 Kin. 7. 49.
[g] Ex. 25. 31, 40. 1 Chr. 28. 12, 19.
[h] 1 Kin. 7. 48.
[i] 1 Kin. 6. 36.
[k] 1 Kin. 7. 39.
[l] See 1 Kin. 7. 40.
[m] 1 Kin. 7. 41.
[n] See 1 Kin. 7. 20.
[o] 1 Kin. 7. 27, 43.

---

[1] That is, *He shall establish.*
[2] That is, *In it is strength.*
[3] Heb. *from his brim to his brim.*
[4] Or, *like a lilyflower.*
[5] Heb. *the work of burnt offering.*
[6] Or, *bowls.*
[7] Or, *bowls.*
[8] Heb. *finished to make.*
[9] Heb. *upon the face.*
[1] Or, *caldrons.*

---

ginning of the word translated "in the oracle," supplied "as." But we have no reason to suppose there were any "chains" or
"festoons" in the "oracle" or most Holy
Place.

IV. 1. The supplementary character of
Chronicles is here once more apparent. The
author of Kings had omitted to record the
dimensions of the Brazen Altar. It stood
in the great court (2 Chr. vi. 12, 13).

3. For "oxen" we find in 1 K. vii. 24,
"knops" or "gourds." An early copyist,
not comprehending the comparatively rare
word here used for "gourd," and expecting

to hear of oxen, as soon as the molten sea
was mentioned, changed the reading.

5. *three thousand baths*] See 1 K. vii. 23
note. It is quite possible that either here
or in Kings the text may have been accidentally corrupted.

7. *according to their form*] Rather, "**after
their manner**" (cp. *v.* 20). There is no allusion to the shape of the candlesticks, which
were made, no doubt, after the pattern of
the original candlestick of Moses.

8. The number of the tables (see *v.* 19)
and of the basons, is additional to the information contained in Kings.

p 1 Kin. 7.
14, 45.
q 1 Kin. 7 46.

r 1 Kin. 7.17.

s 1 Kin. 7.
48, 49, 50
t Ex. 25. 30.

u Ex. 27. 20,
21.
x Ex. 25. 31,
&c.

a 1 Kin. 7.51.

b 1 Kin. 8. 1,
&c.

c 2 Sam 6.12.
d 1 Kin. 8. 2.
e See ch. 7.
8, 9, 10.

f Deut. 10. 2,
5.
ch. 6. 11.

16 The pots also, and the shovels, and the fleshhooks, and all their instruments, did *p*Huram his father make to king Solomon for
17 the house of the LORD of ¹bright brass. *q*In the plain of Jordan did the king cast them, in the ²clay ground between Succoth
18 and Zeredathah. ¶ *r*Thus Solomon made all these vessels in great abundance: for the weight of the brass could not be found out.
19 And *s*Solomon made all the vessels that *were for* the house of God, the golden altar also, and the tables whereon *t*the shew-
20 bread *was set;* moreover the candlesticks with their lamps, that they should burn *u*after the manner before the oracle, of pure
21 gold; and *x*the flowers, and the lamps, and the tongs, *made he of*
22 gold, *and* that ³perfect gold; and the snuffers, and the ⁴basons, and the spoons, and the censers, *of* pure gold: and the entry of the house, the inner doors thereof for the most holy *place,* and the
5 doors of the house of the temple, *were of* gold. THUS *a*all the work that Solomon made for the house of the LORD was finished: and Solomon brought in *all* the things that David his father had dedicated; and the silver, and the gold, and all the instruments,
2 put he among the treasures of the house of God. ¶ *b*Then Solomon assembled the elders of Israel, and all the heads of the tribes, the chief of the fathers of the children of Israel, unto Jerusalem, to bring up the ark of the covenant of the LORD
3 *c*out of the city of David, which *is* Zion. *d*Wherefore all the men of Israel assembled themselves unto the king *e*in the feast
4 which *was* in the seventh month. And all the elders of Israel
5 came; and the Levites took up the ark. And they brought up the ark, and the tabernacle of the congregation, and all the holy vessels that *were* in the tabernacle, these did the priests *and* the
6 Levites bring up. Also king Solomon, and all the congregation of Israel that were assembled unto him before the ark, sacrificed sheep and oxen, which could not be told nor numbered for
7 multitude. And the priests brought in the ark of the covenant of the LORD unto his place, to the oracle of the house, into the
8 most holy *place, even* under the wings of the cherubims: for the cherubims spread forth *their* wings over the place of the ark, and the cherubims covered the ark and the staves thereof above.
9 And they drew out the staves *of the ark,* that the ends of the staves were seen from the ark before the oracle; but they were
10 not seen without. And ⁵there it is unto this day. *There was* nothing in the ark save the two tables which Moses *f*put *therein*

¹ Heb. *made bright,* or, *scoured.*
² Heb. *thicknesses of the ground.*
³ Heb. *perfections of gold.*
⁴ Or, *bowls.*
⁵ Or, *they are there,* as 1 Kin. 8. 8.

---

16. *Huram his father*] Or, "**Huram his master-workman**" (ii. 13 note).

17. *Zeredathah*] Or, Zarthan (marg. ref.). The writer of Chronicles probably uses the name which the place bore in his own day.

19. *the tables*] A single table only is mentioned in 1 K. vii. 48; 2 Chr. xxix. 18. It is supposed that Solomon made ten similar tables, any one of which might be used for the Shewbread; but that the bread was never placed on more than one table at a time.

22. *the entry of the house*] The text is, by some, corrected by 1 K. vii. 50, "the *hinges*" of the doors of the house, &c.

V. This chapter contains one important addition only to the narrative of Kings (marg. reff.); namely, the account of the circumstances under which the manifestation of the Divine Presence took place (*vv.* 11-13).

4. *the Levites took up the ark*] *i.e.* such of the Levites as were also priests (cp. *v.* 7; 1 K. viii. 3).

9. *from the ark*] Or, according to a different reading here and according to 1 K. viii. 8, some read, "the ends of the staves were seen from the Holy Place."

there it is unto this day] This should be corrected as in the margin.

at Horeb, [1]when the LORD made *a covenant* with the children of
11 Israel, when they came out of Egypt.   ¶ And it came to pass,
when the priests were come out of the holy *place:* (for all the
priests *that were* [2]present were sanctified, *and* did not *then* wait
12 by course : *g*also the Levites *which were* the singers, all of them
of Asaph, of Heman, of Jeduthun, with their sons and their
brethren, *being* arrayed in white linen, having cymbals and
psalteries and harps, stood at the east end of the altar, *h*and with
them an hundred and twenty priests sounding with trumpets :)
13 it came even to pass, as the trumpeters and singers *were as* one,
to make one sound to be heard in praising and thanking the
LORD ; and when they lifted up *their* voice with the trumpets
and cymbals and instruments of musick, and praised the LORD,
saying, [i]For *he is* good ; for his mercy *endureth* for ever : that
then the house was filled with a cloud, *even* the house of the
14 LORD; so that the priests could not stand to minister by reason
of the cloud: [k]for the glory of the LORD had filled the house of
God.

CHAP. 6. THEN [a]said Solomon, The LORD hath said that he would
2 dwell in the [b]thick darkness.   But I have built an house of
3 habitation for thee, and a place for thy dwelling for ever.   And
the king turned his face, and blessed the whole congregation of
4 Israel: and all the congregation of Israel stood.   ¶And he said,
Blessed *be* the LORD God of Israel, who hath with his hands
fulfilled *that* which he spake with his mouth to my father David,
5 saying, Since the day that I brought forth my people out of the
land of Egypt I chose no city among all the tribes of Israel to
build an house in, that my name might be there ; neither chose
6 I any man to be a ruler over my people Israel : [c]but I have
chosen Jerusalem, that my name might be there ; and [d]have
7 chosen David to be over my people Israel.   Now [e]it was in the
heart of David my father to build an house for the name of the
8 LORD God of Israel.   But the LORD said to David my father,
Forasmuch as it was in thine heart to build an house for my
9 name, thou didst well in that it was in thine heart : notwithstanding thou shalt not build the house ; but thy son which shall
come forth out of thy loins, he shall build the house for my
10 name.   The LORD therefore hath performed his word that he
hath spoken : for I am risen up in the room of David my father,
and am set on the throne of Israel, as the LORD promised, and
have built the house for the name of the LORD God of Israel.
11 And in it have I put the ark, [f]wherein *is* the covenant of the
12 LORD, that he made with the children of Israel.   ¶[g]And he
stood before the altar of the LORD in the presence of all the con-
13 gregation of Israel, and spread forth his hands : for Solomon
had made a brasen scaffold, of five cubits [3]long, and five cubits
broad, and three cubits high, and had set it in the midst of the
court : and upon it he stood, and kneeled down upon his knees
before all the congregation of Israel, and spread forth his hands
14 toward heaven, and said, ¶O LORD God of Israel, [h]*there is* no God
like thee in the heaven, nor in the earth ; which keepest covenant,
and *shewest* mercy unto thy servants, that walk before thee with

g 1 Chr. 25. 1.

h 1Chr.15.21.

i Ps. 136.
See 1 Chr.
16. 34, 41.

k Ex. 40. 35.
ch. 7. 2.

a 1 Kin. 8.
12–50.
b Lev. 16. 2.

c ch. 12. 13.
d 1 Chr. 23.4.
e 2 Sam. 7. 2.
1 Chr. 17. 1.
& 28. 2.

f ch. 5. 10.
g 1 Kin. 8.22.

h Ex. 15. 11.
Deut. 4. 39.
& 7. 9.

---

[1] Or, *where*.   [2] Heb. *found*.   [3] Heb. *the length thereof, &c.*

---

13. *even the house of the* LORD] Or, according to another reading (LXX.), which re-
moves the superfluousness of these words—

"The house was filled with a cloud of the
glory of the LORD."
    VI. **1–39.** Cp. Kings (marg. reff.).

*1 Chr. 22. 9.

15 all their hearts: *thou which hast kept with thy servant David my father that which thou hast promised him ; and spakest with thy mouth, and hast fulfilled *it* with thine hand, as *it is* this day.

16 Now therefore, O LORD God of Israel, keep with thy servant David my father that which thou hast promised him, saying,

k 2 Sam. 7.
12, 16.
1 Kin. 2. 4.
& 6. 12.
ch. 7. 18.
l Ps. 132. 12.

*k*¹ There shall not fail thee a man in my sight to sit upon the throne of Israel ; *l*yet so that thy children take heed to their

17 way to walk in my law, as thou hast walked before me. Now then, O LORD God of Israel, let thy word be verified, which thou

18 hast spoken unto thy servant David. ¶ But will God in very deed dwell with men on the earth ? *m*behold, heaven and the heaven of heavens cannot contain thee ; how much less this house which

m ch. 2. 6.
Isai. 66. 1.
Acts 7. 49.

19 I have built ! Have respect therefore to the prayer of thy servant, and to his supplication, O LORD my God, to hearken unto the cry and the prayer which thy servant prayeth before thee :

20 that thine eyes may be open upon this house day and night, upon the place whereof thou hast said that thou wouldest put thy name there ; to hearken unto the prayer which thy servant

21 prayeth ²toward this place. Hearken therefore unto the supplications of thy servant, and of thy people Israel, which they shall ³make toward this place : hear thou from thy dwelling-

22 place, *even* from heaven ; and when thou hearest, forgive. ¶ If a man sin against his neighbour, ⁴and an oath be laid upon him to make him swear, and the oath come before thine altar in this

23 house ; then hear thou from heaven, and do, and judge thy servants, by requiting the wicked, by recompensing his way upon his own head ; and by justifying the righteous, by giving

24 him according to his righteousness. ¶ And if thy people Israel ⁵be put to the worse before the enemy, because they have sinned against thee ; and shall return and confess thy name, and pray

25 and make supplication before thee ⁶in this house ; then hear thou from the heavens, and forgive the sin of thy people Israel, and bring them again unto the land which thou gavest to them

n 1 Kin. 17. 1.

26 and to their fathers. ¶ When the *n*heaven is shut up, and there is no rain, because they have sinned against thee ; *yet* if they pray toward this place, and confess thy name, and turn from

27 their sin, when thou dost afflict them ; then hear thou from heaven, and forgive the sin of thy servants, and of thy people Israel, when thou hast taught them the good way, wherein they should walk ; and send rain upon thy land, which thou hast

o ch. 20. 9.

28 given unto thy people for an inheritance. ¶ If there *o*be dearth in the land, if there be pestilence, if there be blasting, or mildew, locusts, or caterpillers ; if their enemies besiege them ⁷in the cities of their land ; whatsoever sore or whatsoever sickness

29 *there be : then* what prayer *or* what supplication soever shall be made of any man, or of all thy people Israel, when every one shall know his own sore and his own grief, and shall spread forth

30 his hands ⁸in this house : then hear thou from heaven thy dwelling place, and forgive, and render unto every man according unto all his ways, whose heart thou knowest ; (for thou only

p 1 Chr. 28. 9.

31 *p*knowest the hearts of the children of men :) that they may fear thee, to walk in thy ways, ⁹so long as they live ¹in the land

32 which thou gavest unto our fathers. ¶ Moreover concerning the

Heb. *There shall not a man be cut off.*
² Or, *in this place.*
³ Heb. *pray.*
⁴ Heb. *and he require an*

oath of him.
⁵ Or, *be smitten.*
⁶ Or, *toward.*
⁷ Heb. *in the land of their gates.*

⁸ Or, *toward this house.*
⁹ Heb. *all the days which.*
¹ Heb. *upon the face of the land.*

stranger, ^qwhich is not of thy people Israel, but is come from a far country for thy great name's sake, and thy mighty hand, and 33 thy stretched out arm; if they come and pray in this house; then hear thou from the heavens, *even* from thy dwelling place, and do according to all that the stranger calleth to thee for; that all people of the earth may know thy name, and fear thee, as *doth* thy people Israel, and may know that [1]this house which I have 34 built is called by thy name. ¶ If thy people go out to war against their enemies by the way that thou shalt send them, and they pray unto thee toward this city which thou hast chosen, and 35 the house which I have built for thy name; then hear thou from the heavens their prayer and their supplication, and maintain 36 their [2]cause. ¶ If they sin against thee, (for *there is* ^rno man which sinneth not,) and thou be angry with them, and deliver them over before *their* enemies, and [3]they carry them away cap- 37 tives unto a land far off or near; yet *if* they [4]bethink themselves in the land whither they are carried captive, and turn and pray unto thee in the land of their captivity, saying, We have sinned, 38 we have done amiss, and have dealt wickedly: if they return to thee with all their heart and with all their soul in the land of their captivity, whither they have carried them captives, and pray toward their land, which thou gavest unto their fathers, and *toward* the city which thou hast chosen, and toward the 39 house which I have built for thy name: then hear thou from the heavens, *even* from thy dwelling place, their prayer and their supplications, and maintain their [5]cause, and forgive thy people 40 which have sinned against thee. ¶ Now, my God, let, I beseech thee, thine eyes be open, and *let* thine ears be attent [6]unto the 41 prayer *that is made* in this place. Now ^stherefore arise, O LORD God, into thy ^tresting place, thou, and the ark of thy strength: let thy priests, O LORD God, be clothed with salvation, and 42 thy saints ^urejoice in goodness. O LORD God, turn not away the face of thine anointed: ^xremember the mercies of David thy servant.

CHAP. 7. NOW ^awhen Solomon had made an end of praying, the ^bfire came down from heaven, and consumed the burnt offering and the sacrifices; and ^cthe glory of the LORD filled the house. 2 ^dAnd the priests could not enter into the house of the LORD, 3 because the glory of the LORD had filled the LORD's house. And when all the children of Israel saw how the fire came down, and the glory of the LORD upon the house, they bowed themselves with their faces to the ground upon the pavement, and wor- shipped, and praised the LORD, ^esaying, For *he is* good; ^ffor his 4 mercy *endureth* for ever. ¶ ^gThen the king and all the people

Marginal references:

q John 12. 20.
Acts 8. 27.

r Prov. 20. 9.
Eccles. 7. 20.
Jam. 3. 2.
1 John 1. 8.

s Ps. 132. 8,
9, 10, 16.
t 1 Chr. 28. 2.

u Neh. 9. 25.

x Ps. 132. 1.
Isai. 55. 3.

a 1 Kin. 8. 54.
b Judg. 6. 21.
1 Kin. 18. 38.
1 Chr. 21. 26.
c 1 Kin. 8.
10, 11.
ch. 5. 13, 14.
Ezek. 10. 3, 4.
d ch. 5. 14.
e ch. 5. 13.
Ps. 136. 1.
f 1 Chr. 16.
41.
ch. 20. 21.
g 1 Kin. 8.
62, 63.

[1] Heb. *thy name is called upon this house.*
[2] Or, *right.*
[3] Heb. *they that take them captives carry them away.*
[4] Heb. *bring back to their heart.*
[5] Or, *right.*
[6] Heb. *to the prayer of this place.*

40-42. In Kings, a different conclusion takes the place of these verses. The docu- ment from which both writers copied con- tained the full prayer of dedication, which each gives in a somewhat abbreviated form.

41. *thy resting place*] i.e. the Holy of Holies. Solomon follows closely the words of David his father, spoken probably when he brought the Ark into Jerusalem. See marg. reff.

42. *turn not away the face of thine anointed*]

i.e. make him not to hide his face through shame at having his prayers rejected (cp. 1 K. ii. 16 note).

the mercies of David] i.e. "God's mercies towards David."

VII. 1. *the fire came down from heaven*] As in the time of Moses on the dedication of the Tabernacle (Lev. ix. 24). The fact is omitted from the narrative of Kings; but omission is not contradiction.

5 offered sacrifices before the LORD. And king Solomon offered a sacrifice of twenty and two thousand oxen, and an hundred and twenty thousand sheep: so the king and all the people

ʰ 1 Chr. 15. 16.

6 dedicated the house of God. ʰAnd the priests waited on their offices: the Levites also with instruments of musick of the LORD, which David the king had made to praise the LORD, because his mercy *endureth* for ever, when David praised ¹by their

ⁱ ch. 5. 12.
ᵏ 1 Kin. 8. 64.

ministry; and ⁱthe priests sounded trumpets before them, and

7 all Israel stood. Moreover ᵏSolomon hallowed the middle of the court that *was* before the house of the LORD: for there he offered burnt offerings, and the fat of the peace offerings, because the brasen altar which Solomon had made was not able to receive the burnt offerings, and the meat offerings, and the fat.

ˡ 1 Kin. 8. 65.

8 ¶ ˡAlso at the same time Solomon kept the feast seven days, and all Israel with him, a very great congregation, from the entering

ᵐ Josh. 13. 3.

9 in of Hamath unto ᵐthe river of Egypt. And in the eighth day they made ²a solemn assembly: for they kept the dedication of

ⁿ 1 Kin. 8. 66.

10 the altar seven days, and the feast seven days. And ⁿon the three and twentieth day of the seventh month he sent the people away into their tents, glad and merry in heart for the goodness that the LORD had shewed unto David, and to Solo-

ᵒ 1 Kin. 9. 1, &c.

11 mon, and to Israel his people. Thus ᵒSolomon finished the house of the LORD, and the king's house: and all that came into Solomon's heart to make in the house of the LORD, and in

12 his own house, he prosperously effected. ¶And the LORD appeared to Solomon by night, and said unto him, I have heard thy prayer, ᵖand have chosen this place to myself for an house

ᵖ Deut. 12. 5.
ᵍ ch. 6. 26, 28.

13 of sacrifice. ᵍIf I shut up heaven that there be no rain, or if I command the locusts to devour the land, or if I send pestilence

14 among my people; if my people, ³which are called by my name,

ʳ Jam. 4. 10.
ˢ ch. 6. 27, 30.
ᵗ ch. 6. 40.

shall ʳhumble themselves, and pray, and seek my face, and turn from their wicked ways; ˢthen will I hear from heaven, and

15 will forgive their sin, and will heal their land. Now ᵗmine eyes shall be open, and mine ears attent ⁴unto the prayer *that*

ᵘ 1 Kin. 9. 3. ch. 6. 6.

16 *is made* in this place. For now have ᵘI chosen and sanctified this house, that my name may be there for ever: and mine eyes

ˣ 1 Kin. 9. 4, &c.

17 and mine heart shall be there perpetually. ˣAnd as for thee, if thou wilt walk before me, as David thy father walked, and do according to all that I have commanded thee, and shalt

18 observe my statutes and my judgments; then will I stablish the throne of thy kingdom, according as I have covenanted with

ʸ ch. 6. 16.

David thy father, saying, ʸ⁵There shall not fail thee a man

---

¹ Heb. *by their hand.*
² Heb. *a restraint.*
³ Heb. *upon whom my*
name *is called.*
⁴ Heb. *to the prayer of this place.*
⁵ Heb. *There shall not be cut off to thee.*

---

8. *Solomon kept the feast*] i.e. Solomon kept at this same time, not the Feast of the Dedication only, but also the Feast of Tabernacles. The former lasted seven days, from the 8th of Tisri to the 15th, the latter also seven days, from the 15th to the 22nd. On the day following the people were dismissed (v. 10).

11. The narrative now runs parallel with 1 K. ix. 1–9, but is more full, and presents less of verbal agreement. Verses 13–15 are additional to the earlier record.

12. *an house of sacrifice*] This expression does not elsewhere occur. Its meaning, however, is clear. God declares that Solomon's Temple is the place whereunto all Israelites were commanded to bring their Burnt-offerings and sacrifices (see Deut. xii. 5, 6).

15. *the prayer that is made in this place*] Lit. as in the margin. The unusual phrase includes the two cases of prayers offered *in* (vi. 24) and *toward* (vi. 34, 38) the Sanctuary.

19 *to be* ruler in Israel. ^{z}But if ye turn away, and forsake my
statutes and my commandments, which I have set before you,
20 and shall go and serve other gods, and worship them; then
will I pluck them up by the roots out of my land which I have
given them; and this house, which I have sanctified for my
name, will I cast out of my sight, and will make it *to be* a pro-
21 verb and a byword among all nations.   And this house, which
is high, shall be an astonishment to every one that passeth by
it; so that he shall say, ^{a}Why hath the LORD done thus unto
22 this land, and unto this house?   And it shall be answered, Because they forsook the LORD God of their fathers, which brought
them forth out of the land of Egypt, and laid hold on other gods,
and worshipped them, and served them: therefore hath he
brought all this evil upon them.

CHAP. 8.   AND ^{a}it came to pass at the end of twenty years, wherein
Solomon had built the house of the LORD, and his own house,
2 that the cities which Huram had restored to Solomon, Solomon
built them, and caused the children of Israel to dwell there.
3 ¶ And Solomon went to Hamath-zobah, and prevailed against
4 it. ^{b}And he built Tadmor in the wilderness, and all the store
5 cities, which he built in Hamath.   Also he built Beth-horon the
upper, and Beth-horon the nether, fenced cities, with walls,
6 gates, and bars; and Baalath, and all the store cities that Solomon had, and all the chariot cities, and the cities of the horsemen, and ^{1}all that Solomon desired to build in Jerusalem, and
7 in Lebanon, and throughout all the land of his dominion. ${}^c As$
for all the people *that were* left of the Hittites, and the Amorites, and the Perizzites, and the Hivites, and the Jebusites,
8 which *were* not of Israel, *but* of their children, who were left
after them in the land, whom the children of Israel consumed
9 not, them did Solomon make to pay tribute until this day.   But
of the children of Israel did Solomon make no servants for his
work; but they *were* men of war, and chief of his captains, and
10 captains of his chariots and horsemen.   And these *were* the chief
of king Solomon's officers, *even* ^{d}two hundred and fifty, that bare
11 rule over the people.   ¶ And Solomon ^{e}brought up the daughter
of Pharaoh out of the city of David unto the house that he had
built for her: for he said, My wife shall not dwell in the house
of David king of Israel, because *the places are* ^{2}holy, whereunto
12 the ark of the LORD hath come.   ¶ Then Solomon offered burnt
offerings unto the LORD on the altar of the LORD, which he had
13 built before the porch, even after a certain rate ^{f}every day, offering according to the commandment of Moses, on the sabbaths,
and on the new moons, and on the solemn feasts, ^{g}three times in
the year, *even* in the feast of unleavened bread, and in the feast

Marginal references:
z Lev. 26. 14, 33. Deut. 28. 15, 36, 37.
a Deut. 29. 24. Jer. 22. 8, 9.
a 1 Kin. 9. 10, &c.
b 1 Kin. 9. 17, &c.
c 1 Kin. 9. 20, &c.
d See 1 Kin. 9. 23.
e 1 Kin. 3. 1. & 7. 8. & 9. 24.
f Ex. 29. 38. Num. 28. 3, 9, 11, 26. & 29. 1, &c.
g Ex. 23. 14. Deut. 16. 16.

---

^{1} Heb. *all the desire of Solomon which he desired to build.* ^{2} Heb. *holiness.*

VIII. Cp. the reff. to 1 Kings.

2. *the cities which Huram had restored to Solomon*] These cities had not been mentioned previously by the writer of Chronicles, who, however, seems to assume that the fact of their having been given by Hiram to Solomon is known to his readers. See 1 K. ix. 11–13.

3. *Hamath-zobah*] Usually identified with the "great Hamath" (Am. vi. 2); the capital of Cœle-Syria; but probably a town

of Zobah otherwise unknown, which revolted from Solomon, and was reduced to subjection.

5. *built*] "Rebuilt," or "repaired" (as in v. 2). The two Beth-horons were both ancient cities (see Josh. x. 10 note).

10. On the number cp. 1 K. v. 16 note.

11. *of Pharaoh*] Here again the writer of Chronicles assumes in his reader a knowledge of the facts recorded in the marg. reff.

14 of weeks and in the feast of tabernacles. And he appointed, according to the order of David his father, the ʰcourses of the priests to their service, and ⁱthe Levites to their charges, to praise and minister before the priests, as the duty of every day required: the ᵏporters also by their courses at every gate: for 15 ¹so had David the man of God commanded. And they departed not from the commandment of the king unto the priests and Levites concerning any matter, or concerning the treasures. 16 Now all the work of Solomon was prepared unto the day of the foundation of the house of the LORD, and until it was finished. 17 *So* the house of the LORD was perfected. ¶ Then went Solomon to ˡEzion-geber, and to ²Eloth, at the sea side in the land of 18 Edom. ᵐAnd Huram sent him by the hands of his servants ships, and servants that had knowledge of the sea; and they went with the servants of Solomon to Ophir, and took thence four hundred and fifty talents of gold, and brought *them* to king Solomon.

CHAP. **9.** AND ᵃwhen the queen of Sheba heard of the fame of Solomon, she came to prove Solomon with hard questions at Jerusalem, with a very great company, and camels that bare spices, and gold in abundance, and precious stones: and when she was come to Solomon, she communed with him of all that 2 was in her heart. And Solomon told her all her questions: and there was nothing hid from Solomon which he told her not. 3 And when the queen of Sheba had seen the wisdom of Solomon, 4 and the house that he had built, and the meat of his table, and the sitting of his servants, and the attendance of his ministers, and their apparel; his ³cupbearers also, and their apparel; and his ascent by which he went up into the house of the LORD; 5 there was no more spirit in her. And she said to the king, *It was* a true ⁴report which I heard in mine own land of thine ⁵acts, 6 and of thy wisdom: howbeit I believed not their words, until I came, and mine eyes had seen *it:* and, behold, the one half of the greatness of thy wisdom was not told me: *for* thou ex-7 ceedest the fame that I heard. Happy *are* thy men, and happy *are* these thy servants, which stand continually before thee, and 8 hear thy wisdom. Blessed be the LORD thy God, which delighted in thee to set thee on his throne, *to be* king for the LORD thy God: because thy God loved Israel, to establish them for ever, therefore made he thee king over them, to do judgment and 9 justice. And she gave the king an hundred and twenty talents

---

¹ Heb. *so was the com-
mandment of David the
man of God.*

² Or, *Elath*, Deut. 2. 8.
2 Kin. 14. 22.

³ Or, *butlers.*

⁴ Heb. *word.*

⁵ Or, *sayings.*

---

14. *the man of God*] This phrase, so common in Kings (see Introduction to Kings, p. 264 n. 4), is rare in Chronicles, and is applied only to Moses (1 Chr. xxiii. 14), David, and one other Prophet (xxv. 7, 9).

18. It has been supposed that these ships were conveyed from Tyre to Ezion-geber, either (1) round the continent of Africa, or (2) across the isthmus of Suez. But the writer probably only means that ships were given by Hiram to Solomon *at this time*, and in connexion with the Ophir enterprise. These vessels may have been deli-

vered at Joppa, and have been there carefully studied by the Jewish shipwrights, who then proceeded to Ezion-geber, and, assisted by Phœnicians, constructed ships after their pattern.

four hundred and fifty talents] "Four hundred and *twenty* talents" in Kings (1 K. ix. 28). One or other of the two texts has suffered from that corruption to which numbers are so especially liable.

IX. 1–12. The narrative here is parallel with that in marg. ref., from which it varies but little, and to which it adds nothing.

of gold, and of spices great abundance, and precious stones: neither was there any such spice as the queen of Sheba gave
10 king Solomon. ¶ And the servants also of Huram, and the servants of Solomon, *b* which brought gold from Ophir, brought
11 *c* algum trees and precious stones. And the king made *of the* algum trees [1] [2] terraces to the house of the LORD, and to the king's palace, and harps and psalteries for singers: and there
12 were none such seen before in the land of Judah. ¶ And king Solomon gave to the queen of Sheba all her desire, whatsoever she asked, beside *that* which she had brought unto the king. So she turned, and went away to her own land, she and her
13 servants. ¶ Now the weight of gold that came to Solomon in one year was six hundred and threescore and six talents of gold;
14 beside *that which* chapmen and merchants brought. And all the kings of Arabia and [3] governors of the country brought gold
15 and silver to Solomon. And king Solomon made two hundred targets *of* beaten gold: six hundred *shekels* of beaten gold went
16 to one target. And three hundred shields *made he of* beaten gold: three hundred *shekels* of gold went to one shield. And
17 the king put them in the house of the forest of Lebanon. Moreover the king made a great throne of ivory, and overlaid it with
18 pure gold. And *there were* six steps to the throne, with a footstool of gold, *which were* fastened to the throne, and [4] stays on each side of the sitting place, and two lions standing by the
19 stays: and twelve lions stood there on the one side and on the other upon the six steps. There was not the like made in any
20 kingdom. And all the drinking vessels of king Solomon *were of* gold, and all the vessels of the house of the forest of Lebanon *were of* [5] pure gold: [6] none *were of* silver; it was *not* any thing
21 accounted of in the days of Solomon. For the king's ships went to Tarshish with the servants of Huram: every three years once came the ships of Tarshish bringing gold, and silver, [7] ivory,
22 and apes, and peacocks. ¶ And king Solomon passed all the
23 kings of the earth in riches and wisdom. And all the kings of the earth sought the presence of Solomon, to hear his wisdom,
24 that God had put in his heart. And they brought every man his present, vessels of silver, and vessels of gold, and raiment, harness, and spices, horses, and mules, a rate year by year.
25 And Solomon *d* had four thousand stalls for horses and chariots, and twelve thousand horsemen; whom he bestowed in the cha-
26 riot cities, and with the king at Jerusalem. *e* And he reigned over all the kings *f* from the [8] river even unto the land of the
27 Philistines, and to the border of Egypt. *g* And the king [9] made silver in Jerusalem as stones, and cedar trees made he as the

b ch. 8. 18.

c 1 Kin. 10. 11, *almug trees.*

d 1 Kin. 4. 26. & 10. 26. ch. 1. 14.
e 1 Kin. 4. 21.
f Gen. 15. 18. Ps. 72. 8.
g 1 Kin. 10. 27. ch. 1. 15.

[1] Or. *stairs.*
[2] Heb. *highways.*
[3] Or, *captains.*
[4] Heb. *hands.*
[5] Heb. *shut up.*
[6] Or, there was *no silver* in them.
[7] Or, *elephants' teeth.*
[8] That is, *Euphrates.*
[9] Heb. *gave.*

11. *terraces*] Rather, as in the margin, "stairs" (see 1 K. x. 12 note).

12. *beside that which she had brought unto the king*] It is difficult to assign any sense to these words as they now stand in the Hebrew text. A slight alteration will give the meaning: "Beside that which the king had brought for her;" which is in conformity with 1 K. x. 13.

15, 16. Comparing 1 K. x. 16, 17, it follows from the two passages together that the "pound of gold" was equal to 100 shekels.

18. The footstool (not mentioned in Kings) was an essential appendage to an Oriental throne; it appears everywhere in the Egyptian, Assyrian, and Persian sculptures.

23. *all the kings of the earth*] Rather, "all the kings of the **land**;" all the monarchs, that is, whose dominions were included in Solomon's empire (see 1 K. iv. 21).

ʰ 1Kin.10.28.
ch. 1. 16.
ⁱ 1Kin.11.41.

ᵏ 1Kin.11.29.
ˡ ch. 12. 15.
& 13. 22.
ᵐ 1 Kin. 11.
42, 43.

ᵃ 1 Kin. 12.
1, &c.

ᵇ 1Kin.11.40.

28 sycomore trees that *are* in the low plains in abundance. ʰAnd they brought unto Solomon horses out of Egypt, and out of all
29 lands. ¶ ⁱNow the rest of the acts of Solomon, first and last, *are* they not written in the ¹book of Nathan the prophet, and in the prophecy of ᵏAhijah the Shilonite, and in the visions of
30 ˡIddo the seer against Jeroboam the son of Nebat? ᵐAnd Solo-
31 mon reigned in Jerusalem over all Israel forty years. And Solomon slept with his fathers, and he was buried in the city of David his father: and Rehoboam his son reigned in his stead.

Chap. 10. AND ᵃRehoboam went to Shechem ; for to Shechem
2 were all Israel come to make him king. And it came to pass, when Jeroboam the son of Nebat, who *was* in Egypt, ᵇwhither he had fled from the presence of Solomon the king, heard *it*,
3 that Jeroboam returned out of Egypt. And they sent and called him. So Jeroboam and all Israel came and spake to Rehoboam,
4 saying, Thy father made our yoke grievous: now therefore ease thou somewhat the grievous servitude of thy father, and his
5 heavy yoke that he put upon us, and we will serve thee. And
6 he said unto them, Come again unto me after three days. And the people departed. ¶ And king Rehoboam took counsel with the old men that had stood before Solomon his father while he yet lived, saying, What counsel give ye *me* to return answer to
7 this people? And they spake unto him, saying, If thou be kind to this people, and please them, and speak good words to them,
8 they will be thy servants for ever. But he forsook the counsel which the old men gave him, and took counsel with the young men that were brought up with him, that stood before him.
9 And he said unto them, What advice give ye that we may return answer to this people, which have spoken to me, saying, Ease
10 somewhat the yoke that thy father did put upon us? And the young men that were brought up with him spake unto him, saying, Thus shalt thou answer the people that spake unto thee, saying, Thy father made our yoke heavy, but make thou *it* somewhat lighter for us ; thus shalt thou say unto them, My
11 little *finger* shall be thicker than my father's loins. For whereas my father ²put a heavy yoke upon you, I will put more to your yoke: my father chastised you with whips, but I *will chastise*
12 *you* with scorpions. ¶ So Jeroboam and all the people came to Rehoboam on the third day, as the king bade, saying, Come again
13 to me on the third day. And the king answered them roughly ;
14 and king Rehoboam forsook the counsel of the old men, and answered them after the advice of the young men, saying, My father made your yoke heavy, but I will add thereto: my father chastised you with whips, but I *will chastise you* with scorpions.

---

¹ Heb. *words*.   ² Heb. *laded*.

---

28. *and out of all lands*] An addition to the words in Kings. The principal countries would no doubt be Arabia and Armenia—the former always famous for its excellent breed ; the latter mentioned in Ezekiel (xxvii. 14) as trading with horses in the fairs of Tyre.

29. *the book of Nathan* &c.] On the "books" here mentioned, see Introduction to Chronicles, p. 447 *n.* 2.

We hear nothing of Iddo in Kings ; but he is mentioned below twice (xii. 15,

xiii. 22). In the latter of these passages he is called not "the seer," but "the prophet." He seems to have been the author of three works :—(1) Visions against Jeroboam ; (2) A book of genealogies ; and (3) A commentary or history. According to some he was identical with Oded, the father of Azariah, who prophesied in the reign of Asa (see xv. 1 note).

X.–XI. 4. The narrative of Kings (marg. ref.) is repeated with only slight verbal differences.

15 So the king hearkened not unto the people : ^cfor the cause was of God, that the LORD might perform his word, which he spake by the ^dhand of Ahijah the Shilonite to Jeroboam the son of
16 Nebat. ¶And when all Israel *saw* that the king would not hearken unto them, the people answered the king, saying,

What portion have we in David ?
And *we have* none inheritance in the son of Jesse:
Every man to your tents, O Israel :
And now, David, see to thine own house.

17 So all Israel went to their tents. But *as for* the children of Israel that dwelt in the cities of Judah, Rehoboam reigned over
18 them. ¶Then king Rehoboam sent Hadoram that *was* over the tribute ; and the children of Israel stoned him with stones, that he died. But king Rehoboam ¹made speed to get him up to *his*
19 chariot, to flee to Jerusalem. ^eAnd Israel rebelled against the house of David unto this day.

CHAP. 11. AND ^awhen Rehoboam was come to Jerusalem, he gathered of the house of Judah and Benjamin an hundred and fourscore thousand chosen *men*, which were warriors, to fight against Israel, that he might bring the kingdom again to Reho-
2 boam. But the word of the LORD came ^bto Shemaiah the man
3 of God, saying, Speak unto Rehoboam the son of Solomon, king of Judah, and to all Israel in Judah and Benjamin, saying,
4 Thus saith the LORD, Ye shall not go up, nor fight against your brethren : return every man to his house : for this thing is done of me. And they obeyed the words of the LORD, and returned
5 from going against Jeroboam. ¶And Rehoboam dwelt in Jeru-
6 salem, and built cities for defence in Judah. He built even
7 Beth-lehem, and Etam, and Tekoa, and Beth-zur, and Shoco,
8, 9 and Adullam, and Gath, and Mareshah, and Ziph, and Ado-
10 raim, and Lachish, and Azekah, and Zorah, and Aijalon, and Hebron, which *are* in Judah and in Benjamin fenced cities.
11 And he fortified the strong holds, and put captains in them,
12 and store of victual, and of oil and wine. And in every several city *he put* shields and spears, and made them exceeding strong,
13 having Judah and Benjamin on his side. ¶And the priests and the Levites that *were* in all Israel ²resorted to him out of all their
14 coasts. For the Levites left ^ctheir suburbs and their possession, and came to Judah and Jerusalem : for ^dJeroboam and his sons

Margin references:
^c 1 Sam. 2. 25.
1 Kin. 12. 15, 24.
^d 1 Kin. 11. 29.
^e 1 Kin. 12. 19.
^a 1 Kin. 12. 21, &c.
^b ch. 12. 5.
^c Num. 35. 2.
^d ch. 13. 9.

¹ Heb. *strengthened himself.*   ² Heb. *presented themselves to him.*

---

5. Rehoboam was between two dangers : on the north he might be attacked by Jeroboam, on the south by Jeroboam's ally, Egypt. From this side was the greater peril, and therefore out of the fifteen cities fortified, all but three were on the southern or western frontier, where Egypt would be most likely to attack.

6, 7. See Josh. xv., notes to *vv.* 33–36, 48–51, 58, 59.

For Adullam see 1 Sam. xxii. 1 note. It was in the near neighbourhood of Socoh (Josh. xv. 35) ; but its site cannot be actually fixed. It was a place of great antiquity (Gen. xxxviii. 1).

8. For Gath, see Josh. xiii. 3 note. Its native king, Achish (1 K. ii. 39), is to be regarded, not as an independent monarch, but as one of the many vassal-kings over

whom Solomon reigned (ix. 23). For Mareshah, see Josh. xv. 44 ; for Ziph, do. *v.* 55.

9, 10. The site of Adoraim is uncertain. For Lachish, see Josh. x. 3 ; Azekah, do. *v.* 10 ; Zorah, do. xv. 33 ; Aijalon, do. x. 12 ; Hebron, do. xiv. 15. No one of the cities was really within the limits of the tribe of Benjamin. The writer uses the phrase "Judah and Benjamin " merely as the common designation of the southern kingdom (cp. *vv.* 12 and 23).

14. Jeroboam probably confiscated the Levitical lands for the benefit of this new priesthood. Under these circumstances the priests and Levites emigrated in large numbers to the southern kingdom ; an act which was followed by a general emigration of the more pious Israelites (*v.* 16).

* 1 Kin.12.31.
& 13. 33.
& 14. 9.
Hos. 13. 2.
f 1 Cor.10.20.
g 1 Kin.12.28.
h See ch.
15. 9.
& 30. 11, 18.
i ch. 12. 1.

had cast them off from executing the priest's office unto the
15 LORD : *and he ordained him priests for the high places, and for
16 f the devils, and for g the calves which he had made.   h And after
them out of all the tribes of Israel such as set their hearts to
seek the LORD God of Israel came to Jerusalem, to sacrifice
17 unto the LORD God of their fathers.   So they i strengthened the
kingdom of Judah, and made Rehoboam the son of Solomon
strong, three years : for three years they walked in the way of
18 David and Solomon.   ¶ And Rehoboam took him Mahalath the
daughter of Jerimoth the son of David to wife, and Abihail the
19 daughter of Eliab the son of Jesse ; which bare him children ;
20 Jeush, and Shamariah, and Zaham.   And after her he took

k 1 Kin. 15.
2. She is
called Mi-
chaiah the
daughter of
Uriel,
ch. 13. 2.
l See Deut.
21.15, 16,17.

k Maachah the daughter of Absalom ; which bare him Abijah,
21 and Attai, and Ziza, and Shelomith.   And Rehoboam loved
Maachah the daughter of Absalom above all his wives and his
concubines : (for he took eighteen wives, and threescore concubines ; and begat twenty and eight sons, and threescore daugh-
22 ters.)   And Rehoboam l made Abijah the son of Maachah the
chief, to be ruler among his brethren : for he thought to make
23 him king.   And he dealt wisely, and dispersed of all his children throughout all the countries of Judah and Benjamin, unto
every fenced city : and he gave them victual in abundance. And
he desired [1] many wives.

a ch. 11. 17.
b 1 Kin. 14.
22, 23, 24.
c 1 Kin. 14.
24, 25.

CHAP. 12. AND a it came to pass, when Rehoboam had established
the kingdom, and had strengthened himself, b he forsook the law
2 of the LORD, and all Israel with him.   c And it came to pass, that
in the fifth year of king Rehoboam Shishak king of Egypt came
up against Jerusalem, because they had transgressed against the
3 LORD, with twelve hundred chariots, and threescore thousand
horsemen : and the people were without number that came with

[1] Heb. a multitude of wives.

---

15. the high places] i.e. the two sanctuaries
at Dan and Bethel.
   for the devils] Lit. "for the goats :" probably the word is used (as in Lev. xvii. 7)
for objects of idolatrous worship generally.
   17. three years] i.e. during the first three
years of Rehoboam's reign.   In the fourth
year an apostasy took place, which neutral-
ised all the advantages of the immigration
(marg. ref.).   In the fifth the apostasy was
punished by the invasion and success of
Shishak (xii. 2).
   18. This is probably an extract from the
"genealogies" of Iddo (xii. 15).
   As Jerimoth is not mentioned among the
legitimate sons of David (1 Chr. iii. 1-8,
xiv. 4-7), he must have been the child of a
concubine.
   Abihail was probably the "grand-daughter," not "daughter," of Eliab (1 Sam. xvi.
6, xvii. 13 ; 1 Chr. ii. 13).
   20. Maachah the daughter of Absalom]
Rather, "grand-daughter" (1 K. xv. 2
note).
   22. Jeush was probably the eldest of Rehoboam's sons, and should naturally and
according to the provisions of the Law
Deut. xxi. 15-17) have been his heir.   But
Rehoboam's affection for Maachah led him
to transgress the Law.

23. Rehoboam's wisdom was shown—(1)
In dispersing his other sons instead of allowing them to remain together in Jerusalem, where they might have joined in a plot
against Abijah, as Adonijah and his brothers
had done against Solomon (1 K. i. 5-10) ; (2)
In giving his sons positions which might well
content them and prevent them from being
jealous of Abijah.
   he desired many wives] [Cp. v. 21].   Some
prefer to connect the words with the preceding words.   If so, they denote another
point in which Rehoboam was careful to
please his sons.
   XII. This chapter runs parallel with
Kings (marg. ref.), but considerably en-
larges the narrative.
   1. all Israel with him] i.e. "all Judah and
Benjamin"—all the Israelites of those two
tribes.
   2. Shishak...came up...because they had
transgressed]   The writer speaks from a
divine, not a human, point of view.   Shishak's motive in coming up was to help
Jeroboam, and to extend his own influence.
   3. twelve hundred chariots] This number
is not unusual (cp. Ex. xiv. 7 ; 1 K. x. 26).
Benhadad brought 1200 chariots into the
field against Shalmaneser II. ; and Ahab had

him out of Egypt; [d]the Lubims, the Sukkiims, and the Ethi-
4 opians. And he took the fenced cities which *pertained* to Judah,
5 and came to Jerusalem. ¶ Then came [e]Shemaiah the prophet
to Rehoboam, and *to* the princes of Judah, that were gathered
together to Jerusalem because of Shishak, and said unto them,
Thus saith the LORD, [f]Ye have forsaken me, and therefore have
6 I also left you in the hand of Shishak. Whereupon the princes
of Israel and the king [v]humbled themselves; and they said,
7 [h]The LORD *is* righteous. And when the LORD saw that they
humbled themselves, [i]the word of the LORD came to Shemaiah,
saying, They have humbled themselves; *therefore* I will not
destroy them, but I will grant them [1]some deliverance; and my
wrath shall not be poured out upon Jerusalem by the hand of
8 Shishak. Nevertheless [k]they shall be his servants; that they
may know [l]my service, and the service of the kingdoms of the
9 countries. ¶ [m]So Shishak king of Egypt came up against Jerusalem, and took away the treasures of the house of the LORD,
and the treasures of the king's house; he took all: he carried
10 away also the shields of gold which Solomon had [n]made. Instead
of which king Rehoboam made shields of brass, and committed
them [o]to the hands of the chief of the guard, that kept the
11 entrance of the king's house. And when the king entered into
the house of the LORD, the guard came and fetched them, and
12 brought them again into the guard chamber. And when he
humbled himself, the wrath of the LORD turned from him, that
he would not destroy *him* altogether : [2]and also in Judah things
13 went well. ¶ So king Rehoboam strengthened himself in Jerusalem, and reigned : for [p]Rehoboam *was* one and forty years
old when he began to reign, and he reigned seventeen years in
Jerusalem, [q]the city which the LORD had chosen out of all the
tribes of Israel, to put his name there. And his mother's name
14 *was* Naamah an Ammonitess. And he did evil, because he
15 [3]prepared not his heart to seek the LORD. ¶ Now the acts of
Rehoboam, first and last, *are* they not written in the [4]book of
Shemaiah, the prophet, [r]and of Iddo the seer concerning genealogies ? [s]And *there were* wars between Rehoboam and Jero-

Marginal references:
[d] ch. 16. 8.
[e] ch. 11. 2.
[f] ch. 15. 2.
[v] Jam. 4. 10.
[h] Ex. 9. 27.
[i] 1 Kin. 21.
28, 29.
[k] See Isai.
26. 13.
[l] Deut. 28.
47, 48.
[m] 1 Kin. 14.
25, 26.
[n] 1 Kin. 10.
16, 17.
ch. 9. 15, 16.
[o] 2Sam.8.18.
[p]1Kin.14.21.
[q] ch. 6. 6.
[r] ch. 9. 29.
& 13. 22.
[s] 1Kin.14.30.

---

[1] Or, *a little while.*
[2] Or, *and yet in Judah there*
were good things: See
Gen. 18. 24. & 1 Kin. 14.
13. ch. 19. 3.
[3] Or, *fixed.*
[4] Heb. *words.*

---

at the same time a force of 2000 chariots
(cp. 1 K. xx. 1 note).

The Lubims or "Libyans" (Dan. xi. 43),
were a people of Africa, distinct from the
Egyptians and the Ethiopians dwelling in
their immediate neighbourhood. They were
called *Ribu* or *Libu* by the Egyptians. See
Gen. x. 13.

Sukkiims] This name does not occur elsewhere. The LXX., who rendered the word
"Troglodytes," regarded the Sukkiim probably as the "cave-dwellers" along the
western shore of the Red Sea ; but the conjecture that the word means "tent-dwel-
lers" is plausible, and would point rather
to a tribe of Arabs (Scenitæ).

4. See 1 K. xiv. 25 note.

6. *they said, The* LORD *is righteous*] *i.e.*
they acknowledged the justice of the sentence
which had gone forth against them (*v.* 5).

7. Cp. the repentance of Ahab (marg.
ref.) and that of the Ninevites (Jonah iii.
5-10), which produced similar revocations
of divine decrees that had been pronounced
by the mouth of a Prophet.

some deliverance] Rather, "deliverance
for a short space" (see marg.). Because of
the repentance, the threat of *immediate* destruction was withdrawn ; but the menace was
still left impending, that the people might be
the more moved to contrition and amend-
ment.

8. *that they may know my service, and the
service of the kingdom*] *i.e.* that they may
contrast the light burthen of the theocracy
with the heavy yoke of a foreign monarch.

14. *he prepared not his heart, &c.*] See
margin. Rehoboam's sin was want of earnestness and consistency.

16 boam continually. And Rehoboam slept with his fathers, and was buried in the city of David: and *t*Abijah his son reigned in his stead.

CHAP. 13. NOW *a*in the eighteenth year of king Jeroboam began 2 Abijah to reign over Judah. He reigned three years in Jerusalem. His mother's name also *was* *b*Michaiah the daughter of Uriel of Gibeah. ¶And there was war between Abijah and 3 Jeroboam. And Abijah [1]set the battle in array with an army of valiant men of war, *even* four hundred thousand chosen men : Jeroboam also set the battle in array against him with eight hundred thousand chosen men, *being* mighty men of valour.

4 ¶And Abijah stood up upon mount *c*Zemaraim, which *is* in mount Ephraim, and said, Hear me, thou Jeroboam, and all 5 Israel; ought ye not to know that the LORD God of Israel *d*gave the kingdom over Israel to David for ever, *even* to him and to 6 his sons *e*by a covenant of salt? Yet Jeroboam the son of Nebat, the servant of Solomon the son of David, is risen up, and hath 7 *f*rebelled against his lord. And there are gathered unto him *g*vain men, the children of Belial, and have strengthened themselves against Rehoboam the son of Solomon, when Rehoboam was young and tenderhearted, and could not withstand them. 8 And now ye think to withstand the kingdom of the LORD in the hand of the sons of David ; and ye *be* a great multitude, and there are with you golden calves, which Jeroboam *h*made you for 9 gods. *i*Have ye not cast out the priests of the LORD, the sons of Aaron, and the Levites, and have made you priests after the manner of the nations of *other* lands? *k*so that whosoever cometh [2]to consecrate himself with a young bullock and seven rams, 10 *the same* may be a priest of *them that are* no gods. But as for us, the LORD *is* our God, and we have not forsaken him ; and the priests, which minister unto the LORD, *are* the sons of Aaron, 11 and the Levites *wait* upon *their* business : *l*and they burn unto the LORD every morning and every evening burnt sacrifices and sweet incense : the *m*shewbread also *set they in order* upon the pure table ; and the candlestick of gold with the lamps thereof, *n*to burn every evening : for we keep the charge of the 12 LORD our God ; but ye have forsaken him. And, behold, God himself *is* with us for *our* captain, *o*and his priests with sounding trumpets to cry alarm against you. O children of Israel, *p*fight ye not against the LORD God of your fathers; for ye shall

[1] Heb. *bound together.*   [2] Heb. *to fill his hand:* See Exod. 29. 1.   Lev. 8. 2.

XIII. The history of Abijah's reign is here related far more fully than in Kings (marg. ref.), especially as regards his war with Jeroboam.

2. See 1 K. xv. 2 note.

3. It has been proposed to change the numbers, here and in *v.* 17, into 40,000, 80,000, and 50,000 respectively — partly because these smaller numbers are found in many early editions of the Vulgate, but mainly because the larger ones are thought to be incredible. The numbers accord well, however, with the census of the people taken in the reign of David (1 Chr. xxi. 5), joined to the fact which the writer has related (xi. 13–17), of a considerable subsequent emigration from the northern kingdom into the southern one.

The total adult male population at the time of the census was 1,570,000. The total of the fighting men now is 1,200,000. This would allow for the aged and infirm 370,000, or nearly a fourth of the whole. And in *v.* 17, our author may be understood to mean that this was the entire Israelite loss in the course of the war, which probably continued through the whole reign of Abijah.

9. *seven rams*] "A bullock and *two* rams" was the offering which God had required at the original consecration of the sons of Aaron (Ex. xxix. 1 ; Lev. viii. 2). Jeroboam, for reasons of his own, enlarged the sacrifice, and required it at the consecration of every priest.

Marginal notes (left column):

t 1Kin.14.31, *Abijam.*

a 1 Kin. 15. 1, &c.

b See ch. 11. 20.

c Josh.18.22.

d 2 Sam. 7. 12, 13, 16.

e Num.18.19.

f 1Kin.11.26. & 12. 20. *g* Judg. 9. 4.

h 1Kin.12.28. & 14. 9. Hos. 8. 6. *i* ch.11.14,15. *k* Ex. 29. 35.

l ch. 2. 4.

m Lev. 24. 6.

n Ex. 27. 20, 21. Lev. 24. 2, 3. *o* Num. 10. 8.

p Acts 5. 39.

13 not prosper. ¶ But Jeroboam caused an ambushment to come
about behind them: so they were before Judah, and the ambush-
14 ment *was* behind them. And when Judah looked back, behold,
the battle *was* before and behind: and they cried unto the LORD,
15 and the priests sounded with the trumpets. Then the men of
Judah gave a shout: and as the men of Judah shouted, it came
to pass, that God ⁹smote Jeroboam and all Israel before Abijah   *q* ch. 14. 12.
16 and Judah. And the children of Israel fled before Judah: and
17 God delivered them into their hand. And Abijah and his people
slew them with a great slaughter: so there fell down slain of
18 Israel five hundred thousand chosen men. ¶ Thus the children
of Israel were brought under at that time, and the children of
Judah prevailed, ʳbecause they relied upon the LORD God of   *r* 1Chr. 5. 20.
19 their fathers. And Abijah pursued after Jeroboam, and took   Ps. 22. 5.
cities from him, Beth-el with the towns thereof, and Jeshanah
with the towns thereof, and ˢEphrain with the towns thereof.   *s* Josh. 15. 9.
20 Neither did Jeroboam recover strength again in the days of
21 Abijah: and the LORD ᵗstruck him, and ᵘhe died. But Abijah   *t* 1Sam.25.39.
waxed mighty, and married fourteen wives, and begat twenty   *u* 1Kin.14.20.
22 and two sons, and sixteen daughters. ¶ And the rest of the acts
of Abijah, and his ways, and his sayings, *are* written in the
¹story of the prophet ˣIddo.   *x* ch. 12. 15.

CHAP. 14. SO Abijah slept with his fathers, and they buried him
in the city of David: and ᵃAsa his son reigned in his stead. In   *a* 1 Kin. 15.
2 his days the land was quiet ten years. And Asa did *that which*   8, &c.
3 *was* good and right in the eyes of the LORD his God: for he took
away the altars of the strange *gods*, and ᵇthe high places, and   *b* See
4 ᶜbrake down the ²images, ᵈand cut down the groves: and com-   1 Kin. 15. 14.
manded Judah to seek the LORD God of their fathers, and to do   ch. 15. 17.
5 the law and the commandment. Also he took away out of all   *c* Ex. 34. 13.
the cities of Judah the high places and the ³images: and the   *d* 1 Kin. 11.7.
6 kingdom was quiet before him. ¶ And he built fenced cities in
Judah: for the land had rest, and he had no war in those years;
7 because the LORD had given him rest. Therefore he said unto
Judah, Let us build these cities, and make about *them* walls,
and towers, gates, and bars, *while* the land *is* yet before us;

---

¹ Or, *commentary*.   ² Heb. *statues*.   ³ Heb. *sun images*.

---

17. *slain*] The word means strictly
"pierced," and will include both the killed
and the wounded. It is translated
"wounded" in Lam. ii. 12.

18. *brought under*] "Humbled" or "defeated," not reduced to subjection.

19. Jeshanah is probably identical with
the "Isanas" of Josephus, where a battle
took place in the war between Antigonus
and Herod; but its situation cannot be
fixed. For Ephrain, see Josh. xviii. 23
note.

20. Jeroboam's death was a judgment
upon him for his sins. Chronologically
speaking, his death is here out of place, for
he outlived Abijah at least two years (cp.
marg. ref. and 1 K. xv. 9); but the writer,
not intending to recur to his history, is
naturally led to carry it on to its termination.

XIV. 1. *Asa his son reigned*] If Rehoboam was (1 K. xii. 8 note) not more than

21 at his accession, Asa, when he mounted
the throne, must have been a mere boy, not
more than 10 or 11.

the land was quiet ten years] The great
blow struck by Abijah (xiii. 15-19), his alliance with Syria (1 K. xv. 19), and the
rapid succession of sovereigns in Israel
during the earlier part of Asa's reign (do.
vv. 25-33), would naturally prevent disturbance on the part of the northern kingdom.
The tender age of Asa himself would be a
bar to warlike enterprises on the part of
Judah.

5. *images*] See marg., *sun-images;* and
Lev. xxvi. 30 note.

7. *the land is yet before us*] *i.e.* "unoccu-
pied by an enemy"—"the land is open to
us to go where we please." Cp. Gen. xiii.
9. The fortification of the strongholds
would be an act of rebellion against Egypt,
and it might be expected that the Egyptians
would endeavour to put a stop to it.

because we have sought the LORD our God, we have sought *him*, and he hath given us rest on every side. So they built and 8 prospered. And Asa had an army *of men* that bare targets and spears, out of Judah three hundred thousand; and out of Benjamin, that bare shields and drew bows, two hundred and four-

e ch. 16. 8.

9 score thousand : all these *were* mighty men of valour. ¶ *e* And there came out against them Zerah the Ethiopian with an host of a thousand thousand, and three hundred chariots; and came

f Josh. 15.44.

10 unto *f* Mareshah. Then Asa went out against him, and they set the battle in array in the valley of Zephathah at Mareshah.

g Ex. 14. 10.
ch. 13. 14.
Ps. 22. 5.
h 1 Sam.14.6.
i 1 Sam.17.45.
Prov. 18. 10.

11 And Asa *g* cried unto the LORD his God, and said, LORD, *it is* *h* nothing with thee to help, whether with many, or with them that have no power: help us, O LORD our God; for we rest on thee, and *i* in thy name we go against this multitude. O LORD,

12 thou *art* our God; let not *1* man prevail against thee. So the

k ch. 13. 15.

LORD *k* smote the Ethiopians before Asa, and before Judah; and

13 the Ethiopians fled. And Asa and the people that *were* with

l Gen. 10. 19.
& 20. 1.

him pursued them unto *l* Gerar: and the Ethiopians were overthrown, that they could not recover themselves; for they were *2* destroyed before the LORD, and before his host; and they

14 carried away very much spoil. And they smote all the cities

m Gen. 35. 5.
ch. 17. 10.

round about Gerar; for *m* the fear of the LORD came upon them : and they spoiled all the cities; for there was exceeding

15 much spoil in them. They smote also the tents of cattle, and carried away sheep and camels in abundance, and returned to Jerusalem.

1 Or, *mortal man.*   *2* Heb. *broken.*

---

8. The men of Judah served as heavy-armed troops, while the Benjamites were light-armed. Their numbers accord well with those of xiii. 3. As the boundaries of Judah had been enlarged (xiii. 19), and as for ten years at least there had been no war (xiv. 1), the effective force had naturally increased. It was 400,000; it is now 580,000.

9. Zerah the Ethiopian is probably Usarken (Osorkon) II., the third king of Egypt after Shishak, according to the Egyptian monuments. Osorkon II. may have been by birth an Ethiopian, for he was the son-in-law, not the son, of the preceding monarch, and reigned in right of his wife. The object of the expedition would be to bring Judæa once more under the Egyptian yoke.

an host of a thousand thousand] This is the largest collected army of which we hear in Scripture ; but it does not exceed the known numbers of other Oriental armies in ancient times. Darius Codomannus brought into the field at Arbela a force of 1,040,000 ; Xerxes crossed into Greece with certainly above a million of combatants.

10. The " valley of Zephathah " — not elsewhere mentioned—is probably the broad Wady which opens out from Mareshah (marg. ref.) in a north-westerly direction, leading into the great Philistine plain. Zerah, on the advance of Asa, drew off into the wider space of the Wady, where he could use his horsemen and chariots.

11. *it is nothing &c.*] *i.e.* "Thou canst as easily help the weak as the strong."

12. The defeat of Zerah is one of the most remarkable events in the history of the Jews. On no other occasion did they meet in the field and overcome the forces of either of the two great monarchies between which they were placed. It was seldom that they ventured to resist, unless behind walls. Shishak, Sennacherib, Esarhaddon, Nebuchadnezzar, were either unopposed or only opposed in this way. On the one other occasion on which they took the field—under Josiah against Necho—their boldness issued in a most disastrous defeat (2 Chr. xxxv. 20-24). Now, however, under Asa, they appear to have gained a complete victory over Egypt. The results which followed were most striking. The Southern power could not rally from the blow, and, for above three centuries made no further effort in this direction. Assyria, growing in strength, finally, under Sargon and Sennacherib, penetrated to Egypt itself. All fear of Egypt as an aggressive power ceased ; and the Israelites learnt instead to lean upon the Pharaohs for support (2 K. xvii. 4, xviii. 21; Isai. xxx. 2-4, &c.). Friendly ties alone connected the two countries : and it was not till B.C. 609 that an Egyptian force again entered Palestine with a hostile intention.

14. *then smote all the cities round about Gerar*] The Philistines of these parts had,

CHAP. **15.** AND ^athe Spirit of God came upon Azariah the son of
2 Oded: and he went out ¹to meet Asa, and said unto him, Hear ye
me, Asa, and all Judah and Benjamin; ^bThe LORD is with you,
while ye be with him; and ^cif ye seek him, he will be found of
3 you; but ^dif ye forsake him, he will forsake you. Now ^efor a
long season Israel *hath been* without the true God, and without
4 ^fa teaching priest, and without law. But ^gwhen they in their
trouble did turn unto the LORD God of Israel, and sought him,
5 he was found of them. And ^hin those times *there was* no peace
to him that went out, nor to him that came in, but great vexa-
6 tions *were* upon all the inhabitants of the countries. ⁱAnd
nation was ²destroyed of nation, and city of city: for God did
7 vex them with all adversity. Be ye strong therefore, and let
not your hands be weak: for your work shall be rewarded.
8 ¶ And when Asa heard these words, and the prophecy of Oded
the prophet, he took courage, and put away the ³abominable
idols out of all the land of Judah and Benjamin, and out of the
cities ^kwhich he had taken from mount Ephraim, and renewed
the altar of the LORD, that *was* before the porch of the LORD.
9 And he gathered all Judah and Benjamin, and ^lthe strangers
with them out of Ephraim and Manasseh, and out of Simeon:
for they fell to him out of Israel in abundance, when they saw
10 that the LORD his God *was* with him. So they gathered themselves together at Jerusalem in the third month, in the fifteenth
11 year of the reign of Asa. ^mAnd they offered unto the LORD
⁴the same time, of ⁿthe spoil *which* they had brought, seven
12 hundred oxen and seven thousand sheep. And they ^oentered
into a covenant to seek the LORD God of their fathers with all
13 their heart and with all their soul; ^pthat whosoever would not
seek the LORD God of Israel ^qshould be put to death, whether
14 small or great, whether man or woman. And they sware unto
the LORD with a loud voice, and with shouting, and with trum-
15 pets, and with cornets. And all Judah rejoiced at the oath:

Reference column (right margin):
^a Num. 24. 2.
Judg. 3. 10.
ch. 20. 14.
& 24. 20.
^b Jam. 4. 8.
^c ver. 4, 15.
1 Chr. 28. 9.
ch. 33. 12. 13.
Jer. 29. 13.
Matt. 7. 7.
^d ch. 24. 20.
^e Hos. 3. 4
^f Lev. 10. 11.
^g Deut. 4. 29.
^h Judg. 5. 6.
ⁱ Matt. 24. 7.

^k ch. 13. 19.

^l ch. 11. 16.

^m ch. 14. 15.
ⁿ ch. 14. 13.
^o 2 Kin. 23 3.
ch. 34. 31.
Neh. 10. 29.
^p Ex. 22. 20.
^q Deut. 13.
5, 9, 15.

---

¹ Heb. *before Asa.*   ³ Heb. *abominations.*
² Heb. *beaten in pieces.*   ⁴ Heb. *in that day.*

---

it is probable, accompanied Zerah in his
expedition.

XV. **1.** Oded is by some identified with
Iddo, the prophet and historian of the two
preceding reigns. In the Hebrew the two
names differ very slightly.

3. "Israel" here is used generally for the
whole people of God; and the reference is
especially to the many apostasies in the days
of the Judges, which were followed by repentance and deliverance.

6. The allusion is probably to the de-
structions recorded in Judges ix. 45, xx. 33–
48.

8. Some versions have "the prophecy of
Azariah the son of Oded," which is perhaps
the true reading.

9. *strangers* &c.] *i.e.* "Israelites of the
tribes of Ephraim and Manasseh." The
separation of the two kingdoms had made
their Israelite brethren "strangers," or
"foreigners," to Judah.

10. *in the third month*] *i.e.* the month

Sivan (Esth. viii. 9), corresponding with our
June.

11. The prevalence of the number seven
in the religious system of the Jews has been
often noticed. Seven bullocks and seven
rams were a common offering (Num. xxix.
32; 1 Chr. xv. 26; 2 Chr. xxix. 21; Job
xlii. 8; Ezek. xlv. 23). In the larger sacrifices, however, it is seldom that we find the
number seven at all prominent (cp. xxx.
24; xxxv. 7–9; 1 K. viii. 63).

12. Solemn renewals of the original Covenant which God made with their fathers in
the wilderness (Ex. xxiv. 3–8) occur from
time to time in the history of the Jews,
following upon intervals of apostasy. This
renewal in the reign of Asa is the first on
record. The next falls three hundred years
later in the reign of Josiah. There is a
third in the time of Nehemiah (see marg.
reff.). On such occasions, the people bound
themselves by a solemn oath to observe all
the directions of the Law, and called down
God's curse upon them if they forsook it.

ʳ ver. 2.

ˢ 1 Kin. 15. 13.

ᵗ ch. 14. 3, 5.
1 Kin. 15. 14,
&c.

ᵃ 1 Kin. 15.
17, &c.
From the
rending of
the ten
tribes from
Judah, over
which Asa
was now
king.
ᵇ ch. 15. 9.

ᶜ 1 Kin. 16. 1.
ch. 19. 2.
ᵈ Isai. 31. 1.
Jer. 17. 5.
ᵉ ch. 14. 9.

for they had sworn with all their heart, and ʳsought him with their whole desire; and he was found of them: and the LORD 16 gave them rest round about. ¶ And also *concerning* ˢMaachah the ¹mother of Asa the king, he removed her from *being* queen, because she had made an ²idol in a grove: and Asa cut down her idol, and stamped *it*, and burnt *it* at the brook Kidron. 17 But ᵗthe high places were not taken away out of Israel: never- 18 theless the heart of Asa was perfect all his days. And he brought into the house of God the things that his father had dedicated, and that he himself had dedicated, silver, and gold, and vessels. 19 And there was no *more* war unto the five and thirtieth year of the reign of Asa.

CHAP. 16. IN the six and thirtieth year of the reign of Asa ᵃBaasha king of Israel came up against Judah, and built Ramah, ᵇto the intent that he might let none go out or come in to Asa king 2 of Judah. Then Asa brought out silver and gold out of the treasures of the house of the LORD and of the king's house, and sent to Ben-hadad king of Syria, that dwelt at ³Damascus, say- 3 ing, *There is* a league between me and thee, as *there was* between my father and thy father: behold, I have sent thee silver and gold; go, break thy league with Baasha king of Israel, that he 4 may depart from me. And Ben-hadad hearkened unto king Asa, and sent the captains of ⁴his armies against the cities of Israel; and they smote Ijon, and Dan, and Abel-maim, and all 5 the store cities of Naphtali. And it came to pass, when Baasha heard *it*, that he left off building of Ramah, and let his work 6 cease. Then Asa the king took all Judah; and they carried away the stones of Ramah, and the timber thereof, wherewith Baasha was building; and he built therewith Geba and Mizpah. 7 And at that time ᶜHanani the seer came to Asa king of Judah, and said unto him, ᵈBecause thou hast relied on the king of Syria, and not relied on the LORD thy God, therefore is the host 8 of the king of Syria escaped out of thine hand. Were not ᵉthe

---

¹ That is, *grandmother*,   ² Heb. *horror.*   ⁴ Heb. *which were his.*
   1 Kin. 15. 2, 10.   ³ Heb. *Darmesek.*

---

17. Comparing this verse with marg. reff., it would seem that in xiv. 3, 5 the intention and endeavours of the monarch are in the writer's mind, while here he is speaking of the practice of the people. However earnestly the most pious monarchs sought to root out the high-place worship, they failed of complete success. Cp. a similar discrepancy, to be similarly explained, in the history of Jehoshaphat (xvii. 6, and xx. 33).

the heart of Asa was perfect all his days] Not that Asa was sinless (see xvi. 2-10, 12); but that he was free from the sin of idolatry, and continued faithful to Jehovah all his life.

19. *the five and thirtieth year of the reign of Asa*] This cannot be reconciled with the chronology of Kings (1 K. xvi. 8): and the suggestion in the marg. implies the adoption of a mode of marking time unknown either to himself or any other Scriptural writer. It is supposed that the figures here and in xvi. 1 are corrupt, and that in both verses

"twentieth" should replace "thirtieth." The attack of Baasha would then have been made in the last year of Asa's reign; and ten years of peace would have followed Asa's victory over Zerah.

XVI. 1-6. This passage runs parallel with Kings (marg. ref.).

3. Cp. 1 K. xv. 19 note.

4. *Abel-maim*] Or, "Abel-beth-maachah" (1 K. xv. 20). It was one of the towns most exposed to attack when an invader entered Israel from the north, and was taken from Pekah by Tiglath-pileser (2 K. xv. 29).

store cities] See 1 K. ix. 19 note.

7-10. The rebuke of Hanani and his imprisonment by Asa, omitted by the writer of Kings, are among the most important of the additions to Asa's history for which we are indebted to the author of Chronicles.

7. *escaped out of thine hand*] Hanani means, "Hadst thou been faithful, and opposed in arms the joint host of Israel and Syria, instead of bribing the Syrian king to desert to thy side, the entire host would

Ethiopians and *f*the Lubims ¹a huge host, with very many chariots and horsemen? yet, because thou didst rely on the
9 LORD, he delivered them into thine hand. *g*For the eyes of the LORD run to and fro throughout the whole earth, ²to shew himself strong in the behalf of *them* whose heart *is* perfect toward him. Herein *h*thou hast done foolishly: therefore from hence-
10 forth *i*thou shalt have wars. Then Asa was wroth with the seer, and *k*put him in a prison house; for *he was* in a rage with him because of this *thing.* And Asa ³oppressed *some* of the
11 people the same time. ¶*l*And, behold, the acts of Asa, first and last, lo, they *are* written in the book cf the kings of Judah and
12 Israel. ¶And Asa in the thirty and ninth year of his reign was diseased in his feet, until his disease *was* exceeding *great:* yet in his disease he *m*sought not to the LORD, but to the physicians.
13 *n*And Asa slept with his fathers, and died in the one and fortieth
14 year of his reign. And they buried him in his own sepulchres, which he had ⁴made for himself in the city of David, and laid him in the bed which was filled *o*with sweet odours and divers kinds *of spices* prepared by the apothecaries' art: and they made *p*a very great burning for him.

CHAP. 17. AND *a*Jehoshaphat his son reigned in his stead, and
2 strengthened himself against Israel. And he placed forces in all the fenced cities of Judah, and set garrisons in the land of Judah, and in the cities of Ephraim, *b*which Asa his father had taken.
3 And the LORD was with Jehoshaphat, because he walked in the first ways ⁵of his father David, and sought not unto Baalim;
4 but sought to the LORD God of his father, and walked in his
5 commandments, and not after *c*the doings of Israel. Therefore the LORD stablished the kingdom in his hand; and all Judah *d*⁶brought to Jehoshaphat presents; *e*and he had riches and
6 honour in abundance. And his heart ⁷was lifted up in the ways

f ch. 12. 3.

g Job 34. 21.
Prov. 5. 21.
& 15. 3.
Jer. 16. 17.
& 32. 19.
Zech. 4. 10.
h 1 Sam. 13.
13.
i 1Kin.15.32.
k ch. 18. 26.
Jer. 20. 2.
Matt. 14. 3.
l 1 Kin.15.23.

m Jer. 17. 5.
n 1Kin.15.24.

o Gen. 50. 2.
Mark 16. 1.
John 19. 39,
40.
p ch. 21. 19.
Jer. 34. 5.
a 1Kin.15.24.

b ch. 15. 8.

c 1Kin.12.28.

d 1 Sam. 10,
27.
1 Kin. 10. 25.
e 1Kin.10.27.
ch. 18. 1.

---

¹ Heb. *in abundance.*
² Or. *strongly to hold with them, &c.*
³ Heb. *crushed.*
⁴ Heb. *digged.*
⁵ Or, *of his father,* and
of David.
⁶ Heb. *gave.*
⁷ That is, *was encouraged.*

---

have been delivered into thy hand, as was Zerah's. But now it is escaped from thee. Thou hast lost a glorious opportunity."

9. *from henceforth thou shalt have wars*] As peace had been the reward of Asa's earlier faith (xiv. 5, xv. 5), so his want of faith was now to be punished by a period of war and disturbance.

10. *in a prison house*] Or, "in the stocks." Cp. 1 K. xxii. 26, 27.

12. *yet in his disease he sought not* &c.] Rather, "and also in his disease he sought not." Not only in his war with Baasha, but also when attacked by illness, Asa placed undue reliance upon the aid of man.

14. The explanation of the plural—"sepulchres"—will be seen in 1 K. xiii. 30 note.

The burning of spices in honour of a king at his funeral was customary (cp. marg. reff.).

XVII. 1. Jehoshaphat ascended the throne in the fourth year of Ahab (1 K. xxii. 41), probably after that monarch had contracted his alliance with the royal family

of Sidon, and before he was engaged in war with Syria. It was thus not unnatural that Jehoshaphat should begin his reign by strengthening himself against a possible attack on the part of his northern neighbour.

3. *the first ways of his father David*] The LXX. and several Hebrew MSS. omit "David," which has probably crept in from the margin; for David's "first ways" are nowhere else contrasted with his later ways. The real meaning of the writer is, that Jehoshaphat followed the example set by his father Asa in his earlier years (xiv., xv.).

Baalim] On the plural form, see 1 K. xviii. 18 note.

4. *the doings of Israel*] i.e. the specially idolatrous doings of the time—the introduction and establishment of the worship of Baal and the groves.

5. *presents*] i.e. "free-will offerings," in addition to the regular taxes. See 1 Sam. x. 27.

6. *his heart was lifted up*] This expression generally occurs in a bad sense (Deut. viii. 14; 2 Chr. xxvi. 16; Ps. cxxxi. 1; Prov.

ƒ 1Kin.22 43.
ch. 15. 17.
& 19. 3.
& 20. 33.
ν ch. 15. 3.

h ch. 35. 3.
Neh. 8. 7.

i Gen. 35. 5.

k 2 Sam. 8. 2.

l Judg.5.2,9.

m ver. 2.

of the LORD: moreover ƒhe took away the high places and groves
7 out of Judah.   ¶ Also in the third year of his reign he sent to
his princes, even to Ben-hail, and to Obadiah, and to Zechariah, and
to Nethaneel, and to Michaiah, ν to teach in the cities of Judah.
8 And with them he sent Levites, even Shemaiah, and Nethaniah,
and Zebadiah, and Asahel, and Shemiramoth, and Jehonathan,
and Adonijah, and Tobijah, and Tob-adonijah, Levites; and
9 with them Elishama and Jehoram, priests. h And they taught
in Judah, and had the book of the law of the LORD with them,
and went about throughout all the cities of Judah, and taught
10 the people.   ¶ And i the fear of the LORD 1 fell upon all the
kingdoms of the lands that were round about Judah, so that they
11 made no war against Jehoshaphat.   Also some of the Philistines
k brought Jehoshaphat presents, and tribute silver; and the Arabians brought him flocks, seven thousand and seven hundred rams,
12 and seven thousand and seven hundred he goats.   And Jehoshaphat waxed great exceedingly; and he built in Judah 2 castles, and
13 cities of store.   And he had much business in the cities of Judah:
and the men of war, mighty men of valour, were in Jerusalem.
14 ¶ And these are the numbers of them according to the house of
their fathers : Of Judah, the captains of thousands; Adnah the
chief, and with him mighty men of valour three hundred thou-
15 sand.   And 3 next to him was Jehohanan the captain, and with
16 him two hundred and fourscore thousand.   And next him was
Amasiah the son of Zichri, l who willingly offered himself unto
the LORD ; and with him two hundred thousand mighty men of
17 valour.   And of Benjamin ; Eliada a mighty man of valour,
and with him armed men with bow and shield two hundred thou-
18 sand.   And next him was Jehozabad, and with him an hundred
19 and fourscore thousand ready prepared for the war.   These
waited on the king, beside m those whom the king put in the fenced
cities throughout all Judah.

1 Heb. was.   2 Or, palaces.   3 Heb. at his hand.

---

xviii. 12); but here it must be taken differently. The margin "was encouraged" expresses fairly the true meaning. He first
began by setting an example of faithfulness
to Jehovah. He then proceeded to use his
best endeavours to extirpate idolatry.
  he took away the high places] Cp. xx. 33,
and see xv. 17 note.
  7. The princes were not sent as teachers
themselves, but had the duty committed to
them of seeing that the people were taught.
The actual teachers were the priests and
Levites of v. 8.
  9. There is no reasonable doubt that this
"book of the law" was the Pentateuch—
nearly, if not quite, in the shape in which
we now have it. Copies of the whole Law
were, no doubt, scarce ; and therefore Jehoshaphat's commission took care to carry a
copy with them.
  11. some of the Philistines brought Jehoshaphat presents] i.e. "some of the Philistines were among his tributaries." Cp. 2
Sam. viii. 2 ; 1 K. iv. 21.
  tribute silver] Or, "much silver"—lit.
"silver of burthen."

the Arabians] The Arab tribes who bordered Judæa to the south and the south-
east paid Jehoshaphat a fixed tribute in
kind. Cp. 2 K. iii. 4 note.
  14. the captains of thousands; Adnah the
chief] Lit. "princes of thousands, Adnah
the prince." The writer does not mean that
Adnah (or Johohanan, v. 15) was in any
way superior to the other "princes," but
only that he was one of them.
  three hundred thousand] This number, and
those which follow in vv. 15-18, have been
with good reason regarded as corrupt by
most critics. For—(1) They imply a mini-
mum population of 1480 to the square mile,
which is more than three times greater than
that of any country in the known world.
(2) They produce a total just double that of
the next largest estimate of the military
force of Judah, the 580,000 of xiv. 8. (3)
They are professedly a statement, not of the
whole military force, but of the force maintained at Jerusalem (v. 13; cp. v. 19). It is
probable that the original numbers have
been lost, and that the loss was supplied by
a scribe, who took xiv. 8 as his basis.

CHAP. 18. NOW Jehoshaphat *a* had riches and honour in abund-
2 ance, and *b* joined affinity with Ahab. *c* And ¹after *certain* years
he went down to Ahab to Samaria. And Ahab killed sheep and
oxen for him in abundance, and for the people that *he had* with
him, and persuaded him to go up *with him* to Ramoth-gilead.
3 And Ahab king of Israel said unto Jehoshaphat king of Judah,
Wilt thou go with me to Ramoth-gilead ? And he answered
him, I *am* as thou *art*, and my people as thy people; and *we will*
4 *be* with thee in the war. ¶ And Jehoshaphat said unto the king
of Israel, *d* Enquire, I pray thee, at the word of the LORD to day.
5 Therefore the king of Israel gathered together of prophets four
hundred men, and said unto them, Shall we go to Ramoth-gilead
to battle, or shall I forbear ? And they said, Go up; for God will
6 deliver *it* into the king's hand. But Jehoshaphat said, *Is there*
not here a prophet of the LORD ²besides, that we might enquire
7 of him ? And the king of Israel said unto Jehoshaphat, *There
is* yet one man, by whom we may enquire of the LORD : but I
hate him ; for he never prophesied good unto me, but always
evil: the same *is* Micaiah the son of Imla. And Jehoshaphat said,
8 Let not the king say so. And the king of Israel called for one
of his ³officers, and said, ⁴Fetch quickly Micaiah the son of Imla.
9 ¶ And the king of Israel and Jehoshaphat king of Judah sat
either of them on his throne, clothed in *their* robes, and they
sat in a ⁵void place at the entering in of the gate of Samaria ;
10 and all the prophets prophesied before him. And Zedekiah
the son of Chenaanah had made him horns of iron, and said,
Thus saith the LORD, With these thou shalt push Syria until
11 ⁶they be consumed. And all the prophets prophesied so, saying,
Go up to Ramoth-gilead, and prosper: for the LORD shall deliver
12 *it* into the hand of the king. ¶ And the messenger that went
to call Micaiah spake to him, saying, Behold, the words of the
prophets *declare* good to the king ⁷with one assent ; let thy word
therefore, I pray thee, be like one of their's, and speak thou
13 good. And Micaiah said, *As* the LORD liveth, *e* even what my God
14 saith, that will I speak. And when he was come to the king,
the king said unto him, Micaiah, shall we go to Ramoth-gilead
to battle, or shall I forbear? And he said, Go ye up, and prosper,
15 and they shall be delivered into your hand. And the king said
to him, How many times shall I adjure thee that thou say
16 nothing but the truth to me in the name of the LORD ? ˙Then
he said, I did see all Israel scattered upon the mountains, as
sheep that have no shepherd: and the LORD said, These have
no master ; let them return *therefore* every man to his house
17 in peace. And the king of Israel said to Jehoshaphat, Did I
not tell thee *that* he would not prophesy good unto me, ⁸but
18 evil ? Again he said, Therefore hear the word of the LORD ; I
saw the LORD sitting upon his throne, and all the host of heaven
19 standing on his right hand and *on* his left. And the LORD said,
Who shall entice Ahab king of Israel, that he may go up and
fall at Ramoth-gilead ? And one spake saying after this manner,

a ch. 17. 5.
b 2 Kin. 8.18.
c 1 Kin. 22.
2, &c.

d 1 Sam. 23.
2, 4, 9.
2 Sam. 2. 1.

e Num. 22.
18, 20, 35.
& 23. 12, 26.
& 24. 13.
1 Kin. 22. 14.

---

¹ Heb. *at the end of years.*
² Heb. *yet,* or, *more.*
³ Or, *eunuchs.*
⁴ Heb. *Hasten.*
⁵ Or, *floor.*
⁶ Heb. thou *consume them.*
⁷ Heb. *with one mouth.*
⁸ Or, *but for evil?*

XVIII. The present chapter runs parallel with Kings, which it closely follows, only
adding a few touches.
  2. *after certain years*] In Jehoshaphat's

seventeenth year (1 K. xxii. 51), not less
than eight years after the marriage (marg.
ref. note).

20 and another saying after that manner. Then there came out
a _f_ spirit, and stood before the LORD, and said, I will entice him.
21 And the LORD said unto him, Wherewith? And he said, I will
go out, and be a lying spirit in the mouth of all his prophets.
And _the LORD_ said, Thou shalt entice _him_, and thou shalt also
22 prevail: go out, and do _even_ so. Now therefore, behold, _g_ the
LORD hath put a lying spirit in the mouth of these thy prophets,
23 and the LORD hath spoken evil against thee. ¶ Then Zedekiah
the son of Chenaanah came near, and _h_ smote Micaiah upon the
cheek, and said, Which way went the Spirit of the LORD from
24 me to speak unto thee? And Micaiah said, Behold, thou shalt
see on that day when thou shalt go ¹into ²an inner chamber to
25 hide thyself. Then the king of Israel said, Take ye Micaiah,
and carry him back to Amon the governor of the city, and to
26 Joash the king's son; and say, Thus saith the king, _i_ Put this
fellow in the prison, and feed him with bread of affliction and
27 with water of affliction, until I return in peace. And Micaiah
said, If thou certainly return in peace, _then_ hath not the LORD
28 spoken by me. And he said, Hearken, all ye people. ¶ So
the king of Israel and Jehoshaphat the king of Judah went
29 up to Ramoth-gilead. And the king of Israel said unto Jehoshaphat, I will disguise myself, and will go to the battle; but
put thou on thy robes. So the king of Israel disguised himself;
30 and they went to the battle. Now the king of Syria had commanded the captains of the chariots that _were_ with him, saying,
Fight ye not with small or great, save only with the king of
31 Israel. And it came to pass, when the captains of the chariots
saw Jehoshaphat, that they said, It _is_ the king of Israel. Therefore they compassed about him to fight: but Jehoshaphat cried
out, and the LORD helped him; and God moved them _to depart_
32 from him. For it came to pass, that, when the captains of the
chariots perceived that it was not the king of Israel, they turned
33 back again ³from pursuing him. And a _certain_ man drew a
bow ⁴at a venture, and smote the king of Israel ⁵between the
joints of the harness: therefore he said to his chariot man,
Turn thine hand, that thou mayest carry me out of the host;
34 for I am ⁶wounded. And the battle increased that day: howbeit
the king of Israel stayed _himself_ up in _his_ chariot against the
Syrians until the even: and about the time of the sun going down
he died.

CHAP. 19. AND Jehoshaphat the king of Judah returned to his house
2 in peace to Jerusalem. And Jehu the son of Hanani _a_ the seer

_f_ Job 1. 6.

_g_ Job 12. 16.
Isai. 19. 14.
Ezek. 14. 9.

_h_ Jer. 20. 2.
Mark 14. 65.
Acts 23. 2.

_i_ ch. 16. 10.

_a_ 1 Sam. 9. 9.

¹ Or, _from chamber to chamber._
² Heb. _a chamber in a chamber._
³ Heb. _from after him._
⁴ Heb. _in his simplicity._
⁵ Heb. _between the joints and_
between the breast plate.
⁶ Heb. _made sick._

---

31. _and the LORD helped him_, &c.] There
is nothing correspondent to this passage in
Kings. It is a pious reflection on the part
of the author, who traces all deliverance to
its real divine source.

XIX. This chapter is entirely additional
to Kings, and of great interest. It deals
with three matters only, (1) The rebuke
addressed to Jehoshaphat by the Prophet
Jehu (_vv._ 1-3), (2) Jehoshaphat's religious
reformation (_v._ 4), and (3) his reform of the
judicial system (_vv._ 5-11).

1. _Jehoshaphat...returned to his house in
peace_] With the battle of Ramoth-Gilead,
and the death of Ahab, the war came to an
end. The combined attack of the two kings
having failed, their troops had been withdrawn, and the enterprise in which they
had joined relinquished. The Syrians, satisfied with their victory, did not press on the
retreating foe, or carry the war into their
enemies' country.

2. _Jehu...went out to meet him_] Cp. xv. 2.
The monarch was therefore rebuked **at the**

went out to meet him, and said to king Jehoshaphat, Shouldest thou help the ungodly, and *b*love them that hate the LORD? *b* Ps. 139. 21.
3 therefore *is* *c*wrath upon thee from before the LORD. Neverthe- *c* ch. 32. 25.
less there are *d*good things found in thee, in that thou hast taken *d* ch. 17. 4, 6.
away the groves out of the land, and hast *e*prepared thine heart See ch.12.12.
4 to seek God. ¶ And Jehoshaphat dwelt at Jerusalem: and *1*he *e* ch. 30. 19.
went out again through the people from Beer-sheba to mount Ezra 7. 10.
Ephraim, and brought them back unto the LORD God of their
5 fathers. And he set judges in the land throughout all the fenced
6 cities of Judah, city by city, and said to the judges, Take heed
what ye do: for *f*ye judge not for man, but for the LORD, *g*who *f* Deut. 1. 17.
7 *is* with you *2*in the judgment. Wherefore now let the fear of *g* Ps. 82. 1.
the LORD be upon you; take heed and do *it :* for *h*there *is* no Eccles. 5. 8.
iniquity with the LORD our God, nor *i*respect of persons, nor *h* Deut. 32. 4.
8 taking of gifts. ¶ Moreover in Jerusalem did Jehoshaphat *k*set *i* Deut.10.17.
of the Levites, and *of* the priests, and of the chief of the fathers Job 34. 19.
of Israel, for the judgment of the LORD, and for controversies, Rom. 2. 11.
9 when they returned to Jerusalem. And he charged them, saying, Gal. 2. 6.
Thus shall ye do *l*in the fear of the LORD, faithfully, and with a Col. 3. 25.
10 perfect heart. *m*And what cause soever shall come to you of 1 Pet. 1. 17.
your brethren that dwell in their cities, between blood and blood, ch. 17. 8.
between law and commandment, statutes and judgments, ye shall *l* 2 Sam.23.3.
even warn them that they trespass not against the LORD, and *m* Deut. 17.
so *n*wrath come upon *o*you, and upon your brethren: this do, 8, &c.
*n*Num.16.46.
o Ezek. 3. 18.

---

1 Heb. *he returned and went out.*   *2* Heb. *in the matter of judgment.*

---

earliest possible moment, and in the most effective way, as he was entering his capital at the head of his returning army. Jehu, thirty-five years previously, had worked in the northern kingdom, and prophesied against Baasha (1 K. xvi. 1–7), but had now come to Jerusalem, as Prophet and historian (cp. xx. 34).

shouldest thou help &c.] As a matter of mere human policy, the conduct of Jehoshaphat in joining Ahab against the Syrians was not only justifiable but wise and prudent. And the reasonings upon which such a policy was founded would have been unexceptionable but for one circumstance. Ahab was an idolater, and had introduced into his kingdom a false religion of a new and most degraded type. This should have led Jehoshaphat to reject his alliance. Military success could only come from the blessing and protection of Jehovah, which such an alliance, if persisted in, was sure to forfeit.

4. Jehoshaphat, while declining to renounce the alliance with Israel (cp. 2 K. iii. 7 note), was careful to show that he had no sympathy with idolatry, and was determined to keep his people, so far as he possibly could, free from it. He therefore personally set about a second reformation, passing through the whole land, from the extreme south to the extreme north (xiii. 19).

5. What exact change Jehoshaphat made in the judicial system of Judah (Deut. xvi.

18; 1 Chr. xxiii. 4), it is impossible to determine. Probably he found corruption widely spread (*v.* 7), and the magistrates in some places tainted with the prevailing idolatry. He therefore made a fresh appointment of judges throughout the whole country; concentrating judicial authority in the hands of a few, or creating superior courts in the chief towns ("fenced cities"), with a right of appeal to such courts from the village judge.

8. The "fathers of Israel" are the heads of families; the "chief of the fathers" are the great patriarchal chiefs, the admitted heads of great houses or clans. They were now admitted to share in the judicial office which seems in David's time to have been confined to the Levites (1 Chr. xxiii. 4).

for the judgment of the LORD, *and for controversies*] By the former are meant disputed cases concerning the performance of religious obligations. In "controversies" are included all the ordinary causes, whether criminal or civil.

when they returned to Jerusalem] Rather, "and they returned to Jerusalem," a clause which if detached from the previous words and attached to *v.* 9, gives a satisfactory sense.

10. The Jews who "dwelt in the cities," if dissatisfied with the decision given by the provincial judges, might therefore remove the cause to Jerusalem, as to a court of appeal.

p 1Chr.23.30.

q ch. 15. 2.

a Gen. 14. 7.
b Josh.15.62.
c ch. 19. 3.
d Ezra 8. 21.
Jer. 36. 9.
Jonah 3. 5.

e Deut. 4. 39.
Josh. 2. 11.
1 Kin. 8. 23.
Matt. 6. 9.
f Ps. 47. 2, 8.
Dan. 4. 17,
25, 32.
g 1Chr.29.12.
Ps. 62. 11.
Matt. 6. 13.
h Gen. 17. 7.
Ex. 6. 7.
i Ps. 44. 2.
k Isai. 41. 8.
Jam. 2. 23.
l 1 Kin. 8.
33, 37.
ch. 6. 28, 29,
30.
m ch. 6. 20.
n Deut. 2. 4,
9, 19.
o Num.20.21.
p Ps. 83. 12.

11 and ye shall not trespass. And, behold, Amariah the chief priest *is* over you *p* in all matters of the LORD; and Zebadiah the son of Ishmael, the ruler of the house of Judah, for all the king's matters: also the Levites *shall be* officers before you. ¹Deal courageously, and the LORD shall be *q* with the good.

CHAP. 20. IT came to pass after this also, *that* the children of Moab, and the children of Ammon, and with them *other* beside 2 the Ammonites, came against Jehoshaphat to battle. Then there came some that told Jehoshaphat, saying, There cometh a great multitude against thee from beyond the sea on this side Syria; and, behold, they *be* *a* in Hazazon-tamar, which *is* *b* En- 3 gedi. And Jehoshaphat feared, and set ²himself to *c* seek the 4 LORD, and *d* proclaimed a fast throughout all Judah. And Judah gathered themselves together, to ask *help* of the LORD: even out of all the cities of Judah they came to seek the LORD.

5 And Jehoshaphat stood in the congregation of Judah and Jeru- 6 salem, in the house of the LORD, before the new court, and said, O LORD God of our fathers, *art* not thou *e* God in heaven? and *f* rulest *not* thou over all the kingdoms of the heathen? and *g* in thine hand *is there not* power and might, so that none is 7 able to withstand thee? *Art* not thou *h* our God, ³ *who* *i* didst drive out the inhabitants of this land before thy people Israel, 8 and gavest it to the seed of Abraham *k* thy friend for ever? And they dwelt therein, and have built thee a sanctuary therein for 9 thy name, saying, *l* If, *when* evil cometh upon us, *as* the sword, judgment, or pestilence, or famine, we stand before this house, and in thy presence, (for thy *m* name *is* in this house,) and cry 10 unto thee in our affliction, then thou wilt hear and help. And now, behold, the children of Ammon and Moab and mount Seir, whom thou *n* wouldest not let Israel invade, when they came out of the land of Egypt, but *o* they turned from them, and destroyed 11 them not; behold, *I say*, how they reward us, *p* to come to cast

¹ Heb. *Take courage and do.*   ² Heb. *his face.*   ³ Heb. *thou.*

---

11. In religious causes, Amariah, the High-Priest, was to preside over the court; in civil or criminal causes, Zebadiah was to be president. And to Levites, other than the judges, he assigned the subordinate offices about the court.

XX. The narrative in *vv.* 1–30 is entirely additional to Kings; in *vv.* 31–37, it runs parallel with 1 K. xxii. 41–49.

1. The present Hebrew (and English) text mentions the Ammonites twice over. Hence some adopt a different reading and translate "the children of Ammon, and with them certain of the Maonites," &c. Cp. *v.* 10; Judg. x. 12; 1 Chr. iv. 41 notes.

2. Translate, "from beyond the sea, from Edom." The "sea" intended is, of course, the Dead Sea. "Syria" (Aram) is probably a mistake of a copyist for "Edom" (cp. 2 Sam. viii. 12 note).

On Engedi, see 1 Sam. xxiii. 29 note.

3. General fasts had been previously observed by the Israelites (*e.g.* Judg. xx. 26; 1 Sam. vii. 6); but we do not hear of any fast having been "proclaimed" by authority before this.

5. *the new court*] In Solomon's Temple

there were two courts. One of these had probably been renovated by Jehoshaphat or by his father, Asa (xv. 8), and was known as "the new court."

6–9. Jehoshaphat's appeal is threefold— (1) to God omnipotent (*v.* 6); (2) to "our God;" (3) the God especially *of this house* the Temple.

7. *Abraham thy friend*] Historically, this is the first use of this remarkable expression, afterwards repeated ˙ (marg. reff.). The ground of the expression is to be found principally in Gen. xviii. 23–33, where Abraham spoke with God as a man with his friend (cp. Ex. xxxiii. 11).

8, 9. The appeal recalls Solomon's prayer (marg. reff.), which God had formally accepted by sending down fire from heaven to consume the accompanying offering.

10. The Maonites of *v.* 1 are here, and in *vv.* 22, 23, called the "children" or inhabitants "of mount Seir." Hence we may gather that they were a tribe of Edomites, the inhabitants, probably, of a city Maon (now *Ma'an*) on the eastern side of the *Waḍy el-Arabah*.

us out of thy possession, which thou hast given us to inherit.
12 O our God, wilt thou not *q*judge them? for we have no might   *q* 1Sam.3.13.
against this great company that cometh against us; neither
13 know we what to do: but *r*our eyes *are* upon thee. And all   *r* Ps. 25. 15.
Judah stood before the LORD, with their little ones, their wives,   & 121. 1, 2.
14 and their children. ¶ Then upon Jahaziel the son of Zechariah,   & 123. 1, 2.
the son of Benaiah, the son of Jeiel, the son of Mattaniah, a   & 141. 8.
Levite of the sons of Asaph, *s*came the Spirit of the LORD in   *s* Num. 11.
15 the midst of the congregation; and he said, Hearken ye, all   25, 26.
Judah, and ye inhabitants of Jerusalem, and thou king Je-   & 24. 2.
hoshaphat, Thus saith the LORD unto you, *t*Be not afraid nor   ch. 15. 1.
dismayed by reason of this great multitude; for the battle *is*   & 24. 20.
16 not your's, but God's. To morrow go ye down against them: *t* Ex. 14. 13, 14.
behold, they come up by the *1*cliff of Ziz; and ye shall find   Deut. 1. 29, 30.
them at the end of the *2*brook, before the wilderness of Jeruel.   & 31. 6, 8.
17 *u*Ye shall not *need* to fight in this *battle:* set yourselves, stand ye   ch. 32. 7.
still, and see the salvation of the LORD with you, O Judah and   *u* Ex. 14. 13, 14.
Jerusalem: fear not, nor be dismayed; to morrow go out
18 against them: *x*for the LORD *will be* with you. And Jehosha-   *x* Num.14. 9.
phat *y*bowed his head with *his* face to the ground: and all   ch. 15. 2.
Judah and the inhabitants of Jerusalem fell before the LORD,   & 32. 8.
19 worshipping the LORD. And the Levites, of the children of the   *y* Ex. 4. 31.
Kohathites, and of the children of the Korhites, stood up to
20 praise the LORD God of Israel with a loud voice on high. ¶ And
they rose early in the morning, and went forth into the wilderness of Tekoa: and as they went forth, Jehoshaphat stood and
said, Hear me, O Judah, and ye inhabitants of Jerusalem;
*z*Believe in the LORD your God, so shall ye be established;   *z* Isai. 7. 9.
21 believe his prophets, so shall ye prosper. And when he had
consulted with the people, he appointed singers unto the LORD,
*a*and *3*that should praise the beauty of holiness, as they went   *a* 1Chr.16.29.
out before the army, and to say, *b*Praise the LORD; *c*for his   *b* 1Chr.16.34.
22 mercy *endureth* for ever. *4*And when they began *5*to sing and   Ps. 136. 1.
to praise, *d*the LORD set ambushments against the children of   *c* 1Chr.16.41.
Ammon, Moab, and mount Seir, which were come against   ch. 5. 13.
23 Judah; and *6*they were smitten. For the children of Ammon   & 7. 3, 6.
and Moab stood up against the inhabitants of mount Seir, utterly   *d* Judg.7. 22.
to slay and destroy *them:* and when they had made an end of   1 Sam.14.20.
the inhabitants of Seir, every one helped *7*to destroy another.

---

1 Heb. *ascent.*	*4* Heb. *And in the time that*	*6* Or, *they smote one an-*
2 Or, *valley.*	*they, &c.*	*other.*
3 Heb. *praisers.*	*5* Heb. *in singing and praise.*	*7* Heb. *for the destruction.*

---

14. "Mattaniah" is thought to be a corrupt reading for "Nethaniah," who is mentioned among the sons of Asaph in 1 Chr.
xxv. 2, 12.

15–17. The Prophet uses words familiar
to the people, and connected with several
great deliverances (see marg. reff.).

16. By the "cliff (or, rather,—as in marg.
—ascent) of Ziz," we must understand the
mountain path which leads up from Engedi
across the elevated tract still known as *El-
Husasah,* in the direction of Tekoa (*v.* 20).

at the end of the brook] Rather, "at the
end of the gulley," or dry torrent-course.
No name like Jeruel has been as yet found
in this district.

20. Tekoa (2 Sam. xiv. 2 note) lay on the
borders of the desert which skirts the highlands of Judæa towards the east. The
town was built on a hill of a considerable
height.

21. *praise the beauty of holiness*] Some
render, "in the beauty of holiness"—*i.e.* in
rich apparel and ornaments suitable to a
holy occasion. Cp. Ps. xxix. 2.

22. *the LORD set ambushments*] These
liers in wait have been regarded as Angels
employed by God to confuse the host and
cause its destruction, so that the Moabites
and Ammonites first united to destroy the
Edomites, and then turned upon each
other.

24 And when Judah came toward the watch tower in the wilderness, they looked unto the multitude, and, behold, they *were*
25 dead bodies fallen to the earth, and ¹none escaped. And when Jehoshaphat and his people came to take away the spoil of them, they found among them in abundance both riches with the dead bodies, and precious jewels, which they stripped off for themselves, more than they could carry away: and they were
26 three days in gathering of the spoil, it was so much. And on the fourth day they assembled themselves in the valley of ²Berachah; for there they blessed the LORD: therefore the name of the same place was called, The valley of Berachah, unto this
27 day. ¶ Then they returned, every man of Judah and Jerusalem, and Jehoshaphat in the ³forefront of them, to go again to Jeru-

Neh. 12. 43. salem with joy; for the LORD had *e*made them to rejoice over
28 their enemies. And they came to Jerusalem with psalteries
f ch. 17. 10. 29 and harps and trumpets unto the house of the LORD. And *f*the fear of God was on all the kingdoms of *those* countries, when they had heard that the LORD fought against the enemies of
g ch. 15. 15. 30 Israel. So the realm of Jehoshaphat was quiet: for his *g*God
Job 34. 29. 31 gave him rest round about. ¶ *h*And Jehoshaphat reigned over
h 1 Kin. 22. 41, &c. Judah: *he was* thirty and five years old when he began to reign, and he reigned twenty and five years in Jerusalem. And his
32 mother's name *was* Azubah the daughter of Shilhi. And he walked in the way of Asa his father, and departed not from it,
33 doing *that which was* right in the sight of the LORD. Howbeit
i See ch.17.6. *i*the high places were not taken away: for as yet the people
k ch. 12. 14. had not *k*prepared their hearts unto the God of their fathers.
& 19. 3. 34 ¶ Now the rest of the acts of Jehoshaphat, first and last, behold,
l 1 Kin. 16. they *are* written in the ⁴book of Jehu the son of Hanani, *l*who
1, 7. 35 ⁵*is* mentioned in the book of the kings of Israel. ¶ And after
m 1 Kin. 22. this *m*did Jehoshaphat king of Judah join himself with Ahaziah
48, 49. 36 king of Israel, who did very wickedly: ⁶and he joined himself with him to make ships to go to Tarshish: and they made the
37 ships in Ezion-gaber. Then Eliezer the son of Dodavah of Mareshah prophesied against Jehoshaphat, saying, Because thou hast joined thyself with Ahaziah, the LORD hath broken thy
*n*1Kin.22.48. works. *n*And the ships were broken, that they were not able
o ch. 9. 21. to go *o*to Tarshish.
*a*1Kin.22.50. **CHAP. 21.** NOW *a*Jehoshaphat slept with his fathers, and was buried with his fathers in the city of David. And Jehoram his

---

¹ Heb. there was *not an* escaping.
² That is, *Blessing.*
³ Heb. *head.*
⁴ Heb. *words.*
⁵ Heb. *was made to ascend.*
⁶ At first Jehoshaphat was unwilling, 1 Kin. 22. 49.

---

24. The march of Judah from Jerusalem would take five or six hours. By the time they reached the watch-towers in the wilderness of Jeruel was all over.

25. *riches with the dead bodies*] Several MSS. give another reading:—"riches, **and garments.**"

26. *the valley of Berachah*] Probably, the *Wady Bereikut*, which lies at a short distance from Tekoa towards the north-west.

33. The latter clause of this verse helps to reconcile the first clause with the statement that Jehoshaphat "took away the high places" (see xv. 17 note).

34. *who is mentioned* &c.] Words which are now generally thought to mean "whose

work was inserted into the Book of the Kings."

of Israel] "Israel" is probably used here inexactly for "Judah" (cp. xii. 6, xxi. 2, 4).

35. *after this*] Jehoshaphat's history had been formally completed (*v.* 34). Consequently we can lay no stress on the note of time contained in the words "after this," which are detached from the context whereto they originally referred. On the history (*vv.* 35–37) see marg. reff. and notes.

XXI. **1.** Jehoram's *sole* reign now began. (See 2 K. viii. 16 note). His eight years (*v.* 5) must be counted from the time of his association, in his father's 23rd year.

2 son ¹reigned in his stead. And he had brethren the sons of
Jehoshaphat, Azariah, and Jehiel, and Zechariah, and Azariah,
and Michael, and Shephatiah: all these *were* the sons of Jehosh-
3 aphat king of Israel. And their father gave them great gifts
of silver, and of gold, and of precious things, with fenced cities
in Judah: but the kingdom gave he to ²Jehoram; because he
4 *was* the firstborn. Now when Jehoram was risen up to the
kingdom of his father, he strengthened himself, and slew all his
brethren with the sword, and *divers* also of the princes of Israel.
5 ¶ ᵇJehoram *was* thirty and two years old when he began to
6 reign, and he reigned eight years in Jerusalem. And he walked
in the way of the kings of Israel, like as did the house of Ahab:
for he had the daughter of ᶜAhab to wife: and he wrought *that*
7 *which was* evil in the eyes of the LORD. Howbeit the LORD
would not destroy the house of David, because of the covenant
that he had made with David, and as he promised to give a
8 ³light to him and to his ᵈsons for ever. ¶ ᵉIn his days the
Edomites revolted from under the ⁴dominion of Judah, and
9 made themselves a king. Then Jehoram went forth with his
princes, and all his chariots with him: and he rose up by night,
and smote the Edomites which compassed him in, and the cap-
10 tains of the chariots. So the Edomites revolted from under the
hand of Judah unto this day. The same time *also* did Libnah
revolt from under his hand; because he had forsaken the LORD
11 God of his fathers. ¶ Moreover he made high places in the mountains of Judah, and caused the inhabitants of Jerusalem to
12 ᶠcommit fornication, and compelled Judah *thereto*. ¶ And there
came a writing to him from Elijah the prophet, saying, Thus
saith the LORD God of David thy father, Because thou hast not
walked in the ways of Jehoshaphat thy father, nor in the ways
13 of Asa king of Judah, but hast walked in the way of the kings
of Israel, and hast ᵍmade Judah and the inhabitants of Jeru-

b In consort,
2 Kin. 8. 17,
&c.

c ch. 22. 2.

d 2 Sam. 7.
12, 13.
1 Kin. 11. 36.
2 Kin. 8. 19.
Ps. 132. 11,
&c.
e 2 Kin. 8.
20, &c.

f Lev. 17. 7.
& 20. 5.
ver. 13.

g ver. 11.

---

¹ Alone.
² Jehoram made partner
of the kingdom with his
father, 2 Kin. 8. 16.
³ Heb. *lamp*, or, *candle*.
⁴ Heb. *hand*.

---

3. Jehoshaphat departed from Rehoboam's policy (xi. 23 note), actually making
over to his sons the "fenced cities" in
which they dwelt. This, it is probable, provoked the jealousy of Jehoram, and induced him to put them to death (*v.* 4).

because he was the firstborn] Cp. Deut. xxi.
15-17. Exceptions to this rule in the northern and southern kingdoms are Solomon,
where divine appointment superseded the
natural order, Abijah (xi. 22 note), and Jehoahaz (2 K. xxiii. 30 note).

4. The execution of several "princes of
Israel" (*i.e.* of Judah; see xx. 34 note) implies that Jehoram's brothers found supporters among the chief men of the country,
and that Jehoram's sole sovereignty was
not established without a struggle.

11. See 2 K. viii. 18. The writer of Kings
only tells us in general terms that Jehoram
"did evil in the sight of the Lord," and
"walked in the way of the house of Ahab."
Here, in *vv.* 11 and 13, we have particulars
of his idolatry. Jehoram, it seems, seduced
by the evil influence of his wife—Athaliah,

the daughter of Ahab—permitted the introduction of Baal-worship, idolatrous
altars in various high places, groves
(Asherahs), images, and pillars; the people
were not only allowed, but compelled to
take part in the new rites. "To commit
fornication" is a common metaphor, signifying idolatry or spiritual unfaithfulness
(cp. 2 K. ix. 22 note).

12. This is the only notice which we have
of Elijah in Chronicles. As a Prophet of the
northern kingdom, he engaged but slightly
the attention of the historian of the southern one. The notice shows that Elijah did
not confine his attention to the affairs of his
own state, but strove to check the progress
of idolatry in Judah. And it proves that
he was alive after the death of Jehoshaphat
(*v.* 13); a fact bearing (1) upon the chronological order of 2 K. ii. 1 (see note), and (2)
showing that Elisha, who prophesied in the
time of Jehoshaphat (2 K. iii. 11-19) commenced his public ministry before his master's translation.

h Ex. 34. 15.
Deut. 31. 16.
i 1 Kin. 16.
31—33.
2 Kin. 9. 22.
k ver. 4.
l ver. 18. 19.

m 1 Kin. 11.
11, 23.

n ch. 24. 7.

o ver. 15.

p ch. 16. 14.

salem to *h*go a whoring, like to the *i*whoredoms of the house
of Ahab, and also hast *k*slain thy brethren of thy father's house,
14 *which were* better than thyself: behold, with ¹a great plague will
the LORD smite thy people, and thy children, and thy wives,
15 and all thy goods: and thou *shalt have* great sickness by *l*disease of thy bowels, until thy bowels fall out by reason of the
16 sickness day by day.. ¶Moreover the LORD *m*stirred up against
Jehoram the spirit of the Philistines, and of the Arabians, that
17 *were* near the Ethiopians: and they came up into Judah, and
brake into it, and ²carried away all the substance that was found
in the king's house, and *n*his sons also, and his wives: so that there
was never a son left him, save ³Jehoahaz, the youngest of his
18 sons. ¶⁴And after all this the LORD smote him *o*in his bowels
19 with an incurable disease. And it came to pass, that in process
of time, after the end of two years, his bowels fell out by reason
of his sickness: so he died of sore diseases. And his people made
20 no burning for him, like *p*the burning of his fathers. Thirty and
two years old was he when he began to reign, and he reigned
in Jerusalem eight years, and departed ⁵without being desired.
Howbeit they buried him in the city of David, but not in the
sepulchres of the kings.

a 2 Kin. 8.
24, &c.
See ch. 21.
17.
ver. 6.
b ch. 21. 17.
c See 2 Kin.
8. 26.
d ch. 21. 6.

CHAP. **22.** AND the inhabitants of Jerusalem made *a*Ahaziah his
youngest son king in his stead: for the band of men that came
with the Arabians to the camp had slain all the *b*eldest. So
2 Ahaziah the son of Jehoram king of Judah reigned. *c*Forty
and two years old *was* Ahaziah when he began to reign, and he
reigned one year in Jerusalem. His mother's name also *was*
3 *d*Athaliah the daughter of Omri. He also walked in the ways of
the house of Ahab: for his mother was his counsellor to do
4 wickedly. Wherefore he did evil in the sight of the LORD like
the house of Ahab: for they were his counsellors after the death
5 of his father to his destruction. He walked also after their

e 2 Kin. 8.
28, &c.
f 2 Kin. 9. 15.

counsel, and *e*went with Jehoram the son of Ahab king of Israel
to war against Hazael king of Syria at Ramoth-gilead: and the
6 Syrians smote Joram. *f*And he returned to be healed in Jezreel
because of the wounds ⁶which were given him at Ramah, when
he fought with Hazael king of Syria. ¶And ⁷Azariah the son of
Jehoram king of Judah went down to see Jehoram the son of
7 Ahab at Jezreel, because he was sick. And the ⁸destruction of
Ahaziah *g*was of God by coming to Joram: for when he was
come, he *h*went out with Jehoram against Jehu the son of
Nimshi, *i*whom the LORD had anointed to cut off the house of

g Judg. 14. 4.
1 Kin. 12. 15.
ch. 10. 15.
h 2 Kin. 9. 21.
i 2 Kin. 9. 6, 7.

¹ Heb. *a great stroke.*
² Heb. *carried captive:* See
ch. 22. 1.
³ Or, *Ahaziah,* ch. 22. 1,
or, *Azariah,* ch. 22. 6.

⁴ His son, *Ahaziah Prorex,*
2 Kin. 9. 29, soon after.
⁵ Heb. *without desire,* Jer.
22. 18.
⁶ Heb. *wherewith they*

wounded him.
⁷ Otherwise called *Ahaziah,* ver. 1. and *Jehoahaz,* ch. 21. 17.
⁸ Heb. *treading down.*

---

14. The fulfilment of the threat is given
in *vv.* 16, 17.

16. *the Arabians, that were near the Ethiopians*] Probably Joktanian Arabs from the
neighbourhood of the Cushites. Southern
Arabia was originally occupied by Cushites,
or Ethiopians (Gen. x. 7), whose descendants
still exist in a remnant of the Himyaritic
Arabs.

17. *Jehoahaz*] The writer of Chronicles
calls him indifferently Jehoahaz and Aha-

ziah, which are equivalent names (2 K. viii.
24 note).

20. *not in the sepulchres of the kings*]
Compare the similar treatment of Joash
(xxiv. 25) and Ahaz (xxviii. 27).

XXII. 2. For 42 read 22 (marg. ref.).
Ahaziah's father, Jehoram, was but forty
when he died (xxi. 20).

7. *the destruction of Ahaziah was of God*]
i.e. his untimely end was a judgment upon
him for his idolatry.

8 Ahab. And it came to pass, that, when Jehu was [k]executing judgment upon the house of Ahab, and [l]found the princes of Judah, and the sons of the brethren of Ahaziah, that ministered
9 to Ahaziah, he slew them. [m]And he sought Ahaziah: and they caught him, (for he was hid in Samaria,) and brought him to Jehu: and when they had slain him, they buried him: Because, said they, he *is* the son of Jehoshaphat, who [n]sought the LORD with all his heart. So the house of Ahaziah had no power to
10 keep still the kingdom. ¶[o]But when Athaliah the mother of Ahaziah saw that her son was dead, she arose and destroyed
11 all the seed royal of the house of Judah. But [p]Jehoshabeath, the daughter of the king, took Joash the son of Ahaziah, and stole him from among the king's sons that were slain, and put him and his nurse in a bedchamber. So Jehoshabeath, the daughter of king Jehoram, the wife of Jehoiada the priest, (for she was the sister of Ahaziah,) hid him from Athaliah, so that
12 she slew him not. And he was with them hid in the house of God six years: and Athaliah reigned over the land.

CHAP. 23. AND [a]in the seventh year Jehoiada strengthened himself, and took the captains of hundreds, Azariah the son of Jeroham, and Ishmael the son of Jehohanan, and Azariah the son of Obed, and Maaseiah the son of Adaiah, and Elishaphat
2 the son of Zichri, into covenant with him. And they went about in Judah, and gathered the Levites out of all the cities of Judah, and the chief of the fathers of Israel, and they came to Jerusa-
3 lem. And all the congregation made a covenant with the king in the house of God. And he said unto them, Behold, the king's son shall reign, as the LORD hath [b]said of the sons of David.
4 This *is* the thing that ye shall do; A third part of you [c]entering on the sabbath, of the priests and of the Levites, *shall be* porters
5 of the [1]doors; and a third part *shall be* at the king's house; and a third part at the gate of the foundation: and all the people
6 *shall be* in the courts of the house of the LORD. But let none come into the house of the LORD, save the priests, and [d]they that minister of the Levites; they shall go in, for they *are* holy:

[k] 2 Kin. 10.
10, 11.
[l] 2 Kin. 10.
13. 14.
[m] 2 Kin. 9.
27, at *Megiddo* in the
kingdom of *Samaria.*
[n] ch. 17. 4.

[o] 2 Kin. 11.
1, &c.

[p] 2 Kin. 11.
2, *Jehosheba.*

[a] 2 Kin. 11.
4, &c.

[b] 2 Sam. 7.12.
1 Kin. 2. 4.
& 9. 5.
ch. 6. 16.
& 7. 18.
& 21. 7.
[c] 1 Chr. 9. 25.

[d] 1 Chr. 23.
28, 29.

[1] Heb. *thresholds.*

---

9. Cp. marg. ref. Ahaziah after remaining a while at Megiddo, removed to Samaria, where his wounds could be better cared for and concealment might be easier; Jehu's emissaries discovered him there; they took him to Jehu, who happened at the time to be at Megiddo; and then and there Jehu put him to death. The narrative here is therefore supplementary to that of 2 Kings, and finds its proper place between the clause, "He fled to Megiddo," and the words "and died there."

and when they had slain him, they buried him] Jehu's emissaries slew him but allowed his servants to bury him (see 2 K. ix. 28).

no power &c.] As Ahaziah was but twenty-three at his death (*v.* 2 note), he had no grown-up son to take the crown.

10-12. Cp. marg. ref. and notes.

XXIII. Cp. the history in Kings (marg. ref.). Both accounts were probably drawn from a common source. The writer of

Kings treated the points of civil and historic importance, the later author of Chronicles collected the notices of the part taken in the transactions by the sacred order to which he probably belonged.

1. The five names do not occur in Kings; only, and incidentally, the five divisions of the royal guard (2 K. xi. 5 note).

2. Jehoiada was unwilling to trust the success of the revolution wholly and entirely to the royal body-guard. Accordingly, the captains collected from the cities of Judah a strong body of Levites and the chief of the fathers of Israel (*i.e.* "Judah," see xx. 34 note) who were brought up to Jerusalem.

3. By "all the congregation" here is meant the persons referred to in *r.* 2.

4. The writer of Chronicles relates the orders that were given to the Levites, the author of Kings those received by the royal body-guard (2 K. xi. 5 note).

6. *keep the watch of the* LORD] *i.e.* guard

7 but all the people shall keep the watch of the LORD. And the
Levites shall compass the king round about, every man with his
weapons in his hand; and whosoever *else* cometh into the house,
he shall be put to death: but be ye with the king when he
8 cometh in, and when he goeth out. ¶ So the Levites and all
Judah did according to all things that Jehoiada the priest had
commanded, and took every man his men that were to come in
on the sabbath, with them that were to go *out* on the sabbath:

See 1 Chr. 24 & 25.

9 for Jehoiada the priest dismissed not *e*the courses. Moreover
Jehoiada the priest delivered to the captains of hundreds spears,
and bucklers, and shields, that *had been* king David's, which
10 *were* in the house of God. And he set all the people, every man
having his weapon in his hand, from the right [1]side of the [2]temple
to the left side of the temple, along by the altar and the temple,
11 by the king round about. Then they brought out the king's

f Deut.17.18.

son, and put upon him the crown, and *f gave him* the testimony,
and made him king. And Jehoiada and his sons anointed him,
12 and said, [3]God save the king. Now when Athaliah heard the
noise of the people running and praising the king, she came to
13 the people into the house of the LORD: and she looked, and,
behold, the king stood at his pillar at the entering in, and the
princes and the trumpets by the king: and all the people of the
land rejoiced, and sounded with trumpets, also the singers with

g 1 Chr. 25.8.

instruments of musick, and *g*such as taught to sing praise.
Then Athaliah rent her clothes, and said, [4]Treason, Treason.
14 Then Jehoiada the priest brought out the captains of hundreds
that were set over the host, and said unto them, Have her forth
of the ranges: and whoso followeth her, let him be slain with the
sword. For the priest said, Slay her not in the house of the

h Neh. 3. 28.

15 LORD. So they laid hands on her; and when she was come to
the entering *h*of the horse gate by the king's house, they slew her
16 there. ¶ And Jehoiada made a covenant between him, and between
all the people, and between the king, that they should be the
17 LORD's people. Then all the people went to the house of Baal,
and brake it down, and brake his altars and his images in pieces,

i Deut. 13.9.

18 and *i*slew Mattan the priest of Baal before the altars. Also
Jehoiada appointed the offices of the house of the LORD by the

k 1 Chr. 23. 6, 30, 31. & 24. 1.
l Num. 28. 2.
m 1 Chr. 26. 1, &c.

hand of the priests the Levites, whom David had *k*distributed in
the house of the LORD, to offer the burnt offerings of the LORD,
as *it is* written in the *l*law of Moses, with rejoicing and with
19 singing, *as it was ordained* [5]by David. And he set the *m*porters
at the gates of the house of the LORD, that none *which was* un-

---

[1] Heb. *shoulder.*   [3] Heb. *Let the king live.*   [5] Heb. *by the hands of*
[2] Heb. *house.*   [4] Heb. *Conspiracy.*   *David,* 1 Chr. 25. 2, 6.

---

against any attempt that might be made by
the Baal-worshippers to force their way
through the courts into the Temple.

7. Cp. 2 K. xi. 8, 11. The soldiers and
the Levites in the Temple were probably intermixed in about equal proportions.

8. *and took every man his men* &c.] *i.e.*
the relief, already organised by Jehoiada
into three bodies (*vv.* 4, 5), was further
strengthened by the members of the out-
going "course," who were associated in the
work to be done.

13. *at the entering in*] *i.e.* at, or near, the

opening from the main chamber of the
Temple into the Holy of Holies.

16. *between him,* &c.] In 2 K. xi. 17 the
covenant is said to have been made "between the LORD," &c. To the writer of
Chronicles Jehoiada was God's representative, and received the pledges of king and
people.

18. *the priests the Levites*] Rather, with
the Versions, "the priests **and** the Levites."
It was the duty of the priests alone to offer
the Burnt offerings (Num. xviii. 1–7), and of
the Levites alone to praise God with singing
and music (1 Chr. xxiii. 5, xxv. 1–7).

20 clean in any thing should enter in. [n]And he took the captains of hundreds, and the nobles, and the governors of the people, and all the people of the land, and brought down the king from the house of the LORD: and they came through the high gate into the king's house, and set the king upon the throne of the 21 kingdom. And all the people of the land rejoiced: and the city was quiet, after that they had slain Athaliah with the sword.

CHAP. 24. JOASH [a]*was* seven years old when he began to reign, and he reigned forty years in Jerusalem. His mother's name 2 also *was* Zibiah of Beer-sheba. And Joash [b]did *that which was* right in the sight of the LORD all the days of Jehoiada the priest.

3 And Jehoiada took for him two wives; and he begat sons and 4 daughters. ¶ And it came to pass after this, *that* Joash was 5 minded [1]to repair the house of the LORD. And he gathered together the priests and the Levites, and said to them, Go out unto the cities of Judah, and [c]gather of all Israel money to repair the house of your God from year to year, and see that ye 6 hasten the matter. Howbeit the Levites hastened *it* not. ¶ [d]And the king called for Jehoiada the chief, and said unto him, Why hast thou not required of the Levites to bring in out of Judah and out of Jerusalem the collection, *according to the commandment* of [e]Moses the servant of the LORD, and of the con- 7 gregation of Israel, for the [f]tabernacle of witness? For [g]the sons of Athaliah, that wicked woman, had broken up the house of God; and also all the [h]dedicated things of the house 8 of the LORD did they bestow upon Baalim. And at the king's commandment [i]they made a chest, and set it without at the 9 gate of the house of the LORD. And they made [2]a proclamation through Judah and Jerusalem, to bring in to the LORD [k]the collection *that* Moses the servant of God *laid* upon Israel in the 10 wilderness. And all the princes and all the people rejoiced, and brought in, and cast into the chest, until they had made an 11 end. Now it came to pass, that at what time the chest was brought unto the king's office by the hand of the Levites, and [l]when they saw that *there was* much money, the king's scribe and the high priest's officer came and emptied the chest, and took it, and carried it to his place again. Thus they did day by 12 day, and gathered money in abundance. And the king and Jehoiada gave it to such as did the work of the service of the house of the LORD, and hired masons and carpenters to repair the house of the LORD, and also such as wrought iron and brass 13 to mend the house of the LORD. So the workmen wrought, and

[n]2 Kin. 11. 19.

[a]2 Kin. 11. 21. & 12. 1, &c.
[b]See ch. 26. 5.

[c]2 Kin. 12. 4.
[d]2 Kin. 12. 7.

[e]Ex. 30. 12, 13, 14, 16.
[f]Num. 1. 50. Acts 7. 44.
[g]ch. 21. 17.
[h]2 Kin. 12. 4.

[i]2 Kin. 12. 9.

[k]ver. 6.

[l]2 Kin. 12. 10.

---

[1]Heb. *to renew.*   [2]Heb. *a voice.*

---

20. *the high gate*] See 2 K. xi. 19 note.

XXIV. This chapter is parallel with 2 K. xii., but treats the matters common to both narratives in a different and, apparently, supplemental way.

2. Jehoiada lived after the accession of Joash at least 23 years (2 K. xii. 6). Thus the idolatries of Joash (*v.* 18) were confined to his last 10 or 15 years.

3. Athaliah's destruction of the seed royal had left Joash without a natural successor, and his marriage at the earliest suitable age, was, therefore, a matter of state policy. One of his wives in question was probably "Jehoaddan of Jerusalem,"

the mother of Amaziah (xxv. 1), who must have been taken to wife by Joash as early as his 21st year.

6. It appears from 2 K. xii. 4 that Joash had assigned to the restoration-fund two other payments also.

11. *the king's scribe...came and emptied,* &c.] Rather, " the king's scribe came...and **they** emptied" &c. *i.e.* the Levites who brought the chest from the Temple emptied it in the presence of the scribe.

13. *they set the house of God in his state*] Some prefer, "they **set up** the house of God in its (old) **measure**" or "**proportions.**"

¹the work was perfected by them, and they set the house of God
14 in his state, and strengthened it. And when they had finished
it, they brought the rest of the money before the king and Je-

hoiada, *m*whereof were made vessels for the house of the LORD,
even vessels to minister, and ²to offer *withal*, and spoons, and
vessels of gold and silver. And they offered burnt offerings
in the house of the LORD continually all the days of Jehoiada.
15 ¶ But Jehoiada waxed old, and was full of days when he died;
16 an hundred and thirty years old *was he* when he died. And they
buried him in the city of David among the kings, because he
had done good in Israel, both toward God, and toward his house.
17 Now after the death of Jehoiada came the princes of Judah,
and made obeisance to the king. Then the king hearkened unto
18 them. And they left the house of the LORD God of their fathers,

and served *n*groves and idols: and *o*wrath came upon Judah and
19 Jerusalem for this their trespass. Yet he *p*sent prophets to
them, to bring them again unto the LORD; and they testified
20 against them: but they would not give ear. ¶ And *q*the Spirit
of God ³came upon Zechariah the son of Jehoiada the priest,
which stood above the people, and said unto them, Thus saith
God, *r*Why transgress ye the commandments of the LORD, that
ye cannot prosper? *s*because ye have forsaken the LORD, he
21 hath also forsaken you. And they conspired against him, and
*t*stoned him with stones at the commandment of the king in
22 the court of the house of the LORD. Thus Joash the king
remembered not the kindness which Jehoiada his father had
done to him, but slew his son. And when he died, he said,
23 The LORD look upon *it*, and require *it*. ¶ And it came to pass

⁴at the end of the year, *that* *u*the host of Syria came up against
him: and they came to Judah and Jerusalem, and destroyed
all the princes of the people from among the people, and sent

---

¹ Heb. *the healing went up upon the work.*	² Or, *pestils.*	⁴ Heb. *in the revolution of the year.*	
	³ Heb. *clothed,* as Judg. 6. 34.		

---

15. *an hundred and thirty years old*] Most critics suppose the number in the text to be corrupt, and suggest in its stead 103 or 83.

16. *they buried him in the city of David among the kings*] This unparalleled honour, due in part to the respect felt for Jehoiada's religious character, was probably, also, in part attributable to his connexion with the royal family through his wife (xxii. 11), and to the fact that, for 10 or 12 years, he had practically held the kingly office.

toward his house] "*i.e.* toward God's house," the Temple.

17. The nobles had taken part in the revolution which placed Joash on the throne (xxiii. 2, 13, 20), but probably on political rather than on religious grounds. They might dislike the rule of a woman and a foreigner without participating in the zeal of Jehoiada for purity of religion. They now petitioned for a toleration of idolatry, not for a return to the condition of things which prevailed under Athaliah. No doubt they carried a considerable party with them; but the Temple-worship continued, as

appears from the history of Zechariah (*v*. 20). Nor is the king taxed personally with idolatry.

20. *stood above the people*] Zechariah, the High-Priest, took up an elevated position, perhaps on the steps of the inner court, which was elevated above the outer court, where the people would be.

21. *in the court of the house of the* LORD] "Between the Altar and the Temple," or directly in front of the Temple porch, if it be this Zechariah of whom our Lord speaks (Matt. xxiii. 35). A horror of the impious deed long possessed the Jews, who believed that the blood could not be effaced, but continued to bubble on the stones of the court, like blood newly shed, until the Temple was entered, just prior to its destruction, by Nebuzaradan.

22. *the* LORD *look upon it and require it*] Cp. Gen. ix. 5, xlii. 22; and contrast the words of Christ (Luke xxiii. 34), and of St. Stephen (Acts vii. 60). Zechariah's prayer was prophetic (see *vv*. 23, 25; Luke xi. 51).

23. On the unusual character of this expedition, see marg. ref. note.

24 all the spoil of them unto the king of [1] Damascus. For the army of the Syrians [x] came with a small company of men, and the LORD [y] delivered a very great host into their hand, because they had forsaken the LORD God of their fathers. So they

25 [z] executed judgment against Joash. ¶ And when they were departed from him, (for they left him in great diseases,) [a] his own servants conspired against him for the blood of the [b] sons of Jehoiada the priest, and slew him on his bed, and he died: and they buried him in the city of David, but they buried him not

26 in the sepulchres of the kings. And these are they that conspired against him; [2] Zabad the son of Shimeath an Ammonitess,

27 and Jehozabad the son of [3] Shimrith a Moabitess. Now *concerning* his sons, and the greatness of [c] the burdens *laid* upon him, and the [4] repairing of the house of God, behold, they *are* written in the [5] story of the book of the kings. [d] And Amaziah his son reigned in his stead.

CHAP. 25. AMAZIAH [a] *was* twenty and five years old *when* he began to reign, and he reigned twenty and nine years in Jerusalem. And his mother's name *was* Jehoaddan of Jerusalem.

2 And he did *that which was* right in the sight of the LORD, [b] but

3 not with a perfect heart. [c] Now it came to pass, when the kingdom was [6] established to him, that he slew his servants that had

4 killed the king his father. But he slew not their children, but *did* as *it is* written in the law in the book of Moses, where the LORD commanded, saying, [d] The fathers shall not die for the children, neither shall the children die for the fathers, but every

5 man shall die for his own sin. ¶ Moreover Amaziah gathered Judah together, and made them captains over thousands, and captains over hundreds, according to the houses of *their* fathers, throughout all Judah and Benjamin: and he numbered them [e] from twenty years old and above, and found them three hundred thousand choice *men, able* to go forth to war, that could

6 handle spear and shield. He hired also an hundred thousand mighty men of valour out of Israel for an hundred talents of

7 silver. But there came a man of God to him, saying, O king, let not the army of Israel go with thee; for the LORD *is* not

8 with Israel, *to wit, with* all the children of Ephraim. But if thou wilt go, do *it*, be strong for the battle: God shall make thee fall before the enemy: for God hath [f] power to help, and to cast

9 down. And Amaziah said to the man of God, But what shall

Right margin references:
[x] Lev. 26. 8.
Deut. 32. 30.
Isai. 30. 17.
[y] Lev. 26. 25.
Deut. 28. 25.
[z] ch. 22. 8.
Isai. 10. 5.
[a] 2 Kin. 12. 20.
[b] ver. 21.

[c] 2 Kin. 12. 18.

[d] 2 Kin. 12. 21.

[a] 2 Kin. 14. 1, &c.

[b] See 2 Kin. 14. 4. ver. 14.
[c] 2 Kin. 14. 5, &c.

[d] Deut. 24. 16. 2 Kin. 14. 6. Jer. 31. 30. Ezek. 18. 20.

[e] Num. 1. 3.

[f] ch. 20. 6.

---

[1] Heb. *Darmesek.*
[2] Or, *Jozachar,* 2 Kin. 12. 21.
[3] Or, *Shomer.*
[4] Heb. *founding.*
[5] Or, *commentary.*
[6] Heb. *confirmed upon him.*

---

24. *they executed judgment against Joash*] By defeating his army, slaying his nobles, and pressing on against Jerusalem, &c. (2 K. xii. 18 note).

27. *the greatness of the burdens laid upon him*] Or, "And the **multitude of burdens uttered against** him." "Burdens" (2 K. ix. 25 note) are prophetical denunciations of coming evil.

the repairing] See marg. rendering. Joash's repairs extended to the very base of the Temple building.

the story of the book of the kings] See Introduction to Chronicles, p. 447, *n.* 2.

XXV. This chapter is evidently taken to a large extent from the same document

as Kings (marg. ref. and notes). At the same time it contains large and important additions ;—*e.g. vv.* 5-10, 13-16.

5. *three hundred thousand*] Asa's army had been nearly twice as numerous, amounting to 580,000 (xiv. 8). The diminution was due, in part, to wars (xxi. 8, 16, xxiv. 23, 24); in part, to the general decadence of the kingdom.

8. If the present text be regarded as sound, this passage must be taken ironically. But most recent commentators supply a second negative, and render—" But go thou alone, act, be strong for the battle—God shall then **not** make thee to fall."

we do for the hundred talents which I have given to the ¹army
of Israel? And the man of God answered, *The LORD is able*
10 to give thee much more than this. Then Amaziah separated
them, *to wit*, the army that was come to him out of Ephraim,
to go ²home again: wherefore their anger was greatly kindled
11 against Judah, and they returned home ³in great anger. ¶ And
Amaziah strengthened himself, and led forth his people, and
went to *the valley of salt, and smote of the children of Seir*
12 ten thousand. And *other* ten thousand *left* alive did the children
of Judah carry away captive, and brought them unto the top of
the rock, and cast them down from the top of the rock, that they
13 all were broken in pieces. But ⁴the soldiers of the army which
Amaziah sent back, that they should not go with him to battle,
fell upon the cities of Judah, from Samaria even unto Beth-
horon, and smote three thousand of them, and took much spoil.
14 ¶ Now it came to pass, after that Amaziah was come from the
slaughter of the Edomites, that *he brought the gods of the*
children of Seir, and set them up *to be* *his gods, and bowed*
down himself before them, and burned incense unto them.
15 Wherefore the anger of the LORD was kindled against Amaziah,
and he sent unto him a prophet, which said unto him, Why hast
thou sought after *the gods of the people, which* *could not*
16 deliver their own people out of thine hand? And it came to
pass, as he talked with him, that *the king* said unto him, Art
thou made of the king's counsel? forbear; why shouldest thou
be smitten? Then the prophet forbare, and said, I know that
God hath ⁵*determined to destroy thee, because thou hast done*
17 this, and hast not hearkened unto my counsel. ¶ Then *Amaziah*
king of Judah took advice, and sent to Joash, the son of
Jehoahaz, the son of Jehu, king of Israel, saying, Come, let
18 us see one another in the face. And Joash king of Israel sent
to Amaziah king of Judah, saying, The ⁶thistle that *was* in
Lebanon sent to the cedar that *was* in Lebanon, saying, Give
thy daughter to my son to wife: and there passed by ⁷a wild
19 beast that *was* in Lebanon, and trode down the thistle. Thou
sayest, Lo, thou hast smitten the Edomites; and thine heart
lifteth thee up to boast: abide now at home; why shouldest
thou meddle to *thine* hurt, that thou shouldest fall, *even* thou,

g Prov. 10. 22.

h 2 Kin. 14. 7.

i See ch. 23.
23.
k Ex. 20. 3, 5.

l Ps. 96. 5.
m ver. 11.

n 1 Sam. 2. 25.
o 2 Kin. 14.
8, 9, &c.

---

¹ Heb. *band.*
² Heb. *to their place.*
³ Heb. *in heat of anger.*
⁴ Heb. *the sons of the band.*
⁵ Heb. *counselled.*
⁶ Or, *furze bush*, or, *thorn.*
⁷ Heb. *a beast of the field.*

---

10. Such a dismissal could not fail to
arouse great indignation. The Israelites
would suppose themselves dismissed because
their good faith was suspected. On the
consequences of their indignation, see *v.* 13.

11. *the children of Seir*] *i.e.* the Edomites
(marg. ref. *h.*).

12. *the top of the rock*] Rather, "the
height of Selah" (or, Petra), near which
the battle was probably fought. On the
cruel features of the Edomite wars, see 1 K.
xi. 15; Ezek. xxv. 12; Obad. 14.

13. To revenge the insult (*v.* 10), the
troops of Joash proceeded southwards and
ravaged all the Jewish towns and villages
between the Israelitish frontier and Beth-

horon. This invasion probably took place
while Amaziah was still in Edom.

14. The practice of carrying off the images
of the gods from a conquered country, or
city, as trophies of victory, was common
among the nations of the East. Sometimes
as with the Romans, the object was worship,
especially when the gods were previously
among those of the conquering country, and
the images had the reputation of peculiar
sanctity.

16. *Art thou made of the king's counsel?*]
A subtle irony:—"Have I made thee one of
my council? If not, what entitles thee to
offer thy advice?"

For the fulfilment of the prophecy, see
vv. 22-24, 27.

20 and Judah with thee? But Amaziah would not hear; for [p]it [p] 1 Kin.12.15.
came of God, that he might deliver them into the hand *of their* ch. 22. 7.
21 *enemies*, because they [q]sought after the gods of Edom. So [q] ver. 14.
Joash the king of Israel went up; and they saw one another in
the face, *both* he and Amaziah king of Judah, at Beth-shemesh,
22 which *belongeth* to Judah. And Judah was [1]put to the worse
23 before Israel, and they fled every man to his tent. And Joash
the king of Israel took Amaziah king of Judah, the son of Joash,
the son of [r]Jehoahaz, at Beth-shemesh, and brought him to [r] See ch. 21.
Jerusalem, and brake down the wall of Jerusalem from the gate 17.
24 of Ephraim to [2]the corner gate, four hundred cubits. And *he* & 22. 1, 6.
took all the gold and the silver, and all the vessels that were
found in the house of God with Obed-edom, and the treasures
of the king's house, the hostages also, and returned to Samaria.
25 ¶ [s]And Amaziah the son of Joash king of Judah lived after the [s] 2 Kin.14.17.
death of Joash son of Jehoahaz king of Israel fifteen years.
26 Now the rest of the acts of Amaziah, first and last, behold, *are*
they not written in the book of the kings of Judah and Israel?
27 Now after the time that Amaziah did turn away [3]from following
the LORD they [4]made a conspiracy against him in Jerusalem;
and he fled to Lachish: but they sent to Lachish after him, and
28 slew him there. And they brought him upon horses, and buried
him with his fathers in the city of [5]Judah.

CHAP. 26. THEN all the people of Judah took [a][6]Uzziah, who *was* [a] 2 Kin. 14.
sixteen years old, and made him king in the room of his father 21, 22.
2 Amaziah. He built Eloth, and restored it to Judah, after that & 15. 1, &c.
3 the king slept with his fathers. Sixteen years old *was* Uzziah
when he began to reign, and he reigned fifty and two years in
Jerusalem. His mother's name also *was* Jecoliah of Jerusalem.
4 And he did *that which was* right in the sight of the LORD, accord-
5 ing to all that his father Amaziah did. And [b]he sought God in the [b] See ch. 24.
days of Zechariah, who [c]had understanding [7]in the visions of 2.
God: and as long as he sought the LORD, God made him to [c] Gen. 41. 15.
Dan. 1. 17.
6 prosper. And he went forth and [d]warred against the Philistines, & 2. 19.
and brake down the wall of Gath, and the wall of Jabneh, and & 10. 1.
[d] Isai. 14. 29.
the wall of Ashdod, and built cities [8]about Ashdod, and among
7 the Philistines. And God helped him against [e]the Philistines, [e] ch. 21. 16.
and against the Arabians that dwelt in Gur-baal, and the

---

[1] Heb. *smitten.*
[2] Heb. *the gate of it that looketh.*
[3] Heb. *from after.*
[4] Heb. *conspired a conspiracy.*
[5] That is, *The city of David,* as it is 2 Kin. 14. 20.
[6] Or, *Azariah.*
[7] Heb. *in the seeing of God.*
[8] Or, *in* the country *of Ashdod.*

---

27. *after the time* &c.] The writer means
that the violent death of Amaziah followed
on his apostasy, not closely in point of time
—for it must have been at least fifteen years
after (*v.* 25)—nor as, humanly speaking,
caused by it; but, in the way of a divine
judgment, his death was a complete fulfilment of the prophecy of *v.* 16.

XXVI. Nearly the whole of this chapter
is additional to the narrative in Kings
(marg. ref.). It is not too much to say that
we are indebted to Chronicles for our whole
conception of the character of Uzziah, and
for nearly our whole knowledge of the events
of his reign.

1. *Uzziah*] This form of the name is found
uniformly in Chronicles (except 1 Chr. iii.

12) and in the Prophets. The writer of
Kings prefers the form Azariah. Uzziah
has been regarded as a phonetic corruption
of the real name used by the common
people.

**5. *who had understanding in the visions of
God*]** Another reading, supported by the
LXX., and some ancient Versions, is :—
"who instructed him in the fear of God."

6. Uzziah's expedition was the natural
sequel to the Edomite war of Amaziah
(xxv. 11), which crushed the most formidable of all the tribes of the south. On
Jabneh see Josh. xv. 11 note; and on
Ashdod see Josh. xiii. 3 note.

7. On the Mehunims or Maonites, see
Judges x. 12 note.

ᶠ 2 Sam. 8. 2.
ch. 17. 11.

ᵍ 2 Kin. 14. 13.
Neh. 3. 13,
19, 32.
Zech. 14. 10.

ʰ Deut. 32. 15.

ⁱ Deut. 8. 14.
ch. 25. 19.
ᵏ So 2 Kin.
16. 12, 13.
ˡ 1 Chr. 6. 10.

8 Mehunims. And the Ammonites ᶠgave gifts to Uzziah: and his name ¹spread abroad *even* to the entering in of Egypt; for he 9 strengthened *himself* exceedingly. ¶ Moreover Uzziah built towers in Jerusalem at the ᵍcorner gate, and at the valley gate, 10 and at the turning *of the wall*, and ²fortified them. Also he built towers in the desert, and ³digged many wells: for he had much cattle, both in the low country, and in the plains: husbandmen *also*, and vine dressers in the mountains, and in 11 ⁴Carmel: for he loved ⁵husbandry. ¶ Moreover Uzziah had an host of fighting men, that went out to war by bands, according to the number of their account by the hand of Jeiel the scribe and Maaseiah the ruler, under the hand of Hananiah, *one* of the 12 king's captains. The whole number of the chief of the fathers of the mighty men of valour *were* two thousand and six hun- 13 dred. And under their hand *was* ⁶an army, three hundred thousand and seven thousand and five hundred, that made war with 14 mighty power, to help the king against the enemy. And Uzziah prepared for them throughout all the host shields, and spears, and helmets, and habergeons, and bows, and ⁷slings *to cast* stones. 15 And he made in Jerusalem engines, invented by cunning men, to be on the towers and upon the bulwarks, to shoot arrows and great stones withal. And his name ⁸spread far abroad; for he 16 was marvellously helped, till he was strong. ¶ But ʰwhen he was strong, his heart was ⁱlifted up to *his* destruction: for he transgressed against the LORD his God, and ᵏwent into the temple of the LORD to burn incense upon the altar of incense. 17 And ˡAzariah the priest went in after him, and with him four-

---

¹ Heb. *went*.
² Or, *repaired*.
³ Or, *cut out many cisterns*.
⁴ Or, *Fruitful fields*.
⁵ Heb. *ground*.
⁶ Heb. *the power of an army*.
⁷ Heb. *stones of slings*.
⁸ Heb. *went forth*.

---

10. *he built towers in the desert*] Refuges for the flocks and the herdsmen in the wild pasture country on the borders of the Holy Land, especially towards the south and south-east.

wells] The marginal translation is preferable. Judæa depends largely for its water-supply on reservoirs in which the rain-fall is stored. These are generally cut in the natural rock, and covered at top.

for he had much cattle, &c.] Some prefer, "for he had much cattle **there, and** in the low country, and **on the downs**," with allusion to three pasture districts—(1) The "wilderness," or high tract to the south and south-east, extending from the western shores of the Dead Sea to the vicinity of Beersheba; (2) The "low country," or maritime plain on the west, between the hills of Judæa and the sea; and (3) The "downs," or rich grazing land beyond the Jordan, on the plateau of Gilead. Uzziah's possession of this last-named district must have been connected with the submission of the Ammonites (see *v.* 8).

in the mountains, and in Carmel] These terms describe Judæa Proper — the hilly tract between the low maritime plain on the one side, and the wilderness and Jordan valley on the other. By "Carmel" we must understand, not the mountain of that name, which belonged to Samaria, but the cultivated portions of the Judæan hill-tract (see margin).

13. Cp. xxv. 5. It will be seen that Uzziah had not added much to the military strength of the nation by his conquests. His army exceeds that of his father Amaziah by 7500 men only.

14. The sling was used in war by the Assyrians, the Egyptians, the Persians, the Greeks, Romans, and others. Its employment by the Benjamites appears from Judg. xx. 16, and by the ten tribes, a century before Uzziah, from 2 K. iii. 25.

15. Uzziah's engines seem to have corresponded respectively to the Roman *balista* and *catapulta*. The *balista*, which threw stones, was known to the Assyrians as early as the time of Sardanapalus I., the contemporary of Jehoshaphat. The catapult is not represented either on the Assyrian or the Egyptian sculptures. It would seem on the whole most probable that both kinds of engines were invented in Assyria and introduced from thence into Palestine.

16. *to his destruction*] Rather, "**to do wickedly**." Uzziah appears to have deliberately determined to invade the priest's office (marg. ref. *m*), thus repeating the sin of Korah, Dathan, and Abiram (Num. xvi. 1-35).

18 score priests of the LORD, *that were* valiant men : and they withstood Uzziah the king, and said unto him, *It* ᵐ*appertaineth* not unto thee, Uzziah, to burn incense unto the LORD, but to the ⁿpriests the sons of Aaron, that are consecrated to burn incense : go out of the sanctuary ; for thou hast trespassed ; neither *shall it be* for
19 thine honour from the LORD God. Then Uzziah was wroth, and *had* a censer in his hand to burn incense : and while he was wroth with the priests, ᵒthe leprosy even rose up in his forehead before the priests in the house of the LORD, from beside the in-
20 cense altar. And Azariah the chief priest, and all the priests, looked upon him, and, behold, he *was* leprous in his forehead, and they thrust him out from thence ; yea, himself ᵖhasted also
21 to go out, because the LORD had smitten him. �q And Uzziah the king was a leper unto the day of his death, and dwelt in a ʳ¹several house, *being* a leper ; for he was cut off from the house of the LORD : and Jotham his son *was* over the king's house,
22 judging the people of the land. ¶ Now the rest of the acts of Uzziah, first and last, did ˢIsaiah the prophet, the son of Amoz,
23 write. ᵗSo Uzziah slept with his fathers, and they buried him with his fathers in the field of the burial which *belonged* to the kings ; for they said, He *is* a leper : and Jotham his son reigned in his stead.

CHAP. 27. JOTHAM ᵃ*was* twenty and five years old when he began to reign, and he reigned sixteen years in Jerusalem. His mother's
2 name also *was* Jerushah, the daughter of Zadok. And he did *that which was* right in the sight of the LORD, according to all that his father Uzziah did : howbeit he entered not into the
3 temple of the LORD. And ᵇthe people did yet corruptly. He built the high gate of the house of the LORD, and on the wall of
4 ²Ophel he built much. Moreover he built cities in the mountains of Judah, and in the forests he built castles and towers.
5 He fought also with the king of the Ammonites, and prevailed against them. And the children of Ammon gave him the same year an hundred talents of silver, and ten thousand measures

m Num. 16. 40. & 18. 7.
n Ex. 30. 7, 8.

o Num. 12. 10. 2 Kin. 5. 27.

p As Esth. 6. 12.
q 2 Kin. 15. 5.
r Lev. 13. 46. Num. 5. 2.

s Isai. 1. 1.
t 2 Kin. 15. 7. Isai. 6. 1.

a 2 Kin. 15. 32, &c.

b 2 Kin. 15. 35.

¹ Heb. *free.*   ² Or, *The tower,* ch. 33. 14. Neh. 3. 26.

20. Death was denounced by the Law against those who invaded the office of the priest ; and death had been the actual punishment of Korah and his company. Uzziah feared lest from him also the extreme penalty should be exacted, and therefore hasted to quit the sacred building where his bare presence was a capital crime.

21. *a several house*] See marg. ref. *q* note ; and cp. Ps. lxxxviii., which is supposed by some to refer to Uzziah.

22. *the acts of Uzziah...did Isaiah...write*] Most critics regard Isaiah as about 20 when Uzziah died. He must, then, have written his history of Uzziah's reign from documents and accounts of others, rather than from his own knowledge.

23. *in the field of the burial*] i.e. in the same piece of ground, but in a separate sepulchre. As the Law separated off the leper from his fellows during life (Lev. xiii. 46), so Jewish feeling required that he should remain separate even in death.

XXVII. This short chapter runs parallel

with 2 Kings (marg. ref.), and is taken mainly from the same source or sources which it amplifies.

3. Ophel was the name given to the long, narrowish, rounded spur or promontory, which intervenes between the central valley of Jerusalem (the Tyropœon) and the Kidron, or valley of Jehoshaphat. The anxiety of Uzziah and Jotham to fortify their territory indicates a fear of external attack, which at this time was probably felt mainly in connexion with Samaria and Syria (2 K. xv. 37 note). The faithless trust put in fortifications was rebuked by the prophets of the time (Hos. viii. 14 ; Isai. ii. 15).

5. The Ammonites, who had submitted to Uzziah (xxvi. 8), revolted against Jotham. This revolt he firmly repressed ; and, to punish it, he exacted a high rate of tribute for the three years following the termination of the war. The productiveness of the Ammonite country in grain, which is here indicated, has been remarked upon as extraordinary by modern travellers.

of wheat, and ten thousand of barley. ¹So much did the children of Ammon pay unto him, both the second year, and the
6 third. So Jotham became mighty, because he ²prepared his
7 ways before the LORD his God. ¶Now the rest of the acts of
Jotham, and all his wars, and his ways, lo, they *are* written in
8 the book of the kings of Israel and Judah. He was five and
twenty years old when he began to reign, and reigned sixteen
*c*2Kin.15.38. 9 years in Jerusalem. *c*And Jotham slept with his fathers, and
they buried him in the city of David : and Ahaz his son reigned
in his stead.

a 2 Kin. 16.2. **CHAP. 28.** AHAZ *a was* twenty years old when he began to reign,
and he reigned sixteen years in Jerusalem: but he did not *that
which was* right in the sight of the LORD, like David his father :
2 for he walked in the ways of the kings of Israel, and made also
b Ex. 34. 17. 3 *b*molten images for *c*Baalim. Moreover he ³burnt incense in
Lev. 19. 4.
c Judg. 2. 11. *d*the valley of the son of Hinnom, and burnt *c*his children in the
*d*2Kin.23.10. fire, after the abominations of the heathen whom the LORD had
e Lev. 18. 21.
ch. 33. 6. 4 cast out before the children of Israel. He sacrificed also and
burnt incense in the high places, and on the hills, and under
f Isai. 7. 1. 5 every green tree. Wherefore *f*the LORD his God delivered him
g 2 Kin. 16. into the hand of the king of Syria ; and they *g*smote him, and
5, 6.
carried away a great multitude of them captives, and brought
them to ⁴Damascus. And he was also delivered into the hand of
6 the king of Israel, who smote him with a great slaughter. For
*h*2Kin.15.27. *h*Pekah the son of Remaliah slew in Judah an hundred and
twenty thousand in one day, *which were* all ⁵valiant men ;
7 because they had forsaken the LORD God of their fathers. And
Zichri, a mighty man of Ephraim, slew Maaseiah the king's son,
and Azrikam the governor of the house, and Elkanah *that was*
8 ⁶next to the king. And the children of Israel carried away
i ch. 11. 4. captive of their *i*brethren two hundred thousand, women, sons,
and daughters, and took also away much spoil from them, and
9 brought the spoil to Samaria. ¶But a prophet of the LORD was
k Ps. 69. 26. there, whose name *was* Oded : and he went out before the host
Isai. 10. 5.
& 47. 6. that came to Samaria, and said unto them, Behold, *k*because the
Ezek. 25.12, LORD God of your fathers was wroth with Judah, he hath de-
15.
& 26. 2. livered them into your hand, and ye have slain them in a rage
Obad.10,&c.
Zech. 1. 15. 10 *that l*reacheth up unto heaven. And now ye purpose to keep
l Ezra 9. 6.
Rev. 18. 5. | ¹ Heb. *This.* | ³ Or, *offered sacrifice.* | ⁵ Heb. *sons of valour.* |
| ² Or, *established.* | ⁴ Heb. *Darmesek.* | ⁶ Heb. *the second to the king.* |

XXVIII. This chapter is *supplemental*
in character. The writer seems to assume
that the narrative of Kings (marg. ref.) is
known, and is mainly anxious to add points
which the author of that narrative has
omitted.

2. *images for Baalim*] Or, to serve as
Baalim, *i.e* as representatives of the different forms or characters of the chief
Phœnician deity.

3. Cp. 2 K. xvi. 3 note.

4. *He sacrificed also &c.*] Cp. 2 K. xvi. 4.

5. The two battles here mentioned, one
with Rezin (king of Syria), and the other
with Pekah (king of Israel) are additions
to the narrative of the writer of Kings
(marg. ref. *g*). The events of the Syro-
Israelite war were probably spread over
several years.

6. The fearful loss here described may
have been due to a complete defeat followed
by panic.

7. Maaseiah was either an officer called
"the king's son" (cp. 1 K. xxii. 26), or
perhaps a son of Jotham, since Ahaz could
hardly have had a son old enough to take
part in the battle (cp. *v.* 1).

Elkanah, as "second to the king," was
probably the chief of the royal counsellors.

9. Nothing more is known of this Oded.
Cp. xv. 1.

he went out before the host] Rather, "He
went out **to meet** the host," as the same
phrase is translated in xv. 2.

a rage that reacheth up to heaven] *i.e.* not
merely an exceedingly great and violent
rage, but one that has displeased God.

10. *are there not with you...sins against the*

under the children of Judah and Jerusalem for [m]bondmen and bondwomen unto you: *but are there* not with you, even with you.
11 sins against the LORD your God? Now hear me therefore, and deliver the captives again, which ye have taken captive of your
12 brethren: [n]for the fierce wrath of the LORD *is* upon you. Then certain of the heads of the children of Ephraim, Azariah the son of Johanan, Berechiah the son of Meshillemoth, and Jehizkiah the son of Shallum, and Amasa the son of Hadlai,
13 stood up against them that came from the war, and said unto them, Ye shall not bring in the captives hither: for whereas we have offended against the LORD *already*, ye intend to add *more* to our sins and to our trespass: for our trespass is great, and *there*
14 *is* fierce wrath against Israel. So the armed men left the captives
15 and the spoil before the princes and all the congregation. And the men [o]which were expressed by name rose up, and took the captives, and with the spoil clothed all that were naked among them, and arrayed them, and shod them, and [p]gave them to eat and to drink, and anointed them, and carried all the feeble of them upon asses, and brought them to Jericho, [q]the city of palm trees, to their brethren: then they returned to
16 Samaria. ¶ [r]At that time did king Ahaz send unto the kings of
17 Assyria to help him. For again the Edomites had come and
18 smitten Judah, and carried away [1]captives. [s]The Philistines also had invaded the cities of the low country, and of the south of Judah, and had taken Beth-shemesh, and Ajalon, and Gederoth, and Shocho with the villages thereof, and Timnah with the villages thereof, Gimzo also and the villages thereof: and they
19 dwelt there. For the LORD brought Judah low because of Ahaz king of [t]Israel; for he [u]made Judah naked, and transgressed
20 sore against the LORD. And [x]Tilgath-pilneser king of Assyria came unto him, and distressed him, but strengthened him not.

[m] Lev. 25.39, 42, 43, 46.

[n] Jam. 2. 13.

[o] ver. 12.

[p] 2 Kin. 6.22. Prov. 25. 21, 22. Luke 6. 27. Rom. 12. 20.
[q] Deut. 34. 3. Judg. 1. 16.
[r] 2 Kin. 16.7.
[s] Ezek. 16. 27, 57.

[t] ch. 21. 2.
[u] Ex. 32. 25.
[x] 2 Kin.15.29. & 16. 7, 8, 9.

[1] Heb. *a captiv'ty.*

LORD?] The ten tribes had fallen away from the true faith far more completely and more hopelessly than the two. It was not for them to press hard against their erring brothers, and aggravate their punishment.

12. "Ephraim" is used here in the generic sense so common in the Prophets, as synonymous with the ten tribes.

15. Jericho, which lies much farther from Samaria than many points of the territory of Judah, was perhaps selected because the captives had been carried off principally from this point; or because there may have been less danger of falling in with portions of Pekah's army on this than on the direct route.

17. The Edomites took advantage of the reverses of Ahaz, and were perhaps in league with Rezin (see 2 K. xvi. 6 note). The pitilessness of Edom, and her readiness to turn against Judah in any severe distress, is noticed and sternly rebuked by the Prophets (Am. i. 11; Ezek. xxxv. 5; Obad. 10-14, &c.).

18. Philistia also, eager to retaliate the blows she had received from Uzziah (xxvi. 6), seized her opportunity. Ajalon and Shocho were among the cities fortified by

Rehoboam (xi. 7, 10); Beth-shemesh (Josh. xv. 10) was famous as the scene of Amaziah's defeat (xxv. 21). Gimzo, which is not elsewhere mentioned in Scripture has been probably identified with the modern *Jimzu*, a large village about 2½ miles from *Ludd* (the ancient Lydda).

19. *Ahaz king of Israel*] An instance of the lax use of the word "Israel" (xii. 6, xxi. 2). It is simply equivalent to "king of Judah."

he made Judah naked] Lit. "he **had caused licentiousness** in Judah"—*i.e.* he had allowed Judah to break loose from all restraints of true religion, and to turn to any idolatry that they preferred (*vv.* 2-4). In this and in the following expression there is implied an apostasy resembling the unfaithfulness of a wife.

20. *Tilgath-pilneser*] This form of the name is doubly corrupt. See the properly Hebraized form in 2 K. xv. 29.

distressed him, but strengthened him not] This statement, and that at the end of *v.* 21, is supplemental to, and not contradictory of, 2 K. xvi. 9. Here it is the writer's object to note that the material assistance rendered by Tiglath-pileser to Ahab, was no

21 For Ahaz took away a portion *out* of the house of the LORD, and
out of the house of the king, and of the princes, and gave *it* unto
22 the king of Assyria: but he helped him not.   ¶ And in the time
of his distress did he trespass yet more against the LORD: this
23 *is that* king Ahaz.   For *y* he sacrificed unto the gods of ¹ Damascus, which smote him: and he said, Because the gods of the
kings of Syria help them, *therefore* will I sacrifice to them, that
z they may help me.   But they were the ruin of him, and of all
24 Israel.   And Ahaz gathered together the vessels of the house
of God, and cut in pieces the vessels of the house of God, *a* and
shut up the doors of the house of the LORD, and he made him
25 altars in every corner of Jerusalem.   And in every several city
of Judah he made high places ² to burn incense unto other gods,
26 and provoked to anger the LORD God of his fathers.   ¶ *b* Now
the rest of his acts and of all his ways, first and last, behold,
they *are* written in the book of the kings of Judah and Israel.
27 And Ahaz slept with his fathers, and they buried him in the
city, *even* in Jerusalem: but they brought him not into the
sepulchres of the kings of Israel: and Hezekiah his son reigned
in his stead.

CHAP. 29. HEZEKIAH *a* began to reign *when he was* five and
twenty years old, and he reigned nine and twenty years in
Jerusalem.   And his mother's name *was* Abijah, the daughter
2 *b* of Zechariah.   And he did *that which was* right in the sight of
3 the LORD, according to all that David his father had done.   He
in the first year of his reign, in the first month, *c* opened the
4 doors of the house of the LORD, and repaired them.   And he
brought in the priests and the Levites, and gathered them
5 together into the east street, and said unto them, Hear me, ye
Levites, *d* sanctify now yourselves, and sanctify the house of the
LORD God of your fathers, and carry forth the filthiness out of
6 the holy *place*.   For our fathers have trespassed, and done *that
which was* evil in the eyes of the LORD our God, and have forsaken him, and have *e* turned away their faces from the habita-
7 tion of the LORD, and ³ turned *their* backs.   *f* Also they have

Marginal notes:

y See ch. 25.
14.

z Jer. 44. 17,
18.
a See ch. 29.
3, 7.

b 2 Kin. 16.
19, 20.

a 2 Kin. 18. 1.

b ch. 26. 5.

c See ch. 28.
24.
ver. 7.

d 1 Chr. 15. 12.
ch. 35. 6.

e Jer. 2. 27.
Ezek. 8. 16.
f ch. 28. 24.

---

¹ Heb. *Darmesek*.   ² Or, *to offer*.   ³ Heb. *given the neck*.

---

real "help" or "strength," but rather a
cause of " distress."
23. His adoption of the Syrian gods,
Hadad, Rimmon, and others, as objects of
worship, no doubt preceded the destruction
of Damascus by the Assyrians (2 K. xvi.
9).
Israel] *i.e.* "Judah;" so in *v.* 27. Cp.
v. 19.
24. Cp. 2 K. xvi. 17 note. The Temple-
worship was suspended, the lamps put out,
and the doors shut, to prevent the priests
from entering. The Jews still celebrate a
yearly fast in commemoration of this time
of affliction.
altars] As the one Altar for sacrifice,
which alone the Law allowed, symbolized
the doctrine of one God, so these many
altars spoke unmistakeably of the all-em-
bracing polytheism affected by Ahaz.
XXIX. The treatment of Hezekiah's
reign by the author of Chronicles is in
marked contrast with that followed in the

Book of Kings. The writer of Kings
describes mainly civil affairs; the author
of Chronicles gives a full account of Hezekiah's religious reformation. Chapters
xxix.-xxxi. contain matter, therefore, which
is almost wholly new.
3. By "the first month" is meant (cp.
xxx. 2, 3) the month of Nisan, the first of
the Jewish sacred year, not necessarily the
first month of Hezekiah's reign.
4. *the east street*] Rather, some open space
before the eastern gate of the outer Temple
Court is intended.
5. *sanctify now yourselves*] Cp. marg. ref.
Hezekiah follows David's example, knowing,
probably, that the priests had in the preceding time of idolatry contracted many de-
filements.
The "filthiness," or "uncleanness" (*v.*
16), might consist, in part, of mere dust and
dirt, in part, of idolatrous objects introduced by Ahaz before he finally shut up the
Temple (2 K. xvi. 10-16).

shut up the doors of the porch, and put out the lamps, and have not burned incense nor offered burnt offerings in the holy *place*
8 unto the God of Israel. Wherefore the *ᵍ*wrath of the LORD was upon Judah and Jerusalem, and he hath delivered them to ¹trouble, to astonishment, and to *ʰ*hissing, as ye see with your
9 eyes. For, lo, *ⁱ*our fathers have fallen by the sword, and our sons and our daughters and our wives *are* in captivity for this.
10 Now *it is* in mine heart to make *ᵏ*a covenant with the LORD God of Israel, that his fierce wrath may turn away from us.
11 My sons, ²be not now negligent: for the LORD hath *ˡ*chosen you to stand before him, to serve him, and that ye should
12 minister unto him, and ³burn incense. ¶Then the Levites arose, Mahath the son of Amasai, and Joel the son of Azariah, of the sons of the Kohathites: and of the sons of Merari, Kish the son of Abdi, and Azariah the son of Jehalelel: and of the Gershonites; Joah the son of Zimmah, and Eden the son of
13 Joah: and of the sons of Elizaphan; Shimri, and Jeiel: and of
14 the sons of Asaph; Zechariah, and Mattaniah: and of the sons of Heman; Jehiel, and Shimei: and of the sons of Jeduthun;
15 Shemaiah, and Uzziel. And they gathered their brethren, and *ᵐ*sanctified themselves, and came, according to the commandment of the king, ⁴by the words of the LORD, *ⁿ*to cleanse the
16 house of the LORD. And the priests went into the inner part of the house of the LORD, to cleanse *it*, and brought out all the uncleanness that they found in the temple of the LORD into the court of the house of the LORD. And the Levites took *it*, to
17 carry *it* out abroad into the brook Kidron. Now they began on the first *day* of the first month to sanctify, and on the eighth day of the month came they to the porch of the LORD: so they sanctified the house of the LORD in eight days; and in the
18 sixteenth day of the first month they made an end. Then they went in to Hezekiah the king, and said, We have cleansed all the house of the LORD, and the altar of burnt offering, with all the vessels thereof, and the shewbread table, with all the
19 vessels thereof. Moreover all the vessels, which king Ahaz in his reign did *ᵒ*cast away in his transgression, have we prepared and sanctified, and, behold, they *are* before the altar of
20 the LORD. ¶Then Hezekiah the king rose early, and gathered the rulers of the city, and went up to the house of the LORD.
21 And they brought seven bullocks, and seven rams, and seven lambs, and seven he goats, for a *ᵖ*sin offering for the kingdom,

ᵍ ch. 24. 18.

ʰ Jer. 18. 16
& 19. 8.
& 25. 9, 18.
& 29. 18.
ⁱ ch. 28. 5,
6. 8, 17.
ᵏ ch. 15. 12.
ˡ Num. 3. 6.
& 8. 14.
& 18. 2, 6.

ᵐ ver. 5.
ⁿ 1 Chr. 23. 28.

ᵒ ch. 28. 24.

ᵖ Lev. 4. 3, 14.

---

¹ Heb. *commotion*, Deut. 28. 25. ² Or, *be not now deceived*. ³ Or, *offer sacrifice*. ⁴ Or, *in the business of the LORD*, ch. 30. 12.

---

8. *he hath delivered them to...hissing*] See 1 K. ix. 8 note. It was an expression which Hezekiah might naturally use, for it had occurred in a prophecy of Micah (vi. 16), his contemporary and monitor (Jer. xxvi. 18, 19), which was probably uttered towards the close of the reign of Ahaz. In Jeremiah the phrase becomes common (marg. reff.).

12, 13. On the triple division of the Levites, see 1 Chr. xxiii. 6; and on the musical Levites, see 1 Chr. xxv. 1-6.

13. The descendants of Elizaphan — a grandson of Kohath (Ex. vi. 22), and chief of the Kohathites at the time of the census in the Wilderness (Num. iii. 30)—appear at

all times to have formed a distinct branch of the Kohathites with special privileges (1 Chr. xv. 8).

15. *by the words of the* LORD] Rather, as suggested in the margin, "According to the commandment of the king *in the business* (or **matters**) of the Lord."

16. The "inner part" means here, not the Holy of Holies in particular, but the interior generally. The priests alone might enter the Temple building. The Levites might penetrate no further than the inner court.

21. Hezekiah commenced his restoration of the Jehovah-worship with an unusually comprehensive Sin-offering, embracing the

and for the sanctuary, and for Judah. And he commanded the priests the sons of Aaron to offer *them* on the altar of the LORD.

22 So they killed the bullocks, and the priests received the blood, and *q* sprinkled *it* on the altar: likewise, when they had killed the rams, they sprinkled the blood upon the altar: they killed also the lambs, and they sprinkled the blood upon the altar.

23 And they brought ¹forth the he goats *for* the sin offering before the king and the congregation; and they laid their *r* hands upon

24 them: and the priests killed them, and they made reconciliation with their blood upon the altar, *s* to make an atonement for all Israel: for the king commanded *that* the burnt offering and the

25 sin offering *should be made* for all Israel. *t* And he set the Levites in the house of the LORD with cymbals, with psalteries, and with harps, *u* according to the commandment of David, and of *x* Gad the king's seer, and Nathan the prophet: *v* for *so was*

26 the commandment ²of the LORD ³by his prophets. And the Levites stood with the instruments *z* of David, and the priests

27 with *a* the trumpets. And Hezekiah commanded to offer the burnt offering upon the altar. And ⁴when the burnt offering began, *b* the song of the LORD began *also* with the trumpets, and

28 with the ⁵instruments *ordained* by David king of Israel. And all the congregation worshipped, and the ⁶singers sang, and the trumpeters sounded: *and all this continued* until the burnt offer-

29 ing was finished. And when they had made an end of offering, *c* the king and all that were ⁷present with him bowed themselves,

30 and worshipped. Moreover Hezekiah the king and the princes commanded the Levites to sing praise unto the LORD with the words of David, and of Asaph the seer. And they sang praises with gladness, and they bowed their heads and worshipped.

31 ¶ Then Hezekiah answered and said, Now ye have ⁸consecrated yourselves unto the LORD, come near and bring sacrifices and *d* thank offerings into the house of the LORD. And the congregation brought in sacrifices and thank offerings; and as many

Left margin references:
q Lev. 8. 14, 15, 19, 24. Heb. 9. 21.

r Lev. 4. 15, 24.

s Lev. 14. 20.

t 1 Chr. 16. 4. & 25. 6.

u 1 Chr. 23. 5. & 25. 1. ch. 8. 14. *x* 2 Sam. 24. 11. *y* ch. 30. 12. *z* 1 Chr. 23. 5. Amos 6, 5. *a* Num. 10. 8, 10. 1 Chr. 15. 24. & 16. 6. *b* ch. 23. 18.

c ch. 20. 18.

d Lev. 7. 12

---

¹ Heb. *near.*
² Heb. *by the hand of the* LORD.
³ Heb. *by the hand of.*
⁴ Heb. *in the time.*
⁵ Heb. *hands of instruments.*
⁶ Heb. *song.*
⁷ Heb. *found.*
⁸ Or, *filled your hand,* ch. 13. 9.

---

four chief kinds of sacrificial animals, and seven animals of each kind : he intended to atone for the sins, both conscious and unconscious, of the king, the priests, the people of Judah, and the people of Israel. After the completion of these expiatory rites, he proceeded to the offering of the Burnt-offering (*v.* 27).

23. *the he goats for the sin offering*] Rather, "the he goats **of the sin offering** "—that portion of the Sin offering which had been reserved to the last.

24. *all Israel*] Hezekiah aimed at reuniting once more the whole people of Israel, if not into a single state, yet, at any rate, into a single religious communion. The northern kingdom was in a condition approaching to anarchy. The end was evidently approaching. Hoshea, the king contemporary with Hezekiah (2 K. xviii. 1), ruled, not as an independent monarch, but as an Assyrian feudatory (do. xvii. 3). Under these circumstances Hezekiah designed to invite the re-

volted tribes to return, if not to their old temporal, at least to their old spiritual, allegiance (xxx. 5-10). In order, therefore, to prepare the way for this return, he included "all Israel" in the expiatory sacrifice, by which he prefaced his restoration of the old worship.

27. All had hitherto been preparatory. Now Hezekiah gave orders that "*the* burnt offering"—*i.e.* the daily morning sacrifice— should be offered upon the Brazen Altar in front of the porch, thus restoring and reinstituting the regular Temple-service. A burst of music gave notice to the people of the moment when the old worship recommenced.

31. Hezekiah addresses, not the priests, but the congregation :—"Now that by the atoning sacrifice which has been offered for you, you are consecrated once more to be a holy people to the Lord, approach with confidence and offer your free-will offerings as of old."

32 as were of a free heart burnt offerings. And the number of the burnt offerings, which the congregation brought, was three-score and ten bullocks, an hundred rams, *and* two hundred
33 lambs: all these *were* for a burnt offering to the LORD. And the consecrated things *were* six hundred oxen and three thousand
34 sheep. But the priests were too few, so that they could not flay all the burnt offerings: wherefore *e*their brethren the Levites ¹did help them, till the work was ended, and until the *other* priests had sanctified themselves: *f*for the Levites *were* more *g*upright in heart to sanctify themselves than the priests.
35 And also the burnt offerings *were* in abundance, with *h*the fat of the peace offerings, and *i*the drink offerings for *every* burnt offering. So the service of the house of the LORD was set in
36 order. And Hezekiah rejoiced, and all the people, that God had prepared the people: for the thing was *done* suddenly.

CHAP. **30.** AND Hezekiah sent to all Israel and Judah, and wrote letters also to Ephraim and Manasseh, that they should come to the house of the LORD at Jerusalem, to keep the passover unto
2 the LORD God of Israel. For the king had taken counsel, and his princes, and all the congregation in Jerusalem, to keep the
3 passover in the second *a*month. For they could not keep it *b*at that time, *c*because the priests had not sanctified themselves sufficiently, neither had the people gathered themselves together
4 to Jerusalem. And the thing ²pleased the king and all the
5 congregation. So they established a decree to make proclamation throughout all Israel, from Beer-sheba even to Dan, that they should come to keep the passover unto the LORD God of Israel at Jerusalem: for they had not done *it* of a long *time in*
6 *such sort* as it was written. ¶ So the posts went with the letters ³from the king and his princes throughout all Israel and Judah, and according to the commandment of the king, saying, Ye children of Israel, *d*turn again unto the LORD God of Abraham, Isaac, and Israel, and he will return to the remnant of you,
7 that are escaped out of the hand of *e*the kings of Assyria. And

e ch. 35. 11.

f ch. 30. 3.
g Ps. 7. 10.
h Lev. 3. 16.
i Num. 15. 5, 7, 10.

a Num. 9. 10, 11.
b Ex. 12. 6, 18.
c ch. 29. 34.

d Jer. 4. 1. Joel 2. 13.

e 2 Kin. 15. 19, 29.

---

¹ Heb. *strengthened them*. ² Heb. *was right in the eyes of the king*. ³ Heb. *from the hand*.

---

burnt offerings] The term thus translated is applied especially to those victims which were to be *wholly* consumed upon the Altar. In the "sacrifices," or Peace offerings generally, and the "thank offerings"—a particular kind of Peace offering (Lev. vii. 12)— the greater part of the victim belonged to, and was consumed by, the worshipper. Hence, to offer "burnt offerings," was indicative of a "free heart."

34. *the Levites were more upright &c.*] See marg. ref. Urijah, the High-Priest, had participated to some extent in the impieties of Ahaz (2 K. xvi. 10–16). He and many of the priests may, therefore, have looked coldly on the reforming zeal of Hezekiah.

XXX. **1.** Cp. xxix. 24 note.

2. *in the second month*] Hezekiah and his counsellors considered that the permission of the Law (see marg. ref.) might, under the circumstances, be extended to the whole people. It had been found impossible to complete the cleansing of the Temple till

the fourteenth day of the first month was past (xxix. 17). It was, therefore, determined to defer it to the 14th of the second month, which allowed time for the priests generally to purify themselves, and for proclamation of the festival to be made throughout all Israel.

3. *at that time*] i.e. in the first month, at the time of the events mentioned in ch. xxix.

5. *they had not done it* &c.] Some prefer, "they had not kept it in full numbers, as it was written"—*i.e.* "they (the Israelites of the northern kingdom) had not (for some while) kept the Passover in full numbers, as the Law required."

6. *the posts went*] The bearers of the letters were probably the "runners" who formed a portion of the king's body-guard (2 K. x. 25 note).

the kings of Assyria] Pul, Tiglath-pileser, and Shalmaneser may all be referred to in this passage (cp. marg. ref. and 2 K. xvii. 3). The passage by no means implies that

J Ezek. 20. 18.

g ch. 29. 8
h Deut. 10. 16.

i ch. 29. 10.

k Ps. 106. 46.

l Ex. 34. 6.

m Isai. 55. 7.

n ch. 36. 16.
o So ch. 11. 16.
ver. 18, 21.
p Phil. 2. 13.
q ch. 29. 25.

r ch. 28. 24.

s ch. 29. 34.

be not ye *f*like your fathers, and like your brethren, which trespassed against the LORD God of their fathers, *who* therefore 8 *g*gave them up to desolation, as ye see. Now [1]be ye not *h*stiff-necked, as your fathers *were*, *but* [2]yield yourselves unto the LORD, and enter into his sanctuary, which he hath sanctified for ever: and serve the LORD your God, *i*that the fierceness of 9 his wrath may turn away from you. For if ye turn again unto the LORD, your brethren and your children *shall find* *k*compassion before them that lead them captive, so that they shall come again into this land: for the LORD your God *is* *l*gracious and merciful, and will not turn away *his* face from you, if ye 10 *m*return unto him. ¶So the posts passed from city to city through the country of Ephraim and Manasseh even unto Zebulun: but *n*they laughed them to scorn, and mocked them. 11 Nevertheless *o*divers of Asher and Manasseh and of Zebulun 12 humbled themselves, and came to Jerusalem. Also in Judah *p*the hand of God was to give them one heart to do the commandment of the king and of the princes, *q*by the word of the 13 LORD. ¶And there assembled at Jerusalem much people to keep the feast of unleavened bread in the second month, a very 14 great congregation. And they arose and took away the *r*altars that *were* in Jerusalem, and all the altars for incense took they 15 away, and cast *them* into the brook Kidron. Then they killed the passover on the fourteenth *day* of the second month: and the priests and the Levites were *s*ashamed, and sanctified themselves, and brought in the burnt offerings into the house of the 16 LORD. And they stood in [3]their place after their manner, according to the law of Moses the man of God: the priests sprinkled the blood, *which they received* of the hand of the Levites.

---

[1] Heb. *harden not your necks.*   [2] Heb. *give the hand:* See 1 Chr. 29. 24. Ezra 10. 19.   [3] Heb. *their standing.*

---

the fall of Samaria and final captivity of the Israelites had as yet taken place.

10. Ephraim and Manasseh are mentioned as the two tribes nearest to Judah, Zebulun as one of the furthest off.

11. Cp. *v.* 18. Hence five of the ten tribes certainly sent representatives. Two—Reuben and Gad—were in Captivity. One—Dan—was absorbed into Judah. Simeon and Naphtali, which alone remained, seem to have been more than ordinarily idolatrous (xxxiv. 6).

14. The continuance of the idolatrous altars to this time shows that Hezekiah had been more anxious to construct than to destroy, to establish the Jehovah-worship than to root out idolatry. Now, however, that the more important work was done, the Temple open, and the daily service restored, attention could be turned to the secondary object of removing from the city all traces of the late apostasy.

15. The laggart priests and Levites, who from want of zeal for the Jehovah-worship, or from actual inclination to idolatry, had neglected to purify themselves (*v.* 3 and marg. ref.), were now shamed by the general ardour, and sanctified themselves for the Paschal festival.

and brought in the burnt offerings] Received them, *i.e.* from the offerers at the doors of the inner court, and took them up to the Brazen Altar in front of the porch. No part of the Burnt offerings was ever taken inside the Temple building.

16. *after their manner*] According to the Mishna, the custom was for the priests to stand in two rows extending from the Altar to the outer court, where the people were assembled. As each offerer slew his lamb the blood was caught in a bason, which was handed to the nearest priest, who passed it on to his neighbour, and he to the next; the blood was thus conveyed to the Altar, at the base of which it was thrown by the last priest in the row. While basons full of blood were thus passed up, empty basons were passed down in a constant succession, so that there was no pause or delay.

which they received of the hand of the Levites] Ordinarily, the blood was received at the hand of the offerer. But the greater number of the Israelites (*v.* 17) who had come to keep the feast were involved in some ceremonial or moral defilement, from which there had not been time for them to purify themselves. On account of this uncleanness, they did not slay their own

17 For *there were* many in the congregation that were not sanctified: [t]therefore the Levites had the charge of the killing of
the passovers for every one *that was* not clean, to sanctify *them*
18 unto the LORD. For a multitude of the people, *even* [u]many of
Ephraim, and Manasseh, Issachar, and Zebulun, had not cleansed
themselves, [x]yet did they eat the passover otherwise than it was
written. But Hezekiah prayed for them, saying, The good LORD
19 pardon every one that [y]prepareth his heart to seek God, the
LORD God of his fathers, though *he be* not *cleansed* according to
20 the purification of the sanctuary. And the LORD hearkened to
21 Hezekiah, and healed the people. ¶ And the children of Israel
that were [1]present at Jerusalem kept [z]the feast of unleavened
bread seven days with great gladness: and the Levites and
the priests praised the LORD day by day, *singing* with [2]loud
22 instruments unto the LORD. And Hezekiah spake [3]comfortably
unto all the Levites [a]that taught the good knowledge of the
LORD: and they did eat throughout the feast seven days, offering peace offerings, and [b]making confession to the LORD God
23 of their fathers. ¶ And the whole assembly took counsel to
keep [c]other seven days: and they kept *other* seven days with
24 gladness. For Hezekiah king of Judah [4d]did give to the congregation a thousand bullocks and seven thousand sheep; and
the princes gave to the congregation a thousand bullocks and
ten thousand sheep: and a great number of priests [e]sanctified
25 themselves. And all the congregation of Judah, with the priests
and the Levites, and all the congregation [f]that came out of
Israel, and the strangers that came out of the land of Israel,
26 and that dwelt in Judah, rejoiced. So there was great joy in
Jerusalem: for since the time of Solomon the son of David
27 king of Israel *there was* not the like in Jerusalem. Then the
priests the Levites arose and [g]blessed the people: and their
voice was heard, and their prayer came *up* to [5]his holy dwelling
place, *even* unto heaven.

CHAP. 31. NOW when all this was finished, all Israel that were
[6]present went out to the cities of Judah, and [a]brake the
[7]images in pieces, and cut down the groves, and threw down the
high places and the altars out of all Judah and Benjamin, in
Ephraim also and Manasseh, [8]until they had utterly destroyed

[t] ch. 29. 34.

[u] ver. 11.

[x] Ex. 12. 43, &c.
[y] ch. 19. 3.

[z] Ex. 12. 15. & 13. 6.

[a] Deut.33.10. ch. 17. 9. & 35. 3.
[b] Ezra 10. 11.

[c] See 1 Kin. 8. 65.
[d] ch. 35. 7, 8.

[e] ch. 29. 34.

[f] ver. 11, 13.

[g] Num. 6. 23.

[a] 2 Kin. 18.4.

---

[1] Heb. *found.*
[2] Heb. *instruments of strength.*
[3] Heb. *to the heart of all,*

&c. Isai. 40. 2.
[4] Heb. *lifted up,* or, *offered.*
[5] Heb. *the habitation of his holiness,* Ps. 68. 5.

[6] Heb. *found.*
[7] Heb. *statues,* ch. 30. 14.
[8] Heb. *until to make an end.*

---

lambs, but delegated the office to the Levites.

22. The "knowledge" intended is perhaps chiefly ritualistic and musical—such
knowledge as enabled them to conduct the
service of the Sanctuary satisfactorily.

they did eat throughout the feast] Lit.
"they did *eat the feast;*" *i.e.* "they kept
the Feast," which was essentially kept by
the eating of unleavened bread. The Levites kept the Feast during the full term
appointed for it, never failing in their
duties, but taking their part day after day,
both in the sacrifice of the victims and in
singing praises to God.

23. *to keep other seven days*] This was a
voluntary addition to the requirements of

the Law—the fruit and sign of the abound-
ing zeal which characterised the time. Hezekiah and the princes probably proposed
it to the people, and presented them with
sacrificial animals.

25. *the strangers*] See xv. 9 note.

26. *since the time of Solomon*] Cp. vii. 8-
10.

XXXI. 1. Jerusalem had been cleansed
(xxx. 14); now the land had to be purged.
Hezekiah therefore gave his sanction to a
popular movement directed as much against
the "high places" which had been maintained since the times of the patriarchs, as
against the remnants of the Baal-worship, as
or the innovations of Ahaz. See 2 K. xviii. 4
note. The invasion of the northern king-

them all. Then all the children of Israel returned, every man 2 to his possession, into their own cities. ¶ And Hezekiah appointed ^bthe courses of the priests and the Levites after their courses, every man according to his service, the priests and Levites ^cfor burnt offerings and for peace offerings, to minister, and to give thanks, and to praise in the gates of the tents of 3 the LORD. *He appointed* also the king's portion of his substance for the burnt offerings, *to wit*, for the morning and evening burnt offerings, and the burnt offerings for the sabbaths, and for the new moons, and for the set feasts, as *it is* written in the ^dlaw 4 of the LORD. ¶ Moreover he commanded the people that dwelt in Jerusalem to give the ^eportion of the priests and the Levites, 5 that they might be encouraged in ^fthe law of the LORD. And as soon as the commandment ¹came abroad, the children of Israel brought in abundance ^gthe firstfruits of corn, wine, and oil, and ²honey, and of all the increase of the field; and the tithe of all 6 *things* brought they in abundantly. And *concerning* the children of Israel and Judah, that dwelt in the cities of Judah, they also brought in the tithe of oxen and sheep, and the ^htithe of holy things which were consecrated unto the LORD their God, and 7 laid *them* ³by heaps. In the third month they began to lay the foundation of the heaps, and finished *them* in the seventh month. 8 And when Hezekiah and the princes came and saw the heaps, 9 they blessed the LORD, and his people Israel. Then Hezekiah questioned with the priests and the Levites concerning the heaps.

Marginal references:

^b 1 Chr. 23. 6. & 24. 1.

^c 1 Chr. 23. 30, 31.

^d Num. 23, & 29.

^e Num. 18. 8, &c. *f* Mal. 2. 7.

^g Ex. 22. 29. Neh. 13. 12.

^h Lev. 27. 30. Deut. 14. 28.

---

¹ Heb. *brake forth.*   ² Or, *dates.*   ³ Heb. *heaps, heaps.*

---

dom "Ephraim and Manasseh" by a tumultuous crowd from the southern one, and the success which attended the movement, can only be explained by the state of weakness into which the northern kingdom had fallen (see note on xxix. 24).

2. *the tents*] Lit. "the camps." The Temple is called the "camp of Jehovah" by an apt metaphor: the square enclosure, with its gates and stations, its guards and porters, its reliefs, its orderly arrangement, and the tabernacle, or tent, of the great commander in the midst, very much resembled a camp.

3. *the king's portion*] Amid the general neglect of the observances commanded by the Law, the tithe system had naturally fallen into disuse. Hezekiah revived it; and, to encourage the people to give what was due, cheerfully set the example of paying the full proportion from his own considerable possessions (cp. xxxii. 28, 29). His tithe was, it seems, specially devoted to the purposes mentioned in this verse (cp. marg. ref.). There were needed for these purposes in the course of the year nearly 1100 lambs, 113 bullocks, 37 rams, and 30 goats, besides vast quantities of flour, oil, and wine for the accompanying Meat and Drink offerings.

4. *that they might be encouraged* &c.] *i.e.* to devote themselves wholly to their proper work, the service of the Sanctuary and the teaching of God's Law (xvii. 7-9), and not engage in secular occupations. Cp. Neh. xiii. 10-14.

5. *honey*] See marg. It is doubtful whether bee-honey was liable to first-fruits. The sort here intended may therefore be that which, according to Josephus, was manufactured from dates.

6. By "the children of Israel" in *v.* 5, seem to be intended the inhabitants of Jerusalem only (see *v.* 4); by "the children of Israel and Judah that dwelt in the cities of Judah" in this verse, seem to be meant the Jews of the country districts and the Israelites who dwelt among them (xxx. 25). Of these two classes, the first brought both first-fruits and tithes of *all things*; while the others, who had not been included in the command (*v.* 4), brought in first-fruits and paid the tithe of sheep and oxen only, and of the things which they had vowed to God.

7. *the third month*] Cp. xxix. 3, xxx. 2, 13. The events hitherto described—the destruction of the high-places, the re-appointment of the courses, and the re-establishment of the tithes—followed so closely upon the Passover, that a month had not elapsed from the conclusion of the Feast before the gifts began to pour in. In the seventh month the harvest was completed; and the last tithes and first-fruits of the year would naturally come in then.

9. "Hezekiah questioned" in order to know whether the ministering priests and Levites had had their maintenance out of the tithes, and whether the accumulation which he saw was clear surplus.

10 And Azariah the chief priest of the house of Zadok answered
him, and said, *Since the people began to bring the offerings into
the house of the LORD, we have had enough to eat, and have left
plenty: for the LORD hath blessed his people; and that which is
11 left is this great store. ¶ Then Hezekiah commanded to prepare
12 ¹chambers in the house of the LORD; and they prepared them, and
brought in the offerings and the tithes and the dedicated things
faithfully: *over which Cononiah the Levite was ruler, and
13 Shimei his brother was the next. And Jehiel, and Azaziah, and
Nahath, and Asahel, and Jerimoth, and Jozabad, and Eliel, and
Ismachiah, and Mahath, and Benaiah, were overseers ²under
the hand of Cononiah and Shimei his brother, at the commandment of Hezekiah the king, and Azariah the ruler of the house
14 of God. And Kore the son of Imnah the Levite, the porter
toward the east, was over the freewill offerings of God, to distribute the oblations of the LORD, and the most holy things.
15 And ³next him were Eden, and Miniamin, and Jeshua, and
Shemaiah, Amariah, and Shecaniah, in *the cities of the priests,
in their ⁴set office, to give to their brethren by courses, as well
16 to the great as to the small: beside their genealogy of males,
from three years old and upward, even unto every one that
entereth into the house of the LORD, his daily portion for their
17 service in their charges according to their courses; both to the
genealogy of the priests by the house of their fathers, and the
Levites ᵐfrom twenty years old and upward, in their charges by
18 their courses; and to the genealogy of all their little ones, their
wives, and their sons, and their daughters, through all the congregation: for in their ⁵set office they sanctified themselves in
19 holiness: also of the sons of Aaron the priests, which were in
ⁿthe fields of the suburbs of their cities, in every several city,

i Mal. 3. 10.

k Neh. 13.13.

i Josh. 21. 9.

m 1 Chr. 23.
24, 27.

n Lev. 25. 34.
Num. 35. 2.

---

¹ Or, storehouses.
² Heb. at the hand.
³ Heb. at his hand.
⁴ Or, trust, 1 Chr. 9. 22.
⁵ Or, trust.

---

10. If this Azariah was the same as he
who resisted Uzziah (xxvi. 17–20), he must
have held his office at least 33 years. Cp.
xxvii. 1, xxviii. 1.

the LORD *hath blessed his people*] *i.e.* God
has made the harvest unusually abundant,
and hence the great amount of tithes and
first-fruits.

14. *the porter toward the east*] *i.e.* the
chief door-keeper at the east gate, where
the proper number of the porters was six (1
Chr. xxvi. 17).

the most holy things] The Sin-offerings and
Trespass-offerings (Lev. vi. 25, vii. 1–6).

15. *the cities of the priests*] *i.e.* the Levitical
cities (cp. marg. ref.). Of these, some had
gone to decay, while others, as Libnah and
Beth-shemesh (xxi. 10, xxviii. 18), had been
lost, so that the original number, thirteen,
was now, apparently, reduced to six.

in their set office] Rather, as in marg.
These six Levites were stationed at the
Levitical cities, with the trust following
committed to them.

16. *beside their genealogy of males*, &c.]
Some translate—"Excepting the list of
males," &c. *i.e.* they distributed to all the
members of the priestly families, excepting

to those who at the time were performing
the duties of their office at Jerusalem.
These persons no doubt obtained their share
at the Temple itself.

17. *both to the genealogy of the priests* &c.]
Some prefer—"And as for the list of the
priests, it was according to the houses of
their fathers, and that of the Levites was
from twenty years," &c. The writer states
the nature of the lists which guided the
officers who made the distributions. Three
lists are enumerated—one of the priests
made out according to families; one of the
Levites, including all above 20 years of age
(see marg. ref.), and made out according to
courses; and a third (*v.* 18) of the priestly
and Levitical families.

18. *and to the genealogy of all their little ones*,
&c.] Or, "And as to the list of all their
little ones, their wives, their sons, and their
daughters, it extended to the whole body;
for they dealt with the holy things faithfully."

19. The country priests and Levites are
here distinguished from those who dwelt in
the towns. The writer means to note that
not even were they neglected.

o ver. 12, 13,
14, 15.
the men that were *o*expressed by name, to give portions to all
the males among the priests, and to all that were reckoned by
20 genealogies among the Levites.   ¶ And thus did Hezekiah

p 2 Kin.20.3.
throughout all Judah, and *p*wrought *that which was* good and
21 right and truth before the LORD his God.   And in every work
that he began in the service of the house of God, and in the law,
and in the commandments, to seek his God, he did *it* with all
his heart, and prospered.

a Isai. 36. 1,
&c.
CHAP. 32. AFTER *a*these things, and the establishment thereof,
Sennacherib king of Assyria came, and entered into Judah, and
encamped against the fenced cities, and thought ¹to win them
2 for himself.   And when Hezekiah saw that Sennacherib was
3 come, and that ²he was purposed to fight against Jerusalem, he
took counsel with his princes and his mighty men to stop the
waters of the fountains which *were* without the city: and they
4 did help him.   So there was gathered much people together, who
stopped all the fountains, and the brook that ³ran through the
midst of the land, saying, Why should the kings of Assyria come,

b Isai. 22. 9,
10.
c ch. 25. 23.
d 2 Sam. 5. 9.
1 Kin. 9. 15.
5 and find much water?   Also *b*he strengthened himself, *c*and
built up all the wall that was broken, and raised *it* up to the
towers, and another wall without, and repaired *d*Millo *in* the
6 city of David, and made ⁴darts and shields in abundance.   And
he set captains of war over the people, and gathered them
together to him in the street of the gate of the city, and ⁵spake

e Deut. 31. 6.
f ch. 20. 15.
7 comfortably to them, saying, *e*Be strong and courageous, *f*be
not afraid nor dismayed for the king of Assyria, nor for all the

g 2 Kin.6.16.
h Jer. 17. 5.
1 John 4. 4.
i ch. 13. 12.
Rom. 8. 31.
multitude that *is* with him: for *g*there *be* more with us than with
8 him: with him *is* an *h*arm of flesh; but *i*with us *is* the LORD
our God to help us, and to fight our battles.   And the people
⁶rested themselves upon the words of Hezekiah king of Judah.

k 2 Kin.18.17.
9 ¶ *k*After this did Sennacherib king of Assyria send his servants
to Jerusalem, (but he *himself laid siege* against Lachish, and all
his ⁷power with him,) unto Hezekiah king of Judah, and unto

l 2 Kin.18.19.
10 all Judah that *were* at Jerusalem, saying, *l*Thus saith Senna-

---

¹ Heb. *to break them up.*
² Heb. *his face* was *to war.*
³ Heb. *overflowed.*

⁴ Or, *swords*, or, *weapons.*
⁵ Heb. *spake to their heart,*
   ch. 30. 22. Isai. 40. 2.

⁶ Heb. *leaned.*
⁷ Heb. *dominion.*

XXXII. 1. *the establishment thereof*] Lit.
"the *faithfulness* thereof"—or, in other
words, "after these things had been faithfully accomplished."

Verses 1–8 form a passage supplementary
to 2 K. xviii. 13–16.

3. *to stop the waters* &c.] Cp. *v.* 30.
Hezekiah's object was probably twofold—
to hide the springs outside the city in order
to distress the Assyrians, and to convey
their water underground into the city, in
order to increase his own supply during the
siege.

4. The "brook" intended is probably not
the Kidron, but the natural water-course of
the Gihon, which ran down the Tyropœon
valley (cp. 1 K. i. 3 note).

5. The breaches in the wall of Jerusalem
were not entirely due to the old hostility of
Joash (marg. ref.); but may have been
caused either by neglect and carelessness in
the reign of Ahaz (ch. xxviii.), or by the

simple process of natural decay.   Hezekiah
pulled down houses for the purpose of his
repairs (Isai. xxii. 10).

On Millo, see marg. reff. notes.

6. *the street of the gate* &c.] Or, "the
square at the gate" (cp. xxix. 4 note).   The
gate intended is probably that of Ephraim
(xxv. 23)—the great northern gate, opposite
the "Camp of the Assyrians"—represented
by the modern Damascus gate.

7. On the language, cp. the marg. reff.;
for details, see Isai. xxii. 5–13, xxix. 3.

8. The faith, which Hezekiah's words express, presently wavered, died away, and
was succeeded by despair and submission
(cp. 2 K. xviii. 14–16 notes).

9–22 The author of Chronicles com-
presses into thirteen verses the history
which occupies in Kings a chapter and a
half (2 K. xviii. 17, xix.; where see notes).

10. *in the siege*] Perhaps "in **straitness**"
(cp. Jer. xix 9).   Jerusalem is thought by

cherib king of Assyria, Whereon do ye trust, that ye abide [1]in
11 the siege in Jerusalem? Doth not Hezekiah persuade you to
give over yourselves to die by famine and by thirst, saying,
[m]The LORD our God shall deliver us out of the hand of the king
12 of Assyria? [n]Hath not the same Hezekiah taken away his
high places and his altars, and commanded Judah and Jerusalem, saying, Ye shall worship before one altar, and burn
13 incense upon it? Know ye not what I and my fathers have
done unto all the people of *other* lands? [o]were the gods of the
nations of those lands any ways able to deliver their lands out
14 of mine hand? Who *was there* among all the gods of those
nations that my fathers utterly destroyed, that could deliver
his people out of mine hand, that your God should be able to
15 deliver you out of mine hand? Now therefore [p]let not Hezekiah deceive you, nor persuade you on this manner, neither yet
believe him: for no god of any nation or kingdom was able to
deliver his people out of mine hand, and out of the hand of my
fathers: how much less shall your God deliver you out of mine
16 hand? And his servants spake yet *more* against the LORD God,
17 and against his servant Hezekiah. ¶ [q]He wrote also letters to
rail on the LORD God of Israel, and to speak against him, saying, [r]As the gods of the nations of *other* lands have not delivered
their people out of mine hand, so shall not the God of Hezekiah
18 deliver his people out of mine hand. [s]Then they cried with a
loud voice in the Jews' speech unto the people of Jerusalem
[t]that *were* on the wall, to affright them, and to trouble them;
19 that they might take the city. And they spake against the God
of Jerusalem, as against the gods of the people of the earth,
20 *which were* [u]the work of the hands of man. ¶ [x]And for this *cause*
Hezekiah the king, and [y]the prophet Isaiah the son of Amoz,
21 prayed and cried to heaven. [z]And the LORD sent an angel,
which cut off all the mighty men of valour, and the leaders and
captains in the camp of the king of Assyria. So he returned
with shame of face to his own land. And when he was come
into the house of his god, they that came forth of his own bowels
22 [2]slew him there with the sword. Thus the LORD saved Hezekiah
and the inhabitants of Jerusalem from the hand of Sennacherib
the king of Assyria, and from the hand of all *other*, and guided
23 them on every side. And many brought gifts unto the LORD
to Jerusalem, and [3a]presents to Hezekiah king of Judah: so
that he was [b]magnified in the sight of all nations from thence-
24 forth. ¶ [c]In those days Hezekiah was sick to the death, and
prayed unto the LORD: and he spake unto him, and he [4]gave
25 him a sign. But Hezekiah [d]rendered not again according to

[m] 2 Kin. 18. 30.
[n] 2 Kin. 18. 22.
[o] 2 Kin.18.33, 34, 35.
[p] 2 Kin.18.29.
[q] 2 Kin.19.9.
[r] 2 Kin.19.12.
[s] 2 Kin.18.28.
[t] 2 Kin. 18. 26, 27, 28.
[u] 2 Kin.19.18.
[x] 2 Kin.19.15.
[y] 2 Kin. 19.
2, 4.
[z] 2 Kin. 19. 35, &c.
[a] ch. 17. 5.
[b] ch. 1. 1.
[c] 2 Kin. 20.1.
Isai. 38. 1.
[d] Ps. 116. 12.

[1] Or, *in the strong hold.*   [3] Heb. *precious things.*   [4] Or, *wrought a miracle*
[2] Heb. *made him fall.*   *for him.*

some to have been not so much besieged at
this time, as distressed and straitened for
supplies, because the Assyrians were masters of the open country.
    13. *fathers*] *i.e.* "predecessors." Senna-
cherib really belonged to a dynasty that had
only furnished one king before himself.
    22. *guided them* &c.] A slight alteration
of the existing text gives the sense—"gave
them rest round about;" a common expression in Chronicles (xv. 15, xx. 30).

24. Cp. 2 K. xx. and notes. The "sign"
is not (as in marg.) the miraculous cure, but
the going back of the shadow on the dial of
Ahaz (see *v.* 31).
    25. *his heart was lifted up*] Cp. marg.
ref. Hezekiah's pride was shown in his un-
necessarily exhibiting his treasures to the
ambassadors from Babylon (see 2 K. xx.
13).
    there was wrath upon him] Cp. 2 K. xx.
17, 18.

e ch. 26. 16.
Hab. 2. 4.
f ch. 24. 18.
g Jer. 26. 18,
19.
h 2 Kin. 20. 19.

the benefit *done* unto him; for *e*his heart was lifted up: *f*therefore there was wrath upon him, and upon Judah and Jerusalem.
26 *g*Notwithstanding Hezekiah humbled himself for [1]the pride of his heart, *both* he and the inhabitants of Jerusalem, so that the wrath of the LORD came not upon them *h*in the days of Hezekiah.
27 ¶And Hezekiah had exceeding much riches and honour: and he made himself treasuries for silver, and for gold, and for precious stones, and for spices, and for shields, and for all
28 manner of [2]pleasant jewels; storehouses also for the increase of corn, and wine, and oil; and stalls for all manner of beasts,
29 and cotes for flocks. Moreover he provided him cities, and possessions of flocks and herds in abundance: for *i*God had

*i*1 Chr. 29. 12.
k Is. 22. 9. 11.

30 given him substance very much. *k*This same Hezekiah also stopped the upper watercourse of Gihon, and brought it straight down to the west side of the city of David. And Hezekiah
31 prospered in all his works. Howbeit in *the business of* the

l 2 Kin. 20. 12.
Isai. 39. 1.

[3]ambassadors of the princes of Babylon, who *l*sent unto him to enquire of the wonder that was *done* in the land, God left him,

m Deut. 8. 2.

to *m*try him, that he might know all *that was* in his heart.
32 ¶Now the rest of the acts of Hezekiah, and his [4]goodness, be-

n Isai. 36, &
37, & 38, & 39.
o 2 Kin. 18, &
19, & 20.
p 2 Kin. 20. 21.
q Prov. 10. 7.
a 2 Kin. 21.
1, &c.
b Deut. 18. 9.
2 Chr. 28. 3.
c 2 Kin. 18. 4.
ch. 30. 14.
& 31. 1.
& 32. 12.
d Deut. 16. 21.
e Deut. 17. 3.
f Deut. 12. 11.
1 Kin. 8. 29.
& 9. 3.
ch. 6. 6.
& 7. 16.
g ch. 4. 9.
h Lev. 18. 21.
Deut. 18. 10.
2 Kin. 23. 10.
ch. 28. 3.
Ezek. 23. 37,
39.
i Deut. 18. 10,
11.

hold, they *are* written in *n*the vision of Isaiah the prophet, the son of Amoz, *and* in the *o*book of the kings of Judah and Israel.
33 *p*And Hezekiah slept with his fathers, and they buried him in the [5]chiefest of the sepulchres of the sons of David: and all Judah and the inhabitants of Jerusalem did him *q*honour at his death. And Manasseh his son reigned in his stead.
Chap. 33. MANASSEH *a was* twelve years old when he began to
2 reign, and he reigned fifty and five years in Jerusalem: but did *that which was* evil in the sight of the LORD, like unto the *b*abominations of the heathen, whom the LORD had cast out
3 before the children of Israel. For [6]he built again the high places which Hezekiah his father had *c*broken down, and he reared up altars for Baalim, and *d*made groves, and worshipped
4 *e*all the host of heaven, and served them. Also he built altars in the house of the LORD, whereof the LORD had said, *f*In
5 Jerusalem shall my name be for ever. And he built altars for all the host of heaven *g*in the two courts of the house of the
6 LORD. *h*And he caused his children to pass through the fire in the valley of the son of Hinnom: *i*also he observed times, and

[1] Heb. *the lifting up.* [3] Heb. *interpreters.* [5] Or, *highest.*
[2] Heb. *instruments of desire.* [4] Heb. *kindnesses.* [6] Heb. *he returned and built.*

---

26. *Hezekiah humbled himself*] Perhaps this is the self-humiliation of which Jeremiah speaks (marg. ref.) as following on a certain prophecy uttered by Micah. The prophecy (iii. 12) is by some referred to the earlier part of the reign of Hezekiah; but there is nothing to show that it was not delivered about this time.

30. See *v.* 3 note. Either then or afterwards, Hezekiah conducted the water of this spring by an underground channel down the Tyropœon valley to a pool or reservoir (marg. ref.).

32. *and in the book*] The "and" is not in the original. The meaning is, that the acts were recorded in the prophecy of Isaiah, which formed a part of the compilation

known as "the Book of the Kings of Judah and Israel." See Introduction, p. 447.

33. *the chiefest of the sepulchres*] Most modern commentators render—"*on the ascent to* the sepulchres;" but some think that an excavation above all the other tombs,—in the same repository, but at a higher level (see marg.)—is intended. The catacomb of David was full; and the later princes had sepulchres quite distinct from the old burial-place (see xxxiii. 20; 2 K. xxi. 18, 26, xxiii. 30).

XXXIII. Cp. reff. and notes. The author of Chronicles differs chiefly from Kings in additions (see 2 K. xxi. 17 note). The central part of this chapter (*vv.* 11–19) is almost entirely new matter.

used enchantments, and used witchcraft, and ^kdealt with a
familiar spirit, and with wizards: he wrought much evil in the
7 sight of the LORD, to provoke him to anger. And ^lhe set a
carved image, the idol which he had made, in the house of God,
of which God had said to David and to Solomon his son, In
^mthis house, and in Jerusalem, which I have chosen before all
8 the tribes of Israel, will I put my name for ever: ⁿneither will
I any more remove the foot of Israel from out of the land which
I have appointed for your fathers; so that they will take heed
to do all that I have commanded them, according to the whole
law and the statutes and the ordinances by the hand of Moses.
9 ¶ So Manasseh made Judah and the inhabitants of Jerusalem to
err, *and* to do worse than the heathen, whom the LORD had
10 destroyed before the children of Israel. And the LORD spake to
Manasseh, and to his people: but they would not hearken.
11 ^oWherefore the LORD brought upon them the captains of the
host ¹of the king of Assyria, which took Manasseh among the
thorns, and ^pbound him with ²fetters, and carried him to Ba-
12 bylon. And when he was in affliction, he besought the LORD
his God, and ^qhumbled himself greatly before the God of his
13 fathers, and prayed unto him: and he was ^rintreated of him,
and heard his supplication, and brought him again to Jerusalem
into his kingdom. Then Manasseh ^sknew that the LORD he *was*
14 God. ¶ Now after this he built a wall without the city of David,
on the west side of ^tGihon, in the valley, even to the entering in
at the fish gate, and compassed ^uabout ³Ophel, and raised it up
a very great height, and put captains of war in all the fenced
15 cities of Judah. And he took away ^xthe strange gods, and the
idol out of the house of the LORD, and all the altars that he had
built in the mount of the house of the LORD, and in Jerusalem,
16 and cast *them* out of the city. And he repaired the altar of the
LORD, and sacrificed thereon peace offerings and ^ythank offerings, and commanded Judah to serve the LORD God of Israel.
17 ^zNevertheless the people did sacrifice still in the high places, *yet*
18 unto the LORD their God only. ¶ Now the rest of the acts of
Manasseh, and his prayer unto his God, and the words of ^athe

k 2 Kin.21.6.

l 2 Kin. 21.7.

m Ps.132.14.
n 2 Sam.7.10.

o Deut.28.36.

p Job 36. 8.
Ps.107.10,11.
q 1 Pet. 5. 6.
r 1 Chr. 5. 20
Ezra 8. 23.
s Ps. 9. 16.
Dan. 4. 25.
t 1 Kin. 1. 33.
u ch. 27. 3.

x ver. 3, 5, 7.

y Lev. 7. 12.

z ch. 32. 12.

a 1 Sam. 9. 9.

¹ Heb. *which were the king's.*   ² Or, *chains.*   ³ Or, *The tower.*

---

7. *the idol*] *i.e.* the Asherah (2 K. xxi. 7
note), which receives here (and in Ezek.
viii. 3, 5) the somewhat unusual name of
semel, which some regard as a proper name,
and compare with the Greek Σεμέλη.

11. The Assyrian monuments contain no
record of this expedition; but there can be
little doubt that it fell into the reign of
Esarhaddon (2 K. xix. 37 note), who reigned
at least thirteen years. Esarhaddon mentions Manasseh among his tributaries; and
he was the only king of Assyria who, from
time to time, held his court at Babylon.

among the thorns] Translate — " **with
rings ;** " and see 2 K. xix. 28 note.

14. Rather, " he built **the outer wall of**
the city of David **on the west of Gihon-in-
the-valley.**" The wall intended seems to
have been that towards the north-east,
which ran from the vicinity of the modern
Damascus gate across the valley of Gihon,

to the "fish-gate" at the north-east corner
of the "city of David."

We may gather from this verse that, late
in his reign, Manasseh revolted from the
Assyrians, and made preparations to resist
them if they should attack him. Assyria
began to decline in power about B.C. 647,
and from that time her outlying provinces
would naturally begin to fall off. Manasseh
reigned till B.C. 642.

17. Cp. 2 K. xxi. 2, xviii. 4 notes.

18. The "prayer of Manasseh," preserved
to us in some MSS. of the LXX., has no
claim to be considered the genuine utterance of the Jewish king. It is the composition of a Hellenistic Jew, well acquainted
with the Septuagint, writing at a time probably not much anterior to the Christian
era.

the words of the seers that spake to him] See
2 K. xxi. 11-15.

seers that spake to him in the name of the LORD God of Israel,
19 behold, they *are written* in the book of the kings of Israel. His
prayer also, and *how God* was intreated of him, and all his sins,
and his trespass, and the places wherein he built high places,
and set up groves and graven images, before he was humbled:
20 behold, they *are* written among the sayings of ¹the seers. ᵇSo
Manasseh slept with his fathers, and they buried him in his own
21 house: and Amon his son reigned in his stead. ¶ᶜAmon *was*
two and twenty years old when he began to reign, and reigned
22 two years in Jerusalem. But he did *that which was* evil in the
sight of the LORD, as did Manasseh his father: for Amon sacrificed unto all the carved images which Manasseh his father
23 had made, and served them; and humbled not himself before
the LORD, ᵈas Manasseh his father had humbled himself; but
24 Amon ²trespassed more and more. ᵉAnd his servants con-
25 spired against him, and slew him in his own house. But the
people of the land slew all them that had conspired against king
Amon; and the people of the land made Josiah his son king in
his stead.

CHAP. 34. JOSIAH ᵃ*was* eight years old when he began to reign,
2 and he reigned in Jerusalem one and thirty years. And· he did
that which was right in the sight of the LORD, and walked in the
ways of David his father, and declined *neither* to the right hand,
3 nor to the left. For in the eighth year of his reign, while he
was yet young, he began to ᵇseek after the God of David his
father: and in the twelfth year he began ᶜto purge Judah and
Jerusalem ᵈfrom the high places, and the groves, and the carved
4 images, and the molten images. ᵉAnd they brake down the
altars of Baalim in his presence; and the ³images, that *were* on
high above them, he cut down; and the groves, and the carved
images, and the molten images, he brake in pieces, and made
dust *of them*, ᶠand strowed *it* upon the ⁴graves of them that had
5 sacrificed unto them. And he ᵍburnt the bones of the priests
6 upon their altars, and cleansed Judah and Jerusalem. And *so
did he* in the cities of Manasseh, and Ephraim, and Simeon, even
7 unto Naphtali, with their ⁵mattocks round about. And when

ᵇ2Kin.21.18.
ᶜ2 Kin. 21. 19, &c.
ᵈ ver. 12.
ᵉ 2 Kin. 21. 23, 24.
ᶜ 2 Kin. 22. 1, &c.
ᵇ ch. 15. 2.
ᶜ 1 Kin.13. 2.
ᵈ ch. 33. 17, 22.
ᵉ Lev. 26. 30. 2 Kin. 23. 4.
ᶠ 2 Kin. 23. 6.
ᵍ 1 Kin.13. 2.

¹ Or, *Hosai.*
² Heb. *multiplied trespass.*
³ Or, *sun images.*
⁴ Heb. *face of the graves.*
⁵ Or, *mauls.*

in the book of the kings of Israel] The writer of Chronicles usually speaks of "the book of the kings of Judah and Israel" (or "Israel and Judah"). Here he designates the same compilation by a more compendious title, without (apparently) any special reason for the change. Cp. xx. 34.

19. *the seers*] Most moderns adopt the translation given in the margin of the Authorised Version, making Hosai (or rather, Chozai) a proper name. The point is a doubtful one.

XXXIV. Cp. the parallel history of 2 K. xxii. and xxiii. 1-30 notes; the writer here being more full on the celebration of the Passover. The only approach to a discrepancy between the two narratives is with respect to the time of the religious reformation, which the writer of Chronicles distinctly places before, the author of Kings after, the repair of the Temple. The best

explanation seems to be, that the author of Kings has departed from the chronological order, to which he makes no profession of adhering.

3. *he began to purge Judah*] Jeremiah's first prophecies (Jer. ii. and iii.) appear to have been coincident with Josiah's earlier efforts to uproot idolatry, and must have greatly strengthened his hands.

4. *the images*] Marg. *sun-images.* See Lev. xxvi. 30 note.

6. The power of Assyria being now (B.C. 629-624) greatly weakened, if not completely broken, Josiah aimed not merely at a religious reformation, but at a restoration of the kingdom to its ancient limits (2 K. xxiii. 19 note).

with their mattocks &c.] Or "in their desolate places" (cp. Ps. cix. 10). Another reading gives the sense, "he *proved their houses* round about."

he had broken down the altars and the groves, and had [h]beaten the graven images [1]into powder, and cut down all the idols throughout all the land of Israel, he returned to Jerusalem.

8 ¶ Now [i]in the eighteenth year of his reign, when he had purged the land, and the house, he sent Shaphan the son of Azaliah, and Maaseiah the governor of the city, and Joah the son of Joahaz

9 the recorder, to repair the house of the LORD his God. And when they came to Hilkiah the high priest, they delivered [k]the money that was brought into the house of God, which the Levites that kept the doors had gathered of the hand of Manasseh and Ephraim, and of all the remnant of Israel, and of all Judah and

10 Benjamin; and they returned to Jerusalem. And they put *it* in the hand of the workmen that had the oversight of the house of the LORD, and they gave it to the workmen that wrought in

11 the house of the LORD, to repair and amend the house: even to the artificers and builders gave they *it*, to buy hewn stone, and timber for couplings, and [2]to floor the houses which the kings of

12 Judah had destroyed. And the men did the work faithfully: and the overseers of them *were* Jahath and Obadiah, the Levites, of the sons of Merari; and Zechariah and Meshullam, of the sons of the Kohathites, to set *it* forward; and *other of* the

13 Levites, all that could skill of instruments of musick. Also *they were* over the bearers of burdens, and *were* overseers of all that wrought the work in any manner of service: [l]and of the Levites

14 *there were* scribes, and officers, and porters. ¶ And when they brought out the money that was brought into the house of the LORD, Hilkiah the priest [m]found a book of the law of the LORD

15 *given* [3]by Moses. And Hilkiah answered and said to Shaphan the scribe, I have found the book of the law in the house of the

16 LORD. And Hilkiah delivered the book to Shaphan. And Shaphan carried the book to the king, and brought the king word back again, saying, All that was committed [4]to thy ser-

17 vants, they do *it*. And they have [5]gathered together the money that was found in the house of the LORD, and have delivered it into the hand of the overseers, and to the hand of the workmen.

18 Then Shaphan the scribe told the king, saying, Hilkiah the priest hath given me a book. And Shaphan read [6]it before the

19 king. And it came to pass, when the king had heard the words

20 of the law, that he rent his clothes. And the king commanded Hilkiah, and Ahikam the son of Shaphan, and [7]Abdon the son of Micah, and Shaphan the scribe, and Asaiah a servant of the

21 king's, saying, Go, enquire of the LORD for me, and for them that are left in Israel and in Judah, concerning the words of

Margin references:
[h] Deut. 9. 21.
[i] 2 Kin. 22. 3.
[k] See 2 Kin. 12. 4, &c.
[l] 1 Chr. 23. 4, 5.
[m] 2 Kin. 22. 8, &c.

---

[1] Heb. *to make powder.*
[2] Or, *to rafter.*
[3] Heb. *by the hand of.*
[4] Heb. *to the hand of.*
[5] Heb. *poured out,* or, *melted.*
[6] Heb. *in it.*
[7] Or, *Achbor,* 2 Kin. 22. 12.

---

11. The "houses" intended are either the "chambers" which surrounded the Temple on three sides (1 K. vi. 5), or outbuildings attached to the courts. The "kings of Judah" intended are, no doubt, Manasseh and Amon.

13. *of the Levites there were scribes*] Hitherto the word "scribe" has never been used to designate a class (cp. 1 K. iv. 3). But here an order of scribes, forming a distinct division of the Levitical body, has been instituted. The class itself probably origi-nated in the reign of Hezekiah (cp. Prov. xxv. 1); and it is probably to the rise of this class that we are indebted for the preserva-tion of so many prophecies belonging to Hezekiah's time, while the works of almost all previous Prophets—Ahijah, Iddo, She-maiah, Jehu, the son of Hanani, and pro-bably many others—have perished.

21. *for them that are left in Israel and in Judah*] Cp. the words in Kings (2 K. xxii. 13). In both records the intention is to show that the king regarded the ten tribes

the book that is found: for great *is* the wrath of the LORD that is poured out upon us, because our fathers have not kept the word of the LORD, to do after all that is written in this book.

22 ¶ And Hilkiah, and *they* that the king *had appointed*, went to Huldah the prophetess, the wife of Shallum the son of ⁿTikvath, the son of ¹Hasrah, keeper of the ²wardrobe; (now she dwelt in Jerusalem ³in the college:) and they spake to her to that

23 *effect.* And she answered them, Thus saith the LORD God of

24 Israel, Tell ye the man that sent you to me, Thus saith the LORD, Behold, I will bring evil upon this place, and upon the inhabitants thereof, *even* all the curses that are written in the

25 book which they have read before the king of Judah: because they have forsaken me, and have burned incense unto other gods, that they might provoke me to anger with all the works of their hands; therefore my wrath shall be poured out upon

26 this place, and shall not be quenched. And as for the king of Judah, who sent you to enquire of the LORD, so shall ye say unto him, Thus saith the LORD God of Israel *concerning* the

27 words which thou hast heard; Because thine heart was tender, and thou didst humble thyself before God, when thou heardest his words against this place, and against the inhabitants thereof, and humbledst thyself before me, and didst rend thy clothes, and weep before me; I have even heard *thee* also, saith the

28 LORD. Behold, I will gather thee to thy fathers, and thou shalt be gathered to thy grave in peace, neither shall thine eyes see all the evil that I will bring upon this place, and upon the inhabitants of the same. So they brought the king word again.

29 ¶ ^oThen the king sent and gathered together all the elders of

30 Judah and Jerusalem. And the king went up into the house of the LORD, and all the men of Judah, and the inhabitants of Jerusalem, and the priests, and the Levites, and all the people, ⁴great and small: and he read in their ears all the words of the book of the covenant that was found in the house of the LORD.

31 And the king stood in ^phis place, and made a covenant before the LORD, to walk after the LORD, and to keep his commandments, and his testimonies, and his statutes, with all his heart, and with all his soul, to perform the words of the covenant

32 which are written in this book. And he caused all that were ⁵present in Jerusalem and Benjamin to stand *to it.* And the inhabitants of Jerusalem did according to the covenant of

33 God, the God of their fathers. And Josiah took away all the ^qabominations out of all the countries that *pertained* to the children of Israel, and made all that were present in Israel to serve, *even* to serve the LORD their God. ^r*And* all his days

Margin notes:
ⁿ 2 Kin. 22. 14.
^o 2 Kin. 23. 1, &c.
^p 2 Kin. 11. 14. ch. 6. 13.
^q 1 Kin. 11. 5.
^r Jer. 3. 10.

---

¹ Or, *Harhas.*
² Heb. *garments.*
³ Or, *in the school, or, in the second part.*
⁴ Heb. *from great even to small.*
⁵ Heb. *found.*

---

as being under his care, no less than the two.

30. The writer has characteristically substituted "Levites" for the "prophets" of 2 K. xxiii. 2. No doubt Josiah was accompanied by priests, Prophets, and Levites, but the writer of Kings thought it enough to mention the two former, and merged the Levites in the mass of the people. The writer of Chronicles, on the other hand, thinks the presence of Levites too important

to be omitted, and as the Prophets could be but few in number, passes them over.

32. *and Benjamin*] It is scarcely possible that the text here can be sound. "Benjamin" is never put in contrast with "Jerusalem," but always with Judah. The reading may be corrected from the parallel passage 2 K. xxiii. 3; "And he caused all those that were present in Jerusalem to stand **to the covenant.**"

33. *all his days they departed not*] This

they departed not [1]from following the LORD, the God of their fathers.

CHAP. 35. MOREOVER [a]Josiah kept a passover unto the LORD in Jerusalem : and they killed the passover on the [b]fourteenth
2 *day* of the first month. And he set the priests in their [c]charges, and [d]encouraged them to the service of the house of the LORD,
3 and said unto the Levites [e]that taught all Israel, which were holy unto the LORD, [f]Put the holy ark [g]in the house which Solomon the son of David king of Israel did build ; [h]*it shall* not *be a burden upon your* shoulders: serve now the LORD your God,
4 and his people Israel, and prepare *yourselves* by the [i]houses of your fathers, after your courses, according to the [k]writing of David king of Israel, and according to the [l]writing of Solomon
5 his son. And [m]stand in the holy *place* according to the divisions of [2]the families of the fathers of your brethren [3]the people,
6 and *after* the division of the families of the Levites. So kill the passover, and [n]sanctify yourselves, and prepare your brethren, that *they* may do according to the word of the LORD by the hand
7 of Moses. ¶ And Josiah [4][o]gave to the people, of the flock, lambs and kids, all for the passover offerings, for all that were present, to the number of thirty thousand, and three thousand
8 bullocks : these *were* of the king's substance. And his princes [5]gave willingly unto the people, to the priests, and to the Levites : Hilkiah and Zechariah and Jehiel, rulers of the house of God, gave unto the priests for the passover offerings two thousand
9 and six hundred *small cattle*, and three hundred oxen. Conaniah also, and Shemaiah and Nethaneel, his brethren, and Hashabiah and Jeiel and Jozabad, chief of the Levites, [6]gave unto the Levites for passover offerings five thousand *small cattle*, and
10 five hundred oxen. ¶ So the service was prepared, and the priests [p]stood in their place, and the Levites in their courses,
11 according to the king's commandment. And they killed the passover, and the priests [q]sprinkled *the* blood from their hands,
12 and the Levites [r]flayed *them*. And they removed the burnt offerings, that they might give according to the divisions of the

a 2 Kin. 23. 21, 22.
b Ex. 12. 6. Ezra 6. 19.
c ch. 23 18. Ezra 6. 18.
d ch. 29. 5,11.
e Deut. 33. 10. ch. 30. 22. Mal. 2. 7.
f See ch. 34. 14.
g ch. 5. 7.
h 1 Chr. 23. 26.
i 1 Chr. 9. 10.
k 1 Chr. 23, & 24, 25, & 26.
l ch. 8. 14.
m Ps. 134. 1.
n ch. 29. 5, 15. & 30. 3, 15. Ezra 6. 20.
o ch. 30. 24.

p Ezra 6. 18.

q ch. 29. 22.
r See ch. 29. 34.

---

[1] Heb. *from after.*
[2] Heb. *the house of the fathers.*
[3] Heb. *the sons of the people.*
[4] Heb. *offered.*
[5] Heb. *offered.*
[6] Heb. *offered.*

---

must be understood in the letter rather than in the spirit. There was no open idolatry in the reign of Josiah, but the reformation was seeming rather than real, superficial rather than searching and complete (cp. marg. ref.).

XXXV. **3.** *Put the holy ark* &c.] The Ark of the Covenant may have been temporarily removed from the Holy of Holies while Josiah effected necessary repairs.

it shall not be a burden upon your shoulders] The removing and replacing the Ark Josiah means " shall not henceforth be your duty. The Ark shall remain undisturbed in the Holy of Holies. You shall return to your old employments, to the service of God and the instruction of the people."

5. The sense of this verse probably is :— "So divide yourselves that, for every distinct family among the people who come to the Passover, there shall be a portion of a Levitical family to minister."

6. *prepare your brethren*, &c.] *i.e.* "as you minister to your brethren the people, by killing and flaying their offerings and handing the blood to the priests, instruct them how they are to eat the Passover acceptably." It is implied that many would be ignorant of the requirements of the Law.

7–11. See marg. reff. and note.

8. *his princes*] *i.e.* his *ecclesiastical* princes, the chief men of the priests and Levites. For the poor families of their own order the leading priests furnished both Passover-cattle and cattle for Thank-offerings. The chief Levites acted similarly towards the poor Levitical families.

12. *they removed the burnt offerings*] They separated from the paschal lambs those parts which were to be burnt on the Altar. These parts they gave to the offerers, who took them up to the Altar and handed them to the officiating priests.

*Lev. 3. 3.

families of the people, to offer unto the LORD, as *it is* written [s]in
13 the book of Moses. And so *did they* with the oxen. And they

[t] Ex. 12. 8, 9.
Deut. 16. 7.
[u] 1 Sam. 2.
13, 14, 15.

[t]roasted the passover with fire according to the ordinance : but
the *other* holy *offerings* [u]sod they in pots, and in caldrons, and
14 in pans, and [l]divided *them* speedily among all the people. And
afterward they made ready for themselves, and for the priests :
because the priests the sons of Aaron *were busied* in offering of
burnt offerings and the fat until night ; therefore the Levites
prepared for themselves, and for the priests the sons of Aaron.
15 And the singers the sons of Asaph *were* in their [2]place, accord-

[x] 1 Chr. 25.
1, &c.
[y] 1 Chr. 9.
17, 18.
& 26. 14, &c.

ing to the [x]commandment of David, and Asaph, and Heman,
and Jeduthun the king's seer ; and the porters [y]*waited* at every
gate ; they might not depart from their service ; for their
16 brethren the Levites prepared for them. So all the service of
the LORD was prepared the same day, to keep the passover, and
to offer burnt offerings upon the altar of the LORD, according to
17 the commandment of king Josiah. And the children of Israel
that were [3]present kept the passover at that time, and the feast

[z] Ex. 12. 15.
& 13. 6.
ch. 30. 21.
[a] 2 Kin. 23.
22, 23.

18 of [z]unleavened bread seven days. ¶ And [a]there was no passover like to that kept in Israel from the days of Samuel the
prophet ; neither did all the kings of Israel keep such a passover
as Josiah kept, and the priests, and the Levites, and all Judah
and Israel that were present, and the inhabitants of Jerusalem.
19 In the eighteenth year of the reign of Josiah was this passover

[b] 2Kin.23.29.
Jer. 46. 2.

20 kept. ¶ [b] After all this, when Josiah had prepared the [4]temple,
Necho king of Egypt came up to fight against Charchemish by
21 Euphrates : and Josiah went out against him. But he sent ambassadors to him, saying, What have I to do with thee, thou king
of Judah ? *I come* not against thee this day, but against [5]the
house wherewith I have war : for God commanded me to make
haste : forbear thee from *meddling with* God, who *is* with me,
22 that he destroy thee not. Nevertheless Josiah would not turn

[c] So 1 Kin.
22. 30.

his face from him, but [c]disguised himself, that he might fight
with him, and hearkened not unto the words of Necho from the
mouth of God, and came to fight in the valley of Megiddo.
23 And the archers shot at king Josiah ; and the king said to his

---

[1] Heb. *made* them *run*.   [3] Heb. *found*.   [5] Heb. *the house of my war*.
[2] Heb. *station*.   [4] Heb. *house*.

---

15. *they might not depart*] The singers and
porters remained at their posts, while other
Levites sacrificed for them and brought
them their share of the lambs.

20. *After all this*] *i.e.* thirteen years after,
B.C. 608. See 2 K. xxiii. 28, 29 notes.

21. *the house wherewith I have war*] Necho
viewed Babylon as the successor and representative of Assyria—the hereditary enemy
of Egypt—and he means that he is merely
continuing an old hostility with which Josiah has nothing to do. No doubt the Assyrian and Egyptian armies had often passed
up and down Syria by the coast route,
without approaching Jerusalem, or even
touching the soil of Judæa.

*God commanded me to make haste : forbear
thee from meddling with God*] These are
remarkable words in the mouth of a heathen ; but ancient inscriptions show that the
Egyptian kings, in a certain sense, acknow-

ledged a single supreme god, and considered
their actions to be inspired by him. [*e.g.*
The god Tum (cp. the name of his city,
Pithom, Ex. i. 11 note) was worshipped as
ankh, "the living One" (cp. "Jehovah")].
Hence Necho merely expressed himself as
Egyptian kings were in the habit of doing.

22. *disguised himself*] Cp. marg. ref. But
most modern critics are dissatisfied with
this sense in this place, and prefer to render
"equipped himself ;" or—with the LXX.—
adopt another reading, and render "took
courage."

the words of Necho from the mouth of God]
The author apparently regarded Necho's
words as actually prophetic—a warning to
which Josiah ought to have listened—sent
him by God to make him pause—though not
spoken by divine inspiration, or in consequence of any supernatural revelation of
the Divine will to the Egyptian king.

24 servants, Have me away; for I am 'sore [1]wounded. [d]His ser-   [d] 2 Kin. 23.
vants therefore took him out of that chariot, and put him in the   30.
second chariot that he had; and they brought him to Jerusalem,
and he died, and was buried [2]in *one of* the sepulchres of his
fathers. And [e]all Judah and Jerusalem mourned for Josiah.   [e] Zech.12.11.
25 And Jeremiah [f]lamented for Josiah: and [g]all the singing men   [f] Lam. 4. 20.
and the singing women spake of Josiah in their lamentations to   [g] See Matt.
this day, [h]and made them an ordinance in Israel: and, behold,   9. 23.
26 they *are* written in the lamentations.   ¶ Now the rest of the acts   [h] Jer. 22. 20.
of Josiah, and his [3]goodness, according to *that which was* written
27 in the law of the LORD, and his deeds, first and last, behold,
they *are* written in the book of the kings of Israel and Judah.
CHAP. **36.** THEN [a]the people of the land took Jehoahaz the son   [a] 2 Kin. 23.
of Josiah, and made him king in his father's stead in Jerusalem.   30, &c.
2 Jehoahaz *was* twenty and three years old when he began to
3 reign, and he reigned three months in Jerusalem. And the
king of Egypt [4]put him down at Jerusalem, and [5]condemned
the land in an hundred talents of silver and a talent of gold.
4 And the king of Egypt made Eliakim his brother king over
Judah and Jerusalem, and turned his name to Jehoiakim. And
Necho took Jehoahaz his brother, and carried him to Egypt.
5 ¶ [b]Jehoiakim *was* twenty and five years old when he began to   [b] 2 Kin. 23.
reign, and he reigned eleven years in Jerusalem: and he did *that*   36, 37.
6 *which was* evil in the sight of the LORD his God. [c]Against him   [c] 2 Kin.24.1.
came up Nebuchadnezzar king of Babylon, and bound him in   Foretold,
7 [6]fetters, to [d]carry him to Babylon. [e]Nebuchadnezzar also   Hab. 1. 6.
carried of the vessels of the house of the LORD to Babylon, and   [d] See
8 put them in his temple at Babylon. Now the rest of the acts   2 Kin. 24. 6.
of Jehoiakim, and his abominations which he did, and that   Jer.22.18,19.
which was found in him, behold, they *are* written in the book of   & 36. 30.
the kings of Israel and Judah: and [7]Jehoiachin his son reigned   [e] 2 Kin. 24.
9 in his stead.   ¶ [f]Jehoiachin *was* eight years old when he began   13.
to reign, and he reigned three months and ten days in Jerusalem: Dan. 1. 1, 2.
   & 5. 2.
   [f] 2 Kin. 24. 8.

[1] Heb. *made sick,* 1 Kin. 22.   [3] Heb. *kindnesses.*   [6] Or, *chains.*
   34.   [4] Heb. *removed him.*   [7] Or, *Jeconiah,* 1 Chr. 3.
[2] Or, *among the sepulchres.*   [5] Heb. *mulcted.*   16. or, *Coniah,* Jer. 22.24.

Cp. the "prophecy" of Caiaphas, John xi.
51.
   24. The fate of Josiah was unprecedented.
No king of Judah had, up to this time,
fallen in battle. None had left his land at
the mercy of a foreign conqueror. Hence
the extraordinary character of the mourning (cp. Zech. xii. 11–14).
   25. Some find Jeremiah's lament in the
entire Book of Lamentations; others in a
part of it (ch. iv.). But most critics are of
opinion that the lament is lost. Days of
calamity were commemorated by lamentations on their anniversaries, and this among
the number. The "Book of Dirges" was a
collection of such poems which once existed
but is now lost.
   and made them an ordinance] Rather,
" and **they** made them an ordinance," they
i.e. who had authority to do so, not the
minstrels.
   XXXVI. The narrative runs parallel
with 2 Kings (marg. ref.) as far as *v.* 13.
The writer then omits the events following,

and substitutes a sketch in which the moral
and didactic element preponderates over the
historical.
   7. *in his temple*] Cp. "the house of *his
god*" (Dan. i. 2). Nebuchadnezzar's inscriptions show him to have been the especial
votary of Merodach, the Babylonian Mars.
His temple, which the Greeks called the
temple of Belus, was one of the most magnificent buildings in Babylon. Its ruins
still remain in the vast mound, called *Babil,*
which is the loftiest and most imposing of
the "heaps" that mark the site of the ancient city.
   his abominations which he did] See Jer.
vii. 9, 30, 31, xix. 3-13, xxv. 1 &c.; Jehoiakim appears to have restored all the
idolatries which Josiah his father had swept
away.
   9. *eight years old*] Rather, eighteen (see
marg. ref.). Jehoiachin had several wives
and (apparently) at least one child (Jer.
xxii. 28), when, three months later, he was
carried captive to Babylon.

10 and he did *that which was* evil in the sight of the LORD. And
¹when the year was expired, ⁹king Nebuchadnezzar sent, and
brought him to Babylon, ʰwith the ²goodly vessels of the house
of the LORD, and made ³ⁱZedekiah his brother king over Judah
11 and Jerusalem. ¶ᵏZedekiah *was* one and twenty years old when
12 he began to reign, and reigned eleven years in Jerusalem. And
he did *that which was* evil in the sight of the LORD his God, *and*
humbled not himself before Jeremiah the prophet *speaking* from
13 the mouth of the LORD. And ˡhe also rebelled against king
Nebuchadnezzar, who had made him swear by God: but he
ᵐstiffened his neck, and hardened his heart from turning unto
14 the LORD God of Israel. ¶ Moreover all the chief of the priests,
and the people, transgressed very much after all the abominations of the heathen; and polluted the house of the LORD which
15 he had hallowed in Jerusalem. ⁿAnd the LORD God of their
fathers sent to them ⁴by his messengers, rising up ⁵betimes, and
sending; because he had compassion on his people, and on his
16 dwelling place: but ᵒthey mocked the messengers of God, and
ᵖdespised his words, and ᑫmisused his prophets, until the ʳwrath
of the LORD arose against his people, till *there was* no ⁶remedy.
17 ˢTherefore he brought upon them the king of the Chaldees, who
ᵗslew their young men with the sword in the house of their
sanctuary, and had no compassion upon young man or maiden,
old man, or him that stooped for age: he gave *them* all into his
18 hand. ᵘAnd all the vessels of the house of God, great and
small, and the treasures of the house of the LORD, and the treasures of the king, and of his princes; all *these* he brought to
19 Babylon. ˣAnd they burnt the house of God, and brake down
the wall of Jerusalem, and burnt all the palaces thereof with
20 fire, and destroyed all the goodly vessels thereof. And ⁷ʸthem
that had escaped from the sword carried he away to Babylon;
ᶻwhere they were servants to him and his sons until the reign of
21 the kingdom of Persia: to fulfil the word of the LORD by the

Margin references (left column):
⁹ 2 Kin. 24.
10—17.
ʰ Dan.1.1,2.
& 5. 2.
ⁱ Jer. 37. 1.
ᵏ 2 Kin. 24.
18.
Jer.52.1,&c.

ˡ Jer. 52. 3.
Ezek. 17. 12,
13.
ᵐ 2 Kin. 17.
14.

ⁿ Jer.25. 3,4.
& 35. 15.
& 44. 4.

ᵒ Jer.5.12,13.
ᵖ Prov. 1. 25,
30.
ᑫ Jer. 32. 3.
& 38. 6.
Matt. 23. 34.
ʳ Ps. 74. 1.
& 79. 5.
ˢ Deut.28.49.
2 Kin. 25. 1,
&c.
Ezra 9. 7.
ᵗ Ps. 74. 20.
& 79. 2, 3.
ᵘ 2 Kin. 25.
13, &c.
ˣ 2 Kin.25.9.
Ps. 74. 6, 7.
& 79. 1, 7.
ʸ 2Kin.25.11.
ᶻ Jer. 27. 7.

¹ Heb. *at the return of the year.*
² Heb. *vessels of desire.*
³ Or, *Mattaniah, his father's*
⁴ Heb. *by the hand of his messengers.*
⁵ That is, *continually and*
brother, 2 Kin. 24. 17.
carefully.
⁶ Heb. *healing.*
⁷ Heb. *the remainder from the sword.*

10. *when the year was expired*] Lit. as in
the margin, *i.e.* at the return of the season
for military expeditions. The expedition
against Jehoiakim took place probably late
in the autumn of one year, that against Jehoiachin early in the spring of the next.
Strictly speaking, Zedekiah was uncle to
Jehoiachin, being the youngest of the sons
of Josiah (marg. note and ref.). He was
nearly of the same age with Jehoiachin, and
is called here his "brother" (cp. Gen. xiv.
14).
12. On Zedekiah's character, see 2 K.
xxiv. 19 note.
13. The oath of allegiance was taken
when he was first installed in his kingdom.
On Zedekiah's sin in breaking his oath, see
Ezek. xvii. 18-20, xxi. 25.
14. *polluted the house of the LORD*] Towards the close of Zedekiah's reign idolatrous rites of several different kinds were
intruded into the sacred precincts of the
Temple (cp Ezek. viii. 10-16).

16. *misused his prophets*] Rather, "scoffed
at his prophets." The allusion is to verbal
mockery, not to persecution.
17. The fearful slaughter took place at
the capture of the city, in the courts of the
Temple itself (Ezek. ix. 6, 7; cp. Lam. ii.
7, 20).
20. *servants*] Or, "slaves." They were
probably employed by Nebuchadnezzar in
the forced labour which his great works
necessitated.
his sons] The word probably includes all
Nebuchadnezzar's successors in the independent sovereignty of Babylon.
21. See marg. reff. The seventy years of
desolation prophesied by Jeremiah, commenced in the fourth year of Jehoiakim
(Jer. xxv. 1 and 12; cp. Dan. i. 1), or B.C.
605; and should therefore have terminated,
if they were fully complete, in B.C. 536. As,
however, the historical date of the taking of
Babylon by Cyrus is B.C. 538, or two years
earlier, it has been usual to suppose that the

mouth of [a] Jeremiah, until the land [b] had enjoyed her sabbaths : *for* as long as she lay desolate [c] she kept sabbath, to fulfil three-22 score and ten years. ¶ [d] Now in the first year of Cyrus king of Persia, that the word of the LORD *spoken* by the mouth of [e] Jeremiah might be accomplished, the LORD stirred up the spirit of [f] Cyrus king of Persia, that he made a proclamation throughout 23 all his kingdom, and *put it* also in writing, saying, [g] Thus saith Cyrus king of Persia, All the kingdoms of the earth hath the LORD God of heaven given me; and he hath charged me to build him an house in Jerusalem, which *is* in Judah. Who *is there* among you of all his people? The LORD his God *be* with him, and let him go up.

[a] Jer. 25. 9, 11, 12. & 26. 6, 7. & 29. 10.
[b] Lev. 26. 34, 35, 43. Dan. 9. 2.
[c] Lev. 25, 4, 5.
[d] Ezra 1. 1.
[e] Jer. 25. 12, 13.
& 29. 10. & 33. 10, 11, 14.
[f] Isai. 44. 28.
[g] Ezra 1. 2, 3.

Jews reckoned "the reign of the kingdom of Persia" as commencing two years after the capture of Babylon, on the death or supersession of "Darius the Mede." But the term "seventy" may be taken as a *round* number, and the prophecy as sufficiently fulfilled by a desolation which lasted sixty-eight years.

until the land had enjoyed her sabbaths] Between the time of Moses and the com-

mencement of the Captivity, there had been (about) 70 occasions on which the Law of the sabbatical year (Lev. xxv. 4–7) had been violated.

22. This and the next verse are repeated at the commencement of the book of Ezra (i. 1–3), which was, it is probable, originally a continuation of Chronicles, Chronicles and Ezra together forming one work. See Introduction, p. 448.

E Z R A .

INTRODUCTION.

THOUGH the Books of Ezra and Nehemiah were undoubtedly regarded as one Book in two parts, both by the Jewish Church and by the early Christian Fathers, yet the judgment of modern criticism, that they were originally two distinct works, seems to be, on the whole, deserving of acceptance.

The object of the writer of Ezra is to give an account of the return from the Captivity, and of the subsequent fortunes of the Palestinian Jews until the eighth year of Artaxerxes Longimanus, B.C. 457. The matters to which he directs attention are three only:—(1) The number, family, and (to some extent) the names of those who returned from Babylonia with Ezra and with Zerubbabel (ii., viii. 1–20); (2) The rebuilding of the Temple and the circumstances connected therewith (i., iii. – vii.); and (3) The misconduct of the returned Jews in respect of mixed marriages, and the steps taken by Ezra in consequence (ix., x.).

The Book of Ezra is made up of two completely distinct sections. (a) In i.–vi., the writer treats of the return from the Captivity and of the events following (B.C. 538–516), or a period of twenty-three years. It belongs to the time when Zerubbabel was governor of Judæa, Jeshua High-Priest, and Zechariah and Haggai Prophets. (b) vii. – end. This relates the commission given to Ezra by Artaxerxes in the seventh year of his reign (B.C. 458), the journey of Ezra to Jerusalem, and his proceedings there (April, B.C. 458–April, B.C. 457). There is thus a gap of fifty-seven years between the first section of the Book and the second; from which it appears that the writer of the second portion cannot well have been a witness of the events recorded in the first.

Jewish tradition ascribes the authorship of the whole Book to Ezra. Modern critics generally admit that Ezra was the original and sole author of the entire second section (vii.–x.), but consider him the compiler of the first (i.–vi.) from state documents, national records, and lists. It is probable that the Book of Ezra was composed soon after the arrangements with respect to the mixed marriages had been completed; i.e. in B.C. 457 or 456.

In character the Book of Ezra is historical, and like Chronicles, it lays great stress on the externals of religion; it gives special prominence to the Levites, and exhibits a genealogical bias; it lays down very distinctly the general principle of a special Providence (viii. 22); and it applies this principle to particular points of the history not unfrequently.

In style Ezra more resembles Daniel than any other Book of Scripture, always excepting Chronicles. This may be accounted for by these two writers being both Babylonian Jews. The work contains also a considerable number of proper names and words which are either known or suspected to be Persian,[1] and altogether, the language is such as might have been looked for under the circumstances of the time, when the contact into which the Jews had been brought with the Babylonians and the Persians had naturally introduced among them a good many foreign words and modes of speech.

The text of Ezra is not in a good condition. The general bearing of the narrative is, however, untouched by slight blemishes which affect chiefly such minute points as the names and numbers of those who returned from the Captivity, the weight and number of the sacrificial vessels, and the like.

---

[1] The following are the proper names, certainly Persian, which occur in Ezra: Cyrus, Darius, Ahasuerus, Artaxerxes, Mithredath (Mithridates), Persia, and Achmetha (Ecbatana). To these may be added, as probably Persian, Rehum, Shimshai, Tatnai, Shetharboznai, and Tabeel. Persian words, not belonging to the class of proper names, which may be recognized in Ezra are the following: *ganza* or *gaza*, "treasury" (v. 17, vi. 1, vii. 20); *ganzabara* or *gazabara*, "treasurer" (i. 8); *khshatrapâ*, "satrap" (viii. 36); *angara*, "a letter" (iv. 8); *nipishta*, the same (iv. 7); *patigama*, "an edict" (iv. 17); *apatama* (?), "at last" (iv. 13); *tarsata*, name of an office, literally, "the feared" (ii. 63); *usfrana*, "speedily, diligently, abundantly" (v. 8, vi. 8; &c.); and *darkon*, or perhaps *darkemon*, a gold coin, a "daric" (viii 27).

THE BOOK

OF

E Z R A.

CHAP. 1. NOW in the first year of Cyrus king of Persia, that the word of the LORD *a*by the mouth of Jeremiah might be fulfilled, the LORD stirred up the spirit of Cyrus king of Persia, *b*that he
1 made a proclamation throughout all his kingdom, and *put it*
2 also in writing, saying, ¶ Thus saith Cyrus king of Persia, The LORD God of heaven hath given me all the kingdoms of the earth; and he hath *c*charged me to build him an house at Jeru-
3 salem, which *is* in Judah. Who *is there* among you of all his people? his God be with him, and let him go up to Jerusalem, which *is* in Judah, and build the house of the LORD God of
4 Israel, (*d*he *is* the God,) which *is* in Jerusalem. And whosoever remaineth in any place where he sojourneth, let the men of his place 2help him with silver, and with gold, and with goods, and with beasts, beside the freewill offering for the house of God
5 that *is* in Jerusalem. ¶ Then rose up the chief of the fathers of Judah and Benjamin, and the priests, and the Levites, with all *them* whose spirit *e*God had raised, to go up to build the house of
6 the LORD which *is* in Jerusalem. And all they that *were* about them 3strengthened their hands with vessels of silver, with gold, with goods, and with beasts, and with precious things, beside all
7 *that* was willingly offered. ¶*f*Also Cyrus the king brought forth the vessels of the house of the LORD, *g*which Nebuchadnezzar had brought forth out of Jerusalem, and had put them
8 in the house of his gods; even those did Cyrus king of Persia bring forth by the hand of Mithredath the treasurer, and num-
9 bered them unto *h*Sheshbazzar, the prince of Judah. And this *is* the number of them: thirty chargers of gold, a thousand

a 2 Chr. 36.
22, 23.
Jer. 25. 12.
& 29. 10.
b ch. 5.13,14.

c Isai. 44. 28.
& 45. 1, 13.

d Dan. 6. 26.

e Phil. 2. 13.

f ch. 5. 14.
& 6. 5.
g 2 Kin. 24.
13.
2 Chr. 36. 7.

h See ch. 5.
14.

1 Heb. *caused a voice to pass.*   2 Heb. *lift him up.*   3 That is, *helped them.*

I. 1. By the first year of Cyrus is to be understood the first year of his sovereignty over the Jews, or B.C. 538.

2. *The* LORD *God of heaven*] Or, "Jehovah, the God of Heaven." In the original Persian, the document probably ran—"Ormazd, the God of Heaven." The Hebrew transcript took "Jehovah" as the equivalent of "Ormazd." The Persian notion of a single Supreme Being — Ahura-Mazda, "the much-knowing, or much-bestowing Spirit"—did, in fact, approach nearly to the Jewish conception of Jehovah.

hath given me all the kingdoms &c.] There is a similar formula at the commencement of the great majority of Persian inscriptions.

he hath charged me to build him an house] It is a reasonable conjecture that, on the capture of Babylon, Cyrus was brought into contact with Daniel, who drew his attention to the prophecy of Isaiah (xliv. 28); and that Cyrus accepted this prophecy as a "charge" to rebuild the Temple.

4. *let the men of his place help him*] *i.e.*

"Let the heathen population help him" (see *v.* 6).

the freewill offering] Probably that made by Cyrus himself (*vv.* 7–11).

5. Only a portion of the Israelites took advantage of the permission of Cyrus. Many remained in Babylon, since they were disinclined to relinquish their property. They who returned were persons whom God had especially stirred up to make sacrifices for His glory.

7. *the house of his gods*] Rather, "of his god" (Dan. i. 2), *i.e.* Merodach, "his lord" (see 2 Chr. xxxvi. 7 note).

8. *Mithredath*] Or, "Mithridates." The occurrence of this name, which means "given by Mithra," or "dedicated to Mithra," is an indication that the Sun-worship of the Persians was at least as old as the time of Cyrus.

Sheshbazzar] *i.e.* Zerubbabel. On his royal descent, see 1 Chr. iii. 19 note.

9. *chargers*] The word in the original thus translated occurs only in this passage. Its meaning is doubtful. Some derive it

10 chargers of silver, nine and twenty knives, thirty basons of gold, silver basons of a second *sort* four hundred and ten, *and* other 11 vessels a thousand. All the vessels of gold and of silver *were* five thousand and four hundred. All *these* did Sheshbazzar bring up with *them of* [1] the captivity that were brought up from Babylon unto Jerusalem.

c Neh. 7. 6, &c.

b 2 Kin. 24. 14, 15, 16. & 25. 11. 2 Chr. 36. 20.

CHAP. 2. NOW *a* these *are* the children of the province that went up out of the captivity, of those which had been carried away, *b* whom Nebuchadnezzar the king of Babylon had carried away unto Babylon, and came again unto Jerusalem and Judah, every 2 one unto his city ; which came with Zerubbabel : Jeshua, Nehemiah, [2] Seraiah, [3] Reelaiah, Mordecai, Bilshan, [4] Mizpar, Bigvai, [5] Rehum, Baanah. ¶ The number of the men of the people of 3 Israel : the children of Parosh, two thousand an hundred seventy 4 and two. The children of Shephatiah, three hundred seventy

c See Neh. 7. 10. *d* Neh. 7. 11.

5 and two. The children of Arah, *c* seven hundred seventy and 6 five. The children of *d* Pahath-moab, of the children of Jeshua 7 *and* Joab, two thousand eight hundred and twelve. The children 8 of Elam, a thousand two hundred fifty and four. The children 9 of Zattu, nine hundred forty and five. The children of Zaccai, 10 seven hundred and threescore. The children of [6] Bani, six hun- 11 dred forty and two. The children of Bebai, six hundred twenty 12 and three. The children of Azgad, a thousand two hundred 13 twenty and two. The children of Adonikam, six hundred sixty 14 and six. The children of Bigvai, two thousand fifty and six. 15, 16 The children of Adin, four hundred fifty and four. The 17 children of Ater of Hezekiah, ninety and eight. The children 18 of Bezai, three hundred twenty and three. The children of 19 [7] Jorah, an hundred and twelve. The children of Hashum, two 20 hundred twenty and three. The children of [8] Gibbar, ninety and 21 five. The children of Beth-lehem, an hundred twenty and 22, 23 three. The men of Netophah, fifty and six. The men of 24 Anathoth, an hundred twenty and eight. The children of 25 [9] Azmaveth, forty and two. The children of Kirjath-arim, Chephirah, and Beeroth, seven hundred and forty and three. 26 The children of Ramah and Gaba, six hundred twenty and one. 27, 28 The men of Michmas, an hundred twenty and two. The 29 men of Beth-el and Ai, two hundred twenty and three. The

[1] Heb. *the transportation.*
[2] Or, *Azariah*, Neh. 7. 7.
[3] Or, *Raamiah.*
[4] Or, *Mispereth.*
[5] Or, *Nehum.*
[6] Or, *Binnui*, Neh. 7. 15.
[7] Or, *Hariph*, Neh. 7. 24.
[8] Or, *Gibeon*, Neh. 7. 25.
[9] Or, *Beth-azmaveth*, Neh. 7. 28.

---

from a Heb. root, "to hollow out," and translate "cup" or "vessel."

knives] This is another doubtful word, only used here. The etymology points to some employment of basket-work.

11. The sum of the numbers as they stand in the present Hebrew text is 2499, instead of 5400. In the Apocryphal book of Esdras the sum given is 5469, and with this sum the items in that place exactly agree (1 Esd. ii. 13, 14). Most commentators propose to correct Ezra by the passage of Esdras ; but the items of Esdras are improbable. Probably the sum total in the present passage has suffered corruption.

II. 1. *the province*] Judæa was no longer a kingdom, but a mere "province" of

Persia. "The children of the province " are the Israelites who returned to Palestine, as distinct from those who remained in Babylonia and Persia.

every one unto his city] That is, to the city whereto his forefathers had belonged. Of course, in the few cases where this was not known (*vv.* 59–62), the plan could not be carried out.

Two other copies of the list following have come down to us, one in Neh. vii. 7–69, the other in 1 .Esd. v. 8–43. All seem to have been taken from the same original document, and to have suffered more or less from corruption. Where two out of the three agree, the reading should prevail over that of the third.

30 children of Nebo, fifty and two. The children of Magbish, an
31 hundred fifty and six. The children of the other *e*Elam, a thou-   *e* See ver. 7.
32 sand two hundred fifty and four. The children of Harim, three
33 hundred and twenty. The children of Lod, [1]Hadid, and Ono,
34 seven hundred twenty and five. The children of Jericho, three
35 hundred forty and five. The children of Senaah, three thousand
36 and six hundred and thirty. ¶The priests: the children of
   *f*Jedaiah, of the house of Jeshua, nine hundred seventy and   *f* 1 Chr. 24.7.
37 three. The children of *g*Immer, a thousand fifty and two.   *g* 1 Chr. 24.14.
38 The children of *h*Pashur, a thousand two hundred forty and   *h* 1 Chr. 9.12.
39 seven. The children of *i*Harim, a thousand and seventeen.   *i* 1 Chr. 24. 8.
40 ¶ The Levites: the children of Jeshua and Kadmiel, of the
41 children of [2]Hodaviah, seventy and four. The singers: the
42 children of Asaph, an hundred twenty and eight. The children
   of the porters: the children of Shallum, the children of Ater,
   the children of Talmon, the children of Akkub, the children of
   Hatita, the children of Shobai, *in* all an hundred thirty and
43 nine. ¶*k*The Nethinims: the children of Ziha, the children of   *k* 1 Chr. 9. 2.
44 Hasupha, the children of Tabbaoth, the children of Keros, the
45 children of [3]Siaha, the children of Padon, the children of Leba-
46 nah, the children of Hagabah, the children of Akkub, the chil-
   dren of Hagab, the children of [4]Shalmai, the children of Hanan,
47 the children of Giddel, the children of Gahar, the children of
48 Reaiah, the children of Rezin, the children of Nekoda, the
49 children of Gazzam, the children of Uzza, the children of Paseah,
50 the children of Besai, the children of Asnah, the children of
51 Mehunim, the children of [5]Nephusim, the children of Bakbuk,
52 the children of Hakupha, the children of Harhur, the children
53 of [6]Bazluth, the children of Mehida, the children of Harsha, the
   children of Barkos, the children of Sisera, the children of Tha-
54, 55 mah, the children of Neziah, the children of Hatipha. ¶The
   children of *l*Solomon's servants: the children of Sotai, the   *l* 1 Kin. 9. 21.
56 children of Sophereth, the children of [7]Peruda, the children
57 of Jaalah, the children of Darkon, the children of Giddel, the
   children of Shephatiah, the children of Hattil, the children of
58 Pochereth of Zebaim, the children of [8]Ami. All the *m*Nethi-   *m* Josh. 9. 21,
   nims, and the children of *n*Solomon's servants, *were* three hun-   27.
59 dred ninety and two. ¶And these *were* they which went up from   1 Chr. 9. 2.
   Tel-melah, Tel-harsa, Cherub, [9]Addan, *and* Immer: but they   *n* 1 Kin. 9.21.
   could not shew their father's house, and their [1]seed, whether
60 they *were* of Israel: the children of Delaiah, the children of
   Tobiah, the children of Nekoda, six hundred fifty and two.
61 And of the children of the priests: the children of Habaiah, the
   children of Koz, the children of Barzillai; which took a wife of
   the daughters of *o*Barzillai the Gileadite, and was called after their   *o* 2 Sam. 17.
62 name: these sought their register *among* those that were reckoned   27.

---

[1] Or, *Harid*, as it is in   [3] Or, *Sia*.   [7] Or, *Peruda*, Neh. 7. 57.
   some copies.   [4] Or, *Shamlai*.   [8] Or, *Amon*, Neh. 7. 59.
[2] Or, *Judah*, ch. 3. 9. called   [5] Or, *Nephishesim*.   [9] Or, *Addon*, Neh. 7. 61.
   also *Hodevah*, Neh. 7. 43.   [6] Or, *Bazlith*, Neh. 7. 54.   [1] Or, *pedigree*.

---

43. *The Nethinims*] The *hieroduli* or
sacred slaves, "given" to the Levites to
assist them in their work (see 1 Chr. ix. 2
note).

   59. Tel-melah, Tel-harsa, Cherub, Addan,
and Immer, were probably cities, or villages,

of Babylonia, at which the Jews here spoken
of had been settled. The first and third
have been reasonably identified with the
Thelmé and Chiripha of Ptolemy. Of the
rest nothing is known at present.

p Num. 3.10.

q Lev. 22. 2,
10, 15, 16.
r Num. 27.
21.
s Neh. 7. 66,
&c.

t Neh. 7. 70.

u 1Chr.26.20.

x ch. 6.16,17.
Neh. 7. 73.

a Matt. 1. 12.
& Luke 3. 27,
called
Salathiel.
b Deut. 12. 5.

c Num. 28. 3,
4.

by genealogy, but they were not found: *p* therefore [1] were they, 63 as polluted, put from the priesthood. And the [2] Tirshatha said unto them, that they *q* should not eat of the most holy things, till there stood up a priest with *r* Urim and with Thummim. 64 ¶ *s* The whole congregation together *was* forty and two thousand 65 three hundred *and* threescore, beside their servants and their maids, of whom *there were* seven thousand three hundred thirty and seven: and *there were* among them two hundred singing 66 men and singing women. Their horses *were* seven hundred 67 thirty and six; their mules, two hundred forty and five; their camels, four hundred thirty and five; *their* asses, six thousand 68 seven hundred and twenty. ¶ *t* And *some* of the chief of the fathers, when they came to the house of the LORD which *is* at Jerusalem, offered freely for the house of God to set it up in his 69 place : they gave after their ability unto the *u* treasure of the work threescore and one thousand drams of gold, and five thou-70 sand pound of silver, and one hundred priests' garments. ¶ *x* So the priests, and the Levites, and *some* of the people, and the singers, and the porters, and the Nethinims, dwelt in their cities, and all Israel in their cities.

CHAP. 3. AND when the seventh month was come, and the children of Israel *were* in the cities, the people gathered themselves toge-2 ther as one man to Jerusalem. Then stood up [3] Jeshua the son of Jozadak, and his brethren the priests, and [4] Zerubbabel the son of *a* Shealtiel, and his brethren, and builded the altar of the God of Israel, to offer burnt offerings thereon, as *it is b* written 3 in the law of Moses the man of God. And they set the altar upon his bases; for fear *was* upon them because of the people of those countries : and they offered burnt offerings thereon unto the LORD, *even c* burnt offerings morning and evening.

[1] Heb. *they were polluted from the priesthood.*
[2] Or, *governor* : See Neh. 8. 9.
[3] Or, *Joshua*, Hag. 1. 1. & 2. 2. Zech. 3. 1.
[4] Called *Zorobabel*, Matt. 1. 12. Luke 3. 27.

---

63. *the Tirshatha*] *i.e.* Zerubbabel. See margin. The word is probably old Persian, though it does not occur in the cuneiform inscriptions. Some derive it from a root "to fear." See Introduction. p. 570 *n.* 1.

a priest with Urim and with Thummim] See Ex. xxviii. 30 note. According to the Rabbinical writers, the second Temple permanently lacked this glory of the first. Zerubbabel, it would seem by the present passage (cp. Neh. vii. 65), expected that the loss would be only temporary.

64. The sum total is given without any variation by Ezra, by Nehemiah (marg. ref.), and by Esdras (1 Esd. v. 41), who adds, that in this reckoning only those of twelve years of age and upward were counted.

It is curious that the total 42,360, is so greatly in excess of the items. Ezra's items make the number 29,818 ; Nehemiah's 31,089, Esdras, 33,950. Probably the original document was in places illegible, and the writers were forced to make omissions.

69. The numbers here and in Nehemiah (marg. ref.) vary.

70. *all Israel*] That Israelites of the ten tribes returned to Palestine with Zerubbabel is apparent, (1) from 1 Chr. ix. 3 ; (2) from the enumeration of *twelve* chiefs (Neh. vii. 7 ; 1 Esd. v. 8) ; and (3) from various expressions in Ezra (ii. 2, 59, iii. 1).

III. 1. *the seventh month*] *i.e.* the month Tisri (nearly our September), the most sacred month in the Jewish year (Ex. xxiii. 16 ; Lev. xxiii. 24–41).

2. Jeshua, the High-Priest, was the son of Jozadak, who was carried into captivity by Nebuchadnezzar (1 Chr. vi. 15).

Zerubbabel was really the son of Pedaiah, Shealtiel's (or Salathiel's) younger brother. But Shealtiel having no sons, and the royal line being continued in the person of his nephew, Zerubbabel, the latter was accounted Shealtiel's son.

3. *upon his bases*] They restored *the old* Altar of Burnt-offerings, which stood directly in front of the Temple-porch, upon the old foundation. This became apparent on the clearing away of the ruins, and on a careful examination of the site.

4 [d]They kept also the feast of tabernacles, [e]as *it is* written, and
[f]offered the daily burnt offerings by number, according to the
5 custom, [1]as the duty of every day required; and afterward
offered the [g]continual burnt offering, both of the new moons,
and of all the set feasts of the LORD that were consecrated, and
of every one that willingly offered a freewill offering unto the
6 LORD. From the first day of the seventh month began they to
offer burnt offerings unto the LORD. But [2]the foundation of
7 the temple of the LORD was not *yet* laid. They gave money
also unto the masons, and to the [3]carpenters; and [h]meat, and
drink, and oil, unto them of Zidon, and to them of Tyre, to
bring cedar trees from Lebanon to the sea of [i]Joppa, [k]according
8 to the grant that they had of Cyrus king of Persia. ¶Now in
the second year of their coming unto the house of God at Jerusalem, in the second month, began Zerubbabel the son of Shealtiel, and Jeshua the son of Jozadak, and the remnant of their
brethren the priests and the Levites, and all they that were
come out of the captivity unto Jerusalem; [l]and appointed the
Levites, from twenty years old and upward, to set forward the
9 work of the house of the LORD. Then stood [m]Jeshua *with* his
sons and his brethren, Kadmiel and his sons, the sons of [4]Judah,
[5]together, to set forward the workmen in the house of God: the
sons of Henadad, *with* their sons and their brethren the Levites.
10 And when the builders laid the foundation of the temple of the
LORD, [n]they set the priests in their apparel with trumpets, and
the Levites the sons of Asaph with cymbals, to praise the LORD,
11 after the [o]ordinance of David king of Israel. [p]And they sang
together by course in praising and giving thanks unto the LORD;
[q]because *he is* good, [r]for his mercy *endureth* for ever toward
Israel. And all the people shouted with a great shout, when
they praised the LORD, because the foundation of the house of
12 the LORD was laid. [s]But many of the priests and Levites and
chief of the fathers, *who were* ancient men, that had seen the
first house, when the foundation of this house was laid before
their eyes, wept with a loud voice; and many shouted aloud for
13 joy: so that the people could not discern the noise of the shout
of joy from the noise of the weeping of the people: for the
people shouted with a loud shout, and the noise was heard
afar off.

[d] Neh. 8. 14, 17.
Zech. 14. 16, 17.
[e] Ex. 23. 16.
[f] Num. 29. 12, &c.
[g] Ex. 29. 38.
Num. 28. 3, 11, 19, 26.
& 29. 2, 8, 13.

[h] 1 Kin. 5. 6, 9.
2 Chr. 2. 10.
Acts 12. 20.
[i] 2 Chr. 2. 16.
Acts 9. 36.
[k] ch. 6. 3.

[l] 1 Chr. 23. 24, 27.

[m] ch. 2. 40.

[n] 1 Chr. 16 5, 6, 42.

[o] 1 Chr.6.31.
& 16. 4.
& 25. 1.
[p] Ex. 15. 21.
2 Chr. 7. 3.
Neh. 12. 24.
[q] 1Chr.16.34.
Ps. 136. 1.
[r] 1Chr.16.41.
Jer. 33. 11.
[s] See
Hag. 2. 3.

[1] Heb. *the matter of the day in his day.*
[2] Heb. *the temple of the LORD was not yet founded.*
[3] Or, *workmen.*
[4] Or, *Hodaviah*, ch. 2. 40.
[5] Heb. *as one.*

7. *according to the grant*] *i.e.* in accordance with the permission granted them by
Cyrus to rebuild their Temple (i. 1-4).
8. *unto the house of God*] *i.e.* to the place
where the house of God had been, and where
God was believed still to have His special
dwelling.
and appointed the Levites] This is the emphatic clause of the present verse. Though
so small a number of Levites had returned
from Babylon (ii. 40), yet they were especially singled out to be entrusted with the
task of superintending and advancing the
building of the Temple.
9. *Jeshua*] See marg. ref. Not the High-
Priest, but the head of one of the two Levitical houses which had returned.

together] The Hebrew phrase is very emphatic—"they stood up **as one man.**"
10. *they set the priests*] Or, according to
another reading, "The priests stood."
the Levites the sons of Asaph] *i.e.* "such of
the Levites as were descendants of Asaph."
It would seem as if no descendants of
Heman or Jeduthun had returned.
12. *wept...shouted...for joy*] Cp. marg. ref.
and Zech. iv. 10. It is implied that the
dimensions of the second Temple were
smaller than those of the first. Hence the
feeling of sorrow which came upon some.
They, however, who had not seen the former Temple, and so could not contrast the
two, naturally rejoiced to see the Sanctuary
of their religion begin to rise from its ruins.

CHAP. 4. NOW when *a*the adversaries of Judah and Benjamin heard that [1]the children of the captivity builded the temple 2 unto the LORD God of Israel; then they came to Zerubbabel, and to the chief of the fathers, and said unto them, Let us build with you: for we seek your God, as ye *do;* and we do sacrifice unto him *b*since the days of Esar-haddon king of Assur, which 3 brought us up hither. But Zerubbabel, and Jeshua, and the rest of the chief of the fathers of Israel, said unto them, *c*Ye have nothing to do with us to build an house unto our God; but we ourselves together will build unto the LORD God of Israel, 4 as *d*king Cyrus the king of Persia hath commanded us. Then *e*the people of the land weakened the hands of the people of 5 Judah, and troubled them in building, and hired counsellors against them, to frustrate their purpose, all the days of Cyrus king of Persia, even until the reign of Darius king of Persia. 6 And in the reign of [2]Ahasuerus, in the beginning of his reign, wrote they *unto him* an accusation against the inhabitants of 7 Judah and Jerusalem. ¶And in the days of Artaxerxes wrote [3]Bishlam, Mithredath, Tabeel, and the rest of their [4]companions, unto Artaxerxes king of Persia; and the writing of the letter *was* written in the Syrian tongue, and interpreted in the Syrian 8 tongue. Rehum the chancellor and Shimshai the [5]scribe wrote a letter against Jerusalem to Artaxerxes the king in this sort: 9 Then *wrote* Rehum the chancellor, and Shimshai the scribe, and the rest of their [6]companions; *f*the Dinaites, the Apharsath-

[1] Heb. *the sons of the transportation.*   [3] Or, *in peace.*   [5] Or, *secretary.*
[2] Heb. *Ahashverosh.*   [4] Heb. *societies.*   [6] Chald. *societies.*

IV. **1.** *adversaries*] *i.e.* the Samaritans, a mixed race, partly Israelite but chiefly foreign, which had replaced to some extent the ancient inhabitants after they were carried into Captivity by Sargon (see 2 K. xvii. 6 note).

2. Cp. 2 K. xvii. 24–28 notes.

since the days] Esar-haddon reigned from B.C. 681–668. Thus the Samaritans speak of what had taken place at least 130 years previously. There appear to have been at least three colonisations of Samaria by the Assyrian kings. The first is mentioned in 2 K. xvii. 24. Later in his reign Sargon added to these first settlers an Arabian element. Some thirty or forty years afterwards, Esarhaddon, his grandson, largely augmented the population by colonists drawn especially from the south-east parts of the Empire (*v.* 10). Thus the later Samaritans were an exceedingly mixed race.

3. *Ye have nothing to do with us*] Because the Samaritans had united idolatrous rites with the worship of Jehovah (2 K. xvii. 29–41). To have allowed them a share in restoring the Temple would have been destructive of all purity of religion.

as king Cyrus...commanded us] The exact words of the edict gave the right of building exclusively to those who should "go up" from Babylonia to Judæa (i. 3).

5. *hired counsellors*] Rather, "bribed" officials at the Persian court to interpose delays and create difficulties, in order to hinder the work.

Darius] *i.e.* Darius the son of Hystaspes

6. *Ahasuerus*] Or, Cambyses, the son and successor of Cyrus. Persian kings had often two names.

7. *Artaxerxes*] Gomates, the Pseudo-Smerdis. He succeeded Cambyses (B.C. 521), and reigned seven months, when he was deposed and executed by Darius Hystaspis.

written in the Syrian tongue, &c.] Or, "**written in Syriac characters and translated into Syriac.**" On the use of this tongue as a medium of communication between the Jews and their Eastern neighbours, see 2 K. xviii. 26 note.

8. *the chancellor*] Lit. "lord of judgment;" the title, apparently, of the Persian governor of the Samaritan province. Every Persian governor was accompanied to his province by a "royal scribe" or "secretary," who had a separate and independent authority.

9, 10. These verses form the superscription or address of the letter (*v.* 11, &c.) sent to Artaxerxes.

The Dinaites were probably colonists from *Dayan*, a country often mentioned in the Assyrian inscriptions as bordering on Cilicia and Cappadocia. No satisfactory explanation can be given of the name Apharsathchites (see v. 6 note). The Tarpelites were colonists from the nation which

chites, the Tarpelites, the Apharsites, the Archevites, the Baby-
10 lonians, the Susanchites, the Dehavites, *and* the Elamites, *g* and
the rest of the nations whom the great and noble Asnapper
brought over, and set in the cities of Samaria, and the rest *that*
11 *are* on this side the river, *h* and ¹ at such a time. ¶ This *is* the
copy of the letter that they sent unto him, *even* unto Artaxerxes
the king; Thy servants the men on this side the river, and at
12 such a time. Be it known unto the king, that the Jews which
came up from thee to us are come unto Jerusalem, building the
rebellious and the bad city, and have ² set up the walls *thereof*,
13 and ³ joined the foundations. Be it known now unto the king,
that, if this city be builded, and the walls set up *again*, *then*
will they not ⁴ pay *i* toll, tribute, and custom, and *so* thou shalt
14 endamage the ⁵ revenue of the kings. Now because ⁶ we have
maintenance from *the king's* palace, and it was not meet for us
to see the king's dishonour, therefore have we sent and certified
15 the king; that search may be made in the book of the records
of thy fathers : so shalt thou find in the book of the records,
and know that this city *is* a rebellious city, and hurtful unto
kings and provinces, and that they have ⁷ moved sedition ⁸ within
the same of old time : for which cause was this city destroyed.
16 We certify the king that, if this city be builded *again*, and the
walls thereof set up, by this means thou shalt have no portion
17 on this side the river. ¶ *Then* sent the king an answer unto
Rehum the chancellor, and *to* Shimshai the scribe, and *to* the
rest of their ⁹ companions that dwell in Samaria, and *unto* the

g ver. 1.

h So ver. 11.
17.
& ch. 7. 12.

i ch. 7. 24.

---

¹ Chald. *Cheeneth*.
² Or, *finished*.
³ Chald.*sewed together*.
⁴ Chald. *give*.
⁵ Or, *strength*.
⁶ Chald. *we are salted with the salt of the palace*.
⁷ Chald. *made*.
⁸ Chald. *in the midst thereof*.
⁹ Chald. *societies*.

---

the Assyrians called *Tuplai*, the Greeks "Tibareni," and the Hebrews generally "Tubal." (It is characteristic of the later Hebrew language to insert the letter *r* before labials. Cp. *Darmesek* for *Dammesek*, 2 Chr. xxviii. 23 marg.). The Apharsites were probably "the Persians ;" the Archevites, natives of Erech [Warka] (Gen. x. 10): the Susanchites, colonists from Shushan or Susa ; the Dehavites, colonists from the Persian tribe of the Daï ; and the Elamites, colonists from Elam or Elymaïs, the country of which Susa was the capital.

10. Asnapper was perhaps the official employed by Esar-haddon (*v.* 2) to settle the colonists in their new country.

on this side the river] Lit. "beyond the river," a phrase used of Palestine by Ezra, Nehemiah, and in the Book of Kings, as designating the region *west* of the Euphrates.

and at such a time] Rather, "**and so forth.**" The phrase is vague, nearly equivalent to the modern use of *et cetera*. It recurs in marg. reff.

13. *toll, tribute, and custom*] Rather, "**tribute, provision, and toll**" (so *v.* 20). The "tribute" is the money-tax imposed on each province, and apportioned to the inhabitants by the local authorities ; the "provision" is the payment in kind,

which was an integral part of the Persian system ; the "toll" is probably a payment required from those who used the Persian highways.

the revenue] The word thus translated is not found elsewhere, and can only be conjecturally interpreted. Modern commentators regard it as an adverb, meaning "at last," or "in the end," and translate, "**And so at last shall damage be done to the kings.**"

14. *we have maintenance*] See marg. The phrase "to eat a man's salt" is common in the East to this day ; and is applied not only to those who receive salaries, but to all who obtain their subsistence by means of another. The Persian satraps had no salaries, but taxed their provinces for the support of themselves and their courts.

15. *the book of the records*] Cp. Esth. ii. 23, vi. 1, x. 2. The existence of such a "book" at the Persian court is attested also by Ctesias.

of thy fathers] *i.e.* thy predecessors upon the throne, Cambyses, Cyrus, &c. If Artaxerxes was the Pseudo-Smerdis (*v.* 7 note), these persons were not really his "fathers" or ancestors ; but the writers of the letter could not venture to call the king an impostor.

18 rest beyond the river, Peace, and at such a time. The letter
19 which ye sent unto us hath been plainly read before me. And
[1] I commanded, and search hath been made, and it is found that
this city of old time hath [2] made insurrection against kings, and
20 *that* rebellion and sedition have been made therein. There have
been mighty kings also over Jerusalem, which have [k] ruled over
all *countries* [l] beyond the river; and toll, tribute, and custom, was
21 paid unto them. [3] Give ye now commandment to cause these
men to cease, and that this city be not builded, until *another*
22 commandment shall be given from me. Take heed now that ye
fail not to do this : why should damage grow to the hurt of the
23 kings? ¶ Now when the copy of king Artaxerxes' letter *was*
read before Rehum, and Shimshai the scribe, and their companions, they went up in haste to Jerusalem unto the Jews, and
24 made them to cease [4] by force and power. Then ceased the work
of the house of God which *is* at Jerusalem. So it ceased unto
the second year of the reign of Darius king of Persia.

CHAP. 5. THEN the prophets, [a] Haggai the prophet, and [b] Zechariah
the son of Iddo, prophesied unto the Jews that *were* in Judah and
2 Jerusalem in the name of the God of Israel, *even* unto them. Then
rose up [c] Zerubbabel the son of Shealtiel, and Jeshua the son
of Jozadak, and began to build the house of God which *is* at
Jerusalem : and with them *were* the prophets of God helping
3 them. ¶ At the same time came to them [d] Tatnai, governor on
this side the river, and Shethar-boznai, and their companions,
and said thus unto them, [e] Who hath commanded you to build

Marginal references:
[k] 1 Kin. 4. 21.
Ps. 72. 8.
[l] Gen. 15. 18.
Josh. 1. 4.
[a] Hag. 1. 1.
[b] Zech. 1. 1.
[c] ch. 3. 2.
[d] ver. 6.
ch. 6. 6.
[e] ver. 9.

[1] Chald. *by me a decree is set.*
[2] Chald. *lifted up itself.*
[3] Chald. *Make a decree.*
[4] Chald. *by arm and power.*

---

18. *hath been...read*] It is doubtful if the Persian monarchs could ordinarily read. At any rate it was their habit to have documents read to them (cp. Esth. vi. 1). This is still the ordinary practice at Eastern courts.

19. The archives of the Babylonian kingdom would contain accounts of the insurrections raised, or threatened, by Jehoiakim, Jehoiachin, and Zedekiah (2 K. xxiv. 1, 10, 20). It does not appear that there had ever been any rebellion against Persia.

20. *mighty kings* &c.] If this reference can scarcely have been to David or Solomon (see marg. ref.), of whom neither the Babylonian nor the Assyrian archives would be likely to have had any account,—it would probably be to Menahem (2 K. xv. 16) and Josiah (2 Chr. xxxiv. 6, 7, xxxv. 18).

24. *it ceased*] The stoppage of the building by the Pseudo-Smerdis is in complete harmony with his character. He was a Magus, devoted to the Magian elemental worship, and opposed to belief in a personal god. His religion did not approve of temples ; and as he persecuted the Zoroastrian so would he naturally be inimical to the Jewish faith. The building was resumed in the second year of Darius (B.C. 520), and was only interrupted for about two years; since the Pseudo-Smerdis reigned less than a year.

V. 1. Haggai and Zechariah stirred up

Zerubbabel and Jeshua (*v.* 2 ; Hag. i. 14), and warned the people against neglecting the building of the Temple, in order to give themselves to the beautifying of their own houses (see Hag. i. 4, 9). Zechariah was the son of Berechiah, and grandson of Iddo (see marg. ref. ; Mat. xxiii. 35). Cp. a similar application of "son" in the case of Jehu (2 K. ix. 20 note).

in the name of the God of Israel, even unto them] Rather, "in the name of the God of Israel, **which was upon them.**" The two Prophets addressed the Jews, in respect of their being God's people, or, in Hebrew phrase (see Jer. xv. 16 marg.), "having God's name called upon them."

2. *began to build*] *i.e.* "made a second beginning"—recommenced the uncompleted work.

helping them] By infusing zeal into the people (see Hag. i. 12).

3. *governor on this side the river*] Cp. iv. 10 note. Tatnai was apparently satrap of Syria, which included the whole tract west of the Euphrates from Cilicia to the borders of Egypt. Zerubbabel must have been, to some extent, under his authority.

Who hath commanded you to build?] There was no doubt a formal illegality in the conduct of Zerubbabel and Jeshua ; since all edicts of Persian kings continued in force unless revoked by their successors. But they felt justified in disobeying the decree

4 this house, and to make up this wall? ^fThen said we unto *f* ver. 10
them after this manner, What are the names of the men ¹that
5 make this building? But ^gthe eye of their God was upon the *g* See ch. 7.
elders of the Jews, that they could not cause them to cease, till 6, 28.
the matter came to Darius: and then they returned ^hanswer by Ps. 33. 18.
6 letter concerning this *matter*. ¶The copy of the letter that *h* ch. 6, 6.
Tatnai, governor on this side the river, and Shethar-boznai,
ⁱand his companions the Apharsachites, which *were* on this side *i* ch. 4. 9.
7 the river, sent unto Darius the king: they sent a letter unto
him, ²wherein was written thus; Unto Darius the king, all
8 peace. Be it known unto the king, that we went into the province of Judea, to the house of the great God, which is builded
with ³great stones, and timber is laid in the walls, and this work
9 goeth fast on, and prospereth in their hands. Then asked we
those elders, *and* said unto them thus, ^kWho commanded you to *k* ver. 3, 4.
10 build this house, and to make up these walls? We asked their
names also, to certify thee, that we might write the names of
11 the men that *were* the chief of them. And thus they returned
us answer, saying, We are the servants of the God of heaven
and earth, and build the house that was builded these many
years ago, which a great king of Israel builded ^land set up. *l* 1 Kin. 6. 1.
12 But ^mafter that our fathers had provoked the God of heaven *m* 2 Chr. 36.
unto wrath, he gave them into the hand of ⁿNebuchadnezzar 16, 17.
the king of Babylon, the Chaldean, who destroyed this house, *n* 2 Kin.24.2.
13 and carried the people away into Babylon. But in the first year & 25. 8, 9, 11.
of ^oCyrus the king of Babylon *the same* king Cyrus made a *o* ch. 1. 1.
14 decree to build this house of God. And ^pthe vessels also of *p* ch.1.7,8.&
gold and silver of the house of God, which Nebuchadnezzar 6. 5.
took out of the temple that *was* in Jerusalem, and brought them
into the temple of Babylon, those did Cyrus the king take out
of the temple of Babylon, and they were delivered unto *one*,
15 ^qwhose name *was* Sheshbazzar, whom he had made ⁴governor; *q* Hag. 1. 14.
and said unto him, Take these vessels, go, carry them into the & 2. 2, 21.
temple that *is* in Jerusalem, and let the house of God be builded
16 in his place Then came the same Sheshbazzar, *and* ^rlaid the *r* ch. 3. 8, 10.
foundation of the house of God which *is* in Jerusalem: and
since that time even until now hath it been in building, and
17 ^syet it is not finished. Now therefore, if *it seem* good to the *s* ch. 6. 15.
king, ^tlet there be search made in the king's treasure house, *t* ch. 6. 1, 2.
which *is* there at Babylon, whether it be *so*, that a decree was
made of Cyrus the king to build this house of God at Jerusalem, and let the king send his pleasure to us concerning this
matter.

¹ Chald. *that build this* ² Chald. *in the midst where-* ³ Chald. *stones of rolling.*
building? *of.* ⁴ Or, *deputy.*

---

of the Pseudo-Smerdis (iv. 7 note), because
the opposition between his religious views
and those of his successor was matter of
notoriety.
4. *Then said we*] The Septuagint, Syriac,
and Arabic Versions have "Then said
they," which brings this verse into exact
accordance with *v.* 10.
6. Apharsachites, like Apharsites, and
Apharsathchites (iv. 9), are thought by some
to be forms of the word "Persians," which
is applied here generally to the foreign
settlers in Samaria. [Others identify the

first and the third names with the "Pareta-
ceni," a people on the Medo-Persian border.]
8. *great stones*] Lit. as in marg.; *i.e.*
stones so large that they were rolled along,
not carried. Others translate "polished
stones."
16. *since that time even until now*] Sixteen
years—from B.C. 536 to B.C. 520. The adversaries of the Jews here overstep the truth;
since, in point of fact, the work had been
suspended for a while (iv. 24).
17. *let there be search made...at Babylon*]
They perhaps doubted whether proof of the

ᵃ ch. 5. 17.

CHAP. 6. THEN Darius the king made a decree, ᵃand search was made in the house of the ¹rolls, where the treasures were ²laid 2 up in Babylon. And there was found at ³Achmetha, in the palace that *is* in the province of the Medes, a roll, and therein 3 *was* a record thus written : In the first year of Cyrus the king *the same* Cyrus the king made a decree *concerning* the house of God at Jerusalem, Let the house be builded, the place where they offered sacrifices, and let the foundations thereof be strongly laid ; the height thereof threescore cubits, *and* the breadth

ᵇ 1 Kin. 6. 36.

4 thereof threescore cubits ; ᵇ*with* three rows of great stones, and a row of new timber : and let the expences be given out of the

ᶜ ch. 1. 7, 8. & 5. 14.

5 king's house : and also let ᶜthe golden and silver vessels of the house of God, which Nebuchadnezzar took forth out of the temple which *is* at Jerusalem, and brought unto Babylon, be restored, and ⁴brought again unto the temple which *is* at Jerusalem, *every one* to his place, and place *them* in the house of God.

ᵈ ch. 5. 3.

6 ¶ ᵈNow *therefore*, Tatnai, governor beyond the river, Shethar-boznai, and ⁵your companions the Apharsachites, which *are*
7 beyond the river, be ye far from thence : let the work of this house of God alone ; let the governor of the Jews and the elders
8 of the Jews build this house of God in his place. Moreover ⁶I make a decree what ye shall do to the elders of these Jews for the building of this house of God : that of the king's goods, *even* of the tribute beyond the river, forthwith expences be given
9 unto these men, that they be not ⁷hindered. And that which they have need of, both young bullocks, and rams, and lambs, for the burnt offerings of the God of heaven, wheat, salt, wine, and oil, according to the appointment of the priests which *are* at Jerusalem, let it be given them day by day without fail :

ᵉ ch. 7. 23. Jer. 29. 7.

10 ᵉthat they may offer sacrifices ⁸of sweet savours unto the God of

---

¹ Chald. *books.*
² Chald. *made to descend.*
³ Or, *Ecbatana*, or, *in a coffer.*

⁴ Chald. *go.*
⁵ Chald. *their societies.*
⁶ Chald. *by me a decree is*

made.
⁷ Chald. *made to cease.*
⁸ Chald. *of rest.*

---

decree of Cyrus remained in the archives. The Pseudo-Smerdis had had the records in his power for seven months ; and, when he reversed the policy of his predecessors, might have been expected to destroy their edicts. The decree was not found at Babylon, the most natural place for it, but in the provincial capital of Ecbatana, which Tatnai and his friends had not asked Darius to have searched (see vi. 2).

VI. 1. A "house of the rolls" was discovered at Koyunjik, the ancient Nineveh, in 1850—a set of chambers, *i.e.* in the palace devoted exclusively to the storing of public documents. These were in baked clay, and covered the floor to the depth of more than a foot. Such a "house" was probably that at Babylon.

2. "Achmetha" is the "Ecbatana," or "Agbatana," of the Greeks, the Persian name for which, as we find in the Behistun Inscription, was HAGMATANA.

We must suppose that, when Babylon had been searched in vain, the other cities which possessed record-offices were visited, and the decree looked for in them. Ecbatana was the capital of Cyrus.

3. It is difficult to reconcile the dimentions here with expressions in Zechariah (iv. 10), Haggai (ii. 3), and even Ezra (iii. 12), which imply that the second Temple was smaller than the first (cp. 1 K. vi. 2). Perhaps the dimensions here are those which Cyrus required the Jews *not to exceed.*

4 The word translated "row" occurs only in this passage. Some regard it as a "course," and suppose that after every three courses of stone there followed a course of timber. Others understand three "storeys " of stone, with a fourth "storey " of woodwork on the summit (cp. 1 K. vi. 5, 6). Others consider that Cyrus intended to limit the *thickness* of the walls, which were not to exceed a breadth of three rows of stone, with an inner wooden wainscotting.

let the expences be given out of the king's house] *i.e.* "out of the Persian revenue," a portion of the decree which was probably not observed during the later years of Cyrus and during the reign of Cambyses, and hence the burthen fell upon the Jews themselves (ii. 68, 69).

6. This verse gives the words of the de-

11 heaven, and *ᶠ*pray for the life of the king, and of his sons. Also I have made a decree, that whosoever shall alter this word, let timber be pulled down from his house, and being set up, ¹let him be hanged thereon; *ᵍ*and let his house be made a dunghill

12 for this. And the God that hath caused his *ʰ*name to dwell there destroy all kings and people, that shall put to their hand to alter *and* to destroy this house of God which *is* at Jerusalem. I Darius have made a decree; let it be done with speed.

13 ¶ Then Tatnai, governor on this side the river, Shethar-boznai, and their companions, according to that which Darius the king

14 had sent, so they did speedily. *ⁱ*And the elders of the Jews builded, and they prospered through the prophesying of Haggai the prophet and Zechariah the son of Iddo. And they builded, and finished *it*, according to the commandment of the God of Israel, and according to the ²commandment of *ᵏ*Cyrus, and

15 *ˡ*Darius, and *ᵐ*Artaxerxes king of Persia. And this house was finished on the third day of the month Adar, which was in the

16 sixth year of the reign of Darius the king. ¶ And the children of Israel, the priests, and the Levites, and the rest of ³the children of the captivity, kept *ⁿ*the dedication of this house of

17 God with joy, and *ᵒ*offered at the dedication of this house of God an hundred bullocks, two hundred rams, four hundred lambs; and for a sin offering for all Israel, twelve he goats, according

18 to the number of the tribes of Israel. And they set the priests in their *ᵖ*divisions, and the Levites in their *�q*courses, for the service of God, which *is* at Jerusalem; *⁴ʳ*as it is written in the

19 book of Moses. ¶ And the children of the captivity kept the

20 passover *ˢ*upon the fourteenth *day* of the first month. For the priests and the Levites were *ᵗ*purified together, all of them *were* pure, and *ᵘ*killed the passover for all the children of the captivity, and for their brethren the priests, and for themselves.

21 And the children of Israel, which were come again out of captivity, and all such as had separated themselves unto them from

Marginal references:
ᶠ 1 Tim. 2. 1, 2.
ᵍ 2 Kin. 10. 27. Dan. 2. 5. & 3. 29.
ʰ 1 Kin. 9. 3.
ⁱ ch. 5. 1, 2.
ᵏ ch. 1. 1. & 5. 13. ver. 3.
ˡ ch. 4. 24.
ᵐ ch. 7. 1.
ⁿ 1 Kin. 8. 63. 2 Chr. 7. 5.
ᵒ ch. 8. 35.
ᵖ 1 Chr. 24. 1.
q 1 Chr. 23. 6.
ʳ Num. 3. 6. & 8. 9.
ˢ Ex. 12. 6.
ᵗ 2 Chr. 30. 15.
ᵘ 2 Chr. 35. 11.

---

¹ Chald. *let him be destroyed.*
² Chald. *decree.*
³ Chald. *the sons of the transportation.*
⁴ Chald. *according to the writing.*

---

cree of Darius, which was grounded upon, and probably recited, the decree of Cyrus.

11. *being set up, let him be hanged thereon*] Rather, "let him be lifted up and crucified upon it." Crucifixion was the most common form of capital punishment among the Persians.

12. *destroy all*] A similar malediction is found at the end of the great inscription of this same king Darius at Behistun. If any injure the tablet which he has set up, he prays that Ormazd will be their enemy, and that they may have no offspring, and that whatever they do, Ormazd may curse it for them.

to alter and *to destroy this house*] i.e. to alter the decree, and then proceed to destroy the house.

14. *Artaxerxes*] The Artaxerxes of marg. ref. seems to be meant (*i.e.* Longimanus); he was one of those who together with Cyrus and Darius helped forward the *completion* of the work.

15. " Adar " was the twelfth or last month of the Jewish year, corresponding nearly with our March. The sixth year of Darius was B.C. 516–515.

17. Cp. with this modest sacrifice, which suits well "the day of small things" (Zech. iv. 10), the lavish offering of Solomon (marg. ref. *n*).

19. With this verse the writer resumes the use of the Hebrew language, which he had discarded for the Chaldee from iv. 8. With the exception of the letter of Artaxerxes (vii. 12–26), all the remainder of the book is in Hebrew.

20. Some render, "**And the priests were purified; and the Levites, as one man, were all of them pure.**" A contrast is drawn between the universal purity of the Levites and the merely general purity of the priests (2 Chr. xxix. 34, xxx. 3), which made it fitting that the former should undertake the slaughter of *all* the paschal lambs, even of those which the priests were to consume. In later times the ordinary practice was for each head of a family to slay for himself.

the *x*filthiness of the heathen of the land, to seek the LORD God
22 of Israel, did eat, and kept the *y*feast of unleavened bread seven
days with joy: for the LORD had made them joyful, and
*z*turned the heart *a*of the king of Assyria unto them, to
strengthen their hands in the work of the house of God, the God
of Israel.

CHAP. 7. NOW after these things, in the reign of *a*Artaxerxes king
of Persia, Ezra *b*the son of Seraiah, the son of Azariah, the son
2 of Hilkiah, the son of Shallum, the son of Zadok, the son of
3 Ahitub, the son of Amariah, the son of Azariah, the son of
4 Meraioth, the son of Zerahiah, the son of Uzzi, the son of Bukki,
5 the son of Abishua, the son of Phinehas, the son of Eleazar, the
6 son of Aaron the chief priest : this Ezra went up from Babylon ;
and he *was* *c*a ready scribe in the law of Moses, which the LORD
God of Israel had given : and the king granted him all his
request, *d*according to the hand of the LORD his God upon him.
7 *e*And there went up *some* of the children of Israel, and of the
priests, and *f*the Levites, and the singers, and the porters, and
*y*the Nethinims, unto Jerusalem, in the seventh year of Arta-
8 xerxes the king. And he came to Jerusalem in the fifth month,
9 which *was* in the seventh year of the king. For upon the first
day of the first month ¹began he to go up from Babylon, and on
the first *day* of the fifth month came he to Jerusalem, *h*according
10 to the good hand of his God upon him. For Ezra had prepared
his heart to *i*seek the law of the LORD, and to do *it*, and to

¹ Heb. *was the foundation of the going up.*

---

22. *the king of Assyria*] *i.e.* Darius. Assyria had so long been the great monarchy
of western Asia that the sacred writers continue the title to those who had inherited
the old Assyrian power, as first to the Babylonians (2 K. xxiii. 29), and secondly to
the Persians. With similar inexactness we
find Herodotus calling Cyrus "king of the
Medes."

VII. 1. *after these things*] The words
mark an interval of 57 years ; if, with most
commentators, we take Artaxerxes to be
Longimanus. See Introd. p. 569. Three
kings named Artaxerxes, the Greek rendering of the Hebrew Artakhshasta, and the
Persian Artakhshatra, ruled over Persia,
viz.:—Longimanus, Mnemon, and Ochus.
Evidence is in favour of the first being
meant here : he was the grandson of Darius
Hystaspis, Jeshua's contemporary.
The genealogy of Ezra here is incomplete. The time between the Exodus and
Ezra must have exceeded a thousand years,
and cannot have been covered by sixteen
generations. One gap may be filled up
from 1 Chr. vi. 7-10, which supplies six
names between Meraioth and Azariah (*v.* 3) :
another gap probably occurs between Seraiah (*v.* 1) and Ezra himself ; since Seraiah
appears to be the High-Priest of Zedekiah's
time (marg. ref.), who lived at least 130
years before Ezra. Three or four names
are probably wanting in this place. Another name (Meraioth) may be supplied
from 1 Chr. ix. 11, between Zadok and

Ahitub (*v.* 2). These additions would produce twenty-seven generations—a number
nearly sufficient—instead of sixteen.

6. *a ready scribe*] Or, "a ready writer"
(Ps. xlv. 1). The professional scribe was
well known in Egypt from an early date
(see Gen. xxxix. 4 note) ; and under David
and his successors "scribes" were attached
to the Court as the king's secretaries (2 Sam.
viii. 17, xx. 25 ; 2 K. xii. 10, &c.). It was
scarcely, however, till the time of the Captivity that the class to which Ezra belonged
arose. The "scribes" of this time, and of
later Jewish history, were students, interpreters, and copiers of the Law (marg. reff.
and Jer. viii. 8). They retained the knowledge of the old dialect, which was being
rapidly superseded by a new one. The emphatic application of the title "the scribe"
toEzra marks the high honour in which the
office was now held. Its glories threw into
the shade those of the priesthood.
the hand of the LORD...upon him] The use
of this phrase in a good sense is rare elsewhere (cp. 1 K. xviii. 46), but is a favourite
one with both Ezra and Nehemiah (see
marg. reff. ; Neh. ii. 8, 18).

9. The direct distance of Babylon from
Jerusalem is about 520 miles ; and the circuitous route by Carchemish and the Orontes
valley, which was ordinarily taken by armies
or large bodies of men, is about 900 miles.
The time occupied in the journey is long,
and is perhaps to be accounted for by the
dangers alluded to in viii. 22, 31.

11 *k*teach in Israel statutes and judgments. ¶ Now this *is* the copy of the letter that the king Artaxerxes gave unto Ezra the priest, the scribe, *even* a scribe of the words of the command-
12 ments of the LORD, and of his statutes to Israel. Artaxerxes, *l*king of kings, *l*unto Ezra the priest, a scribe of the law of the
13 God of heaven, perfect *peace*, *m*and at such a time. I make a decree, that all they of the people of Israel, and *of* his priests and Levites, in my realm, which are minded of their own free-
14 will to go up to Jerusalem, go with thee. Forasmuch as thou art sent *2*of the king, and of his *n*seven counsellors, to enquire concerning Judah and Jerusalem, according to the law of thy
15 God which *is* in thine hand; and to carry the silver and gold, which the king and his counsellors have freely offered unto
16 the God of Israel, *o*whose habitation *is* in Jerusalem, *p*and all the silver and gold that thou canst find in all the province of Babylon, with the freewill offering of the people, and of the priests, *q*offering willingly for the house of their God which *is*
17 in Jerusalem : that thou mayest buy speedily with this money bullocks, rams, lambs, with their *r*meat offerings and their drink offerings, and *s*offer them upon the altar of the house of
18 your God which *is* in Jerusalem. And whatsoever shall seem good to thee, and to thy brethren, to do with the rest of the
19 silver and the gold, that do after the will of your God. The vessels also that are given thee for the service of the house of
20 thy God, *those* deliver thou before the God of Jerusalem. And whatsoever more shall be needful for the house of thy God, which thou shalt have occasion to bestow, bestow *it* out of the
21 king's treasure house. And I, *even* I Artaxerxes the king, do make a decree to all the treasurers which *are* beyond the river, that whatsoever Ezra the priest, the scribe of the law of the
22 God of heaven, shall require of you, it be done speedily, unto an hundred talents of silver, and to an hundred *3*measures of wheat, and to an hundred baths of wine, and to an hundred
23 baths of oil, and salt without prescribing *how much*. *4*Whatso-ever is commanded by the God of heaven, let it be diligently done for the house of the God of heaven : for why should there
24 be wrath against the realm of the king and his sons ? Also we certify you, that touching any of the priests and Levites, singers,

k ver. 6. 25.
Deut. 33. 10.
Neh. 8. 1—8.
Mal. 2. 7.

l Ezek. 26. 7.
Dan. 2. 37.
m ch. 4. 10.

n Esth. 1. 14.

o 2 Chr. 6. 2.
Ps. 135. 21.
p ch. 8. 25.

q 1 Chr. 29.
6, 9.

r Num. 15.
4--13.
s Deut. 12. 5,
11.

---

1 Or, *to Ezra the priest, a perfect scribe of the law of the God of heaven*, peace, &c.
2 Chald. *from before the king.*
3 Chald. *cors.*
4 Heb. *Whatsoever is of the decree.*

---

12. The title, "king of kings," is assumed by almost all the Persian monarchs in their inscriptions.

perfect peace] "Peace" is not in the ori-ginal, and the word translated "perfect" occurs only in this place. Some prefer to take it as an adjective descriptive of Ezra (see marg.); others (LXX.) as the opening word of the first paragraph of the letter, and give it the meaning, "it is completed."

14. *seven counsellors*] Herodotus relates that there were seven families pre-eminent in Persia, those of the seven conspirators against the Pseudo-Smerdis (iv. 7 note); and it is reasonable to suppose that the heads of these families formed the special council of the king; the "Achæmenidæ," or royal family, being represented by the head

of the branch next in succession to that of the reigning monarch (see marg. ref.).

21. *all the treasurers*] The Persian system of taxing the provinces through the satraps involved the establishment in each province of at least one local treasury.

22. This verse assigns limits to the per-mission of *v.* 20. As the Persian tribute was paid partly in money and partly in kind (see iv. 13 note), the treasuries would be able to supply them as readily as they could furnish money.

23. Lit. as in the margin, *i.e.*, Whatso-ever is commanded in the Law with respect to the Temple service.

24. The decree of Artaxerxes was more favourable to the Jews than those of all previous Persian monarchs. We hear of a

porters, Nethinims, or ministers of this house of God, it shall
not be lawful to impose toll, tribute, or custom, upon them.
25 And thou, Ezra, after the wisdom of thy God, that *is* in thine
hand, *t* set magistrates and judges, which may judge all the
people that *are* beyond the river, all such as know the laws of
26 thy God; and *u* teach ye them that know *them* not. And whosoever will not do the law of thy God, and the law of the king,
let judgment be executed speedily upon him, whether *it be* unto
death, or ¹ to banishment, or to confiscation of goods, or to im-
27 prisonment. ¶ *x* Blessed *be* the LORD God of our fathers, *y* which
hath put *such a thing* as this in the king's heart, to beautify the
28 house of the LORD which *is* in Jerusalem: and *z* hath extended
mercy unto me before the king, and his counsellors, and before
all the king's mighty princes. And I was strengthened as *a* the
hand of the LORD my God *was* upon me, and I gathered together
out of Israel chief men to go up with me.

CHAP. 8. THESE *are* now the chief of their fathers, and *this is* the
genealogy of them that went up with me from Babylon, in the
2 reign of Artaxerxes the king. Of the sons of Phinehas; Gershom: of the sons of Ithamar; Daniel: of the sons of David;
3 *a* Hattush. Of the sons of Shechaniah, of the sons of *b* Pharosh;
Zechariah: and with him were reckoned by genealogy of the
4 males an hundred and fifty. Of the sons of Pahath-moab;
Elihoenai the son of Zerahiah, and with him two hundred males.
5 Of the sons of Shechaniah; the son of Jahaziel, and with him
6 three hundred males. Of the sons also of Adin; Ebed the son
7 of Jonathan, and with him fifty males. And of the sons of
Elam; Jeshaiah the son of Athaliah, and with him seventy
8 males. And of the sons of Shephatiah; Zebadiah the son of
9 Michael, and with him fourscore males. Of the sons of Joab;
Obadiah the son of Jehiel, and with him two hundred and
10 eighteen males. And of the sons of Shelomith; the son of Josi-
11 phiah, and with him an hundred and threescore males. And of
the sons of Bebai; Zechariah the son of Bebai, and with him
12 twenty and eight males. And of the sons of Azgad; Johanan
² the son of Hakkatan, and with him an hundred and ten males.
13 And of the last sons of Adonikam, whose names *are* these,
Eliphelet, Jeiel, and Shemaiah, and with them threescore males.
14 Of the sons also of Bigvai; Uthai, and ³ Zabbud, and with them
15 seventy males. ¶ And I gathered them together to the river
that runneth to Ahava; and there ⁴ abode we in tents three

Side references (left margin):
t Ex. 18. 21, 22.
Deut. 16. 18.
u ver. 10.
2 Chr. 17. 7.
Mal. 2. 7.
Matt. 23.2, 3.
x 1Chr.29.10.
y ch. 6. 22.
z ch. 9. 9.
a See ch.5 5.
& ver. 6, 9.
& ch. 8. 18.
a 1 Chr. 3.22.
b ch. 2. 3.

---

¹ Chald. *to rooting out.*
² Or, *the youngest son.*
³ Or, *Zaccur,* as some read.
⁴ Or, *pitched.*

---

similar exemption of ecclesiastics from tribute, only to a less extent, under the Seleu-
cidæ.

ministers] The rare word here used, which
in Daniel has the sense of "worshippers,"
appears to designate in this place the lowest
class of persons employed in the service of
the Temple.

26. *banishment*] Lit. as in marg. Separation from the congregation is probably intended (cp. x. 8).

27. An abrupt transition from the words
of Artaxerxes to those of Ezra. Cp. a
similar abrupt change in vi. 6. The language alters at the same time from Chaldee

to Hebrew, continuing henceforth to be
Hebrew till the close of the book.

VIII. **2, 3.** Punctuate as follows:—
2. ...of the sons of David, Hattush
of the sons of Shechaniah.
3. Of the sons of Pharosh, Zechariah,
&c.

Hattush, the descendant of David, was the
grandson of Shechaniah (see marg. ref.).
Most of these names (*vv.* 2-14) occur also
as those of heads of families in the list of
the Jews who returned with Zerubbabel (ii.
3-15). The LXX. and Syriac Versions
supply omissions in *vv.* 5, 10.
15. Ahava was both a town and a river

days: and I viewed the people, and the priests, and found there
16 none of the *c*sons of Levi. Then sent I for Eliezer, for Ariel,
for Shemaiah, and for Elnathan, and for Jarib, and for Elnathan, and for Nathan, and for Zechariah, and for Meshullam,
chief men; also for Joiarib, and for Elnathan, men of under-
17 standing. And I sent them with commandment unto Iddo the
chief at the place Casiphia, and [1]I told them what they should
say unto Iddo, *and* to his brethren the Nethinims, at the place
Casiphia, that they should bring unto us ministers for the house
18 of our God. And by the good hand of our God upon us they
*d*brought us a man of understanding, of the sons of Mahli, the
son of Levi, the son of Israel; and Sherebiah, with his sons and
19 his brethren, eighteen; and Hashabiah, and with him Jeshaiah
of the sons of Merari, his brethren and their sons, twenty;
20 *e*also of the Nethinims, whom David and the princes had appointed for the service of the Levites, two hundred and twenty
21 Nethinims: all of them were expressed by name. ¶Then I
*f*proclaimed a fast there, at the river of Ahava, that we might
*g*afflict ourselves before our God, to seek of him a *h*right way for
22 us, and for our little ones, and for all our substance. For *i*I
was ashamed to require of the king a band of soldiers and horsemen to help us against the enemy in the way: because we had
spoken unto the king, saying, *k*The hand of our God *is* upon all
them for *l*good that seek him; but his power and his wrath *is*
23 *m*against all them that *n*forsake him. So we fasted and besought
24 our God for this: and he was *o*intreated of us. ¶Then I separated twelve of the chief of the priests, Sherebiah, Hashabiah,
25 and ten of their brethren with them, and weighed unto them
*p*the silver, and the gold, and the vessels, *even* the offering of
the house of our God, which the king, and his counsellors, and
26 his lords, and all Israel *there* present, had offered: I even
weighed unto their hand six hundred and fifty talents of silver,
and silver vessels an hundred talents, *and* of gold an hundred
27 talents; also twenty basons of gold, of a thousand drams; and
28 two vessels of [2]fine copper, [3]precious as gold. And I said unto
them, Ye *are* *q*holy unto the LORD; the vessels *are* *r*holy also;
and the silver and the gold *are* a freewill offering unto the LORD
29 God of your fathers. Watch ye, and keep *them*, until ye weigh
them before the chief of the priests and the Levites, and chief of
the fathers of Israel, at Jerusalem, in the chambers of the house

c See ch. 7.7.

d Neh. 8. 7.
& 9. 4, 5.

e See ch. 2.
43.

f 2 Chr. 20. 3.
g Lev. 16. 29.
& 23. 29.
Isai. 58. 3, 5.
h Ps. 5. 8.
i So 1 Cor. 9.
15.
k ch. 7. 6, 9,
28.
l Ps.33.18,19.
& 34. 15, 22.
Rom. 8. 28.
m Ps. 34. 16.
n 2 Chr.15. 2.
o 1 Chr. 5. 20.
2 Chr. 33. 13.
Isai. 19. 22.
p ch. 7.15,16.

q Lev. 21. 6,
7, 8.
Deut. 33. 8.
r Lev.22.2,3.
Num. 4. 4,
15, 19, 20.

---

[1] Heb. *I put words in their mouth*: See 2 Sam. 14. 3, 19.

[1] Heb *yellow*, or, *shining brass.*
[3] Heb. *desirable.*

(*v.* 21). The modern name of the place is
Hit. It is famous for its bitumen springs,
and is situated on the Euphrates, at a distance of about 80 miles from Babylon, towards the north-west.

none of the sons of Levi] The Levites appear to have been disinclined to return to
Jerusalem (see iii. 8 note).

17. *Casiphia*] Its situation is wholly unknown; but it cannot have been far from
Ahava.

18. *and Sherebiah*] Either a name has
fallen out before the words "a man of understanding," or the "and" here has crept
into the text by accident. Sherebiah appears
among the most earnest of the Levites under
Nehemiah (marg. reff.).

22. What "enemy" menaced Ezra, and on
what account, is wholly uncertain (cp. *v.* 31).
Perhaps robber-tribes, Arab or Syrian, were
his opponents.

27. *twenty basons of gold, of a thousand
drams*] Not of a thousand drams (*i.e.* darics)
each, but worth altogether a thousand darics. As the value of the daric was about
22 shillings of our money, each bason, or
saucer, would have been worth (apart from
the fashioning) 55*l.*

of fine copper] The word translated "fine,"
which occurs here only, is thought to mean
either "yellow" or "glittering" (see marg.).
Probably the vessels were of *orichalcum*, an
amalgam which was either brass or something nearly approaching to brass, but which

30 of the LORD. So took the priests and the Levites the weight of the silver, and the gold, and the vessels, to bring *them* to Jeru-
31 salem unto the house of our God. ¶ Then we departed from the river of Ahava on the twelfth *day* of the first month, to go

unto Jerusalem : and *s*the hand of our God was upon us, and he delivered us from the hand of the enemy, and of such as lay in

t Neh. 2. 11.   32 wait by the way. And we *t*came to Jerusalem, and abode there
33 three days. Now on the fourth day was the silver and the gold

u ver. 26, 30.   and the vessels *u*weighed in the house of our God by the hand of Meremoth the son of Uriah the priest; and with him *was* Eleazar the son of Phinehas; and with them *was* Jozabad the
34 son of Jeshua, and Noadiah the son of Binnui, Levites; by number *and* by weight of every one : and all the weight was
35 written at that time. *Also* the children of those that had been

x So ch.6.17.   carried away, which were come out of the captivity, *x*offered burnt offerings unto the God of Israel, twelve bullocks for all Israel, ninety and six rams, seventy and seven lambs, twelve he goats *for* a sin offering : all *this was* a burnt offering unto the

y ch. 7. 21.   36 LORD. And they delivered the king's *y*commissions unto the king's lieutenants, and to the governors on this side the river : and they furthered the people, and the house of God.

CHAP. 9. NOW when these things were done, the princes came to me, saying, The people of Israel, and the priests, and the

a ch. 6. 21.   Levites, have not *a*separated themselves from the people of the
Neh. 9. 2.   lands, *b*doing* according to their abominations, *even* of the
b Deut. 12.   Canaanites, the Hittites, the Perizzites, the Jebusites, the
30, 31.   Ammonites, the Moabites, the Egyptians, and the Amorites.

c Ex. 34. 16.   2 For they have *c*taken of their daughters for themselves, and for
Deut. 7. 3.   their sons : so that the *d*holy seed have *e*mingled themselves
Neh. 13. 23.   with the people of *those* lands : yea, and the hand of the princes and
d Ex. 19. 6.   3 rulers hath been chief in this trespass. And when I heard this
& 22. 31.   thing, *f*I rent my garment and my mantle, and plucked off the
Deut. 7. 6.   hair of my head and of my beard, and sat down *g*astonied.
& 14. 2.   4 Then were assembled unto me every one that *h*trembled at the
r 2 Cor. 6. 14.   words of the God of Israel, because of the transgression of those
f Job 1. 20.   that had been carried away; and I sat astonied until the *i*even-
g Ps. 143. 4.   5 ing sacrifice. ¶ And at the evening sacrifice I arose up from my
h ch. 10. 3.   *l*heaviness; and having rent my garment and my mantle, I fell
Isai. 66. 2.   upon my knees, and *k*spread out my hands unto the LORD my
i Ex. 29. 39.

k Ex.9.29,33.
l Dan. 9. 7, 8.   6 God, and said, O my God, I am *l*ashamed and blush to lift up

1 Or, *affliction.*

---

was very rarely produced in the ancient world, and, when produced, was regarded as highly valuable.

31. The Jews with Ezra left Babylon on the first day of the first month (vii. 9). They reached Ahava in nine days, and, having remained there three (*v.* 15), quitted it, and resumed their journey on the twelfth. They reached Jerusalem on the first day of the fifth month (vii. 9), four months after the departure from Babylon.

35. Cp. marg. ref. The idea of offerings for all Israel pervades in this case the entire sacrifice, with the exception of the lambs, whose number (77) is peculiar, and has not been accounted for.

36. *the king's commissions*] *i.e.* the orders

issued to all governors of provinces near Judæa by Artaxerxes, given in vii. 21–24.

the king's lieutenants] Lit. "**the king's satraps.**" The word is used in its strict sense, referring to the chief rulers of Persian provinces, from which the "governors" or rulers of smaller districts are distinguished.

IX. **1.** *abominations*] The mixed marriages had prevented that complete separation of the people of God from the idolatrous rites, or "abominations," which the Law required, and which was necessary for purity of religion. See 1 K. xi. 2 note.

3. Plucking out the hair with the hands, so common among the classical nations, is, comparatively speaking, rarely mentioned as practised by Asiatics.

my face to thee, my God: for [m]our iniquities are increased over
our head, and our [1]trespass is [n]grown up unto the heavens.
7 Since the days of our fathers *have* [o]we *been* in a great trespass
unto this day; and for our iniquities [p]have we, our kings, *and*
our priests, been delivered into the hand of the kings of the
lands, to the sword, to captivity, and to a spoil, and to [q]con-
8 fusion of face, as *it is* this day. And now for a [2]little space
grace hath been *shewed* from the LORD our God, to leave us a
remnant to escape, and to give us [3]a nail in his holy place, that
our God may [r]lighten our eyes, and give us a little reviving in
9 our bondage. [s]For we *were* bondmen; [t]yet our God hath not
forsaken us in our bondage, but [u]hath extended mercy unto us
in the sight of the kings of Persia, to give us a reviving, to set
up the house of our God, and [4]to repair the desolations thereof,
10 and to give us [x]a wall in Judah and in Jerusalem. And now, O
our God, what shall we say after this? for we have forsaken thy
11 commandments, which thou hast commanded [5]by thy servants
the prophets, saying, The land, unto which ye go to possess it,
is an unclean land with the [y]filthiness of the people of the lands,
with their abominations, which have filled it [6]from one end to
12 another with their uncleanness. Now therefore [z]give not your
daughters unto their sons, neither take their daughters unto
your sons, [a]nor seek their peace or their wealth for ever: that
ye may be strong, and eat the good of the land, and [b]leave *it* for
13 an inheritance to your children for ever. And after all that
is come upon us for our evil deeds, and for our great trespass, seeing that thou our God [c7]hast punished us less than
our iniquities *deserve*, and hast given us *such* deliverance as
14 this; should we [d]again break thy commandments, and [e]join in
affinity with the people of these abominations? wouldest not
thou be [f]angry with us till thou hadst consumed *us*, so that
15 *there should be* no remnant nor escaping? O LORD God of Israel,
[g]thou *art* righteous: for we remain yet escaped, as *it is* this day:
behold, we *are* [h]before thee [i]in our trespasses: for we cannot
[k]stand before thee because of this.

[m] Ps. 38. 4.
[n] 2 Chr. 28.9.
Rev. 18. 5.
[o] Ps. 106. 6.
Dan.9.5.6,8.
[p] Deut.28.36,
64.
Neh. 9. 30.
[q] Dan. 9.7,8.

[r] Ps. 13. 3.
& 34. 5.
[s] Neh. 9. 36.
[t] Ps. 136. 23.
[u] ch. 7. 28.

[x] Isai. 5. 2.

[y] ch. 6. 21.

[z] Ex. 23, 32.
& 34. 16.
Deut. 7. 3.
[a] Deut. 23. 6.
[b] Prov.13.22.
& 20. 7.

[c] Ps. 103. 10.

[d] John 5. 14.
2Pet.2.20,21.
[e] ver. 2.
Neh. 13. 23,
27.
[f] Deut. 9. 8.
[g] Neh. 9.33.
Dan. 9. 14.
[h] Rom. 3. 19.
[i] 1 Cor.15.17.
[k] Ps. 130.3.

[1] Or, *guiltiness.*
[2] Heb. *moment.*
[3] Or, *a pin :* that is, *a constant and sure abode :* So
Isai. 22. 23.
[4] Heb. *to set up.*
[5] Heb. *by the hand of thy servants.*
[6] Heb. *from mouth to mouth :* as 2 Kin. 21. 16.
[7] Heb.*hast withheld beneath our iniquities.*

---

7. Very similar in tone to this are the
confessions of Nehemiah (Neh. ix. 29-35)
and of Daniel (marg. reff.). The Captivity
had done its work by deeply convincing of
sin the nation that had been proud and
self-righteous previously.
8. The "little space" was above sixty
years, counting from the second year of
Darius (iv. 24), or about eighty, counting
from the first year of Cyrus (i. 1). This
does not seem to Ezra much in the life of a
nation.
a remnant to escape] Rather, "a remnant
that has escaped." The "remnant" is the
new community that has returned from the
Captivity.
a nail] Cp. marg. note and ref. The metaphor is probably drawn from a tent-pin,
which is driven into the earth to make the
tent firm and secure.

9. *we were bondmen*] Rather, "we are
bondmen" (cp. marg. ref.). The Israelites,
though returned from the Captivity, were
still "bondmen." The Persian monarch
was their absolute lord and master.
11. *saying*] The words which follow in
this verse are not quoted from any previous
book of Scripture, but merely give the general sense of numerous passages. Cp. marg
reff.
13. *deliverance*] Or, "remnant," as in
v. 8.
15. Some take "righteous" to mean
here "kind" or "merciful." Others give
it the more usual sense of "just," and understand the full meaning of the passage to
be, "Thou art righteous, and hast punished
us, because of our sin, the contraction of
forbidden marriages, so that we are a mere
remnant of what was once a great people."

a Dan. 9. 20.
b 2 Chr. 20. 9.

c Neh.13. 27.

d 2Chr.34.31.

e ch. 9. 4.
f Deut.7. 2,3.

g 1Chr.28.10.
h Neh. 5. 12.

i Deut. 9. 18.

k See 1 Sam.
12. 18.

l Josh. 7. 19.
Prov. 28. 13.

CHAP. 10. NOW *a*when Ezra had prayed, and when he had confessed, weeping and casting himself down *b*before the house of God, there assembled unto him out of Israel a very great congregation of men and women and children : for the people 2 [1] wept very sore. And Shechaniah the son of Jehiel, *one* of the sons of Elam, answered and said unto Ezra, We have *c*trespassed against our God, and have taken strange wives of the people of the land : yet now there is hope in Israel concerning 3 this thing. Now therefore let us make *d*a covenant with our God [2]to put away all the wives, and such as are born of them, according to the counsel of my lord, and of those that *e*tremble at *f*the commandment of our God ; and let it be done according 4 to the law. Arise ; for *this* matter *belongeth* unto thee : we also 5 *will be* with thee : *g*be of good courage, and do *it*. ¶ Then arose Ezra, and made the chief priests, the Levites, and all Israel, *h*to 6 sware. Then Ezra rose up from before the house of God, and went into the chamber of Johanan the son of Eliashib : and *when* he came thither, he *i*did eat no bread, nor drink water : for he mourned because of the transgression of them that had 7 been carried away. And they made proclamation throughout Judah and Jerusalem unto all the children of the captivity, that 8 they should gather themselves together unto Jerusalem ; and that whosoever would not come within three days, according to the counsel of the princes and the elders, all his substance should be [3]forfeited, and himself separated from the congrega-9 tion of those that had been carried away. ¶ Then all the men of Judah and Benjamin gathered themselves together unto Jerusalem within three days. It *was* the ninth month, on the twentieth *day* of the month ; and *k*all the people sat in the street of the house of God, trembling because of *this* matter, 10 and for [4]the great rain. And Ezra the priest stood up, and said unto them, Ye have transgressed, and [5]have taken strange wives, 11 to increase the trespass of Israel. Now therefore *l*make confession unto the LORD God of your fathers, and do his pleasure :

[1] Heb. *wept a great weeping.*   [3] Heb. *devoted.*   [5] Heb. *have caused to dwell,*
[2] Heb. *to bring forth.*   [4] Heb. *the showers.*   *or, have brought back.*

X. 1., *before the house of God*] *i.e.* in front of the Temple, praying towards it (1 K. viii. 30, 35 ; Dan. vi. 10), and thus in the sight of all the people who happened at the time to be in the great court.

2. Jehiel was one of those who had taken an idolatrous wife (*v.* 26) ; and Shechaniah had therefore had the evil brought home to him.

3. *let it be done according to the law*] *i.e.* let a formal "bill of divorcement" be given to each foreign wife, whereby she will be restored to the condition of an unmarried woman, and be free to wed another husband (see Deut. xxiv. 1, 2). The facility of divorce among the Jews is well known. According to many of the Rabbis, a bill of divorcement might be given by the husband for the most trivial cause. Thus no legal difficulty stood in the way of Shechaniah's proposition ; and Ezra regarded it as neces-

sary for the moral and religious welfare of the people.

6. The "chamber of Johanan" was probably one of those attached externally to the Temple (see 1 K. vi. 5, 6). Eliashib was the grandson of Jeshua (iii. 2), and was High-Priest under Nehemiah (Neh. iii. 1). He could assign chambers in the Temple to whomsoever he pleased (see Neh. xiii. 4, 5).

8. *separated from the congregation*] *i.e.* "excommunicated" (cp. Ex. xii. 19 ; Num. xix. 20, &c.). The power assigned to Ezra is stated in vii. 25, 26.

9. *it was the ninth month*] Or, our December, a time when rain falls heavily in Palestine : four months, therefore, after Ezra's arrival in Jerusalem (cp. vii. 9).

the street] Rather, "**the court**," the "broad," "spacious, place" (cp. 2 Chr. xxix. 4 note).

and ^mseparate yourselves from the people of the land, and from m ver. 3.
12 the strange wives. ¶ Then all the congregation answered and
13 said with a loud voice, As thou hast said, so must we do. But
the people *are* many, and *it is* a time of much rain, and we are
not able to stand without, neither *is this* a work of one day or
two: for ¹we are many that have transgressed in this thing.
14 Let now our rulers of all the congregation stand, and let all
them which have taken strange wives in our cities come at
appointed times, and with them the elders of every city, and the
judges thereof, until ⁿthe fierce wrath of our God ²for this n 2 Chr.30.8.
15 matter be turned from us. ¶ Only Jonathan the son of Asahel
and Jahaziah the son of Tikvah ³were employed about this
matter: and Meshullam and Shabbethai the Levite helped them.
16 And the children of the captivity did so. ¶ And Ezra the priest,
with certain chief of the fathers, after the house of their fathers,
and all of them by *their* names, were separated, and sat down in
17 the first day of the tenth month to examine the matter. And
they made an end with all the men that had taken strange wives
18 by the first day of the first month. ¶ And among the sons of
the priests there were found that had taken strange wives:
namely, of the sons of Jeshua the son of Jozadak, and his
19 brethren; Maaseiah, and Eliezer, and Jarib, and Gedaliah. And
they ^ogave their hands that they would put away their wives; o 2Kin.10.15.
and *being* ^pguilty, *they offered* a ram of the flock for their tres- 1 Chr. 29. 24.
2 Chr. 30. 8.
20 pass. And of the sons of Immer; Hanani, and Zebadiah. p Lev.6. 4, 6.
21 And of the sons of Harim; Maaseiah, and Elijah, and Shemaiah,
22 and Jehiel, and Uzziah. And of the sons of Pashur; Elioenai,
23 Maaseiah, Ishmael, Nethaneel, Jozabad, and Elasah. ¶ Also of
the Levites; Jozabad, and Shimei, and Kelaiah, (the same *is*
24 Kelita,) Pethahiah, Judah, and Eliezer. Of the singers also;
Eliashib: and of the porters; Shallum, and Telem, and Uri.
25 ¶ Moreover of Israel: of the sons of Parosh; Ramiah, and Je-
ziah, and Malchiah, and Miamin, and Eleazar, and Malchijah,
26 and Benaiah. And of the sons of Elam; Mattaniah, Zechariah,
27 and Jehiel, and Abdi, and Jeremoth, and Eliah. And of the
sons of Zattu; Elioenai, Eliashib, Mattaniah, and Jeremoth,
28 and Zabad, and Aziza. Of the sons also of Bebai; Jehohanan,
29 Hananiah, Zabbai, *and* Athlai. And of the sons of Bani; Meshullam, Malluch, and Adaiah, Jashub, and Sheal, and Ramoth.
30 And of the sons of Pahath-moab; Adna, and Chelal, Benaiah,
Maaseiah, Mattaniah, Bezaleel, and Binnui, and Manasseh.
31 And *of* the sons of Harim; Eliezer, Ishijah, Malchiah, She-
32, 33 maiah, Shimeon, Benjamin, Malluch, *and* Shemariah. Of the
sons of Hashum; Mattenai, Mattathah, Zabad, Eliphelet, Jere-
34 mai, Manasseh, *and* Shimei. Of the sons of Bani; Maadai,
35, 36 Amram, and Uel, Benaiah, Bedeiah, Chelluh, Vaniah, Mere-

---

¹ Or, *we have greatly of-*
fended in this thing.   ² Or, *till this matter* be dispatched.   ³ Heb. *stood.*

---

15. Some translate, "**Nevertheless** Jonathan the son of Asahel and Jahaziah the
son of Tikvah **opposed this.**" The opposition was useless (*v.* 16).
17. The business occupied the commission full two months. In some cases, it
may be presumed, they had to summon persons before them who did not wish to part
with their foreign wives; in all, they had
to assure themselves that the wives were
foreign; finally, they had in every case
where they decreed a divorce to make out
the "writing of divorcement" (*v.* 3).
18–43. Cp. with the list in ch. ii.
19. *they gave their hands*] *i.e.* "solemnly
pledged themselves" (cp. marg. reff.).

37, 38 moth, Eliashib, Mattaniah, Mattenai, and Jaasau, and Bani,
39 and Binnui, Shimei, and Shelemiah, and Nathan, and Adaiah,
40, 41 ¹Machnadebai, Shashai, Sharai, Azareel, and Shelemiah, She-
42, 43 mariah, Shallum, Amariah, *and* Joseph. Of the sons of
    Nebo; Jeiel, Mattithiah, Zabad, Zebina, Jadau, and Joel,
44 Benaiah. All these had taken strange wives : and *some* of them
    had wives by whom they had children.

¹ Or, *Mabnadebai,* according to some copies.

---

44. The guilty persons were, it would seem, 113 in number. They comprised four members of the High-Priest's family, thirteen other priests, ten Levites, and eighty-six lay Israelites belonging to at least ten distinct families. The fact noted in the second clause of the verse must have increased the difficulty of Ezra's task.

NEHEMIAH.

INTRODUCTION.

In the earliest form of the Hebrew Canon known to us the Books of Ezra and Nehemiah were united in one, under the name of "The Book of Ezra."[1] After a while a division was made, and the two Books which we now recognise were distinguished as "the first" and "the second Book of Ezra."[2] Later still—probably not till towards the close of the fourth century—the second Book of Ezra came to be known as "the Book of Nehemiah."[3]

2. The Book of Nehemiah is composed of four quite distinct sections :—

(I.) Chs. i.-vii. containing the record of the twentieth year of Artaxerxes (or B.C. 445–444), but composed by Nehemiah at least twelve years later (v. 14).

(II.) The second section of the work consists of chs. viii.--x., and contains a narrative of some events belonging to the autumn of B.C. 444. In this portion Nehemiah is spoken of in the third person ; he is called "the Tirshatha," whereas in the earlier chapters his title is always *pechah* (" governor ") ; and

Ezra holds the first and most prominent position. The style of this portion of the Book is markedly different from that of the earlier and later chapters ;[1] and critics are generally agreed that it is not from the hand of Nehemiah. Some assign it to Ezra ; others conjecture Zadok (or Zidkijah), Nehemiah's scribe or secretary (xiii. 13), to have been the author.

(III.) xi.-xii. 26, which consists of six important lists.

Lists 1 (xi. 1–24) and 2 (xi. 25-36) are probably either the work of Nehemiah himself or documents drawn up by his orders.

Of the other lists (xii.1–26) some may have been drawn up in the time (or even by the hand) of Nehemiah, and incorporated by him into his work as documents having an intrinsic value, though not connected very closely with the subject-matter of his history. But the list in *vv.* 10, 11 cannot in its present shape have proceeded from his hand, or from that of a contemporary, since it mentions Jaddua, who lived about a century later than Nehemiah.[5] Neither can

---

[1] See p. 569.
[2] By Origen (about A.D. 230).
[3] By Jerome.
[4] Nehemiah's parenthetic prayers are wholly wanting in this section. His favourite term for the "nobles" (*khorim*) does not occur. The characteristic phrases, "God of heaven," and "the good hand of God," are absent. God is called "Jehovah" or "Jehovah Elohim," almost as often as simply "Elohim," whereas Nehe-

miah uses "Jehovah" and "Jehovah Elohim," only once, each of them (i. 5, v. 13). Express mention of the Law of Moses, rare with Nehemiah (only xiii. 1), is constant in this section.

[5] Jaddua's High-priesthood is placed by some between B.C. 366 and 336 ; but Josephus brings down his date to B.C. 333, since he makes him meet Alexander after Issus.

vv. 22, 23 intruded between the fifth and sixth lists—lists closely interconnected—belong to Nehemiah's time, since they contain a mention of both Jaddua and Darius Codomannus, his contemporary. [6] Possibly, the list in question and the intruded verses may have proceeded from the same hand.

The section may therefore be regarded as the compilation of Nehemiah himself, with the exception of *vv.* 11, 22, 23, which must have been added a century later. Or, it was first added at that period. In either case the writer must equally be considered to have drawn the lists from contemporary State archives (see xii. 23).

(IV.) xii. 27--end. This section contains an account of the dedication of the wall, and of certain reforms which Nehemiah effected after his return from Babylon in B.C. 432-- 431. It is allowed on all hands to be, in the main, the work of Nehemiah,[7] and written soon after the events—probably in B.C. 431 or 430.

It is perhaps on the whole most probable that the various sections composing the "Book of Nehemiah" were collected by Nehemiah himself, who had written, at any rate, two of them (i.--vii. 5, xii.27-- xiii. 31). Having composed these two separate memoirs, and having perhaps drawn up also certain lists, he adopted from without an account of some religious transactions belonging to his first period, and, inserting this in its proper place, prefixed to the whole work the title, "The words of Nehemiah, the son of Hachaliah," as fitly designating its main contents. His work, thus formed, was subsequently added to by Jaddua, or a writer of that time, who inserted into it xii. 11, 22, 23. Or, possibly, this late writer may first have formed the Book into a whole. The date of the compilation would, in the former case, be about B.C. 430 ; in the latter, about a century later.

The authenticity of the history contained in the Book of Nehemiah is generally admitted : and the condition of the text is generally good.

---

[6] This is the usual identification of "Darius the Persian" (xii. 22, see note). The expression, "*the Persian*," is probably an indication that the passage was written after the Greek rule had set in, or later than B.C. 331.

[7] It possesses such characteristics of his style and manner as the designation of God exclusively by the name of Elohim, the use of parenthetic prayers (xiii. 14, 22, 29, 31), the exact knowledge of localities (xii. 31-39), &c.

THE BOOK

OF

NEHEMIAH.

CHAP. 1. THE words of *a* Nehemiah the son of Hachaliah. ¶And
it came to pass in the month Chisleu, in the twentieth year, as I
2 was in Shushan the palace, that Hanani, one of my brethren,
came, he and *certain* men of Judah; and I asked them concerning the Jews that had escaped, which were left of the cap-
3 tivity, and concerning Jerusalem. And they said unto me, The
remnant that are left of the captivity there in the province *are*
in great affliction and reproach: *b*the wall of Jerusalem also *c*is
4 broken down, and the gates thereof are burned with fire. ¶And
it came to pass, when I had heard these words, that I sat down
and wept, and mourned *certain* days, and fasted, and prayed
5 before the God of heaven, and said, I beseech thee, *d*O LORD
God of heaven, the great and terrible God, *e*that keepeth
covenant and mercy for them that love him and observe his
6 commandments: let thine ear now be attentive, and *f* thine eyes
open, that thou mayest hear the prayer of thy servant, which I
pray before thee now, day and night, for the children of Israel
thy servants, and *g*confess the sins of the children of Israel,
which we have sinned against thee: both I and my father's
7 house have sinned. *h* We have dealt very corruptly against
thee, and have *i*not kept the commandments, nor the statutes,
nor the judgments, which thou commandedst thy servant Moses.
8 Remember, I beseech thee, the word that thou commandedst
thy servant Moses, saying, *k If* ye transgress, I will scatter you
9 abroad among the nations: *l*but *if* ye turn unto me, and keep
my commandments, and do them; *m*though there were of you
cast out unto the uttermost part of the heaven, *yet* will I gather
them from thence, and will bring them unto the place that I
10 have chosen to set my name there. *n* Now these *are* thy servants and thy people, whom thou hast redeemed by thy great
11 power, and by thy strong hand. O Lord, I beseech thee, *o* let
now thine ear be attentive to the prayer of thy servant, and to
the prayer of thy servants, who *p*desire to fear thy name: and
prosper, I pray thee, thy servant this day, and grant him mercy
in the sight of this man. For I was the king's *q*cupbearer.

a ch. 10. 1.

b ch. 2. 17.
c 2Kin.25.10.

d Dan. 9. 4.
e Ex. 20. 6.

f 1 Kin.8.28,
29.
2 Chr. 6. 40.
Dan. 9.17,18.
g Dan. 9. 20.

h Ps. 106. 6.
Dan. 9. 5.
i Deut.28.15.

k Lev. 26. 33.
Deut. 4. 25,
26, 27.
& 28. 64.
l Lev. 26. 39,
&c.
Deut. 4. 29,
30, 31.
& 30. 2.
m Deut.30.4.
n Deut. 9. 29.
Dan. 9. 15.
o ver. 6.
p Isai. 26. 8.
Heb. 13. 18.
q ch. 2. 1.

I. 1. *The words of Nehemiah the son of*
Hachaliah] The prophetical books commence generally with a title of this kind
(see Jer. i. 1); but no other extant Historical Book begins thus. Nehemiah, while
attaching his work to Ezra, perhaps marked
in this manner the point at which his own
composition commenced. See Introd. p. 592.

Chisleu] The ninth month, corresponding
to the end of November and beginning of
December.

in the twentieth year] *i.e.* of Artaxerxes
Longimanus (B.C. 465-425). Cp. ii. 1.

Shushan the palace] Cp. Esth. i. 2, 5 &c.;
Dan. viii. 2. Shushan, or Susa, was the
ordinary residence of the Persian kings.
'The palace" or acropolis was a distinct

quarter of the city, occupying an artificial
eminence.

2. Hanani seems to have been an actual
brother of Nehemiah (vii. 2).

3. The attempt to rebuild the wall in the
time of the Pseudo-Smerdis (Ezra iv. 12-24)
had been stopped. It still remained in
ruins. The Assyrian sculptures show that
it was the usual practice to burn the
gates.

4. *the God of heaven*] This title of the
Almighty, which is Persian rather than
Jewish (see 2 Chr. xxxvi. 23; Ezra i. 2 note,
vi. 10, vii. 12, 21), is a favourite one with
Nehemiah, who had been born and brought
up in Persia.

11. A Persian king had numerous cup-

CHAP. 2. AND it came to pass in the month Nisan, in the twentieth
year of *a*Artaxerxes the king, *that* wine *was* before him : and
*b*I took up the wine, and gave *it* unto the king. Now I had not
2 been *beforetime* sad in his presence. Wherefore the king said
unto me, Why *is* thy countenance sad, seeing thou *art* not sick ?
this *is* nothing *else* but *c*sorrow of heart. Then I was very sore
3 afraid, and said unto the king, *d*Let the king live for ever : why
should not my countenance be sad, when *e* the city, the place of
my fathers' sepulchres, *lieth* waste, and the gates thereof are
4 consumed with fire ? Then the king said unto me, For what
dost thou make request ? So I prayed to the God of heaven.
5 And I said unto the king, If it please the king, and if thy servant have found favour in thy sight, that thou wouldest send me
unto Judah, unto the city of my fathers' sepulchres, that I may
6 build it. And the king said unto me, (the [1] queen also sitting
by him,) For how long shall thy journey be ? and when wilt
thou return ? So it pleased the king to send me ; and I set him
7 *f*a time. Moreover I said unto the king, If it please the king,
let letters be given me to the governors beyond the river, that
8 they may convey me over till I come into Judah ; and a letter
unto Asaph the keeper of the king's forest, that he may give
me timber to make beams for the gates of the palace which
*appertained g*to the house, and for the wall of the city, and for
the house that I shall enter into. And the king granted me,
9 *h*according to the good hand of my God upon me. ¶ Then I came
to the governors beyond the river, and gave them the king's
letters. Now the king had sent captains of the army and horse-
10 men with me. When Sanballat the Horonite, and Tobiah the

a Ezra 7. 1.
b c'i. 1. 11.

c Prov.15.13.
d 1 Kin.1.31.
Dan. 2. 4.
& 5. 10.
& 6. 6, 21.
e ch. 1. 3,

f ch. 5. 14.
& 13. 6.

g ch. 3. 7.

h Ezra 5. 5.
& 7. 6, 9, 28.
ver. 18.

[1] Heb. *wife.*

bearers, each of whom probably discharged
the office in his turn.

II. 1. Nisan was the name given by the
Persian Jews to the month previously called
" Abib," the first month of the Jewish
year, or that which followed the vernal
equinox. It fell four months after Chisleu
(i. 1).

the twentieth year] As Artaxerxes ascended the throne in B.C. 465, his twentieth
year would correspond to B.C. 445-444.

2. *I was very sore afraid*] A Persian subject was expected to be perfectly content so
long as he had the happiness of being with
his king. A request to quit the court was
thus a serious matter.

3. *the city...of my fathers' sepulchres*] We
may conclude from this that Nehemiah was
of the tribe of Judah, as Eusebius and Jerome say that he was.

4. *I prayed to the God of heaven*] Mentally
and momentarily, before answering the
king.

6. *the queen*] Though the Persian kings
practised polygamy, they had always one
chief wife, who alone was recognised as
" queen." The chief wife of Longimanus
was Damaspia.

I set him a time] Nehemiah appears to
have stayed at Jerusalem twelve years from
his first arrival (v. 14) ; but he can scarcely

have mentioned so long a term to the king.
Probably his leave of absence was prolonged
from time to time.

8. *the king's forest*] Rather, **park.** The
word used (*pardes ;* cp. παράδεισος, found only
here, in Eccl. ii. 5, and in Cant. iv. 13), is
of Persian, or at any rate of Aryan origin.
The Persians signified by *pariyadeza* a
walled enclosure, ornamented with trees,
either planted or of natural growth, and
containing numerous wild animals. The
" paradise " here mentioned must have been
in the neighbourhood of Jerusalem, and
may have corresponded to the earlier "gardens of Solomon."

the palace] Rather, " the **fortress.**" The
word in the original has the double meaning of " palace " and " fortress," the fact
being that in ancient times palaces were
always fortified. " The fortress which appertained to the house " or Temple is here
first spoken of. Under the Romans it was
called " Antonia."

10. The name Sanballat is probably Babylonian, the first element being the same
which commences " Sennacherib," viz.
"Sin," the Moon-God, and the second
balatu, " eminent " (?), which is found in
the Assyrian name, Bel-balatu. As a Horonite, he was probably a native of one of
the Bethhorons, the upper or the lower

servant, the Ammonite, heard *of it*, it grieved them exceedingly that there was come a man to seek the welfare of the children of
11 Israel. ¶ So I *i* came to Jerusalem, and was there three days. *i* Ezra 8. 32.
12 And I arose in the night, I and some few men with me; neither told I *any* man what my God had put in my heart to do at Jerusalem: neither *was there any* beast with me, save the beast that
13 I rode upon. And I went out by night *k* by the gate of the valley, *k* 2 Chr. 26,9. even before the dragon well, and to the dung port, and viewed the ch. 3. 13. walls of Jerusalem, which were *l* broken down, and the gates *l* ch. 1. 3.
14 thereof were consumed with fire. Then I went on to the *m* gate & ver. 17. of the fountain, and to the king's pool: but *there was* no place *m* ch. 3. 15.
15 for the beast *that was* under me to pass. Then went I up in the night by the *n* brook, and viewed the wall, and turned back, and *n* 2 Sam. 15.
16 entered by the gate of the valley, and *so* returned. And the Jer. 31. 40. rulers knew not whither I went, or what I did; neither had I as yet told *it* to the Jews, nor to the priests, nor to the nobles, nor
17 to the rulers, nor to the rest that did the work. Then said I unto them, Ye see the distress that we *are* in, how Jerusalem *lieth* waste, and the gates thereof are burned with fire: come, and let us build up the wall of Jerusalem, that we be no more
18 *o* a reproach. Then I told them of *p* the hand of my God which *o* ch. 1. 3. was good upon me; as also the king's words that he had spoken Ps. 44. 13. unto me. And they said, Let us rise up and build. So they Jer. 24. 9.
19 *q* strengthened their hands for *this* good *work*. ¶ But when San- Ezek. 5. 14, ballat the Horonite, and Tobiah the servant, the Ammonite, and & 22. 4. Geshem the Arabian, heard *it*, they *r* laughed us to scorn, and *p* ver. 8. despised us, and said, What *is* this thing that ye do? *s* will ye *q* 2 Sam. 2.7.
20 rebel against the king? Then answered I them, and said unto & 79. 4. them, The God of heaven, he will prosper us; therefore we his & 80. 6. servants will arise and build: *t* but ye have no portion, nor right, *t* Ezra 4. 3. nor memorial, in Jerusalem.

CHAP. 3. THEN *a* Eliashib the high priest rose up with his brethren *a* ch. 12. 10. the priests, *b* and they builded the sheep gate; they sanctified it, *b* John 5. 2

(see Josh. xvi. 3, 5; 2 Chr. viii. 5), and therefore born within the limits of the old kingdom of Samaria. Tobiah seems to have been an Ammonite slave, high in the favour of Sanballat, whom he probably served as secretary (vi. 17-19) and chief adviser.

it grieved them] Cp. Ezra iv. 4-24, v. 6-17. The revival of Jerusalem as a great and strong city, which was Nehemiah's aim, was likely to interfere with the prosperity, or at any rate the eminence, of Samaria.

13. *the gate of the valley*] A gate opening on the valley of Hinnom, which skirted Jerusalem to the west and south. The exact position is uncertain; as is also that of "the dragon well."

the dung port] The gate by which offal and excrements were conveyed out of the city, and placed eastward of the valley-gate.

14. *the gate of the fountain*] A gate on the eastern side of the Tyropœon valley, not far from the pool of Siloam (probably "the king's pool." Cp. iii. 15).

15. *the brook*] The Kidron watercourse, which skirted the city on the east.

turned back] *i.e.* he turned *westward*, and having made the circuit of the city, re-entered by the valley-gate.

16. *the rulers*] The principal authorities of the city, in the absence of the special governor.

the rest that did the work] *i.e.* "the labouring class that (afterwards) actually built the wall."

18. *the king's words*] These have not been given; but the royal permission to restore the walls is implied in ii. 5, 6.

19. *Geshem the Arabian*] The discovery that Sargon peopled Samaria in part with an Arab colony explains why Arabs should have opposed the fortification of Jerusalem.

III. 1. Eliashib (cp. marg. ref.) was the grandson of Joshua, the High-Priest contemporary with Zerubbabel.

the sheep gate] This was a gate in the eastern wall, not far from the pool of Bethesda, marg. ref., which was perhaps originally a sheep-pool.

The exact line which the writer follows in describing the circuit of the wall will probably be always a matter of dispute. According to the view here taken, the line

c ch. 12. 39.
d Jer. 31. 38.
Zech. 14. 10.
e Ezra 2. 34.
f 2 Chr.33.14.
ch. 12. 39.
Zeph. 1. 10.
g See ch. 6.1.
& 7. 1.

h Judg. 5. 23.
i ch. 12. 39.

k ch. 2. 8.

l ch. 12. 38.

and set up the doors of it ; ^ceven unto the tower of Meah they
2 sanctified it, unto the tower of ^dHananeel. And ¹next unto
him builded ^ethe men of Jericho. And next to them builded
3 Zaccur the son of Imri. ¶^fBut the fish gate did the sons of
Hassenaah build, who *also* laid the beams thereof, and ^gset up
4 the doors thereof, the locks thereof, and the bars thereof. And
next unto them repaired Meremoth the son of Urijah, the son
of Koz. And next unto them repaired Meshullam the son of
Berechiah, the son of Meshezabeel. And next unto them re-
5 paired Zadok the son of Baana. And next unto them the Tekoites repaired ; but their nobles put not their necks to ^hthe
6 work of their Lord. ¶Moreover ⁱthe old gate repaired Jehoiada
the son of Paseah, and Meshullam the son of Besodeiah ; they
laid the beams thereof, and set up the doors thereof, and the
7 locks thereof, and the bars thereof. And next unto them repaired Melatiah the Gibeonite, and Jadon the Meronothite, the
men of Gibeon, and of Mizpah, unto the ^kthrone of the governor
8 on this side the river. Next unto him repaired Uzziel the son
of Harhaiah, of the goldsmiths. Next unto him also repaired
Hananiah the son of *one of* the apothecaries, and they ²fortified
9 Jerusalem unto the ^lbroad wall. And next unto them repaired
Rephaiah the son of Hur, the ruler of the half part of Jeru-
10 salem. And next unto them repaired Jedaiah the son of Haru-
maph, even over against his house. And next unto him repaired
11 Hattush the son of Hashabniah. Malchijah the son of Harim,
and Hashub the son of Pahath-moab, repaired the ³other piece,

---

¹ Heb. *at his hand.*　　² Or, *left Jerusalem unto*　　³ Heb. *second measure.*
　　　　　　　　　the broad wall.

described commences near the pool of
Bethesda, on the east of the city, and is
traced thence, first, northwards, then west-
wards, then southwards, and finally eastwards, as far as the pool of Siloam (*v.* 15).
From this point, it seems to the writer of
this note that the line of the *outer* wall is
not followed, but, instead of this, the inner
wall of the "city of David," which included the Temple, is traced. This wall is
followed northwards from the pool of
Siloam, past the "sepulchres of David"
and Hezekiah's pool to the "armoury" (*v.*
19) at its north-west corner ; it is then followed eastwards to "the tower which lieth
out from the king's house" (*v.* 25) ; from
this it is carried southwards, along the
western edge of the Kidron valley to the
"*great* tower which lieth out" (*v.* 27), and
then south-westwards to the point at which
it commenced near Siloam (*v.* 27). The
special wall of the "city of David" being
thus completed, the writer finishes his entire account by filling up the small interval
between the north-east angle of this fortification and the "sheep-gate" (*vv.* 28-32),
from which he started.

they sanctified it] The priests commenced
the work with a formal ceremony of consecration. When the work was completed,
there was a solemn dedication of the entire
circuit (see xii. 27-43).

The tower of Hananeel is often men-

tioned ; that of Meah, or rather Hammeah,
or "the Hundred," in Nehemiah only.
Both towers must have been situated towards the north-eastern corner of the city.

2. The people of each provincial town
were set to work for the most part on the
portion of the wall nearest their city. Thus
"the men of Jericho," were employed at
the north-east corner of Jerusalem.

3. *the fish gate*] The gate through which
fish from the Jordan and the Sea of Galilee
entered Jerusalem ; a gate in the north
wall, a little to the east of the modern Damascus gate.

locks] The word used (here and in *vv.* 6,
13-15) is thought to mean rather a "cross-
bar" than a lock, while that translated
"bars" is regarded as denoting the "hooks"
or "catches" which held the cross-bar at
its two ends.

5. *Tekoites*] See 2 Sam. xiv. 2 note.

6. *the old gate*] Either the modern Damascus gate, the main entrance to the city
on the north side ; or a gate a little further
eastward.

7. *unto the throne* &c.] The meaning is
thought to be "the men of Gibeon and Mizpah, who, though they worked for Nehemiah, were not under his government, but
belonged to the jurisdiction of the governor
on this side the river."

11. *the other piece*] Rather, "**another
piece**" (as in *vv.* 19, 21, 27, 30). It is con-

12 ^mand the tower of the furnaces. And next unto him repaired   ^m ch. 12. 38.
    Shallum the son of Halohesh, the ruler of the half part of Jeru-
13 salem, he and his daughters. ¶ ⁿThe valley gate repaired   ⁿ ch. 2. 13.
    Hanun, and the inhabitants of Zanoah; they built it, and set
    up the doors thereof, the locks thereof, and the bars thereof,
14 and a thousand cubits on the wall unto ^othe dung gate. ¶ But   ^o ch. 2. 13.
    the dung gate repaired Malchiah the son of Rechab, the ruler of
    part of Beth-haccerem ; he built it, and set up the doors thereof,
15 the locks thereof, and the bars thereof. ¶ But ^pthe gate of the   ^p ch. 2. 14.
    fountain repaired Shallun the son of Col-hozeh, the ruler of
    part of Mizpah ; he built it, and covered it, and set up the doors
    thereof, the locks thereof, and the bars thereof, and the wall of
    the pool of ^qSiloah by the king's garden, and unto the stairs   ^q John 9. 7.
16 that go down from the city of David. After him repaired Ne-
    hemiah the son of Azbuk, the ruler of the half part of Beth-zur,
    unto *the place* over against the sepulchres of David, and to the
17 ^rpool that was made, and unto the house of the mighty. After   ^r 2 Kin. 20.
    him repaired the Levites, Rehum the son of Bani. Next unto   20.
    him repaired Hashabiah, the ruler of the half part of Keilah, in   Isai. 22. 11.
18 his part. After him repaired their brethren, Bavai the son of
19 Henadad, the ruler of the half part of Keilah. And next to
    him repaired Ezer the son of Jeshua, the ruler of Mizpah,
    another piece over against the going up to the armoury at the
20 ^sturning *of the wall*. After him Baruch the son of ¹Zabbai   ^s 2 Chr. 26.9.
    earnestly repaired the other piece, from the turning *of the wall*
21 unto the door of the house of Eliashib the high priest. After
    him repaired Meremoth the son of Urijah the son of Koz an-
    other piece, from the door of the house of Eliashib even to
22 the end of the house of Eliashib. And after him repaired the
23 priests, the men of the plain. After him repaired Benjamin
    and Hashub over against their house. After him repaired Aza-

¹ Or, *Zaccai.*

---

jectured that a verse has fallen out in which
Malchijah's and Hashub's "first piece" was
mentioned.

the tower of the furnaces] Either a tower
at the north-western angle of the city ; or,
midway in the western wall. The origin of
the name is uncertain.

13. Zanoah lay west of Jerusalem, at the
distance of about ten miles (Josh. xv. 34
note).

15. The "pool of Siloah" lies at the
south-western foot of the Temple hill, near
the lower end of the Tyropœon. It appears
to have been at all times beyond the line of
the city wall, but was perhaps joined to the
city by a fortification of its own.

the king's garden] See 2 K. xxv. 4 note.

the stairs] A flight of steps, still to be
seen, led from the low valley of the Tyropœon
up the steep sides of Ophel to the "city of
David," which it reached probably at a
point not far south of the Temple.

16. *Beth-zur*] Now *Beit-sur*, on the road
from Jerusalem to Hebron (Josh. xv. 58).

By "the sepulchres of David" must be
understood the burial place in which David
and the kings his descendants to the time
of Hezekiah were interred. This was an

excavation in the rock, in the near vicinity
of the Temple (Ezek. xliii. 7-9), and on its
western side. The position of the burial-
place was well known until the destruction
of the city by Titus ; but modern research
has not yet discovered it.

the pool] Probably that made by Hezekiah in the Tyropœon valley, west of the
Temple area (marg. ref.).

17-30. The constant mention of "priests,"
"Levites," and Nethinims," sufficiently indicates that the writer is here concerned
with the sacerdotal quarter, that immediately about the Temple.

18. *Bavai*] Or, "Binnui" (*v.* 24, x. 9).

the armoury at the turning of the wall] Lit.
"the armoury of the corner." The north-
western corner of the special wall of the
"city of David" seems to be intended. See
v. 1 note.

20. *the other piece*] Rather, "**another**
piece." The notice of Baruch's first piece,
like that of Malchijah's and Hashub's (*v.*
11), seems to have slipped out of the text.

22. The word here translated "plain" is
applied in the rest of Scripture almost exclusively to the *Ghor* or Jordan valley.
Cp., however, xii. 28.

riah the son of Maaseiah the son of Ananiah by his house.
24 After him repaired Binnui the son of Henadad another piece,
from the house of Azariah unto *t*the turning *of the wall,* even
25 unto the corner. Palal the son of Uzai, over against the turning
of the wall, and the tower which lieth out from the king's high
house, that *was* by the *u*court of the prison. After him Pe-
26 daiah the son of Parosh. Moreover *x*the Nethinims ¹dwelt in
*y*²Ophel, unto *the place* over against *z*the water gate toward the
27 east, and the tower that lieth out. After them the Tekoites repaired another piece, over against the great tower that lieth out,
28 even unto the wall of Ophel. ¶ From above the *a*horse gate re-
29 paired the priests, every one over against his house. After
them repaired Zadok the son of Immer over against his house.
After him repaired also Shemaiah the son of Shechaniah, the
30 keeper of the east gate. After him repaired Hananiah the son
of Shelemiah, and Hanun the sixth son of Zalaph, another
piece. After him repaired Meshullam the son of Berechiah
31 over against his chamber. After him repaired Malchiah the
goldsmith's son unto the place of the Nethinims, and of the
merchants, over against the gate. Miphkad, and to the ³going
32 up of the corner. And between the going up of the corner
unto the sheep gate repaired the goldsmiths and the merchants.

CHAP. 4. BUT it came to pass, *a*that when Sanballat heard that we
builded the wall, he was wroth, and took great indignation, and
2 mocked the Jews. And he spake before his brethren and the
army of Samaria, and said, What do these feeble Jews? will
they ⁴fortify themselves? will they sacrifice? will they make
an end in a day? will they revive the stones out of the heaps of
3 the rubbish which are burned? Now *b*Tobiah the Ammonite
was by him, and he said, Even that which they build, if a fox
4 go up, he shall even break down their stone wall. *c*Hear, O our
God; for we are ⁵despised: and *d*turn their reproach upon
their own head, and give them for a prey in the land of cap-
5 tivity: and *e*cover not their iniquity, and let not their sin be

¹ Or, which *dwelt in Ophel,* repaired *unto.* ² Or, *The tower.* ³ Or, *corner-chamber.* ⁴ Heb. *leave to themselves.* ⁵ Heb. *despite.*

t ver. 19.
v Jer. 32. 2.
& 33. 1.
& 37. 21.
x Ezra 2. 43.
ch. 11. 21.
y 2 Chr. 27.3.
z ch. 8. 1, 3.
& 12. 37.
a 2 Kin.11.16.
2 Chr. 23. 15.
Jer. 31. 40.
a ch. 2.10,19.
b ch. 2. 10,19.
c Ps.123.3,4.
d Ps. 79. 12.
Prov. 3. 34.
e Ps.69.27,28.
& 109. 14, 15.
Jer. 18. 23.

24. *the turning of the wall*] The north-eastern angle of the "city of David" seems here to be reached. At this point a tower "lay out" (*v.* 25), or projected extraordi-narily, from the wall, being probably a watch-tower commanding the Kidron valley and all the approaches to the city from the south-east, the east, and the north-east.

25. The "king's high house" is almost certainly the old palace of David, which was on the Temple hill, and probably oc-cupied a position directly north of the Temple.

that was by the court of the prison] Prisons were in old times adjuncts of palaces. The palace of David must have had its prison; and the "prison gate" (xii. 39) was clearly in this quarter.

26. The marg. reading is better. On the Nethinims see 1 Chr. ix. 2 note.

Ophel was the slope south of the Tem-ple (see marg. ref. *y* note); and the water-gate, a gate in the eastern wall, either

for the escape of the superfluous water from the Temple reservoirs, or for the in-troduction of water from the Kidron valley when the reservoirs were low.

27. The foundations of an outlying tower near the south-east angle of the Temple area in this position have been recently dis-covered.

28. "The horse gate" was on the east side of the city, overlooking the Kidron valley. It seems to have been a gate by which horses approached and left the old palace, that of David, which lay north of the Temple (*v.* 25).

31. *the gate Miphkad*] Not elsewhere mentioned. It must have been in the east, or north-east, wall, a little to the south of the "sheep-gate."

IV. 4. The parenthetic prayers of Nehe-miah form one of the most striking charac-teristics of his history. Here we have the first. Other examples are v. 19, vi. 9, 14, xiii. 14, 22, 29, 31.

blotted out from before thee : for they have provoked *thee* to
6 anger before the builders. So built we the wall ; and all the
wall was joined together unto the half thereof : for the people
7 had a mind to work. ¶ But it came to pass, *that* ʄwhen Sanballat, and Tobiah, and the Arabians, and the Ammonites, and
the Ashdodites, heard that the walls of Jerusalem ¹ were made
up, *and* that the breaches began to be stopped, then they were
8 very wroth, and ᵍconspired all of them together to come *and* to
9 fight against Jerusalem, and ² to hinder it. Nevertheless ʰwe
made our prayer unto our God, and set a watch against them
10 day and night, because of them. And Judah said, The strength
of the bearers of burdens is decayed, and *there is* much rubbish ;
11 so that we are not able to build the wall. And our adversaries
said, They shall not know, neither see, till we come in the midst
12 among them, and slay them, and cause the work to cease. And
it came to pass, that when the Jews which dwelt by them came,
they said unto us ten times, ³ From all places whence ye shall
13 return unto us *they will be upon you.* Therefore set I ⁴ in the
lower places behind the wall, *and* on the higher places, I even
set the people after their families with their swords, their spears,
14 and their bows. And I looked, and rose up, and said unto the
nobles, and to the rulers, and to the rest of the people, ⁱ Be not
ye afraid of them : remember the Lord, *which is* ᵏgreat and
terrible, and ˡfight for your brethren, your sons, and your
15 daughters, your wives, and your houses. ¶ And it came to pass,
when our enemies heard that it was known unto us, ᵐand God
had brought their counsel to nought, that we returned all of us
16 to the wall, every one unto his work. And it came to pass from
that time forth, *that* the half of my servants wrought in the
work, and the other half of them held both the spears, the
shields, and the bows, and the habergeons ; and the rulers *were*
17 behind all the house of Judah. They which builded on the
wall, and they that bare burdens, with those that laded, *every*
one with one of his hands wrought in the work, and with the
18 other *hand* held a weapon. For the builders, every one had his
sword girded ⁵ by his side, and *so* builded. And he that sounded
19 the trumpet *was* by me. And I said unto the nobles, and to the
rulers, and to the rest of the people, The work *is* great and

ʄ ver. 1.

ᵍ Ps. 83. 3, 4,
5.
ʰ Ps. 50. 15.

ⁱ Num. 14. 9
Deut. 1. 29.
ᵏ Deut. 10. 17.
ˡ 2 Sam. 10.
12.

ᵐ Job 5. 12.

---

¹ Heb. *ascended.*
² Heb. *to make an error to*
    it.
³ Or, *That from all places*
    ye must return to us.
⁴ Heb. *from the lower parts*
of the place, &c.
⁵ Heb. *on his loins.*

---

6. *unto the half thereof*] *i.e.* to half the intended *height.*

7. *the Arabians* &c.] Probably a band, composed largely of Arabians, Ammonites, and Ashdodites, which Sanballat maintained as a guard to his person, and which formed a portion of "the army of Samaria" (*v.* 2). A quarrel between such a band and the people of Jerusalem might be overlooked by the Persian king.

9. *because of them*] Or, " **over against them,**" *i.e.* opposite to the place where they were encamped, probably on the north side of the city.

12. *ten times*] *i.e.* repeatedly.
From all places &c.] Better as in margin.
The Jews who dwelt on the Samaritan border, came to Jerusalem and tried to withdraw their contingents of workmen from the work, representing to them the impending danger, and saying, "You must return to your homes, and so escape it."

13. *the lower places*] The places where those within the walls had the least advantage of elevation, the naturally weak places, where an enemy was likely to make his attack.

16. *habergeons*] Or, "coats of mail." Coats of mail were common in Assyria from the ninth century B.C., and in Egypt even earlier. They were made of thin laminæ of bronze or iron, sewn upon leather or linen, and overlapping one another.

large, and we are separated upon the wall, one far from another.
20 In what place *therefore* ye hear the sound of the trumpet, resort
21 ye thither unto us: *n*our God shall fight for us.   ¶ So we laboured in the work: and half of them held the spears from the
22 rising of the morning till the stars appeared.   Likewise at the
same time said I unto the people, Let every one with his servant
lodge within Jerusalem, that in the night they may be a guard
23 to us, and labour on the day.   So neither I, nor my brethren,
nor my servants, nor the men of the guard which followed me,
none of us put off our clothes ¹*saving that* every one put them
off for washing.

CHAP. 5. AND there was a great *a*cry of the people and of their
2 wives against their *b*brethren the Jews.   For there were that
said, We, our sons, and our daughters, *are* many: therefore we
3 take up corn *for them*, that we may eat, and live.   *Some* also
there were that said, We have mortgaged our lands, vineyards,
and houses, that we might buy corn, because of the dearth.
4 There were also that said, We have borrowed money for the
5 king's tribute, *and that upon* our lands and vineyards.   Yet now
*c*our flesh *is* as the flesh of our brethren, our children as their
children: and, lo, we *d*bring into bondage our sons and our
daughters to be servants, and *some* of our daughters are brought
unto bondage *already:* neither *is it* in our power *to redeem them;*
6 for other men have our lands and vineyards.   ¶ And I was very
7 angry when I heard their cry and these words.   Then ²I consulted with myself, and I rebuked the nobles, and the rulers,
and said unto them, *e*Ye exact usury, every one of his brother.
8 And I set a great assembly against them.   And I said unto
them, We after our ability have *f*redeemed our brethren the
Jews, which were sold unto the heathen; and will ye even sell
your brethren? or shall they be sold unto us?   Then held they
9 their peace, and found nothing *to answer.*   Also I said, It *is* not
good that ye do: ought ye not to walk *g*in the fear of our God
10 *h*because of the reproach of the heathen our enemies?   I likewise, *and* my brethren, and my servants, might exact of them
11 money and corn: I pray you, let us leave off this usury.   Restore, I pray you, to them, even this day, their lands, their

Marginal references (left column):
n Ex. 14. 14, 25.
Deut. 1. 30.
& 3. 22.
& 20. 4.
Josh. 23. 10.

a Isai. 5. 7.
b Lev. 25. 35, 36, 37.
Deut. 15. 7.

c Isai. 58. 7.
d Lev. 25. 39.

e Ex. 22 25.
Lev. 25. 36.
Ezek. 22. 12.
f Lev. 25. 48.

g Lev. 25. 33.
h 2 Sam. 12. 14.
Rom. 2. 24.
1 Pet. 2. 12.

---

¹ Or, *every one* went *with his weapon for water.*   See Judg. 5. 11.   ² Heb. *my heart consulted in me.*

---

22. *Let every one...lodge within Jerusalem*]
i.e. "Let none return to his own village
or city at night, but let all take their rest
in Jerusalem."
23. *saving* &c.] The text here is probably
unsound.   It yields no satisfactory sense.
See margin.
V. 2. *are many*] A slight emendation
brings this verse into exact parallelism with
the next, and gives the sense—"We have
pledged our sons and our daughters, that we
might get corn, and eat and live." Cp. *v.* 5.
4. *the king's tribute*] The tax payable to
the Persian monarch (cp. Ezra iv. 13 ; Esth.
x. 1).   In ancient times heavy taxation was
often productive of debt and distress.
5. The power of a father to sell his
daughter into slavery is expressly mentioned in the Law (Ex. xxi. 7).   The power

to sell a son appears from this passage.   In
either case the sale held good for six years
only, or until the next year of jubilee
(marg. reff.).
7. *Ye exact usury*] The phrase is peculiar
to Nehemiah, and is best explained by the
context, which shows the practice of the
rich Jews at the time to have been not so
much to lend on usury as to lend on mort-
gage and pledge.
8. Nehemiah contrasts his own example
with that of the rich Jews.   He had spent
money in redeeming some countrymen in
servitude among the heathen; they were
causing others to be sold into slavery among
the Jews.
10. *I...might exact*] Nehemiah had lent,
but not upon pledge.
11. *the hundredth part of the money* &c.]

vineyards, their oliveyards, and their houses, also the hundredth *part* of the money, and of the corn, the wine, and the oil, that
12 ye exact of them. ¶ Then said they, We will restore *them*, and will require nothing of them; so will we do as thou sayest. Then I called the priests; *i* and took an oath of them, that they
13 should do according to this promise. Also *k* I shook my lap, and said, So God shake out every man from his house, and from his labour, that performeth not this promise, even thus be he shaken out, and *l* emptied. And all the congregation said, Amen, and praised the LORD. *l* And the people did according to this
14 promise. ¶ Moreover from the time that I was appointed to be their governor in the land of Judah, from the twentieth year *m* even unto the two and thirtieth year of Artaxerxes the king, *that is*, twelve years, I and my brethren have not *n* eaten the
15 bread of the governor. But the former governors that *had been* before me were chargeable unto the people, and had taken of them bread and wine, beside forty shekels of silver; yea, even their servants bare rule over the people : but *o* so did not I, be-
16 cause of the *p* fear of God. Yea, also I continued in the work of this wall, neither bought we any land : and all my servants *were*
17 gathered thither unto the work. Moreover *there were q* at my table an hundred and fifty of the Jews and rulers, beside those that came unto us from among the heathen that *are* about us.
18 Now *that r* which was prepared *for me* daily *was* one ox *and* six choice sheep; also fowls were prepared for me, and once in ten days store of all sorts of wine : yet for all this *s* required not I the bread of the governor, because the bondage was heavy upon
19 this people. *t* Think upon me, my God, for good, *according to* all that I have done for this people.

CHAP. 6. NOW it came to pass, *a* when Sanballat, and Tobiah, and
2 Geshem the Arabian, and the rest of our enemies, heard that I had builded the wall, and *that* there was no breach left therein ; (*b* though at that time I had not set up the doors upon the gates ;)
2 that Sanballat and Geshem *c* sent unto me, saying, Come, let us meet together in *some one of* the villages in the plain of *d* Ono.
3 But they *e* thought to do me mischief. And I sent messengers unto them, saying, I *am* doing a great work, so that I cannot come down : why should the work cease, whilst I leave it, and
4 come down to you ? Yet they sent unto me four times after

i Ezra 10. 5.
Jer. 34. 8, 9.
k Matt.10.14.
Acts 13. 51.
& 18. 6.

l 2 Kin. 23.3.

m ch. 13. 6.
n 1 Cor. 9. 4, 15.

o 2 Cor.11.9.
& 12. 13.
p ver. 9.

q 2 Sam. 9.7.
1 Kin.18.19.

r 1 Kin.4.22.

s ver. 14, 15.

t ch. 13. 22.

a ch. 2.10,19.
& 4. 1, 7.

b ch. 3. 1, 3.
c Prov. 26.
24, 25.
d 1 Chr. 8.12.
ch. 11. 35.
e Ps. 37. 12, 32.

---

¹ Heb. *empty*, or, *void*.   ² Or, *Gashmu*, ver. 6.

---

i.e. the interest. It is conjectured that the hundredth part was payable *monthly*, or, in other words, that interest was taken at the rate of twelve per cent. The Law altogether disallowed the taking of interest from Israelites (see Ex. xxii. 25; Lev. xxv. 36, &c.).

13. *I shook my lap*] Cp. marg. reff. By "lap" is meant a fold in the bosom of the dress, capable of serving as a pocket. Cp. Isai. xlix. 22 marg.

14. *have not eaten the bread of the governor*] *i.e.* "have not, like other Persian governors, lived at the expense of the people under my government." See Ezra iv. 14 note.

15. *forty shekels of silver*] A daily sum from the entire province. For such a table

as that kept by Nehemiah (*v.* 18), this would be a very moderate payment.

16. *I continued...land*] *i.e.* — "I took my share in the work of the wall, as general superintendent. I did not take advantage of the general poverty to buy poor men's plots of ground."

18. Cp. the far grander provision for Solomon's table (marg. ref.).

VI. **1.** *upon the gates*] Rather, "**in the gates.**" This work would naturally be delayed to the last.

2. The choice made of Ono, on the skirts of Benjamin, 25 or 30 miles from Jerusalem, as the meeting-place, was, no doubt, in order to draw Nehemiah to a distance from his supporters, that so an attack might be made on him with a better chance of success.

5 this sort; and I answered them after the same manner. Then
sent Sanballat his servant unto me in like manner the fifth time
6 with an open letter in his hand; wherein *was* written, It is

reported among the heathen, and ¹Gashmu saith *it*, *ᶠthat* thou
and the Jews think to rebel : for which cause thou buildest the
wall, that thou mayest be their king, according to these words.
7 And thou hast also appointed prophets to preach of thee at
Jerusalem, saying, *There is* a king in Judah : and now shall it
be reported to the king according to these words. Come now
8 therefore, and let us take counsel together. Then I sent unto
him, saying, There are no such things done as thou sayest, but
9 thou feignest them out of thine own heart. For they all made
us afraid, saying, Their hands shall be weakened from the work,
that it be not done. Now therefore, O *God,* strengthen my
10 hands. ¶Afterward I came unto the house of Shemaiah the son
of Delaiah the son of Mehetabeel, who *was* shut up ; and he said,
Let us meet together in the house of God, within the temple,
and let us shut the doors of the temple : for they will come to
11 slay thee ; yea, in the night will they come to slay thee. And I
said, Should such a man as I flee ? and who *is there,* that, *being*
as I *am,* would go into the temple to save his life ? I will not
12 go in. And, lo, I perceived that God had not sent him ; but

g Ezek. 13. 22. that *ᵍ*he pronounced this prophecy against me : for Tobiah and
13 Sanballat had hired him. Therefore *was* he hired, that I should
be afraid, and do so, and sin, and *that* they might have *matter*

h ch. 13. 39. 14 for an evil report, that they might reproach me. *ʰ*My God,
think thou upon Tobiah and Sanballat according to these their

i Ezek. 13. 17. works, and on the *ⁱ*prophetess Noadiah, and the rest of the
15 prophets, that would have put me in fear. ¶So the wall was
finished in the twenty and fifth *day* of *the month* Elul, in fifty

k ch. 2. 10. 16 and two days. And it came to pass, that *ᵏ*when all our enemies
& 4. 1, 7. heard *thereof,* and all the heathen that *were* about us saw *these*
& 6. 1. *l* Ps. 126. 2. *things,* they were much cast down in their own eyes : for *ˡ*they
17 perceived that this work was wrought of our God. ¶Moreover
in those days the nobles of Judah ²sent many letters unto
18 Tobiah, and *the letters* of Tobiah came unto them. For *there were*
many in Judah sworn unto him, because he *was* the son in law

---

¹ Or, *Geshem,* ver. 1.   ² Heb. *multiplied their letters passing to Tobiah.*

---

5. The letter was "open," in order that
the contents might be generally known, and
that the Jews, alarmed at the threats contained in it, might refuse to continue the
work.

10. *who ·was shut up*] On account, probably, of some legal uncleanness. Cp. Jer.
xxxvi. 5.

11. *would go into the temple to save his
life*] Rather, "could go into the temple
and live." For a layman to enter the
Sanctuary was a capital offence (see Num.
xviii. 7).

12. The existence of a party among the
Jews who sided with Sanballat and lent
themselves to his schemes, is here for the
first time indicated. Cp. *vv.* 14, 17–19,
xiii. 4, 5, 28.

14. Noadiah is not elsewhere mentioned.
The examples of Miriam, Deborah, Huldah,
and Anna, show that the prophetical gift

was occasionally bestowed upon women (2
K. xxii. 14 note).

15. *Elul*] The sixth month, corresponding
to the latter part of August and the beginning of September.

in fifty and two days] Josephus states that
the repairs of the wall occupied two years
and four months. But Nehem.ah's narrative is thoroughly consistent with itself,
and contains in it nothing that is improbable. The walls everywhere existed at
the time that he commenced his task, and
only needed repairs. The work was par-
titioned among at least thirty-seven working
parties, who laboured simultaneously, with
material ready at hand ; and, notwithstanding all menaces, uninterruptedly.

18. Though Tobiah is called "the servant" or "slave" (ii. 10, 19), and was perhaps a bought slave of Sanballat's, yet he
was in such a position that Jewish nobles

of Shechaniah the son of Arah ; and his son Johanan had taken
19 the daughter of Meshullam the son of Berechiah. Also they
reported his good deeds before me, and uttered my ¹words to
him. *And* Tobiah sent letters to put me in fear.

CHAP. 7. NOW it came to pass, when the wall was built, and I
had *a*set up the doors, and the porters and the singers and the   *a* ch. 6. 1.
2 Levites were appointed, that I gave my brother Hanani, and
Hananiah the ruler *b*of the palace, charge over Jerusalem : for   *b* ch. 2. 8
3 he *was* a faithful man, and *c*feared God above many. And I   *c* Ex. 18. 21.
said unto them, Let not the gates of Jerusalem be opened until
the sun be hot; and while they stand by, let them shut the
doors, and bar *them :* and appoint watches of the inhabitants of
Jerusalem, every one in his watch, and every one *to be* over
4 against his house. Now the city *was* ²large and great : but the
5 people *were* few therein, and the houses *were* not builded. ¶ And
my God put into mine heart to gather together the nobles, and
the rulers, and the people, that they might be reckoned by
genealogy. And I found a register of the genealogy of them
6 which came up at the first, and found written therein, *d*These   *d* Ezra 2. 1,
are the children of the province, that went up out of the cap-   &c.
tivity, of those that had been carried away, whom Nebuchadnezzar the king of Babylon had carried away, and came again to
7 Jerusalem and to Judah, every one unto his city ; who came
with Zerubbabel, Jeshua, Nehemiah, ³Azariah, Raamiah, Naha-
mani, Mordecai, Bilshan, Mispereth, Bigvai, Nehum, Baanah.
The number, *I say*, of the men of the people of Israel *was this ;*
8 ¶ The children of Parosh, two thousand an hundred seventy and
9 two. The children of Shephatiah, three hundred seventy and
10, 11 two. The children of Arah, six hundred fifty and two. The
children of Pahath-moab, of the children of Jeshua and Joab,
12 two thousand and eight hundred *and* eighteen. The children of
13 Elam, a thousand two hundred fifty and four. The children of
14 Zattu, eight hundred forty and five. The children of Zaccai,
15 seven hundred and threescore. The children of ⁴Binnui, six
16 hundred forty and eight. The children of Bebai, six hundred
17 twenty and eight. The children of Azgad, two thousand three
18 hundred twenty and two. The children of Adonikam, six hun-
19 dred threescore and seven. The children of Bigvai, two thou-

¹ Or, *matters.*   ³ Or, *Seraiah :* See Ezra   ⁴ Or, *Bani.*
² Heb. *broad in spaces.*   2. 2.

---

readily contracted affinity with him. This
is quite in harmony with the practice of
the East, where slaves often fill high positions and make grand marriages.

VII. 1. As the watch of the Temple
had hitherto been kept by porters, singers,
and Levites (1 Chr. xxvi. 1–19), so now the
watch of the entire city was committed to
men of the same three classes, their experience pointing them out as the fittest persons.

2. *my brother Hanani*] See i. 2.

the ruler of the palace] Or, " the governor
of the fortress." See marg. ref. note.

he] *i.e.* Hananiah.

3. *until the sun be hot*] An unusual pre-
caution. The ordinary practice in the East
is to open town gates at sunrise.

4. *the people were few*] The number of
those who returned with Zerubbabel was no
more than 42,360 (*v.* 66). With Ezra had
come less than 2000 (Ezra viii. 1-20).

5. It is argued by some that the entire
catalogue which follows (*vv.* 7-73) is not the
register of them "which came up *at the
first*," but of the Jewish people in Nehemiah's time. Verse 7 and Ezra ii. 2 are,
however, very positive in their support of
the usual view ; and some of the arguments against it are thought to be met by
considering the Nehemiah of *v.* 7 and Ezra
ii. 2 a person different from Nehemiah the
governor ; and "Tirshatha" an official title
likely to have belonged to others besides
Nehemiah (Ezra ii. 63 note.)

20 sand threescore and seven. The children of Adin, six hundred
21 fifty and five. The children of Ater of Hezekiah, ninety and
22 eight. The children of Hashum, three hundred twenty and
23 eight. The children of Bezai, three hundred twenty and four.
24, 25 The children of ¹Hariph, an hundred and twelve. The
26 children of ²Gibeon, ninety and five. The men of Beth-lehem
27 and Netophah, an hundred fourscore and eight. The men of
28 Anathoth, an hundred twenty and eight. The men of ³Beth-
29 azmaveth, forty and two. The men of ⁴Kirjath-jearim, Che-
30 phirah, and Beeroth, seven hundred forty and three. The men
31 of Ramah and Gaba, six hundred twenty and one. The men of
32 Michmas, an hundred and twenty and two. The men of Beth-el
33 and Ai, an hundred twenty and three. The men of the other

e See ver.12. 34 Nebo, fifty and two. The children of the other *e*Elam, a thou-
35 sand two hundred fifty and four. The children of Harim, three
36 hundred and twenty. The children of Jericho, three hundred
37 forty and five. The children of Lod, Hadid, and Ono, seven
38 hundred twenty and one. The children of Senaah, three thou-
39 sand nine hundred and thirty. ¶ The priests : the children of

f 1 Chr. 24.7. *f* Jedaiah, of the house of Jeshua, nine hundred seventy and
g 1 Chr. 24.14. 40 three. The children of *g*Immer, a thousand fifty and two.
h See 1 Chr. 41 The children of *h*Pashur, a thousand two hundred forty and
9. 12. 42 seven. The children of *i*Harim, a thousand and seventeen.
& 24. 9.
i 1 Chr. 24. 8. 43 ¶ The Levites : the children of Jeshua, of Kadmiel, *and* of the
44 children of ⁵Hodevah, seventy and four. The singers : the chil-
45 dren of Asaph, an hundred forty and eight. The porters : the
children of Shallum, the children of Ater, the children of Talmon, the children of Akkub, the children of Hatita, the children
46 of Shobai, an hundred thirty and eight. ¶ The Nethinims : the
children of Ziha, the children of Hashupha, the children of
47 Tabbaoth, the children of Keros, the children of ⁶Sia, the chil-
48 of Padon, the children of Lebana, the children of Hagaba, the
49 children of ⁷Shalmai, the children of Hanan, the children of Giddel,
50 the children of Gahar, the children of Reaiah, the children of
51 Rezin, the children of Nekoda, the children of Gazzam, the
52 children of Uzza, the children of Phaseah, the children of Besai,
53 the children of Meunim, the children of ⁸Nephishesim, the children of Bakbuk, the children of Hakupha, the children of
54 Harhur, the children of ⁹Bazlith, the children of Mehida, the
55 children of Harsha, the children of Barkos, the children of
56 Sisera, the children of Tamah, the children of Neziah, the chil-
57 dren of Hatipha. ¶ The children of Solomon's servants : the
children of Sotai, the children of Sophereth, the children of
58 ¹Perida, the children of Jaala, the children of Darkon, the chil-
59 dren of Giddel, the children of Shephatiah, the children of
Hattil, the children of Pochereth of Zebaim, the children of
60 ²Amon. All the Nethinims, and the children of Solomon's ser-

k Ezra 2. 59. 61 vants, *were* three hundred ninety and two. ¶ *k*And these *were*
they which went up *also* from Tel-melah, Tel-haresha, Cherub,
³Addon, and Immer : but they could not shew their father's
62 house, nor their ⁴seed, whether they *were* of Israel. The children
of Delaiah, the children of Tobiah, the children of Nekoda, six
63 hundred forty and two. ¶ And of the priests : the children of

Habaiah, the children of Koz, the children of Barzillai, which took *one* of the daughters of Barzillai the Gileadite to wife, and
64 was called after their name. These sought their register *among* those that were reckoned by genealogy, but it was not found :
65 therefore were they, as polluted, put from the priesthood. And [l]the Tirshatha said unto them, that they should not eat of the most holy things, till there stood *up* a priest with Urim and
66 Thummim. ¶The whole congregation together *was* forty and
67 two thousand three hundred and threescore, beside their man-servants and their maidservants, of whom *there were* seven thousand three hundred thirty and seven : and they had two
68 hundred forty and five singing men and singing women. Their horses, seven hundred thirty and six : their mules, two hundred
69 forty and five : *their* camels, four hundred thirty and five : six
70 thousand seven hundred and twenty asses. ¶And [2]some of the chief of the fathers gave unto the work. [l]The Tirshatha gave   [l] ch. 8. 9.
to the treasure a thousand drams of gold, fifty basons, five
71 hundred and thirty priests' garments. And *some* of the chief of
the fathers gave to the treasure of the work [m]twenty thousand   [m] So Ezra 2.
drams of gold, and two thousand and two hundred pound of   69.
72 silver. And *that* which the rest of the people gave *was* twenty thousand drams of gold, and two thousand pound of silver, and
73 threescore and seven priests' garments. ¶So the priests, and the Levites, and the porters, and the singers, and *some* of the people, and the Nethinims, and all Israel, dwelt in their cities ; [n]and when the seventh month came, the children of Israel *were*   [n] Ezra 3. 1.
in their cities.

CHAP. 8. AND all [a]the people gathered themselves together as one   [a] Ezra 3. 1.
man into the street that *was* [b]before the water gate ; and they   [b] ch. 3. 26.
spake unto Ezra the [c]scribe to bring the book of the law of   [c] Ezra 7. 6.
2 Moses, which the LORD had commanded to Israel. And Ezra the priest brought [d]the law before the congregation both of men   [d] Deut.31.11,
and women, and all [3]that could hear with understanding, [e]upon   12.
3 the first day of the seventh month. And he read therein before   [e] Lev. 23. 24.
the street that *was* before the water gate [4]from the morning

---

[1] Or, *the governor*, ch. 8. 9.   [3] Heb. *that understood in*   [4] Heb. *from the light.*
[2] Heb. *part.*   *hearing.*

70-73. Compared with Ezra ii. 69 there is considerable difference between the totals for gold, silver, and garments. The usual explanation is that of corruption in the one or the other of the passages.

73. *dwelt in their cities*] Nehemiah's quotation from Zerubbabel's register ends here, and the narration of events in Jerusalem in his own day is resumed from *v.* 3. The narrative (viii.-x.) appears from internal evidence to be by a different author (see Introduction, p. 591).

The last two clauses of *v.* 73 should stand as the beginning of ch. viii. (as in the LXX.). The text would then run :—

" And when the seventh month was come, and the children of Israel were in their cities, the whole people gathered themselves together as one man," &c. Cp. marg. ref.

VIII. **1.** *the street*] Rather, " **the square** " or " **court**." So in *v.* 16 (cp. Ezra x. 9). The

court seems to have been one between the eastern gate of the Temple and the water-gate in the city-wall. It would thus lie within the modern Haram area.

Ezra the scribe] This is the first mention of Ezra in the present book, and the first proof we have had that he was contemporary with Nehemiah. Probably he returned to the court of Artaxerxes soon after effecting the reforms which he relates in Ezra x., and did not revisit Jerusalem till about the time when the walls were completed, or after an absence of more than ten years. It was natural for the people to request him to resume the work of exposition of the Law to which he had accustomed them on his former visit (Ezra vii. 10, 25).

2. *upon the first day of the seventh month*] The day of the "feast of Trumpets" (see marg. ref. note). The gathering together of the people, spoken of in *v.* 1, was probably to keep this feast.

until midday, before the men and the women, and those that could understand; and the ears of all the people *were attentive* 4 unto the book of the law. And Ezra the scribe stood upon a [1]pulpit of wood, which they had made for the purpose; and beside him stood Mattithiah, and Shema, and Anaiah, and Urijah, and Hilkiah, and Maaseiah, on his right hand; and on his left hand, Pedaiah, and Mishael, and Malchiah, and Hashum, 5 and Hashbadana, Zechariah, *and* Meshullam. And Ezra opened the book in the [2]sight of all the people; (for he was above all the people;) and when he opened it, all the people *f* stood up: 6 and Ezra blessed the LORD, the great God. And all the people *g* answered, Amen, Amen, with *k* lifting up their hands: and they *i* bowed their heads, and worshipped the LORD with *their* 7 faces to the ground. Also Jeshua, and Bani, and Sherebiah, Jamin, Akkub, Shabbethai, Hodijah, Maaseiah, Kelita, Azariah, Jozabad, Hanan, Pelaiah, and the Levites, *k* caused the people 8 to understand the law: and the people *stood* in their place. So they read in the book in the law of God distinctly, and gave the 9 sense, and caused *them* to understand the reading. ¶ *l* And Nehemiah, which *is* [3]the Tirshatha, and Ezra the priest the scribe, *m* and the Levites that taught the people, said unto all the people, *n* This day *is* holy unto the LORD your God; *o* mourn not, nor weep. For all the people wept, when they heard the 10 words of the law. Then he said unto them, Go your way, eat the fat, and drink the sweet, *p* and send portions unto them for whom nothing is prepared: for *this* day *is* holy unto our LORD: neither be ye sorry; for the joy of the LORD is your strength. 11 So the Levites stilled all the people, saying, Hold your peace, 12 for the day *is* holy; neither be ye grieved. And all the people went their way to eat, and to drink, and to *q* send portions, and to make great mirth, because they had *r* understood the words that were declared unto them. ¶ And on the second day were gathered together the chief of the fathers of all the people, the priests, and the Levites, unto Ezra the scribe, even [4]to under- 14 stand the words of the law. And they found written in the law

f Judg. 3. 20.

g 1 Cor. 14. 16.
h Lam. 3. 41.
1 Tim. 2. 8.
i Ex. 4. 31.
2 Chr. 20. 18.
k Lev. 10. 11.
Deut. 33. 10.
2 Chr. 17. 7, 8, 9.
Mal. 2. 7.
l Ezra 2. 63.
ch. 7. 65.
& 10. 1.
m 2 Chr. 35. 3.
ver. 8.
n Lev. 23. 24.
Num. 29. 1.
o Deut. 16. 14, 15.
Eccles. 3. 4.
p Esth. 9. 19, 22.
Rev. 11. 10.

q ver. 10.

r ver. 7, 8.

---

[1] Heb. *tower of wood.*
[2] Heb. *eyes.*
[3] Or, *the governor.*
[4] Or, *that they might in-*
struct *in the words of the law.*

---

4. The thirteen persons mentioned were probably the chief priests of the course which was at the time performing the Temple service.

5. *stood up*] The attitude of attention and respect. Cp. the existing practice of the Christian Church at the reading of the Gospel for the day.

7. The names here (and in ix. 4, 5, x. 9) seem not to be the personal appellations of individuals, but rather designations of Levitical families, the descendants respectively of Jeshua, &c., who lived not later than the time of Zerubbabel (vii. 43, xii. 8).

8. *gave the sense*] Either by rendering the Hebrew into the Aramaic dialect, or perhaps simply by explaining obscure words or passages.

caused them to understand] Either "they (the people) understood what was read;" or, "they (the Levites) expounded as they read."

9. *Nehemiah, which is the Tirshatha*] Hitherto Nehemiah has called himself *pechah* (v. 14, 15, 18), which is the ordinary word for "governor." Now for the first time he is called "the Tirshatha" (see Ezra ii. 63 note.)

the people wept &c.] Because the Law brought vividly before them their sins of omission and commission. In *v.* 10 the Jews were not forbidden to be sorry for their sins, but only prohibited from marring with the expression of their sorrow a festive occasion.

10. The "sending of portions" to the poor is not distinctly mentioned in any but the later historical Scriptures (cp. marg. reff.). The practice naturally grew out of this injunction of the Law (Deut. xvi. 11, 14).

13. *to understand*] Rather, "to consider."

14. The Feast of Tabernacles had fallen into abeyance either entirely, or as regarded the dwelling in booths (*v.* 17), since

which the LORD had commanded ¹ by Moses, that the children of Israel should dwell in ˢbooths in the feast of the seventh month :
15 and ᵗthat they should publish and proclaim in all their cities, and ᵘin Jerusalem, saying, Go forth unto the mount, and ˣfetch olive branches, and pine branches, and myrtle branches, and palm branches, and branches of thick trees, to make booths, as
16 *it is* written. So the people went forth, and brought *them*, and made themselves booths, every one upon the ʸroof of his house, and in their courts, and in the courts of the house of God, and in the street of the ᶻwater gate, ᵃand in the street of the gate of
17 Ephraim. And all the congregation of them that were come again out of the captivity made booths, and sat under the booths : for since the days of Jeshua the son of Nun unto that day had not the children of Israel done so. And there was very
18 ᵇgreat gladness. Also ᶜday by day, from the first day unto the last day, he read in the book of the law of God. And they kept the feast seven days ; and on the eighth day *was* ²a solemn assembly, ᵈaccording unto the manner.

CHAP. 9. NOW in the twenty and fourth day of ᵃthis month the children of Israel were assembled with fasting, and with sack-
2 clothes, ᵇand earth upon them. And ᶜthe seed of Israel separated themselves from all ³strangers, and stood and confessed
3 their sins, and the iniquities of their fathers. And they stood up in their place, and ᵈread in the book of the law of the LORD their God *one* fourth part of the day ; and *another* fourth part they
4 confessed, and worshipped the LORD their God. ¶Then stood up upon the ⁴stairs, of the Levites, Jeshua, and Bani, Kadmiel, Shebaniah, Bunni, Sherebiah, Bani, *and* Chenani, and cried with
5 a loud voice unto the LORD their God. Then the Levites, Jeshua, and Kadmiel, Bani, Hashabniah, Sherebiah, Hodijah, Shebaniah, *and* Pethahiah, said, Stand up *and* bless the LORD your God for ever and ever : and blessed be ᵉthy glorious name, which is
6 exalted above all blessing and praise. ᶠThou, *even* thou, *art* LORD alone ; ᵍthou hast made heaven, ʰthe heaven of heavens, with ⁱall their host, the earth, and all *things* that *are* therein, the seas, and all that *is* therein, and thou preservest them all ; and

s Lev. 23. 34, 42.
t Deut. 16. 13.
t Lev. 23. 4.
u Deut.16.16.
x Lev. 23.40.

y Deut. 22. 8.

z ch. 12. 37.
a 2Kin.14.13.
ch. 12. 39.

b 2Chr.30 21.
c Deut.31.10, &c.

d Lev. 23.36.
Num. 29. 35.
a ch. 8. 2.

b Josh. 7. 6.
1 Sam. 4. 12.
2 Sam. 1. 2.
Job 2. 12.
c Ezra 10.11.
ch. 13. 3, 30.
d ch. 8. 7, 8.

e 1 Chr.29.13.
f 2 Kin.19.15, 19.
Ps. 86. 10.
Isai. 37, 16.
g Gen. 1. 1.
Ex. 20. 11.
Rev. 14. 7.
h Deut.10.14.
1 Kin. 8. 27.
i Gen. 2. 1.

¹ Heb. *by the hand of.*
² Heb. *a restraint.*
³ Heb. *strange children.*
⁴ Or, *scaffold.*

the time when it was kept by Zerubbabel (Ezra iii. 4). It is evident that the observance of the Law, impossible during the captivity, was restored slowly and with difficulty after the return.

15. *the mount*] The "mount of Olives" is probably intended.

pine branches] Rather, "branches of the **wild olive.**" The actual trees named by the Law may have become scarce. It was probably considered that the spirit of the command was kept if branches of trees similar in general character to those named in Leviticus were employed.

17. It is not the intention of the writer to state that the Feast of Tabernacles had not been kept from the time of Joshua until this occasion (see 1 K. viii. 2, 65 ; Ezra iii. 4) ; but that there had been *no such* celebration as this since Joshua's time. Cp. 2 K. xxiii. 22 ; 2 Chr. xxxv. 18.

IX. 1. The festival lasted from the 15th day of the 7th month to the 21st. The 22nd day was a day of solemn observance (viii. 18). One day seems to have been allowed the people for rest ; and then the work of repentance, for which they had shown themselves ready (viii. 9), was taken in hand, and a general fast was proclaimed.

4. The LXX. and Vulgate remove the comma after "stairs." By the "stairs (or scaffold) of the Levites" is to be understood an elevated platform from which they could the better address and lead the people (cp. viii. 4).

5. *Stand up*] The people had knelt to confess and to worship God (*v.* 3). They were now to take the attitude proper for praise. Cp. throughout the marg. reff.

6. *the host of heaven worshippeth thee*] *i.e.* the angels. See 1 K. xxii. 19 ; Ps. ciii. 21.

7 the host of heaven worshippeth thee.   ¶ Thou *art* the LORD the
God, who didst choose [k] Abram, and broughtest him forth out of
8 Ur of the Chaldees, and gavest him the name of [l] Abraham ; and
foundest his heart [m] faithful before thee, and madest a [n] covenant
with him to give the land of the Canaanites, the Hittites, the
Amorites, and the Perizzites, and the Jebusites, and the Gir-
gashites, to give *it*, I *say*, to his seed, and [o] hast performed thy
9 words ; for thou *art* righteous : [p] and didst see the affliction of
our fathers in Egypt, and [q] heardest their cry by the Red sea ;
10 and [r] shewedst signs and wonders upon Pharaoh, and on all his
servants, and on all the people of his land : for thou knewest
that they [s] dealt proudly against them.   So didst thou [t] get thee
11 a name, as *it is* this day.   [u] And thou didst divide the sea before
them, so that they went through the midst of the sea on the dry
land ; and their persecutors thou threwest into the deeps, [x] as a
12 stone into the mighty waters.   Moreover thou [y] leddest them in
the day by a cloudy pillar ; and in the night by a pillar of fire,
13 to give them light in the way wherein they should go.   ¶ [a] Thou
camest down also upon mount Sinai, and spakest with them
from heaven, and gavest them [b] right judgments, and [1] true
14 laws, good statutes and commandments : and madest known
unto them thy [c] holy sabbath, and commandedst them precepts,
15 statutes, and laws, by the hand of Moses thy servant : and
[d] gavest them bread from heaven for their hunger, and [e] broughtest forth water for them out of the rock for their thirst, and
promisedst them that they should [f] go in to possess the land
16 [2] which thou hadst sworn to give them.   ¶ [g] But they and our
fathers dealt proudly, and [h] hardened their necks, and hearkened
17 not to thy commandments, and refused to obey, [i] neither were
mindful of thy wonders that thou didst among them ; but
hardened their necks, and in their rebellion appointed [k] a captain
to return to their bondage : but thou *art* [3] a God ready to pardon,
[l] gracious and merciful, slow to anger, and of great kindness,
18 and forsookest them not.   Yea, [m] when they had made them a
molten calf, and said, This *is* thy God that brought thee up out
19 of Egypt, and had wrought great provocations ; yet thou in thy
[n] manifold mercies forsookest them not in the wilderness : the
[o] pillar of the cloud departed not from them by day, to lead them in
the way ; neither the pillar of fire by night, to shew them light,
20 and the way wherein they should go.   ¶ Thou gavest also thy
[p] good spirit to instruct them, and withheldest not thy [q] manna
21 from their mouth, and gavest them [r] water for their thirst. Yea,
[s] forty years didst thou sustain them in the wilderness, so *that*
they lacked nothing ; their [t] clothes waxed not old, and their feet
22 swelled not.   Moreover thou gavest them kingdoms and nations,
and didst divide them into corners : so they possessed the land of
[u] Sihon, and the land of the king of Heshbon, and the land of
23 Og king of Bashan.   [x] Their children also multipliedst thou as

Left margin references:
[k] Gen. 11. 31.
[l] Gen. 17. 5.
[m] Gen. 15. 6.
[n] Gen. 12. 7.

[o] Josh. 23. 14.
[p] Ex. 2. 25.
[q] Ex. 14. 10.
[r] Ex. 7—14 chapters.

[s] Ex. 18. 11.
[t] Ex. 9. 16.
Isai. 63. 12.
Jer. 32. 20.
Dan. 9. 15.
[u] Ex. 14. 21.
Ps. 78. 13.
[x] Ex. 15. 5.
[y] Ex. 13. 21.
[a] Ex. 19. 20.

[b] Ps. 19. 8.
Rom. 7. 12.

[c] Gen. 2. 3.
Ex. 20. 8.

[d] Ex. 16. 14.
John 6. 31.
[e] Ex. 17. 6.
Num. 20. 9, &c.
[f] Deut. 1. 8.
[g] Ps. 106. 6.
[h] Deut. 31. 27.
2 Kin. 17. 14.
Jer. 19. 15.
[i] Ps. 78. 11.
[k] Num. 14. 4.

[l] Ex. 34. 6.
Num. 14. 18.
Ps. 86. 5.
Joel 2. 13.
[m] Ex. 32. 4.

[n] ver. 27.
Ps. 106. 45.
[o] Ex. 13. 21.
Num. 14. 14.
1 Cor. 10. 1.

[p] Num. 11. 17.
Isai. 63. 11.
[q] Ex. 16. 15.
Josh. 5. 12.
[r] Ex. 17. 6.
[s] Deut. 2. 7.
[t] Deut. 8. 4.

[u] Num. 21. 21, &c.
[x] Gen. 22. 17.

---

[1] Heb. *laws of truth.*
[2] Heb. *which thou hadst*
[ ] lift up thine hand to give them, Num. 14. 30.
[3] Heb. *a God of pardons.*

---

17. *In their rebellion*] The LXX. and
several MSS. have " in Egypt " (the words
in the original differing by one letter only),
and translate—" And appointed a captain
to return to their bondage in Egypt."
Cp. marg. ref. The appointment of a leader
is here regarded as made, whereas we are
only told in Numbers that it was proposed.
22. *Thou didst divide them into corners*]
i.e. parts of the Holy Land ; or as some
prefer " thou didst **distribute them on all
sides.**"

the stars of heaven, and broughtest them into the land, concerning which thou hadst promised to their fathers, that they should
24 go in to possess *it*. So *y*the children went in and possessed the land, and *z*thou subduedst before them the inhabitants of the land, the Canaanites, and gavest them into their hands, with their kings, and the people of the land, that they might do with
25 them ¹as they would. And they took strong cities, and a *a*fat land, and possessed *b*houses full of all goods, ²wells digged, vineyards, and oliveyards, and ³fruit trees in abundance : so they did eat, and were filled, and *c*became fat, and delighted
26 themselves in thy great *d*goodness. ¶ Nevertheless they *e*were disobedient, and rebelled against thee, and *f*cast thy law behind their backs, and slew thy *g*prophets which testified against them to turn them to thee, and they wrought great
27 provocations. *h*Therefore thou deliveredst them into the hand of their enemies, who vexed them : and in the time of their trouble, when they cried unto thee, thou *i*heardest *them* from heaven ; and according to thy manifold mercies *k*thou gavest them saviours, who saved them out of the hand of their
28 enemies. But after they had rest, *⁴l*they did evil again before thee : therefore leftest thou them in the hand of their enemies, so that they had the dominion over them : yet when they returned, and cried unto thee, thou heardest *them* from heaven ; and
*m*many times didst thou deliver them according to thy mercies ;
29 and testifiedst against them, that thou mightest bring them again unto thy law : yet they *n*dealt proudly, and hearkened not unto thy commandments, but sinned against thy judgments, (*o*which if a man do, he shall live in them ;) and
⁵withdrew the shoulder, and hardened their neck, and would
30 not hear. Yet many years didst thou ⁶forbear them, and testifiedst *p*against them by thy spirit ⁷*q*in thy prophets : yet would they not give ear : *r*therefore gavest thou them into the
31 hand of the people of the lands. Nevertheless for thy great mercies' sake *s*thou didst not utterly consume them, nor forsake
32 them ; for thou *art* *t*a gracious and merciful God. ¶ Now therefore, our God, the great, the *u*mighty, and the terrible God, who keepest covenant and mercy, let not all the ⁸trouble seem little before thee, ⁹that hath come upon us, on our kings, on our princes, and on our priests, and on our prophets, and on our fathers, and on all thy people, *x*since the time of the kings of
33 Assyria unto this day. Howbeit *y*thou *art* just in all that is brought upon us ; for thou hast done right, but *z*we have done
34 wickedly : neither have our kings, our princes, our priests, nor our fathers, kept thy law, nor hearkened unto thy commandments and thy testimonies, wherewith thou didst testify against
35 them. For they have *a*not served thee in their kingdom, and in

y Josh. 1. 2, &c.
z Ps. 44. 2, 3.

a Num. 13. 27.
Deut. 8. 7.
Ezek. 20. 6.
b Deut. 6. 11.
c Deut.32.15.
d Hos. 3. 5.
e Judg. 2. 11. 12.
Ezek. 20. 21.
f 1 Kin. 14. 9.
g Matt.23.37.
Acts 7. 52.
h Judg. 2. 14.
Ps. 106. 41.
i Ps. 106. 44.
k Judg. 2.18.
& 3. 9.
l So Judg. 3—6 chapters.

m Ps.106.43.

n ver. 16.

o Lev. 18. 5.
Ezek. 20. 11.
Rom. 10. 5.
Gal. 3. 12.
p 2 Kin. 17. 13.
2 Chr. 36.15.
Jer. 7. 25.
q See Acts 7. 51.
1 Pet. 1. 11.
2 Pet. 1. 21.
r Isai. 5. 5.
s Jer. 4. 27.
t ver. 17.
u Ex. 34. 6,7.

x 2 Kin.17.3.

y Ps.119.137.
Dan. 9. 14.
z Ps. 106. 6.
Dan.9.5, 6,8.

a Deut.28.47.

---

¹ Heb. *according to their will.*
² Or, *cisterns.*
³ Heb. *tree of food.*
⁴ Heb. *they returned to do evil.*
⁵ Heb. *they gave a withdrawing shoulder,* Zech. 7. 11.
⁶ Heb. *protract over them.*
⁷ Heb. *in the hand of thy prophets.*
⁸ Heb. *weariness.*
⁹ Heb. *that hath found us.*

---

25. *became fat.*] *i.e.* "grew proud," or "wanton"—a phrase only occurring here, in marg. ref., and in Jer. v. 28.
delighted themselves] Rather, "luxuriated." The word in the original does not occur elsewhere ; but cognate terms make the sense clear.

26. *slew thy prophets*] Cp. 1 K. xviii. 4, xix. 10 ; 2 Chr. xxiv. 21. Jewish tradition further affirms that more than one of the great Prophets (*e.g.* Isaiah, Jeremiah, and Ezekiel) were martyred by their countrymen.
27. *thou gavest them saviours*] See Judg. iii. 15 &c.

^bthy great goodness that thou gavest them, and in the large and ^cfat land which thou gavest before them, neither turned they 36 from their wicked works. Behold, ^dwe *are* servants this day, and *for* the land that thou gavest unto our fathers to eat the fruit thereof and the good thereof, behold, we *are* servants in it : 37 and ^eit yieldeth much increase unto the kings whom thou hast set over us because of our sins : also they have ^fdominion over our bodies, and over our cattle, at their pleasure, and we *are* in great 38 distress. And because of all this we ^gmake a sure covenant, and write it ; and our princes, Levites, *and* priests, ^{1h}seal *unto it.*

CHAP. 10. NOW ²those that sealed *were,* ^aNehemiah, ³the Tirshatha, 2 ^bthe son of Hachaliah, and Zidkijah, ^cSeraiah, Azariah, Jere- 3, 4 miah, Pashur, Amariah, Malchijah, Hattush, Shebaniah, Mal- 5, 6 luch, Harim, Meremoth, Obadiah, Daniel, Ginnethon, Baruch, 7, 8 Meshullam, Abijah, Mijamin, Maaziah, Bilgai, Shemaiah : 9 these *were* the priests. And the Levites : both Jeshua the son of 10 Azaniah, Binnui of the sons of Henadad, Kadmiel ; and their 11 brethren, Shebaniah, Hodijah, Kelita, Pelaiah, Hanan, Micha, 12, 13 Rehob, Hashabiah, Zaccur, Sherebiah, Shebaniah, Hodijah, 14 Bani, Beninu. The chief of the people ; ^dParosh, Pahath-moab, 15, 16 Elam, Zatthu, Bani, Bunni, Azgad, Bebai, Adonijah, Bigvai, 17, 18 Adin, Ater, Hizkijah, Azzur, Hodijah, Hashum, Bezai, 19, 20 Hariph, Anathoth, Nebai, Magpiash, Meshullam, Hezir, 21, 22 Meshezabeel, Zadok, Jaddua, Pelatiah, Hanan, Anaiah, 23, 24 Hoshea, Hananiah, Hashub, Hallohesh, Pileha, Shobek, 25, 26 Rehum, Hashabnah, Maaseiah, and Ahijah, Hanan, Anan, 27, 28 Malluch, Harim, Baanah. ¶ ^eAnd the rest of the people, the priests, the Levites, the porters, the singers, the Nethinims, ^fand all they that had separated themselves from the people of the lands unto the law of God, their wives, their sons, and their daughters, every one having knowledge, and having under- 29 standing ; they clave to their brethren, their nobles, ^gand entered into a curse, and into an oath, ^hto walk in God's law, which was given ⁴ by Moses the servant of God, and to observe and do all the commandments of the LORD our Lord, and his judgments 30 and his statutes ; and that we would not give ⁱour daughters unto the people of the land, nor take their daughters for our 31 sons : ^kand *if* the people of the land bring ware or any victuals on the sabbath day to sell, *that* we would not buy it of them on the sabbath, or on the holy day : and *that* we would leave the 32 ^lseventh year, and the ^mexaction of ⁵every debt. ¶ Also we made ordinances for us, to charge ourselves yearly with the third part of a shekel for the service of the house of our God ;

¹ Heb. are *at the sealing,* or, *sealed.*   ² Heb. *at the sealings,* ch. 9. 38.   ³ Or, *the governor.*   ⁴ Heb. *by the hand of.*   ⁵ Heb. *every hand.*

---

38. *seal unto it*] The exact force of the phrase used is doubtful ; but its general sense must be that the classes named took part in the sealing. It was usual in the East to authenticate covenants by appending the seals of those who were parties to them (see Jer. xxxii. 10).

X. 1. The "Zidkijah" of this passage is probably the same as "Zadok" (xiii. 13). "Zadok" is expressly called "the scribe," and it was probably as the scribe who drew up the document that "Zidkijah" signed it immediately after Nehemiah.

2-8. The names are not personal, but designate families. The seal of the High-priestly house of Seraiah was probably appended either by Ezra or Eliashib, who both belonged to it.

31. *bring ware ... on the sabbath day*] Compare xiii. 16, where this desecration of the Sabbath is shown to have commonly taken place.

leave the seventh year &c.] *i.e.* "let the land rest in the sabbatical year" (marg. reff.) and give up the "pledge-taking" (*v.* 2-10).

32. *the third part of a shekel*] This ap-

33 for ⁿthe shewbread, and for the ^ocontinual meat offering, and for the continual burnt offering, of the sabbaths, of the new moons, for the set feasts, and for the holy *things*, and for the sin offerings to make an atonement for Israel, and *for* all the work

34 of the house of our God. ¶ And we cast the lots among the priests, the Levites, and the people, ^pfor the wood offering, to bring *it* into the house of our God, after the houses of our fathers, at times appointed year by year, to burn upon the

35 altar of the LORD our God, ^qas *it is* written in the law: and ^rto bring the firstfruits of our ground, and the firstfruits of all fruit of all trees, year by year, unto the house of the LORD:

36 also the firstborn of our sons, and of our cattle, as *it is* written ^sin the law, and the firstlings of our herds and of our flocks, to bring to the house of our God, unto the priests

37 that minister in the house of our God: ^tand *that* we should bring the firstfruits of our dough, and our offerings, and the fruit of all manner of trees, of wine and of oil, unto the priests, to the chambers of the house of our God; and ^uthe tithes of our ground unto the Levites, that the same Levites

38 might have the tithes in all the cities of our tillage. And the priest the son of Aaron shall be with the Levites, ^xwhen the Levites take tithes: and the Levites shall bring up the tithe of the tithes unto the house of our God, to ^ythe chambers, into the

39 treasure house. For the children of Israel and the children of Levi ^zshall bring the offering of the corn, of the new wine, and the oil, unto the chambers, where *are* the vessels of the sanctuary, and the priests that minister, and the porters, and the singers: ^aand we will not forsake the house of our God.

CHAP. 11. AND the rulers of the people dwelt at Jerusalem: the rest of the people also cast lots, to bring one of ten to dwell in Jerusalem ^athe holy city, and nine parts *to dwell* in *other* cities.

2 And the people blessed all the men, that ^bwillingly offered them-

3 selves to dwell at Jerusalem. ¶ ^cNow these *are* the chief of the province that dwelt in Jerusalem: but in the cities of Judah dwelt every one in his possession in their cities, *to wit*, Israel, the priests, and the Levites, and ^dthe Nethinims, and ^ethe

4 children of Solomon's servants. And ^fat Jerusalem dwelt *certain* of the children of Judah, and of the children of Benjamin. ¶ Of the children of Judah; Athaiah the son of Uzziah, the son of Zechariah, the son of Amariah, the son of Shephatiah, the

ⁿ Lev. 24. 5, &c.
2 Chr. 2. 4.
^o See Num. 28, & 29.

^p ch. 13. 31.
Isai. 40. 16.

^q Lev. 6. 12.
^r Ex. 23. 19.
& 34. 26.
Lev. 19. 23.
Num. 18. 12.
Deut. 26. 2.
^s Ex. 13. 2, 12, 13.
Lev. 27. 26, 27.
Num. 18. 15, 16.
^t Lev. 23. 17.
Num. 15. 19.
& 18. 12, &c.
Deut. 18. 4.
& 26. 2.
^u Lev. 27. 30.
Num. 18. 21, &c.
^x Num. 18. 26.
^y 1 Chr. 9. 26.
2 Chr. 31. 11.
^z Deut. 12. 6, 11.
2 Chr. 31. 12.
ch. 13. 12.
^a ch. 13. 10, 11.

^a ver. 18.
Matt. 4. 5.
& 27. 53.
^b Judg. 5. 9.
^c 1 Chr. 9. 2, 3.

^d Ezra 2. 43.
^e Ezra 2. 55.
^f 1 Chr. 9. 3, &c.

pears to have been the first occasion on which an annual payment towards the maintenance of the Temple service and fabric was established. The half-shekel of the Law (Ex. xxx. 13) was paid only at the time of a census (which rarely took place), and was thus not a recurring tax. In after-times the annual payment was raised from the third of a shekel to half a shekel (Matt. xvii. 24).

34. No special provision was made by the Law, by David, or by Solomon, for the supply of wood necessary to keep fire ever burning upon the Altar. Nehemiah established a system by which the duty of supplying the wood was laid as a burthen in turn on the various clans or families, which were regarded as constituting the nation. The lot was used to determine the order

in which the several families should perform the duty. A special day (the 14th of the fifth month, according to Josephus) was appointed for the bringing in of the supply; and this day was after a time regarded as a high festival, and called "the feast of the Wood-offering."

XI. 1. *to bring one of ten*] Artificial enlargements of capitals by forcible transfers of population to them, were not unusual in ancient times. Syracuse became a great city, about B.C. 500, in this way. Tradition ascribed the greatness of Rome, in part, to this cause.

4-19. See marg. reff. notes. Both accounts appear to be extracts from a public official register which Nehemiah caused to be made of his census. The census itself seems to have been confined to the dwellers

g Gen. 33. 29,
Pharez.

5 son of Mahalaleel, of the children of *g*Perez; and Maaseiah the son of Baruch, the son of Col-hozeh, the son of Hazaiah, the son of Adaiah, the son of Joiarib, the son of Zechariah, the son 6 of Shiloni. All the sons of Perez that dwelt at Jerusalem *were* 7 four hundred threescore and eight valiant men. And these *are* the sons of Benjamin; Sallu the son of Meshullam, the son of Joed, the son of Pedaiah, the son of Kolaiah, the son of Maas- 8 eiah, the son of Ithiel, the son of Jesaiah. And after him 9 Gabbai, Sallai, nine hundred twenty and eight. And Joel the son of Zichri *was* their overseer: and Judah the son of Senuah

h 1 Chr. 9.
10, &c.

10 *was* second over the city. ¶ *h*Of the priests: Jedaiah the son of 11 Joiarib, Jachin. Seraiah the son of Hilkiah, the son of Me- shullam, the son of Zadok, the son of Meraioth, the son of 12 Ahitub, *was* the ruler of the house of God. And their brethren that did the work of the house *were* eight hundred twenty and two: and Adaiah the son of Jeroham, the son of Pelaliah, the son of Amzi, the son of Zechariah, the son of Pashur, the son 13 of Malchiah, and his brethren, chief of the fathers, two hundred forty and two: and Amashai the son of Azareel, the son of 14 Ahasai, the son of Meshillemoth, the son of Immer, and their brethren, mighty men of valour, an hundred twenty and eight: and their overseer *was* Zabdiel, ¹the son of *one of* the great men. 15 ¶ Also of the Levites: Shemaiah the son of Hashub, the son 16 of Azrikam, the son of Hashabiah, the son of Bunni; and Shabbethai and Jozabad, of the chief of the Levites, ²*had* the

i 1 Chr.26.29.

17 oversight of *i*the outward business of the house of God. And Mattaniah the son of Micha, the son of Zabdi, the son of Asaph, *was* the principal to begin the thanksgiving in prayer: and Bakbukiah the second among his brethren, and Abda the son 18 of Shammua, the son of Galal, the son of Jeduthun. All the

k ver. 1.

Levites in *k*the holy city *were* two hundred fourscore and four. 19 Moreover the porters, Akkub, Talmon, and their brethren that 20 kept ³the gates, *were* an hundred seventy and two. ¶ And the

---

¹ Or, *the son of Haggedolim.*   ² Heb. were over.   ³ Heb. *at the gates.*

---

at Jerusalem. The subjoined table ex- hibits the differences between the accounts of the entire population of Jerusalem as given in Nehemiah and in Chronicles:—

	1 Chronicles.	Nehemiah.
Tribe of Judah: —		
Of Pharez . .	..	468
Of Zerah . . .	690	..
Tribe of Benjamin: —	956	928
Tribe of Levi: —		
Priests . . .	1760	1192
Levites . . .	..	284
Porters . .	212	172

According to Nehemiah's numbers, sup- plemented from Chronicles, the entire adult male population of the city was 3734, which would give a total population of 14,936. According to Chronicles, supplemented from Nehemiah, the adult males were 4370, and consequently the entire population, 17,480. As the Nethinims and the Israelites of Ephraim and Manasseh (1 Chr. ix. 3) are not included in either list, we may conclude that the actual number of the inhabitants, after the efforts recorded in *vv.* 1, 2, was not much short of 20,000.

16. *the outward business of the house of God*] Such as the collection of the newly imposed tax (x. 32), the providing of the regular sacrifices, the renewal of vestments, and the like.

17. *the principal to begin the thanksgiving*] *i.e.* "the precentor," or "leader of the choir."

20. The returned community, though consisting mainly of members of the two tribes, represented the entire people of Israel. The ground, however, which they

residue of Israel, of the priests, *and* the Levites, *were* in all the
21 cities of Judah, every one in his inheritance. *l*But the Nethinims
dwelt in ¹Ophel : and Ziha and Gispa *were* over the Nethinims.
22 ¶ The overseer also of the Levites at Jerusalem *was* Uzzi the
son of Bani, the son of Hashabiah, the son of Mattaniah, the
son of Micha. Of the sons of Asaph, the singers *were* over the
23 business of the house of God. For *m*it *was* the king's commandment concerning them, that ²a certain portion should be
24 for the singers, due for every day. ¶ And Pethahiah the son of
Meshezabeel, of the children of *n*Zerah the son of Judah, *was*
25 *o*at the king's hand in all matters concerning the people. ¶ And
for the villages, with their fields, *some* of the children of Judah
dwelt at *p*Kirjath-arba, and *in* the villages thereof, and at
Dibon, and *in* the villages thereof, and at Jekabzeel, and *in* the
26 villages thereof, and at Jeshua, and at Moladah, and at Beth-
27 phelet, and at Hazar-shual, and at Beer-sheba, and *in* the
28 villages thereof, and at Ziklag, and at Mekonah, and in the
29 villages thereof, and at En-rimmon, and at Zareah, and at
30 Jarmuth, Zanoah, Adullam, and *in* their villages, at Lachish,
and the fields thereof, at Azekah, and *in* the villages thereof.
And they dwelt from Beer-sheba unto the valley of Hin-
31 nom. ¶ The children also of Benjamin ³from Geba dwelt ⁴at
Michmash, and Aija, and Beth-el, and *in* their villages,
32, 33 *and* at Anathoth, Nob, Ananiah, Hazor, Ramah, Gittaim,
34, 35 Hadid, Zeboim, Neballat, Lod, and Ono, *q*the valley of
36 craftsmen. ¶ And of the Levites *were* divisions *in* Judah, *and*
in Benjamin.

CHAP. 12. NOW these *are* the *a*priests and the Levites that went
up with Zerubbabel the son of Shealtiel, and Jeshua : *b*Seraiah,

l See ch.3.26.

m See Ezra
6. 8, 9.
& 7. 20, &c.

n Gen. 38.
30, *Zarah.*
o 1 Chr.18.17.
& 23. 28.
p Josh.14.15.

q 1 Chr. 4. 14.

a Ezra 2.1, 2.
b See ch. 10.
2–8.

¹ Or, *The tower.*
² Or, *a sure ordinance.*
³ Or, *of Geba.*
⁴ Or, *to Michmash.*

---

occupied, was not the whole land, but that
which had constituted the kingdom of
Judah.

21. Ophel, the southern spur of the Temple hill, having a wall of its own (iii. 27)
might be reckoned either in Jerusalem or
outside it. Here it is made a separate
place.

22. The business intended was probably
the *internal* business, as distinct from the
" outward business " (*v.* 16) : a part of which
was the apportionment of the royal bounty
among the members of the choir (*v.* 23).

23. The goodwill of Artaxerxes towards
the ministers employed in the Temple service, had been previously shown by his
exempting them from taxation of every
kind (Ezra vii. 24). Now, it would seem,
he had gone further and assigned to the
singers an allowance from the royal revenue.

24. It is difficult to say what office Pethahiah filled. So far as we know, the only
regular officers under the Persian system
of government were the satrap, the sub-
satrap, the permanent royal secretary, the
commandant, and the occasional commis-
sary.

25. *Kirjath-arba*] *i.e.* Hebron. In the
absence of the Hebrews during the Cap-

tivity the place had recovered its old name
(Josh. xv. 13).

26–35. Many of the places mentioned in
these verses are mentioned in Josh. xv.
27–39, xviii. 21–28.

36. *of the Levites were divisions*] *i.e.*
" the Levites were scattered among various
towns both in Judah and Benjamin."

XII. This chapter is made up of two
portions : (*a*) lists of the leading priests and
Levites at different periods (*vv.* 1-26) : (*b*)
the dedication of the wall of Jerusalem
(*vv.* 27-47). This latter passage is certainly
from the pen of Nehemiah, and was written
probably about B.C. 433. The lists included
in (*a*) are four : (1) the chief priestly and
Levitical families which returned to Jerusalem (*vv.* 1-9) ; (2) the succession of the
High Priests from Jeshua to Jaddua (*vv.*
10, 11) ; (3) the actual heads of the priestly
families in the time of the High-Priest
Joiakim (*vv.* 12-21) ; (4) the chief Levitical
families at the same period (*vv.* 24-26). Of
these lists Nos. 1, 3, and 4, may have been
drawn up in the time of Nehemiah, but
No. 2 in its present form must be much
later. See Introduction, p. 591.

1. *the priests*] The number of the names
here given, which is 22, is probably to

c Luke 1. 5.

d Ezra 3. 2.
Hag. 1. 1.
Zech. 3. 1.
e ch. 11. 17.

f 1 Chr. 9.
14, &c.

g 1 Chr. 23,
& 25, & 26.
h Ezra 3. 11.

2, 3 Jeremiah, Ezra, Amariah, [1]Malluch, Hattush, [2]Shechaniah,
4, 5 [3]Rehum, [4]Meremoth, Iddo, [5]Ginnetho, cAbijah, [6]Miamin,
6, 7 [7]Maadiah, Bilgah, Shemaiah, and Joiarib, Jedaiah, [8]Sallu,
Amok, Hilkiah, Jedaiah. These *were* the chief of the priests
8 and of their brethren in the days of dJeshua. Moreover the
Levites : Jeshua, Binnui, Kadmiel, Sherebiah, Judah, *and*
Mattaniah, c*which was* over [9]the thanksgiving, he and his
9 brethren. Also Bakbukiah and Unni, their brethren, *were* over
10 against them in the watches. ¶And Jeshua begat Joiakim,
11 Joiakim also begat Eliashib, and Eliashib begat Joiada, and
12 Joiada begat Jonathan, and Jonathan begat Jaddua. ¶And in
the days of Joiakim were priests, the chief of the fathers : of
13 Seraiah, Meraiah ; of Jeremiah, Hananiah ; of Ezra, Meshullam ;
14 of Amariah, Jehohanan ; of Melicu, Jonathan ; of Shebaniah,
15, 16 Joseph ; of Harim, Adna ; of Meraioth, Helkai ; of Iddo,
17 Zechariah ; of Ginnethon, Meshullam ; of Abijah, Zichri ; of
18 Miniamin, of Moadiah, Piltai ; of Bilgah, Shammua ; of She-
19 maiah, Jehonathan ; and of Joiarib, Mattenai ; of Jedaiah,
20, 21 Uzzi ; of Sallai, Kallai ; of Amok, Eber ; of Hilkiah, Hasha-
22 biah ; of Jedaiah, Nethaneel. ¶The Levites in the days of
Eliashib, Joiada, and Johanan, and Jaddua, *were* recorded chief
of the fathers : also the priests, to the reign of Darius the Per-
23 sian. The sons of Levi, the chief of the fathers, *were* written in
the book of the fchronicles, even until the days of Johanan the
24 son of Eliashib. ¶And the chief of the Levites : Hashabiah,
Sherebiah, and Jeshua the son of Kadmiel, with their brethren
over against them, to praise *and* to give thanks, gaccording to
the commandment of David the man of God, hward over against

---

[1] Or, *Melicu*, ver. 14.
[2] Or, *Shebaniah*, ver. 14.
[3] Or, *Harim*, ver. 15.
[4] Or, *Meraioth*, ver. 15.

[5] Or, *Ginnethon*, ver. 16.
[6] Or, *Miniamin*, ver. 17.
[7] Or, *Moadiah*, ver. 17.

[8] Or, *Sallai*, ver. 20.
[9] That is, *the psalms of thanksgiving.*

---

be connected with that of the Davidic
"courses," which was 24 (1 Chr. xxiv. 7–18).
Eight names are identical with those of the
heads in David's time. On comparing the
present list with that of the families who
sealed to Nehemiah's covenant (x. 2–8), we
shall find that the first sixteen recur in that
document nearly in the same order ; but
that the last six are absent from it. It
would seem that as these six declined to
seal to Nehemiah's covenant, they were
placed below the rest here in a sort of supplementary list. Note especially the "and"
which connects the second part of the lists
with the earlier part, both in v. 6 and in
v. 19.

8. Of the Levitical houses here mentioned,
three only returned at first, those of Jeshua,
Kadmiel, and Judah or Hodevah (vii. 43).
The others must have returned subsequently.

10, 11. The six generations of High-
Priests covered a little more than two centuries (B.C. 538–333), or a little under thirty-
five years to a generation. Jaddua was the
High-Priest who (according to Josephus)
had an interview with Alexander shortly
after the battle of Issus.

22, 23. These verses interrupt the account
of the church officers in the time of Joiakim,
resumed in v. 24. They appear to be an
addition to the original text, made about
the time of Alexander the Great, when the
Books of Chronicles, Ezra, and Nehemiah
would seem to have first taken their existing shape. The same writer who introduced
these verses, probably also added v. 11 to
the original text.

Darius the Persian] Probably Darius
Codomannus (B.C. 336–331), the antagonist
of Alexander the Great. See Introduction,
p. 592, n. 2.

23. This passage shows that the practice
of keeping a record of public events in state
archives was continued after the return
from the Captivity, at least to the time of
Johanan, the son, *i.e.* "the grandson," of
Eliashib.

24. *Jeshua the son of Kadmiel*] If the
reading be sound, this Jeshua must have
been the head of the Levitical family of
Kadmiel in the time of Joiakim ; but (cp.
viii. 7, ix. 4), some read "Jeshua, Bani,
Kadmiel," &c.

ward over against ward] *i.e.* "alternately,"
one part of the choir answering the other.

25 ward. Mattaniah, and Bakbukiah, Obadiah, Meshullam, Talmon, Akkub, *were* porters keeping the ward at the [1]thresholds
26 of the gates. These *were* in the days of Joiakim the son of Jeshua, the son of Jozadak, and in the days of Nehemiah *i*the
27 governor, and of Ezra the priest, *k*the scribe. ¶ And at *l*the dedication of the wall of Jerusalem they sought the Levites out of all their places, to bring them to Jerusalem, to keep the dedication with gladness, *m*both with thanksgivings, and with
28 singing, *with* cymbals, psalteries, and with harps. And the sons of the singers gathered themselves together, both out of the plain country round about Jerusalem, and from the villages of
29 Netophathi; also from the house of Gilgal, and out of the fields of Geba and Azmaveth: for the singers had builded them vil-
30 lages round about Jerusalem. And the priests and the Levites purified themselves, and purified the people, and the gates, and
31 the wall. ¶ Then I brought up the princes of Judah upon the wall, and appointed two great *companies of them that gave* thanks, *whereof* *n*one went on the right hand upon the wall, *o*toward the
32 dung gate: and after them went Hoshaiah, and half of the
33, 34 princes of Judah, and Azariah, Ezra, and Meshullam, Judah,
35 and Benjamin, and Shemaiah, and Jeremiah, and *certain* of the priests' sons *p*with trumpets; *namely,* Zechariah the son of Jonathan, the son of Shemaiah, the son of Mattaniah, the son
36 of Michaiah, the son of Zaccur, the son of Asaph: and his brethren, Shemaiah, and Azarael, Milalai, Gilalai, Maai, Nethaneel, and Judah, Hanani, with *q*the musical instruments of
37 David the man of God, and Ezra the scribe before them. *r*And at the fountain gate, which was over against them, they went up by *s*the stairs of the city of David, at the going up of the wall, above the house of David, even unto *t*the water gate east-
38 ward. ¶ *u*And the other *company of them that gave* thanks went over against *them*, and I after them, and the half of the people

i ch. 8. 9.

k Ezra 7. 6, 11.
l Deut. 20. 5.
Ps. 30, title.
m 1 Chr.25.6.
2 Chr. 5. 13.
& 7. 6.

n See ver.38.
o ch. 2. 13.
& 3. 13.

p Num. 10. 2, 8.

q 1 Chr. 23.5.
r ch. 2. 14.
& 3. 15.
s ch. 3. 15.
t ch. 3. 26.
& 8. 1, 3, 16.
u See ver.31.

[1] Or, *treasuries*, or, *assemblies*.

---

25. In 1 Chr. ix. 17, 24, 26, four families of porters only are mentioned; *six* are implied here, in vii. 45, and in Ezra ii. 42. From 1 Chr. xxvi. 14-19 it appears that the Temple had four chief gates, fronting the cardinal points, and two minor ones, " towards Asuppim," and " at Parbar."

27. *the dedication of the wall*] The ceremony had been deferred for the space of nearly twelve years (xiii. 6). Perhaps Nehemiah required an express permission from the Persian king before he could venture on a solemnity which might have been liable to misrepresentation.

out of all their places] *i.e.* out of the various cities of Judah and Benjamin in which they dwelt (xi. 36).

28. *the plain country round about Jerusalem*] Perhaps the valleys of Hinnom and Jehoshaphat, which enclose Jerusalem on three sides, are intended.

the villages of Netophathi] Rather, as in 1 Chr. ix. 16. Netophah lay near Bethlehem (1 Chr. ii. 54), and is perhaps represented by the modern *Antubeh*.

29. *the house of Gilgal*] Or, "Beth-Gilgal"

—probably the Gilgal north of Jerusalem (now *Jiljilia*).

31. *I brought up*] Note the resumption of the first person, which has been laid aside since vii. 5, and which is continued now to the end of the Book. It is generally allowed that we have here once more a memoir by Nehemiah himself.

The two "companies" or choirs, having ascended the wall on its western face, near the modern Jaffa Gate, stood looking eastward towards the city and Temple; then the southern choir, being on the *right*, commenced the circuit of the southern wall, while the choir upon the left proceeded round the northern wall (*vv.* 38-39), till both met on the eastern wall, between the water and the prison gates.

34. "Judah and Benjamin" are the lay people of those two tribes.

37. *above the house of David*] This choir or procession went above (or beyond) the old palace of David, following the line described in iii. 16-26, on their way to the eastern wall.

*ch. 3. 11.
*ch. 3. 8.
*2Kin.14.13.
ch. 8. 16.
*ch. 3. 6.
*ch. 3. 3.
*ch. 3. 1.
*ch. 3. 32.
*Jer. 32. 2.

upon the wall, from beyond *the tower of the furnaces even unto
39 *the broad wall; *and from above the gate of Ephraim, and
above *the old gate, and above *the fish gate, *and the tower of
Hananeel, and the tower of Meah, even unto *the sheep gate:
40 and they stood still in *the prison gate.   ¶ So stood the two
companies of them that gave thanks in the house of God, and I,
41 and the half of the rulers with me: and the priests; Eliakim,
Maaseiah, Miniamin, Michaiah, Elioenai, Zechariah, and Ha-
42 naniah, with trumpets; and Maaseiah, and Shemaiah, and
Eleazar, and Uzzi, and Jehohanan, and Malchijah, and Elam,
and Ezer.   And the singers ¹sang loud, with Jezrahiah their
43 overseer.   Also that day they offered great sacrifices, and rejoiced: for God had made them rejoice with great joy: the
wives also and the children rejoiced: so that the joy of Jeru-

*2 Chr. 31.
11, 12.
ch. 13. 5, 12,
13.

44 salem was heard even afar off.   ¶ *And at that time were some
appointed over the chambers for the treasures, for the offerings,
for the firstfruits, and for the tithes, to gather into them out of
the fields of the cities the portions ²of the law for the priests
and Levites: ³for Judah rejoiced for the priests and for the
45 Levites ⁴that waited.   And both the singers and the porters
kept the ward of their God, and the ward of the purification,

*1 Chr. 25,
& 26.
*1 Chr. 25.
1, &c.
2 Chr. 29. 30.

46 *according to the commandment of David, and of Solomon his
son.   For in the days of David *and Asaph of old there were
chief of the singers, and songs of praise and thanksgiving unto
47 God.   And all Israel in the days of Zerubbabel, and in the days
of Nehemiah, gave the portions of the singers and the porters,
every day his portion: *and they ⁵sanctified holy things unto the

*Num. 18.
21, 24.
*Num.18.26.

Levites; *and the Levites sanctified them unto the children of
Aaron.

*Deut. 31.
11, 12.
2 Kin. 23. 2.
ch. 8. 3, 8.
& 9. 3.
Isai. 34. 16.
*Deut. 23. 3,
4.
*Num. 22. 5.
Josh. 24. 9,
10.
*Num.23.11.
& 24. 10.
Deut. 23. 5.
*ch. 9. 2,
& 10. 28.

CHAP. 13. ON that day *⁶they read in the book of Moses in the
⁷audience of the people; and therein was found written, *that
the Ammonite and the Moabite should not come into the congre-
2 gation of God for ever; because they met not the children of Israel with bread and with water, but *hired Balaam against them,
that he should curse them: *howbeit our God turned the curse
3 into a blessing.   Now it came to pass, when they had heard the
law, *that they separated from Israel all the mixed multitude.
4 ¶ And before this, Eliashib the priest, *having the oversight of

---

¹ Heb. made their voice to   ³ Heb. for the joy of   ⁶ Heb. there was read.
   be heard.   Judah.   ⁷ Heb. ears.
² That is, appointed by the   ⁴ Heb. that stood.   ⁸ Heb. being set over, ch.
   law.   ⁵ That is, set apart.   12. 44.

---

44. *Judah rejoiced*] Judah's satisfaction
with the priests and Levites took the shape
of increased offerings, more ample tithes,
and the like, whence the appointment of
treasuries and treasurers became necessary.

45. *the ward of the purification*] The observances with respect to purification. Cp.
1 Chr. xxiii. 28.

47. The intention is to compare the religious activity and strictness of Nehemiah's
time with that which had prevailed under
Zerubbabel, as described by Ezra (vi. 16,
22). It is implied that the intermediate
period had been a time of laxity.

   they sanctified holy things &c.] *i.e.* "the
people paid their tithes regularly to the

Levites, and the Levites paid the tithe of
the tithes to the priests."

   XIII. **1.** *On that day*] Or, "at that
time," as in xii. 44.

   By "the Book of Moses" is probably
meant the entire Pentateuch.

   3. A separation like that made by Ezra,
some twenty years previously (Ezr. x. 15-
44), seems to be intended.   The heathen
wives were divorced and sent back, with
their offspring, to their own countries.

   4. The relations of Eliashib, the High-
Priest (iii. 1), with Tobiah and Sanballat
will account for the absence of any reference to him either in chs. viii.-x., or in
xii. 27-47.

the chamber of the house of our God, *was* allied unto Tobiah :
5 and he had prepared for him a great chamber, *f* where aforetime   *f* ch. 12. 44.
they laid the meat offerings, the frankincense, and the vessels,
and the tithes of the corn, the new wine, and the oil, ¹*g* which   *g* Num. 18.
was commanded *to be given* to the Levites, and the singers, and   21, 24.
6 the porters ; and the offerings of the priests. But in all this *time*
was not I at Jerusalem : *h* for in the two and thirtieth year of   *h* ch. 5. 14.
Artaxerxes king of Babylon came I unto the king, and ²after
7 certain days ³obtained I leave of the king : and I came to Jerusalem, and understood of the evil that Eliashib did for Tobiah,
in *i* preparing him a chamber in the courts of the house of God.   *i* ver. 1, 5.
8 And it grieved me sore : therefore I cast forth all the household
9 stuff of Tobiah out of the chamber. Then I commanded, and
they *k* cleansed the chambers : and thither brought I again the   *k* 2 Char. 29.
vessels of the house of God, with the meat offering and the frank-   5, 15, 16, 18.
10 incense. ¶ And I perceived that the portions of the Levites had
l not been given *them :* for the Levites and the singers, that did   *l* Mal. 3. 8.
11 the work, were fled every one to *m* his field. Then *n* contended I   *m* Num.35.2.
with the rulers, and said, *o* Why is the house of God forsaken ?   *n* ver. 17, 25.
And I gathered them together, and set them in their ⁴place.   Prov. 28. 4.
  o ch. 10. 39.
12 *p* Then brought all Judah the tithe of the corn and the new wine   *p* ch. 10. 38,
13 and the oil unto the ⁵treasuries. *q* And I made treasurers over   39.
the treasuries, Shelemiah the priest, and Zadok the scribe, and   & 12. 44.
of the Levites, Pedaiah : and ⁶next to them *was* Hanan the son   *q* 2Chr.31.12.
of Zaccur, the son of Mattaniah : for they were counted *r* faith-   ch. 12. 44.
ful, and ⁷their office *was* to distribute unto their brethren.   *r* ch. 7. 2.
  1 Cor. 4. 2.
14 *s* Remember me, O my God, concerning this, and wipe not out   *s* ver. 22, 31.
my ⁸good deeds that I have done for the house of my God,   ch. 5. 19.
15 and for the ⁹offices thereof. ¶ In those days saw I in Judah
some treading wine presses *t* on the sabbath, and bringing in   *t* Ex. 20. 10.
sheaves, and lading asses ; as also wine, grapes, and figs, and all
manner of burdens, *u* which they brought into Jerusalem on the   *u* ch. 10. 31.
sabbath day : and I testified *against them* in the day wherein
16 they sold victuals. There dwelt men· of Tyre also therein,

---

¹ Heb. *the commandment of*   ³ Or, *I earnestly requested.*   ⁷ Heb. it was *upon them.*
  the Levites.   ⁴ Heb. *standing.*   ⁸ Heb. *kindnesses.*
² Heb. *at the end of days.*   ⁵ Or, *storehouses.*   ⁹ Or, *observations.*
   ⁶ Heb. *at their hand.*

---

the chamber] The entire outbuilding, or "lean-to," which surrounded the Temple on three sides (1 K. vi. 5-10).

allied] *i.e.* "connected by marriage." Tobiah was married to a Jewess (vi. 18), who may have been a relation of Eliashib ; and his son Johanan was married to another (do.), of whom the same may be said.

5. *the offerings of the priests*] *i.e.* "the portion of the offerings assigned for their sustenance to the priests."

6. *Artaxerxes king of Babylon*] See i. 1. Cp. Ezr. vi. 22, where Darius Hystaspis is called "king of Assyria."

after certain days] Or, "at the end of a year," which is a meaning that the phrase often has (Ex. xiii. 10 ; Lev. xxv. 29, 30 ; Num. ix. 22). Nehemiah probably went to the court at Babylon in B.C. 433, and returned to Jerusalem B.C. 432.

9. *the chambers*] The "great chamber"

assigned to Tobiah (*v.* 5) contained, it would seem, more than one apartment.

10. &c. During Nehemiah's absence there had been a general falling away, and there was danger of a complete national apostasy.

11. *I gathered them together*] Nehemiah gathered the Levites from their lands, and reinstated them in their set offices.

15. The desecration of the Sabbath is first brought into prominence among the sins of the Jewish people by Jeremiah (Jer. xvii. 21-27). It could not but have gained ground during the Captivity, when foreign masters would not have allowed the cessation of labour for one day in seven. On the return from the Captivity, the sabbatical rest appears to have been one of the institutions most difficult to re-establish.

in the day] Some render, "**concerning** the day."

16. Friendly relations subsisted between

which brought fish, and all manner of ware, and sold on the
17 sabbath unto the children of Judah, and in Jerusalem. ˣThen
I contended with the nobles of Judah, and said unto them,
What evil thing *is* this that ye do, and profane the sabbath day?
18 ʸDid not your fathers thus, and did not our God bring all this
evil upon us, and upon this city? yet ye bring more wrath
19 upon Israel by profaning the sabbath. ¶And it came to pass,
that when the gates of Jerusalem ᶻbegan to be dark before
the sabbath, I commanded that the gates should be shut, and
charged that they should not be opened till after the sabbath:
ᵃand *some* of my servants set I at the gates, *that* there should
20 no burden be brought in on the sabbath day. So the merchants
and sellers of all kind of ware lodged without Jerusalem once
21 or twice. Then I testified against them, and said unto them,
Why lodge ye ¹about the wall? if ye do *so* again, I will lay
hands on you. From that time forth came they no *more* on
22 the sabbath. And I commanded the Levites that ᵇthey should
cleanse themselves, and *that* they should come *and* keep
the gates, to sanctify the sabbath day. ᶜRemember me, O
my God, *concerning* this also, and spare me according to the
23 ²greatness of thy mercy. ¶In those days also saw I Jews
that ³ᵈhad married wives of Ashdod, of Ammon, *and* of Moab:
24 and their children spake half in the speech of Ashdod, and
⁴could not speak in the Jews' language, but according to the
25 language ⁵of each people. And I ᵉcontended with them, and
⁶cursed them, and smote certain of them, and plucked off their
hair, and made them ᶠswear by God, *saying*, Ye shall not give
your daughters unto their sons, nor take their daughters unto
26 your sons, or for yourselves. ᵍDid not Solomon king of Israel
sin by these things? yet ʰamong many nations was there no
king like him, ⁱwho was beloved of his God, and God made him
king over all Israel: ᵏnevertheless even him did outlandish
27 women cause to sin. Shall we then hearken unto you to do all
this great evil, to ˡtransgress against our God in marrying
28 strange wives? And *one* of the sons ᵐof Joiada, the son of
Eliashib the high priest, *was* son in law to Sanballat the
29 Horonite: therefore I chased him from me. ⁿRemember them,
O my God, ⁷because they have defiled the priesthood, and ᵒthe

ˣ ver. 11.

ʸ Jer. 17. 21,
22, 23.

ᶻ Lev. 23. 32.

ᵃ Jer. 17. 21,
22.

ᵇ ch. 12. 30.

ᶜ ver. 14, 31.

ᵈ Ezra 9. 2.

ᵉ ver. 11.
Prov. 28. 4.

ᶠ Ezra 10. 5.
ch. 10. 29, 30.

ᵍ 1 Kin. 11.
1, &c.
ʰ 1 Kin. 3. 13.
2 Chr. 1. 12.
ⁱ 2 Sam. 12.
24.
ᵏ 1 Kin. 11.
4, &c.
ˡ Ezra 10. 2.
ᵐ ch. 12. 10,
22.

ⁿ ch. 6. 14.

ᵒ Mal. 2. 4,
11, 12.

¹ Heb. *before the wall?*
² Or, *multitude.*
³ Heb. *had made to dwell*
with them.
⁴ Heb. *they discerned not to speak.*
⁵ Heb. *of people and people.*
⁶ Or, *reviled them.*
⁷ Heb. *for the defilings.*

---

the Phœnicians and the Jews, after the
Captivity (Ezra iii. 7). It was, however, a
new fact, and one pregnant with evil consequences, that the Tyrians should have
established a permanent colony at Jerusalem. Its influence on the other inhabitants
weakened the hold of the Law upon men's
consciences, and caused it to be transgressed
continually more and more openly.

19. The gates were closed at the sunset of
the day before the Sabbath; since the
Sabbath was regarded as commencing on
the previous evening.

21. The lodging of the merchants with
their merchandise just outside Jerusalem
during the Sabbath, marked their im-

patience for the moment when they might
bring their wares in. This was thought by
Nehemiah to be unseemly, and to have an
irreligious tendency.

22. *I commanded the Levites*] At first
Nehemiah had employed his own retinue
(*v.* 19) in the work of keeping the gates.
He now assigned the duty to the Levites,
as one which properly belonged to them,
since the object of the regulation was the
due observance of the Sabbath.

24. *the speech of Ashdod*] The Philistine
language, which was akin to that of Egypt.

according to the language of each people]
The children spoke a mixed dialect, half
Philistine, half Hebrew.

30 covenant of the priesthood, and of the Levites. *p*Thus cleansed
I them from all strangers, and *q*appointed the wards of the priests
31 and the Levites, every one in his business; and for *r*the wood
offering, at times appointed, and for the firstfruits. *s*Remember me, O my God, for good.

p ch. 10. 30.
q ch. 12. 1,
&c.
r ch. 10. 31.
s ver. 14, 22.

---

30. *the wards*] Rather, "the **offices** or observances." Nehemiah's arrangement is
probably that described in xi. 10-22.

ESTHER.

INTRODUCTION.

THE Book of Esther is entitled by the Jews, "the volume of Esther," or simply "the volume." Anciently it was always written on a separate roll, which was read through at the feast of Purim. The Greek translators retained only "Esther," which thus became the ordinary title among Christians.

1. There is much controversy concerning the date of "Esther." The extreme minuteness of the details and vividness of the portraits in "Esther" certainly suggest the hand of a contemporary far more decidedly than any occasional expressions suggest a composer who lived long after the events commemorated : and the tone of the Book is in accord with the history which it narrates, and is not unlike that of Zechariah. Therefore, on the whole, there is no sufficient ground for placing the composition of Esther later than that of Chronicles, Ezra, and Nehemiah, or the time of Artaxerxes Longimanus. On the other hand, there is no ground for regarding Esther as earlier than the other post-Captivity Historical Books—much less for placing it in the reign of Xerxes. Assuming Ahasuerus to be Xerxes (see § 3), it may be said that both the opening sentence and the conclusion of the work indicate that the reign of Xerxes was over. Consequently the earliest date that can reasonably be assigned to the Book is B.C. 464 ; and it is, on the whole,

most probable that it was composed twenty or thirty years later (B.C. 444–434).

2. There are no means of determining who was the author of "Esther." He was not Ezra. He may have been Mordecai, or, more probably, a younger contemporary of Mordecai's.

The author, whoever he was, almost certainly wrote in Persia, where he had access to the royal archives, which contained an account, more or less full, of the transactions he was desirous of recording. Much also must have been derived from personal observation,[1] and from communications with Mordecai and (perhaps) Esther.[2]

The Book is more purely a Historical Book than any other in Scripture. Its main scope is simply to give an account of the circumstances under which the Feast of Purim was instituted. The absence of the name of God, and the slightness of the religious and didactic elements are marked characteristics. The author's Persian breeding, together probably with other circumstances, has prevented his sharing the ordinary Jewish

---

[1] As the description of Susa (i. 5, 6), that of the royal posts (viii. 10, 14), of Mordecai's apparel (do. 15), and the like.

[2] E.g. The genealogy of Mordecai (ii. 5), his private communications with Esther (do. 10, 11, 20, 22) and Hatach (iv. 6–16).

spirit of local attachment, while at the same time it has taught him a reticence with respect to the doctrines of his religion very unusual with his countrymen.

The narrative is striking and graphic ; the style remarkably chaste and simple ; and the sentences clear and unambiguous. The vocabulary, on the contrary, is, as might have been expected, not altogether pure, a certain number of Persian words being employed,[3] and also a few terms characteristic of the later Hebrew or " Chaldee " dialect.

3. The authenticity of the history of Esther has been impugned ; but the main circumstances of the narrative, which at first sight appear improbable, are not so if the peculiarly extravagant and capricious character of the Persian monarch be taken into account. Etymologically, the name Ahasuerus is identical with the Persian *Khshay-arsha* and the Greek Xerxes ; and it is to this particular Persian monarch that the portrait of Ahasuerus exhibits a striking similarity. The chronological notices in the work also exactly fit this monarch's history ; and the entire representation of the Court and kingdom is suitable to his time and character. That we have no direct profane confirmation of the narrative of Esther must be admitted, for the identity of Mordecai with Matacas (see ii. 5) is too doubtful to be relied upon ; but that we have none, is sufficiently accounted for by the fact that the accounts of the reign of Xerxes after his sixth year, and more particularly of his domestic life, are scanty in the extreme, the native records being silent, and the Greek writers concerning themselves almost entirely with those public events which bore upon the history of Greece. " Esther " is, in fact, the sole authority for the period and circumstances of which it treats ; if untrue, it might have easily been proved to be untrue at the time when it was published, by reference to the extant " book of the chronicles of the kings of Media and Persia," which it quotes (ii. 23, x. 2). It has, moreover, always been regarded by the Jews as an authentic account of the great deliverance which they celebrate annually by the feast of Purim.

4. In the Septuagint version occur " additions " to Esther consisting of five principal passages.[4]

Their unauthenticity is very evi-

---

[3] The language of Esther is even more impregnated with Persian than that of Ezra. Several Persian words, as *akhashdarpan, genez (g'naz), iggereth (iggera)*, and *pithgam (pithgama)*, are common to both Books. In addition to these, Esther has, besides some words of doubtful origin, the following list of terms, almost certainly Persian :—*akhashteranim*, "royal ; " *karpas*, "cotton ; " *kether* "crown ; " *partemim*, "nobles ; " *pathshegen*, "a copy, a transcript ; " and *pûr*, "the lot."

[4] 1. The first is introductory. It is dated in the second year of Ahasuerus, and contains (*a*) the pedigree of Mordecai, an anticipation of ii. 5 ; (*b*) a dream which he is supposed to have had ; (*c*) an account of the conspiracy of the two eunuchs and Mordecai's discovery of it ; (*d*) a statement that Mordecai was at once rewarded with gifts ; and (*e*) a statement that Haman wished ill to Mordecai and his people on account of the affair of the eunuchs. 2. The second occurs after iii. 13, and consists of a pretended translation of the letter sent out by Ahasuerus at the request of Haman. 3. The third follows on the close of ch. iv., and comprises (*a*) a long prayer ascribed to Mordecai ; (*b*) another still longer prayer ascribed to Esther ; and (*c*) an expanded account of Esther's venturing before the king unsummoned, in lieu of v. 1, 2. 4. The

dent. They contradict the original document, and are quite different in tone and style from the rest of the Book.

The principal intention of the "additions" is clear enough. They aim at giving a thoroughly religious character to a work in which, as originally written, the religious element was latent or only just perceptible. On the whole we may conclude that the Greek book of Esther, as we have it, was composed in the following way :— first a translation was made of the Hebrew text, honest for the most part, but with a few very short additions and omissions ; then the markedly religious portions were added, the opening passage, the prayers of Mordecai and Esther, the exordium to ch. v., the religious touches in ch. vi. (*vv.* 1 and 13) ; and the concluding verses of ch. x. Finally, the "letters of Ahasuerus" were composed by a writer more familiar than most Hellenists with the true spirit of the Greek tongue, and these, being accepted as genuine, were inserted in chs. iii. and viii.

---

fourth is interposed between *vv.* 13 and 14 of ch. viii., and consists of a pretended copy of the letter sent out in the king's name by Mordecai. 5. The fifth and last occurs at the close of ch. x. It comprises (*a*) Mordecai's application of his dream to the events ; (*b*) his appointment of the days of Purim as a permanent festival ; and (*c*) an epilogue stating that the Greek version of Esther was brought (to Alexandria) in the fourth year of Ptolemy and Cleopatra by a certain Dositheus, a priest, and was said by him to have been translated by a certain Lysimachus, of Jerusalem.

THE BOOK

OF

ESTHER.

a Ezra 4. 6.
Dan. 9. 1.
b ch. 8. 9.
c Dan. 6. 1.
d 1 Kin. 1.16.
e Neh. 1. 1.
f Gen. 40. 20.
ch. 2. 18.
Mark 6. 21.

CHAP. 1. NOW it came to pass in the days of *a*Ahasuerus, (this *i* Ahasuerus which reigned, *b*from India even unto Ethiopia,
2 *c*over an hundred and seven and twenty provinces :) *that* in those days, when the king Ahasuerus *d*sat on the throne of his
3 kingdom, which *was* in *e*Shushan the palace, in the third year of his reign, he *f*made a feast unto all his princes and his servants; the power of Persia and Media, the nobles and princes of the
4 provinces, *being* before him : when he shewed the riches of his glorious kingdom and the honour of his excellent majesty many
5 days, *even* an hundred and fourscore days. ¶And when these days were expired, the king made a feast unto all the people that were ¹present in Shushan the palace, both unto great and small, seven days, in the court of the garden of the king's
6 palace; *where were* white, green, and ²blue, *hangings*, fastened with cords of fine linen and purple to silver rings and pillars

g See ch. 7. 8.
Ezek. 23. 41.
Amos 2. 8.
& 6. 4.

of marble : *g*the beds *were of* gold and silver, upon a pave-
7 ment ³of red, and blue, and white, and black, marble. And they gave *them* drink in vessels of gold, (the vessels being diverse one from another,) and ⁴royal wine in abundance, ⁵according
8 to the state of the king. And the drinking *was* according to the law; none did compel : for so the king had appointed to all the officers of his house, that they should do according to every
9 man's pleasure. Also Vashti the queen made a feast for the women *in* the royal house which *belonged* to king Ahasuerus.

---

¹ Heb. *found.*
² Or, *violet.*
³ O*r*, *of porphyre, and marble, and alabaster, and stone of blue colour.*
⁴ Heb. *wine of the kingdom.*
⁵ Heb. *according to the hand of the king.*

I. 1. *Ahasuerus*]. Xerxes, the son of Darius Hystaspis. His empire is rightly described as from India even unto Ethiopia. The satrapies of Darius Hystaspis reached 29 in number, and the nations under Xerxes were about 60. The 127 "provinces" include probably "sub-satrapies" and other smaller divisions of the great governments.

3. *in the third year*]. In this year, B.C. 483, Xerxes assembled the governors of provinces at Susa, in connexion with his contemplated expedition against Greece.

the nobles] Lit. "the first men." The Hebrew word used is one adopted from the Persian.

5. Feasts on this extensive scale were not unusual in the East. Cyrus is said on one occasion to have feasted "all the Persians." Even ordinarily, the later Persian monarchs entertained at their table 15,000 persons.

6. Rather, "where was an **awning of fine white cotton and violet**." White and blue (or violet) were the royal colours in Persia. Such awnings as are here described were very suitable to the pillared halls and porches

of a Persian summer-palace, and especially to the situation of that of Susa.

the beds] Rather, "**couches**" or "**sofas**," on which the guests reclined at meals.

a pavement &c.] See margin. It is generally agreed that the four substances named are stones; but to identify the stones, or even their colours, is difficult.

8. *according to the law*] An exception to the ordinary practice of compulsory drinking had been made on this occasion by the king's order.

9. *Vashti*] If Ahasuerus be Xerxes, Vashti should be Amestris, whom the Greeks regarded as the only legitimate wife of that monarch, and who was certainly married to him before he ascended the throne. The name may be explained either as a corruption of Amestris, or as a title, *vahishta*, (Sanskr. *vasishtha*, the superlative of *vasu*, "sweet"); and it may be supposed that the disgrace recorded (*vv.* 19-21, see note) was only temporary; Amestris in the later part of Xerxes' reign recovering her former dignity.

10 ¶ On the seventh day, when *the heart of the king was merry with wine, he commanded Mehuman, Biztha, ‘Harbona, Bigtha, and Abagtha, Zethar, and Carcas, the seven [1] chamberlains that
11 served in the presence of Ahasuerus the king, to bring Vashti the queen before the king with the crown royal, to shew the people and the princes her beauty : for she *was* [2] fair to look on.
12 But the queen Vashti refused to come at the king's commandment [3] by *his* chamberlains : therefore was the king very wroth,
13 and his anger burned in him. ¶ Then the king said to the *k* wise men, *l* which knew the times, (for so *was* the king's
14 manner toward all that knew law and judgment : and the next unto him *was* Carshena, Shethar, Admatha, Tarshish, Meres, Marsena, *and* Memucan, the *m* seven princes of Persia and Media, *n* which saw the king's face, *and* which sat the first in the king-
15 dom ;) [4] What shall we do unto the queen Vashti according to law, because she hath not performed the commandment of
16 the king Ahasuerus by the chamberlains? And Memucan answered before the king and the princes, Vashti the queen hath not done wrong to the king only, but also to all the princes, and to all the people that *are* in all the provinces of
17 the king Ahasuerus. For *this* deed of the queen shall come abroad unto all women, so that they shall *o* despise their husbands in their eyes, when it shall be reported, The king Ahasuerus commanded Vashti the queen to be brought in before
18 him, but she came not. *Likewise* shall the ladies of Persia and Media say this day unto all the king's princes, which have heard of the deed of the queen. Thus *shall there arise* too much con-
19 tempt and wrath. [5] If it please the king, let there go a royal commandment [6] from him, and let it be written among the laws of the Persians and the Medes, [7] that it be not altered, That Vashti come no more before king Ahasuerus ; and let the king
20 give her royal estate [8] unto another that is better than she. And when the king's decree which he shall make shall be published throughout all his empire, (for it is great,) all the wives shall *p* give to their husbands honour, both to great and small.
21 ¶ And the saying [9] pleased the king and the princes ; and the
22 king did according to the word of Memucan : for he sent letters

h 2 Sam. 13. 28.
i ch. 7. 9.

k Jer. 10. 7. Dan. 2. 12. Matt. 2. 1.
l 1 Chr. 12. 32.
m Ezra 7. 14.
n 2 Kin. 25. 19.

o Eph. 5. 33.

p Eph. 5. 33. Col. 3. 18. 1 Pet. 3. 1.

[1] Or, *eunuchs.*
[2] Heb. *good of countenance.*
[3] Heb. *which* was *by the hand of* his *eunuchs.*
[4] Heb. *What to do.*
[5] Heb. *If it be good with the king.*
[6] Heb. *from before him.*
[7] Heb. *that it pass not away,* ch. 8. 8. Dan. 6.
8. 12. 15.
[8] Heb. *unto her companion.*
[9] Heb. *was good in the eyes of the king.*

---

11. *to bring Vashti the queen*] This command, though contrary to Persian customs, is not out of harmony with the character of Xerxes ; and is evidently related as something strange and unusual. Otherwise the queen would not have refused to come.

13. *wise men &c.*] Not "astrologers," who were unknown in Persia ; but rather men of practical wisdom, who knew the facts and customs of former times.

for so was the king's manner] Some render, "for so was the king's **business laid before** all that knew law &c."

14. In Marsena we may perhaps recognise the famous Mardonius, and in Admatha, Xerxes' uncle, Artabanus.

the seven princes] There were seven fa-

milies of the first rank in Persia, from which alone the king could take his wives. Their chiefs were entitled to have free access to the monarch's person. See marg. ref. note.

18. Translate — "Likewise shall the princesses of Persia and Media, which have heard of the deed of the queen, say this day unto all the king's princes."

19. *that it be not altered*] Cp. marg. reff. This was the theory. Practically, the monarch, if he chose, could always dispense with the law. It was therefore quite within his power to restore Vashti to her queenly dignity notwithstanding the present decree, if he so pleased.

22. *he sent letters*] The Persian system of posts incidentally noticed in the present

into all the king's provinces, ^qinto every province according to the writing thereof, and to every people after their language, that every man should ^rbear rule in his own house, and [1] that *it* should be published according to the language of every people.

Chap. 2. AFTER these things, when the wrath of king Ahasuerus was appeased, he remembered Vashti, and what she had done,
2 and ^awhat was decreed against her. Then said the king's servants that ministered unto him, Let there be fair young virgins
3 sought for the king : and let the king appoint officers in all the provinces of his kingdom, that they may gather together all the fair young virgins unto Shushan the palace, to the house of the women, [2] unto the custody of [3] Hege the king's chamberlain, keeper of the women; and let their things for purification be
4 given *them :* and let the maiden which pleaseth the king be queen instead of Vashti. And the thing pleased the king ; and
5 he did so. ¶ Now in Shushan the palace there was a certain Jew, whose name *was* Mordecai, the son of Jair, the son of
6 Shimei, the son of Kish, a Benjamite ; ^bwho had been carried away from Jerusalem with the captivity which had been carried away with [4]Jeconiah king of Judah, whom Nebuchadnezzar the
7 king of Babylon had carried away. And he [5] brought up Hadassah, that *is*, Esther, ^chis uncle's daughter : for she had

---

[1] Heb. *that one should pub- l'sh it according to the language of his people.*

[2] Heb. *unto the hand.*
[3] Or, *Hegai*, ver. 8.

[4] Or, *Jehoiachin*, 2 Kin. 24. 6.
[5] Heb. *nourished*, Eph.6.4.

Book (iii. 12-15 ; viii. 9-14), is in entire harmony with the accounts of Herodotus and Xenophon.

into every province according to the writing thereof] The practice of the Persians to address proclamations to the subject-nations in their own speech, and not merely in the language of the conqueror, is illustrated by the bilingual and trilingual inscriptions of the Achæmenian monarchs, from Cyrus to Artaxerxes Ochus, each inscription being of the nature of a proclamation.

The decree was not unnecessary. The undue influence of women in domestic, and even in public, matters is a feature of the ancient Persian monarchy. Atossa completely ruled Darius. Xerxes himself was, in his later years, shamefully subject to Amestris. The example of the court would naturally infect the people. The decree therefore would be a protest, even if ineffectual, against a real and growing evil.

and that it should be published &c.] Render, " and *speak the language of his own people ;*" in the sense that the wife's language, if different from her husband's, should in no case be allowed to prevail in the household.

II. **1-11.** These events must belong to the time between the great assembly held at Susa in Xerxes' third year (B.C. 483), and the departure of the monarch on his expedition against Greece in his fifth year, B.C. 481.

3. *th: house of the women*] i.e. the "gynæceon," or "haram"—always an essential part of an Oriental palace (Cp. 1 K. vii. 8).

In the Persian palaces it was very extensive, since the monarchs maintained, besides their legitimate wives, as many as 300 or 400 concubines (cp. *v.* 14).

5. Mordecai, the eunuch (*vv.* 7, 11), has been conjectured to be the same as Matacas, who, according to Ctesias, was the most powerful of the eunuchs during the latter portion of the reign of Xerxes. Mordecai's line of descent is traced from a certain Kish, carried off by Nebuchadnezzar in B.C. 598— the year of Jeconiah's captivity—who was his great-grandfather. The four generations, Kish, Shimei, Jair, Mordecai, correspond to the known generations in other cases, e.g. :—

High-priests.	Kings of Persia.	Royal stock of Judah.
Seraiah	Cambyses	Jeconiah
Jozadak	Cyrus	Salathiel
Jeshua	Darius	Zerubbabel
Joiakim	Xerxes	Hananiah

The age of Mordecai at the accession of Xerxes may probably have been about 30 or 40 ; that of Esther, his first cousin, about 20.

7. Hadassah ("myrtle") would seem to have been the Hebrew, and Esther the Persian, name of the damsel. Esther is

neither father nor mother, and the maid *was* [1] fair and beautiful; whom Mordecai, when her father and mother were dead, took for
8 his own daughter. ¶ So it came to pass, when the king's commandment and his decree was heard, and when many maidens were [d] gathered together unto Shushan the palace, to the custody of Hegai, that Esther was brought also unto the king's
9 house, to the custody of Hegai, keeper of the women. And the maiden pleased him, and she obtained kindness of him; and he speedily gave her her [e] things for purification, with [2] such things as belonged to her, and seven maidens, *which were* meet to be given her, out of the king's house: and [3] he preferred her and her
10 maids unto the best *place* of the house of the women. [f] Esther had not shewed her people nor her kindred: for Mordecai had
11 charged her that she should not shew *it*. And Mordecai walked every day before the court of the women's house, [4] to know how
12 Esther did, and what should become of her. ¶ Now when every maid's turn was come to go in to king Ahasuerus, after that she had been twelve months, according to the manner of the women, (for so were the days of their purifications accomplished, *to wit*, six months with oil of myrrh, and six months with sweet odours, and with *other* things for the purifying of
13 the women;) then thus came *every* maiden unto the king; whatsoever she desired was given her to go with her out of the house
14 of the women unto the king's house. In the evening she went, and on the morrow she returned into the second house of the women, to the custody of Shaashgaz, the king's chamberlain, which kept the concubines: she came in unto the king no more, except the king delighted in her, and that she were called
15 by name. ¶ Now when the turn of Esther, [g] the daughter of Abihail the uncle of Mordecai, who had taken her for his daughter, was come to go in unto the king, she required nothing but what Hegai the king's chamberlain, the keeper of the women, appointed. And Esther obtained favour in the
16 sight of all them that looked upon her. So Esther was taken unto king Ahasuerus into his house royal in the tenth month, which *is* the month Tebeth, in the seventh year of his reign.
17 And the king loved Esther above all the women, and she ob-

[d] ver. 3.

[e] ver. 3, 12.

[f] ver. 20.

[g] ver. 7.

---

[1] Heb. *fair of form and good of countenance.*
[2] Heb. *her portions.*
[3] Heb. *he changed her.*
[4] Heb. *to know the peace.*

---

thought to be connected through the Zend with ἀστήρ, "star." But there is not at present any positive evidence of the existence in Old Persian of a kindred word.

10. The Persians had no special contempt for the Jews; but, of course, they despised more or less all the subject races. Esther, with her Aryan name, may have passed for a native Persian.

11. Mordecai occupied, apparently, a humble place in the royal household. He was probably one of the porters or doorkeepers at the main entrance to the palace (*v.* 21).

14. *the second house of the women*] *i.e.* Esther returned to the "house of the women," but not to the same part of it. She became an inmate of the "second house," or "house of the concubines," under the superintendence of a distinct officer, Shaashgaz.

15. *she required nothing*] The other virgins perhaps loaded themselves with precious ornaments of various kinds, necklaces, bracelets, earrings, anklets, and the like. Esther let Hegai dress her as he would.

16. Tebeth (cp. the corresponding Egyptian month, *Tobi* or *Tubi*), corresponded nearly to our January.

in the seventh year of his reign] In December, B.C. 479, or January, B.C. 478. Xerxes quitted Sardis for Susa in, or soon after, September, B.C. 479. It has been regarded as a "difficulty" that Vashti's place, declared vacant in B.C. 483, was not supplied till the end of B.C. 479, four years afterwards. But as two years out of the four had been occupied by the Grecian expedition, the objection cannot be considered very weighty.

h ch. 1. 3.

tained grace and [1] favour [2]in his sight more than all the virgins;
so that he set the royal crown upon her head, and made her queen
18 instead of Vashti. Then the king [h] made a great feast unto all
his princes and his servants, *even* Esther's feast; and he made a
[3] release to the provinces, and gave gifts, according to the state
19 of the king. ¶ And when the virgins were gathered together

i ver. 21.
ch. 3. 2.
k ver. 10.

20 the second time, then Mordecai sat [i]in the king's gate. [k]Esther
had not *yet* shewed her kindred nor her people; as Mordecai had
charged her : for Esther did the commandment of Mordecai,
21 like as when she was brought up with him. ¶ In those days,
while Mordecai sat in the king's gate, two of the king's chamberlains, [4]Bigthan and Teresh, of those which kept [5] the door,
were wroth, and sought to lay hand on the king Ahasuerus.

l ch. 6. 2.

22 And the thing was known to Mordecai, [l]who told *it* unto Esther
the queen ; and Esther certified the king *thereof* in Mordecai's
23 name. And when inquisition was made of the matter, it was
found out; therefore they were both hanged on a tree : and it

m ch. 6. 1.

was written in [m]the book of the chronicles before the king.

CHAP. 3. AFTER these things did king Ahasuerus promote Haman

a Num. 24.7.

the son of Hammedatha the [a]Agagite, and advanced him, and
2 set his seat above all the princes that *were* with him. And all

b ch. 2. 19.

the king's servants, that *were* [b]in the king's gate, bowed, and
reverenced Haman : for the king had so commanded concerning

c ver. 5.
Ps. 15. 4.
d ver. 2.

3 him. But Mordecai [c]bowed not, nor did *him* reverence. Then
the king's servants, which *were* in the king's gate, said unto
Mordecai, Why transgressest thou the [d]king's commandment ?
4 Now it came to pass, when they spake daily unto him, and he
hearkened not unto them, that they told Haman, to see whether
Mordecai's matters would stand : for he had told them that he

e ver. 2.
ch. 5. 9.
f Dan. 3. 19.
g Ps. 83. 4.

5 *was* a Jew. And when Haman saw that Mordecai [e]bowed not,
6 nor did him reverence, then was Haman [f]full of wrath. And he
thought scorn to lay hands on Mordecai alone; for they had
shewed him the people of Mordecai : wherefore Haman [g]sought

---

[1] Or, *kindness.*   [3] Heb. *rest.*   [5] Heb. *the threshold.*
[2] Heb. *before him.*   [4] Or, *Bigthana,* ch. 6. 2.

---

18. *a release*] Either remission of taxation, or of military service, or of both.

19. *when the virgins* &c.] Rather, "when
virgins" &c. The words begin a new paragraph. There was a second collection of
virgins (after that of *v.* 8), and it was at the
time of this second collection that Mordecai
had the good fortune to save the king's
life.

21. Conspiracies inside the palace were
ordinary occurrences in Persia. Xerxes was
ultimately murdered by Artabanus, the
captain of the guard, and Aspamitras, a
chamberlain and eunuch.

23. *both hanged on a tree*] i.e. "crucified"
or "impaled"—the ordinary punishment of
rebels and traitors in Persia.

the book of the chronicles] Ctesias drew his
Persian history from them, and they are
often glanced at by Herodotus.

III. 1. The name, Haman, is probably
the same as the classical Omanes, and in
ancient Persian, *Umana,* an exact equivalent of the Greek "Eumenes." Hammedatha is perhaps the same as *Madâta* or

Mahaldta, an old Persian name signifying
"given by (or to) the moon."

the Agagite] The Jews generally understand by this expression "the descendant of
Agag," the Amalekite monarch of 1 Sam.
xv. Haman, however, by his own name,
and the names of his sons (ix. 7-9) and his
father, would seem to have been a genuine
Persian.

The classical writers make no mention of
Haman's advancement ; but their notices of
the reign of Xerxes after B.C. 479 are exceedingly scanty.

2. Mordecai probably refused the required prostration, usual though it was, on
religious grounds. Hence his opposition led
on to his confession that he was a Jew
(*v.* 4).

4. *whether Mordecai's matters would stand*]
Rather, "whether Mordecai's **words** would
hold good"—whether, that is, his excuse,
that he was a Jew, would be allowed as a
valid reason for his refusal.

6. *to destroy all the Jews*] In the East
massacres of a people, a race, a class, have

to destroy all the Jews that *were* throughout the whole kingdom
7 of Ahasuerus, *even* the people of Mordecai. ¶ In the first month,
that *is*, the month Nisan, in the twelfth year of king Ahasuerus,
h they cast Pur, that *is*, the lot, before Haman from day to day,   *h* ch. 9. 24.
and from month to month, *to* the twelfth *month*, that *is*, the
8 month Adar. And Haman said unto king Ahasuerus, There is
a certain people scattered abroad and dispersed among the people
in all the provinces of thy kingdom; and *i* their laws *are* diverse   *i* Ezra 4. 13.
from all people; neither keep they the king's laws: therefore it   Acts 16. 20.
9 *is* not *1* for the king's profit to suffer them. If it please the king,
let it be written *2* that they may be destroyed: and I will *3* pay
ten thousand talents of silver to the hands of those that have
the charge of the business, to bring *it* into the king's treasuries.
10 And the king *k* took *l* his ring from his hand, and gave it unto   *k* Gen. 41. 42.
Haman the son of Hammedatha the Agagite, the Jews' *4* enemy.   *l* ch. 8. 2, 8.
11 And the king said unto Haman, The silver *is* given to thee, the
people also, to do with them as it seemeth good to thee.
12 ¶ *m* Then were the king's *5* scribes called on the thirteenth day of   *m* ch. 8. 9.
the first month, and there was written according to all that
Haman had commanded unto the king's lieutenants, and to the
governors that *were* over every province, and to the rulers of
every people of every province *n* according to the writing thereof,   *n* ch. 1. 22.
and *to* every people after their language; *o* in the name of king   & 8. 9.
13 Ahasuerus was it written, and sealed with the king's ring. And   *o* 1 Kin.21.8.
the letters were *p* sent by posts into all the king's provinces,   ch. 8. 8, 10.
to destroy, to kill, and to cause to perish, all Jews, both young   *p* ch. 8. 10.
and old, little children and women, *q* in one day, *even* upon the   *q* ch. 8. 12,
&c.

---

1 Heb. *meet*, or, *equal.*   *3* Heb. *weigh.*   *5* Or, *secretaries.*
2 Heb. *to destroy them.*   *4* Or, *oppressor,* ch. 7. 6.

---

at all times been among the incidents of
history, and would naturally present themselves to the mind of a statesman. The
Magophonia, or the great massacre of the
Magi at the accession of Darius Hystaspis,
was an event not then fifty years old, and
was commemorated annually. A massacre
of the Scythians had occurred about a century previously.

7. *In the first month* &c.] *i.e.* in March or
April of B.C. 474.

"Pur" is supposed to be an Old Persian
word etymologically connected with the
Latin *pars*, and signifying "part" or "lot."
The practice of casting lots to obtain a
lucky day obtains still in the East, and is
probably extremely ancient. A lot seems
to have been cast, or a throw of some kind
made, for each day of the month and each
month of the year. The day and month
which obtained the best throws were then
selected. Assyrian calendars note lucky
and unlucky days as early as the eighth
century B.C. Lots were in use both among
the Oriental and the classical nations from
a remote antiquity.

"Adar," the twelfth month, corresponds
nearly to our March. It seems to have derived its name from *ádar*, "splendour,"
because of the brightness of the sun and the
flowers at that time.

9. *ten thousand talents of silver*] Accord-

ing to Herodotus, the regular revenue of
the Persian king consisted of 14,560 silver
talents; so that, if the same talent is intended, Haman's offer would have exceeded
two-thirds of a year's revenue (or two and
a half millions sterling). Another Persian
subject, Pythius, once offered to present
Xerxes with four millions of gold darics, or
about four millions and a half of our money.

11. *The silver is given to thee*] Some understand this to mean that Xerxes refused
the silver which Haman had offered to him;
but the passage is better explained as a
grant to him of all the property of such
Jews as should be executed (*v.* 13).

12. *on the thirteenth day*] Haman had,
apparently (cp. *v.* 7 with *v.* 13), obtained by
his use of the lot the 13th day of Adar as
the lucky day for destroying the Jews.
This may have caused him to fix on the 13th
day of another month for the commencement of his enterprise. The Jews throughout the empire had thus from nine to eleven
months' warning of the peril which threatened them.

13. The Jews at present keep three days,
the 13th, the 14th, and the 15th of Adar, as
connected with "the feast of Purim;" but
they make the 13th a fast, commemorative
of the fast of Esther (iv. 16), and keep the
feast itself on the 14th and 15th.

thirteenth *day* of the twelfth month, which *is* the month Adar,
14 and *ʳto take* the spoil of them for a prey. *ˢThe copy of the
writing for a commandment to be given in every province was
published unto all people, that they should be ready against
15 that day. The posts went out, being hastened by the king's
commandment, and the decree was given in Shushan the palace.
And the king and Haman sat down to drink ; but *ᵗthe city Shushan was perplexed.

Chap. 4. WHEN Mordecai perceived all that was done, Mordecai
*ᵃrent his clothes, and put on sackcloth *ᵇwith ashes, and went
out into the midst of the city, and *ᶜcried with a loud and a bitter
2 cry ; and came even before the king's gate : for none *might* enter
3 into the king's gate clothed with sackcloth. And in every province, whithersoever the king's commandment and his decree
came, *there was* great mourning among the Jews, and fasting,
and weeping, and wailing ; and ¹many lay in sackcloth and
4 ashes. ¶ So Esther's maids and her ²chamberlains came and told
it her. Then was the queen exceedingly grieved ; and she sent
raiment to clothe Mordecai, and to take away his sackcloth from
5 him : but he received *it* not. Then called Esther for Hatach,
one of the king's chamberlains, ³whom he had appointed to
attend upon her, and gave him a commandment to Mordecai, to
6 know what it *was*, and why it *was*. So Hatach went forth to
Mordecai unto the street of the city, which *was* before the king's
7 gate. And Mordecai told him of all that had happened unto
him, and of *ᵈthe sum of the money that Haman had promised
to pay to the king's treasuries for the Jews, to destroy them.
8 Also he gave him *ᵉthe copy of the writing of the decree that was
given at Shushan to destroy them, to shew *it* unto Esther, and
to declare *it* unto her, and to charge her that she should go in
unto the king, to make supplication unto him, and to make re-
9 quest before him for her people. And Hatach came and told
10 Esther the words of Mordecai. ¶ Again Esther spake unto
11 Hatach, and gave him commandment unto Mordecai ; all the
king's servants, and the people of the king's provinces, do know,
that whosoever, whether man or woman, shall come unto the
king into *ᶠthe inner court, who is not called, *ᵍthere is one law of
his to put *him* to death, except such *ʰto whom the king shall
hold out the golden sceptre, that he may live : but I have not
12 been called to come in unto the king these thirty days. And they
13 told to Mordecai Esther's words. ¶ Then Mordecai commanded
to answer Esther, Think not with thyself that thou shalt escape

ʳ ch. 8.11.
ˢ ch. 8.13,14.

ᵗ See ch. 8.
15.
Prov. 29. 2.

ᵃ 2 Sam.1.11.
ᵇ Josh. 7. 6.
Ezek. 27. 30.
ᶜ Gen. 27. 34.

ᵈ ch. 3. 9.

ᵉ ch. 3. 14,15.

ᶠ ch. 5. 1.
ᵍ Dan. 2. 9.
ʰ ch. 5. 2.
& 8. 4.

---

¹ Heb. *sackcloth and ashes
were laid under many*,　　² Heb. *eunuchs*.　　Isai. 58. 5. Dan. 9. 3.　　³ Heb. *whom he had set before her*.

---

15 *Shushan was perplexed*] Susa was now
the capital of Persia, and the main residence of the Persians of high rank. These,
being attached to the religion of Zoroaster,
would naturally sympathise with the Jews,
and be disturbed at their threatened destruction. Even apart from this bond of
union, the decree was sufficiently strange
and ominous to " perplex " thoughtful
citizens.

IV. 2. *none might enter into the king's gate
clothed with sackcloth*] This law is not elsewhere mentioned ; but its principle—that
nothing of evil omen is to be obtruded on

the monarch—has been recognized throughout the East in all ages.

4. *Esther's maids...told it her*] Esther's
nationality and her relationship to Mordecai were probably by this time known to
her attendants, though still concealed from
the king. See vii. 4.

11. *the golden sceptre*] In all the numerous
representations of Persian kings at Persepolis the monarch holds a long tapering
staff (probably the sceptre of Esther) in his
right hand. It was death to intrude on the
privacy of the Persian king uninvited.

14 in the king's house, more than all the Jews. For if thou altogether holdest thy peace at this time, *then* shall there [1]enlarge-
ment and deliverance arise to the Jews from another place; but
thou and thy father's house shall be destroyed: and who knoweth
whether thou art come to the kingdom for *such* a time as this?
15, 16 ¶ Then Esther bade *them* return Mordecai *this answer*, Go,
gather together all the Jews that are [2]present in Shushan, and
fast ye for me, and neither eat nor drink *i*three days, night or
day: I also and my maidens will fast likewise; and so will I go
in unto the king, which *is* not according to the law: *k*and if I
17 perish, I perish. So Mordecai [3]went his way, and did according
to all that Esther had commanded him.

CHAP. **5.** NOW it came to pass *a*on the third day, that Esther put
on *her* royal *apparel*, and stood in *b*the inner court of the king's
house, over against the king's house: and the king sat upon his
royal throne in the royal house, over against the gate of the
2 house. And it was so, when the king saw Esther the queen
standing in the court, *that* *c*she obtained favour in his sight:
and *d*the king held out to Esther the golden sceptre that *was* in
his hand. So Esther drew near, and touched the top of the
3 sceptre. Then said the king unto her, What wilt thou, queen
Esther? and what *is* thy request? *e*it shall be even given thee
4 to the half of the kingdom. And Esther answered, If *it seem*
good unto the king, let the king and Haman come this day unto
5 the banquet that I have prepared for him. Then the king said,
Cause Haman to make haste, that he may do as Esther hath
said. So the king and Haman came to the banquet that Esther
6 had prepared. ¶ *f*And the king said unto Esther at the banquet
of wine, *g*What *is* thy petition? and it shall be granted thee:
and what *is* thy request? even to the half of the kingdom it shall
7 be performed. Then answered Esther, and said, My petition
8 and my request *is;* If I have found favour in the sight of the
king, and if it please the king to grant my petition, and [4]to perform my request, let the king and Haman come to the banquet
that I shall prepare for them, and I will do to morrow as the

i See ch. 5.1.

k See Gen. 43. 14.

a See ch. 4. 16.
b See ch. 4. 11.
& ch. 6. 4.

c Prov. 21.1.
d ch. 4. 11.
& 8. 4.

e So Mark 6. 23.

f ch. 7. 2.
g ch. 9. 12.

---

[1] Heb. *respiration*, Job 9. 18.
[2] Heb. *found*.
[3] Heb. *passed*.
[4] Heb. *to do*.

---

14. *from another place*] *i.e.* "from some
other quarter." Mordecai probably concluded from the prophetical Scriptures that
God would not allow His people to be destroyed before His purposes with respect to
them were accomplished, and was therefore
satisfied that deliverance would arise from
one quarter or another.
thou and thy father's house shall be destroyed]
i.e. "a divine vengeance will overtake thee
and thine, if thou neglectest thy plain duty."
Though the *name* of God is not contained in
the Book of Esther, there is in this verse
distinct tacit allusion to God's promises,
and to the direction of human events by
Divine Providence.
16. Again the religious element ihews
itself. Esther's fast could have no object
but to obtain God's favour and protection
in the dangerous course on which she was
about to enter.
V. 1. *over against the gate*] This is the

usual situation of the throne in the "throne-
room" of an Oriental palace. The monarch, from his raised position, can see into
the court through the doorway opposite to
him, which is kept open.
3. *it shall be even given thee* &c.] Xerxes,
on another occasion, when pleased with one
of his wives, offered to grant her any request
whatever, without limitation. Cp. marg.
ref.
4. Esther seems to have been afraid to
make her real request of Xerxes too
abruptly. She concluded that the king
would understand that she had a real petition in the background, and would recur to
it, as in fact he did (*v.* 6, vii. 2).
6. *the banquet of wine*] After the meats
were removed, it was customary in Persia
to continue the banquet for a considerable
time with fruits and wine. During this
part of the feast, the king renewed his
offer.

9 king hath said. ¶ Then went Haman forth that day joyful and
with a glad heart: but when Haman saw Mordecai in the king's

h ch. 3. 5.

i So 2 Sam.
13. 22.

gate, *h*that he stood not up, nor moved for him, he was full of
10 indignation against Mordecai. Nevertheless Haman *i*refrained
himself: and when he came home, he sent and *l*called for his
11 friends, and Zeresh his wife. And Haman told them of the

k ch. 9. 7,&c.

glory of his riches, and *k*the multitude of his children, and all
the things wherein the king had promoted him, and how he had

l ch. 3. 1.

*l*advanced him above the princes and servants of the king.
12 Haman said moreover, Yea, Esther the queen did let no man
come in with the king unto the banquet that she had prepared
but myself; and to morrow am I invited unto her also with the
13 king. Yet all this availeth me nothing, so long as I see Mor-
14 decai the Jew sitting at the king's gate. Then said Zeresh his

m ch. 7. 9.

n ch. 6. 4.

wife and all his friends unto him, Let a *2m*gallows be made of
fifty cubits high, and to morrow *n*speak thou unto the king that
Mordecai may be hanged thereon: then go thou in merrily with
the king unto the banquet. And the thing pleased Haman; and

o ch. 7. 10.

he caused *o*the gallows to be made.

CHAP. 6. ON that night *3*could not the king sleep, and he com-

a ch. 2. 23.

manded to bring *a*the book of records of the chronicles; and
2 they were read before the king. And it was found written, that
Mordecai had told of *4*Bigthana and Teresh, two of the king's
chamberlains, the keepers of the *5*door, who sought to lay hand
3 on the king Ahasuerus. ¶ And the king said, What honour and
dignity hath been done to Mordecai for this? Then said the
king's servants that ministered unto him, There is nothing done
4 for him. And the king said, Who *is* in the court? Now Haman

b See ch. 5. 1.

c ch. 5. 14.

was come into *b*the outward court of the king's house, *c*to speak
unto the king to hang Mordecai on the gallows that he had pre-
5 pared for him. And the king's servants said unto him, Behold,
Haman standeth in the court. And the king said, Let him come
6 in. So Haman came in. And the king said unto him, What
shall be done unto the man *6*whom the king delighteth to honour?
Now Haman thought in his heart, To whom would the king
7 delight to do honour more than to myself? And Haman answered the king, For the man *7*whom the king delighteth to
8 honour, *8*let the royal apparel be brought *9*which the king *useth*

1 Heb. *caused to come.*
2 Heb. *tree.*
3 Heb. *the king's sleep fled away.*
4 Or, *Bigthan, ch. 2. 21.*

5 Heb. *threshold.*
6 Heb. *in whose honour the king delighteth.*
7 Heb. *in whose honour the king delighteth.*

8 Heb. *Let them bring the royal apparel.*
9 Heb. *wherewith the king clotheth himself.*

---

9. *he stood not up, nor moved for him*] This
was undoubtedly a serious breach of Persian etiquette, and may well have angered
Haman.

10. *Zeresh*] This name is probably connected with the Zend *zara*, "gold." Cp. the
Greek "Chrysis."

11. *the multitude of his children*] Herodotus tells us that, "next to prowess in
arms, it was regarded as the greatest proof
of manly excellence in Persia to be the
father of many sons." Haman had ten
sons (marg. ref.)

14. A gallows, in the ordinary sense, is
scarcely intended, since hanging was not a
Persian punishment. The intention, no
doubt, was to crucify (ii. 23 note) or impale

Mordecai; and the pale or cross was to be
75 feet high, to make the punishment more
conspicuous.

speak thou unto the king &c.] Requests for
leave to put persons to death were often
made to Persian kings by their near relatives, but only rarely by others.

VI. **3.** It was a settled principle of the
Persian government that "Royal Benefac-
tors" were to receive an adequate reward.
The names of such persons were placed
on a special roll, and care was taken that
they should be properly recompensed,
though they sometimes waited for months
or years before they were recompensed.

8. The honours here proposed by Haman were such as Persian monarchs rarely

to wear, and ^dthe horse that the king rideth upon, and the crown

9 royal which is set upon his head : and let this apparel and horse be delivered to the hand of one of the king's most noble princes, that they may array the man *withal* whom the king delighteth to honour, and ¹bring him on horseback through the street of the city, ^eand proclaim before him, Thus shall it be done to the

10 man whom the king delighteth to honour. Then the king said to Haman, Make haste, *and* take the apparel and the horse, as thou hast said, and do even so to Mordecai the Jew, that sitteth at the king's gate : ²let nothing fail of all that thou hast spoken.

11 Then took Haman the apparel and the horse, and arrayed Mordecai, and brought him on horseback through the street of the city, and proclaimed before him, Thus shall it be done unto the

12 man whom the king delighteth to honour. ¶ And Mordecai came again to the king's gate. But Haman ^fhasted to his house

13 mourning, ^gand having his head covered. And Haman told Zeresh his wife and all his friends every *thing* that had befallen him. Then said his wise men and Zeresh his wife unto him, If Mordecai *be* of the seed of the Jews, before whom thou hast begun to fall, thou shalt not prevail against him, but shalt surely

14 fall before him. And while they *were* yet talking with him, came the king's chamberlains, and hasted to bring Haman unto ^hthe banquet that Esther had prepared.

CHAP. 7. SO the king and Haman came ³to banquet with Esther

2 the queen. And the king said again unto Esther on the second day ^aat the banquet of wine, What *is* thy petition, queen Esther ? and it shall be granted thee : and what *is* thy request ? and it

3 shall be performed, *even* to the half of the kingdom. Then Esther the queen answered and said, If I have found favour in thy sight, O king, and if it please the king, let my life be given

4 me at my petition, and my people at my request : for we are ^bsold, I and my people, ⁴to be destroyed, to be slain, and to perish. But if we had been sold for bondmen and bondwomen, I had held my tongue, although the enemy could not counter-

5 vail the king's damage. Then the king Ahasuerus answered and said unto Esther the queen, Who is he, and where is he,

6 ⁵that durst presume in his heart to do so ? And Esther said, ^cThe adversary and enemy *is* this wicked Haman. Then Haman

7 was afraid ⁷before the king and the queen. ¶ And the king arising from the banquet of wine in his wrath *went* into the palace garden : and Haman stood up to make request for his life to Esther the queen ; for he saw that there was evil determined

8 against him by the king. Then the king returned out of the palace garden into the place of the banquet of wine ; and Haman

Marginal references:
^d 1 Kin. 1. 33.
^e Gen. 41. 13.
^f 2 Chr. 26. 20.
^g 2 Sam. 15. 30.
Jcr. 14. 3, 4.
^h ch. 5. 8.
^a ch. 5. 6.
^b ch. 3. 9. & 4. 7.

---

¹ Heb. *cause him to ride.*
² Heb. *suffer not a whit to fall.*
³ Heb. *to drink.*
⁴ Heb. *that they should destroy, and kill, and cause to perish.*
⁵ Heb. *whose heart hath filled him.*
⁶ Heb. *The man adversary.*
⁷ Or, *at the presence of.*

---

allowed to subjects. Each act would have been a capital offence if done without permission. Still we find Persian monarchs allowing their subjects in these or similar acts under certain circumstances.

12. It is quite consonant with Oriental notions that Mordecai, after receiving the extraordinary honours assigned him, should return to the palace and resume his former humble employment.

VII. 4. The king now learnt, perhaps for the first time, that his favourite was a Jewess.

although the enemy &c.] *i.e.* "although the enemy (Haman) would not (even in that case) compensate (by his payment to the treasury) for the king's loss of so many subjects."

8. Like the Greeks and Romans, the Persians reclined at their meals on sofas or couches. Haman, in the intensity of his

c ch. 1. 6.

d Job 9. 24.

e ch. 1. 10.

f ch. 5. 14.
Ps. 7. 16.
Prov. 11. 5, 6.

g Ps. 37. 35,
36.
Dan. 6. 24.

a ch. 2. 7.

b ch. 3. 10.

c ch. 4. 11.
& 5. 2.

d Neh. 2. 3.
ch. 7. 4.

e ver. 1.
Prov. 13. 22.

f Dan. 6. 8,
12, 15.
g ch. 3. 12.

h ch. 1. 1.

was fallen upon c the bed whereon Esther _was_. Then said the king, Will he force the queen also ¹before me in the house? As the word went out of the king's mouth, they d covered Ha-
9 man's face. And e Harbonah, one of the chamberlains, said before the king, Behold also, f the ²gallows fifty cubits high, which Haman had made for Mordecai, who had spoken good for the king, standeth in the house of Haman. Then the king said,
10 Hang him thereon. So g they hanged Haman on the gallows that he had prepared for Mordecai. Then was the king's wrath pacified.

CHAP. 8. ON that day did the king Ahasuerus give the house of Haman the Jews' enemy unto Esther the queen. And Mordecai came before the king; for Esther had told a what he _was_ unto
2 her. And the king took off b his ring, which he had taken from Haman, and gave it unto Mordecai. And Esther set Mordecai
3 over the house of Haman. ¶ And Esther spake yet again before the king, and fell down at his feet, ³ and besought him with tears to put away the mischief of Haman the Agagite, and his
4 device that he had devised against the Jews. Then c the king held out the golden sceptre toward Esther. So Esther arose,
5 and stood before the king, and said, If it please the king, and if I have found favour in his sight, and the thing _seem_ right before the king, and I _be_ pleasing in his eyes, let it be written to reverse ⁴the letters devised by Haman the son of Hammedatha the Agagite, ⁵which he wrote to destroy the Jews which _are_ in all
6 the king's provinces: for how can I ⁶endure to see d the evil that shall come unto my people? or how can I endure to see the
7 destruction of my kindred? Then the king Ahasuerus said unto Esther the queen and to Mordecai the Jew, Behold, e I have given Esther the house of Haman, and him they have hanged upon the gallows, because he laid his hand upon the Jews.
8 Write ye also for the Jews, as it liketh you, in the king's name, and seal _it_ with the king's ring: for the writing which is written in the king's name, and sealed with the king's ring, f may no
9 man reverse. ¶ g Then were the king's scribes called at that time in the third month, that _is_, the month Sivan, on the three and twentieth _day_ thereof; and it was written according to all that Mordecai commanded unto the Jews, and to the lieutenants, and the deputies and rulers of the provinces which _are_ h from India

---

¹ Heb. _with me._
² Heb. _tree._
³ Heb. _and she wept, and besought him._
⁴ Heb. _the device._
⁵ Or, _who wrote._
⁶ Heb. _be able that I may see._

---

supplication, had thrown himself upon the couch at Esther's feet.

they covered Haman's face] The Macedonians and the Romans are known to have commonly muffled the heads of prisoners before executing them. It may have been also a Persian custom.

VIII. 1. _give the house of Haman_] Confiscation of goods accompanied public execution in Persia as in other Oriental countries.

2. _his ring_] _i.e._ the royal signet by which the decrees of the government were signed.

over the house of Haman] Not only the building and the furniture, but the household—the vast train of attendants of all

kinds that was attached to the residence of a Persian noble.

3. Though Haman was dead, his work was not yet undone. The royal decree had gone forth, and, according to Persian notions, could not be directly recalled or reversed (_v._ 8). Mordecai did not dare, without express permission from the king, to take any steps even to stay execution. And Esther, being in favour, once more took the initiative.

8. _Write...as it liketh you_ &c.] [See i. 19 note. Practically, Ahasuerus reversed the "device" of Haman].

9. Sivan corresponds nearly to our June; it was the second month from the issue of the first edict (iii. 12).

unto Ethiopia, an hundred twenty and seven provinces, unto every province *according to the writing thereof, and unto every people after their language, and to the Jews according to their

10 writing, and according to their language. *And he wrote in the king Ahasuerus' name, and sealed *it* with the king's ring, and sent letters by posts on horseback, *and* riders on mules, camels,

11 *and* young dromedaries: wherein the king granted the Jews which *were* in every city to gather themselves together, and to stand for their life, to destroy, to slay, and to cause to perish, all the power of the people and province that would assault them, *both* little ones and women, and *to take* the spoil of them for a

12 prey, *upon one day in all the provinces of king Ahasuerus, *namely*, upon the thirteenth *day* of the twelfth month, which *is*

13 the month Adar. *The copy of the writing for a commandment to be given in every province *was* ¹published unto all people, and that the Jews should be ready against that day to

14 avenge themselves on their enemies. *So* the posts that rode upon mules *and* camels went out, being hastened and pressed on by the king's commandment. And the decree was given at

15 Shushan the palace. ¶ And Mordecai went out from the presence of the king in royal apparel of ²blue and white, and with a great crown of gold, and with a garment of fine linen and

16 purple: and *the city of Shushan rejoiced and was glad. The

17 Jews had *light, and gladness, and joy, and honour. And in every province, and in every city, whithersoever the king's commandment and his decree came, the Jews had joy and gladness, a feast *and a good day. And many of the people of the land *became Jews; for *the fear of the Jews fell upon them.

CHAP. 9. NOW *a* in the twelfth month, that *is*, the month Adar, on the thirteenth day of the same, *b* when the king's commandment and his decree drew near to be put in execution, in the day that the enemies of the Jews hoped to have power over them, (though it was turned to the contrary, that the Jews *c* had rule

2 over them that hated them;) the Jews *d* gathered themselves together in their cities throughout all the provinces of the king Ahasuerus, to lay hand on such as *e* sought their hurt: and no man could withstand them; for *f* the fear of them fell upon all

i ch. 1. 22.
& 3. 12.

k 1 Kin.21.8.
ch. 3. 12, 13.

l See ch. 9.
10, 15, 16.
m ch. 3. 13,
&c.
& 9. 1.
n ch. 3. 14,
15.

o See ch. 3.
15.
Prov. 29. 2.
p Ps. 97. 11.

q 1 Sam.25.8.
ch. 9. 19, 22.
r Ps. 18. 43.
s Gen. 35. 5.
Ex. 15. 16.
Deut. 2. 25.
& 11. 25.
ch. 9. 2.
a ch. 8. 12.
b ch. 3. 13.
c 2 Sam. 22.
41.
d ch. 8. 11.
& ver. 16.
e Ps. 71. 13,
24.
f ch. 8. 17.

¹ Heb. *revealed.*   ² Or, *violet.*

---

10. *riders on mules, camels, and young dromedaries*] Most moderns translate "riders upon *coursers and mules, the offspring of mares;* " but the words translated "mules" and "mares," are of very doubtful signification, since they scarcely occur elsewhere. The real meaning of the clause must remain doubtful; perhaps the true translation is, "riders upon **coursers of the king's stud,** offspring of high-bred steeds." So *v.* 14.

11. This fresh decree allowed the Jews to stand on their defence, and to kill all who attacked them. It has been pronounced incredible, that any king would thus have sanctioned civil war in all the great cities of his empire; but some even of the more sceptical critics allow that *Xerxes* might not improbably have done so.

14. *being hastened*] Between Sivan, the third month (June), when the posts went out, and Adar, the twelfth month (March), when the struggle was to take place, the interval would be one of above eight months; but all haste was made, with the object of their being no misunderstanding.

15. See i. 6 note. The "crown" was not a crown like the king's, but a mere golden band or coronet.

a garment] Or, "an inner robe." The tunic or inner robe of the king was of purple, striped with white.

17. *became Jews*] Joined the nation as proselytes, so casting in their lot with them.

IX. 1. *drew near*] Or, "arrived," or "**reached the time** "specified (iii. 13, viii. 12).

3 people. And all the rulers of the provinces, and the lieutenants, and the deputies, and [1] officers of the king, helped the Jews; 4 because the fear of Mordecai fell upon them. For Mordecai *was* great in the king's house, and his fame went out throughout all the provinces: for this man Mordecai *g* waxed greater 5 and greater. ¶ Thus the Jews smote all their enemies with the stroke of the sword, and slaughter, and destruction, and did 6 [2] what they would unto those that hated them. And in Shushan 7 the palace the Jews slew and destroyed five hundred men. And 8 Parshandatha, and Dalphon, and Aspatha, and Poratha, and 9 Adalia, and Aridatha, and Parmashta, and Arisai, and Aridai, 10 and Vajezatha, *h* the ten sons of Haman the son of Hammedatha, the enemy of the Jews, slew they; *i* but on the spoil laid they 11 not their hand. ¶ On that day the number of those that were 12 slain in Shushan the palace [3] was brought before the king. And the king said unto Esther the queen, The Jews have slain and destroyed five hundred men in Shushan the palace, and the ten sons of Haman; what have they done in the rest of the king's provinces? now *k* what *is* thy petition? and it shall be granted thee: or what *is* thy request further? and it shall be done. 13 Then said Esther, If it please the king, let it be granted to the Jews which *are* in Shushan to do to morrow also *l* according unto this day's decree, and [4] let Haman's ten sons *m* be 14 hanged upon the gallows. And the king commanded it so to be done: and the decree was given at Shushan; and they 15 hanged Haman's ten sons. For the Jews that *were* in Shushan *n* gathered themselves together on the fourteenth day also of the month Adar, and slew three hundred men at Shushan; *o* but 16 on the prey they laid not their hand. ¶ But the other Jews that *were* in the king's provinces *p* gathered themselves together, and stood for their lives, and had rest from their enemies, and slew of their foes seventy and five thousand, *q* but they 17 laid not their hands on the prey, on the thirteenth day of the month Adar; and on the fourteenth day [5] of the same rested 18 they, and made it a day of feasting and gladness. But the Jews that *were* at Shushan assembled together *r* on the thirteenth *day* thereof, and on the fourteenth thereof; and on the fifteenth *day* of the same they rested, and made it a day of feasting and glad- 19 ness. Therefore the Jews of the villages, that dwelt in the

b 2 Sam. 3. 1.
1 Chr. 11. 9.
Prov. 4. 18.

h ch. 5. 11.
Job 18. 19.
& 27. 13, 14,
15.
Ps. 21. 10.
i See ch. 8.
11.

k ch. 5. 6.
& 7. 2.

l ch. 8. 11.
m 2 Sam. 21.
6, 9.

n ver. 2.
& ch. 8. 11.
o ver. 10.

p ver. 2.
& ch. 8. 11.
q See ch. 8.
11.

r ver. 11. 15.

---

[1] Heb. *those which did the business that* belonged *to the king.*
[2] Heb. *according to their will.*
[3] Heb. *came.*
[4] Heb. *let men hang.*
[5] Heb. *in it.*

---

3. *all the rulers...helped the Jews*] i.e. the Persians, who formed the standing army which kept the Empire in subjection, and were at the disposal of the various governors of provinces, took the Jews' side. The enemies of the Jews (*e.g. v.* 16) were almost entirely to be found among the idolatrous people of the subject nations, for whose lives neither the Persians generally, nor their monarchs, cared greatly.

6. By "Shushan the palace (or the fort)," is probably meant the whole of the upper town, which occupied an area of above a hundred acres, and contained many residences besides the actual palace. The Jews would not have ventured to shed blood within the palace-precincts.

7-10. Most of these names are Persian, and readily traceable to Old Persian roots.

10. *on the spoil laid they not their hand*] As they might have done (see marg. ref.).

15. *Shushan*] Here probably the lower town, which lay east of the upper one, and was of about the same size (cp. *v.* 6 note).

16. *seventy and five thousand*] The LXX. gives the number as fifteen thousand; and this amount seems more in proportion to the 800 slain in Susa.

18. See iii. 13 note.

19. *the Jews of the villages* &c.] Rather, "the Jews of the **country districts,**" that dwelt in the **country towns,**" as distinguished from those who dwelt in the metropolis.

unwalled towns, made the fourteenth day of the month Adar *a day of* gladness and feasting, [t]and a good day, and of
20 [u]sending portions one to another. ¶And Mordecai wrote these things, and sent letters unto all the Jews that *were* in all the
21 provinces of the king Ahasuerus, *both* nigh and far, to stablish *this* among them, that they should keep the fourteenth day of the month Adar, and the fifteenth day of the same, yearly,
22 as the days wherein the Jews rested from their enemies, and the month which was [x]turned unto them from sorrow to joy, and from mourning into a good day: that they should make them days of feasting and joy, and of [y]sending portions one
23 to another, and gifts to the poor. And the Jews undertook to do as they had begun, and as Mordecai had written unto
24 them; because Haman the son of Hammedatha the Agagite, the enemy of all the Jews, [z]had devised against the Jews to destroy them, and had cast Pur, that *is*, the lot, to [1]consume
25 them, and to destroy them; but [2][a]when *Esther* came before the king, he commanded by letters that his wicked device, which he devised against the Jews, should [b]return upon his own head, and that he and his sons should be hanged on the gallows.
26 Wherefore they called these days Purim after the name of [3]Pur. Therefore for all the words of [c]this letter, and *of that* which they had seen concerning this matter, and which had come unto
27 them, the Jews ordained, and took upon them, and upon their seed, and upon all such as [d]joined themselves unto them, so as it should not [4]fail, that they would keep these two days according to their wr.ting, and according to their *appointed* time every
28 year; and *that* these days *should be* remembered and kept throughout every generation, every family, every province, and every city; and *that* these days of Purim should not [5]fail from among the Jews, nor the memorial of them [6]perish from their seed.
29 ¶ Then Esther the queen, [e]the daughter of Abihail, and Mordecai the Jew, wrote with [7]all authority, to confirm this [f]second
30 letter of Purim. And he sent the letters unto all the Jews, to [g]the hundred twenty and seven provinces of the kingdom of
31 Ahasuerus, *with* words of peace and truth, to confirm these days of Purim in their times *appointed*, according as Mordecai the Jew and Esther the queen had enjoined them, and as they had decreed [8]for themselves and for their seed, the matters of [h]the
32 fastings and their cry. And the decree of Esther confirmed these matters of Purim; and it was written in the book.

CHAP. 10. AND the king Ahasuerus laid a tribute upon the land,

s Deut. 16.11, 14.
t ch. 8. 17.
u ver. 22.
Neh. 8.10,12.

x Ps. 30. 11.

y ver. 19.
Neh. 8. 11.

z ch. 3. 6, 7.

a ver. 13. 14.
ch. 7. 5, &c.
& 8. 3, &c.
b ch. 7. 10.
Ps. 7. 16.

c ver. 20.

d ch. 8. 17.
Isai. 56. 3, 6.
Zech. 2. 11.

e ch. 2. 15.
f See ch. 8.10.
& ver. 20.

g ch. 1. 1.

h ch. 4. 3, 16.

---

[1] Heb. *crush*.	[4] Heb. *pass*	[7] Heb. *all strength*.
[2] Heb. *when she came.*	[5] Heb. *pass.*	[8] Heb. *for their souls.*
[3] That is, *Lot.*	[6] Heb. *be ended.*	

---

29. *this second letter of Purim*] Mordecai's first letter (*v.* 20) was to some extent tentative, a recommendation. The Jews generally having accepted the recommendation (*vv.* 23, 27), he and Esther now wrote a second letter which was mandatory.

31. *the matters of the fastings and their cry*] The Jews of the provinces had added to the form of commemoration proposed by Mordecai certain observances with respect to fasting and wailing, and Mordecai's second letter sanctioned these.

32. As "the book" elsewhere in Esther

always means a particular book—"the book of the chronicles of the kings of Media and Persia"—(ii. 23, vi. 1, x. 2) it seems best to give it the same sense here.

X. 1. *a tribute*] Perhaps an allusion to some fresh arrangement of the tribute likely to have followed on the return of Xerxes from Greece.

upon the isles of the sea] Cyprus, Aradus, the island of Tyre, Platea, &c., remained in the hands of the Persians after the victories of the Greeks, and may be the "isles" here intended.

a Gen. 10. 5.
Ps. 72. 10.
Isai. 24. 15.
b ch. 8. 15.
& 9. 4.

c Gen. 41. 40.
2 Chr. 28. 7.

d Neh. 2. 10.
Ps. 122. 8, 9.

2 and *upon* ^athe isles of the sea. And all the acts of his power and of his might, and the declaration of the greatness of Mordecai, ^bwhereunto the king ¹advanced him, *are* they not written in the book of the chronicles of the kings of Media and Persia? 3 For Mordecai the Jew *was* ^cnext unto king Ahasuerus, and great among the Jews, and accepted of the multitude of his brethren, ^dseeking the wealth of his people, and speaking peace to all his seed.

¹ Heb. *made him great.*

---

2. *power and...might*] In the later years of Xerxes his " power and might " were chiefly shewn in the erection of magnificent buildings, more especially at Persepolis. He abstained from military expeditions.

kings of Media and Persia] Media takes precedence of Persia because the kingdom of Media had preceded that of Persia, and in the " book of the Chronicles " its history came first.

3. *Mordecai...was next unto king Ahasuerus*] See ii. 5 note. Artabanus (i. 14 note) was favourite towards the end of Xerxes' reign, *i.e.* in his 20th and 21st years.